The Editor

ANDREW D. HADFIELD is Professor of English at the University of Sussex and visiting Professor at the University of Granada. He is the author of a number of works on early modern literature, including *Edmund Spenser: A Life* (Oxford University Press, 2012); *Shakespeare and Republicanism* (Cambridge University Press, 2005; paperback, 2008); and *Spenser's Irish Experience: Wilde Fruyt and Salvage Soyl* (Oxford, 1997). He was editor of *Renaissance Studies* (2006–11) and is a regular reviewer for the *Times Literary Supplement*.

ANNE LAKE PRESCOTT is Professor of English, emerita, at Barnard College, Columbia University. The author of *French Poets and the English Renaissance* and *Imagining Rabelais in Renaissance England* as well as of many articles (including ten entries in *The Spenser Encyclopedia*), she is a past president of The Spenser Society, The Sixteenth Century Society, and The John Donne Society, and is currently co-editor of *Spenser Studies*.

W. W. NORTON & COMPANY, INC.
Also Publishes

A NORTON CRITICAL EDITION

Edmund Spenser's Poetry

AUTHORITATIVE TEXTS

CRITICISM

Fourth Edition

Selected and Edited by

ANDREW D. HADFIELD
UNIVERSITY OF SUSSEX

ANNE LAKE PRESCOTT
BARNARD COLLEGE, EMERITA
COLUMBIA UNIVERSITY

W • W • NORTON & COMPANY • *New York* • *London*

W. W. Norton & Company has been independent since its founding in 1923, when William Warder Norton and Mary D. Herter Norton first published lectures delivered at the People's Institute, the adult education division of New York City's Cooper Union. The firm soon expanded its program beyond the Institute, publishing books by celebrated academics from America and abroad. By midcentury, the two major pillars of Norton's publishing program—trade books and college texts—were firmly established. In the 1950s, the Norton family transferred control of the company to its employees, and today—with a staff of four hundred and a comparable number of trade, college, and professional titles published each year—W. W. Norton & Company stands as the largest and oldest publishing house owned wholly by its employees.

Printed in the United States of America

Manufacturing by Courier-Westford
Composition by Westchester Book Service
Production Manager: Sean Mintus

Library of Congress Cataloging-in-Publication Data

Spenser, Edmund, 1552?–1599.
[Poems. Selections]
Edmund Spenser's poetry : authoritative texts, criticism / selected and edited by Andrew D. Hadfield, University Of Sussex; Anne Lake Prescott, Barnard College, Emerita, Columbia University.—Fourth edition.
pages cm.—(A Norton critical edition)
New to this edition's collection of primary texts are Mother Hubberds tale from the 1591 Complaints, The ruines of Rome, and Spenser's translation of Joachim Du Bellay's Antiquitez. Also new are sixteen additions to the critical material, including commentaries by C.S. Lewis, Martha Craig, Gordon Teskey, Jeff Dolven, David Wilson-Okamura, and Jennifer Summit.
Includes bibliographical references.
ISBN 978-0-393-92785-6 (pbk.)
1. Spenser, Edmund, 1552?–1599—Criticism and interpretation.
I. Hadfield, Andrew, editor. II. Prescott, Anne Lake, date, editor.
III. Title.
PR2352.H33 2013
821'.3—dc23

2012050215

W. W. Norton & Company, Inc., 500 Fifth Avenue, New York, NY 10110
wwnorton.com

W. W. Norton & Company Ltd., Castle House, 75/76 Wells Street, London W1T 3QT

1 2 3 4 5 6 7 8 9 0

For A. C. Hamilton,
Spenser scholar and friend

Contents

Preface to the Fourth Edition

The world of Spenser scholarship, as of literary scholarship in general, has changed a great deal since the Third Edition of *Edmund Spenser's Poetry*, and not just because of shifts in scholarly and critical interests. Those shifts include a surge of interest in how a text's paratexts (preface, poems by the author's or the printer's friends, marginalia, etc.) as well as its *mise en page* (the arrangement of the text, the fonts, the size of the print, the placement of the illustrations, and so forth) relate in multiple ways to our less-recent-but-still-lively concern for poetry's relation to gender, for example, or to political, economic, and cultural power. The increased attention to early modern religion, not least to the persistence of Catholicism in officially Protestant England, has affected Spenser studies, as has a continuing attention to the dawn of English transoceanic colonial enterprise, although the full rush upon the Americas, let alone upon Asia and Africa, was yet to come, and the English slave trade was still in its infancy. Granted Spenser's career as a government functionary in Ireland during Elizabeth's efforts to subdue—and in her view civilize—that island, the role of Irish events, customs, and geography in Spenser's imagination has attracted fresh investigation. Those interested in gay, lesbian, and queer studies also have material to consider here, and ecocriticism has begun to notice Spenser. Those new to this poet should always bear in mind that his work is allegory, and indeed its subtlety is another topic of recent concern. Spenserian allegory, to be sure, is not a matter of one-to-one correspondence, but it remains wise to bear in mind the many ways in which *The Faerie Queene* is not a novel.

Just as relevant to the editors' task as recent shifts in scholarly emphases has been the increased presence in literary scholarship of the Internet and the accompanying proliferation of online bibliographies, discussion groups, and downloadable scholarship offering back issues of many academic journals. E-journals, often with essays or reviews relevant to Spenser studies, are now available to many. Such developments are as important to us as the expansion of print was to Spenser's generation. It remains useful, we believe, to gather some particularly valuable critical essays to include in this Norton Critical Edition and likewise to offer a bibliography for further reading. Eliminating some fine modern essays in order to make room for new ones has been painful, as has been the decision to omit some older remarks on Spenser, which are so many and varied that it seemed best to retain a minimum and to remind our readers that many have been collected (see the bibliography under Hefner and Radcliffe). Readers will be aware, moreover, that it is possible to find references to much work on Spenser that we omit here on the Modern Language Association Database, often with links to such websites as JSTOR or Project

Muse. Those who want to see what the original editions look like can find them on "Early English Books Online" or, for later early modern editions, imitations, allusions, and book sales that include Spenser's works, on the website "Eighteenth Century Collections Online." We recognize that many readers will not have easy access to such resources, but that they exist at all has meant a huge shift in what modern research entails.

In revising or replacing the Third Edition's footnotes, and in response to suggestions from others, we have shifted our editorial approach, often excising commentary that might spoil the experience of reading Spenser, especially *The Faerie Queene*, for the first time. Recent work on Spenser has tended to stress the degree to which his romance/epic is not so much illustrative of the virtues in action as it is interrogative and exploratory, interested in demonstrating the complexity and limitations of the virtue in question and allowing each virtue's representative but fallible knight to misread, become confused, err, misdeem, and in some cases even fail a little, if only so as to show the need for the virtue in the book that follows. (Yes, be holy, but show some temperance so as to avoid the zeal that is tearing much of Europe apart; yes, be friendly, but remember that friendship can too easily blunt the sword of justice.) It is perhaps this same reluctance to be morally simple that makes Spenser often delay telling us exactly what is going on or who is who, leaving us just as puzzled or perhaps just as mistaken as are the poem's chief figures themselves and thus giving us something like the experience of the knights associated with this or that virtue. If it takes us some time to identify that man with the beads and book who seems so friendly when the Redcrosse Knight first meets him, we can thus share in that same knight's confusion; Spenser will clarify things for the knight and for us as we read on. Are we confused? So are Spenser's knights. We all get lost. Have patience . . . The editors have, however, provided information that Spenser probably assumed his best readers would have at their fingertips but that even experienced modern readers are less likely to have in mind, and often we have cited scholarly works that provide help when that help, often of a specific nature, might be beyond what a quick search of the Web could readily provide. For the same reason that we have usually postponed commenting on a figure's identity until Spenser himself reveals it, we have, as in the Third Edition, placed the Editors' Notes after, not before, the texts on which they comment and have felt freer than in the notes to offer our own views or readings. We cannot stop those to whom Spenser is new from reading the Editors' Notes first, but for pleasure's sake we urge postponement. And, on the theory that serious students of Spenser will have the wit to consult it for themselves, we have dropped some allusions in the notes that cite (but do not quote) the invaluable multi-authored *Spenser Encyclopedia*.

For this edition we have, reluctantly, dropped *Colin Clouts Come Home Againe* and have not restored the Second Edition's *Fowre Hymnes*. We have added *Mother Hubberds Tale* from the 1591 *Complaints*, a text "called in" by the authorities, almost certainly because its allegory takes a remarkably imprudent aim at William Cecil, Lord Burleigh. It is interesting to see how close to the wind Spenser dared sail and also to see how he modifies this mix of medieval beast fable and more recent anticourt satire. We have included *The Ruines of Rome*, also from *Complaints*, in part because this translation of Joachim Du Bellay's *Antiquitez* offers readers a chance to see Spenser the translator at work and in part because of a continuing interest in how the English, like many other early modern nations or communities, thought about Rome and *imperium*—but also about Time's power to crunch and erode buildings and empires. Is Rome's collapse a warning and a tragedy? Does not that same collapse also make room for modern literatures and empire?

As we finished preparing this Norton Critical Edition, Oxford University Press was planning to publish a new multivolume edition of Spenser (we thank Professors Joseph Loewenstein and David Lee Miller, two of its editors, for their advice, particularly on textual issues). Although the Variorum edition published by Johns Hopkins University Press and edited by Edwin Greenlaw et al. will long remain valuable, the new Oxford edition will be not just a monument to scholarship but an entire mountain range of fresh expertise. The texts reproduced here are based on the 1596 *Faerie Queene* and the shorter poems on those works' first editions, but we have sometimes emended the punctuation by consulting later editions and we have made u/v and i/j conform to modern spelling. We have not modernized the spelling itself, because that would diminish the impression Spenser wanted to give of a modern English often incorporating an older quasi-Chaucerian vocabulary and because early modern English, with its indifference to "correct" spelling, could subtly imply puns (e.g., "travail" and "travel," "sun" and "son") that became harder to suggest as orthography became orthodox. For this edition we have dropped the "textual notes" because the Oxford edition will have rendered them out of date, but on a few occasions we note different readings in different editions. Unfamiliar words are glossed in the margin.

It remains only to thank others who have helped with this volume: Judith H. Anderson and other erudite members of the Sidney-Spenser list gave needed advice and information; Sean Henry sent several pages on early modern lions; Roger Kuin (editor of Sir Philip Sidney's correspondence) offered fine rhetorical advice on the Editors' Notes; Lydia Kirsopp Lake shared her learning on classical matters; and Rivka Genesen, our editor at W. W. Norton, has been the very Platonic Idea of encouraging patience. Mere thanks, however, would hardly express the degree of our obligation to A. C. Hamilton, the chief editor of *The Spenser Encyclopedia*, whose edition of *The Faerie Queene* is unsurpassed and whose scholarship has illuminated Spenser for more than two generations. With gratitude and affection we dedicate this volume to him.

Edmund Spenser: A Chronology

1553/4	Spenser born in London
1561–69	At the Merchant Taylors' School (founded 1561), under its first headmaster, the educator Richard Mulcaster. Contributes a number of verse translations from French to the 1569 English edition of Jan van der Noot's *Theatre [for] Voluptuous Worldlings*.
1569–76	At Cambridge as a "sizar" of Pembroke Hall; friendship with Gabriel Harvey. Earns a BA in 1573 and an MA in 1576.
ca. 1578	Secretary to John Young (formerly master of Pembroke), bishop of Rochester (in Kent).
1579	Marriage to Machabyas Chylde, mother of Sylvanus. Associated with Sir Philip Sidney and his circle; for a time may have been in the employ of Sidney's uncle, Robert Dudley, earl of Leicester. *The Shepheardes Calender* published.
1580	Publication of letters between Spenser and Harvey (two by Spenser). At work on *The Faerie Queene*. Appointed secretary to the lord deputy of Ireland, Lord Grey of Wilton, with whom he departs for Ireland in August.
1581	Awarded the post of clerk in chancery for faculties, a sinecure previously held by Lodowick Bryskett, clerk of the council in Munster; retains the post until 1588.
1582	Leases the property of New Abbey, in County Kildare; a commissioner of muster for the county in 1583 and 1584.
1584	Appointed deputy clerk of the Council of Munster.
ca. 1588	Occupies Kilcolman, an estate of some three thousand acres, situated between Limerick and Cork, in Munster.
1589	To England and the court of Queen Elizabeth with Sir Walter Raleigh (proprietor of Inchiquin, an estate of forty-two thousand acres thirty miles southeast of Kilcolman). *The Faerie Queene* I–III entered in the Stationers' Register, December.
1590	*The Faerie Queene* I–III published, with the *Letter to Raleigh* appended.
1591	The queen grants Spenser an annual pension of £50 for life. *Daphnaïda* and *Complaints* published. Returns to Ireland, probably in the spring.
1594	Marriage to Elizabeth Boyle, mother of Peregrine, probably in Youghal.
1595	*Colin Clouts Come Home Againe* and *Amoretti and Epithalamion* published.
1596	*The Faerie Queene* I–VI, *Fowre Hymnes*, and *Prothalamion* published. Probably in England to oversee the printing of at least the later books of *The Faerie Queene*.

1598 The prose tract *A Vewe of the present state of Irelande* (first published in 1633) entered in the Stationers' Register, April. Insurrection in northern and western Ireland spreads into Munster; Kilcolman sacked by the rebels. Spenser takes refuge in Cork, whence he carries letters from Sir Thomas Norris (lord president of Munster), to the Privy Council in London, arriving on December 24.

1599 Dies in Westminster on January 13 and is buried in Westminster Abbey.

1609 *The Faerie Queene* published, together with the *Cantos of Mutabilitie*.

The Texts of
THE POEMS

THE FAERIE QVEENE.

Diſpoſed into twelue bookes,

Faſhioning

XII. Morall vertues.

LONDON

Printed for VVilliam Ponſonbie.

1596.

TO
THE MOST HIGH,
MIGHTIE
And
MAGNIFICENT
EMPRESSE RENOVV-
MED FOR PIETIE, VER-
TVE, AND ALL GRATIOVS
GOVERNMENT ELIZABETH BY
THE GRACE OF GOD QVEENE
OF ENGLAND FRAVNCE AND
IRELAND AND OF VIRGI-
NIA, DEFENDOVR OF THE
FAITH, &c. HER MOST
HVMBLE SERVAVNT
EDMVND SPENSER
DOTH IN ALL HV-
MILITIE DEDI-
CATE, PRE-
SENT
AND CONSECRATE THESE
HIS LABOVRS TO LIVE
VVITH THE ETERNI-
TIE OF HER
FAME.

The First Booke of The Faerie Queene

Contayning
The Legende of the Knight of the Red Crosse,
or
Of Holinesse

1

Lo I the man, whose Muse whilome° did maske, — *formerly*
As time her taught, in lowly Shepheards weeds,[1]
Am now enforst a far unfitter taske.
For trumpets sterne to chaunge mine Oaten reeds,
And sing of Knights and Ladies gentle deeds;
Whose prayses having slept in silence long,
Me, all too meane, the sacred Muse areeds° — *counsels*
To blazon broad[2] emongst her learnéd throng:
Fierce warres and faithfull loves shall moralize my song.

2

Helpe then, O holy Virgin chiefe of nine,[3]
Thy weaker° Novice to performe thy will, — *too weak*
Lay forth out of thine everlasting scryne° — *chest for records*
The antique rolles, which there lye hidden still,
Of Faerie knights and fairest Tanaquill,[4]
Whom that most noble Briton Prince[5] so long
Sought through the world, and suffered so much ill,
That I must rue his undeservéd wrong:
O helpe thou my weake wit, and sharpen my dull tong.

3

And thou most dreaded impe[6] of highest Jove,
Faire Venus sonne, that with thy cruell dart
At that good knight so cunningly didst rove,° — *shoot*
That glorious fire it kindled in his hart,
Lay now thy deadly Heben° bow apart, — *ebony*
And with thy mother milde come to mine ayde:

1. Lines 1–4 imitate verses that Servius (fourth century B.C.E.) says Virgil's first editors removed from the start of the *Aeneid*; medieval and Renaissance manuscripts or editions often quote them. The lines announce a transition from pastoral to epic, although Spenser would have known that the transition included the *Georgics*; the name, like that of his own St. George, implies working with or deriving from the earth. Line 5 then paraphrases the start of Ariosto's *Orlando Furioso*.
2. I.e., to proclaim.
3. Perhaps Clio, muse of history (see I.xi.5 and III.iii.4), or perhaps Calliope, muse of eloquence and epic; perhaps a composite.
4. Gloriana, i.e., Elizabeth I. The humanist Vives (1492–1540) thought "Caia Tanaquill," whom legend called the wife of the Roman king Tarquinus Priscus, was the true pattern of a noble queen.
5. I.e., Arthur.
6. Child, i.e., Cupid, god of love.

Come both, and with you bring triumphant Mart,[7]
In loves and gentle jollíties arrayd,
After his murdrous spoiles and bloudy rage allayd.

4

And with them eke,° O Goddesse heavenly bright,[8] — *also*
Mirrour of grace and Majestie divine,
Great Lady of the greatest Isle, whose light
Like Phoebus lampe throughout the world doth shine,
Shed thy faire beames into my feeble eyne,
And raise my thoughts too humble and too vile,° — *lowly*
To thinke of that true glorious type° of thine, — *pattern*
The argument of mine afflicted° stile: — *humble*
The which to heare, vouchsafe, O dearest dred[9] a-while.

Canto I

The Patron of true Holinesse,
Foule Errour doth defeate:
Hypocrisie him to entrappe,
Doth to his home entreate.

1

A Gentle Knight was pricking° on the plaine, — *riding briskly*
Y cladd in mightie armes and silver shielde,[1]
Wherein old dints of deepe wounds did remaine,
The cruell markes of many a bloudy fielde;
Yet armes till that time did he never wield:
His angry steede did chide his foming bitt,
As much disdayning to the curbe to yield:
Full jolly° knight he seemd, and faire did sitt, — *gallant*
As one for knightly giusts° and fierce encounters fitt. — *tourneys*

2

But on his brest a bloudie Crosse he bore,
The deare remembrance of his dying Lord,
For whose sweete sake that glorious badge he wore,
And dead as living[2] ever him adored:
Upon his shield the like was also scored,
For soveraine hope, which in his helpe he had:
Right faithfull true he was in deede and word,
But of his cheere° did seeme too solemne sad;° — *countenance / grave*
Yet nothing did he dread, but ever was ydrad.° — *dreaded*

7. Mars, god of war, and Venus's lover.
8. I.e., Queen Elizabeth.
9. Object of reverence and awe.
1. Cf. Ephesians 6.11–7: "Put on the whole armour of God, that ye may be able to stand against the wiles of the devil. . . . Above all, taking the shield of faith, wherewith ye shall be able to quench all the fiery darts of the wicked." Redcrosse's armor is that of every Christian. On this scene, see Anderson this Norton Critical Edition.
2. Revelation 1.18: "I am he that liveth, and was dead; and, behold, I am alive for evermore."

3

Upon a great adventure he was bond,
That greatest Gloriana to him gave,
That greatest Glorious Queene of Faerie lond,
To winne him worship,° and her grace to have, *honor*
Which of all earthly things he most did crave;
And ever as he rode, his hart did earne° *yearn*
To prove his puissance in battell brave
Upon his foe, and his new force to learne;
Upon his foe, a Dragon[3] horrible and stearne.

4

A lovely Ladie[4] rode him faire beside,
Upon a lowly Asse more white then snow,
Yet she much whiter, but the same did hide
Under a vele, that wimpled° was full low, *folded*
And over all a blacke stole she did throw,
As one that inly mournd: so was she sad,
And heavie sat upon her palfrey slow;
Seeméd in heart some hidden care she had,
And by her in a line° a milke white lambe she lad.° *leash / led*

5

So pure an innocent, as that same lambe,
She was in life and every vertuous lore,
And by descent from Royall lynage came
Of ancient Kings and Queenes, that had of yore
Their scepters stretcht from East to Westerne shore,
And all the world in their subjection held;
Till that infernall feend with foule uprore
Forwasted all their land, and them expeld:
Whom to avenge, she had this Knight from far compeld.° *summoned*

6

Behind her farre away a Dwarfe[5] did lag,
That lasie seemd in being ever last,
Or wearied with bearing of her bag
Of needments at his backe. Thus as they past,
The day with cloudes was suddeine overcast,

3. Cf. Revelation 20.2: ". . . the dragon, that old serpent, which is the devil, and Satan. . . ."
4. The ass suggests humility (cf. Jesus's lowly mount in John 12.14 and Mathew 21.5) and that the lady has a lamb with her recalls not only Jesus's lamblike innocence (see John 1.29) but also, for Spenser's readers, the lamb often depicted accompanying the maiden whom St. George rescues from the dragon, particularly in illustrations of Voragine's *Legenda Aurea* or *Golden Legend*, scorned by sterner Protestants but still widely read.
5. The dwarf for many readers suggests common sense, practical understanding, reason, or whatever accoutrements and matters this lady's "needments" might include; he does not figure in the traditional St. George tales or dramas.

And angry Jove an hideous storme of raine
Did poure into his Lemans lap[6] so fast,
That every wight° to shrowd° it did constrain, *creature / cover*
And this faire couple eke to shroud themselves were
fain.° *eager*

7

Enforst to seeke some covert nigh at hand,
A shadie grove not far away they spide,
That promist ayde the tempest to withstand:
Whose loftie trees yclad with sommers pride,
Did spred so broad, that heavens light did hide,
Not perceable with power of any starre:
And all within were pathes and alleies wide,
With footing worne, and leading inward farre:
Faire harbour° that them seemes; so in they entred arre. *shelter*

8

And foorth they passe, with pleasure forward led,
Joying to heare the birdes sweete harmony,
Which therein shrouded from the tempest dred,
Seemd in their song to scorne the cruell sky.
Much can° they prayse the trees so straight and hy,[7] *did*
The sayling Pine, the Cedar proud and tall,
The vine-prop Elme, the Poplar never dry,
The builder Oake, sole king of forrests all,
The Aspine good for staves, the Cypresse funerall.

9

The Laurell, meed° of mightie Conquerours *reward*
And Poets sage, the Firre that weepeth still,
The Willow worne of forlorne Paramours,
The Eugh° obedient to the benders will, *yew*
The Birch for shaftes, the Sallow for the mill,
The Mirrhe sweete bleeding in the bitter wound,[8]
The warlike Beech, the Ash for nothing ill,
The fruitfull Olive, and the Platane° round, *plane-tree*
The carver Holme,° the Maple seeldom inward sound. *holly*

6. I.e., into the lap of his beloved, the earth.
7. Chaucer's *Parliament of Fowls* 176–82 is the immediate source for this catalog of trees; the convention has its roots in Ovid's *Metamorphoses* 10.90–105.
8. Sweet gum flows from the tree when its bark is cut; because of its association with Christ's birth and death (Matthew 2.11 and Mark 15.23; cf. the *OED*), myrrh recalls the trees in Paradise and the "tree" on which Christ was crucified. Ovid tells how Myrrha slept with her father and when turned into a tree, gave birth to Adonis through a rent in her bark (*Metamorphoses* 10.298–514).

10

Led with delight, they thus beguile the way,
Untill the blustring storme is overblowne;
When weening° to returne, whence they did stray, *expecting*
They cannot finde that path, which first was showne,
But wander too and fro in wayes unknowne,
Furthest from end then, when they neerest weene,
That makes them doubt, their wits be not their owne:
So many pathes, so many turnings seene,
That which of them to take, in diverse° doubt they been.[9] *distracting*

11

At last resolving forward still to fare,
Till that some end they finde or° in or out, *either*
That path they take, that beaten seemd most bare,
And like to lead the labyrinth about;° *out of*
Which when by tract° they hunted had throughout, *track*
At length it brought them to a hollow cave,
Amid the thickest woods. The Champion stout
Eftsoones° dismounted from his courser brave, *forthwith*
And to the Dwarfe a while his needlesse spere he gave.

12

"Be well aware," quoth then that Ladie milde,
"Least suddaine mischiefe ye too rash provoke:
The danger hid, the place unknowne and wilde,
Breedes dreadfull doubts: Oft fire is without smoke.
And perill without show: therefore your stroke
Sir knight with-hold, till further triall made."
"Ah Ladie," said he, "shame were to revoke
The forward footing for° an hidden shade: *because of*
Vertue gives her selfe light, through darkenesse for to wade."

13

"Yea but," quoth she, "the perill of this place
I better wot° then you, though now too late *know*
To wish you backe returne with foule disgrace,
Yet wisedome warnes, whilest foot is in the gate,
To stay the steppe, ere forcéd to retrate.
This is the wandring wood, this Errours den,
A monster vile, whom God and man does hate:
Therefore I read° beware." "Fly fly," quoth then *advise*
The fearefull Dwarfe: "this is no place for living men."

9. The labyrinth of forest paths suggests a world of multiplicity and matter. In Plato's *Timaeus* the Creation begins when the One makes the many.

14

But full of fire and greedy hardiment,° *boldness*
The youthfull knight could not for ought be staide,
But forth unto the darksome hole he went,
And lookéd in: his glistring armor made
A litle glooming light, much like a shade,
By which he saw the ugly monster plaine,
Halfe like a serpent horribly displaide,
But th'other halfe did womans shape retaine,[1]
Most lothsom, filthie, foule, and full of vile disdaine.

15

And as she lay upon the durtie ground,
Her huge long taile her den all overspred,
Yet was in knots and many boughtes° upwound, *coils*
Pointed with mortall sting. Of her there bred
A thousand yong ones, which she dayly fed,
Sucking upon her poisonous dugs, eachone
Of sundry shapes, yet all ill favoréd:
Soone as that uncouth° light upon them shone, *unaccustomed*
Into her mouth they crept, and suddain all were gone.

16

Their dam upstart, out of her den effraide,
And rushéd forth, hurling her hideous taile
About her curséd head, whose folds displaid
Were stretcht now forth at length without entraile.° *coiling*
She lookt about, and seeing one in mayle
Arméd to point,° sought backe to turne againe; *completely*
For light she hated as the deadly bale,° *injury*
Ay wont in desert darknesse to remaine,
Where plaine none might her see, nor she see any plaine.

17

Which when the valiant Elfe perceived, he lept
As Lyon fierce upon the flying pray,
And with his trenchand° blade her boldly kept *sharp*
From turning backe, and forcéd her to stay:
Therewith enraged she loudly gan to bray,° *cry out*
And turning fierce, her speckled taile advaunst,
Threatning her angry sting, him to dismay:
Who nought aghast, his mightie hand enhaunst:° *raised*
The stroke down from her head unto her shoulder glaunst.

1. In medieval and Renaissance depictions, Eden's serpent was sometimes given a female head, and the locusts in Revelation 9.7–10 have men's faces, scorpion tails, and "hair as the hair of women." Classical monsters, too, often have female elements: Error may recall in particular the snake goddess in Hesiod's *Theogony* 297–300.

18

Much daunted with that dint, her sence was dazd,
Yet kindling rage, her selfe she gathered round,
And all attonce her beastly body raizd
With doubled forces high above the ground:
Tho° wrapping up her wrethéd sterne arownd, *then*
Lept fierce upon his shield, and her huge traine° *tail*
All suddenly about his body wound,
That hand or foot to stirre he strove in vaine:
God helpe the man so wrapt in Errours endlesse traine.[2]

19

His Lady sad to see his sore constraint,
Cride out, "Now now Sir knight, shew what ye bee,
Add faith unto your force, and be not faint:
Strangle her, else she sure will strangle thee."
That when he heard, in great perplexitie,
His gall did grate[3] for griefe° and high disdaine, *anger*
And knitting all his force got one hand free,
Wherewith he grypt her gorge° with so great paine, *throat*
That soone to loose her wicked bands did her constraine.

20

Therewith she spewd out of her filthy maw
A floud of poyson horrible and blacke,
Full of great lumpes of flesh and gobbets raw,
Which stunck so vildly, that it forst him slacke
His grasping hold, and from her turne him backe:
Her vomit full of bookes and papers[4] was,
With loathly frogs and toades, which eyes did lacke,
And creeping sought way in the weedy gras:
Her filthy parbreake° all the place defiléd has.[5] *vomit*

21

As when old father Nilus gins to swell
With timely° pride above the Aegyptian vale, *seasonal*
His fattie° waves do fertile slime outwell, *rich*
And overflow each plaine and lowly dale:
But when his later spring gins to avale,° *subside*
Huge heapes of mudd he leaves, wherein there breed

2. Some readers hear a pun on "error" and "knight errant": Redcrosse has both wandered and erred, even if here immobilized. Compare Milton's fallen Adam and Eve as they leave Eden with "wand'ring steps."
3. I.e., his gall bladder (once considered the source of choleric passion) was violently disturbed.
4. I.e., Catholic propaganda directed against Elizabeth I and the established church; by extension, the often virulent literature of religious controversy.
5. Revelation 16.13: "I saw three unclean spirits like frogs come out of the mouth of the dragon, and out of the mouth of the beast, and out of the mouth of the false prophet." The margin of the 1560 Geneva translation identifies them as lying agents of the Pope.

Ten thousand kindes of creatures partly male
And partly female of his fruitfull seed;[6]
Such ugly monstrous shapes elswhere may no man reed.° *see*

22

The same so sore annoyéd has the knight,
That welnigh chokéd with the deadly stinke,
His forces faile, ne can no longer fight.
Whose corage when the feend perceived to shrinke,
She pouréd forth out of her hellish sinke
Her fruitfull curséd spawne of serpents small,
Deforméd monsters, fowle, and blacke as inke,
Which swarming all about his legs did crall,
And him encombred sore, but could not hurt at all.

23

As gentle Shepheard in sweete even-tide.
When ruddy Phoebus gins to welke° in west, *fade, sink*
High on an hill, his flocke to vewen wide,
Markes which do byte their hasty supper best;
A cloud of combrous gnattes do him molest,
All striving to infixe their feeble stings,
That from their noyance he no where can rest,
But with his clownish° hands their tender wings *rustic*
He brusheth oft, and oft doth mar their murmurings.

24

Thus ill bestedd,° and fearefull more of shame, *situated*
Then of the certaine perill he stood in,
Halfe furious unto his foe he came,
Resolved in minde all suddenly to win,
Or soone to lose, before he once would lin;° *cease*
And strooke at her with more then manly force,
That from her body full of filthie sin
He raft° her hatefull head without remorse; *cut away*
A streame of cole black bloud forth gushéd from her corse.

25

Her scattred brood, soone as their Parent deare
They saw so rudely falling to the ground,
Groning full deadly, all with troublous feare,
Gathred themselves about her body round,
Weening their wonted entrance to have found
At her wide mouth: but being there withstood

6. Ovid, *Metamorphoses* 1.416–37, is the likely source for Spenser's comments on spontaneous generation, although numerous classical writers refer to the fertility of Nile mud, e.g., Plutarch and Diodorus Siculus.

They flockéd all about her bleeding wound,
And suckéd up their dying mothers blood,
Making her death their life, and eke her hurt their good.

26

That detestable sight him much amazde,
To see th'unkindly Impes[7] of heaven accurst,
Devoure their dam; on whom while so he gazd,
Having all satisfide their bloudy thurst,
Their bellies swolne he saw with fulnesse burst,
And bowels gushing forth: well worthy end
Of such as drunke her life, the which them nurst;
Now needeth him no lenger labour spend,
His foes have slaine themselves, with whom he should contend.

27

His Ladie seeing all, that chaunst, from farre
Approcht in hast to greet his victorie,
And said, "Faire knight, borne under happy starre,
Who see your vanquisht foes before you lye:
Well worthy be you of that Armorie,° *armor*
Wherein ye have great glory wonne this day,
And prooved your strength on a strong enimie,
Your first adventure: many such I pray,
And henceforth ever wish, that like succeed it may."

28

Then mounted he upon his Steede againe,
And with the Lady backward sought to wend;° *turn, go*
That path he kept, which beaten was most plaine,
Ne ever would to any by-way bend,
But still did follow one unto the end,
The which at last out of the wood them brought.
So forward on his way (with God to frend)° *as a friend*
He passéd forth, and new adventure sought;
Long way he travelléd, before he heard of ought.

29

At length they chaunst to meet upon the way
An aged Sire, in long blacke weedes° yclad, *garments*
His feete all bare, his beard all hoarie gray,
And by his belt his booke he hanging had;
Sober he seemde, and very sagely sad,° *grave*
And to the ground his eyes were lowly bent,
Simple in shew, and voyde of malice bad,
And all the way he prayéd, as he went,
And often knockt his brest, as one that did repent.

7. Unnatural offspring.

30

He faire the knight saluted, louting° low, *bowing*
Who faire him quited,° as that courteous was: *responded in kind*
And after askéd him, if he did know
Of straunge adventures, which abroad did pas.
"Ah my deare Sonne," quoth he, "how should, alas,
Silly° old man, that lives in hidden cell, *simple*
Bidding° his beades all day for his trespas, *telling*
Tydings of warre and worldly trouble tell?
With holy father sits not with such things to mell.° *meddle*

31

"But if of daunger which hereby doth dwell,
And homebred evill ye desire to heare,
Of a straunge man I can you tidings tell,
That wasteth all this countrey farre and neare."
"Of such," said he, "I chiefly do inquere,
And shall you well reward to shew the place,
In which that wicked wight his dayes doth weare:° *spend*
For to all knighthood it is foule disgrace,
That such a curséd creature lives so long a space."

32

"Far hence," quoth he, "in wastfull° wildernesse *desolate*
His dwelling is, by which no living wight
May ever passe, but thorough great distresse."
"Now," sayd the Lady, "draweth toward night,
And well I wote,° that of your later° fight *know / recent*
Ye all forwearied be: for what so strong,
But wanting rest will also want of might?
The Sunne that measures heaven all day long,
At night doth baite° his steedes the Ocean waves emong. *refresh*

33

"Then with the Sunne take Sir, your timely rest,
And with new day new worke at once begin:
Untroubled night they say gives counsell best."
"Right well Sir knight ye have adviséd bin,"
Quoth then that aged man; "the way to win
Is wisely to advise: now day is spent;
Therefore with me ye may take up your In° *lodging*
For this same night." The knight was well content:
So with that godly father to his home they went.

34

A little lowly Hermitage it was,
Downe in a dale, hard by a forests side,
Far from resort of people, that did pas

In travell to and froe: a little wyde° *apart*
There was an holy Chappell edifyde,° *built*
Wherein the Hermite dewly wont° to say *was accustomed*
His holy things each morne and eventyde:
Thereby a Christall streame did gently play,
Which from a sacred fountaine welléd forth alway.

35

Arrivéd there, the little house they fill,
Ne looke for entertainement, where none was:
Rest is their feast, and all things at their will;
The noblest mind the best contentment has.
With faire discourse the evening so they pas:
For that old man of pleasing wordes had store,
And well could file his tongue as smooth as glas;
He told of Saintes and Popes, and evermore
He strowd° an Ave-Mary[8] after and before. *scattered*

36

The drouping Night thus creepeth on them fast,
And the sad humour loading their eye liddes,
As messenger of Morpheus on them cast
Sweet slombring deaw,[9] the which to sleepe them biddes.
Unto their lodgings then his guestes he riddes° *conducts*
Where when all drownd in deadly° sleepe he findes, *deathlike*
He to his study goes, and there amiddes
His Magick bookes and arts of sundry kindes,
He seekes out mighty charmes, to trouble sleepy mindes.

37

Then choosing out few wordes most horrible,
(Let none them read) thereof did verses frame,
With which and other spelles like terrible,
He bad awake blacke Plutoes griesly Dame,[1]
And curséd heaven, and spake reprochfull shame
Of highest God, the Lord of life and light;
A bold bad man, that dared to call by name
Great Gorgon,[2] Prince of darknesse and dead night,
At which Cocytus quakes, and Styx[3] is put to flight.

8. I.e., a "Hail Mary"; it is now clear that the "beades" of stanza 30 are a rosary.
9. I.e., Night draws close to them as the cold and wet humor (i.e., in older medical theory "phlegm") weighs down their eyelids, and, like a messenger from Morpheus (god of sleep), throws sweet soporific dew on them.
1. I.e., Proserpine.
2. I.e., Demogorgon, who "the hideous Chaos keepes" (IV.ii.47). Spenser's conception of this figure as a mysterious and terrible prince of darkness is probably based on passages in Boccaccio's *De Genealogia Deorum Gentilium* (Venice, 1472; Basel, 1532), one of two such works on which Spenser regularly depends; the other is Natalis Comes's *Mythologiae* (Venice, 1551).
3. Styx, Cocytus, Acheron, Phlegethon, and Lethe are the rivers of Hades. The flies in stanza 38 suggest Beëlzebub, "Lord of the Flies."

38

And forth he cald out of deepe darknesse dred
Legions of Sprights, the which like little flyes
Fluttring about his ever damnéd hed,
A-waite whereto their service he applyes.
To aide his friends, or fray° his enimies: *frighten*
Of those he chose out two, the falsest twoo,
And fittest for to forge true-seeming lyes;
The one of them he gave a message too,
The other by him selfe staide other worke to doo.

39

He making speedy way through sperséd° ayre, *dispersed*
And through the world of waters wide and deepe,
To Morpheus house[4] doth hastily repaire.
Amid the bowels of the earth full steepe,
And low, where dawning day doth never peepe,
His dwelling is; there Tethys[5] his wet bed
Doth ever wash, and Cynthia[6] still doth steepe
In silver deaw his ever-drouping hed,
Whiles sad Night over him her mantle black doth spred.

40

Whose double gates he findeth lockéd fast,
The one faire framed of burnisht Yvory,[7]
The other all with silver overcast;
And wakefull dogges before them farre do lye,
Watching to banish Care their enimy,
Who oft is wont to trouble gentle Sleepe.
By them the Sprite doth passe in quietly,
And unto Morpheus comes, whom drownéd deepe
In drowsie fit he findes: of nothing he takes keepe.° *notice*

41

And more, to lulle him in his slumber soft,
A trickling streame from high rocke tumbling downe
And ever-drizling raine upon the loft,
Mixt with a murmuring winde, much like the sowne° *sound*
Of swarming Bees, did cast him in a swowne.° *swoon*
No other noyse, nor peoples troublous cryes,
As still are wont t'annoy the walléd towne,
Might there be heard: but carelesse Quiet lyes,
Wrapt in eternall silence farre from enemyes.

4. Spenser's primary source for this episode is *Metamorphoses* 11.592–632.
5. The wife of Ocean, in classical tradition; here the ocean.
6. Goddess of the moon and, as the Letter to Raleigh makes clear, often a representation of Elizabeth.
7. Homer (*Odyssey* 19.562–67) and Virgil (*Aeneid* 6.893–96) refer to the twin portals of Sleep: truthful dreams pass through the gate of horn, false dreams through that of ivory.

42

The messenger approching to him spake,
 But his wast° wordes returnd to him in vaine: *wasted*
 So sound he slept, that nought mought him awake.
 Then rudely he him thrust, and pusht with paine,
 Whereat he gan to stretch: but he againe
 Shooke him so hard, that forcéd him to speake.
 As one then in a dreame, whose dryer braine[8]
 Is tost with troubled sights and fancies weake,
He mumbled soft, but would not all his silence breake.

43

The Sprite then gan more boldly him to wake,
 And threatned unto him the dreaded name
 Of Hecate.[9] whereat he gan to quake,
 And lifting up his lumpish° head, with blame *heavy*
 Halfe angry askéd him, for what he came.
 "Hither," quoth he, "me Archimago[1] sent,
 He that the stubborne Sprites can wisely tame,
 He bids thee to him send for his intent° *purpose*
A fit false dreame, that can delude the sleepers sent."° *senses*

44

The God obayde, and calling forth straight way
 A diverse° dreame out of his prison darke, *distracting*
 Delivered it to him, and downe did lay
 His heavie head, devoide of carefull carke,° *concerns*
 Whose sences all were straight benumbd and starke.° *rigid*
 He backe returning by the Yvorie dore,
 Remounted up as light as chearefull Larke,
 And on his litle winges the dreame he bore
In hast unto his Lord, where he him left afore.

45

Who all this while with charmes and hidden artes,
 Had made a Lady of that other Spright,
 And framed of liquid ayre her tender partes
 So lively,° and so like in all mens sight, *lifelike*

8. I.e., whose brain has become dry and hence filled with too much dried black bile, both the product and cause of too many images and "fancies."
9. Patroness of witchcraft and crossroads.
1. As this canto's "Argument" indicates, Archimago signifies hypocrisy, including what many feared was Catholics' willingness to lie about their loyalities. The name puns on two Reformation claims: as "arch-magus," Archimago embodies the deluding power of magic (Protestants said Catholic beliefs about the Mass confused religion and magic), and as "arch-image" he represents, in the Protestant view, an idolatrous worship of saints and images. The evil magician in hermit's disguise is found in medieval romance, but Archimago recalls the disguised hermit in Ariosto's *Orlando Furioso* 2.12–13 and the enchanter Malagigi in Tasso's *Rinaldo* 1.31.

That weaker° sence it could have ravisht quight:[2] *too weak*
The maker selfe for all his wondrous witt,
Was nigh beguiléd with so goodly sight:
Her all in white he clad, and over it
Cast a blacke stole, most like to seeme for Una fit.[3]

46

Now when that ydle° dreame was to him brought, *unsubstantial*
Unto that Elfin knight he bad him fly,
Where he slept soundly void of evill thought,
And with false shewes abuse his fantasy,° *imagination*
In sort as he him schooléd privily:
And that new creature borne without her dew,
Full of the makers guile, with usage sly
He taught to imitate that Lady trew,
Whose semblance she did carrie under feignéd hew.° *form*

47

Thus well instructed, to their worke they hast,
And comming where the knight in slomber lay,
The one upon his hardy head him plast,
And made him dreame of loves and lustfull play,
That nigh his manly hart did melt away,
Bathéd in wanton blis and wicked joy:
Then seeméd him his Lady by him lay,
And to him playnd,° how that false wingéd boy *complained*
Her chast hart had subdewd, to learne Dame pleasures toy.

48

And she her selfe of beautie soveraigne Queene,
Faire Venus seemde unto his bed to bring
Her, whom he waking evermore did weene
To be the chastest flowre, that ay° did spring *ever*
On earthly braunch, the daughter of a king,
Now a loose Leman° to vile service bound: *paramour*
And eke the Graces[4] seeméd all to sing,
Hymen iô Hymen, dauncing all around,
Whilst freshest Flora her with Yvie[5] girlond crownd.

2. The creation of such figures by evil enchanters is a regular feature of medieval romance: Archimago's "new creature" is "borne without her dew," i.e., unnaturally. Cf. Apollo's creation (*Iliad* 5.449–50) of a phantom resembling Aeneas, or the fashioning by Juno (*Aeneid* 10.637–44) of a shadowy Aeneas, "like dreams that befool the sleeping senses."
3. Finally, Una is identified by name, one signifying "One" and presumably all or much that implies, whether the one truth, the one true church, or unity itself in a world of the many.
4. The Graces are Aglaia, Thalia, and Euphrosyne, who collectively personify grace and beauty. Cf. VI.x.21–24.
5. The plant of Bacchus, god of wine. *Flora*: goddess of flowers and springtime. Cf. E.K.'s Glosse to "March": "the Goddesse of flowres, but indede (as saith Tacitus) a famous harlot, which with the abuse of her body having gotten great riches, made the people of Rome her heyre. . . ."

49

In this great passion of unwonted° lust, *unaccustomed*
Or wonted feare of doing ought amis,
He started up, as seeming to mistrust
Some secret ill, or hidden foe of his:
Lo there before his face his Lady is,
Under blake stole hyding her bayted hooke,
And as halfe blushing offred him to kis,
With gentle blandishment and lovely looke,
Most like that virgin true, which for her knight him took.

50

All cleane dismayd to see so uncouth° sight, *unseemly*
And halfe enragéd at her shameless guise,
He thought have slaine her in his fierce despight:° *indignation*
But hasty heat tempring with sufferance wise,
He stayde his hand, and gan himselfe advise
To prove his sense, and tempt her faignéd truth.
Wringing her hands in wemens pitteous wise,
Tho can° she weepe, to stirre up gentle ruth,° *did / pity*
Both for her noble bloud, and for her tender youth.

51

And said, "Ah Sir, my liege Lord and my love,
Shall I accuse the hidden cruell fate,
And mightie causes wrought in heaven above,
Or the blind God, that doth me thus amate,° *dismay*
For° hopéd love to winne me certaine hate? *instead of*
Yet thus perforce he bids me do, or die.
Die is my dew: yet rew my wretched state
You, whom my hard avenging destinie
Hath made judge of my life or death indifferently.[6]

52

"Your owne deare sake forst me at first to leave
My Fathers kingdome," There she stopt with teares;
Her swollen hart her speach seemd to bereave,
And then againe begun, "My weaker yeares
Captived to fortune and frayle worldly feares,
Fly to your faith for succour and sure ayde:
Let me not dye in languor and long teares."
"Why Dame," quoth he, "what hath ye thus dismayd?
What frayes° ye, that were wont to comfort me affrayd?" *frightens*

6. Spenser's readers would have noted the parody of the Petrarchan clichés then becoming even more popular in England.

53

"Love of your self," she said, "and deare° constraint *dire*
Lets me not sleepe, but wast the wearie night
In secret anguish and unpittied plaint,
Whiles you in carelesse sleepe are drownéd quight."
Her doubtfull° words made that redoubted knight *questionable*
Suspect her truth: yet since no'untruth he knew,
Her fawning love with foule disdainefull spight
He would not shend,° but said, "Deare dame I rew, *reprove*
That for my sake unknowne such griefe unto you grew.

54

"Assure your selfe, it fell not all to ground;
For all so deare as life is to my hart,
I deeme your love, and hold me to you bound;
Ne let vaine feares procure your needlesse smart,
Where cause is none, but to your rest depart."
Not all content, yet seemd she to appease° *cease*
Her mournefull plaintes, beguiléd of her art,
And fed with words, that could not chuse but please,
So slyding softly forth, she turnd as to her ease.

55

Long after lay he musing at her mood,
Much grieved to thinke that gentle Dame so light,° *frivolous*
For whose defence he was to shed his blood.
At last dull wearinesse of former fight
Having yrockt a sleepe his irkesome spright,° *mind, spirit*
That troublous dreame gan freshly tosse his braine,
With bowres, and beds, and Ladies deare delight:
But when he[7] saw his labour all was vaine,
With that misforméd spright he backe returnd againe.

Canto II

The guilefull great Enchaunter parts
The Redcrosse Knight from Truth:
Into whose stead faire falshood steps,
And workes him wofull ruth.° *harm*

1

By this the Northerne wagoner had set
His sevenfold teme behind the stedfast starre,[1]

7. I.e., the dream.
1. I.e., the constellation Boötes ("the ox-driver") has "set" the seven stars of "the Plough" (Ursa Major) behind the unmoving North Star. Since Ursa Major never "sets," this placement may suggest that Arcturus, chief star in Boötes, has risen and hitched his plow to the North Star to start work. If so, and with dawn near, the time would be early fall. Some linked Arcturus to Arthur, while as a plowman Boötes recalls the name "George" (in Greek, "earth-tiller"). Boötes is steadfast in plowing (cf. Luke 9.62), but Job 4.8 warns not to "plow iniquity and sow wickedness."

That was in Ocean waves yet never wet,
But firme is fixt, and sendeth light from farre
To all, that in the wide deepe wandring arre:
And cheerefull Chaunticlere with his note shrill
Had warnéd once, that Phoebus fiery carre[2]
In hast was climbing up the Easterne hill,
Full envious that night so long his roome did fill.

2

When those accurséd messengers of hell,
That feigning dreame, and that faire-forgéd Spright
Came to their wicked maister, and gan tell
Their bootelesse° paines, and ill succeeding night: *useless*
Who all in rage to see his skilfull might
Deluded so, gan threaten hellish paine
And sad Prosérpines wrath, them to affright.
But when he saw his threatning was but vaine,
He cast about, and searcht his balefull° bookes againe. *deadly*

3

Eftsoones he tooke that miscreated faire,
And that false other Spright, on whom he spred
A seeming body of the subtile aire,
Like a young Squire, in loves and lusty-hed
His wanton dayes that ever loosely led,
Without regard of armes and dreaded fight:
Those two he tooke, and in a secret bed,
Covered with darknesse and misdeeming° night, *misleading*
Them both together laid, to joy in vaine delight.

4

Forthwith he runnes with feignéd faithfull hast
Unto his guest, who after troublous sights
And dreames, gan now to take more sound repast,° *repose*
Whom suddenly he wakes with fearefull frights,
As one aghast with feends or damnéd sprights,
And to him cals, "Rise rise unhappy Swaine,
That here wex° old in sleepe, whiles wicked wights *grows*
Have knit themselves in Venus shamefull chaine;
Come see, where your false Lady doth her honour staine."

5

All in amaze he suddenly up start
With sword in hand, and with the old man went;
Who soone him brought into a secret part,
Where that false couple were full closely ment° *joined*
In wanton lust and lewd embracément:

2. The chariot of the sun. *Chaunticlere*: Chanticleer, the generic name for a rooster.

Which when he saw, he burnt with gealous fire,
The eye of reason was with rage yblent,° *blinded*
And would have slaine them in his furious ire,
But hardly° was restreinéd of that aged sire. *with difficulty*

6

Returning to his bed in torment great,
And bitter anguish of his guiltie sight,
He could not rest, but did his stout heart eat,
And wast his inward gall with deepe despight,
Yrkesome° of life, and too long lingring night. *tired*
At last faire Hesperus[3] in highest skie
Had spent his lampe, and brought forth dawning light,
Then up he rose, and clad him hastily;
The Dwarfe him brought his steed: so both away do fly.[4]

7

Now when the rosy-fingred Morning faire,
Weary of aged Tithones[5] saffron bed,
Had spred her purple robe through deawy aire,
And the high hils Titan[6] discoveréd,
The royall virgin shooke off drowsy-hed,
And rising forth out of her baser° bowre, *humble*
Lookt for her knight, who far away was fled,
And for her Dwarfe, that wont to wait each houre;
Then gan she waile and weepe, to see that woefull stowre.° *plight*

8

And after him she rode with so much speede
As her slow beast could make; but all in vaine:
For him so far had borne his light-foot steede,
Prickéd with wrath and fiery fierce disdaine,
That him to follow was but fruitlesse paine;
Yet she her weary limbes would never rest,
But every hill and dale, each wood and plaine
Did search, sore grievéd in her gentle brest,
He so ungently left her, whom she lovéd best.

9

But subtill Archimago, when his guests
He saw divided into double parts,
And Una wandring in woods and forrests,

3. The evening star (the planet Venus); in this context a herald of the morning.
4. Spenser's readers with a taste for numerology would have noted that the duplicitous Archimago divides Una from Redcrosse in Canto ii. As a slanderous "diabolos" figure he has in effect a forked tongue.
5. Husband of Aurora, goddess of the dawn.
6. The sun.

Th'end of his drift,° he praisd his divelish arts, *plot*
That had such might over true meaning harts;
Yet rests not so, but other meanes doth make,
How he may worke unto her further smarts:
For her he hated as the hissing snake,
And in her many troubles did most pleasure take.

10

He then devisde himselfe how to disguise;
For by his mightie science° he could take *knowledge*
As many formes and shapes in seeming wise,° *in appearance*
As ever Proteus[7] to himselfe could make:
Sometime a fowle, sometime a fish in lake,
Now like a foxe, now like a dragon fell,° *cruel*
That of himselfe he oft for feare would quake,
And oft would flie away. O who can tell
The hidden power of herbes, and might of Magicke spell?

11

But now seemde best, the person to put on
Of that good knight, his late beguiléd guest:
In mighty armes he was yclad anon,
And silver shield: upon his coward brest
A bloudy crosse, and on his craven crest
A bounch of haires discolourd° diversly: *dyed*
Full jolly knight he seemde, and well addrest,
And when he sate upon his courser free,° *noble*
Saint George himself ye would have deeméd him to be.

12

But he the knight, whose semblaunt° he did beare, *likeness*
The true Saint George was wandred far away,
Still flying from his thoughts and gealous feare;
Will was his guide, and griefe led him astray.
At last him chaunst to meete upon the way
A faithlesse Sarazin° all armed to point, *Saracen*
In whose great shield was writ with letters gay
Sans foy:[8] large of limbe and every joint
He was, and caréd not for God or man a point.

13

He had a faire companion of his way,
A goodly Lady clad in scarlot red,[9]

7. A sea god who could change himself into many shapes, including those of water and fire (cf. *Odyssey* 4.398–424).
8. "Faithlessness," or false faith.
9. The lady recalls the "purple clothed woman on the seven hills" of Revelation 17.4, "arrayed in purple and scarlet colour, and decked with gold and precious stones and pearls, having a

Purfled° with gold and pearle of rich assay, *decorated*
And like a Persian mitre on her hed
She wore, with crownes and owches° garnishéd, *brooches*
The which her lavish lovers to her gave;
Her wanton palfrey all was overspred
With tinsell trappings, woven like a wave,
Whose bridle rung with golden bels and bosses° brave. *studs*

14

With faire disport° and courting dalliaunce *diversion*
She intertainde her lover all the way:
But when she saw the knight his speare advaunce,
She soone left off her mirth and wanton play,
And bad her knight addresse him to the fray:
His foe was nigh at hand. He prickt with pride
And hope to winne his Ladies heart that day,
Forth spurréd fast: adowne his coursers side
The red bloud trickling staind the way, as he did ride.

15

The knight of the Redcrosse when him he spide,
Spurring so hote with rage dispiteous,° *unpitying*
Gan fairely couch° his speare, and towards ride: *lower*
Soone meete they both, both fell and furious,
That daunted with their forces hideous,
Their steeds do stagger, and amazéd stand,
And eke themselves too rudely rigorous,
Astonied° with the stroke of their owne hand, *stunned*
Do backe rebut,° and each to other yeeldeth land. *recoil*

16

As when two rams stird with ambitious pride,
Fight for the rule of the rich fleecéd flocke,
Their hornéd fronts so fierce on either side
Do meete, that with the terrour of the shocke
Astonied both, stand sencelesse as a blocke,
Forgetfull of the hanging victory:
So stood these twaine, unmovéd as a rocke,
Both staring fierce, and holding idely
The broken reliques of their former cruelty.

17

The Sarazin sore daunted with the buffe
Snatcheth his sword, and fiercely to him flies;
Who well it wards, and quyteth° cuff with cuff: *returns*

---

golden cup in her hand full of abominations and filthiness of her fornication." Protestants often equated her with papal Rome. That her "mitre" is Persian shows again the occasional merging of Roman Catholicism with ancient "oriental" wealth and early modern Islamic power (Robinson 2007 has relevant images).

Each others equall puissaunce envies,
And through their iron sides with cruell spies° *glances*
Does seeke to perce: repining° courage yields *angry*
No foote to foe. The flashing fier flies
As from a forge out of their burning shields,
And streames of purple bloud new dies the verdant fields.

18

"Curse on that Crosse," quoth then the Sarazin,
"That keepes thy body from the bitter fit;[1]
Dead long ygoe I wote thou haddest bin,
Had not that charme from thee forwarnéd° it: *guarded*
But yet I warne thee now assuréd sitt,
And hide thy head." Therewith upon his crest
With rigour so outrageous he smitt,
That a large share° it hewd out of the rest, *piece*
And glauncing downe his shield, from blame° *harm*
him fairely blest.° *preserved*

19

Who thereat wondrous wroth, the sleeping spark
Of native vertue° gan eftsoones revive, *power*
And at his haughtie helmet making mark,
So hugely stroke, that it the steele did rive,
And cleft his head. He tumbling downe alive,
With bloudy mouth his mother earth did kis,
Greeting his grave: his grudging° ghost did strive *complaining*
With the fraile flesh: at last it flitted is,
Whither the soules do fly of men, that live amis.

20

The Lady when she saw her champion fall,
Like the old ruines of a broken towre,
Staid not to waile his woefull funerall,
But from him fled away with all her powre;
Who after her as hastily gan scowre,° *run*
Bidding the Dwarfe with him to bring away
The Sarazins shield, signe of the conqueroure.
Her soone he overtooke, and bad to stay,
For present cause was none of dread her to dismay.

21

She turning backe with ruefull countenaunce,
Cride, "Mercy mercy Sir vouchsafe to show
On silly° Dame, subject to hard mischaunce, *innocent*
And to your mighty will." Her humblesse low

1. I.e., the throes of death. The scene may raise the issue of how a sign relates to the thing signified.

In so ritch weedes and seeming glorious show,
Did much emmove his stout heroicke heart,
And said, "Deare dame, your suddein overthrow
Much rueth° me; but now put feare apart, *grieves*
And tell, both who ye be, and who that tooke your part."

22

Melting in teares, then gan she thus lament;
"The wretched woman, whom unhappy howre
Hath now made thrall to your commandément,
Before that angry heavens list to lowre,° *frown*
And fortune false betraide me to your powre,
Was (O what now availeth that I was!)
Borne the sole daughter of an Emperour,
He that the wide West under his rule has,
And high hath set his throne, where Tiberis[2] doth pas.

23

"He in the first flowre of my freshest age,
Betrothéd me unto the onely haire° *heir*
Of a most mighty king, most rich and sage;
Was never Prince so faithfull and so faire,
Was never Prince so meeke and debonaire;° *gracious*
But ere my hopéd day of spousall shone,
My dearest Lord fell from high honours staire,
Into the hands of his accurséd fone,° *foes*
And cruelly was slaine, that shall I ever mone.

24

"His blesséd body spoild of lively breath,[3]
Was afterward, I know not how, convaid° *removed*
And fro me hid: of whose most innocent death
When tidings came to me unhappy maid,
O how great sorrow my sad soule assaid.° *afflicted*
Then forth I went his woefull corse to find,
And many yeares throughout the world I straid,
A virgin widow, whose deepe wounded mind
With love, long time did languish as the striken hind.

25

"At last it chauncéd this proud Sarazin
To meete me wandring, who perforce me led
With him away, but yet could never win
The Fort, that Ladies hold in soveraigne dread.
There lies he now with foule dishonour dead,

2. The river Tiber, in Rome. The claim to rule "the wide West" contrasts with that of Una's parents, whose "scepters stretcht from East to Westerne shore" (I.i.5).
3. I.e., bereft of the breath of life. The emphasis on death and loss associates Rome with Christ's dead body. Cf. John 20.2.

Wretched man, wretched tree; whose nature weake,
A cruell witch her curséd will to wreake,
Hath thus transformd, and plast in open plaines,
Where Boreas[1] doth blow full bitter bleake,
And scorching Sunne does dry my secret vaines:
For though a tree I seeme, yet cold and heat me pains."

34

"Say on Fradubio then, or° man, or tree," *whether*
Quoth then the knight, "by whose mischievous arts
Art thou misshapéd thus, as now I see?
He oft finds med'cine, who his griefe imparts;° *makes known*
But double griefs afflict concealing harts,
As raging flames who striveth to suppresse."
"The author then," said he, "of all my smarts,
Is one Duessa[2] a false sorceresse,
That many errant° knights hath brought to wretchednesse. *wandering*

35

"In prime of youthly yeares, when corage hot
The fire of love and joy of chevalree
First kindled in my brest, it was my lot
To love this gentle Lady, whom ye see,
Now not a Lady, but a seeming tree;
With whom as once I rode accompanyde,
Me chauncéd of a knight encountred bee,
That had a like° faire Lady by his syde, *similarly*
Like a faire Lady, but did fowle Duessa hyde.

36

"Whose forgéd beauty he did take in hand,[3]
All other Dames to have exceeded farre;
I in defence of mine did likewise stand,
Mine, that did then shine as the Morning starre:
So both to battell fierce arraungéd arre,
In which his harder° fortune was to fall *too hard*
Under my speare: such is the dye° of warre: *hazard*
His Lady left as a prise martiall,° *spoil of battle*
Did yield her comely person, to be at my call.

37

"So doubly loved of Ladies unlike faire,
Th'one seeming such, the other such indeede,
One day in doubt I cast° for to compare, *resolved*
Whether° in beauties glorie did exceede; *which one*

1. The north wind.
2. I.e., of double essence; two-faced.
3. I.e., he maintained.

A Rosy girlond was the victors meede.° *reward*
Both seemde to win, and both seemde won to bee,
So hard the discord was to be agreede.
Fraelissa° was as faire, as faire mote bee, *Frailty*
And ever false Duessa seemde as faire as shee.

38

"The wicked witch now seeing all this while
The doubtfull ballaunce equally to sway,
What not by right, she cast to win by guile,
And by her hellish science raisd straight way
A foggy mist, that overcast the day,
And a dull blast, that breathing on her face,
Dimméd her former beauties shining ray,
And with foule ugly forme did her disgrace:° *disfigure*
Then was she faire alone, when none was faire in place.[4]

39

"Then cride she out, 'Fye, fye, deforméd wight,
Whose borrowed beautie now appeareth plaine
To have before bewitchéd all mens sight;
O leave her soone, or let her soone be slaine.'
Her loathly visage viewing with disdaine,
Eftsoones I thought her such, as she me told,
And would have kild her; but with faignéd paine,
The false witch did my wrathfull hand withhold;
So left her, where she now is turnd to treén mould.[5]

40

"Thens forth I tooke Duessa for my Dame,
And in the witch unweeting° joyd long time, *unwittingly*
Ne ever wist, but that she was the same,
Till on a day (that day is every Prime,° *spring*
When Witches wont do penance for their crime)
I chaunst to see her in her proper hew,° *shape*
Bathing her selfe in origane and thyme.[6]
A filthy foule old woman I did vew,
That ever to have toucht her, I did deadly rew.

41

"Her neather partes misshapen, monstruous,
Were hidd in water, that I could not see,
But they did seeme more foule and hideous,
Then womans shape man would beleeve to bee.

4. I.e., when none present was fair; or, perhaps, when none present was fair in place of her.
5. Form of a tree.
6. Herbs valued for their powers of healing skin disorders (such as Duessa's, described in I.viii.47).

12

Full fast she fled, ne ever lookt behynd,
As if her life upon the wager lay,[4]
And home she came, whereas her mother blynd
Sate in eternall night: nought could she say,
But suddaine catching hold, did her dismay
With quaking hands, and other signes of feare:
Who full of ghastly fright and cold affray,° *terror*
Gan shut the dore. By this arrivéd there
Dame Una, wearie Dame, and entrance did requere.° *request*

13

Which when none yeelded, her unruly Page
With his rude clawes the wicket open rent,
And let her in; where of his cruell rage
Nigh dead with feare, and faint astonishment,[5]
She found them both in darkesome corner pent;
Where that old woman day and night did pray
Upon her beades devoutly penitent;
Nine hundred *Pater nosters* every day,
And thrise nine hundred *Aves* she was wont to say.[6]

14

And to augment her painefull pennance more,
Thrise every weeke in ashes she did sit,
And next her wrinkled skin rough sackcloth wore,
And thrise three times did fast from any bit:° *bite (of food)*
But now for feare her beads she did forget.
Whose needlesse dread for to remove away,
Faire Una framéd words and count'nance fit:
Which hardly° doen, at length she gan them pray, *with difficulty*
That in their cotage small, that night she rest her may.

15

The day is spent, and commeth drowsie night,
When every creature shrowdéd is in sleepe;
Sad Una downe her laies in wearie plight,
And at her feet the Lyon watch doth keepe:
In stead of rest, she does lament, and weepe
For the late losse of her deare lovéd knight,
And sighes, and grones, and evermore does steepe

4. I.e., as if her life were at stake.
5. I.e., amazed and terrified (at the sight of the lion, Una's "Page") to the point of fainting away.
6. The "Pater Noster" is the Lord's Prayer and the "Ave" is the "Hail Mary," the Latin and the large numbers suggesting what Protestants mocked as a Catholic tradition of offering merely rote prayers, although the Lord's Prayer retains a place in most Christian practice. Protestants rejected the "Ave Maria" because it was offered to the Virgin and not directly to God, although Mary herself, revered as the mother of Jesus, continues to figure in Protestant worship and literature.

Her tender brest in bitter teares all night,
All night she thinks too long, and often lookes for light.

16

Now when Aldeboran was mounted hie
Above the shynie Cassiopeias chaire,[7]
And all in deadly sleepe did drownéd lie,
One knockéd at the dore, and in would fare;
He knockéd fast, and often curst, and sware,
That readie entrance was not at his call:
For on his backe a heavy load he bare
Of nightly stelths and pillage severall,° *of various kinds*
Which he had got abroad by purchase° criminall. *acquisition*

17

He was to weete[8] a stout and sturdie thiefe,
Wont to robbe Churches of their ornaments,
And poore mens boxes° of their due reliefe, *almsboxes*
Which given was to them for good intents;
The holy Saints of their rich vestiments
He did disrobe, when all men carelesse slept,
And spoild the Priests of their habiliments,° *vestments*
Whiles none the holy things in safety kept;
Then he by cunning sleights in at the window crept.

18

And all that he by right or wrong could find,
Unto this house he brought, and did bestow
Upon the daughter of this woman blind,
Abessa daughter of Corceca slow,[9]
With whom he whoredome usd, that few did know,
And fed her fat with feast of offerings,
And plentie, which in all the land did grow;
Ne sparéd he to give her gold and rings:
And now he to her brought part of his stolen things.

19

Thus long the dore with rage and threats he bet,° *beat*
Yet of those fearefull women none durst rize,
The Lyon frayéd° them, him in to let: *frightened*

7. Aldebaran is a star in Taurus. If the time is well after midnight, the season would be autumn. Cassiopeia, Andromeda's mother, boasted of her daughter's beauty, thus offending the Nereids; the gods ordained that Andromeda should be sacrificed to a sea monster (she was saved by Perseus). When Cassiopeia stirred up trouble anew, Poseidon placed her among the stars.
8. In fact.
9. Abessa's name (from *abesse*, "to be absent, to lack being") suggests the Augustinian view of evil as ontological deprivation. "Abessa" connotes "abbess." Filled with superstitious dread, Corceca ("blindness of heart") recalls Ephesians 4.17–18: "Walk not as other Gentiles walk, in the vanity of their mind, Having the understanding darkened, being alienated from the life of God through the ignorance that is in them, because of the blindness of their heart." Kirkrapine ("church-robber") gives Abessa the plunder that her absence permits him to seize.

He would no longer stay him to advize,° *consider*
But open breakes the dore in furious wize,
And entring is; when that disdainfull beast
Encountring fierce, him suddaine doth surprize,
And seizing cruell clawes on trembling brest,
Under his Lordly foot him proudly hath supprest.

20

Him booteth not resist,[1] nor succour call,
His bleeding hart is in the vengers° hand, *avenger's*
Who streight him rent in thousand peeces small,
And quite dismembred hath: the thirstie land
Drunke up his life; his corse left on the strand.° *ground*
His fearefull friends weare out the wofull night,
Ne dare to weepe, nor seeme to understand
The heavie hap,° which on them is alight,° *lot / fallen*
Affraid, least to themselves the like mishappen might.

21

Now when broad day the world discovered° has, *revealed*
Up Una rose, up rose the Lyon eke,
And on their former journey forward pas,
In wayes unknowne, her wandring knight to seeke,
With paines farre passing that long wandring Greeke,
That for his love refuséd deitie;[2]
Such were the labours of this Lady meeke,
Still seeking him, that from her still did flie,
Then furthest from her hope, when most she weened nie.° *believed near*

22

Soone as she parted thence, the fearefull twaine,
That blind old woman and her daughter deare
Came forth, and finding Kirkrapine there slaine,
For anguish great they gan to rend their heare,
And beat their brests, and naked flesh to teare.
And when they both had wept and wayld their fill,
Then forth they ranne like two amazéd deare,
Halfe mad through malice, and revenging will,
To follow her, that was the causer of their ill.

23

Whom overtaking, they gan loudly bray,
With hollow howling, and lamenting cry,
Shamefully at her rayling all the way,
And her accusing of dishonesty,° *unchastity*
That was the flowre of faith and chastity;

1. I.e., it is useless for him to resist.
2. Odysseus preferred reunion with his wife Penelope to the immortality offered by Calypso.

And still amidst her rayling, she[3] did pray,
That plagues, and mischiefs, and long misery
Might fall on her, and follow all the way,
And that in endlesse error° she might ever stray. *wandering*

24

But when she saw her prayers nought prevaile,
She backe returnéd with some labour lost;
And in the way as she did weepe and waile,
A knight her met in mighty armes embost,° *encased*
Yet knight was not for all his bragging bost,° *boast*
But subtill Archimag, that Una sought
By traynes° into new troubles to have tost: *deceptive plots*
Of that old woman tydings he besought,
If that of such a Ladie she could tellen ought.

25

Therewith she gan her passion to renew,
And cry, and curse, and raile, and rend her heare,
Saying, that harlot she too lately knew,
That causd her shed so many a bitter teare,
And so forth told the story of her feare:
Much seeméd he to mone her haplesse chaunce,
And after for that Ladie did inquere;
Which being taught, he forward gan advaunce
His fair enchaunted steed, and eke his charméd launce.

26

Ere long he came, where Una traveild slow,
And that wilde Champion wayting her besyde:
Whom seeing such, for dread he durst not show
Himselfe too nigh at hand, but turnéd wyde° *aside*
Unto an hill; from whence when she him spyde,
By his like seeming shield, her knight by name
She weend it was,[4] and towards him gan ryde:
Approchingnigh, she wist° it was the same, *believed*
And with faire fearefull humblesse° towards him shee came. *humility*

27

And weeping said, "Ah my long lackéd Lord,
Where have ye bene thus long out of my sight?
Much fearéd I to have been quite abhord,
Or ought° have done, that ye displeasen might, *aught*
That should as death unto my deare hart light.[5]
For since mine eye your joyous sight did mis,

3. I.e., Corceca.
4. I.e., by his shield, which seemed to be that of Redcrosse.
5. I.e., that should be a deathlike blow to my sad heart.

44

And all the way, with great lamenting paine.
  And piteous plaints she filleth his dull° eares, *deaf*
  That stony hart could riven have in twaine,
  And all the way she wets with flowing teares:
  But he enraged with rancor, nothing heares.
  Her servile beast yet would not leave her so,
  But followes her farre off, ne ought he feares,
  To be partaker of her wandring woe,
  More mild in beastly kind,° then that her beastly foe. *nature*

Canto IV

To sinfull house of Pride, Duessa
guides the faithfull knight,
Where brothers death to wreak° Sansjoy *avenge*
doth chalenge him to fight.

1

Young knight, what ever that dost armes professe,
  And through long labours huntest after fame,
  Beware of fraud, beware of ficklenesse,
  In choice, and change of thy deare lovéd Dame,
  Least thou of her beleeve too lightly blame,
  And rash misweening° doe thy hart remove: *misunderstanding*
  For unto knight there is no greater shame,
  Then lightnesse and inconstancie in love;
That doth this Redcrosse knights ensample plainly prove.

2

Who after that he had faire Una lorne,° *left*
  Through light misdeeming° of her loialtie, *misjudging*
  And false Duessa in her sted had borne,
  Calléd Fidess', and so supposd to bee;
  Long with her traveild, till at last they see
  A goodly building, bravely garnishéd,° *adorned*
  The house of mightie Prince it seemd to bee:
  And towards it a broad high way that led,
All bare through peoples feet, which thither traveiléd.[1]

3

Great troupes of people traveild thitherward
  Both day and night, of each degree and place,° *rank*
  But few returnéd, having scapéd hard,° *with difficulty*
  With balefull beggerie, or foule disgrace,
  Which ever after in most wretched case,
  Like loathsome lazars,° by the hedges lay. *lepers*

1. Cf. Matthew 7.13: "For wide is the gate, and broad is the way, that leadeth to destruction, and many there be which go in thereat."

Thither Duessa bad him bend his pace:
For she is wearie of the toilesome way,
And also nigh consuméd is the lingring day.

4

A stately Pallace built of squaréd bricke,
Which cunningly was without morter laid,
Whose wals were high, but nothing strong, nor thick,
And golden foile all over them displaid,
That purest skye with brightnesse they dismaid:
High lifted up were many loftie towres,
And goodly galleries farre over laid° *placed above*
Full of faire windowes, and delightfull bowres;
And on the top a Diall told the timely° howres.[2] *measured*

5

It was a goodly heape° for to behould, *building*
And spake the praises of the workmans wit,° *skill*
But full great pittie, that so faire a mould° *structure*
Did on so weake foundation ever sit:
For on a sandie hill, that still did flit,° *give way*
And fall away, it mounted was full hie,
That every breath of heaven shakéd it:
And all the hinder parts, that few could spie,
Were ruinous and old, but painted cunningly.[3]

6

Arrivéd there they passéd in forth right;
For still to all the gates stood open wide,
Yet charge of them was to a Porter hight° *committed*
Cald Malvenu,[4] who entrance none denide:
Thence to the hall, which was on every side
With rich array and costly arras dight.° *decked*
Infinite sorts of people did abide
There waiting long, to win the wishéd sight
Of her, that was the Lady of that Pallace bright.

2. Medieval and Renaissance allegorists enjoyed describing evil and good courts or cities, influenced by the Bible and Augustine's *City of God*. This parody of Gloriana's Cleopolis recalls Alcina's house in *Orlando Furioso* 6.59; for an illustrated city of "disordered livers," see also Stephen Batman's *Travayled Pylgrime* (1569): a knight rides his horse Will into a house of vanity and sex, escaping versions of Error only to find Pride.
3. The stanza may owe something to Chaucer's House of Fame, founded on ice ("a feble fundament / To bilden on a place hye," 3.1132–33); but the primary reference is to Matthew 7.26–27: "every one that heareth these sayings of mine and doeth them not, shall be likened unto a foolish man, which built his house upon the sand."
4. The allegorized court-of-love tradition influences Spenser's account of the House of Pride and of the contrasting House of Holiness. Malvenu's name is the opposite of *bienvenu* (welcome) and of *Bel-accueil*, a name often given to the porter in court-of-love allegories.

7

By them they passe, all gazing on them round.[5]
And to the Presence° mount; whose glorious vew — *reception chamber*
Their frayle amazéd senses did confound:
In living Princes court none ever knew
Such endlesse richesse, and so sumptuous shew;
Ne Persia selfe, the nourse of pompous pride
Like ever saw. And there a noble crew
Of Lordes and Ladies stood on every side,
Which with their presence faire, the place much beautifide.

8

High above all a cloth of State was spred,
And a rich throne, as bright as sunny day,
On which there sate most brave embellishéd
With royall robes and gorgeous array,
A mayden Queene, that shone as Titans ray,[6]
In glistring gold, and peerelesse pretious stone:
Yet her bright blazing beautie did assay° — *attempt*
To dim the brightnesse of her glorious throne,
As envying her selfe, that too exceeding shone.

9

Exceeding shone, like Phoebus fairest child,[7]
That did presume his fathers firie wayne,° — *chariot*
And flaming mouthes of steedes unwonted° wilde — *unusually*
Through highest heaven with weaker° hand to rayne; — *too weak*
Proud of such glory and advancement vaine,
While flashing beames do daze his feeble eyen,
He leaves the welkin° way most beaten plaine, — *heavenly*
And rapt° with whirling wheeles, inflames the skyen, — *carried away*
With fire not made to burne, but fairely for to shyne.

10

So proud she shynéd in her Princely state,
Looking to heaven; for earth she did disdayne,
And sitting high; for lowly° she did hate: — *lowliness*
Lo underneath her scornefull feete, was layne
A dreadfull Dragon with an hideous trayne,° — *tail*
And in her hand she held a mirrhour bright,
Wherein her face she often vewéd fayne,

5. I.e., the crowd around gazing on them.
6. "Titans ray" refers to the sun's brightness (as is usual in Spenser's work), but it here recalls the Titans' wars against the Olympian gods (cf. Hesiod, *Theogony* 617–735).
7. Phaëthon, whose reckless driving of his father's chariot threatened to set the world afire; Jove killed him with lightning (*Metamorphoses* 2.1–400).

And in her selfe-loved semblance tooke delight;
For she was wondrous faire, as any living wight.[8]

11

Of griesly Pluto she the daughter was,
And sad Proserpina the Queene of hell;
Yet did she thinke her pearelesse worth to pas
That parentage, with pride so did she swell,
And thundring Jove, that high in heaven doth dwell,
And wield the world, she claymèd for her syre,
Or if that any else did Jove excell:
For to the highest she did still aspyre,
Or if ought higher were then that, did it desyre.

12

And proud Lucifera[9] men did her call,
That made her selfe a Queene, and crownd to be,
Yet rightfull kingdome she had none at all,
Ne heritage of native soveraintie,
But did usurpe with wrong and tyrannie
Upon the scepter, which she now did hold:
Ne ruld her Realmes with lawes, but pollicie,° *political cunning*
And strong advisement of six wisards old,
That with their counsels bad her kingdome did uphold.

13

Soone as the Elfin knight in presence came,
And false Duessa seeming Lady faire,
A gentle Husher,° Vanitie by name *usher*
Made rowme, and passage for them did prepaire:
So goodly brought them to the lowest staire
Of her high throne, where they on humble knee
Making obeyssance, did the cause declare,
Why they were come, her royall state to see,
To prove° the wide report of her great Majestee. *confirm*

14

With loftie eyes, halfe loth to looke so low,
She thankèd them in her disdainefull wise,
Ne other grace vouchsafèd them to show
Of Princesse worthy, scarse them bad arise.
Her Lordes and Ladies all this while devise° *make ready*
Themselves to setten forth to straungers sight:

8. Like many Renaissance images of pride, in literature and the visual arts, Lucifera holds a mirror.
9. Lucifera's name links her with Lucifer (i.e., "light-bearer," recalling his original brightness in Heaven); she rules her usurped realm by "pollicie" and magic rather than by statesmanship allied with true religion. She is presumably the opposite of that other "mayden Queene," Elizabeth, but some suspect that Spenser's satire does not quite exempt his monarch and her court.

At neighbours wealth, that made him ever sad;
For death it was, when any good he saw,
And wept, that cause of weeping none he had,
But when he heard of harme, he wexéd wondrous glad.

31

All in a kirtle of discolourd say[4]
He clothéd was, ypainted full of eyes;
And in his bosome secretly there lay
An hatefull Snake, the which his taile uptyes° *coils*
In many folds, and mortall sting implyes.° *enfolds*
Still as he rode, he gnasht his teeth, to see
Those heapes of gold with griple° Covetyse, *greedy*
And grudgéd at the great felicitie
Of proud Lucifera, and his owne companie.

32

He hated all good workes and vertuous deeds,
And him no lesse, that any like did use,° *practice*
And who with gracious bread the hungry feeds,[5]
His almes for want of faith he doth accuse;
So every good to bad he doth abuse:° *pervert*
And eke the verse of famous Poets witt
He does backebite, and spightfull poison spues
From leprous mouth on all, that ever writt:
Such one vile Envie was, that fifte in row did sitt.[6]

33

And him beside rides fierce revenging Wrath,
Upon a Lion, loth for to be led;
And in his hand a burning brond° he hath, *sword*
The which he brandisheth about his hed;
His eyes did hurle forth sparkles fiery red,
And staréd sterne on all, that him beheld,
As ashes pale of hew and seeming ded;
And on his dagger still his hand he held,
Trembling through hasty rage, when choler° in him sweld. *anger*

34

His ruffin° raiment all was staind with blood, *disarranged*
Which he had spilt, and all to rags yrent,° *torn*
Through unadvizéd rashnesse woxen wood;° *mad*
For of his hands he had no governement,° *control*
Ne cared for[7] bloud in his avengément:

4. In a multicolored woolen outer garment.
5. I.e., graciously feeds the hungry with bread.
6. Here merely one of Pride's attendants, Envy elsewhere in Spenser's work is a threatening and insidious figure, the enemy of true poets. Cf. VI.i.8 and "Blatant Beast."
7. I.e., shrank from.

Him litle answerd th'angry Elfin knight;
He never meant with words, but swords to plead his right.

43

But threw his gauntlet as a sacred pledge,
His cause in combat the next day to try:
So been they parted both, with harts on edge,
To be avenged each on his enimy.
That night they pas in joy and jollity,
Feasting and courting both in bowre and hall;
For Steward was excessive Gluttonie,
That of his plenty pouréd forth to all:
Which doen,° the Chamberlain Slowth did to rest them call. *done*

44

Now whenas darkesome night had all displayd
Her coleblacke curtein over brightest skye,
The warlike youthes on dayntie couches layd,
Did chace away sweet sleepe from sluggish eye,
To muse on meanes of hopéd victory.
But whenas Morpheus had with leaden mace
Arrested all that courtly company,
Up-rose Duessa from her resting place,
And to the Paynims lodging comes with silent pace.

45

Whom broad awake she finds, in troublous fit,° *mood*
Forecasting, how his foe he might annoy,
And him amoves° with speaches seeming fit: *arouses*
"Ah deare Sans joy, next dearest to Sans foy,
Cause of my new griefe, cause of my new joy,
Joyous, to see his ymage in mine eye,
And greeved, to thinke how foe did him destroy,
That was the flowre of grace and chevalrye;
Lo his Fidessa to thy secret faith I flye."

46

With gentle wordes he can° her fairely greet, *did*
And bad say on the secret of her hart.
Then sighing soft, "I learne that litle sweet
Oft tempred is," quoth she, "with muchell° smart: *much*
For since my brest was launcht° with lovely dart *pierced*
Of deare Sansfoy, I never joyéd howre,
But in eternall woes my weaker° hart *too weak*
Have wasted, loving him with all my powre,
And for his sake have felt full many an heavie stowre.° *grief*

47

"At last when perils all I weenéd past,
And hoped to reape the crop of all my care,
Into new woes unweeting I was cast,
By this false faytor,° who unworthy ware — *impostor*
His worthy shield, whom he with guilefull snare
Entrappéd slew, and brought to shamefull grave.
Me silly° maid away with him he bare, — *innocent*
And ever since hath kept in darksome cave,
For that° I would not yeeld, that° to Sans foy I gave. — *because / what*

48

"But since faire Sunne hath sperst° that lowring clowd, — *dispersed*
And to my loathéd life now shewes some light,
Under your beames I will me safely shrowd,
From dreaded storme of his disdainfull spight:
To you th'inheritance belongs by right
Of brothers prayse, to you eke longs° his love. — *belongs*
Let not his love, let not his restlesse spright
Be unrevenged, that calles to you above
From wandring Stygian shores,[3] where it doth endlesse move."

49

Thereto said he, "Faire Dame be nought dismaid
For sorrowes past; their griefe is with them gone:
Ne yet of present perill be affraid;
For needlesse feare did never vantage° none, — *aid*
And helplesse° hap it booteth not to mone. — *unavoidable*
Dead is Sans foy, his vitall paines are past,
Though greevéd ghost for vengeance deepe do grone:
He lives, that shall him pay his dewties° last, — *rites*
And guiltie Elfin bloud shall sacrifice in hast."

50

"O but I feare the fickle freakes,"° quoth shee, — *whims*
"Of fortune false, and oddes of armes in field."
"Why dame," quoth he, "what oddes can ever bee,
Where both do fight alike, to win or yield?"
"Yea but," quoth she, "he beares a charméd shield,
And eke enchaunted armes, that none can perce,
Ne none can wound the man, that does them wield."
"Charmd or enchaunted," answerd he then ferce,° — *fiercely*
"I no whit reck, ne you the like need to reherce.° — *recount*

3. The banks of the river Styx, in the underworld.

For all for prayse and honour he did fight.
Both stricken strike, and beaten both do beat,
That from their shields forth flyeth firie light,
And helmets hewen deepe, shew marks of eithers might.

8

So th'one for wrong, the other strives for right:
As when a Gryfon[4] seizéd° of his pray, *in possession*
A Dragon fiers encountreth in his flight,
Through widest ayre making his ydle way,
That would his rightfull ravine° rend away: *booty*
With hideous horrour both together smight,
And souce° so sore, that they the heavens affray: *strike*
The wise Southsayer seeing so sad° sight, *ominous*
Th'amazéd vulgar tels of warres and mortall fight.

9

So th'one for wrong, the other strives for right,
And each to deadly shame would drive his foe:
The cruell steele so greedily doth bight
In tender flesh, that streames of bloud down flow,
With which the armes, that earst° so bright did show, *at first*
Into a pure vermillion now are dyde:
Great ruth in all the gazers harts did grow,
Seeing the goréd woundes to gape so wyde,
That victory they dare not wish to either side.

10

At last the Paynim chaunst to cast his eye,
His suddein° eye, flaming with wrathfull fyre, *darting*
Upon his brothers shield, which hong thereby:
Therewith redoubled was his raging yre,
And said, "Ah wretched sonne of wofull syre,
Doest thou sit wayling by black Stygian lake,
Whilest here thy shield is hangd for victors hyre,° *reward*
And sluggish german° doest thy forces slake,° *brother / abate*
To after-send his foe, that him may overtake?[5]

11

"Goe caytive° Elfe, him quickly overtake, *base*
And soone redeeme from his long wandring woe;
Goe guiltie ghost, to him my message make,
That I his shield have quit° from dying foe." *taken back*

4. The griffon, referred to by Herodotus (*Histories* 3.116) as guarding deposits of gold in the northern parts of Europe, combines the body of a lion with the head and wings of an eagle; "but a griffoun" (as Sir John Mandeville wrote in the fourteenth century) "hath a body greater than viii Lyons," and is stronger than one hundred eagles (*Travels*, ed. J. Bramont [London, 1928] 195).
5. Cf. Aeneas, who, momentarily inclined to spare the defeated Turnus, is again roused to fury by the sight of the dead Pallas's sword belt on the shoulder of Turnus (*Aeneid* 12.941–49).

Therewith upon his crest he stroke him so,
That twise he reeléd, readie twise to fall;
End of the doubtfull battell deeméd tho° *then*
The lookers on, and lowd to him gan call
The false Duessa, "Thine the shield, and I, and all."

12

Soone as the Faerie heard his Ladie speake,
Out of his swowning dreame he gan awake,
And quickning° faith, that earst was woxen weake, *vitalizing*
The creeping deadly cold away did shake:
Tho moved with wrath, and shame, and Ladies sake,
Of all attonce he cast° avengd to bee, *resolved*
And with so'exceeding furie at him strake,
That forcéd him to stoupe upon his knee;
Had he not stoupéd so, he should have cloven bee.

13

And to him said, "Goe now proud Miscreant,
Thy selfe thy message doe° to german deare, *give*
Alone he wandring thee too long doth want:
Goe say, his foe thy shield with his doth beare."
Therewith his heavie hand he high gan reare,
Him to have slaine; when loe a darkesome clowd
Upon him fell: he no where doth appeare,
But vanisht is. The Elfe him cals alowd,
But answer none receives: the darknes him does shrowd.[6]

14

In haste Duessa from her place arose,
And to him running said, "O prowest° knight, *bravest*
That ever Ladie to her love did chose,
Let now abate the terror of your might,
And quench the flame of furious despight,
And bloudie vengeance; lo th'infernall powres
Covering your foe with cloud of deadly night,
Have borne him thence to Plutoes balefull bowres.
The conquest yours, I yours, the shield, and glory yours."

15

Not all so satisfide, with greedie eye
He sought all round about, his thirstie blade
To bath in bloud of faithlesse enemy;
Who all that while lay hid in secret shade:
He standes amazéd, how he thence should fade.

6. Spenser might have found in Virgil (or Homer) similar measures taken by a god to protect a favorite (cf. *Aeneid* 5.810–12; *Iliad* 3.380); more probably the episode is based on Armida's protection of Rambaldo from the wrath of Tancred, in Tasso, *Gerusalemme Liberata* 7.44–45.

If old Aveugles sonnes so evill heare?[2]
Or who shall not great Nightés children scorne,
When two of three her Nephews are so fowle forlorne?

24

"Up then, up dreary Dame, of darknesse Queene,
Go gather up the reliques of thy race,
Or else goe them avenge, and let be seene,
That dreaded Night in brightest day hath place,
And can the children of faire light deface"° *destroy*
Her feeling speeches some compassion moved
In hart, and chaunge in that great mothers face:
Yet pittie in her hart was never proved° *felt*
Till then: for evermore she hated, never loved.

25

And said, "Deare daughter rightly may I rew
The fall of famous children borne of mee,
And good successes, which their foes ensew:° *attend*
But who can turne the streame of destinee,
Or breake the chayne of strong necessitee,
Which fast is tyde to Joves eternall seat?[3]
The sonnes of Day he favoureth, I see,
And by my ruines thinkes to make them great:
To make one great by others losse, is bad excheat.° *gain*

26

"Yet shall they not escape so freely all;
For some shall pay the price of others guilt:
And he the man that made Sansfoy to fall,
Shall with his owne bloud price° that he hath spilt. *pay for*
But what art thou, that telst of Nephews kilt?"
"I that do seeme not I, Duessa am,"
Quoth she, "how ever now in garments gilt,
And gorgeous gold arayd I to thee came;
Duessa I, the daughter of Deceipt and Shame."

27

Then bowing downe her agéd backe, she kist
The wicked witch, saying; "In that faire face
The false resemblance of Deceipt, I wist° *knew*
Did closely lurke; yet so true-seeming grace
It carried, that I scarse in darkesome place

2. I.e., if Aveugle's sons are so evilly treated. *Aveugles*: Aveugle ("blindness" or "darkness"), the son of Night.
3. Homer's is the first reference to the "golden rope" of Zeus, suspended from heaven, to which gods, mortals, and the entire universe are attached (*Iliad* 8.18–27). Elsewhere Spenser employs the image to signify the harmony that informs the universe and links the actions of the virtuous (I.ix.I), or, parodically, to represent the struggle for position and power (II.vii.46–47).

And with greene braunches strowing all the ground,
Do worship her, as Queene, with olive girlond cround.

14

And all the way their merry pipes they sound,
That all the woods with doubled Eccho ring,
And with their hornéd feet do weare° the ground, *trample*
Leaping like wanton kids in pleasant Spring.
So towards old Sylvanus they her bring;
Who with the noyse awakéd, commeth out,
To weet the cause, his weake steps governing,
And aged limbs on Cypresse stadle° stout, *staff*
And with an yvie twyne his wast is girt about.

15

Far off he wonders, what them makes so glad.
Or Bacchus merry fruit they did invent,[8]
Or Cybeles franticke rites[9] have made them mad;
They drawing nigh, unto their God present
That flowre of faith and beautie excellent.
The God himselfe vewing that mirrhour rare,[1]
Stood long amazd, and burnt in his intent;° *gaze*
His owne faire Dryope now he thinkes not faire,
And Pholoe[2] fowle, when her to this he doth compaire.

16

The woodborne people fall before her flat,
And worship her as Goddesse of the wood;
And old Sylvanus selfe bethinkes° not, what *concludes*
To thinke of wight so faire, but gazing stood,
In doubt to deeme her borne of earthly brood;
Sometimes Dame Venus selfe he seemes to see,
But Venus never had so sober mood;
Sometimes Diana he her takes to bee,
But misseth bow, and shaftes, and buskins° to her knee. *boots*

17

By vew of her he ginneth to revive
His ancient love, and dearest Cyparisse,[3]

8. I.e., whether they had found the grapes that, as wine, make men merry.
9. The Great Mother Cybele, goddess of Earth and upholder of cities, was a Near Eastern deity known to the Greeks as Rhea, daughter of Gea and wife of Kronos (Saturn). She was worshipped with rites led by castrated priests performing orgiastic dances to brass and percussion instruments. For the Romans (and presumably for Spenser) she was patron and symbol of the westward passage of culture and empire. See Catullus's 63d Ode.
1. I.e., that mirror of heavenly beauty.
2. A nymph loved by Pan; *Dryope*: the wife of Faunus. Spenser apparently considered the names of Faunus, Pan, and Sylvanus interchangeable.
3. According to Ovid, Cyparissus, the beloved of Apollo, was changed by the god into a cypress (*Metamorphoses* 10.106–42); in Comes's version, he is associated rather with Sylvanus (*Mythologiae* 5.10).

And calles to mind his pourtraiture alive,[4]
How faire he was, and yet not faire to this,
And how he slew with glauncing dart amisse
A gentle Hynd, the which the lovely boy
Did love as life, above all worldly blisse;
For griefe whereof the lad n'ould° after joy, *would not*
But pynd away in anguish and selfe-wild annoy.° *grief*

18

The wooddy Nymphes, faire Hamadryades
Her to behold do thither runne apace,
And all the troupe of light-foot Naiades,[5]
Flocke all about to see her lovely face:
But when they vewéd have her heavenly grace,
They envie her in their malitious mind,
And fly away for feare of fowle disgrace:
But all the Satyres scorne their woody kind,
And henceforth nothing faire, but her on earth they find.

19

Glad of such lucke, the luckelesse lucky maid,
Did her content to please their feeble eyes,
And long time with that salvage people staid,
To gather breath in many miseries.
During which time her gentle wit she plyes,
To teach them truth, which worshipt her in vaine,° *foolishly*
And made her th'Image of Idolatryes;
But when their bootlesse zeale she did restraine
From her own worship, they her Asse would worship fayn.°[6] *eagerly*

20

It fortunéd a noble warlike knight[7]
By just occasion to that forrest came,
To seeke his kindred, and the lignage right,° *true*
From whence he tooke his well deservéd name:
He had in armes abroad wonne muchell fame,
And fild far landes with glorie of his might,
Plaine, faithfull, true, and enimy of shame,
And ever loved to fight for Ladies right,
But in vaine glorious frayes he litle did delight.

4. I.e., his appearance when he was alive.
5. Naiads, nymphs of lakes and rivers, thought to have prophetic powers. *Hamadryades*: hamadryads, tree nymphs who cannot outlive the trees they inhabit.
6. Spenser may be revising a popular emblem (cf. Alciato, *Emblemata* 7) in which an ass bearing a statue of Isis thinks the crowd is worshipping him.
7. The parentage of this forest-born and well-intentioned hybrid recalls the common folklore theme of a mortal's mating with an otherworldly being. Typically, Spenser delays naming a newly introduced figure (see stanza 28).

To tell the sad sight, which mine eies have red:° *seen*
These eyes did see that knight both living and eke ded."

37

That cruell word her tender hart so thrild,° *pierced*
That suddein cold did runne through every vaine,
And stony horrour all her sences fild
With dying fit, that downe she fell for paine.
The knight her lightly rearéd up againe,
And comforted with curteous kind reliefe:
Then wonne from death, she bad him tellen plaine
The further processe° of her hidden griefe; *account*
The lesser pangs can beare, who hath endured the chiefe.

38

Then gan the Pilgrim thus, "I chaunst this day,
This fatall day, that shall I ever rew,
To see two knights in travell on my way
(A sory sight) arraunged in battell new,[8]
Both breathing vengeaunce, both of wrathfull hew:
My fearefull flesh did tremble at their strife,
To see their blades so greedily imbrew,° *thrust*
That drunke with bloud, yet thristed after life:
What more? the Redcrosse knight was slaine with Paynim knife."

39

"Ah dearest Lord," quoth she, "how might that bee,
And he the stoutest knight, that ever wonne?° *engaged in battle*
"Ah dearest dame," quoth he, "how might I see
The thing, that might not be, and yet was donne?"
"Where is," said Satyrane, "that Paynims sonne,
That him of life, and us of joy hath reft?"
"Not far away," quoth he, "he hence doth wonne° *remain*
Foreby a fountaine, where I late him left
Washing his bloudy wounds, that through the steele were cleft."

40

Therewith the knight thence marchéd forth in hast,
Whiles Una with huge heavinesse° opprest, *grief*
Could not for sorrow follow him so fast;
And soone he came, as he the place had ghest,
Whereas that Pagan proud him selfe did rest,
In secret shadow by a fountaine side:
Even he it was, that earst would have supprest° *ravished*
Faire Una: whom when Satyrane espide,
With fowle reprochfull words he boldly him defide.

8. I.e., striking the first blows of their encounter.

41

And said, "Arise thou curséd Miscreaunt,
That hast with knightlesse guile and trecherous train° *deceit*
Faire knighthood fowly shaméd, and doest vaunt
That good knight of the Redcrosse to have slain:
Arise, and with like treason now maintain
Thy guilty wrong, or else thee guilty yield."
The Sarazin this hearing, rose amain,° *at once*
And catching up in hast his three square° shield, *triangular*
And shining helmet, soone him buckled to the field.

42

And drawing nigh him said, "Ah misborne° Elfe, *basely born*
In evill houre thy foes thee hither sent,
Anothers wrongs to wreake upon thy selfe:[9]
Yet ill thou blamest me, for having blent° *defiled*
My name with guile and traiterous intent;
That Redcrosse knight, perdie,° I never slew, *truly*
But had he beene, where earst his armes were lent,
Th'enchaunter vaine his errour should not rew:
But thou his errour shalt, I hope now proven trew."[1]

43

Therewith they gan, both furious and fell,
To thunder blowes, and fiersly to assaile
Each other bent° his enimy to quell, *determined*
That with their force they perst both plate and maile,
And made wide furrowes in their fleshes fraile,
That it would pitty° any living eie. *bring pity to*
Large floods of bloud adowne their sides did raile:° *flow*
But floods of bloud could not them satisfie:
Both hungred after death: both chose to win, or die.

44

So long they fight, and fell revenge pursue,
That fainting each, themselves to breathen let,
And oft refreshéd, battell oft renue:
As when two Bores with rancling malice met,
Their gory sides fresh bleeding fiercely fret,° *gnaw, tear*
Til breathlesse both them selves aside retire,
Where foming wrath, their cruell tuskes they whet,
And trample th'earth, the whiles they may respire;
Then backe to fight againe, new breathéd and entire.° *refreshed*

9. I.e., to draw upon yourself the consequences of another's wrongs.
1. I.e. [in reference to I.iii.33–39], your experience at my hands shall now, I hope, confirm Archimago's foolishness in venturing to fight me.

45

So fiersly, when these knights had breathéd once,
They gan to fight returne, increasing more
Their puissant force, and cruell rage attonce,
With heapéd strokes more hugely, then before,
That with their drerie° wounds and bloody gore — *gory*
They both deforméd, scarsely could be known.
By this sad Una fraught with anguish sore,
Led with their noise, which through the aire was thrown,
Arrived, where they in erth their fruitles bloud had sown.

46

Whom all so soone as that proud Sarazin
Espide, he gan revive the memory
Of his lewd lusts, and late attempted sin,
And left the doubtfull° battell hastily, — *undecided*
To catch her, newly offred to his eie:
But Satyrane with strokes him turning, staid,
And sternely bad him other businesse plie,
Then hunt the steps of pure unspotted Maid:
Wherewith he all enraged, these bitter speaches said.

47

"O foolish faeries sonne, what furie mad
Hath thee incenst, to hast thy dolefull fate?
Were it not better, I that Lady had,
Then that thou hadst repented it too late?
Most sencelesse man he, that himselfe doth hate,
To love another. Lo then for thine ayd
Here take thy lovers token on thy pate."
So they to fight; the whiles the royall Mayd
Fled farre away, of that proud Paynim sore afrayd.

48

But that false Pilgrim, which that leasing° told, — *falsehood*
Being in deed old Archimage, did stay
In secret shadow, all this to behold,
And much rejoyoéd in their bloudy fray:
But when he saw the Damsell passe away
He left his stond,° and her pursewd apace, — *place*
In hope to bring her to her last decay.° — *destruction*
But for to tell her lamentable cace,
And eke this battels end, will need another place.

Canto VII

The Redcrosse knight is captive made
By Gyaunt proud opprest,
Prince Arthur meets with Una greatly
with those newes distrest.

1

What man so wise, what earthly wit so ware,° *wary*
As to descry° the crafty cunning traine, *discover*
By which deceipt doth maske in visour faire,
And cast° her colours dyéd deepe in graine, *dispose*
To seeme like Truth, whose shape she well can faine,
And fitting gestures to her purpose frame,
The guiltlesse man with guile to entertaine?° *receive*
Great maistresse of her art was that false Dame,
The false Duessa, clokéd with Fidessaes name.

2

Who when returning from the drery Night,
She fownd not in that perilous house of Pryde,
Where she had left, the noble Redcrosse knight,
Her hopéd pray, she would no lenger bide,
But forth she went, to seeke him far and wide.
Ere long she fownd, whereas he wearie sate,
To rest him selfe, foreby° a fountaine side, *near*
Disarméd all of yron-coted Plate,[1]
And by his side his steed the grassy forage ate.

3

He feedes upon the cooling shade, and bayes° *bathes*
His sweatie forehead in the breathing wind,
Which through the trembling leaves full gently playes
Wherein the cherefull birds of sundry kind
Do chaunt sweet musick, to delight his mind:
The Witch approching gan him fairely greet,
And with reproch of carelesnesse° unkind *neglect*
Upbrayd, for leaving her in place unmeet,° *unfitting*
With fowle words tempring faire, soure gall with hony sweet.

4

Unkindnesse past, they gan of solace treat,° *speak*
And bathe in pleasaunce of the joyous shade,
Which shielded them against the boyling heat,
And with greene boughes decking a gloomy glade,
About the fountaine like a girlond made;
Whose bubbling wave did ever freshly well,
Ne ever would through fervent° sommer fade: *hot*
The sacred Nymph, which therein wont to dwell,
Was out of Dianes favour, as it then befell.

1. Erasmus warns in his *Enchiridion* (trans. William Tyndale in 1533 as *The Manual of the Christian Knight*) to beware of escaping vice only to fall into self-congratulatory vanity. The armor that Redcrosse removes may well recall that which Paul urges Christians to wear (see note on Canto I.1.2).

5

The cause was this: one day when Phoebe[2] fayre
With all her band was following the chace,
This Nymph, quite tyred with heat of scorching ayre
Sat downe to rest in middest of the race:
The goddesse wroth gan fowly her disgrace,° *scold, revile*
And bad the waters, which from her did flow,
Be such as she her selfe was then in place.° *that place*
Thenceforth her waters waxéd dull and slow,
And all that drunke thereof, did faint and feeble grow.

6

Hereof this gentle knight unweeting was,
And lying downe upon the sandie graile,° *gravel*
Drunke of the streame, as cleare as cristall glas;
Eftsoones his manly forces gan to faile,
And mightie strong was turnd to feeble fraile.
His chaungéd powres at first themselves not felt,
Till crudled° cold his corage° gan assaile, *congealing / vigor*
And chearefull° bloud in faintnesse chill did melt, *lively*
Which like a fever fit through all his body swelt.° *raged*

7

Yet goodly court he made still to his Dame,
Pourd out in loosnesse on the grassy grownd,
Both carelesse of his health, and of his fame:
Till at the last he heard a dreadfull sownd,
Which through the wood loud bellowing, did rebownd,
That all the earth for terrour seemd to shake,
And trees did tremble. Th'Elfe therewith astownd,° *amazed*
Upstarted lightly from his looser make,° *companion*
And his unready weapons gan in hand to take.

8

But ere he could his armour on him dight,° *put*
Or get his shield, his monstrous enimy
With sturdie steps came stalking in his sight,
An hideous Geant horrible and hye,[3]
That with his talnesse seemd to threat the skye,
The ground eke gronéd under him for dreed;

2. Diana, goddess of the moon. While this episode seems original with Spenser, lines 8–9 recall Ovid's fountain of Salmacis, whose waters enfeebled bathers (*Metamorphoses* 4.286–87).
3. The physiology of this "Geant" (the spelling recalls the mother of giants, Gaea, "Earth") and his appearance just as the unarmed Redcrosse dallies with Duessa on the grass ("all flesh is grass," says Isaiah 40.6) may associate him with monitory earthquakes, which Renaissance science blamed on air trapped underground, and with earthy lust. He is made of "earthly slime," perhaps recalling his fellow foundling George ("earth-tiller") and Adam ("red earth"). Spenser's culture found giants fascinating, often thought them as once or still real, and associated them with the archaic and rebellious. On this giant's sexual overtones, see J. W. Schroeder in *ELH* 29 (1962); on giants and earthquakes, see S. K. Heninger in *ELH* 26 (1959).

His living like saw never living eye,
Ne durst behold: his stature did exceed
The hight of three the tallest sonnes of mortall seed.

9

The greatest Earth his uncouth mother was,
And blustring Aeolus[4] his boasted sire,
Who with his breath, which through the world doth pas,
Her hollow womb did secretly inspire,° *breathe into*
And fild her hidden caves with stormie yre,
That she conceived; and trebling the dew time,
In which the wombes of women do expire,° *gestate*
Brought forth this monstrous masse of earthly slime,
Puft up with emptie wind, and fild with sinfull crime.

10

So growen great through arrogant delight
Of th'high descent, whereof he was yborne,
And through presumption of his matchlesse might,
All other powres and knighthood he did scorne.
Such now he marcheth to this man forlorne,
And left to losse:° his stalking steps are stayed° *destruction / steadied*
Upon a snaggy Oke, which he had torne
Out of his mothers bowelles, and it made
His mortall mace, wherewith his foemen he dismayde.

11

That when the knight he spide, he gan advance
With huge force and insupportable mayne,[5]
And towardes him with dreadfull fury praunce;
Who haplesse, and eke hopelesse, all in vaine
Did to him pace, sad battaile to darrayne,° *undertake*
Disarmd, disgrast, and inwardly dismayde,
And eke so faint in every joynt and vaine,
Through that fraile° fountaine, which him feeble made, *weakening*
That scarsely could he weeld his bootlesse single blade.[6]

12

The Geaunt strooke so maynly° mercilesse, *mightily*
That could have overthrowne a stony towre,
And were not heavenly grace, that him did blesse,° *preserve*
He had beene pouldred° all, as thin as flowre: *pulverized*
But he was wary of that deadly stowre,° *peril*
And lightly lept from underneath the blow:
Yet so exceeding was the villeins powre,

4. God of the winds.
5. Irresistible strength.
6. I.e., sword alone, without the aid of armor or shield.

That with the wind it did him overthrow,
And all his sences stound,° that still he lay full low. *stunned*

13

As when that divelish yron Engine[7] wrought
In deepest Hell, and framd by Furies skill,
With windy Nitre and quick° Sulphur fraught,° *inflammable / filled*
And ramd with bullet round, ordaind to kill,
Conceiveth fire, the heavens it doth fill
With thundring noyse, and all the ayre doth choke,
That none can breath, nor see, nor heare at will,
Through smouldry cloud of duskish stincking smoke,
That th'onely breath[8] him daunts, who hath escapt the stroke.

14

So daunted when the Geaunt saw the knight,
His heavie hand he heavéd up on hye,
And him to dust thought to have battred quight,
Untill Duessa loud to him gan crye;
"O great Orgoglio,[9] greatest under skye,
O hold thy mortall hand for Ladies sake,
Hold for my sake, and do him not to dye,
But vanquisht thine eternall bondslave make,
And me thy worthy meed unto thy Leman° take." *mistress*

15

He hearkned, and did stay from further harmes,
To gayne so goodly guerdon,° as she spake: *reward*
So willingly she came into his armes,
Who her as willingly to grace° did take, *favor*
And was possesséd of his new found make.° *companion*
Then up he tooke the slombred sencelesse corse,
And ere he could out of his swowne awake,
Him to his castle brought with hastie forse,
And in a Dongeon deepe him threw without remorse.

16

From that day forth Duessa was his deare,
And highly honourd in his haughtie eye,
He gave her gold and purple pall° to weare, *robe*
And triple crowne[1] set on her head full hye,
And her endowd with royall majestye:
Then for to make her dreaded more of men,

7. I.e., cannon.
8. I.e., the blast alone.
9. Italian for "pride." The giant's name would offer possibilities to Spenser's readers ranging from the arrogance of the Spanish Armada to papal ambition to swelling sexuality to the deadly sin of spiritual pride.
1. Symbolic of papal power.

And peoples harts with awfull terrour tye,
A monstrous beast[2] ybred in filthy fen
He chose, which he had kept long time in darksome den.

17

Such one it was, as that renowméd Snake[3]
Which great Alcides in Stremona slew,
Long fostred in the filth of Lerna lake,
Whose many heads out budding ever new,
Did breed him endlesse labour to subdew:
But this same Monster much more ugly was;
For seven great heads out of his body grew,
An yron brest, and backe of scaly bras,
And all embrewd° in bloud, his eyes did shine as glas. *stained, defiled*

18

His tayle was stretchéd out in wondrous length,
That to the house of heavenly gods it raught,° *reached*
And with extorted powre, and borrowed strength,
The ever-burning lamps from thence it brought,
And prowdly threw to ground, as things of nought;
And underneath his filthy feet did tread
The sacred things, and holy heasts° foretaught. *commandments*
Upon this dreadfull Beast with sevenfold head
He set the false Duessa, for more aw and dread.

19

The wofull Dwarfe, which saw his maisters fall,
Whiles he had keeping of his grasing steed,
And valiant knight become a caytive° thrall, *captive*
When all was past, tooke up his forlorne weed,° *equipment*
His mightie armour, missing most at need;
His silver shield, now idle maisterlesse;
His poynant° speare, that many made to bleed, *sharp*
The ruefull moniments° of heavinesse, *memorials*
And with them all departes, to tell his great distresse.

20

He had not travaild long, when on the way
He wofull Ladie, wofull Una met,
Fast flying from the Paynims greedy pray,° *clutch*
Whilest Satyrane him from pursuit did let:° *prevent*

2. The description of Duessa's beast echoes passages in Revelation: "I saw a woman sit upon a scarlet coloured beast, full of names of blasphemy, having seven heads and ten horns" (17.3) and "behold a great red dragon, having seven heads and ten horns, and seven crowns upon his heads . . . [whose] tail drew the third part of the stars of heaven, and did cast them to the earth . . . [he is] that old serpent, called the Devil, and Satan, which deceiveth the whole world" (12.3–4, 9).
3. To destroy the Lernean hydra, a nine-headed beast of the swamps, was the second of twelve labors assigned to Hercules (also called Alcides). Una is one; the beast is multiple.

Who when her eyes she on the Dwarfe had set,
And saw the signes, that deadly tydings spake,
She fell to ground for sorrowfull regret,
And lively breath her sad brest did forsake,
Yet might her pitteous hart be seene to pant and quake.

21

The messenger of so unhappie newes,
Would faine have dyde: dead was his hart within,
Yet outwardly some little comfort shewes:
At last recovering hart, he does begin
To rub her temples, and to chaufe her chin,
And every tender part does tosse and turne:
So hardly he the flitted life does win,° *prevail upon*
Unto her native prison[4] to retourne:
Then gins her grievéd ghost° thus to lament and mourne. *spirit*

22

"Ye dreary instruments of dolefull sight,[5]
That doe this deadly spectacle behold,
Why do ye lenger feed on loathéd light,
Or liking find to gaze on earthly mould,° *form*
Sith cruell fates the carefull° threeds unfould, *full of care*
The which my life and love together tyde?
Now let the stony dart of senselesse cold
Perce to my hart, and pas through every side,
And let eternall night so sad sight fro me hide.

23

"O lightsome day, the lampe of highest Jove,
First made by him, mens wandring wayes to guyde,
When darknesse he in deepest dongeon drove,
Henceforth thy hated face for ever hyde,
And shut up heavens windowes shyning wyde:
For earthly sight can nought but sorrow breed,
And late repentance, which shall long abyde.
Mine eyes no more on vanitie shall feed,
But seeléd up with death, shall have their deadly meed."° *reward*

24

Then downe againe she fell unto the ground;
But he her quickly rearéd up againe:
Thrise did she sinke adowne in deadly swownd,
And thrise he her revived with busie paine:
At last when life recovered had the raine,° *rule*
And over-wrestled his strong enemie,

4. I.e., the body.
5. I.e., eyes.

On top of greene Selinis[8] all alone,
With blossomes brave bedeckéd daintily;
Whose tender locks do tremble every one
At every little breath, that under heaven is blowne.

33

His warlike shield[9] all closely covered was,
Ne might of mortall eye be ever seene;
Not made of steele, nor of enduring bras,
Such earthly mettals soone consuméd bene:
But all of Diamond perfect pure and cleene° — *clear*
It framéd was, one massie entire mould,
Hewen out of Adamant° rocke with engines keene, — *diamond-hard*
That point of speare it never percen could,
Ne dint of direfull sword divide the substance would.

34

The same to wight he never wont disclose,
But° when as monsters huge he would dismay, — *except*
Or daunt unequall armies of his foes,
Or when the flying heavens he would affray;° — *frighten*
For so exceeding shone his glistring ray,
That Phoebus golden face it did attaint,° — *dim, darken*
As when a cloud his beames doth over-lay;
And silver Cynthia wexéd pale and faint,
As when her face is staynd with magicke arts constraint.° — *force*

35

No magicke arts hereof had any might,
Nor bloudie wordes of bold Enchaunters call,
But all that was not such, as seemd in sight,
Before that shield did fade, and suddeine fall:
And when him list the raskall routes°, appall, — *crowds*
Men into stones therewith he could transmew,° — *change*
And stones to dust, and dust to nought at all;
And when him list the prouder lookes subdew,
He would them gazing blind, or turne to other hew.° — *form*

36

Ne let it seeme, that credence this exceedes,
For he that made the same, was knowne right well
To have done much more admirable deedes.
It Merlin was, which whylome° did excell — *formerly*
All living wightes in might of magicke spell:
Both shield, and sword, and armour all he wrought

8. Virgil refers to "the city of palms, Selinus," in Asia Minor (*Aeneid* 3.705).
9. Arthur's shield is very like Atlante's in Ariosto, *Orlando Furioso* 2.55–56; but this shield, proof against the arts of enchanters, also recalls the Pauline armor of Ephesians 6.16.

For this young Prince, when first to armes he fell;° *came*
But when he dyde, the Faerie Queene it brought
To Faerie lond, where yet it may be seene, if sought.

37

A gentle youth, his dearely lovéd Squire
His speare of heben° wood behind him bare, *ebony*
Whose harmefull head, thrice heated in the fire,
Had riven many a brest with pikehead square;
A goodly person, and could menage° faire *control*
His stubborne steed with curbéd canon bit,[1]
Who under him did trample as the aire,[2]
And chauft, that any on his backe should sit;
The yron rowels into frothy fome he bit.

38

When as this knight nigh to the Ladie drew,
With lovely° court he gan her entertaine; *loving*
But when he heard her answeres loth, he knew
Some secret sorrow did her heart distraine:° *oppress*
Which to allay, and calme her storming paine,
Faire feeling words he wisely gan display,
And for her humour fitting purpose faine,[3]
To tempt the cause it selfe for to bewray;
Wherewith emmoved, these bleeding words she gan to say.

39

"What worlds delight, or joy of living speach
Can heart, so plunged in sea of sorrowes deepe,
And heapéd with so huge misfortunes, reach?
The carefull° cold beginneth for to creepe, *afflicting*
And in my heart his yron arrow steepe,
Soone as I thinke upon my bitter bale:° *grief*
Such helplesse harmes yts better hidden keepe,
Then rip up° griefe, where it may not availe, *lay bare*
My last left comfort is, my woes to weepe and waile."

40

"Ah Ladie deare," quoth then the gentle knight,
Well may I weene,° your griefe is wondrous great; *believe*
For wondrous great griefe groneth in my spright,
Whiles thus I heare you of your sorrowes treat.
But wofull Ladie let me you intrete,
For to unfold the anguish of your hart:
Mishaps are maistred by advice discrete,

1. Smooth round bit.
2. I.e., tread lightly and eagerly.
3. I.e., suited his speech and demeanor to her sorrowful mood.

And counsell mittigates the greatest smart;
Found never helpe, who never would his hurts impart."

41

"O but," quoth she, "great griefe will not be tould,
And can more easily be thought, then said."
"Right so," quoth he, "but he, that never would,
Could never: will to might gives greatest aid."
"But griefe," quoth she, "does greater grow displaid,
If then it find not helpe, and breedes despaire."
"Despaire breedes not," quoth he, "where faith is staid."° *firm*
"No faith so fast," quoth she, "but flesh does paire."° *impair*
"Flesh may empaire," quoth he, "but reason can repaire."

42

His goodly reason, and well guided speach
So deepe did settle in her gratious thought,
That her perswaded to disclose the breach,
Which love and fortune in her heart had wrought,
And said; "Faire Sir, I hope good hap hath brought
You to inquire the secrets of my griefe,
Or that your wisedome will direct my thought,
Or that your prowesse can me yield reliefe:
Then heare the storie sad, which I shall tell you briefe.

43

"The forlorne Maiden, whom your eyes have seene
The laughing stocke of fortunes mockeries,
Am th'only daughter of a King and Queene,
Whose parents deare, whilest equall° destinies *impartial*
Did runne about,[4] and their felicities
The favourable heavens did not envy,
Did spread their rule through all the territories,
Which Phison and Euphrates floweth by,
And Gehons golden waves doe wash continually.[5]

44

"Till that their cruell curséd enemy,
An huge great Dragon horrible in sight,
Bred in the loathly lakes of Tartary,° *Tartarus (Hell)*
With murdrous ravine,° and devouring might *destruction*
Their kingdome spoild, and countrey wasted quight:
Themselves, for feare into his jawes to fall,
He forst to castle strong to take their flight,

4. I.e., did revolve.
5. Pison, Gihon, Hiddekel, and Euphrates are the four rivers of Paradise (Genesis 2.10–14).

Where fast embard in mightie brasen wall,
He has them now foure yeres[6] besieged to make them thrall.

45

"Full many knights adventurous and stout
Have enterprizd° that Monster to subdew; *undertaken*
From every coast that heaven walks about,
Have thither come the noble Martiall crew,
That famous hard atchievements still pursew,
Yet never any could that girlond win,
But all still shronke,° and still he greater grew: *quailed, fell back*
All they for want of faith, or guilt of sin,
The pitteous pray of his fierce crueltie have bin.

46

"At last yledd with farre reported praise,
Which flying fame throughout the world had spred,
Of doughtie knights, whom Faery land did raise,
That noble order hight° of Maidenhed,[7] *called*
Forthwith to court of Gloriane I sped,
Of Gloriane great Queene of glory bright,
Whose kingdomes seat Cleopolis[8] is red,° *named*
There to obtaine some such redoubted knight,
That Parents deare from tyrants powre deliver might.

47

"It was my chance (my chance was faire and good)
There for to find a fresh unprovéd knight,
Whose manly hands imbrewed° in guiltie blood *stained*
Had never bene, ne ever by his might
Had throwne to ground the unregarded° right: *unrespected*
Yet of his prowesse proofe he since hath made
(I witnesse am) in many a cruell fight;
The groning ghosts of many one dismaide
Have felt the bitter dint of his avenging blade.

48

"And ye the forlorne reliques of his powre,
His byting sword, and his devouring speare,
Which have enduréd many a dreadfull stowre,° *conflict*
Can speake his prowesse, that did earst you beare,
And well could rule: now he hath left you heare,
To be the record of his ruefull losse,

6. The Book of Revelation refers to the dragon's persecution of "the woman clothed with the sun" who "fled into the wilderness, where she had a place prepared of God, that they should feed her there a thousand two hundred and threescore days" (12.1–6).
7. I.e., maidenhood, recalling Queen Elizabeth's virginity; its sign is the head of a maid. The Order parallels England's Order of the Garter, headed by the monarch, in which knights wear insignia that include a figure of George slaying the dragon.
8. "Famed City" or "City of Glory," counterpart of London (but see I.x.58, note).

And of my dolefull disaventurous deare:° *harm, loss*
O heavie record of the good Redcrosse,
Where have you left your Lord, that could so well you tosse?° *wield*

49

"Well hopéd I, and faire beginnings had,
That he my captive languour should redeeme,[9]
Till all unweeting, an Enchaunter bad
His sence abusd, and made him to misdeeme
My loyalty, not such as it did seeme;
That rather death desire, then such despight.[1]
Be judge ye heavens, that all things right esteeme,
How I him loved, and love with all my might,
So thought I eke of him, and thinke I thought aright.

50

"Thenceforth me desolate he quite forsooke,
To wander, where wilde fortune would me lead,
And other bywaies he himselfe betooke,
Where never foot of living wight did tread,
That brought not backe the balefull body dead,[2]
In which him chauncéd false Duessa meete,
Mine onely° foe, mine onely deadly dread, *particular*
Who with her witchcraft and misseeming° sweete, *deception*
Inveigled him to follow her desires unmeete.° *improper*

51

"At last by subtill sleights she him betraid
Unto his foe, a Gyant huge and tall,
Who him disarméd, dissolute,° dismaid, *enfeebled*
Unwares surprisèd, and with mightie mall° *club*
The monster mercilesse him made to fall,
Whose fall did never foe before behold;
And now in darkesome dungeon, wretched thrall,
Remedilesse, for aie° he doth him hold; *ever*
This is my cause of griefe, more great, then may be told."

52

Ere she had ended all, she gan to faint:
But he her comforted and faire bespake,
"Certes, Madame, ye have great cause of plaint,
That stoutest heart, I weene, could cause to quake.
But be of cheare, and comfort to you take:
For till I have acquit° your captive knight, *set free*
Assure your selfe, I will you not forsake."

9. I.e., that he should relieve my condition, captive to sadness (by freeing my parents from the grip of the dragon).
1. I.e., I would prefer death to the outrage of being thought disloyal.
2. I.e., that returned alive.

His chearefull words revived her chearelesse spright,
So forth they went, the Dwarfe them guiding ever right.

Canto VIII

Faire virgin to redeeme her deare
brings Arthur to the fight:
Who slayes the Gyant, wounds the beast,
and strips Duessa quight.

1

Ay me, how many perils doe enfold
The righteous man, to make him daily fall?
Were not, that heavenly grace doth him uphold,
And stedfast truth acquite him out of all.
Her love is firme, her care continuall,
So oft as he through his owne foolish pride,
Or weaknesse is to sinfull bands° made thrall: *bonds*
Else should this Redcrosse knight in bands have dyde,
For whose deliverance she this Prince doth thither guide.

2

They sadly traveild thus, untill they came
Nigh to a castle builded strong and hie:
Then cryde the Dwarfe, "lo yonder is the same,
In which my Lord my liege doth lucklesse lie,
Thrall to that Gyants hatefull tyrannie:
Therefore, deare Sir, your mightie powres assay."
The noble knight alighted by and by[1]
From loftie steede, and bad the Ladie stay,
To see what end of fight should him befall that day.

3

So with the Squire, th'admirer of his might,
He marchéd forth towards that castle wall;
Whose gates he found fast shut, ne living wight
To ward the same, nor answere commers call.
Then tooke that Squire an horne of bugle° small, *wild ox*
Which hong adowne his side in twisted gold,
And tassels gay. Wyde wonders over all
Of that same hornes great vertues weren told,
Which had approvéd° bene in uses manifold. *demonstrated*

4

Was never wight, that heard that shrilling sound,
But trembling feare did feele in every vaine;
Three miles it might be easie heard around,
And Ecchoes three answerd it selfe againe:

1. I.e., immediately.

No false enchauntment, nor deceiptfull traine
Might once abide the terror of that blast,
But presently° was voide and wholly vaine:[2] *at once*
No gate so strong, no locke so firme and fast,
But with that percing noise flew open quite, or brast.° *burst*

5

The same before the Geants gate he blew,
That all the castle quakéd from the ground,
And every dore of freewill open flew.
The Gyant selfe dismaiéd with that sownd,
Where he with his Duessa dalliance° fownd, *amorous play*
In hast came rushing forth from inner bowre,
With staring countenance sterne, as one astownd,
And staggering steps, to weet, what suddein stowre° *disturbance*
Had wrought that horror strange, and dared his dreaded powre.

6

And after him the proud Duessa came,
High mounted on her manyheaded beast,
And every head with fyrie tongue did flame,
And every head was crownéd on his creast,
And bloudie mouthéd with late cruell feast.
That when the knight beheld, his mightie shild
Upon his manly arme he soone addrest,° *placed*
And at him fiercely flew, with courage fild,
And eger greedinesse° through every member thrild. *desire*

7

Therewith the Gyant buckled him to fight,
Inflamed with scornefull wrath and high disdaine,
And lifting up his dreadfull club on hight,
All armed with ragged snubbes° and knottie graine, *snags*
Him thought at first encounter to have slaine.
But wise and warie was that noble Pere,
And lightly leaping from so monstrous maine,° *power*
Did faire avoide the violence him nere;
It booted nought, to thinke, such thunderbolts to beare.

8

Ne shame he thought to shunne so hideous might:
The idle° stroke, enforcing furious way, *futile*
Missing the marke of his misayméd sight
Did fall to ground, and with his heavie sway° *force*
So deepely dinted in the driven clay,

2. The magic horn of Astolfo also terrified evildoers (*Orlando Furioso* 15.14), but this one recalls the ram's horn of Joshua (Joshua 6.5); it also has the power of those who preach God's word: "their sound went into all the earth, and their words unto the ends of the world" (Romans 10.15–18).

That three yardes deepe a furrow up did throw:
The sad earth wounded with so sore assay,° *assault*
Did grone full grievous underneath the blow,
And trembling with strange feare, did like an earthquake show.

9

As when almightie Jove in wrathfull mood,
To wreake° the guilt of mortall sins is bent, *punish*
Hurles forth his thundring dart with deadly food,° *feud*
Enrold in flames, and smouldring dreriment,
Through riven cloudes and molten firmament;
The fierce threeforkéd engin° making way, *weapon*
Both loftie towres and highest trees hath rent,
And all that might his angrie passage stay,
And shooting in the earth, casts up a mount of clay.

10

His boystrous° club, so buried in the ground, *massive*
He could not rearen up againe so light,° *easily*
But that the knight him at avantage found,
And whiles he strove his combred clubbe to quight° *free*
Out of the earth, with blade all burning bright
He smote off his left arme, which like a blocke
Did fall to ground, deprived of native might;
Large streames of bloud out of the trunckéd stocke
Forth gushéd, like fresh water streame from riven rocke.

11

Dismaiéd with so desperate deadly wound,
And eke impatient of[3] unwonted paine,
He loudly brayd with beastly yelling sound,
That all the fields rebellowéd againe;
As great a noyse, as when in Cymbrian plaine[4]
An heard of Bulles, whom kindly rage[5] doth sting,
Do for the milkie mothers want complaine,[6]
And fill the fields with troublous bellowing,
The neighbour woods around with hollow murmur ring.

12

That when his deare Duessa heard, and saw
The evill stownd,° that daungerd her estate, *peril*
Unto his aide she hastily did draw
Her dreadfull beast, who swolne with bloud of late
Came ramping forth with proud presumpteous gate,
And threatned all his heads like flaming brands.

3. I.e., agonized by.
4. Jutland, once called the Cimbric peninsula after its supposedly original inhabitants.
5. I.e., natural passion.
6. I.e., lament the cows' absence.

But him the Squire made quickly to retrate,
Encountring fierce with single° sword in hand, *only*
And twixt him and his Lord did like a bulwarke stand.

13

The proud Duessa full of wrathfull spight,
And fierce disdaine, to be affronted so,
Enforst her purple beast with all her might
That stop° out of the way to overthroe, *obstacle*
Scorning the let° of so unequall foe: *hindrance*
But nathemore° would that courageous swayne *never the more*
To her yeeld passage, gainst his Lord to goe,
But with outrageous strokes did him restraine,
And with his bodie bard the way atwixt them twaine.

14

Then tooke the angrie witch her golden cup,[7]
Which still she bore, replete with magick artes;
Death and despeyre did many thereof sup,
And secret poyson through their inner parts,
Th'eternall bale of heavie wounded harts:
Which after charmes and some enchauntments said,
She lightly sprinkled on his weaker° parts; *too weak*
Therewith his sturdie courage soone was quayd,° *daunted*
And all his senses were with suddeine dread dismayd.

15

So downe he fell before the cruell beast,
Who on his necke his bloudie clawes did seize,
That life nigh crusht out of his panting brest:
No powre he had to stirre, nor will to rize.
That when the carefull° knight gan well avise,° *watchful / notice*
He lightly left the foe, with whom he fought,
And to the beast gan turne his enterprise;
For wondrous anguish in his hart it wrought,
To see his lovéd Squire into such thraldome brought.

16

And high advauncing his bloud-thirstie blade,
Stroke one of those deforméd heads so sore,
That of his puissance proud ensample made;[8]
His monstrous scalpe° downe to his teeth it tore, *skull*
And that misforméd shape mis-shapéd more:
A sea of bloud gusht from the gaping wound,
That her gay garments staynd with filthy gore,

7. The golden cup of Revelation, which Protestant polemic often associated with the Catholic Mass and hence with magic and illusion. Duessa's cup also recalls that of Circe, whose drugs turned men to swine (*Odyssey* 10). Cf. the chalice of Fidelia (I.x.13).
8. "And I saw one of [the beast's] heads as it were wounded to death" (Revelation 13.3).

And overflowéd all the field around;
That over shoes in bloud he waded on the ground.

17

Thereat he roaréd for exceeding paine,
That to have heard, great horror would have bred,
And scourging th'emptie ayre with his long traine,
Through great impatience° of his grievéd hed — *agony*
His gorgeous ryder from her loftie sted
Would have cast downe, and trod in durtie myre,
Had not the Gyant soone her succouréd;
Who all enraged with smart and franticke yre,
Came hurtling in full fierce, and forst the knight retyre.

18

The force, which wont in two to be disperst,
In one alone left° hand he new unites, — *remaining*
Which is through rage more strong then both were erst;
With which his hideous club aloft he dites,° — *raises*
And at his foe with furious rigour smites,
That strongest Oake might seeme to overthrow:
The stroke upon his shield so heavie lites,
That to the ground it doubleth him full low:
What mortall wight could ever beare so monstrous blow?

19

And in his fall his shield, that covered was,
Did loose his vele by chaunce, and open flew:
The light whereof, that heavens light did pas,° — *surpass*
Such blazing brightnesse through the aier threw,
That eye mote not the same endure to vew.
Which when the Gyaunt spyde with staring eye,
He downe let fall his arme, and soft withdrew
His weapon huge, that heavéd was on hye
For to have slaine the man, that on the ground did lye.

20

And eke the fruitfull-headed° beast, amazed — *many-headed*
At flashing beames of that sunshiny shield,
Became starke blind, and all his senses dazed,
That downe he tumbled on the durtie field,
And seemed himselfe as conqueréd to yield.[9]
Whom when his maistresse proud perceived to fall,
Whiles yet his feeble feet for faintnesse reeld,
Unto the Gyant loudly she gan call,
"O helpe Orgoglio, helpe, or else we perish all."

9. Similarly the brightness of Ruggiero's shield, when displayed, overthrows his opponents (*Orlando Furioso* 22).

21

At her so pitteous cry was much amooved
Her champion stout, and for to ayde his frend,
Againe his wonted angry weapon prooved:° *tried*
But all in vaine: for he has read his end
In that bright shield, and all their forces spend
Themselves in vaine: for since that glauncing° sight, *dazzling*
He hath no powre to hurt, nor to defend;
As where th'Almighties lightning brond does light,
It dimmes the dazéd eyen, and daunts the senses quight.

22

Whom when the Prince, to battell new addrest,
And threatning high his dreadfull stroke did see,
His sparkling blade about his head he blest,° *brandished*
And smote off quite his right leg by the knee,
That downe he tombled; as an aged tree;[1]
High growing on the top of rocky clift,
Whose hartstrings with keene steele nigh hewen be,
The mightie trunck halfe rent, with ragged rift
Doth roll adowne the rocks, and fall with fearefull drift.° *force*

23

Or as a Castle[2] rearéd high and round,
By subtile engins and malitious slight° *trickery*
Is underminéd from the lowest ground,
And her foundation forst,° and feebled quight, *shattered*
At last downe falles, and with her heapéd hight
Her hastie ruine does more heavie° make, *forceful*
And yields it selfe unto the victours might;
Such was this Gyaunts fall, that seemd to shake
The stedfast globe of earth, as it for feare did quake.

24

The knight then lightly leaping to the pray,
With mortall steele him smot againe so sore,
That headlesse his unweldy bodie lay,
All wallowd in his owne fowle bloudy gore,
Which flowéd from his wounds in wondrous store.
But soone as breath out of his breast did pas,
That huge great body, which the Gyaunt bore,
Was vanisht quite, and of that monstrous mas
Was nothing left, but like an emptie bladder was.

1. The simile has many classical analogues; see, e.g., *Aeneid* 2.626–31.
2. If the defeat of Orgoglio recalls that of the Spanish Armada there may be a pun on "Castle"/ Castile.

25

Whose grievous fall, when false Duessa spide,
  Her golden cup she cast unto the ground,
  And crownéd mitre rudely threw aside;
  Such percing griefe her stubborne hart did wound,
  That she could not endure that dolefull stound,° *sorrow*
  But leaving all behind her, fled away:
  The light-foot Squire her quickly turnd around,
  And by hard meanes enforcing her to stay,
So brought unto his Lord, as his deservéd pray.

26

The royall Virgin, which beheld from farre,
  In pensive plight, and sad perplexitie,
  The whole atchievement° of this doubtfull warre, *course*
  Came running fast to greet his victorie,
  With sober gladnesse, and myld modestie,
  And with sweet joyous cheare him thus bespake;
  "Faire braunch of noblesse, flowre of chevalrie,
  That with your worth the world amazéd make,
How shall I quite° the paines, ye suffer for my sake? *pay for*

27

"And you[3] fresh bud of vertue springing fast,
  Whom these sad eyes saw nigh unto deaths dore,
  What hath poore Virgin for such perill past,
  Wherewith you to reward? Accept therefore
  My simple selfe, and service evermore;
  And he that high does sit, and all things see
  With equall° eyes, their merites to restore,° *impartial / reward*
  Behold what ye this day have done for mee,
And what I cannot quite, requite° with usuree.° *repay / interest*

28

"But sith the heavens, and your faire handeling° *conduct*
  Have made you maister of the field this day,
  Your fortune maister eke with governing,° *active control*
  And well begun end all so well, I pray,
  Ne let that wicked woman scape away;
  For she it is, that did my Lord bethrall,
  My dearest Lord, and deepe in dongeon lay,
  Where he his better dayes hath wasted all.
O heare, how piteous he to you for ayd does call."

3. I.e., the Squire.

29

Forthwith he gave in charge unto his Squire,
That scarlot whore to keepen carefully;
Whiles he himselfe with greedie° great desire *eager*
Into the Castle entred forcibly,
Where living creature none he did espye;
Then gan he lowdly through the house to call:
But no man cared to answere to his crye.
There raignd a solemne silence over all,
Nor voice was heard, nor wight was seene in bowre or hall.

30

At last with creeping crooked pace forth came
An old old man, with beard as white as snow,
That on a staffe his feeble steps did frame,° *support*
And guide his wearie gate both too and fro:
For his eye sight him failéd long ygo,
And on his arme a bounch of keyes he bore,
The which unuséd rust did overgrow:
Those were the keyes of every inner dore,
But he could not them use, but kept them still in store.

31

But very uncouth sight was to behold,
How he did fashion his untoward° pace, *awkward*
For as he forward mooved his footing old,
So backward still was turnd his wrincled face,
Unlike to men, who ever as they trace,° *walk*
Both feet and face one way are wont to lead.
This was the auncient keeper of that place,
And foster father of the Gyant dead;
His name Ignaro[4] did his nature right aread.° *indicate*

32

His reverend haires and holy gravitie
The knight much honord, as beseeméd well;[5]
And gently askt, where all the people bee,
Which in that stately building wont to dwell.
Who answerd him full soft, he could not tell.
Againe he askt, where that same knight was layd,
Whom great Orgoglio with his puissaunce fell
Had made his caytive thrall; againe he sayde,
He could not tell: ne ever other answere made.

4. Ignorance: his backward-turned face indicates a preoccupation with the past, perhaps including the Law of the Old Testament.
5. I.e., as was proper.

33

Then askéd he, which way he in might pas:
He could not tell, againe he answeréd.
Thereat the curteous knight displeaséd was,
And said, "Old sire, it seemes thou hast not red° — *recognized*
How ill it sits° with that same silver hed — *accords*
In vaine to mocke, or mockt in vaine to bee:
But if thou be, as thou art pourtrahéd
With natures pen, in ages grave degree,
Aread° in graver wise, what I demaund of thee." — *tell*

34

His answere likewise was, he could not tell.
Whose sencelesse speach, and doted° ignorance — *senile*
When as the noble Prince had markéd well,
He ghest his nature by his countenance,
And calmd his wrath with goodly temperance.
Then to him stepping, from his arme did reach
Those keyes, and made himselfe free enterance.
Each dore he opened without any breach;° — *forcing*
There was no barre to stop, nor foe him to empeach.° — *oppose*

35

There all within full rich arayd he found,
With royall arras° and resplendent gold. — *tapestry*
And did with store of every thing abound,
That greatest Princes presence° might behold. — *person*
But all the floore (too filthy to be told)
With bloud of guiltlesse babes, and innocents trew,
Which there were slaine, as sheepe out of the fold,
Defiléd was, that dreadfull was to vew,
And sacred° ashes over it was strowéd new. — *accursed*

36

And there beside of marble stone was built
An Altare, carved with cunning imagery,
On which true Christians bloud was often spilt,
And holy Martyrs often doen to dye,[6]
With cruell malice and strong tyranny:
Whose blessed sprites from underneath the stone
To God for vengeance cryde continually,
And with great griefe were often heard to grone,
That hardest heart would bleede, to heare their piteous mone.[7]

6. I.e., put to death.
7. "I saw under the altar the souls of them that were slain for the word of God, and for the testimony which they held: And they cried with a loud voice, saying, How long, O Lord, holy and true, dost thou not judge and avenge our blood on them that dwell on the earth?" (Revelation 6.9–10). The scriptural echoes in stanzas 35–36 (cf. Matthew 2.16) further associate Arthur with Christ.

37

Through every rowme he sought, and every bowr,
But no where could he find that wofull thrall:
At last he came unto an yron doore,
That fast was lockt, but key found not at all
Emongst that bounch, to open it withall;
But in the same a little grate was pight,° *placed*
Through which he sent his voyce, and lowd did call
With all his powre, to weet, if living wight
Were houséd therewithin, whom he enlargen° might. *free*

38

Therewith an hollow, dreary, murmuring voyce
These piteous plaints and dolours did resound;
"O who is that, which brings me happy choyce° *chance*
Of death, that here lye dying every stound,° *moment*
Yet live perforce in balefull darkenesse bound?
For now three Moones have changéd thrice their hew,° *shape*
And have been thrice hid underneath the ground,
Since I the heavens chearefull face did vew,
O welcome thou, that doest of death bring tydings trew."

39

Which when that Champion heard, with percing point
Of pitty deare° his hart was thrilléd sore, *grievous*
And trembling horrour ran through every joynt,
For ruth of gentle knight so fowle forlore.° *lost*
Which shaking off, he rent that yron dore,
With furious force, and indignation fell;
Where entred in, his foot could find no flore,
But all a deepe descent, as darke as hell,
That breathéd ever forth a filthie banefull smell.

40

But neither darkenesse fowle, nor filthy bands,
Nor noyous° smell his purpose could withhold, *poisonous*
(Entire affection hateth nicer° hands) *too fastidious*
But that with constant zeale, and courage bold,
After long paines and labours manifold,
He found the meanes that Prisoner up to reare;
Whose feeble thighes, unhable to uphold
His pinéd° corse, him scarse to light could beare, *wasted*
A ruefull spectacle of death and ghastly drere.° *wretchedness*

41

His sad dull eyes deepe sunck in hollow pits,
Could not endure th'unwonted sunne to view;
His bare thin cheekes for want of better bits,° *food*

And empty sides deceivéd° of their dew, *defrauded*
Could make a stony hart his hap to rew;
His rawbone armes, whose mighty brawnéd bowrs° *muscles*
Were wont to rive steele plates, and helmets hew,
Were cleane consumed, and all his vitall powres
Decayd, and all his flesh shronk up like withered flowres.[8]

42

Whom when his Lady saw, to him she ran
With hasty joy: to see him made her glad,
And sad to view his visage pale and wan,
Who earst in flowres of freshest youth was clad.
Tho° when her well of teares she wasted had, *then*
She said, "Ah dearest Lord, what evill starre
On you hath fround, and pourd his influence bad,
That of your selfe ye thus berobbéd arre,
And this misseeming hew[9] your manly looks doth marre?

43

"But welcome now my Lord, in wele or woe,
Whose presence I have lackt too long a day;
And fie on Fortune mine avowéd foe,
Whose wrathfull wreakes° them selves do now alay. *revenges*
And for these wrongs shall treble penaunce pay
Of treble good: good growes of evils priefe."° *experience*
The chearelesse man, whom sorrow did dismay,
Had no delight to treaten° of his griefe; *speak*
His long enduréd famine needed more reliefe.

44

"Faire Lady," then said that victorious knight,[1]
"The things, that grievous were to do, or beare,
Them to renew,° I wote, breeds no delight; *recall*
Best musicke breeds delight in loathing eare:
But th'onely good, that growes of passéd feare,
Is to be wise, and ware° of like agein. *wary*
This dayes ensample hath this lesson deare
Deepe written in my heart with yron pen,
That blisse may not abide in state of mortall men.

45

"Henceforth sir knight, take to you wonted strength,
And maister these mishaps with patient might;

8. Breaking down an infernal iron door so as mercifully to lead a captive back to the light recalls the Harrowing of Hell as described in the apocryphal but popular Gospel of Nicodemus. The belief that while he was dead Christ liberated the righteous who lived before his time is, however, older than this composite text from the fourth or fifth century. I.x.40 explicitly associates the redemption of prisoners with Christ's rescue operation.
9. I.e., unseemly appearance.
1. I.e., Arthur.

Loe where your foe lyes stretcht in monstrous length,
And loe that wicked woman in your sight,
The roote of all your care, and wretched plight,
Now in your powre, to let her live, or dye."
"To do her dye," quoth Una, "were despight,° *spiteful*
And shame t'avenge so weake an enimy;
But spoile° her of her scarlot robe, and let her fly." *deprive*

46

So as she bad, that witch they disaraid,
And robd of royall robes, and purple pall,
And ornaments that richly were displaid;
Ne sparéd they to strip her naked all.
Then when they had despoild her tire° and call,° *attire / headdress*
Such as she was, their eyes might her behold,
That her misshapéd parts did them appall,
A loathly, wrinckled hag, ill favoured, old,
Whose secret filth good manners biddeth not be told.[2]

47

Her craftie head was altogether bald,
And as in hate of honorable eld,° *age*
Was overgrowne with scurfe and filthy scald;° *scabby disease*
Her teeth out of her rotten gummes were feld,° *fallen*
And her sowre breath abhominably smeld;
Her driéd dugs, like bladders lacking wind,
Hong downe, and filthy matter from them weld;
Her wrizled° skin as rough, as maple rind, *wrinkled*
So scabby was, that would have loathd° all womankind. *disgusted*

48

Her neather parts, the shame of all her kind,[3]
My chaster° Muse for shame doth blush to write; *very chaste*
But at her rompe she growing had behind
A foxes taile, with dong all fowly dight;° *smeared*
And eke her feet most monstrous were in sight;
For one of them was like an Eagles claw,
With griping talaunts° armd to greedy fight, *talons*
The other like a Beares uneven° paw.[4] *rough*
More ugly shape yet never living creature saw.

2. Alcina is likewise revealed to the disenchanted Ruggiero in *Orlando Furioso* 7.71–73; see Revelation 17.16: "these shall hate the whore, and shall make her desolate and naked."
3. This phrase has received sometimes vexed commentary. What "her kind" means is not fully clear: witchy, female, or human? One older word for the genitalia of both sexes is "pudenda": the shameful parts (the dirty bits), those that modesty bids us cover, so are we to read this as sexism or more general commentary on humankind's fallen condition?
4. "And the . . . feet [of the beast] were as the feet of a bear" (Revelation 13.2). Like the fox, falsehood is crafty; like eagle and bear, rapacious and brutal.

49

Which when the knights beheld, amazd they were,
And wondred at so fowle deforméd wight.
"Such then," said Una, "as she seemeth here,
Such is the face of falshood, such the sight
Of fowle Duessa, when her borrowed light
Is laid away, and counterfesaunce° knowne." *deception*
Thus when they had the witch disrobéd quight,
And all her filthy feature° open showne, *form*
They let her goe at will, and wander wayes unknowne.

50

She flying fast from heavens hated face,
And from the world that her discovered wide,° *widely*
Fled to the wastfull wildernesse apace,
From living eyes her open shame to hide,
And lurkt in rocks and caves long unespide.
But that faire crew of knights, and Una faire
Did in that castle afterwards abide,
To rest them selves, and weary powres repaire,
Where store they found of all, that dainty was and rare.

Canto IX

His loves and lignage Arthur tells:
The knights knit friendly bands:
Sir Trevisan flies from Despayre,
Whom Redcrosse knight withstands.

1

O goodly golden chaine,[1] wherewith yfere° *together*
The vertues linkéd are in lovely wize:
And noble minds of yore allyéd were,
In brave poursuit of chevalrous emprize,° *enterprise*
That none did others saféty despize,
Nor aid envy° to him, in need that stands, *begrudge*
But friendly each did others prayse devize
How to advaunce with favourable hands,
As this good Prince redeemd the Redcrosse knight from bands.

2

Who when their powres, empaird through labour long,
With dew repast they had recuréd° well, *restored*
And that weake captive wight now wexéd strong,
Them list no lenger there at leasure dwell,

1. See I.v.25, note. Chaucer, following Boethius, speaks of "the faire cheyne of love" with which "the Firste Moevere" linked the elements ("Knightes Tale," 2987–92) and also of love, "that with an holsom alliaunce / Halt peples joyned, as hym lest hem gye, / Love, that knetteth lawe of compaignie; / And couples doth in vertue for to dwelle" (*Troilus and Criseyde* 3.1746–49).

But forward fare, as their adventures fell,° *befell*
But ere they parted, Una faire besought
That straunger knight his name and nation tell;
Least so great good, as he for her had wrought,
Should die unknown, and buried be in thanklesse thought.

3

"Faire virgin," said the Prince, "ye me require
A thing without the compas° of my wit: *scope*
For both the lignage and the certain Sire,
From which I sprong, from me are hidden yit.
For all so soone as life did me admit
Into this world, and shewéd heavens light,
From mothers pap I taken was unfit.° *unsuitably*
And streight delivered to a Faery knight,
To be upbrought in gentle thewes° and martiall might. *manners*

4

"Unto old Timon[2] he me brought bylive,° *immediately*
Old Timon, who in youthly yeares hath beene
In warlike feates th'expertest man alive,
And is the wisest now on earth I weene;
His dwelling is low in a valley greene,
Under the foot of Rauran[3] mossy hore,° *gray*
From whence the river Dee as silver cleene° *pure*
His tombling billowes rolls with gentle rore:
There all my dayes he traind me up in vertuous lore.

5

"Thither the great Magicien Merlin came,
As was his use, ofttimes to visit me:
For he had charge my discipline to frame,
And Tutours nouriture° to oversee. *training*
Him oft and oft I askt in privitie,
Of what loines and what lignage I did spring:
Whose aunswere bad me still assuréd bee,
That I was sonne and heire unto a king,
As time in her just terme[4] the truth to light should bring."

6

"Well worthy impe,"° said then the Lady gent,° *scion / gentle*
"And Pupill fit for such a Tutours hand.
But what adventure, or what high intent
Hath brought you hither into Faery land,
Aread° Prince Arthur, crowne of Martiall band?" *tell*

2. "Honor." Either the "Faery knight" of stanza 3 (perhaps Malory's Sir Ector) or, more probably, Merlin brought the child to Timon.
3. A hill in western Wales.
4. I.e., in due course.

"Full hard it is," quoth he, "to read° aright — *discern*
The course of heavenly cause, or understand
The secret meaning of th'eternall might,
That rules mens wayes, and rules the thoughts of living wight.[5]

7

"For whither he through fatall° deepe foresight — *prophetic*
Me hither sent, for cause to me unghest,
Or that fresh bleeding wound, which day and night
Whilome° doth rancle in my riven brest, — *incessantly*
With forcéd fury following his° behest, — *its*
Me hither brought by wayes yet never found,
You to have helpt I hold my selfe yet blest."
"Ah curteous knight," quoth she, "what secret wound
Could ever find,° to grieve the gentlest hart on ground?" — *succeed*

8

"Deare Dame," quoth he, "you sleeping sparkes awake,
Which troubled once, into huge flames will grow,
Ne ever will their fervent fury slake,
Till living moysture into smoke do flow,
And wasted° life do lye in ashes low. — *consumed*
Yet sithens° silence lesseneth not my fire, — *since*
But told it flames, and hidden it does glow,
I will revele, what ye so much desire:
Ah Love, lay downe thy bow, the whiles I may respire.° — *breathe*

9

"It was in freshest flowre of youthly yeares,
When courage first does creepe in manly chest,
Then first the coale of kindly° heat appeares — *natural*
To kindle love in every living brest;
But me had warnd old Timons wise behest,° — *bidding*
Those creeping flames by reason to subdew,
Before their rage grew to so great unrest,
As miserable lovers use to rew,
Which still wex old in woe, whiles woe still wexeth new.

10

"That idle name of love, and lovers life,
As losse of time, and vertues enimy
I ever scornd, and joyd to stirre up strife,
In middest of their mournfull Tragedy,
Ay wont to laugh, when them I heard to cry,
And blow the fire, which them to ashes brent:° — *burned*
Their God himselfe,[6] grieved at my libertie,

5. "How unsearchable are his judgments, and his ways past finding out" (Romans 11.33).
6. I.e., Cupid.

Shot many a dart at me with fiers intent,
But I them warded all with wary government.° *self-discipline*

11

"But all in vaine: no fort can be so strong,
Ne fleshly brest can arméd be so sound,
But will at last be wonne with battrie long,
Or unawares at disavantage found;
Nothing is sure, that growes on earthly ground:
And who most trustes in arme of fleshly might,
And boasts, in beauties chaine not to be bound,
Doth soonest fall in disaventrous° fight, *disastrous*
And yeeldes his caytive neck to victours most despight.[7]

12

"Ensample make of him your haplesse joy,
And of my selfe now mated,° as ye see; *overcome*
Whose prouder° vaunt that proud avenging boy *too proud*
Did soone pluck downe, and curbd my libertie.
For on a day prickt° forth with jollitie *urged*
Of looser° life, and heat of hardiment,° *too loose / boldness*
Raunging the forest wide on courser free,
The fields, the floods, the heavens with one consent
Did seeme to laugh on me, and favour mine intent.

13

"For-wearied with my sports, I did alight
From loftie steed, and downe to sleepe me layd;
The verdant gras my couch did goodly dight,° *make*
And pillow was my helmet faire displayd:
Whiles every sence the humour sweet embayd,° *pervaded*
And slombring soft my hart did steale away,
Me seeméd, by my side a royall Mayd
Her daintie limbes full softly down did lay:
So faire a creature yet saw never sunny day.[8]

14

"Most goodly glee° and lovely blandishment° *pleasure / flattery*
She to me made, and bad me love her deare,
For dearely sure her love was to me bent,
As when just time expiréd should appeare.
But whether dreames delude, or true it were,
Was never hart so ravisht with delight,
Ne living man like words did ever heare,

7. I.e., greatest outrage.
8. Celtic folklore or its literary echoes provided Spenser with the outlines of this episode, based on the liaison established by some elf or fairy with a mortal creature.

23

The Redcrosse knight toward him crosséd fast,
To weet, what mister° wight was so dismayd: *kind of*
There him he finds all sencelesse and aghast,
That of him selfe he seemd to be afrayd;
Whom hardly he from flying forward stayd,
Till he these wordes to him deliver might;
"Sir knight, aread who hath ye thus arayd,
And eke from whom make ye this hasty flight:
For never knight I saw in such misseeming° plight." *unseemly*

24

He answerd nought at all, but adding new
Feare to his first amazment, staring wide
With stony eyes, and hartlesse hollow hew,[2]
Astonisht stood, as one that had aspide
Infernall furies, with their chaines untide.
Him yet againe, and yet againe bespake
The gentle knight; who nought to him replide,
But trembling every joynt did inly quake,
And foltring tongue at last these words seemd forth to shake.

25

"For Gods deare love, Sir knight, do me not stay;
For loe he comes, he comes fast after mee."
Eft° looking backe would faine have runne away; *again*
But he him forst to stay, and tellen free
The secret cause of his perplexitie:
Yet nathemore° by his bold hartie speach, *not at all*
Could his bloud-frosen hart emboldned bee,
But through his boldnesse rather feare did reach,° *penetrate*
Yet forst, at last he made through silence suddein breach.

26

"And am I now in safetie sure," quoth he,
"From him, that would have forcéd me to dye?
And is the point of death now turnd fro mee,
That I may tell this haplesse history?"
"Feare nought:" quoth he, "no daunger now is nye."
"Then shall I you recount a ruefull cace,"
Said he, "the which with this unlucky eye
I late beheld, and had not greater grace
Me reft from it, had bene partaker of the place.[3]

2. I.e., despondent, vacant expression.
3. I.e., would have shared my companion's fate.

27

"I lately chaunst (Would I had never chaunst)
With a faire knight to keepen companee,
Sir Terwin hight, that well himselfe advaunst
In all affaires, and was both bold and free,
But not so happie as mote happie bee:
He loved, as was his lot, a Ladie gent,
That him againe° loved in the least degree: *in return*
For she was proud, and of too high intent,° *aspiration*
And joyd to see her lover languish and lament.

28

"From whom returning sad and comfortlesse,
As on the way together we did fare,
We met that villen (God from him me blesse°) *protect*
That curséd wight, from whom I scapt whyleare,° *lately*
A man of hell, that cals himselfe Despaire:[4]
Who first us greets, and after faire areedes° *tells*
Of tydings strange, and of adventures rare:
So creeping close, as Snake in hidden weedes,
Inquireth of our states, and of our knightly deedes.

29

"Which when he knew, and felt our feeble harts
Embost° with bale,° and bitter byting griefe, *exhausted / sorrow*
Which love had launchéd with his deadly darts,
With wounding words and termes of foule repriefe,° *reproach*
He pluckt from us all hope of due reliefe,
That earst us held in love of lingring life;
Then hopelesse hartlesse, gan the cunning thiefe
Perswade us die, to stint° all further strife: *end*
To me he lent this rope, to him a rustie knife.

30

"With which sad instrument of hastie death,
That wofull lover, loathing lenger light,
A wide way made to let forth living breath.
But I more fearefull, or more luckie wight,
Dismayd with that deforméd dismall sight,
Fled fast away, halfe dead with dying feare:

4. The theme of despair recurs in many Renaissance texts, e.g., Skelton's *Magnyfycence*, Sackville's "Induction" in *The Mirror for Magistrates*, and "The Legend of Cordelia" (in the *Mirror's* 1574 edition), which may have contributed details to Spenser's Despair and his wasted landscape. The "disease of desperation" was also a subject for religious and medical works. In *The Anatomy of Melancholy* (1621), Robert Burton describes it as "a most pernicious sin, wherewith the Devil seeks to entrap men . . . The part affected is the whole soul" (3.4.2.2). It especially overwhelms the distressed "if their bodies be predisposed by melancholy, they [be] religiously given, and have tender consciences" (3.4.2.3). Spenser makes his Despair a master rhetorician, and his readers would have recognized a number of the techniques that this most serious of sins exploits.

Ne yet assured of life by you, Sir knight,
Whose like infirmitie like chaunce may beare:
But God you never let his charméd speeches heare."[5]

31

"How may a man," said he, "with idle speach
Be wonne, to spoyle° the Castle of his health?" *deprive*
"I wote," quoth he, "whom triall late did teach,
That like would not[6] for all this worldés wealth:
His subtill tongue, like dropping honny, mealt'th° *melts*
Into the hart, and searcheth every vaine,
That ere one be aware, by secret stealth
His powre is reft,° and weaknesse doth remaine. *taken away*
O never Sir desire to try° his guilefull traine." *test*

32

"Certes,"° said he, "hence shall I never rest, *surely*
Till I that treachours art have heard and tride;
And you Sir knight, whose name mote° I request, *might*
Of grace do me unto his cabin guide."
"I that hight Trevisan," quoth he, "will ride
Against my liking backe, to doe you grace:
But nor for gold nor glee° will I abide *glitter*
By you, when ye arrive in that same place;
For lever° had I die, then see his deadly face." *rather*

33

Ere long they come, where that same wicked wight
His dwelling has, low in an hollow cave,
Farre underneath a craggie clift ypight,° *placed*
Darke, dolefull, drearie, like a greedie grave,
That still for carrion carcases doth crave:
On top whereof aye dwelt the ghastly Owle,
Shrieking his balefull note, which ever drave
Farre from that haunt all other chearefull fowle;
And all about it wandring ghostes did waile and howle.

34

And all about old stockes° and stubs of trees, *stumps*
Whereon nor fruit, nor leafe was ever seene,
Did hang upon the ragged rocky knees;° *crags*
On which had many wretches hangéd beene,
Whose carcases were scattered on the greene,
And throwne about the cliffs. Arrivéd there,
That bare-head knight for dread and dolefull teene,° *grief*

5. I.e., may God keep you from ever hearing his enchanted discourse.
6. I.e., would not (again) do the like.

Would faine have fled, ne durst approchen neare,
But th'other forst him stay, and comforted in feare.

35

That darkesome cave they enter, where they find
That curséd man, low sitting on the ground,
Musing full sadly in his sullein mind;
His griesie° lockes, long growen, and unbound, *gray*
Disordred hong about his shoulders round,
And hid his face; through which his hollow eyne
Lookt deadly dull, and staréd as astound;
His raw-bone cheekes through penurie and pine,° *inner torment*
Were shronke into his jawes, as° he did never dine. *as if*

36

His garment nought but many ragged clouts,° *shreds of clothing*
With thornes together pind and patchéd was,
The which his naked sides he wrapt abouts;
And him beside there lay upon the gras
A drearie corse, whose life away did pas,
All wallowd in his owne yet luke-warme blood,
That from his wound yet welléd fresh alas;
In which a rustie knife fast fixéd stood,
And made an open passage for the gushing flood.

37

Which piteous spectacle, approving° trew *confirming*
The wofull tale that Trevisan had told,
When as the gentle Redcrosse knight did vew,
With firie zeale he burnt in courage bold,
Him to avenge, before his bloud were cold,
And to the villein said, "Thou damnéd wight,
The author of this fact,° we here behold, *deed*
What justice can but judge against thee right,
With thine owne bloud to price° his bloud, here shed *pay for*
in sight."

38

"What franticke fit," quoth he, "hath thus distraught
Thee, foolish man, so rash a doome° to give?[7] *judgment*
What justice ever other judgement taught,
But he should die, who merites not to live?
None else to death this man despayring drive,
But his owne guiltie mind deserving death.
Is then unjust to each his due to give?
Or let him die, that loatheth living breath?
Or let him die at ease, that liveth here uneath?° *uneasily*

7. Despair draws his arguments chiefly from classical Stoicism and from sayings in the Old Testament concerning God's justice; he omits mention of God's mercy.

39

"Who travels by the wearie wandring way,
To come unto his wishéd home in haste,
And meetes a flood, that doth his passage stay,
Is not great grace to helpe him over past,
Or free his feet, that in the myre sticke fast?
Most envious man, that grieves at neighbours good,
And fond,° that joyest in the woe thou hast, *foolish*
Why wilt not let him passe, that long hath stood
Upon the banke, yet wilt thy selfe not passe the flood?

40

"He there does now enjoy eternall rest
And happie ease, which thou doest want and crave,
And further from it daily wanderest:
What if some litle paine the passage have,
That makes fraile flesh to feare the bitter wave?
Is not short paine well borne, that brings long ease,
And layes the soule to sleepe in quiet grave?
Sleepe after toyle, port after stormie seas,
Ease after warre, death after life does greatly please."

41

The knight much wondred at his suddeine° wit, *quick*
And said, "The terme of life is limited,
Ne may a man prolong, nor shorten it;
The souldier may not move from watchfull sted,° *position*
Nor leave his stand, untill his Captaine bed."° *directs*
"Who life did limit by almightie doome,"
Quoth he, "knowes best the termes establishéd;
And he, that points° the Centonell his roome,° *appoints / station*
Doth license him depart at sound of morning droome.[8]

42

"Is not his deed, what ever thing is donne,
In heaven and earth? did not he all create
To die againe? all ends that was begonne.
Their times in his eternall booke of fate
Are written sure, and have their certaine date.
Who then can strive with strong necessitie,
That holds the world in his° still chaunging state, *its*
Or shunne the death ordaynd by destinie?
When houre of death is come, let none aske whence, nor why.

8. I.e., the morning drum that gives the sentinel permission to leave. Despair's response paraphrases Cicero on the advice of Pythagoras (*De Senectute* 20). The temptation to rest, to a premature Sabbath, would have resonated with Spenser's many readers who imagined life as a pilgrimage or battle, two common analogies for the Christian life.

43

"The lenger life, I wote the greater sin,
The greater sin, the greater punishment:
All those great battels, which thou boasts to win,
Through strife, and bloud-shed, and avengément,
Now praysd, hereafter deare thou shalt repent:
For life must life, and bloud must bloud repay.[9]
Is not enough thy evill life forespent?° *already spent*
For he, that once hath misséd the right way,
The further he doth goe, the further he doth stray.

44

"Then do no further goe, no further stray,
But here lie downe, and to thy rest betake,
Th'ill to prevent, that life ensewen may.[1]
For what hath life, that may it lovéd make,
And gives not rather cause it to forsake?
Feare, sicknesse, age, losse, labour, sorrow, strife,
Paine, hunger, cold, that makes the hart to quake;
And ever fickle fortune rageth rife,
All which, and thousands mo° do make a loathsome life. *more*

45

"Thou wretched man, of death hast greatest need,
If in true ballance thou wilt weigh thy state:
For never knight, that daréd warlike deede,
More lucklesse disaventures did amate.° *daunt, cast down*
Witnesse the dongeon deepe, wherein of late
Thy life shut up, for death so oft did call;
And though good lucke prolongéd hath thy date,° *life span*
Yet death then, would the like mishaps forestall,
Into the which hereafter thou maiest happen fall.

46

"Why then doest thou, O man of sin, desire
To draw thy dayes forth to their last degree?
Is not the measure of thy sinfull hire
High heapéd up with huge iniquitie,
Against the day of wrath,[2] to burden thee?
Is not enough, that to this Ladie milde
Thou falséd hast thy faith with perjurie,
And sold thy selfe to serve Duessa vilde,° *vile*
With whom in all abuse thou hast thy selfe defilde?

9. "Whoso sheddeth man's blood, by man shall his blood be shed" (Genesis 9.6). The stanza's opening lines appear to derive from a poem in *Tottel's Miscellany*, ed. Hyder Rollins (Cambridge, MA, 1965), no. 174.
1. I.e., that the remainder of your life may bring.
2. I.e., Doomsday.

47

"Is not he just, that all this doth behold
From highest heaven, and beares an equall° eye? *impartial*
Shall he thy sins up in his knowledge fold,
And guiltie be of thine impietie?
Is not his law, Let every sinner die:
Die shall all flesh?[3] what then must needs be donne,
Is it not better to doe willinglie,
Then linger, till the glasse be all out ronne?
Death is the end of woes: die soone, O faeries sonne."

48

The knight was much enmovéd with his speach,
That as a swords point through his hart did perse,
And in his conscience made a secret breach,
Well knowing true all, that he did reherse,° *recount*
And to his fresh remembrance did reverse° *recall*
The ugly vew of his deforméd crimes,
That all his manly powres it did disperse,
As he were charméd with inchaunted rimes,
That oftentimes he quakt, and fainted oftentimes.

49

In which amazement, when the Miscreant
Perceivéd him to waver weake and fraile,
Whiles trembling horror did his conscience dant,° *daunt*
And hellish anguish did his soule assaile,
To drive him to despaire, and quite to quaile,° *be dismayed*
He shewed him painted in a table° plaine, *picture*
The damnéd ghosts, that doe in torments waile,
And thousand feends that doe them endlesse paine
With fire and brimstone, which for ever shall remaine.

50

The sight whereof so throughly him dismaid,
That nought but death before his eyes he saw,
And ever burning wrath before him laid,
By righteous sentence of th'Almighties law:
Then gan the villein him to overcraw,° *exult over*
And brought unto him swords, ropes, poison, fire,
And all that might him to perdition draw;
And bad him choose, what death he would desire:
For death was due to him, that had provokt Gods ire.

51

But when as none of them he saw him take,
He to him raught° a dagger sharpe and keene, *held out*

3. "All flesh shall perish together, and man shall turn again into dust" (Job 34.15).

And gave it him in hand: his hand did quake,
And tremble like a leafe of Aspin greene,
And troubled bloud through his pale face was seene
To come, and goe with tydings from the hart,
As it a running messenger had beene.
At last resolved to worke his finall smart,
He lifted up his hand, that backe againe did start.

52

Which when as Una saw, through every vaine
The crudled° cold ran to her well of life,[4] *congealing*
As in a swowne: but soone relived° againe, *recovered*
Out of his hand she snatcht the curséd knife,
And threw it to the ground, enragéd rife,° *deeply*
And to him said, "Fie, fie, faint harted knight,
What meanest thou by this reprochfull strife?
Is this the battell, which thou vauntst to fight
With that fire-mouthéd Dragon, horrible and bright?

53

"Come, come away, fraile, feeble, fleshly wight,[5]
Ne let vaine words bewitch thy manly hart,
Ne divelish thoughts dismay thy constant spright.
In heavenly mercies hast thou not a part?
Why shouldst thou then despeire, that chosen art?
Where justice growes, there grows eke greater grace,
The which doth quench the brond of hellish smart,
And that accurst hand-writing doth deface.° *blot out*
Arise, Sir knight arise, and leave this curséd place."

54

So up he rose, and thence amounted° streight. *mounted (his horse)*
Which when the carle° beheld, and saw his guest *churl*
Would safe depart, for all his subtill sleight,
He chose an halter from among the rest,
And with it hung himselfe, unbid° unblest. *not prayed for*
But death he could not worke himselfe thereby;
For thousand times he so himselfe had drest,° *made ready*
Yet nathelesse it could not doe him die,
Till he should die his last, that is eternally.

4. I.e., her heart.
5. Una's terse language recalls the shield of faith by which "ye shall be able to quench all the fiery darts of the wicked" (Ephesians 6.16) and the significance of Christ's death, "Blotting out the handwriting of ordinances that was against us" (Colossians 2.14).

Canto X

Her faithfull knight faire Una brings
to house of Holinesse,
Where he is taught repentance, and
the way to heavenly blesse.° *bliss*

1

What man is he, that boasts of fleshly might,
And vaine assurance of mortality,° *mortal life*
Which all so soone, as it doth come to fight,
Against spirituall foes, yeelds by and by,[1]
Or from the field most cowardly doth fly?
Ne let the man ascribe it to his skill,
That thorough grace hath gainéd victory.
If any strength we have, it is to ill,
But all the good is Gods, both power and eke will.[2]

2

By that, which lately hapned, Una saw,
That this her knight was feeble, and too faint;
And all his sinews woxen weake and raw,° *unready*
Through long enprisonment, and hard constraint,
Which he enduréd in his late restraint,
That yet he was unfit for bloudie fight:
Therefore to cherish him with diets daint,° *dainty*
She cast to bring him, where he chearen° might, *be refreshed*
Till he recovered had his° late decayéd plight. *from his*

3

There was an auntient house not farre away,
Renowmd throughout the world for sacred lore,
And pure unspotted life: so well they say
It governd was, and guided evermore,
Through wisedome of a matrone grave and hore;° *gray-haired*
Whose onely joy was to relieve the needes
Of wretched soules, and helpe the helpelesse pore:
All night she spent in bidding of her bedes;[3]
And all the day in doing good and godly deedes.

1. I.e., at once.
2. "For by grace are ye saved through faith; and that not of yourselves: it is the gift of God: Not of works, lest any man should boast" (Ephesians 2.8–9). In the context of Reformation polemic, the insistence that spiritual victory is due to God, not to human "skill," is a Protestant emphasis.
3. I.e., saying her prayers (a "bead" was originally a prayer to be counted on a string of what we now call "beads"). Spenser's "beads" might well recall the rosary to his readers; the presence of such seemingly Catholic elements in this house of Holinesse has sometimes puzzled readers and provoked commentary. That this as yet unnamed matron prays in private and does good openly suits Matthew 6.5–6.

4

Dame Caelia[4] men did her call, as thought
From heaven to come, or thither to arise,
The mother of three daughters, well upbrought
In goodly thewes,° and godly exercise: *discipline*
The eldest two most sober, chast, and wise,
Fidelia and Speranza virgins were,
Though spousd,° yet wanting wedlocks solemnize; *betrothed*
But faire Charissa to a lovely fere° *mate*
Was linckéd, and by him had many pledges dere.[5]

5

Arrivéd there, the dore they find fast lockt;
For it was warely watchéd night and day,
For feare of many foes: but when they knockt,
The Porter opened unto them streight way:
He was an aged syre, all hory gray,
With lookes full lowly cast, and gate full slow,
Wont on a staffe his feeble steps to stay,
Hight Humiltá.[6] They passe in stouping low;
For streight and narrow was the way, which he did show.[7]

6

Each goodly thing is hardest to begin,
But entred in a spacious court they see,
Both plaine, and pleasant to be walkéd in,
Where them does meete a francklin° faire and free, *freeman, landowner*
And entertaines with comely courteous glee,
His name was Zele, that him right well became,
For in his speeches and behaviour hee
Did labour lively to expresse the same,
And gladly did them guide, till to the Hall they came.

7

There fairely them receives a gentle Squire,
Of milde demeanure, and rare courtesie,
Right cleanly clad in comely sad° attire; *sober*
In word and deede that shewed great modestie,
And knew his good° to all of each degree, *proper behavior*
Hight Reverence. He them with speeches meet
Does faire entreat; no courting nicetie,° *affectation*

4. "Heavenly."
5. I.e., many children. The daughters' names mean Faith, Hope, and Charity (or "spiritual love"). "And now abideth faith, hope, charity, these three; but the greatest of these is charity" (1 Corinthians 13.13).
6. Humility.
7. "Knock, and it shall be opened unto you" (Matthew 7.7), but "Strait is the gate, and narrow is the way, which leadeth unto life, and few there be that find it" (7.14).

But simple true, and eke unfainéd sweet,
As might become a Squire so great persons to greet.

8

And afterwards them to his Dame he leades,
That aged Dame, the Ladie of the place:
Who all this while was busie at her beades:
Which doen, she up arose with seemely grace,
And toward them full matronely did pace.
Where when that fairest Una she beheld,
Whom well she knew to spring from heavenly race,
Her hart with joy unwonted inly sweld,
As feeling wondrous comfort in her weaker eld.° *old age*

9

And her embracing said, "O happie earth,
Whereon thy innocent feet doe ever tread,
Most vertuous virgin borne of heavenly berth,
That to redeeme thy woefull parents head,
From tyrans rage, and ever-dying dread,[8]
Hast wandred through the world now long a day;
Yet ceasest not thy wearie soles to lead,
What grace hath thee now hither brought this way?
Or doen thy feeble feet unweeting° hither stray? *unwittingly*

10

"Strange thing it is an errant° knight to see *wandering*
Here in this place, or any other wight,
That hither turnes his steps. So few there bee,
That chose the narrow path, or seeke the right:
All keepe the broad high way, and take delight
With many rather for to go astray,
And be partakers of their evill plight,
Then with a few to walke the rightest way;
O foolish men, why haste ye to your owne decay?"

11

"Thy selfe to see, and tyred limbs to rest,
O matrone sage," quoth she, "I hither came,
And this good knight his way with me addrest,° *directed*
Led with thy prayses and broad-blazéd fame,
That up to heaven is blowne." The auncient Dame
Him goodly greeted in her modest guise,
And entertaynd them both, as best became,
With all the court'sies, that she could devise,
Ne wanted ought, to shew her bounteous or wise.

8. I.e., continual fear of death, or fear of eternal death.

12

Thus as they gan of sundry things devise,° *discourse*
Loe two most goodly virgins came in place,
Ylinkéd arme in arme in lovely° wise, *loving*
With countenance demure, and modest grace,
They numbred even steps and equall pace:
Of which the eldest, that Fidelia hight,
Like sunny beames threw from her Christall face,
That could have dazd the rash beholders sight,
And round about her head did shine like heavens light.

13

She was araiéd all in lilly white,
And in her right hand bore a cup of gold,
With wine and water fild up to the hight,
In which a Serpent did himselfe enfold,
That horrour made to all, that did behold;
But she no whit did chaunge her constant mood:° *expression*
And in her other hand she fast did hold
A booke, that was both signd and seald with blood,
Wherein darke things were writ, hard to be understood.[9]

14

Her younger sister, that Speranza hight,
Was clad in blew, that her beseeméd well;
Not all so chearefull seeméd she of sight,
As was her sister; whether dread did dwell,
Or anguish in her hart, is hard to tell:
Upon her arme a silver anchor lay,
Whereon she leanéd ever, as befell:
And ever up to heaven, as she did pray,
Her stedfast eyes were bent, ne swarvéd other way.[1]

15

They seeing Una, towards her gan wend,
Who them encounters with like courtesie;
Many kind speeches they betwene them spend,
And greatly joy each other well to see:
Then to the knight with shamefast° modestie *humble*
They turne themselves, at Unaes meeke request,
And him salute with well beseeming glee;

9. The portraits of Fidelia and Speranza share details with images of faith and hope in emblematic literature and art, notably emblem books like those of Ripa, Alciato, and Whitney. Fidelia's cup recalls Moses's elevation of the brazen serpent (Numbers 21.8–9), which St. John reads typologically as the lifting up of "the Son of man" (John 3.14). Serpents, despite the behavior of one in Eden, can be symbols of healing and—because they cast their skins—of renewal. Jesus says to have the wisdom of the serpent as well as the innocence of the dove (Matthew 10.16). This cup suggests Holy Communion, encompassing death and life. She holds the New Testament, "signd and seald" with Christ's blood. Cf. Peter 3.16.
1. "Which hope we have as an anchor of the soul, both sure and stedfast" (Hebrews 6.19).

Who faire them quites,° as him beseeméd best, *responds to*
And goodly gan discourse of many a noble gest.° *feat of arms*

16

Then Una thus; "But she your sister deare,
The deare Charissa where is she become?[2]
Or wants she health, or busie is elsewhere?"
"Ah no," said they, "but forth she may not come:
For she of late is lightned of her wombe,
And hath encreast the world with one sonne more,
That her to see should be but troublesome."
"Indeede," quoth she, "that should her trouble sore,
But thankt be God, and her encrease so[3] evermore."

17

Then said the aged Caelia, "Deare dame,
And you good Sir, I wote that of your toyle,
And labours long, through which ye hither came,
Ye both forwearied° be: therefore a whyle *tired out*
I read° you rest, and to your bowres recoyle."° *advise / retire*
Then calléd she a Groome, that forth him led
Into a goodly lodge, and gan despoile° *disrobe*
Of puissant armes, and laid in easie bed;
His name was meeke Obedience rightfully ared.° *understood*

18

Now when their wearie limbes with kindly° rest, *natural*
And bodies were refresht with due repast,
Faire Una gan Fidelia faire request,
To have her knight into her schoolehouse plaste,
That of her heavenly learning he might taste,
And heare the wisedome of her words divine.
She graunted, and that knight so much agraste,° *favored*
That she him taught celestiall discipline,[4]
And opened his dull eyes, that light mote in them shine.

19

And that her sacred Booke, with bloud[5] ywrit,
That none could read, except she did them teach,
She unto him discloséd every whit,
And heavenly documents° thereout did preach, *teaching*
That weaker wit of man could never reach,
Of God, of grace, of justice, of free will,
That wonder was to heare her goodly speach:

2. I.e., where is she?
3. I.e., may God increase her in that way.
4. I.e., holy laws.
5. I.e., Christ's blood.

For she was able, with her words to kill,
And raise againe to life[6] the hart, that she did thrill.° *pierce*

20

And when she list poure out her larger spright[7]
She would commaund the hastie Sunne to stay,
Or backward turne his course from heavens hight;
Sometimes great hostes of men she could dismay,
Dry-shod to passe, she parts the flouds in tway;
And eke huge mountaines from their native seat
She would commaund, themselves to beare away,
And throw in raging sea with roaring threat.
Almightie God her gave such powre, and puissance great.

21

The faithfull knight now grew in litle space,
By hearing her, and by her sisters lore,
To such perfection of all heavenly grace,
That wretched world he gan for to abhore,
And mortall life gan loath, as thing forlore,° *abandoned*
Greeved with remembrance of his wicked wayes,
And prickt with anguish of his sinnes so sore,
That he desirde to end his wretched dayes:
So much the dart of sinfull guilt the soule dismayes.

22

But wise Speranza gave him comfort sweet,
And taught him how to take assuréd hold
Upon her silver anchor, as was meet;
Else had his sinnes so great, and manifold
Made him forget all that Fidelia told.
In this distresséd doubtfull agonie,
When him his dearest Una did behold,
Disdeining life, desiring leave to die,
She found her selfe assayld with great perplexitie.

23

And came to Caelia to declare her smart,
Who well acquainted with that commune plight,
Which sinfull horror[8] workes in wounded hart,
Her wisely comforted all that she might,
With goodly counsell and advisement right;
And streightway sent with carefull diligence,
To fetch a Leach,° the which had great insight *physician*

6. "For the letter killeth, but the spirit giveth life" (2 Corinthians 3.6).
7. I.e., higher power. Here Old Testament events (Joshua 10.12; 2 Kings 20.10; Judges 7.7; Exodus 14.21–31) are followed by a reference to Matthew 21.21: "Jesus answered . . . if ye shall say unto this mountain, Be thou removed, and be thou cast into the sea; it shall be done."
8. I.e., horror of sin.

In that disease of grievéd conscience,
And well could cure the same; His name was Patience.

24

Who comming to that soule-diseaséd knight,
Could hardly him intreat,° to tell his griefe: *persuade*
Which knowne, and all that noyd° his heavie spright *troubled*
Well searcht, eftsoones he gan apply reliefe
Of salves and med'cines, which had passing priefe,[9]
And thereto added words of wondrous might:
By which to ease he him recuréd briefe,° *quickly*
And much aswaged the passion° of his plight, *suffering*
That he his paine endured, as seeming now more light.

25

But yet the cause and root of all his ill,
Inward corruption, and infected sin,
Not purged nor heald, behind remainéd still,
And festring sore did rankle yet within,
Close creeping twixt the marrow and the skin.
Which to extirpe,° he laid him privily *root out*
Downe in a darkesome lowly place farre in,
Whereas he meant his corrosives to apply,
And with streight° diet tame his stubborne malady. *strict*

26

In ashes and sackcloth he did array
His daintie corse, proud humors[1] to abate,
And dieted with fasting every day,
The swelling of his wounds to mitigate,
And made him pray both earely and eke late:
And ever as superfluous flesh did rot
Amendment readie still at hand did wayt,
To pluck it out with pincers firie whot,° *hot*
That soone in him was left no one corrupted jot.

27

And bitter Penance with an yron whip,
Was wont him once to disple° every day: *discipline*
And sharpe Remorse his heart did pricke and nip,
That drops of bloud thence like a well did play;
And sad Repentance uséd to embay° *bathe*
His bodie in salt water smarting sore,
The filthy blots of sinne to wash away.[2]

9. I.e., surpassing power.
1. I.e., pride. "Humors" suggests that his body's physical "humors" also need rebalancing; medical theory stressed the ties between mind and body.
2. "Wash me throughly from mine iniquity, and cleanse me from my sin" (Psalms 51.2).

So in short space they did to health restore
The man that would not live, but earst° lay at deathes dore. *formerly*

28

In which his torment often was so great,
That like a Lyon he would cry and rore,
And rend his flesh, and his owne synewes eat.
His owne deare Una hearing evermore
His ruefull shriekes and gronings, often tore
Her guiltlesse garments, and her golden heare,
For pitty of his paine and anguish sore;
Yet all with patience wisely she did beare;
For well she wist, his crime could else be never cleare.° *cleansed*

29

Whom thus recovered by wise Patience,
And trew Repentance they to Una brought:
Who joyous of his curéd conscience,
Him dearely kist, and fairely eke besought
Himselfe to chearish, and consuming thought
To put away out of his carefull brest.
By this Charissa, late in child-bed brought,
Was woxen strong, and left her fruitfull nest;
To her faire Una brought this unacquainted guest.[3]

30

She was a woman in her freshest age,[4]
Of wondrous beauty, and of bountie° rare, *virtue*
With goodly grace and comely personage,
That was on earth not easie to compare;
Full of great love, but Cupids wanton snare
As hell she hated, chast in worke and will;
Her necke and breasts were ever open bare,
That ay thereof her babes might sucke their fill;
The rest was all in yellow robes arayéd still.

31

A multitude of babes about her hong,
Playing their sports, that joyd her to behold,
Whom still she fed, whiles they were weake and young,
But thrust them forth still, as they wexéd old:
And on her head she wore a tyre° of gold, *headdress*
Adornd with gemmes and owches° wondrous faire, *jewels*

3. "Though I have all faith, so that I could remove mountains, and have not charity, I am nothing" (1 Corinthians 13.2).
4. The description of Charissa includes classical elements: Hymen, the god of marriage, traditionally wore yellow (cf. *Metamorphoses* 10.1), and doves were sacred to Venus.

Whose passing price uneath was to be told,[5]
And by her side there sate a gentle paire
Of turtle doves, she sitting in an yvorie chaire.

32

The knight and Una entring, faire her greet,
And bid her joy of that her happie brood;
Who them requites with court'sies seeming meet,° *appropriate*
And entertaines with friendly chearefull mood.
Then Una her besought, to be so good,
As in her vertuous rules to schoole her knight,
Now after all his torment well withstood,
In that sad° house of Penaunce, where his spright *grave*
Had past the paines of hell, and long enduring night.

33

She was right joyous of her just request,
And taking by the hand that Faeries sonne,
Gan him instruct in every good behest,
Of love, and righteousnesse, and well to donne,[6]
And wrath, and hatred warély to shonne,
That drew on men Gods hatred, and his wrath,
And many soules in dolours° had fordonne:° *misery / ruined*
In which when him she well instructed hath,
From thence to heaven she teacheth him the ready path.

34

Wherein his weaker° wandring steps to guide, *too weak*
An auncient matrone she to her does call,
Whose sober lookes her wisedome well descride:° *revealed*
Her name was Mercie, well knowne over all,
To be both gratious, and eke liberall:
To whom the carefull charge of him she gave,
To lead aright, that he should never fall
In all his wayes through this wide worldés wave,
That Mercy in the end his righteous soule might save.

35

The godly Matrone by the hand him beares
Forth from her presence, by a narrow way,
Scattred with bushy thornes, and ragged breares,° *briers*
Which still before him she removed away,
That nothing might his ready passage stay:
And ever when his feet encombred were,
Or gan to shrinke, or from the right to stray,

5. I.e., whose surpassing value might scarcely be estimated.
6. I.e., well-doing.

She held him fast, and firmely did upbeare,
As carefull Nourse her child from falling oft does reare.

36

Eftsoones unto an holy Hospitall,° *retreat, sanctuary*
That was fore° by the way, she did him bring, *close*
In which seven Bead-men[7] that had vowed all
Their life to service of high heavens king
Did spend their dayes in doing godly thing:
Their gates to all were open evermore,
That by the wearie way were travelling,
And one sate wayting° ever them before, *watching*
To call in commers-by, that needy were and pore.

37

The first of them that eldest was, and best,° *chief*
Of all the house had charge and governement,
As Guardian and Steward of the rest:
His office was to give entertainement
And lodging, unto all that came, and went:
Not unto such, as could him feast againe,
And double quite,° for that he on them spent, *repay*
But such, as want of harbour° did constraine: *shelter*
Those for Gods sake his dewty was to entertaine.

38

The second was as Almner° of the place, *distributor of alms*
His office was, the hungry for to feed,
And thristy give to drinke, a worke of grace:
He feard not once him selfe to be in need,
Ne cared to hoord for those, whom he did breede:[8]
The grace of God he layd up still in store,
Which as a stocke° he left unto his seede; *resource*
He had enough, what need him care for more?
And had he lesse, yet some he would give to the pore.

39

The third had of their wardrobe custodie,
In which were not rich tyres,° nor garments gay, *attire*
The plumes of pride, and wings of vanitie,
But clothés meet to keepe keene could° away, *cold*
And naked nature seemely to aray;
With which bare wretched wights he dayly clad,
The images of God in earthly clay;

7. Properly, men who pray for others' spiritual welfare, these "Bead-men" are dedicated to serving the bodily needs of others. Opposed to the Seven Deadly Sins, they perform the traditional seven "Corporal Works of Mercy."
8. I.e., his own family.

And if that no spare cloths to give he had,
His owne coate he would cut, and it distribute glad.

40

The fourth appointed by his office was,
Poore prisoners to relieve with gratious ayd,
And captives to redeeme with price of bras,° *money*
From Turkes and Sarazins, which them had stayd;° *held captive*
And though they faultie were, yet well he wayd,
That God to us forgiveth every howre
Much more then that, why° they in bands were layd, *for which*
And he that harrowd hell with heavie stowre,
The faultie soules from thence brought to his heavenly bowre.

41

The fift had charge sicke persons to attend,
And comfort those, in point of death which lay;
For them most needeth comfort in the end,
When sin, and hell, and death do most dismay
The feeble soule departing hence away.
All is but lost, that living we bestow,° *store up*
If not well ended at our dying day.
O man have mind of that last bitter throw;° *throe*
For as the tree does fall, so lyes it ever low.

42

The sixt had charge of them now being dead,
In seemely sort their corses to engrave,° *bury*
And deck with dainty flowres their bridall bed,
That to their heavenly spouse[9] both sweet and brave° *handsome*
They might appeare, when he their soules shall save.
The wondrous workemanship of Gods owne mould,° *image*
Whose face he made, all beasts to feare, and gave
All in his hand, even dead we honour should.
Ah dearest God me graunt, I dead be not defould.° *defiled*

43

The seventh now after death and buriall done,
Had charge the tender Orphans of the dead
And widowes ayd, least they should be undone:° *ruined*
In face of judgement[1] he their right would plead,
Ne ought the powre of mighty men did dread
In their defence, nor would for gold or fee
Be wonne their rightfull causes downe to tread:

9. I.e., Christ, spouse of the individual soul as well as of the Church (the collective body of all the faithful).
1. I.e., in the court of law.

And when they stood in most necessitee,
He did supply their want, and gave them ever free.° *freely*

44

There when the Elfin knight arrivéd was,
The first and chiefest of the seven, whose care
Was guests to welcome, towardes him did pas:
Where seeing Mercie, that his steps up bare,° *supported*
And alwayes led, to her with reverence rare
He humbly louted° in meeke lowlinesse, *bowed*
And seemely welcome for her did prepare:
For of their order she was Patronesse,
Albe° Charissa were their chiefest founderesse. *although*

45

There she awhile him stayes, him selfe to rest,
That to the rest more able he might bee:
During which time, in every good behest
And godly worke of Almes and charitee
She him instructed with great industree;
Shortly therein so perfect he became,
That from the first unto the last degree,
His mortall life he learnéd had to frame
In holy righteousnesse, without rebuke or blame.

46

Thence forward by that painfull way they pas,
Forth to an hill, that was both steepe and hy;
On top whereof a sacred chappell was,
And eke a litle Hermitage thereby,
Wherein an aged holy man did lye,
That day and night said his devotion,
Ne other worldly busines did apply;° *pursue*
His name was heavenly Contemplation;
Of God and goodnesse was his meditation.[2]

47

Great grace that old man to him given had;
For God he often saw from heavens hight,
All° were his earthly eyen both blunt° and bad, *although / dim*
And through great age had lost their kindly° sight, *natural*
Yet wondrous quick and persant° was his spright, *piercing*
As Eagles eye, that can behold the Sunne.[3]
That hill they scale with all their powre and might,

2. In the episode that follows, Spenser may recall the moral refreshment and strength received by Ariosto's Rinaldo on the "Hill of Hope" (*Rinaldo* 11.56–65).
3. An attribute of eagles in medieval bestiaries: see Chaucer, *Parliament of Fowls* 330–31: "There myghte men the royal egle fynde, / That with his sharpe lok perseth the sonne . . ."

That his frayle thighes nigh wearie and fordonne° *exhausted*
Gan faile, but by her helpe the top at last he wonne.

48

There they do finde that godly aged Sire,
With snowy lockes adowne his shoulders shed,
As hoarie frost with spangles doth attire
The mossy braunches of an Oke halfe ded.
Each bone might through his body well be red,° *seen*
And every sinew seene through° his long fast: *in consequence of*
For nought he cared his carcas long unfed;
His mind was full of spirituall repast,
And pyned° his flesh, to keepe his body low and chast. *starved*

49

Who when these two approching he aspide,
At their first presence grew agrievéd sore,
That forst him lay his heavenly thoughts aside:
And had he not that Dame respected more,° *greatly*
Whom highly he did reverence and adore,
He would not once have movéd for the knight.
They him saluted standing far afore;° *before*
Who well them greeting, humbly did requight,
And askéd, to what end they clomb° that tedious height. *had climbed*

50

"What end," quoth she, "should cause us take such paine,
But that same end, which every living wight
Should make his marke,° high heaven to attaine? *aim*
Is not from hence the way, that leadeth right
To that most glorious house, that glistreth bright
With burning starres, and everliving fire,
Whereof the keyes are to thy hand behight° *entrusted*
By wise Fidelia? she doth thee require,
To shew it to this knight, according° his desire." *granting*

51

"Thrise happy man," said then the father grave,
"Whose staggering steps thy steady hand doth lead,
And shewes the way, his sinfull soule to save.
Who better can the way to heaven aread,° *direct*
Then thou thy selfe, that was both borne and bred
In heavenly throne, where thousand Angels shine?
Thou doest the prayers of the righteous sead° *offspring*
Present before the majestie divine,
And his avenging wrath to clemencie incline.

52

"Yet since thou bidst, thy pleasure shalbe donne.
Then come thou man of earth,[4] and see the way,
That never yet was seene of Faeries sonne,
That never leads the traveiler astray,
But after labours long, and sad delay,
Brings them to joyous rest and endlesse blis.
But first thou must a season fast and pray,
Till from her bands the spright assoiléd° is, *set free*
And have her strength recured° from fraile infirmitis." *recovered*

53

That done, he leads him to the highest Mount,[5]
Such one, as that same mighty man of God,
That bloud-red billowes like a walléd front
One either side disparted with his rod,
Till that his army dry-foot through them yod,° *went*
Dwelt fortie dayes upon; where writ in stone
With bloudy letters by the hand of God,
The bitter doome of death and balefull mone° *grief*
He did receive, whiles flashing fire about him shone.[6]

54

Or like that sacred hill,[7] whose head full hie,
Adornd with fruitfull Olives all arownd,
Is, as it were for endlesse memory
Of that deare Lord, who oft thereon was fownd,
For ever with a flowring girlond crownd:
Or like that pleasaunt Mount[8] that is for ay
Through famous Poets verse each where° renownd, *everywhere*
On which the thrise three learnéd Ladies play
Their heavenly notes, and make full many a lovely lay.

55

From thence, far off he unto him did shew
A litle path, that was both steepe and long,
Which to a goodly Citie[9] led his vew;

4. Contemplation refers to Redcrosse's fleshly humanity but also plays on the etymology of "George," the name by which he identifies him in stanza 61.
5. Cf. that "high mountain" to which the angel carried John "in the spirit" to show him "that great city, the holy Jerusalem, descending out of heaven from God" (Revelation 21.10).
6. God gave Moses the Ten Commandments on Mount Sinai (Exodus 24.16–18); as the still binding "letters" of the Law, in this theology, they bring death to fallen human beings unless released by God's grace working through Christ's sacrifice.
7. The Mount of Olives, where Jesus prayed before his crucifixion.
8. Parnassus, where the nine muses gathered. E. K.'s "Argument" to "October" calls poetry a "divine gift and heavenly instinct not to bee gotten by laboure and learning, but adorned with both: and poured into the witte by . . . celestiall inspiration."
9. The New Jerusalem, whose "light was like unto a stone most precious, even like a jasper stone, clear as crystal; . . . and the twelve gates were twelve pearls; every several gate was of one pearl: and the street of the city was pure gold, as it were transparent glass" (Revelation 21.11, 21).

Whose wals and towres were builded high and strong
Of perle and precious stone, that earthly tong
Cannot describe, nor wit of man can tell;
Too high a ditty° for my simple song; *theme*
The Citie of the great king hight it well,
Wherein eternall peace and happinesse doth dwell.

56

As he thereon stood gazing, he might see
The blessed Angels to and fro descend
From highest heaven, in gladsome companee,
And with great joy into that Citie wend,
As commonly° as friend does with his frend. *sociably*
Whereat he wondred much, and gan enquere,
What stately building durst so high extend
Her loftie towres unto the starry sphere,
And what unknowen nation there empeopled° were. *settled*

57

"Faire knight," quoth he, "Hierusalem that is,
The new Hierusalem, that God has built
For those to dwell in, that are chosen his,
His chosen people purged from sinfull guilt,
With pretious bloud, which cruelly was spilt
On curséd tree, of that unspotted lam,
That for the sinnes of all the world was kilt:[1]
Now are they Saints all in that Citie sam,° *together*
More deare unto their God, then younglings to their dam."

58

"Till now," said then the knight, "I weenéd well,
That great Cleopolis,[2] where I have beene,
In which that fairest Faerie Queene doth dwell,
The fairest Citie was, that might be seene;
And that bright towre all built of christall cleene,° *pure*
Panthea,[3] seemd the brightest thing, that was:
But now by proofe all otherwise I weene;
For this great Citie that does far surpas,
And this bright Angels towre quite dims that towre of glas."

59

"Most trew," then said the holy aged man;
"Yet is Cleopolis for earthly frame,° *structure*

1. "Behold the Lamb of God, which taketh away the sin of the world" (John 1.29).
2. The city of earthly glory; at once an ideal counterpart of Elizabeth's London and a symbolic image of the highest attainment within the reach of the fallen human race unaided by direct divine intervention.
3. The ideal counterpart of either Westminster Abbey or one of Elizabeth's residences near London.

The fairest peece, that eye beholdén can:
And well beseemes all knights of noble name,
That covet in th'immortall booke of fame
To be eternizéd, that same to haunt,° *frequent*
And doen their service to that soveraigne Dame,
That glorie does to them for guerdon° graunt: *reward*
For she is heavenly borne, and heaven may justly vaunt.[4]

60

"And thou faire ymp, sprong out from English race,
How ever now accompted° Elfins sonne, *accounted*
Well worthy doest thy service for her grace,° *favor*
To aide a virgin desolate foredonne.
But when thou famous victorie hast wonne,
And high emongst all knights hast hong thy shield,
Thenceforth the suit° of earthly conquest shonne, *pursuit*
And wash thy hands from guilt of bloudy field:
For bloud can nought but sin, and wars but sorrowes yield.

61

"Then seeke this path, that I to thee presage,° *point out*
Which after all to heaven shall thee send;
Then peaceably thy painefull pilgrimage
To yonder same Hierusalem do bend,
Where is for thee ordaind a blessed end:
For thou emongst those Saints, whom thou doest see,
Shalt be a Saint, and thine owne nations frend
And Patrone: thou Saint George shalt calléd bee,
Saint George of mery England, the signe of victoree."[5]

62

"Unworthy wretch," quoth he, "of so great grace,
How dare I thinke such glory to attaine?"
"These that have it attaind, were in like cace,"
Quoth he, "as wretched, and lived in like paine."
"But deeds of armes must I at last be faine,° *willing*
And Ladies love to leave so dearely bought?"
"What need of armes, where peace doth ay remaine,"

4. I.e., she may justly boast of her heavenly descent.
5. Although Aelfric's ninth-century *Lives of the Saints* includes St. George, Spenser's conception of England's patron saint draws on a tradition stemming from the *Legenda Aurea* (translated by Caxton in 1487), an allied pictorial tradition, and suggestions in folklore of the mysterious circumstances attending the infancy and youth of mortals singled out for a glorious destiny. Spenser's most significant (and Protestant) change was to make George a lover and future husband; in older versions, and despite traces of his archaic role as a fertility figure, he remains celibate until his martyrdom. Stephen Hawes, too, had combined a dragon fight, religious allegory, and love interest. Some Protestants, though, viewed George with skepticism and thought his cult pagan or "papist" nonsense; thus Barnaby Googe's *Shippe of Safegarde* (1569) sets a picture of St. George and the dragon in the Land of Heresy. He was, however, England's patron saint; his red cross on a white background is the English flag, and he is the saint associated with the Order of the Garter.

Said he, "and battailes none are to be fought?
As for loose loves are° vaine, and vanish into nought." *they are*

63

"O let me not," quoth he, "then turne againe
Backe to the world, whose joyes so fruitlesse are;
But let me here for aye in peace remaine,
Or streight way on that last long voyage fare,
That nothing may my present hope empare."° *impair*
"That may not be," said he, "ne maist thou yit
Forgo that royall maides bequeathéd care,° *charge*
Who did her cause into thy hand commit,
Till from her curséd foe thou have her freely quit."° *released*

64

"Then shall I soone," quoth he, "so God me grace,
Abet° that virgins cause disconsolate, *maintain*
And shortly backe returne unto this place,
To walke this way in Pilgrims poore estate.
But now aread, old father, why of late
Didst thou behight° me borne of English blood, *call*
Whom all a Faeries sonne doen nominate?"° *name, consider*
"That word shall I," said he, "avouchen° good, *prove*
Sith to thee is unknowne the cradle of thy brood.

65

"For well I wote, thou springst from ancient race
Of Saxon kings, that have with mightie hand
And many bloudie battailes fought in place
High reard their royall throne in Britane land,
And vanquisht them, unable to withstand:
From thence a Faerie thee unweeting reft,° *stole away*
There as thou slepst in tender swadling band,
And her base Elfin brood there for thee left.
Such men do Chaungelings call, so chaunged by Faeries theft.

66

"Thence she thee brought into this Faerie lond,
And in an heapéd furrow did thee hyde,
Where thee a Ploughman all unweeting fond,
As he his toylesome teme that way did guyde,
And brought thee up in ploughmans state to byde,° *remain*
Whereof Georgos he thee gave to name,[6]
Till prickt with courage, and thy forces pryde,

6. Ovid describes the discovery, by an Etrurian ploughman, of Tages, son of the earth; Tages was destined to instruct his nation in the art of prophecy (*Metamorphoses* 15.558–59). Since George's name associates him with Adam ("red earth"), to call him *Saint* George suggests a new identity. Spenser here and elsewhere destinguishes between Saxons (Germanic) and Britons (Celt).

To Faery court thou cam'st to seeke for fame,
And prove thy puissaunt armes, as seemes thee best became."° *suited*

67

"O holy Sire," quoth he, "how shall I quight° *repay*
The many favours I with thee have found,
That hast my name and nation red° aright, *told*
And taught the way that does to heaven bound?"° *go*
This said, adowne he lookéd to the ground,
To have returnd, but dazéd were his eyne,
Through passing° brightnesse, which did quite confound *surpassing*
His feeble sence, and too exceeding shyne.
So darke are earthly things compard to things divine.

68

At last whenas himselfe he gan to find,° *recover*
To Una back he cast him to retire;
Who him awaited still with pensive mind.
Great thankes and goodly meed° to that good syre, *reward*
He thence departing gave for his paines hyre.[7]
So came to Una, who him joyed to see,
And after litle rest, gan him desire,
Of her adventure mindfull for to bee.
So leave they take of Caelia, and her daughters three.

Canto XI

The knight with that old Dragon fights
two dayes incessantly:
The third him overthrowes, and gayns
most glorious victory.[1]

I

High time now gan it wex° for Una faire, *become*
To thinke of those her captive Parents deare,
And their forwasted kingdome to repaire:[2]
Whereto whenas they now approachéd neare,
With hartie words her knight she gan to cheare,
And in her modest manner thus bespake;
"Deare knight, as deare, as ever knight was deare,
That all these sorrowes suffer for my sake,
High heaven behold the tedious toyle, ye for me take.

7. I.e., as recompense for his trouble.
1. That the dragon fight takes three days would have recalled Christ's Passion to Spenser's readers, although how the details should be read and the degree to which George is Christlike have been debated. The Passion and Christ's consequent victory over sin and death was sometimes read as a battle: William Dunbar (1460–1530), e.g., wrote of the Resurrection, "Done is a battell on the dragon blak."
2. I.e., to restore to health their kingdom, laid waste by "that old Dragon."

2

"Now are we come unto my native soyle,
And to the place, where all our perils dwell;
Here haunts that feend, and does his dayly spoyle,
Therefore henceforth be at your keeping[3] well,
And ever ready for your foeman fell.
The sparke of noble courage now awake,
And strive your excellent selfe to excell;
That shall ye evermore renowméd make,
Above all knights on earth, that batteill undertake."

3

And pointing forth, "lo yonder is," said she,
"The brasen towre in which my parents deare
For dread of that huge feend emprisond be,
Whom I from far see on the walles appeare,
Whose sight my feeble soule doth greatly cheare:
And on the top of all I do espye
The watchman wayting tydings glad to heare,
That O my parents might I happily
Unto you bring, to ease you of your misery."

4

With that they heard a roaring hideous sound,
That all the ayre with terrour filléd wide,
And seemd uneath° to shake the stedfast ground. *almost*
Eftsoones that dreadfull Dragon they espide,
Where stretcht he lay upon the sunny side
Of a great hill, himselfe like a great hill.
But all so soone, as he from far descride
Those glistring armes, that heaven with light did fill,
He rousd himselfe full blith,° and hastned them untill.° *joyfully / toward*

5

Then bad the knight his Lady yede° aloofe,° *go / up high*
And to an hill her selfe with draw aside,
From whence she might behold that battailles proof° *trial*
And eke be safe from daunger far descryde:° *observed*
She him obayd, and turnd a little wyde.° *aside*
Now O thou sacred Muse,[4] most learnéd Dame,
Faire ympe of Phoebus, and his aged bride,
The Nourse of time, and everlasting fame,
That warlike hands ennoblest with immortall name;

3. I.e., on your guard.
4. Here Clio, Muse of history. Departing from the tradition that Jove begot the Muses (cf. Hesiod, *Theogony* 53–62), Spenser reads Comes as making Apollo their father (*Mythologiae* 4.10).

6

O gently come into my feeble brest,
Come gently, but not with that mighty rage,
Wherewith the martiall troupes thou doest infest,° *arouse, inspire*
And harts of great Heroës doest enrage,
That nought their kindled courage may aswage,
Soone as thy dreadfull trompe begins to sownd;
The God of warre with his fiers equipage° *equipment*
Thou doest awake, sleepe never he so sownd,
And scaréd nations doest with horrour sterne astownd.° *petrify*

7

Faire Goddesse lay that furious fit° aside, *martial inspiration*
Till I of warres and bloudy Mars do sing,[5]
And Briton fields with Sarazin bloud bedyde,
Twixt that great faery Queene and Paynim king,
That with their horrour heaven and earth did ring,
A worke of labour long, and endlesse prayse.
But now a while let downe that haughtie° string, *lofty*
And to my tunes thy second tenor[6] rayse,
That I this man of God his godly armes may blaze.° *proclaim*

8

By this the dreadfull Beast[7] drew nigh to hand,
Halfe flying, and halfe footing in his hast,
That with his largenesse measuréd much land,
And made wide shadow under his huge wast;° *girth*
As mountaine doth the valley overcast.
Approching nigh, he rearéd high afore° *in front*
His body monstrous, horrible, and vast,
Which to increase his wondrous greatnesse more,
Was swolne with wrath, and poyson, and with bloudy gore.

9

And over, all[8] with brasen scales was armd,
Like plated coate of steele, so couchéd neare,[9]
That nought mote perce, ne might his corse be harmd
With dint of sword, nor push of pointed speare;
Which as an Eagle, seeing pray appeare,
His aery plumes doth rouze,° full rudely dight,° *shake / arrayed*
So shakéd he, that horrour was to heare,

5. Perhaps an allusion to Spenser's intended epic "of politicke vertues in [Arthur's] person, after that hee came to be king."
6. I.e., lower strain, perhaps reflecting Plato's distinction (*Republic* 3.399) between the Dorian mode, suited to courageous men in war, and the more restrained Phrygian mode.
7. Compare, especially, the "serpent sacred to Mars" that Ovid's Cadmus overcame (*Metamorphoses* 3.31–94).
8. I.e., over the greater part of his body.
9. I.e., closely set.

For as the clashing of an Armour bright,
Such noyse his rouzéd scales did send unto the knight.

10

His flaggy° wings when forth he did display, *drooping*
Were like two sayles, in which the hollow wynd
Is gathered full, and worketh speedy way:
And eke the pennes,° that did his pineons bynd, *feathers, quills*
Were like mayne-yards, with flying canvas lynd,
With which whenas him list the ayre to beat,
And there by force unwonted passage find,
The cloudes before him fled for terrour great,
And all the heavens stood still amazéd with his threat.

11

His huge long tayle wound up in hundred foldes,
Does overspred his long bras-scaly backe,
Whose wreathéd boughts° when ever he unfoldes, *coils*
And thicke entangled knots adown does slacke,
Bespotted as with shields of red and blacke,
It sweepeth all the land behind him farre,
And of three furlongs does but litle lacke;
And at the point two stings in-fixéd arre,
Both deadly sharpe, that sharpest steele exceeden farre.

12

But stings and sharpest steele did far exceed[1]
The sharpnesse of his cruell rending clawes;
Dead was it sure, as sure as death in deed,
What ever thing does touch his ravenous pawes,
Or what within his reach he ever drawes.
But his most hideous head my toung to tell
Does tremble: for his deepe devouring jawes
Wide gapéd, like the griesly mouth of hell,
Through which into his darke abisse all ravin° fell. *prey*

13

And that° more wondrous was, in either jaw *what*
Three ranckes of yron teeth enraungéd were,
In which yet trickling bloud and gobbets raw
Of late devouréd bodies did appeare,
That sight thereof bred cold congealéd feare:
Which to increase, and all atonce to kill,
A cloud of smoothering smoke and sulphur seare° *burning*
Out of his stinking gorge° forth steeméd still, *maw*
That all the ayre about with smoke and stench did fill.

1. I.e., were far exceeded by.

14

His blazing eyes, like two bright shining shields,
Did burne with wrath, and sparkled living fyre;
As two broad Beacons, set in open fields,
Send forth their flames farre off to every shyre,
And warning give, that enemies conspyre,
With fire and sword the region to invade;
So flamed his eyne with rage and rancorous yre:
But farre within, as in a hollow glade,
Those glaring lampes were set, that made a dreadfull shade.

15

So dreadfully he towards him did pas,° *pace*
Forelifting up aloft his speckled brest,
And often bounding on the bruséd gras,
As for great joyance of his newcome guest.
Eftsoones he gan advance his haughtie crest,
As chaufféd° Bore his bristles doth upreare, *angry*
And shoke his scales to battell readie drest;
That made the Redcrosse knight nigh quake for feare,
As bidding bold defiance to his foeman neare.[2]

16

The knight gan fairely couch° his steadie speare, *rest, aim*
And fiercely ran at him with rigorous might:
The pointed steele arriving rudely theare,
His harder° hide would neither perce, nor bight, *too hard*
But glauncing by forth passéd forward right;
Yet sore amovéd with so puissant push,
The wrathfull beast about him turnéd light,° *quickly*
And him so rudely passing by, did brush
With his long tayle, that horse and man to ground did rush.

17

Both horse and man up lightly rose againe,
And fresh encounter towards him addrest:
But th'idle stroke yet backe recoyld in vaine,
And found no place his deadly point to rest.
Exceeding rage enflamed the furious beast,
To be avengéd of so great despight;° *outrage*
For never felt his imperceable brest
So wondrous force, from hand of living wight;
Yet had he proved° the powre of many a puissant knight. *tested*

2. I.e., the dragon shook his scales in defiance.

18

Then with his waving wings displayéd wyde,
Himselfe up high he lifted from the ground,
And with strong flight did forcibly divide
The yielding aire, which nigh too feeble found
Her flitting partes, and element unsound,° *weak*
To beare so great a weight: he cutting way
With his broad sayles, about him soaréd round:
At last low stouping with unweldie sway,[3]
Snatcht up both horse and man, to beare them quite away.

19

Long he them bore above the subject plaine,[4]
So farre as Ewghen° bow a shaft may send, *yew*
Till struggling strong did him at last constraine,
To let them downe before his flightés end:
As hagard° hauke presuming to contend *wild*
With hardie fowle, above his hable° might, *powerful*
His wearie pounces° all in vaine doth spend, *talons*
To trusse° the pray too heavie for his flight; *seize*
Which comming downe to ground, does free it selfe by fight.

20

He so disseizéd of his gryping grosse,[5]
The knight his thrillant° speare againe assayd *piercing*
In his bras-plated body to embosse,° *plunge*
And three mens strength unto the stroke he layd;
Wherewith the stiffe beame quakéd, as affrayd,
And glauncing from his scaly necke, did glyde
Close under his left wing, then broad displayd.
The percing steele there wrought a wound full wyde,
That with the uncouth° smart the Monster lowdly cryde. *unfamiliar*

21

He cryde, as raging seas are wont to rore,
When wintry storme his wrathfull wreck does threat,
The rolling billowes beat the ragged shore,
As they the earth would shoulder from her seat,
And greedie gulfe does gape, as he would eat
His neighbour element in his revenge:
Then gin the blustring brethren[6] boldly threat,
To move the world from off his stedfast henge,° *axis*
And boystrous battell make, each other to avenge.

3. I.e., ponderous force.
4. I.e., the plain below.
5. I.e., freed of his heavy gripful.
6. I.e., the winds.

22

The steely head stucke fast still in his flesh,
Till with his cruell clawes he snatcht the wood,
And quite a sunder broke. Forth flowéd fresh
A gushing river of blacke goarie blood,
That drownéd all the land, whereon he stood;
The streame thereof would drive a water-mill.
Trebly augmented was his furious mood
With bitter sense° of his deepe rooted ill, *feeling*
That flames of fire he threw forth from his large nosethrill.

23

His hideous tayle then hurléd he about,
And therewith all enwrapt the nimble thyes
Of his froth-fomy steed, whose courage stout
Striving to loose the knot, that fast him tyes,
Himselfe in streighter bandes too rash implyes,[7]
That to the ground he is perforce constraynd
To throw his rider: who can° quickly ryse *did*
From off the earth, with durty bloud distaynd,° *stained*
For that reprochfull fall right fowly he disdaynd.

24

And fiercely tooke his trenchand° blade in hand, *sharp*
With which he stroke so furious and so fell,
That nothing seemd the puissance could withstand:
Upon his crest the hardned yron fell,
But his more hardned crest was armd so well,
That deeper dint therein it would not make;
Yet so extremely did the buffe him quell,° *dismay*
That from thenceforth he shund the like to take,
But when he saw them come, he did them still forsake.° *avoid*

25

The knight was wrath to see his stroke beguyld,° *foiled*
And smote againe with more outrageous might;
But backe againe the sparckling steele recoyld,
And left not any marke, where it did light;
As if in Adamant rocke it had bene pight.° *struck*
The beast impatient of his smarting wound,
And of so fierce and forcible despight,° *injury*
Thought with his wings to stye° above the ground; *rise*
But his late wounded wing unserviceable found.

26

Then full of griefe and anguish vehement,
He lowdly brayd, that like was never heard,

7. I.e., too quickly entangles.

And from his wide devouring oven sent
A flake° of fire, that flashing in his beard, — *flash*
Him all amazd, and almost made affeard:
The scorching flame sore swingéd° all his face, — *singed*
And through his armour all his bodie seard,
That he could not endure so cruell cace,
But thought his armes to leave, and helmet to unlace.

27

Not that great Champion of the antique world,[8]
Whom famous Poetes verse so much doth vaunt,
And hath for twelve huge labours high extold,
So many furies and sharpe fits did haunt,
When him the poysoned garment did enchaunt
With Centaures bloud, and bloudie verses charmed,
As did this knight twelve thousand dolours° daunt, — *sufferings*
Whom fyrie steele now burnt, that earst° him armed, — *before*
That erst him goodly armed, now most of all him harmed.

28

Faint, wearie, sore, emboyléd, grievéd, brent° — *burned*
With heat, toyle, wounds, armes, smart, and inward fire
That never man such mischiefes did torment;
Death better were, death did he oft desire,
But death will never come, when needes require.
Whom so dismayd when that his foe beheld,
He cast to suffer him no more respire,° — *rest, take breath*
But gan his sturdie sterne° about to weld,° — *tail / lash*
And him so strongly stroke, that to the ground him feld.

29

It fortunéd (as faire it then befell)
Behind his backe unweeting,° where he stood, — *unnoticed*
Of auncient time there was a springing well,
From which fast trickled forth a silver flood,
Full of great vertues, and for med'cine good.
Whylome,° before that curséd Dragon got — *formerly*
That happie land, and all with innocent blood
Defyld those sacred waves, it rightly hot° — *was called*
The Well of Life,[9] ne yet his° vertues had forgot. — *its*

8. Hercules suffered agony when he put on Nessus's robe, soaked in poisoned blood; by the will of Jove, he put off mortality and took his place in the stars (*Metamorphoses* 9.134–270).
9. "And he shewed me a pure river of water of life, clear as crystal, proceeding out of the throne of God and of the Lamb. In the midst of the street of it, and on either side of the river, was there the tree of life, which bare twelve manner of fruits, and yielded her fruit every month: and the leaves of the tree were for the healing of the nations" (Revelation 22.1–2). Well and tree, narrowly interpreted, signify the sacraments of baptism and communion, for some scholars; others see a more general symbol of grace.

30

For unto life the dead it could restore,
And guilt of sinfull crimes cleane wash away,
Those that with sicknesse were infected sore,
It could recure, and aged long decay
Renew, as one were borne that very day.
Both Silo[1] this, and Jordan did excell,
And th'English Bath, and eke the german Spau,
Ne can Cephise, nor Hebrus match this well:
Into the same the knight backe overthrowen, fell.

31

Now gan the golden Phoebus for to steepe
His fierie face in billowes of the west,
And his faint steedes watred in Ocean deepe,
Whiles from their journall° labours they did rest, *daily*
When that infernall Monster, having kest° *cast*
His wearie foe into that living well,
Can° high advance his broad discoloured brest, *did*
Above his wonted pitch,° with countenance fell, *height*
And clapt his yron wings, as victor he did dwell.° *remain*

32

Which when his pensive Ladie saw from farre,
Great woe and sorrow did her soule assay,° *assail*
As weening that the sad end of the warre,
And gan to highest God entirely° pray, *earnestly*
That fearéd chance from her to turne away;
With folded hands and knees full lowly bent
All night she watcht, ne once adowne would lay
Her daintie limbs in her sad dreriment,
But praying still did wake, and waking did lament.

33

The morrow next gan early to appeare,
That° Titan[2] rose to runne his daily race; *when*
But early ere the morrow next gan reare
Out of the sea faire Titans deawy face,
Up rose the gentle virgin from her place,
And lookéd all about, if she might spy
Her lovéd knight to move his manly pace:[3]
For she had great doubt of his safèty,
Since late she saw him fall before his enemy.

1. All these waters were known, whether in scripture ("the pool of Siloam" in John 9.7; the cleansing powers of Jordan in 2 Kings 5.10–14), or in classical accounts (the river Cephissus, in Pliny, *Historia Naturalis* 2.106.230; the pure Hebrus, in Horace, *Epistles* 1.16.13), or, in the case of Bath and Spa, for their curative power or their purity.
2. The sun.
3. I.e., actively recovering.

34

At last she saw, where he upstarted brave
Out of the well, wherein he drenchéd lay;
As Eagle fresh out of the Ocean wave,[4]
Where he hath left his plumes all hoary gray,
And deckt himselfe with feathers youthly gay,
Like Eyas° hauke up mounts unto the skies, *young*
His newly budded pineons to assay,
And marveiles at himselfe, still as he flies:
So new this new-borne knight to battell new did rise.

35

Whom when the damnéd feend so fresh did spy,
No wonder if he wondred at the sight,
And doubted, whether his late enemy
It were, or other new supplieéd knight.
He, now to prove his late renewéd might,
High brandishing his bright deaw-burning[5] blade,
Upon his crested scalpe so sore did smite,
That to the scull a yawning wound it made:
The deadly dint his dulléd senses all dismaid.

36

I wote not, whether the revenging steele
Were hardned with that holy water dew,
Wherein he fell, or sharper edge did feele,
Or his baptizéd hands now greater° grew; *stronger*
Or other secret vertue did ensew;
Else never could the force of fleshly arme,
Ne molten mettall in his bloud embrew:° *plunge*
For till that stownd° could never wight him harme, *moment*
By subtilty, nor slight,° nor might, nor mighty charme. *trickery*

37

The cruell wound enragéd him so sore,
That loud he yelded° for exceeding paine; *shrieked*
As hundred ramping Lyons seemed to rore,
Whom ravenous hunger did thereto constraine:
Then gan he tosse aloft his stretchéd traine,
And therewith scourge the buxome° aire so sore, *unresisting*
That to his force to yeelden it was faine;° *forced*
Ne ought° his sturdie strokes might stand afore, *anything*
That high trees overthrew, and rocks in peeces tore.

4. "When the eagle grows old . . . then he goes in search of a fountain, and . . . he flies up to the height of heaven. . . . Then at length, diving down into the fountain, he dips himself three times in it, and instantly he is renewed with a great vigour of plumage and splendor of vision. Do the same thing, O man. . . . Seek for the spiritual fountain of the Lord and . . . then your youth will be renewed like the eagle's" (*The Bestiary, A Book of Beasts* 105–17).
5. I.e., gleaming with "that holy water dew" (stanza 36).

38

The same advauncing high above his head,
With sharpe intended° sting so rude him smot, *extended*
That to the earth him drove, as stricken dead
Ne living wight would have him life behot.[6]
The mortall sting his angry needle shot
Quite through his shield, and in his shoulder seasd,
Where fast it stucke, ne would there out be got:
The griefe thereof him wondrous sore diseasd,° *troubled*
Ne might his ranckling paine with patience be appeasd.

39

But yet more mindfull of his honour deare,
Then of the grievous smart, which him did wring,° *torment*
From loathéd soile he can° him lightly reare, *did*
And strove to loose the farre infixéd sting:
Which when in vaine he tryde with struggeling,
Inflamed with wrath, his raging blade he heft,° *raised*
And strooke so strongly, that the knotty string
Of his huge taile he quite a sunder cleft,
Five joynts thereof he hewd, and but the stump him left.

40

Hart cannot thinke, what outrage, and what cryes,
With foule enfouldred° smoake and flashing fire, *black as a thundercloud*
The hell-bred beast threw forth unto the skyes,
That all was coveréd with darknesse dire:
Then fraught with rancour, and engorgéd° ire, *choking, congested*
He cast at once him to avenge for all,
And gathering up himselfe out of the mire,
With his uneven wings did fiercely fall
Upon his sunne-bright shield, and gript it fast withall.

41

Much was the man encombred with his hold,
In feare to lose his weapon in his paw,
Ne wist yet, how his talants° to unfold; *talons*
Nor harder was from Cerberus[7] greedie jaw
To plucke a bone, then from his cruell claw
To reave° by strength the gripéd gage° away: *seize / prize*
Thrise he assayd it from his foot to draw,
And thrise in vaine to draw it did assay,
It booted nought to thinke, to robbe him of his pray.

6. I.e., thought him alive.
7. Cf. I.v.34 and note.

42

Tho° when he saw no power might prevaile, *then*
His trustie sword he cald to his last aid,
Wherewith he fiercely did his foe assaile,
And double blowes about him stoutly laid,
That glauncing fire out of the yron plaid;
As sparckles from the Andvile° use to fly, *anvil*
When heavie hammers on the wedge are swaid;° *struck*
Therewith at last he forst him to unty° *loosen*
One of his grasping feete, him to defend thereby.

43

The other foot, fast fixéd on his shield,
Whenas no strength, nor stroks mote him constraine
To loose, ne yet the warlike pledge to yield,
He smot thereat with all his might and maine,
That nought so wondrous puissance might sustaine;
Upon the joynt the lucky steele did light,
And made such way, that hewd it quite in twaine;
The paw yet misséd not his minisht° might, *lessened*
But hong still on the shield, as it at first was pight.° *placed*

44

For griefe thereof, and divelish despight,
From his infernall fournace forth he threw
Huge flames, that dimméd all the heavens light,
Enrold in duskish smoke and brimstone blew;
As burning Aetna from his boyling stew° *cauldron*
Doth belch out flames, and rockes in peeces broke,
And ragged ribs of mountaines molten new,
Enwrapt in coleblacke clouds and filthy smoke,
That all the land with stench, and heaven with horror choke.

45

The heate whereof, and harmefull pestilence
So sore him noyd,° that forst him to retire *troubled*
A little backward for his best defence,
To save his bodie from the scorching fire,
Which he from hellish entrailes did expire.° *breathe out*
It chaunst (eternall God that chaunce did guide)
As he recoyléd backward, in the mire
His nigh forwearied feeble feet did slide,
And downe he fell, with dread of shame sore terrifide.

46

There grew a goodly tree him faire beside,
Loaden with fruit and apples rosie red,
As they in pure vermilion had beene dide,

Whereof great vertues over all[8] were red:° *known*
For happie life to all, which thereon fed,
And life eke everlasting did befall:
Great God it planted in that blessed sted° *place*
With his almightie hand, and did it call
The Tree of Life, the crime of our first fathers fall.[9]

47

In all the world like was not to be found,
Save in that soile, where all good things did grow,
And freely sprong out of the fruitfull ground,
As incorrupted° Nature did them sow, *untainted*
Till that dread Dragon all did overthrow.
Another like faire tree[1] eke grew thereby,
Whereof who so did eat, eftsoones did know
Both good and ill: O mornefull memory:
That tree through one mans fault hath doen us all to dy.

48

From that first tree forth flowd, as from a well,
A trickling streame of Balme,[2] most soveraine
And daintie deare,[3] which on the ground still fell,
And overflowéd all the fertill plaine,
As it had deawéd bene with timely° raine: *seasonable*
Life and long health that gratious° ointment gave, *full of grace*
And deadly woundes could heale, and reare againe
The senselesse corse appointed° for the grave. *made ready*
Into that same he fell: which did from death him save.

49

For nigh thereto the ever damnéd beast
Durst not approch, for he was deadly made,[4]
And all that life preservéd, did detest:
Yet he it oft adventured° to invade. *endeavored*
By this the drouping day-light gan to fade,
And yeeld his roome to sad succeeding night,
Who with her sable mantle gan to shade
The face of earth, and wayes of living wight,
And high her burning torch set up in heaven bright.

8. I.e., everywhere.
9. Adam was expelled from Eden "lest he put forth his hand, and take also of the tree of life, and eat, and live for ever" (Genesis 3.22); his "crime" is responsibility for the consequent denial of this tree (mentioned again in Revelation 22.2) to all humankind.
1. The tree of the knowledge of good and evil.
2. Some read this balm as signifying Christ's redeeming blood, or the wine of Communion, or more generally divine grace. In the apocryphal Gospel of Nicodemus, Seth heals his father, Adam, with "oil" flowing from "the tree of mercy."
3. I.e., choicely precious.
4. I.e., death was his being and essence.

50

When gentle Una saw the second fall
  Of her deare knight, who wearie of long fight,
  And faint through losse of bloud, moved not at all,
  But lay as in a dreame of deepe delight,
  Besmeard with pretious Balme, whose vertuous° might *efficacious*
  Did heale his wounds, and scorching heat alay,
  Againe she stricken was with sore affright,
  And for his safetie gan devoutly pray;
And watch the noyous° night, and wait for joyous day. *harmful*

51

The joyous day gan early to appeare,
  And faire Aurora from the deawy bed
  Of aged Tithone gan her selfe to reare,
  With rosie cheekes, for shame as blushing red;
  Her golden lockes for haste were loosely shed
  About her eares, when Una her did marke
  Clymbe to her charet, all with flowers spred,
  From heaven high to chase the chearelesse darke;
With merry note her loud salutes the mounting larke.

52

Then freshly up arose the doughtie knight,
  All healéd of his hurts and woundés wide,
  And did himselfe to battell readie dight;
  Whose early foe awaiting him beside
  To have devourd, so soone as day he spyde,
  When now he saw himselfe so freshly reare,
  As if late fight had nought him damnifyde,° *harmed*
  He woxe dismayd, and gan his fate to feare;
Nathlesse° with wonted rage he him advauncéd neare. *nevertheless*

53

And in his first encounter, gaping wide,
  He thought attonce him to have swallowd quight,
  And rusht upon him with outragious pride;
  Who him r'encountring fierce, as hauke in flight,
  Perforce rebutted° backe. The weapon bright *drove*
  Taking advantage of his open jaw,
  Ran through his mouth with so importune° might, *violent*
  That deepe emperst his darksome hollow maw,
And back retyrd,° life bloud forth with all did draw.[5] *withdrawn*

5. St. George usually wields a spear, but his weapon here recalls the sword issuing from the mouth of the righteous warrior named "Faithful and True" in Revelation 19.11–16; Redcrosse aims this sword (usually interpreted as God's Word) at the dragon's mouth, out of which had come destruction, some readers would recall, when the Father of Lies spoke through Eden's serpent.

54

So downe he fell, and forth his life did breath,
That vanisht into smoke and cloudés swift;
So downe he fell, that th'earth him underneath
Did grone, as feeble so great load to lift;
So downe he fell, as an huge rockie clift,
Whose false° foundation waves have washt away, *insecure*
With dreadfull poyse° is from the mayneland rift, *crash*
And rolling downe, great Neptune doth dismay;
So downe he fell, and like an heapéd mountaine lay.

55

The knight himselfe even trembled at his fall,
So huge and horrible a masse it seemed;
And his deare Ladie, that beheld it all,
Durst not approch for dread, which she misdeemed,° *misjudged*
But yet at last, when as the direfull feend
She saw not stirre, off-shaking vaine affright,
She nigher drew, and saw that joyous end:
Then God she praysd, and thankt her faithfull knight,
That had atchieved so great a conquest by his[6] might.

Canto XII

Faire Una to the Redcrosse knight
betrouthéd is with joy:
Though false Duessa it to barre
her false sleights doe imploy.

1

Behold I see the haven nigh at hand,
To which I meane my wearie course to bend;
Vere° the maine shete, and beare up with[1] the land, *shift*
The which afore is fairely to be kend,° *seen*
And seemeth safe from stormes, that may offend;
There this faire virgin wearie of her way
Must landed be, now at her journeyes end:
There eke my feeble barke° a while may stay, *ship*
Till merry wind and weather call her thence away.[2]

2

Scarsely had Phoebus in the glooming East
Yet harnesséd his firie-footed teeme,
Ne reard above the earth his flaming creast,
When the last deadly smoke aloft did steeme,

6. I.e., God's and/or that of Redcrosse; cf. II.i.33.
1. Steer toward.
2. The nautical metaphor with which Spenser opens and concludes this canto (and which recurs at the end of Book II) is a traditional introductory device; widely employed by classical authors, it appears also in Dante's *Paradiso* 2.1–15 and in Chaucer's *Troilus and Criseyde* 2.1–7.

That signe of last outbreathéd life did seeme
Unto the watchman on the castle wall;
Who thereby dead that balefull Beast did deeme,
And to his Lord and Ladie lowd gan call,
To tell, how he had seene the Dragons fatall fall.

3

Uprose with hastie joy, and feeble speed
That aged Sire, the Lord of all that land,
And lookéd forth, to weet, if true indeede
Those tydings were, as he did understand,
Which whenas true by tryall he out fond,° *found*
He bad to open wyde his brazen gate,
Which long time had bene shut, and out of hond[3]
Proclaymèd joy and peace through all his state;
For dead now was their foe, which them forrayéd° late. *ravaged*

4

Then gan triumphant Trompets sound on hie,
That sent to heaven the ecchoéd report
Of their new joy, and happie victorie
Gainst him, that had them long opprest with tort,° *wrong*
And fast imprisonéd in siegéd fort.
Then all the people, as in solemne feast,
To him assembled with one full consort,° *company*
Rejoycing at the fall of that great beast,
From whose eternall bondage now they were releast.

5

Forth came that auncient Lord and aged Queene,
Arayd in antique robes downe to the ground,
And sad° habiliments right well beseene;° *sober / becoming*
A noble crew about them waited round
Of sage and sober Peres, all gravely gownd;
Whom farre before did march a goodly band
Of tall young men, all hable° armes to sownd,[4] *able*
But now they laurell braunches bore in hand;
Glad signe of victorie and peace in all their land.

6

Unto that doughtie Conquerour they came,
And him before themselves prostrating low,
Their Lord and Patrone loud did him proclame,
And at his feet their laurell boughes did throw.
Soone after them all dauncing on a row
The comely virgins came, with girlands dight,

3. I.e., at once.
4. I.e., clash in battle.

As fresh as flowres in medow greene do grow,
When morning deaw upon their leaves doth light:
And in their hands sweet Timbrels° all upheld on hight. *tambourines*

7

And them before, the fry° of children young *crowd*
Their wanton° sports and childish mirth did play, *frolicsome*
And to the Maydens sounding tymbrels sung
In well attunéd notes, a joyous lay,
And made delightfull musicke all the way,
Untill they came, where that faire virgin stood;
As faire Diana in fresh sommers day
Beholds her Nymphes, enraunged in shadie wood,
Some wrestle, some do run, some bathe in christall flood.

8

So she beheld those maydens meriment
With chearefull vew; who when to her they came,
Themselves to ground with gratious humblesse bent,
And her adored by honorable name,
Lifting to heaven her everlasting fame:
Then on her head they set a girland greene,
And crownéd her twixt earnest and twixt game;° *jest*
Who in her selfe-resemblance well beseene,[5]
Did seeme such, as she was, a goodly maiden Queene.

9

And after, all the raskall many° ran, *multitude*
Heapéd together in rude rablement,° *confusion*
To see the face of that victorious man:
Whom all admiréd, as from heaven sent,
And gazd upon with gaping wonderment.
But when they came, where that dead Dragon lay,
Stretcht on the ground in monstrous large extent,
The sight with idle° feare did them dismay, *baseless*
Ne durst approch him nigh, to touch, or once assay.

10

Some feard, and fled; some feard and well it faynd;° *concealed*
One that would wiser seeme, then all the rest,
Warnd him not touch, for yet perhaps remaynd
Some lingring life within his hollow brest,
Or in his wombe might lurke some hidden nest
Of many Dragonets, his fruitfull seed;
Another said, that in his eyes did rest

5. I.e., attractively resembling her real self. The next few stanzas, with their gently humorous commentary on crowd behavior, have a curious parallel in an illustration of the Book of Daniel in the 1568 Bishops' Bible, which in addition to a lion's den shows a tiny dragon on its back, ruins in the background, with onlookers gathering to look.

Yet sparckling fire, and bad thereof take heed;
Another said, he saw him move his eyes indeed.

11

One mother, when as her foolehardie chyld
Did come too neare, and with his talants play,
Halfe dead through feare, her litle babe revyld,° *rebuked*
And to her gossips° gan in counsell say; *women friends*
"How can I tell, but that his talants may
Yet scratch my sonne, or rend his tender hand?"
So diversly themeslves in vaine they fray;° *frighten*
Whiles some more bold, to measure him nigh stand,
To prove° how many acres he did spread of land. *determine*

12

Thus flockéd all the folke him round about,
The whiles that hoarie° king, with all his traine, *gray-haired*
Being arrivéd, where that champion stout
After his foes defeasance° did remaine, *defeat*
Him goodly greetes, and faire does entertaine,
With princely gifts of yvorie and gold,
And thousand thankes him yeelds for all his paine.
Then when his daughter deare he does behold,
Her dearely doth imbrace, and kisseth manifold.° *many times*

13

And after to his Pallace he them brings,
With shaumes,° and trompets, and with Clarions sweet; *oboes*
And all the way the joyous people sings,
And with their garments strowes the pavéd street:
Whence mounting up, they find purveyance° meet *provision*
Of all, that royall Princes court became,° *suited*
And all the floore was underneath their feet
Bespred with costly scarlot of great name,° *quality*
On which they lowly sit, and fitting purpose° frame. *discourse*

14

What needs me tell their feast and goodly guize,° *behavior*
In which was nothing riotous nor vaine?
What needs of daintie dishes to devize,° *talk*
Of comely services, or courtly trayne?° *assembly*
My narrow leaves cannot in them containe
The large discourse of royall Princes state.
Yet was their manner then but bare and plaine:
For th'antique world excesse and pride did hate;
Such proud luxurious pompe is swollen up but late.

15

Then when with meates and drinkes of every kinde
Their fervent appetites they quenchéd had,
That auncient Lord gan fit occasion finde,
Of straunge adventures, and of perils sad,
Which in his travell him befallen had,
For to demaund of his renowméd guest:
Who then with utt'rance grave, and count'nance sad,
From point to point, as is before exprest,
Discourst his voyage long, according his request.

16

Great pleasure mixt with pittifull° regard, *sympathetic*
That godly King and Queene did passionate,° *express with feeling*
Whiles they his pittifull adventures heard,
That oft they did lament his lucklesse state,
And often blame the too importune° fate, *severe*
That heapd on him so many wrathfull wreakes:° *injuries*
For never gentle knight, as he of late,
So tosséd was in fortunes cruell freakes;° *whims*
And all the while salt teares bedeawd the hearers cheaks.

17

Then said that royall Pere in sober wise;° *manner*
"Deare Sonne, great beene the evils, which ye bore
From first to last in your late enterprise,
That I note,° whether prayse, or pitty more: *know not*
For never living man, I weene, so sore
In sea of deadly daungers was distrest;
But since now safe ye seiséd° have the shore, *attained*
And well arrivéd are, (high God be blest)
Let us devize of ease and everlasting rest."

18

"Ah dearest Lord," said then that doughty knight,
"Of ease or rest I may not yet devize;
For by the faith, which I to armes have plight,
I bounden am streight after this emprize,° *enterprise*
As that your daughter can ye well advize,
Backe to returne to that great Faerie Queene,
And her to serve six yeares in warlike wize,
Gainst that proud Paynim king, that workes her teene:° *affliction*
Therefore I ought crave pardon, till I there have beene."[6]

6. Betrothed but not yet married, despite a formal betrothal's legally binding nature, George must serve Gloriana for six years, which in much apocalyptic thinking would numerically signify the six thousand years (or less precisely the "ages") paralleling the six days of Creation before the seventh age, the "Millennium," that parallels the first Sabbath and that then yields to eternity. Only then will Christ the bridegroom marry his bride the Church (not the institution but the whole body of believers).

19

"Unhappie falles that hard necessitie,"
Quoth he, "the troubler of my happie peace,
And vowéd foe of my felicitie;
Ne I against the same can justly preace:° *contend*
But since that band° ye cannot now release, *bond*
Nor doen undo; (for vowes may not be vaine)
Soone as the terme of those six yeares shall cease,
Ye then shall hither backe returne againe,
The marriage to accomplish vowd betwixt you twain.

20

"Which for my part I covet to performe,
In sort° as through the world I did proclame, *manner*
That who so kild that monster most deforme,
And him in hardy battaile overcame,
Should have mine onely daughter to his Dame,° *wife*
And of my kingdome heire apparaunt bee:
Therefore since now to thee perteines° the same, *belongs*
By dew desert of noble chevalree,
Both daughter and eke kingdome, lo I yield to thee."

21

Then forth he calléd that his daughter faire,
The fairest Un' his onely daughter deare,
His onely daughter, and his onely heyre;
Who forth proceeding with sad sober cheare,° *countenance*
As bright as doth the morning starre appeare
Out of the East, with flaming lockes bedight,
To tell that dawning day is drawing neare,
And to the world does bring long wishéd light;
So faire and fresh that Lady shewd her selfe in sight.

22

So faire and fresh, as freshest flowre in May;
For she had layd her mournefull stole aside,
And widow-like sad wimple° throwne away, *veil*
Wherewith her heavenly beautie she did hide,
Whiles on her wearie journey she did ride;
And on her now a garment she did weare,
All lilly white, withoutten spot, or pride,° *ornament*
That seemd like silke and silver woven neare,° *closely*
But neither silke nor silver therein did appeare.[7]

7. Cf. "the marriage of the Lamb is come, and his wife hath made herself ready. And to her was granted that she should be arrayed in fine linen, clean and white: for the fine linen is the righteousness of saints" (Revelation 19.7–8). See also Revelation 21.2, 11 and the Song of Solomon 4.7: "Thou art all fair, my love; there is no spot in thee."

23

The blazing brightnesse of her beauties beame,
And glorious light of her sunshyny face
To tell, were as to strive against the streame.
My ragged rimes are all too rude and bace,
Her heavenly lineaments for to enchace.° *be a setting*
Ne wonder; for her owne deare lovéd knight,
All° were she dayly with himselfe in place, *although*
Did wonder much at her celestiall sight:
Oft had he seene her faire, but never so faire dight.° *adorned*

24

So fairely dight, when she in presence came,
She to her Sire made humble reverence,
And bowéd low, that her right well became,
And added grace unto her excellence:
Who with great wisedome, and grave eloquence
Thus gan to say. But eare he thus had said,
With flying speede, and seeming great pretence,° *purpose*
Came running in, much like a man dismaid,
A Messenger with letters, which his message said.

25

All in the open hall amazéd stood,
At suddeinnesse of that unwarie° sight, *unexpected*
And wondred at his breathlesse hastie mood.
But he for nought would stay his passage right,° *direct*
Till fast° before the king he did alight; *close*
Where falling flat, great humblesse he did make,
And kist the ground, whereon his foot was pight;° *placed*
Then to his hands that writ° he did betake,° *document / deliver*
Which he disclosing,° red thus, as the paper spake. *unfolding*

26

"To thee, most mighty king of Eden faire,
Her greeting sends in these sad lines addrest.
The wofull daughter, and forsaken heire
Of that great Emperour of all the West:
And bids thee be advizéd for the best,
Ere thou thy daughter linck in holy band
Of wedlocke to that new unknowen guest:
For he already plighted his right hand
Unto another love, and to another land.

27

"To me sad mayd, or rather widow sad,
He was affiauncéd long time before,
And sacred pledges he both gave, and had,

False erraunt knight, infamous, and forswore:
Witnesse the burning Altars, which° he swore, *by which*
And guiltie heavens of[8] his bold perjury,
Which though he hath polluted oft of yore,
Yet I to them for judgement just do fly,
And them conjure° t'avenge this shamefull injury. *entreat*

28

"Therefore since mine he is, or° free or bond, *whether*
Or false or trew, or living or else dead,
Withhold, O soveraine Prince, your hasty hond
From knitting league with him, I you aread,° *advise*
Ne weene° my right with strength adowne to tread, *think*
Through weakenesse of my widowhed, or woe:
For truth is strong, her rightfull cause to plead,
And shall find friends, if need requireth soe,
So bids thee well to fare, Thy neither friend, nor foe, Fidessa."

29

When he these bitter byting words had red,
The tydings straunge did him abashéd make,
That still he sate long time astonishéd
As in great muse, ne word to creature spake.
At last his solemne silence thus he brake,
With doubtfull eyes fast fixéd on his guest;
"Redoubted knight, that for mine onely sake
Thy life and honour late adventurest,° *hazarded*
Let nought be hid from me, that ought to be exprest.

30

"What meane these bloudy vowes, and idle threats,
Throwne out from womanish impatient mind?
What heavens? what altars? what enragéd heates
Here heapéd up with termes of love unkind,° *unnatural*
My conscience cleare with guilty bands would bind?
High God be witnesse, that I guiltlesse ame.
But if your selfe, Sir knight, ye faultie find,
Or wrappéd be in loves of former Dame,
With crime do not it cover, but disclose the same."

31

To whom the Redcrosse knight this answere sent,
"My Lord, my King, be nought hereat dismayd,
Till well ye wote by grave intendiment,° *consideration*
What woman, and wherefore doth me upbrayd
With breach of love, and loyalty betrayd.
It was in my mishaps, as hitherward

8. I.e., heavens tainted by.

I lately traveild, that unwares I strayd
Out of my way, through perils straunge and hard;
That day should faile me, ere I had them all declard.

32

"There did I find, or rather I was found
Of this false woman, that Fidessa hight,
Fidessa hight the falsest Dame on ground,
Most false Duessa, royall richly dight,
That easie was t' invegle° weaker sight: *deceive*
Who by her wicked arts, and wylie skill,
Too false and strong for earthly skill or might,
Unwares me wrought unto her wicked will,
And to my foe betrayd, when least I fearéd ill."

33

Then steppéd forth the goodly royall Mayd,
And on the ground her selfe prostrating low,
With sober countenaunce thus to him sayd;
"O pardon me, my soveraigne Lord, to show
The secret treasons, which of late I know
To have bene wroght by that false sorceresse.
She onely she it is, that earst did throw
This gentle knight into so great distresse,
That death him did awaite in dayly wretchednesse.

34

"And now it seemes, that she subornéd hath
This craftie messenger with letters vaine,
To worke new woe and improvided scath,[9]
By breaking of the band betwixt us twaine;
Wherein she uséd hath the practicke paine[1]
Of this false footman, clokt with simplenesse,
Whom if ye please for to discover plaine,
Ye shall him Archimago find, I ghesse,
The falsest man alive; who tries shall find no lesse."

35

The king was greatly movéd at her speach,
And all with suddein indignation fraight,° *filled*
Bad on that Messenger rude hands to reach.
Eftsoones the Gard, which on his state did wait,
Attacht° that faitor° false, and bound him strait: *seized / imposter*
Who seeming sorely chauffféd° at his band, *angered*
As chainéd Beare, whom cruell dogs do bait,

9. I.e., unforeseen harm.
1. I.e., cunning pains.

With idle force did faine them to withstand,
And often semblaunce made to scape out of their hand.

36

But they him layd full low in dungeon deepe,
And bound him hand and foote with yron chains.
And with continuall watch did warely keepe;
Who then would thinke, that by his subtile trains
He could escape fowle death or deadly paines?[2]
Thus when that Princes wrath was pacifide,
He gan renew the late forbidden banes,° — *banns of marriage*
And to the knight his daughter deare he tyde,
With sacred rites and vowes for ever to abyde.

37

His owne two hands the holy knots did knit,
That none but death for ever can devide;
His owne two hands, for such a turne° most fit, — *task*
The housling° fire did kindle and provide, — *sacramental*
And holy water thereon sprinckled wide;[3]
At which the bushy Teade° a groome did light, — *torch*
And sacred lampe in secret chamber hide,
Where it should not be quenchéd day nor night,
For feare of evill fates, but burnen ever bright.

38

Then gan they sprinckle all the posts with wine,
And made great feast to solemnize that day;
They all perfumde with frankencense divine,
And precious odours fetcht from far away,
That all the house did sweat with great aray:
And all the while sweete Musicke did apply
Her curious° skill, the warbling notes to play, — *elaborate, exquisite*
To drive away the dull Melancholy;
The whiles one sung a song of love and jollity.[4]

2. "And he laid hold on the dragon, that old serpent, which is the devil, and Satan, and bound him a thousand years. And cast him into the bottomless pit, and shut him up, and set a seal upon him, that he should deceive the nations no more, till the thousand years should be fulfilled: and after that he must be loosed a little season" (Revelation 20.2–13).
3. Some details in this betrothal, like some in Spenser's *Epithalamion*, recall baptismal rites or prayers set for Easter Saturday in the still widely available Sarum Missal, another instance of Spenser's willingness to incorporate Catholic elements into an apparently Protestant allegory; see Harold Weatherby, "Una's Betrothal and the Easter Vigil," *Spenser at Kalamazoo 1984*, ed. Francis Greco (Clarion, PA: Clarion University of Pennsylvania 1984), 6–16. Alternatively, the scene is yet further evidence that England had not yet become thoroughly "Reformed." Ancient weddings, furthermore, could include sacred fire and water: in *Roman Questions* I, Plutarch says that because fire is masculine and active, water feminine and passive, their combination, like marriage, is productive.
4. Cf. *Epithalamion* 242–60.

39

During the which there was an heavenly noise
Heard sound through all the Pallace pleasantly,
Like as it had bene many an Angels voice,
Singing before th'eternall majesty,
In their trinall triplicities on hye;[5]
Yet wist no creature, whence that heavenly sweet° *delight*
Proceeded, yet each one felt secretly
Himselfe thereby reft of his sences meet,° *proper*
And ravishéd with rare impression in his sprite.

40

Great joy was made that day of young and old,
And solemne feast proclaimd throughout the land,
That their exceeding merth may not be told:
Suffice it heare by signes to understand
The usuall joyes at knitting of loves band.
Thrise happy man the knight himselfe did hold,
Possesséd of his Ladies hart and hand,
And ever, when his eye did her behold,
His heart did seeme to melt in pleasures manifold.

41

Her joyous presence and sweet company
In full content he there did long enjoy,
Ne wicked envie, ne vile gealosy
His deare delights were able to annoy:
Yet swimming in that sea of blisfull joy,
He nought forgot, how he whilome had sworne,
In case he could that monstrous beast destroy,
Unto his Farie Queene backe to returne:
The which he shortly did, and Una left to mourne.

42

Now strike your sailes ye jolly Mariners,
For we be come unto a quiet rode,° *anchorage*
Where we must land some of our passengers,
And light this wearie vessell of her lode.
Here she a while may make her safe abode,
Till she repairéd have her tackles spent,° *worn out*
And wants supplide. And then againe abroad
On the long voyage whereto she is bent:
Well may she speede and fairely finish her intent.

5. The song is referable to that sung at the marriage of the Lamb (Revelation 19.6). The "trinall triplicities" are the nine angelic orders, first elaborated in the fifth century by Dionysius the Areopagite.

From The Second Booke of The Faerie Queene

Contayning
The Legend of Sir Guyon
or
Of Temperaunce

1

Right well I wote° most mighty Soveraine, *know*
That all this famous antique history,
Of some th'aboundance of an idle braine
Will judgéd be, and painted forgery,
Rather then matter of just° memory, *well-founded*
Sith none, that breatheth living aire, does know,
Where is that happy land of Faery,
Which I so much do vaunt, yet no where show,
But cite antiquities, which no body can know.[1]

2

But let that man with better sence advize,° *consider*
That of the world least part to us is red:° *known*
And dayly how through hardy enterprize,
Many great Regions are discoveréd,
Which to late age[2] were never mentionéd.
Who ever heard of th'Indian Peru?
Or who in venturous vessell measuréd
The Amazons huge river now found trew?
Or fruitfullest Virginia who did ever vew?[3]

3

Yet all these were, when no man did them know;
Yet have from wisest ages hidden beene:
And later times things more unknowne shall show.
Why then should witlesse man so much misweene° *misjudge*
That nothing is, but that which he hath seene?
What if within the Moones faire shining spheare?
What if in every other starre unseene
Of other worldes he happily° should heare? *by chance*
He wonder would much more: yet such to some appeare.

1. So too, Ariosto (*Orlando Furioso* 7.1–2) warns that his story may not appeal to the ignorant or foolish and so directs his poem to those with intelligence and insight.
2. I.e., to recent times.
3. Sir Walter Raleigh, to whom Elizabeth ("the Virgin Queen") in 1584 granted a patent to establish a "plantation" in America, twice attempted to settle a colony at Roanoke Island in Pamlico Sound. Although the Virginian project was not firmly established until 1607, the Dedication to the 1596 edition of *The Faerie Queene* adds the words "and of Virginia" to her title, which in the 1590 edition reads "Queene of England, France and Ireland." Many scholars find here further evidence that Spenser's epic inscribes hopes, anxieties, and evasions accompanying the start of English colonialism. (Thus one answer to these rhetorical questions might be "kings Atahualpa and Powhatan.")

4

Of Faerie lond yet if he more inquire,
By certaine signes here set in sundry place
He may it find; ne let him then admire,° *wonder*
But yield his sence to be too blunt and bace,
That no'te° without an hound fine footing° trace. *cannot / tracks*
And thou, O fairest Princesse under sky,
In this faire mirrhour maist behold thy face,
And thine owne realmes in lond of Faery,
And in this antique Image thy great auncestry.[4]

5

The which O pardon me thus to enfold
In covert° vele, and wrap in shadowes light, *concealing*
That feeble eyes your glory may behold,
Which else could not endure those beamés bright,
But would be dazled with exceeding light.
O pardon, and vouchsafe with patient eare
The brave adventures of this Faery knight
The good Sir Guyon gratiously to heare,
In whom great rule of Temp'raunce[5] goodly doth appeare.

Canto I

Guyon by Archimage abusd,° *deceived*
The Redcrosse knight awaytes,
Findes Mordant and Amavia slaine
With pleasures poisoned baytes.

1

That cunning Architect[1] of cancred° guile, *malignant*
Whom Princes late displeasure left in bands,
For falséd letters and subornéd wile,[2]
Soone as the Redcrosse knight he understands,
To beene departed out of Eden lands,
To serve againe his soveraine Elfin Queene,
His artes he moves, and out of caytives° hands *menials'*
Himselfe he frees by secret meanes unseene;
His shackles emptie left, him selfe escapéd cleene.

4. I.e., in Gloriana ("this faire mirrhour") is imaged Queen Elizabeth, and in the whole poem ("this antique Image") England and its ruler's high lineage.
5. "Temperance" infolds or evokes many related words and concepts: to temper (as when we plunge metal alternately into fire and cold water), temperament (the body's balance of humors), temporal (suggesting time and measured tempo), tempest (storms often symbolized the blows of fortune that the temperate and tempered person will meet with fortitude), and what we still call good or bad temper; compare moderate, mode, and mood. On how such concepts relate the body to music and physics, see L. Spitzer, *Classical and Christian Ideas of World Harmony* (Baltimore, 1963).
1. I.e., Archimago, whose escape Spenser has foreshadowed in I.xii.36.
2. I.e., forged letters and perjured deceitfulness.

2

And forth he fares full of malicious mind,
To worken mischiefe and avenging woe,
Where ever he that godly knight may find,
His onely hart sore, and his onely foe,
Sith Una now he algates° must forgoe, *entirely*
Whom his victorious hands did earst restore
To native crowne and kingdome late ygoe:[3]
Where she enjoyes sure peace for evermore,
As weather-beaten ship arrived on happie shore.

3

Him therefore now the object of his spight
And deadly food° he makes: him to offend *feud*
By forgéd treason, or by open fight
He seekes, of all his drift° the aymèd end: *plotting*
Thereto his subtile engins° he does bend, *machinations*
His practick° wit, and his faire filéd° tong, *crafty / smooth*
With thousand other sleights: for well he kend,° *knew*
His credit now in doubtfull ballaunce hong;
For hardly could be hurt, who was already stong.

4

Still as he went, he craftie stales° did lay, *snares*
With cunning traines° him to entrap unwares, *schemes*
And privie° spials° plast in all his way, *hidden / spies*
To weete what course he takes, and how he fares;
To ketch him at a vantage in his snares.
But now so wise and warie was the knight
By triall of his former harmes and cares,
That he descride, and shonnéd still his slight:° *trickery*
The fish that once was caught, new bait will hardly bite.

5

Nath'lesse° th'Enchaunter would not spare his paine, *nevertheless*
In hope to win occasion to his will;
Which when he long awaited had in vaine,
He chaungd his minde from one to other ill:
For to all good he enimy was still.
Upon the way him fortunéd to meet,
Faire marching underneath a shady hill,
A goodly knight[4] all armd in harnesse meete,° *proper*
That from his head no place appearéd to his feete.

3. I.e., lately.
4. I.e., Guyon, named in the Proem. Guyon may be (or strive to be) not "temperate" in Aristotle's sense of unmoved by emotion or temptation but rather "continent": capable of passion or temptation but able to resist, although in the church fathers that Spenser might have read such distinction may not be as clear as it is to modern classicists; and, perhaps, how we read his virtue may

6

His carriage was full comely and upright,
His countenaunce demure and temperate,
But yet so sterne and terrible in sight,
That cheard his friends, and did his foes amate:° *dismay*
He was an Elfin borne of noble state,
And mickle worship[5] in his native land;
Well could he tourney and in lists debate,° *contend*
And knighthood tooke of good Sir Huons hand,
When with king Oberon he came to Faerie land.[6]

7

Him als° accompanyd upon the way *also*
A comely° Palmer,[7] clad in blacke attire, *seemly, sober*
Of ripest yeares, and haires all hoarie gray,
That with a staffe his feeble steps did stire,° *steer*
Least his long way his aged limbes should tire:
And if by lookes one may the mind aread,
He seemd to be a sage and sober sire,
And ever with slow pace the knight did lead,
Who taught his trampling steed with equall steps to tread.

8

Such whenas Archimago them did view,
He weenéd well to worke some uncouth° wile, *strange*
Eftsoones untwisting his deceiptfull clew,[8]
He gan to weave a web of wicked guile,
And with faire countenance and flattring stile,
To them approching, thus the knight bespake:
"Faire sonne of Mars, that seeke with warlike spoile,
And great atchievments great your selfe to make,
Vouchsafe to stay your steed for humble misers° sake." *wretch's*

9

He stayd his steed for humble misers sake,
And bad tell on the tenor of his plaint;
Who feigning then in every limbe to quake,

---

change as the book progresses. Spenser would also have known the parable in Plato's *Phaedrus* in which the balanced soul is the charioteer Reason who controls the two horses of docile and wayward instincts. Spenser may Christianize the classical virtue, although to what degree has been debated. The knight's name may pun on the word "guyon" in the *Golden Legend*, where it is associated with St. George and means "wrestler," or on Eden's river "Gihon," a name suggesting temperance; his schoolteacher Richard Mulcaster was apparently fond of wrestling and thought it educational (Wesley 2009).

5. I.e., much honor.
6. Huon, hero of the thirteenth-century romance *Huon of Bordeaux*, was favored by the fairy king Oberon.
7. Technically, a "palmer" is one who has made a pilgrimage to Jerusalem, although the word also applied to a schoolroom assistant who corrects students with a blow on the palm. Spenser may hope to contrast the balanced tread of this well-controlled steed with the feisty horse and rider of Book I and also the Palmer who leads the knight with the dwarf that follows Una.
8. Ball of thread.

Through inward feare, and seeming pale and faint
With piteous mone his percing speach gan paint;
"Deare Lady how shall I declare thy cace,
Whom late I left in langourous° constraint? *sorrowful*
Would God thy selfe now present were in place,
To tell this ruefull tale; thy sight could win thee grace.

10

"Or rather would, O would it had so chaunst,
That you, most noble Sir, had present beene,
When that lewd ribauld° with vile lust advaunst° *ruffian / moved*
Layd first his filthy hands on virgin cleene,° *pure*
To spoile her daintie corse° so faire and sheene,° *body / bright*
As on the earth, great mother of us all,
With living eye more faire was never seene,
Of chastitie and honour virginall:
Witnesse ye heavens, whom she in vaine to helpe did call."

11

"How may it be," said then the knight halfe wroth,
"That knight should knighthood ever so have shent?"° *disgraced*
"None but that saw," quoth he, "would weene for troth,
How shamefully that Maid he did torment.
Her looser° golden lockes he rudely rent, *unbound*
And drew her on the ground, and his sharpe sword,
Against her snowy brest he fiercely bent,
And threatned death with many a bloudie word;
Toung hates to tell the rest, that eye to see abhord."

12

Therewith amovéd from his sober mood,
"And lives he yet," said he, "that wrought this act,
And doen the heavens afford him vitall food?"
"He lives," quoth he, "and boasteth of the fact,[9]
Ne yet hath any knight his courage crackt."
"Where may that treachour then," said he, "be found,
Or by what meanes may I his footing tract?"° *trace*
"That shall I shew," said he, "as sure, as hound
The stricken Deare doth chalenge° by the bleeding wound." *track*

13

He staid not lenger talke, but with fierce ire
And zealous hast away is quickly gone
To seeke that knight, where him that craftie Squire
Supposd to be. They do arrive anone,
Where sate a gentle Lady all alone,
With garments rent, and haire discheveléd,

9. I.e., the rape of "that Maid."

Wringing her hands, and making piteous mone;
Her swollen eyes were much disfiguréd,
And her faire face with teares was fowly blubberéd.

14

The knight approaching nigh, thus to her said,
"Faire Ladie, through foule sorrow ill bedight,[1]
Great pittie is to see you thus dismaid,
And marre the blossome of your beautie bright:
For thy° appease your grief and heavie plight, *therefore*
And tell the cause of your conceivéd° paine. *evident*
For if he live, that hath you doen despight,° *wrong*
He shall you doe due recompence againe,
Or else his wrong with greater puissance maintaine."

15

Which when she heard, as in despightfull wise,[2]
She wilfully her sorrow did augment,
And offred hope of comfort did despise:
Her golden lockes most cruelly she rent,
And scratcht her face with ghastly dreriment,° *grief*
Ne would she speake, ne see, ne yet be seene,
But hid her visage, and her head downe bent,
Either for grievous shame, or for great teene,° *anguish*
As if her hart with sorrow had transfixéd beene.[3]

16

Till her that Squire bespake, "Madame my liefe,° *dear*
For Gods deare love be not so wilfull bent,
But doe vouchsafe now to receive reliefe,
The which good fortune doth to you present.
For what bootes it to weepe and to wayment,° *lament*
When ill is chaunst, but doth the ill increase,
And the weake mind with double woe torment?"
When she her Squire heard speake, she gan appease
Her voluntarie° paine, and feele some secret ease. *willful*

17

Eftsoone she said, "Ah gentle trustie Squire,
What comfort can I wofull wretch conceave,
Or why should ever I henceforth desire,
To see faire heavens face, and life not leave,
Sith that false Traytour did my honour reave?"° *steal*
"False traytour certes," said the Faerie knight,
"I read° the man, that ever would deceave *regard*

1. I.e., stricken.
2. I.e., in malicious fashion.
3. In her behavior the lady (identified in stanza 21) resembles the enchantress in Trissino's *L'Italia Liberata dai Goti* (1548) 4.765 ff.

A gentle Ladie, or her wrong through might:
Death were too little paine for such a foule despight.

18

"But now, faire Ladie, comfort to you make,
And read,° who hath ye wrought this shamefull plight: *tell*
That short° revenge the man may overtake, *speedy*
Where so he be, and soone upon him light."
"Certes," saide she, "I wote not how he hight,° *is called*
But under him a gray steede did he wield,° *control*
Whose sides with dapled circles weren dight;
Upright he rode, and in his silver shield
He bore a bloudie Crosse, that quartred all the field."[4]

19

"Now by my head," said Guyon, "much I muse,° *wonder*
How that same knight should do so foule amis,
Or ever gentle Damzell so abuse:
For may I boldly say, he surely is
A right good knight, and true of word ywis:° *surely*
I present was, and can it witnesse well,
When armes he swore, and streight did enterpris° *undertake*
Th'adventure of the Errant damozell,[5]
In which he hath great glorie wonne, as I heare tell.

20

"Nathlesse he shortly shall againe be tryde,
And fairely quite° him of th'imputed blame, *acquit*
Else be ye sure he dearely shall abyde,° *suffer*
Or make you good amendment for the same:
All wrongs have mends, but no amends of shame.
Now therefore Ladie, rise out of your paine,
And see the salving of your blotted name."[6]
Full loth she seemd thereto, but yet did faine;
For she was inly glad her purpose so to gaine.

21

Her purpose was not such, as she did faine,
Ne yet her person such, as it was seene,
But under simple shew and semblant plaine
Lurckt false Duessa secretly unseene,
As a chast Virgin, that had wrongéd beene:
So had false Archimago her disguisd,
To cloke her guile with sorrow and sad teene;

4. I.e., divided the shield's surface ("field") into quarters.
5. I.e., Una, the wandering maiden.
6. I.e., the vindication of your honor.

And eke himselfe had craftily devised
To be her Squire, and do her service well aguised.° *arrayed*

22

Her late forlorne and naked he had found,
Where she did wander in waste wildernesse,
Lurking in rockes and caves farre under ground,
And with greene mosse covering her nakednesse,
To hide her shame and loathly filthinesse;
Sith her Prince Arthur of proud ornaments
And borrowed beautie spoyld. Her nathelesse
Th'enchaunter finding fit for his intents,
Did thus revest,° and deckt with due habiliments.° *reclothe / attire*

23

For all he did, was to deceive good knights,
And draw them from pursuit of praise and fame,
To slug in slouth and sensuall delights,
And end their daies with irrenowméd° shame. *dishonorable*
And now exceeding griefe him overcame,
To see the Redcrosse thus advauncéd hye;[7]
Therefore this craftie engine° he did frame, *plot*
Against his praise to stir up enmitye
Of such, as vertues like mote unto him allye.[8]

24

So now he Guyon guides an uncouth° way *strange*
Through woods and mountaines, till they came at last
Into a pleasant dale, that lowly lay
Betwixt two hils, whose high heads overplast,° *looming above*
The valley did with coole shade overcast;
Through midst thereof a little river rold,
By which there sate a knight with helme unlast,
Himselfe refreshing with the liquid cold,
After his travell long, and labours manifold.

25

"Loe yonder he," cryde Archimage alowd,
"That wrought the shamefull fact,° which I did shew; *deed*
And now he doth himselfe in secret shrowd,
To flie the vengeance for his outrage dew;
But vaine: for ye shall dearely do him rew,[9]
So God ye speed, and send you good successe;
Which we farre off will here abide to vew."

7. I.e., highly esteemed.
8. I.e., those of similarly virtuous natures, likely to ally themselves with Redcrosse.
9. I.e., make him repent.

So they him left, inflamed with wrathfulnesse,
That streight against that knight his speare he did addresse.° *direct*

26

Who seeing him from farre so fierce to pricke,
His warlike armes about him gan embrace,° *put on*
And in the rest his readie speare did sticke;
Tho° when as still he saw him towards pace, *then*
He gan rencounter him in equall race.
They bene ymet, both readie to affrap,° *strike*
When suddenly that warriour[1] gan abace° *lower*
His threatned speare, as if some new mishap
Had him betidde,° or hidden danger did entrap. *befallen*

27

And cryde, "Mercie Sir knight, and mercie Lord,
For mine offence and heedlesse hardiment,° *boldness*
That had almost committed crime abhord,
And with reprochfull shame mine honour shent,° *disgraced*
Whiles cursèd steele against that badge I bent,
The sacred badge of my Redeemers death,
Which on your shield is set for ornament:"
But his fierce foe his steede could stay uneath,° *with difficulty*
Who prickt with courage kene, did cruell battell breath.

28

But when he heard him speake, streight way he knew
His error, and himselfe inclyning sayd;
"Ah deare Sir Guyon, well becommeth you,
But me behoveth rather to upbrayd,
Whose hastie hand so farre from reason strayd,
That almost it did haynous violence
On that faire image of that heavenly Mayd,[2]
That decks and armes your shield with faire defence:
Your court'sie takes on you anothers due offence."

29

So bene they both attone,° and doen upreare *united*
Their bevers° bright, each other for to greete; *visors*
Goodly comportance° each to other beare, *behavior*
And entertaine themselves with court'sies meet.
Then said the Redcrosse knight, "Now mote I weet,[3]
Sir Guyon, why with so fierce saliaunce,° *assault*
And fell intent ye did at earst me meet;

1. I.e., Guyon. Unlike Sansfoy in I.ii. 18, Guyon knows that St. George's cross is an "ornament," not a "charme."
2. I.e., Gloriana.
3. I.e., may I know.

For sith I know your goodly governaunce,° *restraint*
Great cause, I weene, you guided, or some uncouth chaunce."

30

"Certes," said he, "well mote I shame to tell
The fond encheason,° that me hither led. *occasion*
A false infamous faitour° late befell *villain*
Me for to meet, that seeméd ill bested,° *beleaguered*
And playnd of grievous outrage, which he red° *said*
A knight had wrought against a Ladie gent;
Which to avenge, he to this place me led,
Where you he made the marke of his intent,
And now is fled; foule shame him follow, where he went."

31

So can° he turne his earnest unto game, *knows how*
Through goodly handling and wise temperance.
By this his aged guide in presence came;
Who soone as on that knight his eye did glance,
Eft soones of him had perfect cognizance,[4]
Sith him in Faerie court he late avizd;° *had seen*
And said, "Faire sonne, God give you happie chance,
And that deare Crosse upon your shield devizd,
Wherewith above all knights ye goodly seeme aguizd.° *equipped*

32

"Joy may you have, and everlasting fame,
Of late most hard atchiev'ment by you donne,
For which enrolléd is your glorious name
In heavenly Registers above the Sunne,
Where you a Saint with Saints your seat have wonne:
But wretched we, where ye have left your marke,
Must now anew begin, like° race to runne; *similar*
God guide thee, Guyon, well to end thy warke,
And to the wishéd haven bring thy weary barke."[5]

33

"Palmer," him answeréd the Redcrosse knight,
"His be the praise, that this atchiev'ment wrought,
Who made my hand the organ of his might;
More then goodwill to me attribute nought:
For all I did, I did but as I ought.
But you, faire Sir, whose pageant[6] next ensewes,
Well mote yee thee,° as well can wish your thought, *thrive*

4. Upon the Palmer's return the allegiance of Redcrosse and Guyon is "perfectly" confirmed.
5. The Palmer puns on Guyon's name: to "guy" meant to guide or govern; a "guy" is a ship's guide-rope.
6. I.e., role in life's drama or procession.

That home ye may report thrise happie newes;
For well ye worthie bene for worth and gentle thewes."° *manners*

34

So courteous congé° both did give and take, *farewell*
With right hands plighted, pledges of good will.
Then Guyon forward gan his voyage make,
With his blacke Palmer, that him guided still.
Still he him guided over dale and hill,
And with his steedie° staffe did point his way: *steady*
His race° with reason, and with words his will, *actions*
From foule intemperance he oft did stay,
And suffred not in wrath his hastie steps to stray.

[Although the specific assignment by Gloriana of Guyon's quest (to seek out and capture the enchantress Acrasia) is not described until the end of the second canto, the remainder of Canto i illustrates Acrasia's terrible power over her victims. Guyon and the Palmer encounter the dying Amavia, who has stabbed herself for grief at the death of her husband, Mordant, a victim of Acrasia's evil magic; their child, Ruddymane, dabbles his hands in her blood. Having told her story, Amavia dies; Guyon, assisted by the Palmer, buries the couple, taking a sacred oath to avenge their deaths, but he is unable to cleanse the blood from the hands of Ruddymane. Allegorically, this episode emphasizes the destructive power of intemperate passion in fallen and mortal humanity. Leaving the child in the care of Medina, whose character and conduct exemplify the Aristotelian "Golden Mean" between extremes of "defect" and "excess" (represented by Medina's sisters, Elissa and Perissa), Guyon proceeds on his quest. After an interlude in Canto iii during which the virgin huntress Belphoebe successfully resists the advances of Braggadocchio, a cowardly boaster, Cantos iv–vi chiefly concern the struggles of Guyon against representatives of the irascible or lethargic elements in human nature: Furor, Atin, and the brothers Cymochles and Pyrochles ("Watery" & "Fiery"). Guyon subdues or successfully resists each of these, but he is not proof against the persuasions of Acrasia's servant Phaedria ("immodest Merth"), who conducts him across her "Idle lake." Guyon does not remain in her company; but he has now been deprived of the Palmer's guidance.]

Canto VII

Guyon findes Mammon in a delve,° *pit*
Sunning his threasure hore:° *ancient*
Is by him tempted, and led downe,
To see his secret store.[1]

1. In Matthew 6.24 Jesus says that one cannot worship both God and Mammon (money); Spenser converts a Hebrew noun into a personification. Some find in Guyon's visit a virtuous or even Christlike refusal to trade old chivalry for modern money-grubbing; others think he also yields to rash curiosity or vain self-reliance. Mammon's house may also recall the American gold flowing to Europe from Spanish mines and colonies as well as Virgil's denunciation of the "cursed hunger" for gold (*Aeneid* 3.57) and Ovid's lament that our iron age's "cursed love of gain" accompanied violence and exploitation (*Metamorphoses* 1.131). Since this is also the Underworld, home to Persephone, daughter of Ceres the agricultural goddess, there may be an ironic commentary on gold and grain, wealth and food. Guyon's stay in Mammon's house takes forty stanzas, which for some recalls the Israelites' forty-year wandering or Jesus's forty days in the wilderness. Yet others see an initiatory experience.

1

As Pilot well expert in perilous wave,
That to a stedfast starre his course hath bent,
When foggy mistes, or cloudy tempests have
The faithfull light of that faire lampe yblent,° *obscured*
And covered heaven with hideous dreriment,
Upon his card° and compas firmes his eye, *chart*
The maisters of his long experiment,° *experience*
And to them does the steddy helme apply,
Bidding his wingéd vessell fairely forward fly:

2

So Guyon having lost his trusty guide,
Late left beyond that Ydle lake, proceedes
Yet on his way, of none accompanide;
And evermore himselfe with comfort feedes,
Of his owne vertues, and prayse-worthy deedes.
So long he yode,° yet no adventure found, *went*
Which fame of her shrill trompet worthy reedes.° *declares*
For still he traveild through wide wastfull ground,
That nought but desert wildernesse shewed all around.

3

At last he came unto a gloomy glade,
Covered with boughes and shrubs from heavens light,
Whereas he sitting found in secret shade
An uncouth, salvage,° and uncivile° wight, *savage / wild*
Of griesly hew, and fowle ill favoured sight;° *appearance*
His face with smoke was tand, and eyes were bleard,
His head and beard with sout were ill bedight,° *adorned*
His cole-blacke hands did seeme to have beene seard
In smithes fire-spitting forge, and nayles like clawes appeard.

4

His yron coate all overgrowne with rust,
Was underneath envelopéd with gold,
Whose glistring glosse darkned with filthy dust,
Well yet appearéd, to have beene of old
A worke of rich entayle,° and curious° mould, *carving / intricate*
Woven with antickes° and wild Imagery: *fantastic figures*
And in his lap a masse of coyne he told,° *counted*
And turnéd upsidowne, to feede his eye
And covetous desire with his huge threasury.

5

And round about him lay on every side
Great heapes of gold, that never could be spent:
Of which some were rude owre,° not purifide *ore*

Of Mulcibers devouring element;[2]
Some others were new driven,° and distent° *beaten / extended*
Into great Ingoes,° and to wedges square; *ingots*
Some in round plates withouten moniment;° *markings*
But most were stampt, and in their metall bare
The antique shapes of kings and kesars° straunge and rare. *emperors*

6

Soone as he Guyon saw, in great affright
And hast he rose, for to remove aside
Those pretious hils from straungers envious sight,
And downe them pouréd through an hole full wide,
Into the hollow earth, them there to hide.
But Guyon lightly to him leaping, stayd
His hand, that trembled, as one terrifyde;
And though him selfe were at the sight dismayd,
Yet him perforce restraynd, and to him doubtfull sayd.[3]

7

"What are thou man, (if man at all thou art)
That here in desert hast thine habitaunce,
And these rich heapes of wealth doest hide apart
From the worldes eye, and from her right usaunce?"° *use*
Thereat with staring eyes fixéd askaunce,[4]
In great disdaine, he answerd; "Hardy Elfe,
That darest vew my direfull countenaunce,
I read° thee rash, and heedlesse of thy selfe, *consider*
To trouble my still seate, and heapes of pretious pelfe.

8

"God of the world and worldlings I me call,
Great Mammon,[5] greatest god below the skye,
That of my plenty poure out unto all,
And unto none my graces do envye:° *begrudge*
Riches, renowme, and principality,
Honour, estate, and all this worldés good,
For which men swinck° and sweat incessantly, *toil*
Fro me do flow into an ample flood,
And in the hollow earth have their eternall brood.° *breeding place*

2. I.e., fire, of which Mulciber (Vulcan) was the god.
3. I.e., said to the apprehensive "wight of griesly hew."
4. I.e., with proudly averted eyes.
5. Like Christ in Matthew 4.1–11, Guyon rejects the offer of wealth (stanzas 18, 32, 38), glory (stanza 49), and, possibly, knowledge (stanza 63). Although deprived of the Palmer's aid, and thus relying on "his owne vertues" (stanza 2), Guyon puts up a successful if exhausting resistance and is then tended by an angel (viii. 5; cf. Matthew 4.11). But the scriptural background may also include Christ's words on the charitable use of money: "make ye friends with the unrighteous Mammon" (Luke 16.9; see Tyndale's *Parable of the Unrighteous Mammon* [1528]). Guyon ignores the question of money's right use (cf. Mallette 1989); nor does he engage Mammon's reminder that in a money economy somebody must pay for a knight's equipment.

9

"Wherefore if me thou deigne to serve and sew,° *follow*
At thy commaund lo all these mountaines bee;
Or if to thy great mind, or greedy vew
All these may not suffise, there shall to thee
Ten times so much be numbred francke and free."
"Mammon," said he, "thy godheades vaunt[6] is vaine,
And idle offers of thy golden fee;° *reward*
To them, that covet such eye-glutting gaine,
Proffer thy giftes, and fitter servaunts entertaine.

10

"Me ill besits, that in der-doing armes,[7]
And honours suit° my vowéd dayes do spend, *pursuit*
Unto thy bounteous baytes, and pleasing charmes,
With which weake men thou witchest, to attend:
Regard of worldly mucke doth fowly blend,° *defile*
And low abase the high heroicke spright,
That joyes for crownes and kingdomes to contend;
Faire shields, gay steedes, bright armes be my delight:
Those be the riches fit for an advent'rous knight."

11

"Vaine glorious Elfe," said he, "doest not thou weet,° *know*
That money can thy wantes at will supply?
Shields, steeds, and armes, and all things for thee meet
It can purvay° in twinckling of an eye; *provide*
And crownes and kingdomes to thee multiply.
Do not I kings create, and throw the crowne
Sometimes to him, that low in dust doth ly?
And him that raignd, into his rowme thrust downe,
And whom I lust,° do heape with glory and renowne?" *choose*

12

"All otherwise," said he, "I riches read,° *consider*
And deeme them roote of all disquietnesse;
First got with guile, and then preserved with dread,
And after spent with pride and lavishnesse,
Leaving behind them griefe and heavinesses.[8]
Infinite mischiefes of them do arize,
Strife, and debate, bloudshed, and bitternesse,
Outrageous wrong, and hellish covetize,
That noble heart as great dishonour doth despize.

6. I.e., boastful claim to godhead.
7. I.e., It is not fitting for me, engaged in daring deeds of arms.
8. "But they that will be rich fall into temptation and a snare, and into many foolish and hurtful lusts, which drown men in destruction and perdition. For the love of money is the root of all evil . . ." (1 Timothy 6.9–10).

13

"Ne thine be kingdomes, ne the scepters thine;
But realmes and rulers thou doest both confound,° *destroy*
And loyall truth to treason doest incline;
Witnesse the guiltlesse bloud pourd oft on ground,
The crownéd often slaine, the slayer cround,
The sacred Diademe in peeces rent,
And purple robe goréd with many a wound;
Castles surprizd, great cities sackt and brent:° *burned*
So mak'st thou kings, and gaynest wrongfull governement.

14

"Long were to tell the troublous stormes, that tosse
The private state,° and make the life unsweet: *condition*
Who° swelling sayles in Caspian sea doth crosse, *one who with*
And in frayle wood on Adrian gulfe[9] doth fleet,
Doth not, I weene, so many evils meet."
Then Mammon wexing wroth, "And why then," said,
"Are mortall men so fond and undiscreet,
So evill thing to seeke unto their ayd,
And having not complaine, and having it upbraid?"[1]

15

"Indeede," quoth he, "through fowle intemperaunce,
Frayle men are oft captived to covetise:
But would they thinke, with how small allowaunce
Untroubled Nature doth her selfe suffise,
Such superfluities they would despise,
Which with sad cares empeach° our native joyes: *hinder*
At the well head the purest streames arise:
But mucky filth his braunching armes annoyes,
And with uncomely weedes the gentle wave accloyes.° *clogs*

16

"The antique° world, in his first flowring youth,[2] *ancient*
Found no defect in his Creatours grace,
But with glad thankes, and unreprovéd° truth, *blameless*
The gifts of soveraigne bountie did embrace:
Like Angels life was then mens happy cace;
But later ages pride, like corn-fed steed,
Abusd her plenty, and fat swolne encreace

9. The Adriatic Sea, like the Caspian Sea notorious for storms.
1. I.e., either complain about not having [money], or, if having it, denigrate it. Guyon's reply echoes the distinction made by Boethius (ca. 475–525) between natural needs and "the superfluity of fortune" (*De Consolatione Philosophiae* 2. Prose 5).
2. I.e., the "golden age"; cf. Ovid, *Metamorphoses* 1.90–112, Virgil's fourth eclogue, and Boethius 2. Metre 5.

To all licentious lust, and gan exceed
The measure of her meane,[3] and naturall first need.

17

"Then gan a curséd hand the quiet wombe
Of his great Grandmother with steele to wound,
And the hid treasures in her sacred tombe,
With Sacriledge to dig. Therein he found
Fountaines of gold and silver to abound,
Of which the matter of his huge desire
And pompous pride eftsoones he did compound;
Then avarice gan through his veines inspire° *breathe*
His greedy flames, and kindled life-devouring fire.

18

"Sonne," said he then, "let be thy bitter scorne,
And leave the rudenesse of that antique age
To them, that lived therein in state forlorne;
Thou that doest live in later times, must wage° *hire out*
Thy workes for wealth, and life for gold engage.
If then thee list my offred grace to use,
Take what thou please of all this surplusage;
If thee list not, leave have thou to refuse:
But thing refuséd, do not afterward accuse."

19

"Me list not," said the Elfin knight, "receave
Thing offred, till I know it well be got,
Ne wote° I, but thou didst these goods bereave *know*
From rightfull owner by unrighteous lot,° *division*
Or that bloud guiltinesse or guile them blot."
"Perdy,"° quoth he, "yet never eye did vew, *truly*
Ne toung did tell, ne hand these handled not,[4]
But safe I have them kept in secret mew,° *den*
From heavens sight, and powre of all which them pursew."

20

"What secret place," quoth he, "can safely hold
So huge a masse, and hide from heavens eye?
Or where hast thou thy wonne,° that so much gold *dwelling*
Thou canst preserve from wrong and robbery?"
"Come thou," quoth he, "and see." So by and by
Through that thicke covert he him led, and found
A darkesome way, which no man could descry,° *discover*
That deepe descended through the hollow ground,
And was with dread and horrour compasséd around.

3. I.e., her proper limits.
4. Mammon echoes 1 Corinthians 2.9 on the wondrous things God has prepared for those who love him.

21

At length they came into a larger space,
That stretcht it selfe into an ample plaine,
Through which a beaten broad high way did trace,
That streight did lead to Plutoes griesly raine:[5]
By that wayes side, there sate infernall Payne,
And fast beside him sat tumultuous Strife:
The one in hand an yron whip did straine,° *wield*
The other brandishéd a bloudy knife,
And both did gnash their teeth, and both did threaten life.

22

On thother side in one consort° there sate, *company*
Cruell Revenge, and rancorous Despight,
Disloyall Treason, and hart-burning Hate,
But gnawing Gealosie out of their sight
Sitting alone, his bitter lips did bight,
And trembling Feare still to and fro did fly,
And found no place, where safe he shroud him might,
Lamenting Sorrow did in darknesse lye,
And Shame his ugly face did hide from living eye.

23

And over them sad Horrour with grim hew,° *aspect*
Did alwayes sore, beating his yron wings;
And after him Owles and Night-ravens flew,
The hatefull messengers of heavy things,
Of death and dolour telling sad tidings;
Whiles sad Celeno,[6] sitting on a clift,
A song of bale and bitter sorrow sings,
That hart of flint a sunder could have rift:° *torn*
Which having ended, after him she flyeth swift.

24

All these before the gates of Pluto lay,
By whom they passing, spake unto them nought.
But th'Elfin knight with wonder all the way
Did feed his eyes, and fild his inner thought.
At last him to a litle dore he brought,
That to the gate of Hell, which gapéd wide,
Was next adjoyning, ne them parted ought:[7]
Betwixt them both was but a litle stride,
That did the house of Richesse from hell-mouth divide.

5. I.e., Pluto's horrible kingdom; cf. Virgil's description of Hades' gates (*Aeneid* 6.267–81) or Sackville's "Induction" in *A Mirror for Magistrates*.
6. Chief of the harpies, birds with female faces and torsos often associated with rapacity.
7. I.e., nor did anything separate them.

25

Before the dore sat selfe-consuming Care,
Day and night keeping wary watch and ward,
For feare least Force or Fraud should unaware
Breake in, and spoile° the treasure there in gard: *plunder*
Ne would he suffer Sleepe once thither-ward
Approch, albe° his drowsie den were next; *although*
For next to death is Sleepe to be compard:[8]
Therefore his house is unto his annext;
Here Sleep, there Richesse, and Hel-gate them both betwext.

26

So soone as Mammon there arrived, the dore
To him did open, and affoorded way;
Him followed eke Sir Guyon evermore,
Ne darkenesse him, ne daunger might dismay.
Soone as he entred was, the dore streight way
Did shut, and from behind it forth there lept
An ugly feend, more fowle then dismall day,[9]
The which with monstrous stalke behind him stept,
And ever as he went, dew° watch upon him kept.[1] *proper*

27

Well hopéd he, ere long that hardy guest,
If ever covetous hand, or lustfull eye,
Or lips he layd on thing, that likt° him best, *pleased*
Or ever sleepe his eye-strings did untye,
Should be his pray. And therefore still on hye
He over him did hold his cruell clawes,
Threatning with greedy gripe to do him dye
And rend in peeces with his ravenous pawes,
If ever he transgrest the fatall Stygian lawes.[2]

28

That houses forme within was rude and strong,
Like an huge cave, hewne out of rocky clift,
From whose rough vaut° the ragged breaches° hong, *vault / fractures*
Embost with massy gold of glorious gift,° *quality*
And with rich metall loaded every rift,
That heavy ruine they did seeme to threat;
And over them Arachne[3] high did lift

8. Both Death and Sleep were sons of Night (Hesiod, *Theogony* 211–12).
9. I.e., the day of death.
1. Cf. the "fury" in the ancient Eleusinian mysteries who followed initiates so as to enforce their observance of ritual procedures; See Claudian's *De Raptu Proserpinae* (early fifth century C.E.) or Pausanias's *Description of Greece* (second century C.E.).
2. I.e., the laws of the underworld.
3. After defeating Arachne in a weaving contest, Minerva turned her into a spider (*Metamorphoses* 6.1–145). Here and in *Muiopotmos* Arachne's own envy causes the change. The web, spread for the unwary, shows that this wealth is unused; cf. Christ's parable of the talents (Matthew 25.14–29).

Her cunning web, and spred her subtile° net, *fine-spun*
Enwrappéd in fowle smoke and clouds more blacke then Jet.

29

Both roofe, and floore, and wals were all of gold,
But overgrowne with dust and old decay,
And hid in darkenesse, that none could behold
The hew° thereof: for vew of chearefull day *condition*
Did never in that house it selfe display,
But a faint shadow of uncertain light;
Such as a lamp, whose life does fade away:
Or as the Moone cloathéd with clowdy night,
Does shew to him, that walkes in feare and sad affright.

30

In all that rowme was nothing to be seene,
But huge great yron chests and coffers strong,
All bard with double bends,° that none could weene° *bands / expect*
Them to efforce° by violence or wrong; *force open*
On every side they placéd were along.
But all the ground with sculs was scatteréd,
And dead mens bones, which roundabout were flong,
Whose lives, it seeméd, whilome° there were shed, *formerly*
And their vile carcases now left unburiéd.

31

They forward passe, ne Guyon yet spoke word,
Till that they came unto an yron dore,
Which to them opened of his owne accord,
And shewd of richesse such exceeding store,
As eye of man did never see before;
Ne ever could within one place be found,
Though all the wealth, which is, or was of yore,
Could gathered be through all the world around,
And that above were added to that under ground.

32

The charge thereof unto a covetous Spright
Commaunded was, who thereby did attend,
And warily awaited day and night,
From other covetous feends it to defend,
Who it to rob and ransacke did intend.
Then Mammon turning to that warriour, said;
"Loe here the worldés blis, loe here the end,
To which all men do ayme, rich to be made:
Such grace now to be happy, is before thee laid."

33

"Certes," said he, "I n'ill° thine offred grace, *will not accept*
Ne to be made so° happy do intend: *thus*
Another blis before mine eyes I place,
Another happinesse, another end.
To them, that list, these base regardes° I lend: *concerns*
But I in armes, and in achievements brave,
Do rather choose my flitting houres to spend,
And to be Lord of those, that riches have,
Then them to have my selfe, and be their servile sclave."

34

Thereat the feend his gnashing teeth did grate,
And grieved, so long to lacke his greedy pray;[4]
For well he weenéd,° that so glorious bayte *supposed*
Would tempt his guest, to take thereof assay:° *trial*
Had he so doen, he had him snatcht away,
More light then Culver° in the Faulcons fist. *dove*
Eternall God thee save from such decay.° *ruin*
But whenas Mammon saw his purpose mist,
Him to entrap unwares another way he wist.° *knew*

35

Thence forward he him led, and shortly brought
Unto another rowme, whose dore forthright,
To him did open, as it had beene taught:
Therein an hundred raunges weren pight,° *placed*
And hundred fornaces all burning bright;
By every fornace many feends did bide,
Deforméd creatures, horrible in sight,
And every feend his busie paines applide,
To melt the golden metall, ready to be tride.° *purified*

36

One with great bellowes gathered filling aire,
And with forst wind the fewell did inflame;
Another did the dying bronds° repaire *embers*
With yron toungs, and sprinckled oft the same
With liquid waves, fiers Vulcans rage[5] to tame,
Who maistring them, renewd his former heat;
Some scumd the drosse, that from the metall came;
Some stird the molten owre with ladles great:
And every one did swincke,° and every one did sweat. *labor*

4. I.e., to be so long denied the prey he greedily desired.
5. I.e., fire. Stanzas 35–36 are based on Virgil's account of the Cyclopean forges beneath Mount Etna (*Aeneid* 8.417–54). Mammon's workaholic miners indicate, perhaps, the vanity of works without faith: contrast the untoiling-lilies of the field in Matthew 6.28.

37

But when as earthly wight they present saw,
Glistring in armes and battailous° aray, *warlike*
From their whot worke they did themselves withdraw
To wonder at the sight: for till that day,
They never creature saw, that came that way.
Their staring eyes sparckling with fervent fire,
And ugly shapes did nigh the man dismay,
That were it not for shame, he would retire,
Till that him thus bespake their soveraigne Lord and sire.

38

"Behold, thou Faeries sonne, with mortall eye,
That° living eye before did never see: *what*
The thing, that thou didst crave so earnestly,
To weet, whence all the wealth late shewd by mee,
Proceeded, lo now is reveald to thee.
Here is the fountaine of the worldés good:
Now therefore, if thou wilt enrichéd bee,
Avise° thee well, and chaunge thy wilfull mood, *consider*
Least thou perhaps hereafter wish, and be withstood."

39

"Suffise it then, thou Money God," quoth hee,
"That all thine idle offers I refuse.
All that I need I have; what needeth mee
To covet more, then I have cause to use?
With such vaine shewes thy worldlings vile abuse:° *deceive*
But give me leave to follow mine emprise."° *enterprise*
Mammon was much displeasd, yet no'te° chuse, *could not*
But beare the rigour of his bold mesprise,° *scorn*
And thence him forward led, him further to entise.

40

He brought him through a darksome narrow strait,
To a broad gate, all built of beaten gold:
The gate was open, but therein did wait
A sturdy villein, striding stiffe and bold,
As if that highest God defie he would;
In his right hand an yron club he held,
But he himselfe was all of golden mould,
Yet had both life and sence, and well could weld° *wield*
That curséd weapon, when his cruell foes he queld.

41

Disdayne he calléd was, and did disdaine
To be so cald, and who so did him call:
Sterne was his looke, and full of stomacke° vaine, *arrogance*

His portaunce° terrible, and stature tall, *bearing*
Far passing th'hight of men terrestriall;
Like an huge Gyant of the Titans race,
That made him scorne all creatures great and small,
And with his pride all others powre deface:° *destroy*
More fit amongst blacke fiendes, then men to have his place.

42

Soone as those glitterand° armes he did espye, *glittering*
That with their brightnesse made that darknesse light,
His harmefull club he gan to hurtle° hye, *brandish*
And threaten batteill to the Faery knight;
Who likewise gan himselfe to batteill dight,° *prepare*
Till Mammon did his hasty hand withhold,
And counseld him abstaine from perilous fight:
For nothing might abash the villein bold,
Ne mortall steele emperce his miscreated° mould. *unnatural*

43

So having him with reason pacifide,
And the fiers Carle° commaunding to forbeare, *churl*
He brought him in. The rowme was large and wide,
As it some Gyeld° or solemne Temple weare: *guildhall*
Many great golden pillours did upbeare
The massy roofe, and riches huge sustayne,
And every pillour deckéd was full deare° *expensively*
With crownes and Diademes, and titles vaine,
Which mortall Princes wore, whiles they on earth did rayne.

44

A route° of people there assembled were, *crowd*
Of every sort and nation under skye,
Which with great uprore preacéd° to draw nere *pressed*
To th'upper part, where was advauncéd hye
A stately siege° of soveraigne majestye; *throne*
And thereon sat a woman gorgeous gay,
And richly clad in robes of royaltye,
That never earthly Prince in such aray
His glory did enhaunce, and pompous pride display.

45

Her face right wondrous faire did seeme to bee,
That her broad beauties beam great brightnes threw
Through the dim shade, that all men might it see:
Yet was not that same her owne native hew,° *aspect*
But wrought by art and counterfetted shew,
Thereby more lovers unto her to call;
Nath'lesse most heavenly faire in deed and vew

She by creation was, till she did fall;
Thenceforth she sought for helps, to cloke her crime withall.

46

There, as in glistring glory she did sit,
She held a great gold chaine ylinckéd well,
Whose upper end to highest heaven was knit,
And lower part did reach to lowest Hell;
And all that preace° did round about her swell, *throng*
To catchen hold of that long chaine, thereby
To clime aloft, and others to excell:
That was Ambition, rash desire to sty,° *mount*
And every lincke thereof a step of dignity.[6]

47

Some thought to raise themselves to high degree,
By riches and unrighteous reward,
Some by close shouldring,° some by flatteree; *thrusting aside*
Others through friends, others for base regard;° *bribes*
And all by wrong wayes for themselves prepard.
Those that were up themselves, kept others low,
Those that were low themselves, held others hard,
Ne suffred them to rise or greater grow,
But every one did strive his fellow downe to throw.

48

Which whenas Guyon saw, he gan inquire,
What meant that preace about that Ladies throne,
And what she was that did so high aspire.
Him Mammon answeréd; "That goodly one,
Whom all that folke with such contention,
Do flocke about, my deare, my daughter is;
Honour and dignitie from her alone,
Derivéd are, and all this worldés blis
For which ye men do strive: few get, but many mis.

49

"And faire Philotime[7] she rightly hight,° *is named*
The fairest wight that wonneth° under skye, *lives*
But that this darksome neather world her light
Doth dim with horrour and deformitie,
Worthy of heaven and hye felicitie,
From whence the gods have her for envy thrust:

6. Status, rank. Comes says that the gold chain can signify avarice or ambition, which, though powerful, cannot distract good men (*Mythologiae* 2.4).
7. Philotime (Greek for "love of fame/honor" and apparently here given four syllables) recalls Lucifera (I.iv), daughter of Pluto and Proserpine, although Lucifera is a usurper and Philotime rules her court with pretense and artifice.

But sith thou has found favour in mine eye,
Thy spouse I will her make, if that thou lust,° *desire*
That she may thee advance for workes and merites just."

50

"Gramercy° Mammon," said the gentle knight, *thanks*
"For so great grace and offred high estate;
But I, that am fraile flesh and earthly wight,
Unworthy match for such immortall mate
My selfe well wote, and mine unequall fate;
And were I not, yet is my trouth yplight,° *plighted*
And love avowd to other Lady late,° *lately*
That to remove the same I have no might:
To chaunge love causelesse is reproch to warlike knight."

51

Mammon emmovéd was with inward wrath;
Yet forcing it to faine,[8] him forth thence led
Through griesly shadowes by a beaten path,
Into a gardin goodly garnishéd
With hearbs and fruits, whose kinds mote not be red:° *described*
Not such, as earth out of her fruitfull woomb
Throwes forth to men, sweet and well savouréd,
But direfull deadly blacke both leafe and bloom,
Fit to adorne the dead, and decke the drery toombe.[9]

52

There mournfull Cypresse grew in greatest store,
And trees of bitter Gall, and Heben sad,
Dead sleeping Poppy, and blacke Hellebore,
Cold Coloquintida, and Tetra mad,
Mortall Samnitis, and Cicuta bad,[1]
With which th'unjust Atheniens made to dy
Wise Socrates, who thereof quaffing glad
Pourd out his life, and last Philosophy
To the faire Critias his dearest Belamy.° *intimate*

53

The Gardin of Proserpina this hight;° *was named*
And in the midst thereof a silver seat,[2]
With a thicke Arber goodly over dight,° *covered*
In which she often usd from open heat
Her selfe to shroud, and pleasures to entreat.° *indulge in*

8. I.e., concealing his wrath.
9. The Garden of Proserpina combines elements from the *Odyssey* (the Grove of Persephone, 10.509–40), Claudian, *De Raptu Proserpinae* (the tree bearing golden fruit, 2.290–91), and Comes, *Mythologiae* (the identification of Proserpina with Hecate, goddess of poisons, 3.15).
1. These plants are associated with death or are themselves poisonous; *Cicuta*: hemlock.
2. On this seat Theseus was sentenced to remain "condemned to endlesse slouth by law" (I. v. 35); it may also refer to the forbidden seat of the goddess Demeter in the Eleusinian rites.

Next thereunto did grow a goodly tree,
With braunches broad dispred° and body great, *spread out*
Clothéd with leaves, that none the wood mote see
And loaden all with fruit as thicke as it might bee.

54

Their fruit were golden apples[3] glistring bright,
That goodly was their glory to behold,
On earth like never grew, ne living wight
Like ever saw, but° they from hence were sold;° *unless / taken*
For those, which Hercules with conquest bold
Got from great Atlas daughters, hence began,
And planted there, did bring forth fruit of gold:
And those with which th'Euboean young man wan° *won*
Swift Atalanta, when through craft he her out ran.[4]

55

Here also sprang that goodly golden fruit,
With which Acontius got his lover trew,
Whom he had long time sought with fruitlesse suit:
Here eke that famous golden Apple grew,
The which emongst the gods false Ate threw;
For which th'Idaean Ladies disagreed,
Till partiall Paris dempt° it Venus dew, *adjudged*
And had of her, faire Helen for his meed,° *reward*
That many noble Greekes and Trojans made to bleed.[5]

56

The warlike Elfe much wondred at this tree,
So faire and great, that shadowed all the ground,
And his broad braunches, laden with rich fee,° *wealth*
Did stretch themselves without the utmost bound
Of this great gardin, compast° with a mound, *surrounded*
Which over-hanging, they themselves did steepe,
In a blacke flood which flowed about it round;
That is the river of Cocytus deepe,[6]
In which full many soules do endlesse waile and weepe.

3. To fetch the golden apples of the Hesperides (the daughters of Atlas) was the eleventh of Hercules' twelve labors. For Comes (*Mythologiae* 7.7), the apples symbolize avarice and discord.
4. Atalanta promised to wed anyone who could defeat her in a footrace; losers were killed. Hippomenes (or, some said, Melanion of Euboea, an island near Boeotia) won by casting down golden apples to delay her as she swerved to pick them up (*Metamorphoses* 10.560–680).
5. Acontius won Cydippe by the strategic use of an apple (Ovid, *Heroides* 20–21), which Spenser here makes golden. He also identifies Ate, goddess of discord (rather than the Eris of Greek myth), as the divinity who, angered at not having been invited to the wedding of Thetis and Peleus, threw among the invited goddesses a golden apple inscribed "For the fairest." Juno, Minerva, and Venus asked Paris to judge their contest, held on Mount Ida; his award of the apple to Venus, who had promised him Helen, led to the Trojan War.
6. A river in Hades, traditionally associated with tears and sorrow.

57

Which to behold, he clomb up to the banke
And looking downe, saw many damnéd wights,
In those sad waves, which direfull deadly stanke,
Plongéd continually of° cruell Sprights, *by*
That with their pitteous cryes, and yelling shrights,° *shrieks*
They made the further shore resounden° wide: *echo*
Emongst the rest of those same ruefull sights,
One curséd creature[7] he by chaunce espide,
That drenchéd lay full deepe, under the Garden side.

58

Deepe was he drenchéd to the upmost chin,
Yet gapéd still, as coveting to drinke
Of the cold liquor, which he waded in,
And stretching forth his hand, did often thinke
To reach the fruit, which grew upon the brincke:
But both the fruit from hand, and floud from mouth
Did flie abacke, and made him vainely swinke:
The whiles he sterved° with hunger and with drouth° *starved / thirst*
He daily dyde, yet never throughly dyen couth.[8]

59

The knight him seeing labour so in vaine,
Askt who he was, and what he ment thereby:
Who groning deepe, thus answerd him againe;
"Most curséd of all creatures under skye,
Lo Tantalus, I here tormented lye:
Of whom high Jove wont whylome feasted bee,[9]
Lo here I now for want of food doe dye:
But if that thou be such, as I thee see,
Of grace I pray thee, give to eat and drinke to mee."

60

"Nay, nay, thou greedie Tantalus," quoth he,
"Abide the fortune of thy present fate,
And unto all that live in high degree,° *place*
Ensample be of mind intemperate,
To teach them how to use their present state."
Then gan the curséd wretch aloud to cry,
Accusing highest Jove and gods ingrate,

7. I.e., Tantalus, punished for revealing divine secrets and for killing his son Pelops and serving him at a banquet for the gods. On his torment, see *Odyssey* 11.582–92. Boccaccio (*Genealogiae* 1.14) and Comes call him a figure for avarice; Ovid (*Ars Amatoria* 2.601–606) and Pindar stress his presumption. The setting here recalls Alciato's *Emblemata* 85. Mythographers routinely assumed that Tantalus was a real king about whom poets wove fables; Horace's *Satire* 1.1, from which Spenser may take details, warns that we should not scoff at him, for avarice may be in us too.
8. I.e., could never utterly die.
9. I.e., by whom Jove was formerly feasted.

And eke blaspheming heaven bitterly,
As authour of unjustice, there to let him dye.

61

He lookt a little further, and espyde
Another wretch, whose carkasse deepe was drent° *immersed*
Within the river, which the same did hyde;
But both his hands most filthy feculent,° *befouled*
Above the water were on high extent,° *stretched*
And faynd° to wash themselves incessantly; *tried*
Yet nothing cleaner were for such intent,
But rather fowler seeméd to the eye;
So lost his labour vaine and idle° industry. *futile*

62

The knight him calling, askéd who he was,
Who lifting up his head, him answerd thus:
"I Pilate am the falsest Judge, alas,
And most unjust, that by unrighteous
And wicked doome,° to Jewes despiteous° *judgment / pitiless*
Delivered up the Lord of life to die,
And did acquite a murdrer felonous;° *wicked*
The whiles my hands I washt in puritie,[1]
The whiles my soule was soyld with foule iniquitie."

63

Infinite moe,° tormented in like paine *more*
He there beheld, too long here to be told:
Ne Mammon would there let him long remaine,
For terrour of the tortures manifold,
In which the damnéd soules he did behold,
But roughly him bespake. "Thou fearefull foole,
Why takest not of that same fruit of gold,
Ne sittest downe on that same silver stoole,
To rest thy wearie person, in the shadow coole."

64

All which he did, to doe him deadly fall
In frayle intemperance through sinfull bayt;
To which if he inclinéd had at all,
That dreadfull feend, which did behind him wayt,
Would him have rent in thousand peeces strayt:° *immediately*
But he was warie wise in all his way,
And well perceivéd his deceiptfull sleight,

1. I.e., in token of purity. Pilate "took water, and washed his hands before the multitude, saying, I am innocent of the blood of this just person" (Matthew 27.24). Some said (e.g., in the *Legenda Aurea*) Pilate had avariciously misused public funds.

Ne suffred lust° his safetie to betray; *desire*
So goodly did beguile the Guyler° of the pray. *deceiver*

65

And now he has so long remainéd there,
That vitall powres gan wexe both weake and wan,° *faint*
For want of food, and sleepe, which two upbeare,
Like mightie pillours, this fraile life of man,
That none without the same endurén can.
For now three dayes of men were full outwrought,° *completed*
Since he this hardie enterprize began:
For thy° great Mammon fairely he besought, *therefore*
Into the world to guide him backe, as he him brought.

66

The God, though loth, yet was constraind t'obay,
For lenger time, then that, no living wight
Below the earth, might suffred be to stay:
So backe againe, him brought to living light.
But all so soone as his enfeebled spright° *spirit*
Gan sucke this vitall aire into his brest,
As overcome with too exceeding might,
The life did flit away out of her nest,
And all his senses were with deadly fit opprest.[2]

Canto VIII

Sir Guyon laid in swowne is by
Acrates[1] sonnes despoyld,
Whom Arthur soone hath reskewéd
And Paynim brethren foyld.

1

And is there care in heaven? and is there love
In heavenly spirits to these creatures bace,
That may compassion of their evils move?
There is: else much more wretched were the cace
Of men, then beasts. But O th'exceeding grace
Of highest God, that loves his creatures so,
And all his workes with mercy doth embrace,
That blessed Angels, he sends to and fro,
To serve to wicked man, to serve his wicked foe.[2]

2. Guyon's faint has been much discussed, some seeing parallels to Jonah's sojourn in the whale's "belly of hell" (Jonah 1.17 and 2.1–10) or Jesus's time before the Resurrection "in the heart of the earth" (Matthew 12.40); more numerologically relevant are Jesus's forty days in the wilderness being tempted by Satan, after which angels minister to him (Matthew 4.1–11).

1. I.e., "Intemperance," or badly mixed, imbalanced.

2. Cf. Hebrews 1.14: "Are [the angels] not all ministering spirits, sent forth to minister for them who shall be heirs of salvation?"; and, with reference to the triple temptation of Jesus, Matthew 4.11: "Then the devil leaveth him, and, behold, angels came and ministered unto him."

2

How oft do they, their silver bowers leave,
To come to succour us, that succour want?° *need*
How oft do they with golden pineons, cleave
The flitting skyes, like flying Pursuivant,° *messenger*
Against foule feends to aide us millitant?[3]
They for us fight, they watch and dewly ward,
And their bright Squadrons round about us plant,
And all for love, and nothing for reward:
O why should heavenly God to men have such regard?

3

During the while, that Guyon did abide
In Mammons house, the Palmer, whom whyleare° *earlier*
That wanton Mayd[4] of passage had denide,
By further search had passage found elsewhere,
And being on his way, approchéd neare,
Where Guyon lay in traunce, when suddenly
He heard a voice, that calléd loud and cleare,
"Come hither, come hither, O come hastily;"
That all the fields resounded with the ruefull cry.

4

The Palmer lent his eare unto the noyce,
To weet, who calléd so importunely:° *urgently*
Againe he heard a more efforcéd° voyce, *forceful*
That bad him come in haste. He by and by° *immediately*
His feeble feet directed to the cry;
Which to that shadie delve him brought at last,
Where Mammon earst° did sunne his threasury: *formerly*
There the good Guyon he found slumbring fast
In senselesse dreame; which sight at first him sore aghast.

5

Beside his head there sate a faire young man,
Of wondrous beautie, and of freshest yeares,
Whose tender bud to blossome new began,
And flourish faire above his equall peares;[5]
His snowy front° curléd with golden heares, *forehead*
Like Phoebus face adornd with sunny rayes,
Divinely shone, and two sharpe wingéd sheares,° *wings*
Deckéd with diverse plumes, like painted Jayes,
Were fixéd at his backe, to cut his ayerie wayes.

3. I.e., by warring on our behalf.
4. I.e., Phaedria.
5. I.e., beyond that of other angels in his rank and station.

6

Like as Cupido on Idaean hill,[6]
When having laid his cruell bow away,
And mortall arrowes, wherewith he doth fill
The world with murdrous spoiles and bloudie pray,
With his faire mother he him dights° to play, *prepares*
And with his goodly sisters, Graces three;[7]
The Goddesse pleaséd with his wanton play,
Suffers her selfe through sleepe beguild to bee,
The whiles the other Ladies mind their merry glee.

7

Whom when the Palmer saw, abasht he was
Through fear and wonder, that he nought could say,
Till him the child bespoke, "Long lackt, alas,
Hath bene thy faithfull aide in hard assay,° *trial*
Whiles deadly fit thy pupill doth dismay;° *overcome*
Behold this heavie sight, thou reverend Sire,
But dread of death and dolour doe away;
For life ere long shall to her home retire,
And he that breathlesse seemes, shal corage bold respire.[8]

8

"The charge, which God doth unto me arret,° *entrust*
Of his deare safetie, I to thee commend;° *commit*
Yet will I not forgoe, ne yet forget
The care thereof my selfe unto the end,
But evermore him succour, and defend
Against his foe and mine: watch thou I pray;
For evill is at hand him to offend."° *harm*
So having said, eftsoones he gan display° *spread*
His painted nimble wings, and vanisht quite away.

9

The Palmer seeing his left empty place,
And his slow eyes beguiléd of their sight,
Woxe° sore affraid, and standing still a space, *became*
Gaz'd after him, as fowle escapt by flight;
At last him turning to his charge behight,° *entrusted*
With trembling hand his troubled pulse gan try;
Where finding life not yet dislodgéd quight,
He much rejoyst, and courd° it tenderly, *protected*
As chicken newly hatcht, from dreaded destiny.

6. Probably Mount Ida near Troy where Paris awarded Venus the golden apple.
7. This view of the Graces as daughters of Venus (not merely her handmaids) may derive from Boccaccio 3.22, or Comes 4.13.
8. I.e., shall regain valiant spirit.

[Directed to the scene by Archimago, Pyrochles and Cymochles are about to despatch the unconscious Guyon, but at this juncture Prince Arthur appears. After a fierce encounter with the brothers he kills them both. The episode recalls Arthur's deliverance of Redcrosse in Book I, but in this engagement Arthur's shield remains covered, and the final strokes in the battle are delivered with Guyon's own sword. Having recovered consciousness, Guyon proceeds with Prince Arthur to the house of Temperance.]

Canto IX

The house of Temperance, in which
doth sober Alma dwell,
Besiegd of many foes, whom straunger
knightes to flight compell.

1

Of all Gods workes, which do this world adorne,
There is no one more faire and excellent,
Then is mans body both for powre and forme,
Whiles it is kept in sober government;
But none then it, more fowle and indecent,° *unseemly*
Distempred through misrule and passions bace:
It growes a Monster, and incontinent° *immediately*
Doth loose his dignitie and native grace.
Behold, who list, both one and other[1] in this place.

2

After the Paynim brethren[2] conquered were,
The Briton Prince recov'ring his stolne sword,
And Guyon his lost shield, they both yfere° *together*
Forth passéd on their way in faire accord,
Till him the Prince with gentle court did bord;° *accost*
"Sir knight, mote I of you this curt'sie read,° *request*
To weet° why on your shield so goodly scord *know*
Beare ye the picture of that Ladies head?
Full lively is the semblaunt,° though the substance dead." *resemblance*

3

"Faire Sir," said he, "if in that picture dead
Such life ye read,° and vertue in vaine shew, *perceive*
What mote ye weene, if the trew lively-head[3]
Of that most glorious visage ye did vew?

1. I.e., Alma's House of Temperance and Maleger, whose troops besiege it. The House is an allegory of the temperate human body that holds the four humors in balance and with a tower/head organized by Renaissance understanding of the brain. "Alma" means nurturing, but she is also the "soul" in this body. What "soul" meant was complex, and a secular animating "soul" or spirit was not the same as the soul/spirit from God, although the vocabulary used could be inconsistent and confusing. How the mortal animating soul relates to the body was in Spenser's day a matter of debate. The Cartesian mind/body split was still in the future, but anticipations were already at work.
2. I.e., Pyrochles and Cymochles.
3. I.e., the living original.

But if the beautie of her mind ye knew,
That is her bountie, and imperiall powre,
Thousand times fairer then her mortall hew,° *shape*
O how great wonder would your thoughts devoure,
And infiinite desire into your spirite poure!

4

"She is the mighty Queene of Faerie,
Whose faire retrait° I in my shield do beare; *portrait*
She is the flowre of grace and chastitie,
Throughout the world renowméd far and neare,
My liefe, my liege,[4] my Soveraigne, my deare,
Whose glory shineth as the morning starre,
And with her light the earth enlumines cleare;
Far reach her mercies, and her prayses farre,
As well in state of peace, as puissaunce in warre."

5

"Thrise happy man," said then the Briton knight,
"Whom gracious lot, and thy great valiaunce
Have made thee souldier of that Princesse bright,
Which with her bounty and glad countenance
Doth blesse her servaunts, and them high advaunce.
How many straunge knight hope ever to aspire,
By faithfull service, and meet amenance,° *conduct*
Unto such blisse? sufficient were that hire° *reward*
For losse of thousand lives, to dye at her desire."

6

Said Guyon, "Noble Lord, what meed so great,
Or grace of earthly Prince so soveraine,
But by your wondrous worth and warlike feat
Ye well may hope, and easely attaine?
But were your will, her sold to entertaine,[5]
And numbred be mongst knights of Maydenhed,
Great guerdon,° well I wote, should you remaine, *reward*
And in her favour high be reckonéd,
As Arthegall, and Sophy[6] now beene honoréd."

7

"Certes," then said the Prince, "I God avow,
That sith I armes and knighthood first did plight,
My whole desire hath beene, and yet is now,
To serve that Queene with all my powre and might.

4. I.e., My beloved, my lord.
5. I.e., to accept her pay (and, in effect, become her soldier).
6. Wisdom (Greek), perhaps to have been the hero of a later book; *Arthegall*: patron of Justice, the hero of Book V.

Now hath[7] the Sunne with his lamp-burning light,
Walkt round about the world, and I no lesse,
Sith of that Goddesse I have sought the sight,
Yet no where can her find: such happinesse
Heaven doth to me envy, and fortune favourlesse."

8

"Fortune, the foe of famous chevisaunce° *enterprise*
Seldome," said Guyon, "yields to vertue aide,
But in her way throwes mischiefe and mischaunce,
Whereby her course is stopt, and passage staid.
But you faire Sir, be not herewith dismaid,
But constant keepe the way, in which ye stand;
Which were it not, that I am else delaid
With hard adventure, which I have in hand,
I labour would to guide you through all Faery land."

9

"Gramercy Sir," said he, "but mote I weete,
What straunge adventure do ye now pursew?
Perhaps my succour,[8] or advizement meete
Mote stead° you much your purpose to subdew." *help*
Then gan Sir Guyon all the story shew
Of false Acrasia, and her wicked wiles,
Which to avenge, the Palmer him forth drew
From Faery court. So talkéd they, the whiles
They wasted had much way, and measurd many miles.

10

And now faire Phœbus gan decline in hast
His weary wagon to the Westerne vale,
Whenas they spide a goodly castle, plast
Foreby° a river in a pleasant dale, *near*
Which choosing for that evenings hospitale,° *lodging*
They thither marcht: but when they came in sight,
And from their sweaty Coursers did avale,° *dismount*
They found the gates fast barréd long ere night,
And every loup° fast lockt, as fearing foes despight. *loophole*

11

Which when they saw, they weenéd fowle reproch
Was to them doen, their entrance to forstall,
Till that the Squire gan nigher to approch;
And wind° his horne under the castle wall, *blow*
That with the noise it shooke, as it would fall:
Eftsoones forth lookéd from the highest spire

7. In the 1590 edition the sun passes through seven years, not (as here) one.
8. I.e., my aid given in your behalf; see II.viii.25 ff.

The watch, and lowd unto the knights did call,
To weete, what they so rudely did require.
Who gently° answeréd, They entrance did desire. *courteously*

12

"Fly fly, good knights," said he, "fly fast away
If that your lives ye love, as meete ye should;
Fly fast, and save your selves from neare decay,° *destruction*
Here may ye not have entraunce, though we would:
We would and would againe, if that we could;
But thousand enemies about us rave,
And with long siege us in this castle hould:
Seven yeares[9] this wize they us besiegéd have,
And many good knights slaine, that have us sought to save."

13

Thus as he spoke, loe with outragious cry
A thousand villeins[1] round about them swarmd
Out of the rockes and caves adjoyning nye,
Vile caytive wretches, ragged, rude, deformd,
All threatning death, all in straunge manner armd,
Some with unweldy clubs, some with long speares,
Some rusty knives, some staves in fire warmd.
Sterne was their looke, like wild amazéd steares,
Staring with hollow eyes, and stiffe upstanding heares.

14

Fiersly at first those knights they did assaile,
And drove them to recoile: but when againe
They gave fresh charge, their forces gan to faile,
Unable their encounter to sustaine;
For with such puissaunce and impetuous maine° *force*
Those Champions broke on them, that forst them fly,
Like scattered Sheepe, whenas the Shepheards swaine
A Lyon and a Tigre doth espye,
With greedy pace forth rushing from the forest nye.

15

A while they fled, but soone returnd againe
With greater fury, then before was found;
And evermore their cruell Capitaine
Sought with his raskall routs[2] t'enclose them round,
And overrun to tread them to the ground.

9. John Upton (*The Faerie Queene* 1758) notes the probable influence on II.ix of the *Commentary on The Dream of Scipio*, by the Roman philosopher Macrobius (fl. ca. 400 C.E.), who saw the number seven as controlling and regulatory in human life (*Commentary* 1.6; tr. and ed. W. H. Stahl [New York, 1952]). Compare the proverbial seven ages of the world, the seven stages of man's life (cf. *As You Like It* 2.7.139–66), and the seven deadly sins.
1. I.e., a mob of brutish rabble: Maleger's troop of "passions bace" (1.6).
2. I.e., disreputable gang; the *canaille*.

But soone the knights with their bright-burning blades
Broke their rude troupes, and orders° did confound, *ranks*
Hewing and slashing at their idle shades;
For though they bodies seeme, yet substance from them fades.

16

As when a swarme of Gnats at eventide
Out of the fennes of Allan[3] do arise,
Their murmuring small trompets sounden wide,
Whiles in the aire their clustring army flies,
That as a cloud doth seeme to dim the skies;
Ne man nor beast may rest, or take repast,
For their sharpe wounds, and noyous° injuries, *annoying*
Till the fierce Northerne wind with blustring blast
Doth blow them quite away, and in the Ocean cast.

17

Thus when they had that troublous rout disperst,
Unto the castle gate they come againe,
And entraunce craved, which was deniéd erst.
Now when report of that their perilous paine,
And combrous° conflict, which they did sustaine, *harassing*
Came to the Ladies eare, which there did dwell,
She forth issewéd with a goodly traine
Of Squires and Ladies equipagéd° well, *arrayed*
And entertainéd them right fairely, as befell.[4]

18

Alma[5] she calléd was, a virgin bright;
That had not yet felt Cupides wanton rage,
Yet was she wooed of many a gentle knight,
And many a Lord of noble parentage,
That sought with her to lincke in marriage:
For she was faire, as faire mote ever bee,
And in the flowre now of her freshest age;
Yet full of grace and goodly modestee,
That even heaven rejoycéd her sweete face to see.

19

In robe of lilly white she was arayd,
That from her shoulder to her heele downe raught,
The traine whereof loose far behind her strayd,
Braunchéd° with gold and pearle, most richly wrought, *embroidered*

3. The extensive "Bog of Allen," westward from Dublin, lies between Edenderry and Kildare.
4. I.e., as was fitting.
5. Alma's castle, looking ultimately to scriptural and classical sources (1 Corinthians 6.19; Plato, *Timaeus*), recalls earlier English and French allegories of the body as city or castle, e.g., Langland, *Piers Plowman* 11.2.1–7; Du Bartas, *Divine Weekes* 1.6. Her guided tour of the body, beginning at stanza 21, reflects Platonic tradition (*Timaeus* 69–73) in the ascent from stomach to heart and at length to the head "that all this other worlds worke doth excell" (stanza 47).

And borne of two faire Damsels, which were taught
That service well. Her yellow golden heare
Was trimly woven, and in tresses wrought,
Ne other tyre° she on her head did weare, *headdress*
But crownéd with a garland of sweete Rosiere.° *rosebush*

20

Goodly she entertaind those noble knights,
And brought them up into her castle hall;
Where gentle court and gracious delight
She to them made, with mildnesse virginall,
Shewing her selfe both wise and liberall:° *generous*
There when they rested had a season dew,
They her besought of favour speciall,
Of that faire Castle to affoord them vew;
She graunted, and them leading forth, the same did shew.

21

First she them led up to the Castle wall,
That was so high, as foe might not it clime,
And all so faire, and fensible° withall, *fortified*
Not built of bricke, ne yet of stone and lime,
But of thing like to that Aegyptian slime,
Whereof king Nine whilome built Babell towre;[6]
But O great pitty, that no lenger time
So goodly workemanship should not endure:
Soone it must turne to earth; no earthly thing is sure.

22

The frame thereof seemd partly circulare,
And part triangulare, O worke divine;
Those two the first and last proportions are,
The one imperfect, mortall, feminine;
Th'other immortall, perfect, masculine,
And twixt them both a quadrate was the base,
Proportioned equally by seven and nine;
Nine was the circle set in heavens place,
All which compacted made a goodly diapase.[7]

6. For Ninus (and Nimrod, "the beginning of [whose] Kingdom was Babel," Genesis 10.10) see 1.5.48 and note. The tower of Babel was constructed of "brick for stone, and slime . . . for mortar," (Genesis 11.3); Spenser's "slime" refers to the "dust" and water from which God made man (Genesis 2.7), but also the "loathly crime / That is ingenerate in fleshly slime" (III.vi. 3.4–5; and see I.vii.9.8).

7. The most heavily interpreted stanza in the poem. The circle refers to the head; the triangle to the lower body (legs apart, as in Leonardo da Vinci's Vitruvian Man); and the quadrate (square) to the whole body. The circle is perfect and so divine; the triangle is a symbol of the mortal, together representing male and female characteristics, and so making the figure androgynous. Such proportions also associate the body with the geometrical, numerical, and hence musical cosmos of which a human being is the microcosm. The most famous early commentary is by Sir Kenelm Digby: *Observations on the 22. Stanza in the 9th Canto of the 2d. Book of Spencers Faery Queen* (London, 1644). See also Fowler 1964.

23

Therein two gates[8] were placed seemly well:
The one before, by which all in did pas,
Did th'other far in workmanship excell;
For not of wood, nor of enduring bras,
But of more worthy substance framd it was;
Doubly disparted, it did locke and close,
That when it lockéd, none might thorough pas,
And when it opened, no man might it close,
Still open to their friends, and closéd to their foes.

24

Of hewen stone the porch[9] was fairely wrought,
Stone more of valew, and more smooth and fine,
Then Jet or Marble far from Ireland brought;
Over the which was cast a wandring vine,
Enchaoéd° with a wanton yvie twine. *adorned*
And over it a faire Portcullis hong,
Which to the gate directly did incline,
With comely compasse, and compacture strong,
Neither unseemely short, nor yet exceeding long.

25

Within the Barbican a Porter[1] sate,
Day and night duely keeping watch and ward,
Nor wight, nor word mote passe out of the gate,
But in good order, and with dew regard;
Utteres of secrets he from thence debard,
Bablers of folly, and blazers° of crime. *proclaimers*
His larumbell might lowd and wide be hard,
When cause requird, but never out of time;
Early and late it rong, at evening and at prime.° *sunrise*

26

And round about the porch on every side
Twise sixteen warders[2] sat, all arméd bright
In glistring steele, and strongly fortifide:
Tall yeomen seeméd they, and of great might,
And were enraungéd ready, still for fight.
By them as Alma passéd with her guestes,
They did obeysaunce, as beseeméd right,
And then againe returnéd to their restes:
The Porter eke to her did lout with humble gestes.[3]

8. The mouth and the anus (or "back-gate": 32.7).
9. Porch, vine, "yvie," and portcullis respectively figure the chin, beard, moustache, and well-proportioned nose.
1. The tongue, within the oral cavity.
2. The teeth.
3. I.e., bowed with respectful gestures.

27

Thence she them brought into a stately Hall,[4]
Wherein were many tables faire dispred,
And ready dight with drapets° festivall, *coverings*
Against[5] the viaundes should be ministred.
At th'upper end there sate, yclad in red
Downe to the ground, a comely personage,
That in his hand a white rod menagéd, *wielded*
He Steward was hight Diet; rype of age,
And in demeanure sober, and in counsell sage.

28

And through the Hall there walkéd to and fro
A jolly yeoman, Marshall of the same,
Whose name was Appetite; he did bestow° *place*
Both guestes and meate, when ever in they came,
And knew them how to order without blame,
As him the Steward bad. They both attone° *together*
Did dewty to their Lady, as became;
Who passing by, forth led her guestes anone° *immediately*
Into the kitchin rowme, ne spard for nicenesse none.[6]

29

It was a vaut ybuilt for great dispence,[7]
With many raunges reard along the wall;
And one great chimney, whose long tonnell thence,
The smoke forth threw. And in the midst of all
There placéd was a caudron wide and tall,
Upon a mighty furnace, burning whot,
More whot, then Aetn', or flaming Mongiball:[8]
For day and night it brent, ne ceaséd not,
So long as any thing it in the caudron got.

30

But to delay° the heat, least by mischaunce *temper*
It might breake out, and set the whole on fire,
There added was by goodly ordinaunce,
An huge great paire of bellowes,[9] which did styre
Continually, and cooling breath inspyre.
About the Caudron many Cookes accoyld,° *gathered*
With hookes and ladles, as need did require;
The whiles the viandes in the vessell boyld
They did about their businesse sweat, and sorely toyld.

4. The throat.
5. I.e., for the time when.
6. I.e., nor [was she] held back by fastidious reserve.
7. I.e., a room with an arched roof, designed for grand hospitality; figuratively, the stomach.
8. Both names refer to Mount Aetna, in Sicily.
9. The lungs.

31

The maister Cooke was cald Concoction,[1]
A carefull man, and full of comely guise:
The kitchin Clerke, that hight Digestion,
Did order all th'Achates° in seemely wise, *provisions*
And set them forth, as well he could devise.
The rest had severall offices assind,
Some to remove the scum, as it did rise;
Others to beare the same away did mind;
And others it to use according to his kind.

32

But all the liquour, which was fowle and wast,
Not good nor serviceable else for ought,
They in another great round vessell plast,
Till by a conduit pipe it thence were brought:
And all the rest, that noyous was, and nought,[2]
By secret wayes, that none might it espy,
Was close convaid, and to the back-gate brought,
That clepéd was Port Esquiline,[3] whereby
It was avoided° quite, and throwne out privily. *removed*

33

Which goodly order, and great workmans skill
Whenas those knights beheld, with rare delight,
And gazing wonder they their minds did fill;
For never had they seene so straunge a sight.
Thence backe againe faire Alma led them right,
And soone into a goodly Parlour[4] brought,
That was with royall arras° richly dight, *tapestry*
In which was nothing pourtrahéd, nor wrought,
Not wrought nor pourtrahéd, but easie to be thought.[5]

34

And in the midst thereof upon the floure,
A lovely bevy of faire Ladies sate,
Courted of many a jolly Paramoure,
The which them did in modest wise amate,[6]
And eachone sought his Lady to aggrate:° *please*

1. I.e., the first of three digestive processes recognized in early physiology: digestion in the stomach and intestines. This was thought to precede a second and a third "concoction" (Spenser's "Digestion" and his minions in stanzas 31–32), which converted, by pancreatic fluid and bile, the "chyme" or pulpy matter into the white milky fluid called "chyle," subsequently eliminated through the anus.
2. I.e., was harmful, and useless.
3. The anus. Beyond the Esquiline Gate of ancient Rome lay the city garbage dump. A number of readers have noted the absence of the genitalia and have offered various explanations (one reason, for example, might be to avoid gendering a generalized human body).
4. The heart, seat of the affections.
5. I.e., nothing except that which is easily apprehended by the five senses.
6. I.e., keep company with.

And eke emongst them litle Cupid playd
His wanton sports, being returnéd late
From his fierce warres, and having from him layd
His cruell bow, wherewith he thousands hath dismayd.

35

Diverse delights they found them selves to please;
Some song in sweet consort,° some laught for joy, *harmony*
Some plaid with strawes, some idly sat at ease;
But other some could not abide to toy,
All pleasaunce was to them griefe and annoy:
This fround, that faund, the third for shame did blush,
Another seeméd envious, or coy,
Another in her teeth did gnaw a rush:° *reed*
But at these straungers presence every one did hush.

36

Soone as the gracious Alma came in place,
They all attonce out of their seates arose,
And to her homage made, with humble grace:
Whom when the knights beheld, they gan dispose
Themselves to court, and each a Damsell chose:
The Prince by chaunce did on a Lady light,
That was right faire and fresh as morning rose,
But somwhat sad, and solemne eke in sight,° *appearance*
As if some pensive thought constraind her gentle spright.

37

In a long purple pall,° whose skirt with gold, *robe*
Was fretted all about, she was arayd;
And in her hand a Poplar braunch[7] did hold:
To whom the Prince in curteous manner said;
"Gentle Madame, why 'beene ye thus dismaid,
And your faire beautie do with sadnesse spill?° *spoil*
Lives any, that you hath thus ill apaid?° *pleased*
Or doen you love, or doen you lacke your will?
What ever be the cause, it sure beseemes you ill."

38

"Faire Sir," said she halfe in disdainefull wise,
"How is it, that this word in me ye blame,
And in your selfe do not the same advise?° *perceive*
Him ill beseemes, anothers fault to name,
That may unwares be blotted with the same:
Pensive I yeeld I am, and sad in mind,
Through great desire of glory and of fame;

7. The poplar, traditionally sacred to Hercules (cf. II.v.31), is an emblem of heroic aspiration for glory.

Ne ought I weene are ye therein behind,
That have twelue moneths[8] sought one, yet no where can her find."

39

The Prince was inly moved at her speach,
Well weeting trew, what she had rashly° told; *boldly*
Yet with faire samblaunt° sought to hide the breach, *appearance*
Which chaunge of colour did perforce unfold,
Now seeming flaming whot, now stony cold.
Tho turning soft aside, he did inquire,
What wight she was, that Poplar braunch did hold:
It answered was, her name was Prays-desire,[9]
That by well doing sought to honour to aspire.

40

The whiles, the Faerie knight did entertaine
Another Damsell of that gentle crew,
That was right faire, and modest of demaine,° *demeanor*
But that too oft she chaunged her native hew:
Straunge was her tyre, and all her garment blew,
Close round about her tuckt with many a plight:° *pleat*
Upon her fist the bird, which shonneth° vew,° *shuns / sight*
And keepes in coverts close from living wight,
Did sit, as yet ashamd, how rude Pan did her dight.[1]

41

So long as Guyon with her commonéd,° *conversed*
Unto the ground she cast her modest eye,
And ever and anone with rosie red
The bashfull bloud her snowy cheekes did dye,
That her became, as polisht yvory,
Which cunning Craftesman hand hath overlayd
With faire vermilion or pure Castory.[2]
Great wonder had the knight, to see the mayd
So straungely passionéd, and to her gently sayd,

42

"Faire Damzell, seemeth, by your troubled cheare,
That either me too bold ye weene, this wise
You to molest, or other ill to feare
That in the secret of your hart close lyes,
From whence it doth, as cloud from sea arise.
If it be I, of pardon I you pray;
But if ought else that I mote not devise,° *guess*

8. In the 1590 edition the figure is three years, not one.
9. I.e., the "thought of glorie and of fame" (II.xi.31.8) that inspires Arthur's quest for Gloriana.
1. I.e. (probably), maltreat, abuse sexually. The bird of line 7 may be the owl, dove, or wryneck, but no source for the hints in line 9 has been identified.
2. I.e., red dye derived from the beaver (and thought to have medicinal value).

I will, if please you it discure,° assay, *reveal*
To ease you of that ill, so wisely as I may."

43

She answerd nought, but more abasht for shame,
Held downe her head, the whiles her lovely face
The flashing bloud with blushing did inflame,
And the strong passion mard her modest grace,
That Guyon mervayld at her uncouth° cace: *strange*
Till Alma him bespake, "Why wonder yee
Faire Sir at that, which ye so much embrace?
She is the fountaine of your modestee;
You shamefast are, but Shamefastnesse it selfe is shee."[3]

44

Thereat the Elfe did blush in privitee,
And turnd his face away; but she the same
Dissembled faire, and faynd to oversee.° *overlook*
Thus they awhile with court and goodly game,
Themselves did solace each one with his Dame,
Till that great Ladie thence away them sought,° *invited*
To vew her castles other wondrous frame.
Up to a stately Turret[4] she them brought,
Ascending by ten steps of Alablaster wrought.

45

That Turrets frame most admirable was,
Like highest heaven compasséd around,
And lifted high above this earthly masse,
Which it survewed,° as hils doen lower ground; *overlooked*
But not on ground mote like to this be found,
Not that, which antique Cadmus whylome built
In Thebes, which Alexander did confound;
Nor that proud towre of Troy, though richly guilt,
From which young Hectors bloud by cruell Greekes was spilt.[5]

46

The roofe hereof was arched ouer head,
And deckt with flowers and herbars° daintily; *arbors*
Two goodly Beacons, set in watches stead,[6]
Therein gave light, and flamed continually:

3. As Arthur appropriately companions "Prays-desire," so "Shamefastnesse" is matched with the temperate knight.
4. The head, to which the spinal cord ascends; "ten steps" may signify completion and perfection (Upton 1758).
5. The legendary Cadmus, searching for his sister Europa, and directed by the oracle at Delphi, built the fortress called Cadmea on the site of the future city of Thebes, in Boeotia (*Metamorphoses* 3.1–130). Alexander the Great destroyed the city in c. 335 B.C.E. sparing only the house of Pindar. Astyanax, Hector's son, was thrown from the walls of Troy by the victorious Greeks (*Metamorphoses* 13.415).
6. The eyes serve as watchmen.

For they of living fire most subtilly
Were made, and set in silver sockets bright,
Covered with lids devized of substance sly,° *fine*
That readily they shut and open might.
O who can tell the prayses of that makers might!

47

Ne can I tell, ne can I stay to tell
This parts great workmanship, and wondrous powre,
That all this other worlds worke doth excell,
And likest is unto that heavenly towre,[7]
That God hath built for his owne blesséd bowre.
Therein were diverse roomes, and diverse stages,
But three the chiefest, and of greatest powre,
In which there dwelt three honorable sages,
The wisest men, I weene, that livéd in their ages.[8]

48

Not he,[9] whom Greece, the Nourse of all good arts,
By Phoebus doome, the wisest thought alive,
Might be compared to these by many parts:
Nor that sage Pylian syre,[1] which did survive
Three ages, such as mortall men contrive,
By whose advise old Priams cittie fell,
With these in praise of pollicies° mote strive. *statecraft*
These three in these three roomes did sundry° dwell, *separately*
And counselléd faire Alma, how to governe well.

49

The first of them could things to come foresee:
The next could of things present best advize;
The third things past could keepe in memoree,
So that no time, nor reason could arize,
But that the same could one of these comprize.° *comprehend*
For thy the first did in the forepart sit,
That nought mote hinder his quicke prejudize:[2]
He had a sharpe foresight, and working wit,
That never idle was, ne once could rest a whit.

7. I.e., the towered "goodly Citie" of the New Jerusalem, revealed to Redcrosse in I.x. 55–57.
8. The three wise men respectively figure (1) the creative imagination, of which prescient foresight makes part; (2) the intellective power of the reason, concerned to correlate and assess the significance in present time of evidence provided by the external senses; (3) memory, which retains and records the mass of sense-evidence so provided through time, that its components "may be forth-coming when they are called for by *phantasy* and *reason*" (Burton, *Anatomy of Melancholy* 1.1.2.7).
9. Socrates, identified by the Delphian Oracle as the wisest man alive (*Apology* 21a).
1. Nestor, king of Pylos for three generations (*Iliad* 1.250–52), was senior counsellor to Agamemnon, leader of the Greek forces besieging Troy.
2. I.e., power to forecast and predict.

50

His chamber was dispainted all within,
With sundry colours, in the which were writ
Infinite shapes of things disperséd thin;
Some such as in the world were never yit,
Ne can devizéd be of mortall wit;
Some daily seene, and knowen by their names,
Such as in idle fantasies doe flit:
Infernall Hags, Centaurs, feendes, Hippodames,
Apes, Lions, Aegles, Owles, fooles, lovers, children, Dames.[3]

51

And all the chamber filléd was with flyes,
Which buzzéd all about, and made such sound,
That they encombred all mens eares and eyes,
Like many swarmes of Bees assembled round,
After their hives with honny do abound:
All those were idle thoughts and fantasies,
Devices, dreames, opinions unsound,
Shewes, visions, sooth-sayes,° and prophesies; *predictions*
And all that fainéd is, as leasings,° tales, and lies. *falsehoods*

52

Emongst them all sate he, which wonnéd there,
That hight Phantastes[4] by his nature trew;
A man of yeares yet fresh, as mote appere,
Of swarth complexion, and of crabbéd hew,
That him full of melancholy did shew;
Bent hollow beetle browes, sharpe staring eyes,
That mad or foolish seemd: one by his vew
Mote deeme him borne with ill disposéd skyes,
When oblique Saturne sate in the house of agonyes.

53

Whom Alma having shewéd to her guestes,
Thence brought them to the second roome, whose wals
Were painted faire with memorable gestes,° *deeds*
Of famous Wisards, and with picturals
Of Magistrates, of courts, of tribunals,
Of commen wealthes, of states, of pollicy,
Of lawes, of judgements, and of decretals;° *decrees*

3. Mythological Centaur (half-man, half-horse) and Hippodame (a slip for "hippotame," or sea-horse; or possibly a quiet jest) keep confused company with figures from the nether regions and the natural world.
4. That Phantastes (Greek, "fantasy") appears "mad or foolish," together with his dark complexion and melancholy (black bile) shows the influence of the gloomy planet Saturn as well as an imbalance of the humors. Melancholy, however, was widely thought to promote contemplation and creativity.

All artes, all science, all Philosophy,
And all that in the world was aye thought wittily.[5]

54

Of those that roome was full, and them among
There sate a man of ripe and perfect age,
Who did them meditate all his life long,
That through continuall practise and usage,
He now was growne right wise, and wondrous sage.
Great pleasure had those stranger knights, to see
His goodly reason, and grave personage,° *appearance*
That his disciples both desired to bee;
But Alma thence them led to th'hindmost roome of three.[6]

55

That chamber seeméd ruinous and old,
And therefore was removéd farre behind,
Yet were the wals, that did the same uphold,
Right firme and strong, though somewhat they declind;
And therein sate an old oldman, halfe blind,
And all decrepit in his feeble corse,
Yet lively vigour rested in his mind,
And recompenst him with a better scorse:° *exchange*
Weake body well is changed for minds redoubled forse.

56

This man of infinite remembrance was,
And things foregone through many ages held,
Which he recorded still, as they did pas,
Ne suffred them to perish through long eld,
As all things else, the which this world doth weld,° *control*
But laid them up in his immortall scrine,° *chest*
Where they for ever incorrupted dweld:
The warres he well remembred of king Nine,
Of old Assaracus, and Inachus divine.[7]

57

The yeares of Nestor nothing were to his,
Ne yet Mathusalem, though longest lived;[8]
For he remembred both their infancies:
Ne wonder then, if that he were deprived
Of native strength now, that he them survived.

5. I.e., was ever wisely conceived.
6. It was commonly thought that the back of the brain governed memory; appropriately, Memory's chamber is set behind those of his fellow sages, who meditate on the present or look into the future. Stanzas 55–58 anticipate the account in Canto x of noble deeds and lineage preserved through time "from Brute . . . to Gloriane" (II.x.Arg.).
7. For Ninus see I.v.48, II.ix.21.6, and notes. The Trojan king Assaracus was Aeneas's great-grandfather; Inacus the river god, son of Oceanus and Tethys, was the first king of Argos.
8. "All the dayes of Methuselah were nine hundred sixty and nine years" (Genesis 5.27).

His chamber all was hangd about with rolles,
And old records from auncient times derived,
Some made in books, some in long parchment scrolles,
That were all worme-eaten, and full of canker holes.

58

Amidst them all he in a chaire was set,
Tossing and turning them withouten end;
But for he was unhable them to fet,° *fetch*
A litle boy did on him still attend,
To reach, when ever he for ought did send;
And oft when things were lost, or laid amis,
That boy them sought, and unto him did lend.
Therefore he Anamnestes clepéd is,
And that old man Eumnestes, by their properties.[9]

59

The knights there entring, did him reverence dew
And wondred at his endlesse exercise,
Then as they gan his Librarie to vew,
And antique Registers for to avise,° *notice*
There chauncéd to the Princes hand to rize,
An auncient booke, hight *Briton moniments*,° *records*
That of this lands first conquest did devize,
And old division into Regiments,° *kingdoms*
Till it reducéd was to one mans governments.

60

Sir Guyon chaunst eke on another booke,
That hight *Antiquitie* of *Faerie* lond.
In which when as he greedily did looke,
Th' off-spring° of Elves and Faries there he fond, *origin*
As it delivered was from hond to hond:
Whereat they burning both with fervent fire,
Their countries auncestry to understand,
Craved leave of Alma, and that aged sire,
To read those bookes; who gladly graunted their desire.

[In Anamnestes' chamber the two knights study their respective ancestries in the chronicles of British and Elfin kings, Arthur "quite ravisht with delight," the sober Guyon pleased and moved too (although he has not finished the "great and ample volume" called "Antiquitee of Faery Lond" when Alma summons the pair to supper). Next day, while Arthur remains behind to repel an attack on the castle by its besiegers (and eventually to destroy Maleger), Guyon departs with the Palmer to renew his quest.]

9. The aged Eumnestes (Greek, "good memory") is served by Anamnestes (Greek, "the reminder").

Canto XII

Guyon, by Palmers governance,° *guidance*
passing through perils great,
Doth overthrowe the Bowre of blisse,
and Acrasie[1] defeat.

1

Now gins this goodly frame° of Temperance *structure*
Fairely to rise, and her adornéd hed
To pricke° of highest praise forth to advance, *point*
Formerly grounded, and fast setteled
On firme foundation of true bountihed;° *virtue*
And this brave knight, that for that vertue fights,
Now comes to point of that same perilous sted,[2]
Where Pleasure dwelles in sensuall delights,
Mongst thousand dangers, and ten thousand magick mights.

2

Two dayes now in that sea he sayléd has,
Ne ever land beheld, ne living wight,
Ne ought save perill, still as he did pas:
Tho° when appearéd the third Morrow bright, *then*
Upon the waves to spred her trembling light,
An hideous roaring farre away they heard,
That all their senses filléd with affright,
And streight they saw the raging surges reard
Up to the skyes, that them of drowning made affeard.[3]

3

Said then the Boteman, "Palmer stere aright,
And keepe an even course; for yonder way
We needes must passe (God to us well acquight,)° *preserve*
That is the Gulfe of Greedinesse, they say,
That deepe engorgeth all this worldés pray:
Which having swallowed up excessively,
He soone in vomit up againe doth lay,° *cast*
And belcheth forth his superfluity,
That all the seas for feare do seeme away to fly.

1. I.e., Acrasia, from the Greek for incontinence, or "badly mixed" (*krasis* means blending) and thus badly tempered or moderated. Both the King James and Geneva Bibles translate *akrasia* as "excess": "Wo be to you Scribes and Pharises, hypocrites: for ye make cleane the utter [outer] side of the cup, and of the platter: but within thei are ful of briberie & excesse" (Matthew 23.25).
2. I.e., now directly approaches that dangerous place.
3. For the voyage to the Bower of Bliss, Spenser draws primarily on Homer's *Odyssey* and the *Mythologiae* of Comes; he makes use also of the voyage of Carlo and Ubaldo to Armida's bower, in Tasso, *Gerusalemme Liberata* 15, and, perhaps, the medieval legend of St. Brendan.

4

"On th'other side an hideous Rocke is pight,
Of mightie Magnes stone,[4] whose craggie clift
Depending° from on high, dreadfull to sight, *overhanging*
Over the waves his rugged armes doth lift,
And threatneth downe to throw his ragged rift° *fragment*
On who so commeth nigh; yet nigh it drawes
All passengers, that none from it can shift:
For whiles they fly that Gulfes devouring jawes,
They on this rock are rent, and sunck in helplesse wawes."[5]

5

Forward they passe, and strongly he them rowes,
Untill they nigh unto that Gulfe arrive,
Where streame more violent and greedy growes:
Then he with all his puissance doth strive
To strike his oares, and mightily doth drive
The hollow vessell through the threatfull wave,
Which gaping wide, to swallow them alive,
In th'huge abysse of his engulfing grave,
Doth rore at them in vaine, and with great terror rave.

6

They passing by, that griesly mouth did see,
Sucking the seas into his entralles° deepe, *inner depths*
That seemed more horrible then hell to bee,
Or that darke dreadfull hole of Tartare[6] steepe,
Through which the damnéd ghosts doen often creepe
Backe to the world, bad livers[7] to torment:
But nought that falles into this direfull deepe,
Ne that approcheth nigh the wide descent,
May backe returne, but is condemnéd to be drent.° *drowned*

7

On th'other side, they saw that perilous Rocke,
Threatning it selfe on them to ruinate,° *fall crushingly*
On whose sharpe clifts the ribs of vessels broke,
And shivered ships, which had bene wreckéd late,
Yet stuck, with carkasses exanimate° *lifeless*
Of such, as having all their substance spent
In wanton joyes, and lustes intemperate,[8]
Did afterwards make shipwracke violent,
Both of their life, and fame for ever fowly blent.° *stained*

4. I.e., lodestone, supposed to be found in Magnesia (cf. Lucretius, *De Rerum Natura* 6.909–10).
5. I.e., helplessly sunk beneath the waves. Scylla and Charybdis (*Odyssey* 12).
6. I.e., the cavernous entrance to Tartarus (below Hades), where the rebel Titans were punished.
7. I.e., sinners.
8. Lines 5–9 paraphrase Comes 8.12.

8

For thy,° this hight° The Rocke of vile Reproch, *therefore / is called*
A daungerous and detestable place,
To which nor fish nor fowle did once approch,
But yelling Meawes,° with Seagulles hoarse and bace, *gulls*
And Cormoyrants, with birds of ravenous race,
Which still sate waiting on that wastfull clift,
For spoyle of wretches, whose unhappie cace,
After lost credite and consuméd thrift,
At last them driven hath to this despairefull drift.° *end*

9

The Palmer seeing them in safetie past,
Thus said; "Behold th'ensamples in our sights,
Of lustfull luxurie and thriftlesse wast:
What now is left of miserable wights,
Which spent their looser daies in lewd delights,
But shame and sad reproch, here to be red,° *perceived*
By these rent reliques, speaking their ill plights?
Let all that live, hereby be counselléd,
To shunne Rocke of Reproch, and it as death to dred."

10

So forth they rowéd, and that Ferryman[9]
With his stiffe oares did brush the sea so strong,
That the hoare waters from his frigot° ran, *swift vessel*
And the light bubbles dauncéd all along,
Whiles the salt brine out of the billowes sprong.
At last farre off they many Islands spy,
On every side floting the floods emong:
Then said the knight, "Loe I the land descry,
Therefore old Syre thy course do thereunto apply."

11

"That may not be," said then the Ferryman,
"Least we unweeting hap to be fordonne.° *ruined*
For those same Islands, seeming now and than.[1]
Are not firme lande, nor any certein wonne,[2]
But straggling plots, which to and fro do ronne
In the wide waters: therefore are they hight
The wandring Islands. Therefore doe them shonne;
For they have oft drawne many a wandring wight
Into most deadly daunger and distresséd plight.

9. In *Aeneid* 6.299, Charon ferries the shades of the dead over the Styx to Hades. Comes says he signifies confidence in God's mercy to the dying (3.4).
1. I.e., appearing here and there.
2. I.e., fixed place.

12

"Yet well they seeme to him, that farre doth vew,
Both faire and fruitfull, and the ground dispred
With grassie greene of delectable hew,
And the tall trees with leaves apparelléd,
Are deckt with blossomes dyde in white and red,
That mote the passengers thereto allure;
But whosoever once hath fastenéd
His foot thereon, may never it recure,[3]
But wandreth ever more uncertain and unsure.

13

"As th'Isle of Delos whylome° men report — *formerly*
Amid th' Aegaean sea long time did stray,
Ne made for shipping any certaine port,
Till that Latona[4] traveiling that way,
Flying from Junoes wrath and hard assay,° — *affliction*
Of her faire twins was there deliveréd,
Which afterwards did rule the night and day;
Thenceforth it firmely was establishéd,
And for Apolloes honor highly herriéd."° — *praised*

14

They to him hearken, as beseemeth meete,
And passe on forward: so their way does ly,
That one of those same Islands, which doe fleet° — *float*
In the wide sea, they needes must passen by,
Which seemd so sweet and pleasant to the eye,
That it would tempt a man to touchen there:
Upon the banck they sitting did espy
A daintie damzell, dressing of her heare,
By whom a litle skippet° floting did appeare. — *skiff*

15

She them espying, loud to them can° call, — *did*
Bidding them nigher draw unto the shore;
For she had cause to busie them withall;
And therewith loudly laught: But nathemore
Would they once turne, but kept on as afore:
Which when she saw, she left her lockes undight,
And running to her boat withouten ore,° — *oar*
From the departing land it launchéd light,° — *quickly*
And after them did drive with all her power and might.

3. I.e., repair that error.
4. For the story of Latona (mother of Apollo and Diana), cf. *Metamorphoses* 6.184–218; but Spenser probably used Comes, who notes the instability of the island of Delos at that time (9.6). In Spenser's day, some still believed in floating islands (for which Herodotus and Pliny gave authority).

16

Whom overtaking, she in merry sort
Them gan to bord, and purpose diversly,[5]
Now faining dalliance and wanton sport,
Now throwing forth lewd words immodestly;
Till that the Palmer gan full bitterly
Her to rebuke, for being loose and light:
Which not abiding, but more scornefully
Scoffing at him, that did her justly wite,° *censure*
She turnd her bote about, and from them rowéd quite.

17

That was the wanton Phaedria, which late
Did ferry him over the Idle lake:
Whom nought regarding, they kept on their gate,° *way*
And all her vaine allurements did forsake,
When them the wary Boateman thus bespake;
"Here now behoveth us well to avyse,° *consider*
And of our safétie good heede to take;
For here before a perlous° passage lyes, *dangerous*
Where many Mermayds haunt, making false melodies.

18

"But by the way, there is a great Quicksand,
And a whirlepoole of hidden jeopardy,
Therefore, Sir Palmer, keepe an even hand;
For twixt them both the narrow way doth ly."
Scarse had he said, when hard at hand they spy
That quicksand nigh with water coveréd;
But by the checkéd° wave they did descry *checkered*
It plaine, and by the sea discolouréd:
It calléd was the quicksand of Unthriftyhed.

19

They passing by, a goodly Ship did see,
Laden from far with precious merchandize,
And bravely furnishéd, as ship might bee,
Which through great disaventure, or mesprize,° *error*
Her selfe had runne into that hazardize;
Whose mariners and merchants with much toyle,
Laboured in vaine, to have recured° their prize, *recovered*
And the rich wares to save from pitteous spoyle,
But neither toyle nor travell° might her backe recoyle.° *effort / draw*

5. I.e., to accost, and chat of various things.

20

On th'other side they see that perilous Poole,
That calléd was the Whirlepoole of decay,
In which full many had with haplesse doole° *grief*
Beene suncke, of whom no memorie did stay:
Whose circled waters rapt with whirling sway,[6]
Like to a restlesse wheele, still running round,
Did covet, as they passéd by that way,
To draw their boate within the utmost bound
Of his wide Labyrinth, and then to have them dround.

21

But th'heedfull Boateman strongly forth did stretch
His brawnie armes, and all his body straine,
That th'utmost sandy breach they shortly fetch,[7]
Whiles the dred daunger does behind remaine.
Suddeine they see from midst of all the Maine,
The surging waters like a mountaine rise,
And the great sea puft up with proud disdaine,
To swell above the measure of his guise,° *custom*
As threatning to devoure all, that his powre despise.

22

The waves come rolling, and the billowes rore
Outragiously, as they enragéd were,
Or wrathfull Neptune did them drive before
His whirling charet, for exceeding feare:
For not one puffe of wind there did appeare,
That all the three thereat woxe much afrayd,
Unweeting, what such horrour straunge did reare.° *cause*
Eftsoones they saw an hideous hoast arrayd,
Of huge Sea monsters, such as living sence dismayd.[8]

23

Most ugly shapes, and horrible aspects,
Such as Dame Nature selfe mote feare to see,
Or shame, that ever should so fowle defects
From her most cunning hand escapéd bee;
All dreadfull pourtraicts of deformitee:
Spring-headed Hydraes, and sea-shouldring Whales,
Great whirlpooles, which all fishes make to flee,

6. I.e., gripped by rapid whirling waters.
7. I.e., they soon reach the safety of the beach.
8. Most of the monsters in stanzas 23–24 are found in Pliny's *Natural History* (first century C.E.) or in N. Gesner, *Historia Animalium* (1588). "Whirlpooles," "Scolopendraes," "Monoceros," "Rosmarines" (and the "morse," named after Death), and "Ziffius" are respectively spouting whales, seagoing centipedes or annelid worms, narwhals, walruses, and swordfish. "Wasserman" and "Seasatyre" may be the dolphin and the seal, but more likely mermen.

Bright Scolopendraes, armed with silver scales,
Mighty Monoceros, with immeasuréd° tayles. *enormous*

24

The dreadfull Fish, that hath deserved the name
Of Death, and like him lookes in dreadfull hew,
The griesly Wasserman, that makes his game
The flying ships with swiftnesse to pursew,
The horrible Sea-satyre, that doth shew
His fearefull face in time of greatest storme,
Huge Ziffius, whom Mariners eschew° *avoid*
No lesse, then rockes, (as travellers informe,)
And greedy Rosmarines with visages deforme.

25

All these, and thousand thousands many more,
And more deforméd Monsters thousand fold,
With dreadfull noise, and hollow rombling rore,
Came rushing in the fomy waves enrold,
Which seemed to fly for feare, them to behold:
Ne wonder, if these did the knight appall;
For all that here on earth we dreadfull hold,
Be but as bugs° to fearen babes withall, *imaginary terrors*
Comparéd to the creatures in the seas entrall.° *depths*

26

"Feare nought," then said the Palmer well avized;
"For these same Monsters are not these in deed,
But are into these fearefull shapes disguized
By that same wicked witch, to worke us dreed,
And draw from on this journey to proceede."
Tho lifting up his vertuous° staffe[9] on hye, *powerful, magical*
He smote the sea, which calméd was with speed,
And all that dreadfull Armie fast gan flye
Into great Tethys bosome,[1] where they hidden lye.

27

Quit° from that daunger, forth their course they kept, *freed*
And as they went, they heard a ruefull cry
Of one, that wayld and pittifully wept,
That through the sea the resounding plaints did fly:
At last they in an Island did espy
A seemely Maiden, sitting by the shore,
That with great sorrow and sad agony,

9. Ubaldo, in Tasso's *Gerusalemme* 14.73, bears a similar wand. Noting the significance of Ulysses' voyage, Comes (6.6) says that reason restrains instinct just as wild beasts must be held in check.
1. I.e., into the depths of the sea (cf. I.i.39, and note).

Seeméd some great misfortune to deplore,
And lowd to them for succour calléd evermore.

28

Which Guyon hearing, streight his Palmer bad,
To stere the boate towards that dolefull Mayd,
That he might know, and ease her sorrow sad:
Who him avizing° better, to him sayd; *counselling*
"Faire Sir, be not displeasd, if disobayd:
For ill it were to hearken to her cry;
For she is inly nothing ill apayd,° *pleased*
But onely womanish fine forgery,
Your stubborne° hart t'affect with fraile infirmity. *firm*

29

"To which when she your courage° hath inclind *spirit*
Through foolish pitty, then her guilefull bayt
She will embosome° deeper in your mind, *implant*
And for your ruine at the last awayt."
The knight was ruléd, and the Boateman strayt
Held on his course with stayéd° stedfastnesse, *constant*
Ne ever shruncke, ne ever sought to bayt° *rest*
His tyréd armes for toylesome wearinesse,
But with his oares did sweepe the watry wildernesse.

30

And now they nigh approachéd to the sted,° *place*
Where as those Mermayds dwelt: it was a still
And calmy bay, on th'one side shelteréd
With the brode shadow of an hoarie hill,
On th'other side an high rocke touréd still,
That twixt them both a pleasaunt port they made,
And did like an halfe Theatre fulfill:
There those five sisters[2] had continuall trade,° *occupation*
And used to bath themselves in that deceiptfull shade.

31

They were faire Ladies, till they fondly° strived *foolishly*
With th'Heliconian maides[3] for maistery;
Of whom they over-comen, were deprived
Of their proud beautie, and th'one moyity° *half*
Transformed to fish, for their bold surquedry,° *presumption*
But th'upper halfe their hew° retainéd still, *form*
And their sweet skill in wonted melody;

2. Homer's Sirens (*Odyssey* 12), often equated with mermaids, are the ultimate source for these figures, traditionally three in number; these "five sisters" may indicate the five senses. Comes (7.13) identifies Sirens with voluptuous desire and whatever seduces the irrational part of the soul.
3. I.e., the Muses. This contest is apparently Spenser's own invention.

Which ever after they abusd to ill,
T'allure weake travellers, whom gotten they did kill.

32

So now to Guyon, as he passéd by,
Their pleasaunt tunes they sweetly thus applide;
"O thou faire sonne of gentle Faery,
That art in mighty armes most magnifide
Above all knights, that ever battell tride,
O turne thy rudder hither-ward a while:
Here may thy storme-bet vessell safely ride;
This is the Port of rest from troublous toyle,
The worlds sweet In, from paine and wearisome turmoyle."

33

With that the rolling sea resounding soft,
In his big base them fitly answeréd,
And on the rocke the waves breaking aloft,
A solemne Meane° unto them measuréd, *tenor*
The whiles sweet Zephirus[4] lowd whisteléd
His treble, a straunge kinde of harmony;
Which Guyons senses softly tickeléd,
That he the boateman bad row easily,
And let him heare some part of their rare melody.

34

But him the Palmer from that vanity,
With temperate advice discounselléd,
That they it past, and shortly gan descry
The land, to which their course they leveléd;° *directed*
When suddeinly a grosse fog over spred
With his dull vapour all that desert has,
And heavens chearefull face envelopéd,
That all things one, and one as nothing was,
And this great Universe seemd one confuséd mas.

35

Thereat they greatly were dismayd, ne wist
How to direct their way in darkenesse wide,
But feard to wander in that wastfull mist,
For tombling into mischiefe unespide.
Worse is the daunger hidden, then descride.
Suddeinly an innumerable flight
Of harmefull fowles about them fluttering, cride,
And with their wicked wings them oft did smight,
And sore annoyéd, groping in that griesly night.

4. The west wind, associated by Comes with the stimulation of sexual impulses (4.13). In E. K.'s Glosse to "Aprill," Zephyrus has "soveraigntye of al flowres and greene herbes, growing on earth."

36

Even all the nation of unfortunate° *ill-omened*
And fatall birds about them flockéd were,
Such as by nature men abhorre and hate,
The ill-faste° Owle, deaths dreadfull messengere, *ugly*
The hoars Night-raven, trump of dolefull drere,
The lether-wingéd Bat, dayes enimy,
The ruefull Strich,° still waiting on the bere, *screech owl*
The Whistler° shrill, that who so heares, doth dy, *plover*
The hellish Harpies, prophets of sad destiny.[5]

37

All those, and all that else does horrour breed,
About them flew, and fild their sayles with feare:
Yet stayd they not, but forward did proceed,
Whiles th'one did row, and th'other stifly steare;
Till that at last the weather gan to cleare,
And the faire land it selfe did plainly show.
Said then the Palmer, "Lo where does appeare
The sacred° soile, where all our perils grow; *cursed*
Therefore, Sir knight, your ready armes about you throw."

38

He hearkned, and his armes about him tooke,
The whiles the nimble boate so well her sped,
That with her crooked° keele the land she strooke, *curved*
Then forth the noble Guyon salliéd,
And his sage Palmer, that him governéd;
But th'other by his boate behind did stay.
They marchéd fairly forth, of nought ydred,° *afraid*
Both firmely armd for every hard assay,
With constancy and care, gainst daunger and dismay.

39

Ere long they heard an hideous bellowing
Of many beasts, that roard outrageously,
As if that hungers point, or Venus sting
Had them enragéd with fell surquedry,° *arrogance*
Yet nought they feard, but past on hardily,
Untill they came in vew of those wild beasts:
Who all attonce, gaping full greedily,
And rearing fiercely their upstarting° crests, *bristling*
Ran towards, to devoure those unexpected guests.

5. Celeno, the harpies' leader in Virgil's *Aeneid*, foretold the future in gloomy terms to Aeneas and his followers (3.225–62).

40

But soone as they approcht with deadly threat,
The Palmer over them his staffe upheld,
His mighty staffe, that could all charmes defeat:
Eftsoones their stubborne courages° were queld, *spirits*
And high advauncéd crests downe meekely feld,
In stead of fraying,° they them selves did feare, *terrifying*
And trembled, as them passing they beheld:
Such wondrous powre did in that staffe appeare,
All monsters to subdew to him, that did it beare.

41

Of that same wood it framed was cunningly,
Of which Caduceus whilome was made,
Caduceus the rod of Mercury,[6]
With which he wonts° the Stygian realmes invade, *is accustomed to*
Through ghastly horrour, and eternall shade;
Th' infernall feends with it he can asswage,
And Orcus[7] tame, whom nothing can perswade,
And rule the Furyes, when they most do rage:
Such vertue in his staffe had eke this Palmer sage.

42

Thence passing forth, they shortly do arrive,
Whereas the Bowre of Blisse[8] was situate;
A place pickt out by choice of best alive,
That natures worke by art can imitate:[9]
In which what ever in this worldly state
Is sweet, and pleasing unto living sense,
Or that may dayntiest fantasie aggrate,° *gratify*
Was pouréd forth with plentifull dispence,° *liberality*
And made there to abound with lavish affluence.

43

Goodly it was enclosed round about,
Aswell their entred guestes to keepe within,
As those unruly beasts to hold without;
Yet was the fence thereof but weake and thin;
Nought feard their force, that fortilage° to win, *fortress*
But wisedomes powre, and temperaunces might,[1]

6. In *Odyssey* 10, Mercury helps Ulysses evade Circe's magic; with his rod, described in *Aeneid* 4.242–46, he can summon the dead. Comes (5.5) says he represents divine reason and wisdom.
7. I.e., Pluto.
8. For his Bower, Spenser took descriptive details from Tasso's *Gerusalemme Liberata* 15–16, and from Tissino's romance, *L'Italia Liberata dai Goti*, he derived certain events and characters, including the name "Acratia."
9. I.e., a place selected by the best living artists. In this lovely garden, though, art works by excess (stanza 50), not complementing nature but competing with or merely copying it. So too, the Bower is not temperance's opposite but its sterile parody.
1. I.e., that enclosure, proof against physical force, was vulnerable to wisdom and temperance.

By which the mightiest things efforcéd bin.[2]
And eke the gate was wrought of substaunce light,
Rather for pleasure, then for battery or fight.

44

Yt framéd was of precious yvory,
That seemd a worke of admirable wit;
And therein all the famous history
Of Jason and Medaea was ywrit[3]
Her mighty charmes, her furious loving fit,
His goodly conquest of the golden fleece,
His falséd faith, and love too lightly flit,
The wondred° Argo, which in venturous peece[4] *wonderful*
First through the Euxine seas bore all the flowr of Greece.

45

Ye might have seene the frothy billowes fry° *foam*
Under the ship, as thorough them she went,
That seemd the waves were into yvory,
Or yvory into the waves were sent;
And other where the snowy substaunce sprent° *sprinkled*
With vermell,° like the boyes[5] bloud therein shed, *vermilion*
A piteous spectacle did represent,
And otherwhiles° with gold besprinkeléd; *elsewhere*
Yt seemd th'enchaunted flame, which did Creüsa[6] wed.

46

All this, and more might in that goodly gate
Be red;° that ever open stood to all, *seen*
Which thither came: but in the Porch there sate
A comely personage of stature tall,
And semblaunce° pleasing, more then naturall, *appearance*
That travellers to him seemd to entize;
His looser° garment to the ground did fall, *too loose*
And flew about his heeles in wanton wize,
Not fit for speedy pace, or manly exercize.

47

They in that place him Genius[7] did call:
Not that celestiall powre, to whom the care

2. I.e., are compelled.
3. On Jason's quest (in the ship *Argo*) for the Golden Fleece, and for his subsequent liaison with the sorceress Medea, see the *Argonautica*, by Apollonius of Rhodes (ca. 200 B.C.E.). That the gate is of ivory shows the Bower's falsity; see I.i.40, note.
4. I.e., adventurous vessel.
5. Medea's younger brother Apsyrtus, killed by Jason at her insistence to delay pursuit of the Argonauts.
6. So as to marry Creüsa, Creon's daughter, Jason deserted Medea, who then destroyed Creüsa by sending her a robe that burst into flames when she put it on.
7. Spenser derives Genius, an androgynous god of generation born of Zeus and Earth, as well as the evil spirits in stanza 48 and the wine and flowers used in Genius's cult, chiefly from Comes 4.3. Compare this figure to his better self and fellow "porter" in III.vi.31.

Of life, and generation of all
That lives, pertaines in charge particulare,
Who wondrous things concerning our welfare,
And straunge phantomes doth let us oft forsee,
And oft of secret ill bids us beware:
That is our Selfe, whom though we do not see,
Yet each doth in him selfe it well perceive to bee.

48

Therefore a God him sage Antiquity
Did wisely make, and good Agdistes call:
But this same was to that quite contrary,
The foe of life, that good envyes° to all, *begrudges*
That secretly doth us procure to fall,
Through guilefull semblaunts,° which he makes us see. *illusions*
He of this Gardin had the governall,° *management*
And Pleasures porter was devizd° to bee, *considered*
Holding a staffe in hand for more formalitee.

49

With diverse flowres he daintily was deckt,
And strowéd round about, and by his side
A mighty Mazer° bowle of wine[8] was set, *maple-wood*
As if it had to him bene sacrifide;
Wherewith all new-come guests he gratifide:
So did he eke Sir Guyon passing by:
But he his idle curtesie defide,
And overthrew his bowle disdainfully;
And broke his staffe, with which he charméd semblants sly.[9]

50

Thus being entred, they behold around
A large and spacious plaine, on every side
Strowéd with pleasauns, whose faire grassy ground
Mantled with greene, and goodly beautifide
With all the ornaments of Floraes pride,
Wherewith her mother Art, as halfe in scorne
Of niggard° Nature, like a pompous bride *miserly*
Did decke her, and too lavishly adorne,
When forth from virgin bowre she comes in th'early morne.

51

Thereto the Heavens alwayes Joviall,° *propitious*
Lookt on them lovely,° still in stedfast state, *lovingly*

8. The cup Circe offers Ulysses in *Odyssey* 10 is a model for this bowl, as well as for the golden cup held by Excess (stanza 56). Both vessels may parody the Christian communion cup.
9. I.e., raised deceitful illusions ("guilefull semblaunts").

Ne suffred storme nor frost on them to fall,
Their tender buds or leaves to violate,
Nor scorching heat, nor cold intemperate
T'afflict the creatures, which therein did dwell,
But the milde aire with season moderate
Gently attempred, and disposd so well,
That still it breathéd forth sweet spirit° and holesome smell. *breath*

52

More sweet and holesome, then the pleasaunt hill
Of Rhodope,[1] on which the Nimphe, that bore
A gyaunt babe, her selfe for griefe did kill;
Or the Thessalian Tempe,[2] where of yore
Faire Daphne Phoebus hart with love did gore;
Or Ida, where the Gods loved to repaire,° *resort*
When ever they their heavenly bowres forlore,° *deserted*
Or sweet Parnasse, the haunt of Muses faire;
Or Eden selfe, if ought with Eden mote compaire.

53

Much wondred Guyon at the faire aspect
Of that sweet place, yet suffred no delight
To sincke into his sence, nor mind affect,
But passéd forth, and lookt still forward right,° *straight ahead*
Bridling his will, and maistering his might:
Till that he came unto another gate;
No gate, but like one, being goodly dight
With boughes and braunches, which did broad dilate° *spread out*
Their clasping armes, in wanton wreathings intricate.

54

So fashionéd a Porch with rare device,
Archt over head with an embracing vine,
Whose bounches hanging downe, seemed to entice
All passers by, to tast their lushious wine,
And did themselves into their hands incline,
As freely offering to be gatheréd:
Some deepe empurpled as the Hyacint,[3]
Some as the Rubine,° laughing sweetly red, *ruby*
Some like faire Emeraudes,° not yet well ripenéd. *emeralds*

55

And them amongst, some were of burnisht gold,
So made by art, to beautifie the rest,

1. Traditionally, Jove turned the incestuous nymph Rhodope into a mountain in Thrace to punish the pride that had led her to call herself "Juno" and her brother "Jove" (*Metamorphoses* 6.87–89); her "gyaunt babe," sired by Neptune, gave his name to Mount Athos.
2. The valley in Thessaly where Apollo pursued Daphne (*Metamorphoses* 1.452–567).
3. The jacinth, a gem of blue (or perhaps of reddish-orange) color.

Which did themselves emongst the leaves enfold,
As lurking from the vew of covetous guest,
That the weake bowes, with so rich load opprest,
Did bow adowne, as over-burdenéd.
Under that Porch a comely dame did rest,
Clad in faire weedes,° but fowle disorderéd, *garments*
And garments loose, that seemd unmeet for womanhed.

56

In her left hand a Cup of gold she held,
And with her right the riper° fruit did reach, *overripe*
Whose sappy liquor, that with fulnesse sweld,
Into her cup she scruzd,° with daintie breach *squeezed*
Of her fine fingers, without fowle empeach,[4]
That so faire wine-presse made the wine more sweet:
Thereof she usd to give to drinke to each,
Whom passing by she happenéd to meet:
It was her guise,° all Straungers goodly so to greet. *custom*

57

So she to Guyon offred it to tast;
Who taking it out of her tender hond,
The cup to ground did violently cast,
That all in peeces it was broken fond,° *found*
And with the liquor stainéd all the lond:
Whereat Exeesse exceedingly was wroth,
Yet no'te° the same amend, ne yet withstand, *could not*
But suffered him to passe, all° were she loth; *although*
Who nought regarding her displeasure forward goth.

58

There the most daintie Paradise on ground,
It selfe doth offer to his sober eye,
In which all pleasures plenteously abound,
And none does others happinesse envye:
The painted flowres, the trees upshooting hye,
The dales for shade, the hilles for breathing space,
The trembling groves, the Christall[5] running by;
And that, which all faire workes doth most aggrace,° *add grace to*
The art, which all that wrought, appearéd in no place.[6]

59

One would have thought, (so cunningly, the rude,
And scornéd parts were mingled with the fine,)
That nature had for wantonesse ensued° *imitated*

4. I.e., crushing them daintily with her delicate fingers.
5. I.e., the crystal stream.
6. The final lines of stanza 58, and most of stanza 59, echo Tasso, *Gerusalemme Liberata*, 16.9–10; Tasso's Garden of Armida is the primary model for many passages in stanzas 58–88.

Art, and that Art at nature did repine;° *complain*
So striving each th' other to undermine,
Each did the others worke more beautifie;
So diff'ring both in willes, agreed in fine:[7]
So all agreed through sweete diversitie,
This Gardin to adorne with all varietie.

60

And in the midst of all, a fountaine[8] stood,
Of richest substaunce, that on earth might bee,
So pure and shiny, that the silver flood
Through every channell running one might see;
Most goodly it with curious imageree
Was over-wrought, and shapes of naked boyes,
Of which some seemd with lively jollitee,
To fly about, playing their wanton toyes,° *sports*
Whilest others did them selves embay° in liquid joyes. *bathe*

61

And over all, of purest gold was spred,
A trayle of yvie in his native hew:
For the rich mettall was so colouréd,
That wight, who did not well avised it vew,
Would surely deeme it to be yvie trew:
Low his lascivious armes adown did creepe,
That themselves dipping in the silver dew,
Their fleecy flowres they tenderly did steepe,
Which° drops of Christall seemd for wantones to weepe. *on which*

62

Infinit streames continually did well
Out of this fountaine, sweet and faire to see,
The which into an ample laver° fell, *basin*
And shortly grew to so great quantitie,
That like a little lake it seemd to bee;
Whose depth exceeded not three cubits hight,[9]
That through the waves one might the bottom see,
All paved beneath with Jaspar shining bright,
That seemd the fountaine in that sea did sayle upright.

63

And all the margent round about was set,
With shady Laurell trees, thence to defend° *ward off*
The sunny beames, which on the billowes bet,° *beat*
And those which therein bathéd, mote offend.

7. I.e., at last.
8. Fountain and damsels recall Tasso 15.55–66. Cf. also Archimago's fountain (I.i.34) and the stream from which Redcrosse drinks (I.vii.2–6).
9. About four and a half feet.

As Guyon hapned by the same to wend,
Two naked Damzelles he therein espyde,
Which therein bathing, seeméd to contend,
And wrestle wantonly, ne cared to hyde,
Their dainty parts from vew of any, which them eyde.

64

Sometimes the one would lift the other quight
Above the waters, and then downe againe
Her plong, as over maisteréd by might,
Where both awhile would coveréd remaine,
And each the other from to rise restraine;
The whiles their snowy limbes, as through a vele,
So through the Christall waves appearéd plaine:
Then suddeinly both would themselves unhele,° *disclose*
And th'amarous sweet spoiles to greedy eyes revele.

65

As that faire Starre, the messenger of morne,
His deawy face out of the sea doth reare:
Or as the Cyprian goddesses,[1] newly borne
Of th'Oceans fruitfull froth, did first appeare:
Such seeméd they, and so their yellow heare
Christalline humour° droppéd downe apace. *moisture*
Whom such when Guyon saw, he drew him neare,
And somewhat gan relent° his earnest pace, *slacken*
His stubborne brest gan secret pleasaunce to embrace.

66

The wanton Maidens him espying, stood
Gazing a while at his unwonted guise;° *manner*
Then th'one her selfe low duckéd in the flood,
Abasht, that her a straunger did avise.° *regard*
But th'other rather higher did arise,
And her two lilly paps aloft displayd,
And all, that might his melting hart entise
To her delights, she unto him bewrayd.° *revealed*
The rest hid underneath, him more desirous made.

67

With that, the other likewise up arose,
And her faire lockes, which formerly were bownd
Up in one knot, she low adowne did lose.° *loosen*
Which flowing long and thick, her clothed arownd,
And th'yvorie in golden mantle gownd:

1. Aphrodite (Venus), who, says Hesiod (*Theogony* 197), sprang from foam that issued from the genitals of Uranos after his son Kronos castrated him and threw the member into the ocean. The new goddess came to shore in Cyprus after passing near Cythera.

So that faire spectacle from him was reft,° *withdrawn*
Yet that, which reft it, no lesse faire was fownd:
So hid in lockes and waves from lookers theft,
Nought but her lovely face she for his looking left.

68

Withall she laughéd, and she blusht withall,
That blushing to her laughter gave more grace,
And laughter to her blushing, as did fall:
Now when they spide the knight to slacke his pace,
Them to behold, and in his sparkling face
The secret signes of kindled lust appeare,
Their wanton meriments they did encreace,
And to him beckned, to approch more neare,
And shewd him many sights, that courage cold could reare.[2]

69

On which when gazing him the Palmer saw,
He much rebukt those wandring eyes of his,
And counseld well, him forward thence did draw.
Now are they come nigh to the Bowre of blis
Of her fond favorites so named amis:
When thus the Palmer; "Now Sir, well avise;° *take care*
For here the end of all our travell° is: *arduous journey*
Here wonnes° Acrasia, whom we must surprise, *dwells*
Else she will slip away, and all our drift despise.[3]

70

Eftsoones they heard a most melodious sound,
Of all that mote delight a daintie eare,
Such as attonce might not on living ground,
Save in this Paradise, be heard elswhere:
Right hard it was, for wight, which did it heare,
To read,° what manner musicke that mote bee: *tell*
For all that pleasing is to living eare,
Was there consorted° in one harmonee, *joined*
Birdes, voyces, instruments, windes, waters, all agree.

71

The joyous birdes shrouded° in chearefull shade, *hidden*
Their notes unto the voyce attempred° sweet; *attuned*
Th'Angelicall soft trembling voyces made
To th'instruments divine respondence meet:° *fitting*
The silver sounding instruments did meet° *join*
With the base murmure of the waters fall:
The waters fall with difference discreet,° *suitable*

2. I.e., could arouse sexual desire.
3. I.e., frustrate all our plans.

Now soft, now loud, unto the wind did call:
The gentle warbling wind low answeréd to all.[4]

72

There, whence that Musick seeméd heard to bee,
Was the faire Witch[5] her selfe now solacing,
With a new Lover, whom through sorceree
And witchcraft, she from farre did thither bring:
There she had him now layd a slombering,
In secret shade, after long wanton joyes:
Whilst round about them pleasauntly did sing
Many faire Ladies, and lascivious boyes,
That ever mixt their song with light licentious toyes.

73

And all that while, right over him she hong,
With her false° eyes fast fixéd in his sight, *deceitful*
As seeking medicine, whence she was stong,
Or greedily depasturing° delight: *feeding on*
And oft inclining downe with kisses light,
For feare of waking him, his lips bedewd,
And through his humid eyes did sucke his spright,
Quite molten into lust and pleasure lewd;
Wherewith she sighéd soft, as if his case she rewd.° *pitied*

74

The whiles some one did chaunt this lovely lay;[6]
"Ah see, who so faire thing doest faine° to see, *delight*
In springing flowre the image of thy day;
Ah see the Virgin Rose, how sweetly shee
Doth first peepe forth with bashfull modestee,
That fairer seemes, the lesse ye see her may;
Lo see soone after, how more bold and free
Her baréd bosome she doth broad display;
Loe see soone after, how she fades, and falles away.

75

"So passeth, in the passing of a day,
Of mortall life the leafe, the bud, the flowre,
Ne more doth flourish after first decay,
That earst was sought to decke both bed and bowre,
Of many a Ladie, and many a Paramowre:° *lover*
Gather therefore the Rose, whilest yet is prime,

4. This stanza follows (and revises) *Gerusalemme Liberata* 16.12; Spenser adds voices and instruments to Tasso's birds and murmuring wind.
5. I.e., Acrasia, whose beauty masks and reinforces her power to immerse her victims in an intemperance that leads at last to bestiality (stanza 39). She has indirectly murdered the parents of the "bloody babe" whose wrong Guyon is avenging.
6. The theme of *carpe diem* ("seize the day"), found in Horace and other Latin poets, appears often in Renaissance verse; Spenser follows *Gerusalemme* 16.14–15.

For soone comes age, that will her pride deflowre:
Gather the Rose of love, whilest yet is time,
Whilest loving thou mayst lovéd be with equall crime."° *sin*

76

He ceast, and then gan all the quire of birdes
Their diverse notes t'attune unto his lay,
As in approvance of his pleasing words.
The constant paire heard all, that he did say,
Yet swarvéd not, but kept their forward way,
Through many covert groves, and thickets close,
In which they creeping did at last display° *discover*
That wanton Ladie, with her lover lose,° *wanton*
Whose sleepie head she in her lap did soft dispose.

77

Upon a bed of Roses she was layd,
As faint through heat, or dight to[7] pleasant sin,
And was arayd, or rather disarayd,
All in a vele of silke and silver thin,
That hid no whit her alablaster° skin, *alabaster*
But rather shewd more white, if more might bee:
More subtile web Arachne[8] cannot spin,
Nor the fine nets, which oft we woven see
Of scorchéd deaw, do not in th'aire more lightly flee.° *float*

78

Her snowy brest was bare to readie spoyle
Of hungry eies, which n'ote° therewith be fild, *might not*
And yet through languour of her late sweet toyle,
Few drops, more cleare then Nectar, forth distild,
That like pure Orient perles adowne it trild,° *trickled*
And her faire eyes sweet smyling in delight,
Moystened their fierie beames, with which she thrild
Fraile harts, yet quenchéd not; like starry light
Which sparckling on the silent waves, does seeme more bright.

79

The young man sleeping by her, seemd to bee
Some goodly swayne of honorable place,° *rank*
That certes it great pittie was to see
Him his nobilitie so foule deface;° *disgrace*
A sweet regard, and amiable grace,
Mixéd with manly sternnesse did appeare
Yet sleeping, in his well proportiond face,
And on his tender lips the downy heare
Did now but freshly spring, and silken blossomes beare.

7. I.e., prepared for.
8. Cf. II.vii.28 and note.

80

His warlike armes, the idle instruments
Of sleeping praise, were hong upon a tree,
And his brave shield, full of old moniments,° *knightly signs*
Was fowly ra'st,° that none the signes might see; *razed*
Ne for them, ne for honour caréd hee,
Ne ought, that did to his advauncement tend,
But in lewd loves, and wastfull luxuree,
His dayes, his goods, his bodie he did spend:
O horrible enchantment, that him so did blend.° *blind*

81

The noble Elfe, and carefull Palmer drew
So nigh them, minding nought, but lustfull game,
That suddein forth they on them rusht, and threw
A subtile net,[9] which onely for the same
The skilfull Palmer formally° did frame. *in exact form*
So held them under fast, the whiles the rest
Fled all away for feare of fowler shame.
The faire Enchauntresse, so unwares opprest,° *surprised*
Tryde all her arts, and all her sleights, thence out to wrest.° *twist*

82

And eke her lover strove: but all in vaine;
For that same net so cunningly was wound,
That neither guile, nor force might it distraine.° *tear*
They tooke them both, and both them strongly bound
In captive bandes, which there they readie found:
But her in chaines of adamant he tyde;
For nothing else might keepe her safe and sound,
But Verdant (so he hight) he soon untyde,
And counsell sage in steed thereof to him applyde.[1]

83

But all those pleasant bowres and Pallace brave,° *splendid*
Guyon broke downe, with rigour pittilesse;
Ne ought their goodly workmanship might save
Them from the tempest of his wrathfulnesse,
But that their blisse he turned to balefulnesse:
Their groves he feld, their gardins did deface,
Their arbers spoyle, their Cabinets° suppresse, *bowers*
Their banket houses burne, their buildings race,° *raze*
And of the fairest late, now made the fowlest place.

9. Vulcan threw a net over his wife Venus and her lover Mars, then called the other gods to come laugh at them (cf. *Metamorphoses* 4.169–89).
1. The name "Verdant" suggests "green" (a green that one might argue is liberated in the Garden of Adonis, III.vi); in Verdant's posture some might see a negative pieta, although just as relevant are the often ambivalent Renaissance images showing Venus with a sleeping and unarmed Mars; on such figures see, e.g., Edgar Wind, *Pagan Mysteries in the Renaissance* (New York, 1968).

84

Then led they her away, and eke that knight
They with them led, both sorrowfull and sad:
The way they came, the same retourned they right,
Till they arrivéd, where they lately had
Charmed those wild-beasts, that raged with furie mad.
Which now awaking, fierce at them gan fly,
As in their mistresse reskew, whom they lad;° *led*
But them the Palmer soone did pacify.
Then Guyon askt, what meant those beastes, which there did ly.

85

Said he, "These seeming beasts are men indeed,
Whom this Enchauntresse hath transforméd thus,
Whylome her lovers, which her lusts did feed,
Now turnéd into figures hideous,
According to their mindes like° monstruous."[2] *similarly*
"Sad end," quoth he, "of life intemperate,
And mournefull meed of joyes delicious:
But Palmer, if it mote thee so aggrate;° *please*
Let them returnéd be unto their former state."

86

Streight way he with his vertuous staffe them strooke,
And streight of beasts they comely men became;
Yet being men they did unmanly looke,
And staréd ghastly, some for inward shame,
And some for wrath, to see their captive Dame:
But one above the rest in speciall,
That had an hog beene late, hight Grille[3] by name,
Repinéd greatly, and did him miscall,° *abuse*
That had from hoggish forme him brought to naturall.

87

Said Guyon, "See the mind of beastly man,
That hath so soone forgot the excellence
Of his creation, when he life began,
That now he chooseth, with vile difference,° *change*
To be a beast, and lacke intelligence."
To whom the Palmer thus, "The donghill kind
Delights in filth and foule incontinence:
Let Grill be Grill, and have his hoggish mind,
But let us hence depart, whilest wether serves and wind."

2. This episode is based on *Odyssey* 10; Comes (6.6) says each man whom Circe enchanted became a beast appropriate to the vice he had favored.
3. "He that is filthy, let him be filthy" (Revelation 22.11). "Grill" is from Greek for "pig." In Plutarch's witty *Whether Beasts Have the Use of Reason* (in his *Moralia*), Grill would rather stay a pig than resume life as a sophist philosopher; he and Ulysses chat about temperance. Spenser probably read Greek, but he could have found Grill in Renaissance emblems.

The Third Booke of The Faerie Queene

Contayning
The Legend of Britomartis or Of Chastitie

1

It falles° me here to write of Chastity, *befalls*
That fairest vertue, farre above the rest;
For which what needs me fetch from Faery
Forreine ensamples, it to have exprest?
Sith it is shrinéd in my Soveraines brest,
And formed so lively° in each perfect part, *lifelike*
That to all Ladies, which have it profest,
Need but behold the pourtraict° of her hart, *image*
If pourtrayd it might be by any living art.

2

But living art may not least part expresse,
Nor life-resembling pencill[1] it can paint,
All were it Zeuxis or Praxiteles:[2]
His daedale° hand would faile, and greatly faint, *skillful*
And her perfections with his error taint:
Ne Poets wit, that passeth Painter farre
In picturing the parts of beautie daint,° *delicate*
So hard a workmanship adventure darre,° *dare*
For fear through want of words her excellence to marre.

3

How then shall I, Apprentice of the skill,
That whylome° in divinest wits did raine, *formerly*
Presume so high to stretch mine humble quill?
Yet now my lucklesse lot doth me constraine
Hereto perforce. But O dred Soveraine
Thus farre forth pardon, sith that choicest wit
Cannot your glorious pourtraict figure plaine
That I in colourd showes may shadow° it, *represent*
And antique° praises unto present persons fit. *ancient*

4

But if in living colours, and right hew,° *form*
Your selfe you covet to see picturéd,
Who can it doe more lively, or more trew,
Then that sweet verse, with Nectar sprinckeléd,
In which a gracious servant[3] picturéd

1. I.e., the artist's brush that creates "living art"; the conceit recalls Du Bellay, *Olive* 19.
2. Ancient Greek artists optimizing excellence in painting and sculpture respectively.
3. I.e., Sir Walter Raleigh, whose poem *Cynthia* celebrated Queen Elizabeth.

His Cynthia, his heavens fairest light?
That with his melting sweetnesse ravishéd,
And with the wonder of her beamés bright,
My senses lulléd are in slomber of delight.

5

But let that same delitious° Poet lend — *pleasing*
A little leave unto a rusticke Muse
To sing his mistresse prayse, and let him mend,
If ought amis her liking may abuse:° — *offend*
Ne let his fairest Cynthia refuse,
In mirrours more then one her selfe to see,
But either Gloriana let her chuse,
Or in Belphoebe fashionéd to bee:
In th'one her rule, in th'other her rare chastitee.[4]

Canto I

Guyon encountreth Britomart,
faire Florimell is chaced:
Duessaes traines[1] and Malecastaes
champions are defaced.° — *confounded*

1

The famous Briton Prince and Faerie knight,
After long wayes and perilous paines endured,
Having their wearie limbes to perfect plight° — *health*
Restord, and sory° wounds right well recured, — *painful*
Of the faire Alma greatly were procured,° — *urged*
To make there lenger sojourne and abode;
But when thereto they might not be allured,
From seeking praise, and deeds of armes abrode,
They courteous congé° tooke, and forth together yode.° — *leave / went*

2

But the captived Acrasia he sent,
Because of travell long, a nigher way,
With a strong gard, all reskew to prevent,
And her to Faerie court safe to convay,
That her for witnesse of his hard assay,° — *trial*
Unto his Faerie Queene he might present:

4. It is worth noting that "chastity" need not be "virginity" and that a faithful spouse is "chaste" even if sexually active with his or her mate. Like Milton, Spenser associates the virtue with power and love, not just with avoiding illicit sex. Spenser's "Letter to Raleigh" notes that since the queen "beareth two persons, the one of a most royall Queene or Empresse, the other of a most vertuous and beautifull Lady," he signifies the latter by "Belphoebe, fashioning her name according to your owne excellent conceipt of Cynthia." "Phoebe" and "Cynthia" are both names for chaste Diana, the moon.

1. I.e., schemes. The reference to Duessa may reflect an abandoned plan for Book III. Stanza I refers to Arthur, Guyon, and the latter's defeat of the witch Acrasia; on Alma, see II.ix.

But he him selfe betooke another way,
To make more triall of his hardiment,° *courage*
And seeke adventures, as he with Prince Arthur went.

3

Long so they travellèd through wastefull° wayes, *desolate*
Where daungers dwelt, and perils most did wonne,° *abide*
To hunt for glorie and renowmèd praise;
Full many Countries they did overronne,
From the uprising to the setting Sunne,
And many hard adventures did atchieve;
Of all the which they honour ever wonne,
Seeking the weake oppressèd to relieve,
And to recover right for such, as wrong did grieve.

4

At last as through an open plaine they yode,
They spide a knight, that towards prickèd faire,[2]
And him beside an aged Squire there rode,
That seemed to couch° under his shield three-square, *crouch*
As if that age bad him that burden spare,
And yield it those, that stouter could it wield:
He them espying, gan himselfe prepare,
And on his arme addresse° his goodly shield *make ready*
That bore a Lion passant in a golden field.[3]

5

Which seeing good Sir Guyon, deare besought
The Prince of grace, to let him runne that turne.
He graunted: then the Faery quickly raught° *took up*
His poinant° speare, and sharpely gan to spurne° *piercing / spur*
His fomy steed, whose fierie feete did burne
The verdant grasse, as he thereon did tread;
Ne did the other backe his foot returne,
But fiercely forward came withouten dread,
And bent° his dreadfull speare against the others head. *aimed*

6

They bene ymet, and both their points arrived,
But Guyon drove so furious and fell,° *fiercely*
That seemed both shield and plate it would have rived;° *pierced*
Nathelesse it bore his foe not from his sell,° *saddle*
But made him stagger, as he were not well:

2. I.e., Expertly spurred his horse.
3. I.e. (in heraldry), a lion walking against a gold background; these were the arms of Brute, legendary founder of the British race and ancestor of this knight (III.ix. 38–51).

But Guyon selfe, ere well he was aware,
Nigh a speares length behind his crouper° fell, *crupper*
Yet in his fall so well him selfe he bare,
That mischievous mischance his life and limbes did spare.

7

Great shame and sorrow of that fall he tooke;
For never yet, sith warlike armes he bore,
And shivering[4] speare in bloudie field first shooke,
He found himselfe dishonoréd so sore.
Ah gentlest knight, that ever armour bore,
Let not thee grieve dismounted to have beene,
And brought to ground, that never wast before;
For not thy fault, but secret powre unseene,
That speare enchaunted was, which layd thee on the greene.[5]

8

But weenedst thou[6] what wight thee overthrew,
Much greater griefe and shamefuller regret
For thy hard fortune then thou wouldst renew,
That of a single damzell thou wert met
On equall plaine, and there so hard beset;
Even the famous Britomart[7] it was,
Whom straunge adventure did from Britaine fet,° *bring*
To seeke her lover (love farre sought alas,)
Whose image she had seene in Venus looking glas.[8]

9

Full of disdainefull wrath, he fierce uprose,
For to revenge that foule reprochfull shame,
And snatching his bright sword began to close
With her on foot, and stoutly forward came;
Die rather would he, then endure that same.
Which when his Palmer saw, he gan to feare
His toward perill and untoward blame,[9]

4. I.e., quivering; or, perhaps, able to splinter whatever it strikes.
5. The spear, "made by Magick art of yore" (iii.60), recalls the one Astolfo gives the warrior-maiden Bradamante in Ariosto, *Orlando Furioso* 23.15. Allegorically, the encounter implies that chastity (which for Spenser includes faithful married sexuality) is even more powerful than temperance.
6. I.e., if you knew.
7. Britomart (Cretan for "sweet maid") represents a chastity fulfilled in marriage, while her name connotes a Briton's martial might. Described by Callimachus (third century B.C.E.) as a nymph of Diana, "Britomartis" was also called Dictynna; in ancient Crete, Diana was worshipped under the name Britomartis. Britomart combines elements from several sources: her quest for Arthegall recalls that of Bradamante for Ruggiero in *Orlando Furioso*; her dialogue with her nurse in Canto ii imitates a scene in the pseudo-Virgilian *Ciris*; her courage in Canto xi parallels the victory over fiery lust of the armed virgin Pudicitia ("Chastity") in Prudentius's fourth-century *Psychomachia*; and in conception she resembles Virgil's warrior-maiden Camilla, to whom Spenser refers in iv.2.
8. The crystal ball presented by Merlin to King Ryence; it enabled the viewer to foresee future events (ii. 18–21).
9. I.e., his imminent danger and unlucky injury.

Which by that new rencounter he should reare:° *cause*
For death sate on the point of that enchaunted speare.

10

And hasting towards him gan faire perswade,
Not to provoke misfortune, nor to weene° *expect*
His speares default to mend with cruell blade;
For by his mightie Science° he had seene *knowledge*
The secret vertue° of that weapon keene, *power*
That mortall puissance mote not withstand:
Nothing on earth mote alwaies happie° beene. *successful*
Great hazard were it, and adventure fond,° *foolish*
To loose long gotten honour with one evill hond.° *action*

11

By such good meanes he him discounselléd,° *dissuaded*
From prosecuting his revenging rage;
And eke the Prince like treaty handeléd,[1]
His wrathfull will with reason to asswage,
And laid the blame, not to his carriage,° *conduct*
But to his starting steed, that swarved asyde,
And to the ill purveyance° of his page, *preparation*
That had his furnitures° not firmely tyde: *gear*
So is his angry courage fairely pacifyde.

12

Thus reconcilement was betweene them knit,
Through goodly temperance, and affection chaste,
And either vowd with all their power and wit,° *intelligence*
To let not others honour be defaste,° *disgraced*
Of friend or foe, who ever it embaste,° *dishonored*
Ne armes to beare against the others syde:
In which accord the Prince was also plaste,
And with that golden chaine of concord tyde.
So goodly all agreed, they forth yfere° did ryde. *together*

13

O goodly usage of those antique times,[2]
In which the sword was servant unto right;
When not for malice and contentious crimes,
But all for praise, and proofe of manly might,
The martiall brood° accustoméd to fight: *race*
Then honour was the meed° of victorie, *reward*
And yet the vanquishéd had no despight:

1. I.e., used similar appeals.
2. The placing of this stanza in the narrative recalls that of Ariosto's apostrophe to the virtues of ancient knighthood (*Orlando Furioso* 1.22).

Let later age that noble use envie,° *imitate*
Vile rancour to avoid, and cruell surquedrie.° *arrogance*

14

Long they thus travelléd in friendly wise,
Through countries waste, and eke well edifyde,° *built up*
Seeking adventures hard, to exercise
Their puissance, whylome full dernely° tryde: *grievously*
At length they came into a forrest wyde,
Whose hideous horror and sad trembling sound
Full griesly° seemed: Therein they long did ryde, *grim*
Yet tract° of living creatures none they found, *track*
Save Beares, Lions, and Buls, which roméd them around.

15

All suddenly out of the thickest brush,
Upon a milk-white Palfrey° all alone, *saddle horse*
A goodly Ladie[3] did foreby° them rush, *past*
Whose face did seeme as cleare as Christall stone,
And eke through feare as white as whalés bone:
Her garments all were wrought of beaten gold,
And all her steed with tinsell° trappings shone, *glittering*
Which fled so fast, that nothing mote° him hold, *might*
And scarse them leasure gave, her passing to behold.

16

Still as she fled, her eye she backward threw,
As fearing evill, that pursewd her fast;
And her faire yellow locks behind her flew,
Loosely disperst with puffe of every blast:
All as a blazing starre[4] doth farre outcast
His hearie° beames, and flaming lockes dispred, *hairy*
At sight whereof the people stand aghast:
But the sage wisard telles, as he has red,° *foreseen*
That it importunes° death and dolefull drerihed.° *portends / misery*

17

So as they gazéd after her a while,
Lo where a griesly Foster° forth did rush, *forester*
Breathing out beastly lust her to defile:
His tyreling jade[5] he fiercely forth did push,
Through thicke and thin, both over banke and bush
In hope her to attaine by hooke or crooke,
That from his gorie sides the bloud did gush:

3. The flight of Florimel ("Flower-honey," named in the Proem) recalls that of Angelica in Ariosto's *Orlando Furioso* 1.33–35. Her name and behavior can suggest a fleeting beauty that inspires desire.
4. I.e., a comet—so named because its tail can look like hair (Greek "kom-").
5. I.e., tired nag.

Large were his limbes, and terrible his looke,
And in his clownish° hand a sharp bore speare he shooke. *rustic*

18

Which outrage when those gentle knights did see,
Full of great envie° and fell gealosy,° *indignation / anger*
They stayd not to avise,° who first should bee, *consider*
But all spurd after fast, as they mote fly,
To reskew her from shamefull villany.
The Prince and Guyon equally bylive° *speedily*
Her selfe pursewd, in hope to win thereby
Most goodly meede, the fairest Dame alive:
But after the foule foster Timias did strive.

19

The whiles faire Britomart, whose constant mind,
Would not so lightly follow beauties chace,
Ne reckt° of Ladies Love, did stay behind, *cared*
And them awayted there a certaine space,
To weet° if they would turne backe to that place: *know*
But when she saw them gone, she forward went,
As lay her journey, through that perlous Pace,° *region*
With stedfast courage and stout hardiment;
Ne evill thing she feared, ne evill thing she ment.° *intended*

20

At last as nigh out of the wood she came,
A stately Castle farre away she spyde,
To which her steps directly she did frame.
That Castle was most goodly edifyde,° *built*
And plaste for pleasure nigh that forrest syde:
But faire before the gate a spatious plaine,
Mantled with greene, itselfe did spredden wyde,
On which she saw sixe knights, that did darraine° *prepare*
Fierce battell against one,[6] with cruell might and maine.

21

Mainly° they all attonce upon him laid, *violently*
And sore beset on every side around,
That nigh he breathlesse grew, yet nought dismaid,
Ne ever to them yielded foot of ground
All° had he lost much bloud through many a wound, *although*
But stoutly dealt his blowes, and every way
To which he turnéd in his wrathfull stound,° *assault*
Made them recoile, and fly from dred decay,° *destruction*
That none of all the sixe before, him durst assay.° *engage*

6. I.e., Redcrosse. On holiness's need for chastity, see 1 Corinthians 6.9–20.

22

Like dastard Curres, that having at a bay
  The salvage beast embost° in wearie chace, *cornered*
  Dare not adventure° on the stubborne pray, *rush in*
  Ne byte before, but rome from place to place,
  To get a snatch, when turnéd is his face.
  In such distresse and doubtfull° jeopardy, *fearful*
  When Britomart him saw, she ran a pace° *quickly*
  Unto his reskew, and with earnest cry,
Bad those same sixe forbeare that single enimy.

23

But to her cry they list° not lenden eare, *cared*
  Ne ought the more their mightie strokes surceasse,
  But gathering him round about more neare,
  Their direfull rancour rather did encreasse;
  Till that she rushing through the thickest preasse,
  Perforce disparted their compacted gyre,° *circle*
  And soone compeld to hearken unto peace:
  Tho° gan she myldly of them to inquyre *then*
The cause of their dissention and outrageous yre.

24

Whereto that single knight did answere frame;° *make*
  "These sixe would me enforce by oddes of might,
  To chaunge my liefe,° and love another Dame, *beloved*
  That death me liefer were, then such despight,
  So unto wrong to yield my wrested right:
  For I love one, the truest one on ground,
  Ne list me chaunge; she th'Errant Damzell hight,[7]
  For whose deare sake full many a bitter stownd,° *attack*
I have endured, and tasted many a bloudy wound."

25

"Certes,"° said she, "then bene ye sixe to blame, *surely*
  To weene° your wrong by force to justifie: *expect*
  For knight to leave his Ladie were great shame,
  That faithfull is, and better were to die.
  All losse is lesse, and lesse the infamie,
  Then losse of love to him, that loves but one;
  Ne may love be compeld by maisterie,° *superior force*
  For soone as maisterie comes, sweet love anone° *at once*
Taketh his nimble wings, and soone away is gone."[8]

7. Presumably Una, the wandering damsel.
8. Lines 7–9 are based on Chaucer's "Franklin's Tale," 764–66.

26

Then spake one of those sixe, "There dwelleth here
Within this castle wall a Ladie faire,
Whose soveraine beautie hath no living pere,° *equal*
Thereto so bounteous and so debonaire,
That never any mote with her compaire.
She hath ordaind this law, which we approve,° *make good*
That every knight, which doth this way repaire,° *travel*
In case he have no Ladie, nor no love,
Shall doe unto her service never to remove.

27

"But if he have a Ladie or a Love,
Then must he her forgoe° with foule defame, *give up*
Or else with us by dint of sword approve,° *prove*
That she is fairer, then our fairest Dame,
As did this knight, before ye hither came."
"Perdie,"° said Britomart, "the choise is hard: *indeed*
But what reward had he, that overcame?"
"He should advauncéd be to high regard,"
Said they, "and have our Ladies love for his reward.

28

"Therefore aread° Sir, if thou have a love." *tell*
"Love have I sure," quoth she, "but Lady none;
Yet will I not fro mine owne love remove,
Ne to your Lady will I service done,
But wreake° your wrongs wrought to this knight alone, *avenge*
And prove his cause." With that her mortall speare
She mightily aventred° towards one, *thrust*
And downe him smot, ere well aware he weare,
Then to the next she rode, and downe the next did beare.

29

Ne did she stay, till three on ground she layd,
That none of them himselfe could reare againe;
The fourth was by that other knight dismayd,
All° were he wearie of his former paine, *although*
That now there do but two of six remaine;
Which two did yield, before she did them smight.
"Ah," said she then, "now may ye all see plaine,
That truth is strong, and trew love most of might,
That for his trusty servaunts doth so strongly fight."

30

"Too well we see," said they, "and prove° too well *experience*
Our faulty weaknesse, and your matchlesse might:

For thy;[9] faire Sir, yours be the Damozell,
Which by her owne law to your lot doth light,° *fall*
And we your liege men faith unto you plight."
So underneath her feet their swords they mard,[1]
And after her besought, well as they might,
To enter in, and reape the dew reward:
She graunted, and then in they all together fared.

31

Long were it to describe the goodly frame,
And stately port° of Castle Joyeous, *appearance*
(For so that Castle hight by commune name)
Where they were entertaind with curteous
And comely glee° of many gracious *cheer*
Faire Ladies, and of many a gentle knight,
Who through a Chamber long and spacious,
Eftsoones° them brought unto their Ladies sight, *presently*
That of them cleepéd° was the Lady of delight.[2] *called*

32

But for to tell the sumptuous aray
Of that great chamber, should be labour lost:
For living wit, I weene, cannot display
The royall riches and exceeding cost,° *value*
Of every pillour and of every post:
Which all of purest bullion framéd were,
And with great pearles and pretious stones embost,° *adorned*
That the bright glister of their beamés cleare
Did sparckle forth great light, and glorious did appeare.

33

These straunger knights through passing, forth were led
Into an inner rowme, whose royaltee
And rich purveyance might uneath be red,[3]
Mote Princes place beseeme so deckt to bee.
Which stately manner when as they did see,
The image of superfluous riotize,° *extravagance*
Exceeding much the state of meane degree,[4]
They greatly wondred, whence so sumptuous guize° *way of life*
Might be maintaynd, and each gan diversely devize.° *guess*

9. I.e., therefore.
1. I.e., broke or hacked their sword blades, casting them at her feet.
2. I.e., Malecasta ("badly chaste"), whose luxurious castle recalls similar dwellings in medieval romances.
3. I.e., the luxurious richness of which might scarcely be described.
4. I.e., medium rank or class.

34

The wals were round about apparelléd
With costly clothes of Arras and of Toure,° *Tours*
In which with cunning hand was pourtrahéd
The love of Venus and her Paramoure° *lover*
The faire Adonis, turnéd to a flowre,
A worke of rare device, and wondrous wit.[5]
First did it shew the bitter balefull stowre,° *turmoil*
Which her assayd with many a fervent fit,
When first her tender hart was with his beautie smit.

35

Then with what sleights and sweet allurements she
Entyst the Boy, as well that art she knew,
And wooéd him her Paramoure to be;
Now making girlonds of each flowre that grew,
To crowne his golden lockes with honour dew;° *due*
Now leading him into a secret shade
From his Beauperes,° and from bright heavens vew, *companions*
Where him to sleepe she gently would perswade,
Or bathe him in a fountaine by some covert° glade. *secret*

36

And whilst he slept, she over him would spred
Her mantle, coloured like the starry skyes,
And her soft arme lay underneath his hed,
And with ambrosiall kisses bathe his eyes;
And whilest he bathed, with her two crafty spyes,
She secretly would search each daintie lim,
And throw into the well sweet Rosemaryes,
And fragrant violets, and Pances° trim, *pansies*
And ever with sweet Nectar she did sprinkle him.

37

So did she steale his heedelesse hart away,
And joyd his love in secret unespyde.
But for she saw him bent to cruell play,
To hunt the salvage beast in forrest wyde,
Dreadfull° of daunger, that mote him betyde,° *fearful / befall*
She oft and oft advized him to refraine
From chase of greater° beasts, whose brutish pryde° *too great / spirit*

5. On Venus and Adonis (a young hunter turned by a sorrowful Venus into an anemone after being gored to death by a boar), a myth that Spenser exploits variously in Book III, see Ovid's *Metamorphoses* 10.519–739 as well as Bion's *Lament for Adonis*, from which Spenser borrowed, probably via Ronsard's version, for his 1595 poem on the dead Sidney, *Astrophel*. Cf. also Natalis Comes, *Mythologiae* 5.16. Mythographers often read Adonis as the sun, killed by the boar of winter but rising again when the sun returns north, and Venus as the earth that suffers in his absence.

Mote breede° him scath° unwares: but all in vaine; *bring / harm*
For who can shun the chaunce, that dest'ny doth ordaine?

38

Lo, where beyond he lyeth languishing,° *suffering*
Deadly engoréd of a great wild Bore,
And by his side the Goddesse groveling
Makes for him endlesse mone, and evermore
With her soft garment wipes away the gore,
Which staines his snowy skin with hatefull hew:
But when she saw no helpe might him restore,
Him to a dainty flowre she did transmew,° *transform*
Which in that cloth was wrought, as if it lively° grew. *actually*

39

So was that chamber clad in goodly wize,
And round about it many beds were dight,[6]
As whilome was the antique worldés guize,° *custom*
Some for untimely° ease, some for delight, *unsuitable*
As pleaséd them to use, that use it might:
And all was full of Damzels, and of Squires,
Dauncing and reveling both day and night,
And swimming deepe in sensuall desires,
And Cupid still emongst them kindled lustfull fires.

40

And all the while sweet Musicke did divide° *descant*
Her looser° notes with Lydian[7] harmony; *too loose*
And all the while sweet birdes thereto applide
Their daintie layes and dulcet melody,
Ay° caroling of love and jollity, *always*
That wonder was to heare their trim consort.° *harmony*
Which when those knights beheld, with scornefull eye,
They sdeignéd° such lascivious disport, *disdained*
And loathed the loose demeanure° of that wanton sort. *conduct*

41

Thence they were brought to that great Ladies vew,
Whom they found sitting on a sumptuous bed,
That glistred all with gold and glorious shew,
As the proud Persian Queenes accustoméd:[8]
She seemd a woman of great bountihed,° *virtue*
And of rare beautie, saving that askaunce° *sidewise*

6. I.e., many couches were arranged.
7. In Greek music, the Lydian mode was thought soft, soothing, and pleasant for guests (Plato, *Republic* 3.398); naughty Catullus praises the "laughter" of a "Lydian" lake (*Carmina* 31), but moral Roger Ascham fears that Lydian music will stimulate immorality in youths (*Toxophilus* [1545]).
8. Cf. Duessa (I.ii.13) and Lucifera (I. iv. 7).

Her wanton eyes, ill signes of womanhed,
Did roll too lightly, and too often glaunce,
Without regard of grace, or comely amenaunce.° *behavior*

42

Long worke it were, and needlesse to devize° *describe*
Their goodly entertainement and great glee:
She causéd them be led in curteous wize
Into a bowre, disarméd for to bee,
And chearéd well with wine and spiceree:° *spiced refreshment*
The Redcrosse Knight was soone disarméd there,
But the brave Mayd would not disarméd bee,
But onely vented up her umbriere,[9]
And so did let her goodly visage to appere.

43

As when faire Cynthia, in darkesome night,
Is in a noyous° cloud envelopéd, *noxious*
Where she may find the substaunce thin and light,
Breakes forth her silver beames, and her bright hed
Discovers° to the world discomfited;° *reveals / dejected*
Of the poore traveller, that went astray,
With thousand blessings she is heriéd;° *praised*
Such was the beautie and the shining ray,
With which faire Britomart gave light unto the day.[1]

44

And eke those six, which lately with her fought,
Now were disarmd, and did them selves present
Unto her vew, and company unsought;
For they all seeméd curteous and gent,
And all sixe brethren, borne of one parent,
Which had them traynd in all civilitee,° *courtesy*
And goodly taught to tilt and turnament,[2]
Now were they liegemen to this Lady free,° *noble*
And her knights service ought, to hold of her in fee.[3]

45

The first of them by name Gardante hight,[4]
A jolly person, and of comely vew;° *appearance*
The second was Parlante, a bold knight,

9. I.e., raised the face guard of her helmet.
1. Cf. *Orlando Furioso*, when Bradamante removes her helmet (32.79–80); see III.ix.20, note.
2. A tilt is an encounter between two mounted knights, armed with lances; a tournament involves a number of knights, armed with lances and swords.
3. I.e., owed her knightly service, as their feudal homage.
4. The knights' names ("watching," "speaking," "jesting," "kissing," "drinking," and "nocturnal activity" [with perhaps a pun on Latin *noceo*, "injure"]) suggest the chronology of seduction. Similar figures appear in *The Romance of the Rose* and other medieval stories by, e.g., Boccaccio and Machaut.

And next to him Jocante did ensew;
Basciante did him selfe most curteous shew;
But fierce Bacchante seemd too fell and keene;
And yet in armes Noctante greater grew:
All were faire knights, and goodly well beseene,[5]
But to faire Britomart they all but shadowes beene.

46

For she was full of amiable° grace, *pleasing*
And manly terrour mixéd therewithall,
That as the one stird up affections bace,
So th'other did mens rash desires apall,
And hold them backe, that would in errour fall;
As he, that hath espide a vermeil° Rose, *vermilion*
To which sharpe thornes and breres the way forstall,
Dare not for dread his hardy hand expose,
But wishing it far off, his idle° wish doth lose. *futile*

47

Whom when the Lady saw so faire a wight,
All ignoraunt of her contrary sex,
(For she her weend a fresh and lusty knight)
She greatly gan enamouréd to wex,° *grow*
And with vaine thoughts her falséd° fancy vex: *deceived*
Her fickle hart conceivéd hasty fire,
Like sparkes of fire, which fall in sclender flex,° *flax*
That shortly brent° into extreme desire, *burned*
And ransackt all her veines with passion entire.

48

Eftsoones she grew to great impatience
And into termes of open outrage brust,[6]
That plaine discovered° her incontinence, *revealed*
Ne reckt she, who her meaning did mistrust;
For she was given all to fleshly lust,
And pouréd forth in sensuall delight,
That all regard of shame she had discust,° *shaken off*
And meet° respect of honour put to flight: *proper*
So shamelesse beauty soone becomes a loathly sight.

49

Faire Ladies, that to love captivéd arre,
And chaste desires do nourish in your mind,
Let not her fault your sweet affections marre,
Ne blot the bounty° of all womankind; *goodness*
'Mongst thousands good one wanton Dame to find:

5. I.e., of good appearance.
6. I.e., broke into openly intemperate terms.

Emongst the Roses grow some wicked weeds;
For this was not to love, but lust inclind;
For love does alwayes bring forth bounteous° deeds, *virtuous*
And in each gentle hart desire of honour breeds.[7]

50

Nought so of love this looser° Dame did skill,° *too loose / understand*
But as a coale to kindle fleshly flame,
Giving the bridle to her wanton will,
And treading under foote her honest name:
Such love is hate, and such desire is shame.
Still did she rove at her with crafty glaunce
Of her false eyes, that at her hart did ayme,
And told her meaning in her countenaunce;
But Britomart dissembled it with ignoraunce.[8]

51

Supper was shortly dight° and downe they sat, *set out*
Where they were servéd with all sumptuous fare,
Whiles fruitfull Ceres, and Lyaeus fat[9]
Pourd out their plenty, without spight° or spare:° *grudge / restraint*
Nought wanted there, that dainty was and rare;
And aye the cups their bancks did overflow,
And aye betweene the cups, she did prepare
Way to her love, and secret darts° did throw; *glances*
But Britomart would not such guilfull message know.

52

So when they slakéd had the fervent heat
Of appetite with meates of every sort,
The Lady did faire Britomart entreat,
Her to disarme, and with delightfull sport
To loose her warlike limbs and strong effort,° *power*
But when she mote not thereunto be wonne,
(For she her sexe under that straunge purport° *appearance*
Did use to hide, and plaine apparaunce shonne:)
In plainer wise to tell her grievaunce she begonne.

53

And all attonce discovered her desire
With sighes, and sobs, and plaints, and piteous griefe,
The outward sparkes of her in burning fire;
Which spent in vaine, at last she told her briefe,
That but if[1] she did lend her short° reliefe, *immediate*

7. An apostrophe to women modeled on *Orlando Furioso* 28.1.
8. I.e., pretended not to understand.
9. *Lyaeus*: Bacchus, the god of wine; i.e., food and drink were plentiful. *Ceres*: Demeter the goddess of earth and its fruits.
1. I.e., unless.

And do her comfort, she mote algates° dye. *altogether*
But the chaste damzell, that had never priefe° *experience*
Of such malengine° and fine forgerie,° *guile / deceit*
Did easily beleeve her strong extremitie.

54

Full easie was for her to have beliefe,
Who by self-feeling of her feeble sexe,
And by long triall of the inward griefe,
Wherewith imperious love her hart did vexe,
Could judge what paines do loving harts perplexe.° *torment*
Who meanes no guile, be guiléd soonest shall,
And to faire semblaunce doth light faith annexe;° *add*
The bird, that knowes not the false fowlers call,
Into his hidden net full easily doth fall.

55

For thy she would not in discourteise wise,
Scorne the faire offer of good will profest;
For great rebuke° it is, love to despise, *shame*
Or rudely sdeigne a gentle harts request;
But with faire countenaunce, as beseeméd best,
Her entertaynd,° nath'lesse she inly deemd *treated*
Her love too light, to wooe a wandring guest:
Which she misconstruing, thereby esteemd
That from like° inward fire that outward smoke had steemd. *matching*

56

Therewith a while she her flit° fancy fed, *changeful*
Till she mote winne fit time for her desire,
But yet her wound still inward freshly bled,
And through her bones the false instilléd fire
Did spred it selfe, and venime close° inspire. *secretly*
Tho were the tables taken all away,
And every knight, and every gentle Squire
Gan choose his dame with Basciomani° gay, *hand kissing*
With whom he meant to make his sport and courtly play.

57

Some fell to daunce, some fell to hazardry,° *dicing*
Some to make love, some to make meriment,
As diverse wits to divers things apply;
And all the while faire Malecasta bent
Her crafty engins° to her close intent. *wiles*
By this th'eternall lampes, wherewith high Jove
Doth light the lower world, were halfe yspent,

And the moist daughters of huge Atlas[2] strove
Into the Ocean deepe to drive their weary drove.° *flock*

58

High time it seeméd then for every wight
Them to betake unto their kindly° rest; *natural*
Eftsoones long waxen torches weren light,
Unto their bowres° to guiden every guest: *chambers*
Tho when the Britonesse saw all the rest
Avoided° quite, she gan her selfe despoile,° *departed / disrobe*
And safe commit to her soft fethered nest,
Where through long watch, and late dayes weary toile,
She soundly slept, and carefull thoughts did quite assoile.° *dispel*

59

Now whenas all the world in silence deepe
Yshrowded was, and every mortall wight
Was drownéd in the depth of deadly° sleepe, *deathlike*
Faire Malecasta, whose engrievéd° spright *afflicted*
Could find no rest in such perplexéd plight,
Lightly arose out of her wearie bed,[3]
And under the blacke vele of guilty Night,[4]
Her with a scarlot mantle coveréd,
That was with gold and Ermines faire envelopéd.

60

Then panting soft, and trembling everie joynt,
Her fearfull feete towards the bowre she moved;
Where she for secret purpose did appoynt
To lodge the warlike mayd unwisely loved,
And to her bed approching, first she prooved,° *tested*
Whether she slept or wakt, with her soft hand
She softly felt, if any member mooved,
And lent her wary eare to understand,
If any puffe of breath, or signe of sence she fond.

61

Which whenas none she fond, with easie shift,[5]
For feare least her unwares she should abrayd,° *awaken*
Th'embroderd quilt she lightly up did lift,
And by her side her selfe she softly layd,
Of every finest° fingers touch affrayd; *slightest*
Ne any noise she made, ne word she spake,

2. As nymphs, the Hyades ("the rainers") wept for their dead brother; now they are seven stars in Taurus. Comes (4.7) calls them daughters of Atlas, which may be why Spenser gives them a "drove" as though they were the Hesperides, also daughters of Atlas, who (some said) herded sheep. It is midnight, and hence the spring equinox, March 11 in the Julian Calendar.
3. I.e., from the bed where she had restlessly lain.
4. Night is "guilty" because its dark veil conceals evil things; in Hesiod, *Theogony* 224, Night is the mother of Deceit. Cf. III.iv. 55.
5. I.e., moving softly.

But inly sighed. At last the royall Mayd
Out of her quiet slomber did awake,
And chaungd her weary side, the better ease to take.

62

Where feeling one close couchéd by her side,
She lightly lept out of her filéd° bed, *defiled*
And to her weapon ran, in minde to gride° *pierce*
The loathéd leachour. But the Dame halfe ded
Through suddein feare and ghastly drerihed,° *horror*
Did shrieke alowd, that through the house it rong,
And the whole family° therewith adred,° *household / terrified*
Rashly° out of their rouzéd couches sprong, *hastily*
And to the troubled chamber all in armes did throng.

63

And those six Knights that Ladies Champions,
And eke the Redcrosse knight ran to the stownd,° *uproar*
Halfe armed and halfe unarmd, with them attons:
Where when confusedly they came, they fownd
Their Lady lying on the sencelesse grownd;[6]
On th'other side, they saw the warlike Mayd
All in her snow-white smocke, with locks unbownd,
Threatning the point of her avenging blade,
That with so troublous terrour they were all dismayde.

64

About their Lady first they flockt arownd,
Whom having laid in comfortable couch,
Shortly they reard out of her frosen swownd;° *swoon*
And afterwards they gan with fowle reproch
To stirre up strife, and troublous contecke broch.[7]
But by ensample of the last dayes losse,
None of them rashly durst to her approch,
Ne in so glorious spoile themselves embosse,° *cover*
Her succourd eke the Champion of the bloudy Crosse.

65

But one of those sixe knights, Gardante hight,
Drew out a deadly bow and arrow keene,
Which forth he sent with felonous° despight, *fierce*
And fell intent against the virgin sheene.° *fair*
The mortall steele stayd not, till it was seene
To gore her side, yet was the wound not deepe,
But lightly raséd° her soft silken skin, *grazed*
That drops of purple bloud thereout did weepe,
Which did her lilly smock with staines of vermeil steepe.

6. I.e., lying senseless on the ground.
7. I.e., instigate troublesome discord.

66

Wherewith enraged she fiercely at them flew,
  And with her flaming sword about her layd,
  That none of them foule mischiefe could eschew,[8]
  But with her dreadfull strokes were all dismayd:
  Here, there, and every where about her swayd° *swung*
  Her wrathfull steele, that none mote it abide,° *endure*
  And eke the Redcrosse knight gave her good aid,
  Ay joyning foot to foot, and side to side,
That in short space their foes they have quite terrifide.

67

Tho whenas all were put to shamefull flight,
  The noble Britomartis her arayd,
  And her bright armes about her body dight:° *put on*
  For nothing would she lenger there be stayd,
  Where so loose life, and so ungentle trade° *conduct*
  Was usd of Knights and Ladies seeming gent:
  So earely ere the grosse Earthes gryesy shade;[9]
  Was all disperst out of the firmament,
They tooke their steeds, and forth upon their journey went.

Canto II

The Redcrosse knight to Britomart
  describeth Artegall:
The wondrous myrrhour, by which she
  in love with him did fall.

1

Here have I cause, in men just blame to find,
  That in their proper° prayse too partiall bee, *own*
  And not indifferent° to woman kind, *impartial*
  To whom no share in armes and chevalrie
  They do impart,° ne maken memorie *allow*
  Of their brave gestes° and prowesse martiall; *exploits*
  Scarse do they spare to one or two or three,
  Rowme in their writs; yet the same writing small
Does all their deeds deface,° and dims their glories all. *obscure*

2

But by record of antique times I find,
  That women wont in warres to beare most sway,
  And to all great exploits them selves inclind:
  Of which they still the girlond bore away,
  Till envious Men fearing their rules decay,° *destruction*
  Gan coyne streight° lawes to curb their liberty; *strict*

8. I.e., none could avoid deadly danger.
9. I.e., the grim shades of night.

Yet sith they warlike armes have layd away,
They have exceld in artes and pollicy,° *statecraft*
That now we foolish men that prayse gin eke t'envy.[1]

3

Of warlike puissaunce in ages spent,
Be thou faire Britomart, whose prayse I write,
But of all wisedome be thou precedent,° *model*
O soveraigne Queene, whose prayse I would endite,° *proclaim*
Endite I would as dewtie doth excite;° *move*
But ah my rimes too rude and rugged arre,
When in so high an object they do lite,
And striving, fit to make, I feare do marre:
Thy selfe thy prayses tell, and make them knowen farre.

4

She travelling with Guyon[2] by the way,
Of sundry things faire purpose° gan to find, *discourse*
T'abridg their journey long, and lingring day;
Mongst which it fell into that Faeries mind,
To aske this Briton Mayd, what uncouth° wind, *strange*
Brought her into those parts, and what inquest° *quest*
Made her dissemble her disguiséd kind:° *nature*
Faire Lady she him seemd, like Lady drest,
But fairest knight alive, when arméd was her brest.

5

Thereat she sighing softly, had no powre
To speake a while, ne ready answere make,
But with hart-thrilling throbs and bitter stowre,° *inward turmoil*
As if she had a fever fit, did quake,
And every daintie limbe with horrour shake;
And ever and anone the rosy red,
Flasht through her face, as it had been a flake° *flash*
Of lightning, through bright heaven fulminéd;° *shot forth*
At last the passion past she thus him answeréd.

6

"Faire Sir, I let you weete, that from the howre
I taken was from nourses tender pap,
I have beene trainéd up in warlike stowre,° *combat*
To tossen° speare and shield, and to affrap° *wield / strike*

1. Unlike Ariosto (e.g., *Orlando Furioso* 20.1), Spenser here seems serious in affirming women's martial and political prowess. Such praise was not uncommon in this normally patriarchal culture, as witness Castiglione's *Courtier* III and John Bale's 1548 edition of Elizabeth's *Godly Meditation*, and there was classical precedent in, e.g., Plutarch's *Moralia* (on the "Bravery of Women"). In V.v.25, however, the narrator says that good women know they are "borne to base humilitie." Had Spenser changed his mind between 1590 and 1596? His own beliefs, if any, remain subject to dispute.
2. Apparently a slip on Spenser's part; Redcrosse is meant (cf. stanza 16).

The warlike ryder to his most mishap;
Sithence° I loathéd have my life to lead, *since then*
As Ladies wont, in pleasures wanton lap,
To finger the fine needle and nyce° thread; *delicate*
Me lever° were with point of foemans speare be dead.[3] *rather*

7

"All my delight on deedes of armes is set,
To hunt out perils and adventures hard,
By sea, by land, where so they may be met,
Onely for honour and for high regard,° *concerns*
Without respect° of richesse or reward. *care*
For such intent into these parts I came,
Withouten compasse, or withouten card,° *map*
Far fro my native soyle, that is by name
The greater Britaine,[4] here to seeke for prayse and fame.

8

"Fame blazéd° hath, that here in Faery lond *proclaimed*
Do many famous Knightes and Ladies wonne,° *dwell*
And many straunge adventures to be fond,
Of which great worth and worship° may be wonne; *honor*
Which I to prove, this voyage have begonne.
But mote I weet of you, right curteous knight,
Tydings of one, that hath unto me donne
Late foule dishonour and reprochfull spight,
The which I seeke to wreake,° and Arthegall he hight."[5] *avenge*

9

The word gone out, she backe againe would call,
As her repenting so to have missayd,[6]
But that he it up-taking ere the fall,
Her shortly answeréd; "Faire martiall Mayd
Certes ye misaviséd° beene, t'upbrayd *misinformed*
A gentle knight with so unknightly blame:
For weet ye well of all, that ever playd
At tilt or tourney, or like warlike game,
The noble Arthegall hath ever borne the name.[7]

3. The warrior woman is a traditional literary type; here Spenser may remember Clorinda's training in Tasso's *Gerusalemme Liberata* 2.39–40.
4. I.e., not the "lesser Britaine," or Brittany, in France.
5. I.e., is named Arthegall, who will be the protagonist of Book V, "The Legend of Justice." Geoffrey of Monmouth's *Historia Regum Britanniae* (ca. 1139) refers to "Arthgal of Cargueir [Warwick]" (10.12), but the name also links Arthegall to King Arthur (punning on French "egal," or "equal," to "Arthur) and perhaps also to Arthur, Lord Grey of Wilton, Spenser's chief in Ireland from 1580 to 1582, at whose treatment by the English government the end of Book V may glance. Unlike the Saxon George, Arthegall is a Briton; the "gall" in his name may recall the Gauls or Wales, "Pays de Galles" in French.
6. I.e., as if she repented having spoken thus wrongly.
7. I.e., has ever been most renowned.

10

"For thy great wonder were it, if such shame
Should ever enter in his bounteous° thought, *virtuous*
Or ever do, that mote deserven blame:
The noble courage° never weeneth ought, *spirit*
That may unworthy of it selfe be thought.
Therefore, faire Damzell, be ye well aware,° *wary*
Least that too farre ye have your sorrow sought:
You and your countrey both I wish welfare,
And honour both; for each of other worthy are."

11

The royall Mayd woxe° inly wondrous glad, *grew*
To heare her Love so highly magnifide,
And joyd that ever she affixéd had,
Her hart on knight so goodly glorifide,
How ever finely she it faind to hide:
The loving mother, that nine monethes did beare,
In the deare closet of her painefull side,
Her tender babe, it seeing safe appeare,
Doth not so much rejoyce, as she rejoycéd theare.

12

But to occasion° him to farther talke, *induce*
To feed her humour° with his pleasing stile, *mood*
Her list in strifull termes with him to balke,° *dispute*
And thus replide, "How ever, Sir, ye file
Your curteous tongue, his prayses to compile,
It ill beseemes a knight of gentle sort,
Such as ye have him boasted, to beguile
A simple mayd, and worke so haynous tort,° *wrong*
In shame of knighthood, as I largely° can report. *at length*

13

"Let be[8] therefore my vengeaunce to disswade,
And read,° where I that faytour° false may find." *tell / villain*
"Ah, but if reason faire might you perswade,
To slake your wrath, and mollifie° your mind," *soften*
Said he, "perhaps ye should it better find:
For hardy° thing it is, to weene by might, *bold*
That man to hard conditions to bind,
Or ever hope to match in equall fight,
Whose prowesse paragon[9] saw never living wight.

8. I.e., cease.
9. I.e., the equal of whose prowess.

14

"Ne soothlich° is it easie for to read,° *truly / know*
Where now on earth, or how he may be found;
For he ne wonneth in one certaine stead,° *place*
But restlesse walketh all the world around,
Ay° doing things, that to his fame redound, *always*
Defending Ladies cause, and Orphans right,
Where so he heares, that any doth confound° *persecute*
Them comfortlesse,° through tyranny or might; *helpless*
So is his soveraine honour raisde to heavens hight."

15

His feeling words her feeble sence much pleased,
And softly sunck into her molten° hart; *melting*
Hart that is inly hurt, is greatly eased
With hope of thing, that may allegge° his smart; *alleviate*
For pleasing words are like to Magick art,
That doth the charméd Snake in slomber lay:
Such secret ease felt gentle Britomart,
Yet list the same efforce with faind gainesay,[1]
So dischord oft in Musick makes the sweeter lay.

16

And said, "Sir knight, these idle termes forbeare,
And sith it is uneath° to find his haunt,° *difficult / abode*
Tell me some markes, by which he may appeare,
If chaunce I him encounter paravaunt;° *face to face*
For perdie° one shall other slay, or daunt: *surely*
What shape, what shield, what armes, what steed, what sted,
And what so else his person most may vaunt?"° *display*
All which the Redcrosse knight to point ared,[2]
And him in every part before her fashionéd.

17

Yet him in every part before she knew,
How ever list her now her knowledge faine,° *hide*
Sith him whilome in Britaine she did vew,
To her revealéd in a mirrhour plaine,
Whereof did grow her first engrafféd° paine; *implanted*
Whose root and stalke so bitter yet did tast,
That but the fruit more sweetnesse did containe,
Her wretched dayes in dolour she mote wast,
And yield the pray of love to lothsome death at last.

1. I.e., yet was pleased to intensify that sensation by pretended disagreement.
2. I.e., exactly described.

18

By strange occasion she did him behold,
  And much more strangely gan to love his sight,
  As it in bookes hath written bene of old.
  In Deheubarth that now South-wales is hight,
  What time king Ryence raigned, and dealéd° right, *dispensed*
  The great Magitian Merlin had devized,
  By his deepe science, and hell-dreaded might,
  A looking glasse,[3] right wondrously aguized,° *fashioned*
Whose vertues through the wyde world soone were solemnized.

19

It vertue° had, to shew in perfect sight, *power*
  What ever thing was in the world contaynd,
  Betwixt the lowest earth and heavens hight,
  So that it to the looker appertaynd;
  What ever foe had wrought, or frend had faynd,
  Therein discovered was, ne ought mote pas,
  Ne ought in secret from the same remaynd;
  For thy it round and hollow shapéd was,
Like to the world it selfe, and seemed a world of glas.

20

Who wonders not, that reades° so wonderous worke? *perceives*
  But who does wonder, that has red° the Towre, *considered*
  Wherein th'Aegyptian Phao long did lurke
  From all mens vew, that none might her discoure,° *discover*
  Yet she might all men vew out of her bowre?
  Great Ptolomae[4] it for his lemans° sake *beloved's*
  Ybuilded all of glasse, by Magicke powre,
  And also it impregnable did make;
Yet when his love was false, he with a peaze° it brake. *blow*

21

Such was the glassie globe that Merlin made,
  And gave unto king Ryence for his gard,° *protection*
  That never foes his kingdome might invade,
  But he it knew at home before he hard
  Tydings thereof, and so them still debared.
  It was a famous Present for a Prince,
  And worthy worke of infinite reward,

3. I.e., a crystal ball. In Chaucer's "Squire's Tale" a "mirror of glas" gives the viewer foreknowledge in matters of love or war. Elizabeth's astrologer, Dr. John Dee, apparently had a small one that he consulted when assuring her of her Arthurian lineage and the legitimacy it gave her.

4. Ptolemy II (308–246 B.C.E.), who built the Pharos, Museum, and Library at Alexandria; legend credited him with almost magical ability in working with glass. The next stanza may allude indirectly to recent plots against the queen, such as the 1586 Babington conspiracy, and to the war with Spain.

That treasons could bewray, and foes convince;° *conquer*
Happie this Realme, had it remainéd ever since.

22

One day it fortunéd, faire Britomart
Into her fathers closet to repayre;° *go*
For nothing he from her reserved apart,
Being his onely daughter and his hayre:° *heir*
Where when she had espyde that mirrhour fayre,
Her selfe a while therein she vewd in vaine;
Tho her avizing° of the vertues rare, *thinking*
Which thereof spoken were, she gan againe
Her to bethinke of, that mote to her selfe pertaine.

23

But as it falleth, in the gentlest harts
Imperious Love hath highest set his throne,
And tyrannizeth in the bitter smarts
Of them, that to him buxome° are and prone:° *yielding / submissive*
So thought this Mayd (as maydens use to done)
Whom fortune for her husband would allot,
Not that she lusted after any one;
For she was pure from blame of sinfull blot,
Yet wist° her life at last must lincke in that same knot. *knew*

24

Eftsoones there was presented to her eye
A comely knight, all armed in complete wize,
Through whose bright ventayle° lifted up on hye *visor*
His manly face, that did his foes agrize,° *terrify*
And friends to termes of gentle truce entize,
Lookt foorth, as Phoebus face out of the east,
Betwixt two shadie mountaines doth arize;
Portly° his person was, and much increast *dignified*
Through his Heroicke grace, and honorable gest.° *bearing*

25

His crest was covered with a couchant Hound,
And all his armour seemed of antique mould,° *form*
But wondrous massie and assuréd sound,
And round about yfretted° all with gold, *adorned*
In which there written was with cyphers° old, *letters*
Achilles armes, which Arthegall did win.
And on his shield enveloped sevenfold
He bore a crownéd litle Ermilin,° *ermine*
That deckt the azure field with her faire pouldred° skin.[5] *spotted*

5. Arthegall's helmet displays a greyhound lying down with head alertly raised; his shield's crowned ermine signifies royalty and chastity. Ariosto alludes to Mandricardo's winning of

26

The Damzell well did vew his personage,° *image*
And likéd well, ne further fastned° not, *fixed on*
But went her way; ne her unguilty age
Did weene, unwares, that her unlucky lot
Lay hidden in the bottome of the pot;
Of hurt unwist most daunger doth redound:° *result*
But the false Archer, which that arrow shot
So slyly, that she did not feele the wound,
Did smyle full smoothly at her weetlesse wofull stound.

27

Thenceforth the feather in her loftie crest,
Ruffféd of[6] love, gan lowly to availe,° *bow*
And her proud portance,° and her princely gest, *bearing*
With which she earst tryumphéd, now did quaile:° *falter*
Sad, solemne, sowre, and full of fancies fraile
She woxe; yet wist she neither how, nor why,
She wist not, silly° Mayd, what she did aile, *innocent*
Yet wist, she was not well at ease perdy,° *certainly*
Yet thought it was not love, but some melancholy.

28

So soone as Night had with her pallid hew
Defast° the beautie of the shining sky, *obscured*
And reft from men the worlds desiréd vew,
She with her Nourse adowne to sleepe did lye;
But sleepe full farre away from her did fly:
In stead thereof sad sighes, and sorrowes deepe
Kept watch and ward about her warily,
That nought she did but wayle, and often steepe° *stain*
Her daintie couch with teares, which closely° she did weepe. *secretly*

29

And if that any drop of slombring rest
Did chaunce to still° into her wearie spright, *trickle*
When feeble nature felt her selfe opprest,
Streight way with dreames, and with fantasticke sight
Of dreadfull things the same was put to flight,
That oft out of her bed she did astart,
As one with vew of ghastly feends affright:
Tho gan she to renew her former smart,
And thinke of that faire visage, written in her hart.

Hector's arms (*Orlando Furioso* 14.30–31), but for Arthegall to win those of the Greek Achilles is especially apt, given the legend that Brute, a Trojan, founded Britain (see ix. 46–51). There may also be a psychological dynamic: Britomart's search will lead her from an image to the man himself.

6. I.e., ruffled by.

30

One night, when she was tost with such unrest,
Her aged Nurse, whose name was Glauce hight,[7]
Feeling her leape out of her loathéd nest,
Betwixt her feeble armes her quickly keight,° *caught*
And downe againe in her warme bed her dight;° *placed*
"Ah my deare daughter, ah my dearest dread,
What uncouth fit," said she, "what evil plight
Hath thee opprest, and with sad drearyhead° *grief*
Chaungéd thy lively cheare,° and living made thee dead? *mood*

31

"For not of nought these suddeine ghastly feares
All night afflict thy naturall repose,
And all the day, when as thine equall peares° *companions*
Their fit disports with faire delight doe chose,
Thou in dull corners doest thy selfe inclose,
Ne tastest Princes pleasures, ne doest spred
Abroad thy fresh youthes fairest flowre, but lose
Both leafe and fruit, both too untimely shed,
As one in wilfull bale° for ever buriéd. *grief*

32

"The time, that mortall men their weary cares
Do lay away, and all wilde beastes do rest,
And every river eke his course forbeares,
Then doth this wicked evill thee infest,° *attack*
And rive with thousand throbs thy thrilléd° brest; *pierced*
Like an huge Aetn' of deepe engulféd griefe,
Sorrow is heapéd in thy hollow chest,
Whence forth it breakes in sighes and anguish rife,
As smoke and sulphure mingled with confuséd strife.

33

"Aye me, how much I feare, least love it bee;
But if that love it be, as sure I read° *perceive*
By knowen signes and passions, which I see,
Be it worthy of thy race and royall sead,
Then I avow by this most sacred head
Of my deare foster child, to ease thy griefe,
And win thy will: Therefore away doe° dread; *banish*
For death nor daunger from thy dew reliefe
Shall me debarre, tell me therefore my liefest liefe."° *beloved*

7. This episode draws heavily on the pseudo-Virgilian *Ciris*, in which passion leads a princess—less honorable than Spenser's heroine—to betray her father and kingdom (cf. Ovid, *Metamorphoses* 8); her nurse is the mother of Diana's nymph, Britomartis. Glauce's name (Greek for "gray" and "owl") suits her age and, the owl being sacred to Athena, associates her charge with the armed goddess of war, wisdom, and giant-killing. The old nurse is a common figure from classical literature through the Renaissance, usually sympathetic but often amoral.

34

So having said, her twixt her armés twaine
She straightly° straynd, and colléd° tenderly, *closely / embraced*
And every trembling joynt, and every vaine
She softly felt, and rubbéd busily,
To doe° the frosen cold away to fly; *cause*
And her faire deawy eies with kisses deare
She oft did bath, and oft againe did dry;
And ever her importund,° not to feare *urged*
To let the secret of her hart to her appeare.

35

The Damzell pauzd, and then thus fearefully:
"Ah Nurse, what needeth thee to eke° my paine? *add to*
Is not enough, that I alone doe dye,
But it must doubled be with death of twaine?
For nought for me but death there doth remaine."
"O daughter deare," said she, "despaire no whit;
For never sore, but might a salve obtaine:
That blinded God, which hath ye blindly smit,
Another arrow hath your lovers hart to hit."

36

"But mine is not," quoth she, "like others wound;
For which no reason can find remedy."
"Was never such, but mote the like be found,"
Said she, "and though no reason may apply
Salve to your sore, yet love can higher stye,° *mount*
Then reasons reach, and oft hath wonders donne."
"But neither God of love, nor God of sky
Can doe," said she, "that, which cannot be donne."
"Things oft impossible," quoth she, "seeme, ere begonne."

37

"These idle words," said she, "doe nought asswage
My stubborne smart, but more annoyance° breed, *grief*
For no no usuall fire, no usuall rage° *passion*
It is, O Nurse, which on my life doth feed,
And suckes the bloud, which from my hart doth bleed.
But since thy faithfull zeale lets me not hyde
My crime, (if crime it be) I will it reed.° *tell*
Nor Prince, nor pere it is, whose love hath gryde° *pierced*
My feeble brest of late, and launchéd° this wound wyde. *inflicted*

38

"Nor man it is, nor other living wight;
For then some hope I might unto me draw,
But th'only shade and semblant° of a knight, *likeness*

Whose shape or person yet I never saw,
Hath me subjected to loves cruell law:
The same one day, as me misfortune led,
I in my fathers wondrous mirrhour saw,
And pleaséd with that seeming goodly-hed,° *good appearance*
Unwares the hidden hooke with baite I swallowéd.

39

"Sithens° it hath infixéd faster hold *Since then*
Within my bleeding bowels, and so sore
Now ranckleth in this same fraile fleshly mould,° *body*
That all mine entrailes flow with poysnous gore,
And th'ulcer groweth daily more and more;
Ne can my running sore find remedie,
Other then my hard fortune to deplore,
And languish as the leafe falne from the tree,
Till death make one end of my dayes and miserie."

40

"Daughter," said she, "what need ye be dismayd,
Or why make ye such Monster of your mind?
Of much more uncouth thing I was affrayd;
Of filthy lust, contrarie unto kind.° *nature*
But this affection nothing straunge I find;
For who with reason can you aye° reprove, *ever*
To love the semblant pleasing most your mind,
And yield your heart, whence ye cannot remove?
No guilt in you, but in the tyranny of love.[8]

41

"Not so th'Arabian Myrrhe[9] did set her mind;
Nor so did Biblis spend her pining hart,
But loved their native flesh against all kind,° *nature*
And to their purpose uséd wicked art:
Yet playd Pasiphae a more monstrous part,
That loved a Bull, and learnd a beast to bee;
Such shamefull lusts who loaths not, which depart
From course of nature and of modestie?
Sweet love such lewdnes bands° from his faire companie. *banishes*

42

"But thine my Deare (welfare thy heart my deare)
Though strange beginning had, yet fixéd is

8. Chaste love accords with reason; yet reason cannot match or control love's power (cf. stanza 36).
9. Yielding to passion for her royal father, and aided by her old nurse, Myrrha conceived Adonis (*Metamorphoses* 10.312–518); Biblis slept with her brother; Queen Pasiphae entered a wooden cow made for her by Daedalus and, impregnated by a handsome bull, bore the Minotaur: cf. Boccaccio, *Genealogiae* 4.9–10.

On one, that worthy may perhaps appeare;
And certes seemes bestowéd not amis:
Joy thereof have thou and eternall blis."
With that upleaning on her elbow weake,
Her alablaster° brest she soft did kis, *alabaster*
Which all that while she felt to pant and quake,
As it an Earth-quake were; at last she thus bespake.

43

"Beldame,° your words doe worke me litle ease; *good mother*
For though my love be not so lewdly bent,° *inclined*
As those ye blame, yet may it nought appease
My raging smart, ne ought my flame relent,° *abate*
But rather doth my helpelesse griefe augment.
For they, how ever shamefull and unkind,
Yet did possesse° their horrible intent: *achieve*
Short end of sorrowes they thereby did find;
So was their fortune good, though wicked were their mind.

44

"But wicked fortune mine, though mind be good,
Can have no end, nor hope of my desire,
But feed on shadowes, whiles I die for food,
And like a shadow wexe,° whiles with entire *become*
Affection, I doe languish and expire.
I fonder, then Cephisus foolish child,[1]
Who having vewéd in a fountaine shere° *clear*
His face, was with the love thereof beguild;
I fonder love a shade, the bodie farre exild."

45

"Nought like," quoth she, "for that same wretched boy
Was of himselfe the idle Paramoure;
Both love and lover, without hope of joy,
For which he faded to a watry flowre.
But better fortune thine, and better howre,° *occasion*
Which lov'st the shadow of a warlike knight;
No shadow, but a bodie hath in powre:[2]
That bodie, wheresoever that it light,° *lodges*
May learnéd be by cyphers,° or by Magicke might. *astrological signs*

46

"But if thou may with reason yet represse
The growing evill, ere it strength have got,
And thee abandond wholly doe possesse,
Against it strongly strive, and yield thee not,

1. I.e., Narcissus.
2. I.e., there is no shadow not cast by a body.

Till thou in open field adowne be smot.° *smitten*
But if the passion mayster thy fraile might,
So that needs love or death must be thy lot,
Then I avow to thee, by wrong or right
To compasse° thy desire, and find that lovéd knight." *bring about*

47

Her chearefull words much cheard the feeble spright
Of the sicke virgin, that her downe she layd
In her warme bed to sleepe, if that she might;
And the old-woman carefully displayd° *arranged*
The clothes about her round with busie ayd;
So that at last a little creeping sleepe
Surprisd her sense: She therewith well apayd,° *pleased*
The drunken lampe downe in the oyle did steepe,
And set her by to watch, and set her by to weepe.

48

Earely the morrow next, before that day
His joyous face did to the world reveale,
They both uprose and tooke their readie way
Unto the Church, their prayers to appeale,° *say*
With great devotion, and with litle zeale:
For the faire Damzell from the holy herse° *ceremony*
Her love-sicke hart to other thoughts did steale;
And that old Dame said many an idle verse,
Out of her daughters hart fond fancies to reverse.

49

Returnéd home, the royall Infant[3] fell
Into her former fit; for why, no powre
Nor guidance of her selfe in her did dwell.
But th'aged Nurse her calling to her bowre,° *chamber*
Had gathered Rew, and Savine, and the flowre
Of Camphora, and Calamint, and Dill,
All which she in a earthen Pot did poure,
And to the brim with Colt wood did it fill,
And many drops of milke and bloud through it did spill.[4]

50

Then taking thrise three haires from off her head,
Them trebly breaded° in a threefold lace, *braided*
And round about the pots mouth, bound the thread,
And after having whisperéd a space
Certaine sad words, with hollow voice and bace,

3. I.e., noble maiden, princess.
4. These herbs were thought to cool love; milk and blood propitiate Hecate, patroness of black magic. Glauce's procedures suggest English witchcraft as well as ancient magic ritual.

She to the virgin said, thrise said she it;
"Come daughter come, come; spit upon my face,
Spit thrise upon me, thrise upon me spit;
Th'uneven number for this businesse is most fit."

51

That sayd, her round about she from her turnd,
She turnéd her contrarie to the Sunne,
Thrise she her turnd contrary, and returnd,
All contrary, for she the right did shunne,
And ever what she did, was streight° undonne. *at once*
So thought she to undoe her daughters[5] love:
But love, that is in gentle brest begonne,
No idle charmes so lightly may remove,
That well can witnesse, who by triall it does prove.° *test*

52

Ne ought it mote the noble Mayd avayle,
Ne slake the furie of her cruell flame,
But that she still did waste, and still did wayle,
That through long languour, and hart-burning brame° *longing*
She shortly like a pynéd° ghost became, *wasted*
Which long hath waited by the Stygian strond.[6]
That when old Glauce saw, for feare least blame
Of her miscarriage° should in her be fond, *failure*
She wist not how t'amend, nor how it to withstond.

Canto III

Merlin bewrayes° to Britomart, *reveals*
the state of Artegall.
And shewes the famous Progeny
which from them springen shall.

1

Most sacred fire, that burnest mightily
In living brests, ykindled first above,
Emongst th'eternall spheres and lamping° sky, *resplendent*
And thence pourd into men, which men call Love;
Not that same, which doth base affections move
In brutish minds, and filthy lust inflame,
But that sweet fit, that doth true beautie love,
And choseth vertue for his dearest Dame,
Whence spring all noble deeds and never dying fame.[1]

5. I.e., her ward's.
6. I.e., who still awaits passage on Charon's ferry across the Styx to Hades.
1. In his *Fowre Hymnes*, Spenser develops this distinction between lust and that love for "true beauty" and "vertue." The Book of Chastity does not, though, disparage sexuality per se.

2

Well did Antiquitie a God thee deeme,
That over mortall minds hast so great might,
To order them, as best to thee doth seeme,
And all their actions to direct aright;
The fatall° purpose of divine foresight, *fated*
Thou doest effect in destinéd descents,° *lineages*
Through deepe impression of thy secret might,
And stirredst up th'Heroes high intents,
Which the late world admyres for wondrous moniments.° *memorials*

3

But thy dread darts in none doe triumph more,
Ne braver° proofe in any, of thy powre *finer*
Shew'dst thou, then in this royall Maid of yore,
Making her seeke an unknowne Paramoure,
From the worlds end, through many a bitter stowre:° *encounter*
From whose two loynes thou afterwards did rayse
Most famous fruits of matrimoniall bowre,
Which through the earth have spred their living prayse,
That fame in trompe of gold eternally displayes.

4

Begin then, O my dearest sacred Dame,[2]
Daughter of Phoebus and of Memorie,
That doest ennoble with immortall name
The warlike Worthies, from antiquitie,
In thy great volume of Eternitie:
Begin, O Clio, and recount from hence
My glorious Soveraines goodly auncestrie,
Till that by dew degrees and long protense,° *extension*
Thou have it lastly brought unto her Excellence.

5

Full many wayes within her troubled mind,
Old Glauce cast,° to cure this Ladies griefe: *considered*
Full many waies she sought, but none could find,
Nor herbes, nor charmes, nor counsell, that is chiefe
And choisest med'cine for sicke harts reliefe:
For thy great care she tooke,[3] and greater feare,
Least that it should her turne to foule repriefe,° *reproof*
And sore reproch, when so her father deare
Should of his dearest daughters hard misfortune heare.

2. I.e., Clio, muse of history. The nine "Worthies" were Hector, Alexander, Julius Caesar; Joshua, Daniel, Judas Maccabaeus; Arthur, Charlemagne, and Godfrey of Boulogne.
3. I.e., therefore she was much troubled.

6

At last she her avisd,° that he, which made *recalled*
That mirrhour, wherein the sicke Damosell
So straungely vewéd her straunge lovers shade,
To weet, the learnéd Merlin,[4] well could tell,
Under what coast° of heaven the man did dwell, *region*
And by what meanes his love might best be wrought:
For though beyond the Africk Ismaell,[5]
Or th'Indian Peru he were, she thought
Him forth through infinite endevour to have sought.

7

Forthwith themselves disguising both in straunge
And base attyre, that none might them bewray,
To Maridunum, that is now by chaunge
Of name Cayr-Merdin[6] cald, they tooke their way:
There the wise Merlin whylome wont (they say)
To make his wonne,° low underneath the ground, *dwelling*
In a deepe delve,° farre from the vew of day, *den*
That of no living wight he mote be found,
When so he counseld with his sprights encompast round.

8

And if thou ever happen that same way
To travell, goe to see that dreadfull place:
It is an hideous hollow cave (they say)
Under a rocke that lyes a little space
From the swift Barry, tombling downe apace,
Emongst the woodie hilles of Dynevowre:
But dare thou not, I charge, in any cace,
To enter into that same balefull Bowre,° *cavern*
For fear the cruell Feends should thee unwares devowre.

9

But standing high aloft, low lay thine eare,
And there such ghastly noise of yron chaines,
And brasen Caudrons thou shalt rombling heare,
Which thousand sprights with long enduring paines
Do tosse,° that it will stonne thy feeble braines, *stir up*
And oftentimes great grones, and grievous stounds,° *outcries*

4. For Merlin and his prophecies, Spenser used Geoffrey's *Historia* and Holinshed's *Chronicles*, as well as Malory's *Morte d'Arthur* and Camden's *Britanniae*. Geoffrey combines invention and legend with material from histories such as Bede's *Ecclesiastical History* (731) and William of Malmesbury's history of English kings (ca. 1125). The design of this canto follows Ariosto's story of Bradamante's visit to Merlin's tomb, where she learns about the future (*Orlando Furioso* 3).
5. The African territories held by the Saracens, thought to be descendants of Ishmael.
6. I.e., Carmarthen, in Wales; Merlin's birthplace, according to Geoffrey (6.17). Dynevor Castle, nearby, was the seat of the princes of South Wales.

When too huge toile and labour them constraines:
And oftentimes loud strokes, and ringing sounds
From under that deepe Rocke most horribly rebounds.

10

The cause some say is this: A litle while
Before that Merlin dyde, he did intend,
A brasen wall in compas to compile° *build*
About Cairmardin, and did it commend° *command*
Unto these Sprights, to bring to perfect end.
During which worke the Ladie of the Lake,[7]
Whom long he loved, for him in hast did send,
Who thereby forst his workemen to forsake,
Them bound till his returne, their labour not to slake.° *slacken*

11

In the meane time through that false Ladies traine,° *trickery*
He was surprisd, and buried under beare,° *tomb*
Ne ever to his worke returnd againe:
Nath'lesse those feends may not their worke forbeare,
So greatly his commaundément they feare,
But there doe toyle and travell day and night,
Untill that brasen wall they up doe reare:° *erect*
For Merlin had in Magicke more insight,
Then ever him before or after living wight.

12

For he by words could call out of the sky
Both Sunne and Moone, and make them him obay:
The land to sea, and sea to maineland dry,
And darkesome night he eke could turne to day:
Huge hostes of men he could alone dismay,
And hostes of men of meanest things could frame,
When so him list his enimies to fray.° *terrify*
That to this day for terror of his fame,
The feends do quake, when any him to them does name.

13

And sooth,° men say that he was not the sonne *truly*
Of mortall Syre, or other living wight,
But wondrously begotten, and begonne
By false illusion of a guilefull Spright,
On a faire Ladie Nonne, that whilome hight
Matilda, daughter to Pubidius,
Who was the Lord of Mathravall by right,

7. I.e., Nimue; see Malory's *Morte d'Arthur* 4.1.

And coosen° unto king Ambrosius.[8] *kinsman*
Whence he indued° was with skill so marvellous. *endowed*

14

They here ariving, staid a while without,
Ne durst adventure rashly in to wend,° *go*
But of their first intent gan make new dout
For dread of daunger, which it might portend:
Untill the hardie° Mayd (with love to frend) *bold*
First entering, the dreadfull Mage° there found *magician*
Deepe busiéd bout worke of wondrous end,
And writing strange characters in the ground,
With which the stubborn feends he to his service bound.

15

He nought was movéd at their entrance bold:
For of their comming well he wist afore,
Yet list them bid their businesse to unfold,
As if ought in this world in secret store
Were from him hidden, or unknowne of yore.
Then Glauce thus, "Let not it thee offend,
That we thus rashly through thy darkesome dore,
Unwares° have prest: for either fatall end,[9] *suddenly*
Or other mightie cause us two did hither send."

16

He bad tell on; And then she thus began:
"Now have three Moones with borrowed brothers light,
Thrice shinéd faire, and thrice seemed dim and wan,
Sith° a sore evill, which this virgin bright *since*
Tormenteth, and doth plonge in dolefull plight,
First rooting tooke; but what thing it mote bee,
Or whence it sprong, I cannot read aright:
But this I read, that but if[1] remedee
Thou her afford, full shortly I her dead shall see."

17

Therewith th'Enchaunter softly gan to smyle
At her smooth speeches, weeting inly well,
That she to him dissembled womanish guyle,
And to her said, "Beldame, by that ye tell,
More need of leach-craft° hath your Damozell, *medicine*
Then of my skill: who helpe may have elsewhere,
In vaine seekes wonders out of Magicke spell."

8. Matraval was a town in Montgomeryshire, Wales; but Geoffrey gives no such names, and identifies Merlin's sire only as an "incubus daemon" (6.18). This is also Ariosto's version (*Orlando Furioso* 33.9).
9. I.e., a purpose ordained by fate.
1. I.e., unless.

Th'old woman wox half blanck,[2] those words to heare;
And yet was loth to let her purpose plaine appeare.

18

And to him said, "If any leaches skill,
Or other learnéd meanes could have redrest° *cured*
This my deare daughters deepe engraffféd° ill, *implanted*
Certes I should be loth thee to molest:
But this sad evill, which doth her infest,
Doth course of naturall cause farre exceed,
And houséd is within her hollow brest,
That either seemes some curséd witches deed,
Or evill spright, that in her doth such torment breed."

19

The wisard could no lenger beare her bord,° *talk*
But brusting° forth in laughter, to her sayd; *bursting*
"Glauce, what needs this colourable° word, *deceptive*
To cloke the cause, that hath it selfe bewrayd?
Ne ye faire Britomartis, thus arayd,
More hidden are, then Sunne in cloudy vele;
Whom thy good fortune, having fate obayd,
Hath hither brought, for succour to appele:
The which the powres to thee are pleaséd to revele."

20

The doubtfull° Mayd, seeing her selfe descryde, *apprehensive*
Was all abasht, and her pure yvory
Into a cleare Carnation suddeine dyde;
As faire Aurora rising hastily,
Doth by her blushing tell, that she did lye
All night in old Tithonus frosen bed,
Whereof she seemes ashaméd inwardly.
But her old Nourse was nought dishartered,
But vauntage made of that, which Merlin had ared.° *said*

21

And sayd, "Sith then thou knowest all our griefe,
(For what doest not thou know?) of grace I pray,
Pitty our plaint, and yield us meet° reliefe." *suitable*
With that the Prophet still awhile did stay,
And then his spirite thus gan forth display;° *show*
"Most noble Virgin, that by fatall lore[3]
Hast learned to love, let no whit thee dismay
The hard begin, that meets thee in the dore,
And with sharpe fits thy tender hart oppresseth sore.

2. I.e., became somewhat disconcerted.
3. I.e., fated knowledge.

22

"For so must all things excellent begin,
And eke enrooted deepe must be that Tree,
Whose big embodied braunches shall not lin,° *cease*
Till they to heavens hight forth stretchéd bee.
For from thy wombe a famous Progenie
Shall spring, out of the auncient Trojan blood,[4]
Which shall revive the sleeping memorie
Of those same antique Peres° the heavens brood, *champions*
Which Greeke and Asian rivers stainéd with their blood.

23

"Renowméd kings, and sacred Emperours,
Thy fruitfull Ofspring, shall from thee descend;
Brave Captaines, and most mighty warriours,
That shall their conquests through all lands extend,
And their decayéd kingdomes shall amend:° *restore*
The feeble Britons, broken with long warre,
They shall upreare, and mightily defend
Against their forrein foe, that comes from farre,
Till universall peace compound° all civill jarre. *settle*

24

"It was not, Britomart, thy wandring eye,
Glauncing unwares in charméd looking glas,
But the streight° course of heavenly destiny, *strict*
Led with eternall providence, that has
Guided thy glaunce, to bring his will to pas:
Ne is thy fate, ne is thy fortune ill,
To love the prowest° knight, that ever was. *bravest*
Therefore submit thy wayes unto his will,
And do by all dew meanes thy destiny fulfill."

25

"But read,"° said Glauce, "thou Magitian *tell*
What meanes shall she out seeke, or what wayes take?
How shall she know, how shall she find the man?
Or what needs her to toyle, sith fates can make
Way for themselves, their purpose to partake?"° *accomplish*
Then Merlin thus; "Indeed the fates are firme,
And may not shrinck, though all the world do shake:
Yet ought mens good endevours them confirme,
And guide the heavenly causes to their constant terme.[5]

4. Belief that Britons (Celtic tribes in Britain before the Anglo-Saxon invasions) were descended, through Brute, from Aeneas echoes regularly in the age's literature. But doubt was growing (the debate was politicized as skeptics affirmed a Germanic heritage with a larger role for parliaments). Spenser accepts the legend in II.x.5–13 and III.ix. 38–51 but the prose *View* rejects it.

5. I.e., fixed outcome. Here and in stanzas 21–22, Merlin assumes that virtuous men and women actively cooperate with Providence. Britomart's love for Arthegall, demanding and formative, makes part of her divinely appointed destiny.

26

"The man whom heavens have ordaynd to bee
The spouse of Britomart, is Arthegall.[6]
He wonneth° in the land of Fayeree, *dwells*
Yet is no Fary borne, ne sib° at all *related*
To Elfes, but sprong of seed terrestriall,
And whilome by false Faries stolne away,
Whiles yet in infant cradle he did crall;° *crawl*
Ne other to himselfe is knowne this day,
But that he by an Elfe was gotten° of a Fay. *begot*

27

"But sooth he is the sonne of Gorlois,
And brother unto Cador Cornish king,[7]
And for his warlike feates renowméd is,
From where the day out of the sea doth spring,
Untill the closure° of the Evening. *limit*
From thence, him firmely bound with faithfull band,° *bond*
To this his native soyle thou backe shalt bring,
Strongly to aide his countrey, to withstand
The powre of forrein Paynims,° which invade thy land. *pagans*

28

"Great aid thereto his mighty puissaunce,
And dreaded name shall give in that sad day:
Where also proofe of thy prow° valiaunce *courageous*
Thou then shalt make, t'increase thy lovers pray.
Long time ye both in armes shall beare great sway,
Till thy wombes burden thee from them do call,
And his last fate him from thee take away,
Too rathe° cut off by practise criminall *soon*
Of secret foes, that him shall make in mischiefe° fall. *misfortune*

29

"With thee yet shall he leave for memory
Of his late puissaunce, his Image dead,[8]
That living him in all activity
To thee shall represent. He from the head
Of his coosin Constantius without dread
Shall take the crowne, that was his fathers right,
And there with crowne himselfe in th'others stead:[9]

6. Stanzas 26–28 prepare for the alignment of the Tudors with Britain's ancient rulers that culminates at stanza 49 when Arthegall is connected with Arthur, son of Uther Pendragon and Igerne (wife of Gorlois).
7. According to Geoffrey (9.1, 5), Cador helped Arthur fight the Saxons.
8. I.e., Arthegall's son, the image of his deceased father.
9. Constantine, son of Cador, succeeded Arthur; soon he was killed by his nephew Conan (*Historia* 11.4–5). From this point to the end of the canto, Spenser depends heavily on Geoffrey and Holinshed, diverging occasionally to take account of other chroniclers; now and then he departs altogether from these sources (e.g., Conan's wars with the Mercians in stanza 30, the Saxons' defeat by Careticus in stanza 33, and the manner of Pellite's death in stanza 36).

Then shall he issew forth with dreadfull might,
Against his Saxon foes in bloudy field to fight.

30

"Like as a Lyon, that in drowsie cave
Hath long time slept, himselfe so shall he shake,
And comming forth, shall spred his banner brave
Over the troubled South, that it shall make
The warlike Mertians[1] for feare to quake:
Thrise shall he fight with them, and twise shall win,
But the third time shall faire accordaunce° make: *agreement*
And if he then with victorie can lin,° *cease*
He shall his dayes with peace bring to his earthly In.° *dwelling*

31

"His sonne, hight Vortipore, shall him succeede
In kingdome, but not in felicity;
Yet shall he long time warre with happy speed,° *success*
And with great honour many battels try:° *undertake*
But at the last to th'importunity
Of froward° fortune shall be forst to yield. *perverse*
But his sonne Malgo shall full mightily
Avenge his fathers losse, with speare and shield,
And his proud foes discomfit in victorious field.

32

"Behold the man, and tell me Britomart,
If ay° more goodly creature thou didst see; *ever*
How like a Gyaunt in each manly part
Beares he himselfe with portly° majestee, *dignified*
That one of th'old Heroés seemes to bee:
He the six Islands,[2] comprovinciall° *joined*
In auncient times unto great Britainee,
Shall to the same reduce,° and to him call *restore*
Their sundry kings to do their homage severall.° *diverse*

33

"All which his sonne Careticus awhile
Shall well defend, and Saxons powre suppresse,
Untill a straunger king from unknowne soyle
Arriving, him with multitude oppresse;
Great Gormond,[3] having with huge mightinesse
Ireland subdewd, and therein fixt his throne,

1. An Anglian tribe that established the kingdom of Mercia, in south-central England, in the sixth century.
2. I.e., Iceland, Norway, the Orkneys, Ireland, Gotland, and Dacia (Denmark).
3. In making Gormond a Norwegian king, Spenser follows the *History of Ireland* by Richard Stanyhurst and Edward Campion (included by Holinshed in his *Chronicles*); Geoffrey (11.8) calls him "king of the Africans."

Like a swift Otter, fell° through emptinesse, *fierce*
Shall overswim the sea with many one
Of his Norveyses,° to assist the Britons fone.° *Norwegians / foes*

34

"He in his furie all shall overrunne,
And holy Church with faithlesse hands deface,
That thy sad people utterly fordonne,° *ruined*
Shall to the utmost mountaines fly apace:
Was never so great wast° in any place, *destruction*
Nor so fowle outrage doen by living men:
For all thy Cities they shall sacke and race,° *raze*
And the greene grasse, that groweth, they shall bren,° *burn*
That even the wild beast shall dy in starvéd den.

35

"Whiles thus thy Britons do in languour° pine, *sorrow*
Proud Etheldred[4] shall from the North arise,
Serving th' ambitious will of Augustine,
And passing Dee with hardy enterprise,
Shall backe repulse the valiaunt Brockwell twise,
And Bangor with massacred Martyrs fill;
But the third time shall rew his foolhardise:° *folly*
For Cadwan pittying his peoples ill,
Shall stoutly him defeat, and thousand Saxons kill.

36

"But after him, Cadwallin mightily
On his sonne Edwin all those wrongs shall wreake;° *avenge*
Ne shall availe the wicked sorcery
Of false Pellite, his purposes to breake,
But him shall slay, and on a gallowes bleake
Shall give th'enchaunter his unhappy hire,° *reward*
Then shall the Britons, late dismayd and weake,
From their long vassalage gin to respire,° *recover*
And on their Paynim foes avenge their rankled° ire. *embittered*

37

"Ne shall he yet his wrath so mitigate,
Till both the sonnes of Edwin he have slaine,
Offricke and Osricke, twinnes unfortunate,
Both slaine in battell upon Layburne plaine,
Together with the king of Louthiane,
Hight Adin, and the king of Orkeny
Both joynt partakers of their fatall° paine: *fated*

4. In stanzas 35–39, Spenser alters Geoffrey's names and events to conform with other Welsh and English sources.

But Penda, fearefull of like desteny,
Shall yield him selfe his liegeman, and sweare fealty.

38

"Him shall he make his fatall Instrument,
T'afflict the other Saxons unsubdewd;
He marching forth with fury insolent
Against the good king Oswald, who indewd° *invested*
With heavenly powre, and by Angels reskewd,
All holding crosses in their hands on hye,
Shall him defeate withouten bloud imbrewd:° *spilt*
Of which, that field for endlesse memory,
Shall Hevenfield be cald to all posterity.

39

"Where at Cadwallin wroth, shall forth issew,
And an huge hoste into Northumber lead,
With which he godly Oswald shall subdew,
And crowne with martyrdome his sacred head.
Whose brother Oswin, daunted with like dread,
With price of silver shall his kingdome buy,° *ransom*
And Penda, seeking him adowne to tread,
Shall tread adowne, and do him fowly dye,[5]
But shall with gifts his Lord Cadwallin pacify.

40

"Then shall Cadwallin dye, and then the raine
Of Britons eke with him attonce° shall dye; *forthwith*
Ne shall the good Cadwallader with paine,
Or powre, be hable it to remedy,
When the full time prefixt by destiny.
Shalbe expird of Britons regiment.° *rule*
For heaven it selfe shall their successe envy,
And them with plagues and murrins° pestilent *diseases*
Consume, till all their warlike puissaunce be spent.

41

"Yet after all these sorrowes, and huge hills
Of dying people, during eight yeares space,
Cadwallader not yielding to his ills,
From Armoricke,[6] where long in wretched cace° *state*
He lived, returning[7] to his native place,
Shalbe by vision staid from his intent:
For th'heavens have decreéd, to displace

5. I.e., and Oswin shall defeat Penda (who sought to defeat Oswin) and put him miserably to death.
6. The old name for Brittany, northwestern France.
7. I.e., expecting to return.

The Britons, for their sinnes dew punishment,
And to the Saxons over-give° their government. *give up*

42

"Then woe, and woe, and everlasting woe,
Be to the Briton babe, that shalbe borne,
To live in thraldome of° his fathers foe; *to*
Late King, now captive, late Lord, now forlorne,
The worlds reproch, the cruell victors scorne,
Banisht from Princely bowre° to wastfull° wood: *chamber / desolate*
O who shall helpe me to lament, and mourne
The royall seed, the antique Trojan blood,
Whose Empire lenger here, then ever any stood."[8]

43

The Damzell was full deepe empassionéd,° *moved*
Both for his griefe, and for her peoples sake,
Whose future woes so plaine he fashionéd,
And sighing sore, at length him thus bespake,
"Ah but will heavens fury never slake,° *slacken*
Nor vengeaunce huge relent it selfe at last?
Will not long misery late° mercy make, *at length*
But shall their name for ever be defast,° *destroyed*
And quite from of the earth their memory be rast?° *erased*

44

"Nay but the terme," said he, "is limited,
That in this thraldome Britons shall abide,
And the just revolution[9] measuréd,
That they as Straungers shalbe notified.° *known*
For twise foure hundreth yeares shalbe supplide,
Ere they to former rule restored shalbee,[1]
And their importune° fates all satisfide: *grievous*
Yet during this their most obscuritee,
Their beames shall oft breake forth, that men them faire may see.

45

"For Rhodoricke,[2] whose surname shalbe Great,
Shall of him selfe a brave ensample shew,
That Saxon kings his friendship shall intreat:
And Howell Dha shall goodly well indew
The salvage minds with skill of just and trew;
Then Griffyth Conan also shall up reare

8. Reckoning from the arrival of Brute, supposedly in 1132 B.C.E., to the death of Cadwallader, ca. 690.
9. I.e., exact cycle.
1. I.e., with the reign of Henry VII, who came to the throne in 1485, almost exactly eight hundred years after Cadwallader's death.
2. These Welsh rulers reigned within the period from 843 to 1136. C.E.

His dreaded head, and the old sparkes renew
Of native courage, that his foes shall feare,
Least backe againe the kingdome he from them should beare.° *take*

46

"Ne shall the Saxons selves all peaceably
Enjoy the crowne, which they from Britons wonne
First ill, and after ruléd wickedly:
For ere two hundred yeares be full outronne,
There shall a Raven[3] far from rising Sunne,
With his wide wings upon them fiercely fly,
And bid his faithlesse chickens overrone
The fruitfull plaines, and with fell cruelty,
In their avenge, tread downe the victours surquedry.° *presumption*

47

"Yet shall a third both these, and thine subdew;
There shall a Lyon[4] from the sea-bord wood
Of Neustria come roring, with a crew
Of hungry whelpes, his battailous° bold brood, *warlike*
Whose clawes were newly dipt in cruddy° blood, *clotted*
That from the Daniske Tyrants head shall rend
Th'usurpéd crowne, as if that he were wood,° *mad*
And the spoile of the countrey conqueréd
Emongst his young ones shall divide with bountyhed.° *generosity*

48

"Tho when the terme is full accomplishid,
There shall a sparke of fire,[5] which hath longwhile
Bene in his ashes rakéd up, and hid,
Be freshly kindled in the fruitfull Ile
Of Mona, where it lurkéd in exile;
Which shall breake forth into bright burning flame,
And reach into the house, that beares the stile° *title*
Of royall majesty and soveraigne name;° *reputation*
So shall the Briton bloud their crowne againe reclame.

49

"Thenceforth eternall union shall be made
Betweene the nations different afore,
And sacred Peace shall lovingly perswade
The warlike minds, to learne her goodly lore,° *doctrine*
And civile armes to exercise no more:

3. The (heathen) Danes, who first invaded England in 787 C.E.
4. William I of Normandy.
5. Henry VII was born in Anglesey (Mona), the last British territory possessed by the Welsh prince Llewelyn ap Griffith under the terms of his treaty with Edward I in 1283.

Then shall a royall virgin[6] raine, which shall
Stretch her white rod over the Belgicke shore,
And the great Castle smite so sore with all,
That it shall make him shake, and shortly learne to fall.

50

"But yet the end is not." There Merlin stayd,° *ceased*
As° overcomen of the spirites powre, *as if*
Or other ghastly spectacle dismayd,
That secretly he saw, yet note discoure:[7]
Which suddein fit, and halfe extatick stoure° *paroxysm*
When the two fearefull women saw, they grew
Greatly confuséd in behavioure;
At last the fury° past, to former hew° *seizure / appearance*
Hee turnd againe, and chearefull looks as earst° did shew. *before*

51

Then, when them selves they well instructed had
Of all, that needed them to be inquird,
They both conceiving hope of comfort glad,
With lighter hearts unto their home retird;
Where they in secret counsell close conspird,
How to effect so hard an enterprize,
And to possesse° the purpose they desird: *achieve*
Now this, now that twixt them they did devise,
And diverse plots did frame, to maske in strange disguise.

52

At last the Nourse in her foolhardy wit
Conceived a bold devise,° and thus bespake; *plan*
"Daughter, I deeme that counsell aye most fit,
That of the time doth dew advauntage take;
Ye see that good king Uther now doth make
Strong warre upon the Paynim brethren, hight
Octa and Oza, whom he lately brake
Beside Cayr Verolame, in victorious fight,
That now all Britanie doth burne in armés bright.[8]

53

"That therefore nought our passage may empeach,° *hinder*
Let us in feignéd armes our selves disguize,
And our weake hands (whom need new strength shall teach)

6. Queen Elizabeth, whose navy turned back the galleons (or "great castles") of the Spanish Armada in 1588, and whose troops (from 1585 onward) were actively engaged in the Low Countries against those of Spain (Castile).
7. I.e., would not reveal.
8. These events, described in Geoffrey (8.23), would have taken place about 470–80 C.E., approximately the supposed time of Arthur.

The dreadfull speare and shield to exercize:
Ne certes daughter that same warlike wize° *manner*
I weene, would you misseeme;° for ye bene tall, *not be fitting*
And large of limbe, t'atchieve an hard emprize,
Ne ought ye want,° but skill, which practize small *lack*
Will bring, and shortly make you a mayd Martiall.

54

"And sooth, it ought your courage much inflame,
To heare so often, in that royall hous,
From whence to none inferiour ye came,
Bards tell of many women valorous
Which have full many feats adventurous
Performd, in paragone° of proudest men: *emulation*
The bold Bunduca, whose victorious
Exploits made Rome to quake, stout Guendolen,
Renowméd Martia, and redoubted Emmilen.[9]

55

"And that, which more than all the rest may sway,° *move*
Late dayes ensample, which these eyes beheld,
In the last field before Menevia[1]
Which Uther with those forrein Pagans held,
I saw a Saxon Virgin,[2] the which feld
Great Ulfin thrise upon the bloudy plaine,
And had not Carados her hand withheld
From rash revenge, she had him surely slaine,
Yet Carados himselfe from her escapt with paine."° *difficulty*

56

"Ah read," quoth Britomart, "how is she hight?"
"Faire Angela," quoth she, "men do her call,
No whit lesse faire, then terrible in fight:
She hath the leading of a Martiall
And mighty people, dreaded more then all
The other Saxons, which do for her sake
And love, themselves of her name Angles call.
Therefore faire Infant her ensample make
Unto thy selfe, and equall courage to thee take."

9. Boadicea, queen of the Iceni in southeastern England, led a revolt against the Romans in 61 C.E.; Gwendolen, daughter of Corineus, slew her unfaithful husband in battle and ruled Cornwall for fifteen years; Marcia, wife of the British king Guithelin, was renowned for learning and statecraft; "Emmilen" is perhaps Charlemagne's daughter, but Spenser also gives the name to the mother of Sir Tristram (VI.ii. 29).
1. St. Davids; cf. Geoffrey 8.16.
2. Angela, identified with the Saxon queen for whom England was named; Spenser invented this story or used some now lost source.

57

Her harty° words so deepe into the mynd — *spirited*
Of the young Damzell sunke, that great desire
Of warlike armes in her forthwith they tynd,° — *kindled*
And generous stout courage did inspire,
That she resolved, unweeting° to her Sire, — *unknown*
Advent'rous knighthood on her selfe to don,
And counseld with her Nourse, her Maides attire
To turne into a massy habergeon,° — *coat of mail*
And bad her all things put in readinesse anon.

58

Th'old woman nought, that needed, did omit;
But all things did conveniently purvay:° — *provide*
It fortunéd (so time their turne did fit)[3]
A band of Britons ryding on forray° — *a raid*
Few dayes before, had gotten a great pray° — *booty*
Of Saxon goods, emongst the which was seene
A goodly Armour, and full rich aray,° — *equipment*
Which longed to Angela, the Saxon Queene,
All fretted° round with gold, and goodly well beseene. — *adorned*

59

The same, with all the other ornaments,
King Ryence causéd to be hangéd hy
In his chiefe Church, for endlesse moniments° — *memorials*
Of his successe and gladfull victory:
Of which her selfe avising° readily, — *calling to mind*
In th'evening late old Glauce thither led
Faire Britomart, and that same Armory° — *armor*
Downe taking, her therein appareléd,
Well as she might, and with brave bauldrick° garnishéd — *shoulder belt*

60

Beside those armes there stood a mighty speare,
Which Bladud[4] made by Magick art of yore,
And usd the same in battell aye to beare;
Sith which it had bin here preserved in store,
For his great vertues° provéd long afore: — *powers*
For never wight so fast in sell° could sit, — *saddle*
But him perforce unto the ground it bore:
Both speare she tooke, and shield, which hong by it:
Both speare and shield of great powre, for her purpose fit.

3. I.e., events fell out suitably for their needs
4. A British king renowned for his magic. Britomart's arms combine Saxon and Celtic power.

61

Thus when she had the virgin all arayd,
  Another harnesse,° which did hang thereby, — *set of armor*
  About her selfe she dight, that the young Mayd
  She might in equall armes accompany,
  And as her Squire attend her carefully:
  Tho to their ready Steeds they clombe full light,° — *easily*
  And through back wayes, that none might them espy,
  Covered with secret cloud of silent night,
Themselves they forth convayd, and passéd forward right.

62

Ne rested they, till that to Faery lond
  They came, as Merlin them directed late:
  Where meeting with this Redcrosse knight, she fond
  Of diverse things discourses to dilate,° — *enlarge upon*
  But most of Arthegall, and his estate.° — *condition*
  At last their wayes so fell, that they mote part:
  Then each to other well affectionate,° — *disposed*
  Friendship professéd with unfainéd hart,
The Redcrosse knight diverst, but forth° rode Britomart. — *forward*

Canto IV

Bold Marinell of Britomart,
  Is throwne on the Rich strond:° — *shore*
Faire Florimell of Arthur is
  Long followed, but not fond.° — *found*

1

Where is the Antique glory now become,° — *gone*
  That whilome wont in women to appeare?
  Where be the brave atchievements doen by some?
  Where be the battels, where the shield and speare,
  And all the conquests, which them high did reare,
  That matter made for famous Poets verse,
  And boastfull men so oft abasht to heare?
  Bene they all dead, and laid in dolefull herse?
Or doen they onely sleepe, and shall againe reverse?° — *return*

2

If they be dead, then woe is me therefore:
  But if they sleepe, O let them soone awake:
  For all too long I burne with envy° sore, — *longing*
  To heare the warlike feates, which Homere spake
  Of bold Penthesilee,[1] which made a lake

1. Homer does not mention the Amazon queen Penthesilea, but she appears briefly in *Aeneid* 1.490–95; on Camilla and Orsilochus, see 11.690–98. The Israelite heroine Jaël killed Sisera, a patriotic murder engineered and celebrated by the judge Deborah (Judges 4).

Of Greekish bloud so oft in Trojan plaine;
But when I read, how stout Debora strake
Proud Sisera, and how Camill' hath slaine
The huge Orsilochus, I swell with great disdaine.° *indignation*

3

Yet these, and all that else had puissaunce,
Cannot with noble Britomart compare,
Aswell for glory of great valiaunce,° *valor*
As for pure chastitie and vertue rare,
That all her goodly deeds do well declare.
Well worthy stock, from which the branches sprong,
That in late yeares so faire a blossome bare,
As thee, O Queene, the matter° of my song, *theme*
Whose lignage from this Lady I derive along.° *throughout*

4

Who when through speaches with the Redcrosse knight,
She learnéd had th'estate of Arthegall,
And in each point her selfe informd aright,
A friendly league of love perpetuall
She with him bound, and Congé° tooke withall. *leave*
Then he forth on his journey did proceede,
To seeke adventures, which mote him befall,
And win him worship° through his warlike deed, *renown*
Which alwayes of his paines he made the chiefest meed.° *reward*

5

But Britomart kept on her former course,
Ne ever dofte° her armes, but all the way *took off*
Grew pensive through that amorous discourse,
By which the Redcrosse knight did earst display° *set forth*
Her lovers shape, and chevalrous aray;
A thousand thoughts she fashioned in her mind,
And in her feigning fancie did pourtray
Him such, as fittest she for love could find,
Wise, warlike, personable, curteous, and kind.

6

With such selfe-pleasing thoughts her wound she fed,
And thought so to beguile° her grievous smart; *charm away*
But so her smart was much more grievous bred,
And the deepe wound more deepe engord her hart,
That nought but death her dolour mote depart.° *remove*
So forth she rode without repose or rest,
Searching all lands and each remotest part,
Following the guidance of her blinded guest,[2]
Till that to the sea-coast at length she her addrest.

2. I.e., Cupid, god of love.

7

There she alighted from her light-foot beast,
And sitting downe upon the rocky shore,
Bad her old Squire unlace her lofty creast;° *helmet*
Tho having vewd a while the surges hore,° *gray*
That gainst the craggy clifts did loudly rore,
And in their raging surquedry° disdaynd, *arrogance*
That the fast° earth affronted them so sore, *firm*
And their devouring covetize restraynd,
Thereat she sighéd deepe, and after thus complaynd.[3]

8

"Huge sea of sorrow, and tempestuous griefe,
Wherein my feeble barke° is tosséd long, *vessel*
Far from the hopéd haven of reliefe,
Why do thy cruell billowes beat so strong,
And thy moyst mountaines each on others throng,
Threatning to swallow up my fearefull life?
O do thy cruell wrath and spightfull wrong
At length allay, and stint° thy stormy strife, *cease*
Which in these troubled bowels raignes, and rageth rife.° *strongly*

9

"For else my feeble vessell crazd,° and crackt *weakened*
Through thy strong buffets and outrageous blowes,
Cannot endure, but needs it must be wrackt
On the rough rocks, or on the sandy shallowes,
The whiles that love it steres, and fortune rowes;
Love my lewd° Pilot hath a restlesse mind *unskillful*
And fortune Boteswaine no assurance° knowes, *certainty*
But saile withouten starres gainst tide and wind:
How can they other do, sith both are bold and blind?

10

"Thou God of winds, that raignest in the seas,
That raignest also in the Continent,° *land*
At last blow up some gentle gale of ease,
The which may bring my ship, ere it be rent,° *torn apart*
Unto the gladsome port of her intent:° *purpose*
Then when I shall my selfe in safety see,
A table° for eternall moniment *votive tablet*
Of thy great grace, and my great jeopardee,
Great Neptune, I avow to hallow unto thee."

3. The central conceit of Britomart's "complaint" (likening herself to a ship in a storm) appears often in Renaissance love lyrics, most famously in Petrarch's *Rime* 189 (cf. Wyatt's "My galley charged" and *Amoretti* 34). Cf. Clymène's lament in Ronsard's *Franciade*.

11

Then sighing softly sore, and inly deepe,
She shut up all her plaint in privy° griefe; *secret*
For her great courage° would not let her weepe, *spirit*
Till that old Glauce gan with sharpe repriefe,° *reproof*
Her to restraine, and give her good reliefe,
Through hope of those, which Merlin had her told
Should of her name and nation be chiefe,
And fetch their being from the sacred mould° *form*
Of her immortall wombe, to be in heaven enrold.

12

Thus as she her recomforted, she spyde,
Where farre away one all in armour bright,
With hastie gallop towards her did ryde,
Her dolour soone she ceast, and on her dight
Her Helmet, to her Courser mounting light:
Her former sorrow into suddein wrath,
Both coosen° passions of distroubled spright, *kindred*
Converting, forth she beates the dustie path;
Love and despight° attonce her courage kindled hath. *defiance*

13

As when a foggy mist hath overcast
The face of heaven, and the cleare aire engrost,° *thickened*
The world in darkenesse dwels, till that at last
The watry Southwinde from the seabord cost
Upblowing, doth disperse the vapour lo'st,° *released*
And poures it selfe forth in a stormy showre;
So the faire Britomart having disclo'st
Her clowdy care into a wrathfull stowre,[4]
The mist of griefe dissolved, did into vengeance powre.

14

Eftsoonse her goodly shield addressing° faire, *adjusting*
That mortall speare she in her hand did take,
And unto battell did her selfe prepaire
The knight approching, sternely her bespake;
"Sir knight, that doest thy voyage rashly make
By this forbidden way in my despight,[5]
Ne doest by others death ensample take,
I read° thee soone retyre, whiles thou hast might, *advise*
Least afterwards it be too late to take thy flight."

4. I.e., having relieved her gloomy despondency by an outburst of anger.
5. I.e., in scorn of me.

15

Ythrild° with deepe disdaine of his proud threat, *deeply moved*
She shortly thus: "Fly they, that need to fly;
Words fearen° babes. I meane not thee entreat *frighten*
To passe; but maugre° thee will passe or dy." *in spite of*
Ne lenger stayd for th'other to reply,
But with sharpe speare the rest made dearly° knowne, *resolutely*
Strongly the straunge knight ran, and sturdily,
Strooke her full on the brest, that made her downe
Decline her head, and touch her crouper with her crowne.[6]

16

But she againe° him in the shield did smite *in return*
With so fierce furie and great puissaunce,
That through his threesquare scuchin° percing quite, *shield*
And through his mayléd hauberque,° by mischaunce *coat of mail*
The wicked steele through his left side did glaunce;
Him so transfixéd she before her bore
Beyond his croupe, the length of all her launce,
Till sadly soucing° on the sandie shore, *falling*
He tombled on° an heape, and wallowd in his gore. *in*

17

Like as the sacred Oxe, that carelesse stands,
With gilden hornes, and flowry girlonds crownd,
Proud of his dying honor and deare bands,° *bonds*
Whiles th' altars fume with frankincense arownd,
All suddenly with mortall stroke astownd,° *stunned*
Doth groveling fall, and with his streaming gore
Distaines° the pillours, and the holy grownd, *stains*
And the faire flowres, that deckéd him afore;
So fell proud Marinell upon the pretious shore.

18

The martiall Mayd stayd not him to lament,
But forward rode, and kept her readie way
Along the strond, which as she over-went,° *traversed*
She saw bestrowéd all with rich aray
Of pearles and pretious stones of great assay,° *worth*
And all the gravell mixt with golden owre;° *ore*
Whereat she wondred much, but would not stay
For gold, or perles, or pretious stones an howre,
But them despiséd all; for° all was in her powre. *although*

6. I.e., bent her backward so that her head touched the leather strap behind the saddle.

19

Whiles thus he lay in deadly stonishment,° *swoon*
Tydings hereof came to his mothers eare;
His mother was the blacke-browd Cymoent,[7]
The daughter of great Nereus, which did beare
This warlike sonne unto an earthly peare,° *noble*
The famous Dumarin; who on a day
Finding the Nymph a sleepe in secret wheare,° *place*
As he by chaunce did wander that same way,
Was taken with her love, and by her closely lay.

20

There he this knight of her begot, whom borne
She of his father Marinell did name,[8]
And in a rocky cave as wight forlorne,
Long time she fostred up, till he became
A mightie man at armes, and mickle° fame *much*
Did get through great adventures by him donne:
For never man he suffred by that same
Rich strond to travell, whereas he did wonne,° *dwell*
But that he must do battell with the Sea-nymphes sonne.

21

An hundred knights of honorable name
He had subdewed, and them his vassals made,
That through all Farie lond his noble fame
Now blazéd° was, and feare did all invade,° *proclaimed / afflict*
That none durst passen through that perilous glade.
And to advaunce° his name and glorie more, *heighten*
Her Sea-god syre she dearely° did perswade;° *boldly / entreat*
T'endow her sonne with threasure and rich store,
Bove all the sonnes, that were of earthly wombes ybore.

22

The God did graunt his daughters deare demaund,
To doen° his Nephew in all riches flow; *make*
Eftsoones his heapéd waves he did commaund,
Out of their hollow bosome forth to throw
All the huge threasure, which the sea below
Had in his greedie gulfe devouréd deepe,
And him enrichéd through the overthrow
And wreckes of many wretches, which did weepe,
And often waile their wealth, which he from them did keepe.

7. Cymoent (from Greek, "wave") was one of fifty Nereids (sea nymphs). Her son's conception and her efforts to preserve him recall Thetis's futile attempt to make her son, Achilles, invulnerable (*Metamorphoses* 11.217–65; 13.162–70).
8. Like his parents' names (a sea nymph and a mortal peer named Dumarin, loose French for "of the ocean"), Marinell's name connects him to the sea. Guarding a rich "strond" (strand, or beach) he has wealth.

23

Shortly upon that shore there heapéd was,
Exceeding riches and all pretious things,
The spoyle of all the world, that it did pas
The wealth of th'East, and pompe of Persian kings;
Gold, amber, yvorie, perles, owches,° rings, *brooches*
And all that else was pretious and deare,° *valuable*
The sea unto him voluntary brings,
That shortly he a great Lord did appeare,
As was in all the lond of Faery, or elsewheare.

24

Thereto he was a doughtie dreaded knight,
Tryde often to the scath° of many deare,° *harm / dearly*
That none in equall armes him matchen might,
The which his mother seeing, gan to feare
Least his too haughtie hardines might reare° *cause*
Some hard mishap, in hazard of[9] his life:
For thy she oft him counseld to forbeare
The bloudie battell, and to stirre up strife,
But after all his warre, to rest his wearie knife.° *sword*

25

And for his more assurance,° she inquired *security*
One day of Proteus[1] by his mightie spell,° *magic charm*
(For Proteus was with prophecie inspired)
Her deare sonnes destinie to her to tell,
And the sad end of her sweet Marinell.
Who through foresight of his eternall skill,° *knowledge*
Bad her from womankind to keepe him well:
For of a woman he should have much ill,
A virgin strange and stout° him should dismay, or kill. *bold*

26

For thy she gave him warning every day,
The love of women not to entertaine;° *accept*
A lesson too too hard for living clay,
From love in course of nature to refraine:
Yet he his mothers lore did well retaine,
And ever from faire Ladies love did fly;
Yet many Ladies faire did oft complaine,
That they for love of him would algates° dy: *entirely*
Dy, who so list for him, he was loves enimy.

9. I.e., to endanger.
1. A sea god who could foretell the future and change his shape at will: cf. Ovid, *Metamorphoses* 11.249–56, and Homer, *Odyssey* 4.384ff.

27

But ah, who can deceive his destiny,
Or weene by warning to avoyd his fate?
That when he sleepes in most security,
And safest seemes, him soonest doth amate,° *dismay*
And findeth dew effect or soone or late.
So feeble is the powre of fleshly arme.
His mother bad him womens love to hate,
For she of womans force did feare no harme;
So weening to have armed him, she did quite disarme.

28

This was that woman, this that deadly wound,
That Proteus prophecide should him dismay,
The which his mother vainely° did expound, *wrongly*
To be hart-wounding love, which should assay° *assault*
To bring her sonne unto his last decay.
So tickle° be the termes of mortall state,° *uncertain / condition*
And full of subtile sophismes; which do play
With double senses, and with false debate,
T'approve° the unknowen purpose of eternall fate. *demonstrate*

29

Too true the famous Marinell it fownd,
Who through late triall, on that wealthy Strond
Inglorious now lies in senselesse swownd,
Through heavy° stroke of Britomartis hond. *grievous*
Which when his mother deare did understand,
And heavy tydings heard, whereas she playd
Amongst her watry sisters by a pond,
Gathering sweet daffadillyes, to have made
Gay girlonds, from the Sun their forheads faire to shade;

30

Eftsoones both flowres and girlonds farre away
She flong, and her faire deawy lockes yrent,° *tore*
To sorrow huge she turnd her former play,
And gamesom merth to grievous dreriment:
She threw her selfe downe on the Continent,° *ground*
Ne word did speake, but lay as in a swowne,
Whiles all her sisters did for her lament,
With yelling outcries, and with shrieking sowne;° *sound*
And every one did teare her girlond from her crowne.

31

Soone as she up out of her deadly fit° *swoon*
Arose, she bad her charet° to be brought, *chariot*
And all her sisters, that with her did sit,

Bad eke attonce their charets to be sought;
Tho full of bitter griefe and pensive thought,
She to her wagon clombe;° clombe all the rest, *mounted*
And forth together went, with sorrow fraught.
The waves obedient to their beheast,° *bidding*
Them yielded readie passage, and their rage surceast.

32

Great Neptune stood amazéd at their sight,
Whiles on his broad round backe they softly slid
And eke himselfe mournd at their mournfull plight,
Yet wist not what their wailing ment, yet did
For great compassion of their sorrow, bid
His mightie waters to them buxome° bee: *yielding*
Eftsoones the roaring billowes still abid,° *remained*
And all the griesly° Monsters of the See *horrible*
Stood gaping at their gate, and wondred them to see.

33

A teme of Dolphins raungéd in aray,
Drew the smooth charet of sad Cymoent;
They were all taught by Triton, to obay
To the long raynes, at her commaundément:
As swift as swallowes, on the waves they went,
That their broad flaggie° finnes no fome did reare,° *drooping / raise*
Ne bubbling roundell° they behind them sent; *globule*
The rest of° other fishes drawen weare, *by*
Which with their finny oars the swelling sea did sheare.° *cleave*

34

Soone as they bene arrived upon the brim° *edge*
Of the Rich strond, their charets they forlore,° *left*
And let their teméd fishes softly swim
Along the margent of the fomy shore,
Least they their finnes should bruze, and surbate° sore *chafe*
Their tender feet upon the stony ground:
And comming to the place, where all in gore
And cruddy bloud enwallowéd° they found *tumbled*
The lucklesse Marinell, lying in deadly swound;

35

His mother swownéd thrise, and the third time
Could scarce recovered be out of her paine;
Had she not bene devoyd of mortall slime,° *clay*
She should not then have bene relived° againe, *revived*
But soone as life recovered had the raine,
She made so piteous mone and deare wayment,° *lamentation*
That the hard rocks could scarse from teares refraine,

And all her sister Nymphes with one consent° *harmony*
Supplide her sobbing breaches[2] with sad complement.

36

"Deare image of my selfe," she said, "that is,
The wretched sonne of wretched mother borne,
Is this thine high advauncement, O is this
Th'immortall name, with which thee yet unborne
Thy Gransire Nereus promist to adorne?
Now lyest thou of life and honor reft;° *deprived*
Now lyest thou a lumpe of earth forlorne,
Ne of thy late life memory is left,
Ne can thy irrevocable destiny be weft?° *avoided*

37

"Fond° Proteus, father of false prophecis, *foolish*
And they more fond, that credit to thee give,
Not this the worke of womans hand ywis,° *certainly*
That so deepe wound through these deare members drive.
I fearéd love: but they that love do live,
But they that die, doe neither love nor hate.
Nath'lesse to thee thy folly I forgive,
And to my selfe, and to accurséd fate
The guilt I doe ascribe: deare wisedome bought too late.

38

"O what availes it of immortall seed
To beene ybred and never borne to die?
Farre better I it deeme to die with speed,
Then waste in woe and wailefull miserie.
Who dyes the utmost dolour doth abye,° *suffer*
But who that lives, is left to waile his losse:
So life is losse, and deathe felicitie.
Sad life worse then glad death: and greater crosse
To see friends grave, then dead the grave selfe to engrosse.° *fill*

39

"But if the heavens did his dayes envie,
And my short blisse maligne,° yet mote they well *grudge*
Thus much afford me, ere that he did die
That the dim eyes of my deare Marinell
I mote have closéd, and him bed farewell,
Sith other offices° for mother meet *services*
They would not graunt.
Yet maulgre° them farewell, my sweetest sweet; *in spite of*
Farewell my sweetest sonne, sith we no more shall meet."

2. I.e., the intervals between fits of sobbing.

40

Thus when they all had sorrowéd their fill,
They softly gan to search his griesly wound:
And that they might him handle more at will,
They him disarmed, and spredding on the ground
Their watchet° mantles frindgd with silver round, *pale blue*
They softly wipt away the gelly° blood *clotted*
From th'orifice; which having well upbound,
They pourd in soveraine balme, and Nectar good,
Good both for earthly med'cine, and for heavenly food.

41

Tho when the lilly handed Liagore,[3]
(This Liagore whylome had learnéd skill
In leaches craft, by great Appolloes lore,° *teaching*
Sith her whylome upon high Pindus hill,
He lovéd, and at last her wombe did fill
With heavenly seed, whereof wise Paeon sprong)
Did feele his pulse, she knew their staiéd still
Some litle life his feeble sprites° emong; *spirit*
Which to his mother told, despeire she from her flong.

42

Tho up him taking in their tender hands,
They easily unto her charet beare:
Her teme at her commaundement quiet stands,
Whiles they the corse into her wagon reare,° *raise*
And strow with flowres the lamentable beare.[4]
Then all the rest into their coches clim,° *mount*
And through the brackish waves their passage sheare;
Upon great Neptunes necke they softly swim,
And to her watry chamber swiftly carry him.

43

Deepe in the bottome of the sea, her bowre
Is built of hollow billowes heapéd hye,
Like to thicke cloudes, that threat a stormy showre,
And vauted° all within, like to the sky, *arched*
In which the Gods do dwell eternally:
There they him laid in easie couch well dight;
And sent in haste for Tryphon,[5] to apply
Salves to his wounds, and medicines of might:
For Tryphon of sea gods the soveraine leach is hight.

3. From Greek, "white-armed"; Hesiod calls her a Nereid (*Theogony* 257). Spenser seems to have invented his story of the birth of Paeon, physician to the gods; cf. *Iliad* 5.401–402, 899–901.
4. I.e., the bier and its sad burden.
5. A sea god skilled in healing; Boccaccio says he was the brother of Aesculapius (*De Genealogia Deorum* 7.36).

44

The whiles the Nymphes sit all about him round,
Lamenting his mishap and heavy° plight; *sad*
And oft his mother vewing his wide wound,
Curséd the hand, that did so deadly smight
Her dearest sonne, her dearest harts delight.[6]
But none of all those curses overtooke
The warlike Maid, th'ensample of that might,
But fairely well she thrived, and well did brooke° *persist in*
Her noble deeds, ne her right course for ought forsooke.

45

Yet did false Archimage[7] her still pursew,
To bring to passe his mischievous intent,
Now that he had her singled° from the crew *separated*
Of courteous knights, the Prince, and Faery gent,° *noble*
Whom late in chace of beautie excellent
She left, pursewing that same foster strong;
Of whose foule outrage they impatient,° *angered*
And full of fiery zeale, him followed long,
To reskew her from shame, and to revenge her wrong.

46

Through thick and thin, through mountaines and through plains,
Those two great champions did attonce° pursew *together*
The fearefull damzell, with incessant paines:
Who from them fled, as light-foot hare from vew
Of hunter swift, and sent of houndés trew.
At last they came unto a double way,
Where, doubtfull which to take, her to reskew,
Themselves they did dispart,° each to assay, *separate*
Whether more happie were, to win so goodly pray.

47

But Timias, the Princes gentle Squire,
That Ladies love unto his Lord forlent,° *relinquished*
And with proud envy,° and indignant ire, *indignation*
After that wicked foster fiercely went.
So beene they three three sundry wayes ybent.° *turned*
But fairest fortune to the Prince befell,
Whose chaunce it was, that soone he did repent,° *regret*
To take that way, in which that Damozell
Was fled afore, affraid of him, as feend of hell.

6. Thus Marinell disappears from Book III into the recesses of the wild salt sea. He will be cured by Tryphon in IV.xi.7.
7. See note to the "Argument" of III.i.

48

At last of her farre off he gainéd vew:
Then gan he freshly pricke his fomy steed,
And ever as he nigher to her drew,
So evermore he did increase his speed,
And of each turning still kept warie heed:
Aloud to her he oftentimes did call,
To doe° away vaine doubt, and needlesse dreed: *banish*
Full myld to her he spake, and oft let fall
Many meeke wordes, to stay and comfort her withall.

49

But nothing might relent° her hastie flight; *slacken*
So deepe the deadly feare of that foule swaine° *rustic*
Was earst impresséd in her gentle spright:
Like as a fearefull Dove, which through the raine,° *domain*
Of the wide aire her way does cut amaine,° *rapidly*
Having farre off espyde a Tassell gent,[8]
Which after her his nimble wings doth straine,
Doubleth her haste for feare to be for-hent,° *seized*
And with her pineons cleaves the liquid firmament.

50

With no lesse haste, and eke with no lesse dreed,
That fearefull Ladie fled from him, that ment
To her no evill thought, nor evill deed;
Yet former feare of being fowly shent,° *disgraced*
Carried her forward with her first intent:
And though oft looking backward, well she vewd,
Her selfe freed from that foster insolent,
And that it was a knight, which now her sewd,° *pursued*
Yet she no lesse the knight feard, then that villein rude.

51

His uncouth° shield and straunge armes her dismayd, *unusual*
Whose like in Faery lond were seldome seene,
That fast she from him fled, no lesse affrayd,
Then of wilde beastes if she had chaséd beene:
Yet he her followd still with courage° keene, *spirit*
So long that now the golden Hesperus[9]
Was mounted high in top of heaven sheene,° *bright*
And warned his other brethren joyeous,
To light their blesséd lamps in Joves eternall hous.

8. I.e., a male falcon.
9. The evening star.

52

All suddenly dim woxe the dampish ayre,
And griesly shadowes covered heaven bright,
That now with thousand starres was deckéd fayre;
Which when the Prince beheld, a lothfull sight,
And that perforce, for want of lenger light,
He mote surcease his suit,° and lose the hope — *pursuit*
Of his long labour, he gan fowly wyte° — *chide*
His wicked fortune, that had turnd aslope,° — *awry*
And curséd night, that reft from him so goodly scope.° — *desired object*

53

Tho when her wayes he could no more descry,
But to and fro at disaventure° strayd; — *random*
Like as a ship, whose Lodestarre suddenly
Covered with cloudes, her Pilot hath dismayd;
His wearisome pursuit perforce he stayd,
And from his loftie steed dismounting low,
Did let him forage. Downe himselfe he layd
Upon the grassie ground, to sleepe a throw;° — *while*
The cold earth was his couch, the hard steele his pillow.

54

But gentle Sleepe envyde° him any rest; — *grudged*
In stead thereof sad sorrow, and disdaine
Of his hard hap° did vexe his noble brest, — *lot*
And thousand fancies bet his idle braine
With their light wings, the sights of semblants° vaine: — *illusions*
Oft did he wish, that Lady faire mote bee
His Faery Queene, for whom he did complaine:° — *lament*
Or that his Faery Queene were such, as shee:
And ever hastie Night he blaméd bitterlie.[1]

55

"Night thou foule Mother of annoyance° sad, — *grief*
Sister of heavie death, and nourse of woe,
Which wast begot in heaven, but for thy bad
And brutish shape thrust downe to hell below,
Where by the grim floud of Cocytus slow
Thy dwelling is, in Herebus blacke house[2]
(Blacke Herebus thy husband is the foe
Of all the Gods) where thou ungratious,
Halfe of thy dayes doest lead in horrour hideous.

1. Arthur's lament in stanzas 55–60 structurally balances Britomart's early in the canto. Both belong to the genre of the lover's complaint, often voiced at night (cf. Dido's lament, *Aeneid* 4.522–54 and Clymène's marine speeches in Ronsard's *Franciade* III).
2. Chaos bore Night and Erebus, who dwell in Hades (Hesiod, *Theogony* 123, 669–70).

56

"What had th'eternall Maker need of thee,
The world in his° continuall course to keepe, *its*
That doest all things deface,° ne lettest see *obscure*
The beautie of his worke? Indeed in sleepe
The slouthfull bodie, that doth love to steepe
His lustlesse° limbes, and drowne his baser° mind, *feeble / too base*
Doth praise thee oft, and oft from Stygian deepe
Calles[3] thee, his goddesse in his error blind,
And great Dame Natures handmaide, chearing every kind.

57

"But well I wote, that to an heavy hart
Thou art the root and nurse of bitter cares,
Breeder of new, renewer of old smarts:
In stead of rest thou lendest rayling° teares, *bitter*
In stead of sleepe thou sendest troublous feares,
And dreadfull visions, in the which alive
The drearie image of sad death appeares:
So from the wearie spirit thou doest drive
Desiréd rest, and men of happinesse deprive.

58

"Under thy mantle blacke there hidden lye,
Light-shonning theft, and traiterous intent,
Abhorréd bloudshed, and vile felony,
Shamefull deceipt, and daunger imminent;° *threatening*
Foule horror, and eke hellish dreriment:[4]
All these I wote in thy protection bee,
And light doe shonne, for feare of being shent:° *put to shame*
For light ylike° is lothed of them and thee, *alike*
And all that lewdnesse° love, doe hate the light to see. *wickedness*

59

"For day discovers° all dishonest wayes, *reveals*
And sheweth each thing, as it is indeed:
The prayses of high God he faire displayes
And his large bountie rightly doth areed.° *show*
Dayes dearest children be the blesséd seed,
Which darknesse shall subdew, and heaven win:
Truth is his daughter; he her first did breed,
Most sacred virgin, without spot of sin.[5]
Our life is day, but death with darknesse doth begin.

3. I.e., summons thee from Hades, and calls thee his goddess and the handmaid of Dame Nature.
4. The list of Night's offspring is based on Hesiod, *Theogony* 211–25, or Comes, *Mythologiae* 3.12.
5. More often Truth is called the daughter of Time.

60

"O when will day then turne to me againe,
And bring with him his long expected light?
O Titan, haste to reare thy joyous waine.[6]
Speed thee to spred abroad thy beamés bright,
And chase away this too long lingring night,
Chase her away, from whence she came, to hell.
She, she it is, that hath me done despight:° *wrong*
There let her with the damnéd spirits dwell,
And yeeld her roome to day, that can it governe well."

61

Thus did the Prince that wearie night outweare,° *spend*
In restlesse anguish and unquiet paine:
And earely, ere the morrow did upreare
His deawy head out of the Ocean maine,
He up arose, as halfe in great disdaine,
And clombe unto his steed. So forth he went,
With heavie looke and lumpish° pace, that plaine *dull*
In him bewraid great grudge and maltalent:° *ill will*
His steed eke seemed t'apply° his steps to his intent.° *suit / spirit*

Canto V

Prince Arthur heares of Florimell:
three fosters° Timias wound, *foresters*
Belphebe finds him almost dead,
and reareth out of sownd.° *swoon*

1

Wonder it is to see, in diverse minds,
How diversly love doth his pageants° play, *roles*
And shewes his powre in variable° kinds: *various*
The baser wit,° whose idle thoughts alway *mind*
Are wont to cleave unto the lowly clay,
It stirreth up to sensuall desire,
And in lewd slouth to wast his carelesse day:
But in brave sprite it kindles goodly fire,
That to all high desert° and honour doth aspire. *worth*

2

Ne suffereth it uncomely° idlenesse, *unbecoming*
In his free thought to build her sluggish nest:
Ne suffereth it thought of ungentlenesse,
Ever to creepe into his noble brest,
But to the highest and the worthiest
Lifteth it up, that else would lowly fall:

6. I.e., may the sun soon rise, driving his "waine," his chariot.

It lets not fall, it lets it not to rest:
It lets not scarse this Prince to breath at all,
But to his first poursuit him forward still doth call.

3

Who long time wandred through the forrest wyde,
To finde some issue° thence, till that at last *way out*
He met a Dwarfe, that seeméd terrifyde
With some late perill, which he hardly° past, *with difficulty*
Or other accident, which him aghast,° *terrified*
Of whom he askéd, whence he lately came,
And whither now he travelléd so fast:
For sore he swat,° and running through that same *sweated*
Thicke forest, was bescratcht, and both his feet nigh lame.

4

Panting for breath, and almost out of hart,
The Dwarfe him answerd, "Sir, ill mote I stay
To tell the same. I lately did depart
From Faery court, where I have many a day
Servéd a gentle Lady of great sway,
And high accompt° through out all Elfin land, *reputation*
Who lately left the same, and tooke this way:
Her now I seeke, and if ye understand
Which way she faréd hath, good Sir tell out of hand."[1]

5

"What mister° wight," said he, "and how arayd?" *kind of*
"Royally clad," quoth he, "in cloth of gold,
As meetest may beseeme a noble mayd;
Her faire lockes in rich circlet be enrold,
A fairer wight did never Sunne behold,
And on a Palfrey rides more white then snow,
Yet she her selfe is whiter manifold:
The surest signe, whereby ye may her know,
Is, that she is the fairest wight alive, I trow."

6

"Now certes swaine," said he, "such one I weene,
Fast flying through this forest from her fo,
A foule ill favoured° foster, I have seene; *featured*
Her selfe, well as I might, I reskewd tho,
But could not stay; so fast she did foregoe,° *go on before*
Carried away with wings of speedy feare."
"Ah dearest God," quoth he, "that is great woe,
And wondrous ruth° to all, that shall it heare. *grief*
But can ye read Sir, how I may her find, or where?"

1. I.e., at once.

7

"Perdy me lever° were to weeten that," *rather*
Said he, "then ransome of the richest knight,
Or all the good that ever yet I gat:
But froward° fortune, and too forward Night *reluctant*
Such happinesse did, maulgre, to me spight,[2]
And fro me reft both life and light attone.° *together*
But Dwarfe aread,° what is that Lady bright, *explain*
That through this forest wandreth thus alone;
For of her errour° straunge I have great ruth and mone." *wandering*

8

"That Lady is," quoth he, "where so she bee,
The bountiest° virgin, and most debonaire, *most virtuous*
That ever living eye I weene did see;
Lives none this day, that may with her compare
In stedfast chastitie and vertue rare,
The goodly ornaments of beautie bright;
And is yclepéd° Florimell the faire, *called*
Faire Florimell beloved of many a knight,
Yet she loves none but one, that Marinell is hight.

9

"A Sea-nymphes sonne, that Marinell is hight,
Of my deare Dame is lovéd dearely well;
In other none, but him, she sets delight,
All her delight is set on Marinell;
But he sets nought at all by Florimell:
For Ladies love his mother long ygoe
Did him, they say, forwarne° through sacred spell. *forbid*
But fame° now flies, that of a forreine foe *rumor*
He is yslaine, which is the ground of all our woe.

10

"Five dayes there be, since he (they say) was slaine,
And foure, since Florimell the Court for-went,° *left*
And vowéd never to returne againe,
Till him alive or dead she did invent.° *find*
Therefore, faire Sir, for love of knighthood gent,
And honour of trew Ladies, if ye may
By your good counsell, or bold hardiment,
Or° succour her, or me direct the way; *either*
Do one, or other good, I you most humbly pray.[3]

2. I.e., Fortune and Night, against my will, envied me this happiness.
3. Spenser has allowed an inconsistency between the Dwarfe's account of Florimell's departure from the court and the glimpse (at III. i. 15–16) of Florimell in flight before Marinell's encounter with Britomart.

11

"So may ye gaine to you full great renowme,
Of all good Ladies through the world so wide,
And haply in her hart find highest rowme,
Of whom ye seeke to be most magnifide:
At least eternall meede shall you abide."° *await*
To whom the Prince; "Dwarfe, comfort to thee take,
For till thou tidings learne, what her betide,
I here avow thee never to forsake.
Ill weares he armes, that nill° them use for Ladies sake." *will not*

12

So with the Dwarfe he backe returned againe,
To seeke his Lady, where he mote her find;
But by the way he greatly gan complaine
The want of his good Squire late left behind,
For whom he wondrous pensive grew in mind,
For doubt° of daunger, which mote him betide; *fear*
For him he lovéd above all mankind,
Having him trew and faithfull ever tride,° *proved*
And bold, as ever Squire that waited by knights side.

13

Who all this while full hardly was assayd
Of deadly daunger, which to him betid;° *befell*
For whiles his Lord pursewd that noble Mayd,
After that foster fowle he fiercely rid,° *rode*
To bene avengéd of the shame, he did
To that faire Damzell: Him he chacéd long
Through the thicke woods, wherein he would have hid
His shamefull head from his avengement strong,
And oft him threatned death for his outrageous wrong.

14

Nathlesse the villen° sped him selfe so well, *churl*
Whether through swiftnesse of his speedy beast,
Or knowledge of those woods, where he did dwell,
That shortly he from daunger was releast,
And out of sight escapéd at the least;° *last*
Yet not escapéd from the dew reward
Of his bad deeds, which dayly he increast,
Ne ceaséd not, till him oppresséd hard
The heavy plague, that for such leachours is prepard.

15

For soone as he was vanisht out of sight,
His coward courage gan emboldned bee,

And cast° t'avenge him of that fowle despight, *resolved*
Which he had borne of his bold enimee.
Tho to his brethren came: for they were three
Ungratious children of one gracelesse sire,
And unto them complainéd, how that he
Had uséd bene of that foolehardy Squire;
So them with bitter words he stird to bloudy ire.

16

Forthwith themselves with their sad° instruments *grievous*
Of spoyle and murder they gan arme bylive,° *speedily*
And with him forth into the forest went,
To wreake the wrath, which he did earst revive
In their sterne brests, on him which late did drive
Their brother to reproch and shamefull flight:
For they had vowed, that never he alive
Out of that forest should escape their might;
Vile rancour their rude harts had fild with such despight.

17

Within that wood there was a covert glade,
Foreby° a narrow foord, to them well knowne, *near*
Through which it was uneath° for wight to wade; *difficult*
And now by fortune it was overflowne:
By that same way they knew that Squire unknowne
Mote algates° passe; for thy themselves they set *necessarily*
There in await, with thicke woods over growne,
And all the while their malice they did whet
With cruell threats, his passage through the ford to let.° *prevent*

18

It fortunéd, as they devizéd had,
The gentle Squire came ryding that same way,
Unweeting of their wile and treason bad,
And through the ford to passen did assay;
But that fierce foster, which late fled away,
Stoutly forth stepping on the further shore,
Him boldly bad his passage there to stay,
Till he had made amends, and full restore
For all the damage, which he had him doen afore.

19

With that at him a quiv'ring dart he threw,
With so fell force and villeinous despighte,
That through his haberjeon the forkehead flew,
And through the linkéd mayles° empiercéd quite, *armor rings*
But had no powre in his soft flesh to bite:
That stroke the hardy Squire did sore displease,

But more that him he could not come to smite;
For by no meanes the high banke he could sease,° — *reach*
But laboured long in that deepe ford with vaine disease.° — *distress*

20

And still the foster with his long bore-speare
Him kept from landing at his wishéd will;
Anone one sent out of the thicket neare
A cruell shaft, headed with deadly ill,
And fetheréd with an unlucky quill;
The wicked steele stayd not, till it did light
In his left thigh, and deepely did it thrill:° — *pierce*
Exceeding griefe that wound in him empight,° — *fixed*
But more that with his foes he could not come to fight.

21

At last through wrath and vengeaunce making way,
He on the bancke arrived with mickle° paine, — *much*
Where the third brother him did sore assay,
And drove at him with all his might and maine
A forrest bill,[4] which both his hands did straine;
But warily he did avoide the blow,
And with his speare requited him againe,
That both his sides were thrilléd with the throw,° — *thrust*
And a large streame of bloud out of the wound did flow.

22

He tombling downe, with gnashing teeth did bite
The bitter earth, and bad to let him in
Into the balefull house of endlesse night,
Where wicked ghosts do waile their former sin.
Tho gan the battell freshly to begin;
For nathemore for that spectacle bad,
Did th'other two their cruell vengeaunce blin,° — *cease*
But both attonce on both sides him bested,° — *beset*
And load upon him layd,[5] his life for to have had.

23

Tho when that villain he avized,° which late — *perceived*
Affrighted had the fairest Florimell,
Full of fiers fury, and indignant hate.
To him he turnéd, and with rigour° fell — *force*
Smote him so rudely on the Pannikell,° — *brain pan*
That to the chin he cleft his head in twaine:
Downe on the ground his carkas groveling fell;

4. A digging or pruning implement.
5. I.e., assailed him with blows.

His sinfull soule with desperate disdaine,
Out of her fleshly ferme° fled to the place of paine. *enclosure*

24

That seeing now the onely° last of three, *solitary*
Who with that wicked shaft him wounded had,
Trembling with horrour, as° that did foresee *as one*
The fearefull end of his avengement sad,
Through which he follow should his brethren bad,
His bootelesse bow in feeble hand upcaught,
And therewith shot an arrow at the lad;
Which faintly fluttring, scarce his helmet raught,° *reached*
And glauncing fell to ground, but him annoyéd naught.

25

With that he would have fled into the wood;
But Timias him lightly overhent,° *overtook*
Right as he entring was into the flood,
And strooke at him with force so violent,
That headlesse him into the foord he sent:
The carkas with the streame was carried downe,
But th'head fell backeward on the Continent° *ground*
So mischief fel upon the meaners crowne;[6]
They three be dead with shame, the Squire lives with renowne.

26

He lives, but takes small joy of his renowne;
For of that cruell wound he bled so sore,
That from his steed he fell in deadly swowne;
Yet still the bloud forth gusht in so great store,
That he lay wallowd all in his owne gore.
Now God thee keepe, thou gentlest Squire alive,
Else shall thy loving Lord thee see no more,
But both of comfort him thou shalt deprive,
And eke thy selfe of honour, which thou didst atchive.

27

Providence heavenly passeth living thought,
And doth for wretched mens reliefe make way;
For loe great grace or fortune thither brought
Comfort to him, that comfortlesse now lay.
In those same woods, ye well remember may,
How that a noble hunteresse did wonne,
She, that base Braggadochio did affray,° *frighten*
And made him fast out of the forrest runne;
Belphoebe was her name, as faire as Phoebus sunne.

6. I.e., on those who intended mischief.

28

She on a day, as she pursewd the chace
Of some wild beast, which with her arrowes keene
She wounded had, the same along did trace
By tract° of bloud, which she had freshly seene, *trace*
To have besprinckled all the grassy greene;
By the great persue,° which she there perceaved, *trail of blood*
Well hopéd she the beast engored had beene,
And made more hast, the life to have bereaved:
But ah, her expectation greatly was deceaved.

29

Shortly she came, whereas that woefull Squire
With bloud deforméd,° lay in deadly swownd: *made hideous*
In whose faire eyes, like lamps of quenchéd fire,
The Christall humour° stood congealéd rownd; *fluid*
His locks, like faded leaves fallen to grownd,
Knotted with bloud, in bounches rudely ran,
And his sweete lips, on which before that stownd° *encounter*
The bud of youth to blossome faire began,
Spoild of their rosie red, were woxen pale and wan.

30

Saw never living eye more heavy sight,
That could have made a rocke of stone to rew,
Or rive in twaine: which when that Lady bright
Besides all hope[7] with melting eyes did vew,
All suddeinly abasht she chaungéd hew,
And with sterne horrour backward gan to start:
But when she better him beheld, she grew
Full of soft passion and unwonted smart:
The point of pitty percéd through her tender hart.[8]

31

Meekely she bowéd downe, to weete if life
Yet in his frosen members did remaine,
And feeling by his pulses beating rife,° *strongly*
That the weake soule her seat did yet retaine,
She cast to comfort him with busie paine:
His double folded necke she reard upright,
And rubd his temples, and each trembling vaine;
His mayléd haberjeon she did undight,° *take off*
And from his head his heavy burganet did light.° *remove*

7. I.e., contrary to expectation.
8. The rest of this canto adapts Ariosto's story of Angelica and Medoro (*Orlando Furioso* 19.17–42), although Angelica allows Medoro to "gather the first rose" and Belphoebe reserves "that dainty Rose" (stanza 51). The tale of Timeas, whose name suggests the Greek for "glory," and Belphoebe, whom Spenser's Letter to Raleigh associates with Elizabeth, can be read as alluding to Raleigh's stormy if ostentatiously loving service to the queen. The queen's anger and later partial forgiveness when he impregnated and then married one of her ladies-in-waiting are allegorized in IV.vii–viii.

32

Into the woods thenceforth in hast she went,
To seeke for hearbes, that mote him remedy;
For she of hearbes had great intendiment,° *knowledge*
Taught of the Nymphe, which from her infancy
Her nourcéd had in trew Nobility:
There, whether it divine Tobacco were,
Or Panachaea, or Polygony,[9]
She found, and brought it to her patient deare
Who al this while lay bleeding out his hartbloud neare.

33

The soveraigne weede betwixt two marbles plaine° *smooth*
She pownded small, and did in peeces bruze,° *break*
And then atweene her lilly handés twaine,
Into his wound the juyce thereof did scruze,° *squeeze*
And round about, as she could well it uze,
The flesh therewith she suppled and did steepe,
T'abate all spasme, and soke the swelling bruze,
And after having searcht the intuse° deepe, *contusion*
She with her scarfe did bind the wound from cold to keepe.

34

By this he had sweete life recured° againe, *recovered*
And groning inly deepe, at last his eyes,
His watry eyes, drizling like deawy raine,
He up gan lift toward the azure skies,
From whence descend all hopelesse° remedies: *unexpected*
Therewith he sighed, and turning him aside,
The goodly Mayd full of divinities,
And gifts of heavenly grace he by him spide,
Her bow and gilden quiver lying him beside.

35

"Mercy deare Lord," said he, "what grace is this,
That thou hast shewéd to me sinfull wight,
To send thine Angell from her bowre of blis,
To comfort me in my distresséd plight?
Angell, or Goddesse do I call thee right?
What service may I do unto thee meete,
That hast from darkenesse me returnd to light,
And with thy heavenly salves and med'cines sweete,
Hast drest my sinfull wounds? I kisse thy blessed feete."

9. Raleigh introduced tobacco into England in 1584; Polygony: an astringent root; "Panachaea": an herb with manifold healing properties.

36

Thereat she blushing said, "Ah gentle Squire,
Nor Goddesse I, nor Angell, but the Mayd,
And daughter of a woody° Nymphe, desire — *of the forest*
No service, but thy safety and ayd;
Which if thou gaine, I shalbe well apayd.
We mortall wights whose lives and fortunes bee
To commun accidents still open layd,
Are bound with commun bond of frailtee,
To succour wretched wights, whom we captivéd see."

37

By this her Damzels, which the former chace
Had undertaken after her, arryved,
As did Belphoebe, in the bloudy place,
And thereby deemd the beast had bene deprived
Of life, whom late their Ladies arrow ryved:° — *pierced*
For thy the bloudy tract they follow fast,
And every one to runne the swiftest stryved;
But two of them the rest far overpast,
And where their Lady was, arrivéd at the last.

38

Where when they saw that goodly boy, with blood
Defowléd, and their Lady dresse his wownd,
They wondred much, and shortly understood,
How him in deadly case° their Lady fownd, — *condition*
And reskewéd out of the heavy stownd.° — *plight*
Eftsoones his warlike courser, which was strayd
Farre in the woods, while that he lay in swownd,
She made those Damzels search, which being stayd,
They did him set thereon, and forth with them convayd.° — *removed*

39

Into that forest farre they thence him led,
Where was their dwelling, in a pleasant glade,
With mountaines round about environéd,
And mighty woods, which did the valley shade,
And like a stately Theatre it made,
Spreading it selfe into a spatious plaine.
And in the midst a little river plaide
Emongst the pumy° stones, which seemd to plaine — *pumice*
With gentle murmure, that his course they did restraine.

40

Beside the same a dainty place there lay,
Planted with mirtle trees and laurels greene,

In which the birds song many a lovely lay
Of gods high prayse, and of their loves sweet teene,° *sorrow*
As it an earthly Paradize had beene:
In whose encloséd shadow there was pight
A faire Pavilion, scarcely to be seene,
The which was all within most richly dight,
That greatest Princes living it mote well delight.

41

Thither they brought that wounded Squire, and layd
In easie couch his feeble limbes to rest,
He rested him a while, and then the Mayd
His ready wound with better salves new drest;
Dayly she dresséd him, and did the best
His grievous hurt to garish,° that she might, *cure*
That shortly she his dolour hath redrest,° *healed*
And his foule sore reducéd° to faire plight: *restored*
It she reducéd, but himselfe destroyéd quight.

42

O foolish Physick, and unfruitfull paine,° *effort*
That heales up one and makes another wound:
She his hurt thigh to him recured againe,
But hurt his hart, the which before was sound,
Through an unwary dart, which did rebound° *leap*
From her faire eyes and gracious countenaunce.
What bootes it him from death to be unbound,
To be captivéd in endlesse duraunce° *captivity*
Of sorrow and despaire without aleggeaunce?° *alleviation*

43

Still as his wound did gather, and grow hole,
So still his hart woxe sore, and health decayd:
Madnesse to save a part, and lose the whole.
Still whenas he beheld the heavenly Mayd,
Whiles dayly plaisters to his wound she layd,
So still his Malady the more increast,
The whiles her matchlesse beautie him dismayd.
Ah God, what other could he do at least,
But love so faire a Lady, that his life releast?° *saved*

44

Long while he strove in his courageous brest,
With reason dew the passion to subdew,
And love for to dislodge out of his nest:
Still when her excellencies he did vew,
Her soveraigne bounty,° and celestiall hew,° *goodness / form*
The same to love he strongly was constraind:

But when his meane estate he did revew,
He from such hardy boldnesse was restraind,
And of his lucklesse lot and cruell love thus plaind.

45

"Unthankfull wretch," said he, "is this the meed,
With which her soveraigne mercy thou doest quight?° *repay*
Thy life she savéd by her gracious deed,
But thou doest weene with villeinous despight,° *wrong*
To blot her honour, and her heavenly light.
Dye rather, dye, then so disloyally
Deeme of her high desert,° or seeme so light: *worth*
Faire death it is to shonne more shame, to dy:
Dye rather, dy, then ever love disloyally.

46

"But if to love disloyalty it bee,
Shall I then hate her, that from deathés dore
Me brought? ah farre be such reproch fro mee.
What can I lesse do, then her love therefore,
Sith I her dew reward cannot restore?
Dye rather, dye, and dying do her serve,
Dying her serve, and living her adore;
Thy life she gave, thy life she doth deserve:
Dye rather, dye, then ever from her service swerve.

47

"But foolish boy, what bootes thy service bace
To her, to whom the heavens do serve, and sew?
Thou a meane Squire, of meeke and lowly place,
She heavenly borne, and of celestiall hew.
How then? of all love taketh equall vew:
And doth not highest God vouchsafe to take
The love and service of the basest crew?° *company*
If she will not, dye meekly for her sake;
Dye rather, dye, then ever so faire love forsake."

48

Thus warreid° he long time against his will, *struggled*
Till that through weaknesse he was forst at last,
To yield himselfe unto the mighty ill:
Which as a victour proud, gan ransack fast
His inward parts, and all his entrayles wast,
That neither bloud in face, nor life in hart
It left, but both did quite drye up, and blast;
As percing levin,° which the inner part *lightning*
Of every thing consumes, and calcineth° by art. *pulverizes*

49

Which seeing faire Belphoebe gan to feare,
Least that his wound were inly well not healed,
Or that the wicked steele empoysned were:
Litle she weend, that love he close concealed;
Yet still he wasted, as the snow congealed,
When the bright sunne his beams thereon doth beat;
Yet never he his hart to her revealed,
But rather chose to dye for sorrow great,
Then with dishonorable termes her to entreat.

50

She gracious Lady, yet no paines did spare,
To do him ease, or do him remedy:
Many Restoratives of vertues° rare, *powers*
And costly Cordialles she did apply,
To mitigate his stubborne mallady:
But that sweet Cordiall, which can restore
A love-sick hart, she did to him envy;° *grudge*
To him, and to all th'unworthy world forlore° *forlorn*
She did envy that soveraigne salve, in secret store.

51

That dainty Rose, the daughter of her Morne,
More deare then life she tenderéd, whose flowre
The girlond of her honour did adorne:
Ne suffred she the Middayes scorching powre,
Ne the sharp Northerne wind thereon to showre,
But lappéd° up her silken leaves most chaire,° *folded / dear*
When so the froward skye began to lowre:
But soone as calméd was the Christall aire,
She did it faire dispred, and let to florish faire.

52

Eternall God in his almighty powre,
To make ensample of his heavenly grace,
In Paradize whilome did plant this flowre,
Whence he it fetcht out of her native place,
And did in stocke of earthly flesh enrace,° *implant*
That mortall men her glory should admire:
In gentle Ladies brest, and bounteous race
Of woman kind it fairest flowre doth spire,° *cause to spring*
And beareth fruit of honour and all chast desire.

53

Faire ympes° of beautie, whose bright shining beames *children*
Adorne the world with like to heavenly light,
And to your willes both royalties and Realmes

Subdew, through conquest of your wondrous might,
With this faire flowre your goodly girlonds dight,
Of chastity and vertue virginall,
That shall embellish more your beautie bright,
And crowne your heades with heavenly coronall,
Such as the Angels weare before Gods tribunall.

54

To youre faire selves a faire ensample frame,
Of this faire virgin, this Belphoebe faire,
To whom in perfect love, and spotlesse fame
Of chastitie, none living may compaire:
Ne poysnous Envy justly can empaire
The prayse of her fresh flowring Maidenhead;
For thy she standeth on the highest staire
Of th'honorable stage of womanhead,
That Ladies all may follow her ensample dead.

55

In so great prayse of stedfast chastity,
Nathlesse she was so curteous and kind,
Tempred with grace, and goodly modesty,
That seeméd those two vertues strove to find
The higher place in her Heroick mind:
So striving each did other more augment,
And both encreast the prayse of woman kind,
And both encreast her beautie excellent;
So all did make in her a perfect complement.

Canto VI

The birth of faire Belphoebe and
Of Amoret is told.
The Gardins of Adonis fraught
With pleasures manifold.

1

Well may I weene,° faire Ladies, all this while — *expect*
Ye wonder, how this noble Damozell
So great perfections did in her compile,° — *heap up*
Sith that in salvage forests she did dwell,
So farre from court and royall Citadell,
The great schoolmistresse of all curtesy:
Seemeth that such wild woods should far expell
All civill usage and gentility,
And gentle sprite deforme with rude rusticity.

2

But to this faire Belphoebe in her berth
The heavens so favourable were and free,

Looking with myld aspect upon the earth,
In th'Horoscope of her nativitee,
That all the gifts of grace and chastitee
On her they pouréd forth of plenteous horne;
Jove laught on Venus from his soveraigne see,° *throne*
And Phoebus with faire beames did her adorne,[1]
And all the Graces rockt her cradle being borne.

3

Her berth was of the wombe of Morning dew,[2]
And her conception of the joyous Prime,° *spring*
And all her whole creation did her shew
Pure and unspotted from all loathly crime,
That is ingenerate in fleshly slime.° *clay*
So was this virgin borne, so was she bred,
So was she traynéd up from time to time,[3]
In all chast vertue, and true bounti-hed
Till to her dew perfection she was ripenéd.

4

Her mother was the faire Chrysogonee,
The daughter of Amphisa,[4] who by race
A Faerie was, yborne of high degree,
She bore Belphoebe, she bore in like cace° *condition*
Faire Amoretta in the second place:
These two were twinnes, and twixt them two did share
The heritage of all celestiall grace.
That all the rest it seemed they robbéd bare
Of bountie, and of beautie, and all vertues rare.

5

It were a goodly storie, to declare,
By what straunge accident faire Chrysogone
Conceived these infants, and how them she bare,
In this wild forrest wandring all alone,
After she had nine moneths fulfild and gone:
For not as other wemens commune brood,
They were enwombéd° in the sacred throne *conceived*
Of her chaste bodie, nor with commune food,
As other wemens babes, they suckéd vitall blood.

1. Spenser seems to imply that Jupiter and Venus were "in trine," an astrological "aspect" thought to confer beauty, grace, fidelity, and honesty on those born under its influence. While the sun's "aspect" is not given, its influence was favorable to fortune and high place.
2. "Thy people shall be willing in the day of thy power, in the beauties of holiness from the womb of the morning: thou hast the dew of thy youth" (Psalms 110.3).
3. Thanks to the peculiarities of this conception and birth, Belphoebe was born free of inherent human sinfulness ("loathly crime," or "original sin" in Christian terminology). Stars determine much of a newborn's nature, said many, but education helps shape it and, in Christian thinking, they cannot displace divine will.
4. Would suggest "double nature" in Greek; *Chrysogonee*: Greek for "golden-born."

6

But wondrously they were begot, and bred
Through influence of th'heavens fruitfull ray,
As it in antique bookes is mentionéd.[5]
It was upon a Sommers shynie day,
When Titan faire his beamés did display,
In a fresh fountaine, farre from all mens vew,
She bathed her brest, the boyling heat t' allay;
She bathed with roses red, and violets blew,
And all the sweetest flowres, that in the forrest grew.

7

Till faint through irkesome wearinesse, adowne
Upon the grassie ground her selfe she layd
To sleepe, the whiles a gentle slombring swowne
Upon her fell all naked bare displayd;
The sunne-beames bright upon her body playd,
Being through former bathing mollified,° *softened*
And pierst into her wombe, where they embayd° *suffused*
With so sweet sence and secret power unspide,
That in her pregnant flesh they shortly fructifide.

8

Miraculous may seeme to him, that reades
So straunge ensample of conception;
But reason teacheth that the fruitfull seades
Of all things living, through impression
Of the sunbeames in moyst complexion,[6]
Doe life conceive and quickned are by kynd.° *nature*
So after Nilus inundation,
Infinite shapes of creatures men do fynd,
Informéd° in the mud, on which the Sunne hath shynd.[7] *formed*

9

Great father he of generation
Is rightly cald, th'author of life and light;
And his faire sister[8] for creation
Ministreth matter fit, which tempred right
With heate and humour, breedes the living wight.
So sprong these twinnes in wombe of Chrysogone,
Yet wist° she nought thereof, but sore affright, *knew*

5. Stanzas 6–9 (cf. *Metamorphoses* 1.416–37) prepare for the allegory of life processes in the Garden of Adonis. Like other mythographers, Comes associates Adonis with the sun, "sole author of generation" (*Mythologiae* 4.13).
6. I.e., in a temperament, or physical constitution, dominated by moist "humors."
7. Cf. I.i.21 and note.
8. I.e., the moon, whose light Plutarch considered favorable to the generation and growth of life in plants and animals (*Isis and Osiris* 41).

Wondred to see her belly so upblone,
Which still increast, till she her terme had full outgone.° *completed*

10

Whereof conceiving shame and foule disgrace,
Albe her guiltlesse conscience her cleard,
She fled into the wildernesse a space,
Till that unweeldy burden she had reard,° *brought forth*
And shund dishonor, which as death she feard:
Where wearie of long travell,° downe to rest *labor*
Her selfe she set, and comfortably cheard;
There a sad cloud of sleepe her overkest,° *covered*
And seizéd every sense with sorrow sore opprest.

11

It fortunéd, faire Venus having lost
Her little sonne, the wingéd god of love,
Who for some light displeasure, which him crost,
Was from her fled, as flit° as ayerie Dove, *swift*
And left her blisfull bowre of joy above,
(So from her often he had fled away,
When she for ought him sharpely did reprove,
And wandred in the world in strange aray,
Disguized in thousand shapes, that none might him bewray.)[9]

12

Him for to seeke, she left her heavenly hous,
The house of goodly formes and faire aspects,
Whence all the world derives the glorious
Features of beautie, and all shapes select,
With which high God his workmanship hath deckt;
And searchéd every way, through which his wings
Had borne him, or his tract° she mote detect: *track*
She promist kisses sweet, and sweeter things
Unto the man, that of him tydings to her brings.

13

First she him sought in Court, where most he used
Whylome to haunt, but there she found him not;
But many there she found, which sore accused
His falsehood, and with foule infamous blot
His cruell deedes and wicked wyles did spot:
Ladies and Lords she every where mote heare
Complayning, how with his empoysned shot

9. This episode is based on Tasso's version (in his pastoral drama *Aminta*) of the first *Idyl*, "Love the Runaway," by Moschus (fl. 250 B.C.E.). In his Glosse to "March," E. K. cites "Moschus his Idyllion of wandering love."

Their wofull harts he wounded had whyleare,
And so had left them languishing twixt hope and feare.

14

She then the Citties sought from gate to gate,
And every one did aske, did he him see;
And every one her answerd, that too late
He had him seene, and felt the crueltie
Of his sharpe darts and whot° artillerie; *hot*
And every one threw forth reproches rife
Of his mischievous deedes, and said, That hee
Was the disturber of all civill life,
The enimy of peace, and author of all strife.

15

Then in the countrey she abroad him sought,
And in the rurall cottages inquired,
Where also many plaints to her were brought,
How he their heedlesse harts with love had fyred,
And his false venim through their veines inspyred;
And eke the gentle shepheard swaynes, which sat
Keeping their fleecie flockes, as they were hyred,
She sweetly heard complaine, both how and what
Her sonne had to them doen; yet she did smile thereat.

16

But when in none of all these she him got,
She gan avize,° where else he mote him hyde: *consider*
At last she her bethought, that she had not
Yet sought the salvage woods and forrests wyde,
In which full many lovely Nymphes abyde,
Mongst whom might be, that he did closely lye,[1]
Or that the love of some of them him tyde:
For thy she thither cast° her course t'apply, *resolved*
To search the secret haunts of Dianes company.

17

Shortly unto the wastefull° woods she came, *wild*
Whereas she found the Goddesse with her crew,
After late chace of their embrewéd° game, *blood-stained*
Sitting beside a fountaine in a rew,° *row*
Some of them washing with the liquid dew
From off their dainty limbes the dustie sweat,
And soyle which did deforme their lively hew;
Others lay shaded from the scorching heat;
The rest upon her person gave attendance great.

1. I.e., did secretly lurk.

18

She having hong upon a bough on high
Her bow and painted quiver, had unlaste
Her silver buskins° from her nimble thigh, *high boots*
And her lancke° loynes ungirt, and brests unbraste, *slender*
After her heat the breathing cold to taste;
Her golden lockes, that late in tresses bright
Embreaded were for hindring of her haste,[2]
Now loose about her shoulders hong undight,
And were with sweet Ambrosia all besprinckled light.

19

Soone as she Venus saw behind her backe,
She was ashamed to be so loose surprized,
And woxe halfe wroth against her damzels slacke,
That had not her thereof before avized,° *warned*
But suffred her so carelesly disguized
Be overtaken. Soone her garments loose
Upgath'ring, in her bosome she comprized,° *gathered*
Well as she might, and to the Goddesse rose,
Whiles all her Nymphes did like a girlond her enclose.

20

Goodly she gan faire Cytherea[3] greet,
And shortly askéd her, what cause her brought
Into that wildernesse for her unmeet,
From her sweete bowres, and beds with pleasures fraught:
That suddein change she strange adventure thought.
To whom halfe weeping, she thus answeréd,
That she her dearest sonne Cupido sought,
Who in his frowardnesse from her was fled;
That she repented sore, to have him angeréd.

21

Thereat Diana gan to smile, in scorne
Of her vaine plaint, and to her scoffing sayd;
"Great pittie sure, that ye be so forlorne
Of your gay sonne, that gives ye so good ayd
To your disports: ill mote ye bene apayd."[4]
But she was more engrievéd, and replide;
"Faire sister, ill beseemes it to upbrayd
A dolefull heart with so disdainfull pride;
The like that mine, may be your paine another tide.° *time*

2. I.e., were braided up to prevent them from hindering her speed.
3. I.e., Venus, who rose from sea foam near Cythera, off the southernmost point of Greece; see II.xii.65.
4. I.e., you are ill requited.

22

"As you in woods and wanton wildernesse
Your glory set, to chace the salvage beasts,
So my delight is all in joyfulnesse,
In beds, in bowres, in banckets, and in feasts:
And ill becomes you with your loftie creasts,
To scorne the joy, that Jove is glad to seeke;
We both are bound to follow heavens beheasts,° *commands*
And tend our charges with obeisance meeke:
Spare, gentle sister, with reproch my paine to eeke.° *increase*

23

"And tell me, if that ye my sonne have heard,
To lurke emongst your Nymphes in secret wize;
Or keepe their cabins: much I am affeard,
Least he like one of them him selfe disguize,
And turne his arrowes to their exercize:
So may he long himselfe full easie hide:
For he is faire and fresh in face and guize,
As any Nymph (let not it be envyde.)"° *grudged*
So saying every Nymph full narrowly she eyde.

24

But Phoebe therewith sore was angeréd,
And sharply said; "Goe Dame, goe seeke your boy,
Where you him lately left, in Mars his bed;
He comes not here, we scorne his foolish joy,
Ne lend we leisure to his idle toy:° *play*
But if I catch him in this company,
By Stygian lake I vow, whose sad annoy[5]
The Gods doe dread, he dearely shall abye:° *pay*
Ile clip his wanton wings, that he no more shall fly."

25

Whom when as Venus saw so sore displeased,
She inly sory was, and gan relent,
What she had said: so her she soone appeased,
With sugred words and gentle blandishment,
Which as a fountaine from her sweet lips went,
And welléd goodly forth, that in short space
She was well pleasd, and forth her damzels sent,
Through all the woods, to search from place to place,
If any tract of him or tydings they mote trace.

5. I.e., grievous affliction.

26

To search the God of love, her Nymphes she sent
Throughout the wandring forrest every where:
And after them her selfe eke with her went
To seeke the fugitive, both farre and nere.
So long they sought, till they arrivéd were
In that same shadie covert, whereas lay
Faire Crysogone in slombry traunce whilere:° *lately*
Who in her sleepe (a wondrous thing to say)
Unwares had borne two babes, as faire as springing day.

27

Unwares she them conceived, unwares she bore:
She bore withouten paine, that she conceived
Withouten pleasure; ne her need implore
Lucinaes[6] aide: which when they both perceived,
They were through wonder nigh of sense bereaved,
And gazing each on other, nought bespake:
At last they both agreed, her seeming grieved
Out of her heavy swowne not to awake,
But from her loving side the tender babes to take.

28

Up they them tooke, each one a babe uptooke,
And with them carried, to be fosteréd;
Dame Phoebe to a Nymph her babe betooke,
To be upbrought in perfect Maydenhed,
And of her selfe her name Belphoebe red:° *called*
But Venus hers thence farre away convayd,
To be upbrought in goodly womanhed,
And in her litle loves stead, which was strayd,
Her Amoretta cald, to comfort her dismayd.

29

She brought her to her joyous Paradize,
Where most she wonnes, when she on earth does dwel.
So faire a place, as Nature can devize:
Whether in Paphos,[7] or Cytheron hill,
Or it in Gnidus be, I wote not well;
But well I wote by tryall, that this same
All other pleasant places doth excell,
And calléd is by her lost lovers name,
The Gardin of Adonis,[8] farre renowmd by fame.

6. The goddess of childbirth.
7. Important centers of the cult of Venus were at Paphos (on Cyprus) and at Cnidus, in Asia Minor. The allusion to "Cytheron hill" probably derives from Boccaccio (*Genealogiae* 3.22).
8. In antiquity, a "garden of Adonis" was a pot of quick-growing herbs (see e.g., *Phaedrus* 276b); Erasmus, *Adagia* 1.1.4, says it symbolized what is transitory or fleeting. Spenser's own Garden is in a tradition of earthly paradises such as Homer's Garden of Alcinous (*Odyssey* 7.112–34), Clau-

30

In that same Gardin all the goodly flowres,
Wherewith dame Nature doth her beautifie,
And decks the girlonds of her paramoures,
Are fetcht: there is the first seminarie° *seed plot*
Of all things, that are borne to live and die,
According to their kindes.[9] Long worke it were,
Here to account° the endlesse progenie *list*
Of all the weedes,° that bud and blossome there; *plants*
But so much as doth need, must needs be counted° here. *recounted*

31

It sited was in fruitfull soyle of old,
And girt in with two walles on either side;
The one of yron, the other of bright gold,[1]
That none might thorough breake, nor overstride:
And double gates it had, which opened wide,
By which both in and out men moten° pas; *could*
Th'one faire and fresh, the other old and dride:
Old Genius[2] the porter of them was,
Old Genius, the which a double nature has.

32

He letteth in, he letteth out to wend,
All that to come into the world desire;
A thousand thousand naked babes[3] attend
About him day and night, which doe require,
That he with fleshly weedes° would them attire: *clothes*
Such as him list, such as eternall fate
Ordainéd hath, he clothes with sinfull mire,[4]
And sendeth forth to live in mortall state,
Till they againe returne backe by the hinder gate.

33

After that they againe returnéd beene,
They in that Gardin planted be againe;

---

dian's Cyprian Garden of Venus (*Epithalamion of Honoris and Maria* 49–96), and Nature's garden in Chaucer's *Parliament of Fowls*. Love allegories like *The Romance of the Rose* and Boccaccio's *Teseide* contributed to the tradition. Spenser probably consulted all these as well as Comes 5.16.

9. The loose Neoplatonism of stanzas 30–50 reflects a number of texts, particularly the Myth of Er in Plato's *Republic*, the *Enneads* of Plotinus (or Ficino's commentary), and Arthur Golding's translation of the *Metamorphoses* together with his prefatory epistle. Spenser's account develops in four stages: stanzas 30–35 describe, first in symbolic terms, then more concretely, the cyclical process through which all life passes; stanzas 36–38 emphasize how substance survives all changes of form (a stress found also in works by the French poets Ronsard and Du Bartas); stanzas 39–42 acknowledge the power of mutability; stanzas 43–50 revise the myth of Venus and Adonis.
1. Probably from Claudian 56–57.
2. Cf. II.xii.47 and note.
3. I.e., the "seed principles" of natural life; not souls in the religious sense, for reincarnation and preexistence are not part of Christian doctrine. Cartari, *Imagini degli Dei* (Venice, 1571) 38, has a picture of such "babes" with Time as their porter.
4. I.e., the flesh.

And grow afresh, as they had never seene
Fleshly corruption, nor mortall paine.
Some thousand yeares so doen they there remaine;
And then of him are clad with other hew,° *form*
Or sent into the chaungefull world againe,
Till thither they returne, where first they grew:
So like a wheele around they runne from old to new.[5]

34

Ne needs there Gardiner to set, or sow,
To plant or prune: for of their owne accord
All things, as they created were, doe grow,
And yet remember well the mightie word,
Which first was spoken by th'Almightie lord,
That bad them to increase and multiply.[6]
Ne doe they need with water of the ford,° *stream*
Or of the clouds to moysten their roots dry;
For in themselves eternall moisture they imply.° *contain*

35

Infinite shapes of creatures there are bred,
And uncouth° formes, which none yet ever knew, *strange*
And every sort is in a sundry° bed *separate*
Set by it selfe, and ranckt in comely rew:[7]
Some fit for reasonable soules t'indew,° *put on*
Some made for beasts, some made for birds to weare,
And all the fruitfull spawne of fishes hew
In endlesse rancks along enraungéd were,
That seemed the Ocean could not containe them there.

36

Daily they grow, and daily forth are sent
Into the world, it to replenish more;
Yet is the stocke not lessenéd, nor spent,
But still remaines in everlasting store,
As it at first created was of yore.
For in the wide wombe of the world there lyes,
In hatefull darkenesse and in deepe horrore,
An huge eternall Chaos, which supplyes
The substances of natures fruitfull progenyes.[8]

5. As in Plato's Myth of Er (*Republic* 10); cf. Ovid, *Metamorphoses* 15. 165–72.
6. Genesis 1.22: "And God blessed them, saying, Be fruitful, and multiply." To mix scripture and Platonism was common; cf. Golding's prefatory epistle to his translation of the *Metamorphoses*.
7. I Corinthians 15.39: "All flesh is not the same flesh: but there is one kind of flesh of men, another flesh of beasts, and another of fishes, and another of birds."
8. Boccaccio refers to Chaos in strikingly similar terms (1.2).

37

All things from thence doe their first being fetch,
And borrow matter, whereof they are made,
Which when as forme and feature it does ketch,[9]
Becomes a bodie, and doth then invade° *enter*
The state of life, out of the griesly shade.
That substance is eterne, and bideth° so, *remains*
Ne when the life decayes, and forme does fade,
Doth it consume, and into nothing go,
But chaungéd is, and often altred to and fro.

38

The substance is not chaunged, nor alteréd,
But th'only forme and outward fashion;° *appearance*
For every substance is conditionéd° *bound*
To change her hew, and sundry formes to don,
Meet for her temper and complexion:
For formes are variable and decay,
By course of kind,° and by occasion; *nature*
And that faire flowre of beautie fades away,
As doth the lilly fresh before the sunny ray.

39

Great enimy to it, and to all the rest,
That in the Gardin of Adonis springs,
Is wicked Time, who with his scyth addrest,° *armed*
Does mow the flowring herbes and goodly things,
And all their glory to the ground downe flings,
Where they doe wither, and are fowly mard:
He flyes about, and with his flaggy° wings *drooping*
Beates downe both leaves and buds without regard,
Ne ever pittie may relent° his malice hard. *soften*

40

Yet pittie often did the gods relent,
To see so faire things mard, and spoyléd quight:
And their great mother Venus did lament
The losse of her deare brood, her deare delight:
Her hart was pierst with pittie at the sight,
When walking through the Gardin, them she spyde,
Yet no'te she find redresse for such despight.[1]
For all that lives, is subject to that law:
All things decay in time, and to their end do draw.

9. I.e., when it assumes shape and outline. The word "forme" in stanzas 37–38 seems confusingly at odds with the expressions in stanzas 32 and 35.
1. I.e., she could not repair that injury. Stanza 42 makes clear, though, that Time's effect on the Garden differs from its effect on our world.

41

But were it not, that Time their troubler is,
All that in this delightfull Gardin growes,
Should happie be, and have immortall blis:
For here all plentie, and all pleasure flowes,
And sweet love gentle fits° emongst them throwes, *impulses*
Without fell rancor, or fond gealosie;
Franckly each paramour his leman° knowes, *beloved*
Each bird his mate, ne any does envie
Their goodly meriment, and gay felicitie.

42

There is continuall spring, and harvest there
Continuall, both meeting at one time:
For both the boughes doe laughing blossomes beare,
And with fresh colours decke the wanton Prime,[2]
And eke attonce the heavy trees they clime,
Which seeme to labour under their fruits lode:
The whiles the joyous birdes make their pastime
Emongst the shadie leaves, their sweet abode,
And their true loves without suspition tell abrode.

43

Right in the middest of that Paradise,
There stood a stately Mount,[3] on whose round top
A gloomy grove of mirtle trees did rise,
Whose shadie boughes sharpe steele did never lop,
Nor wicked beasts their tender buds did crop,
But like a girlond compasséd the hight,
And from their fruitfull sides sweet gum did drop,
That all the ground with precious deaw bedight,
Threw forth most dainty odours, and most sweet delight.

44

And in the thickest covert of that shade,
There was a pleasant arbour, not by art,
But of the trees owne inclination made,
Which knitting their rancke° braunches part to part, *dense*
With wanton yvie twyne entrayld° athwart, *interlaced*
And Eglantine, and Caprifole° emong, *honeysuckle*
Fashioned above within their inmost part,
That nether Phoebus beams could through them throng,
Nor Aeolus sharp blast could worke them any wrong.

2. I.e., luxuriant spring.
3. The goddess lies with her young lover in terrain representing her own pubic region; myrtle, the plant of Venus growing on the *mons veneris*, parallels the laurel of poetry and conquest that Spenser perhaps ironically placed in the Bower of Bliss (II.xii). In the 1590 *Faerie Queene* this scene "in the middest of that Paradise" comes at the exact center of Book III.

45

And all about grew every sort of flowre,
To which sad lovers were transformd of yore;
Fresh Hyacinthus,[4] Phoebus paramoure,
And dearest love,
Foolish Narcisse, that likes the watry shore,
Sad Amaranthus,[5]made a flowre but late,
Sad Amaranthus, in whose purple gore
Me seemes I see Amintas[6] wretched fate,
To whom sweet Poets verse hath given endlesse date.

46

There wont faire Venus often to enjoy
Her deare Adonis joyous company,
And reape sweet pleasure of the wanton boy;
There yet, some say, in secret he does ly,
Lappéd in flowres and pretious spycery,
By her hid from the world, and from the skill° *knowledge*
Of Stygian Gods, which doe her love envy;
But she her selfe, when ever that she will,
Possesseth him, and of his sweetnesse takes her fill.

47

And sooth it seemes they say: for he may not
For ever die, and ever buried bee
In balefull night, where all things are forgot;
All° be he subject to mortalitie, *although*
Yet is eterne in mutabilitie,
And by succession made perpetuall,
Transforméd oft, and chaungéd diverslie:
For him the Father of all formes[7] they call;
Therefore needs mote he live, that living gives to all.

48

There now he liveth in eternall blis,
Joying his goddesse, and of her enjoyed:
Ne feareth he henceforth that foe of his,
Which with his cruell tuske him deadly cloyd:° *gored*

4. After accidentally killing the youth Hyacinthus, Apollo made the hyacinth spring from his beloved's blood and bear the marking "AI AI" ("alas"); see *Metamorphoses* 10.163–219 and, on Narcissus, 3.341–511.
5. Greek for "unfading," a flower traditionally symbolizing eternity.
6. Amyntas is a shepherd in Virgil's *Eclogues* 10. The stress on the recent metamorphosis of Amaranthus into a flower and the comparison to "Amintas late" may allude to the much-lamented Philip Sidney, who died fighting in the Netherlands in 1586.
7. Exactly how form relates to matter in the Garden is unclear and has been debated. Since Venus actively "posseseth" Adonis, her relation to him suggests that of form impressing matter, reversing the tradition that form is male and matter female. But Adonis seems also to represent a formal principle that survives through the very multiplicity it prints on matter.

For that wilde Bore,[8] the which him once annoyd,° *injured*
She firmely hath emprisonéd for ay,
That her sweet love his malice mote avoyd,
In a strong rocky Cave, which is they say,
Hewen underneath that Mount, that none him losen° may. *set free*

49

There now he lives in everlasting joy,
With many of the Gods in company,
Which thither haunt,° and with the wingéd boy *frequent*
Sporting himselfe in safe felicity:
Who when he hath with spoiles and cruelty
Ransackt the world, and in the wofull harts
Of many wretches set his triumphes hye,
Thither resorts, and laying his sad darts
Aside, with faire Adonis playes his wanton parts.

50

And his true love faire Psyche[9] with him playes,
Faire Psyche to him lately reconcyld,
After long troubles and unmeet upbrayes,° *reproaches*
With which his mother Venus her revyld,° *scolded*
And eke himselfe her cruelly exyld:
But now in stedfast love and happy state
She with him lives, and hath him borne a chyld,
Pleasure, that doth both gods and men aggrate,° *gratify*
Pleasure, the daughter of Cupid and Psyche late.

51

Hither great Venus brought this infant faire,
The younger daughter of Chrysogonee,[1]
And unto Psyche with great trust and care
Committed her, yfosteréd to bee,
And trainéd up in true feminitee:
Who no lesse carefully her tenderéd,° *cared for*
Then her owne daughter Pleasure, to whom shee
Made her companion, and her lessonéd° *taught*
In all the lore of love, and goodly womanhead.

52

In which when she to perfect ripenesse grew,
Of grace and beautie noble Paragone,° *model*
She brought her forth into the worldés vew,

8. On a solar Adonis and a wintry boar see, e.g., Comes 5.16. That the boar is under the mount of Venus, the *mons veneris*, may suggest, in this anamorphic corporal allegory, that the creature is imprisoned inside Venus's own genitalia.
9. The story of Cupid and Psyche is told by Apuleius in his second-century *Metamorphoses*, trans. W. Adlington as *The Golden Asse* in 1566.
1. I.e., Amoret, whose name includes *amor*, or "love."

To be th'ensample of true love alone,
And Lodestarre of all chaste affectione,
To all faire Ladies, that doe live on ground.
To Faery court she came, where many one
Admyrd her goodly haveour,° and found — *deportment*
His feeble hart wide launchéd° with loves cruell wound. — *pierced*

53

But she to none of them her love did cast,° — *grant*
Save to the noble knight Sir Scudamore,
To whom her loving hart she linkéd fast
In faithfull love, t'abide for evermore,
And for his dearest sake enduréd sore,° — *grievous*
Sore trouble of an hainous enimy;
Who her would forcéd have to have forlore
Her former love, and stedfast loialty,
As ye may elsewhere read that ruefull history.

54

But well I weene, ye first desire to learne,
What end unto that fearefull Damozell,
Which fled so fast from that same foster stearne,
Whom with his brethren Timias slew, befell:
That was to weet, the goodly Florimell;
Who wandring for to seeke her lover deare,
Her lover deare, her dearest Marinell,
Into misfortune fell, as ye did heare,
And from Prince Arthur fled with wings of idle feare.

Canto VII

The witches sonne loves Florimell:
she flyes, he faines° to die. — *desires*
Satyrane saves the Squire of Dames
from Gyants tyrannie.

I

Like as an Hynd forth singled from the heard,
That hath escapéd from a ravenous beast,
Yet flyes away of her owne feet affeard,
And every leafe, that shaketh with the least
Murmure of winde, her terror hath encreast;
So fled faire Florimell from her vaine feare,
Long after she from perill was releast:
Each shade she saw, and each noyse she did heare,
Did seeme to be the same, which she escapt whyleare.[1]

1. Florimell's flight parallels that of Angelica from Rinaldo in *Orlando Furioso* 1.33–34, which itself has models in Horace and Anacreon.

2

All that same evening she in flying spent,
  And all that night her course continewéd:
  Ne did she let dull sleepe once to relent,° *slacken*
  Nor wearinesse to slacke her hast, but fled
  Ever alike, as if her former dred
  Were hard behind, her readie to arrest:° *seize*
  And her white Palfrey having conqueréd
  The maistring raines out of her weary wrest,° *wrist*
Perforce her carriéd, where ever he thought best.

3

So long as breath, and hable° puissance *sufficient*
  Did native courage unto him supply,
  His pace he freshly forward did advaunce,
  And carried her beyond all jeopardy,
  But nought that wanteth rest, can long aby.° *endure*
  He having through incessant travell spent
  His force, at last perforce a downe did ly,
  Ne foot could further move: The Lady gent° *noble*
Thereat was suddein strooke with great astonishment.° *dismay*

4

And forst t'alight, on foot mote algates° fare, *entirely*
  A traveller unwonted to such way:
  Need teacheth her this lesson hard and rare,
  That fortune all in equall launce° doth sway, *balance*
  And mortall miseries doth make her play.
  So long she travelled, till at length she came
  To an hilles side, which did to her bewray
  A little valley, subject to[2] the same,
All covered with thick woods, that quite it overcame.° *spread over*

5

Through the tops of the high trees she did descry
  A litle smoke, whose vapour thin and light,
  Reeking° aloft, uprolléd to the sky: *smoking*
  Which chearefull signe did send unto her sight,
  That in the same did wonne some living wight.
  Eftsoones her steps she thereunto applyde,
  And came at last in weary wretched plight
  Unto the place, to which her hope did guyde,
To find some refuge there, and rest her weary syde.

2. I.e., beneath.

6

There in a gloomy hollow glen she found
A little cottage, built of stickes and reedes
In homely wize, and wald with sods around,
In which a witch did dwell, in loathly weedes,° *garments*
And wilfull want, all carelesse of her needes;
So choosing solitaire to abide,
Far from all neighbours, that her devilish deedes
And hellish arts from people she might hide,
And hurt far off unknowne, whom ever she envide.° *hated*

7

The Damzell there arriving entred in;
Where sitting on the flore the Hag she found,
Busie (as seemed) about some wicked gin:° *scheme*
Who soone as she beheld that suddein stound,° *surprising sight*
Lightly upstarted from the dustie ground,
And with fell looke and hollow deadly gaze
Staréd on her awhile, as one astound,° *stunned*
Ne had one word to speake, for great amaze,
But shewd by outward signes, that dread her sence did daze.

8

At last turning her feare to foolish wrath,
She askt, what devill had her thither brought,
And who she was, and what unwonted° path *unfamiliar*
Had guided her, unwelcoméd, unsought?
To which the Damzell full of doubtfull thought,
Her mildly answered; "Beldame be not wroth
With silly° Virgin by adventure brought *innocent*
Unto your dwelling, ignorant and loth,° *reluctant*
That crave but rowme to rest, while tempest overblo'th."

9

With that adowne out of her Christall eyne
Few trickling teares she softly forth let fall,
That like two Orient pearles, did purely shyne
Upon her snowy cheeke; and therewithall
She sighéd soft, that none so bestiall,
Nor salvage hart, but ruth° of her sad plight *pity*
Would make to melt, or pitteously appall;
And that vile Hag, all° were her whole delight *although*
In mischiefe, was much movéd at so pitteous sight.

10

And gan recomfort her in her rude wyse,
With womanish compassion of her plaint,
Wiping the teares from her suffuséd eyes,

And bidding her sit downe, to rest her faint
And wearie limbs a while. She nothing quaint° *fastidious*
Nor s'deignfull of so homely fashion,
Sith brought she was now to so hard constraint,
Sate downe upon the dusty ground anon,
As glad of that small rest, as Bird of tempest gon.° *passed*

11

Tho gan she gather up her garments rent,° *torn*
And her loose lockes to dight in order dew,
With golden wreath and gorgeous ornament;
Whom such whenas the wicked Hag did vew,
She was astonisht at her heavenly hew,° *appearance*
And doubted her to deeme an earthly wight,
But or° some Goddesse, or of Dianes crew, *either*
And thought her to adore with humble spright;
T'adore thing so divine as beauty, were but right.

12

This wicked woman had a wicked sonne,
The comfort of her age and weary dayes,
A laesie loord,° for nothing good to donne,[3] *lout*
But stretchéd forth in idlenesse alwayes,
Ne ever cast his mind to covet prayse,
Or ply him selfe to any honest trade,
But all the day before the sunny rayes
He used to slug,° or sleepe in slothfull shade: *idle*
Such laesinesse both lewd° and poore attonce him made. *ignorant*

13

He comming home at undertime,° there found *noon*
The fairest creature, that he ever saw,
Sitting beside his mother on the ground;
The sight whereof did greatly him adaw,° *daunt*
And his base thought with terrour and with aw
So inly smot, that as one, which had gazed
On the bright Sunne unwares, doth soone withdraw
His feeble eyne, with too much brightnesse dazed,
So staréd he on her, and stood long while amazed.

14

Softly at last he gan his mother aske,
What mister° wight that was, and whence derived, *kind of*
That in so straunge disguizement there did maske,
And by what accident she there arrived:
But she, as one nigh of her wits deprived,
With nought but ghastly lookes him answeréd,

3. I.e., good for nothing.

Like to a ghost, that lately is revived
From Stygian shores, where late it wanderéd;
So both at her, and each at other wonderéd.

15

But the faire Virgin was so meeke and mild,
That she to them vouchsaféd to embace
Her goodly port,[4] and to their senses vild,° *vile*
Her gentle speach applide, that in short space
She grew familiare in that desert° place. *desolate*
During which time, the Chorle° through her so kind *churl*
And curteise use° conceived affection bace, *demeanour*
And cast° to love her in his brutish mind; *resolved*
No love, but brutish lust, that was so beastly tind.° *kindled*

16

Closely° the wicked flame his bowels brent,° *secretly / burned*
And shortly grew into outrageous fire;
Yet had he not the hart, nor hardiment,
As unto her to utter his desire;
His caytive° thought durst not so high aspire, *base*
But with soft sighes, and lovely semblaunces,° *expressions*
He weened that his affection entire
She should aread; many resemblaunces° *signs of love*
To her he made, and many kind remembraunces.

17

Oft from the forrest wildings° he did bring, *crab apples*
Whose sides empurpled were with smiling red,
And oft young birds, which he had taught to sing
His mistresse prayses, sweetly caroléd,
Girlonds of flowres sometimes for her faire hed
He fine would dight; sometimes the squirell wild
He brought to her in bands, as conqueréd
To be her thrall, his fellow servant vild;
All which, she of him tooke with countenance meeke and mild.

18

But past awhile, when she fit season° saw *time*
To leave that desert mansion, she cast
In secret wize her selfe thence to withdraw,
For feare of mischiefe, which she did forecast
Might be by the witch or that her sonne compast:° *contrived*
Her wearie Palfrey closely, as she might,
Now well recovered after long repast,
In his proud furnitures° she freshly dight, *trappings*
His late miswandred wayes now to remeasure° right. *retrace*

4. I.e., she adopted a gently courteous manner toward them.

19

And earely ere the dawning day appeard,
She forth issewed, and on her journey went;
She went in perill, of each noyse affeard,
And of each shade, that did it selfe present;
For still she fearéd to be overhent,° *overtaken*
Of that vile hag, or her uncivile sonne:
Who when too late awaking, well they kent,° *discovered*
That their faire guest was gone, they both begonne
To make exceeding mone, as they had bene undonne.

20

But that lewd° lover did the most lament *base*
For her depart, that ever man did heare;
He knockt his brest with desperate intent,
And scratcht his face, and with his teeth did teare
His rugged flesh, and rent his ragged heare:
That his sad mother seeing his sore plight,
Was greatly woe begon, and gan to feare,
Least his fraile senses were emperish° quight, *enfeebled*
And love to frenzy turnd, sith love is franticke hight.

21

All wayes she sought, him to restore to plight,
With herbs, with charms, with counsell, and with teares,
But tears, nor charms, nor herbs, nor counsell might
Asswage the fury, which his entrails teares:
So strong is passion, that no reason heares.
Tho when all other helpes she saw to faile,
She turnd her selfe backe to her wicked leares° *lessons*
And by her devilish arts thought to prevaile,
To bring her backe againe, or worke her finall bale.° *harm*

22

Eftsoones out of her hidden cave she cald
An hideous beast,[5] of horrible aspect,
That could the stoutest courage have appald;
Monstrous mishapt, and all his backe was spect° *speckled*
With thousand spots of colours queint elect,[6]
Thereto so swift, that it all beasts did pas:
Like never yet did living eye detect;
But likest it to an Hyena was,
That feeds on womens flesh, as others feede on gras.

5. Stanzas 22–28 are based on the pursuit of Manricardo by a monstrous "orc" in Boiardo, *Orlando Innamorato* (3.3.24 ff.). Medieval bestiaries associate the hyena with changefulness, hypocrisy, sin, and death.
6. I.e., strangely chosen.

23

It forth she cald, and gave it streight in charge,
Through thicke and thin her to pursew apace,
Ne once to stay to rest, or breath at large,
Till her he had attaind, and brought in place,[7]
Or quite devourd her beauties scornefull grace.
The Monster swift as word, that from her went,
Went forth in hast, and did her footing trace
So sure and swiftly, through his perfect sent,° *scent*
And passing speede, that shortly he her overhent.

24

Whom when the fearefull Damzell nigh espide,
No need to bid her fast away to flie;
That ugly shape so sore her terrifide,
That it she shund no lesse, then dread to die,
And her flit° Palfrey did so well apply° *fleet / adapt*
His nimble feet to her conceivéd feare,
That whilest his breath did strength to him supply,
From perill free he her away did beare:
But when his force gan faile, his pace gan wex areare.° *slacken*

25

Which whenas she perceived, she was dismayd
At that same last extremitie° full sore, *adversity*
And of her safetie greatly grew afrayd;
And now she gan approch to the sea shore,
As it befell, that she could flie no more,
But yield her selfe to spoile of greedinesse.
Lightly she leapéd, as a wight forlore,
From her dull horse, in desperate distresse,
And to her feet betooke her doubtfull sickernesse.° *safety*

26

Not halfe so fast the wicked Myrrha[8] fled
From dread of her revenging fathers hond:
Nor halfe so fast to save her maidenhed,
Fled fearefull Daphne on th'Aegaean strond,
As Florimell fled from that Monster yond,
To reach the sea, ere she of him were raught.° *seized*
For in the sea to drowne her selfe she fond,° *tried*
Rather then of the tyrant to be caught:
Thereto feare gave her wings, and neede her courage taught.

7. I.e., back to the witch's abode.
8. For Myrrha, see the note on III.ii.41; Daphne, fleeing from Apollo, was turned into a laurel tree (Ovid, *Metamorphoses* 1.450–567).

27

It fortunéd (high God did so ordaine)
As she arrivéd on the roring shore,
In minde to leape into the mighty maine,
A little boate lay hoving° her before, *floating*
In which there slept a fisher old and pore,
The whiles his nets were drying on the sand;
Into the same she leapt, and with the ore° *oar*
Did thrust the shallop° from the floting strand: *sailboat*
So safetie found at sea, which she found not at land.

28

The Monster ready on the pray to sease,
Was of his forward° hope deceivéd quight; *eager*
Ne durst assay to wade the perlous seas,
But greedily long gaping at the sight,
At last in vaine was forst to turne his flight,
And tell the idle tidings to his Dame:
Yet to avenge his devilish despight,° *malice*
He set upon her Palfrey tired lame,
And slew him cruelly, ere any reskew came.

29

And after having him embowelléd,
To fill his hellish gorge,° it chaunst a knight *maw*
To passe that way, as forth he travelléd;
It was a goodly Swaine, and of great might,
As ever man that bloudy field did fight;
But in vaine sheows,° that wont young knights bewitch, *pretence*
And courtly services tooke no delight,
But rather joyd to be, then seemen sich.° *such*
For both to be and seeme to him was labour lich.° *like*

30

It was to weete the good Sir Satyrane,
That raungd abroad to seeke adventures wilde,
As was his wont in forrest, and in plaine;
He was all armd in rugged steel unfilde,° *unpolished*
As in the smoky forge it was compilde,° *made*
And in his Scutchin° bore a Satyres hed: *shield*
He comming present, where the Monster vilde
Upon that milke-white Palfreyes carkas fed,
Unto his reskew ran, and greedily him sped.

31

There well perceived he, that it was the horse,
Whereon faire Florimell was wont to ride,
That of that feend was rent without remorse:

Much fearéd he, least ought did ill betide
To that faire Mayd, the flowre of womens pride;
For her he dearely lovéd, and in all
His famous conquests highly magnified:° *glorified*
Besides her golden girdle, which did fall
From her in flight, he found, that did him sore apall.° *dismay*

32

Full of sad feare, and doubtfull agony,
Fiercely he flew upon that wicked feend,
And with huge strokes, and cruell battery
Him forst to leave his pray, for to attend
Him selfe from deadly daunger to defend:
Full many wounds in his corrupted flesh
He did engrave,° and muchell bloud did spend, *cut deeply*
Yet might not do him dye, but aye more fresh
And fierce he still appeard, the more he did him thresh.° *strike*

33

He wist not, how him to despoile of life,
Ne how to win the wishéd victory,
Sith him he saw still stronger grow through strife,
And him selfe weaker through infirmity;
Greatly he grew enraged, and furiously
Hurling his sword away, he lightly lept
Upon the beast, that with great cruelty° *ferocity*
Roréd, and ragéd to be under-kept.° *held down*
Yet he perforce him held, and strokes upon him hept.

34

As he that strives to stop a suddein flood,
And in strong banckes his violence enclose,
Forceth it swell above his wonted mood,
And largely overflow the fruitfull plaine,
That all the countrey seemes to be a Maine,° *sea*
And the rich furrowes flote, all quite fordonne:° *ruined*
The wofull husbandman doth lowd complaine,
To see his whole yeares labour lost so soone,
For which to God he made so many an idle boone.° *prayer*

35

So him he held, and did through might amate:° *subdue*
So long he held him, and him bet so long,
That at the last his fiercenesse gan abate,
And meekely stoup unto the victour strong:
Who to avenge the implacable° wrong, *irremediable*
Which he supposéd donne to Florimell,
Sought by all meanes his dolour° to prolong, *pain*

Sith dint of steele his carcas could not quell:
His maker with her charmes had framéd him so well.

36

The golden ribband, which that virgin wore
About her sclender wast, he tooke in hand,
And with it bound the beast, that lowd did rore
For great despight of that unwonted band,
Yet daréd not his victour to withstand,
But trembled like a lambe, fled from the pray,
And all the way him followd on the strand,
As he had long bene learnéd to obay;
Yet never learnéd he such service, till that day.[9]

37

Thus as he led the Beast along the way,
He spide far off a mighty Giauntesse,[1]
Fast flying on a Courser dapled gray,
From a bold knight, that with great hardinesse
Her hard pursewd, and sought for to suppresse;
She bore before her lap a dolefull Squire,
Lying athwart° her horse in great distresse, *across*
Fast bounden hand and foote with cords of wire,
Whom she did meane to make the thrall of her desire.

38

Which whenas Satyrane beheld, in hast
He left his captive Beast at liberty,
And crost the nearest way, by which he cast° *intended*
Her to encounter, ere she passéd by:
But she the way shund nathemore for thy,[2]
But forward gallopt fast; which when he spyde,
His mighty speare he couchéd warily,
And at her ran: she having him descryde,
Her selfe to fight addrest,° and threw her lode aside. *prepared*

39

Like as a Goshauke, that in foote doth beare
A trembling Culver,° having spide on hight *dove*
An Egle, that with plumy wings doth sheare
The subtile ayre, stouping° with all his might, *plunging*
The quarrey throwes to ground with fell despight,
And to the battell doth her selfe prepare:

9. IV.v.3 will associate this sash (then sometimes called a "girdle") with chastity.
1. Judith H. Anderson, "Arthur, Argante, and the Ideal Vision: An Exercise in Speculation and Parody," in *Reading the Allegorical Intertext: Chaucer, Spenser, Shakespeare, Milton* (New York: Fordham UP), 126–34, suggests that this giantess parodies the aging Elizabeth's "notorious exploitation of courtly flirtation."
2. I.e., but she did not turn aside on that account.

So ran the Geauntesse unto the fight;
Her firie eyes with furious sparkes did stare,° *glitter*
And with blasphemous bannes° high God in peeces tare.[3] *oaths*

40

She caught in hand an huge great yron mace,
Wherewith she many had of life deprived,
But ere the stroke could seize° his aymèd place, *attain*
His speare amids her sun-broad shield arrived;
Yet nathemore the steele a sunder rived,
All were the beame° in bignesse like a mast, *spear*
Ne her out of the stedfast sadle drived,
But glauncing on the tempred metall, brast° *burst*
In thousand shivers, and so forth beside her past.

41

Her Steed did stagger with that puissaunt strooke;
But she no more was movèd with that might,
Then it had lighted° on an aged Oke; *fallen*
Or on the marble Pillour, that is pight° *placed*
Upon the top of Mount Olympus hight,
For the brave youthly Champions to assay,
With burning charet wheeles it nigh to smite.[4]
But who that smites it, mars his joyous play,
And is the spectacle of ruinous decay.° *destruction*

42

Yet therewith sore enraged, with sterne regard
Her dreadfull weapon she to him addrest,° *directed*
Which on his helmet martellèd° so hard, *hammered*
That made him low incline his lofty crest,
And bowd his battred visour to his brest:
Wherewith he was so stund, that he n'ote° ryde, *could not*
But reelèd to and fro from East to West:
Which when his cruel enimy espyde,
She lightly unto him adjoynèd side to syde;

43

And on his collar laying puissant hand,
Out of his wavering seat him pluckt perforse,° *forcibly*
Perforse him pluckt, unable to withstand,
Or helpe himselfe, and laying thwart her horse,
In loathly wise like to a carion corse,° *corpse*
She bore him fast away. Which when the knight,
That her pursewèd, saw, with great remorse° *compassion*

3. I.e., dismember the body of Christ with then common oaths such as "swounds" ("his wounds") or "sdeath" ("his death").
4. The assumption that Mount Olympus was the site of the Olympic Games appears also in Sidney's *Apologie for Poetrie*, but Spenser may have been misled by phrasing in Comes 5.1.

He neare was touchéd in his noble spright,
And gan encrease his speed, as she encreast her flight.

44

Whom when as nigh approching she espyde,
She threw away her burden angrily;
For she list° not the battell to abide, *cared*
But made her selfe more light, away to fly:
Yet her the hardy knight pursewd so nye,
That almost in the backe he oft her strake:
But still when him at hand she did espy,
She turnd, and semblaunce of faire fight did make;
But when he stayd, to flight againe she did her take.

45

By this the good Sir Satyrane gan wake
Out of his dreame, that did him long entraunce,
And seeing none in place, he gan to make
Exceeding mone, and curst that cruell chaunce,
Which reft from him so faire a chevisaunce:° *enterprise*
At length he spide, whereas that wofull Squire,
Whom he had reskewéd from captivaunce
Of his strong foe, lay tombled in the myre,
Unable to arise, or foot or hand to styre.° *stir*

46

To whom approching, well he mote perceive
In that foule plight a comely personage,
And lovely face, made fit for to deceive
Fraile Ladies hart with loves consuming rage,
Now in the blossome of his freshest age:
He reard him up, and loosd his yron bands,
And after gan inquire his parentage,
And how he fell into that Gyaunts hands,
And who that was, which chacéd her along the lands.° *countryside*

47

Then trembling yet through feare, the Squire bespake,
"That Geauntesse Argante[5] is behight,
A daughter of the Titans which did make
Warre against heaven, and heapéd hils on hight,
To scale the skyes, and put Jove from his right:
Her sire Typhoeus was, who mad through merth,
And drunke with bloud of men, slaine by his might,

5. The name of this "geauntesse," Argante, suggests the Greek (αργος) for speedy brightness, and the name "Argus" can imply a many-eyed alertness. But Judith Anderson shows the greater relevance of the benign Argante, queen of Avalon, in Layamon's *Brut* (Anderson 2008, 126–34).

Through incest, her of his owne mother Earth
Whilome begot, being but halfe twin of that berth.

48

"For at that berth another Babe she bore,
To weet the mighty Ollyphant[6] that wrought
Great wreake° to many errant knights of yore, *destruction*
And many hath to foule confusion° brought. *ruin*
These twinnes, men say, (a thing far passing thought)
Whiles in their mothers wombe enclosd they were,
Ere they into the lightsome° world were brought, *bright*
In fleshly lust were mingled both yfere,° *together*
And in that monstrous wise did to the world appere.

49

"So lived they ever after in like sin,
Gainst natures law, and good behavioure:° *conduct*
But greatest shame was to that maiden twin,
Who not content so fowly to devoure° *eagerly enjoy*
Her native flesh, and staine her brothers bowre,
Did wallow in all other fleshly myre,
And suffred beasts her body to deflowre:
So whot° she burnéd in that lustfull fyre, *hot*
Yet all that might not slake her sensuall desyre.

50

"But over all the countrey she did raunge,
To seeke young men, to quench her flaming thrust,° *thirst*
And feed her fancy with delightfull chaunge:
Whom so she fittest finds to serve her lust,
Through her maine° strength, in which she most doth trust, *mighty*
She with her brings into a secret Ile,
Where in eternall bondage dye he must,
Or be the vassall of her pleasures vile,
And in all shamefull sort him selfe with her defile.

51

"Me seely° wretch she so at vauntage caught, *simple*
After she long in waite for me did lye,
And meant unto her prison to have brought,
Her lothsome pleasure there to satisfye;
That thousand deathes me lever° were to dye, *rather*
Then breake the vow, that to faire Columbell
I plighted have, and yet keepe stedfastly:

6. Literally, "elephant"; cf. the "geaunt" named "Sire Olifaunt" in Chaucer's comic "Tale of Sir Thopas." The parentage Spenser invents for the twins explains their sexual perversity and pride, vices shared with the Giants and Titans who opposed Zeus's rule.

As for my name, it mistreth° not to tell; *needs*
Call me the Squyre of Dames,[7] that me beseemeth well.

52

"But that bold knight, whom ye pursuing saw
That Geauntesse, is not such, as she seemed,
But a faire virgin, that in martiall law,
And deedes of armes above all Dames is deemed,
And above many knights is eke esteemed,
For her great worth; She Palladine is hight:
She you from death, you me from dread redeemed.
Ne any may that Monster match in fight,
But she, or such as she, that is so chaste a wight."[8]

53

"Her well beseemes that Quest," quoth Satyrane,
"But read, thou Squyre of Dames, what vow is this,
Which thou upon thy selfe hast lately ta'ne?"
"That shall I you recount," quoth he, "ywis,° *certainly*
So be ye pleasd to pardon all amis.
That gentle Lady, whom I love and serve,
After long suit and weary servicis,
Did aske me, how I could her love deserve,
And how she might be sure, that I would never swerve.

54

"I glad by any meanes her grace to gaine,
Bad her commaund my life to save, or spill.° *destroy*
Eftsoones she bad me, with incessaunt paine
To wander through the world abroad at will,
And every where, where with my power or skill
I might do service unto gentle Dames,
That I the same should faithfully fulfill,
And at the twelve monethes end should bring their names
And pledges; as the spoiles of my victorious games.

55

"So well I to faire Ladies service did,
And found such favour in their loving hartes,
That ere the yeare his course had compassid,° *completed*
Three hundred pledges for my good desartes,
And thrise three hundred thanks for my good partes° *conduct*
I with me brought, and did to her present:
Which when she saw, more bent to eke° my smartes, *add to*

7. The Squire comically exemplifies bondage to conventional love codes (cf. *Orlando Furioso* 28).
8. Palladine's name suggests "paladin" (a knightly champion) and the giant-fighter Pallas Athena; she may represent an early version of Britomart.

Then to reward my trusty true intent,
She gan for me devise a grievous punishment.

56

"To weet, that I my travell should resume,
And with like labour walke the world around,
Ne ever to her presence should presume,
Till I so many other Dames had found,
The which, for all the suit I could propound,
Would me refuse their pledges to afford,
But did abide for ever chast and sound."
"Ah gentle Squire," quoth he, "tell at one word,
How many foundst thou such to put in thy record?"

57

"In deed Sir knight," said he, "one word may tell
All, that I ever found so wisely stayd;° *constant*
For onely three they were disposd so well,
And yet three yeares I now abroad have stayd,
To find them out." "Mote I," then laughing sayd
The knight, "inquire of thee, what were those three,
The which thy proffred curtesie denayd?° *rejected*
Or ill they seeméd sure avizd to bee,[9]
Or brutishly brought up, that nev'r did fashions see."

58

"The first which then refuséd me," said hee,
"Certes was but a common Courtisane,
Yet flat refusd to have a do with mee,
Because I could not give her many a Jane."° *coin*
(Thereat full hartely laughed Satyrane).
"The second was an holy Nunne to chose,[1]
Which would not let me be her Chappellane,° *confessor*
Because she knew, she said, I would disclose
Her counsell,° if she should her trust in me repose. *secrets*

59

"The third a Damzell was of low degree,
Whom I in countrey cottage found by chaunce;
Full little weenéd I, that chastitee
Had lodging in so meane a maintenaunce,° *condition*
Yet was she faire, and in her countenance
Dwelt simple truth in seemely fashion.
Long thus I wooed her with dew observaunce,
In hope unto my pleasure to have won;
But was as farre at last, as when I first begon.

9. I.e., either they were foolish.
1. I.e., if you please.

60

"Safe her, I never any woman found,
That chastity did for it selfe embrace,
But were for other causes firme and sound;
Either for want of handsome° time and place, *suitable*
Or else for feare of shame and fowle disgrace.
Thus am I hopelesse ever to attaine
My Ladies love, in such a desperate case.
But all my dayes am like to wast in vaine,
Seeking to match the chaste with th'unchaste Ladies traine."° *company*

61

"Perdy," said Satyrane, "thou Squire of Dames,
Great labour fondly° hast thou hent° in hand, *foolishly / taken*
To get small thankes, and therewith many blames,
That may emongst Alcides[2] labours stand."
Thence backe returning to the former land,° *place*
Where late he left the Beast, he overcame,
He found him not; for he had broke his band,
And was returned againe unto his Dame,
To tell what tydings of faire Florimell became.

Canto VIII

The Witch creates a snowy Lady,
like to Florimell,
Who wronged by Carle° by Proteus saved, *churl*
is sought by Paridell.

1

So oft as I this history record,
My hart doth melt with meere° compassion, *pure*
To thinke, how causelesse of her owne accord[1]
This gentle Damzell, whom I write upon,
Should plongéd be in such affliction,
Without all hope of comfort or reliefe,
That sure I weene, the hardest hart of stone,
Would hardly find° to aggravate her griefe; *choose*
For misery craves rather mercie, then repriefe.° *reproach*

2

But that accurséd Hag, her hostesse late,
Had so enranckled her malitious hart,
That she desyrd th'abridgement of her fate,[2]
Or long enlargement° of her painefull smart. *increase*
Now when the Beast, which by her wicked art

2. Hercules.
1. I.e., through no culpable action on her part.
2. I.e., to shorten the fated term of her life.

Late forth she sent, she backe returning spyde,
Tyde with her broken girdle, it a part
Of her rich spoyles, whom he had earst destroyd,
She weend,° and wondrous gladnesse to her hart applyde. *supposed*

3

And with it running hast'ly to her sonne,
Thought with that sight him much to have relived;° *restored*
Who thereby deeming sure the thing as donne,
His former griefe with furie fresh revived,
Much more then earst, and would have algates rived[3]
The hart out of his brest: for sith her ded
He surely dempt,° himselfe he thought deprived *thought*
Quite of all hope, wherewith he long had fed
His foolish maladie, and long time had misled.

4

With thought whereof, exceeding mad° he grew, *frenzied*
And in his rage his mother would have slaine,
Had she not fled into a secret mew,° *hiding place*
Where she was wont her Sprights to entertaine
The maisters of her art[4] there was she faine° *accustomed*
To call them all in order to her ayde,
And them conjure° upon eternall paine, *charge*
To counsell her so carefully° dismayd, *grievously*
How she might heale her sonne, whose senses were decayd.° *destroyed*

5

By their advise, and her owne wicked wit,
She there devized a wondrous worke to frame,° *construct*
Whose like on earth was never framéd yit,
That even Nature selfe envide the same,
And grudged to see the counterfet should shame
The thing it selfe. In hand she boldly tooke
To make another like the former Dame,
Another Florimell, in shape and looke
So lively° and so like, that many it mistooke. *lifelike*

6

The substance, whereof she the bodie made,
Was purest snow in massie mould congeald,
Which she had gathered in a shadie glade
Of the Riphoean hils,[5] to her reveald
By errant Sprights, but from all men conceald:
The same she tempred with fine Mercury,

3. I.e., entirely torn.
4. The demons who enable her magic; in *Macbeth* the witches call such spirits "masters" (4.1.63).
5. Mountains once supposed to be in the wilds of northern Eurasia.

And virgin wex, that never yet was seald,
And mingled them with perfect vermily,° *vermilion*
That like a lively sanguine° it seemed to the eye. *blood-red*

7

In stead of eyes two burning lampes she set
In silver sockets, shyning like the skyes,
And a quicke moving Spirit did arret° *assign*
To stirre and roll them, like a womans eyes;
In stead of yellow lockes she did devise,
With golden wyre° to weave her curléd head; *metallic thread*
Yet golden wyre was not so yellow thrise° *by a third*
As Florimells faire haire: and in the stead
Of life, she put a Spright to rule the carkasse dead.

8

A wicked Spright yfraught° with fawning guile, *filled*
And faire resemblance above all the rest,
Which with the Prince of Darknesse fell somewhile,
From heavens blisse and everlasting rest;
Him needed not instruct,[6] which way were best
Himselfe to fashion likest Florimell,
Ne how to speake, ne how to use his gest,° *bearing*
For he in counterfeisance° did excell, *deception*
And all the wyles of wemens wits knew passing well.[7]

9

Him shapéd thus, she deckt in garments gay,
Which Florimell had left behind her late,
That who so then her saw, would surely say,
It was her selfe, whom it did imitate,
Or fairer then her selfe, if ought algate
Might fairer be. And then she forth her brought
Unto her sonne, that lay in feeble state;
Who seeing her gan streight° upstart, and thought *at once*
She was the Lady selfe, whom he so long had sought.

10

Tho fast her clipping twixt his armés twaine,
Extremely joyéd in so happie sight,
And soone forgot his former sickly paine;
But she, the more to seeme such as she hight,
Coyly rebutted° his embracement light; *repelled*
Yet still with gentle countenaunce retained,
Enough to hold a foole in vaine delight:

6. I.e., he needed no instruction.
7. The making of the false Florimell, whose pseudo-Petrarchan beauty cloaks immodesty, hints at the danger of magic technology (her ingredients are alchemical and Paracelsean) and of false art and poetry. It may also be relevant that mercury was used to cure syphilis.

Him long she so with shadowes entertained,
As her Creatresse had in charge to her ordained.

11

Till on a day, as he disposéd was
To walke the woods with that his Idole faire,
Her to disport,° and idle time to pas, *entertain*
In th'open freshnesse of the gentle aire,
A knight that way there chauncéd to repaire;° *go*
Yet knight he was not, but a boastfull swaine,
That deedes of armes had ever in despaire,[8]
Proud Braggadocchio, that in vaunting vaine
His glory did repose,° and credit did maintaine. *establish*

12

He seeing with that Chorle so faire a wight,
Deckéd with many a costly ornament,
Much merveiléd thereat, as well he might,
And thought that match a fowle disparagement:° *disgrace*
His bloudie speare eftsoones he boldly bent
Against the silly clowne,° who dead through feare, *rustic*
Fell streight to ground in great astonishment;
"Villein," said he, "this Ladie is my deare,
Dy, if thou it gainesay: I will away her beare."

13

The fearefull Chorle durst not gainesay, nor dooe,
But trembling stood, and yielded him the pray;
Who finding litle leasure her to wooe,
On Tromparts steed her mounted without stay,° *hindrance*
And without reskew led her quite away.
Proud man himselfe then Braggadocchio deemed,
And next to none, after that happie day,
Being possesséd of that spoyle, which seemed
The fairest wight on ground, and most of men esteemed.

14

But when he saw himselfe free from poursute,
He gan make gentle purpose° to his Dame, *discourse*
With termes of love and lewdnesse dissolute;
For he could well his glozing speaches frame
To such vaine uses, that him best became:
But she thereto would lend but light regard,
As seeming sory, that she ever came

8. I.e., from whom true feats of arms could never be expected. The boaster Braggadocchio and his squire Trompart, whose name suggests "trompeur" (French for "deceiver") and trumpet, have been introduced in II.iii.

Into his powre, that uséd her so hard,
To reave° her honor, which she more then life prefard. *take away*

15

Thus as they two of kindnesse° treated long, *love*
There them by chaunce encountred on the way
An arméd knight,[9] upon a courser strong,
Whose trampling feet upon the hollow lay° *ground*
Seeméd to thunder, and did nigh affray
That Capons° courage: yet he lookéd grim, *coward*
And fained to cheare his Ladie in dismay;
Who seemed for feare to quake in every lim,
And her to save from outrage, meekely prayéd him.

16

Fiercely that stranger forward came, and nigh
Approaching, with bold words and bitter threat,
Bad that same boaster, as he mote, on high[1]
To leave to him that Lady for excheat,[2]
Or bide° him battell without further treat.° *endure / parley*
That challenge did too peremptory seeme,
And fild his senses with abashment great;
Yet seeing nigh him jeopardy extreme,
He it dissembled well, and light seemed to esteeme.

17

Saying, "Thou foolish knight, that weenst with words
To steale away, that I with blowes have wonne,
And brought throgh points of many perilous swords:
But if thee list to see thy Courser ronne,
Or prove thy selfe, this sad° encounter shonne, *grievous*
And seeke else° without hazard of thy hed." *elsewhere*
At those proud words that other knight begonne
To wexe exceeding wroth, and him ared° *told*
To turne his steede about, or sure he should be ded.

18

"Sith then," said Braggadocchio, "needes thou wilt
Thy dayes abridge, through proofe of puissance,
Turne we our steedes, that both in equall tilt° *mounted combat*
May meet againe, and each take happie chance."
This said, they both a furlongs mountenance° *distance*
Retyrd their steeds, to ronne in even race:
But Braggadocchio with his bloudie lance

9. I.e., Sir Ferraugh, who is not identified until IV.ii.4.
1. I.e., as loudly as he could.
2. I.e., as his property.

Once having turnd, no more returnd his face,
But left his love to losse, and fled himselfe apace.

19

The knight him seeing fly, had no regard° *care*
Him to poursew, but to the Ladie rode,
And having her from Trompart lightly reard,° *taken up*
Upon his Courser set the lovely lode,
And with her fled away without abode.° *delay*
Well weenéd he, that fairest Florimell
It was, with whom in company he yode,° *went*
And so her selfe did alwaies to him tell;
So made him thinke him selfe in heaven, that was in hell.

20

But Florimell her selfe was farre away,
Driven to great distresse by Fortune straunge,
And taught the carefull° Mariner to play, *full of care*
Sith late mischaunce had her compeld to chaunge
The land for sea, at randon° there to raunge: *random*
Yet there that cruell Queene avengeresse,[3]
Not satisfide so farre her to estraunge
From courtly blisse and wonted happinesse,
Did heape on her new waves of weary wretchednesse.

21

For being fled into the fishers bote,
For refuge from the Monsters crueltie,
Long so she on the mightie maine did flote,
And with the tide drove forward careleslie;
For th'aire was milde, and clearéd was the skie,
And all his windes Dan° Aeolus did keepe, *Master*
From stirring up their stormy enmitie,
As pittying to see her waile and weepe;
But all the while the fisher did securely sleepe.

22

At last when droncke with drowsinesse, he woke,
And saw his drover° drive along the streame, *boat*
He was dismayd, and thrise his breast he stroke,
For marvell of that accident extreame;
But when he saw that blazing beauties beame,
Which with rare light his bote did beautifie,
He marveild more, and thought he yet did dreame
Not well awakt, or that some extasie° *madness*
Assotted° had his sense, or dazéd was his eie. *bewildered*

3. I.e., the goddess Fortuna (Fortune).

23

But when her well avizing,° he perceived — *viewing*
To be no vision, nor fantasticke sight,
Great comfort of her presence he conceived,
And felt in his old courage° new delight — *spirit*
To gin awake, and stirre his frozen spright:
Tho rudely askt her, how she thither came.
"Ah," said she, "father, I note read[4] aright,
What hard misfortune brought me to the same;
Yet am I glad that here I now in safety am.

24

"But thou good man, sith farre in sea we bee,
And the great waters gin apace to swell,
That now no more we can the maine-land see,
Have care, I pray, to guide the cock-bote° well, — *skiff*
Least worse on sea then us on land befell."
Thereat th'old man did nought but fondly° grin, — *foolishly*
And said, his boat the way could wisely tell:
But his deceiptfull eyes did never lin,° — *cease*
To looke on her faire face, and marke her snowy skin.

25

The sight whereof in his congealéd flesh,
Infixt such secret sting of greedy lust,
That the drie withered stocke it gan refresh,
And kindled heat, that soone in flame forth brust:° — *burst*
The driest wood is soonest burnt to dust.
Rudely to her he lept, and his rough hand
Where ill became him, rashly would have thrust,
But she with angry scorne him did withstand,
And shamefully reprovéd for his rudeness fond.

26

But he, that never good nor maners knew,
Her sharpe rebuke full litle did esteeme;
Hard is to teach an old horse amble trew.
The inward smoke, that did before but steeme,
Broke into open fire and rage° extreme, — *passion*
And now he strength gan adde unto his will,
Forcing to doe, that did him fowle misseeme:° — *misbecome*
Beastly he threw her downe, ne cared to spill[5]
Her garments gay with scales of fish, that all did fill.

4. I.e., cannot tell.
5. I.e., nor cared if he stained. Cf. the hermit's assault on Angelica in *Orlando Furioso* 8.30–50.

27

The silly° virgin strove him to withstand, — *innocent*
All that she might, and him in vaine revild:° — *rebuked*
She struggled strongly both with foot and hand,
To save her honor from that villaine vild,
And cride to heaven, from humane helpe exild.
O ye brave knights, that boast this Ladies love,
Where be ye now, when she is nigh defild
Of filthy wretch? well may shee you reprove
Or falshood or of slouth, when most it may behove.[6]

28

But if that thou, Sir Satyran, didst weete,
Or thou, Sir Peridure,[7] her sorie state,
How soone would yee assemble many a fleete,
To fetch from sea, that ye at land lost late;
Towres, Cities, Kingdomes ye would ruinate,° — *ruin*
In your avengement and dispiteous° rage, — *pitiless*
Ne ought your burning fury mote abate;
But° if Sir Calidore[8] could it presage,° — *unless / know of*
No living creature could his cruelty asswage.

29

But sith that none of all her knights is nye,
See how the heavens of voluntary grace,
And soveraine favour towards chastity,
Doe succour send to her distresséd cace:
So much high God doth innocence embrace.° — *protect*
It fortunéd, whilest thus she stifly strove,
And the wide sea importunéd long space
With shrilling shriekes, Proteus[9] abroad did rove,
Along the fomy waves driving his finny drove.

30

Proteus is Shepheard of the seas of yore,
And hath the charge of Neptunes mightie heard;
An aged sire with head all frory° hore, — *frosty*
And sprinckled frost upon his deawy beard:
Who when those pittifull outcries he heard,
Through all the seas so ruefully resound,
His charet swift in haste he thither steard,

6. I.e., when it most behooves you to aid her.
7. In the Welsh *Mabinogion* Peredur is the equivalent of Perceval; Geoffrey of Monmouth calls him a knight of the Round Table (9.12). Spenser may have intended him to be the hero of a later book.
8. The hero of Book VI.
9. At III.iv.25 chiefly a seer, Proteus is here the shape-shifting shepherd of the seas (cf. *Odyssey* 4.456–58 and Virgil. *Georgics* 4.387–95, 406–10). To Boccaccio (*Genealogiae* 7.9), his various forms indicate the passions.

Which with a teeme of scaly Phocas° bound *seals*
Was drawne upon the waves, that foméd him around.

31

And comming to that Fishers wandring bote,
That went at will, withouten carde° or sayle, *chart*
He therein saw that yrkesome sight, which smote
Deepe indignation and compassion frayle° *tender*
Into his hart attonce: streight did he hayle° *drag*
The greedy villein from his hopéd pray,
Of which he now did very litle fayle,
And with his staffe, that drives his Heard astray,
Him bet so sore, that life and sense did much dismay.

32

The whiles the pitteous Ladie up did ryse,
Ruffled and fowly raid° with filthy soyle, *smeared*
And blubbred face with teares of her faire eyes:
Her heart nigh broken was with weary toyle,
To save her selfe from that outrageous spoyle,
But when she lookéd up, to weet, what wight
Had her from so infamous fact assoyle,° *freed*
For shame, but more for feare of his grim sight,
Downe in her lap she hid her face, and loudly shright.° *shrieked*

33

Her selfe not savéd yet from daunger dred
She thought, but chaunged from one to other feare;
Like as a fearefull Partridge, that is fled
From the sharpe Hauke, which her attachéd neare,[1]
And fals to ground, to seeke for succour theare,
Whereas the hungry Spaniels she does spy,
With greedy jawes her readie for to teare;
In such distresse and sad perplexity
Was Florimell, when Proteus she did see thereby.

34

But he endevouréd with speeches milde
Her to recomfort, and accourage bold,
Bidding her feare no more her foeman vilde,
Nor doubt himselfe; and who he was, her told.
Yet all that could not from affright her hold,
Ne to recomfort her at all prevayld;
For her faint heart was with the frozen cold
Benumbd so inly, that her wits nigh fayld,
And all her senses with abashment° quite were quayld.° *fear / overcome*

1. I.e., nearly seized.

35

Her up betwixt his rugged hands he reard,
And with his frory° lips full softly kist, *frosty*
Whiles the cold ysickles from his rough beard,
Droppéd adowne upon her yvorie brest:
Yet he himselfe so busily addrest,° *applied*
That her out of astonishment° he wrought. *insensibility*
And out of that same fishers filthy nest
Removing her, into his charet brought,
And there with many gentle termes her faire besought.

36

But that old leachour, which with bold assault
That beautie durst presume to violate,
He cast° to punish for his hainous fault: *resolved*
Then tooke he him yet trembling sith of late,
And tyde behind his charet, to aggrate° *gratify*
The virgin, whom he had abusde so sore:
So draged him through the waves in scornefull state,
And after cast him up, upon the shore;
But Florimell with him unto his bowre he bore.

37

His bowre is in the bottome of the maine,° *ocean*
Under a mightie rocke, gainst which do rave
The roaring billowes in their proud disdaine,
That with the angry working of the wave,
Therein is eaten out an hollow cave,
That seemes rough Masons hand with engines° keene *tools*
Had long while labouréd it to engrave:° *dig out*
There was his wonne, ne living wight was seene,
Save one old Nymph, hight Panope[2] to keepe it cleane.

38

Thither he brought the sory Florimell,
And entertainéd her the best he might
And Panope her entertaind eke well,
As an immortall mote a mortall wight,
To winne her liking unto his delight:
With flattering words he sweetly wooéd her,
And offeréd faire gifts t'allure her sight,
But she both offers and the offerer
Despysde, and all the fawning of the flatterer.

2. From Greek, "all-seeing." Hesiod makes her a nereid (*Theogony* 250), but as an elderly underwater housekeeper she is Spenser's own creation. In V.iii Florimell, released from watery captivity, will marry her beloved Marinell.

39

Daily he tempted her with this or that,
And never suffred her to be at rest:
But evermore she him refuséd flat,
And all his fainéd kindnesse did detest,
So firmely she had sealéd up her brest.
Sometimes he boasted, that a God he hight:
But she a mortall creature lovéd best:
Then he would make himselfe a mortall wight;
But then she said she loved none, but a Faerie knight.

40

Then like a Faerie knight himselfe he drest;
For every shape on him he could endew:° *endow*
Then like a king he was to her exprest,° *shown*
And offred kingdomes unto her in vew,
To be his Leman° and his Ladie trew: *sweetheart*
But when all this he nothing saw prevaile,
With harder meanes he cast her to subdew,
And with sharpe threates her often did assaile,
So thinking for to make her stubborne courage quaile.

41

To dreadfull shapes he did himselfe transforme,
Now like a Gyant, now like to a feend,
Then like a Centaure, then like to a storme,
Raging within the waves: thereby he weend
Her will to win unto his wishéd end.
But when with feare, nor favour, nor with all
He else could doe, he saw himselfe esteemd,
Downe in a Dongeon deepe he let her fall,
And threatned there to make her his eternall thrall.

42

Eternall thraldome was to her more liefe,° *dear*
Then losse of chastitie, or chaunge of love:
Die had she rather in tormenting griefe,
Then any should of falsenesse her reprove,
Or loosenesse, that she lightly did remove.° *change*
Most vertuous virgin, glory be thy meed,
And crowne of heavenly praise with Saints above,
Where most sweet hymmes of this thy famous deed
Are still emongst them song, that far my rymes exceed.

43

Fit song of Angels caroléd to bee;
But yet what so my feeble Muse can frame,
Shall be t'advaunce° thy goodly chastitee, *praise*

And to enroll thy memorable name,
In th'heart of every honourable Dame,
That they thy vertuous deedes may imitate,
And be partakers of thy endlesse fame.
It yrkes° me, leave thee in this wofull state, *grieves*
To tell of Satyrane, where I him left of late.

44

Who having ended with that Squire of Dames
A long discourse of his adventures vaine,
The which himselfe, then° Ladies more defames, *than*
And finding not th' Hyena to be slaine,
With that same Squire, returnéd backe againe
To his first way. And as they forward went,
They spyde a knight faire pricking on the plaine,
As if he were on some adventure bent,
And in his port appearéd manly hardiment.

45

Sir Satyrane him towards did addresse,
To weet, what wight he was, and what his quest:
And comming nigh, eftsoones he gan to gesse
Both by the burning hart, which on his brest
He bare, and by the colours in his crest,
That Paridell[3] it was. Tho to him yode,° *went*
And him saluting,° as beseeméd best, *greeting*
Gan first inquire of tydings farre abrode;
And afterwardes, on what adventure now he rode.

46

Who thereto answering, said; "The tydings bad,
Which now in Faerie court all men do tell,
Which turnéd hath great mirth, to mourning sad,
Is the late ruine of proud Marinell,
And suddein parture of faire Florimell,
To find him forth: and after her are gone
All the brave knights, that doen in armes excell,
To savegard her, ywandred all alone;
Emongst the rest my lot (unworthy) is to be one."

47

"Ah gentle knight," said then Sir Satyrane,
"Thy labour all is lost, I greatly dread,
That hast a thanklesse service on thee ta'ne,
And offrest sacrifice unto the dead:
For dead, I surely doubt,° thou maist aread *fear*

3. Paridell's name indicates his descent from the Trojan Paris; see ix. 36–37. Comes says, "Nature made [Paris] noble, but a little time joined him with lust" (6.23).

Henceforth for ever Florimell to be,
That all the noble knights of Maydenhead,
Which her adored, may sore repent° with me, *grieve*
And all faire Ladies may for ever sory be."

48

Which words when Paridell had heard, his hew
Gan greatly chaunge, and seemed dismayd to bee;
Then said, "Faire Sir, how may I weene it trew,
That ye doe tell in such uncertaintee?
Or speake ye of report,° or did ye see *rumor*
Just cause of dread, that makes ye doubt so sore?
For perdie else how mote it ever bee,
That ever hand should dare for to engore° *shed*
Her noble bloud? the heavens such crueltie abhore."

49

"These eyes did see, that° they will ever rew *what*
T'have seene," quoth he, "when as a monstrous beast
The Palfrey, whereon she did travell, slew,
And of his bowels made his bloudie feast:
Which speaking token[4] sheweth at the least
Her certaine losse, if not her sure decay:° *destruction*
Besides, that° more suspition encreast, *which*
I found her golden girdle cast astray,° *aside*
Distaynd with durt and bloud, as relique of the pray."

50

"Aye me," said Paridell, "the signes be sad,
And but God turne the same to good soothsay,° *omen*
That Ladies safetie is sore to be drad:° *feared*
Yet will I not forsake my forward way,
Till triall doe more certaine truth bewray."
"Faire Sir," quoth he, "well may it you succeed,
Ne long shall Satyrane behind you stay,
But to the rest, which in this Quest proceed
My labour adde, and be partaker of their speed."° *fortune*

51

"Ye noble knights," said then the Squire of Dames,
"Well may ye speed in so praiseworthy paine:
But sith the Sunne now ginnes to slake his beames,
In deawy vapours of the westerne maine,
And lose° the teme out of his weary waine, *release*
Mote not mislike° you also to abate *ill please*
Your zealous hast, till morrow next againe
Both light of heaven, and strength of men relate:° *bring back*
Which if ye please, to yonder castle turne your gate."° *steps*

4. I.e., eloquent indication.

52

That counsell pleaséd well; so all yfere° *together*
Forth marchéd to a Castle them before,
Where soone arriving, they restrainéd were
Of readie entrance, which ought evermore
To errant knights be commun: wondrous sore
Thereat displeasd they were, till that young Squire
Gan them informe the cause, why that same dore
Was shut to all, which lodging did desire:
The which to let you weet, will further time require.

Canto IX

Malbecco will no straunge knights host,
For peevish gealosie:
Paridell giusts° with Britomart: *jousts*
Both shew their auncestrie.

1

Redoubted knights, and honorable Dames,[1]
To whom I levell° all my labours end, *direct*
Right sore I feare, least with unworthy blames
This odious argument my rimes should shend,° *disgrace*
Or ought your goodly patience offend,
Whiles of a wanton Lady I do write,
Which with her loose incontinence doth blend° *blemish*
The shyning glory of your soveraigne light,
And knighthood fowle defacéd by a faithlesse knight.

2

But never let th'ensample of the bad
Offend the good: for good by paragone° *comparison*
Of evill, may more notably be rad,° *perceived*
As white seemes fairer, matcht with blacke attone;° *together*
Ne all are shaméd by the fault of one:
For lo in heaven, whereas all goodnesse is,
Emongst the Angels, a whole legione
Of wicked Sprights did fall from happy blis;
What wonder then, if one of women all did mis?° *err*

3

Then listen Lordings, if ye list to weet
The cause, why Satyrane and Paridell
Mote not be entertaynd, as seeméd meet,
Into that Castle (as that Squire does tell.)
"Therein a cancred° crabbéd Carle does dwell, *malignant*
That has no skill° of Court nor courtesie, *knowledge*

1. Stanzas 1–2 are based on the opening stanzas of Ariosto, *Orlando Furioso* 28.

Ne cares, what men say of him ill or well;
For all his dayes he drownes in privitie,° *seclusion*
Yet has full large to live, and spend at libertie.

4

"But all his mind is set on mucky pelfe,° *lucre*
To hoord up heapes of evill gotten masse,° *wealth*
For which he others wrongs, and wreckes° himselfe; *harms*
Yet is he linckéd to a lovely lasse,
Whose beauty doth her bounty° far surpasse, *goodness*
The which to him both far unequall yeares,
And also far unlike conditions has;
For she does joy to play emongst her peares,[2]
And to be free from hard restraint and gealous feares.

5

"But he is old, and witheréd like hay,
Unfit faire Ladies service to supply;
The privie° guilt whereof makes him alway *secret*
Suspect her truth, and keepe continuall spy
Upon her with his other blinckéd° eye; *dim*
Ne suffreth he resort° of living wight *visiting*
Approch to her, ne keepe her company,
But in close bowre her mewes° from all mens sight, *shuts up*
Deprived of kindly° joy and naturall delight. *natural*

6

"Malbecco he, and Hellenore she hight,
Unfitly yokt together in one teeme,[3]
That is the cause, why never any knight
Is suffred here to enter, but he seeme
Such, as no doubt of him he neede misdeeme."° *suspect*
Thereat Sir Satyrane gan smile, and say;
"Extremely mad° the man I surely deeme, *crazed*
That weenes with watch and hard restraint to stay° *restrain*
A womans will, which is disposd to go astray.

7

"In vaine he feares that, which he cannot shonne:
For who wotes not, that womans subtiltyes
Can guilen° Argus,[4] when she list misdonne?° *deceive / misbehave*
It is not yron bandes, nor hundred eyes,

2. I.e., to enjoy herself with lively and youthful friends.
3. The jealous old husband, his bored young wife, and the vigorous sophisticate who takes advantage are literary types familiar since ancient times; cf. Chaucer's "Merchant's Tale." Spenser takes details from *Orlando Furioso* 32, but the names of Malbecco (Latin *malus* [bad] and Italian *becco* [goat]: i.e., cuckold), Hellenore, and Paridell parody those of Menelaus, Helen of Troy, and Helen's abductor, Paris.
4. The hundred-eyed monster Juno set to watch Jove's beloved Io (*Metamorphoses* 1.622–723); after Mercury lulled him to sleep with music and story, Juno set his eyes in her peacock's tail.

Nor brasen walls, nor many wakefull spyes,
That can withhold her wilfull wandring feet;
But fast° good will with gentle curtesyes, *firm*
And timely service to her pleasures meet
May her perhaps containe, that else would algates fleet."° *slip away*

8

"Then is he not more mad," said Paridell,
"That hath himselfe unto such service sold,
In dolefull thraldome all his dayes to dwell?
For sure a foole I do him firmely hold,
That loves his fetters, though they were of gold.
But why do we devise of others ill,
Whiles thus we suffer this same dotard old,
To keepe us out, in scorne of his owne will,
And rather do not ransack all, and him selfe kill?"

9

"Nay let us first," said Satyrane, "entreat
The man by gentle meanes, to let us in,
And afterwardes affray with cruell threat,
Ere that we to efforce it do begin:
Then if all fayle, we will by force it win,
And eke reward the wretch for his mesprise,° *insolence*
As may be worthy of his haynous sin."
That counsell pleasd: then Paridell did rise,
And to the Castle gate approcht in quiet wise.

10

Whereat soft knocking, entrance he desyrd.
The good man selfe, which then the Porter playd,
Him answeréd, that all were now retyrd
Unto their rest, and all the keyes convayd
Unto their maister, who in bed was layd,
That none him durst awake out of his dreme;
And therefore them of patience gently prayd.
Then Paridell began to chaunge his theme,
And threatned him with force and punishment extreme.

11

But all in vaine; for nought mote him relent,
And now so long before the wicket fast
They wayted, that the night was forward spent,[5]
And the faire welkin° fowly overcast, *sky*
Gan blowen up a bitter stormy blast,

5. I.e., well advanced. This episode recalls a passage in the *Thebaid* 1.401–81, an epic by the Roman poet Statius (61–ca. 96 C.E.), and also Bradamante's actions outside the Castle of Tristan in *Orlando Furioso* 32.

With shoure and hayle so horrible and dred,
That this faire many° were compeld at last, *company*
To fly for succour to a little shed,
The which beside the gate for swine was orderéd.° *prepared*

12

It fortunéd, soone after they were gone,
Another knight, whom tempest thither brought,
Came to that Castle, and with earnest mone,° *plea*
Like as the rest, late entrance deare besought;
But like so as the rest he prayd for nought,
For flatly he of entrance was refusd,
Sorely thereat he was displeasd, and thought
How to avenge himselfe so sore abusd,
And evermore the Carle of curtesie[6] accusd.

13

But to avoyde th'intollerable stowre,° *storm*
He was compeld to seeke some refuge neare,
And to that shed, to shrowd him from the showre,
He came, which full of guests he found whyleare,° *already*
So as he was not let to enter there:
Whereat he gan to wex exceeding wroth,
And swore, that he would lodge with them yfere,
Or them dislodge, all were they liefe or loth;[7]
And so defide them each, and so defide them both.

14

Both were full loth to leave that needfull tent,° *shed*
And both full loth in darkenesse to debate;
Yet both full liefe him lodging to have lent,
And both full liefe his boasting to abate;
But chiefly Paridell his hart did grate,° *fret*
To heare him threaten so despightfully,
As if he did a dogge to kenell rate,° *scold*
That durst not barke; and rather had he dy,
Then when he was defide, in coward corner ly.

15

Tho hastily remounting to his steed,
He forth issewed; like as a boistrous wind,
Which in th'earthes hollow caves hath long bin hid,
And shut up fast within her prisons blind,° *dark*
Makes the huge element against her kind
To move, and tremble as it were agast,
Until that it an issew forth may find;

6. I.e., of discourtesy.
7. I.e., whether they were willing or not.

Then forth it breakes, and with his furious blast
Confounds both land and seas, and skyes doth overcast.

16

Their steel-hed speares they strongly coucht, and met
Together with impetuous rage and forse,
That with the terrour of their fierce affret,° *encounter*
They rudely drove to ground both man and horse,
That each awhile lay like a sencelesse corse.
But Paridell sore brusèd with the blow,
Could not arise, the counterchaunge to scorse,[8]
Till that young Squire him rearèd from below;
Then drew he his bright sword, and gan about him throw.° *brandish*

17

But Satyrane forth stepping, did them stay
And with faire treatie° pacifide their ire, *speech*
Then when they were accorded° from the fray, *reconciled*
Against that Castles Lord they gan conspire,
To heape on him dew vengeaunce for his hire.° *reward*
They bene agreed, and to the gates they goe
To burne the same with unquenchable fire,
And that uncurteous Carle their commune foe
To do fowle death to dye, or wrap in grievous woe.

18

Malbecco seeing them resolved in deed
To flame the gates, and hearing them to call
For fire in earnest, ran with fearefull° speed, *full of fear*
And to them calling from the castle wall,
Besought them humbly, him to beare with all,[9]
As ignoraunt of servaunts bad abuse,
And slacke attendaunce unto straungers call.
The knights were willing all things to excuse,
Though nought beleved, and entraunce late did not refuse.

19

They bene ybrought into a comely bowre,° *chamber*
And served of all things that mote needfull bee;
Yet secretly their hoste did on them lowre,° *scowl*
And welcomde more for feare, then charitee;
But they dissembled, what they did not see,[1]
And welcomèd themselves. Each gan undight
Their garments wet, and weary armour free,
To dry them selves by Vulcanes flaming light,
And eke their lately bruzèd parts to bring in plight.° *health*

8. I.e., to strike back by way of requital.
9. I.e., to bear with him.
1. I.e., they pretended not to notice his discourtesy.

20

And eke that straunger knight emongst the rest
Was for like need enforst to disaray:
Tho whenas vailéd° was her loftie crest, *lowered*
Her golden locks, that were in tramels° gay *plaits*
Unbounden, did them selves adowne display,
And raught° unto her heeles; like sunny beames, *reached*
That in a cloud their light did long time stay,
Their vapour vaded,° shew their golden gleames, *vanished*
And through the persant aire shoote forth their azure streames.[2]

21

She also dofte her heavy haberjeon,° *coat of mail*
Which the faire feature of her limbs did hyde,
And her well plighted° frock, which she did won° *folded / use*
To tucke about her short, when she did ryde,
She low let fall, that flowd from her lanck° syde *slender*
Downe to her foot, with carelesse° modestee. *simple*
Then of them all she plainly was espyde,
To be a woman wight, unwist° to bee, *unknown*
The fairest woman wight, that ever eye did see.

22

Like as Minerva[3] being late returnd
From slaughter of the Giaunts conqueréd;
Where proud Encelade, whose wide nosethrils burnd
With breathéd flames, like to a furnace red,
Transfixéd with the speare, downe tombled ded
From top of Hemus, by him heapéd hye;
Hath loosd her helmet from her lofty hed,
And her Gorgonian[4] shield gins to untye
From her left arme, to rest in glorious victorye.

23

Which whenas they beheld, they smitten were
With great amazement of so wondrous sight,
And each on other, and they all on her
Stood gazing, as if suddein great affright
Had them surprised. At last avizing° right, *perceiving*
Her goodly personage and glorious hew,° *form*
Which they so much mistooke, they tooke delight

2. This simile appears in *Orlando Furioso* 32.80 and Tasso's *Gerusalemme* 4.29; cf. *Metamorphoses* 14.767–69 (see also III.i.43). The lady knight is identified in stanza 27.
3. "Bellona" in the 1590 edition. In a Glosse to "October," E. K. identifies Bellona with Pallas (Minerva), "godesse of battaile." Some say Pallas transfixed Enceladus, biggest of the Giants, with her spear; others give the victory to Zeus, who put him under a volcano (often identified as Aetna). But it was Typhoeus, not "proud Encelade," whom Zeus overcame on Mount Haemus in Thrace.
4. Minerva wore the snaky-haired head of Medusa, the Gorgon slain by Perseus, on her "aegis" (shield or breastplate); see *Metamorphoses* 4.803.

In their first errour, and yet still anew
With wonder of her beauty fed their hungry vew.

24

Yet note° their hungry vew be satisfide, *might not*
But seeing still the more desired to see,
And ever firmely fixéd did abide
In contemplation of divinitie:
But most they mervaild at her chevalree,
And noble prowesse, which they had approved,° *tested*
That much they faynd° to know, who she mote bee; *desired*
Yet none of all them her thereof amoved,° *stirred*
Yet every one her likte, and every one her loved.

25

And Paridell though partly discontent
With his late fall, and fowle indignity,
Yet was soone wonne his malice to relent,° *soften*
Through gracious regard of her faire eye,
And knightly worth, which he too late did try,° *experience*
Yet triéd did adore. Supper was dight;° *set out*
Then they Malbecco prayd of curtesy,
That of his Lady they might have the sight,
And company at meat, to do them more delight.

26

But he to shift their curious request,
Gan causen,° why she could not come in place; *explain*
Her craséd° health, her late° recourse to rest, *infirm / recent*
And humid evening ill for sicke folkes cace:
But none of those excuses could take place;[5]
Ne would they eate, till she in presence came.
She came in presence with right comely grace,
And fairely them saluted,° as became, *greeted*
And shewd her selfe in all a gentle curteous Dame.

27

They sate to meat, and Satyrane his chaunce
Was her before,[6] and Paridell besyde;
But he him selfe sate looking still askaunce,° *sidewise*
Gainst Britomart, and ever closely eyde
Sir Satyrane, that glaunces might not glyde:
But his blind eye, that syded Paridell,
All his demeasnure° from his sight did hyde: *behavior*
On her faire face so did he feede his fill,
And sent close° messages of love to her at will. *secret*

5. I.e., was acceptable.
6. I.e., was to sit opposite her.

28

And ever and anone, when none was ware,
With speaking lookes, that close embassage° bore, *message*
He roved° at her, and told his secret care: *darted*
For all that art he learnéd had of yore.
Ne was she ignoraunt of that lewd lore,
But in his eye his meaning wisely red,
And with the like him answerd evermore:
She sent at him one firie dart, whose hed
Empoisned was with privy° lust, and gealous dred. *secret*

29

He from that deadly throw° made no defence, *thrust*
But to the wound his weake hart opened wyde;
The wicked engine° through false influence, *device*
Past through his eyes, and secretly did glyde
Into his hart, which it did sorely gryde.° *pierce*
But nothing new to him was that same paine,
Ne paine at all; for he so oft had tryde
The powre thereof, and loved so oft in vaine,
That thing of course[7] he counted,° love to entertaine. *regarded*

30

Thenceforth to her he sought to intimate
His inward griefe, by meanes to him well knowne,
Now Bacchus fruit[8] out of the silver plate° *cup*
He on the table dasht, as overthrowne,
Or of the fruitfull liquor overflowne,
And by the dauncing bubbles did divine,
Or therein write to let his love be showne;
Which well she red out of the learnéd line,
A sacrament prophane in mistery of wine.

31

And when so of his hand the pledge she raught,[9]
The guilty cup she fainéd to mistake,° *let slip*
And in her lap did shed her idle draught,
Shewing desire her inward flame to slake:° *relieve*
By such close signes they secret way did make
Unto their wils, and one eyes watch escape;
Two eyes him needeth, for to watch and wake,
Who lovers will deceive. Thus was the ape,
By their faire handling, put into Malbeccoes cape.[1]

7. I.e., as a usual occurrence.
8. I.e., the wine. Paridell's techniques echo Ovid's *Art of Love* and the epistle from Helen to Paris in his *Heroides* 17.75–90; line 9 suggests that he blasphemously misuses wine in a sort of lustful antieucharist.
9. I.e., when she reached to take the cup from his hand.
1. I.e., they made a fool of him (as in Chaucer, Introduction to "The Prioress's Tale," 1630).

32

Now when of meats and drinks they had their fill,
Purpose° was movéd by that gentle Dame, *proposal*
Unto those knights adventurous, to tell
Of deeds of armes, which unto them became,° *happened*
And every one his kindred, and his name.
Then Paridell, in whom a kindly° pryde *natural*
Of gracious speach, and skill his words to frame
Abounded, being glad of so fit tyde° *occasion*
Him to commend to her, thus spake, of all well eyde.

33

"Troy, that art now nought, but an idle name,
And in thine ashes buried low dost lie,
Though whilome far much greater then thy fame,
Before that angry Gods, and cruell skye
Upon thee heapt a direfull destinie,
What boots it boast thy glorious descent,
And fetch from heaven thy great Genealogie,
Sith all thy worthy prayses being blent,° *stained*
Their of-spring hath embaste, and later glory shent.° *disgraced*

34

"Most famous Worthy of the world, by whome
That warre was kindled, which did Troy inflame,
And stately towres of Ilion whilome
Brought unto balefull ruine, was by name
Sir Paris far renowmd through noble fame,
Who through great prowesse and bold hardinesse,
From Lacedaemon fetcht the fairest Dame,
That ever Greece did boast, or knight possesse,
Whom Venus to him gave for meed of worthinesse.[2]

35

"Faire Helene, flowre of beautie excellent,
And girlond of the mighty Conquerours,
That madest many Ladies deare lament
The heavie losse of their brave Paramours,
Which they far off beheld from Trojan toures,
And saw the fieldes of faire Scamander[3] strowne
With carcases of noble warrioures,
Whose fruitless lives were under furrow sowne,
And Xanthus sandy bankes with bloud all overflowne.

2. See II.vii.55, note.
3. The river Scamander (also called the Xanthus) flowed near Troy.

36

"From him my linage I derive aright,
Who long before the ten yeares siege of Troy,
Whiles yet on Ida he a shepheard hight,
On faire Oenone got a lovely boy,
Whom for remembraunce of her passéd joy,
She of his Father Parius[4] did name;
Who, after Greekes did Priams realme destroy,
Gathred the Trojan reliques saved from flame,
And with them sayling thence, to th'Isle of Paros[5] came.

37

"That was by him cald Paros, which before
Hight Nausa, there he many yeares did raine,
And built Nausicle by the Pontick[6] shore,
The which he dying left next in remaine
To Paridas his sonne.
From whom I Paridell by kin descend;
But for faire Ladies love, and glories gaine,
My native soile have left, my dayes to spend
In sewing° deeds of armes, my lives and labours end." *following*

38

Whenas the noble Britomart heard tell
Of Trojan warres, and Priams Citie sackt,
The ruefull story of Sir Paridell,
She was empassiond at that piteous act,
With zelous envy° of Greekes cruell fact,° *indignation / deed*
Against that nation, from whose race of old
She heard, that she was lineally extract:° *descended*
For noble Britons sprong from Trojans bold,
And Troynovant[7] was built of old Troyes ashes cold.

39

Then sighing soft awhile, at last she thus:
"O lamentable fall of famous towne,
Which raignd so many yeares victorious,
And of all Asie bore the soveraigne crowne,
In one sad night consumd, and throwen downe:
What stony hart, that heares thy haplesse fate,
Is not empierst with deepe compassiowne,
And makes ensample of mans wretched state,
That floures so fresh at morne, and fades at evening late?

4. Oenone's son by Paris was named Corythus, but Paridell (or Spenser) changes it to "Parius" to suit his claim to descend from Trojan royalty.
5. An island in the Aegean Sea.
6. The Black Sea.
7. I.e., London, "New Troy."

40

"Behold, Sir, how your pitifull complaint° *lament*
Hath found another partner of your payne:
For nothing may impresse so deare constraint,° *distress*
As countries cause, and commune foes disdayne.
But if it should not grieve you, backe agayne
To turne your course, I would to heare desyre,
What to Aeneas fell; sith that men sayne
He was not in the Cities wofull fyre
Consumed, but did him selfe to safétie retyre."

41

"Anchyses sonne begot of Venus faire,"
Said he, "out of the flames for safegard fled,
And with a remnant did to sea repaire,
Where he through fatall errour[8] long was led
Full many yeares, and weetlesse° wanderéd *at random*
From shore to shore, emongst the Lybicke° sands, *Lybian*
Ere rest he found. Much there he sufferéd,
And many perils past in forreine lands,
To save his people sad from victours vengefull hands.[9]

42

"At last in Latium[1] he did arrive,
Where he with cruell warre was entertaind
Of th'inland folke, which sought him backe to drive,
Till he with old Latinus was constraind,
To contract wedlock:[2] (so the fates ordaind).
Wedlock contract in bloud, and eke in blood
Accomplishéd, that many deare complaind:
The rivall slaine, the victour through the flood
Escapéd hardly, hardly praisd his wedlock good.

43

"Yet after all, he victour did survive,
And with Latinus did the kingdome part.° *divide*
But after, when both nations gan to strive,
Into their names the title to convart,[3]
His sonne Iülus did from thence depart,
With all the warlike youth of Trojans bloud,
And in long Alba[4] plast his throne apart,

8. I.e., fated wandering; Virgil calls Aeneas "fato profugus" (impelled by fate, *Aeneid* 1.2).
9. Paridell passes rapidly over the earlier wanderings of Aeneas, omitting his love for Dido and descent to Hades so as to stress his final romance and resettlement.
1. Land of the Latins. King Latinus gave his daughter Lavinia in marriage to Aeneas (*Aeneid* 7.267–74); this precipitated war with the Rutulian leader Turnus, to whom she had been promised.
2. I.e., to ally himself through marriage with Lavinia.
3. I.e., to claim sole power.
4. Alba Longa, Latium's oldest town, about twenty miles southeast of Rome. On lulus's move to Alba Longa, see Boccaccio (*Genealogiae* 6.54).

Where faire it florishéd, and long time stoud,
Till Romulus renewing it, to Rome removd."

44

"There there," said Britomart, "a fresh appeard
The glory of the later world to spring,
And Troy againe out of her dust was reard,
To sit in second seat of soveraigne king,
Of all the world under her governing.
But a third kingdome yet is to arise,
Out of the Trojans scatteréd of-spring,
That in all glory and great enterprise,
Both first and second Troy shall dare to equalise.° *equal*

45

"It Troynovant is hight, that with the waves
Of wealthy Thamis[5] washéd is along,
Upon whose stubborne neck, whereat he raves
With roring rage, and sore him selfe does throng,° *press*
That all men feare to tempt his billowes strong,
She fastned hath her foot, which standes so hy,
That it a wonder of the world is song
In forreine landes, and all which passen by,
Beholding it from far, do thinke it threates the skye.

46

"The Trojan Brute did first that Citie found,
And Hygate made the meare° thereof by West, *boundary*
And Overt gate by North: that is the bound
Toward the land; two rivers bound the rest.
So huge a scope at first him seeméd best,
To be the compasse of his kingdomes seat:
So huge a mind could not in lesser rest,
Ne in small meares containe his glory great,
That Albion[6] had conquered first by warlike feat."

47

"Ah fairest Lady knight," said Paridell,
"Pardon I pray my heedlesse oversight,
Who had forgot, that whilome I heard tell
From aged Mnemon,[7] for my wits bene light.
Indeed he said (if I remember right,)
That of the antique Trojan stocke, there grew
Another plant, that raught° to wondrous hight, *reached*
And far abroad his mighty branches threw,
Into the utmost Angle of the world he knew:

5. The Thames, spanned by London Bridge.
6. The island's pre-British name (see Geoffrey 1.16).
7. From Greek, "memory."

48

"For that same Brute, whom much he did advaunce° *praise*
In all his speach, was Sylvius his sonne,[8]
Whom having slaine, through luckles arrowes glaunce
He fled for feare of that he had misdonne,
Or else for shame, so fowle reproch to shonne,
And with him led to sea an youthly trayne,° *company*
Where wearie wandring they long time did wonne,
And many fortunes proved° in th'Ocean mayne, *experienced*
And great adventures found, that now were long to sayne.

49

"At last by fatall° course they driven were *fated*
Into an Island spatious and brode,
The furthest North, that did to them appeare:
Which after rest they seeking far abrode,
Found it the fittest soyle for their abode,
Fruitfull of all things fit for living foode,
But wholy wast, and void of peoples trode,° *footstep*
Save an huge nation of the Geaunts broode,
That fed on living flesh, and druncke mens vitall blood.

50

"Whom he through wearie wars and labours long,
Subdewd with losse of many Britons bold:
In which the great Goëmagot of strong
Corineus, and Coulin of Debon old
Were overthrowne, and layd on th'earth full cold,
Which quakéd under their so hideous masse,
A famous history to be enrold
In everlasting moniments of brasse,
That all the antique Worthies merits far did passe.

51

"His worke great Troynovant, his worke is eke
Faire Lincolne, both renowméd far away,
That who from East to West will endlong° seeke, *from end to end*
Cannot two fairer Cities find this day,
Except Cleopolis: so heard I say
Old Mnemon. Therefore Sir, I greet you well
Your countrey kin,° and you entirely pray *kinsman*
Of pardon for the strife, which late befell
Betwixt us both unknowne." So ended Paridell.

8. I.e., the son of Sylvius. Stanzas 48–51 rely on Geoffrey 1.3–17, who does not, though, say Brute founded Lincoln.

52

But all the while, that he these speaches spent,
Upon his lips hong faire Dame Hellenore,
With vigilant regard, and dew attent,° *attention*
Fashioning worlds of fancies evermore
In her fraile wit, that now her quite forlore:
The whiles unwares away her wondring eye,
And greedy eares her weake hart from her bore:
Which he perceiving, ever privily
In speaking, many false belgardes° at her let fly. *loving looks*

53

So long these knights discourséd diversly,
Of straunge affairs, and noble hardiment,
Which they had past with mickle jeopardy,
That now the humid night was farforth spent,
And heavenly lampes were halfendeale ybrent.[9]
Which th'old man seeing well, who too long thought
Every discourse and every argument,
Which by the houres he measuréd, besought
Them go to rest. So all unto their bowres were brought.

Canto X

Paridell rapeth° Hellenore: *carries off*
Malbecco her pursewes:
Findes emongst Satyres, whence with him
To turne she doth refuse.

1

The morow next, so soone as Phoebus Lamp
Bewrayéd° had the world with early light, *revealed*
And fresh Aurora had the shady damp
Out of the goodly heaven amovéd quight,
Faire Britomart and that same Faerie knight[1]
Uprose, forth on their journey for to wend:
But Paridell complaynd, that his late fight
With Britomart, so sore did him offend° *trouble*
That ryde he could not, till his hurts he did amend.

2

So forth they fared, but he behind them stayd,
Maulgre° his host, who grudgéd grievously, *despite*
To house a guest, that would be needes obayd,
And of his owne him left not liberty:
Might wanting measure moveth surquedry.[2]

9. I.e., half consumed.
1. I.e., Satyrane.
2. I.e., excessive power breeds arrogance.

Two things he fearéd, but the third was death;
That fierce youngmans unruly maistery;
His money, which he loved as living breath;
And his faire wife, whom honest long he kept uneath.° *with difficulty*

3

But patience perforce he must abie,° *endure*
What fortune and his fate on him will lay,
Fond° is the feare, that findes no remedie; *foolish*
Yet warily he watcheth every way,
By which he feareth evill happen may:
So th'evill thinkes by watching to prevent;
Ne doth he suffer her, nor night, nor day,
Out of his sight her selfe once to absent.
So doth he punish her and eke himselfe torment.

4

But Paridell kept better watch, then hee,
A fit occasion for his turne to find:
False love, why do men say, thou canst not see,
And in their foolish fancie feigne thee blind,
That with thy charmes° the sharpest sight doest bind, *spells*
And to thy will abuse? Thou walkest free,
And seest every secret of the mind;
Thou seest all, yet none at all sees thee;
All that is by the working of thy Deitee.

5

So perfect in that art was Paridell,
That he Malbeccoes halfen eye did wyle,[3]
His halfen eye he wiléd wondrous well,
And Hellenors both eyes did eke beguyle,
Both eyes and hart attonce, during the whyle
That he there sojournéd his wounds to heale;
That Cupid selfe it seeing, close did smyle,
To weet how he her love away did steale,
And bad, that none their joyous treason should reveale.

6

The learnéd lover lost no time nor tyde,
That least avantage mote to him afford,
Yet bore so faire a saile, that none espyde
His secret drift,° till he her layd abord. *aim*
When so in open place, and commune bord,° *table*
He fortuned her to meet, with commune speach

3. I.e., fooled his one good eye. Malbecco's damaged sight matches his idolatry toward wife and money.

He courted her, yet bayted° every word, *spoke softly*
That his ungentle hoste n'ote him appeach
Of vile ungentlenesse, or hospitages breach.[4]

7

But when apart (if ever her apart)
He found, then his false engins° fast he plyde, *wiles*
And all the sleights unbosomd in his hart;
He sighed, he sobd, he swownd, he perdy° dyde, *verily*
And cast himselfe on ground her fast° besyde: *close*
Tho when againe he him bethought to live,
He wept, and wayld, and false laments belyde,° *counterfeited*
Saying, but if[5] she Mercie would him give
That he mote algates dye, yet did his death forgive.[6]

8

And otherwhiles with amorous delights,
And pleasing toyes he would her entertaine,
Now singing sweetly, to surprise her sprights,
Now making layes of love and lovers paine,
Bransles,° Ballads, virelayes,° and verses vaine; *dances / songs*
Oft purposes,° oft riddles he devysd, *word games*
And thousands like, which flowéd in his braine,
With which he fed her fancie, and entysd
To take to his new love, and leave her old despysd.

9

And every where he might, and every while
He did her service dewtifull, and sewed° *followed*
At hand with humble pride, and pleasing guile,
So closely yet, that none but she it vewed,
Who well perceivéd all, and all indewed.° *took in*
Thus finely did he his false nets dispred,
With which he many weake harts had subdewed
Of yore, and many had ylike misled:
What wonder then, if she were likewise carriéd?

10

No fort so fensible,° no wals so strong, *fortified*
But that continuall battery will rive,
Or daily siege through dispurvayance° long, *lack of supplies*
And lacke of reskewes will to parley drive;
And Peece,° that unto parley eare will give, *fortress*
Will shortly yeeld it selfe, and will be made

4. I.e., could not accuse him of discourtesy or of conduct unbecoming to a guest.
5. I.e., unless.
6. Spenser parodies medieval and Petrarchan love complaint.

The vassall of the victors will bylive:° *quickly*
That stratageme had oftentimes assayd
This crafty Paramoure, and now it plaine displayd.

11

For through his traines° he her intrappéd hath, *wiles*
That she her love and hart hath wholy sold
To him, without regard of gaine, or scath,° *harm*
Or care of credite, or of husband old,
Whom she hath vowed to dub a faire Cucquold.
Nought wants but time and place, which shortly shee
Devizéd hath, and to her lover told.
It pleaséd well. So well they both agree;
So readie rype to ill, ill wemens counsels bee.

12

Darke was the Evening, fit for lovers stealth,
When chaunst Malbecco busie be elsewhere,
She to his closet° went, where all his wealth *private room*
Lay hid: thereof she countlesse summes did reare,° *take*
The which she meant away with her to beare;
The rest she fyred for sport, or for despight,° *malice*
As Hellene, when she saw aloft appeare
The Trojane flames, and reach to heavens hight
Did clap her hands, and joyéd at that dolefull sight.[7]

13

This second Hellene, faire Dame Hellenore,
The whiles her husband ranne with sory haste,
To quench the flames, which she had tyned° before, *kindled*
Laught at his foolish labour spent in waste;
And ranne into her lovers armes right fast;
Where streight embracéd, she to him did cry,
And call aloud for helpe, ere helpe were past;
For loe that Guest would beare her forcibly,
And meant to ravish her, that rather had to dy.

14

The wretched man hearing her call for ayd,
And readie seeing him with her to fly,
In his disquiet mind was much dismayd:
But when againe he backward cast his eye,
And saw the wicked fire so furiously
Consume his hart, and scorch his Idoles face,
He was therewith distresséd diversly,
Ne wist he how to turne, nor to what place;
Was never wretched man in such a wofull cace.

7. Cf. allusions in *Aeneid* (e.g., 6.517–19) to Helen's conduct when Troy fell.

15

Ay° when to him she cryde, to her he turnd, *always*
And left the fire; love money overcame:
But when he markéd, how his money burnd,
He left his wife; money did love disclame.° *renounce*
Both was he loth to loose his lovéd Dame,
And loth to leave his liefest pelfe behind,
Yet sith he n'ote° save both, he saved that same, *might not*
Which was the dearest to his donghill mind,
The God of his desire, the joy of misers blind.

16

Thus whilest all things in troublous uprore were,
And all men busie to suppresse the flame,
The loving couple need no reskew feare,
But leasure had, and libertie to frame
Their purpost flight, free from all mens reclame;° *recall*
And Night, the patronesse of love-stealth faire,
Gave them safe conduct, till to end they came:
So bene they gone yfeare,° a wanton paire *together*
Of lovers loosely knit, where list them to repaire.

17

Soone as the cruell flames yslakéd° were, *abated*
Malbecco seeing, how his losse did lye,
Out of the flames, which he had quencht whylere
Into huge waves of griefe and gealosye
Full deepe emplongéd was, and drownéd nye,
Twixt inward doole° and felonous° despight; *grief / fierce*
He raved, he wept, he stampt, he lowd did cry,
And all the passions, that in man may light,° *occur*
Did him attonce oppresse, and vex his caytive spright.

18

Long thus he chawd the cud of inward griefe,
And did consume his gall with anguish sore,
Still when he muséd on his late mischiefe,
Then still the smart thereof increaséd more,
And seemed more grievous, then it was before:
At last when sorrow he saw booted° nought, *availed*
Ne griefe might not his love to him restore,
He gan devise, how her he reskew mought,
Ten thousand wayes he cast in his confuséd thought.

19

At last resolving, like a pilgrim pore,
To search her forth, where so she might he fond,
And bearing with him treasure in close° store, *secret*

The rest he leaves in ground: So takes in hond
To seeke her endlong, both by sea and lond.
Long he her sought, he sought her farre and nere,
And every where that he mote understand,
Of knights and ladies any meetings were,
And of eachone he met, he tydings did inquere.

20

But all in vaine, his woman was too wise,
Ever to come into his clouch° againe, *grip*
And he too simple ever to surprise
The jolly° Paridell, for all his paine. *gallant*
One day, as he forpasséd by[8] the plaine
With weary pace, he farre away espide
A couple, seeming well to be his twaine,
Which hovéd° close under a forrest side, *waited*
As if they lay in wait, or else themselves did hide.

21

Well weenéd he, that those the same mote bee,
And as he better did their shape avize,
Him seeméd more their manner did agree;
For th'one was arméd all in warlike wize,
Whom, to be Paridell he did devize;° *guess*
And th'other all yclad in garments light,
Discoloured° like to womanish disguise, *many colored*
He did resemble° to his Ladie bright; *liken*
And ever his faint hart much earnéd° at the sight. *yearned*

22

And ever faine° he towards them would goe, *eagerly*
But yet durst not for dread approchen nie,
But stood aloofe, unweeting what to doe;
Till that prickt forth with loves extremitie,
That is the father of foule gealosy,
He closely nearer crept, the truth to weet:
But, as he nigher drew, he easily
Might scerne,° that it was not his sweetest sweet, *discern*
Ne yet her Belamour,° the partner of his sheet. *lover*

23

But it was scornefull Braggadocchio,
That with his servant Trompart hoverd there,
Sith late he fled from his too earnest foe:
Whom such when as Malbecco spyéd clere,
He turnéd backe, and would have fled arere;° *back*
Till Trompart ronning hastily, him did stay,

8. I.e., passed over.

And bad before his soveraine Lord appere:
That was him loth, yet durst he not gainesay,
And comming him before, low louted° on the lay.° *bowed / lea*

24

The Boaster at him sternely bent his browe,
As if he could have kild him with his looke,
That to the ground him meekely made to bowe,
And awfull terror deepe into him strooke,
That every member of his bodie quooke.° *quaked*
Said he, "Thou man of nought, what doest thou here,
Unfitly furnisht with thy bag and booke,
Where I expected one with shield and spere,
To prove° some deedes of armes upon an equall pere." *try*

25

The wretched man at his imperious speach,
Was all abasht, and low prostrating, said;
"Good Sir, let not my rudenesse be no breach
Unto your patience, ne be ill ypaid;° *displeased*
For I unwares this way by fortune straid,
A silly Pilgrim driven to distresse,
That seeke a Lady," There he suddein staid,
And did the rest with grievous sighes suppresse,
While teares stood in his eies, few drops of bitternesse.

26

"What Ladie, man?" said Trompart, "take good hart,
And tell thy griefe, if any hidden lye;
Was never better time to shew thy smart,
Then now, that noble succour is thee by,
That is the whole worlds commune remedy."
That cheareful word his weake hart much did cheare,
And with vaine hope his spirits faint supply,
That bold he said; "O most redoubted Pere,
Vouchsafe with mild regard a wretches cace to heare."

27

Then sighing sore, "It is not long," said hee,
"Sith I enjoyd the gentlest Dame alive;
Of whom a knight, no knight at all perdee,
But shame of all, that doe for honor strive,
By treacherous deceipt did me deprive;
Through open outrage he her bore away,
And with fowle force unto his will did drive,
Which all good knights, that armes do beare this day;
Are bound for to revenge, and punish if they may.

28

"And you most noble Lord, that can and dare
Redresse the wrong of miserable wight,
Cannot employ your most victorious speare
In better quarrell, then defence of right,
And for a Ladie gainst a faithlesse knight;
So shall your glory be advauncéd° much, *praised*
And all faire Ladies magnifie your might,
And eke my selfe, albe I simple such,[9]
Your worthy paine shall well reward with guerdon rich."

29

With that out of his bouget° forth he drew *pouch*
Great store of treasure, therewith him to tempt;
But he on it lookt scornefully askew,° *sidelong*
As much disdeigning to be so misdempt,° *misjudged*
Or a war-monger° to be basely nempt;° *mercenary / named*
And said, "Thy offers base I greatly loth,
And eke thy words uncourteous and unkempt;° *unpolished*
I tread in dust thee and thy money both,
That, were it not for shame," So turnéd from him wroth.

30

But Trompart, that his maisters humor knew,
In lofty lookes to hide an humble mind,
Was inly tickled with that golden vew,
And in his eare him rounded° close behind: *whispered*
Yet stoupt he not, but lay still in the wind,[1]
Waiting advauntage on the pray to sease;
Till Trompart lowly to the ground inclind,
Besought him his great courage° to appease, *anger*
And pardon simple man, that rash did him displease.

31

Bigge looking like a doughtie Doucepere,[2]
At last he thus; "Thou clod of vilest clay,
I pardon yield, and with thy rudenesse beare;
But weete henceforth, that all that golden pray,
And all that else the vaine world vaunten° may, *boast of*
I loath as doung, ne deeme my dew reward:
Fame is my meed, and glory vertues pray.° *booty*
But minds of mortall men are muchell mard,
And moved amisse with massie mucks unmeet regard.[3]

9. I.e., although I am so humble and lowly.
1. I.e. (in a hawking image), he did not swoop down on the prey, but hovered aloft.
2. One of Charlemagne's twelve peers ("les douze pairs").
3. I.e., men's minds are much marred and misdirected by unbecoming care for cash.

32

"And more, I graunt to thy great miserie
Gratious respect,° thy wife shall backe be sent, *attention*
And that vile knight, who ever that he bee,
Which hath thy Lady reft, and knighthood shent,° *disgraced*
By Sanglamort my sword, whose deadly dent° *blow*
The bloud hath of so many thousands shed,
I sweare, ere long shall dearely it repent;
Ne he twixt heaven and earth shall hide his hed,
But soone he shall be found, and shortly doen be ded."

33

The foolish man thereat woxe wondrous blith,
As if the word so spoken, were halfe donne,
And humbly thankéd him a thousand sith,° *times*
That had from death to life him newly wonne.
Tho forth the Boaster marching, brave begonne
His stolen steed to thunder furiously,
As if he heaven and hell would overronne,
And all the world confound with cruelty,
That much Malbecco joyéd in his jollity.° *gallant show*

34

Thus long they three together traveiléd,
Through many a wood, and many an uncouth way,
To seeke his wife, that was farre wanderéd:
But those two sought nought, but the present pray,
To weete the treasure, which he did bewray,° *reveal*
On which their eies and harts were wholly set,
With purpose, how they might it best betray;
For sith the houre, that first he did them let
The same behold, therewith their keene desires were whet.° *sharpened*

35

It fortunéd as they together fared,
They spide, where Paridell came pricking fast
Upon the plaine, the which himselfe prepared
To giust with that brave straunger knight a cast,° *bout*
As on adventure by the way he past:
Alone he rode without his Paragone,° *companion*
For having filcht her bels, her up he cast
To the wide world, and let her fly alone,
He nould be clogd.[4] So had he servéd many one.

4. I.e., having taken his pleasure, and not wanting to be weighed down, he went his own way (a hawking image).

36

The gentle Lady, loose at randon left,
The greene-wood long did walke, and wander wide
At wilde adventure, like a forlorne weft,° *waif*
Till on a day the Satyres her espide
Straying alone withouten groome° or guide; *servant*
Her up they tooke, and with them home her led,
With them as housewife ever to abide,
To milk their gotes, and make them cheese and bred,
And every one as commune good her handeléd.

37

That shortly she Malbecco has forgot,
And eke Sir Paridell, all° were he deare; *although*
Who from her went to seeke another lot,
And now by fortune was arrivéd here,
Where those two guilers with Malbecco were:
Soone as the oldman saw Sir Paridell,
He fainted, and was almost dead with feare,
Ne word he had to speake, his griefe to tell,
But to him louted low, and greeted goodly well.

38

And after askéd him for Hellenore,
"I take no keepe° of her," said Paridell, *care*
"She wonneth in the forrest there before."
So forth he rode, as his adventure fell;
The whiles the Boaster from his loftie sell° *saddle*
Faynd to alight, something amisse to mend;
But the fresh Swayne would not his leasure dwell,° *await*
But went his way; whom when he passéd kend,[5]
He up remounted light, and after fained to wend.

39

"Perdy nay," said Malbecco, "shall ye not:
But let him passe as lightly, as he came:
For litle good of him is to be got,
And mickle perill to be put to shame.
But let us go to seeke my dearest Dame,
Whom he hath left in yonder forrest wyld:
For of her safety in great doubt I am,
Least salvage beastes her person have despoyld:
Then all the world is lost, and we in vaine have toyld."

40

They all agree, and forward them addrest:
"Ah but," said craftie Trompart, "weete ye well,

5. I.e., when he was sure that Paridell had gone.

That yonder in that wastefull wildernesse
Huge monsters haunt, and many dangers dwell;
Dragons, and Minotaures, and feendes of hell,
And many wilde woodmen, which robbe and rend
All travellers; therefore advise ye well,
Before ye enterprise that way to wend:
One may his journey bring too soone to evill end."

41

Malbecco stopt in great astonishment,° *dismay*
And with pale eyes fast fixéd on the rest,
Their counsell craved, in daunger imminent.
Said Trompart, "You that are the most opprest
With burden of great treasure, I thinke best
Here for to stay in safetie behind;
My Lord and I will search the wide forrest."
That counsell pleaséd not Malbeccoes mind;
For he was much affraid, himselfe alone to find.

42

"Then is it best," said he, "that ye doe leave
Your treasure here in some securitie,
Either fast closéd in some hollow greave,° *thicket*
Or buried in the ground from jeopardie,
Till we returne againe in safetie:
As for us two, least doubt of us ye have,
Hence farre away we will blindfolded lie,
Ne privie be unto your treasures grave."[6]
It pleaséd: so he did. Then they march forward brave.

43

Now when amid the thickest woods they were,
They heard a noyse of many bagpipes shrill,
And shrieking Hububs them approching nere,
Which all the forrest did with horror fill:
That dreadfull sound the boasters hart did thrill,° *pierce*
With such amazement, that in haste he fled,
Ne ever lookéd backe for good or ill,
And after him eke fearefull Trompart sped;
The old man could not fly, but fell to ground halfe ded.

44

Yet afterwards close creeping, as he might,
He in a bush did hide his fearefull hed,
The jolly Satyres full of fresh delight,
Came dauncing forth, and with them nimbly led
Faire Hellenore, with girlonds all bespred,

6. I.e., and not know where your money is hidden.

Whom their May-lady they had newly made:
She proud of that new honour, which they red,° — *declared*
And of their lovely° fellowship full glade, — *loving*
Daunst lively, and her face did with a Lawrell shade.[7]

45

The silly man that in the thicket lay
Saw all this goodly sport, and grievéd sore,
Yet durst he not against it doe or say,
But did his hart with bitter thoughts engore,
To see th'unkindness° of his Hellenore. — *unnatural conduct*
All day they douncéd with great lustihed,
And with their hornéd feet the greene grasse wore,
The whiles their Gotes upon the brouzes° fed, — *twigs*
Till drouping Phoebus gan to hide his golden hed.

46

Tho up they gan their merry pypes to trusse,° — *pack*
And all their goodly heards did gather round,
But every Satyre first did give a busse° — *kiss*
To Hellenore: so busses did abound.
Now gan the humid vapour shed the ground
With perly deaw, and th'Earthés gloomy shade
Did dim the brightnesse of the welkin° round, — *heavens*
That every bird and beast awarnéd made,
To shrowd themselves, while sleepe their senses did invade.

47

Which when Malbecco saw, out of his bush
Upon his hands and feete he crept full light,
And like a Gote emongst the Gotes did rush,
That through the helpe of his faire hornes[8] on hight,
And misty dampe of misconceiving° night, — *misleading*
And eke through likenesse of his gotish beard,
He did the better counterfeite aright:
So home he marcht emongst the hornéd heard,
That none of all the Satyres him espyde or heard.

48

At night, when all they went to sleepe, he vewd,
Whereas his lovely wife emongst them lay,
Embracéd of a Satyre rough and rude,
Who all the night did minde° his joyous play: — *attend to*
Nine times he heard him come aloft ere day,
That all his hart with gealosie did swell;

7. In I.vi, the satyrs instinctively treat the virtuous Una with admiration (if also with ignorant idolatry); here they instinctively treat Hellenore with delighted sensuality.
8. The horns of cuckoldry, first sign of his transformation into Jealousy; Spenser modulates from a fabliau to personification allegory by way of pastoral.

But yet that nights ensample did bewray,
That not for nought his wife them loved so well,
When one so oft a night did ring his matins bell.

49

So closely as he could, he to them crept,
When wearie of their sport to sleepe they fell,
And to his wife, that now full soundly slept,
He whispered in her eare, and did her tell,
That it was he, which by her side did dwell,
And therefore prayd her wake, to heare him plaine.
As one out of a dreame not wakéd well,
She turned her, and returnéd backe againe:
Yet her for to awake he did the more constraine.

50

At last with irkesome trouble she abrayd;° *awakened*
And then perceiving, that it was indeed
Her old Malbecco, which did her upbrayd,
With loosenesse of her love, and loathly deed,
She was astonisht with exceeding dreed,
And would have wakt the Satyre by her syde;
But he her prayd, for mercy, or for meed,
To save his life, ne let him be descryde,
But hearken to his lore, and all his counsell hyde.

51

Tho gan he her perswade, to leave that lewd
And loathsome life, of God and man abhord,
And home returne, where all should be renewd
With perfect peace, and bandes of fresh accord,
And she received againe to bed and bord,
As if no trespasse ever had bene donne:
But she it all refuséd at one word,
And by no meanes would to his will be wonne,
But chose emongst the jolly Satyres still to wonne.° *dwell*

52

He wooéd her, till day spring he espyde;
But all in vaine: and then turnd to the heard,
Who butted him with homes on every syde,
And trode downe in the durt, where his hore° beard *gray*
Was fowly dight,° and he of death afeard. *defiled*
Early before the heavens fairest light
Out of the ruddy East was fully reard,
The heardes out of their foldes were looséd quight,
And he emongst the rest crept forth in sory plight.

53

So soone as he the Prison dore did pas,
He ran as fast, as both his feete could beare,
And never lookéd, who behind him was,
Ne scarsely who before: like as a Beare
That creeping close, amongst the hives to reare° *carry off*
An hony combe, the wakefull dogs espy,
And him assayling, sore his carkasse teare,
That hardly he with life away does fly,
Ne stayes, till safe himselfe he see from jeopardy.

54

Ne stayd he, till he came unto the place,
Where late his treasure he entombéd had,
Where when he found it not (for Trompart bace
Had it purloynéd for his maister bad:)
With extreme fury he became quite mad,
And ran away, ran with himselfe away:
That who so straungely had him seene bestad,° *situated*
With upstart haire, and staring eyes dismay,
From Limbo lake him late escapéd sure would say.

55

High over hilles and over dales he fled,
As if the wind him on his winges had borne,
Ne banck nor bush could stay him, when he sped
His nimble feet, as treading still on thorne:
Griefe, and despight, and gealosie, and scorne
Did all the way him follow hard behind,
And he himself himselfe loathed so forlorne,
So shamefully forlorne of womankind;
That as a Snake, still lurkéd in his wounded mind.

56

Still fled he forward, looking backward still,
Ne stayd his flight, nor fearefull agony,
Till that he came unto a rockie hill,
Over the sea, suspended dreadfully,
That living creature it would terrify,
To looke adowne, or upward to the hight:
From thence he threw himselfe dispiteously,° *pitilessly*
All desperate° of his fore-damnéd spright, *despairing*
That seemed no helpe for him was left in living sight.

57

But through long anguish, and selfe-murdring thought
He was so wasted and forpinéd° quight, *enfeebled*
That all his substance was consumed to nought,

And nothing left, but like an aery Spright,
That on the rockes he fell so flit and light,
That he thereby received no hurt at all,
But chauncéd on a craggy cliff to light;
Whence he with crooked clawes so long did crall,
That at the last he found a cave with entrance small.

58

Into the same he creepes, and thenceforth there
Resolved to build his balefull mansion,
In drery darkenesse, and continuall feare
Of that rockes fall, which ever and anon
Threates with huge ruine him to fall upon,
That he dare never sleepe, but that one eye
Still ope he keepes for that occasion;
Ne ever rests he in tranquillity,
The roring billowes beat his bowre so boystrously.

59

Ne ever is he wont on ought to feed,
But toades and frogs, his pasture° poysonous, *food*
Which in his cold complexion° do breed *constitution*
A filthy bloud, or humour rancorous,
Matter of doubt and dread suspitious,
That doth with curelesse care consume the hart,
Corrupts the stomacke with gall vitious,
Croscuts the liver with internall smart,
And doth transfixe the soule with deathes eternall dart.

60

Yet can he never dye, but dying lives,
And doth himselfe with sorrow new sustaine,
That death and life attonce unto him gives.
And painefull pleasure turnes to pleasing paine.
There dwels he ever, miserable swaine,
Hatefull both to him selfe, and every wight;
Where he through privy griefe, and horrour vaine,
Is woxen so deformed, that he has quight
Forgot he was a man, and Gealosie is hight.

Canto XI

Britomart chaceth Ollyphant,
findes Scudamour distrest:
Assayes the house of Busyrane,[1]
where Loves spoyles are exprest.

1. The name recalls the Egyptian tyrant Busiris, who sacrificed strangers to Zeus; Hercules killed him. For more on this episode see "Readings of the House of Busyrane" in the criticism section of this edition.

1

O hatefull hellish Snake, what furie furst
Brought thee from balefull house of Proserpine,
Where in her bosome she thee long had nurst,
And fostred up with bitter milke of tine,° *affliction*
Fowle Gealosie, that turnest love divine
To joylesse dread, and mak'st the loving hart
With hatefull thoughts to languish and to pine,
And feed it selfe with selfe-consuming smart?
Of all the passions in the mind thou vilest art.

2

O let him far be banishéd away,
And in his stead let Love for ever dwell,
Sweet Love, that doth his golden wings embay° *bathe*
In blesséd Nectar, and pure Pleasures well,
Untroubled of vile feare, or bitter fell.° *rancor*
And ye faire Ladies, that your kingdomes make
In th'harts of men, them governe wisely well,
And of faire Britomart ensample take,
That was as trew in love, as Turtle° to her make.° *dove / mate*

3

Who with Sir Satyrane, as earst ye red,
Forth ryding from Malbeccoes hostlesse hous,
Far off aspyde a young man, the which fled
From an huge Geaunt, that with hideous
And hatefull outrage long him chacéd thus;
It was that Ollyphant, the brother deare
Of that Argante vile and vitious,
From whom the Squire of Dames was reft whylere;
This all as bad as she, and worse, if worse ought were.

4

For as the sister did in feminine
And filthy lust exceede all woman kind,
So he surpasséd his sex masculine,
In beastly use that I did ever find;° *hear of*
Whom when as Britomart beheld behind
The fearefull boy so greedily pursew,
She was emmovéd in her noble mind,
T'employ her puissaunce to his reskew,
And prickéd fiercely forward, where she him did vew.

5

Ne was Sir Satyrane her far behinde,
But with like fiercenesse did ensew° the chace: *follow*
Whom when the Gyaunt saw, he soone resinde

His former suit, and from them fled apace;
They after both, and boldly bad him bace,[2]
And each did strive the other to out-goe,
But he them both outran a wondrous space,
For he was long, and swift as any Roe,° *deer*
And now made better speed, t'escape his fearéd foe.

6

It was not Satyrane, whom he did feare,
But Britomart the flowre of chastity;
For he the powre of chast hands might not beare,
But alwayes did their dread encounter fly:
And now so fast his feet he did apply,
That he has gotten to a forrest neare,
Where he is shrowded in security.
The wood they enter, and search every where,
They searchéd diversely, so both divided were.

7

Faire Britomart so long him followéd,
That she at last came to a fountaine sheare,° *clear*
By which there lay a knight[3] all wallowéd° *grovelling*
Upon the grassy ground, and by him neare
His haberjeon, his helmet, and his speare;
A little off,° his shield was rudely throwne, *aside*
On which the wingéd boy in colours cleare
Depeincted was, full easie to be knowne,
And he thereby, where ever it in field was showne.

8

His face upon the ground did groveling ly,
As if he had bene slombring in the shade,
That the brave Mayd would not for courtesy,
Out of his quiet slomber him abrade,° *arouse*
Nor seeme too suddeinly him to invade:° *intrude on*
Still as she stood, she heard with grievous throb
Him grone, as if his hart were peeces made,
And with most painefull pangs to sigh and sob,
That pitty did the Virgins hart of patience rob.

9

At last forth breaking into bitter plaintes
He said; "O soveraigne Lord that sit'st on hye,
And raignst in blis emongst thy blesséd Saintes,
How suffrest thou such shamefull cruelty,

2. I.e., challenged him.
3. I.e., Scudamour, whose shield bears Cupid's image. The episode that follows is based primarily on Tasso, *Rinaldo* 5.

So long unwreakéd of thine enimy? *unavenged*
Or hast thou, Lord, of good mens cause no heed?
Or doth thy justice sleepe, and silent ly?
What booteth then the good and righteous deed,
If goodnesse find no grace, nor righteousnesse no meed?

10

"If good find grace, and righteousnesse reward,
Why then is Amoret in caytive band,[4]
Sith that more bounteous creature never fared
On foot, upon the face of living land?
Or if that heavenly justice may withstand
The wrongfull outrage of unrighteous men,
Why then is Busirane with wicked hand
Suffred, these seven monethes day in secret den
My Lady and my love so cruelly to pen?[5]

11

"My Lady and my love is cruelly pend
In dolefull darkenesse from the vew of day,
Whilest deadly torments do her chast brest rend,
And the sharpe steele doth rive her hart in tway,
All for she Scudamore will not denay.° *deny*
Yet thou vile man, vile Scudamore art sound,
Ne canst her ayde, ne canst her foe dismay;
Unworthy wretch to tread upon the ground,
For whom so faire a Lady feeles so sore a wound."

12

There an huge heape of singultes° did oppresse *sobs*
His strugling soule, and swelling throbs empeach° *hinder*
His foltring toung with pangs of drerinesse,° *grief*
Choking the remnant of his plaintife speach,
As if his dayes were come to their last reach.° *end*
Which when she heard, and saw the ghastly fit,
Threatning into his life to make a breach,
Both with great ruth and terrour she was smit,
Fearing least from her cage the wearie soule would flit.

13

Tho stooping downe she him amovéd light;
Who therewith somewhat starting, up gan looke,
And seeing him behind a straunger knight,

4. I.e., captive in bonds.
5. Spenser may pun on "to pen" (to enclose, to write), for Amoret's situation is made of clichés from love poetry. Readers have disagreed as to whose imagination generates what Britomart sees: is Amoret upset by Scudamour's attempted masculine mastery, or does her own wavering "wit" (stanza 26) make her fear such mastery? Is there some combination of her doubts and his urgency? Her captivity recalls those of Florimell and Pastorella (in Book VI), but her torture may show how cultural convention can reconstruct the erotic impulse as a cruel prison.

Whereas no living creature he mistooke,[6]
With great indignaunce he that sight forsooke,
And downe againe himselfe disdainefully
Abjecting,° th'earth with his faire forhead strooke: *casting*
Which the bold Virgin seeing, gan apply
Fit medcine to his griefe, and spake thus courtesly.

14

"Ah gentle knight, whose deepe conceivéd griefe
Well seemes t'exceede the powre of patience,
Yet if that heavenly grace some good reliefe
You send, submit you to high providence,
And ever in your noble hart prepense,° *consider*
That all the sorrow in the world is lesse,
Then vertues might, and values° confidence, *valor's*
For who nill bide the burden of distresse,
Must not here thinke to live: for life is wretchednesse.

15

"Therefore, faire Sir, do comfort to you take,
And freely read,° what wicked felon so *tell*
Hath outraged you, and thrald your gentle make.° *mate*
Perhaps this hand may helpe to ease your woe,
And wreake your sorrow on your cruell foe,
At least it faire endevour will apply."
Those feeling wordes so neare the quicke did goe,
That up his head he rearéd easily,
And leaning on his elbow, these few wordes let fly.

16

"What boots it plaine,° that cannot be redrest, *to lament*
And sow vaine sorrow in a fruitlesse eare,
Sith powre of hand, nor skill of learnéd brest,
Ne worldly price cannot redeeme my deare,
Out of her thraldome and continuall feare?
For he the tyraunt, which her hath in ward° *control*
By strong enchauntments and blacke Magicke leare,° *lore*
Hath in a dungeon deepe her close embard,
And many dreadfull feends hath pointed° to her gard. *appointed*

17

"There he tormenteth her most terribly,
And day and night afflicts with mortall paine,
Because to yield him love she doth deny,
Once to me yold,° not to be yold againe.[7] *yielded*

6. I.e., where he had mistakenly thought no one to be.
7. In IV.x, Scudamour tells how he won Amoret and the shield of Love (hence his name) in the Temple of Venus; the story of the wedding, during which Busirane abducts Amoret, is in IV.i.2–4.

But yet by torture he would her constraine
Love to conceive in her disdainfull brest;
Till so she do, she must in doole° remaine, *pain*
Ne may by living meanes be thence relest.° *released*
What boots it then to plaine, that cannot be redrest?"

18

With this sad hersall° of his heavy stresse,° *account / distress*
The warlike Damzell was empassiond sore,
And said; "Sir knight, your cause is nothing lesse,
Then is your sorrow, certes if not more;
For nothing so much pitty doth implore,
As gentle Ladies helplesse misery.
But yet, if please ye listen to my lore,
I will with proofe of last extremity,[8]
Deliver her fro thence, or with her for you dy."

19

"Ah gentlest knight alive," said Scudamore,
"What huge heroicke magnanimity
Dwels in thy bounteous brest? what couldst thou more,
If she were thine, and thou as now am I?
O spare thy happy dayes, and them apply
To better boot,° but let me dye, that ought; *advantage*
More is more losse: one is enough to dy."
"Life is not lost," said she, "for which is bought
Endlesse renowm, that more then death is to be sought."[9]

20

Thus she at length perswaded him to rise,
And with her wend, to see what new successe° *result*
Mote him befall upon new enterprise;
His armes, which he had vowed to disprofesse,° *renounce*
She gathered up and did about him dresse,
And his forwandred steed unto him got:
So forth they both yfere° make their progresse, *together*
And march not past the mountenaunce° of a shot, *distance*
Till they arrived, whereas their purpose they did plot.

21

There they dismounting, drew their weapons bold
And stoutly came unto the Castle gate;
Whereas no gate they found, them to withhold,
Nor ward° to wait at morne and evening late, *porter*
But in the Porch, that did them sore amate,° *dismay*

8. I.e., to the utmost of my strength and spirit.
9. I.e., that is to be sought even at the risk of death.

A flaming fire,[1] ymixt with smouldry smoke,
And stinking Sulphure, that with griesly hate
And dreadfull horrour did all entraunce choke,
Enforcéd them their forward footing to revoke.° *withdraw*

22

Greatly thereat was Britomart dismayd,
Ne in that stownd° wist, how her selfe to beare; *crisis*
For daunger vaine it were, to have assayd
That cruell element, which all things feare,
Ne none can suffer to approchen neare:
And turning backe to Scudamour, thus sayd;
"What monstrous enmity provoke we heare,
Foolhardy as th'Earthes children, the which made
Battell against the Gods? so we a God invade.[2]

23

"Daunger without discretion to attempt,
Inglorious and beastlike is: therefore Sir knight,
Aread what course of you is safest dempt,° *judged*
And how we with our foe may come to fight."
"This is," quoth he, "the dolorous despight,
Which earst to you I playnd: for neither may
This fire be quencht by any wit or might,
Ne yet by any meanes removed away,
So mighty be th'enchauntments, which the same do stay.° *support*

24

"What is there else, but cease these fruitlesse paines,
And leave me to my former languishing?
Faire Amoret must dwell in wicked chaines,
And Scudamore here dye with sorrowing."
"Perdy not so;" said she, "for shamefull thing
It were t'abandon noble chevisaunce,° *enterprise*
For shew of perill, without venturing:
Rather let try extremities of chaunce,
Then enterprisèd prayse for dread to disavaunce."[3]

25

Therewith resolved to prove her utmost might,
Her ample shield she threw before her face,
And her swords point directing forward right,

1. Stanzas 21–25 adapt Tasso's *Rinaldo* 5.58–61 and *Gerusalemme* 13.34–35. There are similar details in R. Johnson's *Seven Champions of Christendom* (printed ca. 1597), notably a fire barrier, found also in fairy stories, and cf. the fourth-century *Psychomachia* of Prudentius, ll. 40–97, in which an armed (and talkative) Chastity defeats a likewise female Lust armed with flames.
2. I.e., like the giants attacking Olympus, we attack Vulcan (god of fire and oft-cuckolded husband of Venus; he was also, as in stanza 26, called Mulciber).
3. I.e., than to retreat fearfully from actions deserving praise.

Assayld the flame, the which eftsoones gave place,
And did it selfe divide with equall space,
That through she passéd; as a thunder bolt
Perceth the yielding ayre, and doth displace
The soring clouds into sad showres ymolt,° *melted*
So to her yold the flames, and did their force revolt.° *withdraw*

26

Whom whenas Scudamour saw past the fire,
Safe and untoucht, he likewise gan assay,
With greedy will, and envious desire,
And bad the stubborne flames to yield him way:
But cruell Mulciber would not obay
His threatfull pride, but did the more augment
His mighty rage, and with imperious sway
Him forst (maulgre) his fiercenesse to relent,
And backe retire, all scorcht and pitifully brent.

27

With huge impatience he inly swelt,° *burned*
More for great sorrow, that he could not pas,
Then for the burning torment, which he felt,
That with fell woodnesse° he effiercéd° was, *madness / enraged*
And wilfully him throwing on the gras,
Did beat and bounse his head and brest full sore;
The whiles the Championesse now entred has
The utmost° rowme, and past the formest dore, *outermost*
The utmost rowme, abounding with all precious store.

28

For round about, the wals yclothéd were
With goodly arras of great majesty,[4]
Woven with gold and silke so close and nere,
That the rich metall lurkéd privily,
As faining to be hid from envious eye;
Yet here, and there, and every where unwares
It shewd it selfe, and shone unwillingly;
Like a discolourd° Snake, whose hidden snares *varicolored*
Through the greene gras his long bright burnisht backe
declares.

29

And in those Tapets° weren fashionéd *tapestries*
Many faire pourtraicts, and many a faire feate,
And all of love, and all of lusty-hed,
As seeméd by their semblaunt did entreat;° *concern*

4. The chief literary basis for stanzas 28–46 is *Metamorphoses* 6.103–28; Spenser also consulted the mythographers, and there are parallels in Renaissance tapestries, paintings, and court pageantry.

And eke all Cupids warres they did repeate,
And cruell battels, which he whilome fought
Gainst all the Gods, to make his empire great;
Besides the huge massacres, which he wrought
On mighty kings and kesars,° into thraldome brought. *emperors*

30

Therein was writ, how often thundring Jove
Had felt the point of his hart-percing dart,
And leaving heavens kingdome, here did rove
In straunge disguize, to slake his scalding smart;
Now like a Ram, faire Helle to pervart,[5]
Now like a Bull, Europa to withdraw:° *carry off*
Ah, how the fearefull Ladies tender hart
Did lively° seeme to tremble, when she saw *actually*
The huge seas under her t'obay her servaunts law.

31

Soone after that into a golden showre
Him selfe he chaunged faire Danaë to vew,
And through the roofe of her strong brasen towre
Did raine into her lap an hony dew,
The whiles her foolish garde, that little knew
Of such deceipt, kept th'yron dore fast bard,
And watcht, that none should enter nor issew;
Vaine was that watch, and bootlesse all the ward,° *guard*
Whenas the God to golden hew° him selfe transfard. *form*

32

Then was he turnd into a snowy Swan,
To win faire Leda to his lovely° trade: *loving*
O wondrous skill, and sweet wit of the man,
That her in daffadillies sleeping made,
From scorching heat her daintie limbes to shade:
Whiles the proud Bird ruffing° his fethers wyde, *ruffling*
And brushing his faire brest, did her invade:
She slept, yet twixt her eyelids closely spyde,
How towards her he rusht, and smiléd at his pryde.

33

Then shewd it, how the Thebane Semelee[6]
Deceived of gealous Juno, did require

5. Helle and her brother, Phrixus, whom their stepmother, Ino, meant to sacrifice to Zeus, were saved when Hermes (Mercury) provided a gold-fleeced flying ram to carry them to safety (although Helle fell into the sea now called the Hellespont); see Ovid, *Fasti* 3.851–76, and Boccaccio, *Genealogiae* 13.68. In 4.68, Boccaccio links the influence of Aries ("the Ram") to the characteristics of Jove as leader and lover; Spenser combines these to make his own myth.
6. See *Metamorphoses* 3.253–309. Jealous of Semele, Juno took the form of her nurse and urged her to ask Jove to make love in all his glory; when he did so, Semele was consumed (but the god placed her embryo son, Bacchus, in his own thigh to gestate).

To see him in his soveraigne majestee,
Armd with his thunderbolts and lightning fire,
Whence dearely she with death bought her desire.
But faire Alcmena[7] better match did make,
Joying his love, in likenesse more entire,° *perfect*
Three nights in one, they say, that for her sake
He then did put, her pleasures lenger to partake.

34

Twise was he seene in soaring Eagles shape,
And with wide wings to beat the buxome° ayre, *yielding*
Once, when he with Asterie[8] did scape,
Againe, when as the Trojane boy[9] so faire
He snatcht from Ida hill, and with him bare:
Wondrous delight it was, there to behould,
How the rude Shepheards after him did stare,
Trembling through feare, least down he fallen should,
And often to him calling, to take surer hould.

35

In Satyres shape Antiopa he snatcht:
And like a fire, when he Aegin' assayd:
A shepheard, when Mnemosyné he catcht:
And like a Serpent to the Thracian mayd.[1]
Whiles thus on earth great Jove these pageaunts° playd, *scenes*
The wingéd boy did thrust into his throne,
And scoffing, thus unto his mother sayd,
"Lo now the heavens obey to me alone,
And take me for their Jove, whiles Jove to earth is gone."

36

And thou, faire Phoebus, in thy colours bright
Wast there enwoven, and the sad distresse,
In which that boy thee plongéd, for despight,
That thou bewrayedst his mothers wantonnesse,
When she with Mars was meynt° in joyfulnesse: *mingled*
For thy° he thrild° thee with a leaden dart, *therefore/pierced*
To love faire Daphne, which thee lovéd lesse:[2]
Lesse she thee loved, then was thy just desart,
Yet was thy love her death, and her death was thy smart.

7. Alcmena conceived Hercules when Jove came to her in the form of her husband, Amphitryon. The fusing of three nights into one may reflect the version in Comes 6.1.
8. Fleeing Jove, Asterie became a quail; he then became an eagle.
9. I.e., Ganymede, young son of Troy's King Tros whom Zeus, in the form of an eagle, snatched up to Olympus to serve as his cup-bearer (cf. *Metamorphoses* 10.144–62). Often read as a homosexual abduction, the myth was sometimes also allegorized as the rapture of mystic contemplation.
1. I.e., Proserpine, known to her Thracian worshippers as Cotytto.
2. On Apollo and Daphne, see *Metamorphoses* 1.450–567. Ovid says Cupid's gold-tipped and lead-tipped arrows inspire love or antipathy respectively; here the "leaden dart" may indicate Apollo's failure in love.

37

So lovedst thou the lusty° Hyacinct, *handsome*
So lovedst thou the faire Coronis deare.[3]
Yet both are of thy haplesse hand extinct,
Yet both in flowres do live, and love thee beare,
The one a Paunce,° the other a sweet breare: *pansy*
For griefe whereof, ye mote have lively seene
The God himselfe rending his golden heare,
And breaking quite his gyrlond ever greene,
With other signes of sorrow and impatient teene.° *woe*

38

Both for those two, and for his owne deare sonne,
The sonne of Climene[4] he did repent,
Who bold to guide the charet of the Sunne,
Himselfe in thousand peeces fondly rent,
And all the world with flashing fier brent;
So like,° that all the walles did seeme to flame. *lifelike*
Yet cruell Cupid, not herewith content,
Forst him eftsoones to follow other game,
And love a Shepheards daughter for his dearest Dame.

39

He lovéd Isse for his dearest Dame,[5]
And for her sake her cattell fed a while,
And for her sake a cowheard vile became,
The servant of Admetus cowheard vile,
Whiles that from heaven he sufferéd exile.
Long were to tell each other lovely fit,° *episode of love*
Now like a Lyon, hunting after spoile,
Now like a Stag, now like a faulcon flit:
All which in that faire arras was most lively writ.

40

Next unto him was Neptune picturéd,
In his divine resemblance wondrous lyke:
His face was rugged, and his hoarie hed
Droppéd with brackish deaw; his three-forkt Pyke
He stearnly shooke, and therewith fierce did stryke
The raging billowes, that on every syde
They trembling stood, and made a long broad dyke,
That his swift charet might have passage wyde,
Which foure great Hippodames° did draw in temewise tyde. *sea horses*

3. On Hyacinth see III.vi.45. Coronis, a victim of Apollo's jealous rage, appears in *Metamorphoses* 2.542–632; Spenser invents her transformation into a sweetbriar.
4. I.e., Phaethon (cf. *Metamorphoses* 2.1–400).
5. Spenser merges two myths: Apollo's appearance as a shepherd to Isse (*Metamorphoses* 6.124) and his nine years as an indentured herdsman to Admetus (see Hyginus, *Fabulae* 50).

41

His sea-horses did seeme to snort amayne,° *violently*
And from their nosethrilles blow the brynie streame,
That made the sparckling waves to smoke agayne,
And flame with gold, but the white fomy creame,
Did shine with silver, and shoot forth his beame.
The God himselfe did pensive seeme and sad,
And hong adowne his head, as he did dreame:
For privy love his brest empiercéd had,
Ne ought but deare Bisaltis[6] ay could make him glad.

42

He lovéd eke Iphimedia deare,
And Aeolus faire daughter Arne hight,
For whom he turnd him selfe into a Steare,
And fed on fodder, to beguile her sight.
Also to win Deucalions daughter bright,[7]
He turned him selfe into a Dolphin fayre;
And like a wingéd horse he tooke his flight,
To snaky-locke Medusa to repayre,
On whom he got faire Pegasus, that flitteth in the ayre.

43

Next Saturne[8] was, (but who would ever weene,
That sullein Saturne ever weend to love?
Yet love is sullein, and Saturnlike seene,
As he did for Erigone it prove,)
That to a Centaure did him selfe transmove.° *transmute*
So prooved it eke that gracious God of wine,
When for to compasse° Philliras hard love, *achieve*
He turnd himselfe into a fruitfull vine,
And into her faire bosome made his grapes decline.

44

Long were to tell the amorous assayes,
And gentle pangues,° with which he makéd meeke *pangs*
The mighty Mars, to learne his wanton playes:
How oft for Venus, and how often eek
For many other Nymphes he sore did shreek,
With womanish teares, and with unwarlike smarts,
Privily moystening his horrid° cheek. *rough*
There was he painted full of burning darts,
And many wide woundes launchéd° through his inner parts. *pierced*

6. I.e., Theophane, changed by Neptune into a ewe that he might, in the form of a ram, outwit her suitors (cf. Hyginus, *Fabulae* 88).
7. I.e., Melantho; for these allusions Spenser depends on *Metamorphoses* 6.116–20 and commentaries by Boccaccio and Comes.
8. The planet Saturn's influence is stern, ominous, and "crabbed" (cf. *Mutabilitie* vii.52). The stanza confuses Bacchus's seduction of Erigone with Saturn's deception of Philyra, mother of the centaur Chiron (*Metamorphoses* 6.125–26). A scribal or printer's error may be to blame.

45

Ne did he spare (so cruell was the Elfe)
His owne deare mother, (ah why should he so?)
Ne did he spare sometime to pricke himselfe,
That he might tast the sweet consuming woe,
Which he had wrought to many others moe.
But to declare the mournfull Tragedyes,
And spoiles, wherewith he all the ground did strow,
More eath° to number, with how many eyes *easy*
High heaven beholds sad lovers nightly theeveryes.

46

Kings Queenes, Lords Ladies, Knights and Damzels gent° *noble*
Were heaped together with the vulgar sort,
And mingled with the raskall rablement,
Without respect of person or of port,° *rank*
To shew Dan° Cupids powre and great effort: *Master*
And round about a border was entrayld,° *entwined*
Of broken bowes and arrowes shivered short,
And a long bloudy river through them rayld,° *flowed*
So lively and so like, that living sence it fayld.

47

And at the upper end of that faire rowme,
There was an Altar built of pretious stone,
Of passing valew, and of great renowme,
On which there stood an Image all alone,
Of massy gold, which with his owne light shone;
And wings it had with sundry colours dight,
More sundry colours, then the proud Pavone[9]
Beares in his boasted fan,° or Iris bright, *tail*
When her discolourd° bow she spreds through heaven bright. *many colored*

48

Blindfold he was, and in his cruèll fist
A mortall bow and arrowes keene did hold,
With which he shot at random, when him list,
Some headed with sad lead, some with pure gold;
(Ah man beware, how thou those darts behold)
A wounded Dragon under him did ly,
Whose hideous tayle his left foot did enfold,
And with a shaft was shot through either eye,
That no man forth might draw, ne no man remedye.

9. I.e., the peacock; Iris is goddess of the rainbow. The combination of images recalls Tasso, *Gerusalemme* 16.24, while the altar suggests idolatry.

49

And underneath his feet was written thus,
Unto the Victor of the Gods this bee:
And all the people in that ample hous
Did to that image bow their humble knee,
And oft committed fowle Idolatree.
That wondrous sight faire Britomart amazed,
Ne seeing could her wonder satisfie,
But ever more and more upon it gazed,
The whiles the passing° brightnes her fraile sences dazed. *surpassing*

50

Tho as she backward cast her busie eye,
To search each secret of that goodly sted,° *place*
Over the dore thus written she did spye
Be bold: she oft it over-red,
Yet could not find what sence it figuréd:
But what so were therein or writ or ment,
She was no whit thereby discouragéd
From prosecuting of her first intent,
But forward with bold steps into the next roome went.

51

Much fairer, then the former, was that roome,
And richlier by many partes° arayd: *degrees*
For not with arras made in painefull° loome, *painstaking*
But with pure gold it all was overlayd,
Wrought with wilde Antickes,° which their follies playd, *grotesque figures*
In the rich metall, as they living were:
A thousand monstrous formes therein were made,
Such as false love doth oft upon him weare,
For love in thousand monstrous formes doth oft appeare.

52

And all about, the glistring walles were hong
With warlike spoiles, and with victorious prayes,° *booty*
Of mighty Conquerours and Captaines strong,
Which were whilome captivéd in their dayes
To cruell love, and wrought their owne decayes:
Their swerds and speres were broke, and hauberques rent;
And their proud girlonds of tryumphant bayes° *laurels*
Troden in dust with fury insolent,
To shew the victors might and mercilesse intent.

53

The warlike Mayde beholding earnestly
The goodly ordinance° of this rich place, *arrangement*

Did greatly wonder, ne could satisfie
Her greedy eyes with gazing a long space,
But more she mervaild that no footings trace,
Nor wight appeared, but wastefull emptinesse,
And solemne silence over all that place:
Straunge thing it seemed, that none was to possesse
So rich purveyance,° ne them keepe with carefulnesse. *provision*

54

And as she lookt about, she did behold,
How over that same dore was likewise writ,
Be bold, be bold, and every where *Be bold*,
That much she muzed, yet could not construe it
By any ridling skill, or commune wit.
At last she spyde at that roomes upper end,
Another yron dore, on which was writ,
Be not too bold; whereto though she did bend
Her earnest mind, yet wist not what it might intend.

55

Thus she there waited untill eventyde,
Yet living creature none she saw appeare:
And now sad shadowes gan the world to hyde,
From mortall vew, and wrap in darkenesse dreare;
Yet nould° she d'off her weary armes, for feare *would not*
Of secret daunger, ne let sleepe oppresse
Her heavy eyes with natures burdein deare,
But drew her selfe aside in sickernesse,° *safety*
And her welpointed° weapons did about her dresse.° *ready / arrange*

Canto XII

The maske of Cupid,[1] and th'enchaunted
Chamber are displayd,
Whence Britomart redeemes faire
Amoret, through charmes decayd.° *weakened*

I

Tho when as chearelesse Night ycovered had
Faire heaven with an universall cloud,
That every wight dismayd with darknesse sad,° *heavy*
In silence and in sleepe themselves did shroud,
She heard a shrilling Trompet sound aloud,
Signe of nigh battell, or got victory;

1. This artfully symmetrical "maske" may revise an early work by Spenser such as the "Court of Cupide" mentioned in the "Epistle" to *The Shepheardes Calender* or the "Pageaunts" noted in the Glosse to "June." It is a "disguising," or pageant, presented (as IV.i.2–3 confirms) at the wedding of Amoret and Scudamour. Its personages, structure, and allegory reflect Tudor court entertainments, which fused mythology, romance, and court-of-love allegory. Specifically, Spenser joins the court-of-love "procession of Cupid" (as in Andreas Capellanus's *De Amore*) to Cupid's "triumph" with his adherents and victims (cf. Petrarch's *Trionfi*).

Nought therewith daunted was her courage proud,
But rather stird to cruell enmity,
Expecting ever, when some foe she might descry.

2

With that, an hideous storme of winde arose,
With dreadfull thunder and lightning atwixt,
And an earth-quake, as if it streight would lose° *loosen*
The worlds foundations from his centre fixt;
A direfull stench of smoke and sulphure mixt
Ensewd, whose noyance fild the fearefull sted,° *place*
From the fourth houre of night untill the sixt;
Yet the bold Britonesse was nought ydred,
Though much emmoved, but stedfast still perseveréd.

3

All suddenly a stormy whirlwind blew
Throughout the house, that clappéd° every dore, *slammed*
With which that yron wicket[2] open flew,
As it with mightie levers had bene tore:
And forth issewd, as on the ready° flore *prepared*
Of some Theatre, a grave personage,
That in his hand a branch of laurell bore,
With comely haveour and count'nance sage,
Yclad in costly garments, fit for tragicke Stage.

4

Proceeding to the midst, he still did stand,
As if in mind he somewhat had to say,
And to the vulgar° beckning with his hand, *common people*
In signe of silence, as to heare a play,
By lively actions he gan bewray
Some argument of matter passionéd;[3]
Which doen, he backe retyréd soft away,
And passing by, his name discoveréd,
Ease, on his robe in golden letters cypheréd.° *written*

5

The noble Mayd, still standing all this vewd,
And merveild at his strange intendiment,° *purpose*
With that a joyous fellowship issewd
Of Minstrals, making goodly meriment,
With wanton Bardes, and Rymers impudent,
All which together sung full chearefully

2. I.e., the "yron dore" in xi.54.
3. I.e., by expressive gestures, he revealed the theme of the coming masque. In Senecan tragedies of the period, dumbshows between the acts indicated the play's progressive action.

A lay of loves delight, with sweet concent:° *harmony*
After whom marcht a jolly company,
In manner of a maske, enrangéd orderly.

6

The whiles a most delitious harmony,
In full straunge notes was sweetly heard to sound,
That the rare sweetnesse of the melody
The feeble senses wholly did confound,
And the fraile soule in deepe delight nigh dround:
And when it ceast, shrill trompets loud did bray,
That their report° did farre away rebound, *echo*
And when they ceast, it gan againe to play,
The whiles the maskers marchéd forth in trim aray.

7

The first was Fancy, like a lovely boy,
Of rare aspect, and beautie without peare;
Matchable either to that ympe of Troy,[4]
Whom Jove did love, and chose his cup to beare,
Or that same daintie lad, which was so deare
To great Alcides, that when as he dyde,
He wailéd womanlike with many a teare,
And every wood, and every valley wyde
He fild with Hylas name; the Nymphes eke Hylas cryde.[5]

8

His garment neither was of silke nor say,° *fine wool*
But painted plumes, in goodly order dight,
Like as the sunburnt Indians do aray
Their tawney bodies, in their proudest plight:° *attire*
As those same plumes, so seemd he vaine and light,
That by his gate° might easily appeare; *gait*
For still he fared as dauncing in delight,
And in his hand a windy fan[6] did beare,
That in the idle aire he moved still here and there.

9

And him beside marcht amorous Desyre,
Who seemd of riper yeares, then th'other Swaine,
Yet was that other swayne this elders syre,
And gave him being, commune to them twaine:
His garment was disguiséd very vaine,[7]

4. I.e., Ganymede.
5. Cf. Theocritus, *Idyl* 13. Accompanying his lover Hercules (often called Alcides) on the Argo, the youth Hylas drowned in a spring during shore leave. See also the *Dictionarium* (1553) of C. Estienne, which has the wailing nymphs.
6. I.e., a fan to stir the breeze.
7. I.e., unusually designed for fashionable display.

And his embrodered Bonet sat awry;
Twixt both his hands few sparkes he close did straine,° *clasp*
Which still he blew, and kindled busily,
That soone they life conceived, and forth in flames did fly.

10

Next after him went Doubt, who was yclad
In a discoloured cote, of straunge disguyse,° *fashion*
That at his backe a brode Capuccio° had, *hood*
And sleeves dependant Albanese-wyse:[8]
He lookt askew with his mistrustfull eyes,
And nicely° trode, as thornes lay in his way, *delicately*
Or that the flore to shrinke he did avyse,° *perceive*
And on a broken reed he still did stay° *support*
His feeble steps, which shrunke, when hard theron he lay.

11

With him went Daunger, clothed in ragged weed,° *garment*
Made of Beares skin, that him more dreadfull made,
Yet his owne face was dreadfull, ne did need
Straunge horrour, to deforme his griesly shade;
A net in th'one hand, and a rustie blade
In th'other was, this Mischiefe, that Mishap;
With th'one his foes he threatned to invade,° *assault*
With th'other he his friends ment to enwrap:
For whom he could not kill, he practizd° to entrap. *plotted*

12

Next him was Feare, all armed from top to toe,
Yet thought himselfe not safe enough thereby,
But feard each shadow moving to and fro,
And his owne armes when glittering he did spy,
Or clashing heard, he fast away did fly,
As ashes pale of hew, and wingyheeld;
And evermore on Daunger fixt his eye,
Gainst whom he alwaies bent° a brasen shield, *directed*
Which his right hand unarméd fearefully did wield.

13

With him went Hope in rancke, a handsome Mayd,
Of chearefull looke and lovely to behold;
In silken samite° she was light arayd, *rich cloth*
And her faire lockes were woven up in gold;
She alway smyld, and in her hand did hold
An holy water Sprinckle,[9] dipt in deowe,° *dew*
With which she sprinckled favours manifold,

8. Hanging down in the Albanian style.
9. An aspergillum, or brush for sprinkling holy water.

On whom she list, and did great liking sheowe,
Great liking unto many, but true love to feowe.

14

And after them Dissemblance, and Suspect
Marcht in one rancke, yet an unequall paire:
For she was gentle, and of milde aspect,
Courteous to all, and seeming debonaire,
Goodly adornéd, and exceeding faire:
Yet was that all but painted, and purloynd,
And her bright browes were deckt with borrowed haire:
Her deedes were forgéd, and her words false coynd,
And alwaies in her hand two clewes° of silke she twynd. *balls*

15

But he was foule, ill favouréd, and grim,
Under his eyebrowes looking still askaunce;° *sideways*
And ever as Dissemblance laught on him,
He lowrd° on her with daungerous° eyeglaunce; *scowled / hard*
Shewing his nature in his countenance;
His rolling eyes did never rest in place,
But walkt each° where, for feare of hid mischaunce, *every*
Holding a lattice[1] still before his face,
Through which he still did peepe, as forward he did pace.

16

Next him went Griefe, and Fury matcht yfere;° *together*
Griefe all in sable sorrowfully clad,
Downe hanging his dull head with heavy chere,° *countenance*
Yet inly being more, then seeming sad:
A paire of Pincers in his hand he had,
With which he pinchéd people to the hart,
That from thenceforth a wretched life they lad,
In wilfull languor and consuming smart,
Dying each day with inward wounds of dolours dart.

17

But Fury was full ill appareiléd
In rags, that naked nigh she did appeare,
With ghastly lookes and dreadfull drerihed;° *horror*
For from her backe her garments she did teare,
And from her head oft rent her snarléd heare:
In her right hand a firebrand she did tosse
About her head, still roming here and there;
As a dismayéd Deare in chace embost,° *hard pressed*
Forgetfull of his safety, hath his right way lost.

1. I.e., a small screen or vizard.

18

After them went Displeasure and Pleasance,
He looking lompish and full sullein sad,
And hanging downe his heavy countenance;
She chearefull fresh and full of joyance glad,
As if no sorrow she ne felt ne drad;° *feared*
That evill matchéd paire they seemed to bee:
An angry Waspe th'one in a viall had,
Th'other in hers an hony-lady° Bee; *honey-laden*
Thus marchéd these sixe couples forth in faire degree.° *order*

19

After all these there marcht a most faire Dame,
Led of two grysie° villeins, th'one Despight,° *grim / outrage*
The other clepéd° Cruelty by name: *called*
She dolefull Lady, like a dreary Spright,
Cald by strong charmes out of eternall night,
Had deathes owne image figurd in her face,
Full of sad signes, fearefull to living sight;
Yet in that horror shewd a seemely grace,
And with her feeble feet did move a comely pace.

20

Her brest all naked, as net° ivory, *pure*
Without adorne of gold or silver bright,
Wherewith the Craftesman wonts° it beautify, *is used to*
Of her dew honour° was despoyléd quight, *covering*
And a wide wound therein (O ruefull sight)
Entrenchéd deepe with knife accurséd keene,
Yet freshly bleeding forth her fainting spright,
(The worke of cruell hand) was to be seene,
That dyde in sanguine red her skin all snowy cleene.

21

At that wide orifice her trembling hart
Was drawne forth, and in silver basin layd,
Quite through transfixéd with a deadly dart,
And in her bloud yet steeming fresh embayd:° *bathed*
And those two villeins, which her steps upstayd,
When her weake feete could scarcely her sustaine,
And fading vitall powers gan to fade,
Her forward still with torture did constraine,
And evermore encreaséd her consuming paine.

22

Next after her the wingéd God himselfe[2]
Came riding on a Lion ravenous,

2. I.e., Cupid.

Taught to abay the menage° of that Elfe, *control*
That man and beast with powre imperious
Subdeweth to his kingdome tyrannous:
His blindfold eyes he bad a while unbind,
That his proud spoyle of that same dolorous
Faire Dame he might behold in perfect kind;° *manner*
Which seene, he much rejoycéd in his cruell mind.

23

Of which full proud, himselfe up rearing hye,
He lookéd round about with sterne disdaine;
And did survay his goodly company:
And marshalling the evill ordered traine,° *assembly*
With that the darts which his right hand did straine,
Full dreadfully he shooke that all did quake,
And clapt on hie his coulourd wingés twaine,
That all his many° it affraide did make: *company*
Tho blinding him againe, his way he forth did take.

24

Behinde him was Reproch, Repentance, Shame;
Reproch the first, Shame next, Repent behind:
Repentance feeble, sorrowfull, and lame:
Reproch despightfull, carelesse, and unkind;
Shame most ill favourd,° bestiall, and blind: *featured*
Shame lowrd, Repentance sighed, Reproch did scould;
Reproch sharpe stings, Repentance whips entwind,
Shame burning brond-yrons in her hand did hold:
All three to each° unlike, yet all made in one mould. *each other*

25

And after them a rude confuséd rout° *mob*
Of persons flockt, whose names is hard to read:° *distinguish*
Emongst them was sterne Strife, and Anger stout,
Unquiet Care, and fond Unthriftihead,° *wastefulness*
Lewd° Losse of Time, and Sorrow seeming dead, *foolish*
Inconstant Chaunge, and false Disloyaltie,
Consuming Riotise,° and guilty Dread *extravagance*
Of heavenly vengeance, faint Infirmitie,
Vile Povertie, and lastly Death with infamie.

26

There were full many moe like° maladies, *similar*
Whose names and natures I note° readen well; *cannot*
So many moe, as there be phantasies
In wavering wemens wit,° that none can tell,° *mind / count*
Or paines in love, or punishments in hell;
All which disguizéd marcht in masking wise,
About the chamber with that Damozell,

And then returnéd, having marchéd thrise,
Into the inner roome, from whence they first did rise.° *emerge*

27

So soone as they were in, the dore streight way
Fast lockéd, driven with that stormy blast,
Which first it opened; and bore all away.
Then the brave Maid, which all this while was plast
In secret shade, and saw both first and last,
Issewéd forth, and went unto the dore,
To enter in, but found it lockéd fast:
It vaine she thought with rigorous uprore
For to efforce,° when charmes had closéd it afore. *force open*

28

Where force might not availe, there sleights and art
She cast° to use, both fit for hard emprize; *purposed*
For thy from that same roome not to depart
Till morrow next, she did her selfe avize,° *resolve*
When, that same Maske againe should forth arize.
The morrow next appeard with joyous cheare,
Calling men to their daily exercize,
Then she, as morrow fresh, her selfe did reare° *arouse*
Out of her secret stand, that day for to out weare.[3]

29

All that day she outwore in wandering,
And gazing on that Chambers ornament,
Till that againe the second evening
Her covered with her sable vestiment,
Wherewith the worlds faire beautie she hath blent:° *obscured*
Then when the second watch was almost past,[4]
That brasen dore flew open, and in went
Bold Britomart, as she had late forecast,° *determined*
Neither of idle shewes, nor of false charmes aghast.

30

So soone as she was entred, round about
She cast her eies, to see what was become
Of all those persons, which she saw without:
But lo, they streight were vanisht all and some,[5]
Ne living wight she saw in all that roome,
Save that same woefull Ladie,[6] both whose hands
Were bounden fast, that did her ill become,

3. I.e., to pass that day.
4. I.e., just before midnight. The "second watch" began at nine and ended at twelve.
5. I.e., one and all.
6. I.e., Amoret. One can read the pillar to which Amoret is bound as the phallic rigidity that she fears or that Scudamour threatens to exert too masterfully; it detumesces in stanza 37.

And her small wast girt round with yron bands,
Unto a brasen pillour, by the which she stands.

31

And her before the vile Enchaunter[7] sate,
Figuring° straunge characters of his art, *drawing*
With living bloud he those characters wrate,
Dreadfully dropping from her dying hart,
Seeming transfixéd with a cruell dart,
And all perforce to make her him to love.
Ah who can love the worker of her smart?
A thousand charmes he formerly did prove;° *try*
Yet thousand charmes could not her stedfast heart remove.

32

Soone as that virgin knight he saw in place,[8]
His wicked bookes in hast he overthrew,
Not caring his long labours to deface,[9]
And fiercely ronning to that Lady trew,
A murdrous knife out of his pocket drew,
The which he thought, for villeinous despight,
In her tormented bodie to embrew:° *plunge*
But the stout Damzell to him leaping light,
His cursed hand withheld, and maisteréd his might.

33

From her, to whom his fury first he ment,° *intended*
The wicked weapon rashly° he did wrest, *quickly*
And turning to her selfe his fell intent,
Unwares° it strooke into her snowie chest, *suddenly*
That little drops empurpled her faire brest.
Exceeding wroth therewith the virgin grew,
Albe the wound were nothing deepe imprest,
And fiercely forth her mortall blade she drew,
To give him the reward for such vile outrage dew.

34

So mightily she smote him, that to ground
He fell halfe dead; next stroke him should have slaine,
Had not the Lady, which by him stood bound,
Dernely° unto her calléd to abstaine, *dismally*
From doing him to dy. For else her paine
Should be remedilesse, sith none but hee,
Which wrought it, could the same recure againe.[1]

7. I.e., Busyrane.
8. I.e., there.
9. I.e., not caring whether he destroyed his long labors.
1. Amoret's request may hint that Busyrane is in some sense a necessary if distorted aspect of Scudamour and the erotic experience, or that he is that experience as it might seem to the uninitiated.

Therewith she stayd her hand, loth stayd to bee;
For life she him envyde,° and longed revenge to see. *begrudged*

35

And to him said, "Thou wicked man, whose meed
For so huge mischiefe, and vile villany
Is death, or if that ought do death exceed,
Be sure, that nought may save thee from to dy,
But if that[2] thou this Dame doe presently° *at once*
Restore unto her health, and former state;
This doe and live, else die undoubtedly."
He glad of life, that lookt for death but late,
Did yield himselfe right willing to prolong his date.° *term of life*

36

And rising up, gan streight to overlooke° *read*
Those curséd leaves, his charmes backe to reverse;
Full dreadfull things out of that balefull booke
He red,° and measured° many a sad verse, *said / chanted*
That horror gan the virgins hart to perse,
And her faire locks up staréd stiffe on end,
Hearing him those same bloudy lines reherse;° *recite*
And all the while he red, she did extend
Her sword high over him, if ought° he did offend. *in any way*

37

Anon she gan perceive the house to quake,
And all the dores to rattle round about;
Yet all that did not her dismaiéd make,
Nor slacke her threatfull hand for daungers dout,° *fear*
But still with stedfast eye and courage stout
Abode,° to weet what end would come of all. *waited*
At last that mightie chaine, which round about
Her tender waste was wound, adowne gan fall,
And that great brasen pillour broke in peeces small.

38

The cruell steele, which thrild her dying hart,
Fell softly forth, as of his owne accord,
And the wyde wound, which lately did dispart° *cleave*
Her bleeding brest, and riven bowels gored,[3]
Was closéd up, as it had not bene bored,
And every part to safety full sound,
As she were never hurt, was soone restored:

2. I.e., unless.
3. I.e., pierced her torn inner parts.

Tho when she felt her selfe to be unbound,
And perfect hole, prostrate she fell unto the ground.[4]

39

Before faire Britomart, she fell prostrate,
Saying, "Ah noble knight, what worthy meed
Can wretched Lady, quit from wofull state,
Yield you in liew of this your gratious deed?
Your vertue selfe her owne reward shall breed,
Even immortall praise, and glory wyde,
Which I your vassall, by your prowesse freed,
Shall through the world make to be notifyde,° *proclaimed*
And goodly well advance,° that goodly well was tryde." *praise*

40

But Britomart uprearing her from ground,
Said, "Gentle Dame, reward enough I weene
For many labours more, then I have found,
This, that in safety now I have you seene,
And meane° of your deliverance have beene: *means*
Henceforth faire Lady comfort to you take,
And put away remembrance of late teene;° *woe*
In stead thereof know, that your loving Make,° *mate*
Hath no lesse griefe enduréd for your gentle sake."

41

She much was cheard to heare him mentiónd,
Whom of all living wights she lovéd best.
Then laid the noble Championesse strong hond
Upon th'enchaunter, which had her distrest
So sore, and with foule outrages opprest:
With that great chaine, wherewith not long ygo
He bound that pitteous Lady prisoner, now relest,
Himselfe she bound, more worthy to be so,
And captive with her led to wretchednesse and wo.

42

Returning backe, those goodly roomes, which erst
She saw so rich and royally arayd,
Now vanisht utterly, and cleane subverst° *overturned*
She found, and all their glory quite decayd,° *destroyed*
That sight of such a chaunge her much dismayd.
Thence forth descending to that perlous° Porch, *perilous*
Those dreadfull flames she also found delayd,° *allayed*

4. The phrase "perfect hole" can provoke varied readings. Does "hole" simply mean "whole"? Is this a pun? Does Amoret discover that she is still "whole" despite her frightening (and sexualized) experience? Is there erotic wordplay on "whole" and "hole" meaning vagina, sometimes called the female "nothing" because of a hole's zero shape?

And quenchéd quite, like a consuméd torch,
That erst all entrers wont so cruelly to scorch.

43

More easie issew now, then entrance late
She found: for now that fainéd° dreadfull flame, *false*
Which chokt the porch of that enchaunted gate,
And passage bard to all, that thither came,
Was vanisht quite, as it were not the same,
And gave her leave at pleasure forth to passe.
Th'Enchaunter selfe, which all that fraud did frame,
To have efforst° the love of that faire lasse, *compelled*
Seeing his worke now wasted deepe engrievéd was.

44

But when the victoresse arrivéd there,
Where late she left the pensife Scudamore,
With her owne trusty Squire, both full of feare,
Neither of them she found where she them lore.° *left*
Thereat her noble hart was stonisht sore;
But most faire Amoret, whose gentle spright
Now gan to feede on hope, which she before
Conceivéd had, to see her owne deare knight,
Being thereof beguyld was fild with new affright.

45

But he sad man, when he had long in drede
Awayted there for Britomarts returne,
Yet saw her not nor signe of her good speed,° *success*
His expectation to despaire did turne,
Misdeeming sure that her those flames did burne;
And therefore gan advize° with her old Squire, *consult*
Who her deare nourslings losse no lesse did mourne,
Thence to depart for further aide t'enquire:
Where let them wend at will, whilest here I doe respire.° *breathe*

[Stanzas 43–45 first appear in the 1596 edition of *The Faerie Queene*. In the edition of 1590, the following stanzas conclude Book III.]

At last she came unto the place, where late
She left Sir Scudamour in great distresse,
Twixt dolour and despight halfe desperate,
Of his loves succour, of his owne redresse,° *relief*
And of the hardie Britomarts successe:
There on the cold earth him now thrown she found,
In wilfull anguish, and dead heavinesse,° *grief*
And to him cald; whose voices knowen sound
Soon as he heard, himself he rearéd light from ground.

There did he see, that most on earth him joyd,
His dearest love, the comfort of his dayes,
Whose too long absence him had sore annoyd,° *troubled*
And wearièd his life with dull delayes:
Straight he upstarted from the loathèd layes,° *ground*
And to her ran with hasty egernesse,
Like as a Deare, that greedily embayes° *bathes*
In the coole soile,° after long thirstinesse, *marsh*
Which he in chace endurèd hath, now nigh breathlesse.

Lightly he clipt her twixt his armès twaine,
And straightly° did embrace her body bright, *closely*
Her body, late the prison of sad paine,
Now the sweet lodge of love and deare delight:
But she faire Lady overcommen quight
Of huge affection, did in pleasure melt,
And in sweete ravishment pourd out her spright:
No word they spake, nor earthly thing they felt,
But like two senceles stocks in long embracement dwelt.

Had ye them seene, ye would have surely thought,
That they had beene that faire Hermaphrodite,[5]
Which that rich Romane of white marble wrought,
And in his costly Bath causd to bee site:
So seemd those two, as growne together quite,
That Britomart halfe envying their blesse,° *bliss*
Was much empassiond° in her gentle° sprite, *moved/noble*
And to her selfe oft wisht like happinesse,
In vaine she wisht, that fate n'ould° let her yet possesse. *would not*

Thus doe those lovers with sweet countervayle,° *exchange*
Each other of loves bitter fruit despoile.
But now my teme begins to faint and fayle,
All woxen weary of their journall° toyle: *daily*
Therefore I will their sweatie yokes assoyle° *release*
At this same furrowes end, till a new day:
And ye faire Swayns, after your long turmoyle,
Now cease your worke, and at your pleasure play;
Now cease your worke; to morrow is an holy day.

5. Cf. *Metamorphoses* 4.285–388. Upon request, the gods fused Salmacis and Hermaphroditus into one creature. The resulting "hermaphrodite," possessing both male and female genitalia, was often read positively as symbolizing marriage but could also be seen as merely interesting and alien (see the voyages of "Sir John Mandeville") or as negatively monstrous (e.g., in Ben Jonson's *Volpone*). Spenser's early readers might have seen in the "rich Romane" with a "costly bath" either Italian decadence or ancient glamour.

A Letter of the Authors

EXPOUNDING HIS WHOLE INTENTION IN THE COURSE OF THIS WORKE: WHICH FOR THAT IT GIVETH GREAT LIGHT TO THE READER, FOR THE BETTER UNDERSTANDING IS HEREUNTO ANNEXED.[1]

To the Right noble, and Valorous, Sir Walter Raleigh knight, Lo. Wardein of the Stanneryes, and her Majesties liefetenaunt of the County of Cornewayll.

Sir knowing how doubtfully all Allegories may be construed, and this booke of mine, which I have entituled the Faery Queene, being a continued Allegory, or darke conceit, I have thought good aswell for avoyding of gealous opinions and misconstructions, as also for your better light in reading thereof, (being so by you commanded,) to discover unto you the general intention and meaning, which in the whole course thereof I have fashioned, without expressing of any particular purposes or by-accidents[2] therein occasioned. The generall end therefore of all the booke is to fashion[3] a gentleman or noble person in vertuous and gentle discipline: Which for that I conceived shoulde be most plausible[4] and pleasing, being coloured with an historicall fiction, the which the most part of men delight to read, rather for variety of matter, then for profite of the ensample: I chose the historye of king Arthure, as most fitte for the excellency of his person, being made famous by many mens former workes, and also furthest from the daunger of envy, and suspition of present time. In which I have followed all the antique Poets historicall, first Homere, who in the Persons of Agamemnon and Ulysses hath ensampled a good governour and a vertuous man, the one in his *Ilias*, and the other in his *Odysseis*: then Virgil, whose like intention was to doe in the person of Aeneas: after him Ariosto comprised them both in his Orlando: and lately Tasso dissevered them againe, and formed both parts in two persons, namely that part which they in Philosophy call Ethice, or vertues of a private man, coloured in his Rinaldo: The other named Politice in his Godfredo.[5] By ensample of which excellente Poets, I labour to pourtraict in Arthure, before he was king, the image of a brave knight, perfected in the twelve private morall vertues, as Aristotle hath devised,[6] the which is the purpose of these first twelve bookes: which if I finde to be well accepted, I may be perhaps encoraged, to frame the other part of polliticke vertues in his person, after that hee came to be king. To some I know this Methode will seeme displeasaunt, which had rather have good discipline delivered

1. This "Letter" was appended to the 1590 edition of *The Faerie Queene* (Books I–III) and dropped from the 1596 edition. Such epistolary commentaries were commonly employed by Renaissance poets to explain or defend their purpose and method; cf. Tasso's account of the allegory in his epic poem *Gerusalemme Liberata*, and Sir John Harington's preface to his translation of Ariosto's *Orlando Furioso* (1591). The degree to which we should read the letter as a sure guide has been debated.
2. Side issues, secondary concerns.
3. I.e., to represent (in a secondary sense, to train or educate).
4. Acceptable, deserving of approval.
5. Lodovico Ariosto (1474–1533) wrote the epic romance *Orlando Furioso*, published in complete form in 1532; Torquato Tasso (1544–1595) published his chivalric romance *Rinaldo* in 1562 and the epic *Gerusalemme Liberata* (centered on the heroic figure of Count Godfredo) in 1581.
6. Aristotle does not actually distinguish twelve moral virtues in the *Nicomachaean Ethics*, but medieval and early sixteenth-century commentators, following Aquinas, had so divided them.

plainly in way of precepts, or sermoned at large, as they use, then thus clowdily enwrapped in Allegoricall devises. But such, me seeme, should be satisfide with the use of these dayes, seeing all things accounted by their showes, and nothing esteemed of, that is not delightfull and pleasing to commune sence. For this cause is Xenophon preferred before Plato, for that the one in the exquisite depth of his judgement, formed a Commune welth such as it should be, but the other in the person of Cyrus and the Persians fashioned a governement such as might best be: So much more profitable and gratious is doctrine by ensample, then by rule.[7] So have I laboured to doe in the person of Arthure: whome I conceive after his long education by Timon, to whom he was by Merlin delivered to be brought up, so soone as he was borne of the Lady Igrayne, to have seene in a dream or vision the Faery Queen, with whose excellent beauty ravished, he awaking resolved to seeke her out, and so being by Merlin armed, and by Timon throughly instructed, he went to seeke her forth in Faerye land. In that Faery Queene I meane glory in my generall intention, but in my particular I conceive the most excellent and glorious person of our soveraine the Queene, and her kingdome in Faery land. And yet in some places els, I doe otherwise shadow[8] her. For considering she beareth two persons, the one of a most royall Queene or Empresse, the other of a most vertuous and beautifull Lady, this latter part in some places I doe expresse in Belphoebe, fashioning her name according to your owne excellent conceipt of Cynthia,[9] (Phoebe and Cynthia being both names of Diana.) So in the person of Prince Arthure I sette forth magnificence in particular, which vertue for that (according to Aristotle and the rest)[1] it is the perfection of all the rest, and conteineth in it them all, therefore in the whole course I mention the deedes of Arthure applyable to that vertue, which I write of in that booke. But of the xii. other vertues, I make xii. other knights the patrones, for the more variety of the history: Of which these three bookes contayn three, The first of the knight of the Redcrosse, in whome I expresse Holynes: The seconde of Sir Guyon, in whome I sette forth Temperaunce: The third of Britomartis a Lady knight, in whome I picture Chastity. But because the beginning of the whole worke seemeth abrupte and as depending upon other antecedents, it needs that ye know the occasion of these three knights severall adventures. For the Methode of a Poet historical is not such, as of an Historiographer.[2] For an Historiographer discourseth of affayres orderly as they were donne, accounting as well the times as the actions, but a Poet thrusteth into the middest, even where it most concerneth him, and there recoursing to the thinges forepaste, and divining of thinges to come, maketh a pleasing Analysis of all. The beginning therefore of my history, if it were to be told by an Historiographer, should be the twelfth booke, which is the last, where I devise that the Faery Queene kept her Annuall

7. This distinction between Xenophon's *Cyropaedia* and Plato's *Republic* recalls Sidney's praise of the poet (who "coupleth the generall notion with the particuler example") at the expense of the philosopher, whose "woordish description . . . dooth neyther strike, pierce, nor possesse the sight of the soule so much as that other dooth."
8. I.e., portray allegorically.
9. Raleigh's fragmentary poem *Cynthia* celebrates Queen Elizabeth.
1. Aristotle has *magnanimity* (greatness of soul). Spenser either confuses the terms or prefers "greatness of doing."
2. I.e., the method employed by an epic poet is not that of the historian.

feaste xii. dayes, uppon which xii. severall dayes, the occasions of the xii. severall adventures hapned, which being undertaken by xii. severall knights, are in these xii books severally handled and discoursed. The first was this. In the beginning of the feast, there presented him selfe a tall clownishe[3] younge man, who falling before the Queen of Faries desired a boone (as the manner then was) which during that feast she might not refuse: which was that hee might have the atchievement of any adventure, which during that feaste should happen, that being graunted, he rested him on the floore, unfitte through his rusticity for a better place. Soone after entred a faire Ladye in mourning weedes, riding on a white Asse, with a dwarfe behind her leading a warlike steed, that bore the Armes of a knight, and his speare in the dwarfes hand. Shee falling before the Queene of Faeries, complayned that her father and mother an ancient King and Queene, had bene by an huge dragon many years shut up in a brasen Castle, who thence suffred them not to yssew: and therefore besought the Faery Queene to assygne her some one of her knights to take on him that exployt. Presently that clownish person upstarting, desired that adventure: whereat the Queene much wondering, and the Lady much gainesaying, yet he earnestly importuned his desire. In the end the Lady told him that unlesse that armour which she brought, would serve him (that is the armour of a Christian man specified by Saint Paul v. Ephes.)[4] that he could not succeed in that enterprise, which being forthwith put upon him with dewe furnitures[5] thereunto, he seemed the goodliest man in al that company, and was well liked of the Lady. And eftesoones[6] taking on him knighthood, and mounting on that straunge Courser, he went forth with her on that adventure: where beginneth the first booke, vz.

A gentle knight was pricking on the playne. &c.

The second day ther came in a Palmer bearing an Infant with bloody hands, whose Parents he complained to have bene slayn by an Enchaunteresse called Acrasia: and therefore craved of the Faery Queene, to appoint him some knight, to performe that adventure, which being assigned to Sir Guyon, he presently went forth with that same Palmer: which is the beginning of the second booke and the whole subject thereof. The third day there came in, a Groome who complained before the Faery Queene, that a vile Enchaunter called Busirane had in hand a most faire Lady called Amoretta, whom he kept in most grievous torment, because she would not yield him the pleasure of her body. Whereupon Sir Scudamour the lover of that Lady presently tooke on him that adventure. But being unable to performe it by reason of the hard Enchauntments, after long sorrow, in the end met with Britomartis, who succoured him, and reskewed his love.

But by occasion hereof, many other adventures are intermedled, but rather as Accidents, then intendments[7]. As the love of Britomart, the

3. I.e., of rustic appearance. Wall 1986 and 1987 deduces from an astronomical reference in II.ii.46 that Gloriana holds her twelve-day feast at Christmastide, traditional time for mumming plays about St. George.
4. Cf. the note on I.i.I.
5. Suitable equipment.
6. Forthwith.
7. I.e., as matters relatively incidental to a central purpose.

overthrow of Marinell, the misery of Florimell, the vertuousnes of Belphoebe, the lasciviousnes of Hellenora, and many the like.

Thus much Sir. I have briefly overronne to direct your understanding to the wel-head[8] of the History, that from thence gathering the whole intention of the conceit, ye may as in a handfull gripe al the discourse, which otherwise may happily[9] seeme tedious and confused. So humbly craving the continuaunce of your honorable favour towards me, and th'eternall establishment of your happines, I humbly take leave.

23. January. 1589.[1]
Yours most humbly affectionate.
Ed. Spenser.

8. Source, spring.
9. By chance.
1. I.e., 1590. In England (until 1752), the official year was reckoned from March 25.

From The Fourth Booke of the Faerie Queene

Containing
The Legend of Cambel and Telamond[1]
or
of Friendship

I

The rugged forhead that with grave foresight
Welds° kingdomes causes, and affaires of state,[2] — *manages*
My looser rimes (I wote) doth sharply wite,° — *blame*
For praising love, as I have done of late,
And magnifying lovers deare debate;
By which fraile youth is oft to follie led,
Through false allurement of that pleasing baite,
That better were in vertues discipled,° — *instructed*
Then with vaine poemes weeds to have their fancies fed.

2

Such ones ill judge of love, that cannot love,
Ne in their frosen hearts feele kindly° flame: — *natural*
For thy° they ought not thing unknowne reprove, — *therefore*
Ne naturall affection faultlesse blame,
For fault of few that have abusd the same.
For it of honor and all vertue is
The roote, and brings forth glorious flowres of fame,
That crowne true lovers with immortall blis,
The meed of them that love, and do not live amisse.

3

Which who so list looke backe to former ages,
And call to count the things that then were donne,
Shall find, that all the workes of those wise sages,
And brave exploits which great Heroés wonne,
In love were either ended or begunne;
Witnesse the father of Philosophie,[3]
Which to his Critias, shaded oft from sunne,

1. Nobody named Telamond appears in Book IV itself; the name may combine Greek *téleios* and Latin *mundus* to mean "perfect world," the harmony that friendship and brotherhood (see IV. ii–iii) aims, although the number of possibly relevant Greek "tel-" words makes it hard to pin down what Spenser may have intended. There was, furthermore, an ancient King Telamon, an Argonaut and friend of Hercules who married the sister of Priam, king of Troy.
2. Many have read these lines as alluding to William Cecil, Lord Burleigh, whose displeasure with Spenser appears to be noted in VI.xii.41. If so, Spenser's implicitly defiant phrases can be compared to the rashness with which he allegorized Burleigh in *Mother Hubberds Tale*. The "looser rimes" suggest the recently published *Amoretti*, and educated readers might well have connected the "rugged forhead" to the "furrowed brow" ("*fronte . . . torva*") of Tragedy as she arrives, carrying a scepter, to rebuke Ovid for writing erotic elegiacs instead of something serious (*Amores* III.i). Spenser appears to appeal over Burleigh's head to Elizabeth, whose court, with the queen's encouragement, had exploited love poetry as a form of courtiership (cf. Marotti 1982).
3. I.e., Socrates, who discoursed on love to Phaedrus (not Critias) under a plane tree (Plato, *Phaedrus* 229a ff.).

Of love full manie lessons did apply,
The which these Stoicke censours cannot well deny.

4

To such therefore I do not sing at all,
But to that sacred Saint my soveraigne Queene,
In whose chast breast all bountie naturall,
And treasures of true love enlockéd beene,
Bove all her sexe that ever yet was seene;
To her I sing of love, that loveth best,
And best is loved of all alive I weene:
To her this song most fitly is addrest,
The Queene of love, and Prince of peace from heaven blest.

5

Which that she may the better deigne to heare,
Do thou dred infant,[4] Venus dearling dove,
From her high spirit chase imperious feare,[5]
And use of awfull Majestie remove:
In sted thereof with drops of melting love,
Deawd with ambrosiall kisses, by thee gotten
From thy sweete smyling mother from above,
Sprinckle her heart, and haughtie courage° soften, *nature*
That she may hearke to love, and reade this lesson often.

[The involved structure of Book IV reflects Spenser's examination of the full reach and scope of the traditional virtue of friendship, even as the convolutions befit the romance form's postponement of closure (Parker 1979; for a deconstructionist view of the poem's "endlesse werke," see Goldberg 1981). The first two cantos focus on friendships true and false; the third, with the story of Cambel and the three sons of Agape, explores friendship's larger role in human relationships. The allegorical narrative thenceforth shows how amity informs and steadies "lovers' deare debate" while helping establish social concord and natural harmony. For C. S. Lewis (1936), Books III and IV constitute "a single book on the subject of love" (338); certainly Book IV carries forward the several narrative strands of Book III. Britomart and Arthegall meet and pledge mutual love (Cantos iv, vi). Belphoebe is reconciled to Timias (Canto viii); in Cantos xi–xii, the marriage of Thames and Medway, magnificently celebrated by the world's rivers, leads to the union of Florimell and Marinell, whose wedding is described in Book V. Finally, Scudamour's story of how he conquered "vertuous Amoret" in the Temple of Venus provides an allegorical set piece retrospectively central not only to this book but to the tapestry of love relationships woven in Books III and IV.]

4. I.e., Cupid.
5. I.e., the power to instill fear and awe.

From The Fifth Booke of the Faerie Queene

Contayning
The Legend of Artegall
or
of Justice

1

So oft as I with state of present time,
The image of the antique world compare,
When as mans age was in his freshest prime,
And the first blossome of faire vertue bare,
Such oddes° I finde twixt those, and these which are, — *difference*
As that, through long continuance of his course,
Me seemes the world is runne quite out of square,[1]
From the first point of his appointed sourse,
And being once amisse growes daily wourse and wourse.

2

For from the golden age, that first was named,
It's now at earst[2] become a stonie one;
And men themselves, the which at first were framed
Of earthly mould, and formed of flesh and bone,
Are now transformèd into hardest stone:
Such as behind their backs (so backward bred)
Were throwne by Pyrrha and Deucalione:[3]
And if then those may any worse be red,° — *imagined*
They into that ere long will be degenderèd.° — *degenerated*

3

Let none then blame me, if in discipline° — *instruction*
Of vertue and of civill uses lore,
I doe not forme them to the common line° — *standard*
Of present dayes, which are corrupted sore,
But to the antique use, which was of yore,
When good was onely for it selfe desyred,
And all men sought their owne, and none no more;
When Justice was not for most meed outhyred,[4]
But simple Truth did rayne, and was of all admyred.

1. I.e., has careered away from its first appointed and ordered course. The phrase "out of square" may wittily refer to turning from the *fourth* book. Spenser's account of the world's decay looks to the myth (cf. Ovid's *Metamorphoses* 1.89–151) of a decline from a "golden" age, by way of silver and brass, to a modern time of "hard iron." The mood is darkened also by a once common belief in the deterioration of the created universe.
2. I.e., at length.
3. Ovid (*Metamorphoses* 1.348–415) tells how Pyrrha and Deucalion, after a flood that destroyed all other human life, were divinely instructed to cast stones behind them, which became people. Spenser's "stonie" age echoes Ovid's dry comment that this explains our stony character.
4. I.e., responsive to the largest bribes.

4

For that which all men then did vertue call,
Is now cald vice; and that which vice was hight,
Is now hight vertue, and so used of all:
Right now is wrong, and wrong that was is right,
As all things else in time are chaungéd quight.
Ne wonder; for the heavens revolution
Is wandred farre from where it first was pight,
And so doe make contrarie constitution
Of all this lower world, toward his dissolution.

5

For who so list into the heavens looke,
And search the courses of the rowling spheares,
Shall find that from the point, where they first tooke
Their setting forth, in these few thousand yeares
They all are wandred much; that plaine appeares.
For that same golden fleecy Ram, which bore
Phrixus and Helle from their stepdames feares,
Hath now forgot, where he was plast of yore,
And shouldred hath the Bull, which fayre Europa bore.[5]

6

And eke the Bull hath with his bow-bent horne
So hardly butted those two twinnes of Jove,
That they have crusht the Crab, and quite him borne
Into the great Nemaean lions grove.[6]
So now all range, and doe at randon rove
Out of their proper places farre away,
And all this world with them amisse doe move,
And all his creatures from their course astray,
Till they arrive at their last ruinous decay.° *destruction*

7

Ne is that same great glorious lampe of light,
That doth enlumine all these lesser fyres,[7]

5. In the pre-Copernican astrological system, because of the "precession [backward movement] of the equinox" (in fact due to the earth's wobble on its axis), the constellations no longer correspond to the astrological signs as devised when the zodiac was first invented. When the sun should enter Aries (the Ram) on the spring equinox, that is, it now enters the constellation Pisces. The counterpart of this is that the signs have moved forward, so that Aries has seemingly invaded the space once inhabited by Taurus (the Bull), and so around the zodiac. Astrologers continued to calculate according to signs, not constellations, but such changes in the heavens were disconcerting. For the tale of Phrixus and Helle, see III.xi.30. Jove became a bull so as to carry off the maiden Europa.
6. That is, Taurus has butted Gemini (the Twins) into the space belonging to Cancer (the Crab), which has in turn moved along the zodiac into the House of Leo (the Lion). Next in the zodiac, as Spenser's readers would have known, is Virgo, the Virgin, or Astraea, goddess of justice who left earth in disgust when the Iron Age arrived; Elizabeth was often associated with her. Becoming a swan, Jove begot Castor and Pollux on Leda. To slay the Nemean Lion was the first of Hercules' twelve labors.
7. In the Ptolomaic pre-Copernican system the stars and planets reflected solar light as they orbited

In better case, ne keepes his course more right,
But is miscaried° with the other Spheres. *strayed*
For since the terme of fourteene hundred yeres,
That learnéd Ptolomae his hight did take,
He is declynéd from that marke of theirs,
Nigh thirtie minutes to the Southerne lake;
That makes me feare in time he will us quite forsake.

8

And if to those Aegyptian wisards old,
Which in star-read° were wont have best insight, *astronomy*
Faith may be given, it is by them told,
That since the time they first tooke the Sunnes hight,
Foure times his place he shifted hath in sight,
And twice hath risen, where he now doth West,° *set*
And wested twice, where he ought rise aright.
But most is Mars amisse of all the rest,
And next to him old Saturne, that was wont be best.[8]

9

For during Saturnes ancient raigne[9] it's sayd,
That all the world with goodnesse did abound:
All lovéd vertue, no man was affrayd
Of force, ne fraud in wight was to be found:
No warre was knowne, no dreadfull trompets sound,
Peace universall rayned mongst men and beasts,
And all things freely grew out of the ground:
Justice sate high adored with solemne feasts,
And to all people did divide° her dred beheasts. *dispense*

10

Most sacred vertue she of all the rest,
Resembling God in his imperiall might;
Whose soveraine powre is herein most exprest,
That both to good and bad he dealeth right,
And all his workes with Justice hath bedight.° *adorned*
That powre he also doth to Princes lend,
And makes them like himselfe in glorious sight,
To sit in his owne seate, his cause to end,° *fulfill*
And rule his people right, as he doth recommend.[1]

---

the Earth. On solar declination, see J. C. Eade, *The Forgotten Sky: A Guide to Astrology in English Literature* (Oxford, 1984); Eade doubts that Spenser was seriously worried, but the issues were becoming troublesome as what Donne called "the new philosophy [science] call[ed] all in doubt."

8. The authority for lines 4–7 is Herodotus, *Histories* 2.142. Before Kepler showed them to be ellipses, planetary orbits were assumed to be normally circular, so observers were puzzled by anomalies in those of Mars and Saturn.

9. I.e., the golden age.

1. Cf. Proverbs 8.15: "By me [i.e., God's wisdom] Kings reign, and princes decree justice."

II

Dread Soverayne Goddesse,[2] that doest highest sit
In seate of judgement, in th'Almighties stead,° *place*
And with magnificke might and wondrous wit
Doest to thy people righteous doome aread,° *proclaim*
That furthest Nations filles with awfull dread,
Pardon the boldnesse of thy basest thrall,
That dare discourse of so divine a read,° *matter*
As thy great justice praysèd over all:
The instrument whereof loe here thy Artegall.

[The association of justice with Elizabeth established in the proem leads to the introduction in V.i of Arthegall, "Champion of true Justice," to whom Astraea taught "all the discipline" of that virtue. The quest assigned him by Gloriana is the overthrow of the tyrant Grantorto ("great wrong" with a pun on "tort"& "twisted") and the restoration of the maiden queen Eirena ("peace," with a pun on "Eire" [Ireland]), a task duly but incompletely accomplished in V.xii. Structurally, Book V returns to the linear form of Books I and II. In V.i–iv, Arthegall (aided by his squire Talus, "an yron man" provided by Astraea) overcomes a succession of figures representing various forms of injustice. In V.v he is himself overcome by Radigund, an Amazon queen who forces him to wear female dress and spin flax (recalling Hercules' servitude to Omphale). Heartened by her vision in Isis Church (Canto vii), Britomart kills Radigund, frees Arthegall, and restores male government. The remainder of Book V (focusing allegorically on foreign policy) narrates the further adventures of Arthegall, instructed by Queen Mercilla (equity, or perhaps the mercy that tempers justice), and of Arthur, whose exploits on behalf of justice are set out in V.viii, x, and xi. Critics have debated the relation of equity to Spenser's view of female sovereignty and to the politics allegorized in Book V, notably the anti-egalitarian violence in V.ii and the suppression of Irish rebels. And many readers are fascinated by the iconography of Britomart's sojourn in Isis Church, central to the moral, historical, and psychological allegory in Book V.]

Canto VII

Britomart comes to Isis Church,
Where shee strange visions sees:
She fights with Radigund, her slaies,
And Artegall thence frees.

I

Nought is on earth more sacred or divine,
That Gods and men doe equally adore,
Then this same vertue, that doth right define:
For th'hevens themselves, whence mortal men implore
Right in their wrongs, are ruled by righteous lore
Of highest Jove, who doth true justice deale
To his inferiour Gods, and evermore

2. I.e., Queen Elizabeth.

Therewith containes° his heavenly Common-weale: *controls*
The skill° whereof to Princes hearts he doth reveale. *understanding*

2

Well therefore did the antique world invent,° *feign*
That Justice was a God of soveraine grace,
And altars unto him, and temples lent,° *gave*
And heavenly honours in the highest place;
Calling him great Osyris, of the race
Of th'old Aegyptian Kings, that whylome were;
With faynéd colours shading[1] a true case:
For that Osyris, whilest he livéd here,
The justest man alive, and truest did appeare.[2]

3

His wife was Isis, whom they likewise made
A Goddesse of great powre and soverainty,
And in her person cunningly did shade
That part of Justice, which is Equity,[3]
Whereof I have to treat here presently.° *now*
Unto whose temple when as Britomart
Arrivéd, shee with great humility
Did enter in, ne would that night depart;
But Talus mote not be admitted to her part.° *side*

4

There she receivéd was in goodly wize
Of many Priests, which duely did attend
Uppon the rites and daily sacrifize,
All clad in linnen robes with silver hemd;
And on their heads with long locks comely kemd,° *combed*
They wore rich Mitres shapéd like the Moone,
To shew that Isis doth the Moone portend;° *signify*
Like as Osyris signifies the Sunne.
For that they both like race in equall justice runne.[4]

1. I.e., (1) obscuring; (2) "shadowing forth."
2. Plutarch, *De Iside* 13, and Diodorus Siculus, *Bibliotheca Historica* 1.11–22, identify Osiris with the sun and Isis with the moon. Both were Egyptian deities, siblings, and spouses; Osiris was torn apart by Typhon (or Set) and Isis then gathered his parts (some said except his penis) to reconstitute him. For the mythology sustaining Book V Spenser drew on materials merging Greek and biblical story, Egyptian religion, and European dynastic legend as found, if sometimes disbelieved, in the forgeries of Annius of Viterbo and the works of Jean Lemaire de Belges. Britomart's sojourn also recalls the initiation of Lucius in Apuleius's *Metamorphoses* 11.4–8.
3. Justice as determined by common law was based on a fairly exact system of offense and retribution or restitution and was closely tied to legal precedent. It was widely recognized that specific circumstances could force either written (statutory) or unwritten (common) law to yield an obviously unjust result, and so the Court of Chancery, nominally under the Lord Chancellor, developed to address these situations, Equity is not the same as mercy, but it does allow for more mitigation than does an exact or precedent-based justice.
4. I.e., the courses of sun and moon are equally precise and regular.

5

The Championesse them greeting, as she could,[5]
Was thence by them into the Temple led;
Whose goodly building when she did behould,
Borne uppon stately pillours, all dispred° *overspread*
With shining gold, and archéd over hed,
She wondred at the workemans passing skill,
Whose like before she never saw nor red;° *imagined*
And thereuppon long while stood gazing still,
But thought, that she thereon could never gaze her fill.

6

Thence forth unto the Idoll they her brought,
The which was framéd all of silver fine,
So well as could with cunning hand be wrought,
And clothéd all in garments made of line,° *linen*
Hemd all about with fringe of silver twine.
Uppon her head she wore a Crowne of gold,
To shew that she had powre in things divine;
And at her feete a Crocodile was rold,
That with her wreathéd taile her middle did enfold.[6]

7

One foote was set uppon the Crocodile,
And on the ground the other fast did stand,
So meaning to suppresse both forgéd guile,
And open force: and in her other hand
She stretchéd forth a long white sclender wand.
Such was the Goddesse; whom when Britomart
Had long beheld, her selfe uppon the land
She did prostrate, and with right humble hart,
Unto her selfe her silent prayers did impart.

8

To which the Idoll as it were inclining,
Her wand did move with amiable looke,
By outward shew her inward sence desining.° *indicating*
Who well perceiving, how her wand she shooke,
It as a token of good fortune tooke.
By this the day with dampe° was overcast, *mist*

5. I.e., as she knew how (decorously).
6. Wearing both gold and silver suggests a combination of lunar and solar powers. On crocodiles see Aptekar (1969) and Alice Miskimin, "Britomart's Crocodile and the Legends of Chastity, in *JEGP* 77.1 (1978): 17–36. This one shows both force and guile, argues Clifford Davidson, indicating that Isis restrains what harms justice, but for those such as Machiavelli both guile and force are required for effective government and its enforcement of justice; see "The Idol of Isis Church," *SP* 66.1 (1969): 70–86. Spenser found crocodiles intriguing; Sean Henry, "How doth the little Crocodile improve his shining Tale: Contextualizing the Crocodile of *Prosopopoia: Or Mother Hubberds Tale SSt* 23 (2008): 153–79, includes a possbily relevant contemporary image of the Armada as a crocodile.

And joyous light the house of Jove forsooke:
Which when she saw, her helmet she unlaste,
And by the altars side her selfe to slumber plaste.

9

For other beds the Priests there uséd none,
But on their mother Earths deare lap did lie,
And bake° their sides uppon the cold hard stone, *harden*
T'enure them selves to sufferaunce° thereby *endurance*
And proud rebellious flesh to mortify.° *subject*
For by the vow of their religion
They tiéd were to stedfast chastity,
And continence of life, that all forgon,° *renounced*
They mote the better tend to their devotion.[7]

10

Therefore they mote not taste of fleshly food,
Ne feed on ought, the which doth bloud containe,
Ne drinke of wine, for wine they say is blood,
Even the bloud of Gyants, which were slaine,
By thundring Jove in the Phlegrean plaine.[8]
For which the earth (as they the story tell)
Wroth with the Gods, which to perpetuall paine
Had damned her sonnes, which gainst them did rebell,
With inward griefe and malice did against them swell.

11

And of their vitall bloud, the which was shed
Into her pregnant bosome, forth she brought
The fruitfull vine, whose liquor blouddy red
Having the mindes of men with fury fraught,
Mote in them stirre up old rebellious thought,
To make new warre against the Gods againe:
Such is the powre of that same fruit, that nought
The fell contagion may thereof restraine,
Ne within reasons rule, her madding mood containe.

12

There did the warlike Maide her selfe repose,
Under the wings of Isis[9] all that night,
And with sweete rest her heavy eyes did close,
After that long daies toile and weary plight.
Where whilest her earthly parts with soft delight

7. For the priests' austere life, see Plutarch, *De Iside* 2.
8. Spenser combines scripture and classical myth. Lines 1–2 echo Genesis 9.4: "But flesh with the life thereof, which is the blood thereof, shall ye not eat"; the rest of the stanza and stanza 11 reflect *Metamorphoses* 1.151–62 and Plutarch, *De Iside* 6.
9. Cf. Psalms 57.1: "in the shadow of thy wings will I make my refuge."

Of sencelesse sleepe did deeply drownéd lie,
There did appeare unto her heavenly spright
A wondrous vision, which did close implie[1]
The course of all her fortune and posteritie.

13

Her seemed, as she was doing sacrifize
To Isis, deckt with Mitre on her hed,
And linnen stole after those Priestés guize,
All sodainely she saw transfiguréd
Her linnen stole to robe of scarlet red,[2]
And Moone-like Mitre to a Crowne of gold,
That even she her selfe much wonderéd
At such a chaunge, and joyéd to behold
Her selfe, adorned with gems and jewels manifold.

14

And in the midst of her felicity,
An hideous tempest seeméd from below,
To rise through all the Temple sodainely,
That from the Altar all about did blow
The holy fire, and all the embers strow
Uppon the ground, which kindled privily,
Into outragious flames[3] unwares did grow,
That all the Temple put in jeopardy
Of flaming, and her selfe in great perplexity.° *concern*

15

With that the Crocodile, which sleeping lay
Under the Idols feete in fearelesse bowre,[4]
Seemed to awake in horrible dismay,
As being troubled with that stormy stowre;° *turmoil*
And gaping greedy wide, did streight devoure
Both flames and tempest: with which growen great,
And swolne with pride of his owne peerelesse powre,
He gan to threaten her likewise to eat;
But that the Goddesse with her rod him backe did beat.

16

Tho turning all his pride to humblesse meeke,
Him selfe before her feete he lowly threw,
And gan for grace and love of her to seeke:

1. I.e., secretly enfold.
2. Scarlet was an imperial color; cf. "Aprill" 57.
3. I.e., flames of desire. "The night before the consummation of her marriage," Olympias, mother of Alexander the Great, "dreamed that a thunderbolt fell upon her body, which kindled a great fire, whose divided flames dispersed themselves all about . . ." (Plutarch, *Lives*, tr. Dryden: "Alexander"). Plutarch adds that "once . . . a serpent was found lying by Olympias as she slept."
4. I.e., fearlessly lay sheltered under the idols feet.

Which she accepting, he so neare her drew,
That of his game[5] she soone enwombéd grew,
And forth did bring a Lion of great might;
That shortly did all other beasts subdew.
With that she wakéd, full of fearefull fright,
And doubtfully dismayd through that so uncouth° sight. *strange*

17

So thereuppon long while she musing lay,
With thousand thoughts feeding her fantasie,
Untill she spide the lampe of lightsome day,
Up-lifted in the porch of heaven hie.
Then up she rose fraught with melancholy,
And forth into the lower parts did pas;
Whereas the Priestes she found full busily.
About their holy things for morrow Mas:[6]
Whom she saluting° faire, faire resaluted was. *greeting*

18

But by the change of her unchearefull looke,
They might perceive, she was not well in plight;
Or that some pensivenesse to heart she tooke.
Therefore thus one of them, who seemed in sight
To be the greatest, and the gravest wight,
To her bespake; "Sir Knight it seemes to me,
That thorough evill rest of this last night,
Or ill apayd,° or much dismayd ye be, *pleased*
That by your change of cheare is easie for to see."

19

"Certes," sayd she, "sith ye so well have spide
The troublous passion of my pensive mind,
I will not seeke the same from you to hide,
But will my cares unfolde, in hope to find
Your aide, to guide me out of errour blind."
"Say on," quoth he, "the secret of your hart:
For by the holy vow, which me doth bind,
I am adjured,° best counsell to impart *sworn*
To all, that shall require my comfort in their smart."

20

Then gan she to declare the whole discourse° *course*
Of all that vision, which to her appeard,

5. I.e., his amorous play.
6. I.e., for the first religious observance next day.

As well as to her minde it had recourse.[7]
All which when he unto the end had heard,
Like to a weake faint-hearted man he fared,° *behaved*
Through great astonishment of that strange sight;
And with long locks up-standing, stifly stared
Like one adawéd° with some dreadfull spright. *terrified*
So fild with heavenly fury,° thus he her behight.° *frenzy / addressed*

21

"Magnificke Virgin, that in queint° disguise *strange*
Of British armes doest maske thy royall blood,
So to pursue a perillous emprize,
How couldst thou weene, through that disguizéd hood,° *covering*
To hide thy state from being understood?
Can from th'immortall Gods ought hidden bee?
They doe thy linage, and thy Lordly brood;° *race*
They doe thy sire, lamenting sore for thee;
They doe thy love, forlorne in womens thraldome see.

22

"The end whereof, and all the long event,° *outcome*
They doe to thee in this same dreame discover.
For that same Crocodile doth represent
The righteous Knight, that is thy faithfull lover,
Like to Osyris in all just endever.
For that same Crocodile Osyris is,
That under Isis feete doth sleepe for ever:
To shew that clemence oft in things amis,
Restraines those sterne behests, and cruell doomes of his.

23

"That Knight shall all the troublous stormes asswage,
And raging flames, that many foes shall reare,
To hinder thee from the just heritage
Of thy sires Crowne, and from thy countrey deare.
Then shalt thou take him to thy lovéd fere,° *mate*
And joyne in equall portion of thy realme.
And afterwards a sonne to him shalt beare,
That Lion-like shall shew his powre extreame:
So blesse thee God, and give thee joyance of thy dreame."

24

All which when she unto the end had heard,
She much was easéd in her troubles thought,
And on those Priests bestowéd rich reward:
And royall gifts of gold and silver wrought,

7. I.e., as well as she could recall it.

She for a present to their Goddesse brought.
Then taking leave of them, she forward went,
To seeke her love, where he was to be sought;
Ne rested till she came without relent° *delay*
Unto the land of Amazons, as she was bent.

From The Sixte Booke of the Faerie Queene

Contayning
The Legend of S. Calidore
or
of Courtesie

I

The waies, through which my weary steps I guyde,
In this delightfull land of Faery,
Are so exceeding spacious and wyde,
And sprinckled with such sweet variety,
Of all that pleasant is to eare or eye,
That I nigh ravisht with rare thoughts delight,
My tedious travell doe forget thereby;
And when I gin to feele decay of might,
It strength to me supplies, and chears my dulléd spright.

2

Such secret comfort, and such heavenly pleasures,
Ye sacred imps, that on Parnasso dwell,[1]
And there the keeping have of learnings threasures,
Which doe all worldly riches farre excell,
Into the mindes of mortall men doe well,° *flow*
And goodly fury° into them infuse; *inspiration*
Guyde ye my footing, and conduct me well
In these strange waies, where never foote did use,° *go, frequent*
Ne none can find, but who was taught them by the Muse.[2]

3

Revele to me the sacred noursery
Of vertue, which with you doth there remaine,
Where it in silver bowre does hidden ly
From view of men, and wicked worlds disdaine.
Since it at first was by the Gods with paine
Planted in earth, being derived at furst
From heavenly seedes of bounty° soveraine, *virtue*
And by them long with carefull labour nurst,
Till it to ripenesse grew, and forth to honour burst.

4

Amongst them all growes not a fayrer flowre,
Then is the bloosme of comely courtesie,[3]

1. I.e., the Muses.
2. Such claims are found from classical times on (cf. Lucretius, *De Rerum Natura* 1.925–26, Ariosto, *Orlando Furioso* 1.1–2, and Milton's Muse, who will pursue "Things unattempted yet in prose or rhyme" [*Paradise Lost* 1.16]).
3. The "courtesy" (incorporating the word "court") that Spenser explores owes something to Aristotle on the man "concerned with the pleasures and pains of social life" who "renders to each class what is befitting" (*Nichomachaean Ethics* 4.6) and something to the old belief that virtuous conduct, not birth, proves nobility (see, e.g., Chaucer's poem "Gentilesse"). Castiglione's *Courtier* explaining how a true gentleman (or lady) acts among rural or "base" people (cf. VI.ix) notes that

Which though it on a lowly stalke doe bowre,° *shelter*
Yet brancheth forth in brave nobilitie,
And spreds it selfe through all civilitie:° *civilized life*
Of which though present age doe plenteous seeme,
Yet being matcht with plaine Antiquitie,
Ye will them all but faynéd showes esteeme,
Which carry colours° faire, that feeble eies misdeeme.° *appearances* *misjudge*

5

But in the triall of true curtesie,
Its now so farre from that, which then it was,
That it indeed is nought but forgerie,
Fashioned to please the eies of them, that pas,
Which see not perfect things but in a glas.[4]
Yet is that glasse so gay,° that it can blynd *brilliant*
The wisest sight, to thinke gold that is bras.
But vertues seat is deepe within the mynd,
And not in outward shows, but inward thoughts defynd.° *determined*

6

But where shall I in all Antiquity
So faire a patterne finde, where may be seene
The goodly praise of Princely curtesie,
As in your selfe, O soveraine Lady Queene,
In whose pure minde, as in a mirrour sheene,° *bright*
It showes, and with her brightnesse doth inflame° *inspire*
The eyes of all, which thereon fixéd beene;[5]
But meriteth indeede an higher name:
Yet so from low to high uplifted is your name.

7

Then pardon me, most dreaded Soveraine,
That from your selfe I doe this vertue bring,
And to your selfe doe it returne againe:
So from the Ocean all rivers spring,
And tribute backe repay as to their King.
Right so from you all goodly vertues well
Into the rest, which round about you ring.
Faire Lords and Ladies, which about you dwell,
And doe adorne your Court, where courtesies excell.

---

behavior can entail a sometimes canny empathy as well as good manners. Some, though, also hear hints of an anticourt satire or complaint and implied commentary explaining the problematic nature of smooth-tongued courtesy and its occasional need for self-serving or kindly fibs and slippery words.

4. Cf. I Corinthians 13.12: "For now we see through a glass, darkly; but then face to face. . . ."
5. One of Spenser's favorite images, perhaps derived from Ficino's commentary on Plato's *Symposium;* cf. 2 Corinthians 3.18: "But we all, with open face beholding as in a glass the glory of the Lord, are changed into the same image from glory to glory. . . ."

[Calidore's quest, described in Canto i as "an endlesse trace," is to find and subdue the Blatant Beast, a many-tongued monster whose poisoned bites afflict men and women in every quarter of the world; as a figure for slander, envious backbiting, and badmouthing of all kinds, the Beast is courtesy's chief enemy. Calidore's adventures are the focus of Cantos i–iii, in which a number of episodes illustrate varieties of courtesy and discourtesy; he does not appear in Cantos iv–viii, which explore courtesy through the adventures of other figures, inducting Arthur, Timias, and Sir Calepine. In Canto ix Spenser resumes Calidore's story: taken by the delights of the pastoral world, the Knight of Courtesy is about to suspend his quest so as to enjoy the pleasures of courtship and the rustic life (some readers have seen his holiday as restorative recreation, others as lax truancy). In the final cantos, he will move from contemplation to action, from smooth words to deeds.]

Canto IX

Calidore hostes° with Meliboe *lodges*
and loves fayre Pastorell;
Coridon envies him, yet he
for ill rewards him well.

1

Now turne againe my teme° thou jolly swayne,[1] *team*
Backe to the furrow which I lately left;
I lately left a furrow, one or twayne
Unploughed, the which my coulter° hath not cleft: *plowshare*
Yet seemed the soyle both fayre and frutefull eft,° *moreover*
As I it past, that were too great a shame,
That so rich frute should be from us bereft;
Besides the great dishonour and defame,
Which should befall to Calidores immortall name.[2]

2

Great travell hath the gentle Calidore
And toyle enduréd, sith I left him last
Sewing° the Blatant beast,[3] which I forbore *pursuing*
To finish then, for other present hast.
Full many pathes and perils he hath past,
Through hils, through dales, throgh forests, and throgh plaines

1. Spenser's poetic powers, personified as bullocks or horses pulling his plow to suit a rustic sojourn and, says DeNeef 1982, to suggest a Virgilian Georgic poetic mode that can mediate between the pastoral and chivalric epic and cultivate the seeds in courtesy's nursery.
2. Calidore (Greek, "beautiful gift," with maybe an overtone of Latin *calidus*, adroit and crafty).
3. Chief model for this monster is the "questing [barking] beast of Malory's *Morte d'Arthur* (1.19, 10.13), which sounded like "thirty couple of hounds questing." *Blatant:* from Latin *blaterare*, "to babble or talk idly." The beast shares features with the parents named in i.7–8: Cerberus (the three-headed dog that guards Hades) and the Chimera (amalgam of lion, goat, and serpent). In vi.12 Spenser gives us yet other parents: "foule Echidna" (a snake goddess) and "Cruell Typhon" (a giant). These creatures, doomed to defeat by Zeus or such heroes as Hercules, are in Hesiod's *Theogony.* In his conversations with William Drummond, Ben Jonson identified the Beast with "Puritans," meaning radical reformers who thought the established church both pagan and papist.

In that same quest which fortune on him cast,[4]
Which he atchievéd to his owne great gaines,
Reaping eternall glorie of his restlesse° paines. *unresting*

3

So sharply he the Monster did pursew,
That day nor night he suffred him to rest,
Ne rested he himselfe but natures dew,
For dread of daunger, not to be redrest,
If he for slouth forslackt° so famous quest. *neglected*
Him first from court he to the citties coursed,° *chased*
And from the citties to the townes him prest,
And from the townes into the countrie forsed,
And from the country back to private farmes he scorsed.[5]

4

From thence into the open fields he fled,
Whereas the Heardes° were keeping of their neat,° *herdsmen / cattle*
And shepheards singing to their flockes, that fed,
Layes of sweete love and youthes delightfull heat:
Him thether eke for all his fearefull threat
He followed fast, and chacéd him so nie,
That to the folds, where sheepe at night doe seat,° *rest*
And to the litle cots,° where shepherds lie *shelters*
In winters wrathfull time, he forcéd him to flie.

5

There on a day as he pursewed the chace,
He chaunst to spy a sort of shepheard groomes,[6]
Playing on pypes,° and caroling apace, *bagpipes*
The whyles their beasts there in the budded broomes° *broom plants*
Beside them fed, and nipt the tender bloomes:
For other worldly wealth they caréd nought.
To whom Sir Calidore yet sweating comes,
And them to tell him courteously besought,
If such a beast they saw, which he had thether brought.

6

They answered him, that no such beast they saw,
Nor any wicked feend, that mote offend
Their happie flockes, nor daunger to them draw:
But if that such there were (as none they kend)
They prayd high God him farre from them to send.
Then one of them him seeing so to sweat,

4. Fortune is much in evidence in Book VI, suiting a story with parallels in late classical romances such as the third-century *Daphnis and Chloe* by Longus.
5. I.e., forced it to leave the open country for private estates and farms.
6. I.e., a company of shepherds.

After his rusticke wise,° that well he weend, *manner*
Offred him drinke, to quench his thirstie heat,
And if he hungry were, him offred eke to eat.

7

The knight was nothing nice,° where was no need, *fastidious*
And tooke their gentle offer: so adowne
They prayd him sit, and gave him for to feed
Such homely what,° as serves the simple clowne,° *thing / rustic*
That doth despise the dainties of the towne.
Tho having fed his fill, he there besyde
Saw a faire damzell, which did weare a crowne
Of sundry flowres, with silken ribbands tyde,
Yclad in home-made greene that her owne hands had dyde.

8

Upon a litle hillocke she was placed
Higher then all the rest, and round about
Environed with a girland, goodly graced,
Of lovely lasses, and them all without[7]
The lustie shepheard swaynes sate in a rout,° *group*
The which did pype and sing her prayses dew,
And oft rejoyce, and oft for wonder shout,
As if some miracle of heavenly hew° *form*
Were downe to them descended in that earthly vew.

9

And soothly sure[8] she was full fayre of face,
And perfectly well shapt in every lim,
Which she did more augment with modest grace,
And comely carriage of her count'nance° trim, *demeanor*
That all the rest like lesser lamps did dim:
Who her admiring as some heavenly wight,
Did for their soveraine goddesse her esteeme,
And caroling her name both day and night,
The fayrest Pastorella her by name did hight.° *call*

10

Ne was there heard, ne was there shepheards swayne
But her did honour, and eke many a one
Burnt in her love, and with sweet pleasing payne
Full many a night for her did sigh and grone:
But most of all the shepheard Coridon
For her did languish, and his deare life spend;° *waste away*
Yet neither she for him, nor other none

7. I.e., outside the ring of maidens.
8. I.e., truly.

Did care a whit, ne any liking lend:° *give*
Though meane her lot, yet higher did her mind ascend.

11

Her whyles Sir Calidore there vewéd well,
And markt her rare demeanure, which him seemed
So farre the meane° of shepheards to excell, *usual average*
As that he in his mind her worthy deemed,
To be a Princes Paragone° esteemed, *consort*
He was unwares surprisd in subtile bands
Of the blynd boy,[9] ne thence could be redeemed
By any skill out of his cruell hands,
Caught like the bird, which gazing still on others stands.[1]

12

So stood he still long gazing thereupon,
Ne any will had thence to move away,
Although his quest[2] were farre afore him gon;
But after he had fed, yet did he stay,
And sate there still, untill the flying day
Was farre forth spent, discoursing diversly
Of sundry things, as fell,° to worke delay; *befell*
And evermore his speach he did apply
To th'heards, but meant them to the damzels fantazy.° *fancy*

13

By this the moystie° night approching fast, *humid*
Her deawy humour° gan on th'earth to shed, *mist*
That warned the shepheards to their homes to hast
Their tender flocks, now being fully fed,
For feare of wetting them before their bed;
Then came to them a good old aged syre,
Whose silver lockes bedeckt his beard and hed,
With shepheards hooke in hand, and fit attyre,
That wild° the damzell rise; the day did now expyre. *bade*

14

He was to weet[3] by common voice esteemed
The father of the fayrest Pastorell,
And of her selfe in very deede so deemed;° *considered*
Yet was not so, but as old stories tell
Found her by fortune, which to him befell,
In th'open fields an Infant left alone,

9. I.e., Cupid.
1. I.e., the lark, caught with a net while it stared in fascination at the hawk held by the fowler.
2. I.e., the object of his quest, the Blatant Beast.
3. I.e., in fact.

And taking up brought home, and nourséd well
As his owne chyld; for other he had none,
That she in tract° of time accompted was his owne. *course*

15

She at his bidding meekely did arise,
And streight unto her litle flocke did fare:
Then all the rest about her rose likewise,
And each his sundrie sheepe with severall° care *separate*
Gathered together, and them homeward bare:
Whylest everie one with helping hands did strive
Amongst themselves, and did their labours share,
To helpe faire Pastorella, home to drive
Her fleecie flocke; but Coridon most helpe did give.

16

But Meliboe[4] (so hight that good old man)
Now seeing Calidore left all alone,
And night arrivéd hard at hand, began
Him to invite unto his simple home;
Which though it were a cottage clad with lome,° *clay*
And all things therein meane, yet better so
To lodge, then in the salvage° fields to rome. *wild*
The knight full gladly soone agreed thereto,
Being his harts owne wish, and home with him did go.

17

There he was welcomed of that honest syre,
And of his aged Beldame° homely well; *wife*
Who him besought himselfe to disattyre,° *take off his armor*
And rest himselfe, till supper time befell.
By which home came the fayrest Pastorell,
After her flocke she in their fold had tyde,
And supper readie dight, they to it fell
With small adoe, and nature satisfyde,
The which doth litle crave contented to abyde.[5]

18

Tho when they had their hunger slakéd well,
And the fayre mayd the table° ta'ne away, *food and drink*
The gentle knight, as he that did excell
In courtesie, and well could doe and say,
For so great kindnesse as he found that day,
Gan greatly thanke his host and his good wife;
And drawing thence his speach another way,

4. From Greek, "honey-toned"; cf. stanza 26.
5. I.e., nature needs little to be contented.

Gan highly to commend the happie life.
Which Shepheards lead, without debate° or bitter strife. *contention*

19

"How much," sayd he, "more happie is the state,
In which ye father here doe dwell at ease,
Leading a life so free and fortunate,
From all the tempests of these worldly seas,
Which tosse the rest in daungerous disease;° *distress*
Where warres, and wreckes, and wicked enmitie
Doe them afflict, which no man can appease,
That certes° I your happinesse envie, *surely*
And wish my lot were plast in such felicitie."

20

"Surely my sonne," then answered he againe,[6]
"If happie, then it is in this intent,° *respect*
That having small, yet doe I not complaine
Of want, ne wish for more it to augment,
But doe my self, with that I have, content;
So taught of nature, which doth litle need
Of forreine helpes to lifes due nourishment:
The fields my food, my flocke my rayment breed;
No better doe I weare, no better doe I feed.

21

"Therefore I doe not any one envy,
Nor am envyde of any one therefore;
They that have much, feare much to loose thereby,
And store of cares doth follow riches store.
The litle that I have, growes dayly more
Without my care,° but onely to attend it; *worry*
My lambes doe every yeare increase their score,
And my flockes father daily doth amend° it. *improve*
What have I, but to praise th'Almighty, that doth send it?

22

"To them, that list,° the worlds gay showes I leave, *desire*
And to great ones such follies doe forgive,° *leave*
Which oft through pride do their owne perill weave,
And through ambition downe themselves doe drive
To sad decay,° that might contented live. *ruin*
Me no such cares nor combrous thoughts offend,° *disturb*
Ne once my minds unmovéd quiet grieve,
But all the night in silver sleepe[7] I spend,
And all the day, to what I list, I doe attend.

6. Stanzas 20–25 may be compared to Tasso, *Gerusalemme* 7.8–13.
7. I.e., soft and enriching sleep (suggesting the moon's silvery influence).

23

"Sometimes I hunt the Fox, the vowéd foe
Unto my Lambes, and him dislodge away;
Sometime the fawne I practise° from the Doe, *devise*
Or from the Goat her kidde how to convay,° *steal away*
Another while I baytes and nets display,
The birds to catch, or fishes to beguyle:
And when I wearie am, I downe doe lay
My limbes in every° shade, to rest from toyle, *any*
And drinke of every brooke, when thirst my throte doth boyle.

24

"The time was once, in my first prime of yeares,
When pride of youth forth prickéd my desire,
That I disdained amongst mine equall peares
To follow sheepe, and shepheards base attire:
For further fortune then I would inquire.° *seek*
And leaving home, to roiall court I sought,° *went*
Where I did sell my selfe for yearely hire,
And in the Princes gardin daily wrought:
There I beheld such vainenesse, as I never thought.

25

"With sight whereof soone cloyd, and long deluded
With idle hopes, which them doe entertaine,
After I had ten yeares my selfe excluded
From native home, and spent my youth in vaine,
I gan my follies to my selfe to plaine,° *lament*
And this sweet peace, whose lacke did then appeare.
Tho backe returning to my sheepe againe,
I from thenceforth have learned to love more deare
This lowly quiet life, which I inherite° here." *possess*

26

Whylest thus he talkt, the knight with greedy eare
Hong still upon his melting mouth attent,[8]
Whose sensefull° words empierst his hart so neare, *sensible*
That he was rapt with double ravishment,
Both of his speach that wrought him great content,
And also of the object of his vew,[9]
On which his hungry eye was alwayes bent;
That twixt his pleasing tongue, and her faire hew,° *form*
He lost himselfe, and like one halfe entrauncéd grew.

8. I.e., attentively listened to his sweetly persuasive speech.
9. I.e., Pastorella.

27

Yet to occasion meanes, to worke his mind,
And to insinuate his harts desire,[1]
He thus replyde; "Now surely syre, I find,
That all this worlds gay showes, which we admire,
Be but vaine shadowes to this safe retyre° — *retirement*
Of life, which here in lowlinesse ye lead,
Fearelesse of foes, or fortunes wrackfull° yre, — *destructive*
Which tosseth states, and under foot doth tread
The mightie ones, affrayd of every chaunges dread.

28

"That even I which daily doe behold
The glorie of the great, mongst whom I won,° — *dwell*
And now have proved,° what happinesse ye hold — *experienced*
In this small plot of your dominion,
Now loath great Lordship and ambition;
And wish the heavens so much had gracéd mee,
As graunt me live in like condition;
Or that my fortunes might transposéd bee
From pitch° of higher place, unto this low degree." — *height*

29

"In vaine," said then old Meliboe, "doe men
The heavens of their fortunes fault accuse,
Sith they know best, what is the best for them:
For they to each such fortune doe diffuse,° — *distribute*
As they doe know each can most aptly use.
For not that, which men covet most, is best,
Nor that thing worst, which men do most refuse;
But fittest is, that all contented rest
With that they hold: each hath his fortune in his brest.[2]

30

"It is the mynd, that maketh good or ill,
That maketh wretch or happie, rich or poore:
For some, that hath abundance at his will,
Hath not enough, but wants in greatest store;
And other, that hath litle, askes no more,
But in that litle is both rich and wise.
For wisedome is most riches; fooles therefore
They are, which fortunes doe by vowes devize,° — *plan to get*
Sith each unto himselfe his life may fortunize."° — *make fortunate*

1. I.e., to exercise thought, and, subtly, also to satisfy his longing.
2. Cf. Juvenal, *Satire* 10. 417–25, and Chaucer, *Troilus and Criseyde* 4.197–201.

31

"Since then in each mans self," said Calidore,
"It is, to fashion his owne lyfes estate,
Give leave awhyle, good father, in this shore
To rest my barcke, which hath bene beaten late
With stormes of fortune and tempestuous fate,
In seas of troubles and of toylesome paine,
That whether quite from them for to retrate
I shall resolve, or backe to turne againe,
I may here with your selfe some small repose obtaine.

32

"Not that the burden of so bold a guest
Shall chargefull° be, or chaunge to you at all; *troublesome*
For your meane food shall be my daily feast,
And this your cabin both my bowre and hall.
Besides for recompence hereof, I shall
You well reward, and golden guerdon give,
That may perhaps you better much withall,
And in this quiet make you safer live."
So forth he drew much gold, and toward him it drive.° *thrust*

33

But the good man, nought tempted with the offer
Of his rich mould,° did thrust it farre away, *dross*
And thus bespake; "Sir knight, your bounteous proffer
Be farre fro me, to whom ye ill display
That mucky masse, the cause of mens decay,
That mote empaire my peace with daungers dread.
But if ye algates° covet to assay *in any case*
This simple sort of life, that shepheards lead,
Be it your owne: our rudenesse to your selfe aread."° *take*

34

So there that night Sir Calidore did dwell,
And long while after, whilest him list remaine,
Dayly beholding the faire Pastorell,
And feeding on the bayt of his owne bane.° *ruin*
During which time he did her entertaine
With all kind courtesies, he could invent;
And every day, her companie to gaine,
When to the field she went, he with her went:
So for to quench his fire, he did it more augment.

35

But she that never had acquainted beene
With such queint° usage, fit for Queenes and Kings, *elegant*
Ne ever had such knightly service seene,

But being bred under base shepheards wings,
Had ever learned to love the lowly things,
Did litle whit regard his courteous guize,° *behavior*
But caréd more for Colins[3] carolings
Then all that he could doe, or ever devize:
His layes, his loves, his lookes she did them all despize.

36

Which Calidore perceiving, thought it best
To chaunge the manner of his loftie looke;° *appearance*
And doffing his bright armes, himself addrest° *clothed*
In shepheards weed, and in his hand he tooke,
In stead of steelehead speare, a shepheards hooke,
That who had seene him then, would have bethought
On Phrygian Paris by Plexippus brooke,[4]
When he the love of fayre Oenone sought,
What time the golden apple was unto him brought.

37

So being clad, unto the fields he went
With the faire Pastorella every day,
And kept her sheepe with diligent attent,° *attention*
Watching to drive the ravenous Wolfe away,
The whylest at pleasure she mote sport and play;
And every evening helping them to fold:
And otherwhiles for need, he did assay
In his strong hand their rugged teats to hold,
And out of them to presse the milke: love so much could.

38

Which seeing Coridon, who her likewise
Long time had loved, and hoped her love to gaine,
He much was troubled at that straungers guize,
And many gealous thoughts conceived in vaine,
That this of all his labour and long paine
Should reap the harvest, ere it ripened were,
That made him scoule, and pout, and oft complaine
Of Pastorell to all the shepheards there,
That she did love a stranger swayne then him more dere.

39

And ever when he came in companie,
Where Calidore was present, he would loure,° *scowl*

3. I.e., Colin Clout, the shepherd poet with whom Spenser associates himself; cf. E. K.'s Glosse to "Januarye," in *The Shepheardes Calender.*
4. Spenser's invention, perhaps derived from a mistaken etymology. *Phrygian Paris*: a Trojan prince whose abduction of Helen started the Trojan War, was a shepherd when young; asked to award a golden apple to the fairest goddess, he chose Venus (the episode was much mythologized as a choice among lives of contemplation, action, and pleasure).

And byte his lip, and even for gealousie
Was readie oft his owne hart to devoure,
Impatient of any paramoure:° *lover*
Who on the other side did seeme so farre
From malicing, or grudging his good houre,[5]
That all he could, he gracéd him with her,
Ne ever shewéd signe of rancour or of jarre.° *quarrelling*

40

And oft, when Coridon unto her brought
Or° litle sparrowes, stolen from their nest, *either*
Or wanton squirrels, in the woods farre sought,
Or other daintie thing for her addrest,° *prepared*
He would commend his guift, and make the best.[6]
Yet she no whit his presents did regard,
Ne him could find to fancie in her brest:
This newcome shepheard had his market mard.° *spoiled*
Old love is litle worth when new is more prefard.

41

One day when as the shepheard swaynes together
Were met, to make their sports and merrie glee,
As they are wont in faire sunshynie weather,
The whiles their flockes in shadowes shrouded bee,
They fell to daunce: then did they all agree,
That Colin Clout should pipe as one most fit;
And Calidore should lead the ring, as hee
That most in Pastorellaes grace did sit.
Thereat frowned Coridon, and his lip closely bit.

42

But Calidore of courteous inclination
Tooke Coridon, and set him in his place,
That he should lead the daunce, as was his fashion;
For Coridon could daunce, and trimly trace[7]
And when as Pastorella, him to grace,
Her flowry garlond tooke from her owne head,
And plast on his, he did it soone displace,
And did it put on Coridons in stead:
Then Coridon woxe° frollicke, that earst seeméd dead. *became*

43

Another time, when as they did dispose° *incline*
To practise games, and maisteries° to try, *contests of strength*
They for their Judge did Pastorella chose;

5. I.e., good fortune.
6. I.e., praise it highly.
7. I.e., precisely execute the dance steps.

A garland was the meed of victory.
There Coridon forth stepping openly,
Did chalenge Calidore to wrestling game:
For he through long and perfect industry,
Therein well practisd was, and in the same
Thought sure t'avenge his grudge, and worke his foe great shame.

44

But Calidore he greatly did mistake;
For he was strong and mightily stiffe pight,[8]
That with one fall his necke he almost brake,
And had he not upon him fallen light,
His dearest joynt[9] he sure had broken quight.
Then was the oaken crowne by Pastorell
Given to Calidore, as his due right;
But he, that did in courtesie excell,
Gave it to Coridon, and said he wonne it well.

45

Thus did the gentle knight himselfe abeare° *conduct*
Amongst that rusticke rout in all his deeds,
That even they, the which his rivals were,
Could not maligne him, but commend him needs:
For courtesie amongst the rudest breeds
Good will and favour. So it surely wrought
With this faire Mayd, and in her mynde the seeds
Of perfect love did sow, that last° forth brought *finally*
The fruite of joy and blisse, though long time dearely bought.

46

Thus Calidore continued there long time,
To winne the love of the faire Pastorell;
Which having got, he uséd without crime° *sin*
Or blamefull blot, but menagéd so well,
That he of all the rest, which there did dwell,
Was favouréd, and to her grace commended.
But what straunge fortunes unto him befell,
Ere he attained the point by him intended,
Shall more conveniently in other place be ended.

Canto X

Calidore sees the Graces daunce,
To Colins melody:
The whiles his Pastorell is led
Into captivity.

8. I.e., solidly built.
9. I.e., presumably, his neck.

1

Who now does follow the foule Blatant Beast,
Whilest Calidore does follow that faire Mayd,
Unmyndfull of his vow and high beheast,° *command*
Which by the Faery Queene was on him layd,
That he should never leave, nor be delayd
From chacing him, till he had it attchieved?
But now entrapt of love, which him betrayd,
He mindeth more, how he may be relieved
With grace from her, whose love his heart hath sore engrieved.

2

That from henceforth he meanes no more to sew° *pursue*
His former quest, so full of toile and paine;
Another quest, another game in vew
He hath, the guerdon° of his love to gaine: *reward*
With whom he myndes° for ever to remaine, *intends*
And set his rest[1] amongst the rusticke sort,
Rather then hunt still after shadowes vaine
Of courtly favour, fed with light° report *empty*
Of every blaste, and sayling alwaies in the port.[2]

3

Ne certes mote he greatly blaméd be,
From so high step to stoupe unto so low.
For who had tasted once (as oft did he)
The happy peace, which there doth overflow,
And proved the perfect pleasures, which doe grow
Amongst poore hyndes,° in hils, in woods, in dales, *rustics*
Would never more delight in painted show
Of such false blisse, as there is set for stales,° *snares*
T'entrap unwary fooles in their eternall bales.° *woe*

4

For what hath all that goodly glorious gaze° *spectacle*
Like to one sight, which Calidore did vew?
The glaunce whereof their dimméd eies would daze,° *dazzle*
That never more they should endure the shew
Of that sunne-shine, that makes them looke askew.° *asquint*
Ne ought in all that world of beauties rare,
(Save onely Glorianaes heavenly hew
To which what can compare?) can it compare;° *rival*
The which as commeth now, by course[3] I will declare.

1. I.e., permanently remain.
2. I.e., never setting sail at all.
3. I.e., in due order, properly.

5

One day as he did raunge the fields abroad,
Whilest his faire Pastorella was elsewhere,
He chaunst to come, far from all peoples troad,° *track*
Unto a place, whose pleasaunce did appere
To passe all others, on the earth which were:
For all that ever was by natures skill
Devized to worke delight, was gathered there,
And there by her were pouréd forth at fill,
As if this to adorne, she all the rest did pill.° *ransack*

6

It was an hill plaste in an open plaine,
That round about was bordered with a wood
Of matchlesse hight, that seemed th'earth to disdaine,
In which all trees of honour stately stood,
And did all winter as in sommer bud,
Spredding pavilions for the birds to bowre,° *shelter*
Which in their lower braunches sung aloud;
And in their tops the soring hauke did towre,° *perch*
Sitting like King of fowles in majesty and powre.

7

And at the foote thereof, a gentle flud° *stream*
His silver waves did softly tumble downe,
Unmard with ragged mosse or filthy mud,
Ne mote wylde beastes, ne mote the ruder clowne° *rustic*
Thereto approch, ne filth mote therein drowne.° *fall*
But Nymphes and Faeries by the bancks did sit,
In the woods shade, which did the waters crowne,
Keeping all noysome° things away from it, *harmful*
And to the waters fall tuning their accents fit.

8

And on the top thereof a spacious plaine
Did spred it selfe, to serve to all delight,
Either to daunce, when they to daunce would faine,° *desire*
Or else to course about their bases light;[4]
Ne ought there wanted, which for pleasure might
Desiréd be, or thence to banish bale:° *sorrow*
So pleasauntly the hill with equall° hight, *even*
Did seeme to overlooke the lowly vale;
Therefore it rightly cleepéd° was mount Acidale.[5] *named*

4. In the game of prisoner's base.
5. Venus was sometimes called "Acidalia" after a spring in Boeotia where the Graces, her handmaids, would bathe. The name may derive from ἀκηδής, "free from care."

9

They say that Venus, when she did dispose° *incline*
Her selfe to pleasaunce, uséd to resort
Unto this place, and therein to repose
And rest her selfe, as in a gladsome port,° *refuge*
Or with the Graces there to play and sport;
That even her owne Cytheron,[6] though in it
She uséd most to keepe her royall court,
And in her soveraine Majesty to sit,
She in regard° hereof refusde and thought unfit. *comparison*

10

Unto this place when as the Elfin Knight
Approcht, him seeméd that the merry sound
Of a shrill pipe he playing heard on hight,° *loudly*
And many feete fast thumping th'hollow ground,
That through the woods their Eccho did rebound.
He nigher drew, to weete what mote it be;
There he a troupe of Ladies dauncing found
Full merrily, and making gladfull glee,
And in the midst a Shepheard piping he did see.

11

He durst not enter into th'open greene,
For dread of them unwares to be descryde,° *observed*
For° breaking of their daunce, if he were seene; *and for*
But in the covert of the wood did byde,
Beholding all, yet of them unespyde.
There he did see, that pleaséd much his sight,
That even he him selfe his eyes envyde,
An hundred naked maidens lilly white,
All raungéd in a ring, and dauncing in delight.

12

All they without were raungéd in a ring,
And daunced round; but in the midst of them
Three other Ladies did both daunce and sing,
The whilest the rest them round about did hemme,
And like a girlond did in compasse stemme.° *encircle*
And in the middest of those same three, was placed
Another Damzell, as a precious gemme,
Amidst a ring most richly well enchaced,° *adorned*
That with her goodly presence all the rest much graced.

6. Perhaps Cythera; but cf. III.vi.29.

13

Looke how the Crowne, which Ariadne[7] wore
Upon her yvory forehead that same day,
That Theseus her unto his bridale bore,
When the bold Centaures made that bloudy fray
With the fierce Lapithes, which did them dismay;° *defeat*
Being now placéd in the firmament,
Through the bright heaven doth her beams display,
And is unto the starres an ornament,
Which round about her move in order excellent.

14

Such was the beauty of this goodly band,
Whose sundry parts were here too long to tell:
But she that in the midst of them did stand,
Seemed all the rest in beauty to excell,
Crownd with a rosie girlond, that right well
Did her beseeme. And ever, as the crew° *company*
About her daunst, sweet flowres, that far did smell,
And fragrant odours they uppon her threw;
But most of all, those three did her with gifts endew.

15

Those were the Graces, daughters of delight,
Handmaides of Venus, which are wont to haunt
Uppon this hill, and daunce there day and night:
Those three to men all gifts of grace do graunt,
And all, that Venus in her selfe doth vaunt,
Is borrowéd of them. But that faire one,
That in the midst was placéd paravaunt,° *pre-eminently*
Was she to whom that shepheard pypt alone,
That made him pipe so merrily, as never none.[8]

16

She was to weete that jolly Shepheards lasse,[9]
Which pipéd there unto that merry rout,° *company*
That jolly shepheard, which there pipéd, was
Poore Colin Clout (who knowes not Colin Clout?)
He pypt apace,° whilest they him daunst about. *briskly*

7. Spenser combines two passages from the *Metamorphoses*. Daughter of King Minos, Ariadne helped Theseus escape Crete after killing the Minotaur hidden in the Labyrinth; finding her abandoned on the isle of Naxos, Dionysus made her his consort and her bridal crown a constellation (VIII. 169–82). The battle of Centaurs and Lapithae, which Theseus joined, took place at the wedding of Hippodamia to Pirithous (XII.210–535).

8. I.e., as no one had ever piped.

9. In the *Calender*'s "Aprill" eclogue, Colin had called "fayre Elisa" a fourth Grace (not an uncommon compliment), but stanza 28, below, will distinguish her from the queen; the precise identity of Colin's inspirational beloved remains unclear. Some detect, in the scene's tension between a shepherd's private piping and a knight's bumbling intrusion, Spenser's doubts concerning his role as an epic poet; some find the intrusion relevant to an Ireland (and England) torn by discourtesy and indifferent to poetry's civilizing role.

Pype jolly shepheard, pype thou now apace
Unto thy love, that made thee low to lout,° *bow*
Thy love is present there with thee in place,
Thy love is there advaunst° to be another Grace. *raised*

17

Much wondred Calidore at this straunge sight
Whose like before his eye had never seene,
And standing long astonishéd in spright,
And rapt with pleasaunce, wist not what to weene;° *think*
Whether it were the traine° of beauties Queene, *assembly*
Or Nymphes, or Faeries, or enchaunted show,
With which his eyes mote have deluded beene.
Therefore resolving, what it was, to know,
Out of the wood he rose, and toward them did go.

18

But soone as he appearéd to their vew,
They vanisht all away out of his sight,
And cleane were gone, which way he never knew;
All save the shepheard, who for fell despight° *anger*
Of that displeasure, broke his bag-pipe quight,
And made great mone for that unhappy° turne. *unlucky*
But Calidore, though no lesse sory wight,
For that mishap, yet seeing him to mourne,
Drew neare, that he the truth of all by him mote learne.

19

And first him greeting, thus unto him spake,
"Haile jolly shepheard, which thy joyous dayes
Here leadest in this goodly merry make,° *making*
Frequented of these gentle Nymphes alwayes,
Which to thee flocke, to heare thy lovely layes;
Tell me, what mote these dainty Damzels be,
Which here with thee doe make their pleasant playes?
Right happy thou, that mayst them freely see:
But why when I them saw, fled they away from me?"

20

"Not I so happy," answerd then that swaine,
"As thou unhappy, which them thence didst chace,
Whom by no meanes thou canst recall againe,
For being gone, none can them bring in place,
But whom they of them selves list so to grace."
"Right sory I," saide then Sir Calidore,
"That my ill fortune did them hence displace.
But since things passéd none may now restore,
Tell me, what were they all, whose lacke thee grieves so sore."

21

Tho gan that shepheard thus for to dilate;° *discourse*
"Then wote thou shepheard, whatsoever thou bee,
That all those Ladies, which thou sawest late,
Are Venus Damzels, all within her fee,° *service*
But differing in honour and degree:
They all are Graces, which on her depend,[1]
Besides a thousand more, which ready bee
Her to adorne, when so she forth doth wend:
But those three in the midst, doe chiefe on her attend.

22

"They are the daughters of sky-ruling Jove,
By him begot of faire Eurynome,[2]
The Oceans daughter, in this pleasant grove,
As he this way comming from feastfull glee,
Of Thetis wedding with Aeacidee,
In sommers shade him selfe here rested weary.
The first of them hight mylde Euphrosyne,
Next faire Aglaia, last Thalia merry:
Sweete Goddesses all three which me in mirth do cherry.° *cheer*

23

"These three on men all gracious gifts bestow,
Which decke the body or adorne the mynde,
To make them lovely or well favoured show,
As comely carriage, entertainement° kynde, *manners*
Sweete semblaunt,° friendly offices that bynde, *demeanor*
And all the complements° of curtesie: *accomplishments*
They teach us, how to each degree and kynde
We should our selves demeane, to low, to hie;
To friends, to foes, which skill men call Civility.

24

"Therefore they alwaies smoothly seeme to smile,
That we likewise should mylde and gentle be,
And also naked are, that without guile
Or false dissemblaunce all them plaine may see,
Simple and true from covert malice free:
And eke them selves so in their daunce they bore,
That two of them still froward° seemed to bee, *turned away*
But one still towards shewed her selfe afore,° *in front*
That good should from us goe, then come in greater store.[3]

1. I.e., who belong to her and make part of her retinue.
2. Cf. Hesiod, *Theogony* 907–11; the notion that Jove sired the Graces after the marriage of Thetis to Peleus, son of Aeacus, is Spenser's.
3. Cf. "Aprill" 109. See Seneca's skeptical but influential comments on the Graces in *De Beneficiis* I.ii–iii and E. Wind, *Pagan Mysteries in the Renaissance* (New York, 1958), ch. 2.

25

"Such were those Goddesses, which ye did see;
But that fourth Mayd, which there amidst them traced,° *danced*
Who can aread,° what creature mote she bee, *say*
Whether a creature, or a goddesse graced
With heavenly gifts from heven first enraced?° *implanted*
But what so sure she was, she worthy was,
To be the fourth with those three other placed:
Yet was she certes but a countrey lasse,
Yet she all other countrey lasses farre did passe.

26

"So farre as doth the daughter of the day,[4]
All other lesser lights in light excell,
So farre doth she in beautyfull array,
Above all other lasses beare the bell,[5]
Ne lesse in vertue that beseemes her well,
Doth she exceede the rest of all her race,
For which the Graces that here wont to dwell,
Have for more honor brought her to this place,
And gracéd her so much to be another Grace.

27

"Another Grace she well deserves to be,
In whom so many Graces gathered are,
Excelling much the meane° of her degree; *average*
Divine resemblaunce, beauty soveraine rare,
Firme Chastity, that spight ne blemish dare,[6]
All which she with such courtesie doth grace,
That all her peres cannot with her compare,
But quite are dimméd, when she is in place.
She made me often pipe and now to pipe apace.

28

"Sunne of the world, great glory of the sky,
That all the earth doest lighten with thy rayes,
Great Gloriana, greatest Majesty,
Pardon thy shepheard, mongst so many layes,
As he hath sung of thee in all his dayes,
To make one minime[7] of they poore handmayd,
And underneath thy feete to place her prayse,

4. Perhaps the sun, but since it is usually male in English poetry, Spenser may mean the morning star, Venus, which reflects the sun's light; in III.iv.59 Truth is Day's daughter.
5. I.e., take the prize.
6. I.e., that neither malice nor slur may injure.
7. I.e., a half-note; also a musician's mark placed in a circle to indicate "perfect (i.e., triple) time." On the technicalities, with an argument that this "minim" perfects the dance, see Seth Weiner, "Minims and Grace Notes: Spenser's Acidalian Vision and Sixteenth-Century Music," *SSt* 5 (1985): 91–112.

That when thy glory shall be farre displayd
To future age of her this mention may be made."

29

When thus that shepheard ended had his speach,
Sayd Calidore; "Now sure it yrketh° mee, *pains*
That to thy blisse I made this luckelesse breach,
As now the author of thy bale° to be, *grief*
Thus to bereave thy loves deare sight from thee:
But gentle Shepheard pardon thou my shame,
Who rashly sought that, which I mote not see."
Thus did the courteous Knight excuse his blame,
And to recomfort him, all comely meanes did frame.

30

In such discourses they together spent
Long time, as fit occasion forth them led;
With which the Knight him selfe did much content,
And with delight his greedy fancy fed,
Both of his words, which he with reason red,° *spoke*
And also of the place, whose pleasures rare
With such regard° his sences ravishéd, *sight*
That thence, he had no will away to fare,
But wisht, that with that shepheard he mote dwelling share.

31

But that envenimd sting,[8] the which of yore,
His poysnous point deepe fixéd in his hart
Had left, now gan afresh to rancle sore,
And to renue the rigour of his smart:
Which to recure, no skill of Leaches° art *physicians*
Mote him availe, but to returne againe
To his wounds worker, that with lovely dart
Dinting° his brest, had bred his restlesse paine, *striking*
Like as the wounded Whale to shore flies from the maine.[9]

32

So taking leave of that same gentle swaine,
He backe returnéd to his rusticke wonne,° *dwelling*
Where his faire Pastorella did remaine:
To whome in sort, as[1] he at first begonne,
He daily did apply him selfe to donne
All dewfull° service voide of thoughts impure: *due*
Ne any paines ne perill did he shonne,

8. I.e., the wound inflicted by Cupid's arrow (1.7; cf. VI.ix. 11.6–9).
9. I.e., from the ocean (natural habitat of the whale).
1. I.e., the same as.

By which he might her to his love allure,
And liking in her yet untaméd heart procure.

33

And evermore the shepheard Coridon,
What ever thing he did her to aggrate,° *please*
Did strive to match with strong contention,
And all his paines did closely emulate;
Whether it were to caroll, as they sate
Keeping their sheepe, or games to exercize,
Or to present her with their labours late;
Through which if any grace chaunst to arize
To him, the Shepheard streight with jealousie did frize.° *turn cold*

34

One day as they all three together went
To the greene wood, to gather strawberies,
There chaunst to them a dangerous accident;
A Tigre[2] forth out of the wood did rise,
That with fell clawes full of fierce gourmandize,° *gluttony*
And greedy mouth, wide gaping like hell gate,
Did runne at Pastorell her to surprize:
Whom she beholding, now all desolate
Gan cry to them aloud, to helpe her all too late.

35

Which Coridon first hearing, ran in hast
To reskue her, but when he saw the feend,
Through cowherd feare he fled away as fast,
Ne durst abide the daunger of the end;
His life he steeméd° dearer then his frend. *reckoned*
But Calidore soone comming to her ayde,
When he the beast saw ready now to rend
His loves deare spoile, in which his heart was prayde,[3]
He ran at him enraged in stead of being frayde.

36

He had no weapon, but his shepheards hooke,
To serve the vengeaunce of his wrathfull will,
With which so sternely he the monster strooke,
That to the ground astonishéd° he fell; *stunned*
Whence ere he could recov'r, he did him quell,° *kill*
And hewing off his head, [he][4] it presented

2. Tigers in Spenser's art are regularly fierce, cruel, and "unkind" (*Amoretti* 56; *FQ passim*); notably, Maleger rides "a Tygre swift and fierce" as he directs his savage band in "restlesse siege" of Alma's castle (II.xi.20.4).
3. I.e., his love's dear body (about to be despoiled), where his heart lies captive as booty.
4. A later conjecture to repair the meter.

Before the feete of the faire Pastorell;
Who scarcely yet from former feare exempted,
A thousand times him thankt, that had her death prevented.

37

From that day forth she gan him to affect,° *love*
And daily more her favour to augment;
But Coridon for cowherdize reject,
Fit to keepe sheepe, unfit for loves content:
The gentle heart scornes base disparagement.[5]
Yet Calidore did not despise him quight,
But usde him friendly for further intent,
That by his fellowship, he colour° might *disguise*
Both his estate, and love from skill° of any wight. *knowledge*

38

So well he wood her, and so well he wrought her,
With humble service, and with daily sute,
That at the last unto his will he brought her;
Which he so wisely well did prosecute,
That of his love he reapt the timely frute,[6]
And joyéd long in close felicity:
Till fortune fraught with malice, blinde, and brute,° *insensible*
That envies lovers long prosperity,
Blew up a bitter storme of foule adversity.

39

It fortunéd one day, when Calidore
Was hunting in the woods (as was his trade)° *custom*
A lawlesse people, Brigants hight of yore,
That never usde to live by plough nor spade,
But fed on spoile and booty, which they made
Upon their neighbours, which did nigh them border,
The dwelling of these shepheards did invade,
And spoyld their houses, and them selves did murder;
And drove away their flocks, with other much disorder.[7]

40

Amongst the rest, the which they then did pray,° *capture*
They spoyld old Melibee of all he had,
And all his people captive led away,
Mongst which this lucklesse mayd away was lad,
Faire Pastorella, sorrowfull and sad,

5. I.e., The true aristocratic temper draws back from union with natures of inferior quality.
6. Coridon had feared such reaping, "ere it ripened were" (VI.ix.38.6).
7. This scene draws on the violence implied by "brigand" (from Italian, "devils") and can also parallel the cannibalistic "salvage nation" in VI.viii.35–49, but the word may also recall the ancient "Briganti," a Celtic tribe that Spenser would have known had inhabited both the Northumbrian border with Scotland and the Cork area in Ireland where he lived; a second-century map by Ptolemy locates the Briganti in both places.

Most sorrowfull, most sad, that ever sight.° *sighed*
Now made the spoile of theeves and Brigants bad,
Which was the conquest of the gentlest Knight,
That ever lived, th'onely° glory of his might. *chief*

41

With them also was taken Coridon,
And carried captive by those theeves away;
Who in the covert of the night, that none
Mote them descry, nor reskue from their pray,
Unto their dwelling did them close° convay. *secretly*
Their dwelling in a little Island was,
Covered with shrubby woods, in which no way
Appeard for people in nor out to pas,
Nor any footing fynde for overgrowen gras.

42

For underneath the ground their way was made,
Through hollow caves, that no man mote discover
For the thicke shrubs, which did them alwaies shade
From view of living wight, and covered over:
But darkenesse dred and daily night did hover
Through all the inner parts, wherein they dwelt.
Ne lightned was with window, nor with lover,[8]
But with continuall candlelight, which delt
A doubtfull sense of things, not so well seene, as felt.

43

Hither those Brigants brought their present pray,
And kept them with continuall watch and ward,
Meaning so soone, as they convenient may,
For slaves to sell them, for no small reward,
To merchants, which them kept in bondage hard,
Or sold againe. Now when faire Pastorell
Into this place was brought, and kept with gard
Of griesly theeves, she thought her self in hell,
Where with such damnéd fiends she should in darknesse dwell.

44

But for to tell the dolefull dreriment,
And pittifull complaints, which there she made,
Where day and night she nought did but lament
Her wretched life, shut up in deadly shade,
And waste her goodly beauty, which did fade
Like to a flowre, that feeles no heate of sunne,
Which may her feeble leaves with comfort glade.° *gladden*
But what befell her in that theevish wonne,
Will in an other Canto better be begonne.

8. I.e., louvre; an opening in the roof to let smoke escape, and to admit light.

Canto XI

The theeves fall out for Pastorell,
Whilest Melibee is slaine:
Her Calidore from them redeemes,
And bringeth backe againe.

I

The joyes of love, if they should ever last,
Without affliction or disquietnesse,
That worldly chaunces° doe amongst them cast, *hazards*
Would be on earth too great a blessednesse,
Liker to heaven, then mortall wretchednesse.
Therefore the wingéd God,[1] to let men weet,
That here on earth is no sure happinesse,
A thousand sowres hath tempred with one sweet,
To make it seeme more deare and dainty,° as is meet. *choice*

2

Like as is now befalne to this faire Mayd,
Faire Pastorell,[2] of whom is now my song,
Who being now in dreadfull darknesse layd,
Amongst those theeves, which her in bondage strong
Detaynd, yet Fortune not with all this wrong
Contented, greater mischiefe on her threw,
And sorrowes heapt on her in greater throng;
That who so heares her heavinesse,° would rew *grief*
And pitty her sad plight, so changed from pleasaunt hew.

3

Whylest thus she in these hellish dens remayned,
Wrappéd in wretched cares and hearts unrest,
It so befell (as Fortune had ordayned)
That he, which was their Capitaine profest,
And had the chiefe commaund of all the rest,
One day as he did all his prisoners vew,
With lustfull eyes, beheld that lovely guest,
Faire Pastorella, whose sad mournefull hew
Like the faire Morning clad in misty fog did shew.

4

At sight whereof his barbarous heart was fired,
And inly burnt with flames most raging whot,
That her alone he for his part desired
Of all the other pray, which they had got,
And her in mynde did to him selfe allot.
From that day forth he kyndnesse to her showed,

1. Cupid (in league with Fortune).
2. The episode of Pastorella's captivity derives from Ariosto, *Orlando Furioso* 12.91 ff.

And sought her love, by all the meanes he mote;
With looks, with words, with gifts he oft her wowed:° *wooed*
And mixéd threats among, and much unto her vowed.

5

But all that ever he could doe or say,
Her constant mynd could not a whit remove,
Nor draw unto the lure of his lewd lay,
To graunt him favour, or afford him love.
Yet ceast he not to sew° and all waies prove,° *plead / try*
By which he mote accomplish his request,
Saying and doing all that mote behove;[3]
Ne day nor night he suffred her to rest,
But her all night did watch, and all the day molest.° *annoy*

6

At last when him she so importune saw,
Fearing least he at length the raines would lend
Unto his lust, and make his will his law,
Sith in his powre she was to foe or frend,[4]
She thought it best, for shadow to pretend
Some shew of favour, by him gracing small,[5]
That she thereby mote either freely wend,° *go*
Or at more ease continue there his thrall:
A little well is lent, that gaineth more withall.

7

So from thenceforth, when love he to her made,
With better tearmes she did him entertaine,
Which gave him hope, and did him halfe perswade,
That he in time her joyaunce should obtaine.[6]
But when she saw, through that small favours gaine,
That further, then she willing was, he prest,
She found no meanes to barre him, but to faine
A sodaine sickenesse, which her sore opprest,
And made unfit to serve his lawlesse mindes behest.

8

By meanes whereof she would not him permit
Once to approach to her in privity,° *private*
But onely mongst the rest by her to sit,
Mourning the rigour of her malady,
And seeking all things meete for remedy.
But she resolved no remedy to fynde,

3. I.e., that might aptly serve his purpose.
4. I.e., since it was in his power to treat her as foe or friend.
5. I.e., by showing him some slight favor.
6. I.e., when he undertook flattering preliminaries (that might lead "in time" to sexual consummation).

Nor better cheare to shew in misery,
Till Fortune would her captive bonds unbynde,
Her sickenesse was not of the body but the mynde.

9

During which space that she thus sicke did lie,
It chaunst a sort° of merchants, which were wount — *company*
To skim those coastes, for bondmen° there to buy, — *slaves*
And by such trafficke after gaines to hunt,
Arrivéd in this Isle though bare and blunt,
T'inquire for slaves; where being readie met
By some of these same theeves at the instant brunt,[7]
Were brought unto their Captaine, who was set
By his faire patients side with sorrowfull regret.

10

To whom they shewéd, how those marchants were
Arrived in place, their bondslaves for to buy,
And therefore prayd, that those same captives there
Mote to them for their most commodity° — *profit*
Be sold, and mongst them sharéd equally.
This their request the Captaine much appalled;
Yet could he not their just demaund deny,
And willéd streight the slaves should forth be called,
And sold for most advantage not to be forstalled.[8]

11

Then forth the good old Melibœ was brought,
And Coridon, with many other moe,
Whom they before in diverse spoyles had caught:
All which he to the marchants sale did showe.
Till some, which did the sundry prisoners knowe,
Gan to inquire for that faire shepherdesse,
Which with the rest they tooke not long agoe,
And gan her forme and feature to expresse,° — *describe*
The more t'augment her price, through praise of comlinesse.

12

To whom the Captaine in full angry wize
Made answere, that the Mayd of whom they spake,
Was his owne purchase and his onely prize,[9]
With which none had to doe, ne ought partake,
But he himselfe, which did that conquest make;
Litle for him to have one silly° lasse: — *simple*
Besides through sicknesse now so wan and weake,

7. I.e., at the moment of their arrival.
8. I.e., not reserving any slaves from sale.
9. I.e., his booty, reserved for him alone.

That nothing meet in marchandise to passe.[1]
So shewed them her, to prove how pale and weake she was.

13

The sight of whom, though now decayd and mard,
And eke but hardly seene by candle-light,
Yet like a Diamond of rich regard,° *value*
In doubtfull shadow of the darkesome night,
With starrie beames about her shining bright,
These marchants fixéd eyes did so amaze,
That what through wonder, and what through delight,
A while on her they greedily did gaze,
And did her greatly like, and did her greatly praize.

14

At last when all the rest them offred were,
And prises° to them placéd at their pleasure, *prices*
They all refuséd in regard of her,[2]
Ne ought would buy, how ever prisd with measure,[3]
Withouten her, whose worth above all threasure
They did esteeme, and offred store of gold.
But then the Captaine fraught with more displeasure,
Bad them be still, his love should not be sold:
The rest take if they would, he her to him would hold.

15

Therewith some other of the chiefest theeves
Boldly him bad such injurie forbeare;
For that same mayd, how ever it him greeves,
Should with the rest be sold before him theare,
To make the prises of the rest more deare.
That with great rage he stoutly doth denay;
And fiercely drawing forth his blade, doth sweare,
That who so hardie hand on her doth lay,
It dearely shall aby,° and death for handsell° pay. *pay / reward*

16

Thus as they words amongst them multiply,
They fall to strokes, the frute of too much talke,
And the mad steele about doth fiercely fly,
Not sparing wight, ne leaving any balke,[4]
But making way for death at large to walke:
Who in the horror of the griesly night,
In thousand dreadful shapes doth mongst them stalke,

1. I.e., not fit for sale.
2. I.e., on account of her (beauty).
3. I.e., however moderately (the rest were) priced.
4. I.e., leaving anyone untouched (as careless farmers may leave a "balke" or ridge of land unploughed).

And makes huge havocke, whiles the candlelight
Out quenchéd, leaves no skill° nor difference of wight. *distinction*

17

Like as a sort of hungry dogs ymet
About some carcase by the common way,
Doe fall together, stryving each to get
The greatest portion of the greedie pray;[5]
All on confuséd heapes themselves assay,° *attack*
And snatch, and byte, and rend, and tug, and teare;
That who them sees, would wonder at their fray,
And who sees not, would be affrayd to heare.
Such was the conflict of those cruell Brigants there.

18

But first of all, their captives they doe kill,
Least they should joyne against the weaker side,
Or rise against the remnant at their will;
Old Melibœ is slaine, and him beside
His aged wife, with many others wide,° *round about*
But Coridon escaping craftily,
Creepes forth of dores, whilst darknes him doth hide,
And flyes away as fast as he can hye,
Ne stayeth leave to take, before his friends doe dye.

19

But Pastorella, wofull wretched Elfe,[6]
Was by the Captaine all this while defended,
Who minding more her safety then himselfe,
His target° alwayes over her pretended;° *shield / stretched*
By meanes whereof, that mote not be amended,
He at the length was slaine, and layd on ground,
Yet holding fast twixt both his armes extended
Fayre Pastorell, who with the selfe same wound
Launcht° through the arme, fell down with him in drerie° swound *pierced / bloody*

20

There lay she covered with confuséd preasse° *heap*
Of carcases, which dying on her fell.
Tho when as he was dead, the fray gan ceasse,
And each to other calling, did compell
To stay their cruell hands from slaughter fell,
Sith they that were the cause of all, were gone.
Thereto they all attonce agreéd well,

5. I.e., the prey for which they greedily fight.
6. I.e., frail creature.

And lighting candles new, gan search anone,
How many of their friends were slaine, how many fone.

21

Their Captaine there they cruelly found kild,
And in his armes the dreary[7] dying mayd,
Like a sweet Angell twixt two clouds uphild:
Her lovely light was dimméd and decayd,
With cloud of death upon her eyes displayd;
Yet did the cloud make even that dimmed light
Seeme much more lovely in that darknesse layd,
And twixt the twinckling of her eye-lids bright,
To sparke out litle beames, like starres in foggie night.

22

But when they moved the carcases aside,
They found that life did yet in her remaine:
Then all their helpes they busily applyde,
To call the soule backe to her home againe;
And wrought so well with labour and long paine,
That they to life recovered her at last.
Who sighing sore, as if her hart in twaine
Had riven bene, and all her hart strings brast,° *torn*
With drearie drouping eyne lookt up like one aghast.

23

There she beheld, that sore her grieved to see,
Her father and her friends about her lying,
Her selfe sole left, a second spoyle to bee
Of those, that having savéd her from dying,
Renewed her death by timely death denying:
What now is left her, but to wayle and weepe,
Wringing her hands, and ruefully loud crying?
Ne caréd she her wound in teares to steepe,° *bathe*
Albe with all their might those Brigants her did keepe.

24

But when they saw her now relived againe,
They left her so, in charge of one the best
Of many worst, who with unkind disdaine
And cruell rigour her did much molest;
Scarse yeelding her due food, or timely rest,
And scarsely suffring her infestred° wound, *infected*
That sore her payned, by any to be drest.
So leave we her in wretched thraldome bound,
And turne we backe to Calidore, where we him found.

7. I.e., dismal, bloody.

25

Who when he backe returnéd from the wood,
And saw his shepheards cottage spoylėd quight,
And his love reft away, he wexed wood,° *frantic*
And halfe enragéd at that ruefull sight,
That even his hart for very fell despight,
And his owne flesh he readie was to teare,
He chauft, he grieved, he fretted, and he sight,° *sighed*
And faréd° like a furious wyld Beare, *acted*
Whose whelpes are stolne away, she being otherwhere.[8]

26

Ne wight he found, to whom he might complaine,
Ne wight he found, of whom he might inquire;
That more increast the anguish of his paine.
He sought the woods; but no man could see there:
He sought the plaines; but could no tydings heare.
The woods did nought but ecchoes vaine rebound;
The playnes all waste and emptie did appeare:
Where wont the shepheards oft their pypes resound,
And feed an hundred flocks, there now not one he found.

27

At last as there he roméd up and downe,
He chaunst one comming towards him to spy,
That seemed to be some sorie simple clowne,° *rustic*
With ragged weedes, and lockes upstaring° hye, *bristling*
As if he did from some late daunger fly,
And yet his feare did follow him behynd:
Who as he unto him approchéd nye,
He mote perceive by signes, which he did fynd,
That Coridon it was, the silly shepherds hynd.

28

Tho to him running fast, he did not stay
To greet him first, but askt where were the rest;
Where Pastorell? who full of fresh dismay,
And gushing forth in teares, was so opprest,
That he no word could speake, but smit his brest,
And up to heaven his eyes fast streming threw.
Whereat the knight amazed, yet did not rest,
But askt againe, what ment that rufull hew:
Where was his Pastorell? where all the other crew?

8. Classical and scriptural passages echo here: 4–6 recall *Iliad* 1.243, "then thou shalt tear thy heart within thee for anger," and perhaps Joel 2.13; 7–9 look to 2 Samuel 17.8, "they be chafed in their minds, as a bear robbed of of her whelps in the field," perhaps also to *Iliad* 18.318–22.

29

"Ah well away," sayd he then sighing sore,
"That ever I did live, this day to see,
This dismall day, and was not dead before,
Before I saw faire Pastorella dye."
"Die? out alas!" then Calidore did cry:
"How could the death dare ever her to quell?° *overcome*
But read° thou shepheard, read what destiny, *tell*
Or other dyrefull hap from heaven or hell
Hath wrought this wicked deed, doe° feare away, and tell." *put*

30

Tho when the shepheard breathéd had a whyle,
He thus began: "Where shall I then commence
This wofull tale? or how those Brigants vyle,
With cruell rage and dreadfull violence
Spoyld all our cots, and caried us from hence?
Or how faire Pastorell should have bene sold
To marchants, but was saved with strong defence?
Or how those theeves, whilest one sought her to hold,
Fell all at ods, and fought through fury fierce and bold.

31

"In that same conflict (woe is me) befell
This fatall chaunce, this dolefull accident,
Whose heavy tydings now I have to tell.
First all the captives, which they here had hent,° *seized*
Were by them slaine by generall consent;
Old Melibœ and his good wife withall
These eyes saw die, and dearely did lament:
But when the lot to Pastorell did fall,
Their Captaine long withstood, and did her death forstall.

32

"But what could he gainst all them doe alone?
It could not boot;° needs mote she die at last: *serve (her)*
I onely scapt through great confusione
Of cryes and clamors, which amongst them past,
In dreadfull darknesse dreadfully aghast;
That better were with them to have bene dead,
Then here to see all desolate and wast
Despoyléd of those joyes and jollyhead,° *merriment*
Which with those gentle shepherds here I wont to lead."

33

When Calidore these ruefull newes had raught,° *grasped*
His hart quite deaded was with anguish great,
And all his wits with doole° were nigh distraught, *grief*

That he his face, his head, his brest did beat,
And death it selfe unto himselfe did threat;
Oft cursing th'heavens, that so cruell were
To her, whose name he often did repeat;
And wishing oft, that he were present there,
When she was slaine, or had bene to her succour nere.

34

But after griefe awhile had had his course,
And spent it selfe in mourning, he at last
Began to mitigate his swelling sourse,[9]
And in his mind with better reason cast,
How he might save her life, if life did last;
Or if that dead, how he her death might wreake,° *avenge*
Sith otherwise he could not mend thing past;
Or if it to revenge he were too weake,
Then for to die with her, and his lives threed to breake.[1]

35

Tho Coridon he prayd, sith he well knew
The readie way unto that theevish wonne,
To wend with him, and be his conduct trew
Unto the place, to see what should be donne.
But he, whose hart through feare was late fordonne,° *overcome*
Would not for ought be drawne to former drede,
But by all meanes the daunger knowne did shonne:
Yet Calidore so well him wrought with meed,[2]
And faire bespoke with words, that he at last agreed.

36

So forth they goe together (God before)
Both clad in shepheards weeds agreeably,° *similarly*
And both with shepheards hookes: But Calidore
Had underneath, him armèd privily.
Tho to the place when they approchèd nye,
They chaunst, upon an hill not farre away,
Some flockes of sheepe and shepheards to espy;
To whom they both agreed to take their way,
In hope there newes to learne, how they mote best assay.° *proceed*

37

There did they find, that which they did not feare,° *expect*
The selfe same flocks, the which those theeves had reft
From Melibœ and from themselves whyleare,
And certaine of the theeves there by them left,

9. I.e., began to moderate his grief.
1. Effectively, to defy the Fates by severing the thread of life (spun and measured by Clotho and Lachesis), an act reserved for Atropos.
2. I.e., (probably) moved him with (promises of) money.

The which for want of heards° themselves then kept. *herdsmen*
Right well knew Coridon his owne late sheepe,
And seeing them, for tender pittie wept:
But when he saw the theeves, which did them keepe,
His hart gan fayle, albe he saw them all asleepe.

38

But Calidore recomforting° his griefe, *consoling*
Though not his feare: for nought may feare disswade,° *remove*
Him hardly° forward drew, whereas the thiefe *boldly*
Lay sleeping soundly in the bushes shade,
Whom Coridon him counseld to invade° *attack*
Now all unwares, and take the spoyle away;
But he, that in his mind had closely° made *secretly*
A further purpose, would not so them slay,
But gently waking them, gave them the time of day.[3]

39

Tho sitting downe by them upon the greene,
Of sundrie things he purpose gan to faine;[4]
That he by them might certaine tydings weene
Of Pastorell, were she alive or slaine.
Mongst which the theeves them questionéd againe,
What mister° men, and eke from whence they were. *kind of*
To whom they answered, as did appertaine,[5]
That they were poore heardgroomes, the which whylere
Had from their maisters fled, and now sought hyre elswhere.

40

Whereof right glad they seemed, and offer made
To hyre° them well, if they their flockes would keepe: *pay*
For they themselves were evill° groomes, they sayd, *unskilled*
Unwont with heards to watch, or pasture sheepe,
But to forray the land, or scoure the deepe.
Thereto they soone agreed, and earnest° tooke, *pledge*
To keepe their flockes for litle hyre and chepe:
For they for better hyre did shortly looke,
So there all day they bode, till light the sky forsooke.

41

Tho when as towards darksome night it drew,
Unto their hellish dens those theeves them brought,
Where shortly they in great acquaintance grew,
And all the secrets of their entrayles[6] sought.
There did they find, contrarie to their thought,

3. I.e., greeted them.
4. I.e., began to make conversation.
5. I.e., as suited their disguise.
6. I.e., either (1) their minds, or, more probably, (2) the inner arrangements of their cave.

That Pastorell yet lived, but all the rest
Were dead, right so as Coridon had taught:
Whereof they both full glad and blyth did rest,
But chiefly Calidore, whom griefe had most possest.

42

At length when they occasion fittest found,
In dead of night, when all the theeves did rest
After a late forray, and slept full sound,
Sir Calidore him armed, as he thought best,
Having of late by diligent inquest,° *search*
Provided him a sword of meanest sort:
With which he streight went to the Captaines nest.
But Coridon durst not with him consort,
Ne durst abide behind, for dread of worse effort.

43

When to the Cave they came, they found it fast:° *locked*
But Calidore with huge resistlesse might,
The dores assayléd, and the locks upbrast.
With noyse whereof the theefe awaking light,° *quickly*
Unto the entrance ran: where the bold knight
Encountring him with small resistance slew;
The whiles faire Pastorell through great affright
Was almost dead, misdoubting least of new[7]
Some uprore were like that, which lately she did vew.

44

But when as Calidore was comen in,
And gan aloud for Pastorell to call,
Knowing his voice although not heard long sin,° *since*
She sudden was revivéd therewithall,
And wondrous joy felt in her spirits thrall:° *thrill*
Like him that being long in tempest tost,
Looking each houre into deathes mouth to fall,
At length espyes at hand the happie cost,° *coast*
On which he safety hopes, that earst feard to be lost.

45

Her gentle hart, that now long season past
Had never joyance felt, nor chearefull thought,
Began some smacke of comfort new to tast,
Like lyfull heat to numméd senses brought,
And life to feele, that long for death had sought;
Ne lesse in hart rejoycéd Calidore,
When he her found, but like to one distraught
And robd of reason, towards her him bore,
A thousand times embrast, and kist a thousand more.

7. I.e., fearing lest again.

46

But now by this, with noyse of late uprore,
The hue and cry was raysèd all about;
And all the Brigants flocking in great store,
Unto the cave gan preasse, nought having dout
Of that was doen, and entred in a rout.° *crowd*
But Calidore in th'entry close did stand,
And entertayning them with courage stout,
Still slew the formost, that came first to hand,
So long till all the entry was with bodies mand.° *piled*

47

Tho when no more could nigh to him approch,
He breathed° his sword, and rested him till day: *rested*
Which when he spyde upon the earth t'encroch,
Through the dead carcases he made his way,
Mongst which he found a sword of better say,° *temper*
With which he forth went into th'open light:
Where all the rest for him did readie stay,
And fierce assayling him, with all their might
Gan all upon him lay: there gan a dreadfull fight.

48

How many flyes in whottest sommers day
Do seize upon some beast, whose flesh is bare,
That all the place with swarmes do overlay,
And with their litle stings right felly° fare; *fiercely*
So many theeves about him swarming are,
All which do him assayle on every side,
And sore oppresse, ne any him doth spare:
But he doth with his raging brond° divide *sword*
Their thickest troups, and round about him scattreth wide.

49

Like as a Lion mongst an heard of dere,
Disperseth them to catch his choysest pray;
So did he fly amongst them here and there,
And all that nere him came, did hew and slay,
Till he had strowd with bodies all the way;
That none his daunger daring to abide,
Fled from his wrath, and did themselves convay
Into their caves, their heads from death to hide,
Ne any left, that victorie to him envide.

50

Then backe returning to his dearest deare,
He her gan to recomfort, all he might,
With gladfull speaches, and with lovely cheare,

And forth her bringing to the joyous light,
Whereof she long had lackt the wishfull sight,
Devized all goodly meanes, from her to drive
The sad remembrance of her wretched plight.
So her uneath[8] at last he did revive,
That long had lyen dead, and made againe alive.

51

This doen, into those theevish dens he went,
And thence did all the spoyles and threasures take,
Which they from many long had robd and rent,
But fortune now the victors meed did make;
Of which the best he did his love betake,° *give to*
And also all those flockes, which they before
Had reft from Melibœ and from his make,° *mate*
He did them all to Coridon restore.
So drove them all away, and his love with him bore.

Canto XII

Fayre Pastorella by great hap° *chance*
her parents understands,
Calidore doth the Blatant beast
subdew, and bynd in bands.

1

Like as a ship, that through the Ocean wyde
Directs her course unto one certaine cost,° *coast*
Is met of many a counter winde and tyde,
With which her wingéd speed is let° and crost, *checked*
And she her selfe in stormie surges tost;
Yet making many a borde, and many a bay,
Still winneth way, ne hath her compasse lost.[1]
Right so it fares with me in this long way,
Whose course is often stayd, yet never is astray.

2

For all that hetherto hath long delayd
This gentle knight, from sewing° his first quest, *pursuing*
Though out of course, yet hath not bene mis-sayd,
To shew the courtesie by him profest,
Even unto the lowest and the least.
But now I come into my course againe,
To his atchievement of the Blatant beast;
Who all this while at will did range and raine,
Whilst none was him to stop, nor none him to restraine.

8. I.e., with difficulty.
1. I.e. (lines 6–7), either (1) reaching many a coast, and (reaching) many (sheltered) bays; or (2) making many a tack, and often turning directly into the wind (as in "turning to bay"), still forges ahead on the correct course.

3

Sir Calidore when thus he now had raught
  Faire Pastorella from those Brigants powre,
  Unto the Castle of Belgard[2] her brought,
  Whereof was Lord the good Sir Bellamoure;
  Who whylome was in his youthes freshest flowre
  A lustie knight, as ever wielded speare,
  And had enduréd many a dreadfull stoure° *encounter*
  In bloudy battell for a Ladie deare,
The fayrest Ladie then of all that living were.

4

Her name was Claribell,[3] whose father hight
  The Lord of Many Ilands, farre renound
  For his great riches and his greater might.
  He through the wealth, wherein he did abound,
  This daughter thought in wedlocke to have bound
  Unto the Prince of Picteland[4] bordering nere,
  But she whose sides before with secret wound
  Of love to Bellamoure empiercéd were,
By all meanes shund to match with any forrein fere.° *mate*

5

And Bellamour againe so well her pleased,
  With dayly service and attendance dew,
  That of her love he was entyrely seized,
  And closely° did her wed, but knowne to few. *secretly*
  Which when her father understood, he grew
  In so great rage, that them in dongeon deepe
  Without compassion cruelly he threw;
  Yet did so streightly° them a sunder keepe, *strictly*
That neither could to company of th'other creepe.

6

Nathlesse Sir Bellamour, whether through grace[5]
  Or secret guifts so with his keepers wrought,
  That to his love sometimes he came in place,
  Whereof her wombe unwist to wight was fraught,[6]
  And in dew time a mayden child forth brought.
  Which she streight way for dread least, if her syre
  Should know thereof, to slay he would have sought,

2. From Italian, "loving look" or "good care." Bellamoure's name in these contexts signifies both "lover of beauty" and "lover of war," as well as "beautiful love." The remainder of Pastorella's story derives chiefly from Boiardo, *Orlando Innamorato* 2.27.25 ff., with details from Tasso, *Rinaldo* 11.94.
3. "Bright beauty."
4. I.e., Scotland, home of the Picts.
5. I.e., the persuasive force of his "gentle" character.
6. I.e., without anyone's knowledge she became pregnant.

Delivered to her handmayd, that for hyre° *payment*
She should it cause be fostred under straunge attyre.[7]

7

The trustie damzell bearing it abrode
Into the emptie fields, where living wight
Mote not bewray the secret of her lode,
She forth gan lay unto the open light
The litle babe, to take thereof a sight.
Whom whylest she did with watrie eyne behold,
Upon the litle brest like christall bright,
She mote perceive a litle purple mold,° *mole*
That like a rose her silken leaves did faire unfold.

8

Well she it markt, and pittiéd the more,
Yet could not remedie her wretched case,
But closing it againe like as before,
Bedeawed with teares there left it in the place:
Yet left not quite, but drew a litle space
Behind the bushes, where she her did hyde,
To weet what mortall hand, or heavens grace
Would for the wretched infants helpe provyde,
For which it loudly cald, and pittifully cryde.

9

At length a Shepheard, which there by did keepe
His fleecie flocke upon the playnes around,
Led with the infants cry, that loud did weepe,
Came to the place, where when he wrappéd found
Th'abandond spoyle, he softly it unbound;
And seeing there, that did° him pittie sore, *made*
He tooke it up, and in his mantle wound;
So home unto his honest wife it bore,
Who as her owne it nurst, and naméd[8] evermore.

10

Thus long continued Claribell a thrall,
And Bellamour in bands, till that her syre
Departed life, and left unto them all.
Then all the stormes of fortunes former yre
Were turnd, and they to freedome did retyre.° *return*
Thenceforth they joyed in happinesse together,
And livéd long in peace and love entyre,
Without disquiet or dislike of ether,
Till time that Calidore brought Pastorella thether.

7. I.e., under false identity.
8. I.e., who thereafter called it her own child.

11

Both whom they goodly well did entertaine;
For Bellamour knew Calidore right well,
And lovéd for his prowesse, sith they twaine
Long since had fought in field. Als Claribell
No lesse did tender the faire Pastorell,
Seeing her weake and wan, through durance° long. *captivity*
There they a while together thus did dwell
In much delight, and many joyes among,
Untill the damzell gan to wex more sound and strong.

12

Tho gan Sir Calidore him to advize° *consider*
Of his first quest, which he had long forlore,° *neglected*
Ashamed to thinke, how he that enterprize,
The which the Faery Queene had long afore
Bequeathed to him, forslackéd had so sore;
That much he fearéd, least reprochfull blame
With foule dishonour him mote blot therefore;
Besides the losse of so much loos° and fame, *renown*
As through the world thereby should glorifie his name.

13

Therefore resolving to returne in hast
Unto so great atchievement, he bethought
To leave his love, now perill being past,
With Claribell, whylest he that monster sought
Throughout the world, and to destruction brought.
So taking leave of his faire Pastorell,
Whom to recomfort, all the meanes he wrought,
With thanks to Bellamour and Claribell,
He went forth on his quest, and did, that him befell.

14

But first, ere I doe his adventures tell,
In this exploite, me needeth to declare,
What did betide to the faire Pastorell,
During his absence left in heavy care,° *sorrow*
Through daily mourning, and nightly misfare:° *grief*
Yet did that auncient matrone all she might,
To cherish her with all things choice and rare;
And her owne handmayd, that Melissa[9] hight,
Appointed to attend her dewly day and night.

15

Who in a morning, when this Mayden faire
Was dighting° her, having her snowy brest *dressing*

9. From Greek ("honeybee"). The priestesses attending the temple of Demeter (Ceres) were so named.

As yet not lacéd, nor her golden haire
Into their comely tresses dewly drest,
Chaunst to espy upon her yvory chest
The rosie marke, which she remembred well
That litle Infant had, which forth she kest,° *cast*
The daughter of her Lady Claribell,
The which she bore, the whiles in prison she did dwell.

16

Which well avizing,° streight she gan to cast *perceiving*
In her conceiptfull° mynd, that this faire Mayd *clever*
Was that same infant, which so long sith past
She in the open fields had loosely layd
To fortunes spoile, unable it to ayd.
So full of joy, streight forth she ran in hast
Unto her mistresse, being halfe dismayd,
To tell her, how the heavens had her graste,
To save her chylde, which in misfortunes mouth was plaste.

17

The sober mother seeing such her mood,
Yet knowing not, what meant that sodaine thro,[1]
Askt her, how mote her words be understood,
And what the matter was, that moved her so.
"My liefe," sayd she, "ye know, that long ygo,
Whilest ye in durance dwelt, ye to me gave
A little mayde, the which ye chylded[2] tho;
The same againe if now ye list to have,
The same is yonder Lady, whom high God did save."

18

Much was the Lady troubled at that speach,
And gan to question streight how she it knew.
"Most certaine markes," sayd she, "do me it teach,
For on her brest I with these eyes did vew
The litle purple rose, which thereon grew,
Whereof her name ye then to her did give.
Besides her countenaunce, and her likely hew,[3]
Matchéd with equall yeares, do surely prieve° *prove*
That yond same is your daughter sure, which yet doth live."

19

The matrone stayd no lenger to enquire,
But forth in hast ran to the straunger Mayd;

1. I.e., that thrilling emotional quiver.
2. I.e., gave birth to.
3. I.e., her similar appearance.

Whom catching greedily for great desire,
Rent up her brest, and bosome open layd,
In which that rose she plainely saw displayd.
Then her embracing twixt her armés twaine,
She long so held, and softly weeping sayd;
"And livest thou my daughter now againe?
And art thou yet alive, whom dead I long did faine?° *imagine*

20

Tho further asking her of sundry things,
And times comparing with their accidents,° *happenings*
She found at last by very certaine signes,
And speaking markes of passéd monuments,[4]
That this young Mayd, whom chance to her presents
Is her owne daughter, her owne infant deare.
Tho wondring long at those so straunge events,
A thousand times she her embracéd nere,
With many a joyfull kisse, and many a melting teare.

21

Who ever is the mother of one chylde,
Which having thought long dead, she fyndes alive,
Let her by proofe of that, which she hath fylde° *felt*
In her owne breast, this mothers joy descrive:° *describe*
For other none such passion can contrive
In perfect forme, as this good Lady felt,
When she so faire a daughter saw survive,
As Pastorella was, that nigh she swelt° *fainted*
For passing° joy, which did all into pitty melt. *surpassing*

22

Thence running forth unto her lovéd Lord,
She unto him recounted, all that fell:
Who joyning joy with her in one accord,
Acknowledged for his owne faire Pastorell.
There leave we them in joy, and let us tell
Of Calidore, who seeking all this while
That monstrous Beast by finall force to quell,° *kill*
Through every place, with restlesse paine and toile
Him followed, by the tract° of his outragious spoile.° *track / ravaging*

23

Through all estates[5] he found that he had past,
In which he many massacres had left,
And to the Clergy now was come at last;

4. I.e., recorded events.
5. I.e., the three estates of clergy, court (subsuming knighthood and the nobility), and commons: all ranks of human life.

In which such spoile, such havocke, and such theft
He wrought, that thence all goodnesse he bereft,
That endlesse were to tell. The Elfin Knight,
Who now no place besides unsought had left,
At length into a Monastere did light,
Where he him found despoyling all with maine and might.[6]

24

Into their cloysters now he broken had,
Through which the Monckes he chacéd here and there,
And them pursued into their dortours° sad, *bed-chambers*
And searchéd all their cels and secrets neare;
In which what filth and ordure did appeare,
Were yrkesome to report; yet that foule Beast
Nought sparing them, the more did tosse and teare,
And ransacke all their dennes from most to least,
Regarding nought religion, nor their holy heast.° *vow*

25

From thence into the sacred Church he broke,
And robd the Chancell, and the deskes downe threw,
And Altars fouléd, and blasphemy spoke,
And th'Images for all their goodly hew,
Did cast to ground, whilest none was them to rew;
So all confounded and disordered there.
But seeing Calidore, away he flew,
Knowing his fatall hand by former feare;
But he him fast pursuing, soone approchéd neare.

26

Him in a narrow place he overtooke,
And fierce assailing forst him turne againe:
Sternely° he turnd againe, when he him strooke *fiercely*
With his sharpe steele, and ran at him amaine
With open mouth, that seeméd to containe
A full good pecke within the utmost brim,
All set with yron teeth in raunges° twaine, *ranks*
That terrifide his foes, and arméd him,
Appearing like the mouth of Orcus[7] griesly grim.

6. The beast's assault on and pillage of monastery and "sacred Church" might seem surprising in a Protestant, but the scene could reflect a by no means unusual dislike of overzealous iconoclasm and dismay at the destruction wrought by the Reformation in both England and Ireland, a violence that had resulted in the loss of art, books, and the turning of lovely buildings into "bare ruined choirs, where late the sweet birds sang" (Shakespeare, Sonnet 73). Spenser may have reflected that monasteries and the contemplative life preceded the corruptions, as he saw them, of the Roman Catholic Church.

7. I.e., Pluto, ruler of Hades.

27

And therein were a thousand tongs empight,° *implanted*
Of sundry kindes, and sundry quality,
Some were of dogs, that barkéd day and night,
And some of cats, that wrawling° still did cry, *caterwauling*
And some of Beares, that groynd° continually, *growled*
And some of Tygres, that did seeme to gren,° *grin*
And snar° at all, that ever passéd by: *snarl*
But most of them were tongues of mortall men,
Which spake reprochfully, not caring where nor when.

28

And them amongst were mingled here and there,
The tongues of Serpents with three forkéd stings,
That spat out poyson and gore bloudy gere° *filth*
At all, that came within his ravenings,
And spake licentious words, and hatefull things
Of good and bad alike, of low and hie;
Ne Kesars° sparéd he a whit, nor Kings, *emperors*
But either blotted them with infamie,
Or bit them with his banefull teeth of injury.° *insult*

29

But Calidore thereof no whit afrayd,
Rencountred him with so impetuous might,
That th'outrage of his violence he stayd,
And bet° abacke, threatning in vaine to bite, *forced*
And spitting forth the poyson of his spight,
That foméd all about his bloody jawes.
Tho rearing up his former° feete on hight, *fore*
He rampt[8] upon him with his ravenous pawes,
As if he would have rent him with his cruell clawes.

30

But he right well aware,° his rage to ward, *alert*
Did cast his shield atweene, and therewithall
Putting his puissaunce forth, pursued so hard,
That backeward he enforcéd him to fall,
And being downe, ere he new helpe could call,
His shield he on him threw, and fast downe held,
Like as a bullocke, that in bloody stall
Of butchers balefull hand to ground is feld,
Is forcibly kept downe, till he be throughly queld.

8. I.e., reared up threateningly.

31

Full cruelly the Beast did rage and rore,
To be downe held, and maystred so with might,
That he gan fret and fome out bloudy gore,
Striving in vaine to rere him selfe upright.
For still the more he strove, the more the Knight
Did him suppresse, and forcibly subdew;
That made him almost mad for fell despight.
He grind,[9] hee bit, he scratcht, he venim threw,
And faréd° like a feend, right horrible in hew. *acted*

32

Or like the hell-borne Hydra, which they faine
That great Alcides whilome overthrew,
After that he had labourd long in vaine,
To crop his thousand heads, the which still new
Forth budded, and in greater number grew.[1]
Such was the fury of this hellish Beast,
Whilest Calidore him under him downe threw;
Who nathemore° his heavy load releast, *never*
But aye the more he raged, the more his powre increast.

33

Tho when the Beast saw, he mote nought availe,° *effect*
By force, he gan his hundred tongues apply,
And sharpely at him to revile and raile,
With bitter termes of shamefull infamy;
Oft interlacing many a forgéd lie,
Whose like he never once did speake, nor heare,
Nor ever thought thing so unworthily:
Yet did he nought for all that him forbeare,° *spare*
But strainéd° him so streightly, that he chokt him neare. *gripped*

34

At last when as he found his force to shrincke,
And rage to quaile,° he tooke a muzzell strong *fail*
Of surest yron, made with many a lincke;
Therewith he muréd° up his mouth along, *closed*
And therein shut up his blasphemous tong,
For never more defaming gentle Knight,
Or unto lovely Lady doing wrong:
And thereunto a great long chaine he tight,° *tied*
With which he drew him forth, even in his own despight.[2]

9. I.e., gnashed his teeth.
1. Hercules, grandson of Alcaeus, needed all his wit and skill (and the help of his servant Iolaus) to slay the nine-headed Lernean Hydra, offspring of Typhon and Echidna (Hesiod, *Theogony* 313–15). See also Hyginus, *Genealogiae* 30.64, and Apollodorus, *Bibliotheca*. The association of Hydra with Hell appears in *Aeneid* 6.576–77.
2. I.e., in spite of his fury.

35

Like as whylome that strong Tirynthian swaine,[3]
Brought forth with him the dreadfull dog of hell,
Against his will fast bound in yron chaine,
And roring horribly, did him compell
To see the hatefull sunne, that he might tell
To griesly Pluto, what on earth was donne,
And to the other damnéd ghosts, which dwell
For aye in darkenesse, which day light doth shonne.
So led this Knight his captyve with like conquest wonne.

36

Yet greatly did the Beast repine at those
Straunge bands, whose like till then he never bore,
Ne ever any durst till then impose,
And chauffféd° inly, seeing now no more — *raged*
Him liberty was left aloud to rore:
Yet durst he not draw backe; nor once withstand
The provéd powre of noble Calidore,
But trembled underneath his mighty hand,
And like a fearefull dog him followed through the land.

37

Him through all Faery land he followed so,
As if he learnéd had obedience long,
That all the people where so he did go,
Out of their townes did round about him throng,
To see him leade that Beast in bondage strong,
And seeing it, much wondred at the sight;
And all such persons, as he earst did wrong,
Rejoycéd much to see his captive plight,
And much admyred[4] the Beast, but more admyred the Knight.

38

Thus was this Monster by the maystring might
Of doughty Calidore, supprest and tamed,
That never more he mote endammadge wight
With his vile tongue, which many had defamed,
And many causelesse causéd to be blamed:
So did he eeke long after this remaine,
Untill that, whether wicked fate so framed,

3. As the last of his twelve labors while serving Eurystheus, in Tiryns, Hercules forced the monstrous dog Cerberus, guardian of Hell-gate, into the upper world (*Iliad* 8.368; *Metamorphoses* 6.408–15).
4. I.e., wondered at.

Or fault of men, he broke his yron chaine,
And got into the world at liberty againe.

39

Thenceforth more mischiefe and more scath° he wrought — *harm*
To mortall men, then he had done before;
Ne ever could by any more° be brought — *again*
Into like bands, ne maystred any more:
Albe that long time after Calidore,
The good Sir Pelleas him tooke in hand,
And after him Sir Lamoracke of yore,[5]
And all his brethren borne in Britaine land;
Yet none of them could ever bring him into band.

40

So now he raungeth through the world againe,
And rageth sore in each degree and state;[6]
Ne any is, that may him now restraine,
He growen is so great and strong of late,
Barking and biting all that him doe bate,° — *attack*
Albe they worthy blame, or cleare of crime:
Ne spareth he most learnéd wits to rate,° — *scold*
Ne spareth he the gentle Poets rime,
But rends without regard of person or of time.

41

Ne may this homely verse, of many meanest,
Hope to escape his venemous despite,
More then my former writs,° all were they cleanest — *writings*
From blamefull blot, and free from all that wite,° — *blame*
With which some wicked tongues did it backebite,
And bring into a mighty Peres displeasure,[7]
That never so deservéd to endite.[8]
Therfore do you my rimes keep better measure,
And seeke to please, that now is counted wisemens threasure.

5. Sir Pelleas and Sir Lamoracke, knights of Arthur's Round Table, appear in Malory's *Morte d'Arthur*, but neither is there connected with the "questing beast."
6. I.e., in every rank and class of society.
7. Presumably Lord Burleigh, the queen's Lord Treasurer, whose displeasure with Spenser's earlier work the poet notices in IV.Pr.1.
8. I.e., that never deserved such censure.

Two Cantos of *Mutabilitie*:

WHICH, BOTH FOR FORME AND MATTER, APPEARE TO BE PARCELL OF SOME FOLLOWING BOOKE OF THE FAERIE QUEENE

(∴)

Under the Legend of Constancie.[1]

Canto VI

Proud Change (not pleasd, in mortall things,
beneath the Moone, to raigne)
Pretends, as well of Gods, as Men,
to be the Soveraine.

1

What man that sees the ever-whirling wheele
Of Change, the which all mortall things doth sway,° *rule*
But that therby doth find, and plainly feele,
How Mutability[2] in them doth play
Her cruell sports, to many mens decay?° *destruction*
Which that to all may better yet appeare,
I will rehearse that whylome° I heard say, *formerly*
How she at first her selfe began to reare,
Gainst all the Gods, and th'empire sought from them
to beare.° *take away*

2

But first, here falleth fittest to unfold
Her antique race and linage ancient,
As I have found it registred of old,
In Faery Land mongst records permanent:
She was, to weet,[3] a daughter by descent
Of those old Titans,[4] that did whylome strive
With Saturnes sonne for heavens regiment.° *rule*
Whom, though high Jove of kingdome did deprive,
Yet many of their stemme° long after did survive. *race*

1. That Spenser meant this fragment for *The Faerie Queene* is probable, if not quite certain, granted this claim by his Matthew Lownes (publisher of the 1609 folio), the stanzaic form, the division into cantos, and comments in vi.37. It is also possible to argue that Spenser meant "Constancie" as a sort of correction to Courtesy's slipperiness, just as Courtesy helps repair the iron harshness of Justice and so forth. Spenser would have heard of and perhaps read *De Constantia* (1583–84) by the great Netherlandish humanist, Justus Lipsius, whose subtitle says it is for times of public calamities.
2. The power of change, personified by Mutability, is not identical with that of time (cf. stanza 8), here imagined as itself subject to change (see vii.47). Astronomical discoveries in the Renaissance reinforced classical affirmations that decay is inevitable (e.g. Ovid, *Metamorphoses* 15.237–51, and Lucretius, *De Rerum Natura* 5); "the ever-whirling wheele of Change," though, also suggests Fortune's wheel.
3. I.e., in fact.
4. The Titans, offspring of Earth, rebelled against their father, Uranos (Sky); their leader Kronos (Saturn) castrated Uranos but was himself deposed by his own son Zeus (Jove); see stanza 27 and cf. Hesiod, *Theogony* 137–210.

3

And many of them, afterwards obtained
Great power of Jove, and high authority;
As Hecate, in whose almighty hand,
He plac't all rule and principality,
To be by her disposéd diversly,
To Gods, and men, as she them list° divide: *chose to*
And drad° Bellona,[5] that doth sound on hie *dreaded*
Warres and allarums unto Nations wide,
That makes both heaven and earth to tremble at her pride.

4

So likewise did this Titanesse aspire,
Rule and dominion to her selfe to gaine;
That as a Goddesse, men might her admire,° *wonder at*
And heavenly honours yield, as to them twaine.[6]
And first, on earth she sought it to obtaine;
Where she such proofe and sad° examples shewed *grievous*
Of her great power, to many ones great paine,
That not men onely (whom she soone subdewed)
But eke all other creatures, her bad dooings rewed.

5

For, she the face of earthly things so changed,
That all which Nature had establisht first
In good estate, and in meet° order ranged, *fitting*
She did pervert, and all their statutes burst:
And all the worlds faire frame (which none yet durst
Of Gods or men to alter or misguide)
She altered quite, and made them all accurst
That God had blest; and did at first provide
In that still happy state for ever to abide.

6

Ne shee the lawes of Nature onely brake,
But eke of Justice, and of Policie;° *government*
And wrong of right, and bad of good did make,
And death for life exchangéd foolishlie:
Since which, all living wights have learned to die,
And all this world is woxen° daily worse. *grown*
O pittious worke of Mutabilitie!
By which, we all are subject to that curse,
And death in stead of life have suckéd from our Nurse.[7]

5. The Roman goddess of war; in Spenser's *Visions of Bellay*, "Typhoeus sister" seems to be Bellona (the Glosse to "October" 115 identifies Bellona as Athena, but no mythographer thought Athena a Titan). *Hecate*: Hesiod (411–53) calls Hecate the only Titan favored by Zeus; mythographers associated her, as goddess of witches, with Persephone and Hades.
6. I.e., Hecate and Bellona.
7. Stanzas 5–6 associate the consequences of Mutability's ambition with those of the Fall.

7

And now, when all the earth she thus had brought
To her behest,° and thrallèd to her might, *bidding*
She gan to cast° in her ambitious thought, *resolve*
T'attempt the empire of the heavens hight,
And Jove himselfe to shoulder from his right.
And first, she past the region of the ayre,
And of the fire, whose substance thin and slight,
Made no resistance, ne could her contraire,° *withstand*
But ready passage to her pleasure did prepaire.

8

Thence, to the Circle of the Moone she clambe,[8]
Where Cynthia[9] raignes in everlasting glory,
To whose bright shining palace straight she came,
All fairely deckt with heavens goodly story;° *rows (of stars)*
Whose silver gates (by which there sate an hory
Old aged Sire, with hower-glasse in hand,
Hight Tyme) she entred, were he liefe or sory:[1]
Ne staide till she the highest stage° had scand,° *level / mounted to*
Where Cynthia did sit, that never still did stand.

9

Her sitting on an Ivory throne shee found,
Drawne of two steeds, th'one black, the other white,[2]
Environd with tenne thousand starres around,
That duly her attended day and night;
And by her side, there ran her Page, that hight
Vesper, whom we the Evening-starre intend:° *call*
That with his Torche, still twinkling like twylight,
Her lightened all the way where she should wend,
And joy to weary wandring travailers did lend:

10

That when the hardy Titanesse beheld
The goodly building of her Palace bright,
Made of the heavens substance, and up-held
With thousand Crystall pillors of huge hight,
Shee gan to burne in her ambitious spright,

8. I.e., climbed to the moon's sphere. Stanzas 8–15 recall Phaethon's disastrous ride across the heavens in the sun chariot of his father, Apollo; to save the earth, Jove killed him with a thunderbolt (*Metamorphoses* 2.1–400).
9. Goddess of the moon. Poets often associated Elizabeth with her, although the queen's motto "Semper Eadem"—"Always the Same"—seems to counter a lunar inconstancy, so this effort to eclipse Cynthia may have political resonance. Meyer (1983) deduces from a lunar eclipse on April 14, 1595, when the planets, positioned like the gods in this scene, "ran altogether" (stanza 15), that Spenser wrote this canto after that date.
1. I.e., whether he were willing or not.
2. Mythographers (e.g., Boccaccio, *Genealogiae* 4.16) say the moon has these horses because she shines sometimes by night and sometimes by day.

And t'envie her that in such glorie raigned.
Eftsoones she cast by force and tortious° might, *wrongful*
Her to displace; and to her selfe to have gained
The kingdome of the Night, and waters by her wained.° *moved*

11

Boldly she bid the Goddesse downe descend,
And let her selfe into that Ivory throne;
For, shee her selfe more worthy thereof wend,° *thought*
And better able it to guide alone:
Whether to men, whose fall she did bemone,
Or unto Gods, whose state she did maligne,° *envy*
Or to th'infernall Powers, her need give lone[3]
Of her faire light, and bounty most benigne,
Her selfe of all that rule shee deemèd most condigne.° *worthy*

12

But shee that had to her that soveraigne seat
By highest Jove assigned, therein to beare
Nights burning lamp, regarded not her threat,
Ne yielded ought for favour or for feare;
But with sterne countenaunce and disdainfull cheare,° *aspect*
Bending her hornèd browes, did put her back:
And boldly blaming her for comming there,
Bade her attonce from heavens coast to pack,
Or at her perill bide the wrathfull Thunders wrack.° *destruction*

13

Yet nathemore° the Giantesse forbare: *not at all*
But boldly preacing-on,° raught forth her hand *advancing*
To pluck her downe perforce° from off her chaire; *by force*
And there-with lifting up her golden wand,
Threatned to strike her if she did with-stand.
Where-at the starres, which round about her blazed,
And eke the Moones bright wagon, still did stand,
All beeing with so bold attempt amazed,
And on her uncouth° habit and sterne looke still gazed. *strange*

14

Mean-while, the lower World, which nothing knew
Of all that chauncèd here, was darkned quite;
And eke the heavens, and all the heavenly crew
Of happy wights, now unpurvaide° of light, *deprived*
Were much afraid, and wondred at that sight;
Fearing least Chaos broken had his chaine,
And brought againe on them eternall night:

3. I.e., she must give.

But chiefely Mercury, that next doth raigne,[4]
Ran forth in haste, unto the king of Gods to plaine.° *complain*

15

All ran together with a great out-cry,
To Joves faire Palace, fixt in heavens hight;
And beating at his gates full earnestly,
Gan call to him aloud with all their might,
To know what meant that suddaine lack of light.
The father of the Gods when this he heard,
Was troubled much at their so strange affright,
Doubting least Typhon[5] were againe upreared,
Or other his old foes, that once him sorely feared.° *frightened*

16

Eftsoones the sonne of Maia forth he sent
Downe to the Circle of the Moone, to knowe
The cause of this so strange astonishment,
And why shee did her wonted course forslowe;° *delay*
And if that any were on earth belowe
That did with charmes or Magick her molest,
Him to attache,° and downe to hell to throwe: *seize*
But, if from heaven it were, then to arrest
The Author, and him bring before his presence prest.° *immediately*

17

The wingd-foot God, so fast his plumes did beat,
That soone he came where-as the Titanesse
Was striving with faire Cynthia for her seat:
At whose strange sight, and haughty hardinesse,° *boldness*
He wondred much, and fearéd her no lesse.
Yet laying feare aside to doe his charge,° *assigned task*
At last, he bade her (with bold stedfastnesse)
Ceasse to molest the Moone to walke at large,[6]
Or come before high Jove, her dooings to discharge.° *account for*

18

And there-with-all, he on her shoulder laid
His snaky-wreathéd Mace,[7] whose awfull power
Doth make both Gods and hellish fiends affraid:
Where-at the Titanesse did sternely lower,° *scowl*
And stoutly answered, that in evill hower
He from his Jove such message to her brought,

4. Mercury (Hermes) was the son of Maia (cf. stanza 16); in Ptolemaic astronomy, the planet Mercury's sphere was next beyond the moon's.
5. The giant Typhon (also called Typhoeus) rebelled against Zeus, who then hurled him down to Tartarus (or, some said, piled Mount Aetna on him).
6. I.e., cease to hinder the moon's free movement.
7. I.e., the caduceus. Cf. II.xii.41.

To bid her leave faire Cynthias silver bower;
Sith shee his Jove and him esteeméd nought,
No more then Cynthia's selfe; but all their kingdoms sought.

19

The Heavens Herald staid not to reply,
But past away, his doings to relate
Unto his Lord; who now in th'highest sky,
Was placéd in his principall Estate,[8]
With all the Gods about him congregate:
To whom when Hermes had his message told,
It did them all exceedingly amate,° *dismay*
Save Jove; who, changing nought his count'nance bold,
Did unto them at length these speeches wise unfold;

20

"Harken to mee awhile yee heavenly Powers;
Ye may remember since th'Earths curséd seed[9]
Sought to assaile the heavens eternall towers,
And to us all exceeding feare did breed:
But how we then defeated all their deed,
Yee all doe knowe, and them destroiéd quite;
Yet not so quite, but that there did succeed
An off-spring of their bloud, which did alite
Upon the fruitfull earth, which doth us yet despite.° *disdain*

21

"Of that bad seed is this bold woman bred,
That now with bold presumption doth aspire
To thrust faire Phoebe from her silver bed,
And eke our selves from heavens high Empire,
If that her might were match to her desire:
Wherefore, it now behoves us to advise° *consider*
What way is best to drive her to retire;
Whether by open force, or counsell wise,
Areed° ye sonnes of God, as best ye can devise." *advise*

22

So having said, he ceast; and with his brow
(His black eye-brow, whose doomefull dreaded beck[1]
Is wont to wield the world unto his vow,° *will*
And even the highest Powers of heaven to check)
Made signe to them in their degrees to speake:
Who straight gan cast° their counsell grave and wise. *consider*

8. I.e., enthroned in his regal aspect.
9. I.e., the giants, who piled Mount Pelion on Mount Ossa to reach Jove (cf. *Metamorphoses* 1.156–62). Spenser seldom distinguishes between Titans and giants, representatives of rebellion against all established order from the cosmological to the political.
1. I.e., his feared nod of command.

Meane-while, th'Earths daughter, thogh she nought did reck
Of Hermes message; yet gan now advise,
What course were best to take in this hot bold emprize.° *undertaking*

23

Eftsoones she thus resolved; that whil'st the Gods
(After returne of Hermes Embassie)
Were troubled, and amongst themselves at ods,
Before they could new counsels re-allie,° *form again*
To set upon them in that extasie,° *astonishment*
And take what fortune time and place would lend:
So, forth she rose, and through the purest sky
To Joves high Palace straight cast° to ascend, *resolved*
To prosecute her plot: Good on-set boads good end.

24

Shee there arriving, boldly in did pass;
Where all the Gods she found in counsell close,° *secret*
All quite unarmed, as then their manner was.
At sight of her they suddaine all arose,
In great amaze, ne wist what way to chose.
But Jove, all fearelesse, forc't them to aby;° *remain*
And in his soveraine throne, gan straight dispose° *arrange*
Himselfe more full of grace and Majestie,
That mote encheare° his friends, and foes mote terrifie. *cheer*

25

That, when the haughty Titanesse beheld,
All° were she fraught with pride and impudence, *although*
Yet with the sight thereof was almost queld;
And inly quaking, seemed as reft of sense,
And voyd of speech in that drad° audience; *dread*
Until that Jove himself, her selfe bespake:
"Speake thou fraile woman, speake with confidence,
Whence art thou, and what doost thou here now make?° *intend*
What idle errand hast thou, earths mansion to forsake?"

26

Shee, halfe confuséd with his great commaund,
Yet gathering spirit of her natures pride,
Him boldly answered thus to his demaund:
"I am a daughter, by the mothers side,
Of her that is Grand-mother magnifide° *glorified*
Of all the Gods, great Earth, great Chaos child.[2]
But by the fathers (be it not envide)

2. Earth is the child of Chaos in Hesiod, *Theogony* 116; Boccaccio terms her "great mother" in *Genealogia* 1.8.

I greater am in bloud (whereon I build)
Then all the Gods, though wrongfully from heaven exiled.

27

"For Titan (as ye all acknowledge must)
Was Saturnes elder brother by birth-right;
Both, sonnes of Uranus: but by unjust
And guilefull meanes, through Corybantes slight,° *trickery*
The younger thrust the elder from his right:[3]
Since which, thou Jove, injuriously hast held
The Heavens rule from Titans sonnes by might;
And them to hellish dungeons downe hast feld:
Witnesse ye Heavens the truth of all that I have teld."

28

Whilst she thus spake, the Gods that gave good eare
To her bold words, and markéd well her grace,
Beeing of stature tall as any there
Of all the Gods, and beautifull of face,
As any of the Goddesses in place,
Stood all astonied, like a sort° of Steeres; *herd*
Mongst whom, some beast of strange and forraine race,
Unwares° is chaunc't, far straying from his peeres: *unexpectedly*
So did their ghastly gaze bewray° their hidden feares. *reveal*

29

Till having pauzed awhile, Jove thus bespake;
"Will never mortall thoughts ceasse to aspire,
In this bold sort, to Heaven claime to make,
And touch celestiall seates with earthly mire?
I would have thought, that bold Procrustes hire,° *reward*
Or Typhons fall, or proud Ixions paine,
Or great Prometheus,[4] tasting of our ire,
Would have suffized, the rest for to restraine;
And warned all men by their example to refraine:

30

"But now, this off-scum of that curséd fry,[5]
Dare to renew the like bold enterprize,

3. According to Renaissance mythographers, Titan (not normally found in older classical mythology) agreed to abdicate in favor of his younger brother, Kronos (Saturn), on condition that Saturn would swallow his own children and so assure Titan's eventual return to power (Comes 2.1, 6.20). But when Saturn's wife, Rhea, bore Zeus, she fooled her husband into swallowing a stone while her attendants, the Corybantes, beat on shields to drown out the baby's cries. "The younger thrust the elder from his right," though applicable to Saturn and Titan, refers primarily to the later overthrow of Saturn by Zeus. The implications are intriguing, for England, like Olympus, was ruled by a dynasty basing its claim partly on the right of conquest.

4. The robber Procrustes ("the stretcher") made guests fit his bed by cutting or stretching their limbs; Theseus destroyed him. On Typhon see stanza 15. For trying to rape Hera (Juno), Ixion was bound in Hades to a whirling wheel. Prometheus stole fire from heaven as a gift to mortals; Jove bound him to a cliff, where a vulture daily consumed his liver (it grew again at night). See Ovid 7.438, 3.303, 4.461, and Hesiod, *Theogony* 521–25.

5. I.e., Mutability, this latest example of rebellious presumption.

And chalenge th'heritage of this our skie;
Whom what should hinder, but that we likewise
Should handle as the rest of her allies,
And thunder-drive to hell?" With that, he shooke
His Nectar-deawéd locks, with which the skyes
And all the world beneath for terror quooke,° *quaked*
And eft° his burning levin-brond° in hand he tooke. *then / lightning bolt*

31

But, when he lookéd on her lovely face,
In which, faire beames of beauty did appeare,
That could the greatest wrath soone turne to grace
(Such sway° doth beauty even in Heaven beare) *power*
He staide his hand: and having changed his cheare,° *mood*
He thus againe in milder wise began;
"But ah! if Gods should strive with flesh yfere,° *together*
Then shortly should the progeny of Man
Be rooted out, if Jove should doe still° what he can.[6] *always*

32

"But thee faire Titans child, I rather weene,° *suppose*
Through some vaine errour or inducement light,
To see that° mortall eyes have never seene; *that which*
Or through ensample of thy sisters might,
Bellona; whose great glory thou doost spight,° *envy*
Since thou hast seene her dreadfull power belowe,
Mongst wretched men (dismaide with her affright)[7]
To bandie Crownes, and Kingdomes to bestowe:
And sure thy worth, no lesse then hers doth seem to showe.

33

"But wote° thou this, thou hardy Titanesse, *know*
That not the worth of any living wight
May challenge ought in Heavens interesse;[8]
Much lesse the Title of old Titans Right:
For, we by Conquest of our soveraine might,
And by eternall doome of Fates decree,
Have wonne the Empire of the Heavens bright;
Which to our selves we hold, and to whom wee
Shall worthy deeme partakers of our blisse to bee.

34

"Then ceasse thy idle claime thou foolish gerle,
And seeke by grace and goodnesse to obtaine
That place from which by folly Titan fell;

6. Psalms 78.38–39: "Yea, many a time turned he his anger away, and did not stir up all his wrath. For he remembered that they were but flesh. . . ."
7. I.e., terror of her.
8. I.e., may lay claim to any part of heaven's dominion or title.

There-to thou maist perhaps, if so thou faine° *desire*
Have Jove thy gratious Lord and Soveraigne."
So, having said, she thus to him replide;
"Ceasse Saturnes sonne, to seeke by proffers vaine
Of idle hopes t'allure mee to thy side,
For to betray my Right, before I have it tride.

35

"But thee, O Jove, no equall° Judge I deeme *impartial*
Of my desert, or of my dewfull° Right; *due*
That in thine owne behalfe maist partiall seeme:
But to the highest him, that is behight
Father of Gods and men by equall might;[9]
To weet, the God of Nature, I appeale."
There-at Jove wexéd wroth, and in his spright
Did inly grudge, yet did it well conceale;
And bade Dan Phoebus Scribe her Appellation° seale. *appeal*

36

Eftsoones the time and place appointed were,
Where all, both heavenly Powers, and earthly wights,
Before great Natures presence should appeare,
For triall of their Titles and best Rights:
That was, to weet, upon the highest hights
Of Arlo-hill[1] (Who knowes not Arlo-hill?)
That is the highest head (in all mens sights)
Of my old father Mole, whom Shepheards quill
Renownéd hath with hymnes fit for a rurall skill.

37

And, were it not ill fitting for this file,° *recital*
To sing of hilles and woods, mongst warres and Knights,
I would abate the sternenesse of my stile,
Mongst these sterne stounds° to mingle soft delights; *clashes*
And tell how Arlo through Dianaes spights
(Beeing of old the best and fairest Hill
That was in all this holy-Islands hights)
Was made the most unpleasant, and most ill.
Meane while, O Clio, lend Calliope thy quill.[2]

38

Whylome,° when Ireland florishéd in fame *formerly*
Of wealths and goodnesse, far above the rest

9. I.e., equally powerful over gods as over men. The god of nature, here described as masculine, appears in vii.5, as Dame Nature; "Whether she man or woman inly were" is uncertain.
1. Galtymore, a peak in the mountain range near Spenser's estate in Ireland; it overlooked the "Golden Vale" of Aherlow. In the person of the shepherd Colin, Spenser mentions "Old father Mole . . . that mountain gray" in *Colin Clouts Come Home Againe* 56–59, 104–15.
2. I.e., let Calliope, borrowing the pen of Clio, Muse of history, tell the story of Faunus and Molanna.

Of all that beare the British Islands name,[3]
The Gods then used (for pleasure and for rest)
Oft to resort there-to, when seemed them best:
But none of all there-in more pleasure found,
Then Cynthia;[4] that is soveraine Queene profest° *acknowledged*
Of woods and forrests, which therein abound,
Sprinkled with wholsom waters, more then most on ground.

39

But mongst them all, as fittest for her game,° *recreation*
Either for chace of beasts with hound or boawe,
Or for to shroude in shade from Phoebus flame,
Or bathe in fountaines that doe freshly flowe,
Or from high hilles, or from the dales belowe,
She chose this Arlo; where shee did resort
With all her Nymphes enrangéd on a rowe,
With whom the woody Gods did oft consort:
For, with the Nymphes, the Satyres love to play and sport.

40

Amongst the which, there was a Nymph that hight
Molanna;[5] daughter of old father Mole,
And sister unto Mulla,[6] faire and bright:
Unto whose bed false Bregog whylome stole,
That Shepheard Colin dearely° did condole, *earnestly*
And made her lucklesse loves well knowne to be.
But this Molanna, were she not so shole,° *shallow*
Were no lesse faire and beautifull then shee:
Yet as she is, a fairer flood may no man see.

41

For, first, she springs out of two marble Rocks,
On which, a grove of Oakes high mounted growes,
That as a girlond seemes to deck the locks
Of som faire Bride, brought forth with pompous° *magnificent*
showes
Out of her bowre,° that many flowers strowes: *chamber*
So, through the flowry Dales she tumbling downe,
Through many woods, and shady coverts° flowes *thickets*
(That on each side her silver channell crowne)
Till to the Plaine she come, whose Valleyes shee doth drowne.

3. Spenser observes in *A Vewe of the Present State of Irelande* that "it is Certaine that Irelande hathe had the use of lettres verye Ancientlye and longe before Englande" (1246–47).
4. I.e., Diana, goddess of the forest.
5. The river Behanna, which rises near Galtymore and eventually joins the Funsheon ("Fanchin" in stanza 44).
6. The river Awbeg; it and the Bregoge flowed by Spenser's estate at Kilcolman. On Mulla and Bregog (Irish, "false"), see *Colin Clouts Come Home Againe* 104–55.

42

In her sweet streames, Diana uséd oft
(After her sweatie chace and toilesome play)
To bathe her selfe; and after, on the soft
And downy grasse, her dainty limbes to lay
In covert° shade, where none behold her may: *secret*
For, much she hated sight of living eye.
Foolish God Faunus, though full many a day
He saw her clad, yet longéd foolishly
To see her naked mongst her Nymphes in privity.[7]

43

No way he found to compasse° his desire. *accomplish*
But to corrupt Molanna, this her maid,
Her to discover for some secret hire:° *reward*
So, her with flattering words he first assaid;
And after, pleasing gifts for her purvaid,° *provided*
Queene-apples,[8] and red Cherries from the tree,
With which he her alluréd and betraid,
To tell what time he might her Lady see
When she her selfe did bathe, that he might secret° bee. *hidden*

44

There-to hee promist, if she would him pleasure
With this small boone, to quit° her with a better; *repay*
To weet, that where-as she had out of measure
Long loved the Fanchin,[9] who by nought did set her,[1]
That he would undertake, for this to get her
To be his Love, and of him likéd well:
Besides all which, he vowed to be her debter
For many moe good turnes then he would tell;
The least of which, this little pleasure should excell.

45

The simple maid did yield to him anone;° *at once*
And eft him placéd where he close might view
That° never any saw, save onely one; *that which*
Who, for his hire to so foole-hardy dew,
Was of his hounds devoured in Hunters hew.[2]
Tho,° as her manner was on sunny day, *then*

7. This episode combines Irish folklore with classical myth, notably the tale of Actaeon, who, while out hunting, inadvertently spied Diana bathing with her nymphs and, turned into a stag by the goddess, was chased and torn apart by his hounds (*Metamorphoses* 3.138–252); and of Arethusa, who, thanks to Diana, escaped the river god Alpheus by becoming a stream that plunges underground to arise again in Sicily (*Metamorphoses* 5.572–641, where the story is told by Calliope; others add that Alpheus follows and rejoins Arethusa).
8. A kind of apple with red flesh; or perhaps a quince.
9. The river Funsheon.
1. I.e., who cared nothing for her.
2. I.e., who, deservedly rewarded for his foolhardiness, was devoured by his hounds in the slaughter that concludes the hunt.

Diana, with her Nymphes about her, drew
To this sweet spring; where, doffing her array,
She bathed her lovely limbes, for Jove a likely pray.

46

There Faunus saw that pleaséd much his eye,
And made his hart to tickle in his brest,
That for great joy of some-what he did spy,
He could him not containe in silent rest;
But breaking forth in laughter, loud profest
His foolish thought. A foolish Faune indeed,
That couldst not hold thy selfe so° hidden blest, *thus*
But wouldest needs thine owne conceit areed.° *make known*
Babblers unworthy been of so divine a meed.° *reward*

47

The Goddesse, all abashéd with that noise,
In haste forth started from the guilty brooke;
And running straight where-as she heard his voice,
Enclosed the bush about, and there him tooke,
Like darréd° Larke; not daring up to looke *terrified*
On her whose sight before so much he sought.
Thence, forth they drew him by the hornes, and shooke
Nigh all to peeces, that they left him nought;
And then into the open light they forth him brought.

48

Like as an huswife, that with busie care
Thinks of her Dairie to make wondrous gaine,
Finding where-as some wicked beast unware° *unexpectedly*
That breakes into her Dayr'house, there doth draine
Her creaming pannes, and frustrate all her paine;
Hath in some snare or gin° set close behind, *trap*
Entrappéd him, and caught into her traine,° *snare*
Then thinkes what punishment were best assigned,
And thousand deathes deviseth in her vengefull mind:

49

So did Diana and her maydens all
Use silly Faunus, now within their baile:° *custody*
They mocke and scorne him, and him foule miscall;
Some by the nose him pluckt, some by the taile,
And by his goatish beard some did him haile:° *pull*
Yet he (poore soule) with patience all did beare;
For, nought against their wils might countervaile:° *resist*
Ne ought he said what ever he did heare;
But hanging downe his head, did like a Mome° appeare. *fool*

50

At length, when they had flouted him their fill,
They gan to cast what penaunce him to give.
Some would have gelt° him, but that same would spill° — *castrated*, *destroy*
The Wood-gods breed, which must for ever live:
Others would through the river him have drive,
And duckéd deepe: but that seemed penaunce light;
But most agreed and did this sentence give,
Him in Deares skin to clad; and in that plight,
To hunt him with their hounds, him selfe save how hee might.

51

But Cynthia's selfe, more angry then the rest,
Thought not enough, to punish him in sport,
And of her shame to make a gamesome jest;
But gan examine him in straighter° sort, — *stricter*
Which of her Nymphes, or other close consort,[3]
Him thither brought, and her to him betraid?
He, much affeard, to her confesséd short,° — *soon*
That 'twas Molanna which her so bewraid.° — *betrayed*
Then all attonce their hands upon Molanna laid.

52

But him (according as they had decreed)
With a Deeres-skin they covered, and then chast
With all their hounds that after him did speed;
But he more speedy, from them fled more fast
Then any Deere: so sore him dread aghast.° — *terrified*
They after followed all with shrill out-cry,
Shouting as they the heavens would have brast:° — *burst*
That all the woods and dales where he did flie,
Did ring againe, and loud reeccho to the skie.

53

So they him followed till they weary were;
When, back returning to Molann' againe,
They, by commaund'ment of Diana, there
Her whelmed with stones.[4] Yet Faunus (for her paine)° — *trouble*
Of her beloved Fanchin did obtaine,
That her he would receive unto his bed.
So now her waves passe through a pleasant Plaine,
Till with the Fanchin she her selfe doe wed,
And (both combined) themselves in one faire river spred.

3. I.e., secret companion.
4. Thus accounting for the shallowness of the river (stanza 40).

54

Nath'lesse,° Diana, full of indignation, *nonetheless*
Thence-forth abandoned her delicious brooke;
In whose sweet streame, before that bad occasion,
So much delight to bathe her limbes she tooke:
Ne onely her, but also quite forsooke.
All those faire forrests about Arlo hid,
And all that Mountaine, which doth over-looke
The richest champian that may else be rid,[5]
And the faire Shure,[6] in which are thousand Salmons bred.

55

Them all, and all that she so deare did way,° *esteem*
Thence-forth she left; and parting from the place,
There-on an heavy haplesse curse did lay,
To weet, that Wolves, where she was wont to space,° *roam*
Should harboured be, and all those Woods deface,
And Thieves should rob and spoile that Coast around.
Since which, those Woods, and all that
goodly Chase,° *hunting ground*
Doth to this day with Wolves and Thieves abound:
Which too-too true that lands in-dwellers since have found.[7]

Canto VII

Pealing,° from Jove, to Natur's Bar, *appealing*
bold Alteration[1] pleades
Large Evidence: but Nature soone
her righteous Doome° areads.° *judgment / delivers*

1

Ah! whither doost thou now thou greater Muse[2]
Me from these woods and pleasing forrests bring?
And my fraile spirit (that dooth oft refuse
This too high flight, unfit for her weake wing)
Lift up aloft, to tell of heavens King
(Thy soveraine Sire) his fortunate successe,
And victory, in bigger° noates to sing, *louder*
Which he obtained against that Titanesse,
That him of heavens Empire sought to dispossesse.

2

Yet sith I needs must follow thy behest,
Doe thou my weaker° wit with skill inspire, *too weak*

5. I.e., the richest plain to be seen anywhere.
6. The river Suir, which flows through the Vale of Aherlow.
7. Cf. *Colin Clouts Come Home Againe* 312–19.
1. I.e., Mutability.
2. Probably Clio, but see I proem 2, note 3.

Fit for this turne; and in my feeble brest
Kindle fresh sparks of that immortall fire,
Which learnéd minds inflameth with desire
Of heavenly things: for, who but thou alone,
That art yborne of heaven and heavenly Sire,
Can tell things doen in heaven so long ygone;
So farre past memory of man that may be knowne.

3

Now, at the time that was before agreed,
The Gods assembled all on Arlo hill;
As well those that are sprung of heavenly seed,
As those that all the other world[3] doe fill,
And rule both sea and land unto their will:
Onely th'infernall Powers might not appeare;
Aswell for horror of their count'naunce ill,
As for th'unruly fiends which they did feare;° *keep in awe*
Yet Pluto and Proserpina[4] were present there.

4

And thither also came all other creatures,
What-ever life or motion doe retaine,
According to their sundry kinds of features;
That Arlo scarsly could them all containe;
So full they filléd every hill and Plaine:
And had not Natures Sergeant (that is Order)[5]
Them well disposéd by his busie paine,° *care*
And raungéd farre abroad in every border,
They would have causéd much confusion and disorder.

5

Then forth issewed (great goddesse) great dame Nature,[6]
With goodly port° and gracious Majesty; *bearing*
Being far greater and more tall of stature
Then any of the gods or Powers on hie:
Yet certes by her face and physnomy,° *countenance*
Whether she man or woman inly were,
That could not any creature well descry:

3. I.e., the earth.
4. Rulers of the underworld.
5. Order is Nature's sergeant, or chief executive attendant, whereas Mutability opposes every law of Nature (vi.5). Significantly, when the seasons and months appear as witnesses at Mutability's own request, they come in proper order and garb; see S. Hawkins, "Mutabilitie and the Cycle of the Months," in W. Nelson, ed., *Form and Convention in the Poetry of Edmund Spenser* (New York, 1961) 76–102.
6. For his "Great dame Nature" Spenser drew on a number of classical and medieval writers (e.g., Plutarch, Boethius, and Jean de Meun), but she chiefly recalls "this noble goddesse Nature" in Chaucer's *Parliament of Fowls* and, probably, "Natura" in the twelfth-century poem *De Planctu Naturae*, by Alain de Lille [Alanus de Insulis], which Chaucer himself cites. Spenser notes both works in stanza 9. The "Nature" to whom all three refer is the natural creative force itself (what philosophers called *Natura naturans*), not the created natural world. Thus she is taller than other gods; she is veiled (to protect mortals from her face's terror or beauty, and perhaps also because we cannot know Nature herself, only her effects); and she encompasses youth and age, being and becoming.

For, with a veile that wimpled° every where, *covered in folds*
Her head and face was hid, that mote to none appeare.

6

That some doe say was so by skill devized,
To hide the terror of her uncouth° hew, *strange*
From mortall eyes that should be sore agrized;° *horrified*
For that her face did like a Lion shew,
That eye of wight could not indure to view:
But others tell that it so beautious was,
And round about such beames of splendor threw,
That it the Sunne a thousand times did pass,° *surpass*
Ne could be seene, but° like an image in a glass. *except*

7

That well may seemen true: for, well I weene
That this same day, when she on Arlo sat,
Her garment was so bright and wondrous sheene,° *fair*
That my fraile wit cannot devize to what
It to compare, nor finde like stuffe to that,
As those three sacred Saints,[7] though else most wise,
Yet on mount Thabor quite their wits forgat,
When they their glorious Lord in strange disguise
Transfigured sawe; his garments so did daze their eyes.

8

In a fayre Plaine upon an equall° Hill, *level*
She placéd was in a pavilion;
Not such as Craftes-men by their idle° skill *vain*
Are wont for Princes states° to fashion: *canopies*
But th'earth her self of her owne motion,
Out of her fruitfull bosome made to growe
Most dainty trees; that, shooting up anon,
Did seeme to bow their bloosming° heads full lowe, *blossoming*
For homage unto her, and like a throne did shew.° *appear*

9

So hard it is for any living wight,
All her array and vestiments to tell,
That old Dan Geffrey (in whose gentle spright
The pure well head of Poesie did dwell)
In his *Foules parley* durst not with it mel,° *meddle*
But it transferd° to Alane,[8] who he thought *referred*
Had in his *Plaint of kindes* described it well:
Which who will read set forth so as it ought,
Go seek he out that Alane where he may be sought.

7. Peter, James, and John, to whom Jesus appeared in transfigured brightness: "his face did shine as the sun, and his raiment was white as the light" (Matthew 17.1–8).
8. Alain de Lille; *Dan Geffrey*: i.e., Master Geoffrey Chaucer.

10

And all the earth far underneath her feete
Was dight with flowres, that voluntary grew
Out of the ground, and sent forth odours sweet,
Tenne thousand mores° of sundry sent and hew, *plants*
That might delight the smell, or please the view:
The which, the Nymphes, from all the brooks thereby
Had gathered, which they at her foot-stoole threw;
That richer seemed then any tapestry,
That Princes bowres adorne with painted imagery.

11

And Mole himselfe, to honour her the more,
Did deck himself in freshest faire attire,
And his high head, that seemeth alwaies hore
With hardned frosts of former winters ire,
He with an Oaken girlond now did tire,° *attire*
As if the love of some new Nymph late seene,
Had in him kindled youthfull fresh desire,
And made him change his gray attire to greene;
Ah gentle Mole! such joyance hath thee well beseene.° *provided*

12

Was never so great joyance since the day,
That all the gods whylome assembled were,
On Haemus hill[9] in their divine array,
To celebrate the solemne bridall cheare,
Twixt Peleus, and dame Thetis pointed° there; *appointed*
Where Phoebus self, that god of Poets hight,
They say did sing the spousall hymne full cleere,
That all the gods were ravisht with delight
Of his celestiall song, and Musicks wondrous might.

13

This great Grandmother of all creatures bred
Great Nature, ever young yet full of eld,° *age*
Still mooving, yet unmovéd from her sted;° *place*
Unseene of any, yet of all beheld;
Thus sitting in her throne as I have teld,
Before her came dame Mutabilitie;
And being lowe before her presence feld,° *prostrated*
With meek obaysance and humilitie,
Thus gan her plaintif Plea, with words to amplifie;

9. The marriage of Peleus and Thetis took place on Mount Pelion; the opening lines in Ovid's account perhaps misled Spenser (cf. *Metamorphoses* 11.229–30).

14

"To thee O greatest goddesse, onely° great, *uniquely*
An humble suppliant loe, I lowely fly
Seeking for Right, which I of thee entreat;
Who Right to all dost deale indifferently,° *impartially*
Damning all Wrong and tortious° Injurie, *wrongful*
Which any of thy creatures doe to other
(Oppressing them with power, unequally)° *unjustly*
Sith of them all thou are the equall mother,
And knittest each to each, as brother unto brother.

15

"To thee therefore of this same Jove I plaine,
And of his fellow gods that faine° to be, *pretend*
That challenge° to themselves the whole worlds raign; *claim*
Of which, the greatest part is due to me,
And heaven it selfe by heritage in Fee[1]
For, heaven and earth I both alike do deeme,
Sith heaven and earth are both alike to thee;
And, gods no more then men thou doest esteeme:
For, even the gods to thee, as men to gods do seeme.

16

"Then weigh, O soveraigne goddesse, by what right
These gods do claime the worlds whole soverainty;
And that° is onely dew unto thy might *that which*
Arrogate to themselves ambitiously:
As for the gods owne principality,° *sovereignty*
Which Jove usurpes unjustly; that to be
My heritage, Jove's self cannot deny,
From my great Grandsire Titan, unto mee,
Derived by dew descent; as is well knowen to thee.

17

"Yet mauger° Jove, and all his gods beside, *despite*
I doe possesse the worlds most regiment;° *rule*
As, if ye please it into parts divide,
And every parts inholders° to convent,° *tenants / convene*
Shall to your eyes appeare incontinent.° *at once*
And first, the Earth (great mother of us all)
That only seems unmoved and permanent,
And unto Mutability not thrall;
Yet is she changed in part, and eeke in generall.[2]

1. I.e., in fee simple, conferring absolute rule.
2. Mutability's arguments and wording in stanzas 17–25 echo Lucretius's *De Rerum Natura* 5, and (particularly) Ovid's *Metamorphoses* 15.

18

"For, all that from her springs, and is ybredde,
How-ever fayre it flourish for a time,
Yet see we soone decay; and, being dead,
To turne again unto their earthly slime:
Yet, out of their decay and mortall crime,° *corruption*
We daily see new creatures to arize;
And of their Winter spring another Prime,° *spring*
Unlike in forme, and changed by strange disguise:
So turne they still about, and change in restlesse wise.

19

"As for her tenants; that is, man and beasts,
The beasts we daily see massacred dy,
As thralls and vassalls unto mens beheasts:
And men themselves doe change continually,
From youth to eld, from wealth to poverty,
From good to bad, from bad to worst of all.
Ne doe their bodies only flit and fly:
But eeke their minds (which they immortall call)
Still change and vary thoughts, as new occasions fall.

20

"Ne is the water in more constant case;
Whether those same on high, or these belowe.
For, th'Ocean moveth stil, from place to place;
And every River still doth ebbe and flowe:
Ne any Lake, that seems most still and slowe,
Ne Poole so small, that can his smoothnesse holde,
When any winde doth under heaven blowe;
With which, the clouds are also tost and rolled;
Now like great hills; and, streight,° like sluces, *immediately*
them unfold.° *open*

21

"So likewise are all watry living wights
Still tost, and turnéd, with continuall change,
Never abyding in their stedfast plights.° *conditions*
The fish, still floting, doe at randon° range, *random*
And never rest; but evermore exchange
Their dwelling places, as the streames them carrie:
Ne have the watry foules a certaine grange,° *abode*
Wherein to rest, ne in one stead° do tarry; *place*
But flitting still doe flie, and still their places vary.

22

"Next is the Ayre: which who feels not by sense
(For, of all sense it is the middle meane)[3]
To flit still? and, with subtill influence
Of his thin spirit, all creatures to maintaine,
In state of life? O weake life! that does leane
On thing so tickle° as th'unsteady ayre; *uncertain*
Which every howre is changed, and altred cleane° *altogether*
With every blast that bloweth fowle or faire:
The faire doth it prolong; the fowle doth it impaire.

23

"Therein the changes infinite beholde,
Which to her creatures every minute chaunce;
Now, boyling hot: streight, friezing deadly cold:
Now, faire sun-shine, that makes all skip and daunce:
Streight, bitter storms and balefull countenance,
That makes them all to shiver and to shake:
Rayne, hayle, and snowe do pay them sad penance,
And dreadfull thunder-claps (that make them quake)
With flames and flashing lights that thousand changes make.

24

"Last is the fire: which, though it live for ever,
Ne can be quenchéd quite; yet, every day,
We see his parts, so soone as they do sever,
To lose their heat, and shortly to decay;
So, makes himself his owne consuming pray.
Ne any living creatures doth he breed:
But all, that are of others bredd, doth slay;
And, with their death, his cruell life dooth feed;
Nought leaving but their barren ashes, without seede.

25

"Thus, all these fower (the which the ground-work bee
Of all the world, and of all living wights)
To thousand sorts of Change we subject see:
Yet are they changed (by other wondrous slights)° *devices*
Into themselves, and lose their native mights;
The Fire to Aire, and th' Ayre to Water sheere,° *clear*
And Water into Earth: yet Water fights
With Fire, and Aire with Earth approaching neere:
Yet all are in one body, and as one appeare.[4]

3. I.e., the medium (for all the senses).
4. These views derive from Ovid's doctrine of the transmutation of elements (*Metamorphoses* 15.237–49), a position rejected by Lucretius (*De Rerum Natura* 1.780–844).

26

"So, in them all raignes Mutabilitie;
How-ever these, that Gods themselves do call,
Of them doe claime the rule and soverainty:
As, Vesta, of the fire aethereall;[5]
Vulcan, of this, with us so usuall;
Ops,[6] of the earth; and Juno of the Ayre;
Neptune, of Seas; and Nymphes, of Rivers all.
For, all those Rivers to me subject are:
And all the rest, which they usurp, be all my share.

27

"Which to approven° true, as I have told, *prove*
Vouchsafe, O goddesse, to thy presence call
The rest which doe the world in being hold:
As, times and seasons of the yeare that fall:
Of all the which, demand in generall,
Or judge thy selfe, by verdit° of thine eye, *verdict*
Whether to me they are not subject all."
Nature did yeeld thereto; and by-and-by,° *immediately*
Bade Order call them all, before her Majesty.

28

So, forth issewed the Seasons of the yeare;[7]
First, lusty Spring, all dight in leaves of flowres
That freshly budded and new bloosmes did beare
(In which a thousand birds had built their bowres
That sweetly sung, to call forth Paramours):
And in his hand a javelin he did beare,
And on his head (as fit for warlike stoures)° *encounters*
A guilt engraven morion° he did weare; *helmet*
That as some did him love, so others did him feare.

29

Then came the jolly Sommer, being dight
In a thin silken cassock° coloured greene, *cloak*
That was unlynéd all, to be more light:
And on his head a girlond well beseene° *ordered*
He wore, from which as he had chaufféd° been *heated*
The sweat did drop; and in his hand he bore
A boawe and shaftes, as he in forrest greene
Had hunted late the Libbard° or the Bore, *leopard*
And now would bathe his limbes, with labor heated sore.

5. I.e., of celestial fire. *Vesta*: Roman goddess of the hearth and, more generally, of consecrated fire; Aeneas transported from Troy the eternal flame sacred to her (*Aeneid* 2.296).
6. Roman goddess of fertility and the ground. Mythographers equated her with the Greek Rhea, consort of Kronos (Saturn) and mother of the Olympian gods.
7. The seasons here owe something to *Metamorphoses* 2.25–30 and 15.199–213, but the procession has the Renaissance style described by A. Fowler, *Triumphal Forms* (Cambridge, 1970).

30

Then came the Autumne all in yellow clad,
As though he joyéd in his plentious store,
Laden with fruits that made him laugh, full glad
That he had banisht hunger, which to-fore° *formerly*
Had by the belly oft him pinchéd sore.
Upon his head a wreath that was enrold° *enfolded*
With eares of corne, of every sort he bore:
And in his hand a sickle he did holde,
To reape the ripened fruits the which the earth had yold.° *yielded*

31

Lastly, came Winter cloathed all in frize,° *rough cloth*
Chattering his teeth for cold that did him chill,
Whil'st on his hoary beard his breath did freese;
And the dull drops that from his purpled bill° *nose*
As from a limbeck° did adown distill. *alembic*
In his right hand a tippéd staffe he held,
With which his feeble steps he stayéd still:° *continually*
For, he was faint with cold, and weak with eld;
That scarse his looséd limbes he hable was to weld.° *move*

32

These, marching softly, thus in order went,
And after them, the Monthes all riding came;[8]
First, sturdy March with brows full sternly bent,
And arméd strongly, rode upon a Ram,
The same which over Hellespontus swam:
Yet in his hand a spade he also hent,° *grasped*
And in a bag all sorts of seeds ysame,° *together*
Which on the earth he strowéd as he went,
And fild her womb with fruitfull hope of nourishment.

33

Next came fresh Aprill full of lustyhed,° *vigor*
And wanton as a Kid whose home new buds:
Upon a Bull[9] he rode, the same which led
Europa floting through th'Argolick fluds:
His hornes were gilden all with golden studs,
And garnishéd with garlonds goodly dight
Of all the fairest flowres and freshest buds
Which th'earth brings forth, and wet he seemed in sight
With waves, through which he waded for his loves delight.

8. In stanzas 32–43, Spenser uses Ovid's *Fasti* and *Metamorphoses* for many details. March leads because until 1752 the official year, in England, began on March 25 (date of the Annunciation to Mary), although like traditional almanacs and social custom, *The Shepheardes Calender* starts with January. As in many Books of Hours, the *Calender's* illustrations include zodiacal signs appropriate for each month; March's ram, for example, represents the sign Aries.
9. The constellation Taurus, here identified with the bull in whose shape Jove abducted Europa, bearing her over the Argolic (i.e., Greek) waves.

34

Then came faire May, the fayrest mayd on ground,
Deckt all with dainties of her seasons pryde,
And throwing flowres out of her lap around:
Upon two brethrens shoulders she did ride,
The twinnes of Leda;[1] which on eyther side
Supported her like to their soveraine Queene.
Lord! how all creatures laught, when her they spide,
And leapt and daunc't as they had ravisht° beene! *enraptured*
And Cupid selfe about her fluttred all in greene.

35

And after her, came jolly June, arrayd
All in greene leaves, as he a Player were;[2]
Yet in his time, he wrought° as well as playd, *worked*
That by his plough-yrons° mote right well appeare: *ploughshares*
Upon a Crab[3] he rode, that him did beare
With crooked crawling steps an uncouth pase,
And backward yode,° as Bargemen wont to fare *went*
Bending their force contrary to their face,
Like that ungracious crew which faines demurest grace.[4]

36

Then came hot July boyling like to fire,
That all his garments he had cast away:
Upon a Lyon[5] raging yet with ire
He boldly rode and made him to obay:
It was the beast that whylome did forray
The Nemaean forrest, till th'Amphytrionide
Him slew, and with his hide did him array;
Behinde his back a sithe,° and by his side *scythe*
Under his belt he bore a sickle circling wide.

37

The sixt was August, being rich arrayd
In garment all of gold downe to the ground:
Yet rode he not, but led a lovely Mayd[6]
Forth by the lilly hand, the which was cround
With eares of come, and full her hand was found;
That was the righteous Virgin, which of old

1. Castor and Pollux, the Gemini.
2. I.e., like an actor garbed as a forest spirit or a "savage" man.
3. I.e., Cancer.
4. I.e., like hypocritical courtiers whose fashion of leaving their lord's presence by walking respectfully backward hides their true feelings. *Bargemen*: London's taxidrivers, who as they rowed passengers up and down the Thames of course faced away from the direction in which they were going.
5. Leo, here identified with the Nemean lion slain by Hercules, whose reputed father was Amphitryon.
6. I.e., Virgo (Astraea, goddess of justice), who left earth in disgust at the corrupt violence of the iron (modern) age; see *Metamorphoses* 1.127–150.

Lived here on earth, and plenty made abound;
But, after Wrong was loved and Justice solde,
She left th'unrighteous world and was to heaven extold.° *raised*

38

Next him, September marchéd eeke on foote;
Yet was he heavy laden with the spoyle
Of harvests riches, which he made his boot,° *booty*
And him enricht with bounty of the soyle:
In his one hand, as fit for harvests toyle,
He held a knife-hook; and in th'other hand
A paire of waights,[7] with which he did assoyle° *determine*
Both more and lesse, where it in doubt did stand,
And equall gave to each as Justice duly scanned.° *judged*

39

Then came October full of merry glee:
For, yet his noule was totty of the must,[8]
Which he was treading in the wine-fats see,[9]
And of the joyous oyle, whose gentle gust° *taste*
Made him so frollick and so full of lust:
Upon a dreadfull Scorpion[1] he did ride,
The same which by Dianaes doom unjust
Slew great Orion: and eeke by his side
He had his ploughing share, and coulter ready tyde.

40

Next was November, he full grosse and fat,
As fed with lard, and that right well might seeme;
For, he had been a fatting° hogs of late, *fattening*
That yet his browes with sweat, did reek and steem,
And yet the season was full sharp and breem;° *cold*
In planting eeke he took no small delight:
Whereon he rode, not easie was to deeme;
For it a dreadfull Centaure[2] was in sight,
The seed of Saturne, and faire Nais, Chiron hight.

41

And after him, came next the chill December:
Yet he through merry feasting which he made,
And great bonfires, did not the cold remember;
His Saviours birth his mind so much did glad:

7. I.e., scales, representing Libra.
8. I.e., his head was giddy from new wine.
9. I.e., the "sea" of the wine vats.
1. Representing Scorpio. Angry at the hunter Orion's boasts, Earth made a scorpion that killed him, but Diana placed him and the scorpion in the stars; others, whom Spenser here follows, said it was Diana herself who had sent the scorpion (see C. Estienne, *Dictionarum*, "Orion").
2. The centaur Chiron, son of Saturn and Philyra (a Naiad), was stellified as Sagittarius, the archer.

Upon a shaggy-bearded Goat[3] he rade,° *rode*
The same wherewith Dan Jove in tender yeares,
They say, was nourisht by th'Idaean mayd;
And in his hand a broad deepe boawle he beares;
Of which, he freely drinks an health to all his peeres.

42

Then came old January, wrappéd well
In many weeds to keep the cold away;
Yet did he quake and quiver like to quell,° *perish*
And blowe his nayles to warme them if he may:
For, they were numbd with holding all the day
An hatchet keene, with which he felléd wood,
And from the trees did lop the needlesse spray:° *branches*
Upon an huge great Earth-pot steane[4] he stood;
From whose wide mouth, there flowéd forth the Romane floud.

43

And lastly, came cold February, sitting
In an old wagon, for he could not ride;
Drawne of two fishes[5] for the season fitting,
Which through the flood before did softly slyde
And swim away: yet had he by his side
His plough and harnesse fit to till the ground,
And tooles to prune the trees, before the pride
Of hasting Prime did make them burgein° round: *bud*
So past the twelve Months forth, and their dew places found.

44

And after these, there came the Day, and Night,
Riding together both with equall pase,
Th'one on a Palfrey blacke, the other white;
But Night had covered her uncomely face
With a blacke veile, and held in hand a mace,
On top whereof the moon and stars were pight,° *placed*
And sleep and darknesse round about did trace:° *walk*
But Day did beare, upon his scepters hight,
The goodly Sun, encompast all with beamés bright.

45

Then came the Howres, faire daughters of high Jove,[6]
And timely Night, the which were all endewed

3. Amalthea nurtured the infant Jove with goat's milk on Mount Ida; the goat became the constellation Capricorn (cf. Comes 7.2).
4. I.e., an earthen water jar, recalling the sign Aquarius, the water bearer; here it originates the river Tiber.
5. The constellation Pisces. It was believed that each of these twelve signs, as the sun (or sometimes the moon) passes through it, governed one part of the human body; Pisces, for example, governed the feet and Aries the head.
6. Like Homer (*Iliad* 5.749) and Ovid (*Fasti* 1.125), Spenser has the Hours attend heaven's gates; Hesiod, though, says their mother was Themis (*Theogony* 900). Cf. *Epithalamion* 98–102.

With wondrous beauty fit to kindle love;
But they were Virgins all, and love eschewed,
That might forslack° the charge to them foreshewed *neglect*
By mighty Jove; who did them Porters make
Of heavens gate (whence all the gods issued)
Which they did dayly watch, and nightly wake° *guard*
By even turnes, ne ever did their charge forsake.

46

And after all came Life, and lastly Death;
Death with most grim and griesly visage seene,
Yet is he nought but parting of the breath;
Ne ought to see, but like a shade to weene,° *conceive*
Unbodiéd, unsouled, unheard, unseene.
But Life was like a faire young lusty boy,
Such as they faine Dan Cupid to have beene,
Full of delightfull health and lively joy,
Deckt all with flowres, and wings of gold fit to employ.

47

When these were past, thus gan the Titanesse;
"Lo, mighty mother, now be judge and say,
Whether in all thy creatures more or lesse
Change doth not raign and beare the greatest sway:
For, who sees not, that Time on all doth pray?° *prey*
But Times do change and move continually.
So nothing here long standeth in one stay:
Wherefore, this lower world who can deny
But to be subject still to Mutabilitie?"

48

Then thus gan Jove; "Right true it is, that these
And all things else that under heaven dwell
Are chaunged of Time, who doth them all disseise° *deprive*
Of being: But, who is it (to me tell)
That Time himselfe doth move and still compell
To keepe his course? Is not that namely wee[7]
Which poure that vertue° from our heavenly cell, *power*
That moves them all, and makes them changéd be?
So them we gods doe rule, and in them also thee."

49

To whom, thus Mutability: "The things
Which we see not how they are moved and swayd,
Ye may attribute to your selves as Kings,
And say they by your secret powre are made:
But what we see not, who shall us perswade?

7. I.e., only we.

But were they so, as ye them faine to be,
Moved by your might, and ordred by your ayde;
Yet what if I can prove, that even yee
Your selves are likewise changed, and subject unto mee?

50

"And first, concerning her that is the first,[8]
Even you faire Cynthia, whom so much ye make
Joves dearest darling, she was bred and nurst
On Cynthus hill,[9] whence she her name did take:
Then is she mortall borne, how-so ye crake,° *brag*
Besides, her face and countenance every day
We changéd see, and sundry forms partake,
Now hornd, now round, now bright, now brown and gray:
So that 'as changefull as the Moone' men use to say.

51

"Next, Mercury, who though he lesse appeare
To change his hew, and alwayes seeme as one;
Yet, he his course doth altar every yeare,
And is of late far out of order gone.[1]
So Venus eeke, that goodly Paragone,° *model of excellence*
Though faire all night, yet is she darke all day;
And Phoebus self, who lightsome is alone,
Yet is he oft eclipséd by the way,
And fills the darkned world with terror and dismay.

52

"Now Mars that valiant man is changéd most:
For, he some times so far runs out of square,
That he his way doth seem quite to have lost,
And cleane without° his usuall sphere to fare; *beyond*
That even these Star-gazers stonisht are
At sight thereof, and damne their lying bookes:
So likewise, grim Sir Saturne oft doth spare° *restrain*
His sterne aspect, and calme his crabbéd lookes:
So many turning cranks° these have, so many crookes. *twists*

53

"But you Dan Jove, that only constant are,
And King of all the rest, as ye do clame,
Are you not subject eeke to this misfare?° *deviation*
Then let me aske you this withouten blame,
Where were ye borne? some say in Crete by name,

8. In the Ptolemaic system, the moon's sphere is nearest to the earth.
9. Traditionally the birthplace of Diana and Apollo, on the island of Delos.
1. Even before Galileo's reports on what his telescope had shown, better astronomical observation had shown that the planets did not behave with the regularity long sought or assumed; such observation had led to the theories, still rejected by most people, advanced by Copernicus.

Others in Thebes, and others other-where;
But wheresoever they comment° the same, *invent*
They all consent that ye begotten were,
And borne here in this world, ne other can appeare.

54

"Then are ye mortall borne, and thrall to me,
Unlesse the kingdome of the sky yee make
Immortall, and unchangeable to bee;
Besides, that power and vertue which ye spake,
That ye here worke, doth many changes take,
And your owne natures change: for, each of you
That vertue have, or° this, or that to make, *either*
Is checkt and changéd from his nature trew,
By others opposition or obliquid view.[2]

55

"Besides, the sundry motions of your Spheares,
So sundry waies and fashions as clerkes° faine, *learned men*
Some in short space, and some in longer yeares;
What is the same but alteration plaine?
Onely the starrie skie doth still remaine:
Yet do the Starres and Signes therein still move,
And even it self is moved, as wizards saine.[3]
But all that moveth, doth mutation love:
Therefore both you and them to me I subject prove.

56

"Then since within this wide great Universe
Nothing doth firme and permanent appeare,
But all things tost and turnéd by transverse:[4]
What then should let,° but I aloft should reare *hinder*
My Trophee, and from all, the triumph beare?
Now judge then (O thou greatest goddesse trew!)
According as thy selfe doest see and heare,
And unto me addoom that[5] is my dew;
That is the rule of all, all being ruled by you."

57

So having ended, silence long ensewed,
Ne Nature to or fro[6] spake for a space,
But with firme eyes affixt, the ground still viewed.
Meane while, all creatures, looking in her face,

2. I.e., each planet's "influence" is counteracted and qualified by the relative position of other planets.
3. I.e., as wise men say, even the sphere of the "fixed stars" moves.
4. I.e., haphazardly.
5. I.e., adjudge that which.
6. I.e., for or against.

Expecting° th'end of this so doubtfull case, *awaiting*
Did hang in long suspence what would ensew,
To whether side should fall the soveraigne place:
At length, she looking up with chearefull view,
The silence brake, and gave her doome in speeches° few. *phrases*

58

"I well consider all that ye have sayd,[7]
And find that all things steadfastnes doe hate
And changéd be: yet being rightly wayd° *weighed*
They are not changéd from their first estate;
But by their change their being doe dilate:° *extend*
And turning to themselves at length againe,
Doe worke their owne perfection so by fate:
Then over them Change doth not rule and raigne;
But they raigne over change, and doe their states maintaine.

59

"Cease therefore daughter further to aspire,
And thee content thus to be ruled by me:
For thy decay° thou seekst by thy desire; *ruin*
But time shall come that all shall changéd bee,
And from thenceforth, none no more change shall see."
So was the Titaness put downe and whist,° *silenced*
And Jove confirmed in his imperiall see.° *throne*
Then was that whole assembly quite dismist,
And Natur's selfe did vanish, whither no man wist.° *knew*

The VIII. Canto, unperfite.° *unfinished.*

1

When I bethinke me on that speech whyleare,° *earlier*
Of Mutability, and well it way.° *consider*
Me seemes, that though she all unworthy were
Of the Heav'ns Rule; yet very sooth to say,
In all things else she beares the greatest sway.
Which makes me loath this state of life so tickle,° *uncertain*
And love of things so vaine to cast away;
Whose flowring pride, so fading and so fickle,
Short Time shall soon cut down with his consuming sickle.

2

Then gin I thinke on that which Nature sayd,
Of that same time when no more Change shall be,

7. Nature acknowledges cosmic change, but not as a blind "ever-whirling wheele" (vi.1); her words recall the Neoplatonic view that change is a "dilation" or expansion by which being fulfills itself (cf. Plotinus, *Enneads* 3.7.4). Boethius says that the divine thought that directs all being is properly called Providence, but that when it is "referred to things that it moves and regulates, then by men in ancient times it was called destiny [i.e., fate]" (4. Prose 6).

But stedfast rest of all things firmely stayd
Upon the pillours of Eternity,
That is contrayr to Mutabilitie:
For, all that moveth, doth in Change delight:
But thence-forth all shall rest eternally
With Him that is the God of Sabbaoth hight.[1]
O that great Sabbaoth God, graunt me that Sabaoths sight.[2]

Editors' Note to *The Faerie Queene*

Spenser's career in print is odd. He began with a great flourish in 1579 with *The Shepheardes Calender* and then *Three Proper, and Wittie, Familiar Letters* between the poet and his close ally, Gabriel Harvey, in 1581. Together these works make the claim that not only was Spenser the new poet whose work could be published in an edition that resembled that of ancient classical authors, with footnotes, commentary and woodcuts, but that his private thoughts were worthy of public knowledge. Yet, after this staggeringly arrogant beginning, he then published nothing until he had reached middle age (Spenser was probably thirty-six or seven in 1590) and had acquired a large landed estate in Ireland and the title of "gentleman." He must have been writing *The Faerie Queene* in this period—along with the *Complaints* and other substantial works—which he developed further in the next eight years before his death.

The Faerie Queene evolved over a protracted period. We know from a comment by Spenser's friend Lodowick Bryskett that an early version circulated in the early 1580s, and the wealth of historical allusions indicate that the text was subsequently revised before it was published in 1590 and 1596. Arguments still rage about which sections might have been written first. A frequently made assumption is that Books II and III were written before Book I, and that the poem started life as a romance that mutated into a religious epic. Book IV looks as if it had been written alongside Book III, suggesting that sections of the second part of the poem were actually written first. Spenser revised the ending of Book III for the second edition of the poem (1596) and removed the hermaphrodite union of Amoret and Scudamore so that their complicated love affair could continue in Book IV, which might indicate that he saw these two books as interrelated. Although most critics agree that Book VI, the book of courtesy, is a late work, as the prologue indicates, some argue that Book V was an early book, given what they think of as its relatively primitive tone and style and reference to events that took place in the 1580s, and that it was then revised to fit into the evolving structure of the poem and to incorporate such later events as Henri de Navarre's conversion to Catholicism (allegorized by Sir Burbon's casting away his shield) in 1593;

1. I.e., called the Lord of Hosts.
2. I.e., the sight of eternal rest. There may be wordplay on "sabaoth" (hosts, as in "Lord God of Hosts) and "sabbath" (the seventh day—and in some Renaissance cosmology the last age before Eternity). Such puns were not unusual because some (mis)read Elizabeth's name as Hebrew for "God's Rest"; see A. C. Hamilton, "Our New Poet," in *Essential Articles for the Study of Edmund Spenser* (Hamden, 972). That the turn to eternity comes in the eighth canto may show Spenser's awareness that in traditional Christian number symbolism the number eight often signified the Resurrection that will follow mortal time.

for others, its stark and brutal style mark it as a late work. The fragment of Book VII that remains, "Two Cantos of Mutabilitie," has generated similar debates. It is often thought of as a late, unfinished work that reflects Spenser's growing sense of anxiety and gloom at the vicissitudes of the world; a minority argues that its Ovidian style marks it as a rediscovered early experiment. We do not know anything about the relationship between the "Two Cantos of Mutability" and the rest of the poem. Most readers favor later composition (Hadfield 2004), as the text seems to allude to the developing situation in the Nine Years War (1594–1603) that threatened Spenser's estate and existence. The Cantos were published after Spenser's death in 1609, probably having found their way into the papers of the printer Matthew Lownes, who appears to have inherited the Spenser manuscripts from Spenser's principal publisher in the 1590s, William Ponsonby. Most scholars also agree that they form the basis of a planned book that never appeared. If they do, however, Spenser departs from his stated plans in the "Letter to Raleigh" and from the narrative progress of the published poem. Moreover, they break off after only two stanzas of the eighth canto. Did Lownes have only a part of the manuscript? Or was this yet another example of Spenser teasing the reader, this time from beyond the grave? We shall almost certainly never know. In the absence of manuscript evidence it is hard to determine how Spenser composed his poem, whether he ever intended to complete his work, whether his plans changed and he left it in a finished state (Neuse 1968), or whether he had always intended to write a much more satisfying and complete work but simply died too soon.

Given the complicated and disputed history of the work, and the sedimentation of different levels of poetic substance, it is hardly surprising that *The Faerie Queene* is such a complicated and controversial poem. It is difficult to imagine how Spenser composed this large, diffuse, and experimental fragment, or how he thought of the whole when it was finally published. It has been assumed that Spenser imagined a work that would establish him as a Protestant moralist, inviting us to follow the triumph of the Redcrosse Knight, who, after defeating the Satanic dragon, is betrothed to Una ready to unite Church and state—and, on a different level of the allegory, anticipating the eventual marriage of Christ and Church. The subsequent books detail the virtues loosely derived from Aristotle—temperance, chastity, friendship, justice, and courtesy—giving the attentive reader the means to live an active spiritual life allied to the best of classical virtues. But whether Spenser ever intended to write a moral tale of Aristotelian virtues, as claimed in the letter to Raleigh, has been disputed by many recent scholars. The letter was appended to the first edition but was not republished in the second edition, so its value as a hermeneutic tool is, unfortunately, in doubt. Spenser was acutely aware of what could be done with paratexts—prefaces, appendices, and other textual apparatus supposedly outside the body of the primary text—and appears to have enjoyed playing games with readers who are tantalized by information about the work that may or may not be true. The letter was perhaps designed to challenge as much as to inform.

It appears likely, following Bennett's painstakingly brilliant analysis and speculative insight (Bennett 1942), that the earliest versions of *The Faerie Queene* were probably based heavily on the Italian romances of

Ariosto and, to a lesser extent, Tasso, making up much of what later appears in Books III and IV. Ariosto's romances move away from the ostensibly central narratives as the heroes get ever more lost and confused in the forests and have to undertake tasks they had not intended, which, in turn, lead the narrator to explain events, stories, and happenings that appear not to have been part of the original plan. Such works are characterized by the narrative process known as "dilation" (Parker 1979), which distinguishes them from the forward-thrusting narrative of the epic with its sense of imperial destiny. In combining both narrative forms, *The Faerie Queene* belongs to a tradition of epic-romance, making it an experimental work designed to push the boundaries of what was possible in English literature (Burrow 1993), and the probable debts to late medieval pilgrimage allegory in Books I and II (Prescott 1989) expand those boundaries yet further.

But this is only to start to deal with the questions that this fascinating and ever-elusive text asks its readers to tackle. *The Faerie Queene* is an exciting and complex work that has always made heavy demands on its readership. Little wonder that even soon after its publication readers appear to have been divided about what it meant and how the poem could be appropriated. On the one hand, there were those who saw Spenser as a royalist author because they believed that he was writing a poem in praise of the monarchy and the establishment. On the other, there were those who hailed Spenser as a radical Protestant at odds with the status quo and keen to explore alternative ideals of life and government. It is this aspect of Spenser's work and reputation that inspired John Milton to hail him as a "better teacher than Scotus or Aquinas" in his exploration of virtue. Spenser's elaborately layered text reveals him to be an experimental writer more akin to iconoclastic modernists than to the sycophantic "arse kissing poet" of Karl Marx's imagination. Working out what *The Faerie Queene* means involves the labor of imaginatively recreating a work written over twenty fraught and dangerous years in the life of a difficult and demanding artist keen to reform and rethink English literature, on his own if necessary.

Spenser used every part of his text—style, rhyme schemes, meter, stanza, typeface—to make his readers think. Even the material that surrounds his poetry—the paratexts—may not be quite what it seems to be. Spenser uses a variety of strategies to put his readers to work, often deliberately misleading us so that truth and falsehood have to be carefully distinguished (Erikson ed. 2005). He adopts a number of disguises himself throughout his literary career—Colin Clout and Immerito, being the two most prominent identities—suggesting that the work can be related to his life, but only as the author chooses to represent it. When Colin Clout appears in *The Faerie Queene* VI.x, his playing has conjured up the Graces, who dance before him. The fourth and central Grace (adding a fourth to the traditional three was a not-uncommon compliment to a lady) is probably a figure of the poet's wife, Elizabeth Boyle, star of *Amoretti* and *The Epithalamion*, and Colin apologizes to the queen for preferring his beloved to her:

> Sunne of the worlde, great glory of the sky,
> That all the earth doest lighten with thy rayes,

> Great *Gloriana*, greatest Majesty,
> Pardon thy shepheard, mongst so many layes,
> As he hath sung of thee in all his dayes,
> To make one minime of they poore handmayd,
> And underneath thy feete to place her prayse,
> That when thy glory shall be farre displayd
> To future age of her this mention may be made. (VI.x.28)

This stanza appears as if it were a polite but firm reminder to the queen that the poet has served her faithfully and is now entitled to praise his wife instead of her. Read another way, it might appear to be rather more pointed, even aggressive, especially if read alongside the stanza in *The Epithalamion* that represents Elizabeth as the moon Cynthia, peering voyeuristically into the bedroom of the newlyweds as if in envy if their happiness (lines 372–89) and perhaps even wondering where the rest of Spenser's epic might be. Elizabeth, as was well known, interfered in the love lives of her courtiers and lost her temper if her favorites secretly married without her blessing, the most notorious case being Sir Walter Raleigh's union with Elizabeth Throckmorton in 1592, an incident allegorized in the second edition of *The Faerie Queene* (IV.vii). Spenser's representation of his own wife superseding the queen in his Book VI deliberately places the reader in a potentially uncomfortable position, made to attend to the poet's divided loyalties to his two mistresses. The episode—along with a host of others—encourages speculation about the relation of the poet's work to his life, and about what might actually be true.

However we think of the poem, Spenser's intention in writing *The Faerie Queene* will always be shrouded in mystery. Although handsome editions of the poem appeared after Spenser's death, the first edition (1590) was a surprisingly modest and unattractive quarto. It would have been obvious to any reader that the poem was a sophisticated and complex work of art, merging the epic tradition of classical Greece and Rome, the Italian romances of Ariosto, Tasso, and Boiardo, and a varied history of religious poetry. However, the poem appeared with no explanatory apparatus, apart from the letter to Raleigh, which was merely appended to the main text. The dedicatory sonnets were messily presented and gave every appearance that they had been assembled at the last possible minute by the author and the printer. This is all the more surprising given the lavish and careful manner in which Spenser's previous major work of poetry, *The Shepheardes Calender*, had been published in 1579. That had appeared with a long introductory letter, an explanatory summary of the argument, woodcuts prefacing each section, and notes explaining key details after each month, supposedly written by one E. K. Had Spenser fallen so spectacularly out of favor in the decade that separated the two works that he now had to make do with second best? Or was the publication of *The Faerie Queene* a cunning ploy by the author?

It is hard to say exactly. Subsequent editions of the poem were all much more attractive in design, easier to read, and expensive. Perhaps this last detail is crucial, as it is possible that Spenser hoped that he could reach a wide audience with his *magnum opus*, and certainly *The Faerie Queene* sold well for such a large and difficult work. We should bear in mind that Spenser was well versed in forms of early modern popular culture, and his works advertise their affinities to a number of "lowbrow" genres—almanacs, popular religious tracts, saints' lives, romances, even pornography—as well as to "highbrow" works of art. The problem is that the one piece of explanatory material, the letter to Raleigh, bears a problematic relationship to the work it purports to illuminate.

The letter claims that the poem was originally conceived as a poem of twelve books, each describing a virtue represented in Aristotle's *Ethics*, and each virtue related (presumably by their representative knights) to twelve annual feast days held by Gloriana, the Faerie Queene. This would indicate that Spenser probably planned the poem to appear in four installments of three books, the poem eventually ending with a grand finale at the court. In the letter Spenser claims that *The Faerie Queene* is a "continued Allegory, or darke conceit," a description that simultaneously hides and reveals its purpose. We learn that the poem stands for something other than its ostensible surface narrative and are encouraged to look for deeper hidden meanings. But we are warned that these meanings may not be straightforward and that we will have to be careful in working out what they are, so we cannot simply abandon the surface meaning if we wish to follow the poem, or concentrate only on key moments that seem to have symbolic force and import. The poem appears to us, as it has to every generation of readers, as a grand puzzle. We are never certain just how seriously we can take any particular image, phrase, or stanza, or whether there is particular symbolic significance at any point.

This is the case from the start of Book I. In the first canto the Redcrosse Knight enters a dark wood and defeats a dragon called Error. He thinks that he has completed his quest, a moment of comic hubris that the poem exploits throughout the rest of its narrative. It is always easy to win battles for which you are prepared and that balance the forces of good and evil so neatly and clearly against each other. The problem is that in defeating Error the knight has destroyed the symbol that made error visible. Errors now lurk everywhere for both knights and readers. When seeking a place to rest, Redcrosse encounters Archimago, who is described in terms that mark him as an adherent of traditional religion:

> At length they chaunst to meet upon the way
> An aged Sire, in long blacke weedes yclad,
> His feete all bare, his beard all hoarie gray,
> And by his belt his booke he hanging had;
> Sober he seemde, and very sagely sad,
> And to the ground his eyes were lowly bent,
> Simple in shew, and voyde of malice bad,
> And all the way he prayéd, as he went,
> And often knockt his brest, as one that did repent. (I.i.29)

The Redcrosse Knight is taken in by Archimago, whose success in all too easily separating the knight from his lady shows just how far Redcrosse is from being a finished article and how painful his journey back to spiritual health must be. Such a reading risks overconfidence, however, and suggests that any reader who thinks that this is the right way to imagine the poem may be as guilty as the knight. What Spenser's work does is present the reader with ever more difficult and challenging issues—religious, ethical, and political—so that distinctions that seemed clear-cut at the start gradually appear more and more complicated and dangerous. By the time we reach Book V, we know that there is justice and there are forces hostile to it, but, as each deploys more and more violent methods, telling the two sides apart is not an easy task. By the time we reach Book VI we cannot be sure that the center holds at all, and the poor confused Knight of Courtesy, Calidore, does not know what he is fighting for or whom he is fighting against. The great challenge—and the great pleasure—of reading *The Faerie Queene* is how we think through the ever more complicated problems with which Spenser confronts us, a challenge that invariably involves our returning to earlier incidents in the poem and rethinking how we read them in the light of later events. The poem is not in all ways timeless, and many of its issues are bound up with the situation of late Elizabethan England. Nevertheless, its style and method have much to teach us about the problems that we will always encounter when we want to consider any series of complex issues, which is just what Milton realized when he heaped such lavish praise on Spenser's qualities as a teacher.

From The Shepheardes Calender†

To His Booke

Goe little booke:[1] thy selfe present,
As child whose parent is unkent:° *unknown*
To him that is the president° *pattern*
Of noblesse and of chevalree,[2]
5 And if that Envie barke at thee,
As sure it will, for succoure flee
Under the shadow of his wing,
And askéd, who thee forth did bring,
A shepheards swaine saye did thee sing,
10 All as his straying flocke he fedde:
And when his honor has thee redde,° *seen*
Crave pardon for my hardyhedde:° *boldness*
But if that any aske thy name,
Say thou wert base° begot with blame: *lowly*
15 For thy° thereof thou takest shame. *therefore*
And when thou art past jeopardee,
Come tell me, what was sayd of mee:
And I will send more after thee.

IMMERITO.[3]

† This set of eclogues' typographical layout, with their important-looking annotations, illustrations, and varying typefaces (not fully replicated in this Norton Critical Edition), may be meant, a bit flashily, to signal association or even competition with Renaissance editions of such important figures as Virgil, the Italian poet Sannazaro, and the French poet Ronsard. The image of the Coliseum in the background may hint at epic hopes after the abandoment of the pastoral pipe.

1. Spenser recalls Chaucer's *Troilus and Criseyde* 5.1786 ("Go, litel bok, go litel myn tragedye"), probably to associate himself with that much-admired poet whom E. K. calls "the Loadestarre of our Language." At the conclusion of the *Calender* Spenser again acknowledges Chaucer ("Envoy" 8–11).
2. I.e., Sir Philip Sidney, nephew of the powerful Robert Dudley, earl of Leicester. In October 1579, Spenser wrote Harvey that "As for the twoo worthy Gentlemen, Master *Sidney* and Master [Edward] *Dyer*, they have me, I thanke them, in some use of familiarity." Such "use" would give Spenser credibility as a significant poet, although his careful wording may possibly exaggerate the degree to which a man of his modest social standing could yet have had the well-born Sidney in "familiarity." Throughout his career, though, Spenser knew that enmity in high places could harm an unprotected poet: compare line 5's barking dog to Book VI's Blatant Beast. This "wing" may be yet another plume/pen pun, even if Sidney had not published any of his writings, but it may also recall biblical allusions (e.g., in Psalms 17 and 91) to the protective shadow of God's wing.
3. I.e,. "The Undeserving One." Later editions retained this pesudonymity until Spenser's collected works appeared in 1611, but interested readers soon knew the author's name.

["E. K."]

[Dedicatory Epistle to *The Shepheardes Calender*]

To the most excellent and learned both orator and poete, MAYSTER GABRIELL HARVEY,[1] his verie special and singular good frend E. K. commendeth the good lyking of this his labour, and the patronage of the new Poete.

Uncouthe unkiste, sayde the olde famous Poete Chaucer: whom for his excellencie and wonderfull skil in making, his scholler Lidgate, a worthy scholler of so excellent a maister, calleth the Loadestarre of our Language: and whom our Colin clout in his Aeglogue[2] calleth Tityrus the God of shepheards, comparing hym to the worthines of the Roman Tityrus Virgile. Which proverbe, myne owne good friend Ma. Harvey, as in that good old Poete it served well Pandares purpose, for the bolstering of his baudy brocage,[3] so very well taketh place in this our new Poete, who for that he is uncouthe (as said Chaucer) is unkist, and unknown to most men, is regarded but of few. But I dout not, so soone as his name shall come into the knowledg of men, and his worthines be sounded in the tromp of fame, but that he shall be not onely kiste, but also beloved of all, embraced of the most, and wondred at of the best. No lesse I thinke, deserveth his wittinesse in devising, his pithinesse in uttering, his complaints of love so lovely, his discourses of pleasure so pleasantly, his pastorall rudenesse, his morall wisenesse, his dewe observing of Decorum[4] everye where, in personages, in seasons, in matter, in speach, and generally in al seemely simplycitie of handeling his matter, and framing his words: the which of many thinges which in him be straunge, I know will seeme the straungest, the words them selves being so auncient, the knitting of them so short and intricate, and the whole Periode and compasse of speache[5] so delightsome for the roundnesse, and so grave for the straungenesse. And firste of the wordes to speake, I graunt they be something hard, and of most men unused, yet both English, and also used of most excellent Authors and most famous Poetes. In whom whenas this our Poet hath bene much traveiled and throughly redd, how could it be, (as that

1. The disputatious, often defensive, and always learned Gabriel Harvey (ca. 1545–1630) was a Fellow of Pembroke Hall, Cambridge, where he and Spenser became friends. Their correspondence, published in 1580 with or without Spenser's cooperation, shows the pair's literary aspirations and their shared interest in English quantitative poetry (i.e., with metrical patterns based, like Latin verse, on the length of syllables rather than on stress). Despite much speculation, the identity of E. K. has not been established to everyone's satisfaction. One Edward Kirke? Harvey? Spenser himself? A collaboration? The errors in E. K.'s commentary remain mystifying.
2. The spelling "Aeglogue" mistakenly suggests "goatherd" in Greek; the more common term was "eclogue" (from the Greek for "chosen, selected"), although Theocritus of Syracuse (third-century B.C.E.) called his pastoral lyrics "Idyls." From these derive the "eclogues" by Virgil, one of whose shepherds, Tityrus, provides Spenser with his name for Chaucer. *Poete Chaucer*: E. K. quotes Chaucer's *Troilus and Criseyde* 1.809 ("Unknowe, unkist, and lost, that is unsought") and Thomas Lydgate (1370–ca. 1451)'s *Fall of Princes* 252; *Loadestarre*: a "lodestar," usually Polaris, is a star used in navigation. *our Colin clout*: a shepherd in the *Calender* and, most scholars assume, a version of Spenser himself.
3. I.e, "pandering," named for Pandarus, Criseyde's corrupt uncle.
4. I.e., his concern for what is fitting and proper in this pastoral context; *wittinesse*: intelligence, skill; *rudenesse*: i.e., his deliberately unpolished rustic style.
5. I.e., the sentence (or a defined group of sentences) and well-crafted course of language.

worthy Oratour[6] sayde) but that walking in the sonne although for other cause he walked, yet needes he mought be sunburnt; and having the sound of those auncient Poetes still ringing in his eares, he mought needes in singing hit out some of theyr tunes. But whether he useth them by such casualtye[7] and custome, or of set purpose and choyse, as thinking them fittest for such rusticall rudenesse of shepheards, eyther for that theyr rough sounde would make his rymes more ragged and rustical, or els because such olde and obsolete wordes are most used of country folke, sure I think, and think I think not amisse, that they bring great grace and, as one would say, auctoritie to the verse. For albe amongst many other faultes it specially be objected of Valla against Livie, and of other against Saluste,[8] that with over much studie they affect antiquitie, as coveting thereby credence and honor of elder yeeres, yet I am of opinion, and eke the best learned are of the lyke, that those auncient solemne wordes are a great ornament both in the one and in the other; the one labouring to set forth in hys worke an eternall image of antiquitie, and the other carefully discoursing matters of gravitie and importaunce. For if my memory fayle not, Tullie[9] in that booke, wherein he endevoureth to set forth the paterne of a perfect Oratour, sayth that ofttimes an auncient worde maketh the style seeme grave, and as it were reverend: no otherwise then we honour and reverence gray heares for a certein religious regard, which we have of old age. Yet nether every where must old words be stuffed in, nor the commen Dialecte and maner of speaking so corrupted therby, that as in old buildings it seme disorderly and ruinous. But all as in most exquisite pictures they use to blaze[1] and portraict not onely the daintie lineaments of beautye, but also rounde about it to shadow the rude thickets and craggy clifts, that by the basenesse of such parts, more excellency may accrew to the principall; for oftimes we fynde ourselves, I knowe not how, singularly delighted with the shewe of such naturall rudenesse, and take great pleasure in that disorderly order. Even so doe those rough and harsh termes enlumine and make more clearly to appeare the brightnesse of brave and glorious words. So ofentimes a dischorde in Musick maketh a comely concordaunce:[2] so great delight tooke the worthy Poete Alceus[3] to behold a blemish in the joynt of a wel shaped body. But if any will rashly blame such his purpose in choyse of old and unwonted words, him may I more justly blame and condemne, or of witlesse headinesse[4] in judging, or of heedelesse hardinesse in condemning; for not marking the compasse of hys bent, he wil judge of the length of his cast.[5] For in my opinion it is one special prayse, of many whych are dew to this Poete, that he hath laboured to restore, as to theyr rightfull heritage such good and naturall English

6. I.e., Cicero; cf. *De Oratore* 2.14.60; *thoroughly redd*: i.e., inasmuch as our poet is widely and thoroughly acquainted (with "those auncient Poetes").
7. Chance.
8. Lorenzo Valla (1405–57) emended the text of *Annales*, by the Roman historian Titus Livius (59 B.C.E.–17 C.E.); Sir John Cheke (1514–1557), Edward VI's tutor and professor of Greek at Cambridge, criticized the use of archaic terms by the Roman historian Sallust (86–34 B.C.E).
9. I.e., Cicero; cf. *De Oratore* 3.38.153. Cicero's full name was Marcus Tullius Cicero.
1. Depict positively.
2. Cf. *The Faerie Queehe*, III.ii.15: "So dischord oft in Musick makes the sweeter lay."
3. Alcaeus, a Greek lyric poet of the seventh century B.C.E.; cf. Cicero, *De Natura Deorum* 1.28.79.
4. I.e., either of witless rashness; *unwonted*: unfamiliar, unusual.
5. I.e., not noting the extent of the artist's purpose, the rash critic foolishly presumes to judge the other's achievement.

words, as have ben long time out of use and almost cleare disherited. Which is the onely cause, that our Mother tonge, which truely of it self is both ful enough for prose and stately enough for verse, hath long time ben counted most bare and barrein of both. Which default when as some endevoured to salve and recure, they patched up the holes with peces and rags of other languages, borrowing here of the french, there of the Italian, every where of the Latine, not weighing how il, those tongues accorde with themselves, but much worse with ours: So now they have made our English tongue, a gallimaufray or hodgepodge of al other speches.[6] Other some not so wel seene[7] in the English tonge as perhaps in other languages, if them happen to here an olde word albeit very naturall and significant, crye out streight way, that we speak no English, but gibbrish, or rather such, as in old time Evanders mother spake.[8] Whose first shame is, that they are not ashamed, in their own mother tonge straungers to be counted and alienes. The second shame no lesse then the first, that what so they understand not, they streight way deeme to be sencelesse, and not at al to be understode. Much like to the Mole in Aesopes fable, that being blynd her selfe, would in no wise be perswaded, that any beast could see. The last more shameful then both, that of their owne country and natural speach, which together with their Nources milk they sucked, they have so base regard and bastard judgement, that they will not onely themselves not labor to garnish and beautifie it, but also repine, that of[9] other it shold be embellished. Like to the dogge in the maunger, that him selfe can eate no hay, and yet barketh at the hungry bullock, that so faine would feede: whose currish kind though cannot be kept from barking, yet I conne[1] them thanke that they refraine from byting.

Now for the knitting of sentences, whych they[2] call the joynts and members therof, and for al the compasse of the speach, it is round without roughnesse, and learned wythout hardnes, such indeede as may be perceived of the leaste, understoode of the moste, but judged onely of the learned. For what in most English wryters useth to be loose, and as it were ungyrt, in this Authour is well grounded, finely framed, and strongly trussed up together. In regard whereof, I scorne and spue out the rakehellye route of our ragged rymers (for so themselves use to hunt the letter)[3] which without learning boste, without judgement jangle, without reason rage and fome, as if some instinct of Poeticall spirite had newly ravished them above the meanenesse of commen capacitie. And being in the middest of all theyr bravery, sodenly eyther for want of matter, or of ryme, or having forgotten theyr former conceipt, they seeme to be so pained and traveiled in theyr remembrance, as it were a woman in childebirth or as that same Pythia, when the traunce came upon her.

6. E. K.'s position recalls Sir John Cheke's opinion (in a letter to Sir Thomas Hoby): "our own tongue should be written clean and pure, unmixed and unmangled with borrowing of other tongues."
7. I.e., skilled.
8. Cf. an anecdote in Aulus Gellius (a Latin grammarian, second century C.E.), *Attic Nights* 1.10.2.
9. By.
1. Can.
2. I.e., rhetoricians.
3. E. K. Satirizes the excessive alliteration that characterized the work of many Elizabethan versifiers; cf. Sidney's allusion (in *An Apologie for Poetrie*) to "coursing of a Letter, as if they were bound to followe the method of a Dictionary."

Os rabidum fera corda domans &c.[4]

Nethelesse[5] let them a Gods name feede on theyr owne folly, so they seeke not to darken the beames of others glory. As for Colin, under whose person the Authour selfe is shadowed, how furre he is from such vaunted titles and glorious showes, both him selfe sheweth, where he sayth.

Of Muses Hobbin. I conne no skill. And,
Enough is me to paint out my unrest, &c.[6]

And also appeareth by the basenesse of the name, wherein, it semeth, he chose rather to unfold great matter of argument covertly, then professing it, not suffice thereto accordingly. Which moved him rather in Aeglogues, then other wise to write, doubting perhaps his habilitie, which he little needed, or mynding to furnish our tongue with this kinde, wherein it faulteth, or following the example of the best and most auncient Poetes, which devised this kind of wryting, being both so base[7] for the matter, and homely for the manner, at the first to trye theyr habilities; and as young birdes, that be newly crept out of the nest, by little first to prove theyr tender wyngs, before they make a greater flyght. So flew Theocritus, as you may perceive he was all ready full fledged. So flew Virgile, as not yet well feeling his winges. So flew Mantuane, as being not full somd.[8] So Petrarque. So Boccace; So Marot, Sanazarus, and also divers other excellent both Italian and French Poetes, whose foting this Author every where followeth, yet so as few, but they be wel sented can trace him out.[9] So finally flyeth this our new Poete, as a bird, whose principals[1] be scarce growen out, but yet as that in time shall be hable to keepe wing with the best.

Now as touching the generall dryft and purpose of his Aeglogues, I mind not to say much, him selfe labouring to conceale it. Onely this appeareth, that his unstayed yougth had long wandred in the common Labyrinth of Love, in which time to mitigate and allay the heate of his passion, or els to warne (as he sayth) the young shepheards .s.[2] his equalls and companions of his unfortunate folly, he compiled these xii. Aeglogues, which for that they be proportioned to the state of the xii. monethes, he termeth the SHEPHEARDS CALENDAR, applying an olde name[3] to a new worke. Hereunto have I added a certain Glosse or scholion for thexposition of old wordes and harder phrases: which maner of glosing and commenting, well I wote, wil seeme straunge and rare in our tongue: yet for somuch as I knew many excellent and proper devises both in wordes and matter would passe in the speedy course of reading, either as unknowen, or as not marked, and that in this kind, as in other we might be equal to

4. "Taming the frenzied mouth and savage heart"; cf. Virgil, *Aeneid* 6.80.
5. Nevertheless.
6. These verses occur in "June" 65, 79.
7. Humble, low; *faulteth*: is deficient.
8. I.e., fledged. *Mantuane*: Baptista Spagnuoli (1448–1516), called Mantuan, who was born in Mantua.
9. To these famous classical and Renaissance poets, some of whom began their careers with pastoral before moving to grander forms, E. K. adds Clément Marot (1496–1544), whose "footing" Spenser indeed follows in "November" and "December."
1. The first two primary feathers of a hawk's wing.
2. *Scilicet*, i.e., namely; *unstayed*: unsteady.
3. I.e., that of *Le Compost et Kalendrier des bergiers* first published at Paris in 1493; a number of English versions had appeared by Spenser's time.

the learned of other nations, I thought good to take the paines upon me, the rather for that by meanes of some familiar acquaintaunce I was made privie to his counsell and secret meaning in them, as also in sundry other works of his. Which albeit I know he nothing so much hateth, as to promulgate, yet thus much have I adventured upon his frendship, him selfe being for long time furre estraunged, hoping that this will the rather occasion him, to put forth divers other excellent works of his, which slepe in silence, as his Dreames, his Legendes, his Court of Cupide, and sondry others;[4] whose commendations to set out, were verye vayne; the thinges though worthy of many, yet being knowen to few. These my present paynes if to any they be pleasurable or profitable, be you judge, mine own good Maister Harvey, to whom I have both in respect of your worthinesse generally, and otherwyse upon some particular and special considerations voued this my labour, and the maydenhead of this our commen frends Poetrie, himselfe having already in the beginning dedicated it to the Noble and worthy Gentleman, the right worshipfull Ma. Phi. Sidney, a special favourer and maintainer of all kind of learning. Whose cause I pray you Sir, yf Envie shall stur up any wrongful accusasion, defend with your mighty Rhetorick and other your rare gifts of learning, as you can, and shield with your good wil, as you ought, against the malice and outrage of so many enemies, as I know wilbe set on fire with the sparks of his kindled glory. And thus recommending the Author unto you, as unto his most special good frend, and my selfe unto you both, as one making singuler account of two so very good and so choise frends, I bid you both most hartely farwel, and commit you and your most commendable studies to the tuicion of the greatest.

Your owne assuredly to be commaunded
E. K.

4. These poems are lost, although possibly part of *The Court of Cupid* survives in *The Faerie Queene*, III.xii.

Januarye

Argument

In this fyrst Aeglogue Colin cloute[1] *a shepheardes boy complaineth him of his unfortunate love, being but newly (as semeth) enamoured of a countrie lasse called* Rosalinde: *with which strong affection being very sore traveled, he compareth his carefull case*[2] *to the sadde season of the yeare, to the frostie ground, to the frosen trees, and to his owne winterbeaten flocke. And lastlye, fynding himselfe robbed of all former pleasaunce and delights, hee breaketh his Pipe*[3] *in peeces, and casteth him selfe to the ground.*

COLIN CLOUTE

A Shepeheards boye (no better doe him call)
When Winters wastful° spight was almost spent, *devastating*
All in a sunneshine day, as did befall,
Led forth his flock, that had bene long ypent.° *pent up*
5 So faynt they woxe,° and feeble in the folde, *grew*
That now unnethes° their feete could them uphold. *scarcely*

1. "A name not greatly used, and yet I have sene a Poesie of M. Skeltons under that title. But indeede the word Colin is Frenche, and used of the French Poete Marot (if he be worthy of the name of a Poete) in a certein Aeglogue. Under which name this Poete secretly shadoweth himself, as sometime did Virgil under the name Tityrus, thinking it much fitter, then such Latine names, for the great unlikelyhoode of the language" [*E. K.'s Glosse*]. E. K. thus locates three sorts of influence: the Roman Virgil's *Eclogue* I, the French Marot's *Eglogue sur le trespas de . . . Dame Loyse de Savoye* (1531, with shepherds named "Colin" and "Thenot"), and the English Skelton's satirical *Collyn Clout* (1521 or 1522; a "clout" is a rag). Spenser's Colin reappears in *Colin Clouts Come Home Againe* and, as a swain who pipes to the Graces, in *The Faerie Queene* VI.x.15–16. E. K.'s (unjust) doubt that Marot is a true "Poete" may be due to Marot's now old-fashioned look, his cheerful self-mockery, and his failure to attempt major forms such as the hymn or epic.
2. I.e., his sorrowful plight; *traveled*: troubled.
3. I.e., the shepherd's reed pipe, not unlike a modern recorder, or the "panpipes," a row of such pipes whose varied notes, thought some Renaissance mythographers, parallel the musical tones and ratios of the cosmos. True, the illustration for "Januarye" shows a smashed bagpipe.

All as the Sheepe, such was the shepeheards looke,
For pale and wanne he was, (alas the while,)
May seeme he lovd, or else some care he tooke:[4]
10 Well couth° he tune his pipe, and frame his stile. *could*
Tho° to a hill his faynting flocke he ledde, *then*
And thus him playnd,° the while his shepe there fedde. *lamented*

"Ye Gods of love, that pitie lovers payne,
(If any gods the paine of lovers pitie:)
15 Looke from above, where you in joyes remaine,
And bowe your eares unto my dolefull dittie.
And Pan thou shepheards God,[5] that once didst love,
Pitie the paines, that thou thy selfe didst prove.° *experience*

"Thou barrein ground, whome winters wrath hath wasted,
20 Art made a myrrhour, to behold my plight:
Whilome° thy fresh spring flowrd, and after hasted *formerly*
Thy sommer prowde with Daffadillies dight.° *decked*
And now is come thy wynters stormy state,
Thy mantle mard, wherein thou maskedst late.

25 "Such rage as winters, reigneth in my heart,
My life bloud friesing with unkindly° cold: *unnatural*
Such stormy stoures° do breede my balefull° smart, *tumults / painful*
As if my yeare were wast,° and woxen old. *lasted*
And yet alas, but now my spring begonne,
30 And yet alas, yt is already donne.

"You naked trees, whose shady leaves are lost,
Wherein the byrds were wont to build their bowre:
And now are clothd with mosse and hoary frost,
Instede of bloosmes, wherwith your buds did flowre:
35 I see your teares, that from your boughes doe raine,
Whose drops in drery° ysicles remaine. *dismal*

"All so my lustfull° leafe is drye and sere, *vigorous*
My timely° buds with wayling all are wasted: *seasonable*
The blossome, which my braunch of youth did beare,
40 With breathéd sighes is blowne away, and blasted
And from mine eyes the drizling teares descend,
As on your boughes the ysicles depend.° *hang*

"Thou feeble flocke, whose fleece is rough and rent,
Whose knees are weake through fast and evill fare:
45 Mayst witnesse well by thy ill governement,[6]
Thy maysters mind is overcome with care.

4. I.e., or else he was afflicted by some sorrow.
5. The horned and goat-legged Pan, god of shepherds, forests, and pastoral poetry, pursued the nymph Syrinx, whose sisters granted her prayer for rescue by turning her into the reeds from which Pan then made his pipe; see Ovid, *Metamorphoses* 1.689–712. Cf. "Aprill" 50–51 and note.
6. I.e., by being badly cared for.

Thou weake, I wanne: thou leane, I quite forlorne:
With mourning pyne I, you with pyning mourne.

"A thousand sithes° I curse that carefull hower, *times*
50 Wherein I longd the neighbour towne to see:
And eke tenne thousand sithes I blesse the stoure,° *moment*
Wherein I sawe so fayre a sight, as shee.
Yet all for naught: such sight hath bred my bane.
Ah God, that love should breede both joy and payne.

55 "It is not Hobbinol,[7] wherefore I plaine,
Albee my love he seeke with dayly suit:
His clownish° gifts and curtsies° I disdaine, *rustic / courtesies*
His kiddes, his cracknelles,° and his early fruit. *biscuits*
Ah foolish Hobbinol, thy gyfts bene vayne:
60 Colin them gives to Rosalind[8] againe.

I love thilke° lasse, (alas why doe I love?) *this*
And am forlorne, (alas why am I lorne?)[9]
Shee deignes° not my good will, but doth reprove, *accepts*
And of my rurall musick holdeth scorne.
65 Shepheards devise° she hateth as the snake, *invention*
And laughes the songes, that Colin Clout doth make.

"Wherefore my pype, albee° rude Pan thou please, *although*
Yet for thou pleasest not, where most I would:

7. "A fained country name, whereby, it being so commune [i.e., common] and usuall, seemeth to be hidden the person of some his very speciall and most familiar freend, whom he entirely and extraordinarily beloved, as peradventure [i.e., perhaps] shall be more largely declared hereafter. In thys place seemeth to be some savour of disorderly love, which the learned call pæderastice [i.e., pederastic]: but it is gathered beside his meaning. For who that hath red Plato his dialogue called Alcybiades, Xenophon and Maximus Tyrius of Socrates opinions, may easily perceive, that such love is muche to be alowed and liked of, specially so meant, as Socrates used it: who sayth, that in deede he loved Alcybiades extremely, yet not Alcybiades person, but his soule, which is Alcybiades owne selfe. And so is pæderastice much to be præferred before gynerastice, that is the love whiche enflameth men with lust toward woman kind. But yet let no man thinke, that herein I stand with Lucian or hys develish disciple Unico Aretino, in defence of execrable and horrible sinnes of forbidden and unlawful fleshlinesse. Whose abominable errour is fully confuted of Perionius, and others" [*E. K.'s Glosse*]. In his Glosse to "September" 176, E. K. explicitly identifies Hobbinol as "Mayster Gabriel Harvey." Plato's most famous, and positive, description of "pederastic" love, including that of Socrates for Alcibiades (although noting an instance of the philosopher's avoidance of intercourse), is in the *Symposium*. To offer information on ancient homoeroticism even while improbably denying its physicality or, in the case of later works, mentioning but then rejecting as models the often indecent satirist Lucian (second century C.E.) or Pietro Aretino (1492–1556), author of obscene sonnets and dialogues admired by Harvey when annotating his books but condemned by him in print, may be typical of all-male communities such as the universities and law courts. Mutual familiarity with classical texts offered a way to speak of matters otherwise forbidden, even if this could mean denying their clear meaning. Peronius (Joachim Perion, d. 1559) had written against Aretino in his *In Petrum Aretinum Oratio* (1551). That "Januarie," like Marlowe's pastoral "Come live with me," owes a good deal to Virgil's Second Eclogue (Corydon vainly loves the boy Alexis, who vainly loves the maid Amaryllis) gives what E. K. says yet more overtones. E. K. cites Virgil's Tityrus (First Eclogue), a poem relevant to Colin's stance in the woodcut as he looks to what is clearly Rome, and perhaps the epic.
8. "A feigned name; which being wel ordered, wil bewray the very name of hys love and mistresse, whom by that name he coloureth" [*E. K.'s Glosse*]. Citing classical and Renaissance instances, E. K. adds, "this generally hath bene a common custome of counterfeicting the names of secret Personages."
9. "A prety Epanorthosis in these two verses, and withall a Paronomasia or playing with the word" [*E. K.'s Glosse*]. The rhetorical figure of epanorthosis "taketh away that that is said, and putteth a more meet word in the place" (H. Peacham, *The Garden of Eloquence* [London, 1593] 172); "paronomasia" is a form of pun.

And thou unlucky Muse, that wontst to ease
70 My musing mynd, yet canst not, when thou should:
Both pype and Muse, shall sore the while abye"[1]
So broke his oaten pype, and downe dyd lye.

By that, the welkéd Phoebus[2] gan availe,° *lower*
His weary waine,° and nowe the frosty Night *wagon*
75 Her mantle black through heaven gan overhaile.° *draw over*
Which seene, the pensife boy halfe in despight
Arose, and homeward drove his sonnéd° sheepe, *sunned*
Whose hanging heads did seeme his carefull case to weepe.

Colins Embleme.

Anchôra Speme.[3]

Februarie

Argument

This Æglogue is rather morall and generall, then bent to any secrete or particular purpose.[1] *It specially conteyneth a discourse of old age, in the per-*

1. I.e., shall dearly pay for that time of failure.
2. I.e., the setting sun.
3. The meaning wherof is, that notwithstande his extreme passion and lucklesse love, yet leaning on hope, he is some what recomforted" [*E. K.'s Glosse*].

1. E. K.'s disclaimer has not prevented speculation about political or ecclesiastical allegory. Specific allusions to actual people may be hard to pin down and would have been dangerous to articulate explicitly (why does the figure with the axe look so female?), but Spenser certainly explores the dynamics of ambition, envy, and repression, doubtless glancing at royal courts; the falling towers and proud peacocks may add psychosexual resonance. As E. K. also implies, this study of generational conflict fits the month of February. That month is early in the traditional astrological and agricultural calendars that Spenser here adopts (and in the Gregorian calendar, soon to be promulgated by the Pope in 1582 even though rejected by the English). But it is late in the equally traditional English civil year that began on March 25. February is both old and young. A set of woodcuts for the Catholic missals still widely found in England shows not the traditional labors but the stages of life through the months. That for February often shows a boys' classroom: the master holds a switch and sometimes a naked-bottomed boy

sone of Thenot *an olde Shepheard, who for his crookednesse and unlustinesse, is scorned of* Cuddie *an unhappy Heardmans boye. The matter very well accordeth with the season of the moneth, the yeare now drouping, and as it were, drawing to his last age. For as in this time of yeare, so then in our bodies there is a dry and withering cold, which congealeth the crudled blood, and frieseth the wetherbeaten flesh, with stormes of Fortune, and hoare frosts of Care. To which purpose the olde man telleth a tale of the Oake and the Bryer, so lively and so feelingly, as if the thing were set forth in some Picture before our eyes, more plainly could not appeare.*

CUDDIE THENOT

Ah for pittie, wil rancke° Winters rage, *violent*
These bitter blasts never ginne t'asswage?° *lessen*
The kene cold blowes through my beaten hyde,
All as I were through the body gryde.° *pierced*
5 My ragged rontes[2] all shiver and shake,
As doen high Towers in an earthquake:
They wont in the wind wagge their wrigle° tailes, *wriggling*
Perke as Peacock: but nowe it avales.[3]

THENOT[4]

Lewdly° complainest thou laesie ladde, *Ignorantly*
10 Of Winters wracke,[5] for making thee sadde.
Must not the world wend in his commun course
From good to badd, and from badde to worse,
From worse unto that° is worst of all, *what*
And then returne to his former fall?[6]
15 Who will not suffer° the stormy time, *endure*
Where will he live tyll the lusty prime°? *spring*
Selfe° have I worne out thrise threttie° yeares, *Myself / thirty*
Some in much joy, many in many teares:
Yet never complained of cold nor heate,
20 Of Sommers flame, nor of Winters threat:
Ne ever was to Fortune foeman,° *enemy*
But gently tooke, that° ungently came. *whatever*
And ever my flocke was my chiefe care,
Winter or Sommer they mought° well fare. *could*

CUDDIE

25 No marveile Thenot, if thou can beare

is being disciplined. The eclogue's vocabulary, alliteration, and (usually) four-beat nine-syllable line may be meant to sound rustic and Chaucerian, a style then suitable to quasi-satirical moral commentary. That Thenot is "crooked" means his body is distorted by age. "Cuddie" was a popular nickname for "Cuthbert," a saint popular in northern England.

2. "Young bullockes" [*E. K.'s Glosse*].
3. Cuddie's calves once wagged their tails proudly but now let them droop, hinting that they and their master suffer "unlustiness" in the cold.
4. "The name of a shepheard in Marot his Ælogues" [*E. K.'s Glosse*]. He means Clément Marot's lament for Louise of Savoy, chief source of Spenser's "November."
5. "Ruine or Violence, whence commeth shipwracke: and not wreake, that is vengeaunce or wrath" [*E. K.'s Glosse*].
6. I.e., circle back to an earlier condition; the included meanings of "fall" musical cadence, a throw at wrestling, the felling of trees, autumn, and the Fall of Man.

Cherefully the Winters wrathfull cheare:° *mood*
For Age and Winter accord full nie,
This chill, that cold, this crooked, that wrye.° *twisted*
And as the lowring Wether lookes downe,
30 So semest thou like good fryday[7] to frowne.
But my flowring youth is foe to frost,
My shippe unwont° in stormes to be tost. *unused*

THENOT

The soveraigne of seas he blames in vaine,
That° once seabeate, will to sea againe.[8] *who*
35 So loytring live you little heardgroomes,[9]
Keeping your beastes in the budded broomes.[1]
And when the shining sunne laugheth once,
You deemen° the Spring is come attonce. *believe*
Tho gynne you, fond° flyes, the cold to scorne, *foolish*
40 And crowing in pypes made of greene corne,[2]
You thinken to be Lords of the yeare.
But eft,° when ye count you freed from feare, *afterward*
Comes the breme° winter with chamfred° browes, *chill / wrinkled*
Full of wrinckles and frostie furrowes:
45 Drerily shooting his stormy darte,
Which cruddles the blood, and pricks the harte.
Then is your careless corage accoied,[3]
Your carefull heards with cold bene annoied.
Then paye you the price of your surquedrie,° *pride*
50 With weeping, and wayling, and misery.

CUDDIE

Ah foolish old man, I scorne thy skill,° *knowledge*
That wouldest me, my springing youngth to spil.° *ruin*
I deeme, thy braine emperished bee
Through rusty elde,° that hath rotted thee: *age*
55 Or sicker° thy head veray tottie° is, *surely / unsteady*
So on thy corbe° shoulder it leanes amisse. *bent*
Now thy selfe hast lost both lopp and topp,
Als my budding braunch thou wouldest cropp:[4]
But were thy yeares greene, as now bene myne,

7. Good Friday, day of Jesus' crucifixion; Lent usually begins in February.
8. "Neptune the God of the seas" [*E. K.'s Glosse*]. The lines that follow (35–50) expand Mantuan's sixth eclogue 19–25.
9. I.e., thus you young herdsmen live idly; as E. K. notes, this passage paraphrases Chaucer's *House of Fame* 1224–26.
1. Broom is a flowering bush.
2. "He compareth careless sluggards or ill husbandmen to flyes [flying insects], that so soone as the sunne shineth or yt wexeth any thing warme, begin to flye abroade, when sodeinly they be overtaken with cold" [*E. K.'s Glosse*]. The pipes are either made of the stalks of early grain ("corn" in England) or, suited to February, blades held between the thumbs and blown on to make noise.
3. I.e., "plucked downe and daunted," says E. K., who calls this passage "A verye excellent and lively description of Winter, so as may be indifferently [i.e. equally well] taken, eyther for Old Age, or for Winter season" [*Glosse*].
4. "Lopp" and "topp" are small branches and twigs. In traditional illustrations of monthly labors, February was often the time for gathering wood.

60 To other delights they would encline.
Tho° wouldest thou learne to caroll of Love, *Then*
And hery° with hymnes thy lasses glove. *praise*
Tho wouldest thou pype of Phyllis[5] prayse:
But Phyllis is myne for many dayes:
65 I wonne her with a gyrdle° of gelt,° *sash / gold*
Embost with buegle about the belt.[6]
Such an one shepeheards woulde make full faine:[7]
Such an one would make thee younge againe.

THENOT

Thou art a fon,° of thy love to boste, *fool*
70 All that is lent to love, wyll be lost.

CUDDIE

Seest, howe brag° yond Bullocke beares, *boastfully*
So smirke,° so smoothe, his prickéd eares? *trim*
His hornes bene as broade, as Rainebowe bent,° *arched*
His dewelap as lythe, as lasse of Kent.
75 See howe he venteth into the wynd.[8]
Weenest of love is not his mynd?
Seemeth thy flocke thy counsell can,[9]
So lustlesse bene they, so weake so wan,
Clothed with cold, and hoary wyth frost.
80 Thy flocks father[1] his corage hath lost:
Thy Ewes, that wont to have blowen bags,[2]
Like wailefull widdowes hangen their crags:° *necks*
The rather° Lambes bene starved° with cold, *early / dead*
All for° their Maister is lustlesse and old. *because*

THENOT

85 Cuddie, I wote thou kenst° little good, *understand*
So vainely t'advaunce thy headlesse hood.[3]
For Youngth is a bubble blown up with breath,
Whose witt is weakenesse, whose wage is death,
Whose way is wildernesse, whose ynne Penaunce,
90 And stoopegallaunt[4] Age the hoste of Greevaunce.

5. "The name of some mayde unknowen, whom Cuddie, whose person is secrete, loved. The name is usuall in Theocritus, Virgile, and Mantuane" [*E. K.'s Glosse*], perhaps hinting that in fact Cuddie stands for some other figure.
6. I.e., embroidered with glass beads on the waistband.
7. I.e., make shepherds well pleased.
8. I.e., "snuffeth in the wind" [*E. K.'s Glosse*], presumably sensing female scent.
9. I.e., your flock seems to know your secrets.
1. "The ramme" [*E. K.'s Glosse*].
2. I.e., swollen udders.
3. Cuddie's hood is empty because, thinks Thenot, he is brainless.
4. I.e., that which humbles a proudly fashionable youth; sometimes applied to low doors that force one to bend down. The rustic Cuddie is no "gallant," but Thenot's warning is meant generally. E. K. calls the passage a "moral and pithy Allegorie of youth, and the lustes thereof, compared to a wearie wayfaring man" [*Glosse*]. Cf. S. Bateman's *Travayled Pylgrime* (1569), in which a lusty youth crosses a wilderness called Age to lie down with Penance in a bedroom called Pain.

But shall I tel thee a tale of truth,
Which I cond° of Tityrus[5] in my youth, *learned*
Keeping his sheepe on the hils of Kent?

CUDDIE

To nought more Thenot, my mind is bent,
95 Then to heare novells of his devise:[6]
They bene so well thewed,[7] and so wise,
What ever that good old man bespake.° *spoke*

THENOT

Many meete° tales of youth did he make, *suitable*
And some of love, and some of chevalrie:
100 But none fitter then this to applie.
Now listen a while, and hearken the end.

There grewe an aged Tree on the greene,[8]
A goodly Oake sometime had it bene,
With armes full strong and largely displayd,[9]
105 But of their leaves they were disarayde:° *stripped*
The bodie bigge, and mightely pight,° *set*
Throughly rooted, and of wonderous hight:
Whilome° had bene the King of the field, *Once*
And mochell mast to the husband did yielde,[1]
110 And with his nuts larded° many swine. *fattened*
But now the gray mosse marred his rine,° *bark*
His bared boughes were beaten with stormes,
His toppe was bald, and wasted with wormes,
His honor decayed, his braunches sere.
115 Hard by his side grewe a bragging brere,° *briar*
Which proudly thrust into Th'element,[2]
And seemed to threat the Firmament.
Yt was embellisht with blossomes fayre,
And thereto aye wonnéd to repayre[3]
120 The shepheards daughters, to gather flowres,
To peinct° their girlonds with his colowres. *paint*
And in his small bushes used to shrowde° *shelter*
The sweete Nightingale singing so lowde:
Which made this foolish Brere wexe so bold,
125 That on a time he cast him[4] to scold,

5. "I suppose he meane[s] Chaucer, whose prayse for pleasaunt tales cannot dye, so long as the memorie of hys name shal live, and the name of Poetrie shal endure" [*E. K.'s Glosse*].
6. I.e., new stories devised by him. A "novel" was a short tale.
7. I.e., "full of morall wisenesse" [*E. K.'s Glosse*].
8. As E. K. notes, the fable is closer in style to Aesop. It is, he adds, "excellente for pleasaunt descriptions, being altogether a certaine Icon or Hypotyposis [vivid description] of disdainfull younkers [youths]" [*Glosse*].
9. I.e., broadly branching outward.
1. I.e., gave many acorns to the farmer.
2. I.e., the air.
3. I.e., were wont to visit; E. K. reads "wonned" as "frequented" [*Glosse*].
4. I.e., he intended, decided.

And snebbe° the good Oake, for he was old.[5] *reprove*
"Why standst there," quoth he, "thou brutish° blocke? *stupid*
Nor for fruict, nor for shadowe serves thy stocke:° *trunk*
Seest, how fresh my flowers bene spredde,
130 Dyed in Lilly white, and Cremsin redde,
With Leaves engrained° in lusty greene, *dyed*
Colours meete to clothe a mayden Queene.[6]
Thy wast bignes but combers the grownd,[7]
And dirks° the beauty of my blossomes rownd. *darkens*
135 The mouldie mosse, which thee accloieth,° *encumbers*
My Sinamon smell too much annoieth.
Wherefore soone I rede° thee, hence remove, *advise*
Least thou the price of my displeasure prove."
So spake this bold brere with great disdaine:
140 Little him answered the Oake againe,
But yielded, with shame and greefe adawed,[8]
That of a weede he was overawed.[9]
Yt chauncéd after upon a day,
The Husbandman selfe° to come that way, *himself*
145 Of custome for to servewe° his grownd, *oversee*
And his trees of state[1] in compasse rownd.
Him when the spitefull brere had espyed,
Causlesse complained, and lowdly cryed
Unto his Lord, stirring up sterne strife.[2]
150 "O my liege Lord,[3] the God of my life,
Pleaseth you ponder your Suppliants plaint,
Caused of wrong, and cruell constraint,
Which I your poore Vassall dayly endure:
And but° your goodnes the same recure,° *unless / redress*
155 Am like for desperate doole° to dye, *pain*
Through felonous force of mine enemie."
Greatly aghast with this piteous plea,
Him rested the goodman on the lea,[4]
And badde the Brere in his plaint proceede.
160 With painted words tho gan this proude weede,
(As most usen Ambitious folke:)
His colowred crime[5] with craft to cloke.
"Ah my soveraigne, Lord of creatures all,
Thou placer of plants both humble and tall,

5. I.e., because the oak was old. E. K. calls his speech "scorneful and very presumptuous" [*Glosse*].
6. Recalling the red-and-white Tudor rose.
7. I.e., your useless bulk merely burdens the ground.
8. I.e., "daunted and confounded" [*E. K.'s Glosse*].
9. Overawed: later editions have "overcrawed," a Northern version of "overcrowed," meaning exulted over, overpowered (*OED*, which cites *Faerie Queene* I.ix.50.5).
1. I.e., "taller trees fitte for timber wood" [*E. K.'s Glosse*]; a "state" was also a statesman.
2. In a *Glosse* E. K. notes that the phrase is from Chaucer; see the opening of "The Plowman's Tale," then thought authentic.
3. "A maner of supplication, wherein is kindly [naturally] coloured the affection and speache of Ambitious men" [*E. K.'s Glosse*].
4. The husbandman sits down on the meadow to listen; in northern dialect a "lea" was a scythe, suitable for leaning on but probably not useful in February.
5. The rhetorically disguised ("colowred") crime is slander, of increased legal interest in Spenser's day (see F. T. Plucknett, *A Concise History of the Common Law* [London, 1956]) and a major theme in his works. The briar commits *scandalum magnatum*: slandering the great.

165 Was not I planted of thine owne hand,
To be the primrose of all thy land,
With flowring blossomes, to furnish the prime,° *spring*
And scarlot berries in Sommer time?
How falls it then, that this faded Oake,
170 Whose bodie is sere, whose braunches broke,
Whose naked Armes stretch unto the fyre,[6]
Unto such tyrannie doth aspire:
Hindering with his shade my lovely light,
And robbing me of the swete sonnes sight?
175 So beate his old boughes my tender side,
That oft the bloud springeth from wounds wyde.[7]
Untimely my flowres forced to fall,
That bene the honor of your Coronall.° *garland*
And oft he lets his cancker wormes° light *caterpillars*
180 Upon my braunches, to worke me more spight:
And oft his hoarie locks[8] downe doth cast,
Where with my fresh flowretts bene defast.[9]
For this, and many more such outrage,
Craving your goodlihead° to aswage° *goodness / diminish*
185 The ranckorous rigour of his might,
Nought aske I, but onely to hold my right:
Submitting me to your good sufferance,° *permission*
And praying to be garded from greevance."
To this the Oake cast him to replie
190 Well as he couth:[1] but his enemie
Had kindled such coles of displeasure,
That the good man noulde stay his leasure,[2]
But home him hasted with furious heate,
Encreasing his wrath with many a threate.
195 His harmefull Hatchet he hent° in hand, *caught*
(Alas, that it so ready should stand)
And to the field alone he speedeth.
(Ay° little helpe to harme there needeth) *Always*
Anger nould let him speake to the tree,
200 Enaunter° his rage mought cooléd bee: *lest*
But to the roote bent his sturdy stroke,
And made many wounds in the wast° Oake. *ruined*
The Axes edge did oft turne againe,
As halfe unwilling to cutte the graine:
205 Seméd, the sencelesse yron dyd feare,
Or to wrong holy eld° did forbeare.° *age / refrain*
For it had bene an auncient tree,

6. "Metaphorically ment of the bare boughes, spoyled of leaves. This colourably [speciously] he speaketh, as adjudging hym to the fyre" [*E. K.'s Glosse*].
7. "Spoken of a blocke, as it were of a living creature, figuratively, and (as they saye) κατ' εἰκασμόν. [as a comparison]" [*E. K.'s Glosse*].
8. "Metaphorically for withered leaves" [*E. K.'s Glosse*].
9. I.e., by which my new little flowers are destroyed; "defaced" also meant abashed and defamed.
1. I.e., as well as he knew how.
2. I.e., would not wait. It was often said of slander that foolish magistrates act with credulous haste upon hearing it; hence the ass's ears on the judge in the lost but often imitated painting of Calumny by Apelles (fourth century B.C.E.).

Sacred with many a mysteree,
And often crost with the priestes crewe,
210 And often halowed with holy water dewe.[3]
But sike° fancies weren foolerie, *such*
And broughten this Oake to this miserye.
For nought mought they quitten° him from decay:° *deliver / ruin*
For fiercely the good man at him did laye.
215 The blocke oft gronéd under the blow,[4]
And sighed to see his neare ouerthrow.
In fine[5] the steele had piercéd his pitth,
Tho downe to the earth he fell forthwith:
His wonderous weight made the grounde to quake,
220 Th'earth shronke under him, and seemed to shake.
There lyeth the Oake, pitied of none.
  Now stands the Brere like a Lord alone,
Puffed up with pryde and vaine pleasaunce:
But all this glee had no continuaunce.
225 For eftsones° Winter gan to approche, *soon*
The blustring Boreas[6] did encroche,
And beate upon the solitarie Brere:
For nowe no succoure was seene him nere.
Now gan he repent his pryde to late:
230 For naked left and disconsolate,
The byting frost nipt his stalke dead,
The watrie wette weighed downe his head,
And heapéd snowe burdned him so sore,
That nowe upright he can stand no more:
235 And being downe, is trodde in the durt
Of cattell, and brouzed, and sorely hurt.
Such was th'end of this Ambitious brere,
For scorning Eld[7]

CUDDIE

Now I pray thee shepheard, tel it not forth:
240 Here is a long tale, and little worth.[8]
So longe have I listened to thy speche,
That graffféd° to the ground is my breche:° *grafted / rump*
My hartblood is welnigh frorne° I feele, *frozen*
And my galage[9] growne fast to my heele:

3. The tree was blessed by the sign of the cross and holy water from a "crewe," a "pott, wherewith the popishe priest used to sprinckle and hallowe the trees from [i.e., against] mischaunce. Such blindnesse was in those times, which the Poete supposeth, to have bene the finall decay of this auncient Oake" [*E. K.'s Glosse*]. By associating the oak with practices abolished by the Reformation, Spenser hints at historical allegory. The tree resembles one in Lucan's *Civil War* 1.136–43 (applied to Caesar's opponent, Pompey), borrowed by Joachim Du Bellay for *Antiquitez* 28 (on ancient Rome) and then translated by Spenser in *The Ruines of Rome* (*Complaints* 1591).
4. "A lively figure, which geveth sence and feeling to unsensible [i.e., incapable of sensory perception] creatures" [*E. K.'s Glosse*].
5. I.e., in the end.
6. "The Northerne wynd, that bringeth the moste stormie weather" [*E. K.'s Glosse*].
7. "And minding (as should seme) to have made ryme to the former verse, he is conningly cutte of[f] by Cuddye, as disdayning to here any more" [*E. K.'s Glosse*].
8. I.e., worth little.
9. I.e., "a startuppe [boot; the word also meant upstart] or clownish [rustic] shoe" [*E. K.'s Glosse*].

245 But little ease of thy lewd° tale I tasted. *worthless*
Hye thee home shepheard, the day is nigh° wasted. *nearly*

Thenots Embleme.

Iddio perche è vecchio,
Fa suoi al suo essempio.[1]

Cuddies Embleme.

Niuno vecchio,
Spaventa Iddio.[2]

Aprill

Argument

This Aeglogue is purposely intended to the honor and prayse of our most gracious sovereigne, Queene Elizabeth. The speakers herein be Hobbinoll and Thenott,[1] *two shepheardes: the which Hobbinoll being before mentioned, greatly to have loved Colin, is here set forth more largely, complayning*[2] *him of that boyes great misadventure in Love, whereby his mynd was*

1. E. K. calls this "a moral of his former tale" and paraphrases the Italian: "God, which is himselfe most aged, being before al ages, and without beginninge, maketh those, whom he loveth like to himselfe, in heaping yeares unto theyre dayes, and blessing them wyth longe lyfe. . . . So the old man checketh the rashheaded boy, for despysing his gray and frostye heares" [*Glosse*].
2. I.e., "No old man fears the Lord" (Italian). Cuddie thus gives a "counterbuff," says E. K., "with a byting and bitter proverbe," for "it was an old opinion, and yet is continued in some mens conceipt [i.e., thought], that men of yeares have no feare of god at al, or not so much as younger folke. For that being rypened with long experience, and having passed many bitter brunts and blastes of vengeaunce, they dread no stormes of Fortune, nor wrathe of Gods, nor daunger of menne, as being eyther by longe and ripe wisedome armed against all mischaunces and adversitie, or with much trouble hardened against all troublesome tydes: lyke unto the Ape, of which is sayd in Æsops fables, that oftentimes meeting the Lyon, he was at first sore aghast and dismayed at the grimnes[s] and austeritie of hys countenance, but at last being acquainted with his lookes, he was so furre from fearing him, that he would familiarly gybe [i.e., joke] and jest with him" [*Glosse*].

1. Elsewhere in the *Calender* Thenot seems, if ambiguously, to represent the wisdom of experience.
2. Lamenting.

alienate and with drawen not onely from him, who moste loved him, but also from all former delightes and studies, aswell in pleasaunt pyping, as conning[3] *ryming and singing, and other his laudable exercises. Whereby he taketh occasion, for proofe of his more excellencie and skill in poetrie, to recorde a songe, which the sayd Colin sometime made in honor of her Majestie, whom abruptely he termeth Elysa.*

THENOT **HOBBINOLL**

Tell me good Hobbinoll, what garres° thee greete?° *makes / weep*
What? hath some Wolfe thy tender Lambes ytorne?
Or is thy Bagpype broke, that soundes so sweete?
Or art thou of thy lovéd lasse forlorne?° *deserted*

5 Or bene thine eyes attempred° to the yeare, *attuned*
Quenching the gasping furrowes thirst with rayne?
Like April shoure, so stremes the trickling teares
Adowne thy cheeke, to quenche thy thristye° payne. *thirsty*

HOBBINOLL

Nor thys, nor that, so muche doeth make me mourne,
10 But for° the ladde,[4] whome long I loyd so deare, *that*
Nowe loves a lasse, that all his love doth scorne:
He plongd in payne, his tresséd° locks dooth teare. *curled*

Shepheards delights he dooth them all forsweare,
Hys pleasaunt Pipe, whych made us meriment,
15 He wylfully hath broke, and doth forbeare
His wonted songs, wherein he all outwent.° *surpassed*

THENOT

What is he for a Ladde,[5] you so lament?
Ys love such pinching payne to them, that prove?° *feel (it)*
And hath he skill to make[6] so excellent,
20 Yet hath so little skill to brydle love?

HOBBINOLL

Colin thou kenst,° the Southerne shepheardes boye:[7] *knowest*
Him Love hath wounded with a deadly darte.
Whilome on him was all my care and joye,
Forcing with gyfts to winne his wanton heart.

3. Learning, studying. "Laudable exercises" are formal expressions of praise: encomiastic poetry.
4. I.e., Colin.
5. E. K. notes that the expression is "a straunge manner of speaking"; he renders it, "What maner of Ladde is he?" [*Glosse*].
6. "To rime and versifye. For in this word making, our olde Englishe Poetes were wont to comprehend all the skil of Poetrye, according to the Greeke woorder ποιειν, to make, whence commeth the name of Poetes" [*E. K.'s Glosse*].
7. "Seemeth hereby that Colin perteyneth to some Southern noble man . . ." [*E. K.'s Glosse*]. "The Southerne shepheardе" may refer to the earl of Leicester, but Spenser is more probably alluding to his own association with Bishop John Young.

25 But now from me hys madding° mynd is starte,° *foolish / broken away*
And woes° the Widdowes daughter of the glenne:[8] *woos*
So nowe fayre Rosalind hath bredde° hys smart, *caused*
So now his frend is chaungéd for a frenne.° *stranger*

THENOT

But if hys ditties bene so trimly dight,[9]
30 I pray thee Hobbinoll, recorde° some one: *sing*
The whiles our flockes doe graze about in sight,
And we close shrowded in thys shade alone.

HOBBINOLL

Contented I: then will I singe his laye[1]
Of fayre Elisa, Queene of shepheardes all:
35 Which once he made, as by a spring he laye,
And tunéd it unto the Waters fall.

"Ye dayntye Nymphs, that in this blesséd Brooke
Doe bathe your brest,
Forsake your watry bowres, and hether looke,
40 At my request:
And eke you Virgins,[2] that on Parnasse dwell,
Whence floweth Helicon the learnéd well,
Helpe me to blaze° *proclaim, depict*
Her worthy praise,
45 Which in her sexe doth all excell.

"Of fayre Elisa be your silver song,
That blesséd wight:
The flowre of Virgins, may shee florish long,
In princely plight.° *condition*
50 For shee is Syrinx daughter without spotte,
Which Pan the shepheards God of her begot:[3]

8. "He calleth Rosalind the Widowes daughter of the glenne, that is, of a country Hamlet or borough, which I thinke is rather sayde to coloure and concele the person, then simply spoken. For it is well knowen, even in spighte of Colin and Hobbinoll, that shee is a Gentle woman of no meane house, nor endewed with anye vulgare and common gifts both of nature and manners: but suche indeede, as neede nether Colin be ashamed to have her made knowne by his verses, nor Hobbinol be greved, that so she should be commended to immortalitie for her rare and singular Vertues" [*E. K.'s Glosse*]. E. K. misunderstands the word "glenne" (a wooded mountain valley).
9. I.e., neatly made.
1. "A songe. As Roundelayes and Virelayes. In all this songe is not to be respected, what the worthinesse of her Majestie deserveth, nor what to the highnes of a Prince is agreeable, but what is moste comely for the meanesse of a shepheards witte, or to conceive, or to utter. And therefore he calleth her Elysa, as through rudenesse tripping in her name: and a shepheards daughter, it being very unfit, that a shepheards boy brought up in the shepefold, should know, or ever seme to have heard of a Queenes roialty" [*E. K.'s Glosse*].
2. I.e., the nine Muses, described by E. K. as "daughters of Apollo and Memorie, whose abode the Poets faine to be on Parnassus, a hill in Grece, for that in that countrye specially florished the honor of all excellent studies" [*Glosse*]. Properly, Helicon was not a "well," but the mountain from which flowed the springs Hippocrene and Aganippe; medieval tradition (as in Chaucer's *Hous of Fame* 521–22, or *Troilus and Criseyde* 3.1809) accounts for E. K.'s reference.
3. E. K., having summarized Ovid's tale of Pan and Syrinx, says that "here by Pan and Syrinx is not to bee thoughte, that the shepehearde simplye meante those Poetical Gods: but rather supposing (as seemeth) her graces progenie to be divine and immortall . . . could devise no parents in his judgement so worthy for her, as Pan the shepeheards God, and his best beloved Syrinx. So that by Pan is here meant the most famous and victorious King, her highnesse Father, late

So sprang her grace
Of heavenly race,
No mortall blemishe may her blotte.

55 "See, where she sits upon the grassie greene,
(O seemely sight)
Yclad in Scarlot like a mayden Queene,
And Ermines white.
Upon her head a Cremosin° coronet, *crimson*
60 With Damaske roses and Daffadillies set:
Bayleaves betweene,
And Primroses greene
Embellish the sweete Violet.

"Tell me, have ye seene her angelick face,
65 Like Phoebe[4] fayre?
Her heavenly haveour,° her princely grace *bearing*
Can you well compare?° *match*
The Redde rose medled° with the White yfere,° *combined / together*
In either cheeke depeincten° lively chere.[5] *depict*
70 Her modest eye,
Her Majestie,
Where have you seene the like, but there?

"I sawe Phoebus thrust out his golden hedde,
Upon her to gaze:
75 But when he sawe, how broade her beames did spredde,
It did him amaze.
He blusht to see another Sunne belowe,
Ne durst againe his fyrye face out showe:
Let him, if he dare,
80 His brightnesse compare
With hers, to have the overthrowe.

"Shewe thy selfe Cynthia with thy silver rayes,
And be not abasht:
When shee the beames of her beauty displayes,
85 O how art thou dasht?
But I will not match her with Latonaes seede,[6]

---

of worthy memorye K. Henry the eyght. And by that name, oftymes (as hereafter appeareth) be noted kings and mighty Potentates: And in some place Christ himselfe, who is the verye Pan and god of Shepheardes" [*Glosse*]. Marot had alluded to a king (Francis I) as Pan.

4. "The Moone, whom the Poets faine to be sister unto Phoebus, that is the Sunne" [*E. K.'s Glosse*]. Born on Cynthus Hill, in the island of Delos (according to legend), she was known also as Cynthia.
5. "By the mingling of the Redde rose and the White, is meant the uniting of the two principall houses of Lancaster and of Yorke: by whose longe discord and deadly debate, this realm many yeares was sore traveiled, and almost cleane decayed. Til the famous Henry the seventh, of the line of Lancaster, taking to wife the most vertuous Princesse Elisabeth, daughter to the fourth Edward of the house of Yorke, begat the most royal Henry the eyght aforesayde, in whom was the firste union of the Whyte Rose and the Redde" [*E. K.'s Glosse*].
6. Niobe, mother of fourteen children, dared to scorn the Titaness Latona, who had given birth only to Apollo and Diana; these two consequently slew all of Niobe's offspring and Zeus turned her into a stone, from which tears forever flow (cf. Ovid, *Metamorphoses* 6.148–312).

Such follie great sorow to Niobe did breede.° *cause*
  Now she is a stone,
  And makes dayly mone,
90 Warning all other to take heede.

"Pan may be proud, that ever he begot
  Such a Bellibone,° *fair maid*
And Syrinx rejoyse, that ever was her lot
  To beare such an one.
95 Soone as my younglings cryen for the dam,
To her will I offer a milkwhite Lamb:
  Shee is my goddesse plaine,° *absolute*
  And I her shepherds swayne,
Albee forswonck and forswatt I am.[7]

100 "I see Calliope[8] speede her to the place,
  Where my Goddesse shines:
And after her the other Muses trace,° *step*
  With their Violines.
Bene they not Bay braunches,[9] which they do beare,
105 All for Elisa in her hand to weare?
  So sweetely they play,
  And sing all the way,
That it a heaven is to heare.

"Lo how finely the graces[1] can it foote
110   To the Instrument:
They dauncen deffly,° and singen soote,° *deftly / sweetly*
  In their meriment.
Wants not a fourth grace, to make the daunce even?
Let that rowme to my Lady be yeven:° *given*
115   She shalbe a grace,
  To fyll the fourth place,
And reigne with the rest in heaven.[2]

"And whither rennes° this bevie of Ladies bright, *runs*
  Raungéd in a rowe?
120 They bene all Ladyes of the lake[3] behight,° *called*

7. I.e., tired from work and bathed in sweat. The expression occurs also in "The Plowman's Tale," a lengthy satire on the clergy, then thought to be by Chaucer. Cf. "Envoy" 10 and note.
8. The Muse of epic poetry; "to whome they assigne the honor of al Poetical Invention, and the firste glorye of the Heroicall verse" [*E. K.'s Glosse*].
9. "The signe of honor and victory, and therfore of myghty Conquerors worn in theyr triumphes, and eke of famous Poets, as saith Petrarch in hys Sonets . . ." [*E. K.'s Glosse*].
1. "Three sisters, the daughters of Jupiter, whose names are Aglaia, Thalia, Euphrosyne. . . . whom the Poetes feyned to be the Goddesses of al bountie and comelines, which therefore (as sayth Theodontius) they make three, to wete, that men first ought to be gracious and bountiful to other freely, then to receive benefits at other mens hands curteously, and thirdly to requite them thankfully: which are three sundry Actions in liberalitye. And Boccace saith, that they be painted naked, (as they were indeede on the tombe of C. Julius Caesar) the one having her backe toward us, and her face fromwarde, as proceeding from us: the other two toward us, noting double thanke to be due to us for the benefit, we have done" [*E. K.'s Glosse*].
2. Cf. *The Faerie Queene* VI.x. 16 and note.
3. "Ladyes of the lake be Nymphes. For it was an olde opinion amongste the Auncient Heathen,

That unto her goe.
Chloris,[4] that is the chiefest Nymph of al,
Of Olive braunches beares a Coronall:° *coronet*
Olives bene for peace,
125 When wars doe surcease:
Such for a Princesse bene principall.° *princely*

"Ye shepheards daughters, that dwell on the greene,
Hye you there apace:° *quickly*
Let none come there, but that Virgins bene,
130 To adorne her grace.
And when you come, whereas shee is in place,
See, that your rudenesse doe not you disgrace:
Binde your fillets° faste, *hair ribbons*
And gird in your waste,
135 For more finesse, with a tawdrie lace.[5]

"Bring hether the Pincke and purple Cullambine,
With Gelliflowres:
Bring Coronations, and Sops in wine,
Worne of Paramoures.° *lovers*
140 Strowe me the ground with Daffadowndillies,
And Cowslips, and Kingcups, and lovéd Lillies:
The pretie Pawnce,
And the Chevisaunce,
Shall match with the fayre flowre Delice.[6]

145 "Now ryse up Elisa, deckéd as thou art,
In royall aray:
And now ye daintie Damsells may depart
Echeone her way,
I feare, I have troubled your troupes to longe:
150 Let dame Eliza thanke you for her song.
And if you come hether,
When Damsines° I gether, *plums*
I will part them all you among."

---

that of every spring and fountaine was a goddesse the Soveraigne. Whiche opinion stucke in the myndes of men not manye yeares sithence, by meanes of certain fine fablers and lowd lyers, such as were the Authors of King Arthure the great and such like, who tell many an unlawfull leasing of the Ladyes of the Lake, that is, the Nymphes. For the word Nymphe in Greeke signifieth Well water, or otherwise a Spouse or Bryde" [*E. K.'s Glosse*]. A "Lady of the Lake" figured in the entertainment presented before Queen Elizabeth at Kenilworth in 1575; cf. *The Faerie Queene* III.iii.10.

4. "The name of a Nymph, and signifieth greenesse, of whome is sayd, that Zephyrus the Westerne wind being in love with her, and coveting her to wyfe, gave her for a dowrie, the chiefedome and soveraigntye of al flowres and greene herbes, growing on earth" [*E. K.'s Glosse*].
5. I.e., to present a finer appearance, with a band of lace or silk (sold during the fair of St. Audrey).
6. Spenser's flower passage, owing something to Marot's Lament for Louise of Savoy 225–36, in turn influenced Milton's *Lycidas. Coronations*: carnations; *Sops in wine*: clove pinks; *Pawnce*: the pansy; *flowre Delice*: fleur de lys (a variety of iris); *Chevisaunce*: not satisfactorily identified, but perhaps a species of wallflower.

THENOT

And was thilk same song of Colins owne making?
155 Ah foolish boy, that is with love yblent;° *blinded*
Great pittie is, he be in such taking,° *plight*
For naught caren, that bene so lewdly bent.[7]

HOBBINOL

Sicker° I hold him, for a greater fon,° *surely / fool*
That loves the thing, he cannot purchase.
160 But let us homeward: for night draweth on,
And twincling starres the daylight hence chase.

Thenots Embleme.[8]

O quam te memorem virgo?

Hobbinols Embleme.

O dea certe.

7. I.e., for they that are so foolishly inclined are quite heedless.
8. "This Poesye is taken out of Virgile [*Aeneid* I.327–28], and there of him used in the person of Aeneas to his mother Venus, appearing to him in likenesse of one of Dianaes damosells: being there most divinely set forth. To which similitude of divinitie Hobbinoll comparing the excelency of Elisa, and being through the worthynes of Colins song, as it were, overcome with the hugenesse of his imagination, brusteth out in great admiration (O quam te memorem virgo?) being otherwise unhable, then by soddein silence, to expresse the worthinesse of his conceipt. Whom Thenot answereth with another part of the like verse, as confirming by his graunt and approvance, that Elisa is no whit inferiour to the Majestie of her, of whome that Poete so boldly pronounced, O dea certe" [*E. K.'s Glosse*].

October†

Argument

In Cuddie[1] *is set out the perfecte paterne of a Poete, whiche finding no maintenaunce of his state and studies, complayneth of the contempte of Poetrie, and the causes thereof: Specially having bene in all ages, and even amongst the most barbarous alwayes of singular accounpt*[2] *and honor, and being indede so worthy and commendable an arte: or rather no arte, but a divine gift and heavenly instinct not to bee gotten by laboure and learning, but adorned with both: and poured into the witte by a certaine ἐνθουσιασμός*[3] *and celestiall inspiration, as the Author hereof els where at large discourseth, in his booke called the English Poete, which booke being lately come to my hands, I mynde also by Gods grace upon further advisement to publish.*

† "This Aeglogue is made in imitation of Theocritus his xvi. Idilion, wherein hee reproved the Tyranne Hiero of Syracuse for his nigardise towarde Poetes, in whome is the power to make men immortal for theyr good dedes, or shameful for their naughty lyfe. And the lyke also is in Mantuane. The style hereof as also that in Theocritus, is more loftye then the rest, and applyed to the heighte of Poeticall witte" [*E. K.'s Glosse*]. In fact, the influence of Theocritus on this eclogue is slight; Spenser's debt to the fifth eclogue of Mantuan is more significant, in structural outline as well as in outlook and detail.

1. "I doubte whether by Cuddie be specified the authour selfe, or some other. For in the eyght Aeglogue the same person was brought in, singing a Cantion of Colins making, as he sayth. So that some doubt, that the persons be different" [*E. K.'s Glosse*].
2. Esteem.
3. "Enthousiasmos," says Plato, is that force in the soul (E. K.'s "divine gift and heavenly instinct"), that good "mania" that, depending on its particular divine source, inspires poetry, religious initiation, prophecy, and love; see his *Phaedrus* 249E and *Ion* 536. Spenser could have read about such "celestiall inspiration" in Plato himself or in a number of Renaissance texts such as Minturno's *De Poeta* (1559) or the Englishman Richard Willes's *De Re Poetica* in his *Poematum Liber* (1573), sig. C1. The "English Poete" to which E. K. refers has not survived. There could be one further ambiguity: Spenser's generation used commas where we would not, and so this "perfecte paterne of a Poete" *may* be a perfect pattern of a poet who is inadequately supported.

PIERS CUDDIE

Cuddie, for shame hold up thy heavye head,
And let us cast° with what delight to chace, *devise*
And weary thys long lingring Phoebus race.[4]
Whilome° thou wont the shepheards laddes to leade, *formerly*
5 In rymes, in ridles, and in bydding base:[5]
Now they in thee, and thou in sleepe art dead.

CUDDIE

Piers, I have pypéd erst so long with payne,
That all mine Oten reedes[6] bene rent and wore:
And my poore Muse hath spent her sparéd store,
10 Yet little good hath got, and much lesse gayne.
Such pleasaunce makes the Grashopper so poore.
And ligge so layd,[7] when Winter doth her straine.° *constrain*

The dapper° ditties, that I wont devise, *pretty*
To feede youthes fancie, and the flocking fry,[8]
15 Delighten much: what I the bett for thy?[9]
They han° the pleasure, I a sclender prise. *have*
I beate the bush, the byrds to them doe flye:
What good thereof to Cuddie can arise?

PIERS

Cuddie, the prayse is better, then the price,
20 The glory eke much greater then the gayne:
O what an honor is it, to restraine
The lust of lawlesse youth with good advice:
Or pricke them forth with pleasaunce of thy vaine,° *poetic vein*
Whereto thou list their traynéd° willes entice.[1] *allured*

25 Soone as thou gynst to sette thy notes in frame,
O how the rurall routes° to thee doe cleave: *crowds*
Seemeth thou dost their soule of sence bereave,[2]

4. I.e., and pass this long day.
5. The game of prisoner's base; or, possibly, poetical contests.
6. E. K.'s Glosse refers to Virgil's term, "avena" (*Eclogue* 1.2); properly "oats," or "oat stalks," the term signifies in Virgil's (and Ovid's) usage a reed or pipe.
7. "Lye so faynt and unlustie" [*E. K's Glosse*]; as in the fable of the ant and the grasshopper.
8. "Frye is a bold Metaphore, forced from the spawning fishes. For the multitude of young fish be called the frye" [*E. K.'s Glosse*.]
9. I.e., in what way am I therefore the better?
1. "This place seemeth to conspyre with Plato, who in his first booke de Legibus sayth, that the first invention of Poetry was of very vertuous intent" [*E. K.'s Glosse*].
2. "What the secrete working of Musick is in the myndes of men, aswell appeareth, hereby, that some of the auncient Philosophers, and those the moste wise, as Plato and Pythagoras held for opinion, that the mynd was made of a certaine harmonie and musicall nombers, for the great compassion and likenes of affection in thone and in the other as also by that memorable history of Alexander: to whom when as Timotheus the great Musitian playd the Phrygian melodie, it is said, that he was distraught with such unwonted fury, that streight way rysing from the table in great rage, he caused himselfe to be armed, as ready to goe to warre (for that musick is very war like:) And immediatly whenas the Musitian chaunged his stroke into the Lydian and Ionique harmony, he was so furr from warring, that he sat as styl, as if he had bene in matters of counsell. Such might is in musick" [*E. K.'s Glosse*].

All as the shepheard,[3] that did fetch his dame
From Plutoes balefull bowre withouten leave:
30 His musicks might the hellish hound did tame.

CUDDIE

So praysen babes the Peacoks spotted traine,
And wondren at bright Argus blazing eye:[4]
But who rewards him ere the more for thy?[5]
Or feedes him once the fuller by a graine?
35 Sike° prayse is smoke, that sheddeth° in the skye, *such / is dispersed*
Sike words bene wynd, and wasten soone in vayne.

PIERS

Abandon then the base and viler clowne,[6]
Lyft up thy selfe out of the lowly dust:
And sing of bloody Mars, of wars, of giusts,° *jousts*
40 Turne thee to those, that weld° the awful crowne. *bear*
To doubted° Knights, whose woundlesse armour[7] rusts, *dreaded*
And helmes unbruzéd wexen° dayly browne. *grow*

There may thy Muse display[8] her fluttryng wing,
And stretch her selfe at large from East to West:
45 Whither thou list in fayre Elisa rest,
Or if thee please in bigger notes to sing,
Advaunce° the worthy whome shee loveth best,[9] *extol*
That first the white beare to the stake did bring.

And when the stubborne stroke of stronger stounds,° *taxing efforts*
50 Has somewhat slackt the tenor of thy string:[1]
Of love and lustihead° tho mayst thou sing, *pleasure*
And carrol lowde, and leade the Myllers rownde,[2]
All° were Elisa one of thilke same ring. *although*
So mought our Cuddies name to Heaven sownde.

3. "Orpheus: of whom is sayd, that by his excellent skil in Musick and Poetry, he recovered his wife Eurydice from hell" [*E. K.'s Glosse*]. The "hellish hound" in line 30 is Cerberus, the three-headed hound guarding the gates of Hades (cf. Ovid, *Metamorphoses* 10.22; Virgil, *Georgics* 4.483).
4. "Juno to [Argus] committed hir husband Jupiter his Paragon Io, because he had an hundred eyes: but afterwarde Mercury wyth hys Musick lulling Argus aslepe, slew him and brought Io away, whose eyes it is sayd that Juno for his eternall memory placed in her byrd the Peacocks tayle. For those coloured spots indeede resemble eyes" [*E. K.'s Glosse*]. Cf. Ovid, *Metamorphoses* 1.622–723.
5. I.e., therefore.
6. I.e., too mean or low rustic. The stanza promises a rise to higher "kinds," i.e., tragedy and epic.
7. "Woundlesse armour," E. K. observes, "unwounded in warre, doe rust through long peace" [*Glosse*].
8. "A poeticall metaphore: whereof the meaning is, that if the Poet list showe his skill in matter of more dignitie, then is the homely Aeglogue, good occasion is him offered of higher veyne and more Heroicall argument, in the person of our most gratious soveraign, whom (as before) he calleth Elisa. Or if mater of knighthoode and chevalrie please him better, that there be many Noble and valiaunt men, that are both worthy of his payne in theyr deserved prayses, and also favourers of hys skil and faculty" [*E. K.'s Glosse*].
9. I.e., the earl of Leicester, whose heraldic device was a bear and "ragged" staff.
1. I.e., slackened the strings of your lyre, lowering its pitch; "that is when thou chaungest thy verse from stately discourse, to matter of more pleasaunce and delight" [*E. K.'s Glosse*].
2. "A kind of daunce" [*E. K.'s Glosse*].

CUDDIE

55 Indeede the Romish Tityrus,[3] I heare,
Through his Mecaenas left his Oaten reede,
Whereon he earst° had taught his flocks to feede, *formerly*
And laboured lands to yield the timely eare,
And eft did sing of warres and deadly drede,
60 So as the Heavens did quake his verse to here.[4]

But ah Mecaenas is yclad in claye,
And great Augustus long ygoe is dead:
And all the worthies liggen° wrapt in leade, *lie*
That matter made for Poets on to play:
65 For ever, who in derring doe[5] were dreade,
The loftie verse of hem was lovéd aye.[6]

But after vertue gan for age to stoupe,
And mighty manhode brought a bedde of ease:[7]
The vaunting Poets found nought worth a pease,° *pea*
70 To put in preace[8] emong the learnéd troupe.
Tho gan the streames of flowing wittes to cease,
And sonnebright honour pend in shamefull coupe.[9]

And if that any buddes of Poesie,
Yet of the old stocke gan to shoote agayne:
75 Or° it mens follies mote be forst to fayne, *either*
And rolle with rest in rymes of rybaudrye:
Or as it sprong, it wither must agayne:
Tom Piper makes us better melodie.[1]

3. "Wel knowen to be Virgile, who by Mecaenas means was brought into the favour of the Emperor Augustus, and by him moved to write in loftier kinde, then he erst had doen" [*E. K.'s Glosse*]. Cf. *The Faerie Queene* I.P.1–4.
4. "In these three verses are the three severall workes of Virgile intended. For in teaching his flocks to feede, is meant his Aeglogues. In labouring of lands, is hys Bucoliques. In singing of wars and deadly dreade, is his divine Aeneis figured" [*E. K.'s Glosse*].
5. I.e., daring deeds.
6. "He sheweth the cause, why Poetes were wont be had in such honor of noble men; that is, that by them their worthines and valor shold through theyr famous Posies be commended to al posterities. Wherfore it is sayd, that Achilles had never bene so famous, as he is, but for Homeres immortal verses. Which is the only advantage, which he had of Hector. . . . And that such account hath bene alwayes made of Poetes, aswell sheweth this that the worthy Scipio in all his warres against Carthage and Numantia had evermore in his company, and that in a most familiar sort the good olde Poet Ennius: as also that Alexander destroying Thebes, when he was enformed that the famous Lyrick Poet Pindarus was borne in that citie, not onely commaunded streightly, that no man should upon payne of death do any violence to that house by fire or otherwise: but also specially spared most, and some highly rewarded, that were of hys kinne. So favoured he the only name of a Poete. Whych prayse otherwise was in the same man no lesse famous, that when he came to ransacking of king Darius coffers, whom he lately had overthrowen, he founde in a little coffer of silver the two bookes of Homers works, as layd up there for special jewells and richesse, which he taking thence, put one of them dayly in his bosome, and thother every night layde under his pillowe" [*E. K.'s Glosse*]. E. K. probably drew these materials from Plutarch's *Life of Alexander* or from Boccaccio.
7. I.e., brought into a passive and helpless state through love of luxurious ease; "he sheweth the cause of contempt of Poetry to be idlenesse and basenesse of mynd" [*E. K.'s Glosse*].
8. I.e., to present for competition.
9. ". . . shut up in slouth, as in a coupe or cage" [*E. K.'s Glosse*].
1. "An Ironicall Sarcasmus, spoken in derision of these rude wits, whych make more account of a ryming rybaud, then of skill grounded upon learning and judgment" [*E. K.'s Glosse*]. "Tom Piper" refers to the piper who accompanied the morris dancers.

PIERS

O pierlesse Poesye, where is then thy place?
80 If nor in Princes pallace thou doe sitt:
(And yet is Princes pallace the most fitt)
Ne brest of baser birth[2] doth thee embrace.
Then make thee winges of thine aspyring wit,
And, whence thou camst, flye backe to heaven apace.[3]

CUDDIE

85 Ah Percy it is all to weake and wanne,
So high to sore, and make so large a flight:
Her peecéd pyneons[4] bene not so in plight,° *condition*
For Colin fittes[5] such famous flight to scanne:° *attempt*
He, were he not with love so ill bedight,° *afflicted*
90 Would mount as high, and sing as soote as Swanne[6]

PIERS

Ah fon,° for love does teach him climbe so hie, *fool*
And lyftes him up out of the loathsome myre:
Such immortall mirrhor,[7] as he doth admire,
Would rayse ones mynd above the starry skie.
95 And cause a caytive corage[8] to aspire,
For lofty love doth loath a lowly eye.

CUDDIE

All otherwise the state of Poet stands,
For lordly love is such a Tyranne fell:
That where he rules, all power he doth expell.[9]
100 The vaunted verse a vacant head demaundes,
Ne wont with crabbéd care the Muses dwell.
Unwisely weaves, that takes two webbes in hand.

Who ever casts to compasse° weightye prise, *attain*
And thinks to throwe out thondring words of threate:
105 Let powre in lavish cups and thriftie° bitts of meate, *nourishing*
For Bacchus fruite is frend to Phoebus wise.[1]

2. ". . . the meaner sort of men" [*E. K.'s Glosse*].
3. I.e., wing your way back to the divine love that inspires the highest poetic "kind."
4. I.e., imperfect, patched wings: "unperfect skil" [*E. K.'s Glosse*].
5. I.e., it is proper for Colin.
6. "The comparison seemeth to be strange: for the swanne hath ever wonne small commendation for her swete singing: but it is sayd of the learned that the swan a little before hir death, singeth most pleasantly, as prophecying by a secrete instinct her neere destinie . . ." [*E. K.'s Glosse*].
7. "Beauty, which is an excellent object of Poeticall spirites . . ." [*E. K.'s Glosse*]. The lover, contemplating the beloved's beauty (which reflects immortal and heavenly beauty), is thereby enabled to rise above earthly concerns, and approach more nearly to divine beauty and love.
8. ". . . a base and abject minde" [*E. K.'s Glosse*].
9. Renaissance sonneteers regularly make use of the Ovidian conceit that love is an arbitrary tyrant whose dictates the lover is powerless to resist.
1. Boccaccio (*De Genealogia Deorum* 5.25) and Comes (*Mythologiae* 5.13) note wine's power to heighten poetic genius (here represented by Phoebus Apollo), although in Plato's *Phaedrus* the wine god Dionysus (Bacchus) presides over religious inspiration.

And when with Wine the braine begins to sweate,
The nombers flowe as fast as spring doth ryse.

Thou kenst not Percie howe the ryme should rage.
110 O if my temples were distaind° with wine,[2] *stained*
And girt in girlonds of wild Yvie twine,
How I could reare the Muse on stately stage,
And teache her tread aloft in bus-kin[3] fine,
With queint Bellona[4] in her equipage.

115 But ah my corage cooles ere it be warme,
For thy, content us in thys humble shade:
Where no such troublous tydes han us assayde,° *assailed*
Here we our slender pipes may safely charme.[5]

PIERS

And when my Gates shall han their bellies layd:[6]
120 Cuddie shall have a Kidde to store his farme.

Cuddies Embleme.

Agitante calescimus illo &c.[7]

2. "He seemeth here to be ravished with a Poetical furie. For (if one rightly mark) the numbers rise so ful, and the verse groweth so big, that it seemeth he hath forgot the meanenesse of shepheards state and stile. . . . Wild yvie . . . is dedicated to Bacchus and therefore it is sayd that the Maenades (that is Bacchus franticke priests) used in theyr sacrifice to carry Thyrsos, which were pointed staves or Javelins, wrapped about with yvie" [*E. K.'s Glosse*]. The word "furie" was regularly used to mean madness, including the madness of inspiration, and did not in such cases connote anger.
3. The high boot traditionally worn by the actors of Greek tragedy.
4. "Strange Bellona; the goddesse of battaile, that is Pallas, which may therfore wel be called queint for that (as Lucian saith) when Jupiter hir father was in traveile of her, he caused his sonne Vulcane with his axe to hew his head. Out of which leaped forth lustely a valiant damsell armed at all poyntes . . ." [*E. K.'s Glosse*]. Jupiter/Zeus turned his pregnant first wife, Metis ("prudence," "cunning"), into a fly and then swallowed her. The fly made its way to his head and, after birth pangs (E. K.'s "traveile") so severe that Vulcan opened the head with an axe, out sprang the fully adult and armed Pallas Athena, who in her capacity as goddess of war, is called Bellona. "Lustely" means energetically, eagerly.
5. "Temper and order. For Charmes were wont to be made by verses as Ovid sayth" [*E. K.'s Glosse*]. The passage referred to may be *Amores* 3.7.27–30.
6. I.e., when my goats have been delivered of their young.
7. From Ovid, *Fasti* 6.5: *est deus in nobis; agitante calescimus illo* (There is a god in us, by whose movement we are kept warm). "Hereby is meant, as also in the whole course of this Aeglogue, that Poetry is a divine instinct and unnatural rage passing the reache of comen reason. Whom Piers answereth Epiphonematicos as admiring the excellencye of the skyll whereof in Cuddie hee hadde alreadye hadde a taste" [*E. K.'s Glosse*]. The rhetorical figure "epiphonema" is a brief moralizing summary of what has gone before.

November

Argument

In this xi. Aeglogue he bewayleth the death of some mayden of greate bloud, whom he calleth Dido.[1] *The personage is secrete, and to me altogether unknowne, albe of him selfe I often required*[2] *the same. This Aeglogue is made in imitation of Marot his song, which he made upon the death of Loys the frenche Queene.*[3] *But farre passing his reache, and in myne opinion all other the Eglogues of this booke.*

THENOT COLIN

Colin my deare, when shall it please thee sing,
As thou were wont songs of some jouisaunce?° *merriment*
Thy Muse to long slombreth in sorrowing,
Lulléd a sleepe through loves misgovernaunce.
5 Now somewhat sing, whose endles sovenaunce,° *remembrance*
Emong the shepeheards swaines may aye remaine,
Whether thee list thy lovéd lasse advaunce,° *praise*
Or honor Pan with hymnes of higher vaine.° *vein*

COLIN

Thenot, now nis the time of merimake.° *festivity*
10 Nor Pan to herye,° nor with love to playe: *honor*

1. Some have taken Spenser's "Dido," whose other name was Elissa, as an allusion to Elizabeth, perhaps "dead" to England and to Leicester (who had hoped to marry her) because of her marriage negotiations with the French duc d'Alençon [now Anjou]), but the matter remains obscure, and E. K.'s comments on the matter may be a teasing—and successful—call to vain speculation.
2. Requested.
3. This eclogue's opening looks more to Virgil's Eclogue V than to the author of Spenser's chief model for this poem, Marot, whom E. K. again treats dismissively (cf. the Argument for "Januarie"). Marot's father, Jean Marot, had praised Louise as a Dido, the queen of Carthage who, except for her catastrophic affair with Virgil's Aeneas, had been a canny and successful queen.

Sike myrth in May is meetest for to make,
Or summer shade under the cocked° haye. *stacked*
But nowe sadde Winter welkéd[4] hath the day,
And Phoebus weary of his yerely taske,
15 Ystabled hath his steedes in lowlye laye,° *meadow*
And taken up his ynne in Fishes haske.[5]
Thilke sollein° season sadder plight doth aske,° *sullen / require*
And loatheth sike delightes, as thou doest prayse:
The mornefull Muse in myrth now list ne maske,
20 As shee was wont in youngth and sommer dayes.
But if thou algate lust light virelayes,[6]
And looser songs of love to underfong° *undertake*
Who but thy selfe deserves sike Poetes prayse?
Relieve thy Oaten pypes,[7] that sleepen long.

THENOT

25 The Nightingale is sovereigne of song,
Before him sits the Titmose silent bee:[8]
And I unfitte to thrust in skilfull thronge,
Should Colin make judge of my fooleree.
Nay, better learne of hem, that leanéd bee,
30 And han be watered at the Muses well:[9]
The kindlye dewe drops from the higher tree,
And wets the little plants that lowly dwell.
But if sadde winters wrathe and season chill,
Accorde not with thy Muses meriment,
35 To sadder times thou mayst attune thy quill,° *pipe*
And sing of sorrowe and deathes dreeriment.° *grief*
For deade is Dido, dead alas and drent;° *drowned*
Dido the greate shepehearde[1] his daughter sheene.° *fair*
The fayrest May she was that ever went,[2]
40 Her like shee has not left behinde I weene.° *believe*
And if thou wilt bewayle my wofull tene,° *grief*
I shall thee give yond Cosset[3] for thy payne:
And if thy rymes as rownd° and rufull bene, *finished*

4. "Shortned, or empayred. As the moone being in the waine is sayde of Lidgate to welk" [*E. K.'s Glosse*].
5. I.e., the sun's path has edged closer to the horizon. "A haske is a wicker pad, wherein they use to cary fish" [*E. K.'s Glosse*]. Although the sign Pisces roughly corresponds to February, E. K. observes (for reasons that have provoked puzzlement and speculation) that "The sonne reigneth . . . in the signe Pisces all November" [*Glosse*]. No Elizabethan could read that without a pause. At line 37 Thenot refers to Dido's death by drowning, although in the *Aeneid* she burns herself alive from grief at Aeneas's desertion.
6. "A light kind of song" [*E. K.'s Glosse*]; e.g., the rondeau.
7. I.e., take up your reed pipe again. Cf. "October" 8 and note.
8. I.e., it is proper that the titmouse (a small bird not unlike the nuthatch) should be silent in the presence of the nightingale.
9. "For it is a saying of poetes, that they have dronk of the Muses well Castalias . . ." [*E. K.'s Glosse*]. The Castalian spring on Mount Parnassus was sacred to Apollo and the Muses.
1. ". . . some man of high degree, and not, as some vainely suppose, God Pan. The person both of the shephearde and of Dido is unknowen, and closely buried in the authors conceipt. But out of doubt I am, that it is not Rosalind, as some imagin: for he speaketh soone after of her also" [*E. K.'s Glosse*].
2. I.e., the fairest maiden that ever walked.
3. "A lambe brought up without the dam" [*E. K.'s Glosse*].

As those that did thy Rosalind complayne,
45 Much greater gyfts for guerdon thou shalt gayne,
Then Kidde or Cosset, which I thee bynempt:° *promised*
Then up I say, thou jolly shepeheard swayne,
Let not my small demaund be so contempt.° *scorned*

COLIN

Thenot to that I choose, thou doest me tempt,
50 But ah to well I wote my humble vaine,
And howe my rymes bene rugged and unkempt:° *rough*
Yet as I conne, my conning I will strayne.[4]

"Up then Melpomene thou mournefulst Muse of nyne,[5]
Such cause of mourning never hadst afore:
55 Up grieslie ghostes[6] and up my rufull ryme,
Matter of myrth now shalt thou have no more.
For dead shee is, that myrth thee made of yore.
  Dido my deare alas is dead,
  Dead and lyeth wrapt in lead:
60   O heavie herse,[7]
Let streaming teares be pouréd out in store:
    O carefull verse.

"Shepheards, that by your flocks on Kentish downes abyde,
Waile ye this wofull waste° of natures warke: *devastation*
65 Waile we the wight, whose presence was our pryde:
Waile we the wight, whose absence is our carke.° *grief*
The sonne of all the world is dimme and darke:
  The earth now lacks her wonted light,
  And all we dwell in deadly night,
70   O heavie herse.
Breake we our pypes, that shrild as lowde as Larke,
    O carefull verse.

"Why doe we longer live, (ah why live we so long)
Whose better dayes death hath shut up in woe?
75 The fayrest floure our gyrlond all emong,
Is faded quite and into dust ygoe.° *gone*
Sing now ye shepheards daughters, sing no moe
  The songs that Colin made in her prayse,
  But into weeping turne your wanton° layes, *playful*
80   O heavie herse,

4. I.e., yet as well as I know how, I will exert my skill. The dirge starting at line 53 metrically complements and may thus allude to Colin's lay in "Aprill," a poem that clearly glances at Elizabeth.
5. An invocation to Melpomene, "the sadde and waylefull Muse, used of poets in honor of tragedies" [*E. K.'s Glosse*], suitably introduces the elegy.
6. "The maner of tragicall poetes, to call for helpe of furies and damned ghostes: so is Hecuba of Euripides, and Tantalus brought in of Seneca" [*E. K.'s Glosse*]. E. K. is confused: the ghost of Tantalus appears in Seneca's *Thyestes*; the ghost of Polydorus appears in Euripides' *Hecuba*.
7. "The solemne obsequie in funeralles" [*E. K.'s Glosse*].

Now is time to dye. Nay time was long ygoe,
O carefull verse.

"Whence is it, that the flouret of the field doth fade,
And lyeth buryed long in Winters bale:[8]
85 Yet soone as spring his mantle doth displaye,
It floureth fresh, as it should never fayle?
But thing on earth that is of most availe,° *worth*
As vertues braunch and beauties budde,
Reliven° not for any good. *revive*
90 O heavie herse,
The braunch once dead, the budde eke needes must quaile,° *wither*
O carefull verse.[9]

"She while she was (that was, a woful word to sayne)
For beauties prayse and plesaunce had no pere:
95 So well she couth the shepherds entertayne,
With cakes and cracknells° and such country chere. *biscuits*
Ne would she scorne the simple shepheards swaine,
For she would cal hem often heme° *home*
And give hem curds and clouted° Creme. *clotted*
100 O heavie herse,
Als° Colin Cloute she would not once disdayne. *also*
O carefull verse.

"But nowe sike happy cheere is turnd to heavie chaunce,
Such pleasaunce now displast by dolors dint:
105 All Musick sleepes, where death doth leade the daunce,
And shepherds wonted solace is extinct.
The blew in black, the greene in gray is tinct,° *dyed*
The gaudie girlonds[1] deck her grave,
The faded flowres her corse embrave.° *adorn*
110 O heavie herse,
Morne nowe my Muse, now morne with teares besprint.° *besprinkled*
O carefull verse.

"O thou greate shepheard Lobbin,[2] how great is thy griefe,
Where bene the nosegays that she dight° for thee, *made*
115 The colourd chaplets wrought with a chiefe,
The knotted rushrings,[3] and gilte Rosemaree?
For shee deeméd nothing too deere for thee.
Ah they bene all yclad in clay,

8. I.e., winter's harmful power.
9. Lines 83–92 recall Moschus, *Idyl* 3.99–104, but also Job 14.7–10: "For there is hope of a tree, if it be cut down, that it will sprout again, and that the tender branch thereof will not cease. Though the root thereof wax old in the earth, and the stock thereof die in the ground; yet through the scent of water it will bud, and bring forth boughs like a plant. But man dieth, and wasteth away: yea, man giveth up the ghost, and where is he?"
1. "The meaning is, that the things which were the ornaments of her lyfe are made the honor of her funerall, as is used in burialls" [*E. K.'s Glosse*].
2. "The name of a shepherd, which seemeth to have bene the lover and deere frende of Dido" [*E. K.'s Glosse*]. If Dido is identified somehow with Elizabeth, "Lobbin" could well allude to her favorite Robert Dudley, earl of Leicester (1531–1588), whom the queen sometimes called "Robin."
3. "Agreeable for such base gyftes" [*E. K.'s Glosse*].

One bitter blast blewe all away.
120 O heavie herse,
Thereof nought remaynés but the memoree.
O carefull verse.

"Ay me that dreerie death should strike so mortall stroke,
That can undoe Dame Natures kindly° course: *natural*
125 The faded lockes[4] fall from the loftie oke,
The flouds° do gaspe, for dryéd is theyr sourse, *streams*
And flouds of teares flowe in theyr stead perforse.
The mantled medowes mourne,
Theyr sondry colours tourne.
130 O heavie herse,
The heavens doe melt in teares without remorse.
O carefull verse.

"The feeble flocks in field refuse their former foode,
And hang theyr heads, as they would learne to weepe:
135 The beastes in forest wayle as they were woode,° *mad*
Except the Wolves, that chase the wandring sheepe:
Now she is gon that safely did hem keepe,
The Turtle° on the baréd braunch, *turtledove*
Laments the wound, that death did launch.° *inflict*
140 O heavie herse,
And Philomele[5] her song with teares doth steepe.
O carefull verse.

"The water Nymphs, that wont with her to sing and daunce,
And for her girlond Olive braunches beare,
145 Now balefull boughes of Cypres[6] doen advaunce:° *bring*
The Muses, that were wont greene bayes° to weare, *laurels*
Now bringen bitter Eldre braunches seare,[7]
The fatall sisters[8] eke repent,
Her vitall threde so soone was spent.
150 O heavie herse,
Morne now my Muse, now morne with heavie cheare.° *mood*
O carefull verse.

"O trustlesse[9] state of earthly things, and slipper° hope *slippery*
Of mortal men, that swincke° and sweate for nought, *toil*

4. "Dryed leaves. As if Nature her selfe bewayled the death of the mayde" [*E. K.'s Glosse*]. Lines 123–42 exemplify one convention of pastoral elegy in which "all nature mourns" the loved one's loss.
5. "The nightingale: whome the poetes faine once to have bene a ladye of great beauty, till, being ravished by her sisters husbande, she desired to be turned into a byrd of her name" [*E. K.'s Glosse*]. Cf. *Metamorphoses* 6.424–674.
6. "Used of old paynims [i.e., pagans] in the furnishing of their funerall pompe, and properly the signe of all sorrow and heavinesse" [*E. K.'s Glosse*].
7. The elder tree could be unlucky; Judas, ran one legend, hanged himself on an elder (see, e.g., Shakespeare's *Love's Labour's Lost* V.ii for punning allusions).
8. I.e., the Fates: Clotho spins the thread of life; Lachesis measures it; and Atropos cuts it.
9. "A gallant exclamation, moralised with great wisedom, and passionate with great affection" [*E. K.'s Glosse*]. The emphasis of lines 153–62 on the "earthlie" context of Colin's dirge to this point dramatically prepares for the change of key, common to classical and Christian elegy, in the remainder of the poem.

155 And shooting wide, doe misse the markéd scope:° *target*
Now have I learnd (a lesson derely bought)
That nys on earth assuraunce to be sought:
For what might be in earthlie mould,° *form*
That did her buried body hould,
160 O heavie herse,
Yet saw I on the beare° when it was brought *bier*
O carefull verse.

"But maugre° death, and dreaded sisters deadly spight, *in spite of*
And gates of hel, and fyrie furies[1] forse,
165 She hath the bonds broke of eternall night,
Her soule unbodied of the burdenous corpse.
Why then weepes Lobbin so without remorse?° *moderation*
O Lobb, thy losse no longer lament,
Dido nis dead, but into heaven hent.° *taken*
170 O happye herse,
Cease now my Muse, now cease thy sorrowes sourse,° *flow*
O joyfull verse.

"Why wayle we then? why weary we the Gods with playnts,
As if some evill were to her betight?° *befallen*
175 She raignes a goddesse now emong the saintes,
That whilome was the saynt of shepheards light.° *simple*
And is enstalléd nowe in heavens hight.
I see thee blessed soule, I see,[2]
Walke in Elisian fieldes so free.
180 O happy herse,
Might I once come to thee (O that I might)
O joyfull verse.

"Unwise and wretched men to weete whats good or ill,
We deeme of Death as doome of ill desert.[3]
185 But knewe we fooles, what it us bringes until,° *unto*
Dye would we dayly, once it to expert.[4]
No daunger there the shepheard can astert.° *disturb*
Fayre fieldes and pleasaunt layes° there bene, *meadows*
The fieldes ay fresh, the grasse ay greene:
190 O happy herse,
Make hast ye shepheards, thether to revert,° *return*
O joyfull verse.

"Dido is gone afore (whose turne shall be the next?)
There lives shee with the blessed Gods in blisse,

1. The three Furies, Tisiphone, Alecto, and Megaera, daughters of Earth (or of Night), dwelt in the depths of Tartarus; they punished men and women in life and after death. E. K. calls them "the authours of all evill and mischiefe" [*Glosse*]. Cf. *Aeneid* 7.324–26.
2. "A lively icon or representation, as if he saw her in heaven present" [*E. K.'s Glosse*].
3. I.e., as an appropriate recompense for an evil or ill-spent life.
4. I.e., to experience. E. K. cites Plato's *Phaedo* (thinking perhaps of 68–69).

195 There drincks she Nectar with Ambrosia mixt,[5]
And joyes enjoyes, that mortall men doe misse.
The honor now of highest gods she is,
That whilome was poore shepheards pryde,
While here on earth she did abyde.
200 O happy herse,
Ceasse now my song, my woe now wasted° is. *spent*
O joyfull verse."

THENOT

Ay francke shepheard, how bene thy verses meint° *mingled*
With doolful pleasaunce, so as I ne wotte,° *know*
205 Whether rejoyce or weepe for great constrainte?° *distress*
Thyne be the cossette, well hast thow it gotte.
Up Colin up, ynough thou mornéd hast,
Now gynnes to mizzle,° hye we homeward fast. *drizzle*

Colins Embleme.

La mort ny mord.[6]

5. "Feigned to be the drink and food of the gods: ambrosia they liken to manna in Scripture, and nectar to be white like creme . . ." [*E. K.'s Glosse*].
6. "Which is as much to say as, *death biteth not.* For although by course of nature we be borne to dye, and being ripened with age, as with a timely harvest, we must be gathered in time, or els of our selves fall like rotted ripefruite fro the tree: yet death is not to be counted for evill, nor (as the poete sayd a little before) as doome of ill desert. For though the trespasse of the first man brought death into the world, as the guerdon of sinne, yet being overcome by the death of one that dyed for al, it is now made (as Chaucer sayth) the grene path way to life. So that it agreeth well with that was sayd, that Death byteth not (that is) hurteth not at all" [*E. K.'s Glosse*]. Spenser acknowledges his debt to Marot, who called himself "Colin," by adopting the French poet's own motto.

December†

Argument

This Aeglogue (even as the first beganne) is ended with a complaynte of Colin to God Pan. Wherein as weary of his former wayes, he proportioneth his life to the foure seasons of the yeare, comparing hys youthe to the spring time, when he was fresh and free from loves follye. His manhoode to the sommer, which he sayth, was consumed with greate heate and excessive drouth caused throughe a Comet or blasinge starre, by which hee meaneth love, which passion is comenly compared to such flames and immoderate heate. His riper yeares hee resembleth to an unseasonable harveste wherein the fruites fall ere they be rype. His latter age to winters chyll and frostie season, now drawing neare to his last ende.

The gentle shepheard satte beside a springe,
All in the shadowe of a bushye brere,° *briar*
That Colin hight, which wel could pype and singe,
For he of Tityrus[1] his songs did lere.° *learn*
5 There as he satte in secreate shade alone,
Thus gan he make of love his piteous mone.

"O soveraigne Pan thou God of shepheards all,
Which of our tender Lambkins takest keepe:
And when our flocks into mischaunce mought fall,
10 Doest save from mischiefe the unwary sheepe:

† Spenser here follows Marot's *Eglogue au Roy soubs les noms de Pan et Robin* (1539), addressed to King Francis I, from whom Marot sought and often obtained patronage but whose favor he sometimes lost thanks to evangelical views (and psalm translations) that conservative Catholics read as Lutheran. Marot takes much of the description of the poet's youth from an earlier poet, Jean Lemaire de Belges, in his *Illustrations de Gaule*. Francis rewarded Marot with a house.
1. See "Februarie" 92 and note.

Als° of their maisters hast no lesse regarde, *also*
Then of the flocks, which thou doest watch and ward:

"I thee beseche (so be thou deigne to heare,
Rude ditties tund to shepheards Oaten reede,
15 Or if I ever sonet[2] song so cleare,
As it with pleasaunce mought thy fancie feede)
Hearken awhile from thy greene cabinet,° *bower*
The rurall song of carefull° Colinet. *sorrowful*

"Whilome in youth, when flowrd my joyfull spring,
20 Like Swallow swift I wandred here and there:
For heate of heedlesse lust me so did sting,
That I of doubted° daunger had no feare. *fearful*
I went° the wastefull woodes and forest wyde, *walked*
Withouten dreade of Wolves to bene espyed.

25 "I wont to raunge amydde the mazie thickette,
And gather nuttes to make me Christmas game:° *pleasure*
And joyéd oft to chace the trembling Pricket,° *young deer*
Or hunt the hartlesse° hare, til shee were tame. *timid*
What wreakéd° I of wintrye ages waste, *cared*
30 Tho° deeméd I, my spring would ever laste. *then*

"How often have I scaled the craggie Oke,
All to dislodge the Raven of her neste:
Howe have I wearied with many a stroke
The stately Walnut tree, the while the rest
35 Under the tree fell all for nuts at strife:
For ylike° to me was libertee and lyfe. *the same*

"And for I was in thilke same looser yeares,[3]
(Whether the Muse so wrought me from my birth,
Or I tomuch beleeved my shepherd peres)
40 Somedele° ybent to song and musicks[4] mirth. *somewhat*
A good olde shepheard, Wrenock[5] was his name,
Made me by arte more cunning in the same.

"Fro thence I durst in derring doe[6] compare
With shepheards swayne, what ever fedde in field:
And if that Hobbinol right judgement bare,° *held*
45 To Pan his owne selfe pype I neede not yield.
For if the flocking Nymphes did folow Pan,
The wiser Muses after Colin ranne.

2. A little poem or song.
3. I.e., since I was in those, my salad days.
4. "That is poetry, as Terence sayth, *Qui artem tractant musicam* ['those who follow poetic art,' Terence, *Phormio*, Prologue, 17], speaking of poetes" [*E. K.'s Glosse*].
5. Wrenock probably figures Richard Mulcaster (ca. 1530–1611), Spenser's headmaster at the Merchant Taylors' School in London.
6. I.e., daring deeds.

"But ah such pryde at length was ill repayde,
50 The shepheards God (perdie° God was he none) — *by God, certainly*
My hurtlesse pleasaunce did me ill upbraide,
My freedome lorne, my life he lefte to mone.[7]
  Love they him calléd, that gave me checkmate,
  But better mought they have behote° him Hate. — *named*

55 "Tho gan my lovely Spring bid me farewel,
And Sommer season sped him to display
(For love then in the Lyons house[8] did dwell)
The raging fyre, that kindled at his ray.
  A comett stird up that unkindly heate,
60 That reignéd (as men sayd) in Venus[9] seate.

"Forth was I ledde, not as I wont afore,
When choise I had to choose my wandring waye:
But whether luck and loves unbridled lore
Would leade me forth on Fancies bitte to playe,
65 The bush my bedde, the bramble was my bowre,
  The Woodes can witnesse many a wofull stowre.° — *affliction*

"Where I was[1] wont to seeke the honey Bee,
Working her formall rowmes[2] in Wexen frame:
The grieslie° Todestoole growne there mought I see — *ugly*
70 And loathéd Paddocks° lording on the same. — *toads*
  And where the chaunting birds luld me a sleepe,
  The ghastlie Owle her grievous° ynne doth keepe. — *dreary*

"Then as the springe gives place to elder time,
And bringeth forth the fruite of sommers pryde:
75 All° so my age now passéd youngthly pryme, — *even*
To thinges of ryper reason selfe° applyed. — *itself*
  And learnd of lighter timber cotes° to frame, — *shelters*
  Such as might save my sheepe and me from shame.° — *disaster*

"To make fine cages for the Nightingale,
80 And Baskets of bulrushes was my wont:
Who to entrappe the fish in winding sale° — *net*
Was better seene,° or hurtful beastes to hont? — *skilled*
  I learnéd als° the signes of heaven to ken, — *also*
  How Phoebe fayles, where Venus sittes and when.[3]

7. I.e., he did evilly abuse my harmless pleasure; my freedom was lost; he left me a life of lamentation.
8. "He imagineth simply that Cupid, which is Love, had his abode in the whote signe Leo, which is in middest of somer; a pretie allegory, whereof the meaning is that love in him wrought an extraordinarie heate of lust" [*E. K.'s Glosse*].
9. "The goddess of beauty or pleasure. Also a signe in heaven, as it is here taken. So he meaneth that beautie, which hath alwayes aspect to Venus, was the cause of all his unquietnes in love" [*E. K.'s Glosse*].
1. "A fine description of the chaunge of hys lyfe and liking: for all things nowe seemed to hym to have altered their kindly [i.e., natural] course" [*E. K.'s Glosse*]. Cf. "November" 125, and note.
2. I.e., symmetrical compartments.
3. Noting that "Phoebe fayles" refers to the eclipse of the moon, and that "Venus starre" is also

85 "And tryéd time[4] yet taught me greater thinges,
The sodain rysing of the raging seas:
The soothe of byrds by beating of their wings,[5]
The power of herbs, both which can hurt and ease:[6]
And which be wont t'enrage° the restlesse sheepe, *arouse*
90 And which be wont to worke eternall sleepe.

"But ah unwise and witlesse Colin Cloute,
That kydst° the hidden kinds of many a wede: *knew*
Yet kydst not ene° to cure thy sore hart roote, *even*
Whose ranckling wound as yet does rifelye° bleede. *copiously*
95 Why livest thou stil, and yet hast thy deathes wound?
Why dyest thou stil, and yet alive art founde?

"Thus is my sommer worne away and wasted,
Thus is my harvest hastened all to rathe:° *soon*
The care that budded faire, is burnt and blasted,° *withered*
100 And all my hopéd gaine is turnd to scathe.° *loss*
Of all the seede, that in my youth was sowne,
Was nought but brakes° and brambles to be mowne. *bracken*

"My boughes with bloosmes that crownéd were at firste,
And promiséd of timely fruite such store,
Are left both bare and barrein now at erst° *length*
105 The flattring° fruite is fallen to grownd before, *promising*
And rotted, ere they were halfe mellow ripe:
My harvest wast, my hope away dyd wipe.

"The fragrant flowres,[7] that in my garden grewe,
110 Bene withered, as° they had bene gathered long. *as if*
Theyr rootes bene dryéd up for lacke of dewe,
Yet dewed with teares they han be ever among.[8]
Ah who has wrought my° Rosalind this spight, *in my*
To spil° the flowres, that should her girlond dight? *destroy*

115 "And I, that whilome wont to frame° my pype, *direct*
Unto the shifting of the shepheards foote:
Sike follies nowe have gathered as too ripe
And cast hem out, as rotten and unsoote.° *unsweet*

---

called "Hesperus, and Vesper, and Lucifer," E. K. concludes, "All which skill in starres being convenient for shepheardes to knowe. Theocritus and the rest use" [*Glosse*].

4. I.e., life's experiences.
5. "A kind of sooth saying used in elder tymes, which they gathered by the flying of byrds: first (as is sayd) invented by the Thuscanes [i.e., the Etruscans], and from them derived to the Romanes . . ." [*E. K.'s Glosse*]. Cf. Cicero, *De Diviniatione* 1.41.
6. "That wonderous thinges be wrought by herbes, aswell appeareth by the common working of them in our bodies, as also by the wonderful enchauntments and sorceries that have bene wrought by them: insomuch that it is sayde that Circe, a famous sorceresse, turned men into sondry kinds of beastes and monsters, and onely by herbes . . ." [*E. K.'s Glosse*].
7. "Sundry studies and laudable partes of learning, wherein how our Poete is seene, be they witnesse, which are privie to his study" [*E. K.'s Glosse*].
8. I.e., have continually been.

The loser° Lasse I cast° to please nomore, *fickle / resolve*
120 One[9] if I please, enough is me therefore.

"And thus of all my harvest hope I have
Nought reapéd but a weedye crop of care:
Which, when I thought have thresht in swelling sheave,
Cockel° for corne, and chaffe for barley bare° *weeds / bore*
125 Soone as the chaffe should in the fan be fynd,[1]
All was blowne away of the wavering wynd.

"So now my yeare drawes to his latter terme,
My spring is spent, my sommer burnt up quite:
My harveste hasts to stirre up winter sterne,
130 And bids him clayme with rigorous rage hys right.
So nowe he stormes with many a sturdy stoure,° *blast*
So now his blustring blast eche coste doth scoure.° *scourge*

"The carefull cold[2] hath nypt my rugged rynde,
And in my face deepe furrowes eld° hath pight.° *age / placed*
135 My head besprent° with hoary frost I fynd, *sprinkled*
And by myne eie the Crow his clawe dooth wright.
Delight is layd abedde, and pleasure past,
No sonne now shines, cloudes han all overcast.

"Now leave ye shepheards boyes your merry glee,
140 My Muse is hoarse and weary of thys stounde:° *struggle*
Here will I hang my pype upon this tree,
Was never pype of reede did better sounde.
Winter is come, that blowes the bitter blaste,
And after Winter dreerie death does hast.

145 "Gather ye together my little flocke,
My little flock, that was to me so liefe:° *dear*
Let me, ah lette me in your folds ye lock,
Ere the breme° Winter breede you greater griefe. *fierce*
Winter is come, that blowes the balefull breath,
150 And after Winter commeth timely death.

"Adieu delightes,[3] that lulléd me asleepe,
Adieu my deare, whose love I bought so deare:
Adieu my little Lambes and lovéd sheepe,
Adieu ye Woodes that oft my witnesse were:
155 Adieu good Hobbinol, that was so true,
Tell Rosalind, her Colin bids her adieu."

9. I.e., by one view, God; by another, Colin himself.
1. I.e., be made fine; driven off.
2. "For care is sayd to coole the blood" [*E. K.'s Glosse*].
3. "A conclusion of all, where in sixe verses he comprehendeth briefly all that was touched in this booke. In the first verse his delights of youth generally; in the second, his love of Rosalind: in the thyrd, the keeping of sheepe, which is the argument of all Aeglogues: in the fourth, his complaints: and in the last two, his professed friendship and good will to his good friend Hobbinol" [*E. K.'s Glosse*].

Colins Embleme.

[Vivitur ingenio: caetera mortis erunt.][4]

[Envoy]

Loe I have made a Calender for every yeare,
That steele in strength, and time in durance shall outweare:
And if I marked well the starres revolution,
It shall continewe till the worlds dissolution.[1]
5 To teach the ruder shepheard how to feede his sheepe,
And from the falsers° fraud his folded flocke to keepe. *deceiver's*
Goe lyttle Calender, thou hast a free passeporte,
Goe but a lowly gate° emongste the meaner sorte. *gait*
Dare not to match thy pype with Tityrus hys style,[2]
10 Nor with the Pilgrim that the Ploughman playde a whyle;[3]
But followed them farre off, and their high steppes adore,
The better please, the worse despise, I ask no more.

Merce non mercede.[4]

Editors' Note

The Shepheardes Calender was Spenser's first published work, appearing in 1579. It is clearly a work designed to make a statement and so announce the arrival of the new poet who would transform English literature. It evidently succeeded in this aim, as witness Sir Philip Sidney singling it out as one of the few works in English worth reading—along with Chaucer, Langland, and *A Mirror for Magistrates*—in his *Apology for Poetry*, written a few years later. Although Spenser was soon identified as the author, here he assumes the identity of "Immerito" ("the unworthy one"), suggesting that the *Calender* needs to be read as a series of clever games between author and reader. Spenser would not have written a work like this if he had truly thought of himself as an unworthy poet. The reader, opening the volume for the first time, would have found a series of poems unlike any other in English literary history. The twelve eclogues written for each month of the year recall on the one hand the pastoral poems of Virgil, the poet who everyone knew would one day write an epic, and on the other the months of an almanac, bought by everyone eager to know how

4. First deduced from the glosses and added in 1715. "The meaning whereof is, that all thinges perish and come to theyr last end, but workes of learned wits and monuments of poetry abide for ever . . ." [*E. K.'s Glosse*]. The passage is to be found in "Elegiae in Maecenatem" 37–38, part of the *Appendix Vergiliana*, a collection of minor poems attributed to Virgil in Spenser's time. Modern scholars generally agree that "Elegiae in Maecenatum" are not Virgil's.
1. At the end of the *Metamorphoses*, Ovid observes that "neither fire nor sword nor consuming time can destroy" his work (15.871–72).
2. I.e., Chaucer's pen or manner; probably also, by extension, that of Virgil (cf. "October" 55).
3. I.e., either (1) with the Pilgrim, the role played for a time by the Ploughman, or, more probably, (2) with the Pilgrim, who played the role of a Ploughman for a time. If the latter is correct, line 10 refers to William Langland (ca. 1330–ca.1400), author of *Piers Plowman*.
4. "For reward [in the sense of intelligent response] not for hire [or salary]."

to plan the year. To start the year in January recalls those almanacs, for although the legal year still started on March 25 and the astronomical cycle traditionally began when the sun entered Aries on what was then March 11, the "agricultural year," as some called it, began on January 1. The style and language of the poems mark them as distinctly English even as the elaborate notes written by the mysterious "E. K." (quite possibly Spenser himself) suggest that this is a work of great importance, worthy to have such an apparatus, like the great Latin works and only a very few vernacular ones imported from the finest European printers in Venice, Paris, or Munich. This important distinction is highlighted by the use of old-fashioned black letter for the poetry and the Roman font, by now more favored by the educated, for the notes and commentary. The shepherds in the eclogues discuss a variety of subjects, at times lamenting their unhappy love affairs, at others analysing recent dramatic religious changes. The *Calender* intrigued, baffled, and inspired readers at the time—the seventeenth-century Spenserians took their cue from it rather than from *The Faerie Queene*—and it has done so ever since.

The *Calender* itself covers what its readers would have considered to be virtually the whole tradition of English literature as it was then known. The style and content of many of the eclogues contain numerous allusions to Langland and Chaucer, and the "Colin Clout" persona adopted by Spenser recalls John Skelton's most famous literary creation. Skelton was significant as a trickster figure, thanks to the jest book that bore his name; but he was even more important as the unofficial but universally recognized poet laureate of his time, a title Spenser was also afforded, if without royal sanction, by his contemporaries. The style and form of many of the eclogues, which were written in dialogue, and the black-letter type, make the text resemble the recently published eclogues of Barnabe Googe (1563) and George Turberville (1567). Spenser would have known their work, as well as the influential eclogues of Alexander Barclay (ca. 1484–1552). The type is also a conspicuous reference to Chaucer, whose poetry was always produced in black-letter type until the end of the seventeenth century. Whereas Googe and Turbervile produced straightforward black-letter poetic texts on the page, though, Spenser goes beyond what they had achieved in adding an elaborate textual apparatus. They wrote for students and graduates of the Inns of Court (what we would call, roughly, law schools); Spenser deliberately recaptured the familiar and friendly style of their eclogues but also looked to address a much wider readership. The appearance of the book signals a new development in English writing and printing: its constituent elements were familiar enough, but the whole was more than the sum of the parts.

The *Calender* also provides a series of references that deliberately place it within the tradition of major European and classical pastoral poetry. E. K. remarks that the author is just learning to spread his poetic wings and follow the careers of the most celebrated poets: "So flew Theocritus, as you may perceive he was all ready full fledged. So flew Virgile, as not yet well feeling his winges. So flew Mantuane, as being not full somd. So Petrarque. So Boccace; So Marot, Sanazarus, and also divers other excellent both Italian and French Poetes . . . So finally flyeth this our new Poete[.]" If the *Calender* has one obvious underlying model in terms of form, content and the layout of the printed edition, it is Francesco Sansovino's 1571 edition of Jacopo Sannazaro's *Arcadia* (ca. 1489), a work that had a similarly important influence on Sidney's *Arcadia*, the other outstanding English literary work of the 1580s. And, if we then consider that the printed work itself is designed to resemble a humanist edition of a work of Latin or Greek literature or of a classically influenced vernacular text like those by Sannazaro or Pierre de Ronsard, we can see how provocative, unusual, and carefully placed Spenser's first volume truly was.

But the *Calender* has further semantic resonances: those of popular culture and contemporary politics. In many ways the book resembles an almanac, one of the best-selling forms of published work in the early modern period, and one closely linked to autobiographical writing thanks in part to the blank spaces many offered for the owner's own thoughts or records. The almanac was itself a diverse and varied form with an uncertain register, varying from cheap, disposable sheets aimed at a market that included the educated but also a large group of the scarcely literate, to sophisticated and expensive books such as Marcellus Palingenius Stellatus's Neo-Platonic calendar based on the signs of the zodiac, *The Zodiac of Life*, translated by Googe and dedicated to Burleigh in 1576, a book Spenser could scarcely have avoided. Almanacs were intimately bound up with an understanding of the self: individuals mapped the year in terms of their own actions as the sun made its laggard way through the signs of the zodiac, for such texts were closely linked to the popular and controversial discourse of astrology and to the planets' supposed influence on human events and the human body.

Spenser was clearly exploiting this complex and divided heritage in the *Calender*, a book simultaneously gesturing toward a wider audience than most early printed poetry had reached and drawing attention to his mastery of the sources available; the *Calender* is conspicuously both elite and popular. The author's version of himself as Colin Clout is another gesture of studied ambiguity, one that exploits an understanding of England's literary heritage as it was perceived in the 1570s. Although, Colin is a voice of the people confronting the central authorities in the name of the popular will, he had been, as just mentioned, the literary creation of John Skelton, who had likewise alternated between a court and a country identity, as well as able at times to play the fool. In making Colin Clout his own figure, moreover, Spenser was also signalling a debt to Chaucer, imitating Chaucer's self-representation in his poetry, as well as taking on the mantle of Englishness even if, as E. K. points out, the rustic name "Colin" had been adopted by the French Clément Marot, another poet with a complex persona and, like Skelton, willing to look foolish.

In short, the *Calender* is a work of literary pyrotechnics, one that implicitly urges a reader to think about every aspect of poetry: content, form, style, register, texts and emblems, printing, readership, distribution, audience, and so on. The eclogues themselves tell a series of stories that are sometimes connected, sometimes discrete. Often they are provocative and inconclusive, as readers are invited to think of the world of the shepherds in terms of their own. There are a large number of parallels to recent events, most significantly the projected marriage of Elizabeth to the French and Catholic François, duc d'Alençon, a match opposed by many in England, wary of their queen marrying a foreign prince as her half-sister Mary had done. The November eclogue, lamenting the death of Dido, has frequently been read as a dirge for the death of England and her queen should this happen (and, it is sometimes said, an elegiac parallel to the April eclogue, read as an epithalamion for Elizabeth's marriage to England). Such readings are entirely plausible. The *Calender* was published by Hugh Singleton, an aged printer associated with Protestant causes who had not produced a literary work before. Singleton had only one printing press and in 1579 he produced two works, probably working on both at the same time. The other was John Stubbs's *The discoverie of a gaping gulf whereinto England is like to be swallowed by another French mariage, if the Lord forbid not the banes* [banns], *by letting her Majestie see the sin and punishment thereof*, a piece of forthright advice addressed to the queen, urging her to come to her senses and abandon her plans for union with a perfidious Catholic foreigner. For his pains, Stubbs had his right hand severed, although he bravely managed to shout "God save the queen!" before he fainted. The topical allusions that have been detected in the *Calender*, notably by McLane (1991), have much substance, for there is an obvious connection between these works as well as with a widely circulated letter by Sidney urging the queen to avoid this marriage, even if we need to be careful not to reduce Spenser's poëm to its topical relevance.

The *Calender*, opens with Colin Clout, Spenser's alter ego, bemoaning his failing suit for the elusive Rosalind, an eclogue that encourages a biographical reading as Spenser was about to get married when the poem was published (he married Machybyas Childe in St. Margaret's Church, Westminster on October 27, 1579). Colin represents his newfound love for Rosalind as a definitive break with Hobbinol, one that the slightly older man fails to accept:

> It is not *Hobbinol*, wherefore I plaine,
> Albee my love he seeke with dayly suit:
> His clowinish gifts and curtsies I disdaine,
> His kiddes, his cracknelles, and his early fruit.
> Ah foolish Hobbinol, thy gifts bene vayne:
> Colin them gives to Rosalind againe.
> I love thilke lasse, (alas why doe I love?)
> And am forlorne, (alas why am I lorne?)
> Shee deignes not my good will, but doth reprove,
> And of my rurall musick holdeth scorne.
> Shepheards devise she hateth as the snake,
> And laughes the songes, that Colin Clout doth make.
> ("Januarie," ll. 55–66)

Since Hobbinol, as the sequence later makes clear, is Gabriel Harvey, Spenser is announcing here his break with his former Cambridge tutor (Hadfield 2012). The way in which this is done surely suggests that it is a joke, one that Harvey and Spenser's new wife were able to share. When read alongside the equally melancholy descriptions in the November eclogue we realise that we have to be alert readers in order to understand the shifting registers of the collection of poems.

The *Calender*, like all Spenser's subsequent works, makes heavy demands on its readers, pushing the chosen form to the limit in order to elicit complex responses. This is especially true of the eclogues that involve debate, such as the discussion in "Februarie" between the aged Thenot and the younger but unhappy Cuddie, which concludes with Thenot's fable of the oak and the briar. The arrogant and myopic young briar persuades the woodman to cut down the aged oak that overshadows it, only to realize, too late, that the oak had protected it against the harsh winds and storms that eventually destroy the smaller and more vulnerable tree. The allegory is a traditional one of youthful pride receiving its just deserts, a warning to others to respect their elders and learn from the wisdom they have accumulated. But the poem has to be read in terms of the Reformation, despite the disclaimer in the Argument that the eclogue "is rather morall and generall, then bent to any secrete or particular purpose." The oak is described as "Sacred with many a mysteree, / And often crost with the priestes crewe, / And often halowed with holy water dewe." The phrase "priestes crewe" is glossed by E. K. as "holy water pott, wherewith the popishe priest used to sprinckle and hallowe the trees from mischaunce. Such blindnesse was in those times, which the Poete supposeth, to have bene the finall decay of this aunciente Oake." The gloss cannot be taken at face value. It is not the oak's past that destroys it but the hostile intervention of the briar as well as the axe wielded by the suspiciously female-looking figure in the woodcut. If the oak's past had been the cause of its downfall then the briar would have been right to condemn it, not criticized as foolish in the poem. The point may well be that the Reformation must not forget its roots in the past and the need to think through what is good and what is pernicious about the legacy of the pre-Reformation.

The other religious eclogues contain stories that may well be more balanced and nuanced than has often been acknowledged. The argument between Thomalin and Morrell in "Julye" (for which there is, unfortunately, no room in this volume) has often been assumed to validate the position of the lowly Protestant pastor against his more hierarchical colleague, depicted sitting on a mound while Thomalin tends his flock. But the poetry spoken by Morrell, notably his lyrical description of the English rivers, indicates that he may have more to offer than has often been assumed, and the religious dispute should be balanced against other factors. Similarly, in "September" (likewise omitted here for lack of space), which looks like an attack on Catholicism, things may not be what they seem. Its portrait of Bishop Young, Spenser's employer, as "Roffy" describes him as a tireless hunter of wolves, seconded by his dog Lowder, in lines that need not be wholly complimentary. When Lowder is away Roffy catches a wolf in sheep's clothing and "tooke out the Woolfe in his counterfect cote, / And let out the sheepes bloud at his throte." The second line is ambiguous: does it mean that Roffy slit the throat of the false creature? If so, was he acting out of harsh necessity? Or do his actions indicate that he has overstepped the mark and is actually in danger of becoming what he is trying to prevent? The line cannot be read without a suggestion that the forces of the Reformation are in danger of becoming as tainted as those they are opposing. Even the extensive debts to Marot suggest just such ambiguity, for Marot, probably an evangelical Catholic, was accused by some of outright Lutheranism and fled into exile; true, his actual position remains not fully clear, which together with his willingness to clown around may help explain the ambivalence of Englishmen such as E. K. Far from an unproblematic and determined champion of Protestantism (itself a complex matter), then, Spenser's position here, and later, was more subtle and conflicted than many have assumed.

The *Calender* is thus arguably the most spectacular first work by any major figure in English literature. After all, Spenser was well into his twenties when it appeared, considerably older than many of his contemporaries when they first ventured into print. It had obviously taken a long time to write and was based on formidable erudition and doubtless frequent rewriting. It is hardly surprising that this work had such a major impact immediately after publication, that it was often reprinted before joining Spenser's other works in 1611, that it was thought worthy of a Latin translation (Bradner 1935), or that it would play such a significant role in the subsequent history of English letters.

From Complaints

Prosopopoia, or Mother Hubberds Tale

It was the month, in which the righteous Maide,
That for disdaine of sinfull worlds upbraide,° *slander, criticism*
Fled back to heaven, whence she was first conceived,
Into her silver bowre the Sunne received;
And the hot *Syrian* Dog on him awayting,
After the chaféd° Lyons cruell bayting,° *heated / tormenting*
Corrupted had th'ayre with his noysome breath,
And powr'd on th'earth plague, pestilence, and death.[1]
Emongst the rest a wicked maladie
10 Raign'd emongst men, that manie did to die,[2]
Depriv'd of sense and ordinarie reason;
That it to Leaches° seeméd strange and geason.° *doctors / unusual*
My fortune was mongst manie others moe,
To be partaker of their common woe;
And my weake bodie set on fire with griefe,° *pain*
Was rob'd of rest, and naturall reliefe.
In this ill plight, there came to visite mee
Some friends, who sorie my sad case to see,
Began to comfort me in chearfull wise,° *manner*
20 And meanes of gladsome solace to devise.
But seeing kindly° sleep refuse to doe *natural*
His office, and my feeble eyes forgoe,
They sought my troubled sense how to deceave
With talke, that might unquiet fancies reave;° *remove*
And sitting all in seates about me round,
With pleasant tales (fit for that idle stound)[3]
They cast in course to waste° the wearie howres:[4] *occupy, pass*
Some tolde of Ladies, and their Paramoures;
Some of brave Knights, and their renownéd Squires;
30 Some of the Faeries and their strange attires;

1. August. The sun leaves Leo to live in the sign of Virgo (also known as Astraea), finding there Sirius the dog-star, who has been "baiting" the Lion (as might happen in London when dogs "baited" bears as theatrical entertainment). The retreat of the "righteous Maide" to the heavens parallels the departure of Astraea, the goddess of justice, at the start of *The Faerie Queene*, V. This long first sentence is Chaucerian in style, recalling the opening of *The Canterbury Tales* as well as the Chaucerian tradition of poetry that developed in the fifteenth and early sixteenth centuries. The dominance of Sirius gave rise to the phrase "dog days," associated with disease, lethargy, and moral corruption.
2. I.e., caused to die.
3. Period of forced inaction.
4. Telling stories to distract those living in fear of the plague recalls the opening of Boccaccio's *Decameron*.

And some of Giaunts hard to be beleeved,
That the delight thereof me much releeved.
Amongst the rest a good old woman was,
Hight° Mother *Hubberd*, who did farre surpas — *called*
The rest in honest mirth, that seem'd° her well: — *suited*
She when her turne was come her tale to tell,
Tolde of a strange adventure, that betided
Betwixt the Foxe and th'Ape by him misguided;
The which for that my sense it greatly pleased,
40 All were my spirite heavie and diseased,
Ile write in termes,[5] as she the same did say,
So well as I her words remember may.
No Muses aide me needes heretoo to call;
Base is the style, and matter meane° withall. — *low, humble*
Whilome (said she) before the world was civill,[6]
The Foxe and th'Ape disliking of their evill
And hard estate,[7] determinéd to seeke
Their fortunes farre abroad, lyeke with his lyeke:
For both were craftie and unhappie witted;[8]
50 Two fellowes might no where be better fitted.° — *suited*
The Foxe, that first this cause of griefe did finde,
Gan first thus plaine his case with words unkinde.[9]
Neighbour Ape, and my Gossip[1] eke beside,
(Both two sure bands in friendship to be tide,)° — *tied*
To whom may I more trustely complaine
The evill plight, that doth me sore constraine,
And hope thereof to finde due remedie?
Heare then my paine and inward agonie.
Thus manie yeares I now have spent and worne,
60 In meane regard, and basest fortunes scorne,
Dooing my Countrey service as I might,
No lesse I dare saie than the prowdest wight;
And still I hopéd to be up advaunced,
For my good parts; but still it hath mischaunced.
Now therefore that no lenger hope I see,
But froward° fortune still to follow mee, — *contrary, malicious*
And losels° lifted up on high, where I did looke, — *nobodies*
I meane to turne the next leafe of the booke.
Yet ere that anie way I doo betake,
70 I meane my Gossip privie first to make.[2]
Ah my deare Gossip, (answer'd then the Ape,)
Deeply doo your sad words my wits awhape,° — *confound, amaze*
Both for because your griefe doth great appeare,
And eke because my selfe am touchéd neare:

5. I'll convey using her style and language.
6. Civilized. The narrator suggests that this poem deals with the distant past of a barbarous age, but the reader will soon realize that the allegory deals with contemporary issues.
7. I.e., lowly status, condition in life.
8. Having the ability to cause trouble.
9. That is, unnatural, not fitting his nature.
1. I.e., friend, companion.
2. I.e., I plan to tell my friend first.

For I likewise have wasted much good time,
Still wayting to preferment up to clime,
Whilest others alwayes have before me stept,
And from my beard the fat away have swept;[3]
That now unto despaire I gin to growe
80 And meane for better winde about to throwe.[4]
Therefore to me, my trustie friend, aread° *tell, declare*
Thy councell: two is better than one head.
Certes (said he) I meane me to disguize
In some straunge habit, after uncouth wize,[5]
Or like a Pilgrime, or a Lymiter,[6]
Or like a *Gipsen*,° or a Juggeler, *Gypsy*
And so to wander to the worldés ende,
To seeke my fortune, where I may it mend:
For worse than that I have, I cannot meete.
90 Wide is the world I wote, and everie streete
Is full of fortunes, and adventures straunge,
Continuallie subiect unto chaunge.
Say my faire brother now, if this device
Doth like° you, or may you to like entice. *please*
Surely (said th'Ape) it likes me wondrous well;
And would ye not poore fellowship expel,° *refuse*
My selfe would offer you t'accompanie
In this adventures chauncefull jeopardie.° *adventure*
For to wexe olde at home in idlenesse,
100 Is disadventrous,° and quite fortunelesse:° *unfortunate / pointless*
Abroad where change is, good may gotten bee.
The Foxe was glad, and quickly did agree:
So both resolv'd, the morrow next ensuing,
So soone as day appeard to peoples vewing,
On their intended journey to proceede;
And over night, whatso theretoo did neede,
Each did prepare, in readines to bee.
The morrow next, so soone as one might see
Light out of heavens windowes forth to looke,
110 Both their habiliments° unto them tooke, *clothing*
And put themselves (a Gods name) on their way.
Whenas the Ape beginning well to wey° *weigh*
This hard adventure, thus began t'advise;° *consider*
Now read° Sir Reynold,[7] as ye be right wise, *advise*
What course ye weene° is best for us to take, *think*
That for our selves we may a living make.
Whether shall we professe some trade or skill?
Or shall we varie our device at will,
Even as new occasión° appeares? *opportunity*
120 Or shall we tie our selves for certaine yeares

3. I.e., stolen my rightful profits.
4. Choose another direction.
5. Unfamiliar fashion.
6. Mendicant (begging) friar.
7. I.e., Renard the fox.

To anie service, or to anie° place? *one*
For it behoves ere that into the race
We enter, to resolve first hereupon.
Now surely brother (said the Foxe anon)
Ye have this matter motionéd° in season: *mentioned*
For everie thing that is begun with reason
Will come by readie meanes unto his end;
But things miscounselléd must needs miswend.° *go astray*
Thus therefore I advize upon the case,
130 That not to anie certaine trade or place,
Nor anie man we should our selves applie;
For why should he that is at libertie
Make himselfe bond? sith then we are free borne,
Let us all servile base subiection scorne;
And as we bee sonnes of the world so wide,
Let us our fathers heritage divide,
And chalenge° to our selves our portions dew *claim*
Of all the patrimonie, which a few
Now hold in hugger mugger[8] in their hand,
140 And all the rest doo rob of good and land.
For now a few have all and all have nought,
Yet all be brethren ylike dearly bought:[9]
There is no right in this partitión,
Ne was it so by institutión
Ordainéd first, ne by the law of Nature,
But that she gave like blessing to each creture
As well of worldly livelode° as of life, *livelihood*
That there might be no difference nor strife,
Nor ought cald mine or thine: thrice happie then
150 Was the conditión of mortall men.
That was the golden age of *Saturne* old,[1]
But this might better be the world of gold:
For without golde now nothing wilbe got.
Therefore (if please you) this shalbe our plot,° *plan*
We will not be of anie occupation,
Let such vile vassalls borne to base vocation
Drudge in the world, and for their living droyle° *toil, slave*
Which have no wit to live withouten toyle.
But we will walke about the world at pleasure
160 Like two free men, and make our ease our treasure.
Free men some beggers call, but they be free,
And they which call them so more beggers bee:
For they doo swinke° and sweate to feed the other, *work*
Who live like Lords of that which they doo gather,
And yet doo never thanke them for the same,

8. Privately, secretly.
9. I.e., brothers whom all alike Christ had "bought" (redeemed) by his suffering on the Cross.
1. I.e., the age of equality when we lived in harmony with the natural world and with each other, before the earth started to decay to the ages of silver, bronze, and then iron. The most frequently cited source in the Renaissance was Ovid, *Metamorphoses* I.89–150. Spenser, like many other poets, refers to this myth throughout his poetry.

But as their due by Nature doo it clame.
Such will we fashion both our selves to bee,
Lords of the world, and so will wander free
Where so us listeth, uncontrol'd of anie.
170 Hard is our hap,° if we (emongst so manie) *fortune*
Light not on some that may our state° amend; *condition*
Sildome but some good commeth ere the end.
Well seemd the Ape to like this ordinaunce:° *arrangement*
Yet well considering of the circumstaunce,
As pausing in great doubt, awhile he staid,
And afterwards with grave advizement° said; *reflection*
I cannot, my lief° brother, like but well *dear*
The purpose of the complot° which ye tell: *plan, conspiracy*
For well I wot° (compar'd to all the rest *know*
180 Of each degree) that Beggers life is best:
And they that thinke themselves the best of all,
Oft-times to begging are content to fall.
But this I wot withall that we shall ronne
Into great daunger like to bee undonne,
Thus wildly to wander in the worlds eye,
Withouten pasport[2] or good warrantye,
For feare least we like rogues should be reputed,
And for eare markéd beasts abroad be bruted:° *reported*
Therefore I read,° that we our counsells call, *advise*
190 How to prevent this mischiefe ere it fall,
And how we may with most securitie,
Beg amongst those that beggers doo defie.[3]
Right well deere Gossip ye advizéd have,
(Said then the Foxe) but I this doubt will save:
For ere we farther passe, I will devise
A pasport for us both in fittest wize,
And by the names of Souldiers us protect;
That now is thought a civile[4] begging sect.
Be you the Souldier, for you likest are
200 For manly semblance, and small skill in warre:
I will but wayte on you, and as occasion
Falls out, my selfe fit for the same will fashion.
The Pasport ended,° both they forward went, *finished*
The Ape clad Souldierlike, fit for th'intent,
In a blew jacket with a crosse of redd[5]
And manie slits, as if that he had shedd
Much blood throgh many wounds therein receaved,
Which had the use of his right arme bereaved;
Upon his head an old Scotch cap he wore,
210 With a plume feather all to peeces tore:

2. After an act of 1547 vagrants needed to have passports issued by local authorities to travel through most areas. Failure to produce one could result in physical punishment such as branding the ear, as line 188 indicates.
3. That is, hold in contempt.
4. Well ordered, acceptable (an irony, given the public fear of discharged soldiers, who were often still armed, hungry, and unpaid).
5. The cross of red may ironically recall that of St. George, which still figures in the English flag.

His breeches were made after the new cut,
Al Portugese,[6] loose like an emptie gut;
And his hose broken high above the heeling,
And his shooes beaten out with traveling.
But neither sword nor dagger he did beare,
Seemes that no foes revengement he did feare;
In stead of them a handsome bat° he held, *stick*
On which he leanéd, as one farre in elde.° *age*
Shame light on him, that through so false illusion,
220 Doth turne the name of Souldiers to abusion,
And that, which is the noblest mysterie,° *occupation, vocation*
Brings to reproach and common infamie.
Long they thus travailéd, yet never met
Adventure, which might them a working set:
Yet manie waies they sought, and manie tryed;
Yet for their purposes none fit espyed.
At last they chaunst to meete upon the way
A simple husbandman in garments gray;
Yet though his vesture were but meane and bace,
230 A good yeoman he was of honest place,
And more for thrift did care than for gay° clothing: *fancy*
Gay without good, is good hearts greatest loathing.
The Foxe him spying, bad the Ape him dight° *prepare*
To play his part, for loe he was in sight,
That (if he er'd not) should them entertaine,
And yeeld them timely profite for their paine.
Eftsoones the Ape himselfe gan up to reare,
And on his shoulders high his bat to beare,
As if good service he were fit to doo;
240 But little thrift for him he did it too:
And stoutly forward he his steps did straine,
That like a handsome swaine[7] it him became:
When as they nigh approachéd, that good man
Seeing them wander loosly,° first began *carelessly*
T'enquire of custome, what and whence they were?
To whom the Ape, I am a Souldiere,
That late in warres have spent my deerest blood,
And in long service lost both limbs and good,° *goods, property*
And now constrain'd that trade to overgive,[8]
250 I driven am to seeke some meanes to live:
Which might it you in pitie please t'afford,
I would be readie both in deed and word,
To doo you faithfull service all my dayes.
This yron world[9] (that same he weeping sayes)
Brings downe the stowtest hearts to lowest state:
For miserie doth bravest mindes abate,[1]

6. I.e., à la Portuguese, in the Portuguese style.
7. I.e., a rustic gallant.
8. Give up.
9. See note to line 151.
1. Bring down.

And make them seeke for that they wont to scorne,
Of fortune and of hope at once forlorne.
The honest man, that heard him thus complaine,
260 Was griev'd, as he had felt part of his paine;
And well disposd' him some reliefe to showe,
Askt if in husbandrie he ought did knowe,
To plough, to plant, to reap, to rake, to sowe,
To hedge, to ditch, to thrash, to thetch,° to mowe; *thatch*
Or to what labour els he was prepar'd?
For husbands life is labourous and hard.
Whenas the Ape him hard so much to talke
Of labour, that did from his liking balke,[2]
He would have slipt the coller handsomly,[3]
270 And to him said; good Sir, full glad am I,
To take what paines may anie living wight:
But my late maymèd limbs lack wonted might
To doo their kindly° services, as needeth: *natural*
Scarce this right hand the mouth with diet feedeth,
So that it may no painfull worke endure,
Ne to strong labour can it selfe enure.° *accustom*
But if that anie other place you have,
Which askes small paines, but thriftines to save,
Or care to overlooke, or trust to gather,
280 Ye may me trust as your owne ghostly father.[4]
With that the husbandman gan him avize
That it for him were fittest exercise
Cattell to keep, or grounds to oversee;
And askèd him, if he could willing bee
To keep his sheep, or to attend his swyne,
Or watch his mares, or take his charge of kyne?° *cattle*
Gladly (said he) what ever such like paine° *work*
Ye put on me, I will the same sustaine:° *support*
But gladliest I of your fleecie sheepe
290 (Might it you please) would take on me the keep.
For ere that unto armes I me betooke,
Unto my fathers sheepe I usde to looke,
That yet the skill thereof I have not loste:
Thereto right well this Curdog by my coste° *side*
(Meaning the Foxe) will serve, my sheepe to gather,
And drive to follow after their Belwether.[5]
The Husbandman was meanly well content,
Triall to make of his endevourment,° *industry*
And home him leading, lent to him the charge
300 Of all his flocke, with libertie full large,
Giving accompt of th'annuall increce
Both of their lambes, and of their woolly fleece.
Thus is this Ape become a shepheard swaine° *countryman, rustic*

2. I.e., was not something that he was keen on.
3. That is, neatly avoided the task.
4. Spiritual father (i.e., priestly confessor).
5. The head sheep, which carried a bell around its neck.

And the false Foxe his dog. (God give them paine)° — *punishment*
For ere the yeare have halfe his course out-run,
And doo returne from whence he first begun,
They shall him make an ill accompt of thrift.
Now whenas Time flying with wingés swift,
Expiréd had the terme, that these two javels° — *villains*
310 Should render up a reckning of their travels° — *labor*
Unto their master, which it of them sought,
Exceedingly they troubled were in thought,
Ne wist what answere unto him to frame,
Ne how to scape great punishment, or shame,
For their false treason and vile theeverie.
For not a lambe of all their flockes supply
Had they to shew: but ever as they bred,
They slue them, and upon their fleshes fed:
For that disguiséd Dog lov'd blood to spill,
320 And drew the wicked Shepheard to his will.
So twixt them both they not a lambkin left,
And when lambes fail'd, the old sheepes lives they reft;° — *stole, took*
That how t'acquite themselves[6] unto their Lord,
They were in doubt, and flatly set abord.[7]
The Foxe then counsel'd th'Ape, for to require
Respite till morrow, t'answere his desire:
For times delay new hope of helpe still breeds.
The goodman granted, doubting° nought their deeds, — *suspecting*
And bad, next day that all should readie be.
330 But they more subtill meaning° had than he: — *intention*
For the next morrowes meed° they closely° ment, — *profit / secretly*
For feare of afterclaps° for to prevent. — *consequences*
And that same evening, when all shrowded were
In careles sleep, they without care or feare,
Cruelly fell upon their flock in folde,
And of them slew at pleasure what they wolde:
Of which whenas they feasted had their fill,
For a full complement of all their ill,
They stole away, and tooke their hastie flight,
340 Carried in clowdes of all-concealing night.
So was the husbandman left to his losse,
And they unto their fortunes change to tosse.[8]
After which sort they wanderéd long while,
Abusing° manie through their cloakéd guile; — *deceiving*
That at the last they gan to be descryed° — *discerned, discovered*
Of everie one, and all their sleights espyed.
So as their begging now them failéd quyte;
For none would give, but all men would them wyte:° — *blame*
Yet would they take no paines to get their living,
350 But seeke some other way to gaine by giving,

6. Explain themselves.
7. Completely at sea.
8. I.e., buffeted by (the waves of) fortune (continuing the nautical metaphor of previous lines).

Much like to begging but much better named;
For manie beg, which are thereof ashamed.
And now the Foxe had gotten him a gowne,
And th'Ape a cassocke[9] sidelong hanging downe;
For they their occupation meant to change,
And now in other state abroad to range:
For since their souldiers pas° no better spedd, *passport*
They forg'd another, as for Clerkes booke-redd.
Who passing foorth, as their adventures fell,
360 Through manie haps, which needs not here to tell;
At length chaunst with a formall[1] Priest to meete,
Whom they in civill manner first did greete,
And after askt an almes for Gods deare love.
The man straight way his choler up did move,
And with reproachfull tearmes gan them revile,
For following that trade so base and vile;
And askt what license, or what Pas they had?
Ah (said the Ape as sighing wondrous sad)
Its an hard case, when men of good deserving
370 Must either driven be perforce to sterving,
Or askéd for their pas by everie squib,[2]
That list° at will them to revile or snib:° *desires, chooses / reproach*
And yet (God wote)° small oddes° I often see *knows / difference*
Twixt them that aske, and them that askéd bee.
Natheles because you shall not us misdeeme,° *misjudge*
But that we are as honest as we seeme,
Yee shall our pasport at your pleasure see,
And then ye will (I hope) well moovéd° bee. *enlightened*
Which when the Priest beheld, he vew'd it nere,° *closely*
380 As if therein some text he studying were,
But little els (God wote) could thereof skill:° *understand*
For read he could not evidence,° nor will, *documents*
Ne tell a written word, ne write a letter,
Ne make one title worse, ne make one better:
Of such deep learning little had he neede,
Ne yet of Latine, ne of Greeke, that breede
Doubts mongst Divines, and difference of texts,
From whence arise diversitie of sects,
And hatefull heresies, of God abhor'd:[3]
390 But this good Sir did follow the plaine word,
Ne medled with their controversies vaine;
All his care was, his service well to saine,[4]
And to read Homelies upon holidayes:
When that was done, he might attend his playes;
An easie life, and fit high God to please.[5]

9. A priest's gown. A "gown," like being a "clerk," often indicated academic or priestly status, or both.
1. Dignified, prim, and concerned only for externals.
2. Person (insulting).
3. An ironic imitation of this illiterate priest's claim that learning breeds doubts and religious divisions.
4. I.e., to say the church rituals well.
5. Complex satire. Spenser is, of course, condemning ignorant clergy; but is he also suggesting

He having overlookt their pas at ease,
Gan at the length them to rebuke againe,
That no good trade of life did entertaine,
But lost their time in wandring loose abroad,
400 Seeing the world, in which they bootles boad,[6]
Had wayes enough for all therein to live;
Such grace did God unto his creatures give.
Said then the Foxe; who hath the world not tride,° *experienced*
From the right way full eath° may wander wide. *easily*
We are but Novices, new come abroad,
We have not yet the tract of anie troad,[7]
Nor on us taken anie state of life,
But readie are of anie to make preife.[8]
Therefore might please you, which the world have proved,[9]
410 Us to advise, which forth but lately moved,
Of some good course, that we might undertake;
Ye shall for ever us your bondmen° make. *debtors*
The Priest gan wexe halfe proud to be so praide,° *prayed, asked*
And thereby willing to affoord them aide;
It seemes (said he) right well that ye be Clerks,
Both by your wittie words, and by your werks.
Is not that name enough to make a living
To him that hath a whit of Natures giving?
How manie honest men see ye arize
420 Daylie thereby, and grow to goodly prize?
To Deanes, to Archdeacons, to Commissaries,[1]
To Lords, to Principalls, to Prebendaries;[2]
All jolly Prelates, worthie rule to beare,
Who ever them envie: yet spite bites neare.[3]
Why should ye doubt then, but that ye likewise
Might unto some of those in time arise?
In the meane time to live in good estate,
Loving that love,[4] and hating those that hate;
Being some honest Curate, or some Vicker
430 Content with little in condition sicker.° *secure*
Ah but (said th'Ape) the charge is wondrous great,
To feed mens soules, and hath an heavie threat.
To feede mens soules (quoth he) is not in man:
For they must feed themselves, doo what we can.[5]

---

that debate and argument are the natural results of learning and that such consequences must be accepted, tolerated, even encouraged? That this priest attends plays would disgust "Puritan" reformers.

6. Lived pointlessly.
7. I.e., have not yet trodden on them (and chosen one).
8. I.e., to experience, to put to the proof, to test out.
9. I.e., who have experienced ("proved") the world.
1. Employees of a bishop who would oversee parts of his bishopric in his absence (Spenser worked as a secretary for John Young, Bishop of Rochester, in ca.1578–79).
2. Canons (i.e., minor clerics) in a cathedral who were paid for their work. A main object of Protestant satire in the sixteenth century was the holding of multiple offices by clerics more concerned with personal wealth than performing their duties properly. *Principalls*: Heads of religious houses.
3. Probably "although the spiteful might envy and criticize."
4. I.e., loving those who love.
5. A distortion of Christ's instruction that shepherds need to tend their flocks (John 10.11–16), under the guise of Protestant liberation from the corruption of the late medieval Church.

We are but charg'd to lay the meate before:
Eate they that list, we need to doo no more.
But God it is that feedes them with his grace,
The bread of life powr'd downe from heavenly place.
Therefore said he, that with the budding rod
440 Did rule the Jewes,[6] *All shalbe taught of God.*
That same hath Jesus Christ now to him raught,[7]
By whom the flock is rightly fed, and taught:
He is the Shepheard, and the Priest is hee;
We but his shepheard swaines ordain'd to bee.[8]
Therefore herewith doo not your selfe dismay;
Ne is the paines so great, but beare ye may;
For not so great as it was wont of yore,
It's now a dayes, ne halfe so streight and sore:
They whilome uséd duly everie day
450 Their service and their holie things to say,
At morne and even, besides their Anthemes[9] sweete,
Their penie Masses, and their Complynes[1] meete,
Their Dirges, their Trentals, and their shrifts,[2]
Their memories,[3] their singings, and their gifts.
Now all those needlesse works are laid away;
Now once a weeke upon the Sabbath day,
It is enough to doo our small devotion,
And then to follow any merrie motion.° *inclination, impulse*
Ne are we tyde to fast, but when we list,[4]
460 Ne to weare garments base of wollen twist,[5]
But with the finest silkes us to aray,
That before God we may appeare more gay,
Resembling *Aarons* glorie in his place:[6]
For farre unfit it is, that person bace
Should with vile cloaths approach Gods majestie,
Whom no uncleannes may approachen nie:
Or that all men, which anie master serve,
Good garments for their service should deserve;
But he that serves the Lord of hoasts most high,
470 And that in highest place, t'approach him nigh,
And all the peoples prayers to present
Before his throne, as on ambassage° sent *embassy*
Both too and fro, should not deserve to weare

6. I.e., Moses, with the help of Aaron's flowering rod; see Numbers 17.
7. Christ, giver of the New Law, has taken ("raught") the rod of Moses, the Old Law, for himself, and now gives "that same" (the bread of life).
8. A travesty of Protestant understanding of Christ's teaching, which did not absolve ministers from concern for their congregations.
9. Antiphonal singing.
1. The last service of the day; *penie Masses*: Masses given for a fee of a penny.
2. Private confessions; *Dirges*: services for the dead; *Trentals*: a sequence of thirty requiem masses.
3. Commemoration services, especially for the dead.
4. I.e., we go without food only when we wish.
5. One of the key disputes of the early Elizabethan period was that over which clothes a priest should wear (the "vestarian controversy"). Puritans opposed the wearing of the surplice, and many were removed from their positions as a result.
6. Aaron was ordered by God to wear an elaborate priestly costume; see Exodus 39.1–30. George Herbert's poem "Aaron" explores the spiritual significance of the clothes.

A garment better, than of wooll or heare.° *hair*
Beside we may have lying by our sides
Our lovely Lasses, or bright shining Brides:
We be not tyde to wilfull[7] chastitie,
But have the Gospell of free libertie.[8]
By that he ended had his ghostly[9] sermon,
480 The Foxe was well induc'd to be a Parson;
And of the Priest eftsoones gan to enquire,
How to a Benefice[1] he might aspire.
Marie[2] there (said the Priest) is arte indeed.
Much good deep learning one thereout[3] may reed,
For that the ground-worke is, and end of all,
How to obtaine a Beneficiall.[4]
First therefore, when ye have in handsome wise
Your selfe attyréd, as you can devise,
Then to some Noble man your selfe applye,
490 Or other great one in the worldes eye,
That hath a zealous[5] disposition
To God, and so to his religion:
There must thou fashion eke a godly zeale,[6]
Such as no carpers may contrayre reveale:
For each thing fainéd, ought more warie bee.
There thou must walke in sober gravitee,
And seeme as Saintlike as Saint *Radegund*:[7]
Fast much, pray oft, looke lowly on the ground,
And unto everie one doo curtesie meeke:[8]
500 These lookes (nought saying) doo a benefice seeke,
And be thou sure one not to lacke or° long. *before*
But if thee list unto the Court to throng,
And there to hunt after the hopéd pray,
Then must thou thee dispose another way:
For there thou needs must learne, to laugh, to lie,
To face, to forge, to scoffe, to companie,
To crouche, to please, to be a beetle stock[9]
Of thy great Masters will, to scorne, or mock:
So maist thou chaunce mock out a Benefice,[1]
510 Unlesse thou canst one conjure by device,[2]

7. Perverse, for no reason.
8. Protestants urged priests to marry, but here the message is twisted to mean that they should enjoy sexual indulgence.
9. That is, spiritual or religious (doubtless to be heard ironically).
1. Church living. The occupation of numerous offices by absent priests was a common source of criticism, and was much attacked by anticlerical satirists.
2. A common oath: "By [the Virgin] Mary!"
3. I.e., on that subject.
4. A living, or a letter recommending a priest.
5. A word almost always associated with Puritans.
6. A figure named Zele [Zeal] appears in *The Faerie Queene* V.ix.39 to condemn Duessa.
7. Saint Radigund was devoted to the preservation of her virginity, a virtue that enabled her to perform a series of miraculous cures; a far more problematic "Radigund," however, appears in *The Faerie Queene* V.iv.33.
8. I.e., appear humble before everyone.
9. The handle of a hammer, i.e., an instrument that serves others.
1. Gain an ecclesiastical living through playing the fool.
2. By magic.

Or cast a figure[3] for a Bishoprick:
And if one could, it were but a schoole-trick.[4]
These be the wayes, by which without reward
Livings in Court be gotten, though full hard.
For nothing there is done without a fee:
The Courtier needes must recompencéd bee
With a Benevolence, or have in gage[5]
The *Primitias*[6] of your Parsonage:
Scarse can a Bishoprick forpas them by,[7]
520 But that it must be gelt in privitie.[8]
Doo not thou therefore seeke a living there,
But of more private persons seeke elswhere,
Whereas thou maist compound a better penie,[9]
Ne let thy learning question'd be of anie.
For some good Gentleman that hath the right
Unto his Church for to present a wight,
Will cope° with thee in reasonable wise; *bargain*
That if the living yerely doo arise
To fortie pound, that then his yongest sonne
530 Shall twentie have, and twentie thou hast wonne:
Thou hast it wonne, for it is of franke° gift, *free*
And he will care for all the rest to shift;
Both that the Bishop may admit of thee,
And that therein thou maist maintainéd bee.
This is the way for one that is unlern'd
Living to get, and not to be discern'd.
But they that are great Clerkes,° have nearer wayes, *scholars, students*
For learning sake to living them to raise:
Yet manie eke of them (God wote) are driven,
540 T'accept a Benefice in peeces riven.[1]
How saist thou (friend) have I not well discourst
Upon this Common place (though plaine, not wourst)?
Better a short tale, than a bad long shriving.° *confession*
Needes anie more to learne to get a living?
Now sure and by my hallidome[2] (quoth he)
Ye a great master are in your degree:
Great thankes I yeeld you for your discipline,° *teaching, instruction*
And doo not doubt, but duly to encline
My wits theretoo, as ye shall shortly heare.
550 The Priest him wisht good speed,° and well to fare. *luck*
So parted they, as eithers way them led.
But th'Ape and Foxe ere long so well them sped,
Through the Priests holesome counsell lately tought,

3. Cast a horoscope.
4. Academic exercise.
5. As a promise; *Benevolence*: a financial gift.
6. First year's income.
7. Ignore them.
8. Secretly paid for.
9. Get a better deal.
1. Divided between the holder and his patron.
2. I.e., by my holiness (a common oath).

And throgh their own faire handling wisely wroght,
That they a Benefice twixt them obtained;
And craftie Reynold was a Priest ordained;
And th'Ape his Parish Clarke procur'd to bee.
Then made they revell route[3] and goodly glee.
But ere long time had passéd, they so ill
560 Did order their affaires, that th'evill will
Of all their Parishners they had constraind;
Who to the Ordinarie[4] of them complain'd,
How fowlie they their offices abusd',
And them of crimes and heresies accusd';
That Pursivants he often for them sent:
But they neglected his commaundément.
So long persisted obstinate and bolde,
Till at the length he publishéd° to holde — *announced*
A Visitation, and them cyted° thether: — *summoned*
570 Then was high time their wits about to geather;
What did they then, but made a composition° — *financial deal*
With their next neighbor Priest for light condition,[5]
To whom their living they resignéd quight° — *entirely*
For a few pence, and ran away by night.
So passing through the Countrey in disguize,
They fled farre off, where none might them surprize,
And after that long straiéd here and there,
Through everie field and forrest farre and nere;
Yet never found occasion for their tourne,[6]
580 But almost sterv'd, did much lament and mourne.
At last they chaunst to meete upon the way
The Mule, all deckt in goodly rich aray,
With bells and bosses,[7] that full lowdly rung,
And costly trappings, that to ground downe hung.
Lowly they him saluted in meeke wise;
But he through pride and fatnes gan despise
Their meanesse; scarce vouchsafte them to requite.[8]
Whereat the Foxe deep groning in his sprite,
Said, Ah sir Mule, now blesséd be the day,
590 That I see you so goodly and so gay
In your attyres, and eke your silken hyde
Fil'd with round flesh, that everie bone doth hide.
Seemes that in fruitfull pastures ye doo live,
Or fortune doth you secret favour give.

3. Made boisterous revelry (the *OED* cites this line).
4. Bishop of the diocese (or his deputy). Spenser's description of ecclesiastical procedures here is accurate and technical. When the parishioners complain to the bishop, who has the power to judge ecclesiastical cases, he sends out pursuivants (church officers), who order the fox and ape to appear before him. When they fail to appear, he then orders a visitation of the parish, which was an official enquiry to see whether the current incumbents were fit to act as parish priests. To prevent this outcome the fox and ape sell their parish offices to a neighboring priest, compounding their sins.
5. Easy terms.
6. An opportunity for their tricks.
7. Fancy knobs or studs, here probably made of precious metal.
8. Return the greeting.

Foolish Foxe (said the Mule) thy wretched need
Praiseth the thing that doth thy sorrow breed.
For well I weene,° thou canst not but envie — *know*
My wealth, compar'd to thine owne miserie,
That art so leane and meagre waxen late,
600 That scarse thy legs uphold thy feeble gate.° — *gait, steps*
Ay me (said then the Foxe) whom evill hap° — *fortune*
Unworthy in such wretchednes doth wrap,
And makes the scorne of other beasts to bee:
But read° (faire Sir, of grace)[9] from whence come yee? — *tell*
Or what of tidings you abroad doo heare?
Newes may perhaps some good unweeting beare.[1]
From royall Court I lately came (said he)
Where all the braverie° that eye may see, — *showiness, fashion*
And all the happinesse that heart desire,
610 Is to be found; he nothing can admire,
That hath not seene that heavens portracture:[2]
But tidings there is none I you assure,
Save that which common is, and knowne to all,
That Courtiers as the tide doo rise and fall.
But tell us (said the Ape) we doo you pray,
Who now in Court doth beare the greatest sway.
That if such fortune doo to us befall,
We may seeke favour of the best of all.
Marie (said he) the highest now in grace,[3]
620 Be the wilde beasts, that swiftest are in chase;
For in their speedie course and nimble flight
The Lyon[4] now doth take the most delight:
But chieflie, joyes on foote them to beholde,
Enchaste° with chaine and circulet of golde: — *bound*
So wilde a beast so tame ytaught to bee,
And buxome° to his bands is joy to see. — *obedient*
So well his golden Circlet him beseemeth:
But his late chayne his Liege unmeete[5] esteemeth;
For so brave beasts she loveth best to see,
630 In the wilde forrest raunging fresh and free.
Therefore if fortune thee in Court to live,
In case thou ever there wilt hope to thrive,
To some of these thou must thy selfe apply:
Els as a thistle-downe in th'ayre doth flie,
So vainly shalt thou too and fro be tost,
And loose thy labour and thy fruitles cost.[6]
And yet full few, which follow them I see,

9. Through your kindness; please.
1. I.e., unknowingly carry some opportunity or opening.
2. Heavenly image.
3. It is hard to work out exactly to whom the following lines refer, but that may be the point: preferment at court comes through good fortune or the monarch's whims and is just as quickly or arbitrarily lost, so that who is in favor is difficult to determine.
4. The monarch, and apparently, as shown by pronouns several lines later, female (like Elizabeth?).
5. Unsuitable. This might refer to the secret marriages of the earl of Leicester to Lettys Knollys or the earl of Essex to Frances Walsingham, Sir Philip Sidney's widow.
6. Pointless spending.

For vertues bare regard advauncéd bee,
But either for some gainfull° benefit, *profitable*
640 Or that they may for their owne turnes° be fit. *tricks*
Nath'les perhaps ye things may handle soe,
That ye may better thrive than thousands moe.
But (said the Ape) how shall we first come in,
That after we may favour seeke to win?
How els (said he) but with a good bold face,
And with big words, and with a stately pace,
That men may thinke of you in generall,
That to be in you, which is not at all:
For not by that which is, the world now deemeth,
650 (As it was wont) but by that same that seemeth.
Ne do I doubt, but that ye well can fashion
Your selves theretoo, according to occasion:
So fare ye well, good Courtiers may ye bee;
So proudlie neighing from them parted hee.
Then gan this craftie couple to devize,
How for the Court themselves they might aguize:° *dress*
For thither they themselves meant to addresse,
In hope to finde there happier successe.
So well they shifted, that the Ape anon
660 Himselfe had cloathéd like a Gentleman,
And the slie Foxe, as like to be his groome,
That to the Court in seemly sort they come.
Where the fond Ape himselfe uprearing hy
Upon his tiptoes, stalketh stately by,
As if he were some great *Magnifico*,[7]
And boldlie doth amongst the boldest go.
And his man Reynold with fine counterfesaunce° *pretence, counterfeiting*
Supports his credite° and his countenaunce.° *reputation / appearance*
Then gan the Courtiers gaze on everie side,
670 And stare on him, with big lookes basen wide,[8]
Wondring what mister wight[9] he was, and whence:
For he was clad in strange accoustrements,° *clothes*
Fashion'd with queint devises[1] never seene
In Court before, yet there all fashions beene:
Yet he them in newfanglenesse did pas:
But his behaviour altogether was
Alla Turchesca,[2] much the more admyr'd,
And his lookes loftie, as if he aspyr'd
To dignitie,[3] and sdeign'd° the low degree; *disdained, scorned*
680 That all which did such strangenesse° in him see, *aloofness*
By secrete meanes gan of his state[4] enquire,

7. A nobleman or grandee; from the Italian and hence suggesting well-traveled arrogance.
8. As wide as a basin (i.e., big-eyed, stunned, incredulous).
9. "Mister wight": i.e., what kind of person.
1. I.e., cleverly elaborate designs.
2. In a Turkish fashion, typical of the foreign styles affected at court that many English poets satirized.
3. High position, splendid appointment.
4. Social status.

And privily his servant thereto hire:° *bribe*
Who throughly arm'd against such coverture,[5]
Reported unto all, that he was sure
A noble Gentleman of high regard,
Which through the world had with long travel far'd,
And seene the manners of all beasts on ground;
Now here arriv'd, to see if like he found.
Thus did the Ape at first him credit° gaine, *belief, credibility*
690 Which afterwards he wisely did maintaine
With gallant showe, and daylie more augment
Through his fine feates and Courtly complement;
For he could play, and daunce, and vaute,° and spring, *jump*
And all that els pertaines to reveling,
Onely through kindly aptnes of his joynts.
Besides he could doo manie other poynts,
The which in Court him servéd to good stead:
For he mongst Ladies could their fortunes read
Out of their hands, and merie leasings° tell, *lies*
700 And juggle° finely, that became him well: *cheat, delude*
But he so light was at legier demaine,[6]
That what he toucht, came not to light againe;
Yet would he laugh it out, and proudly looke,
And tell them, that they greatly him mistooke.
So would he scoffe them out[7] with mockerie,
For he therein had great felicitie;
And with sharp quips joy'd others to deface,
Thinking that their disgracing did him grace:
So whilst that other like vaine wits he pleased,
710 And made to laugh, his heart was greatly eased.
But the right gentle minde would bite his lip,
To heare the Javell so good men to nip:[8]
For though the vulgar yeeld an open eare,
And common Courtiers love to gybe and fleare[9]
At everie thing, which they heare spoken ill,
And the best speaches with ill meaning spill;° *spoil*
Yet the brave Courtier,[1] in whose beauteous thought
Regard of honour harbours more than ought,° *anything*
Doth loath such base condition, to backbite
720 Anies good name for envie or despite:
He stands on tearmes of honourable minde,
Ne will be carried with the common winde
Of Courts inconstant mutabilitie,
Ne after everie tattling fable flie;
But heares, and sees the follies of the rest,

5. Underhand strategy.
6. Sleight of hand.
7. "Scoff them out" with "countenance" understood: i.e., humiliate or abash them.
8. I.e., the gentle (well born, well bred, well intentioned) wince to hear such a "javel" (rascal) bite at good men. One of many Elizabethan complaints against satirists who doggishly "nip" or snarl.
9. Laugh and sneer.
1. A description of the ideal courtier follows, one based on discussions in Renaissance conduct books.

And thereof gathers for himselfe the best:
He will not creepe, nor crouche° with fainéd face, *stoop*
But walkes upright with comely stedfast pace,
And unto all doth yeeld due curtesie;° *polite bow*
730 But not with kisséd hand belowe the knee,
As that same Apish crue is wont to doo:
For he disdaines himselfe t'embase° theretoo. *lower, degrade*
He hates fowle leasings,° and vile flatterie, *lies*
Two filthie blots in noble Gentrie;[2]
And lothefull idlenes he doth detest,
The canker worme of everie gentle° brest; *well-born*
The which to banish with faire exercise
Of knightly feates, he daylie doth devise:
Now menaging[3] the mouthes of stubborne steedes,
740 Now practising the proofe[4] of warlike deedes,
Now his bright armes assaying, now his speare,
Now the nigh aymėd ring away to beare;[5]
At other times he casts to sew[6] the chace
Of swift wilde beasts, or runne on foote a race,
T'enlarge his breath (large breath in armes most needfull);
Or els by wrestling to wex strong and heedfull,
Or his stiffe armes to stretch with Eughen° bowe, *yew*
And manly legs, still passing too and fro,
Without a gownéd beast him fast beside;[7]
750 A vaine ensample of the *Persian* pride,
Who after he had wonne th'*Assyrian* foe,
Did ever after scorne on foote to goe.[8]
Thus when this Courtly Gentleman with toyle
Himselfe hath weariéd, he doth recoyle° *retire*
Unto his rest, and there with sweete delight
Of Musicks skill revives his toyléd spright,
Or els with Loves, and Ladies gentle sports,
The joy of youth, himselfe he recomforts:
Or lastly, when the bodie list to pause,
760 His minde unto the Muses he withdrawes;
Sweete Ladie Muses, Ladies of delight,
Delights of life, and ornaments of light:
With whom he close confers with wise discourse,
Of Natures workes, of heavens continuall course,
Of forreine lands, of people different,
Of kingdomes change, of divers government,

2. Technically, all noblemen were gentlemen (i.e., with a legal right to a coat of arms), but the "gentry" was distinct from the nobility, if often related to it by blood. Here "noble Gentrie" suggests high birth.
3. A technical term for horsemanship.
4. I.e., trying out, showing.
5. I.e., carrying off a ring with a lance in a tournament (and hence showing good aim).
6. I.e., aims to follow the hunt.
7. Saddled and carefully dressed.
8. Probably a confused memory of Cyrus, king of Persia, who defeated the Babylonian king who ruled the Assyrians; some said Cyrus was always on horseback when not in his palace. The Romans thought the Persians proud, but Xenophon ascribes their liking to stay on horseback rather to their belief that it is good training.

Of dreadfull battailes of renownéd Knights;
With which he kindleth his ambitious sprights
To like desire and praise of noble fame,
770 The onely upshot[9] whereto he doth ayme:
For all his minde on honour fixéd is,
To which he levels° all his purposis, *aims*
And in his Princes service spends his dayes,
Not so much for to gaine, or for to raise
Himselfe to high degree, as for his grace,° *prince*
And in his[1] liking to winne worthie place;
Through due deserts and comely carriáge,
In whatso please employ his personage,
That may be matter meete to gaine him praise;
780 For he is fit to use in all assayes,° *battles, skirmishes*
Whether for Armes and warlike amenaunce,° *conduct, bearing*
Or else for wise and civill governaunce.
For he is practiz'd well in policie,[2]
And thereto doth his Courting[3] most applie:° *devote, apply*
To learne the enterdeale[4] of Princes strange,° *foreign*
To marke th'intent of Counsells, and the change
Of states, and eke of private men somewhile,
Supplanted by fine falshood and faire guile;
Of all the which he gathereth, what is fit
790 T'enrich the storehouse of his powerfull wit,
Which through wise speaches, and grave conference
He daylie eekes,° and brings to excellence. *increases*
Such is the rightfull Courtier in his kinde:° *species, nature*
But unto such the Ape lent not his minde;
Such were for him no fit companions,
Such would descrie° his lewd° conditions: *uncover / worthless*
But the yong lustie gallants he did chose
To follow, meete to whom he might disclose
His witlesse pleasance, and ill pleasing vaine.
800 A thousand wayes he them could entertaine,
With all the thriftles games, that may be found,
With mumming[5] and with masking all around,
With dice, with cards, with balliards° farre unfit, *billiards*
With shuttelcocks, misseeming° manlie wit, *inappropriate*
With courtizans, and costly riotize,
Whereof still somewhat to his share did rize:
Ne, them to pleasure, would he sometimes scorne
A Pandares coate[6] (so basely was he borne);
Thereto he could fine loving verses frame,[7]

9. Mark (in archery).
1. I.e., the prince's.
2. Cunning, political maneuvering.
3. Behavior as a courtier.
4. Verbal strategies.
5. Disguising (mummers' plays required actors to disguise themselves).
6. Acting as a pander (i.e., procuring women for his fellow courtiers); Pandarus was Criseyde's go-between uncle in Chaucer's *Troilus and Criseyde*.
7. One of Spenser's many attacks on poetry written merely for gain; cf. the end of *Faerie Queene* VI (with a parallel in Du Bellay's "Poète courtisanne").

810 And play the Poet oft. But ah, for shame
Let not sweete Poets praise, whose onely pride
Is vertue to advaunce, and vice deride,
Be with the worke of losels° wit defamed, *libertines*
Ne let such verses Poetrie be named:
Yet he the name on him would rashly take,
Maugré° the sacred Muses, and it make *despite*
A servant to the vile affection° *lust*
Of such, as he depended most upon,
And with the sugrie sweete thereof allure
820 Chast Ladies eares to fantasies impure.
To such delights the noble wits he led
Which him reliev'd,° and their vaine humours° fed *rewarded / fancies*
With fruitles follies, and unsound delights.
But if perhaps into their noble sprights
Desire of honor, or brave thought of armes
Did ever creepe, then with his wicked charmes° *songs, verses*
And strong conceipts° he would it drive away, *language, ideas*
Ne suffer it to house there halfe a day.
And whenso love of letters did inspire
830 Their gentle wits, and kindly wise desire,
That chieflie doth each noble minde adorne,
Then he would scoffe at learning, and eke scorne
The Sectaries° thereof, as people base *scholars, followers*
And simple men, which never came in place
Of worlds affaires, but in darke corners mewd,° *hidden*
Muttred of matters, as their bookes them shewd,
Ne other knowledge ever did attaine,
But with their gownes[8] their gravitie maintaine.
From them he would his impudent lewde speach
840 Against Gods holie Ministers oft reach,
And mocke Divines and their professión:
What else then did he by progressión,
But mocke high God himselfe, whom they professe?° *acknowledge, teach*
But what car'd he for God, or godlinesse?
All his care was himselfe how to advaunce,
And to uphold his courtly countenaunce° *appearance*
By all the cunning meanes he could devise;
Were it by honest wayes, or otherwise,
He made small choice:[9] yet sure his honestie
850 Got him small gaines, but shameles flatterie,
And filthie brocage,° and unseemly shifts,° *pimping / devices, plans*
And borowe° base, and some good Ladies gifts: *promises*
But the best helpe, which chiefly him sustain'd,
Was his man Raynolds purchase° which he gain'd. *winnings, loot*
For he was school'd by kinde° in all the skill *nature*
Of close conveyance,[1] and each practise ill

8. I.e., their academic costume.
9. He did not care.
1. Subtle trickery, underhand dealing.

Of coosinage° and cleanly° knaverie, *fraud / clever, subtle*
Which oft maintain'd his masters braverie.[2]
860 Besides he usde another slipprie slight,° *trick*
In taking on himselfe in common sight,
False personages[3] fit for everie sted,° *occasion*
With which he thousands cleanly coosinéd:° *stole*
Now like a Merchant, Merchants to deceave,
With whom his credite he did often leave
In gage,° for his gay° Masters hopelesse dett: *pledge / fancily dressed*
Now like a Lawyer, when he land would lett,
Or sell fee-simples[4] in his Masters name,
Which he had never, nor ought like the same:
Then would he be a Broker,° and draw in *agent*
870 Both wares° and money, by exchange to win: *goods*
Then would he seeme a Farmer, that would sell
Bargaines of woods, which he did lately fell,
Or corne, or cattle, or such other ware,
Thereby to coosin° men not well aware; *con, delude*
Of all the which there came a secret fee
To th'Ape, that he his countenaunce° might bee. *patron, supporter*
Besides all this, he usd' oft to beguile° *deceive*
Poore suters,° that in Court did haunt some while: *suitors*
For he would learne their busines secretly,
880 And then informe his Master hastely,
That he by meanes might cast° them to prevent,° *plan / anticipate*
And beg the sute, the which the other ment.[5]
Or otherwise false Reynold would abuse
The simple Suter,[6] and wish him to chuse
His Master, being one of great regard
In Court, to compas° anie sute not hard, *undertake*
In case his paines were recompenst with reason:[7]
So would he worke the silly man by treason
To buy his Masters frivolous° good will, *worthless*
890 That had not power to doo him good or ill.
So pitifull a thing is Suters state.
Most miserable man, whom wicked fate
Hath brought to Court, to sue for had ywist,[8]
That few have found, and manie one hath mist;
Full little knowest thou that hast not tride,
What hell it is, in suing long to bide:
To loose good dayes, that might be better spent;
To wast long nights in pensive discontent;
To speed to day, to be put back to morrow;
900 To feed on hope, to pine with feare and sorrow;

2. Fine appearance.
3. I.e., disguises.
4. Land that belonged outright to the owner (freehold).
5. I.e., get there first in asking for the favor or reward.
6. I.e., badmouth the foolish or dim-witted man who wants the favor or reward.
7. Providing his labor was reasonably rewarded.
8. "Had I but known" (proverbial).

To have thy Princes grace, yet want her Peeres;[9]
To have thy asking, yet waite manie yeeres;
To fret thy soule with crosses° and with cares; *misfortunes, obstacles*
To eate thy heart through comfortlesse dispaires;
To fawne, to crowche, to waite, to ride, to ronne,
To spend, to give, to want, to be undonne.
Unhappie wight, borne to desastrous end,
That doth his life in so long tendance° spend. *waiting*
Who ever leaves sweete home, where meane° estate *low*
910 In safe assurance, without strife or hate,
Findes all things needfull for contentment meeke;
And will to Court for shadowes vaine to seeke,
Or hope to gaine, himselfe will a daw trie:[1]
That curse God send unto mine enemie.
For none but such as this bold Ape unblest,
Can ever thrive in that unluckie quest;
Or such as hath a Reynold to his man,
That by his shifts his Master furnish can.
But yet this Foxe could not so closely hide
920 His craftie feates, but that they were descride° *perceived*
At length, by such as sate in justice seate,
Who for the same him fowlie did entreate;[2]
And having worthily him punishéd,
Out of the Court for ever banishéd.
And now the Ape wanting his huckster man,[3]
That wont provide his necessaries, gan
To growe into great lacke, ne could upholde
His countenaunce° in those his garments olde; *appearance*
Ne new ones could he easily provide,
930 Though all men him uncaséd[4] gan deride,
Like as a Puppit placéd in a play,
Whose part once past all men bid take away:
So that he driven was to great distresse,
And shortly brought to hopelesse wretchednesse.
Then closely as he might he cast to leave
The Court, not asking any passe or leave;
But ran away in his rent° rags by night, *torn*
Ne ever stayd in place, ne spake to wight,
Till that the Foxe his copesmate° he had found, *accomplice*
940 To whome complayning his unhappy stound,° *time*
At last againe with him in travell joynd,
And with him far'd some better chaunce to fynde.
So in the world long time they wanderéd,
And mickle° want and hardnesse sufferéd; *much*
That them repented much so foolishly[5]

9. I.e., to have the prince's favor but lack that of her advisers; perhaps Spenser's comment on winning a pension from the queen but not the admiration of William Cecil, Lord Burleigh.
1. That is, prove himself a fool.
2. Treat badly.
3. I.e., con man.
4. That is, stripped of his fancy clothes
5. They regretted.

To come so farre to seeke for misery,
And leave the sweetnes of contented home,
Though eating hipps,[6] and drinking watry fome.
Thus as they them complaynéd too and fro,
950 Whilst through the forest rechlesse[7] they did goe,
Lo where they spide, how in a gloomy glade,
The Lyon sleeping lay in secret shade,[8]
His Crowne and Scepter lying him beside,
And having doft for heate his dreadfull° hide: *frightening*
Which when they sawe, the Ape was sore afrayde,
And would have fled with terror all dismayde.
But him the Foxe with hardy words did stay,
And bad him put all cowardize away:
For now was time (if ever they would hope)
960 To ayme their counsels to the fairest scope,° *point, mark*
And them for ever highly to advaunce,
In case the good which their owne happie chaunce
Them freely offred, they would wisely take.
Scarse could the Ape yet speake, so did he quake,
Yet as he could, he askt how good might growe,
Where nought but dread and death do seeme in show.
Now (sayd he) whiles the Lyon sleepeth sound,
May we his Crowne and Mace take from the ground,
And eke his skinne the terror of the wood,
970 Wherewith we may our selves (if we thinke good)
Make Kings of Beasts, and Lords of forests all,
Subject unto that powre imperiall.
Ah but (sayd the Ape) who is so bold a wretch,
That dare his hardy hand to those outstretch:
When as he knowes his meede,° if he be spide, *reward*
To be a thousand deathes, and shame beside?
Fond Ape (sayd then the Foxe) into whose brest
Never crept thought of honor, nor brave gest,° *exploit*
Who will not venture° life a King to be, *risk*
980 And rather rule and raigne in soveraign see,° *throne*
Than dwell in dust inglorious and bace,
Where none shall name the number of his place?[9]
One joyous houre in blisfull happines,
I chose before a life of wretchednes.
Be therefore counselléd herein by me,
And shake off this vile harted cowardree.° *cowardice*
If he awake, yet is not death the next,
For we may coulor it[1] with some pretext
Of this, or that, that may excuse the cryme:
990 Else we may flye; thou to a tree mayst clyme,
And I creepe under ground; both from his reach:

6. Wild rose hips.
7. With no purpose.
8. What follows is a version of Aesop's fable of the ass in the lion's skin.
9. I.e., calculate his (low) social degree.
1. Disguise it.

Therefore be rul'd to doo as I doo teach.
The Ape, that earst° did nought but chill and quake, *first*
Now gan some courage unto him to take,
And was content to attempt that enterprise,
Tickled° with glorie and rash covetise.° *inspired, excited / greed*
But first gan question, whether° should assay° *which / attempt, try*
Those royall ornaments to steale away?
Marie that shall your selfe (quoth he theretoo)
1000 For ye be fine and nimble it to doo;
Of all the beasts which in the forrests bee,
Is not a fitter for this turne than yee:
Therefore, mine owne deare brother take good hart,
And ever thinke a Kingdome is your part.
Loath was the Ape, though praiséd, to adventer,
Yet faintly gan into his worke to enter,
Afraid of everie leafe, that stir'd him by,
And everie stick, that underneath did ly;
Upon his tiptoes nicely° he up went, *carefully, gingerly*
1010 For making noyse,[2] and still his eare he lent
To everie sound, that under heaven blew;
Now went, now stept, now crept, now backward drew,
That it good sport had been him to have eyde:
Yet at the last (so well he him applyde,)
Through his fine handling, and cleanly play,
He all those royall signes had stolne away,
And with the Foxes helpe them borne aside,
Into a secret corner unespide.
Whither whenas they came, they fell at words,
1020 Whether° of them should be the Lord of Lords: *which*
For th'Ape was stryfull,° and ambicious; *argumentative*
And the Foxe guilefull, and most covetous,
That neither pleaséd was, to have the rayne
Twixt them divided into even twaine,[3]
But either (algates)° would be Lords alone: *anyway*
For Love and Lordship bide no paragone.° *rival, equal*
I am most worthie (said the Ape) sith I
For it did put my life in jeopardie:
Thereto I am in person, and in stature
1030 Most like a man, the Lord of everie creature;
So that it seemeth I was made to raigne,
And borne to be a Kingly soveraigne.
Nay (said the Foxe) Sir Ape you are astray:
For though to steale the Diademe away
Were the worke of your nimble hand, yet I
Did first devise the plot by pollicie;° *guile*
So that it wholly springeth from my wit:
For which also I claime my selfe more fit
Than you, to rule: for government of state

2. To avoid making noise.
3. I.e., to have the rule divided between them into two equal parts.

1040 Will without wisedome soone be ruinate.
And where ye claime your selfe for outward shape
Most like a man, Man is not like an Ape
In his chiefe parts, that is, in wit and spirite;
But I therein most like to him doo merite
For my slie wyles and subtill craftinesse,
The title of the Kingdome to possesse.
Nath'les (my brother) since we passéd are
Unto this point, we will appease our jarre,° *dispute*
And I with reason meete will rest content,
1050 That ye shall have both crowne and government,
Upon condition, that ye ruléd bee
In all affaires, and counselléd by mee;
And that ye let none other ever drawe
Your minde from me, but keepe this as a lawe:
And hereupon an oath unto me plight.
The Ape was glad to end the strife so light,° *easily*
And thereto swore: for who would not oft sweare,
And oft unsweare a Diademe to beare?
Then freely up those royall spoyles he tooke,
1060 Yet at the Lyons skin he inly quooke;° *quaked*
But it dissembled,[4] and upon his head
The Crowne, and on his backe the skin he did,° *put*
And the false Foxe him helpéd to array.
Then when he was all dight° he tooke his way *dressed*
Into the forest, that he might be seene
Of the wilde beasts in his new glory sheene.° *resplendent*
There the two first, whome he encountred, were
The Sheepe and th'Asse, who striken both with feare
At sight of him, gan fast away to flye,
1070 But unto them the Foxe alowd did cry,
And in the Kings name bad them both to stay,
Upon the payne that thereof follow may.[5]
Hardly naythles° were they restraynéd so, *however*
Till that the Foxe forth toward them did goe,
And there disswaded them from needlesse feare,
For that the King did favour to them beare;
And therefore dreadles° bad them come to Corte: *unafraid*
For no wild beasts should do them any torte° *wrong*
There or abroad, ne would his majestye
1080 Use them but well, with gracious clemencye,° *mercy, care*
As whome he knew to him both fast and true;[6]
So he perswaded them, with homage due
Themselves to humble to the Ape prostrate,
Who gently to them bowing in his gate,
Receyvéd them with chearefull entertayne.° *treatment*

4. That is, he concealed his fear.
5. Upon the pain of whatever punishment might follow a failure to obey.
6. I.e., since he knew him (the king) to be faithful and loyal to him (the fox); the trick of rousing and then allaying fear is an example of "pollicie," the foxiness that many such as Machiavelli thought a vital part of rulership and others thought morally repellent.

Thenceforth proceeding with his princely trayne,
He shortly met the Tygre, and the Bore,
Which with the simple° Camell ragéd sore — *naïve, innocent*
In bitter words, seeking to take occasion,
1090 Upon his fleshly corpse° to make invasion:° — *body / attack*
But soone as they this mock-King did espy,
Their troublous strife they stinted by and by,[7]
Thinking indeed that it the Lyon was:
He then to prove,° whether his powre would pas — *test*
As currant,[8] sent the Foxe to them streight way,
Commaunding them their cause of strife bewray;° — *reveal*
And if that wrong on eyther side there were,
That he should warne° the wronger to appeare — *summon*
The morrow next at Court, it to defend;
1100 In the meane time upon the King t'attend.
The subtile Foxe so well his message sayd,
That the proud beasts him readily obayd:
Whereby the Ape in wondrous stomack° woxe, — *pride*
Strongly encorag'd by the crafty Foxe;
That King indeed himselfe he shortly thought,
And all the Beasts him fearéd as they ought:
And followéd unto his palaice hye,
Where taking Congé,° each one by and by — *leave*
Departed to his home in dreadfull° awe, — *scared, quaking*
1110 Full of the fearéd sight, which late they sawe.
The Ape thus seizéd of the Regall throne,
Eftsones° by counsell of the Foxe alone, — *soon, shortly*
Gan to provide for all things in assurance,
That so his rule might lenger have endurance.
First to his Gate he pointed° a strong gard, — *appointed*
That none might enter but with issue° hard: — *attempt*
Then for the safegard of his personage,
He did appoint a warlike equipage° — *retinue*
Of forreine beasts, not in the forest bred,
1120 But part by land, and part by water fed;[9]
For tyrannie is with strange° ayde supported. — *foreign*
Then unto him all monstrous beasts resorted
Bred of two kindes, as Griffons, Minotaures,
Crocodiles, Dragons, Beavers, and Centaures:
With those himselfe he strengthned mightelie,
That feare he neede no force of enemie.
Then gan he rule and tyrannize at will,
Like as the Foxe did guide his graceles skill,
And all wylde beasts made vassals of his pleasures,

7. I.e., ceased at once.
8. I.e., would be taken as authentic.
9. The importing of foreign animals recalls English fears earlier in Elizabeth's reign that a foreign consort (such as the duc d'Alençon) might bring with him a military retinue or, more recently, that the queen's still unnamed heir might do so. The radical Catholic rebels against Henri IV ("Sir Burbon" in *The Faerie Queene* V), the beleaguered French king whom Elizabeth was supporting when this poem was published, had garrisoned Paris with Spanish soldiers. Fear of foreign mercenaries was in any case common.

1130 And with their spoyles enlarg'd his private treasures.
No care of justice, nor no rule of reason,
No temperance, nor no regard of season
Did thenceforth ever enter in his minde,
But crueltie, the signe of currish kinde,
And sdeignfull° pride, and wilfull arrogaunce; *dismissive*
Such followes those whom fortune doth advaunce.
But the false Foxe most kindly[1] plaid his part.
For whatsoever mother wit, or arte
Could worke, he put in proofe:° no practise slie, *practice*
1140 No counterpoint[2] of cunning policie,
No reach,° no breach,[3] that might him profit bring, *scheme*
But he the same did to his purpose wring.
Nought suffered he the Ape to give or graunt,
But through his hand must passe the Fiaunt.° *warrant*
All offices, all leases by him lept,° *passed*
And of them all whatso he likte, he kept.
Justice he solde injustice for to buy,
And for to purchase for his progeny.[4]
Ill might it prosper, that ill gotten was,
1150 But so he got it, little did he pas.° *care*
He fed his cubs with fat of all the soyle,
And with the sweete of others sweating toyle,
He crammèd them with crumbs of Benefices,
And fild their mouthes with meeds of malefices,[5]
He cloathèd them with all colours save white,
And loded them with lordships and with might,
So much as they were able well to beare,
That with the weight their backs nigh broken were;[6]
He chaffred° Chayres[7] in which Churchmen were set, *sold*
1160 And breach of lawes to privie ferme[8] did let;° *rent*
No statute so establishèd might bee,
Nor ordinaunce so needfull, but that hee
Would violate, though not with violence,
Yet under colour of the confidence
The which the Ape reposd' in him alone,
And reckned him the kingdomes corner stone.
And ever when he ought° would bring to pas, *anything*
His long experience the platforme° was: *basis*
And when he ought not pleasing would put by,
1170 The cloke was care of thrift, and husbandry,
For to encrease the common treasures store;[9]

1. I.e., according to his [evil] nature; *false Foxe*: this description is often read as an attack on William Cecil, Lord Burghleigh.
2. Actions balanced against each other (a musical metaphor).
3. Breach of the laws.
4. Provide for his offspring.
5. The rewards of evil deeds.
6. Burghleigh's son, the powerful Robert Cecil, who would be chief minister to James I, was a hunchback; he too would earn the dislike of several poets, not least John Donne.
7. I.e., bishoprics.
8. The practice of paying individuals to collect taxes led to massive corruption and overcharging.
9. That is, whenever he ignored or rejected something that displeased him, his cover story was the need to spare public expense.

But his owne treasure he encreaséd more
And lifted up his loftie towres thereby,[1]
That they began to threat the neighbour sky;
The whiles the Princes pallaces fell fast
To ruine: (for what thing can ever last?)
And whilest the other Peeres, for povertie
Were forst their auncient houses to let lie,
And their olde Castles to the ground to fall,
1180 Which their forefathers famous over all
Had founded for the Kingdomes ornament,
And for their memories long moniment.
But he no count made of Nobilitie,
Nor the wilde beasts whom armes did glorifie,
The Realmes chiefe strength and girlond of the crowne.
All these through fainéd crimes he thrust adowne,
Or made them dwell in darknes of disgrace:
For none, but whom he list° might come in place.[2] *wanted*
Of men of armes he had but small regard,
1190 But kept them lowe, and streignéd° verie hard. *restrained*
For men of learning little he esteemed;
His wisedome he above their learning deemed.
As for the rascall Commons[3] least he cared;
For not so common was his bountie shared;
Let God (said he) if please, care for the manie,
I for my selfe must care before els anie:
So did he good to none, to manie ill,
So did he all the kingdome rob and pill,° *pillage*
Yet none durst speake, ne none durst of him plaine;° *complain*
1200 So great he was in grace,[4] and rich through gaine.
Ne would he anie let to have accesse
Unto the Prince, but by his owne addresse:° *introduction*
For all that els did come, were sure to faile,
Yet would he further none but for availe.° *gain*
For on a time the Sheepe, to whom of yore
The Foxe had promiséd of friendship store,
What time[5] the Ape the kingdome first did gaine,
Came to the Court, her case there to complaine,
How that the Wolfe her mortall enemie
1210 Had sithence slaine her Lambe most cruellie;
And therefore crav'd to come unto the King,
To let him knowe the order of the thing.[6]
Soft Gooddie Sheepe[7] (then said the Foxe) not soe:
Unto the King so rash ye may not goe,

1. Burleigh was well known for his ambitious building projects.
2. Be welcomed to high position at court, to receive promotion and favor.
3. I.e., the rabblelike, baseborn, common folk, but with a glance at the House of Commons; technically, "rascal" animals were thin, inferior, or badly developed.
4. I.e., in the ruler's favor ("grace").
5. I.e., when.
6. That is, how things were, what had occurred.
7. "Goody," a condensation of "Good Wife [woman]," was the term of address for older women of the lower classes.

He is with greater matter busiéd,
Than a Lambe, or the Lambes owne mothers hed.
Ne certes may I take it well in part,
That ye my cousin Wolfe so fowly thwart,° *oppose, frustrate*
And seeke with slaunder his good name to blot:
1220 For there was cause, els doo it he would not.
Therefore surcease good Dame, and hence depart.
So went the Sheepe away with heavie hart.
So manie moe, so everie one was used,
That to give largely to the boxe[8] refused.
Now when high *Jove*, in whose almightie hand
The care of Kings, and power of Empires stand,
Sitting one day within his turret hye,
From whence he vewes with his blacklidded eye,
Whatso the heaven in his wide vawte° containes, *vault*
1230 And all that in the deepest earth remaines,
The troubled kingdome of wilde beasts behelde,
Whom not their kindly Sovereigne did welde,
But an usurping Ape with guile suborn'd,° *assisted*
Had all subverst,[9] he sdeignfully° it scorn'd *disdainfully*
In his great heart, and hardly did refraine,
But that with thunder bolts he had him slaine,
And driven downe to hell, his dewest meed:[1]
But him avizing,° he that dreadfull deed *reflecting, considering*
Forbore, and rather chose with scornfull shame
1240 Him to avenge, and blot° his brutish name *stain, sully*
Unto the world, that never after anie
Should of his race be voyd of infamie:
And his false counsellor, the cause of all,
To damne to death, or dole° perpetuall, *suffering, pain*
From whence he never should be quit, nor stal'd.[2]
Forthwith he *Mercurie*[3] unto him cal'd,
And bad him flie with never resting speed
Unto the forrest, where wilde beasts doo breed,° *live*
And there enquiring privily, to learne,
1250 What did of late chaunce to the Lyon stearne,
That he rul'd not the Empire, as he ought;
And whence were all those plaints° unto him brought *complaints*
Of wrongs and spoyles, by salvage beasts committed;
Which done, he bad the Lyon be remitted° *restored*
Into his seate, and those same treachours vile
Be punishéd for their presumptuous guile.
The Sonne of *Maia*[4] soone as he receiv'd
That word, streight with his azure wings he cleav'd[5]
The liquid clowdes, and lucid firmament;

8. Moneybox.
9. Turned upside down.
1. Proper reward.
2. I.e., be liberated or bailed out by a series of payments (*OED* cites this line, calling it figurative).
3. The gods' messenger (also god of clever rhetoric, merchants, and thieves).
4. I.e., Mercury.
5. Went (cut) through.

1260 Ne staid, till that he came with steep descent
Unto the place, where his prescript° did showe. — *instructions, directions*
There stouping[6] like an arrowe from a bowe,
He soft arrivéd on the grassie plaine,
And fairly pacéd forth with easie paine,[7]
Till that unto the Pallace nigh he came.
Then gan he to himselfe new shape to frame,
And that faire face, and that Ambrosiall hew,[8]
Which wonts to decke the Gods immortall crew,° — *company, group*
And beautefie the shinie firmament,
1270 He doft, unfit for that rude rabblement.° — *mob*
So standing by the gates in strange° disguize, — *unwonted, unfamiliar*
He gan enquire of some in secret wize,[9]
Both of the King, and of his government,
And of the Foxe, and his false blandishment:° — *promises*
And evermore he heard each one complaine
Of foule abuses both in realme and raine.[1]
Which yet to prove more true, he meant to see,
And an ey-witnes of each thing to bee.
Tho° on his head his dreadfull hat he dight,[2] — *then*
1280 Which maketh him invisible in sight,
And mocketh th'eyes of all the lookers on,
Making them thinke it but a visión.
Through power of that, he runnes through enemies swerds;
Through power of that, he passeth through the herds
Of ravenous wilde beasts, and doth beguile
Their greedie mouthes of the expected spoyle;
Through power of that, his cunning theeveries
He wonts to worke, that none the same espies;
And through the power of that, he putteth on
1290 What shape he list in apparition.
That on his head he wore, and in his hand
He tooke *Caduceus* his snakie wand,
With which the damnéd ghosts he governeth,
And furies rules, and Tartare[3] tempereth.
With that he causeth sleep to seize the eyes,
And feare° the harts of all his enemyes; — *terrify*
And when him list, an universall night
Throughout the world he makes on everie wight;
As when his Syre with *Alcumena*[4] lay.
1300 Thus dight,° into the Court he tooke his way, — *dressed, equipped*
Both through the gard, which never him descride,
And through the watchmen, who him never spide:

6. Swooping down (often said of hawks).
7. Little effort.
8. Heavenly appearance.
9. I.e., privately, in confidence.
1. Kingdom and government.
2. That is, donned his fearsome hat (presumably the one with wings).
3. Tartarus, the punitive part of the classical underworld; *furies*: In classical mythology, the three Furies were Hades's agents of retribution.
4. Jove forbade the sun to rise for three days so he could spend more time in bed with Alcumena.

Thenceforth he past into each secrete part,
Whereas he saw, that sorely griev'd his hart;
Each place abounding with fowle injuries,
And fild with treasure rackt with[5] robberies:
Each place defilde with blood of guiltles beasts,
Which had been slaine, to serve the Apes beheasts;
Gluttonie, malice, pride, and covetize,
1310 And lawlesnes raigning with riotize;
Besides the infinite extortións,
Done through the Foxes great oppressións,
That the complaints thereof could not be tolde.° *counted*
Which when he did with lothfull° eyes beholde, *reluctant*
He would no more endure, but came his way,
And cast to seeke the Lion, where he may,
That he might worke the avengement° for this shame, *revenge, retribution*
On those two caytives,° which had bred him blame. *villains*
And seeking all the forrest busily,
1320 At last he found, where sleeping he did ly:
The wicked weed, which there the Foxe did lay,
From underneath his head he tooke away,
And then him waking, forcéd up to rize.
The Lion looking up gan him avize,[6]
As one late in a traunce, what had of long
Become of him: for fantasie is strong.
Arise (said *Mercurie*) thou sluggish beast,
That here liest senseles, like the corpse deceast,
The whilste thy kingdome from thy head is rent,
1330 And thy throne royall with dishonour blent:° *stained*
Arise, and doo thy selfe redeeme from shame,
And be aveng'd on those that breed thy blame.
Thereat enragéd, soone he gan upstart,
Grinding his teeth, and grating° his great hart, *striking*
And rouzing up himselfe, for his rough hide
He gan to reach; but no where it espide.
Therewith he gan full terribly to rore,
And chafte at that indignitie right sore.
But when his Crowne and scepter both he wanted,° *missed, lacked*
1340 Lord how he fum'd, and sweld, and rag'd, and panted;
And threatned death, and thousand deadly dolours
To them that had purloyn'd his Princely honours.
With that in hast, disroabéd as he was,
He toward his owne Pallace forth did pas;
And all the way he roaréd as he went,
That all the forrest with astonishment
Thereof did tremble, and the beasts therein
Fled fast away from that so dreadfull din.
At last he came unto his mansión,
1350 Where all the gates he found fast lockt anon,

5. I.e., extorted by.
6. I.e., look around.

And manie warders round about them stood:
With that he roar'd alowd, as he were wood,°	*mad*
That all the Pallace quakéd at the stound,°	*shock*
As if it quite were riven from the ground,
And all within were dead and hartles left;
And th'Ape himselfe, as one whose wits were reft,°	*snatched*
Fled here and there, and everie corner sought,
To hide himselfe from his owne fearéd thought.
But the false Foxe when he the Lion heard,
1360 Fled closely° forth, streightway of death afeard,	*secretly*
And to the Lion came, full lowly creeping,
With fainéd face, and watrie eyne halfe weeping,
T'excuse his former treason and abusion,[7]
And turning all unto the Apes confusion:[8]
Nath'les the royall Beast forbore° beleeving,	*withheld*
But bad him stay at ease[9] till further preeving.°	*proof, evidence*
Then when he saw no entrance to him graunted,
Roaring yet lowder that all harts it daunted,
Upon those gates with force he fiercely flewe,
1370 And rending them in pieces, felly° slewe	*harshly*
Those warders strange,° and all that els he met.	*foreign*
But th'Ape still flying, he no where might get:
From rowme to rowme, from beame to beame he fled
All breathles, and for feare now almost ded:
Yet him at last the Lyon spide, and caught,
And forth with shame unto his judgement brought.
Then all the beasts he causd' assembled bee,
To heare their doome,° and sad ensample° see:	*fate / example*
The Foxe, first Author of that treacherie,
1380 He did uncase,[1] and then away let flie.
But th'Apes long taile (which then he had) he quight
Cut off, and both eares paréd of their hight;
Since which, all Apes but halfe their eares have left,
And of their tailes are utterlie bereft.
So Mother *Hubberd* her discourse did end:
Which pardon me, if I amisse have pend,
For weake was my remembrance it to hold,
And bad her tongue that it so bluntly tolde.

FINIS.

Editors' Note

Mother Hubberds Tale was first published in 1591 as part of the collected volume *Complaints* but is described by the author in his dedicatory epistle to the Ladies Compton and Monteagle as a work "long sithens com-

7. Abuse, wrong.
8. Disadvantage, ruin.
9. Remain free; the lion respects the niceties of the English legal system.
1. Strip off his hide (cf. the stripping of Duessa in *The Faerie Queene*, I. viii. 46–50).

posed in the raw conceipt of my youth." Any modesty topos aside, this is quite plausible, as the poem contains the remnants of a fairly direct allegory of the queen's possible marriage to François, duc d'Alençon, in 1579–80 (see below). Indeed, a number of commentators, following Edwin Greenlaw, have argued that the poem circulated in manuscript in 1580 and that its highly charged political content was responsible for Spenser beating a hasty retreat to Ireland as secretary to Lord Grey in 1580. Such a case is hard to sustain without any corroborating evidence, although it is plausible, especially as we know that *The Faerie Queene* circulated in manuscript before it was published, and there are distinct topical allusions to the events of the early 1580s in the text. Spenser's reasons for going to Ireland will probably always remain obscure unless new documents are discovered. Given the ways in which he announced himself as the new poet ready to transform English letters in 1579, leaving London a year later might seem to be a strange move, so it could have been pragmatic to escape hostility. On the other hand, Spenser was only one of a number of writers with an insecure and uncertain future—Barnabe Rich, Barnabe Googe, and Sir John Davies were others—who sought to exploit the opportunities of acquiring land and wealth in a country that seemed to offer opportunities that were not available in England. It was no accident that Walter Raleigh acquired a vast estate of some 20,000 acres in Munster, nor that Richard Boyle, from relatively humble origins in Kent, acquired the largest fortune in the British Isles through land-dealing in Ireland. Spenser himself acquired an estate of 3000 acres, way beyond what he could have obtained had he remained in England.

What is beyond dispute is that when *Mother Hubberds Tale* was published in 1591 it did cause huge offense and managed to make the author a powerful enemy in William Cecil, Lord Burleigh, Elizabeth's principal minister. A long letter by a Catholic recusant, Thomas Tresham, recently discovered by Richard Peterson, revels in Spenser's discomfort, describing how he is likely to lose the annual £50 pension granted him by the queen and transform him from a poet laureate to a "Poett Lorrell" (fool; see Peterson 1989). Copies of the poem were "called in" and it became risky to own one. Spenser clearly caused a serious controversy, one of a number in the edgy years of the 1590s, when people were especially anxious about the succession and criticism of the monarch and her inner circle of advisers was invariably treated harshly. Eventually, in 1599, after a bitter feud between Thomas Nashe and Spenser's friend and ally, Gabriel Harvey, satire was banned altogether. In fact, the poem was not republished until after the death of Lord Burleigh's son, Robert Cecil, in 1612, suggesting that the reference to the fox making his cubs fat with the spoils of ecclesiastical livings had struck home.

Mother Hubberds Tale is a beast fable, a tale of moral, spiritual, and political corruption set in the "dog days" of August, the opening lines reminding readers of other great works in a similar vein, such as Chaucer's *Canterbury Tales* or Boccaccio's *Decameron*. While the poem contains a number of important topical references, it also demands to be read as a coherent work reflecting on human foibles and failings. It tells the story of the resistible rise of an ape and a fox, narrated by a decent old woman who is one of a number of friends gathered around the ill narrator, hoping to cheer him up in time of plague. The story works so well that the narrator then reproduces it as a poem in rhyming pentameters. The poem contains four sections that chart the progress of the devious couple as they gradually ascend the social ladder, a model that owes much to the familiar genre of medieval estates satire, also a source for *The Canterbury Tales*. As so often in his work Spenser shows that he is a careful reader of Chaucer, who in the 1580s was still the most powerful influence on English poets.

In part one the ape disguises himself as a soldier and the fox as his servant, enabling them to dupe an honest shepherd into letting them look after his flock of sheep (ll. 45–342). Within six months they manage to consume most of them, killing the remainder when they leave. In the second episode (ll. 353–574) the ape disguises himself as a priest and the fox as a scholar and they beg for alms. This episode continues the ecclesiastical satire of *The Shepheardes Calender*, which also suggests that an earlier version might date from the late 1570s or early 1580s. They encounter a hostile priest who is fooled when they produce a false document that supposedly grants them rights to beg. Following the priest's speech on how to obtain an ecclesiastical position, the pair become a priest and a parish clerk respectively until they exploit their positions so seriously that they alienate their parishioners and have to flee just before an official visitation.

Part three (ll. 581–942) turns our attention to the court as the fox and ape reach the apex of society. The ape disguises himself as a gentleman and the fox becomes his groom. Spenser provides the reader with a long description of the ideal courtier (ll. 717–93), which serves only to highlight the appalling behavior of the ape and, by implication, that of the courtiers who fail to notice that he is a fake rather than one of them. As in the hostile portraits of the court in *Colin Clouts Come Home Againe* and *The Faerie Queene* Books V and VI, Spenser demonstrates that he is more of an anticourt than a court poet. The ape proves his "worth" by improving his abilities to cheat, deceive, and exploit his fellow courtiers, performing so well that he and the fox are both forced to leave.

The final episode (ll. 949–1384) sees the ape and the fox going as far as they can possibly go when they steal the crown, sceptre, and skin of a lion, enabling them to impersonate the monarch and his chief adviser. After a squabble, the fox allows the ape to wear the trappings of power, as long as he agrees to be ruled by him. It is easy to see why first Burleigh and then his son would have found this poem so offensive: Burleigh was often represented as the cunning fox who really ruled England behind Elizabeth's back. A number of satires, many written by disaffected and hostile Catholics, portrayed Burleigh as the operator of a sinister *Regnum Cecilium* ("rule of the Cecils"), usurping the legitimate power of the monarch for his own selfish ends. The ape and the fox now rule the animals in the forest in a pitiless and corrupt manner, bending justice to their advantage. They exploit the nobility and appropriate their wealth and they abuse offices of state and church for the same reasons. Whereas earlier the ape and the fox had to flee when their plans became public, there is now no one to stop them until Jove becomes offended by their violations of good kingship and sends Mercury to earth to end their rule.

Mercury wakes the lion up, the criminals are tried and punished and proper order is restored.

Spenser's satirical poem is at once an attack on specific abuses and a comment on the eternal failings of human nature. It is simultaneously an angry poem that demands justice and a resigned work that accepts that the world is unfair because some people are abusive and other are credulous. The difference between the two positions, as in most satirical works, is there for the reader to decide. The subtitle of the poem, *Prosopopoia*, means personification, or, in George Puttenham's words in *The Arte of English Poesie* (1589), "Counterfait inpersonation." We have to decide how close men are to beasts and how useful the reading of human behavior in terms of animal behavior really is. Are men like foxes and apes? Spenser's satirical focus is directed at the court, a common theme in 1590s literature, as the satires of John Donne or Joseph Hall indicate. Indeed much of Spenser's work in this period is clearly attuned to contemporary satirical works, and few other writers have a more negative perception of the court and its influence on life throughout the queen's dominions. We witness the failure of agriculture, the church, culture, and monarchy. Of course, all these are stock themes in satire, but the topical details that Spenser includes at strategic points indicate that he wanted readers to see in the poem what was wrong in their country. One of the readers was, unfortunately, Lord Burleigh, and Spenser ends the second edition of *The Faerie Queene* (1596) with an acknowledgment of how much he felt his satirical forays had cost him. That poem ends with the escape of the unstoppable Blatant Beast, a creature who abuses language itself, threatening to engulf Spenser's poetry:

> Ne may this homely verse, of many meanest,
> Hope to escape his venemous despite,
> More then my former writs, all were they clearest
> From blamefull blot, and free from all that wite,
> With which some wicked tongues did it backebite,
> And bring into a mighty Peres displeasure,
> That never so deserved to endite.
> Therfore do you my rimes keep better measure,
> And seeke to please, that now is counted wisemens threasure.
>
> *FQ*, VI.xii.41

The claim that Spenser intended no harm in *Mother Hubberds Tale* is either foolish or disingenuous, as the poem was clearly designed to cause offense and hit certain key targets very hard. Spenser may well be expressing a genuine outrage and bemusement at the reception of his earlier poem. More likely, he was adopting yet another *faux-naïve* mask, effacing the role of the author so that readers have the burden of satirical work transferred to them.

Mother Hubberds Tale was regarded as a "minor" poem for a long time but has now been generally reclassified as a "shorter" poem. Its central role in Spenser's life is now widely acknowledged, and its status as an ebullient satire full of mock-heroic motifs and episodes—such as Mercury's intervention at the end of the poem—make it a much more exciting and interesting work for readers (McCabe 2006). Richard Rambuss (1993) has provided an ingenious reading that suggests that Spenser is concerned not to reveal the names of allegorical figures in the poem, showing the reader that he knows how to behave at court, i.e., like the fox and ape. However, the poem sailed too close to the wind in its tantalizing use of allegory and earned Spenser opprobrium rather than the employment he desired. Some commentators have studied the poem as an exploration of the problems of writing poetry and the relation between writing and society (Brown 1999). Yet others have attempted to link the attack on corruption in the poem to events in Ireland (Herron 2004), or to Burleigh's establishment of an alternative court at his prodigy house, Theobalds (Danner 2011). However it is read, the poem is a powerful beast fable that had a major influence on the course of English satire in the next two centuries.

The Ruines of Rome: by Bellay

1

Ye heavenly spirites, whose ashie cinders lie
Under deep ruines, with huge walls opprest,
But not your praise, the which shall never die
Through your faire verses, ne in ashes rest;
If so be shrilling[1] voyce of wight° alive — *person*
May reach from hence to depth of darkest hell,
Then let those deep Abysses open rive,[2]
That ye may understand my shreiking yell.
Thrice having seene under the heavens veale° — *veil*
Your toombs devoted° compasse over all,[3] — *hallowed, consecrated*
Thrice unto you with lowd voyce I appeale,
And for your antique furie[4] here doo call,
The whiles° that I with sacred horror[5] sing — *while*
Your glorie, fairest of all earthly thing.

2[6]

Great *Babylon*[7] her haughtie walls will praise,
And sharpéd steeples high shot up in ayre;
Greece will the olde *Ephesian* buildings[8] blaze;° — *trumpet forth*
And *Nylus* nurslings their Pyramides[9] faire;
The same yet vaunting *Greece* will tell the storie
Of *Joves* great Image in *Olympus* placed,[1]

1. Loud, often high pitched, but probably without the modern connotations of "shrill."
2. I.e., let your depths split open.
3. Obscurely put. In Spenser's source, the *Antiquitez,* Joachim Du Bellay has both ritual as well as invocation: "Thrice devoutly circling your tombs."
4. Usually meant not so much anger as madness or, as here, inspiration.
5. Probably more "a thrill of awe" or "imaginative fear" (*OED*) than repugnance.
6. Exploiting the traditional "Seven Wonders of the World," Du Bellay recalls Horace's ode on Tivoli, "Laudarunt alli" ("Others will praise"; Odes I.vii).
7. Babylon was famed for its hanging gardens, a detail Du Bellay includes but Spenser omits; the site of Israelite exile (see Psalm 137), it was one of the powers that the Bible foretold would collapse (Daniel 4) and thus belonged to the "translation of empire." Some associated Babylon with papal Rome.
8. Ephesus (in modern Turkey, but once part of Greek culture) had a temple to Diana.
9. The meter works better with the accent on the second syllable; *nurslings*: the Egyptians, nourished by the Nile.
1. Du Bellay, however, refers not to Olympus but to Olympia, site of a temple to Zeus/Jove.

Mausolus worke will be the *Carians* glorie,[2]
And *Crete* will boast the Labyrinth, now raced;°[3] *razed, erased*
The antique *Rhodian* will likewise set forth
The great Colosse,[4] erect to Memorie;
And what els in the world is of like worth,
Some greater learned wit will magnifie.
But I will sing above all moniments
Seven *Romane* Hils, the worlds 7. wonderments.

3[5]

Thou stranger, which for *Rome* in *Rome* here seekest,
And nought of *Rome* in *Rome* perceiv'st at all,
These same olde walls, olde arches, which thou seest,
Olde Palaces, is that which *Rome* men call.
Behold what wreake,° what ruine, and what wast,° *damage / desolation*
And how that she, which with her mightie powre
Tam'd all the world, hath tam'd herselfe at last,
The pray of time, which all things doth devowre.
Rome now of *Rome* is th'onely funerall,[6]
And onely *Rome* of *Rome* hath victorie;
Ne ought save *Tyber*[7] hastning to his fall
Remaines of all: O worlds inconstancie.
That which is firme doth flit and fall away,
And that° is flitting, doth abide and stay. *what*

4

She,[8] whose high top above the starres did sore,° *soar*
One foote on *Thetis*,[9] th'other on the Morning,
One hand on *Scythia*, th'other on the *More*,[1]
Both heaven and earth in roundnesse compassing,
Jove fearing, least° if she should greater growe, *lest*
The old Giants should once againe uprise,[2]
Her whelm'd with hills, these 7. hils, which be nowe
Tombes of her greatnes, which did threate the skies:
Upon her head he heapt Mount *Saturnal*,

2. Mausolus: a fourth-century B.C.E. king of the Carians on the southeastern coast of modern Turkey; from his huge unfinished tomb at Helicarnassus comes "Mausoleum."
3. Here, King Minos's Labyrinth is now razed; for Du Bellay, "Crete will not forget its old labyrinth."
4. The Colossus of Rhodes, a huge statue of the sun god Helios erected in the third century B.C.E. near the harbor of the Greek isle of Rhodes; half a century later an earthquake felled it.
5. Du Bellay translates a widely admired Neo-Latin epigram by Janus Vitalis.
6. I.e., Rome is its own funeral [monument].
7. The river Tiber, flowing through Rome, "falls" into the sea.
8. Rome and its empire.
9. The sea nymph Thetis, mother of Achilles, who often symbolized the waters where the sun seemingly sinks or rises, here the West. Du Bellay's sonnet parallels a Latin poem in his *Poemata* (1558).
1. Northwest Africa, where Rome had defeated its rival Carthage; here the South. *Scythia*: Northeast of the Black Sea (its borders varied over time) and to the Romans a land of barbarians.
2. A race of giants; born from Earth and the bloodshed when the Titan Saturn castrated his father Uranos (Sky), they fought a doomed war against Zeus and the Olympians. Like many others, Spenser often conflates them with the Titans. Jove put one of the Titans under Aetna, where he sometimes erupts. Here Rome is itself a fallen giant, buried under its own seven hills, which the poet then names.

Upon her bellie th'antique *Palatine*,
Upon her stomacke laid Mount *Quirinal*,
On her left hand the noysome *Esquiline*,[3]
And *Cælian* on the right; but both her feete
Mount *Viminall* and *Aventine* doo meete.

5

Who lists° to see, what ever nature, arte, *wishes*
And heaven could doo, O *Rome*, thee let him see,[4]
In case thy greatnes he can gesse° in harte, *guess*
By that which but the picture is of thee.
Rome is no more: but if the shade° of *Rome* *ghost*
May of the bodie yeeld a seeming sight,
It's like a corse° drawne forth out of the tombe *corpse*
By Magicke skill out of eternall night:
The corpes° of *Rome* in ashes is entombed, *corpse*
And her great spirite rejoynéd to the spirite
Of this great masse,[5] is in the same enwombed;
But her brave writings, which her famous merite
In spight of time, out of the dust doth reare,
Doo make her Idole[6] through the world appeare.

6[7]

Such as the *Berecynthian* Goddesse[8] bright
In her swift charret with high turrets crownde,
Proud that so manie Gods she brought to light;
Such was this Citie in her good daies fownd:
This Citie, more than that great *Phrygian* mother
Renowm'd for fruite of famous progenie,
Whose greatnes by the greatnes of none other,
But by her selfe her equall match could see:
Rome onely might to *Rome* comparéd bee,
And onely *Rome* could make great *Rome* to tremble:
So did the Gods by heavenly doome° decree, *ruling*
That other earthlie power should not resemble
Her that did match the whole earths puissance,° *power*
And did her courage to the heavens advaunce.

7[9]

Ye sacred ruines, and ye tragick sights,[1]
Which onely doo the name of *Rome* retaine,

3. The Esquiline was "noisome" (stinking) because Roman sewers ran there.
4. The opening recalls Petrarch's sonnet to Laura ("Chi vuol veder"), *Rime* 248.
5. The "mass" of the earth, or perhaps of the created cosmos.
6. Image, maybe faintly suggesting "false god" or "superstitiously worshiped effigy."
7. Cf. Virgil's *Aeneid* VI.782–87.
8. I.e., Cybele, also *Magna Mater* (the Great Mother) and the Titanness Rhea, daughter of Gaea and mother of the Olympians, who taught mortals to build cities. Often pictured in a lion-drawn chariot, she wore a crown shaped like a circle of turrets and was accompanied by castrated, orgiastic priests. "Rhea" means "flowing," for the earth is mutable. Berecynthia was a region of Phrygia, in modern Turkey.
9. Du Bellay translates Baldassare Castiglione's sonnet on Rome, "Superbi colli."
1. Perhaps with a pun on "sites"; Du Bellay has "costaux" (low hills).

Olde moniments, which of so famous sprights° *spirits*
The honour yet in ashes doo maintaine:
Triumphant Arcks,° spyres neighbours to the skie, *arches*
That you to see doth th'heaven it selfe appall,[2]
Alas, by little ye to nothing flie,
The peoples fable, and the spoyle of all:
And though your frames[3] do for a time make warre
Gainst time, yet time in time shall ruinate
Your workes and names, and your last reliques[4] marre.
My sad desires, rest therefore moderate:
For if that time make ende of things so sure,
It als° will end the paine, which I endure. *also*

8[5]

Through armes and vassals[6] *Rome* the world subdu'd,
That one would weene,° that one sole Cities strength *think*
Both land and sea in roundnes° had survew'd, *globally*
To be the measure of her bredth and length:[7]
This peoples vertue yet so fruitfull was
Of vertuous nephewes,° that posteritie *offspring, descendants*
Striving in power their grandfathers to passe,
The lowest earth join'd to the heaven hie;
To th'end that having all parts in their power,
Nought from the Romane Empire might be quight,° *quit, free*
And that though time doth Commonwealths devowre,
Yet no time should so low embase° their hight, *lower, humble*
That her head earth'd in her foundations deep,
Should not her name and endles honour keep.[8]

9

Ye cruell starres, and eke° ye Gods unkinde, *also*
Heaven envious, and bitter stepdame Nature,
Be it by fortune, or by course of kinde° *nature*
That ye doo weld° th'affaires of earthlie creature; *wield, govern*
Why have your hands long sithence° traveiled° *since / worked, struggled*
To frame° this world, that doth endure so long? *build, structure*
Or why were not the Romane palaces
Made of some matter no lesse firme and strong?
I say not, as the common voyce doth say,
That all things which beneath the Moone have being

2. Literally to "make pale," metaphorically to dismay.
3. I.e., your remaining structures.
4. Remains; the word might also recall the Catholic saints' "relics" rejected by Protestants.
5. Du Bellay expands a Neo-Latin epigram by the Scottish humanist poet George Buchanan.
6. Du Bellay has "vaisseaux" (vessels, ships), not vassals (subservient helpers).
7. That is, one would suppose Rome to have surveyed (like an engineer or architect) the whole globe when establishing her perimeter.
8. Spenser obscures Du Bellay's allusion: digging the foundations of a temple to Jove, the Romans unearthed a head (*caput*; see Livy, *The Early History of Rome* I.55); hence the *Cap*itol hill, with the implication that Rome would be "head"—*cap*ital—of the world. Spenser's meaning is that Time could not so bury Rome in her own foundations that her name and honor would die.

Are temporall, and subject to decay:[9]
But I say rather, though not all agreeing
With some, that weene the contrarie in thought;
That all this whole[1] shall one day come to nought.

10

As that brave sonne of *Aeson*, which by charmes
Atcheiv'd the golden Fleece in *Colchid* land,
Out of the earth engendred men of armes
Of Dragons teeth, sowne in the sacred sand;[2]
So this brave Towne, that in her youthlie daies
An *Hydra*[3] was of warriours glorious,
Did fill with her renowméd nourslings praise
The firie sunnes both one and other hous:[4]
But they at last, there being then not living
An *Hercules*, so ranke seed[5] to represse;
Emongst themselves with cruell furie striving,
Mow'd downe themselves with slaughter mercilesse;
Renewing in themselves that rage unkinde,° *unnatural*
Which whilom° did those earthborn brethren blinde. *once*

11

Mars[6] shaming° to have given so great head *ashamed*
To his off-spring, that mortall puissaunce° *power*
Puft up with pride of Romane hardie head,° *hardihood, boldness*
Seem'd above heavens powre it selfe to advaunce;
Cooling againe his former kindled heate,
With which he had those Romane spirits fild;
Did blowe new fire, and with enflaméd breath,
Into the Gothicke colde hot rage instil'd:[7]
Then gan that Nation,° th'earths new Giant brood,[8] *tribe, people*
To dart abroad the thunder bolts of warre,
And beating downe these walls with furious mood
Into her mothers bosome,[9] all did marre;° *ruin*

9. Ancient geocentric astronomy held that only the world below the moon (including the lunar surface) is subject to change; Galileo's discovery of sunspots would further ruin the theory.
1. The universe, perhaps with a pun on "hole" furthering the claim that the whole cosmos shall eventually become "nought," nothing, zero.
2. Jason, son of Aeson, sailed with his Argonauts to Colchis (on the Black Sea in modern Georgia), where aided by the sorceress Medea he performed the tasks set by her father the king and won the golden fleece. Threatened by soldiers who grew from the dragon teeth he had been told to sow like seed, he threw a rock into their midst; in their angry confusion they killed each other (Ovid, *Metamorphosis* VII.121–42).
3. Hercules' second labor was killing the Hydra, a many-headed swamp monster that grew two heads for each one cut off. Du Bellay remembers Horace, *Odes* IV.4.61–64, in which Hannibal compares his failed efforts to defeat Rome to fighting the Hydra and the monster of Colchis.
4. I.e., Roman glory spread to both solar "houses" in the extreme east and west.
5. Corrupt offspring or people.
6. Mars, son of Jove and god of war, supposedly fathered Romulus, founder of Rome. The barbarians' destruction of Rome meant that nobody could boast of ruling her empire.
7. I.e., having cooled the once-hot Romans, Mars now heated the cold (because northern) barbarian Goths.
8. I.e., the Germanic tribes resemble the giants (here conflated with the Titans) who warred on Jove.
9. That is, buried the walls in the bosom of Mother Earth and thus ruined all.

To th'end that none, all were it *Jove* his sire[1]
Should boast himselfe of the Romane Empire.

12

Like as whilome° the children of the earth — *once*
Heapt hils on hils, to scale the starrie skie,[2]
And fight against the Gods of heavenly berth,° — *birth*
Whiles *Jove* at them his thunderbolts let flie;
All suddenly with lightning overthrowne,
The furious squadrons downe to ground did fall,
That th'earth under her childrens weight did grone,
And th'heavens in glorie triumpht over all:
So did that haughtie front° which heapéd was — *brow, face*
On those seven Romane hils, it selfe upreare
Over the world, and lift her loftie face
Against the heaven, that gan° her force to feare. — *began*
But now these scornéd fields bemone her fall,
And Gods secure feare not her force at all.

13

Nor the swift furie of the flames aspiring,
Nor the deep wounds of victours raging blade,
Nor ruthlesse spoyle of souldiers blood-desiring,
The which so oft thee (*Rome*) their conquest made;
Ne stroke on stroke of fortune variable,
Ne rust of age hating continuance,° — *long-lastingness*
Nor wrath of Gods, nor spight° of men unstable, — *spite*
Nor thou oppos'd against thine owne puissance;[3]
Nor th'horrible uprore of windes high blowing,
Nor swelling stremes of that God snakie-paced,[4]
Which hath so often with his overflowing
Thee drenchéd,° have thy pride so much abaced;° — *drowned / humbled*
But that this nothing, which they have thee left,
Makes the world wonder, what they have from thee reft.° — *taken*

14

As men in Summer fearles passe the foord,
Which is in Winter lord of all the plaine,
And with his tumbling streames doth beare aboord[5]

1. I.e., Even if he were Jove's father Saturn, the Titan who ate his children in a vain attempt to prevent their replacing him and who thanks to a confusion of his Greek name, *Kronos*, and *chronos* (time), became equated with Father Time. He presided over the Golden Age, which legend said would some day return; his festival was the carnivalesque Saturnalia. Spenser's allusion bears a significant relation to time, destruction, and renewal. Du Bellay, however, has the warring Gothic nation disappear, and "des Dieux le pere" (the father of the gods) is probably "Father Jove," not Saturn.
2. To reach Olympus, the rebel giants heaped Mount Ossa on Mount Pelion.
3. Rome's civil wars that pitted its own power against itself; by the time Spenser wrote, Du Bellay might have seemed to be foretelling France's religious civil wars.
4. The Tiber, sometimes pictured as a semi-recumbent god pouring water from an urn. The giants were said to have snake feet, but Spenser probably means the river's serpentine route.
5. The *OED* cites this as a (unique) example meaning "adrift," but the word could also suggest water bearing the hope and labor with it ("aboard" it) as it flows.

The ploughmans hope, and shepheards labour vaine:[6]
And as the coward beasts use° to despise — *are wont*
The noble Lion after his lives end,
Whetting their teeth, and with vaine foolhardise° — *foolhardiness*
Daring the foe, that cannot him defend:[7]
And as at *Troy* most dastards° of the Greekes — *wretched cowards*
Did brave° about the corpes of *Hector*[8] colde; — *swagger, boast*
So those which whilome wont with pallid cheekes[9]
The Romane triumphs glorie to behold,
Now on these ashie tombes shew boldnesse vaine,[1]
And conquer'd dare the Conquerour disdaine.

15

Ye pallid spirits, and ye ashie ghoasts,
Which joying in the brightnes of your day,
Brought foorth those signes of your presumptuous boasts
Which now their dusty reliques do bewray;° — *reveal, show*
Tell me ye spirits (sith° the darksome river — *since*
Of *Styx*, not passable to soules returning,
Enclosing you in thrice three wards[2] for ever,
Doo not restraine your images still mourning)[3]
Tell me then (for perhaps some one of you
Yet here above him secretly doth hide)[4]
Doo ye not feele your torments to accrewe,° — *increase*
When ye sometimes behold the ruin'd pride
Of these old *Romane* works built with your hands,
Now to become nought els, but heapéd sands?

16

Like as ye see the wrathfull Sea from farre,
In a great mountaine heap't with hideous noyse,
Eftsoones° of thousand billowes shouldred narre,[5] — *soon afterward*
Against a Rocke to breake with dreadfull poyse:° — *impact*
Like as ye see fell *Boreas*[6] with sharpe blast,
Tossing huge tempests through the troubled skie,
Eftsoones having his wide wings spent in wast,[7]
To stop his wearie cariere° suddenly: — *course*

6. Here water is good for crops and bad for sheep; Du Bellay has it give both plowman and shepherd hope.
7. I.e., cannot defend himself.
8. Achilles killed the Trojan Hector, whose body the Greeks mutilated; he then dragged the corpse around Troy's walls three times.
9. Pale with fear and awe.
1. Empty and perhaps also proud.
2. A barrier that can guard and confine.
3. The shades of the dead, once ferried across the Styx (which flowed nine times around Hades), were normally unable to recross the river. Here, although the Styx stops the dead from returning, their images might still appear and speak; "*Doo*:" is either a subjunctive or Spenser, as was once common, uses a plural verb for a singular subject.
4. That is, still hides himself secretly here above. From error or a different mental image, Spenser turns Du Bellay's "dessous" ("below") to "above" ("dessus" in French).
5. I.e., pushed together closely.
6. Greco-Roman god of the north wind.
7. Either in vain or in destruction. The French has Boreas "s'esbanoyant"—diverting himself.

And as ye see huge flames spred diverslie,
Gathered in one up to the heavens to spyre,° *spiral, aspire*
Eftsoones consum'd to fall downe feebily:
So whilom did this Monarchie aspyre
As waves, as winde, as fire spred over all,
Till it by fatall doome adowne did fall.[8]

17

So long as *Joves* great Bird[9] did make his flight,
Bearing the fire with which heaven doth us fray,° *frighten*
Heaven had not feare of that presumptuous might,
With which the Giaunts did the Gods assay.° *try, assail*
But all so soone, as scortching Sunne had brent° *burnt*
His wings, which wont the earth to overspredd,
The earth out of her massie wombe forth sent
That antique horror, which made heaven adredd.[1]
Then was the Germane Raven[2] in disguise
That Romane Eagle seene to cleave asunder,
And towards heaven freshly to arise
Out of these mountaines, now consum'd to pouder.° *dust*
In which the foule° that serves to beare the lightning, *fowl, bird*
Is now no more seen flying, nor alighting.

18[3]

These heapes of stones, these old wals which ye see,
Were first enclosures but of salvage° soyle; *savage*
And these brave° Pallaces which maystred bee *showy, splendid*
Of time,[4] were shepheards cottages somewhile.° *once*
Then tooke the shepheards Kingly ornaments[5]
And the stout hynde° arm'd his right hand with steele: *farmer, yeoman*
Eftsoones their rule of yearely Presidents
Grew great, and sixe months greater a great deele;
Which made perpetuall, rose to so great might,
That thence th'Imperiall Eagle rooting tooke,[6]
Till th'heaven it selfe opposing gainst her might,

8. I.e., fell because of Fate's verdict or sentence. Moving through water, air, and fire, the sonnet ends with earth. '*Monarchie*': alludes to Roman power but also to the "translation of empire" (see Editors' Note).
9. Jove's bird is the eagle, bearer of his thunderbolts and symbol of Rome (and, later, of the Holy Roman Empire). Du Bellay's raven "feindre"—feigns—to be an eagle; Spenser took this as "fendre," to split.
1. I.e., that ancient threat that made Olympus afraid. The French is clearer: the piled-up hills of the earth-born giant rebels recall the hills of Rome. Du Bellay's giants also "violate" the "law"; Hesiod and other ancients had read Jove's assumption of power as the start of rule by law.
2. Representing the Gothic tribes who defeated Rome; Du Bellay may point at the Holy Roman Emperor, Charles V, the papacy's chief rival for geopolitical power, whose troops sacked Rome in 1527.
3. The sonnet echoes passages in Propertius, Ovid, and Buchanan. Tradition gave Rome rustic origins, so the sonnet's irony that since popes are "pastors" (shepherds) Rome has circled back to its pastoral start.
4. I.e., are conquered (mastered) by Time.
5. I.e., shepherds adopted royal dress and accoutrements.
6. Consuls ("Presidents" because presiding) had one-year terms; the term of the late Republic's "dictator" (one issuing dictates, not a despot) had been six months until Julius Caesar made it a lifetime appointment and the Republic soon became an Empire.

Her power to *Peters*[7] successor betooke;
Who sheperdlike, (as fates the same foreseeing)
Doth shew, that all things turne to their first being.

19

All that is perfect, which th'heaven beautifies;
All that's imperfect, borne belowe the Moone;[8]
All that doth feede our spirits and our eies;
And all that doth consume our pleasures soone;
All the mishap,° the which our daies outweares, *ill fortune*
All the good hap° of th'oldest times afore, *luck*
Rome in the time of her great ancesters,
Like a *Pandora*,[9] lockéd long in store.
But destinie this huge *Chaos* turmoyling,[1]
In which all good and evill was enclosed,
Their heavenly vertues from these woes assoyling,° *releasing*
Caried to heaven, from sinfull bondage losed:° *loosed*
But their great sinnes, the causers of their paine,
Under these antique ruines yet remaine.

20

No otherwise than raynie cloud, first fed
With earthly vapours gathered in the ayre,
Eftsoones in compas arch't,[2] to steepe his hed,
Doth plonge himselfe in *Tethys*[3] bosome faire;
And mounting up againe, from whence he came,
With his great bellie spreds the dimméd world,
Till at the last dissolving his moist frame,
In raine, or snowe, or haile he forth is horld;° *hurled*
This Citie, which was first but shepheards shade,
Uprising by degrees, grewe to such height,
That Queene of land and sea her selfe she made.
At last not able to beare so great weight,
Her power disperst, through all the world did vade;° *vanish*
To shew that all in th'end to nought shall fade.

21

The same which *Pyrrhus*, and the puissaunce° *power*
Of *Afrike* could not tame,[4] that same brave Citie,

7. Catholics claimed that the line of popes went back to Jesus's disciple Peter.
8. See note to *Ruines of Rome* 9.11.
9. Angry that the Titan Prometheus ("Foresight") had stolen fire on behalf of men, Zeus sent the first woman, Pandora ("All-gift") to his brother Epimetheus ("Hindsight"); she brought with her a jar (or box) that, when opened, released the ills that afflict us. At the bottom was Hope.
1. Either "turmoyling" modifies Chaos and means "in turmoil" or Destiny is tossing Chaos so as to differentiate its parts, sending the good ones back to the heavens; French "débrouillant" suggests the latter.
2. Arched in a curve as the cloud first picks up moisture, moves across the sky, and falls as rain into the sea.
3. Tethys married her fellow Titan Oceanus and bore the world's rivers and thousands of ocean nymphs; Du Bellay has "Thetis," a nymph, with whom Tethys was often confused.
4. I.e., Rome. In the third century B.C.E. Pyrrhus, ruler of Epirus in northwestern Greece, fought Rome with some success; the African power is Carthage, in modern Tunisia; its general, Hannibal, led soldiers and elephants across the Alps into Italy, nearly defeating Rome.

Which with stout courage arm'd against mischaunce,
Sustein'd the shocke of common enmitie;[5]
Long as her ship tost with so manie freakes,° *caprices*
Had all the world in armes against her bent,
Was never seene, that anie fortunes wreakes[6]
Could breake her course begun with brave intent.
But when the object of her vertue failed,[7]
Her power it selfe against it selfe did arme;[8]
As he that having long in tempest sailed,
Faine would arive, but cannot for the storme,[9]
If too great winde against the port him drive,
Doth in the port it selfe his vessell rive.° *split*

22

When that brave honour of the Latine name,
Which mear'd° her rule with *Africa*, and *Byze*, *measured, limited*
With *Thames* inhabitants of noble fame,
And they which see the dawning day arize;[1]
Her nourslings did with mutinous uprore
Harten° against her selfe, her conquer'd spoile, *embolden*
Which she had wonne from all the world afore,
Of all the world was spoyl'd within a while.[2]
So when the compast[3] course of the universe
In sixe and thirtie thousand yeares is ronne,
The bands[4] of th'elements shall backe reverse
To their first discord, and be quite undonne:
The seedes, of which all things at first were bred,
Shall in great *Chaos* wombe againe be hid.[5]

23

O warie° wisedome of the man, that would *prudent*
That *Carthage* towres from spoile° should be forborne,° *sacking / spared*
To th'end that his victorious people should

5. I.e., a unified or widespread opposition.
6. I.e., destructive acts of Fortune.
7. That is, when her martial prowess lacked an external enemy or object.
8. Probably an allusion to the Roman civil wars.
9. I.e., because of the storm. The sonnet exploits the ancient metaphor of the ship of state (and sometimes of the Church); in Petrarchan poetry the storm-battered ship is usually the lover. This ship reaches port only when hurled into it by a wrecking wind.
1. The sonnet may give four points of the compass: Africa to the south, the Bise (French/Alpine version of Boreas) to the north, Britons to the west ("noble fame" is Spenser's addition), and sunrise in the east.
2. I.e., the world that she had despoiled now despoiled her.
3. I.e., when Time, as in a circle drawn with a compass, completes its course.
4. A complex word: bonds or connective forces but perhaps also restraints or even agreements.
5. An ancient theory held that after the "great year," usually 36,000 years, the skies would return to their first configuration; then the elements again merge, primal chaos returns, and the world starts anew; see Plutarch's "On Fate" in his *Moralia*, trans. Phillip de Lacy and Benedict Einarson (Harvard UP, 1959), VII, p. 317, notes. The "seeds of things," another ancient concept (see, e.g., Lucretius, *De rerum natura* Book II), are the primal particles generating or composing all being and from which new species might yet grow; see *Faerie Queene* III.vi. The sonnet exploits two ancient views of matter: elemental and atomic.

With cancring laisure not be overworne;[6]
He well foresaw, how that the Romane courage,
Impatient of pleasures faint desires,
Through idlenes would turne to civill rage,
And be her selfe the matter of her fires.[7]
For in a people given all to ease,
Ambition is engendred easily;
As in a vicious bodie, grose disease
Soone growes through humours superfluitie.[8]
That came to passe, when swolne with plenties pride,
Nor prince, nor peere, nor kin they would abide.

24[9]

If the blinde furie,° which warres breedeth oft, *madness*
Wonts not[1] t'enrage the hearts of equall° beasts, *similar, related*
Whether they fare on foote, or flie aloft,
Or arméd be with clawes, or scalie creasts;
What fell *Erynnis*[2] with hot burning tongs,
Did grype° your hearts, with noysome° rage imbew'd,° *grip / noxious / inspired*
That each to other working cruell wrongs,
Your blades in your owne bowels you embrew'd?° *stained, defiled*
Was this (ye *Romanes*) your hard destinie?
Or some old sinne, whose unappeaséd[3] guilt
Powr'd vengeance forth on you eternallie?
Or brothers blood, the which at first was spilt
Upon your walls, that God might not endure,
Upon the same to set foundation sure?[4]

25

O that I had the *Thracian* Poets harpe,[5]
For to awake out of th'infernall shade
Those antique *Cæsars*, sleeping long in darke,
The which this auncient Citie whilome made:
Or that I had *Amphions* instrument,
To quicken with his vitall notes accord,° *harmony, agreement*

6. I.e., be eroded by corrupting leisure. The Roman is Publius C. Scipio "Nasica," Consul in 191 B.C.E.
7. That is, turning to civil war she would make herself the fuel for her own combative fire.
8. An excess of any one "humor" (black bile, choler, phlegm, or blood).
9. Based largely on Horace, *Epodes* VII.
1. I.e., is not in the habit of.
2. The Erinyes ("angry ones"), Alecto, Tisiphone, and Megaera, were snake-haired and often bat-winged "furies" sent from Hades to punish wrongdoers.
3. Syntactically, "unappeased" applies to guilt; logically, it applies to God (unless meaning "unpaid for").
4. During the building of Rome Romulus killed his twin, Remus, after the latter defiantly jumped over a wall, a fratricide that could recall Cain and Abel. The slipperiness of anything built on blood had political relevance to history's murderous usurpations (see *Mutabilitie Cantos* VI.i); *foundation*: may echo Luke 6.48–49.
5. Orpheus's music moved trees and rocks. It also persuaded Pluto to release his dead wife Eurydice, but when the musician looked back as he led her home, he lost her. So, says Ovid, he then "set the example" of "giving his love to tender boys" and so was later torn apart by the Maenads—wild female followers of Dionysius; his detached head floated, singing, down the river Hebrus (*Metamorphosis* X.83–85, XI.1ff.).

The stonie joynts of these old walls now rent,° *torn up*
By which th'*Ausonian*° light might be restor'd:[6] *Italian*
Or that at least I could with pencill fine,
Fashion the pourtraicts of these Palacis,
By paterne of great *Virgils* spirit divine;
I would assay° with that which in me is, *try*
To builde with levell of my loftie style,[7]
That which no hands can evermore compyle.° *construct*

26

Who list the Romanes greatnes forth to figure,[8]
Him needeth not to seeke for usage right
Of line, or lead,° or rule,° or squaire, to measure *plumbline / ruler*
Her length, her breadth, her deepnes, or her hight:
But him behooves to vew in compasse round[9]
All that the Ocean graspes in his long armes;
Be it where the yerely starre[1] doth scortch the ground,
Or where colde *Boreas* blowes his bitter stormes.
Rome was th'whole world, and al the world was *Rome*,[2]
And if things nam'd their names doo equalize,° *equal, correspond to*
When land and sea ye name, then name ye *Rome*;
And naming *Rome* ye land and sea comprize:° *include, comprehend*
For th'auncient Plot° of *Rome* displayéd plaine, *plan, blueprint*
The map of all the wide world doth containe.

27

Thou that at *Rome* astonisht dost behold
The antique pride, which menacéd the skie,
These haughtie heapes,[3] these palaces of olde,
These wals, these arcks,° these baths, these temples hie; *arches*
Judge by these ample ruines vew,° the rest *sight*
The which injurious time hath quite outworne,
Since of all workmen helde in reckning best,
Yet these olde fragments are for paternes borne:[4]
Then also marke, how Rome from day to day,
Repayring her decayéd fashión,
Renewes herselfe with buildings rich and gay;
That one would judge, that the *Romaine Dæmon*[5]

6. As Amphion played his lyre, stones rose of their own accord to fortify the city of Thebes.
7. I.e., using his pen/stylus as an architect's "level," with a pun on "style" (manner). Du Bellay, whose mention of Roman architects Spenser drops, has "compass"; Spenser's instruments make lines and squares.
8. That is, figure forth; imagine or present.
9. I.e., he needs to see the whole circumference.
1. The sun, which takes a year to circle through the geocentric ecliptic, scorching the African Sahara.
2. Du Bellay says, "Rome was the world and all the world *is* Rome."
3. Cf. Isaiah 25.2: "thou hast made of a city an heap" (a mere pile); yet these Roman ones are "haughtie" and may suggest heaped up architectural creations.
4. I.e., those builders and architects reckoned to be best use the remains of Roman buildings as patterns.
5. I.e., Rome's genius, or *daimon*, not "demon" in the devilish sense (although, granted Protestant fear of Rome, a demonic overtone might be audible).

Doth yet himselfe with fatall° hand enforce, *destined*
Againe on foote to reare her pouldred° corse. *dusty, pulverized*

28[6]

He that hath seene a great Oke drie and dead,
Yet clad with reliques° of some Trophees olde, *remainders*
Lifting to heaven her aged hoarie° head, *whitened*
Whose foote in ground hath left but feeble holde;
But halfe disbowel'd lies above the ground,
Shewing her wreathed rootes, and naked armes,
And on her trunke all rotten and unsound
Onely supports herselfe for meate° of wormes; *food*
And though she owe her fall to the first winde,
Yet of the devout° people is ador'd, *devoted, reverent*
And manie yong plants spring out of her rinde;[7]
Who such an Oke hath seene let him record° *write, remember*
That such this Cities honour was of yore,
And mongst all Cities florished much more.[8]

29

All that which *Aegypt* whilome did devise,
All that which *Greece* their temples to embrave,° *embellish*
After th'Ionicke, Atticke, Doricke guise,° *manner*
Or *Corinth*[9] skil'd in curious workes to grave;° *sculpt*
All that *Lysippus* practike arte could forme,
Apelles wit, or *Phidias* his skill,[1]
Was wont this auncient Citie to adorne,
And the heaven it selfe with her wide wonders fill;
All that which *Athens* ever brought forth wise,[2]
All that which *Afrike* ever brought forth strange,[3]
All that which *Asie* ever had of prise,[4]
Was here to see. O mervelous great change:
Rome living, was the worlds sole ornament,
And dead, is now the worlds sole moniment.[5]

6. This oak, a tree once sacred to Jove, is taken from Lucan's *Civil Wars* I.135ff, where it represents Caesar's rival, Pompey. Cf. the oaks in "Februarie," *The Shepheardes Calender*, and "Visions of Bellay" 5 in *Complaints* (1591); see also Alciato's emblem on "quercus" (the 1571 edition's commentary cites Lucan).
7. The new shoots recall the felled dream tree in Daniel 4 that foretells Nebuchadnezzar's punishment by God and his power's later renewal. An illustration in the 1568 *Bishops' Bible* shows shoots growing from the dead trunk. See also Luke 3.9: "Now also is the axe laid unto the roote of the trees."
8. Du Bellay uses the present tense in the last line.
9. Styles of ancient Greek architecture, ranging from plain to ornate, that can correlate with literary styles.
1. Phidias (fifth-century B.C.E.) and Lysippus (fourth-century B.C.E.) were Greek sculptors. *Apelles wit*: paintings by Apelles (fourth-century B.C.E.), whose "wit"—his ingenuity—was his ability to fool the eye and to use perspective.
2. The "wise" Greek must be Socrates—wisest, said the Delphic oracle, because he was aware of his ignorance.
3. Africa had a reputation for exotica ("Out of Africa always something new," ran a Roman proverb).
4. Value, price. *Asie*: Asia (for the Romans primarily the Middle and Near East, but for Spenser also India and the East Indies) had long been thought rich with jewels, pearls, ivory, silk, and spices.
5. Du Bellay has "tombeau" (tomb); "moniment" then connoted both monument and warning. To be the world's ornament may recall that that "cosmos" itself means "ornament."

30

Like as the seeded field greene grasse first showes,
Then from greene grasse into a stalke doth spring,
And from a stalke into an eare forth-growes,
Which eare the frutefull graine doth shortly bring;
And as in season due the husband° mowes — *farmer, husbandman*
The waving lockes of those faire yeallow heares,[6]
Which bound in sheaves, and layd in comely rowes,
Upon the naked fields in stackes he reares:
So grew the Romane Empire by degree,
Till that Barbarian hands it quite did spill,° — *destroy*
And left of it but these olde markes to see,
Of which all passers by doo somewhat° pill:° — *something / pilfer*
As they which gleane, the reliques° use° to gather, — *leftovers / are wont to*
Which th'husbandman behind him chanst to scater.

31

That same is now nought but a champian° wide, — *open field*
Where all this worlds pride once was situate.
No blame to thee, whosoever dost abide° — *live*
By *Nile*, or *Gange*, or *Tygre*, or *Euphrate*,[7]
Ne *Afrike* therof guiltie is, nor *Spaine*,
Nor the bolde[8] people by the *Thamis* brincks,° — *banks*
Nor the brave warlicke brood of *Alemaine*,° — *Germany*
Nor the borne Souldier which *Rhine* running drinks:[9]
Thou onely cause, O Civill furie, art
Which sowing in the *Aemathian*[1] fields thy spight,° — *spite*
Didst arme thy hand against thy proper° hart; — *own*
To th'end that when thou wast in greatest hight
To greatnes growne, through long prosperitie,
Thou then adowne might'st fall more horriblie.[2]

32

Hope ye my verses that posteritie
Of age ensuing° shall you ever read? — *future*
Hope ye that ever immortalitie
So meane° Harpes worke may chalenge for her meed?° — *lowly / reward*

6. The farmer mows the yellow (ripe) "hairs" of grain, meaning ears ("ear" is a clump of grains, not an American corncob), maybe also continuing the image set up by "locks." Lines 1–4 recall Jesus's parable in Mark 4.26–29: the Kingdom of Heaven is a field seeded and harvested by God. Here, the barbarians harvest the crop, leaving remnants behind (does "reliques" again hint at the Catholic reverence for saints' relics so despised by Protestants?). For another harvest, see Virgil, *Georgics* I.314–17.
7. The rivers, respectively, of Egypt, India (the Ganges), and Babylonia (Tigris and Euphrates).
8. Spenser's patriotic addition.
9. Du Bellay has "the brave soldier who drinks the Gaulish [Gallic] Rhine," the river that made an often disputed boundary between Germanic and Gallic lands before reaching the North Sea. Spenser omits "Gaulish," and "running" could modify the Rhine (the name is Celtic/Gaulish for "running") or the soldier.
1. Emathia, in Pharsalia, Greek site of Caesar's defeat of Pompey (cf. Lucan, *Civil Wars* 1.1). Here and in *Ruines of Rome* 23 Spenser drops Du Bellay's reminder that Pompey was Caesar's son-in-law.
2. The loose syntax allows a shift of addressee from civil war to Rome.

If under heaven anie endurance were,
These moniments, which not in paper writ,
But in Porphyre[3] and Marble doo appeare,
Might well have hop'd to have obtainéd it.
Nath'les° my Lute, whom *Phoebus* deignd to give, *nevertheless*
Cease not to sound these olde antiquities:
For if that time doo let thy glorie live,
Well maist thou boast, how ever base thou bee,
That thou art first, which of thy Nation song
Th'olde honour of the people gownéd long.[4]

L'Enuoy.[5]

Bellay, first garland of free Poësie
That *France* brought forth, though fruitfull of brave wits,[6]
Well worthie thou of immortalitie,
That long hast traveld° by thy learnéd writs,° *labored / writings*
Olde *Rome* out of her ashes to revive,
And give a second life to dead decayes:° *ruins*
Needes must he all eternitie survive,
That can to other give eternall dayes.
Thy dayes therefore are endles, and thy prayse
Excelling all, that ever went before;
And after thee, gins *Bartas* hie to rayse
His heavenly Muse, th'Almightie to adore.[7]
Live happie spirits, th'honour of your name,
And fill the world with never dying fame.

FINIS.

Editors' Note

In 1558 the French poet Joachim Du Bellay published several sets of verses drawing on his experiences and thoughts while serving as secretary to his cousin Cardinal Jean Du Bellay, ambassador from Francis I to the Pope. The most impressive of these is the *Regrets*, a long sonnet sequence in which the poet laments his absence from France or satiri-

3. A semiprecious purple stone.
4. I.e., the "gens togata"—the race/people dressed in (Roman) togas—to whom, Jove says (*Aeneid* I.275–282) he gave unbounded empire.
5. The envoy makes up for the omission of Du Bellay's dedicatory sonnet to Henri II, restoring the number of sonnets to thirty-three (a double three and the age at which Jesus was crucified), a number that may have had symbolic significance for both poets.
6. Spenser had paraphrased poems by Clément Marot for "November" and "December" in *The Shepheardes Calender* and would have known other French poets who wrote before Du Bellay burst into fame with his splendidly arrogant *Defense et Illustration de la Langue Françoise* (1549); "*free poësie*:" must mean a new kind of poetry with greater sweep and fresh bold energy. Spenser certainly read Pierre de Ronsard, but he never names him.
7. The Huguenot poet Guillaume Salluste, sieur Du Bartas, wrote two once-admired epics, *La Premiere Sepmaine* and *La Seconde Sepmaine* (The first and second "Week," translated by Joshua Sylvester and partially by others, including James I), as well as "L'Uranie," in which the muse Urania (the name means "Heavenly") tells the poet to write Bible-based poetry. Spenser refers to her or to the volume that contained the poem: *La Muse Chrestienne* (1574). *after*: probably means chronologically.

cally reproaches the corruptions he observes in modern Rome. But it was Du Bellay's sonnets on the collapse of ancient Rome (*Les Antiquitez* and its companion poem *Songe*) that drew Spenser's particular attention. Most of *Songe* ("Dream" or "Vision"), which features allegorical images of collapse, overthrow, and decay, had appeared with striking illustrations in *The Theatre for Voluptuous Worldlings* (1569), translated anonymously by a very young Spenser and interpreted in violently anti-Catholic terms by the author Jan van der Noot. Such a reading would have distressed Du Bellay himself, who—whatever his desire for reform—was no Protestant, but it seems to have set the terms for Spenser's later work with these poems. Some years later Spenser revised what he had translated of *Songe*, publishing it in his *Complaints* (1591) as the "Visions of Bellay" and, in the same volume, offering a revised translation of the *Antiquitez* that called this sequence of thirty-three poems *The Ruines of Rome*. Spenser would eventually publish love poetry, but it has been argued that the *Antiquitez* is in its own way a Petrarchan sonnet sequence, that genre so often in explicit tension with epic ambitions, for ancient Rome is the absent other, the object of hopeless longing (cf. Rebhorn 1980).

Ruines may not now be as widely praised as Spenser's *Amoretti*, but its sonnets had an immediate influence on Elizabethan poetry, further encouraging English thought about ancient Rome and its collapse. Both matters were of intense interest in the sixteenth century, and in England Spenser's translations accelerated both this interest and a late Elizabethan fondness for the particular constellation of phrases and images found in the *Ruines*: falling towers, bloodied foundations, eroded or buried walls, Time's appetite for marble, the vain pride of sky-pointing obelisks and pyramids, the struggle to be everything that leads to the emptiness of nothing, and how all this damage and tragedy relate to cultural arrogance, divine displeasure, and the vulnerability of great civilizations to civil war on the one hand and barbarian incursions on the other. As Spenser was putting together the *Complaints*, he and his contemporaries could remember their own civil wars, fear their own nation's vulnerabilities (with an aging heirless queen), and watch as French religious and dynastic conflicts raged fiercely a few miles away. No wonder that phrases from *Ruines* appear in Shakespeare's sonnets, for example (cf. Hieatt 1983), as well as in the verse of Samuel Daniel, Michael Drayton, and Mary Sidney. While such phrases can often be found elsewhere as well, there is no text other than Spenser's *Ruines of Rome* with such a concentration of them.

Behind this influential complex of phrases and concepts lies the old notion of *translatio imperii* (the "translation/movement of empire"), a belief that "empire," the focus of power and influence in the world, has been moving westward since its early days (and which, Du Bellay may have thought, would now move north to France, although it is also possible to read his verse as suggesting that such empire is now over). Such ideas were current in the Middle Ages, often uncomfortably merged with the pseudohistory tracing ancient migrations after the Flood and with legends asserting the Trojan origin of several royal dynasties, including those of France and England. Stories about the transfer of temporal or political power, even though meeting with increased skepticism in the later Renaissance, thus gave various nations reason to assert their potential equality with ancient Rome and gave various poets reason to compete with Virgil's epic on Rome's descent from Troy, although Du Bellay himself almost boasted in the *Regrets* that he was not trying to write like Virgil—or like his friend Ronsard, whose epic *Franciade* Spenser may have read. This competitive concern for the transfer of empire energizes both Du Bellay's *Antiquitez* and Spenser's *Ruines* translation, but the two poets' contexts differ. For Christians, and particularly for Protestants, another major source of thinking about the westward transfer of empire was the Bible's Book of Daniel. Only the Israelite prophet Daniel, we read, can interpret the tyrant Nebuchadnezzar's dream of a giant made, in order from the head down, of gold, silver, brass, and iron—with feet of clay. The metals represent, as the Geneva Bible translation's headnote puts it, "the Babylonians, Persians, Grecians, & Romaines," whose empires are all to be destroyed as power moves west and eventually, said Christian exegetes, will yield to the reign of God. While waiting for this fifth monarchy (which the more apocalyptically minded of Spenser's contemporaries expected to arrive soon), rulers such as Elizabeth could claim that the Roman "imperium" had not vanished, and had certainly not moved to the huge Holy Roman Empire under the Habsburgs, but had dispersed so that the English could claim their part and the queen could indeed be an "empress"—with or without colonies. *The Ruines of Rome*, then, for Spenser as well as for Du Bellay, had both religious and geopolitical significance beyond the spectacle of ruined walls and toppled pride.

Rome's fall, however tragic, however indicative of mutability's cruelty to flesh and cities, thus made room not only for modern poets but also for modern cities and modern empires. For Protestants, moreover, the sight of Rome's fall (especially when ascribed to the same pride that built the obelisks and palaces) was a reminder that modern Rome, the Rome of the Popes and, in anti-Catholic apocalyptic polemic, the Rome of the Whore of Babylon with her cup of abominations and her many-headed beast, would fall too, making room not for English empire but for God's (Protestant) New Jerusalem. Book I of *The Faerie Queene* exploits just such imagery, and although Du Bellay was a Catholic, Spenser could translate his visions of fallen greatness so as to favor the hopes that impelled much English religious interest in Roman ruination, drawing also on the seductive melancholy that the sight of fallen greatness can inspire. Melancholy—but also pleasure in a collapse leaving room for poets such as himself: in both the *Antiquitez* and the *Ruines of Rome* it is possible to hear not just sorrow but a curious satisfaction. (Coldiron 2002, Melehy 2010)

Spenser never forgot such ambiguities or his hope for their future resolution in a world beyond time. Phrases and imagery that he found in Du Bellay's verse reappear periodically in his other poems, often in the *Complaints'* "Ruines of Time" but also in *The Faerie Queene* (Prescott in Anderson 1996). At the end of his epic as we have it, the speaker turns from the spectacle of change to a stability figured as the sort of architecture the author would have remembered from the illustrations in the *Theatre*: in his final lines he prays for the "Sabaoths sight" of "all things firmely "stayd / Upon the pillours of Eternity / That is contrayr to *Mutabilitie*." Just as in the last lines of the poem he added to Du Bellay's sequence Spenser had shifted attention to the more overtly Christian "muse" of Guillaume du Bartas, so too here the French poet's ruined Rome has died and gone to heaven as the New Jerusalem.

Muiopotmos:† or The Fate of the Butterflie

To the right worthy and vertuous Ladie; the La: Carey.[1]

Most brave and bountifull La: for so excellent favours as I have received at your sweet handes, to offer these fewe leaves as in recompence, should be as to offer flowers to the Gods for their divine benefites. Therefore I have determined to give my selfe wholy to you, as quite abandoned from my selfe,[2] and absolutely vowed to your services: which in all right is ever held for full recompence of debt or damage to have the person yeelded. My person I wot wel how little worth it is. But the faithfull minde and humble zeale which I beare unto your La: may perhaps be more of price, as may please you to account and use the poore service thereof; which taketh glory to advance your excellent partes and noble vertues, and to spend it selfe in honouring you: not so much for your great bounty to my self, which yet may not be unminded; nor for name or kindreds sake by you vouchsafed, beeing also regardable; as for that honorable name, which yee have by your brave deserts[3] purchast to your self, and spred in the mouths of al men: with which I have also presumed to grace my verses, and under your name to commend to the world this smal Poeme, the which beseeching your La: to take in worth,[4] and of all things therein according to your wonted graciousnes to make a milde construction,[5] I humbly pray for your happines.

Your La: ever
humbly;
E.S.

I sing of deadly dolorous debate,
Stired up through wrathfull Nemesis despight,° *malice*
Betwixt two mightie ones of great estate,° *status*
Drawne into armes, and proofe° of mortall fight, *trial*
5 Through prowd ambition, and hartswelling hate,
Whilest neither could the others greater might
And sdeignfull° scorne endure; that from small jarre° *haughty / discord*
Their wraths at length broke into open warre.[6]

The roote whereof and tragicall effect,
10 Vouchsafe, O thou the mournfulst Muse of nyne,[7]
That wontst° the tragick stage for to direct, *are accustomed*
In funerall complaints and waylfull tyne,° *sorrow*
Reveale to me, and all the meanes detect,° *reveal*

† From Greek *muia* ("fly") and *potmos* ("fate"). Probably composed in 1590, *Muiopotmos* was published in Spenser's *Complaints* (1591), the collection of poems that the "Printer to the Gentle [well-bred] Reader" calls "meditations of the worlds vanitie, verie grave and profitable."

1. Lady Elizabeth Carey (1551–1618), daughter of Sir John Spencer of Althorpe; in *Colin Clouts Come Home Againe* (1595) she is "Phyllis, the floure of rare perfection" (541–47).
2. I.e., as having given up all thought of self.
3. I.e., your admirable qualities.
4. I.e., to accept indulgently.
5. I.e., to interpret the poem with judicious reserve.
6. Lines 1–8 recall the start of the *Iliad*, in which Homer describes the enmity between Agamemnon and Achilles, naming Apollo as instigator of their quarrel. Spenser's "wrathfull Nemesis" echoes *Metamorphoses* 14.694 and Hesiod's *Theogony* 223. The "two mightie ones" (1.3) may refer to Minerva (Pallas Athena) and Venus (Aphrodite) or to Minerva and Arachne.
7. I.e., Melpomene, Muse of tragedy.

Through which sad Clarion did at last declyne
15 To lowest wretchednes; And is there then
Such rancour in the harts of mightie men?[8]

Of all the race of silver-wingéd Flies° — *insects*
Which doo possesse the Empire of the aire,
Betwixt the centred earth, and azure skies,
20 Was none more favourable,° nor more faire, — *fortunate*
Whilst heaven did favour his felicities,
Then Clarion, the eldest sonne and haire
Of Muscaroll,[9] and in his fathers sight
Of all alive did seeme the fairest wight.° — *creature*

25 With fruitfull hope his aged breast he fed
Of future good, which his yong toward° yeares, — *promising*
Full of brave courage° and bold hardyhed,° — *spirit / courage*
Above th'ensample of his equall peares,
Did largely promise, and to him forered° — *presaged*
30 (Whilst oft his heart did melt in tender teares)
That he in time would sure prove such an one,
As should be worthie of his fathers throne.

The fresh yong flie, in whom the kindly° fire — *natural*
Of lustfull° youngth began to kindle fast, — *vigorous*
35 Did much disdaine to subject his desire
To loathsome sloth, or houres in ease to wast,
But joyed to range abroad in fresh attire;
Through the wide compas of the ayrie coast,° — *region*
And with unwearied wings each part t'inquire° — *explore*
40 Of the wide rule of his renowméd sire.

For he so swift and nimble was of flight,
That from this lower tract° he dared to stie° — *realm / mount*
Up to the clowdes, and thence with pineons light,
To mount aloft unto the Christall skie,
45 To vew the workmanship of heavens hight:
Whence downe descending he along would flie
Upon the streaming rivers, sport to finde;
And oft would dare to tempt° the troublous winde. — *test*

So on a Summers day, when season milde
50 With gentle calme the world has quieted,
And high in heaven Hyperions fierie childe[1]
Ascending, did his beames abroad dispred,
Whiles all the heavens on lower creatures smilde;
Yong Clarion with vauntfull lustie head,[2]

8. Cf. *Aeneid* 1.11: "Can such anger dwell in divine hearts?" The narrator's high-flown language signals the mock-heroic style.
9. From Latin *musca* ("fly"), *Clarion*: a trumpet, derives from Latin *clarus* ("bright"; "renowned," worthy of Fame's trumpet).
1. I.e., Apollo.
2. I.e., with boastful eagerness.

55 After his guize° did cast° abroad to fare; *custom / resolve*
And theretoo gan his furnitures° prepare. *equipment*

His breastplate first, that was of substance pure,
Before his noble heart he firmely bound,
That mought his life from yron death assure,
60 And ward his gentle corpes° from cruell wound: *body*
For it by arte was framéd, to endure
The bit of balefull steele and bitter stownd,° *assault*
No lesse than that, which Vulcane made to shield
Achilles life from fate of Troyan field.[3]

65 And then about his shoulders broad he threw
An hairie hide of some wilde beast, whom hee
In salvage forrest by adventure° slew, *chance*
And reft° the spoyle his ornament to bee: *took*
Which spredding all his backe with dreadfull vew,° *appearance*
70 Made all that him so horrible did see,
Thinke him Alcides[4] with the Lyons skin,
When the Naemean Conquest he did win.

Upon his head his glistering Burganet,° *helmet*
The which was wrought by wonderous device,
75 And curiously engraven, he did set:
The mettall was of rare and passing price;° *value*
Not Bilbo[5] steele, nor brasse from Corinth fet,° *brought*
Nor costly Oricalche° from strange° Phoenice; *brass / distant*
But such as could both Phoebus arrowes ward,
80 And th'hayling darts of heaven beating hard.

Therein two deadly weapons fixt he bore,
Strongly outlancéd° towards either side, *out-thrust*
Like two sharpe speares, his enemies to gore:
Like as a warlike Brigandine, applyde° *prepared*
85 To fight, layes forth her threatfull pikes[6] afore,
The engines° which in them sad death doo hyde: *weapons*
So did this flie outstretch his fearefull hornes,
Yet so as him their terrour more adornes.

Lastly his shinie wings as silver bright,
90 Painted with thousand colours, passing farre
All Painters skill, he did about him dight:° *draw*
Not halfe so manie sundrie colours arre
In Iris[7] bowe, ne heaven doth shine so bright,
Distinguishéd with manie a twinckling starre,

3. The arming of the hero is an epic convention: cf. *Iliad* 11.15–46, and *Aeneid* 12.87–89. For the shield of Achilles, cf. *Iliad* 18.478–617.
4. Hercules. Cf. *The Faerie Queene* V.Pr.6, and note.
5. Bilbao, on the northern coast of Spain.
6. I.e., the rams with which such small galleys were equipped.
7. Goddess of the rainbow. Cf. *Aeneid* 4.700–701.

95 Nor Junoes Bird[8] in her ey-spotted traine
So manie goodly colours doth containe.

Ne (may it be withouten perill spoken)
The Archer God, the sonne of Cytheree,[9]
That joyes on wretched lovers to be wroken,° *avenged*
100 And heapéd spoyles of bleeding harts to see,
Beares in his wings so manie a changefull token.[1]
Ah my liege Lord, forgive it unto mee,
If ought against thine honour I have tolde;
Yet sure those wings were fairer manifolde.

105 Full manie a Ladie faire, in Court full oft
Beholding them, him secretly envide,
And wisht that two such fannes, so silken soft,
And golden faire, her Love would her provide;
Or that when them the gorgeous Flie had doft,
110 Some one that would with grace be gratifide,° *rewarded*
From him would steale them privily° away, *secretly*
And bring to her so precious a pray.

Report is that dame Venus on a day,
In spring when flowres doo clothe the fruitful ground,
115 Walking abroad with all her Nymphes to play,
Bad her faire damzels flocking her arownd,
To gather flowres, her forhead to array:
Emongst the rest a gentle Nymph was found,
Hight° Astery,[2] excelling all the crewe *named*
120 In curteous usage,° and unstainéd hewe. *behavior*

Who being nimbler joynted than the rest,
And more industrious, gatheréd more store
Of the fields honour, than the others best;
Which they in secret harts envying sore,
125 Tolde Venus, when her as the worthiest
She praisd, that Cupide (as they heard before)
Did lend her secret aide, in gathering
Into her lap the children of the spring.

Whereof the Goddesse gathering jealous feare,
130 Not yet unmindfull,° how not long agoe *forgetful*
Her sonne to Psyche[3] secrete love did beare,
And long it close° concealed, till mickle° woe *secretly / much*
Thereof arose, and manie a rufull teare;

8. I.e., the peacock.
9. I.e., Cupid, the son of Venus (Cythera).
1. I.e., such various patternings.
2. Cf. *The Faerie Queene* III.xi.34, and note. Arachne, challenging Athena's claim to mastery in weaving, made Asterie ("gripped by the struggling eagle") part of her tapestry; cf. *Metamorphoses* 6.108. While Spenser alludes in lines 131–33 to the myth of Cupid and Psyche (see *The Faerie Queene* III.vi.50, and note), the metamorphosis of Astery is essentially his own invention.
3. In Greek, "psyche" means both "soul" and "butterfly."

Reason with sudden rage did overgoe,[4]
135 And giving hastie credit to th'accuser,
Was led away of° them that did abuse her. *by*

Eftsoones° that Damzel by her heavenly might, *forthwith*
She turned into a wingéd Butterflie,
In the wide aire to make her wandring flight;
140 And all those flowres, with which so plenteouslie
Her lap she filléd had, that bred her spight,
She placéd in her wings, for memorie
Of her pretended crime, though crime none were:
Since which that flie them in her wings doth beare.

145 Thus the fresh Clarion being readie dight,° *attired*
Unto his journey did himselfe addresse,
And with good speed began to take his flight:
Over the fields in his franke° lustinesse, *vigorous*
And all the champion° he soaréd light, *plain*
150 And all the countrey wide he did possesse,
Feeding upon their pleasures bounteouslie,
That none gainsaid, nor none did him envie.

The woods, the rivers, and the medowes green,
With his aire-cutting wings he measured wide,
155 Ne did he leave the mountaines bare unseene,
Nor the ranke grassie fennes° delights untride. *marshes*
But none of these, how ever sweete they beene,
Mote please his fancie, nor him cause t'abide:
His choicefull° sense with everie change doth flit. *fickle*
160 No common things may please a wavering wit.° *mind*

To the gay gardins his unstaid° desire *shifting*
Him wholly caried, to refresh his sprights:
There lavish Nature in her best attire,
Powres forth sweete odors, and alluring sights;
165 And Arte with her contending, doth aspire
T'excell the naturall, with made delights:
And all that faire or pleasant may be found,
In riotous excesse doth there abound.

There he arriving, round about doth flie,
170 From bed to bed, from one to other border,
And takes survey with curious busie eye,
Of everie flowre and herbe there set in order;
Now this, now that he tasteth tenderly,
Yet none of them he rudely doth disorder,
175 Ne with his feete their silken leaves deface;° *harm*
But pastures on the pleasures of each place.

4. I.e., quick rage overcame reason.

And evermore with most varietie,
And change of sweetnesse (for all change is sweete)
He casts° his glutton sense to satisfie, *seeks*
180 Now sucking of the sap of herbe most meete,° *proper*
Or of the deaw, which yet on them does lie,
Now in the same bathing his tender feete:
And then he pearcheth on some braunch thereby,
To weather him, and his moyst wings to dry.

185 And then againe he turneth to his play,
To spoyle° the pleasures of that Paradise:[5] *ravage*
The wholsome Saulge,° and Lavender still gray, *sage*
Ranke smelling Rue, and Cummin good for eyes,
The Roses raigning in the pride of May,
190 Sharpe Isope,° good for greene wounds remedies, *hyssop*
Faire Marigoldes, and Bees alluring Thime,
Sweete Marjoram, and Daysies decking prime.° *spring*

Coole Violets, and Orpine growing still,[6]
Embathéd Balme, and chearfull Galingale,
195 Fresh Costmarie, and breathfull Camomill,
Dull Poppie, and drink-quickning Setuale,
Veyne-healing Verven, and hed-purging Dill,
Sound Savorie, and Bazill hartie-hale,
Fat Colworts, and comforting Perseline,
200 Colde Lettuce, and refreshing Rosmarine.[7]

And whatso else of vertue good or ill
Grewe in this Gardin, fetcht from farre away,
Of everie one he takes, and tastes at will,
And on their pleasures greedily doth pray.
205 Then when he hath both plaid, and fed his fill,
In the warme Sunne he doth himselfe embay,° *bask*
And there him rests in riotous suffisaunce° *abundance*
Of all his gladfulnes, and kingly joyaunce.

What more felicitie can fall to creature,
210 Than to enjoy delight with libertie,
And to be Lord of all the workes of Nature,
To raine in th'aire from earth to highest skie,
To feed on flowres, and weeds of glorious feature,
To take what ever thing doth please the eie?
215 Who rests not pleaséd with such happines,
Well worthie he to taste of wretchednes.

5. The catalogue of small plants in lines 187–200 glances at and presumably parodies the traditional tree catalogue; cf. *The Faerie Queene* I.i.8–9.
6. "Orpine" is commonly known in England as "live-long."
7. Among the less familiar plants in this stanza, "galingale" was used as a condiment (e.g., by Chaucer's Cook: cf. *The Canterbury Tales*, "General Prologue" 381); costmary, camomile, and vervain are aromatic medicinal herbs; "setuale" is the modern valerian, used as a drug. Colewort is a kind of cabbage; perseline either parsley or purslane, a succulent herb.

But what on earth can long abide in state?[8]
Or who can him assure of happie day;
Sith morning faire may bring fowle evening late,
220 And least mishap the most blisse alter may?
For thousand perills lie in close° awaite — *secret*
About us daylie, to worke our decay;° — *destruction*
That none, except a God, or God him guide,
May them avoyde, or remedie provide.

225 And whatso heavens in their secret doome° — *judgment*
Ordainéd have, how can fraile fleshly wight
Forecast, but it must needs to issue come?
The sea, the aire, the fire, the day, the night,
And th'armies of their creatures all and some[9]
230 Do serve to them, and with importune° might — *grievous*
Warre against us the vassals of their will.
Who then can save, what they dispose to spill?[1]

Not thou, O Clarion, though fairest thou
Of all thy kinde, unhappie happie Flie,
235 Whose cruell fate is woven even now
Of° Joves owne hand, to worke thy miserie: — *by*
Ne may thee helpe the manie hartie vow,
Which thy olde Sire with sacred pietie
Hath powréd forth for thee, and th'altars sprent:° — *sprinkled*
240 Nought may thee save from heavens avengément.

It fortunéd (as heavens had behight)° — *ordained*
That in this gardin, where yong Clarion
Was wont to solace him,° a wicked wight — *himself*
The foe of faire things, th'author of confusion,
245 The shame of Nature, the bondslave of spight,
Had lately built his hatefull mansion,
And lurking closely, in awayte now lay,
How he might anie in his trap betray.

But when he spide the joyous Butterflie
250 In this faire plot dispacing° too and fro, — *moving*
Fearles of foes and hidden jeopardie,
Lord how he gan for to bestirre him tho,° — *then*
And to his wicked worke each part applie:
His heart did earne° against his hated foe, — *rage*
255 And bowels so with ranckling poyson swelde,
That scarce the skin the strong contagion helde.

The cause why he this Flie so malicéd,
Was (as in stories it is written found)

8. I.e., can long remain secure.
9. I.e., one and all.
1. I.e., what they ordain to destruction.

For that his mother which him bore and bred,
260 The most fine-fingred workwoman on ground,
Arachne, by his meanes was vanquishéd
Of Pallas, and in her owne skill confound,° *overcome*
When she with her for excellence contended,
That wrought her shame, and sorrow never ended.

265 For the Tritonian Goddesse[2] having hard° *heard*
Her blazéd° fame, which all the world had filled, *proclaimed*
Came downe to prove° the truth, and due reward *test*
For her prais-worthie workmanship to yeild;
But the presumptuous Damzel rashly dared
270 The Goddesse selfe to chalenge to the field,
And to compare° with her in curious° skill *vie / intricate*
Of workes with loome, with needle, and with quill.° *spool*

Minerva did the chalenge not refuse,
But deigned with her the paragon to make:[3]
275 So to their worke they sit, and each doth chuse
What storie she will for her tapet° take. *tapestry*
Arachne figured° how Jove did abuse *showed*
Europa like a Bull, and on his backe
Her through the sea did beare; so lively seene,
280 That it true Sea, and true Bull ye would weene:° *suppose*

She seemed still backe unto the land to looke,
And her play-fellowes aide to call, and feare
The dashing of the waves, that° up she tooke *so that*
Her daintie feete, and garments gathered neare:
285 But (Lord) how she in everie member shooke,
When as the land she saw no more appeare,
But a wilde wildernes of waters deepe:
Then gan she greatly to lament and weepe.

Before the Bull she pictured wingéd Love,
290 With his yong brother Sport, light fluttering
Upon the waves, as each had been a Dove;
The one his bowe and shafts, the other Spring° *youth*
A burning Teade° about his head did move, *torch*
As in their Syres new love both triumphing.° *exulting*
295 And manie Nymphes about them flocking round,
And manie Tritons, which their hornes did sound.

And round about, her worke she did empale° *enclose*
With a faire border wrought of sundrie flowres,
Enwoven with an Yvie winding trayle:
300 A goodly worke, full fit for Kingly bowres,
Such as Dame Pallas, such as Envie pale,

2. According to legend, Minerva was reared by the sea god Triton.
3. I.e., to accept the (challenge of) comparison.

That al good things with venemous tooth devowres,
Could not accuse. Then gan the Goddesse bright
Her selfe likewise unto her worke to dight.° *prepare*

305 She made the storie of the olde debate,
Which she with Neptune did for Athens trie:° *engage in*
Twelve Gods doo sit around in royall state,
And Jove in midst with awfull Majestie,
To judge the strife betweene them stirréd late:
310 Each of the Gods by his like visnomie° *visage*
Eathe° to be knowen; but Jove above them all, *easy*
By his great lookes and power Imperiall.

Before them stands the God of Seas in place,
Clayming that sea-coast Citie as his right,
315 And strikes the rockes with his three-forkéd mace;
Whenceforth issues a warlike steed in sight,
The signe by which he chalengeth° the place, *claims*
That° all the Gods, which saw his wondrous might *so that*
Did surely deeme the victorie his due:
320 But seldome seene, forejudgment proveth true.

Then to her selfe she gives her Aegide shield,[4]
And steelhed speare, and morion° on her hedd, *helmet*
Such as she oft is seene in warlicke field:
Then sets she forth, how with her weapon dredd
325 She smote the ground, the which streight foorth did yield
A fruitfull Olyve tree, with berries spredd,
That all the Gods admired; then all the storie
She compast° with a wreathe of Olyves hoarie. *encircled*

Emongst those leaves she made a Butterflie,
330 With excellent device and wondrous slight,° *art*
Fluttring among the Olives wantonly,° *playfully*
That seemed to live, so like it was in sight:
The velvet nap which on his wings doth lie,
The silken downe with which his backe is dight,
335 His broad outstretchéd hornes, his hayrie thies,
His glorious colours, and his glistering° eies. *shining*

Which when Arachne saw, as over as overlaid,° *overwhelmed*
And masteréd with workmanship so rare,
She stood astonied long, ne ought gainesaid,
340 And with fast fixéd eyes on her did stare,
And by her silence, signe of one dismaid,
The victorie did yeeld her as her share:
Yet did she inly fret, and felly° burne, *fiercely*
And all her blood to poysonous rancor turne.

4. I.e., her shield with the symbolic and protective device of the "aegis."

345 That shortly from the shape of womanhed
Such as she was, when Pallas she attempted,° *challenged*
She grew to hideous shape of dryrihed,° *horror*
Pinéd with griefe of follie late repented:
Eftsoones her white streight legs were alteréd
350 To crooked crawling shankes, of marrowe empted,
And her faire face to fowle and loathsome hewe
And her fine corpes° to a bag of venim grewe.[5] *body*

This curséd creature, mindfull of that olde
Enfestred grudge, the which his mother felt,
355 So soone as Clarion he did beholde,
His heart with vengefull malice inly swelt,
And weaving straight a net with manie a folde
About the cave, in which he lurking dwelt,
With fine small cords about it stretchéd wide,
360 So finely sponne, that scarce they could be spide.

Not anie damzell, which her° vaunteth most *herself*
In skilfull knitting of soft silken twyne;
Nor anie weaver, which his worke doth boast
In dieper,[6] in damaske, or in lyne;° *linen*
365 Nor anie skiled in workmanship embost;[7]
Nor anie skiled in loupes of fingring fine,
Might in their divers cunning° ever dare, *skill*
With this so curious networke to compare.

Ne doo I thinke, that that same subtil gin,° *net*
370 The which the Lemnian God[8] framde craftflie,
Mars sleeping with his wife to compasse in,
That all the Gods with common mockerie
Might laugh at them, and scorne their shamefull sin,
Was like to this. This same he did applie,
375 For to entrap the careles Clarion,
That ranged each where without suspition.

Suspition of friend, nor feare of foe,
That hazarded° his health, had he at all, *threatened*
But walkt at will, and wandred too and fro,
380 In the pride of his freedome principall:° *princely*
Little wist° he his fatall future woe, *knew*
But was secure, the liker he to fall.

5. Spenser's version of Arachne's transformation differs from that in Ovid's *Metamorphoses* 6.1–145. There Minerva, outraged by Arachne's artistic prowess and by her embarrassingly truthful depiction of the gods' deceits and misdeeds, destroys the tapestry; when Arachne attempts suicide the goddess, with mingled sternness and pity, changes her to a spider, a creature that still, notes Ovid, can weave. In Spenser's poem it is Arachne's own envy that causes her self-transformation and produces the (supposed) enmity between spiders and butterflies.
6. A fabric patterned with small repeated designs.
7. I.e., in the art (in embroidery) of richly elaborate decoration.
8. I.e., Vulcan (Hephaestus), who was thrown down from Olympus by Jove; after falling for an entire day, he came to earth on the Aegean isle of Lemnos. For the story of his entrapment of his wife Venus and her lover Mars, see *Metamorphoses* 4.176–89.

He likest is to fall into mischaunce,
That is regardles of his governaunce.° *conduct*

385 Yet still Aragnoll[9] (so his foe was hight) ° *named*
Lay lurking covertly him to surprise,
And all his gins that him entangle might,
Drest° in good order as he could devise. *arranged*
At length the foolish Flie without foresight,
390 As he that did all daunger quite despise,
Toward those parts came flying careleslie,
Where hidden was his hatefull enemie.

Who seeing him, with secrete joy therefore
Did tickle inwardly in everie vaine,
395 And his false hart fraught with all treasons store,
Was filled with hope, his purpose to obtaine:
Himselfe he close upgathered more and more
Into his den, that his deceiptfull traine° *snare*
By his there being might not be bewraid,° *revealed*
400 Ne anie noyse, ne anie motion made.

Like as a wily Foxe, that having spide,
Where on a sunnie banke the Lambes doo play,
Full closely° creeping by the hinder side, *secretly*
Lyes in ambushment of° his hopéd pray, *for*
405 Ne stirreth limbe, till seeing readie tide,[1]
He rusheth forth, and snatcheth quite away
One of the litle yonglings unawares:
So to his worke Aragnoll him prepares.

Who now shall give unto my heavie eyes
410 A well of teares, that all may overflow?
Or where shall I finde lamentable cryes,
And mournfull tunes enough my griefe to show?
Helpe O thou Tragick Muse, me to devise
Notes sad enough, t'expresse this bitter throw:° *throe*
415 For loe, the drerie stownd° is now arrived, *moment*
That of all happines hath us deprived.

The luckles Clarion, whether cruell Fate,
Or wicked Fortune faultles him misled,
Or some ungracious blast out of the gate
420 Of Aeoles raine perforce him drove on hed,[2]
Was (O sad hap° and howre unfortunate) *lot*
With violent swift flight forth cariéd
Into the curséd cobweb, which his foe
Had framéd for his finall overthroe.

9. From Latin *aranea* (or perhaps *araneolus*), "spider."
1. I.e., the right moment.
2. I.e., (some blast from the gate) of the kingdom of Aeolus [god of the winds] drove him headlong.

425 There the fond° Flie entangled, strugled long, *foolish*
Himselfe to free thereout; but all in vaine.
For striving more, the more in laces strong
Himselfe he tide, and wrapt his wingés twaine
In lymie° snares the subtill loupes among; *sticky*
430 That in the ende he breathelesse did remaine,
And all his yougthly forces idly spent,
Him to the mercie of th'avenger lent.° *gave*

Which when the greisly° tyrant did espie, *horrible*
Like a grimme Lyon rushing with fierce might
435 Out of his den, he seizéd greedelie
On the resistles pray, and with fell spight,
Under the left wing stroke° his weapon slie *struck*
Into his heart, that his deepe groning spright
In bloodie streames foorth fled into the aire,
440 His bodie left the spectacle of care.[3]

Editors' Note

Spenser's *Complaints*, the collection including *Muiopotmos*, appeared in 1591 and, good evidence shows (Peterson 1989), was "called in" by the authorities, doubtless because the powerful William Cecil, Lord Burleigh, almost certainly the frowning owner of the "rugged forhead" in the Proem to *The Faerie Queene's* Book IV, had recognized himself as an object of satire in *Mother Hubberds Tale* (see the Editors' Note to that poem in this Norton Critical Edition). *Complaints*, although not including *Mother Hubberd*, was reprinted by Matthew Lownes for his 1611 folio edition of Spenser's *Works*, by which time both Spenser and Burleigh were long dead. In 1612 Cecil's equally powerful son Robert died and *Mother Hubberd* was added to later printings of Spenser's works.

If *Mother Hubberd* was an astonishingly imprudent work, is there any such risky allegory in *Muiopotmos*? In his prefatory letter, Spenser asks Lady Carey to "make a milde construction" of the poem, unavoidably implying that some might read it with a suspicious "construction." Various scholars have identified various possibilities, but even without specific persons in mind Spenser certainly takes aim, as he had in *The Shepheardes Calender*'s "Februarie" and again in *Mother Hubberds Tale*, at the rivalries and jealousies of court life as well as at the lazy frivolities, the fluttery and—in Renaissance terms—unmanly care for appearance and self-presentation that might expose an incautious courtier to poisoned tongues and even violence. Clarion's very name suggests self-trumpeting. *Muiopotmos* thus fits comfortably into a lively tradition of anticourt satire to which a number of writers on the Continent had contributed and that in Renaissance England stretched from Skelton and Wyatt to John Donne and Shakespeare and beyond (*Hamlet*'s foppish Osric makes a good Clarion). Courtiers are all too often butterflies: all

3. So Virgil concludes the *Aeneid*: "[Turnus's] limbs relax and grow cold; and his moaning spirit flies resentfully into the shades" (12.951–52).

color and carelessness, unable to focus, unwilling to work, and blind to danger. Does Spenser's butterfly recall anybody in particular? That is hard to say. Spiders, on the other hand, work—if not for a living then for the queen—but what they produce from their innards is gray and dangerous to others. Again, identifying any particular court spider is difficult. Butterflies are more attractive than spiders, to be sure, even if they do not generate anything useful to themselves or others. In their colorful uselessness, armed only with their own frail body parts, might they recall those other pretty but unproductive creatures, poets? Are spiders killjoy if hard-working "Puritans"? Or are butterflies, rather, the frivolous courtier poets at whom Spenser will scoff at the very end of Book VI of *The Faerie Queene*? One powerful figure in the backstory of *Muiopotmos* is Minerva, that famous and armed virgin goddess. We have no evidence that this poem vexed England's own armed virgin queen, or the Cecils for that matter, but the poem seems to signal relevance to life at court even if Spenser leaves working out any particulars to the reader.

Muiopotmos starts with a parody of the *Aeneid*'s opening lines, and we soon meet a hero-butterfly armed to what in a real hero would be the teeth as Spenser sings of arms and the insect (a takeoff on "*Arma virumque cano*"). The poem is, then, a mock epic, a send-up of the very genre in which Spenser was working as he penned the second half of *The Faerie Queene*. In a culture so fascinated with defining or exploring various genres, in which poetry was not personal effusion but imitation and revision of established "kinds," generic parody was irresistible. This is an Aesopian or medieval beast fable that is also a sequel to Ovid's tale of Arachne's metamorphosis and at the same time a parody of the genre most admired in the Renaissance. Like many mock epics, *Muiopotmos* may have elements of the paradoxical encomium, although it is more cautionary than celebratory. Writers had long amused themselves by writing about small or negative matters as though they were worth praise or at least attention, whether baldness, a nut, debt, folly, "nothing," red herrings, even cuckoldry. And, in France, the Pléiade poet Rémy Belleau had sent a friend an Anacreontic poem on the butterfly, that pretty painted representative of earthly transience.

Muiopotmos is, in its parodic way, the story not only of jealous betrayal and incautious idleness but also of a fall from greatness. In this regard it suits the recent fashion for the complaint—and hence deserves its place in *Complaints*. Like fallen Rome or Verlame (in the *Complaints*' "Ruines of Time") Clarion has tumbled down. So we can find a context for the poem in such works as *The Mirror for Magistrates* (1559 et seq.) with its grieving statesmen whose misfortunes may have more than one cause—fate, fortune, their own incaution, or the malice of others. Spenser also wrote near the start of another version of the complaint tradition, one in which a woman is raised not by prowess or birth but by an essentially useless beauty and then loses everything. Just as Spenser was readying *Complaints* for the press, Samuel Daniel was readying his own lament by Rosamond, a once great royal mistress, taken up by mere beauty to high if illegitimate place and now recounting her fall to the sympathetic narrator. Such laments, whether by statesmen or by fallen women, suit Spenser's career-long interest in mutability as well as in the threat to poetry of hypocrisy and arrogance in high places.

Muiopotmos, then, is a witty but also complex poem, entertaining us by its glance at a number of traditions and "kinds" even as it (perhaps) invites readers to wonder if anyone at Elizabeth's court might seem a Clarion—or an Aragnoll—and if poets are useless but pretty flutterers or web-weaving spiders who can wound the great when the great aren't looking. Or both.

Amoretti and Epithalamion

Amoretti†

Sonnet 1

Happy ye leaves[1] when as° those lilly hands, *when*
Which hold my life in their dead doing[2] might,
Shall handle you and hold in loves soft bands,
Lyke captives trembling at the victors sight.
5 And happy lines, on which with starry light,
Those lamping° eyes will deigne sometimes to look *shining*
And reade the sorrowes of my dying spright,° *spirit*
Written with teares in harts close° bleeding book. *secret*
And happy rymes bathed in the sacred brooke
10 Of Helicon[3] whence she derivéd is,
When ye behold that Angels blesséd looke,
My soules long lackéd foode, my heavens blis.
Leaves, lines, and rymes, seeke her to please alone,
Whom if ye please, I care for other none.° *none other*

Sonnet 2

Unquiet thought, whom at the first I bred
Of th'inward bale° of my love pinéd° hart: *woe / tormented*
And sithens° have with sighes and sorrowes fed, *since*
Till greater then my wombe thou woxen° art: *grown*
5 Breake forth at length out of the inner part,
In which thou lurkest lyke to vipers brood:[4]
And seeke some succour° both to ease my smart *aid*
And also to sustayne thy selfe with food.
But if in presence of that fayrest proud[5]
10 Thou chance to come, fall lowly at her feet:
And with meeke humblesse° and afflicted° mood, *humility / dejected*
Pardon for thee, and grace for me intreat.

† Italian for "little loves."
1. Pages, singly or bound, but also recalling Petrarch's laurel wreath. The pun initiates *Amoretti's* themes of binding, fame, victory, and time (garlands symbolize both time and eternal glory). Like Petrarch's, the opening sonnet gives an impression of being written after the others and is thus retrospective as well as introductory.
2. I.e., death-dealing.
3. The Hippocrene Spring on Mount Helicon, sacred to the Muses, inspires poetry.
4. Vipers were thought to gnaw their way out of their mother, killing her.
5. I.e., proud lady.

Which if she graunt, then live, and my love cherish:
If not, die soone, and I with thee will perish.

Sonnet 3

The soverayne beauty which I doo admyre,[6]
Witnesse the world how worthy to be prayzed:
The light wherof hath kindled heavenly fyre,
In my fraile spirit by her from baseness raysed.
5 That being now with her huge brightnesse dazed,° *dazzled*
Base thing I can no more endure to view:
But looking still on her I stand amazed,
At wondrous sight of so celestiall hew.° *figure*
So when my toung would speak her praises dew,[7]
10 It stoppéd is with thoughts astonishment:
And when my pen would write her titles[8] true,
It ravisht is with fancies[9] wonderment:
Yet in my hart I then both speake and write
The wonder that my wit cannot endite.[1]

Sonnet 4

New yeare forth looking out of Janus gate,[2]
Doth seeme to promise hope of new delight;
And bidding th'old Adieu, his passéd date[3]
Bids all old thoughts to die in dumpish° spright. *sad*
5 And calling forth out of sad Winters night,
Fresh love, that long hath slept in cheerlesse bower:
Wils him awake, and soone about him dight° *prepare*
His wanton wings and darts of deadly power.[4]
For lusty spring now in his timely howre,
10 Is ready to come forth him[5] to receive:
And warnes the Earth with divers° colord flowre, *sundry*
To decke hir selfe, and her faire mantle weave.
Then you faire flowre, in whom fresh youth doth raine,
Prepare your selfe new love to entertaine.

6. "Admire" and "wonder at," from Latin *admiror.*
7. That which is due her praiseworthiness or those praises due her.
8. I.e., correct descriptive names; also the lawful claims of a "soverayne" beauty to which witnesses can testify. As so often, Spenser's language has legal implications.
9. "Fancy" is our image-making faculty; many viewed it with suspicion as liable to mislead the reason.
1. I.e., express or, more precisely, dictate.
2. Two-faced Janus, bringer of harmony, was god of gates; even before the Julian calendar, his month, January, had replaced March as the start of the Roman year (in Ovid's *Fasti* 1.161–64, Janus explains that midwinter sees the sun renewed). "New yeare," who need not be New Year's Day itself, is too soon for spring, but he looks "forth" toward it. Possibly Spenser means March 25, when the year's number officially changed; this, however, makes "passéd date" (1.3) hard to identify. In the allegory itself New Year asks Cupid to wake up and meet the coming Spring.
3. Either the recent January 1 or the now-elapsed dead of winter; in either case the year's turn teaches the lady to prepare for love.
4. Cupid will put on his wings and the arrows that make us "die" for love.
5. I.e., Cupid.

Sonnet 5

Rudely[6] thou wrongest my deare harts desire,
In finding fault with her too portly° pride: *stately*
The thing which I doo most in her admire,
Is of the world unworthy most envide.[7]
5 For in those lofty lookes is close implide,[8]
Scorn of base things, and sdeigne° of foule dishonor: *disdain*
Thretning rash eies which gaze on her so wide,° *unrestrainedly*
That loosely they ne° dare to looke upon her. *not*
Such pride is praise, such portlinesse is honor,
10 That boldned innocence beares in hir eies:
And her faire countenance like a goodly banner,
Spreds in defiaunce of all enemies.
Was never in this world ought° worthy tride,[9] *anything*
Without some spark of such self-pleasing pride.

Sonnet 6

Be nought° dismayd that her unmovéd mind *nothing*
Doth still persist in her rebellious pride:
Such love not lyke to lusts of baser kynd,
The harder wonne, the firmer will abide.
5 The durefull[1] Oake whose sap is not yet dride
Is long ere it conceive the kindling fyre:
But when it once doth burne, it doth divide° *dispense*
Great heat, and makes his flames to heaven aspire.
So hard it is to kindle new desire,
10 In gentle brest that shall endure for ever:
Deepe is the wound that dints the parts entire[2]
With chast affects,° that naught but death can sever. *desires*
Then thinke not long in taking litle paine,
To knit the knot, that ever shall remaine.[3]

Sonnet 7

Fayre eyes, the myrrour of my mazéd[4] hart,
What wondrous vertue° is contaynd in you, *power*
The which both lyfe and death forth from you dart
Into the object of your mighty view?[5]
5 For when ye mildly looke with lovely hew,° *appearance*

6. I.e., without learning or sophistication. If not the lover himself, the addressee is a critical bystander, a standard figure in love poetry.
7. I.e., is most envied or denigrated by the unworthy world, or is most unworthily disparaged by the world.
8. I.e., enfolded and included, but also logically necessitated.
9. I.e., attempted; also, experienced and tested.
1. Perhaps "lasting"; but "hard" (oak is dense and, when green, slow to burn). Spenser allows wordplay on "harder" and "endure."
2. I.e., that strikes an impression on intact interior organs (such as the heart).
3. I.e., marriage; note the play on "knot" and "not" in 1.13.
4. I.e., amazed; also, put into a maze or labyrinth. Reflecting and mediating, mirrors fascinated Renaissance love poets, particularly Neoplatonists.
5. Vision was widely believed to emanate from the eye and affect the object viewed; hence the comparison of glances to arrows or lightning.

Then is my soule with life and love inspired:
But when ye lowre, or looke on me askew,
Then doe I die, as one with lightning fyred.
But since that lyfe is more then death desyred,
10 Looke ever lovely, as becomes you best,
That your bright beams of° my weak eies admyred, *by*
May kindle living fire within my brest.
Such life should be the honor of your light,
Such death the sad ensample° of your might. *example*

Sonnet 8[6]

More then most faire, full of the living fire
Kindled above unto the maker[7] neere:
No eies but joyes, in which al powers conspire
That to the world naught else be counted deare.
5 Thrugh your bright beams doth not the blinded guest
Shoot out his darts to base affections wound?[8]
But Angels come to lead fraile mindes to rest
In chast desires on heavenly beauty bound.
You frame my thoughts and fashion me within,
10 You stop my toung, and teach my hart to speake,
You calme the storme that passion did begin,
Strong thrugh your cause, but by your vertue weak.[9]
Dark is the world where your light shinéd never;
Well is he borne that may behold you ever.

Sonnet 9

Long-while I sought to what I might compare
Those powrefull eies, which lighten my dark spright,
Yet find I nought on earth to which I dare
Resemble° th'ymage of their goodly light. *liken*
5 Not to the Sun: for they doo shine by night;
Nor to the Moone: for they are changéd never;
Nor to the Starres: for they have purer sight;
Nor to the fire: for they consume not ever;
Nor to the lightning: for they still° persever;° *always / continue*
10 Nor to the Diamond: for they are more tender;
Nor unto Christall.[1] for nought may them sever;° *break*
Nor unto glasse: such basenesse mought° offend her; *might*
Then to the Maker selfe they likest be,
Whose light doth lighten° all that here we see.[2] *illuminate*

6. This Neo-Platonic sonnet, with a "Shakespearean" rhyme scheme, seems to have been composed before Spenser went to Ireland in 1580 (Cummings 1964) and so was not originally addressed to Elizabeth Boyle, object of the lover's affections in *Amoretti* (see Editors' Note). Such recycling was not uncommon.
7. I.e., God.
8. The syntax is ambiguous; the sense is that through the lady's eyes Cupid sends wounding arrows that create unworthy desires.
9. The storm is strong thanks to her but is moderated by her virtue's power.
1. I.e., quartz, more fragile than diamond and less common than glass.
2. Cf. "a light to lighten the gentiles" (Luke 2.32), said at evening prayer.

Sonnet 10[3]

Unrighteous Lord of love,[4] what law is this,
That me thou makest thus tormented be?
The whiles she lordeth in licentious° blisse — *lawless*
Of her freewill, scorning both thee and me.
5 See how the Tyrannesse doth joy to see
The huge massácres which her eyes do make:
And humbled harts brings captives unto thee;[5]
That thou of° them mayst mightie vengeance take. — *against*
But her proud hart doe thou a little shake
10 And that high look, with which she doth comptroll° — *dominate*
All this worlds pride bow to a baser make,° — *mate*
And al her faults in thy black booke enroll:
That I may laugh at her in equall sort,
As she doth laugh at me and makes my pain her sport.[6]

Sonnet 11

Dayly when I do seeke and sew° for peace, — *sue*
And hostages doe offer for my truth.[7]
She cruell warriour doth her selfe addresse
To battell, and the weary war renew'th.
5 Ne wilbe mooved with reason or with rewth,° — *pity*
To graunt small respit to my restlesse° toile: — *ceaseless*
But greedily her fell° intent poursewth,° — *cruel / pursues*
Of my poore life to make unpittied spoile.
Yet my poore life, all sorrowes to assoyle,° — *release*
10 I would her yield,[8] her wrath to pacify:
But then she seekes with torment and turmoyle,
To force me live and will not let me dy.
All paine hath end and every war hath peace,
But mine no price nor prayer may surcease.° — *discontinue*

Sonnet 12

One day I sought with her hart-thrilling° eies — *piercing*
To make a truce, and termes to entertaine.[9]
All fearelesse then of so false enimies,
Which sought me to entrap in treasons traine.[1]
5 So as I then disarméd did remaine,

3. Based on Petrarch, *Rime* 121; cf. Wyatt's "Behold, love." Spenser adds allusions to tyranny and, more significantly, to a violence that may glance at the bloody situation in Ireland. See Fleming 2001, who notes that while many Renaissance love poets ascribe cruelty to the beloved, in *Amoretti* Spenser goes further than most.
4. I.e., Cupid as ruler and lawgiver; the lover asks why he permits subversion.
5. Like an ancient or feudal warrior, the lady brings her captives (lovers' hearts) to present to her lord, Cupid. To imagine erotic pursuit as a war was common; see, e.g., Ovid's *Amores* I.9 ("Every lover's a warrior . . . and Cupid has his GHQ").
6. An alexandrine; cf. *Amoretti* 45.
7. I.e., integrity and troth; the lover is like a vanquished leader giving hostages to guarantee a treaty.
8. I.e., give up my life to her.
9. I.e., negotiate a treaty.
1. I.e., a treacherous snare.

A wicked ambush which lay hidden long
In the close° covert° of her guilefull eyen, *secret / thicket*
Thence breaking forth did thick about me throng.
Too feeble I t'abide the brunt° so strong, *onslaught*
10 Was forst to yeeld my selfe into their hands:
Who me captiving streight° with rigorous wrong, *tightly*
Have ever since me kept in cruell bands.
So Ladie now to you I doo complaine,
Against your eies that justice I may gaine.

Sonnet 13

In that proud port,° which her so goodly graceth, *bearing*
Whiles her faire face she reares up to the skie:
And to the ground her eie-lids low embaseth,° *lowers*
Most goodly temperature[2] ye may descry,
5 Myld humblesse mixt with awfull° majesty, *awesome*
For looking on the earth whence she was borne,[3]
Her minde remembreth her mortalitie,
What so is fayrest shall to earth returne.
But that same lofty countenance seemes to scorne
10 Base thing, and thinke how she to heaven may clime:
Treading downe earth as lothsome and forlorne,[4]
That hinders heavenly thoughts with drossy° slime. *impure*
Yet lowly still vouchsafe to looke on me,
Such lowlinesse shall make you lofty be.

Sonnet 14

Retourne agayne, my forces late dismayd,
Unto the siege by you abandoned quite:
Great shame it is to leave like one afrayd,
So fayre a peece[5] for one repulse so light.
5 Gaynst such strong castles needeth[6] greater might,
Then those small forts which ye were wont belay;[7]
Such haughty mynds enured to hardy° fight, *bold*
Disdayne to yield unto the first assay.° *attack*
Bring therefore all the forces that ye may,
10 And lay incessant battery to her heart:
Playnts, prayers, vowes, ruth, sorrow, and dismay,
Those engins can the proudest love convert.° *turn*

2. At its simplest, "temperature" is the mixture of elements in body, rational soul, and behavior. Spenser often plays with cognates of "temper" such as "time" (Latin *tempus*), "tempered" (cf. *Amoretti* 1. 21), "temperance," and "tempest" (symbol of time or fortune). His most extensive treatment of these related concepts is Book II of *The Faerie Queene*.
3. She is descended from Adam, made of clay; her "humblesse" recalls Latin *humus*, earth, but her "port" echoes Ovid, who says the gods gave "a face uplifted to the stars" only to humankind (*Metamorphoses* 1.86). The lady tempers this upward-gazing nobility with an awareness of mortality.
4. Suggests both abandoned and lost.
5. I.e., fortress. "Piece" was also a decent term for a person of either sex.
6. I.e., there needs.
7. I.e., besiege; also, to make fast.

And if those fayle fall downe and dy before her,
So dying live, and living do adore her.

Sonnet 15[8]

Ye tradefull Merchants that with weary toyle,
Do seeke most pretious things to make your gain:
And both the Indias[9] of their treasures spoile,° *despoil*
What needeth you to seeke so farre in vaine?
5 For loe my love doth in her selfe containe
All this worlds riches that may farre be found;
If Saphyres, loe her eies be Saphyres plaine,
If Rubies, loe hir lips be Rubies sound:
If Pearles, hir teeth be pearles both pure and round;
10 If Yvorie, her forhead yvory weene,[1]
If Gold, her locks are finest gold on ground,° *earth*
If silver, her faire hands are silver sheene:° *shining*
But that which fairest is, but few behold,
Her mind adornd with vertues manifold.

Sonnet 16

One day as I unwarily did gaze
On those fayre eyes my loves immortall light:
The whiles my stonisht° hart stood in amaze,° *astonished / puzzlement amazement*
Through sweet illusion[2] of her lookes delight,
5 I mote° perceive how in her glauncing sight, *could*
Legions of loves[3] with little wings did fly:
Darting their deadly arrowes fyry bright,
At every rash beholder passing by.
One of those archers closely° I did spy, *covertly*
10 Ayming his arrow at my very hart:
When suddenly with twincle° of her eye, *blink*
The Damzell broke his misintended dart.
Had she not so doon, sure I had bene slayne,
Yet as it was, I hardly scap't with paine.[4]

Sonnet 17

The glorious pourtraict of that Angels face,
Made to amaze weake mens confuséd skil:
And this worlds worthlesse glory to embase,° *humble*
What pen, what pencill can expresse her fill?° *fully*
5 For though he colours could devize at will,

8. From Desportes, *Diane* 1.32; Spenser adds a couplet on the lady's inwardness. The poem is a "blazon," detailing a lady's qualities by a series of comparisons or depictions; some blazons focus on one feature, like Maurice Scève's famous poem on his mistress's eyebrow ("Sourcil tractif").
9. The East and West Indies.
1. An imperative: ween (i.e., think) her forehead is ivory.
2. I.e., deceptive appearance; also, perhaps, mockery or teasing.
3. Her eyebeams contain "amoretti."
4. I.e., barely escaped, and only with hurt.

And eke his learnéd hand at pleasure guide,
Least° trembling it his workmanship should spill,° *lest / ruin*
Yet many wondrous things there are beside.
The sweet eye-glaunces, that like arrowes glide,
10 The charming smiles, that rob sence from the hart:
The lovely pleasance[5] and the lofty pride,
Cannot expresséd be by any art.
A greater craftesmans hand thereto doth neede,
That can expresse the life of things indeed.

Sonnet 18

The rolling wheele that runneth often round,
The hardest steele in tract of time doth teare:
And drizling drops that often doe redound,° *overflow*
The firmest flint doth in continuance weare.[6]
5 Yet cannot I, with many a dropping teare,
And long intreaty, soften her hard hart:
That she will once vouchsafe my plaint to heare,
Or looke with pitty on my payneful smart.
But when I pleade, she bids me play my part,
10 And when I weep, she sayes teares are but water:
And when I sigh, she sayes I know the art,[7]
And when I waile, she turnes hir selfe to laughter.
So doe I weepe, and wayle, and pleade in vaine,
Whiles she as steele and flint doth still remayne.

Sonnet 19

The merry Cuckow, messenger of Spring,
His trompet shrill hath thrise already sounded:
That warnes al lovers wayt upon their king,[8]
Who now is comming forth with, girland crounéd.
5 With noyse whereof the quyre° of Byrds resounded *choir*
Their anthemes sweet devizéd of loves prayse,
That all the woods theyr ecchoes back rebounded,[9]
As if they knew the meaning of their layes.
But mongst them all which did Loves honor rayse
10 No word was heard of° her that most it ought,° *from / owed*
But she his precept proudly disobayes,
And doth his ydle[1] message set at nought.
Therefore O love, unlesse she turne to thee
Ere Cuckow end, let her a rebell be.[2]

5. I.e., pleasantness; also, a shady garden enclosure for sitting and walking, a contrast with her "lofty pride."
6. I.e., drops that fall continually will wear down flint. Surprise that a lady can resist erosion was common; less so is this one's spirited mockery.
7. It is not clear who speaks: either the lady says the lover knows the art of wooing with sighs or she says she herself sees this art for what it is.
8. I.e., Cupid.
9. Cf. the refrain of *Epithalamion*.
1. I.e., ineffective; and Cupid was said to like idleness.
2. I.e., be legally declared a rebel against Lord Cupid.

Sonnet 20

In vaine I seeke and sew° to her for grace, *sue*
And doe myne humbled hart before her poure:
The whiles her foot she in my necke doth place,
And tread my life downe in the lowly floure.° *floor*
5 And yet the Lyon that is Lord of power,
And reigneth over every beast in field,
In his most pride disdeigneth to devoure
The silly lambe that to his might doth yield.[3]
But she more cruell and more salvage wylde,
10 Then either Lyon or the Lyonesse:
Shames not[4] to be with guiltlesse bloud defylde,
But taketh glory in her cruelnesse.
Fayrer then fayrest, let none ever say
That ye were blooded in a yeelded pray.[5]

Sonnet 21

Was it the worke of nature or of Art,
Which tempred so the feature of her face,
That pride and meeknesse mixt by equall part,
Doe both appeare t'adorne her beauties grace?
5 For with mild pleasance, which doth pride displace,
She to her love doth lookers eyes allure.[6]
And with sterne countenance back again doth chace
Their looser lookes that stir up lustes impure.
With such strange termes her eyes she doth inure,[7]
10 That with one looke she doth my life dismay:
And with another doth it streight recure,° *recover*
Her smile me drawes, her frowne me drives away.
Thus doth she traine[8] and teach me with her lookes,
Such art of eyes I never read in bookes.

Sonnet 22[9]

This holy season fit to fast and pray,
Men to devotion ought to be inclynd:
Therefore, I lykewise on so holy day;[1]

3. Lions were thought magnanimous; see Pliny, *Natural History* 8.19. In famous lines, the Roman poet Martial wrote (*Epigrams* 1.22) that just as lions let hares go, so the great spare the humble. The lover is a "silly" (innocent) lamb.
4. I.e., is not ashamed.
5. Only bad sportsmen kill prey that gives up. It is tempting to read "blooded" as the smearing of a novice hunter with blood from a first kill, but the *OED*'s citations of this sense are modern.
6. I.e., draws observers' eyes to love her.
7. I.e., accustoms her eyes to use peculiar and foreign "terms" (words; also negotiable conditions). "Inure" also meant put into legal effect.
8. Probably "draw along," rather than "educate and discipline," so as to sustain the paradox that her eyes both entice and instruct.
9. The start of a Lenten sequence of forty-seven sonnets (see Editors' Note). Poets such as Desportes, whose *Diane* 1.43 *Amoretti* 22 resembles, had promised a temple or sung of love on a holy day (cf. Petrarch, *Rime* 3).
1. Ash Wednesday, first day of Lent; in 1594 it fell on February 13. The phrasing recalls texts in the prayerbook (Johnson 1990), while the sacrifice and "ire" echo Psalm 51 and the "Commination against Sinners" appointed for this day.

For my sweet Saynt[2] some service fit will find.
5 Her temple fayre is built within my mind,
In which her glorious ymage placéd is,
On which my thoughts doo day and night attend
Lyke sacred priests that never thinke amisse.
There I to her as th'author of my blisse,
10 Will builde an altar to appease her yre:
And on the same my hart will sacrifise,
Burning in flames of pure and chast desyre:
The which vouchsafe O goddesse to accept,
Amongst thy deerest relicks to be kept.

Sonnet 23

Penelope for her Ulisses sake,
Devized a Web her wooers to deceave:
In which the worke that she all day did make
The same at night she did againe unreave:[3]
5 Such subtile craft my Damzell doth conceave,° *devise*
Th'importune° suit of my desire to shonne:[4] *importunate*
For all that I in many dayes doo weave,
In one short houre I find by her undonne.
So when I thinke to end that° I begonne, *what*
10 I must begin and never bring to end:
For with one looke she spils° that long I sponne,[5] *destroys*
And with one word my whole years work doth rend.[6]
Such labour like the Spyders web I fynd,
Whose fruitlesse worke is broken with least wynd.

Sonnet 24

When I behold that beauties wonderment,
And rare perfection of each goodly part:
Of natures skill the onely complement,
I honor and admire the makers art.
5 But when I feele the bitter balefull° smart, *deadly*
Which her fayre eyes unwares° doe worke in mee, *unwittingly*
That death out of theyr shiny beames doe dart,
I thinke that I a new Pandora see,[7]

2. By "saints" Elizabethan Protestants often meant those chosen by God for salvation, but the word could also mean, often negatively, postbiblical figures canonized by the Catholic church and the objects of particular scorn to more radical reformers; "ymage," "relicks," and "goddesse" would, to many readers, connote "popish" idolatry and superstition.
3. During the absence of her husband, Odysseus, Penelope assured her many suitors that she would choose one after she had finished weaving a shroud for the hero Laertes; then every night she undid what she had woven that day (Homer, *Odyssey* 2). Web: the product of weaving, tying it to a set of related words or concepts such as "textile," "text," or "trap."
4. I.e., elude; she imagines a cunning way to evade his desire's urgent pleading.
5. I.e., what I took a long time to spin.
6. This line has fed debate over how the courtship's duration relates to the poetry's time scheme.
7. Pandora, "all-gifted," was forged by Zeus's smith Hephaestus (Vulcan) and graced by all the gods. Angry at the trickster Prometheus for giving mankind fire, Zeus sent her to him and his brother Epimetheus, slyly supplying her with a box enclosing evils and plagues (Hesiod, *Theogony* 507–616, who adds, "This was the origin of the damnable race of women"); some poets used her name to represent perfection, but here she is a scourge. Spenser replaces Zeus's jealous fury at human knowledge with divine disgust at human sin.

Whom all the Gods in councell did agree,
10 Into this sinfull world from heaven to send:
That she to wicked men a scourge should bee,
For all their faults with which they did offend.
But since ye are my scourge I will intreat,
That for my faults ye will me gently beat.

Sonnet 25

How long shall this lyke dying lyfe[8] endure,
And know no end of her[9] owne mysery:
But wast and weare away in termes° unsure, *conditions*
Twixt feare and hope depending° doubtfully? *suspended*
5 Yet better were attonce to let me die,
And shew the last ensample of your pride:
Then to torment me thus with cruelty,
To prove your powre, which I too wel have tride.° *experienced*
But yet if in your hardned brest ye hide
10 A close° intent at last to shew me grace: *secret*
Then all the woes and wrecks which I abide,° *undergo*
As meanes of blisse I gladly wil embrace;
And wish that more and greater they might be,
That greater meede° at last may turne to mee. *reward*

Sonnet 26

Sweet is the Rose, but growes upon a brere;° *briar*
Sweet is the Junipere, but sharpe his bough;
Sweet is the Eglantine, but pricketh nere;
Sweet is the firbloome, but his braunches rough.
5 Sweet is the Cypresse, but his rynd is tough,
Sweet is the nut, but bitter is his pill;
Sweet is the broome-flowre, but yet sowre enough;
And sweet is Moly, but his root is ill.[1]
So every sweet with soure is tempred still,° *always*
10 That° maketh it be coveted the more: *which*
For easie things that may be got at will,
Most sorts of men doe set but little store.
Why then should I accoumpt of little paine,
That endlesse pleasure shall unto me gaine?[2]

Sonnet 27

Faire proud, now tell me, why should faire be proud,
Sith° all worlds glorie is but drosse uncleane? *since*
And in the shade of death it selfe shall shroud,° *clothe*
How ever now thereof ye little weene.

8. I.e., a life that is more like dying.
9. I.e., life's.
1. The black-rooted, purple-blossomed, and milky flower that Hermes gave Odysseus as protection against the sorceress Circe (Homer, *Odyssey* 10). For some it signified temperance, for others an erudite eloquence (cf. Andrea Alciato, *Emblemata* #182).
2. I.e., take account of minor pain/work that will gain me endless pleasure.

5 That goodly Idoll now so gay beseene,
Shall doffe her fleshes borowd fayre attyre:[3]
And be forgot as it[4] had never beene,
That many now much worship° and admire. *honor*
Ne any then shall after it inquire,
10 Ne any mention shall thereof remaine:
But° what this verse, that never shall expyre, *except*
Shall to you purchas with her thankles paine.[5]
Faire, be no lenger proud of that° shall perish, *what*
But that which shal you make immortall, cherish.

Sonnet 28

The laurell leafe, which you this day doe weare,
Gives me great hope of your relenting mynd:
For since it is the badg which I doe beare,
Ye bearing it doe seeme to me inclind.[6]
5 The powre thereof, which ofte in me I find,
Let it lykewise your gentle brest inspire
With sweet infusion, and put you in mind
Of that proud mayd, whom now those leaves attyre:
Proud Daphne scorning Phaebus lovely fyre,
10 On the Thessalian shore from him did flee:
For which the gods in theyr revengefull yre
Did her transforme into a laurell tree.
Then fly no more fayre love from Phebus chace,° *pursuit*
But in your brest his leafe and love embrace.[7]

Sonnet 29

See how the stubborne damzell doth deprave° *misinterpret*
My simple meaning with disdaynfull scorne:
And by the bay° which I unto her gave, *laurel*
Accoumpts my selfe her captive quite forlorne.
5 "The bay," quoth she, "is of the victours borne,
Yielded them by the vanquisht as theyr meeds,° *rewards*
And they[8] therewith doe poetes heads adorne,
To sing the glory of their famous deedes."
But sith she will the conquest challeng needs,[9]
10 Let her accept me as her faithfull thrall,° *slave*
That her great triumph which my skill exceeds,

3. I.e., her lovely *eidolon* or image that wears flesh like a borrowed dress will have to take it off.
4. Probably "it" is the "Idoll," genderless without its "attyre."
5. I.e., will obtain for you with effort that receives no thanks.
6. In ancient times laurel was worn by victors, but Petrarch, who called his lady Laura, adopted it for poets. Cf. Ronsard, *Astrée* 11, in which the lady wears it to show her power.
7. Ovid (*Metamorphoses* 1.452–567) tells how thanks to divine mercy the nymph Daphne escaped Apollo by becoming a laurel; the god took her foliage as a badge. With only minimal precedent, Spenser mischievously departs from tradition: Cupid had shot Daphne with a leaden arrow of antipathy.
8. Possibly the laurels; more likely the victors, who then in turn crown with bay the poets who will make them famous. Spenser puts into the lady's mouth this reminder that poets can reward patronage.
9. I.e., since she must needs claim victory.

I may in trump of fame blaze° over all. *proclaim*
Then would I decke her head with glorious bayes,
And fill the world with her victorious prayse.

Sonnet 30[1]

My love is lyke to yse, and I to fyre;
How comes it then that this her cold so great
Is not dissolved through my so hot desyre,
But harder growes the more I her intreat?
5 Or how comes it that my exceeding heat
Is not delayd° by her hart frosen cold: *quenched*
But that I burne much more in boyling[2] sweat,
And feele my flames augmented manifold?
What more miraculous thing may be told,
10 That fire which all thing melts, should harden yse:
And yse which is congeald with sencelesse cold,
Should kindle fyre by wonderfull devyse?° *contrivance*
Such is the powre of love in gentle° mind, *noble*
That it can alter all the course of kynd.° *Nature*

Sonnet 31

Ah why hath nature to so hard a hart,
Given so goodly giftes of beauties grace?
Whose pryde depraves° each other better part, *spoils*
And all those pretious ornaments deface.[3]
5 Sith to all other beastes of bloody race,
A dreadfull countenaunce she given hath:
That with theyr terrour al the rest may chace,
And warne to shun the daunger of theyr wrath.
But my proud one doth worke the greater scath,° *harm*
10 Through sweet allurement of her lovely hew.° *shape*
That she the better may in bloody bath
Of such poore thralls her cruell hands embrew.° *stain*
But did she know how ill these two accord,
Such cruelty she would have soone abhord.

Sonnet 32

The paynefull° smith with force of fervent heat, *painstaking*
The hardest yron soone doth mollify,° *soften*
That with his heavy sledge he can it beat,
And fashion to what he it list apply.[4]
5 Yet cannot all these flames in which I fry,
Her hart more harde then yron soft° awhit: *soften*
Ne all the playnts and prayers with which I

1. Cf. Petrarch *Rime* 202 and its many offspring.
2. Perhaps a pun on boil/Boyle.
3. I.e., defaces; acceptable grammar in Spenser's time.
4. I.e., whatever he wants to turn it into and use it for; "apply" had its modern sense but also meant "bend."

Doe beat on th'andvyle° of her stubberne wit: *anvil*
But still the more she fervent sees my fit;[5]
10 The more she frieseth in her wilfull pryde:
And harder growes the harder she is smit,° *struck*
With all the playnts which to her be applyde.
What then remaines but I to ashes burne,
And she to stones at length all frosen turne?

Sonnet 33

Great wrong I doe, I can it not deny,
To that most sacred Empresse my dear dred,[6]
Not finishing her Queene of faery,
That mote enlarge her living prayses dead:[7]
5 But lodwick, this of grace to me aread:[8]
Doe ye not thinck th'accomplishment of it,
Sufficient worke for one mans simple head,
All° were it as the rest but rudely writ. *even*
How then should I without another wit,
10 Thinck ever to endure so tædious toyle?
Sins that this one[9] is tost with troublous fit,
Of a proud love, that doth my spirite spoyle.° *ravage*
Ceasse then, till she vouchsafe to grawnt me rest,
Or lend you me another living brest.

Sonnet 34[1]

Lyke as a ship that through the Ocean wyde,
By conduct of some star doth make her way,
Whenas a storme hath dimd her trusty guyde,
Out of her course doth wander far astray:
5 So I whose star, that wont with her bright ray
Me to direct, with cloudes is overcast,
Doe wander now in darknesse and dismay,
Through hidden perils round about me plast.
Yet hope I well, that when this storme is past
10 My Helice the lodestar of my life[2]

5. I.e., my paroxysm of activity, pain, and possibly lunacy; a "fit" was also a section of a poem.
6. Elizabeth I: dear but held in awe, and "Empresse" because she claimed Ireland, France, Virginia, and (like other Renaissance rulers) a share of Rome's ancient *imperium* and later ecclesiastical authority.
7. *Faerie Queene* IV–VI appeared the following year, 1596. It is "her" book because as Gloriana she is its heroine, and it will broaden and preserve her praise after she is dead.
8. I.e., be so good as to advise me. *Lodwick*: i.e., Lodowick Bryskett. Earlier amatory collections had likewise included poems to friends, commenting on current events or implying a tension between public and private life. Like Spenser, Petrarch, Du Bellay, and Ronsard had defended a turn from epic to love poetry or, with Ovid as a witty precedent, the refusal even to attempt heroic verse; in *Delia* (1592) Samuel Daniel will not imitate *The Faerie Queene* ("Let others sing of knights and paladins"). See Ovid's *Amores* I.i, in which Cupid steals a syllable and forces the poet to change heroic dactylic hexameter for elegiacs.
9. I.e., this wit, the one in love.
1. Comparing a lover to a storm-tossed sailor was a favorite Petrarchan conceit (e.g., *Rime* 189, translated by Wyatt as "My galley chargéd with forgetfulness"), deployed on the Continent by both male and female poets; Spenser had many models.
2. Helice (which can sound like "Eliza") is a name for Ursa Major and also a city at the foot of

Will shine again, and looke on me at last,
With lovely light to cleare my cloudy grief.
Till then I wander carefull[3] comfortlesse,
In secret sorow and sad pensivenesse.

Sonnet 35

My hungry eyes through greedy covetize
Still° to behold the object of their paine, *always*
With no contentment can themselves suffize:° *satisfy*
But having pine and having not complaine.[4]
5 For lacking it, they cannot lyfe sustayne,
And having it, they gaze on it the more:
In their amazement lyke Narcissus vaine
Whose eyes him starved: so plenty makes me poore.[5]
Yet are mine eyes so fillėd with the store
10 Of that faire sight, that nothing else they brooke,° *endure*
But lothe the things which they did like before,
And can no more endure on them to looke.
All this worlds glory seemeth vayne to me,
And all their showes but shadowes saving she.

Sonnet 36

Tell me when shall these wearie woes have end,
Or shall their ruthlesse torment never cease:
But al my dayes in pining languor spend,
Without hope of aswagement or release:
5 Is there no meanes for me to purchace peace,
Or make agreement with her thrilling° eyes: *piercing*
But that their cruelty doth still increace,
And dayly more augment my miseryes?
But when ye have shewed all extremityes,
10 Then thinke how litle glory ye have gayned,
By slaying him, whose lyfe though ye despyse,
Mote° have your life in honour long maintayned. *might*
But by his death which some perhaps will mone,
Ye shall condemnėd be of many a one.

Sonnet 37

What guyle is this, that those her golden tresses
She doth attyre under a net of gold:

Helicon. Perhaps that is why Spenser uses it and not "Cynosure" (Ursa Minor), which in fact has the pole (or lode) star used in navigation. Chaucer ("Knight's Tale," ed. Robinson, 2059) also confuses the names.
3. I.e., full of care.
4. His eyes suffer longingly in seeing the lady who makes them hurt, but they complain when they cannot see her.
5. Ovid tells (*Metamorphoses* 3.339–509) how Narcissus so loved his own reflection that he ignored the nymph Echo (who faded to a mere voice) and would not eat. Lamenting that "inopem me copia fecit" ("plenty makes me poor"), he became a flower—a narcissus.

And with sly skill so cunningly them dresses,
That which is gold or heare, may scarse be told?
5 Is it that mens frayle eyes, which gaze too bold,
She may entangle in that golden snare:
And being caught may craftily enfold
Theyr weaker harts, which are not wel aware?
Take heed therefore, myne eyes, how ye doe stare
10 Henceforth too rashly on that guilefull net,
In which if ever ye entrappéd are,
Out of her bands ye by no meanes shall get.
Fondnesse° it were for any being free,[6] *madness*
To covet fetters, though they golden bee.

Sonnet 38

Arion, when through tempests cruel wracke,
He forth was thrown into the greedy seas:
Through the sweet musick which his harp did make
Allured a Dolphin him from death to ease.[7]
5 But my rude musick, which was wont to please
Some dainty eares, cannot with any skill
The dreadfull tempest of her wrath appease,
Nor move the Dolphin from her stubborne will,
But in her pride she dooth persever still,
10 All carelesse° how my life for her decayse: *uncaring*
Yet with one word she can it save or spill,° *destroy*
To spill were pitty, but to save were prayse.
Chose rather to be praysd for dooing good,
Then to be blamed for spilling guiltlesse blood.

Sonnet 39

Sweet smile, the daughter of the Queene of love,[8]
Expressing all thy mothers powrefull art,
With which she wonts to temper° angry Joue, *moderate*
When all the gods he threats with thundring dart:[9]
5 Sweet is thy vertue,° as thy selfe sweet art,[1] *power*
For when on me thou shinedst late in sadnesse,
A melting pleasance ran through every part,
And me revivéd with hart-robbing gladnesse.[2]
Whylest rapt with joy resembling heavenly madnes,
10 My soule was ravisht quite as in a traunce:
And feeling thence no more her sorowes sadnesse,

6. I.e., anyone being free or, subtly different, any free being.
7. Arion was a famous musician whom sailors robbed and forced into the sea; charmed by his farewell shipboard recital, a passing dolphin carried him to shore, showing the power of song (cf. Herodotus, *Persian Wars* 1.23–24). Here Arion escapes a tempest, not thieves, but storms in turn often symbolized misfortune.
8. I.e., Venus.
9. Thunderbolts, forged by Vulcan for the ruler of the gods.
1. I.e., as thou thyself art sweet.
2. Before William Harvey discovered that blood circulates, it was thought that passions draw it to and from the heart: fear sends blood to succor the constricted organ, but here joy sends it outward—the lover may be flushed with happiness.

Fed on the fulnesse of that chearefull glaunce.
More sweet than Nectar or Ambrosiall meat,° *food*
Seemd every bit which thenceforth I did eat.

Sonnet 40

Mark when she smiles with amiable cheare,° *expression*
And tell me whereto can ye lyken it:
When on each eyelid sweetly doe appeare
An hundred Graces as in shade to sit.[3]
5 Lykest it seemeth in my simple wit
Unto the fayre sunshine in somers day:
That when a dreadfull storme away is flit,
Thrugh the broad world doth spred his goodly ray:
At sight whereof each bird that sits on spray,
10 And every beast that to his den was fled,
Comes forth afresh out of their late dismay,
And to the light lift up theyr drouping hed.
So my storme-beaten hart likewise is cheared,
With that sunshine when cloudy looks are cleared.

Sonnet 41

Is it her nature or is it her will,[4]
To be so cruell to an humbled foe?
If nature, then she may it mend with skill:
If will, then she at will may will forgoe.
5 But if her nature and her wil be so,
That she will plague the man that loves her most:
And take delight t'encrease a wretches woe,
Then all her natures goodly guifts are lost.
And that same glorious beauties ydle boast,
10 Is but a bayt such wretches to beguile,
As being long in her loves tempest tost,
She meanes at last to make her piteous° spoyle. *pitiable*
O fayrest fayre let never it be named,
That so fayre beauty was so fowly shamed.

Sonnet 42

The love which me so cruelly tormenteth,
So pleasing is in my extreamest paine:
That all the more my sorrow it augmenteth,
The more I love and doe embrace my bane.° *destruction*
5 Ne doe I wish (for wishing were but vaine)
To be acquit° fro my continuall smart: *free*
But joy her thrall for ever to remayne,[5]

3. I.e., as though a hundred Graces were sitting in the shade (as a rule there were three, attending Venus; cf. *The Shepheardes Calender* "April" and *The Faerie Queene* VI.x.15.21–24).
4. A psychological faculty needing Reason to guide it lest it become runaway whim or stubborn egoism; on the word's occasional sexual meaning see *Amoretti* 67 and note.
5. I.e., rejoice to remain ever her slave.

And yield for pledge my poore captyvéd hart;
The which that it from her may never start,° *move*
10 Let her, yf please her, bynd with adamant[6] chayne:
And from all wandring loves which mote pervart[7]
His[8] safe assurance, strongly it restrayne.
Onely let her abstaine from cruelty,
And doe° me not before my time to dy. *make*

Sonnet 43[9]

Shall I then silent be or shall I speake?
And if I speake, her wrath renew I shall:
And if I silent be, my hart will breake,
Or chokéd be with overflowing gall.
5 What tyranny is this both my hart to thrall,° *enslave*
And eke my toung with proud restraint to tie;
That nether I may speake nor thinke at all,
But like a stupid stock° in silence die? *stump*
Yet I my hart with silence secretly
10 Will teach to speak, and my just cause to plead:
And eke mine eies with meeke humility,
Love-learnéd[1] letters to her eyes to read.
Which her deep wit, that true harts thought can spel,° *read*
Wil soone conceive, and learne to cónstrue well.[2]

Sonnet 44

When those renouméd° noble Peres of Greece, *renowned*
Thrugh stubborn pride amongst themselves did jar° *quarrel*
Forgetfull of the famous golden fleece,
Then Orpheus[3] with his harp theyr strife did bar.° *check*
5 But this continuall cruell civill warre,
The which my selfe against my selfe doe make,
Whilest my weak powres of passions warreid° arre, *afflicted*
No skill can stint nor reason can aslake.° *abate*
But when in hand my tunelesse harp I take,
10 Then doe I more augment my foes despight,° *scorn*
And griefe renew, and passions doe awake
To battaile fresh against my selfe to fight.
Mongst whome the more I seeke to settle peace,
The more I fynd their malice to increace.

6. I.e., diamond or, less probably, lodestone.
7. I.e., corrupt; also, turn aside.
8. I.e., his heart's.
9. The first and third quatrains adapt Tasso's "Se taccio, il duol s'avanza."
1. I.e., teach my eyes to send letters taught by love and learnéd concerning it.
2. I.e., will soon comprehend by making an inward image of the matter and learning to interpret it correctly.
3. The poet Orpheus sailed to Argos with Jason's crew of celebrities, singing away their bad temper. The story is told by Apollonius (*Argonautica* 1), but Spenser probably used Natalis Comes *Mythologiae* (Venice, 1551) 7.14.

Sonnet 45

Leave lady in your glasse of christall clene,
Your goodly selfe for evermore to vew:
And in my selfe, my inward selfe I meane,
Most lively lyke behold your semblant trew:[4]
5 Within my hart, though hardly it can shew
Thing so divine to vew° of earthly eye, *sight*
The fayre Idea[5] of your celestiall hew° *shape*
And every part remaines immortally:
And were it not that through your cruelty,
10 With sorrow dimméd and deformd it were,
The goodly ymage of your visnomy,° *face*
Clearer then christall would therein appere.
But if your selfe in me ye playne will see,
Remove the cause by which your fayre beames darkned be.[6]

Sonnet 46

When my abodes° prefixéd time is spent,[7] *visit*
My cruell fayre streight bids me wend my way:
But then from heaven most hideous stormes are sent
As willing me against her will to stay.
5 Whom then shall I or heaven or her obay?
The heavens know best what is the best for me:
But as she will, whose will my life doth sway,
My lower heaven, so it perforce must bee.
But ye high hevens, that all this sorowe see,
10 Sith all your tempests cannot hold me backe:
Aswage your stormes, or else both you and she
Will both together me too sorely wrack.
Enough it is for one man to sustaine
The stormes, which she alone on me doth raine.

Sonnet 47

Trust not the treason of those smyling lookes,
Untill ye have theyr guylefull traynes° well tryde.° *snares / examined*
For they are lyke but unto golden hookes,
That from the foolish fish theyr bayts doe hyde:
5 So she with flattring smyles weake harts doth guyde
Unto her love, and tempte to theyr decay,° *destruction*
Whome being caught she kills with cruell pryde,
And feeds at pleasure on the wretched pray:
Yet even whylst her bloody hands them slay,
10 Her eyes looke lovely and upon them smyle:

4. I.e., see your lifelike resemblance.
5. In diction loosely recalling the Neoplatonic "forms" in God's mind and visible only to the intellect; this "idea" is the image of the lady in the lover's inmost self, albeit deformed (l. 10) by his grief.
6. An alexandrine.
7. I.e., when my visit's set time is up.

That they take pleasure in her cruell play,
And dying doe them selves of payne beguyle.[8]
O mighty charm which makes men love theyr bane,[9]
And thinck they dy with pleasure, live with payne.

Sonnet 48

Innocent paper, whom too cruell hand
Did make the matter to avenge her yre:
And ere she could thy cause wel understand,
Did sacrifize unto the greedy fyre.[1]
5 Well worthy thou to have found better hyre,° *payment*
Then so bad end for hereticks ordayned:
Yet heresy nor treason didst conspire,
But plead thy maisters cause unjustly payned.[2]
Whom she, all carelesse° of his griefe, constrayned *uncaring*
10 To utter forth the anguish of his hart:
And would not heare, when he to her complayned
The piteous passion° of his dying smart. *suffering*
Yet live for ever, though against her will,
And speake her good,[3] though she requite it ill.

Sonnet 49

Fayre cruell, why are ye so fierce and cruell?
Is it because your eyes have powre to kill?
Then know that mercy is the mighties jewell,
And greater glory thinke to save, then spill:[4]
5 But if it be your pleasure and proud will,
To shew the powre of your imperious eyes:
Then not on him that never thought you ill,
But bend your force against your enemyes.
Let them feele th'utmost of your crueltyes,
10 And kill with looks, as Cockatrices[5] doo:
But him that at your footstoole humbled lies,
With mercifull regard, give mercy too.
Such mercy shal you make admyred to be,[6]
So shall you live by giving life to me.

Sonnet 50

Long languishing in double malady,
Of my harts wound and of my bodies griefe,
There came to me a leach° that would apply *doctor*

8. As they die, the hearts elude or charm away pain.
9. I.e., poison; more generally, ruin.
1. Cf. *Amoretti* 22's sacrifice.
2. I.e., tortured into confessing, like a heretic or traitor.
3. I.e., speak well of her; or speak to her benefit.
4. I.e., think you get more glory by preserving than by destroying.
5. Fabulous serpents with lethal eyebeams, born of roosters' eggs.
6. I.e., shall make you be admired.

Fit medicines[7] for my bodies best reliefe.
5 "Vayne man," quod I, "that hast but little priefe,° *experience*
In deep discovery of the mynds disease,
Is not the hart of all the body chiefe?
And rules the members as it selfe doth please?[8]
Then with some cordialls[9] seeke first to appease
10 The inward languour of my wounded hart,
And then my body shall have shortly ease:
But such sweet cordialls passe Physitions art."
Then my lyfes Leach[1] doe you your skill reveale,
And with one salve both hart and body heale.

Sonnet 51

Doe I not see that fayrest ymages
Of hardest Marble are of purpose made?[2]
For that they should endure through many ages,
Ne let theyr famous moniments to fade.
5 Why then doe I, untrainde in lovers trade,
Her hardnes blame which I should more commend?
Sith never ought was excellent assayde,
Which was not hard t'atchive and bring to end.[3]
Ne ought so hard, but he that would attend,[4]
10 Mote soften it and to his will allure:
So doe I hope her stubborne hart to bend,
And that it then more stedfast will endure.
Onely my paines wil be the more to get her,
But having her, my joy wil be the greater.

Sonnet 52

So oft as homeward I from her depart,
I goe lyke one that having lost the field,
Is prisoner led away with heavy hart,
Despoyld of warlike armes and knowen shield.[5]
5 So doe I now my selfe a prisoner yeeld,
To sorrow and to solitary paine:
From presence of my dearest deare exylde,
Longwhile alone in languor to remaine.
There let no thought of joy or pleasure vaine,
10 Dare to approch, that may my solace breed:
But sudden° dumps[6] and drery sad disdayne *unpremeditated*
Of all worlds gladnesse more my torment feed.

7. "Medicine" has two syllables.
8. Sager authorities such as St. Paul said the head should in turn rule the body.
9. Potions good for the heart (from Latin *cor*, heart).
1. I.e., the lady.
2. I.e., are not the fairest statues deliberately made of the hardest marble?
3. I.e., nothing excellent was ever attempted that was not hard to accomplish.
4. I.e., pay attention and apply himself; the word also means "wait."
5. I.e., recognized coat of arms.
6. Doleful pieces of music.

So I her absens will my penaunce make,
That of her presens I my meed° may take. *reward*

Sonnet 53

The Panther knowing that his spotted hyde
Doth please all beasts, but that his looks them fray.° *terrify*
Within a bush his dreadfull head doth hide,
To let them gaze whylest° he on them may pray.[7] *until / prey*
5 Right so my cruell fayre with me doth play,
For with the goodly semblant° of her hew° *image / form*
She doth allure me to mine owne decay,° *ruin*
And then no mercy will unto me shew.
Great shame it is, thing so divine in view,° *appearance*
10 Made for to be the worlds most ornament,
To make the bayte her gazers to embrew:
Good shames to be to ill an instrument.[8]
But mercy doth with beautie best agree,
As in theyr maker[9] ye them best may see.

Sonnet 54

Of this worlds Theatre in which we stay,[1]
My love lyke the Spectátor ydly sits,
Beholding me that all the pageants play,
Disguysing diversly my troubled wits.
5 Sometimes I joy when glad occasion fits,
And mask[2] in myrth lyke to a Comedy:
Soone after when my joy to sorrow flits,
I waile and make my woes a Tragedy.
Yet she beholding me with constant eye,[3]
10 Delights not in my merth nor rues° my smart.° *pities / hurt*
But when I laugh she mocks, and when I cry
She laughes, and hardens evermore her hart.
What then can move her? if nor merth nor mone,° *moan*
She is no woman, but a sencelesse stone.[4]

Sonnet 55[5]

So oft as I her beauty doe behold,
And therewith doe her cruelty compare,
I marvaile of what substance was the mould° *material*

7. See Pliny, *Natural History* 8.23. *Panther*: usually meant a spotted leopard.
8. I.e., it shames goodness (or goodness is ashamed) to be evil's instrument.
9. I.e., God.
1. A favorite Renaissance theme derived in part from Lucian's *Menippos* and further popularized by Erasmus's *Praise of Folly* (Norton 1989 ed., 28); cf. Shakespeare, *As You Like It* 2.7.139.
2. Put on a mask; also, act in a masque, an élite entertainment with symbolic costumes or "guises."
3. Noteworthy in that women were often called inconstant; Elizabeth I defied the same stereotype with her motto *semper eadem:* "ever the same."
4. Some readers (e.g., Martz 1961) hear a friendly and self-mocking humor; if so, cf. Philip Sidney's *Astrophil and Stella* 45.
5. The sonnet relies on the theory that the world is made of four elements: earth, air, fire, and water.

The which her made attonce so cruell faire.
5 Not earth; for her high thoghts more heavenly are,
Not water; for her love doth burne like fyre:
Not ayre; for she is not so light or rare,[6]
Not fyre; for she doth friese with faint desire.
Then needs another Element inquire
10 Whereof she mote be made; that is the skye.
For to the heaven her haughty lookes aspire:
And eke her mind is pure immortall hye.
Then sith to heaven ye lykened are the best,
Be lyke in mercy as in all the rest.

Sonnet 56

Fayre ye be sure,° but cruell and unkind, *surely*
As is a Tygre that with greedinesse
Hunts after bloud, when he by chance doth find
A feeble beast, doth felly° him oppresse. *cruelly*
5 Fayre be ye sure, but proud and pittilesse,
As is a storme, that all things doth prostrate:
Finding a tree alone all comfortlesse,
Beats on it strongly it to ruinate.
Fayre be ye sure, but hard and obstinate,
10 As is a rocke amidst the raging floods:
Gaynst which a ship of succour desolate,[7]
Doth suffer wreck both of her selfe and goods.
That ship, that tree, and that same beast am I,
Whom ye doe wreck, doe ruine, and destroy.[8]

Sonnet 57

Sweet warriour[9] when shall I have peace with you?
High time it is, this warre now ended were:
Which I no lenger can endure to sue,° *wage*
Ne your incessant battry more to beare:
5 So weake my powres, so sore my wounds appeare,
That wonder is how I should live a jot,
Seeing my hart through-launchéd° every where *pierced*
With thousand arrowes, which your eies have shot:
Yet shoot ye sharpely still, and spare me not,
10 But glory thinke[1] to make these cruel stoures.° *battles*
Ye cruell one, what glory can be got,
In slaying him that would live gladly yours?
Make peace therefore, and graunt me timely grace,[2]
That al my wounds wil heale in little space.[3]

6. I.e., rarefied; Spenser puns on "light," which can mean sexually lax.
7. I.e., utterly without help.
8. These *vers rapportés* summarize the images in reverse order.
9. A famous Petrarchan oxymoron; cf. *Rime* 17, "O dolce mia guerrera."
1. I.e., you think it glorious.
2. I.e., pity me before I perish.
3. I.e., soon.

Sonnet 58
By her that is most assured to her selfe.[4]

Weake is th'assurance that weake flesh reposeth
In her[5] owne powre, and scorneth others ayde:
That soonest fals when as she most supposeth
Her selfe assurd, and is of nought affrayd.
5 All flesh is frayle, and all her strength unstayd,
Like a vaine[6] bubble blowen up with ayre:
Devouring tyme and changeful chance haue prayd° *ravaged*
Her glories pride that none may it repayre.
Ne none so rich or wise, so strong or fayre,
10 But fayleth trusting on his owne assurance:
And he that standeth on the hyghest stayre
Fals lowest: for on earth nought hath enduraunce.
Why then doe ye proud fayre, misdeeme so farre,
That to your selfe ye most assuréd arre?

Sonnet 59[7]

Thrise happie she, that is so well assured
Unto her selfe and setled so in hart:
That nether will for better be allured
Ne feard° with worse to any chaunce to start,[8] *affrighted*
5 But like a steddy ship doth strongly part
The raging waves and keepes her course aright:
Ne ought for tempest doth from it depart,
Ne ought for fayrer weathers false delight.
Such selfe assurance need not feare the spight
10 Of grudging foes, ne favour seek of friends:
But in the stay[9] of her owne stedfast might,
Nether to one her selfe nor other bends.
Most happy she that most assured doth rest,
But he most happy who such one loves best.

Sonnet 60

They that in course of heavenly spheares are skild,
To every planet point° his sundry° yeare:[1] *appoint / particular*
In which her[2] circles voyage is fulfild,
As Mars in three score yeares doth run his spheare.

4. A puzzle. Does "by" mean "concerning," or is the poem said "by" the lady speaking "to herself"? Possibly, the title was intended for the following poem. The speaker's thoughts on human frailty echo biblical passages such as Isaiah 40.6–7 and 1 Corinthians 10.12.
5. I.e., the flesh's.
6. Both empty and proud; cf. Orgoglio in *The Faerie Queene* I.vii–viii.
7. Either the lady's reply or the lover's new perspective.
8. Obscurely put; the sense is that no misfortune will make her swerve.
9. I.e., guidance and support. A "stay" is a ship's rope.
1. I.e., one full revolution around the earth in the geocentric system. Spenser gives Mars an orbit of sixty years, not the correct seventy-nine, perhaps because he has spent sixty sonnets warring for the lady.
2. I.e., the sphere's; some said the crystal spheres that held the planets were guided by sirens or other beings imagined as female.

5 So since the wingéd God his planet cleare,
Began in me to move, one yeare is spent.[3]
The which doth longer unto me appeare,
Then al those fourty which my life outwent.[4]
Then by that count, which lovers books invent,
10 The spheare of Cupid fourty yeares containes,
Which I have wasted in long languishment,
That seemd the longer for my greater paines.
But let my loves fayre Planet short her wayes
This yeare ensuing,° or else short my dayes.[5] *following*

Sonnet 61

The glorious image of the makers beautie,
My soverayne saynt, the Idoll of my thought,[6]
Dare not henceforth above the bounds of dewtie,
T'accuse of pride, or rashly blame for ought.
5 For being as she is divinely wrought,
And of the brood of Angels hevenly borne:
And with the crew of blesséd Saynts upbrought,
Each of which did her with theyr guifts adorne;
The bud of joy, the blossome of the morne,
10 The beame of light, whom mortal eyes admyre:
What reason is it then but she should scorne
Base things that to her love too bold aspire?
Such heavenly formes ought rather worshipt be,[7]
Then dare be loved by men of meane degree.

Sonnet 62

The weary yeare his race now having run,
The new begins his compast course[8] anew:
With shew of morning mylde he hath begun,
Betokening peace and plenty to ensew.° *follow*
5 So let us, which° this chaunge of weather vew, *who*
Chaunge eeke our mynds and former lives amend,
The old yeares sinnes forepast let us eschew,
And fly the faults with which we did offend.
Then shall the new yeares joy forth freshly send,
10 Into the glooming° world his gladsome ray: *dark*
And all these stormes which now his beauty blend,° *pollute*

3. Spenser jokingly invents a planetary sphere for Cupid—the lover's body; it has been turning for a year.
4. I.e., went through. Spenser must have been about forty in 1594 (for the relevance of his age, see D. Cheney 1983); forty also recalls Lent and the Israelite trek to the Promised Land.
5. The lady, too, has a sphere. The lover asks her to shorten its orbit—to hurry; then Cupid and she will come into planetary conjunction. Or else, he says, shorten his days (by killing him with grief).
6. Lines 1–2 are the object of the imperative "dare" in 3: he orders himself not to accuse or blame his saint.
7. "Worship" could then mean honor, but as in *Amoretti* 22 Spenser perhaps plays, for one reason or another, with the idolatry and image-worship that Protestants condemned.
8. I.e., his curved path; Spenser almost certainly means it is March 25, start of the new civil year, also called "Lady Day" in honor of the angel's annunciation to Mary that she was to bear Jesus.

Shall turne to caulmes and tymely cleare away.
So, likewise love, cheare you your heavy spright,
And chaunge old yeares annoy to new delight.

Sonnet 63[9]

After long stormes and tempests sad assay,[1]
Which hardly[2] I enduréd heretofore,
In dread of death and daungerous dismay,
With which my silly° barke was tosséd sore:° *frail / grievously*
5 I doe at length descry the happy shore,
In which I hope ere long for to arryve:
Fayre soyle it seemes from far and fraught° with store° *laden / plenty*
Of all that deare and daynty is alyve.
Most happy he that can at last atchyve
10 The joyous safety of so sweet a rest.[3]
Whose least delight sufficeth to deprive
Remembrance of all paines which him opprest.
All paines are nothing in respect of[4] this,
All sorrowes short that gaine eternall blisse.

Sonnet 64[5]

Comming to kisse her lyps, (such grace I found)
Me seemd I smelt a gardin of sweet flowres:
That dainty odours from them threw around,
For damzels fit to decke their lovers bowres.
5 Her lips did smell lyke unto Gillyflowers,[6]
Her ruddy cheekes lyke unto Roses red:
Her snowy browes lyke budded Bellamoures,[7]
Her lovely eyes lyke Pincks but newly spred,
Her goodly bosome lyke a Strawberry bed,
10 Her neck lyke to a bounch of Cullambynes:° *columbines*
Her brest lyke lillyes, ere theyr leaves be shed,
Her nipples[8] lyke yong blossomd Jessemynes:° *jasmines*
Such fragrant flowres doe give most odorous smell,
But her sweet odour did them all excell.

Sonnet 65

The doubt which ye misdeeme,° fayre love, is vaine, *misconceive*
That fondly° feare to loose your liberty, *foolishly*

9. Cf. *Amoretti* 34; the expectation of safe harbor rewrites Petrarchan tradition.
1. I.e., assault; also trial and testing.
2. I.e., barely and with hardship.
3. Cf. *Epithalamion* 424. Here and in *The Faerie Queene* VII. 8.2 Spenser may pun on "Elizabeth" in the then common if mistaken belief (see e.g., Camden, *Remains Concerning Britain* [1605; 1974] 102) that it is Hebrew for Lord's (Eli) rest (Sabbath): Elizabeth = "eternall bliss."
4. I.e., compared to; also, in view of (Latin *respectare*, see).
5. The manner is that of the Bible's Song of Solomon, usually read as a duet by Christ and his Church (the body of believers). Greeting a lady on the lips was common.
6. A variety of pink, smelling of clove.
7. Unidentified; the name means "beautiful love."
8. Later Elizabethan necklines sometimes revealed much of the bosom, a fashion favored by the queen and connoting virginity (J. Nunn, *Fashion in Costume* [New York, 1984] 39).

When loosing one, two liberties ye gayne,
And make him bond that bondage earst dyd fly.
5 Sweet be the bands, the which true love doth tye,
Without constraynt or dread of any ill.[9]
The gentle° birde feeles no captivity *noble*
Within her cage, but singes and feeds her fill.
There pride dare not approch, nor discord spill° *destroy*
10 The league twixt them,[1] that loyal love hath bound:
But simple truth and mutuall good will
Seekes with sweet peace to salve each others wound.
There fayth doth fearlesse dwell in brasen towre,
And spotlesse pleasure builds her sacred bowre.

Sonnet 66

To all those happy blessings which ye have,
With plenteous hand by heaven upon you thrown,
This one disparagement° they to you gave, *disgrace*
That ye your love lent to so meane a one.
5 Yee whose high worths surpassing paragon° *comparison*
Could not on earth have found one fit for mate,
Ne but in heaven matchable to none,
Why did ye stoup unto so lowly state?°[2] *rank*
But ye thereby much greater glory gate,
10 Then had ye sorted° with a princes pere: *mated*
For now your light doth more it selfe dilate,° *enlarge*
And in my darknesse greater doth appeare.
Yet since your light hath once elumind me,
With my reflex yours shall encreaséd be.[3]

Sonnet 67[4]

Lyke as a huntsman after weary chace,
Seeing the game from him escapt away,
Sits downe to rest him in some shady place,
With panting hounds beguiléd of their pray:
5 So after long pursuit and vaine assay,° *attempt*
When I all weary had the chace forsooke,
The gentle deare returnd the selfe-same way,
Thinking to quench her thirst at the next° brooke. *nearby*

9. The claim that love liberates even as it binds parallels a belief that God's "service is perfect freedom" (Morning Prayer's Collect for Peace).
1. I.e., those whom: the lovers.
2. I.e., you whose incomparable worthiness could not have found anyone on earth unsuitable as a mate, you who are fit to be matched only with someone in heaven, why did you stoop to someone of such low status? In the calendrical scheme that many find (most elaborately Larsen 1997) it is now Good Friday.
3. Without radiation of his own, the lover will reflect hers and thus add to her glory. It is the first full moon after the equinox (March 11 in the old Julian calendar) that determines the date of Easter, so the lady's "dilation" of light suits the season.
4. Unlike Petrarch in *Rime* 190 (trans. Wyatt as "Whoso list to hunt . . ."), the lover catches the deer. Dasenbrock (1991) cites Tasso's "Questa fera gentil," although not even Tasso captures the prey. For an analogous poem by Marguerite de Navarre and a context for the deer, see Prescott 1985, excerpted in this Norton Critical Edition, p. 860–64.

There she beholding me with mylder looke,[5]
10 Sought not to fly, but fearelesse still did bide:
Till I in hand her yet halfe trembling tooke,
And with her owne goodwill hir fyrmely tyde.[6]
Strange thing me seemd to see a beast so wyld,
So goodly wonne with her owne will beguyld.[7]

Sonnet 68

Most glorious Lord of lyfe that on this day,[8]
Didst make thy triumph over death and sin:
And having harrowd hell didst bring away
Captivity thence captive[9] us to win:
5 This joyous day, deare Lord, with joy begin,
And grant that we for whom thou diddest dye,
Being with thy deare blood clene washt from sin,
May live for ever in felicity.
And that thy love we weighing worthily,
10 May likewise love thee for the same againe:
And for thy sake that all lyke deare didst buy,[1]
With love may one another entertayne.
So let us love, deare love, lyke as we ought,[2]
Love is the lesson which the Lord us taught.

Sonnet 69[3]

The famous warriors of the anticke world,
Used Trophees to erect in stately wize:° *manner*
In which they would the records have enrold,
Of theyr great deeds and valarous emprize.° *undertaking*
5 What trophee then shall I most fit devize,
In which I may record the memory
Of my loves conquest, peerelesse beauties prise,
Adorned with honour, love, and chastity.
Even this verse vowd to eternity,
10 Shall be thereof immortall moniment:
And tell her prayse to all posterity,
That may admire such worlds rare wonderment:° *marvel*

5. It is syntactically unclear who has the "mylder looke."
6. Deer were then often netted and bound, not immediately shot, after being caught.
7. Cf. line 4, where the dogs are "beguiléd" (cheated, tricked out of) their prey. *Will*: a complex word, for it meant not only the psychological faculty involving intention, wish, and choice but also, in some contexts, erotic desire and even the genitalia. It is highly unlikely that Spenser wishes here to be as indecently funny as is Shakespeare in Sonnet 135, but "will" permits readers to hear a recognition of the erotic in the lady's surrender.
8. I.e., Easter, which in 1594 fell on March 31. Lines 1–12 incorporate phrases from the Bible, the authorized prayer book, and the Catholic "Sarum Missal" (Prescott 1985, Larsen 1997).
9. Cf. "led captivity captive" in Psalm 68 and Ephesians 4.8. Before the Easter resurrection, said tradition, Christ sacked ("harrowed") Hell to free those destined for or worthy of salvation.
1. I.e., redeemed all alike lovingly, and at great cost (in its primary sense here, "deare" is an adverb).
2. I.e., as we should and as we owe. The couplet anticipates the gospel reading for the June 11 wedding day (Kaske 1977).
3. Compare Du Bellay, *Olive* 34.

The happy purchase° of my glorious spoile,° — *acquisition / plunder*
Gotten at last with labour and long toyle.[4]

Sonnet 70

Fresh spring the herald of loves mighty king,
In whose cote-armour[5] richly are displayd
All sorts of flowers the which on earth do spring
In goodly colours gloriously arrayd:
5 Goe to my love, where she is carelesse layd,
Yet in her winters bowre not well awake:
Tell her the joyous time wil not be staid
Unlesse she doe him by the forelock take.[6]
Bid her therefore her selfe soone ready make,
10 To wayt on love[7] amongst his lovely crew:
Where every one that misseth then her make,° — *mate*
Shall be by him amearst° with penance dew. — *punished*
Make hast therefore sweet love, whilest it is prime,° — *spring*
For none can call againe the passéd time.

Sonnet 71

I joy to see how in your drawen work,[8]
Your selfe unto the Bee ye doe compare;
And me unto the Spyder that doth lurke,
In close awayt° to catch her unaware. — *ambush*
5 Right so your selfe were caught in cunning snare
Of a deare foe, and thralléd° to his love: — *enslaved*
In whose streight° bands ye now captivéd are — *tight*
So firmely, that ye never may remove.
But as your worke is woven all about[9]
10 With woodbynd flowers and fragrant Eglantine.[1]
So sweet your prison you in time shall prove,° — *find*
With many deare delights bedeckéd fyne.
And all thensforth eternall peace shall see,
Betweene the Spyder and the gentle Bee.

Sonnet 72[2]

Oft when my spirit doth spred her bolder winges,
In mind to mount up to the purest sky:
It down is weighd with thoght of earthly things
And clogd with burden of mortality,[3]

4. He did not, strictly, win the lady, yet Paul calls Christ's resurrection our "victory" (1 Corinthians 15).
5. A herald's formal costume; Spring precedes Cupid to announce his decrees.
6. Opportunity is proverbially bald behind: grab his forelock as he passes or miss your chance.
7. I.e., to attend and serve Love.
8. Tapestry work done by drawing out threads to form patterns.
9. The 1595 edition has "above."
1. Wild rose; *woodbynd*: honeysuckle. Both plants are emblems of pleasing entanglement. Donald Cheney (1980) suggests that "*bee*" and "*spider*" allude to *Boyle* and *Spenser*.
2. The opening lines adapt Tasso's "L'alma vaga."
3. A common emblematic image; cf. Alciato 121. Often the winged figure with a clog (a weighted chain) symbolized ambition hampered by poverty.

5 Where when that soverayne beauty it doth spy,
Resembling heavens glory in her light:
Drawne with sweet pleasures bayt, it back doth fly,
And unto heaven forgets her former flight.
There my fraile fancy fed with full delight,
10 Doth bath in blisse and mantleth most at ease:[4]
Ne thinks of other heaven, but how it might
Her harts desire with most contentment please.
Hart need not wish none other happinesse,
But here on earth to have such hevens blisse.

Sonnet 73[5]

Being my selfe captyvéd here in care,
My hart, whom none with servile bands can tye,
But the fayre tresses of your golden hayre,
Breaking his prison forth to you doth fly.
5 Lyke as a byrd that in ones hand doth spy
Desiréd food, to it doth make his flight:
Even so my hart, that wont on your fayre eye
To feed his fill, flyes backe unto your sight.
Doe you him take, and in your bosome bright,
10 Gently encage, that he may be your thrall:
Perhaps he there may learne with rare delight,
To sing your name and prayses over all.
That it hereafter may you not repent,
Him lodging in your bosome to have lent.

Sonnet 74

Most happy letters framed by skilfull trade,
With which that happy name[6] was first desynd:
The which three times thrise happy hath me made,
With guifts of body, fortune and of mind.
5 The first my being to me gave by kind,° *nature*
From mothers womb derived by dew descent,
The second is my sovereigne Queene most kind,
That honour and large richesse to me lent.
The third my love, my lives last ornament,
10 By whom my spirit out of dust was raysed:
To speake her prayse and glory excellent,
Of all alive most worthy to be praysed.
Ye three Elizabeths for ever live,
That three such graces did unto me give.

Sonnet 75

One day I wrote her name upon the strand,° *beach*
But came the waves and washéd it away:

4. I.e., stretches wings and legs to ease them (a term from hawking).
5. An increasingly free adaptation of Tasso's "Donna, poichè fortuna."
6. I.e., the nine letters of "Elizabeth."

Agayne I wrote it with a second hand,
But came the tyde, and made my paynes his pray.° *prey*
5 "Vayne man," sayd she, "that doest in vaine assay
A mortall thing so to immortalize,
For I my selve shall lyke to this decay,
And eek my name bee wypéd out lykewize."
"Not so," quod I, "let baser things devize° *contrive*
10 To dy in dust, but you shall live by fame:
My verse your vertues rare shall eternize,
And in the hevens wryte your glorious name.
Where whenas death shall all the world subdew,
Our love shall live, and later life renew."

Sonnet 76[7]

Fayre bosome fraught with vertues richest tresure,
The neast of love, the lodging of delight:
The bowre of blisse,[8] the paradice of pleasure,
The sacred harbour of that hevenly spright:
5 How was I ravisht with your lovely sight,
And my frayle thoughts too rashly led astray?
Whiles diving deepe through amorous insight,
On the sweet spoyle of beautie they did pray.
And twixt her paps° like early fruit in May, *nipples*
10 Whose harvest seemd to hasten now apace:
They loosely did theyr wanton winges display,
And there to rest themselves did boldly place.
Sweet thoughts I envy your so happy rest,
Which oft I wisht, yet never was so blest.

Sonnet 77

Was it a dreame, or did I see it playne,
A goodly table of pure yvory:
All spred with juncats,° fit to entertayne *delicacies*
The greatest Prince with pompous roialty?
5 Mongst which there in a silver dish did ly
Twoo golden apples of unvalewd° price: *inestimable*
Far passing those which Hercules came by,
Or those which Atalanta did entice.[9]
Exceeding sweet, yet voyd of sinfull vice,
10 That many sought yet none could ever taste,
Sweet fruit of pleasure brought from paradice

7. *Amoretti* 76 and 77 derive loosely from Tasso's "Il seno di madonna."
8. A contrast with the deceptive bower in *The Faerie Queene* II.x. Severer readers have taken the thoughts here and in *Amoretti* 77 as signs of lapse or aggression; the lover only calls them rash (possibly because premature) and could cite in their defense Proverbs 5.19: "Let [your wife] be as the loving hind . . . let her breasts satisfy thee at all times."
9. On an island garden west of North Africa grew golden apples guarded by a dragon and tended by the Hesperides, daughters of the evening star Hesperus (alternatively, of Atlas); Hercules stole some as one of his labors. Atalanta would marry only a man able to outrace her (losers were executed). Venus gave Hippomenes three gold apples with which to distract her while she ran; he won (Ovid, *Metamorphoses* 10).

By Love himselfe and in his garden plaste.
Her brest that table was so richly spredd,
My thoughts the guests, which would thereon have fedd.

Sonnet 78

Lackyng my love I go from place to place,
Lyke a young fawne that late hath lost the hynd.[1]
And seeke each where, where last I sawe her face,
Whose ymage yet I carry fresh in mynd.[2]
5 I seeke the fields with her late footing synd,[3]
I seeke her bowre with her late presence deckt,
Yet nor in field nor bowre I her can fynd:
Yet field and bowre are full of her aspect.
But when myne eyes I thereunto direct,
10 They ydly back returne to me agayne,
And when I hope to see theyr trew obiect,
I fynd my selfe but fed with fancies vayne.
Ceasse then myne eyes, to seeke her selfe to see,
And let my thoughts behold her selfe in mee.

Sonnet 79

Men call you fayre, and you doe credit° it, *believe*
For that your selfe ye dayly such doe see:
But the trew fayre,° that is the gentle wit, *beauty*
And vertuous mind, is much more praysd of° me. *by*
5 For all the rest, how ever fayre it be,
Shall turne to nought and loose that glorious hew:° *appearance*
But onely that[4] is permanent and free
From frayle corruption, that doth flesh ensew.° *attend*
That is true beautie: that doth argue you
10 To be divine and borne of heavenly seed:
Derived from that fayre Spirit,[5] from whom al true
And perfect beauty did at first proceed.
He onely fayre, and what he fayre hath made,
All other fayre lyke flowres untymely fade.[6]

1. C.f. Horace's comparison of his timidly unwilling Chloé to a trembling fawn seeking its mother (*Odes* 1.23).
2. If Spenser still wants us to remember the church calendar, he may also hope we recall that while awaiting the return of their absent bridegroom (Christ), Christians harbor the Spirit inside them (John 14.16). In any case, Spenser reworks a Petrarchan theme of absence.
3. I.e., bearing signs (footprints) of her recent presence, perhaps with overtones of the vestigial "signs" of God still legible in the natural world; see E. Curtius, *European Literature and the Latin Middle Ages* (Princeton, 1953) ch. 16.
4. I.e., that true beauty of wit and mind, but the syntax allows other readings.
5. I.e., God as the Holy Spirit.
6. I.e., only God is beautiful—he and the things he has made beautiful (or made beautifully); all other beauty fades too soon, like flowers.

Sonnet 80[7]

After so long a race as I have run
Through Faery land, which those six books compile,° *comprise*
Give leave to rest me being halfe fordonne,° *exhausted*
And gather to my selfe new breath awhile.
5 Then as a steed refreshéd after toyle,
Out of my prison I will breake anew:
And stoutly° will that second worke assoyle,° *boldly / release*
With strong endevour and attention dew.
Till then give leave to me in pleasant mew[8]
10 To sport my muse, and sing my loves sweet praise:
The contemplation of whose heavenly hew,
My spirit to an higher pitch will rayse.
But let her prayses yet be low and meane,[9]
Fit for the handmayd of the Faery Queene.

Sonnet 81[1]

Fayre is my love, when her fayre golden heares,
With the loose wynd ye waving chance to marke.[2]
Fayre when the rose in her red cheekes appeares,
Or in her eyes the fyre of love does sparke.
5 Fayre when her brest lyke a rich laden barke,
With pretious merchandize she forth doth lay:
Fayre when that cloud of pryde, which oft doth dark
Her goodly light, with smiles she drives away.
But fayrest she, when so she doth display
10 The gate with pearles and rubyes richly dight:° *adorned*
Throgh which her words so wise do make their way
To beare the message of her gentle spright:
The rest be works of natures wonderment,
But this the worke of harts astonishment.

Sonnet 82

Joy of my life, full oft for loving you
I blesse my lot, that was so lucky placed:
But then the more your owne mishap I rew,
That are so much by so meane love embased.° *degraded*
5 For had the equall° hevens so much you graced *equitable*
In this as in the rest, ye mote invent
Som hevenly wit, whose verse could have enchased[3]

7. *Amoretti* 80 helps date the composition of *The Faerie Queene* IV–VI, although Spenser may have revised before publication in 1596; apparently in 1594 he hoped, or wished to seem he hoped, to write *The Faerie Queene* VII–XII.
8. I.e., confinement; also a cage for a molting hawk as it grows new feathers.
9. I.e., common, but also moderate (as in "golden mean"); cf. *The Faerie Queene* VI.x.28 and note.
1. Spenser adapts Tasso's "Bella è la donna mia," adding his own conclusion.
2. I.e., when you happen to notice her hair waving in the loose wind; evidently her hair is also loose, as suited unwed women.
3. I.e., put in a setting, like a jewel, so as to show it to advantage; the word also meant to enclose.

Your glorious name in golden moniment.
But since ye deignd so goodly to relent
10 To me your thrall, in whom is little worth,
That little that I am, shall all be spent,
In setting your immortall prayses forth.
Whose lofty argument uplifting me,
Shall lift you up unto an high degree.

Sonnet 83[4]

My hungry eyes, through greedy covetize,
Still° to behold the object of theyr payne: *always*
With no contentment can themselues suffize,° *satisfy*
But having pine, and having not complayne.
5 For lacking it, they cannot lyfe sustayne,
And seeing it,[5] they gaze on it the more:
In theyr amazement lyke Narcissus vayne
Whose eyes him starved: so plenty makes me pore.
Yet are myne eyes so filléd with the store
10 Of that fayre sight, that nothing else they brooke:° *endure*
But loath the things which they did like before,
And can no more endure on them to looke.
All this worlds glory seemeth vayne to me,
And all theyr shewes but shadowes saving° she. *except*

Sonnet 84[6]

Let not one sparke of filthy lustfull fyre[7]
Breake out, that may her sacred peace molest:
Ne one light glance of sensuall desyre
Attempt to work her gentle mindes unrest.
5 But pure affections bred in spotlesse brest,
And modest thoughts breathd from wel tempred sprites,
Goe visit her in her chast bowre of rest,
Accompanyde with ángelick delightes.
There fill your selfe with those most joyous sights,
10 The which my selfe could never yet attayne:
But speake no word to her of these sad plights,
Which her too constant stiffenesse doth constrayn.° *enforce*
Onely behold her rare perfection,[8]
And blesse your fortunes fayre election.

Sonnet 85

The world that cannot deeme° of worthy things, *judge*
When I doe praise her, say I doe but flatter:

4. Almost identical to *Amoretti* 35; the repetition may be an error by Spenser or his printer, but it fits some numerological or calendrical schemes and its new context may subtly modify its meaning.
5. In *Amoretti* 35 the eyes "have"; here they "see."
6. The opening adapts Tasso, "Uom di non pure fiamme."
7. I.e., a sexual urge that ignores her virtue, spirit, or feelings; as he elsewhere makes clear, Spenser did not disdain physical desire except when misdirected or untimely.
8. In Elizabethan verse the suffix "-tion" was often disyllabic.

So does the Cuckow, when the Mavis[9] sings,
Begin his witlesse note apace to clatter.
5 But they that skill not of so heavenly matter,
All that they know not, envy or admyre,
Rather then envy let them wonder at her,
But not to deeme of her desert aspire:[1]
Deepe in the closet of my parts entyre,° *interior*
10 Her worth is written with a golden quill:
That me with heavenly fury[2] doth inspire,
And my glad mouth with her sweet prayses fill.
Which when as fame in her shrill trump shal thunder,
Let the world chose to envy or to wonder.

Sonnet 86

Venemous toung tipt with vile adders sting,
Of that selfe kynd with which the Furies fell
Theyr snaky heads doe combe, from which a spring
Of poysoned words and spitefull speeches well.[3]
5 Let all the plagues and horrid paines of hell,
Upon thee fall for thine accurséd hyre:° *punishment*
That with false forgéd° lyes, which thou didst tel, *feigned*
In my true love did stirre up coles of yre,
The sparkes whereof let kindle thine own fyre,
10 And catching hold on thine owne wicked hed
Consume thee quite, that didst with guile conspire
In my sweet peace such breaches to have bred.
Shame be thy meed,° and mischiefe thy reward, *payment*
Dew° to thy selfe that it for me prepard.[4] *due*

Sonnet 87

Since I did leave the presence of my love,
Many long weary dayes I have outworne:
And many nights, that slowly seemd to move
Theyr sad protract° from evening untill morne. *duration*
5 For when as day the heaven doth adorne,
I wish that night the noyous° day would end: *vexatious*
And when as night hath us of light forlorne,° *deprived*
I wish that day would shortly reascend.
Thus I the time with expectation spend,

9. I.e., song thrush. Now the lover denigrates the traditionally adulterous cuckoo that in *Amoretti* 19 was Spring's messenger.
1. Those ignorant of heavenly matters respond to what they do not understand with either wonder or envy; so let them wonder at rather than envy the lady, and not try to judge her merit.
2. I.e., divine madness, Platonic language for inspiration infused by the Muses; cf. Plato's *Phaedrus*.
3. Spenser merges the Furies (Hades' enforcers, the Erinyes) with a common image of Envy as a snaky-haired hag chewing a viper and spewing slander (cf. Ovid, *Metamorphoses* 2.760ff. and Alciato, *Emblemata* 71). Perhaps Spenser was slandered to Elizabeth Boyle, but he may also need to find new causes for the pain that sonnet sequences fed on. If the religious subtext still operates, readers can recall that Jesus told his followers to expect slander.
4. I.e., the shame you prepared for me is due instead to you. Cf. Psalms 57, in which David says his slanderers will fall into the traps they set for him.

10 And faine° my griefe with chaunges to beguile, *desiring*
That[5] further seemes his terme still to extend,
And maketh every minute seeme a myle.
So sorrow still° doth seeme too long to last, *always*
But joyous houres doo fly away too fast.

Sonnet 88

Since I have lackt the comfort of that light,
The which was wont to lead my thoughts astray,
I wander as in darknesse of the night,
Affrayd of every dangers least dismay.° *threat*
5 Ne ought I see, though in the clearest day,
When others gaze upon theyr shadowes vayne.[6]
But th'onely[7] image of that heavenly ray,
Whereof some glance doth in mine eie remayne.
Of which beholding the Idæa playne,
10 Through contemplation of my purest part,
With light thereof I doe my selfe sustayne,
And thereon feed my love-affamisht hart.
But with such brightnesse whylest I fill my mind,
I starve my body and mine eyes doe blynd.

Sonnet 89[8]

Lyke as the Culver° on the baréd bough, *dove*
Sits mourning for the absence of her mate:
And in her songs sends many a wishfull vow,
For his returne that seemes to linger late.
5 So I alone now left disconsolate,
Mourne to my selfe the absence of my love:
And wandring here and there all desolate,
Seek with my playnts to match that mournful dove:
Ne joy of ought that under heaven doth hove° *abide*
10 Can comfort me, but her owne joyous sight:
Whose sweet aspect° both God and man can move, *sight*
In her unspotted pleasauns[9] to delight.
Dark is my day, whyles her fayre light I mis,
And dead my life that wants° such lively blis. *lacks*

5. I.e., my effort to elude my sorrow by changing my desires seems only to extend its duration; if we take "faine" as "feign," he means he pretends to delude grief by looking for change.
6. The shadows are "vayne" because made by mere physical light; cf. Plato's allegory in which those who prefer appearance watch shadows on a firelit cave wall (*Republic* 7). The lady's light is transcendently real; with sparkles of it still in his eyes, the lover can see her divine form when he looks in his soul, feeding his heart. For religious parallels, cf. "in thy light shall we see light" (Psalms 36.9).
7. I.e., but only the image.
8. Doves symbolize fidelity, and if betrothed the lovers are now legally "mated." The bare branch suggests winter; perhaps, despite the June date of *Epithalamion*, Spenser refers to the Advent season of waiting, or at least to chilly weather, so as to recall a liturgical circle that bends back toward its cold beginning.
9. I.e., pleasantness; also a garden's pleasure area. Dove and garden together recall the lovers in the Song of Solomon: there the groom is a singing dove (2.12) and the bride an enclosed garden (4.12).

[Anacreontics]†

[1]

In youth, before I waxéd old,
The blynd boy, Venus baby,
For want of cunning made me bold,
In bitter hyve to grope for honny.

5 But when he saw me stung and cry,
He tooke his wings and away did fly.

[2][1]

As Diane hunted on a day,
She chaunst to come where Cupid lay,
his quiver by his head:
10 One of his shafts she stole away,
And one of hers did close° convay, *secretly*
into the others stead:° *place*
With that love wounded my loves hart,
but Diane beasts with Cupids dart.[2]

[3][3]

15 I Saw in secret to my Dame,
How little Cupid humbly came:
and sayd to her, "All hayle, my mother."
But when he saw me laugh, for shame
His face with bashfull blood did flame,
20 not knowing Venus from the other.
"Then never blush, Cupid," quoth I,
"for many have erred in this beauty."[4]

[4][5]

Upon a day, as love lay sweetly slumbring
all in his mothers lap:

† In the first edition these lyrics lack titles and any indication that they are separate poems. Many call them "Anacreontics" because they resemble poems wrongly ascribed to Anacreon (sixth century B.C.E.), singer of boys and wine who died at eighty-five after, some said, choking on a grape seed. Henri Estienne's 1554 edition of *Anacreontea* started a fashion for them. True, a wine-and-roses manner and a taste for self-consciously exquisite erotic anecdotes preceded the recovery of "Anacreon," and Spenser adapts two epigrams by the older poet Clément Marot. Nevertheless these Anacreontics signal stylish and learned elegance.

1. Based on Marot's 1538 First Book of epigrams #63, "L'Enfant Amour" (Rigolot ed. I.448).
2. Cupid shot the lady's heart with the huntress Diana's arrow (making her chaste), whereas Diana shot animals with Cupid's arrow (inflaming them sexually). "Beasts" is the object of the understood "wounded."
3. A close translation of Marot's "Amour trouva celle," #128 in the 1638 Second Book of epigrams (Rigolot ed. I.466)
4. I.e., have mistaken my lady for Venus. "Quoth" then sounded like "quote" and the first syllable of "beauty" could be pronounced "bo," as in French, so the rhyme works.
5. The story of Cupid and the bee was popular. Renaissance versions derive finally from a poem by Bion or Moschus once attributed to Theocritus, or from an ancient imitation first printed in the 1554 *Anacreontea*. Spenser follows Tasso's "Mentre in grembo" for two stanzas and then, with a glance at Ronsard and others, goes his own way (Hutton 1941).

25 A gentle Bee with his loud trumpet murm'ring,
  about him flew by hap.° *chance*
Whereof when he was wakened with the noyse,
  and saw the beast so small:
"Whats this," quoth he, "that gives so great a voyce,
30   that wakens men withall?
In angry wize° he flyes about, *manner*
  and threatens all with corage stout.° *doughty*

To whom his mother closely° smiling sayd, *privately*
  twixt earnest and twixt game:
35 "See thou thy selfe likewise art lyttle made,
  if thou regard° the same. *behold*
And yet thou suffrest neyther gods in sky,
  nor men in earth to rest:
But when thou art disposéd cruelly,
40   theyr sleepe thou doost molest.
Then eyther change thy cruelty,
  or give lyke leave unto the fly."[6]

Nathlesse the cruell boy not so content,
  would needs the fly pursue:
45 And in his hand with heedlesse hardiment,° *boldness*
  him caught for to subdue.
But when on it he hasty hand did lay,
  the Bee him stung therefore:
"Now out alasse," he cryde, "and welaway,"[7]
50   I wounded am full sore:
The fly that I so much did scorne,
  hath hurt me with his little horne."

Unto his mother straight he weeping came,
  and of his griefe complayned:
55 Who could not chose° but laugh at his fond game, *choose*
  though sad to see him pained.
"Think now," quod she, "my sonne how great the smart
  of those whom thou dost wound:
Full many thou hast prickéd to the hart,
60   that pitty never found:[8]
Therefore henceforth some pitty take,
  when thou doest spoyle° of lovers make." *pillage*

She tooke him streight full pitiously lamenting,
  and wrapt him in her smock:
65 She wrapt him softly, all the while repenting,[9]
  that he the fly did mock.
She drest his wound and it embaulmed[1] wel

6. Any winged insect.
7. "Out alas" and "welaway" were common expressions of anguish.
8. I.e., who never had mercy from you.
9. In modern grammar a misplaced participle; it is Cupid who repents.
1. I.e., anointed with ointment.

with salve of soveraigne might:
And then she bathed him in a dainty well,
70 the well of deare delight.
Who would not oft be stung as this,
to be so bathed in Venus blis?

The wanton boy was shortly wel recured° *recovered*
of that his malady:
75 But he soone after fresh againe enured° *commenced*
his former cruelty.
And since that time he wounded hath my selfe
with his sharpe dart of love:
And now forgets the cruell carelesse elfe
80 his mothers heast° to prove:° *bidding / do*
So now I languish till he please
my pining anguish to appease.

Epithalamion†

[1]

Ye learned sisters[1] which have oftentimes
Beene to me ayding, others to adorne:
Whom ye thought worthy of your gracefull rymes,
That even the greatest did not greatly scorne
5 To heare theyr names sung in your simple layes,
But joyéd in theyr prayse.
And when ye list your owne mishaps to mourne,
Which death, or love, or fortunes wreck did rayse,
Your string could soone to sadder tenor° turne, *mood*
10 And teach the woods and waters to lament
Your dolefull dreriment.° *grief*
Now lay those sorrowfull complaints aside,
And having all your heads with girland crownd,
Helpe me mine owne loves prayses to resound,° *celebrate*
15 Ne let the same of° any be envide: *by*
So Orpheus[2] did for his owne bride,
So I unto my selfe alone will sing,
The woods shall to me answer and my Eccho ring.

† Literally, Greek for "before the bedchamber," the first known use of the term in English. Spenser's most famous model or precedent was an epithalamion by the Roman poet Catullus (*Carmina* #61) together with the following a dialogue between "youths" and "maidens" (*Carmina* #62), both with refrains invoking Hymen, the torch-bearing god of weddings. The genre became fashionable in the Renaissance: Jean Salmon Macrin published a *Livre des épithalames* in 1531 and Jan van der Noot, for whom Spenser had translated the verse in the *Theatre for Worldlings*, wrote one in Dutch.

1. The nine Muses.
2. Cf. *Amoretti* 40; the singer Orpheus moved Pluto to release the dead Eurydice, but he lost her again when he broke a promise not to look back as he led her home.

[2]

Early before the worlds light giving lampe,
20 His golden beame upon the hils doth spred,
Having disperst the nights unchearefull dampe,
Doe ye awake, and with fresh lusty hed,[3]
Go to the bowre° of my belovéd love, *chamber*
My truest turtle dove,
25 Bid her awake; for Hymen is awake,
And long since ready forth his maske to move,
With his bright Tead° that flames with many a flake,° *torch / spark*
And many a bachelor to waite on him,
In theyr fresh garments trim.
30 Bid her awake therefore and soone her dight,° *dress*
For lo the wishéd day is come at last,
That shall for al the paynes and sorrowes past,
Pay to her usury of long delight:
And whylest she doth her dight,
35 Doe ye to her of joy and solace° sing, *pleasure*
That all the woods may answer and your eccho ring.

[3]

Bring with you all the Nymphes that you can heare[4]
Both of the rivers and the forrests greene:
And of the sea that neighbours to her neare,
40 Al with gay girlands goodly wel beseene.[5]
And let them also with them bring in hand,
Another gay girland
For my fayre love of lillyes and of roses,
Bound truelove wise with a blew silke riband.[6]
45 And let them make great store of bridale poses,° *posies*
And let them eeke° bring store of other flowers *also*
To deck the bridale bowers.
And let the ground whereas her foot shall tread,
For feare the stones her tender foot should wrong
50 Be strewed with fragrant flowers all along,
And diapred lyke the discolored mead:[7]
Which done, doe at her chamber dore awayt,
For she will waken strayt,° *straightway*
The whiles doe ye this song unto her sing,
55 The woods shall to you answer and your Eccho ring.

3. I.e., vigor.
4. I.e., that can hear you.
5. I.e., attractively adorned; *sea*: could be the coastal waters near Yougal, near where Elizabeth Boyle had relatives (cf. Larsen 1997, note).
6. Symbolizing the fidelity of true love.
7. I.e., diversely adorned like the varicolored meadows.

[4]

Ye Nymphes of Mulla[8] which with carefull heed,
The silver scaly trouts doe tend full well,
And greedy pikes which use therein to feed,
(Those trouts and pikes all others doo excell)
60 And ye likewise which keepe the rushy lake,
Where none doo fishes take,
Bynd up the locks the which hang scatterd light,
And in his waters which your mirror make,
Behold your faces as the christall bright,
65 That when you come whereas my love doth lie,
No blemish she may spie.
And eke ye lightfoot mayds which keepe the deere,[9]
That on the hoary mountayne use to towre,[1]
And the wylde wolves which seeke them to devoure,[2]
70 With your steele darts doo chace from comming neer
Be also present heere,
To helpe to decke her and to help to sing,
That all the woods may answer and your eccho ring.

[5]

Wake, now my love, awake;[3] for it is time,
75 The Rosy Morne long since left Tithones[4] bed,
All ready to her silver coche to clyme,
And Phoebus gins to shew his glorious hed.
Hark how the cheerefull birds do chaunt theyr laies
And carroll of loves praise.
80 The merry Larke hir mattins° sings aloft, *morning song*
The thrush replyes, the Mavis descant playes,[5]
The Ouzell° shrills, the Ruddock° warbles soft, *blackbird / robin*
So goodly all agree with sweet consent,
To this dayes merriment.
85 Ah my deere love why doe ye sleepe thus long,
When meeter° were that ye should now awake, *more fitting*
T'awayt the comming of your joyous make,° *mate*
And hearken to the birds lovelearnéd song,
The deawy leaves among.
90 For they of joy and pleasance to you sing,
That all the woods them answer and theyr eccho ring.

8. The river Awbeg, near Spenser's Irish estate of Kilcolman; cf. *Mutabilitie* vi.41.
9. In the 1611 edition the maids keep the "dore" (door), doubtless the printer's mistake.
1. A hawking term meaning "to soar"; here, "to frequent high places."
2. Cf. *Mutabilitie* vi.55 and note.
3. Cf. the Song of Solomon 2.10–13; the Song was read as an allegory of the love between Christ and "the faithful soule or his Church . . . appointed to be his spouse" (headnote in the Geneva translation). The Elizabethan prayerbook says marriage was "instituted of God in paradise" and signifies "the mystical union, that is betwixt Christ and his Church."
4. The husband of Aurora, goddess of the dawn; cf. Homer, *Iliad* 11.1–12.
5. I.e., the thrush carols the melody. Such bird consorts were conventional in medieval poetry; cf. Chaucer's *Romance of the Rose* 655–68.

[6]

My love is now awake out of her dreame,
And her fayre eyes like stars that dimméd were
With darksome cloud, now shew theyr goodly beams
95 More bright then Hesperus[6] his head doth rere.
Come now ye damzels, daughters of delight,
Helpe quickly her to dight,
But first come ye fayre houres[7] which were begot
In Joves sweet paradice, of Day and Night,
100 Which doe the seasons of the yeare allot,
And al that ever in this world is fayre
Doe make and still° repayre. *continually*
And ye three handmayds of the Cyprian Queene,[8]
The which doe still adorne her beauties pride,
105 Helpe to addorne my beautifullest bride:
And as ye her array, still throw betweene° *at intervals*
Some graces to be seene,
And as ye use to Venus, to her sing,
The whiles the woods shal answer and your eccho ring.

[7]

110 Now is my love all ready forth to come,
Let all the virgins therefore well awayt,
And ye fresh boyes that tend upon her groome
Prepare your selves; for he is comming strayt.
Set all your things in seemely good aray
115 Fit for so joyfull day,
The joyfulst day that ever sunne did see.
Faire Sun, shew forth thy favourable ray,
And let thy lifull° heat not fervent be *life-giving*
For feare of burning her sunshyny face,
120 Her beauty to disgrace.° *mar*
O fayrest Phoebus, father of the Muse,[9]
If ever I did honour thee aright,
Or sing the thing, that mote° thy mind delight, *might*
Doe not thy servants simple boone° refuse, *request*
125 But let this day let this one day be myne,
Let all the rest be thine.
Then I thy soverayne prayses loud wil sing,
That all the woods shal answer and theyr eccho ring.

6. The evening star, usually but not always Venus; as in *Prothalamion* 164, Spenser associates Hesperus with the morning star (usually Venus).
7. On the Hours, see *Mutabilitie* vii.45; cf. Comes (*Mythologiae* 4.16), who says the Hours control the seasons and preserve natural beauty. See also Hieatt 1960, 32–41.
8. I.e., the Graces (Aglaia, Euphrosyne, and Thalia) attendant on Venus, who was born from sea-foam near Cyprus (the foam, said one tradition, came from the genitals of Uranos after his son Cronos castrated him).
9. Usually Spenser agrees with Hesiod (*Theogony* 77) in making Jove the Muses' sire; to call Apollo their father may show the influence of some other source or a willingness to modify tradition.

[8]

Harke how the Minstrels gin to shrill aloud
130 Their merry Musick that resounds from far,
The pipe, the tabor, and the trembling Croud,[1]
That well agree withouten breach or jar.° *discord*
But most of all the Damzels doe delite,
When they their tymbrels° smyte, *tambourines*
135 And thereunto doe daunce and carrol sweet,
That all the sences they doe ravish quite,
The whyles the boyes run up and downe the street,
Crying aloud with strong confuséd noyce,
As if it were one voyce.
140 *Hymen iô Hymen, Hymen* they do shout,
That even to the heavens theyr shouting shrill
Doth reach, and all the firmament doth fill,
To which the people standing all about,
As in approvance doe thereto applaud
145 And loud advaunce her laud,[2]
And evermore they *Hymen Hymen* sing,
That al the woods them answer and theyr eccho ring.

[9]

Loe where she comes along with portly° pace, *stately*
Lyke Phoebe[3] from her chamber of the East,
150 Arysing forth to run her mighty race,[4]
Clad all in white, that seemes° a virgin best. *suits*
So well it her beseemes that ye would weene
Some angell she had beene.
Her long loose yellow locks lyke golden wyre,
155 Sprinckled with perle, and perling[5] flowres a tweene,
Doe lyke a golden mantle her attyre,
And being crownéd with a girland greene,
Seeme lyke some mayden Queene.[6]
Her modest eyes abashéd to behold
160 So many gazers, as on her do stare,
Upon the lowly ground affixéd are.
Ne dare lift up her countenance too bold,
But blush to heare her prayses sung so loud,
So farre from being proud.
165 Nathlesse° doe ye still loud her prayses sing. *nevertheless*
That all the woods may answer and your eccho ring.

1. I.e., bagpipe (cf. *The Faerie Queene* VI.x.18), drum, and fiddle, used in Irish popular music.
2. I.e., sing her praises.
3. Diana, virgin goddess of the moon.
4. In Psalm 19 the sun rises like "a bridegroom coming out of his chamber, and rejoiceth as a strong man to run a race."
5. Winding; or perhaps lacework flowers.
6. Perhaps gracefully recalling Elizabeth I; cf. *Amoretti* 74.

[10]

Tell me ye merchants daughters did ye see
So fayre a creature in your towne before,
So sweet, so lovely, and so mild as she,
170 Adornd with beautyes grace and vertues store,° *wealth*
Her goodly eyes lyke Saphyres shining bright,
Her forehead yvory white,
Her cheekes lyke apples which the sun hath rudded,° *reddened*
Her lips lyke cherryes charming men to byte,
175 Her brest like to a bowle of creame uncrudded,° *uncurdled*
Her paps lyke lyllies budded,
Her snowie necke lyke to a marble towre,[7]
And all her body like a pallace fayre,
Ascending uppe with many a stately stayre,
180 To honors seat and chastities sweet bowre.[8]
Why stand ye still ye virgins in amaze,
Upon her so to gaze,
Whiles ye forget your former lay to sing,
To which the woods did answer and your eccho ring.

[11]

185 But if ye saw that which no eyes can see,
The inward beauty of her lively spright,[9]
Garnisht with heavenly guifts of high degree,
Much more then would ye wonder at that sight,
And stand astonisht lyke to those which red° *saw*
190 Medusaes mazeful hed.[1]
There dwels sweet love and constant chastity,
Unspotted fayth and comely womanhood,
Regard of honour and mild modesty,
There vertue raynes as Queene in royal throne,
195 And giveth lawes alone.
The which the base affections[2] doe obay,
And yeeld theyr services unto her will,
Ne thought of thing uncomely° ever may *unbecoming*
Thereto approch to tempt her mind to ill.
200 Had ye once seene these her celestial threasures,
And unrevealéd pleasures,
Then would ye wonder and her prayses sing,
That al the woods should answer and your echo ring.

7. "Thy neck is as a tower of ivory" (Song of Solomon 7.4); the allusion concludes a catalogue of attractions drawing on classical and Renaissance conventions. Comparing a woman to a building or city (or vice versa) was traditional.
8. I.e., to the head, seat of reason and of the higher faculties generally.
9. I.e., living spirit; soul.
1. All who looked directly at Medusa, a Gorgon whose hair Athena had turned into what could look like a maze of snakes, became stone. The comparison might seem shocking, perhaps the result of erotic anxiety, but other Renaissance writers had read Medusa as signifying the spiritual beauty that produces awed fear (Young 1973).
2. I.e., the lower passions.

[12]

Open the temple gates unto my love,
205 Open them wide that she may enter in,[3]
And all the postes adorne as doth behove,[4]
And all the pillours deck with girlands trim,
For to recyve this Saynt[5] with honour dew,
That commeth in to you.
210 With trembling steps and humble reverence,
She commeth in, before th'almighties vew,
Of her ye virgins learne obedience,
When so ye come into those holy places,
To humble your proud faces;
215 Bring her up to th'high altar, that she may
The sacred ceremonies there partake,
The which do endlesse matrimony make,
And let the roring Organs loudly play
The praises of the Lord in lively notes,
220 The whiles with hollow throates
The Choristers the joyous Antheme sing,
That al the woods may answere and their eccho ring.

[13]

Behold whiles she before the altar stands
Hearing the holy priest that to her speakes
225 And blesseth her with his two happy hands,[6]
How the red roses flush up in her cheekes,
And the pure snow with goodly vermill° stayne, *vermilion*
Like crimsin dyde in grayne,[7]
That even th'Angels which continually,
230 About the sacred Altare doe remaine,
Forget their service and about her fly,
Ofte peeping in her face that seemes more fayre,
The more they on it stare.
But her sad° eyes still fastened on the ground, *grave*
235 Are governéd with goodly modesty,
That suffers not one looke to glaunce awry,
Which may let in a little thought unsownd.° *immodest*
Why blush ye love to give to me your hand,
The pledge of all our band?° *bond*
240 Sing ye sweet Angels, Alleluya sing,
That all the woods may answere and your eccho ring.

3. "Open yee the gates, that the righteous nation which keepeth the truth may enter in" (Isaiah 26.2). Cf. Psalms 14.7, often read as referring to Christ.
4. I.e., adorn the doorposts, as is fitting. Symbolic decoration of doorposts (e.g., with myrtle, sacred to Venus) was common at ancient weddings.
5. In Protestant terminology, a "saint" was anyone assured of salvation.
6. I.e., hands that bestow happiness by virtue of the priest's blessing—and the priest may be happy.
7. I.e., thoroughly; fast.

[14]

Now al is done; bring home the bride againe,
Bring home the triumph of our victory,
Bring home with you the glory of her gaine,[8]
245 With joyance bring her and with jollity.
Never had man more joyfull day then this,
Whom heaven would heape with blis.
Make feast therefore now all this live long day,
This day for ever to me holy is,
250 Poure out the wine without restraint or stay,
Poure not by cups, but by the belly full,
Poure out to all that wull,° *will*
And sprinkle all the postes and wals with wine,[9]
That they may sweat, and drunken be withall.
255 Crowne ye God Bacchus with a coronall,° *garland*
And Hymen also crowne with wreathes of vine,
And let the Graces daunce unto the rest;
For they can doo it best:
The whiles the maydens doe theyr carroll sing,
260 To which the woods shal answer and theyr eccho ring.

[15]

Ring ye the bels,[1] ye yong men of the towne,
And leave your wonted° labors for this day: *usual*
This day is holy; doe ye write it downe,
That ye for ever it remember may.
265 This day the sunne is in his chiefest hight,
With Barnaby the bright;[2]
From whence declining daily by degrees,
He somewhat loseth of his heat and light,
When once the Crab behind his back he sees.[3]
270 But for this time it ill ordainéd was,
To chose the longest day in all the yeare,
And shortest night, when longest fitter weare:
Yet never day so long, but late° would passe. *at last*
Ring ye the bels, to make it weare away,
275 And bonefiers make all day,
And daunce about them, and about them sing
That all the woods may answer, and your eccho ring.

8. I.e., the glory of having gained her.
9. A traditional practice at Roman weddings.
1. Either an artful "change ringing" or random enthusiastic ringing of bells.
2. St. Barnabas's Day, June 11, was the summer solstice in the old calendar; bells and bonfires had long greeted the solstice (or Midsummer's Day, June 24); but many now called them "papist," and in England the fun was dying out (D. Cressy, *Bonfires and Bells* [Berkeley, 1989]). Lines 263–64 fall at the poem's "golden section" (the point at which dividing the poem would give two parts with a ratio equaling that of the larger part to the whole (Chinitz 1991).
3. On the solstice the sun is about to quit the "house" of Gemini (the Twins) for Cancer (the Crab) and daylight will slowly diminish; he will see the Crab at his back because in the old system he daily travels 359° while the fixed stars turn a full 360°, allowing the zodiac's houses one by one to overtake him. Or, because the houses no longer in fact coincide with their constellations, Spenser may mean that Sol is leaving Cancer (cf. *The Faerie Queene* V. Pr.).

[16]

Ah when will this long weary day have end,
And lende me leave to come unto my love?
280 How slowly do the houres theyr numbers spend?
How slowly does sad Time his feathers move?
Hast thee O fayrest Planet[4] to thy home
Within the Westerne fome:
Thy tyred steedes long since have need of rest.
285 Long though it be, at last I see it gloome,° *grow dark*
And the bright evening star with golden creast
Appeare out of the East.
Fayre childe of beauty, glorious lampe of love
That all the host of heaven in rankes doost lead,
290 And guydest lovers through the nightés dread,
How chearefully thou lookest from above,
And seemst to laugh atweene thy twinkling light
As joying in the sight
Of these glad many which for joy doe sing,
295 That all the woods them answer and their echo ring.

[17]

Now ceasse ye damsels your delights forepast;
Enough is it, that all the day was youres:
Now day is doen, and night is nighing fast:
Now bring the Bryde into the brydall boures.
300 Now night is come, now soone her disaray,° *undress*
And in her bed her lay;
Lay her in lillies and in violets,
And silken courteins over her display,
And odourd° sheetes, and Arras coverlets.[5] *perfumed*
305 Behold how goodly my faire love does ly
In proud humility;
Like unto Maia,[6] when as Jove her tooke,
In Tempe, lying on the flowry gras,
Twixt sleepe and wake, after she weary was,
310 With bathing in the Acidalian brooke.
Now it is night, ye damsels may be gon,
And leave my love alone,
And leave likewise your former lay to sing:
The woods no more shal answere, nor your echo ring.

[18]

315 Now welcome night, thou night so long expected,
That long daies labour doest at last defray,° *pay for*

4. I.e., the sun, in the Ptolemaic system a planet circling the earth.
5. Fine tapestry spreads.
6. Loveliest of Atlas's seven daughters (later stellified as the Pleiades), Maia bore Mercury (Hermes) to Jove; allusions to Tempe and "the Acidalian brooke" may derive from a hint in Comes, *Mythologiae* 5.5). Since it is now night, the refrain shifts to the negative.

And all my cares, which cruell love collected,
Hast sumd in one, and cancelléd for aye:
Spread thy broad wing over my love and me,
320 That no man may us see,
And in thy sable mantle us enwrap,
From feare of perrill and foule horror free.
Let no false treason seeke us to entrap,
Nor any dread disquiet once annoy
325 The safety of our joy:
But let the night be calme and quietsome,
Without tempestuous storms or sad afray:° *fear*
Lyke as when Jove with fayre Alcmena lay,
When he begot the great Tirynthian groome:
330 Or lyke as when he with thy selfe did lie,
And begot Majesty.[7]
And let the mayds and yongmen cease to sing:
Ne let the woods them answer, nor theyr eccho ring.

[19]

Let no lamenting cryes, nor dolefull teares,
335 Be heard all night within nor yet without:
Ne let false whispers, breeding hidden feares,
Breake gentle sleepe with misconceivéd dout.° *fear*
Let no deluding dreames, nor dreadful sights
Make sudden sad affrights;
340 Ne let housefyres, nor lightnings helpelesse harmes,
Ne let the Pouke,[8] nor other evill sprights,
Ne let mischivous witches with theyr charmes,
Ne let hob Goblins, names whose sence we see not,
Fray° us with things that be not. *terrify*
345 Let not the shriech Oule,[9] nor the Storke be heard:
Nor the night Raven that still° deadly yels, *continually*
Nor damnéd ghosts cald up with mighty spels,
Nor griesly vultures make us once affeard:
Ne let th'unpleasant Quyre of Frogs still croking
350 Make us to wish theyr choking.
Let none of these theyr drery accents sing;
Ne let the woods them answer, nor theyr eccho ring.

[20]

But let stil Silence trew night watches keepe,
That sacred peace may in assurance rayne,
355 And tymely sleep, when it is tyme to sleepe,

7. Tradition calls Hercules (who dwelt at Tiryns, in Argolis) the son of Jove and Alcmena: cf. *Metamorphoses* 9.23–26. Spenser says Majesty's parents were Jove and Night, but Ovid identifies them as Honor and Reverence (*Fasti* 5.23).

8. Puck (Hobgoblin or Robin Goodfellow) was usually thought a malicious spirit. Spenser's wishes have analogues in other epithalamia but also echo the traditional pre-Reformation blessing of the bed in which the priest banishes illusory demons (Prescott 1985).

9. Screech owls and ravens are birds of ill omen. The stork is listed with these and other "unclean" birds in Deuteronomy 14.12–18; Ovid says it "claps its rattling bill" (*Metamorphoses* 6.97).

May poure his limbs forth on your pleasant playne,
The whiles an hundred little wingéd loves,[1]
Like divers fethered doves,
Shall fly and flutter round about your bed,
360 And in the secret darke, that none reproves,
Their prety stealthes shal worke, and snares shal spread
To filch away sweet snatches of delight,
Conceald through covert night.
Ye sonnes of Venus, play your sports at will,
365 For greedy pleasure, carelesse of your toyes,° *amorous dallying*
Thinks more upon her paradise of joyes,
Then what ye do, albe it good or ill.
All night therefore attend your merry play,
For it will soone be day:
370 Now none doth hinder you, that say or sing,
Ne will the woods now answer, nor your Eccho ring.

[21]

Who is the same, which at my window peepes?
Or whose is that faire face, that shines so bright,
Is it not Cinthia,[2] she that never sleepes,
375 But walkes about high heaven al the night?
O fayrest goddesse, do thou not envy
My love with me to spy:
For thou likewise didst love, though now unthought,[3]
And for a fleece of woll,° which privily, *wool*
380 The Latmian shephard once unto thee brought,
His pleasures with thee wrought.
Therefore to us be favorable now;
And sith of wemens labours thou hast charge,[4]
And generation goodly dost enlarge,
385 Encline thy will t'effect our wishfull vow,
And the chast wombe informe with timely seed,
That may our comfort breed:
Till which we cease our hopefull hap[5] to sing,
Ne let the woods us answere, nor our Eccho ring.

[22]

390 And thou great Juno, which with awful° might *awe-inspiring*
The lawes of wedlock still dost patronize,

1. I.e., little winged cupids ("amoretti," in fact), playful figures in the Anacreontic style that often flutter in Renaissance love poetry; Spenser may have known those (and other details) in Du Bellay's 1559 *Epithalame* for Marguerite de France (McPeek 1936).
2. Goddess of the moon, Diana.
3. I.e., not thought of. Cynthia loved Endymion, a shepherd whom Jove put into perpetual sleep; he lies in a cave on Mount Latmus, in Asia Minor, where she can kiss him. Some said she had children by him; others read the sleep and kisses as religious contemplation or astronomical discovery (Comes, *Mythologiae* 4.8). Virgil (*Georgics* 3.391–93) says Pan gave the fleece, but Spenser follows later mythography.
4. Both Diana and Juno were invoked as Lucina, goddess who "brings to light" and thus presides over childbirth.
5. I.e., the lot for which we hope.

And the religion° of the faith first plight — *sanctity*
With sacred rites hast taught to solemnize:
And eeke for comfort often calléd art
395 Of women in their smart,° — *pains*
Eternally bind thou this lovely° band, — *loving*
And all thy blessings unto us impart.
And thou glad Genius,[6] in whose gentle hand,
The bridale bowre and geniall bed[7] remaine,
400 Without blemish or staine,
And the sweet pleasures of theyr loves delight
With secret ayde doest succour and supply,
Till they bring forth the fruitfull progeny,
Send us the timely fruit of this same night.
405 And thou fayre Hebe,[8] and thou Hymen free,
Grant that it may so be.
Til which we cease your further prayse to sing,
Ne any woods shal answer, nor your Eccho ring.

[23]

And ye high heavens, the temple of the gods,
410 In which a thousand torches flaming bright
Doe burne, that to us wretched earthly clods,
In dreadful darknesse lend desiréd light:
And all ye powers which in the same[9] remayne,
More then we men can fayne,° — *imagine*
415 Poure out your blessing on us plentiously,
And happy influence upon us raine,
That we may raise a large posterity,
Which from the earth, which they may long possesse,
With lasting happinesse,
420 Up to your haughty pallaces may mount,
And for the guerdon° of theyr glorious merit — *reward*
May heavenly tabernacles there inherit,
Of blessed Saints for to increase the count.
So let us rest, sweet love, in hope of this,[1]
425 And cease till then our tymely joyes to sing,
The woods no more us answer, nor our eccho ring.

[24]

Song[2] made in lieu of many ornaments,
With which my love should duly have bene dect,° — *adorned*

6. The god of birth and generation; cf. *The Faerie Queene* II.xii.47 and III.vi.31–32.
7. I.e., generative as well as pleasant bed (with a play on the god's name).
8. Daughter of Juno, and cupbearer to the gods; Spenser, following Ovid and Renaissance mythographers, regards her as goddess of youth and rejuvenation (cf. *Metamorphoses* 9.397–401).
9. I.e., in the heavens; *powers*: may refer both to the ninefold angelic hierarchy and to stellar "influences" on us.
1. The rhyme is defective; see Editors' Note. The prayer for children echoes the marriage service.
2. The envoy addresses the poem itself, the tangled syntax eventuating in a syntactically ambiguous imperative ordering it to be both decoration and "moniment" (the word means memorial, but can connote "warning").

Which cutting off through hasty accidents;[3]
430 Ye would not stay your dew time to expect,° *await*
But promist both to recompens,
Be unto her a goodly ornament,
And for short time an endlesse moniment.° *memorial*

Editors' Note

Amoretti and *Epithalamion* were published together in 1595, the former arranged one sonnet to a page and with a new title page for the marriage hymn. After the sonnets come some little lyrics conventionally called, although not by Spenser, the "Anacreontics" (on their nature and origin see the notes). The resulting structure (sonnet sequence, then a change of tone—what a chef might call a palate cleanser—and then a longer poem) follows the precedent set by Samuel Daniel in his *Delia* and used by various Elizabethan poets. The long poem was often a "complaint," but Spenser offers a triumphant marriage song, an epithalamion, a form going back to Catullus and the Romans. Spenser's was the first in English and, unlike those by his classical predecessors, sung by the poet to his own wife. It is true that Spenser was not the first in the Renaissance to address sonnets and an epithalamion to a wife, rather than to a mistress or to somebody else's bride, for in France Jean Salmon Macrin had written sonnets and epithalamia to his beloved Gelonis. True also that the exiled Ovid had lamented in *Tristia* his exile-enforced distance from the by now old wife he loved and true that Michelangelo's friend Vitoria Colonna had written sonnets on her deceased husband. Nevertheless, Spenser's sequence offered English readers something unusual as well as powerful.

Most critics agree that Spenser's sonnets allude to his courtship of Elizabeth Boyle and that the *Epithalamion* celebrates his marriage (his second) to that lady in the summer of 1594, most probably at Youghal in County Cork or at his home in Kilcolman. A few sonnets were doubtless written earlier and addressed to some other women or woman, for Renaissance poets were happy to recycle their verse, and *Amoretti* 8 is found in a manuscript put together before 1580. The reference in *Amoretti* 74 to a beloved named Elizabeth, a pattern of calendrical allusions in the sonnets that must refer to the Easter season of 1594 (the year of Spenser's marriage), and the reference in *Epithalamion* to the summer solstice, which in the unreformed Julian calendar that England stubbornly used until 1752, fell on June 11: all these associate this set of poems with Spenser's own biography and reinforce the common assumption that at some point during 1594 or early 1595 he composed new verses and reworked some older ones to make a sequence of striking originality.

The sonnet sequence itself, if not begun by Petrarch then established by him as a rich genre imitated by both men such as Tasso or Desportes and women such as Gaspara Stampa or Louise Labé on the Continent, had entered England with Anne Lock's 1560 paraphrase of Psalm 51. The amatory sequence, although not written in what we—stricter in our definitions—would call sonnets, enters with Thomas

3. Perhaps alluding to an unexpected change in wedding plans, but see Editors' Note.

Watson's *Hekatompathia*, a sequence heavily indebted to Continental poets but also to a pattern set by the twelfth-century Andreas Capellanus and Petrarch himself in which erotic desire is followed by repentance or a surge heavenward (Ovid's often satirical *Ars Amatoria* had itself turned from advice on how to seduce women to a *Remedia Amoris* on how to fall out of love). Spenser turns instead to marriage. After all, marriage is one answer to poor Astrophil's recognition that despite all his efforts at learning idealism from his lady, "Desire still cries, 'give me some food'" (Philip Sidney, *Astrophil and Stella* 71). Or, as Paul put it, "It is better to marry than to burn" (1 Corinthians 7) and most sonneteers had burned with little or no serious hope. Spenser's bride can yield honorably, chastely, and pleasurably, but Laura and Stella cannot.

The English had long noticed Petrarch himself, of course, as witness Chaucer's paraphrase of the *Rime* in *Troilus and Criseyde*'s "Canticus Troili" (I.400–20), and the English poetry written by duc Charles d'Orléans while a prisoner in England.[1] But it was Philip Sidney's *Astrophil and Stella* and Samuel Daniel's *Delia* that first introduced the cleverly organized Petrarchan sonnet sequence into English, followed soon by Henry Constable's *Diana*, Drayton's *Idea's Mirror*, and Thomas Lodge's *Phillis*, to name only the most famous. They share with Petrarch himself a sense of the divided self, a mixture of physical desire and idealization, and sometimes a pseudonym for the lady that can inspire wordplay or allusion (e.g., Petrarch's laurel/gold/breath Laura, Sidney's starry "Stella," and conceivably Boyle, then pronounced "bile"), a clever conceit—an ingenious and elaborate metaphor or notion—as the basis of a mere fourteen-line poem (thus sometimes edging the sonnet into the epigram), and glances—direct or from the eye's corner—at a political situation. Such a glance would not be surprising, for whatever the true affection and desire that doubtless lay behind some sonneteering, the performance of Petrarchan desire played a part in England's political life as the queen and those who sought her favor collaborated in fashioning her as a mistress to be courted and her courtiers as lovelorn wooers.[2] Spenser's exploitation of this connection is complex, however. The praise of Elizabeth's name in *Amoretti* 74 combines with praise of Spenser's mother and beloved, both also named Elizabeth, but one might hear some nervousness, real or judiciously assumed, in *Amoretti*'s vow to continue *The Faerie Queene* and even in the glimpse with which "Cynthia," who so often in Elizabethan poetry evokes Elizabeth, peeps through the bedroom window during Spenser's wedding night (*Epithalamion* stanza 21). Is the moon goddess wondering where her epic has gone amidst all this connubial bliss? And who is the "Latmian shephard" whom once she loved? Love for the Elizabethans was not exclusively private; nor was political life without *eros*.

Spenser is in full conversation with this Petrarchan tradition, one now inflected by the idealisms of Neoplatonism that can partly assuage the pain of erotic refusal but also by an ironic and even self-mocking wit that pushes intriguingly against what was sometimes (and sometimes not) a

1. On Charles, see A. E. B. Coldiron, *Canon, Period, and the Poetry of Charles of Orleans* (Ann Arbor: University of Michigan Press, 2000).
2. See especially Arthur Marotti, "'Love is not Love': Elizabethan Sonnet Sequences and the Social Order," *ELH* 49 (1982): 396–428.

genuine anguish. To write longingly to a beloved whom the writer could legitimately win and even marry, rather than attempting through verse to seduce another person's spouse (like Philip Sidney) or to enlist Eros when one is (like Philippe Desportes) in holy orders was, for Spenser, one way to shake off or modify such tradition. Spenser modifies it yet further, if with psychologically complex overtones (Sanchez 2011), by tracing how a good woman's own erotic nature can be aroused without dishonor, thus applying Reformation thought on sex and marriage to Petrarchan tradition, for Protestants tended to elevate married sexuality above celibacy, and inexperienced readers should be reminded that chastity is not the same as virginity, for a faithful wife is chaste even if sexually active. (Renaissance medical theory held that conception could not take place without sexual pleasure.) Nobody before Spenser had written so organized and ingenious a set of poems that triumphs over Petrarch by catching Petrarch's speeding deer and steering a storm-tossed ship into the harbor that Petrarch cannot find, bows to Plato but brushes him aside so as to celebrate married love and the hope for babies, establishes a complex Ovidian irony and semi-Ovidian relation to the epic (Pugh 2005, Stapleton 2008), and writes of a beloved who has spirit and wit of her own and indeed who, some readers have found, shares with her lover a mutual sense of play (e.g., Martz 1961). This last may be important, for a number of poems sound very different depending on whether one takes them straight, so to speak, or with an ear out for affectionate self-mockery. A little exaggerated Petrarchism might amuse a clever young woman, not least one who can tease her middle-aged lover as the two bend over her embroidery (*Amoretti* 71), force him out of the house and into the rain (46), challenge his reading of his own emblem, the laurel (29), and refuse to take his histrionics seriously (54).

Individual elements in this combination of accomplishments had precedent, but not the combination, not the range. Nor is there much precedent for the sheer ingenuity with which Spenser exploits numerical and calendrical patterning.[3] He was not the first to associate love for a lady with the calendar, for Petrarch had done that, although in his last poem leaving the 365 days of the year for eternity, and Du Bellay had in effect made an olive wreath for his *Olive* (1549/1551) by connecting his sequence to the liturgical year. In England Giles Fletcher had written his more secular *Licia* (1592) as a year's worth of sonnets that heat and chill with the seasons.[4] But Spenser goes further, giving Elizabeth Boyle as many sonnets as there are feast days and Sundays in the Book of Common Prayer and including into *Amoretti* a set of sonnets that moves from Ash Wednesday to the legal new year that in England started on Lady Day (March 25) in the Julian Calendar and then, after exactly the right number of "days"/sonnets (the forty of Lent plus Sundays), celebrates Easter on what in 1594 would have been March 31. The couple is separated for a while at the end of *Amoretti*, if only because, as has been said, the sonnet sequence is uneasy with closure (Neely 1978), but after some more numerologically clever footwork the

3. Those writing on Spenser's calendrical patterning (Kaske 1978 doing so more skeptically), include Hieatt 1960, Dunlop 1980, Thompson 1985, Fukuda 1988, Prescott 1995, Johnson 1990, and Larsen 1997.

4. Anne Prescott, "Licia's Temple: Giles Fletcher the Elder and Number Symbolism," *Renaissance and Reformation* 2 (1978): 170–81.

sequence moves to a marriage song with twenty-four stanzas in 365 lines, 359 of these (the sun's lagging path that creates the seasons in the old system) before a stanza referring to "short time," and all this with a refrain that changes to the negative exactly so as to divide the poem into segments correlating with the hours of day and night on June 11 in southwest Ireland.

Epithalamion begins and ends in quiet and partial solitude with a gradually accumulating and then diminishing noisy bustle even as the pagan names give way to Christian and then revert, in part, to the pagan (Wickert 1968). One scholar, moreover, has detected in the structure the ratios of the "golden section" (Chinitz 1991). There are further puzzles, too, for Spenser can incorporate here, as he had done at the end of *The Faerie Queene* I, elements of the Catholic Sarum Missal, and the sort of merriment he describes would hardly please England's more solemn-minded radical Protestants. Here, as in *The Faerie Queene*, Spenser is less easy to categorize than many readers once thought.

Nor, as we hope we have shown, is his love poetry easy to categorize. Spenser pushes against generic expectations in ways with serious but positive implications for his views of love and God, love and sexuality, love and marriage, love and politics, even love and war in Ireland (Fleming 2001) but also with a degree of playfulness that can invite in return a playful postmodernist response (Kuin 1987). Also giving his love poetry depth, however, are traces of unease and conflict that do not subtract from its joy and eventual triumph but that are an inevitable part of human erotic experience, including the anticipation of marriage. When a hind lets herself be bound, and only after the hunter has ceased for the moment his aggressive pursuit, what does she expect? Real hinds may well be killed (like the Christ who in the next sonnet makes his triumph over death?). What happens to women who give themselves up? The joy of marriage, often, but also the pain of childbearing and submission to a husband? The deer is tied in bonds that both constrict and liberate—we still say that to marry is to "get hitched," although that same hitching, that shared yoke, can liberate us from much else. Spenser's poetry, moreover, can hint at Eros's occasional narcissism, manipulation, and aggression (Loewenstein 1987), even if the poet's aim is chiefly to celebrate it and his own victory as a lover.

No wonder that Spenser adapts for himself the old prayer that in Catholic days was said by the priest over the marriage bed, asking that it be free from the demons of illusion (see *Epithalamion* stanza 19 and note). Marriage is a liminal moment, with all the anxieties that such moments bring—literally liminal when the groom in modern custom carries the bride over the threshold, the *limen*. Monsters like those of stanza 19 can lurk under thresholds and bridges. That victory in love and marriage can bring stress, then, is no surprise. And there are other odd touches. Spenser compares himself at the start of the marriage hymn to Orpheus, but Orpheus, great singer though he was, lost his wife almost as soon as he gained her. Perhaps it is true that there is a little elegy in the epithalamion (Schenck 1988), both requiring flowers and both marking a transition. One can cry at both weddings and funerals. And yet the final impression of Spenser's *Amoretti and Epithalamion* is joyful, whatever those woods that echo his song and then fall silent may conceal. The poet's awareness that human love can mix with fear, cruelty, violence, grief, or deceit makes his affirmations of its legitimacy and beauty all the more powerfully moving.

Prothalamion†

I

Calme was the day, and through the trembling ayre,
Sweete breathing Zephyrus did softly play,
A gentle spirit, that lightly did delay° — *temper*
Hot Titans beames, which then did glyster° fayre: — *shine*
5 When I whom sullein care,
Through discontent of my long fruitlesse stay
In Princes Court, and expectation vayne
Of idle hopes, which still doe fly away,
Like empty shaddowes, did aflict my brayne,
10 Walkt forth to ease my payne
Along the shoare of silver streaming Themmes,[1]
Whose rutty° Bancke, the which his River hemmes, — *rooty*
Was paynted all with variable° flowers, — *various*
And all the meades adornd with daintie gemmes,
15 Fit to decke maydens bowres,
And crowne their Paramours,° — *lovers*
Against the Brydale day, which is not long:[2]
Sweete Themmes runne softly, till I end my Song.

2

There, in a Meadow, by the Rivers side,
20 A Flocke of Nymphes I chauncéd to espy,
All lovely Daughters of the Flood° thereby, — *river*
With goodly greenish locks all loose untyde,
As each had bene a Bryde,
And each one had a little wicker basket,
25 Made of fine twigs entrayléd curiously, — *interlaced*
In which they gathered flowers to fill their flasket:° — *basket*
And with fine Fingers, cropt full feateously[3]
The tender stalkes on hye.
Of every sort, which in that Meadow grew,

† The term, Greek for "preliminary nuptial song," is the invention of Spenser, who subtitles it "A Spousall Verse." Printed in 1596, it celebrates the approaching marriage of Elizabeth and Catherine Somerset, daughters of Edward Somerset, earl of Worcester, to Henry Guildford and William Petre, respectively. The refrain achieved particular fame when T. S. Eliot quoted it in *The Wasteland*.

1. To recount what the narrator observes as he or she walks out of town, often near a river, long remained conventional; Nashe's pornographic "Choice of Valentines," written but not published two years or so after this poem, parodies the convention.
2. I.e., in anticipation of the bridal day, which is not far off.
3. I.e., and with a delicate touch, plucked most dextrously.

30 They gathered some; the Violet pallid blew,
The little Dazie, that at evening closes,
The virgin Lillie, and the Primrose trew,
With store° of vermeil° Roses, *abundance / scarlet*
To decke their Bridegromes posies,° *bouquets*
35 Against the Brydale day, which was not long:
Sweete Themmes runne softly, till I end my Song.

3

With that, I saw two Swannes of goodly hewe,° *appearance*
Come softly swimming downe along the Lee;[4]
Two fairer Birds I yet did never see:
40 The snow which doth the top of Pindus[5] strew,
Did never whiter shew,
Nor Jove himselfe when he a Swan would be
For love of Leda, whiter did appeare.[6]
Yet Leda was they say as white as he,
45 Yet not so white as these, nor nothing neare;
So purely white they were,
That even the gentle streame, the which them bare,
Seemed foule to[7] them, and bad his billowes spare° *forbear*
To wet their silken feathers, least they might
50 Soyle their fayre plumes with water not so fayre
And marre their beauties bright,
That shone as heavens light,
Against their Brydale day, which was not long:
Sweete Themmes runne softly, till I end my Song.

4

55 Eftsoones° the Nymphes, which now had Flowers their fill, *presently*
Ran all in haste, to see that silver brood,[8]
As they came floating on the Christal Flood.
Whom when they sawe, they stood amazéd still,
Their wondring eyes to fill,
60 Them seemed they never saw a sight so fayre,
Of Fowles so lovely, that they sure did deeme
Them heavenly borne, or to be that same payre
Which through the Skie draw Venus silver Teeme,[9]
For sure they did not seeme
65 To be begot of any earthly Seede,
But rather Angels or of Angels breede:° *race*
Yet were they bred of Somers-heat[1] they say,

4. Possibly ambiguous: the word "lea" means grassy meadow but a river Lea flows into the Thames. Swans were regularly to be seen on the Thames; these represent the brides.
5. Properly refers to the mountainous western boundary of the Thessalian plain, in Greece. Ovid often alludes to Pindus's height (e.g., *Metamorphoses* 2.225).
6. Cf. *Metamorphoses* 6.109; and *The Faerie Queene* III.xi.32.
7. I.e., compared with.
8. I.e., that silvery pair of noble lineage.
9. Traditionally, the chariot of Venus was drawn through the air by swans; cf. *Metamorphoses* 10.717–18.
1. Spenser puns on the ladies' surname.

In sweetest Season, when each Flower and weede° *plant*
The earth did fresh aray,
70 So fresh they seemed as day,
Even as their Brydale day, which was not long:
Sweete Themmes runne softly, till I end my Song.

5

Then forth they all out of their baskets drew,
Great store of Flowers, the honour° of the field, *glory*
75 That to the sense did fragrant odours yeild,
All which upon those goodly Birds they threw,
And all the Waves did strew,
That like old Peneus Waters[2] they did seeme,
When downe along by pleasant Tempes shore
80 Scattred with Flowres, through Thessaly they streeme,
That they appeare through Lillies plenteous store,
Like a Brydes Chamber flore:
Two of those Nymphes, meane while, two Garlands bound,
Of freshest Flowres which in that Mead° they found, *meadow*
85 The which presenting all in trim Array,
Their snowie Foreheads[3] therewithall they crownd,
Whil'st one did sing this Lay,
Prepared against that Day,
Against their Brydale day, which was not long:
90 Sweete Themmes runne softly, till I end my Song.

6

"Ye gentle Birdes, the worlds faire ornament,
And heavens glorie, whom this happie hower
Doth leade unto your lovers blisfull bower,
Joy may you have and gentle hearts content
95 Of your loves couplement:° *union*
And let faire Venus, that is Queene of love,
With her heart-quelling Sonne upon you smile,
Whose smile they say, hath vertue° to remove *power*
All Loves dislike, and friendships faultie guile
100 For ever to assoile.[4]
Let endlesse Peace your steadfast hearts accord,° *harmonize*
And blesséd Plentie wait upon your bord,° *table*
And let your bed with pleasures chast abound,
That fruitfull issue may to you afford,[5]
105 Which may your foes confound,
And make your joyes redound,° *overflow*

2. The Peneus river flows through the vale of Tempe, in Thessaly, between Mount Ossa and Mount Olympus to the sea; Spenser probably recalls Catullus, *Odes* 64.278–88.
3. I.e., those of the swans.
4. I.e., has power to remove all cause for aversion in love, and to dispel forever the offensive guile that may undermine friendship. Venus appears as beneficent overseer of marriage in Claudian, *Epithalamium de Nuptiis Honorii Augusti* 190–287, and (with her son) in Statius, *Silvae* 1.2.162–93.
5. I.e., be given.

Upon your Brydale day, which is not long:
Sweete Themmes run softlie, till I end my Song."

7

So ended she; and all the rest around
110 To her redoubled that her undersong,[6]
Which said, their bridale daye should not be long.
And gentle Eccho from the neighbour ground,
Their accents did resound.
So forth those joyous Birdes did passe along,
115 Adowne the Lee, that to them murmurde low,
As he would speake, but that he lackt a tong.
Yet did by signes his glad affection show,
Making his streame run slow.
And all the foule which in his flood did dwell
120 Gan flock about these twaine. that did excell
The rest, so far, as Cynthia[7] doth shend° — *shame, overgo*
The lesser starres. So they enrangéd° well, — *ordered*
Did on those two attend,
And their best service lend,° — *give*
125 Against their wedding day, which was not long:
Sweete Themmes run softly, till I end my song.

8

At length they all to mery London came,
To mery London, my most kyndly Nurse,
That to me gave this Lifes first native sourse:
130 Though from another place I take my name,
An house of auncient fame.[8]
There when they came, whereas those bricky towres,[9]
The which on Themmes brode aged backe doe ryde,
Where now the studious Lawyers have their bowers
135 There whylome° wont the Templer Knights to byde, — *formerly*
Till they decayd[1] through pride:
Next whereunto there standes a stately place,[2]
Where oft I gaynéd giftes and goodly grace
Of that great Lord, which therein wont to dwell,
140 Whose want too well now feeles my freendles case:

6. I.e., reechoed the refrain of her song. Fowler 1975 comments on the functions of this "anomalous" stanza, which breaks the zodiacal sequence and is otherwise formally exceptional, within the poem's larger pattern.

7. I.e., Diana, goddess of the moon, called Cynthia from Mount Cynthus (on the island of Delos), her birthplace. It is easy to detect a polite allusion to Elizabeth.

8. Born and bred in London, Spenser associates himself with the Spencers of Althorp in Northamptonshire (cf. also *Colin Clouts Come Home Againe* 536–55), who claimed descent from the ancient house of Despencer.

9. I.e., the Temple, between Fleet Street and the north bank of the Thames; originally the London residence of the Knights Templar. When that order was suppressed by Edward II, the property passed to the Knights of St. John, and was subsequently leased to the students of English common law.

1. I.e., until their downfall.

2. I.e., Leicester House, London residence of "that great Lord" the earl of Leicester, Spenser's patron in 1579–80. When, after the earl's death in 1588, the estate passed into the possession of Robert Devereux, second earl of Essex, the building was called Essex House.

But Ah here fits° not well — *suits*
Olde woes but joyes to tell
Against the bridale daye, which is not long:
Sweete Themmes runne softly, till I end my Song.

9

145 Yet therein now doth lodge a noble Peer,[3]
Great Englands glory and the Worlds wide wonder,
Whose dreadfull name, late through all Spaine did thunder,
And Hercules two pillors standing neere,
Did make to quake and feare:
150 Faire branch of Honor, flower of Chevalrie,
That fillest England with thy triumphs fame,
Joy have thou of thy noble victorie,
And endlesse happinesse of thine owne name
That promiseth the same:[4]
155 That through thy prowesse and victorious armes,
Thy country may be freed from forraine harmes:
And great Elisaes glorious name may ring
Through al the world, filled with thy wide Alarmes,
Which some brave muse may sing
160 To ages following,[5]
Upon the Brydale day, which is not long:
Sweete Themmes runne softly, till I end my Song.

10

From those high Towers, this noble Lord issuing,
Like Radiant Hesper[6] when his golden hayre
165 In th'Ocean billowes he hath Bathéd fayre,
Descended to the Rivers open viewing,
With a great traine ensuing.[7]
Above the rest were goodly to bee seene
Two gentle Knights[8] of lovely face and feature
170 Beseeming well the bower of anie Queene,
With gifts of wit and ornaments of nature,
Fit for so goodly stature:
That like the twins of Jove[9] they seemed in sight,
Which decke the Bauldricke of the Heavens bright[1]
175 They two forth pacing to the Rivers side,
Received those two faire Brides, their Loves delight,

3. I.e., the earl of Essex, who (together with Sir Walter Raleigh) had in June 1596, overwhelmed a Spanish fleet at Cadiz, plundered the city, and forced the destruction of forty-odd merchantmen together with their enormously valuable cargoes. Cadiz lies some fifty miles northwest from the Straits of Gibraltar, anciently known as the Pillars of Hercules.
4. Spenser puns on "Devereux" (family name of the earl of Essex) and "hereux," French for "fortunate."
5. I.e., through all the world, everywhere touched by your active and wide-ranging spirit, which some gifted poet (e.g., Spenser) may celebrate for times to come.
6. I.e., Hesperus, the morning star in this context; see *Aeneid* 8.589–91.
7. I.e., attended by an extensive retinue.
8. The bridegrooms-to-be, Henry Guildford and William Petre.
9. I.e., Castor and Pollux, the Gemini.
1. I.e., the zodiac (regarded as a belt studded with stars).

Which at th'appointed tyde,° *time*
Each one did make his Bryde,
Against their Brydale day, which is not long:
180 Sweete Themmes runne softly, till I end my Song.

Editors' Note

Spenser's *Prothalamion* (1596) praises in ten eighteen-line stanzas—a semicircle of verses to compare with *Epithalamion*'s 365 circle of long lines—a wedding's aristocratic and good-looking participants even as the poet himself enjoys somewhat grouchy solitude and asks the usually noisy Thames to be quiet while he sings. The festive activities he is praising and their attendant sounds accumulate, and by the poem's end the onlooker Spenser is celebrating not only the participants but also the earl of Essex, a relative of the two brides and now a powerful royal favorite.

On November 8, 1596, Elizabeth and Catherine Somerset, the daughters of Edward Somerset, fourth earl of Worcester, married Henry Guildford and William Petre, respectively. The wedding took place at London's Essex House, in the Strand. The poet may have been acquainted with relatives of the brides' family, and we do not know the story behind his celebration, but a hope to win more patronage from Essex himself may have been a motive. It is a commonplace of some Spenser scholarship, if one subject to challenge, that as the poet aged he came to have doubts about epic ambition and his role as a national poet; hence the little satirical kick at the end of Book VI of *The Faerie Queene* and what can look like that same book's pastoral regression atop Mount Acidale as Colin Clout pipes to the Graces and his own beloved. It is possible to hear in *Prothalamion*, however, a suggestion to Essex and his like that Spenser is ready to sing of mighty deeds and not just pipe like a shepherd on fairyland's grassy hilltops (cf. P. Cheney 1993, 25–45). The reference to "some brave muse" that might "sing" Elizabeth and the salvation of her realm thanks to the victory of Essex and Sir Walter Raleigh over the Spanish at Cadiz has struck some as the Renaissance equivalent of a job application.

True, one can also hear tensions when pressuring the poem's wording (for example, "against their Brydale day" means "anticipating" that day, but to some ears "against" might whisper bridal reluctance). Perhaps, too, the poet shows ambivalence toward the city itself when telling its famous river to cease the noise that readers familiar with London would know was generated by its increased commerce and manufacture. A "softly" silent Thames would thus occlude the role of money and trade in the city's greatness, economic interests that had in part inspired the conflict between Spain and England and hence the victory at Cadiz. For Spenser, then, chivalric heroics and modern commerce were uneasy companions in both the recent Virginian adventures and the continuing war in Ireland (Owens 2007, who suggests that the "silver streaming Themmes" might even suggest a flow of cash). And at least one reader (Alastair Fowler 1975) thinks that the poem not only moves from the solitary and discontented walk at the start—a walk through a landscape that in a typical Renaissance way combines pagan demidivinities with local allusions—to the bustle and heroics of the end but also does so in stanzas that make numerological and astrological patterns.

Rivers have always fascinated poets. Both mutable (like Time, they flow) and often steady (Rome is gone, says Du Bellay in a sonnet that Spenser translated for the *Ruines of Rome*, but the Tiber remains), they are moving in every sense. The Thames is London's great river but it also offers access both to the landscape upstream and to the rest of the world as it debouches into the North Sea, even as it can remember when London was Troynovant and was there in the time of the Templars (on whom see Canto 9). Both geographically and temporally the Thames invites poetic meditation. No wonder that the antiquary William Leland had published a *Cygnea Cantio* ("Swan Song") in 1545 or that his great successor William Camden wrote a poem *De Connubio Tamis et Isis* ("On the Marriage of Thames and Isis" [Isis is the river, not the goddess]) in 1586. In 1590 William Vallans produced *A Tale of Two Swannes* (sensibly complimenting Burleigh in passing) in which swans and their cygnets swim along English streams that Vallans annotates by reference to the early British history that Spenser likewise recounts in *The Faerie Queene* II.x and III.ix. The Thames is not just pretty—it carries history and archaeology with it. So Spenser had precedent, to say nothing of poems by Continental writers praising their own rivers, although nobody was doing so in England with such beauty and complexity. In a 1580 letter to Gabriel Harvey, Spenser mentions his intention to write an "*Epithalamion Thamesis*," together with an account of "all the rivers throughout Englande, whyche came to the wedding," but we do not know how that lost poem relates to anything published later.[1]

Nor do we know what Spenser would have published had he lived longer. The complete Book of Constancy? At least he did not survive to see Essex's attempted political coup or his consequent disgrace and execution in what he might have read as another triumph of Mutabilitie, another bend in the river.

1. In *Three proper and wittie familiar Letters* (London, 1580). Vallans, who notes the old legend that swans sing just before they die, reports seeing an "*Epithalamion Thamesis* in Latin verse" and its equivalent in English that begged the author(s) to publish; such poems, if they existed, have vanished. For Spenser's extant river-marriage, see *The Faerie Queene* IV.xi, in which the Thames weds the Medway.

CRITICISM

Early Critical Views

WILLIAM CAMDEN

[The Death of Spenser]†

The rebellion in Ireland now flamed forth dangerously, as I will declare anon, after I shall first have related what countrymen of ours of worthiest memorie died this yeere [1598/9]. And they were no more than 3, except the Lord Burghley already mentioned: and those three of the number of the most learned, and no lesse renowned than Fame that blazed them.

The first was Thomas Stapleton, Doctor of Divinitie, brought up in New Colledge at Oxford, and ordinarie professor of Divinity and controversies in the Universitie of Douay. . . . Another was Richard Cosins a Cambridge man, Doctor of Law, Deane of the Arches. . . . The third was Edmund Spenser, a Londoner by birth, and a Scholler also of the University of Cambridge, borne under so favourable an aspect of the Muses, that he surpassed all the English poets of former times, not excepting even Chaucer himselfe, his Country man. But by a fate peculiar to Poets, he alwaies struggled with poverty, though he were Secretary to the Lord Grey, Lord Deputy of Ireland. For scarce had hee there gotten a solitary place and leisure to write, when hee was by the Rebels cast out of his dwelling, despoyled of his goods, and returned into England, a poore man, where shortly after hee dyed, and was interred at Westminster, neere to Chaucer, at the charges of the Earle of Essex, his Hearse being carried by Poets, and mournefull Verses and Poems thrown into his Tombe.

SAMUEL TAYLOR COLERIDGE

[Spenser's Art]‡

There is this difference, among many others, between Shakspeare and Spenser:—Shakspeare is never colored by the customs of his age; what appears of contemporary character in him is merely negative; it is just not something else. He has none of the fictitious realities of the classics, none of the grotesquenesses of chivalry, none of the allegory of the middle

† From *Annales, or The History of the most Renowned and Victorious Princesse Elizabeth, late Queen of England . . . written in Latin and translated into English, by R. N[orton] . . .* [London] 1635. Camden (1551–1623), antiquary and historian, was also the author of *Britannia* (1586), a Latin topographical history of England (first English tr. 1610), dedicated to Lord Burleigh.

‡ From the third in "A Course of Lectures" (1818); the published versions of these lectures are based on notes arranged by H. N. Coleridge. Cf. *Coleridge's Miscellaneous Criticism*, ed. T. M. Raysor (Cambridge, MA, 1936), 32–38.

ages; there is no sectarianism either of politics or religion, no miser, no witch,—no common witch,—no astrology—nothing impermanent of however long duration; but he stands like the yew-tree in Lorton vale, which has known so many ages that it belongs to none in particular; a living image of endless self-reproduction, like the immortal tree of Malabar. In Spenser the spirit of chivalry is entirely predominant, although with a much greater infusion of the poet's own individual self into it than is found in any other writer. He has the wit of the southern with the deeper inwardness of the northern genius.

No one can appreciate Spenser without some reflection on the nature of allegorical writing. The mere etymological meaning of the word, allegory,—to talk of one thing and thereby convey another,—is too wide. The true sense is this,—the employment of one set of agents and images to convey in disguise a moral meaning, with a likeness to the imagination, but with a difference to the understanding,—those agents and images being so combined as to form a homogeneous whole. This distinguishes it from metaphor, which is part of an allegory. But allegory is not properly distinguishable from fable, otherwise than as the first includes the second, as a genus its species; for in a fable there must be nothing but what is universally known and acknowledged, but in an allegory there may be that which is new and not previously admitted. The pictures of the great masters, especially of the Italian schools, are genuine allegories. Amongst the classics, the multitude of their gods either precluded allegory altogether, or else made every thing allegory, as in the Hesiodic Theogonia; for you can scarcely distinguish between power and the personification of power. The Cupid and Psyche of, or found in, Apuleius, is a phenomenon. It is the Platonic mode of accounting for the fall of man. The Battle of the Soul by Prudentius[1] is an early instance of Christian allegory.

Narrative allegory is distinguished from mythology as reality from symbol; it is, in short, the proper intermedium between person and personification. Where it is too strongly individualized, it ceases to be allegory; this is often felt in the Pilgrim's Progress, where the characters are real persons with nicknames. Perhaps one of the most curious warnings against another attempt at narrative allegory on a great scale, may be found in Tasso's account of what he himself intended in and by his Jerusalem Delivered.

As characteristic of Spenser, I would call your particular attention in the first place to the indescribable sweetness and fluent projection of his verse, very clearly distinguishable from the deeper and more interwoven harmonies of Shakspeare and Milton. This stanza is a good instance of what I mean:—

> Yet she, most faithfull ladie, all this while
> Forsaken, wofull, solitarie mayd,
> Far from all peoples preace, as in exile,
> In wildernesse and wastfull deserts strayd
> To seeke her knight; who, subtily betrayd
> Through that late vision which th' enchaunter wrought,
> Had her abandond; she, of nought affrayd,

1. Latin (Christian) poet of the fourth century C.E. [*Editors*].

Through woods and wastnes wide him daily sought,
Yet wished tydinges none of him unto her brought.
[*F.Q.*, I.iii.3]

2. Combined with this sweetness and fluency, the scientific construction of the metre of the Faery Queene is very noticeable. One of Spenser's arts is that of alliteration, and he uses it with great effect in doubling the impression of an image:—

In *w*ildernesse and *w*astful deserts—
Through *w*oods and *w*astnes wilde,—
They passe the bitter *w*aves of Acheron,
Where many *s*oules *s*it *w*ailing *w*oefully,
And come to *f*iery *f*lood of *Ph*alegeton,
Whereas the damned ghosts in torments fry,
And with *s*harp *s*hrilling *s*hrieks doth bootlesse cry,—&c.
[*F.Q.*, I.v. 33]

He is particularly given to an alternate alliteration, which is, perhaps, when well used, a great secret in melody:—

A *r*amping lyon *r*ushed suddenly,—
And *s*ad to *s*ee her sorrowful constraint,—
And on the grasse her *d*aintie *l*imbes *d*id *l*ay,—&c.
[*F.Q.*, I.iii.5]

You can not read a page of the Faery Queene, if you read for that purpose, without perceiving the intentional alliterativeness of the words; and yet so skilfully is this managed, that it never strikes any unwarned ear as artificial, or other than the result of the necessary movement of the verse.

3. Spenser displays great skill in harmonizing his descriptions of external nature and actual incidents with the allegorical character and epic activity of the poem. Take these two beautiful passages as illustrations of what I mean:—[Quotes from I.ii.1–2, and I.v.2].

Observe also the exceeding vividness of Spenser's descriptions. They are not, in the true sense of the word, picturesque; but are composed of a wondrous series of images, as in our dreams. Compare the following passage with any thing you may remember in *pari materia*[2] in Milton or Shakspeare:—[Quotes I.vii. 31–32].

4. You will take especial note of the marvellous independence and true imaginative absence of all particular space or time in the Faery Queene. It is in the domains neither of history or geography; it is ignorant of all artificial boundary, all material obstacles; it is truly in land of Faery, that is, of mental space. The poet has placed you in a dream, a charmed sleep, and you neither wish, nor have the power, to inquire where you are, or how you got there. It reminds me of some lines of my own:—

Oh! would to Alla!
The raven or the sea-mew were appointed
To bring me food!—or rather that my soul
Might draw in life from the universal air!
It were a lot divine in some small skiff
Along some ocean's boundless solitude

2. I.e., "in similar vein" [*Editors*].

> To float forever with a careless course
> And think myself the only being alive![3]

Indeed Spenser himself, in the conduct of his great poem, may be represented under the same image, his symbolizing purpose being his mariner's compass:—

> As pilot well expert in perilous wave,
> That to a stedfast starre his course hath bent,
> When foggy mistes or cloudy tempests have
> The faithfull light of that faire lampe yblent,
> And coverd Heaven with hideous dreriment;
> Upon his card and compas firmes his eye,
> The maysters of his long experiment,
> And to them does the steddy helme apply,
> Bidding his winged vessell fairely forward fly.
> [II.vii.1]

So the poet through the realms of allegory.

5. You should note the quintessential character of Christian chivalry in all his characters, but more especially in his women. The Greeks, except, perhaps, in Homer, seem to have had no way of making their women interesting, but by unsexing them, as in the instances of the tragic Medea, Electra, &c. Contrast such characters with Spenser's Una, who exhibits no prominent feature, has no particularization, but produces the same feeling that a statue does, when contemplated at a distance:—

> From her fayre head her fillet she undight,
> And layd her stole aside: her angels face,
> As the great eye of Heaven, shyned bright,
> And made a sunshine in the shady place;
> Did never mortal eye behold such heavenly grace.
> [I.iii.4]

6. In Spenser we see the brightest and purest form of that nationality which was so common a characteristic of our elder poets. There is nothing unamiable, nothing contemptuous of others, in it. To glorify their country—to elevate England into a queen, an empress of the heart—this was their passion and object; and how dear and important an object it was or may be, let Spain, in the recollection of her Cid,[4] declare! There is a great magic in national names. What a damper to all interest is a list of native East Indian merchants! Unknown names are non-conductors; they stop all sympathy. No one of our poets has touched this string more exquisitely than Spenser; especially in his chronicle of the British Kings,[5] and the marriage of the Thames with the Medway,[6] in both which passages the mere names constitute half the pleasure we receive. To the same feeling we must in particular attribute Spenser's sweet reference to Ireland:—

3. From Coleridge's drama *Remorse* 4.3 [*Editors*].
4. Rodrigo Diaz de Bivar, "el Cid" (ca. 1030–1099), national hero of Spain [*Editors*].
5. *The Faerie Queene* II.x [*Editors*].
6. *The Faerie Queene* IV.xi [*Editors*].

Ne thence the Irishe rivers absent were;
Sith no lesse famous than the rest they be, &c.
* * * * * * * *
And Mulla mine, whose waves I whilom taught to weep.
[IV.xi.40–41]

And there is a beautiful passage of the same sort in the Colin Clout's Come Home Again:—

"One day," quoth he, "I sat, as was my trade,
Under the foot of Mole," &c. [56–57]

Lastly, the great and prevailing character of Spenser's mind is fancy under the conditions of imagination, as an ever-present but not always active power. He has an imaginative fancy, but he has not imagination, in kind or degree, as Shakspeare and Milton have; the boldest effort of his powers in this way is the character of Talus.[7] Add to this a feminine tenderness and almost maidenly purity of feeling, and above all, a deep moral earnestness which produces a believing sympathy and acquiescence in the reader, and you have a tolerably adequate view of Spenser's intellectual being.

7. Arthegall's servant, "made of yron mould," in *The Faerie Queene* V [*Editors*].

MODERN AND CONTEMPORARY CRITICISM

C. S. LEWIS

[Edmund Spenser's Platonized Protestantism]†

* * *

Formally considered, the *Faerie Queene* is the fusion of two kinds, the medieval allegory and the more recent romantic epic of the Italians. Because it is allegory, and allegory neither strictly religious nor strictly erotic but universal, every part of the poet's experience can be brought in: because it is romantic epic, a certain unity is immediately imposed on all that enters it, for all is embodied in romantic adventures. 'Faerie land' itself provides the unity—a unity not of plot but of *milieu. A priori* the ways of Faerie Land might seem 'so exceeding spatious and wide' that such a unity amounted to nothing, but this is not found to be so. Few poems have a greater harmony of atmosphere. The multiplicity of the stories, far from impairing the unity, supports it; for just that multiplicity, that packed fullness of 'vehement adventures', is the quality of Faerie Land; as tragedy is the quality of Hardy's Wessex.

When I last wrote about the *Faerie Queene* some fifteen years ago, I do not think I sufficiently emphasized the originality and fruitfulness of this structural invention. Perhaps it can be best brought out by considering the problems it solves. Spenser, let us say, has experienced in himself and observed in others sensual temptation; frivolous gallantry; the imprisonment and frustration of long, serious, and self-condemned passions; happy love; and religious melancholy. You could, perhaps, get all this into a lengthy, biographical novel, but that form did not exist in his time. You could get it into half a dozen plays; but only if your talent were theatrical, and only if you were ready to see these states of the heart (which were Spenser's real concern) almost smothered by the Elizabethan demands for an exciting plot and comic relief. But in Faerie Land it is all quite simple. All the states become people or places in that country. You meet the first in the Bower of Acrasia, the second in Malecasta's castle, the third in the House of Busirane, the fourth on Mount Acidale, and the fifth in Orgoglio's dungeons and Despair's cave. And this is not scissors and paste work. Such bowers, such castles, such ogres are just what we require to meet in Faerie Land: they are as necessary for filling the country as the country is for accommodating them. Whatever incidental faults the poem may have, it has, so to speak, a healthy constitution: the matter and the form fit each other like hand and glove.

This primary structural idea is reinforced by two others, the first internal to each book, and the second striding across from book to book through the whole poem. Thus in each book Spenser decided that there should be what I have called an 'allegorical core' (or shrine, or inner stage) where the theme of that book would appear disentangled from the complex adventures and reveal its unity: the House of Holiness in I, the House of Alma in II, the Garden of Adonis in III, the Temple of Venus in

† From C. S. Lewis, *English Literature in the Sixteenth Century, Excluding Drama* (Oxford: Oxford University Press, 1954), pp. 380–93.

IV, the Church of Isis in V, Mount Acidale in VI, and the whole appeal of Mutabilitie in the unfinished book. (Since the position of the core within the book is variable, no conclusion can be based on the numbering of those two cantos.) Next in dignity to the core in each book comes the main allegorical story of the book (Guyon's or Calidore's quest). Beyond that is a loose fringe of stories which may be fully allegorical (like Scudamore's visit to the cottage of Care) or merely typical (like Paridell's seduction of Hellenore) or not allegorical at all (like the story told by the Squire of Dames to Satyrane). Thus the appearance, so necessary to the poem's quality, of pathless wandering is largely a work of deliberate and successful illusion. Spenser, for reasons I have indicated, may not always know where he is going as regards the particular stories: as regards the symphony of moods, the careful arrangement of different degrees of allegory and different degrees of seriousness, he is always in command.

The second of the subordinate structural ideas is, of course, the quest of Arthur for Gloriana. In approaching Spenser's Arthur we must empty our minds of many associations. Very few places in Spenser's work show with certainty the influence of Malory, and most of them come late; in the Fifth Book of the *Faerie Queene* or the *State of Ireland*. His Merlin can be fully accounted for by Ariosto. If he had not used the form *Igrayne* (for Geoffrey's *Igerne*) in the *Letter to Raleigh* we might almost conclude that he had never met Malory's book till late in life. But the truth is that Malory's Arthur would not serve the Elizabethans' turn. He was too closely connected with the old religion and too little connected with later English history. The Arthur whom Camden in 1586 pointed out as suitable matter for a poet was a different figure. The same blood flowed in his veins as in Elizabeth's. In opposing the Saxons he had very nearly been opposing the Pope. At Henry VII's coronation the Red Dragon of Cadwallader had been advanced, and Henry's son was named Arthur (as Bacon says) 'in honour of the British race of which himself was'. Arthur's conquests supported our claims to Ireland. There may even have been in Spenser's mind associations of a more homely and *bourgeois* sort. Mulcaster in later life—and perhaps when Spenser sat under him—belonged to an archers' club in London who called themselves the knights not of King Arthur but of *Prince* (the *magnificent* Prince) Arthur.

Such an Arthur belonged to the antiquaries and to the patriots far more than to Malory; but even from this new Arthur Spenser turned away. He invented *enfances* for his hero which had no precedent either in Tudor or in medieval tradition. His Arthur was to be a lover endlessly seeking an unknown mistress whom he had loved in a vision. For that theme he was presumably indebted to *Arthur of Little Britain*; whose hero, it must be remembered, was not the British king at all. But it is in Spenser that the myth of the visionary mistress effectively enters modern literature. His prince is the precursor of Novalis's Heinrich, of Alastor, and of Keats's Endymion. Allegorically, we are told, he is Magnificence; and it is clear that, in so far as this means anything Aristotelian, it means Aristotle's Magnanimity. He is seeking Gloriana who is glory, and glory is honour, and honour is the goal of Aristotle's Magnanimous Man. The name of his foster-father, Timon, underlines this. But then glory and honour are difficult words. We found in Douglas's *Palace* that the sight of true Honour was the vision of God. We know, if we are Christians, that glory is what awaits the faithful in heaven. We know, if we are Platonists—and a reading of Boethius would make us Platonists enough for this—that every inferior good attracts us only by being an image of the single real good. The false Florimell attracts by being like the true, the true Florimell by being like Beauty itself. Earthly glory would never have moved us but by being a shadow or *idolon* of the Divine Glory, in which we are called to participate. Gloriana is 'the idole of her Makers great magnificence'. The First Fair is desired in all that is desired. It is only, I think, in the light of such conceptions that the quest of Spenser's Arthur can be understood. Arthur is an embodiment of what Professor Nygren calls 'Eros religion', the thirst of the soul for the Perfection beyond the created universe. Only this explains the terms in which Spenser describes his preliminary vision of Gloriana (I.ix). The laughter of all Nature, the grassy bed shared with the 'royall Mayd', the ravishing words ('no living man like wordes did ever heare') must, it seems to me, be taken for a picture not of nascent ambition and desire for fame but either of natural or celestial love; and they are certainly not simply a picture of the former. Only this explains the scene in which Arthur pursues Florimell (III. i, iv). Those who accuse him of inconstancy forget that he had seen the glory only in a vision by night. Hence, following Florimell,

> Oft did he wish that Lady faire mote bee
> His Faery Queene for whom he did complaine,
> Or that his Faery Queene were such as shee (III. iv. 54).

The best parallel to this is the repeated (and always disappointed) belief of the Trojans in *Aeneid*, III, that they have already found the *mansuram urbem*. It is in the very nature of the Platonic quest and the Eros religion that the soul cannot know her true aim till she has achieved it. The seeker must advance, with the possibility at each step of error, beyond the false Florimells to the true, and beyond the true Florimell to the Glory. Only such an interpretation will explain the deep seriousness and the explicitly religious language of Arthur's subsequent soliloquy (55–60).

We must not, of course, forget that Gloriana is also Queen Elizabeth. This was much less chilling and shocking to the sixteenth century than it is to us. Quite apart from any prudent desire to flatter his prince (in an age when flattery had a ceremonial element in it) or from any romantic loyalty which he may have felt and probably did feel as an individual, Spenser new that even outside poetry all reigning sovereigns were *ex officio* vicegerents and images of God. No orthodox person doubted that in this sense Elizabeth was 'an idole' of the divine magnificence. It is also easy to misunderstand the sentence 'Gloriana is Elizabeth'. She *is* Elizabeth in a sense which does not prevent Belphoebe from also being Elizabeth nor Elizabeth from being also a remote, unborn descendant of Arthegall and Britomart who are contemporaries of Gloriana. Modern readers, trained on a strict *roman-à-clef* like Dryden's *Absalom*, hardly know how to sit lightly enough to what is called the 'historical allegory' in Spenser. 'Historical parallels' or 'fugitive historical allusions' would be better names. The scene we have just been discussing is a good example. Arthur may at some moments and in some senses 'be' Leicester: but the poet is certainly not meaning to proclaim to the public that Elizabeth had shared her favourite's bed.[1] (For though Arthur met Gloriana in a vision, it was not quite a vision: there was 'pressed gras where she had lyen'.) In general it must be remembered that the identifications of Gloriana and Belphoebe are the only two in the whole poem that have Spenser's authority. That of Duessa was made so early that we may take it for certain. As for the rest, it is well to remember Spenser's own warning 'how doubtfully all allegories may be construed'. He can never have expected most of his historical meanings to be clear to more than a privileged minority of readers: it is reasonable to suppose that he seldom wrote a canto which depended on them for its main interest. No poet would embark his fame in such an unseaworthy vessel Nor do I think that attempts in our own day to recover such meanings are at all likely to be fruitful. Great learning and skill have been spent on them. Every increase in our knowledge suggests a fresh allegory. If historical parallels were harder to come by they would convince more; but their multiplicity rather suggests to me how hard it is for a poet to feign an event which will not resemble some real event—or half a dozen real events.

In addition to the structural elements which I have already mentioned, Spenser at one time thought of stiffening his poem by dovetailing into it the Virtues out of Aristotle's *Ethics*. He was thinking that way when he wrote the Letter to Raleigh as a preface for Fragment A. Presumably he had not though of Aristotle when he wrote Book I, and had ceased thinking of Aristotle when he decided to write a legend of Constancy. Aristotle's doctrine of the Mean is (rather dully) allegorized in II. ii. But the Aristotelian influence on Spenser is fitful and superficial. The *Ethics* was not at all his kind of book. His treatment of Justice suggests that he had forgotten, or never read, most of what Aristotle says about it.

Hitherto I have been speaking about the structural or (in that sense) 'poetic' ideas of the *Faerie Queene*, the inventions which make it the poem it is. Critics often, however, speak of a poet's 'ideas' in quite a different sense, meaning his opinions or (in extreme cases) his philosophy. These are not often so important in a work of art as its 'idea' or 'ideas' in the first sense; the first two books of *Gulliver* depend much more on the 'idea' of big and little men than on any great novelty or profundity in Swift's 'ideas' about politics and ethics. Spenser's thought, however, has been so variously estimated that we cannot pass it over without some discussion.

Some scholars believe that in parts of the *Faerie Queene* they can find Spenser systematically expounding the doctrines of a school. But if so, the school can hardly be defined as anything narrower than Platonized Protestantism. He certainly believes in Predestination. 'Why shouldst thou then despeire, that chosen art?' says Una to the Redcrosse Knight (I. ix. 53). But this will hardly make Spenser Calvinist as distinct from Lutheran, nor either as distinct from Augustinian, or simply Pauline. It is also true that the virtues we meet in the House of Holiness—Humility, Zeal, Reverence, Faith, Hope, Charity, Mercy, and Contemplation—can all be paralleled in Calvin's *Institutio*; but they are not arranged in the same order, and the things themselves would be likely to occur in any Christian teaching whatever. It is argued, again, that the quests on which

1. A friend points out that, after all, nothing but 'words' is said to have passed between Arthur and Gloriana. This makes the ice a little less thin: but nothing like thick enough for safe skating.

the faerie knights are engaged, and especially the scene (i. x. 63) in which Contemplation commands St. George to turn back from the vision of the New Jerusalem and finish the 'royal maides bequeathed care', reflect the activism of Protestant (and, particularly, Calvinist) ethics and its rejection of the contemplative life. They may: but it is not certain. The quests of the knights are after all allegorical. A combat with Error or with the Old Dragon does not necessarily symbolize the active life. St. George's return from the mountain of Contemplation is quite as close to the return of Plato's 'guardians' (*Republic*, 519 d et seq.) as to anything in Protestant theology. And in any case, St. George in the poem must return because the story must go on. It is equally true that Spenser asserts total depravity ('If any strength we have, it is to ill', i. x. i) and 'loathes' this world 'this state of life so tickle' (*Mut.* viii. i), and that this fits well enough with Calvinist theology. But hardly less well with Lutheran. Indeed expressions very similar can be found in nearly all Christian writers. And something not unlike them can be found even in Platonism. When scholars claim that there is a profound difference of temper between Platonism and these world-renouncing attitudes, I do not know what they mean. There is difference of course; but few pagan systems adapt themselves so nearly to total depravity and *contemptus mundi* as the Platonic. The emotional overtones of the words 'Renaissance Platonism' perhaps help us to forget that Plato's thought is at bottom other-worldly, pessimistic, and ascetic; far more ascetic than Protestantism. The natural universe is for Plato, a world of shadows, of Helens false as Spenser's false Florimell (*Rep.* 586 a–c); the soul has come into it at all only because she lost her wings in a better place (*Phaedr.* 246 d–248 e); and the life of wisdom, while we are here, is a practice or exercise of death (*Phaed.* 80 d–81 a).

I am not arguing that Spenser was not a Calvinist. *A priori* it is very likely that he was. But his poetry is not so written as to enable us to pick out his own beliefs in distinct separation from kindred beliefs. When a modern writer is didactic he endeavours, like Shaw or M. Sartre, to throw his own 'ideas' into sharp relief, distinguishing them from the orthodoxy which he wants to attack. Spenser is not at all like that. Political circumstances lead him at times to stress his opposition to Roman Christianity; and if pressed, he would no doubt admit that where the pagan doctors differed from the Christian, the pagan doctors were wrong. But in general he is concerned with agreements, not differences. He is, like nearly all his contemporaries, a syncretist. He never dreamed of expounding something he could call 'his philosophy'. His business was to embody in moving images the common wisdom. It is this that may easily arouse distrust of him in a modern reader. We feel that the man who could weld together, or think that he had welded together, so many diverse elements, Protestant, chivalric, Platonic, Ovidian, Lucretian, and pastoral, must have been very vague and shallow in each. But here we need to remember the difference between his basic assumption and ours. It is scepticism, despair of objective truth, which has trained us to regard diverse philosophies as historical phenomena, 'period pieces', not to be pitted against one another but each to be taken in its purest form and savoured on the historical palate. Thinking thus, we despise syncretism as we despise Victorian Gothic. Spenser could not feel thus, because he assumed from the outset that the truth about the universe was knowable and in fact known. If that were so, then of course you would expect agreements between the great teachers of all ages just as you expect agreements between the reports of different explorers. The agreements are the important thing, the useful and interesting thing. Differences, far from delighting us as precious manifestations of some unique temper or culture, are mere errors which can be neglected. Such intellectual optimism may be mistaken; but granted the mistake, a sincere and serious poet is bound to be, from our point of view, a syncretist. I believe that Sidney and Shakespeare are in this respect like Spenser, and to grasp this is one of the first duties of their critics. I do not think Shakespeare wrote a single line to express 'his' ideas. What some call his philosophy, he would have called common knowledge.

It is this that makes the thought of the *Faerie Queene*, as Professor Osgood says, 'somehow unmeasurable'. Spenser expected his readers to find in it not his philosophy but their own experience—everyone's experience—loosened from its particular contexts by the universalizing power of allegory. It is, no doubt, true that Spenser was far from being an exact thinker or a precise scholar in any department of human knowledge. Whatever he had tried to write would have had a certain vagueness about it. But most poetry is vague about something. In Milton the theology is clear, the images vague. In Racine the passions and the logic of events are clear, but the 'manners' vague and generalized. What is clear in Spenser is the image; Pyrochles beating the water while he cries 'I burne, I burne, I burne', or Disdain strutting, crane-like, on tiptoes, with legs that break but do not bleed, and as good as new, still glaring and still tiptoed, when he has been set up again. That is why it is at once so true and so misleading to call his poetry dream-like; its images have the violent clarity and precision which we often find in actual dreams, but not the dimness and evasiveness which the overtones of the word *dream-like* (based more on waking reverie than real dreaming) usually call up. These images are not founded on, but merely festooned with, philosophical conceptions. In IV. x we can find, if that is our interest, the following: (1) Love as friendship; (2) Venus distinct from Love (or Cupid) as mother from son; (3) Love (Eros) as the brother of Hate (Eris) derived ultimately from Empedocles (32); (4) the hermaphroditic Venus whose obscure origins have been studied by Miss J. W. Bennett (41); (5) Love naturalistically conceived in lines adapted from Lucretius (44 et seq.). But Spenser did not set out by collecting these concepts, still less by attempting a philosophical synthesis of them. His theme is courtship and his model is medieval erotic allegory. How a gentle knight found the island fortress of true love and overcame its defenders and won meek Amoret—that is the substance. And that is all clear and vivid—the bridge with its corbes and pendants, the door where the porter Doubt peeps 'through a crevis small', the ubiquitous sound of running water, the inner paradise, the Loves fluttering round the statue, and the capture of the beloved. The philosophical matter merely adds a suggestion of depth, as if shadows of old thought played about the temple: just as fugitive memories of Donne or Dante or Patmore or Meredith might play about our own minds during a real love affair. I do not mean that Spenser thought of it quite in that way. He was too serious and too syncretistic. Everything that the wise had said about Love was worth attending to. He would not have said 'Let us shade in here a little Platonism and there a little Epicureanism'. He would have said 'Proclus *in Timaeum* doth report . . . Orpheus hath it thus . . . read the like in that place of Ficinus'. But the result is much the same. It produces that depth or thickness which is one of the excellences of the *Faerie Queene*.

This is why work on Spenser's philosophical and iconographical background seems to me so much more rewarding than work on his historical allegory. But though such studies are enrichments they are not necessary for all readers. For those who can surrender themselves simply to the story Spenser himself will provide guidance enough. The allegory that really matters is usually unmistakable. Hazlitt can hardly have meant what he said on that subject. Few poets are so radically allegorical as Spenser: it is significant that one of the few words he has given to our language, Braggadocchio, though intended by him as the name of a man, has become the name of a quality. But it is not impossible that many who thought they were obeying Hazlitt have read the poetry aright. They receive the allegory so easily that they forget they have done so, as a man in health is unaware of breathing.

It has been the fate of the *Faerie Queene* to be attacked where it is strongest. The plan, the story, the invention are triumphant. If they have faults, they are such faults as never deterred any reader except those who dislike romance and would not be allured to read it by any perfections.

In his own day Spenser's narrative technique was highly individual; it has proved so widely serviceable in later fiction that we ignore this. The opening ('A gentle knight was pricking on the playne') seems to us the most ordinary thing in the world. We have seen a hundred novels begun in the same way; 'Dombey sat in the corner of the darkened room in the great armchair by the bedside', or 'It was early on a fine summer's day near the end of the eighteenth century when a young man of genteel appearance', &c. This method—the immediate presentation of a figure already in action—was not, however, the method of Spenser's predecessors and contemporaries. He had perhaps no perfect model of it except in Heliodorus; and Shakespeare, in his two narrative pieces, is almost his only follower within the sixteenth century. Homer is not quite so direct. Chaucer's *Troilus* does not show us Criseyde kneeling to Hector until line 105. The *Canterbury Tales* do not reach concrete particulars till line 20. Sackville's *Induction* begins with eleven stanzas of description and reflection. In the *Barons Wars* we wade through pages of political prolegomena to reach anything like a scene. *Hero and Leander* hardly becomes a story before line 156. Ariosto does not rise from synopsis to real presentation till his tenth stanza. And the promise of Spenser's opening line is kept in the canto that follows. Nineteenth-century critics, bred on *Marmion* and *The Bride of Abydos*, might think it leisurely; to an Elizabethan, reading it for the first time, the businesslike progression, the absence of what schoolboys call 'gas', must have appeared almost startling. Every line adds. We feel at once that the author has a tale to tell. The business-like progression creates faith. Hence, as Hazlitt (with my italics) says, 'In reading the Faery Queen, you *see* a little withered old man by a wood-side opening a wicket, a giant, and a dwarf', &c.

No critics seem to me farther astray than those who deny that Spenser is an essentially narrative poet. No one loves him who does not love his story; outside the proems to the books and cantos he scarcely writes a line that is not for the story's sake. His style is to be judged as the style of a story-teller. This is one reason why, though eminently a poet of Golden matter, he does not at all continuously exemplify the Golden manner. There is unfortunately another reason: Spenser at times relapses into the vices of the Drab Age.

We therefore have to distinguish three conditions of his style, two good, and one bad. Here is a specimen of the bad:

> Tho when they had long time there taken rest,
> Sir Arthegall, who all this while was bound
> Upon an hard adventure yet in quest,
> Fit time for him thence to depart it found (iv. vi. 42).

It might come from the *Mirror for Magistrates.* Not one word into speaks to the senses or to the emotions. It is dry information, far worse than prose because the language has been cruelly racked to fit it into metre. That is Spenser in his Drab condition. Here is Spenser in his Golden condition:

> By this the Northerne wagoner had set
> His sevenfold teme behind the stedfast starre
> That was in Ocean waves yet never wet
> But firme is fixed and sendeth light from farre
> To all that in the wide deep wandring are . . . (i. ii. i).

That is plain gold; the unsubtle yet delicious flow, the frank (yet here not excessive) alliteration, the frequent images, the Homeric echoes. The last line here, like the last line of the previous example, has an inversion. Yet the effect is quite different. The one, with its clustered consonants and emotional flatness, is felt as mere clumsiness; the other, coming in a line full of melody and calling up great distances, adds a chant-like solemnity. But thirdly, there is Spenser not Golden, not sugared at all (in his manner) but thoroughly good, pressing his tale:

> And there beside of marble stone was built
> An Altare carv'd with cunning ymagery,
> On which trew Christians blood was often spilt . . . (i. viii. 36).

Or again:

> He durst not enter into th' open greene
> For dread of them unawares to be descryde,
> For breaking of their daunce if he were seene;
> But in the covert of the wood did byde,
> Beholding all. . . . (vi. x. ii.).

It is as direct as good medieval verse: not to be lingered over, carrying us equably forward. Much of the *Faerie Queene* is like that; a 'poetry of statement'. The typical Spenserian line tells you what somebody did or wore or where he went. Thus Spenser both falls beneath the Golden norm by defect and is also free to go outside for his own good purposes. We class him among Golden poets for his matter—the whole story is a Golden invention—and because he can often command the Golden style. His lapses into the Drab cannot be palliated in the poem, however we may excuse them historically in the man. But his successful departures from the Golden manner are an added excellence. In an age when poetry was soon to be almost too poetical, he kept open the great thoroughfare of verse for long-distance travellers in workday clothes. Thus, while he touches hands with the pure Golden poets, he also touches hands with Chaucer, Byron, and Crabbe. Wordsworth acknowledged him as a model.

It will be noticed that speeches in the *Faerie Queene* are usually bad if they are meant to express personal passion, and good if they are essentially chants or meditations. The more nearly Spenser approaches to drama the less he succeeds. He does not know the rhetoric of the passions and substitutes that of the schools. This is because he is not the poet of passions but of moods. I use that word to mean those prolonged states of the 'inner weather' which may colour our world for a week or even a month. That is what Spenser does best. In reading him we are reminded not of falling in love but of being in love; not of the moment which brought despair but of the despair which followed it; not of our sudden surrenders to temptation but of our habitual vices; not of religious conversion but of the religious life. Despite the apparent remoteness of his scenes, he is, far more than the dramatists, the poet of ordinary life, of the thing that goes on. Few of us have been in Lear's situation or Hamlet's: the houses and bowers and gardens of the *Faerie Queene*, both good and evil, are always at hand.

From what has been said it follows that those who wish to attack Spenser will be wise to concentrate on his style. There alone he is seriously vulnerable. I have made no attempt to conceal or defend those places where, on any view, he must be admitted to write dully, shrilly, or clumsily. But we come to something more controversial when we consider that quality which, in his best passages no less than in his worst, will alienate many modern readers—the absence of pressure or tension. There are, indeed, metrical variations, more numerous than we always remember. But the general effect is tranquil; line by line, unremarkable. His voice never breaks, he does not pluck you by the elbow, unexpected collocations of ideas do not pour out red hot. There is no irony or ambiguity. Some now would deny the name of poetry to writing of which this must be admitted. Let us not dispute about the name. It is more important to realize that this style (when it is true to itself) is suitable for Spenser's purpose. He needs to create a certain quiet in our minds. The great images, the embodiments, as I have said, of moods or whole phases of experience, rise best if we are not flurried. A still, brooding attention, not a perpetual excitement, is what he demands. It is also probably true that the lack of tension in his verse reflects the lack of tension in his mind. His poetry does not express (though of course it often presents) discord and struggle: it expresses harmony. No poet, I think, was ever less like an Existentialist. He discovered early what things he valued, and there is no sign that his allegiance ever wavered. He was of course often, perhaps usually, disappointed. The actual court did not conform to his standard of courtesy: mutability, if philosophically accepted from the outset, might yet prove unexpectedly bitter to the taste. But disappointment is not necessarily conflict. It did not for Spenser discredit the things of which he was disappointed. It might breed melancholy or indignation, but not doubt. Why, after all, should it? Spenser inherited the Platonic and Christian dualism: heaven was set over against earth, being against becoming, eternity against time. He knew from the outset that the lower, half-unreal world must always fail to copy its archetype exactly. The worst that experience could do was to show that the degree of failure was greater than one had anticipated. If he had thought that the objects of his desire were merely 'ideals', private, subjective constructions of his own mind, then the actual world might have thrown doubt on those ideals. But he thought no such thing. The Existentialist feels *Angst* because he thinks that man's nature (and therefore his relation to all things) has to be created or invented, without guidance, at each moment of decision. Spenser thought that man's nature was given, discoverable, and discovered; he did not feel *Angst*. He was often sad: but not, at bottom, worried. To many of my readers such a state of mind must appear a total illusion. If they cannot suspend their disbelief, they should leave Spenser alone; there are plenty of other authors to read. They must not, however, suppose that he was under an illusion about the historical world. That is not where he differs from them. He differs from them in thinking that it is not the whole story. His tranquillity is a robust tranquillity that 'tolerates the indignities of time', refusing (if we may put the matter in his terms) to be deceived by them, recognizing them as truths, indeed, but only the truths of 'a foolish world'. He would not have called himself 'the poet of our waking dreams': rather the poet of our waking.

What, then, should be our final judgement of Spenser? That question is, in one sense, unanswerable; in another, almost too easy to be worth asking. Among those who shared, or still share, the culture for which he wrote, and which he helped to create, there is no dispute about his greatness. He never, while that culture lasted, suffered any eclipse comparable to that which Donne suffered in the eighteenth century, or Pope in the nineteenth. There are only minor fluctuations in his fame. Even for Rymer he is among the men 'whose intellectuals were of so great a making' that they may outlast 'founders of empires'. Even Dryden acknowledges that 'no man was ever born with so great a genius'. Pope imitated him as if he were an ancient. Within the older English tradition he is only less secure and central than Shakespeare and Milton. But of course this gives us no assurance that he will be mentioned a hundred years hence. His world has ended and his fame may end with it. To attempt an agreed estimate across the chasms that have now opened would be futile. There may—or may not—come a time when the culture for which Spenser wrote and the culture which is now replacing it can be compared, by men to whom English is a dead language, as coolly as we now compare two periods of ancient Egyptian history. At present it is not possible. We can only say that those who in any degree belong to the old culture still find in the ordered exuberance of the *Faerie Queene* an invigorating refreshment which no other book can supply. Doctor I. A. Richards's conception of a poem as a health-giving adjustment of impulses may not cover all poetry—I am not sure. But it certainly covers the *Faerie Queene*. Perhaps that is why, though it may fail to gain some readers, it seldom loses those it has once gained. I never meet a man who says that he *used to* like the *Faerie Queene*.

MARTHA CRAIG

The Secret Wit of Spenser's Language†

The language of *The Faerie Queene* to most modern readers seems alien and unaccountable. Spenser seems to have overlooked the expressive possibilities of idiomatic speech revealed so magnificently by Shakespeare and devised an artificial language which, in contrast to the artificialities of Milton's language in *Paradise Lost*, seems less significant and less forceful than the ordinary language it replaces. Many qualities may seem unfortunate, but perhaps the most vitiating are the archaisms and an apparently purposeless distortion of words. Even after careful study, Spenser's archaism seems superficial and specious, consisting more in odd spellings and grammatical forms than in a genuine rejuvenation of obsolete words that are needed because they are particularly meaningful or expressive. And his liberties with language, the coinages and peculiar forms seem willful and meaningless; alteration of words for the sake of rhyme seems to betray not only lack of resourcefulness but irresponsibility. It is no exaggeration to say that for many readers the language of *The Faerie Queene* is at best merely curious or quaint, at worst hollow and contorted. And this is especially puzzling because the faults seem not only bad but often utterly gratuitous.

* * *

The qualities of style that seem puzzling may be accounted for more adequately if, in place of the specific recommendations of the Pleiade, we consult a more fundamental view of language and reality which the recommendations of the Pleiade only in part represent, that is, the Platonic or "Platonistic" view. A useful document to study in this connection is Plato's *Cratylus*, useful because as an abstract exposition of the fundamental view, it makes the view explicit.

The *Cratylus* is cited prominently by two of Spenser's mentors in their works on language, and references to the dialogue elsewhere during the Renaissance suggest that Plato's discussion had a certain vogue.[1] Spenser must surely have been aware of it and the view of language it presents. The specific question of influence is not primary to an understanding of his poem, however. The dialogue is important to the modern reader as a rationale to account for Spenser's linguistic impulses and to disclose the attitude toward language which *The Faerie Queene* presupposes.

In the *Cratylus* Socrates sets forth the view that words must be not merely conventional and arbitrary, as many believe, but in fact "correct" and "true." For if there is such a thing as reality and knowledge of it, our statements must be about reality, and they must be true to it. And if statements as a whole are to be true, the parts, that is, the words of which

† From Paul J. Alpers, ed., *Elizabethan Poetry: Modern Essays in Criticism* (London: Oxford University Press, 1967), pp. 447–72. The original footnotes have been slightly edited. Reprinted by permission of Oxford University Press.

1. Richard Mulcaster, Spenser's master at the Merchant Taylors' School, cites the *Cratylus* in the peroration to the first part of his *Elementarie*, 1582, proving the existence and importance of "right names" (ed. E. T. Campagnac, Oxford, 1925, p. 188).

they are composed must be true as well. Or, on the analogy of a craft like weaving or cutting, speaking is an action performed for a certain purpose and must be done not according to our own opinion or arbitrary whim but according to nature. We must have the proper instrument correctly suited to the task. In the craft of weaving, the instrument is the shuttle used to separate the web. In the craft of speaking, the instrument is the word.

The instruments of a craft are originally made by someone; so words, too, must have been constructed by an original law-giver or name-maker. An instrument that is good must be constructed according to an ideal. The one who judges whether this has been done successfully, who superintends, is the one who uses the instrument; the carpenter judges the awl. In the case of words the one who judges is the one who knows how to ask and answer questions, who knows how to use words, that is, the dialectician.

What, then, is the principle of "correctness" in words? Socrates says that he does not have the money for a course with the Sophists, so he suggests that the poets be consulted instead. For the modern student of Plato, this advice is tinged with irony, but the Renaissance Platonist, who took at face value the description of poetic inspiration in the *Ion*, Marsilio Ficino, for example, accepts and even approves of the appeal to the poets.

> After thus carefully inquiring from whom the correctness of names, that is, the proper principle by which they are constituted, is to be learned, he mocks the Sophists, and he leads us rather to the poets, not just any of them but the divine ones, as if they had received the true names of things from the gods, among whom are the true names.[2]

In a similar spirit, the Ramist logic acknowledged no fundamental distinction between dialectic and poetry. In respect to words as well as ideas, the poet ideally is a dialectician; he has divinely inspired insight into the truth.

If we consult the poet Homer, we discover that correctness of words consists in revealing the nature of the things named. Words reveal reality through their etymologies. The composition of "Agamemnon," for example, shows that he is admirable (*agastos*) for enduring (*menein*); the derivation of "Atreus" shows that he is the destructive one (*atēros*). Words contain within them little self-explanatory statements. The subject of the statement is the word itself, the predicate is the elemental word or words from which it is made, what we would call the morphemes. Words are "true" because they imply a true statement.

The Ramists on these grounds even introduced etymologizing into logic. Words are a form of argument because the "notation" or etymology of the word bears some logical relation to the "notion" of the thing. "A woman is a woe man because shee worketh a man woe."[3] As the Ramist

2. Marsilio Ficino, "In Cratylum" (Torino, 1959, a reproduction of *Opera Omnia*, Basilea, 1576), II, i, p. 1311, trans. by the author. Cf. Richard Wills, *De Re Poetica*, ed. Fowler, p. 73:

> So Plato, when he inquires in *Cratylus* who are learned in the true names of things, with good reason ridicules the sophists, and judges it necessary to go to the poets—not indiscriminately to all of them, but to such as are divine; as if they had learned the true names of things from the gods.

3. Abraham Fraunce, *Lawier's Logike*, 1588 I, xii, p. 57.

discussion reveals, the "etymology" here is not necessarily the grammatical one, for this may not furnish a second term: we can not make a significant statement out of "argument" from "argue." The etymology required is the "logical" one which "explains the cause why this name is imposed for this thing."[4] That is, the "etymology" or "true" word is not historically true but philosophically true, and it is not the function of the grammarian but the dialectician to interpret words. Often philosophically true turns out to be what we would simply call "fanciful," but neither Plato nor the Renaissance Platonists had any definite standard for distinguishing the two nor any desire to do so.

The names of Spenser's characters are clearly philosophic and true, for they reveal the nature of the one named through the etymology. The heroes' names, like the names of Homer's heroes, are "composed according to a certain allegorical rationale," as Ficino would say. Belphoebe is the "beautiful, pure one," Artegall is the "art of justice." As a poet-dialectician Spenser also interprets given words truly and philosophically through etymology. Magnificence is not properly conspicuous consumption but "doing great deeds" as the etymology shows.

When a suitable etymology is not apparent in the current form of a word, Socrates looks to its archaic form or other archaic words to see if they are more suggestive, for if language has been handed down from some original name-maker, words may have been corrupted in the course of time. If so, the early form should be the right one (*Cratylus* 418–19). Through his theory of language Plato in fact acts out the etymology of "etymology": the true explanation of words is in their origin. The original name-maker in Plato is really a metaphor for whatever principle of order and reason there may be in language. The search for older forms is a search for the true forms that are ideally expressive.

Plato's etymologizing expedient explains the sort of archaizing Spenser does in *The Faerie Queene*. Through archaism Spenser carries out the basic Platonic metaphor of the poem, the metaphor of the antique world, a time in the past when the world was more rational and comprehensible, an ideal time, "ideal" not because there was no evil or difference, but because evil and difference could be more readily perceived and understood. The purpose of his archaisms is not primarily to enlarge his vocabulary, the concern of the Pleiade, but to make it more flexible and expressive. The archaic forms and form words, "-en" endings, "y-" prefixes, and expressions like "ywis" act as a sort of solvent of language, dissolving ordinary patterns and the reader's usual expectation. With archaism established as a mode of diction, Spenser is free to pick out archaic forms that are more suggestive of philosophic meaning.

The action of Spenser's heroes in *The Faerie Queene* continually unfolds an "etymological" rationale, the secret wit of reality which his language is devised to disclose. Nothing, therefore, could be more misleading than the opinion that Spenser's language is negligible in our reading of the poem. In fact "etymological" associations of language are a constant guide to the

4. Fraunce, I, xii, p. 51. "Grammatica notatio exponit vocū adsignificationē Logica vero causam explicat, cur hoc nomen huic rei sit impositū." "Nomina sunt argumenta, non quatenus ad rem significandam referuntur, sed quatenus referuntur vel inter se mutuo, ut coniugata: vel ad suae originis interpretationem, quae Notatio dicitur. Sed sic non considerantur ut nomina, id est symbola, sed ut res quędam, seu *onta* quędam. Piscator."

implicit meaning of the poem and form the very principle of its organization. From the beginning, the poem evolves according to such a rationale: for example, in the action of Book I, a *hero* inspired by *eros* (these terms are explicitly connected in the *Cratylus*, 398 D and make up a traditional "etymology") rides forth as a knight *errant*. His first adventure as a knight errant is, naturally, an encounter with Errour: he defeats her but then proceeds to err through eros, the misplaced affections of his "heroicke" heart.[5] So misled, he goes to the house of Pride from which he emerges safely, only to err again in the *arrogance* of Orgoglio, the presumptuous spirit, the *airs* of man. He is then redeemed from Orgoglio by *Arthur*, the *ardor* and the *art* or efficacy of grace. Yet again he almost errs in *despair* before he is led to the house of Holiness by *Una* where he is restored to *wholeness* and the whole of *holiness* is symbolically revealed.

The action thus proceeds by a series of etymological puns, yet their presence is frequently unobtrusive; the wit appears to us as a secret wit. At the opening of the poem when the knight, his lady, and the dwarf enter the "covert" to find shelter from the storm, we enter into their vision of things. The traditional catalogue of trees becomes a dramatic record of enthrallment, the process of being "led with delight" and so beguiled. The trees, clad with summer's "pride," conceal "heavens light" and the guiding star: what is simply "farre" seems "faire." We are warned by Una that "This is the wandring wood, this *Errours den*," and the double meaning of "knot's and "boughtes" (bouts) anticipate the implication of the knight's encounter with this tortuous beast. Yet the climactic pun drawing so deeply upon the very wit of the language itself takes us by surprise: "God helpe the man so wrapt in *Errours* endlesse traine."

With the killing of Errour the knight's first encounter is complete. He proves that he is not in this sense an errant knight: he is not subject to a form of error which, as the language re-asserts again and again, can be made "plaine." He proves worthy of the "Armorie" which first won his heroic heart.

The action then proceeds to show that the knight is "errant," however, in another sense made fully clear when the word is at last used in Fradubio's speech, he is subject to Duessa or duplicity. "The author then (said he) of all my smarts,/ Is one *Duessa* a false sorceresse, / That many errant knights hath brought to wretchednesse" (I. ii. 34. 7–9). "*Duessa*" is, of course, associated with *duo*, two to suggest her doubleness or deceit but

5. The "heroicke" spirit is an erotic one, Amor and Mars natural companions, as the ambiguity of "courage" and "heart" in the poem confirms. This idea is first suggested in the proem to Book I but is most explicitly elaborated in the defense of love in the proem to Book IV.

> Which who so list looke backe to former ages,
> And call to count the things that then were donne,
> Shall find, that all the workes of those wise sages,
> And brave exploits which great Heroes wonne,
> In love were either ended or begunne:
> Witnesse the father of Philosophie,
> Which to his *Critias*, shaded oft from sunne,
> Of love full manie lessons did apply,
> The which these Stoicke censours cannot well deny.
> IV. Proem, iii

The appearance of "*Critias*" suggests a comparable ambiguity. He is Socrates' chosen, a critic who is not a censour like the Stoics but a discerner, one for whom' "philosophie" is the love of wisdom and the wisdom of love, the erotic heroism of the mind.

also with Greek *dus*, bad, ill and *duē*, misery to suggest the wretchedness she brings.

The Red Cross Knight is parted from Una, the one truth, by Archimago, the arch magician, and can be because "*Archimago*" in his "Hermitage" is the architect of images, of delusive likenesses. Archimago sends to "*Morpheus*," the former or fashioner, for a "diverse" or, etymologically, misleading dream, subtler and more seductive than the "diverse doubt" of Errour because the threat then made "plaine" now becomes an ambiguous "plaint." The "doubtfull words" of the dreamlady make the "redoubted knight / Suspect her truth." Yet "since no' untruth he knew," he is not seduced but interprets her appeal in an honorable way. Sheer ambiguity can not destroy him because if the evil is truly ambiguous, the interpreter must ascertain or supply it, and the knight as "redoubted," reverent as well as revered, has no such evil in him to supply. Archimago must create a definite false illusion of Una as unfaithful which exploits the knight's virtue, his love of her. Una and the Red Cross are thus divided into "double parts" or separated through duplicity and Una left "wandring," the end of Archimago's "drift," leaving the Red Cross to Duessa's wiles.

The nature of the Red Cross Knight's susceptibility is then further dramatized by the difference between Duessa and Sans Foy. The Red Cross defeats Sans Foy; it is not a complete loss of faith on his part which is leading him astray. But he errs, he falls prey to Duessa as Fidessa, a superficially perfect semblance of faith, through his impulse to love, the "heroicke" character of his stout heart. His love for Duessa is certainly a crude bedazzlement revealed in the way he looks her up and down, and in respect to him she is "*Fidessa*" or little faith, but it is significant that his faith is not lost primarily but misplaced: he always believes but he may misbelieve.

The analysis of error which began in the "wandring wood" is completed in the encounter with Fradubio, metamorphosed into a tree or an instance of error in its more refined and significant sense. In the symbolic plant the meaning of the action which began with the earlier "plaints" is "plast in open plaines" (I. ii. 32. 9; 33. 6) and made explicit. Fradubio like the Red Cross was overcome not by doubt per se but by guile, the guile to which doubt as an indeterminate state of mind makes him prey. When he tried to judge between his lady and Duessa, "the doubtfull ballaunce" swayed equally; doubt itself determines in no way. So Duessa intervened with an act of misrepresentation, obscuring his lady in a fog. Fradubio suggests *dubius*, doubting, and reflects its dangers; more specifically, though, he is the victim of "fraud" (I. iv. I. 3), the active evil to which the uncommitted state of doubt makes him vulnerable.

The Red Cross Knight misled by Archimago's Duessa next appears at the house of Pride, implicitly the palace of hypocrisy, as playfully derived from *Hyper chrysos*, covered over with gold.[6]

6. Fraunce, I, xii, p. 57, derives "Hypocrisis, of *hypo*," (for *hyper*, it seems) "which is over, and *chrysos*, gold, because hypocrites bee cloaked with a golden shew overcast." He regards this as a "monkish" and ignorant definition, however, and gives the proper one as *hypokrinomai*, to dissemble.

> A stately Pallace built of squared bricke,
> Which cunningly was without morter laid,
> Whose wals were high, but nothing strong, nor thick,
> And golden foile all over them displaid,
> That purest skye with brightnesse they dismaid.
>
> I. iv. 4

It is a house, as the *Bible* suggests, not on the strait but the broad way and built on sand, but it is "painted cunningly." The porter *"Malvenu,"* a parody of *bienvenu* or welcome, greets them, prefiguring the evil that will come. Then *"Lucifera"* appears, the bringer of light who like Phaeton proudly burns and bedazzles with light intended "fairely for to shyne" or *phaēthōn* (I. iv. 9.9).

In the pageant of the Seven Deadly Sins which follows Spenser's wit is comically farfetched in keeping with the gaudy cartoon quality of the parade. The first sin *"Idlenesse,"* dressed like a monk in "habit blacke, and amis thin," which may by some extravagant puns suggest the poet's condemnation, carries his "Portesse," but unfortunately the prayer book is only a "portesse" only carried and rarely read. Certainly the "wayne" is poorly led with such a vacuous and inattentive fellow guiding its "way." Idlenesse "esloynes" himself and challenges "essoyne" "from worldly cares," (*soins* in French); the legal terms suggest his Jesuitical invocation of the letter of the law to free him ironically for "lawlesse riotise."

Gluttony follows with the long fine neck of a crane; "gluttony" in Latin is derived from *glutire*, to swallow. He is depicted as Silenus the satyr (*satur*, full); his drunken "corse" reflects the course he leads. Lechery, who appears on the traditional goat, *caper*, is true to that depiction, capricious; his "whally" eyes, white of wall eyes, are the goat's eye or *oeil de chèvre* in French.[7]

Envy is presented primarily as a vile mouth, stressed by the rare form "chaw" for jaw to reiterate his endless malicious and mordant backbiting. His gown of satin as "discolourd say" seems to pun on the vicious things he says; the snake he carries in his bosom "implyes" his mortal sting. Envy's gown "ypainted full of eyes" reflects the root meaning of envy in Latin, *invidia*, the evil eye. He eyes all with hatred but particularly looks at his precursor "Covetyse" or avarice with covet eyes, reflecting their close connection.

Wrath is depicted through associations in English as rash or rathe; his is a "*hasty* rage." And when Satan tries to drive this "laesie teme" of evils, Idleness is called *"Slowth,"* spelled as if derived from "slow."

The pride of the Red Cross Knight is mettle, spirit and courage (I. x. 66. 7), zeal, not the pride of this house. As the inhabitants go forth to sport, he estranges himself from their "joyaunce vaine" and therefore encounters Sans Joy. By the defeat of Sans Joy he reveals that it is only vain joy, proud and empty pleasure that he is estranged from, however; though his "cheere" seems initially "too solemne sad," his solemnity is not a puritanical joylessness but reverence.

The Red Cross Knight's Dwarf discovers those who have "mortgaged" (I. v. 46. 4) their lives or literally pledged their lives to death through pride and warns his master who escapes. The Dwarf, who is always the

7. Randle Cotgrave, *A Dictionarie of the French and English Tongues* (London, 1611).

"wary" dwarf, the "carefull" dwarf, seems—in part through association with the archaic term "dwere," meaning doubt or dread—to symbolize not common sense as critics have believed but the fear implicit in the reverence of holiness. His first speech of warning epitomizes his nature: "Fly fly (quoth then / The fearefull Dwarfe:) this is no place for living men." (I. i. 13. 8–9).

The Red Cross escapes the house of Pride only to encounter pride in another form, Orgoglio. According to mythographers pride is derived from heaven and earth, *ex aethere et terra*, but Spenser corrects this through a series of puns to suggest that pride as symbolized by Orgoglio is not from heaven and earth but merely from earth and air. As a "Geant" Orgoglio is born of *Gea*, the earth, but his "boasted sire" is "blustring Aeolus" from *aella*, stormy wind, and *aiolos*, shifting, changeable. Pride is man's earthliness blown up by the vicissitudes of his mortal circumstance. Aeolus "secretly inspired" the earth with "stormy yre," a form which suggests both ire and air, creating Orgoglio. Orgoglio takes "arrogant delight," again with a suggestion of air, in his "high descent," but such descent suggests not true divinity but rather how far he has fallen. Orgoglio thus suggests Greek *orgaein* to swell, to teem, and *orgē*, temperament, wrath, passion, as well as the Italian *orgoglio*, pride.

This association of Orgoglio with air apparently alludes to the Prince of the Power of the Air in *Ephesians*, chapter II, and explains why an encounter with Orgoglio succeeds the Red Cross Knight's rejection of the house of Pride. In *Ephesians* Paul recalls that all men once followed

> the course of this world, according to the Prince of the Power of the Air, the spirit that now worketh in the children of disobedience: Among whom also we all had our conversation in times past in the lusts of our flesh, fulfilling the desires of the flesh and of the mind; and were by nature the children of wrath, even as others. But God, who is rich in mercy, for his great love wherewith he loved us, even when we were dead in sins, hath quickened us together with Christ. . . . For by grace are ye saved through faith; and that not of yourselves: It is the gift of God: Not of works, lest any man should boast. (Authorized Version. The earlier translations contain the same key phrases.)

When he leaves the house of Pride, the Red Cross Knight, wearied by the ordeal, disarms and sits down to rest by a fountain; he thus puts off the armor of faith, to which Spenser in the prefatory letter ascribes all his success, and fails to stand, according to the teaching of *Ephesians* (chapter VI, verses 10ff.), having done all in the whole armor of God. Instead, like the natural man or the child of wrath in *Ephesians*, he indulges the desires of the flesh and the mind by bathing in the pleasure of the shade, listening to the music of the birds, and taking solace with his lady. He drinks from the fountain, the antithesis of the well of life which is later to renew him in his battle with the dragon, for this makes all who drink from it feeble and faint. It comes from a nymph who "tyr'd with heat of scorching ayre" like the knight sat down in the midst of her race, making the goddess Diana "wroth." So disarmed, the knight encounters Orgoglio. The monster, boasting of his high descent and matchless might, symbolizes the knight's pride and the divine wrath such pride arouses: the pride of indulging himself in the confidence of his achievement. Duessa intercedes with Orgoglio begging him not to destroy her knight but to make him an "eternal bondslave," the thrall of pride in works, especially works as a sign of "high descent," of election. And he is so enthralled, erring in the arrogance of the Prince of the Power of the Air, until he is redeemed by grace.

The Red Cross is redeemed from the wrath of Orgoglio by Arthur, symbol of the ardor and art of God's grace. Arthur represents not the magnanimity of God, his potentiality or etymologically his great spirit, but his magnificence, his actuality or etymologically his doing great deeds. Arthur's image and geneology are resplendent with the glory of such greatness. He appears with a headpiece like an almond tree on the top of "greene *Selinis*"; "*Selinis*" in Greek resembles *selinon*, the plant from which the chaplets of victors in the ancient games were made; Virgil calls its "palmosa Selinus" (*Aeneid* III. 705).

* * *

When Arthur appears to save the Red Cross Knight, the poet proclaims the "goodly golden chaine" by which the virtues are linked in love, and each hero aids the other. This chain is literally "concord," the cord that ties all things together (cf. III. i. 12. 8) through *con* and *cor*, the uniting of the heroes' hearts.

Arthur departs in search of the Faerie Queene whom he discovered in the revelation of a dream, the antithesis of the Red Cross Knight's dream delusion contrived by Archimago in canto one. The Red Cross and Una set off and are soon accosted by a knight fleeing a ghastly sight, the sight, we soon learn, of Despair. The knight Trevisan with his head disarmed and a rope about his neck approaches looking back continually in fear. His steed flies with winged heels "As he had beene a fole of *Pegasus* his kind."

The myth of Pegasus and Bellerophon, according to mythographers, signifies the importance of neither exulting too much in good fortune, nor sorrowing too much in adversity since God is the governor of all. Bellerophon, over-elated by his success, decided to fly to the sun on his horse, Pegasus, but he was struck down for such pride by Jupiter and so taught the true limits and proper temperament of man. Both "Trevisan" and his companion "Terwin" reflect the topsy-turvy fate and temperament of Bellerophon in his fall. "Trevisan," however, sees (*viso*) and escapes.

God brought such a disaster upon Bellerophon, according to mythographers, to reveal his true source and sustainer. As the poet asserts in the opening stanza of the next canto, "all the good is Gods, both power and eke will." But God is good, as his name itself implies, and he is merciful to man. The "fole" (I. ix. 21. 9) or foal of Pegasus, and his rider, is also a fool thus in his "foltring" (ix. 24. 9) terror of despair.

Pegasus is traditionally the symbol of poetry; the tradition is germane to the depiction of Despair, for his victim Terwin is a victim of Petrarchan despair in love, so closely associated with poetry, and, more important, Despair's appeal is through the power of rhetoric. The Red Cross Knight is nearly overwhelmed by the poetry of Despair, almost charmed by the "inchaunted" rhyme of the "Miscreant," the unbeliever who miscreates or distorts his argument, evoking doom by the omission of God's grace, insisting that the knight will eternally err: "For he, that once hath missed the right way, / The further he doth goe, the further he doth stray." Even the knight's response is the traditional literary one; he begins to "tremble like a leafe of Aspin greene" (the only use of this figure in the poem.)

Like most of the evils in Book I, Despair is associated with division and doubleness. The main accusation he brings is that the Red Cross was false to his faith and served "Duessa." The term first appears in Book I when Una is originally "from her knight divorced in despaire" (I. iii. 2. 8); she herself remains faithful, but she is "forsaken, wofull, solitarie" through his error, his displaced faith. Spenser seems to suggest that despair is the dis-spirited state which occurs when Una or the one truth of grace and the Red Cross Knight are divided or dispaired. At any rate it is Una who now rescues the Red Cross from the rhetoric of Despair, calling him away from vain words and "the accurst hand-writing" of God's justice to action and grace.

The knight then proceeds to the house of Holiness where the whole of holiness is symbolized. In this house he is taught repentence and the way to "heavenly blesse," according to the argument of the canto. The spelling distinguishes "blesse" from "blisse," though the two were often identified in Elizabethan English and come ultimately from the same etymological source. The Bower of Bliss thus lies in contrast to the house of Holiness as the house of Unblessed Bliss, an ironic *Eden* or garden of pleasure in Hebrew. The excess of *"Acrasia"* which we see there is implicitly contrasted with the abundance of *"Charissa." "Acrasia"* is presented in Book II as a perversion of *charis* or true grace; she "depastures" delight, a term Spenser coined, as the ironic pastor in her bower who takes life rather than nourishing it, destroying her worshippers.

In the house of Holiness Saint George at last gains his name and full identity as his sainthood is foreseen. He learns that he like Arthur is a changeling. Arthur was taken from his mother and delivered to the faery knight "old Timon" thus, it seems, being taught by time, as Achilles was taught by Cheiron, son of Chronos. Saint George, however, was found where a faerie left him in the furrow of a field.

> Thence she thee brought into this Faerie lond,
> And in an heaped furrow did thee hyde,
> Where thee a Ploughman all unweeting fond,
> As he his toylesome teme that way did guyde,
> And brought thee up in ploughmans state to byde,
> Whereof *Georgos* he thee gave to name;
> Till prikt with courage, and thy forces pryde,
> To Faery court thou cam'st to seeke for fame,
> And prove thy puissaunt armes, as seemes thee best became.
>
> I. x. 76

"Georgos" is derived from the Greek term for plowman as "Adam" was derived from the Hebrew term for earth. The etymology suggests their ultimate affinity in the moral allegory. It suggests, too, in retrospect that the earthly giant *"Orgoglio"* is George himself, inspired or blown up with the air of arrogance to which every man in his weakness may succumb.

The etymology of St. George functions also in a very different way: it presents an allusion to English literary history and the career of "holiness" as a topic for poetry. The truth of holiness was lost but then "fond" or found again as invention, matter for poetry in *Piers Plowman*, substantiating the traditional name of the English saint as "ploughman" or man of the soil. Spenser eventually returns the topic to the simple, rural world through the career of "grace" in the poem. "Of Court it seemes, men Courtesie doe call" (VI. i. 1), but Spenser eventually corrects this to show that the court is the source of false courtesy, of "courting;" true "courtesy" is a form of "grace" which thrives best not at court but in the pastoral milieu, or pastoral ideal, of Book VI.

Spenser's secret wit suggests not only the moral implication of the action but political and social instances which substantiate and exemplify. * * *

* * *

DAVID LEE MILLER

[Dan Edmund Meets the Romantics]†

Spenser's peculiar sensibility has eluded many readers over the centuries. His use of Sir Thopas, for example—at once sublime and ridiculous—has moved critics to suggest that Spenser missed the humor of Chaucer's burlesque, that he had no gift for narrative, or that he worked somehow inadvertently, which is rather like saying that Renoir became an impressionist because he could not draw lines. This tendency to underestimate the sophistication of the poem's design goes hand in hand with a tendency to identify the narrative voice as the author's, and consequently to assume that everything the narrator says should be taken at face value. The "Spenser" created by such assumptions was earnest, idealistic, sentimental, and learned but not very clever; a lover of beauty and old books so carried away by his own music he was apt to lose track of the story. In short, he was "Dan Edmund": the comically inept figure Chaucer always pretended to be, though gifted with special powers of song.

This picture of Spenser made the poem easier to read. Without Dan Edmund to take us by the hand, it is a lot harder to know which meanings we can trust. The opening of Book I, Canto iii, is a case in point. After Redcrosse abandons Una at the start of Canto ii, the story follows his exploits with Sansfoy, Duessa, and Fradubio before returning to the wanderings of Una. Spenser marks the transition back to Una by opening Canto iii in his standard manner, for as editors since Upton (1758) have observed, he "usually begins his canto with some moral reflection, agreeable to his subject" (*Var.* 1.206):

> Nought is there vnder heau'ns wide hollownesse,
> That moues more deare compassion of mind,
> Then beautie brought t'vnworthie wretchednesse
> Through enuies snares or fortunes freakes vnkind:
> I, whether lately through her brightnes blynd,
> Or through alleageance and fast fealty,
> Which I do owe vnto all womankynd,

† From "*The Faerie Queene* (1590)" in Bart van Es, ed., *A Critical Companion to Spenser Studies* (New York: Palgrave Macmillan, 2006), 151–55. Reprinted by permission of Palgrave Macmillan.

Feele my hart perst with so great agony,
When such I see, that all for pitty I could dy.
(I.iii.1)

Like Chaucer's Dan Geoffrey, the narrator in these lines casts himself as a humble servant of women—too humble indeed to put himself forward as a lover, but deeply susceptible to beauty in distress. What seems to be missing, when we look through the eyes of Romantic and Victorian readers, is a sense of comedy, a feel for some ironic distance between the poet and the earnest naivety of his narrator. The opening line offers a keynote for this response, since heaven will seem hollow either to the "Forsaken, wofull, solitarie mayd . . . in exile" (I.iii.3.2–3) or to the reader who finds his empathy quickened by her distress. This pathos, reinforced by the music of the phrase "heau'ns wide hollowness," would be sharply qualified by ironic distancing of the sort we associate with Chaucer.

As the *Variorum* shows, readers of this passage from Coleridge to the early twentieth century respond to the "plenilune loveliness" of the "tender stanzas" that open Canto iii much as Dan Edmund responds to Una's beauty in distress (Cory 1917, cited in *Var.* 1.206). Leigh Hunt (1844, cited in *Var.* 1.206–7) offers a note of dissent: quoting Coleridge on "the indescribable sweetness and fluent projections" of Spenser's verse as illustrated in Stanza 3, Hunt objects that there are better examples to be found. He is right. What distinguishes the passage is not its sheer beauty (though it is beautiful) but its pathos—and, more specifically, its gender politics. Romantic critics typically rhapsodize over three qualities in Spenser: his imagery, his verbal music, and his heroines. Emile Legouis (1924, cited in *Var.* 3.392) illustrates the first tendency—"fortune made him a painter in verse"—while Edward Dowden (1888, cited in *Var.* 3.384) illustrates the last: "They rejoice, they sorrow; fears and hopes play through the life blood in their cheeks; they are tender, indignant, pensive, ardent; they know the pain the bliss of love; they are wise with the lore of purity, and loyalty, and fortitude."

None of these critics notices the equivocation in lines 5–6 of the stanza quoted: the narrator is pierced with agony, he tells us, either because of the allegiance he owes to "all womankynd," or because "her brightness" (beauty's?) has blinded him. This blurring of motives repeats a key feature of Redcrosse's response in the previous canto to Duessa, who simulates Una's pathos as well as her virtue:

In this sad plight, friendlesse, vnfortunate,
Now miserable I *Fidessa* dwell,
Crauing of you in pitty of my state,
To do none ill, if please ye not do well.
(II.ii.26.1–4)

Line four with its singsong rhythm sounds just a little too pat, but Redcrosse hears no warning bell. Instead he responds like a Romantic critic:

He in great passion al this while did dwell,
More busying his quick eies, her face to view,
Then his dull eares, to heare what shee did tell,
And said, Faire Lady hart of flint would rew
The vndeserued woes and sorrowes, which ye shew.
(I.ii.26.5–9)

The conventional masculine response to imperiled beauty thrives on the bad faith of disavowed egotism and imperfectly repressed sexual desire. Duessa knows this, and uses her knowledge repeatedly to manipulate Redcrosse. In the closing stanza of Canto ii she distracts him from Fradubio's warning by pretending to faint: "Her vp he tooke, too simple and too trew, / And oft her kist" (45.7–8). As commentators always notice, the phrase "too simple and too trew" is adroitly suspended between the knight and his lady, applying to each in very different senses.

This stanza directly precedes the opening of Canto iii, already quoted. Since Una is not actually mentioned until the *second* stanza, Duessa/Fidessa remains tantalizingly available in stanza one as a point of reference for beauty brought to wretchedness—a gambit that extends the ambiguity already in play at the close of Canto ii. This possibility makes the narrator's equivocation in lines 5–6 seem less innocuous, and may even turn our sense of the stanza on its head. In place of clichéd sentiment embroidered with hyperbole, we find a passage that tempts us to recreate the Redcrosse Knight's error as part of the reading process. And the alternatives are not just different. As the critic Paul de Man writes in another context, "The two readings have to engage each other in direct confrontation, for the one reading is precisely the error denounced by the other and has to be undone by it" (1979, 12). The Romantic reading, here, is denounced and undone by an ironic reading.

The difference between these responses depends on our sense of the narrator. The ironic possibility is subdued, not emphasized by any pointed stylistic device: indeed, the most attention-getting flourish of the stanza is probably the sonorous music of its opening line, which (as we have seen) cues a sentimental identification with suffering beauty. By contrast, the signals for a more ironic reading include a juxtaposition we might ignore, since it spans the break between cantos, and a skeptical take on line 5, with its hint that the narrator's response to beauty may inhibit his powers of perception. The ironic reading also borrows an assumption from reader-response criticism, the idea that if a text invites misunderstandings, even momentarily, these misunderstandings are meaningful as part of the reading process.

Modern criticism recognizes such mixed signals as a pervasive element of *The Faerie Queene*. The text offers a profusion of cues, often muted, that invite incompatible responses. Many other questions are therefore bound up with our sense of the narrative voice: What values does the poem convey? How deliberate are its effects? How deep do its ironies go, and how frequent are they? The best answer to such questions was provided by critic and poet William Empson in remarks directed not to the character of the narrator but to the stylistic qualities of the Spenserian stanza—specifically its "use of diffuseness as an alternative to, or peculiar branch of, ambiguity." In the course of what must be the finest page and a half ever written on Spenser's style, Empson remarks that

> you have to yield yourself to [the stanza] very completely to take in the variety of its movement, and, at the same time, there is no need to concentrate the elements of the situation into a judgment as if for action. As a result of this, when there are ambiguities of idea, it is whole civilizations rather than details of the moment which are

> their elements; he can pour into the even dreamwork of his fairyland Christian, classical, and chivalrous materials with an air, not of ignoring their differences, but of holding all their systems of value floating as if at a distance, so as not to interfere with one another, in the prolonged and diffused energies of his mind. (1930, 34)

If we shift this evocation of the author's mind back in the direction of the text, we may wish to add that differences among systems of value are often experienced precisely in and through details of the moment. We may even want to insist that concentrating elements into a judgment can be productive because it activates what is latent in the text, bringing floating systems of value into contact to reveal that they *do* sometimes interfere with one another. Thus in the passage we have examined, an Augustinian warning against carnal understanding interferes with the chivalric ethos of fealty to womankind. Activating this latent conflict of values lets us see in the poem a prophetic critique of the neo-chivalric sexual politics of Romantic and Victorian critics.

Now a skeptical reader might object that in the process I am describing it is we, not the poet or the text, who trigger the clash of values. This is true: readers activate or repress what is latent. But as I mentioned earlier, a distinctive feature of Spenserian authorship is its separation of *invention* from *authority*. That authority, ceded in the first instance to Elizabeth, necessarily passes to each new reader who picks up a copy of *The Faerie Queene*. When Spenser "defers" the meaning of his text, he is deferring *to us*. I have argued elsewhere that he does so quite self-consciously, going so far as to build into the poem an allegory of the way readers construct his authorship (1996).

This deferral of authority has as its corollary the openness, the suspension of judgment, that Empson finds in Spenser. The term "dreamwork" is particularly suggestive of this uncensored ease with which radically incompatible networks of value and feeling pass into the text. This is not only a quality of mind, however; it is also a formal feature of the allegory. Perhaps I may dream of a librarian. She has my sister's name, with long hair braided like my first wife's, but she is saying things that remind me of a particularly scary colleague, and wearing a dress the color of ripe watermelon, like one I saw once on my babysitter when I was very small. Such a fusion of recent and archaic memories would be the result of what Freud calls dreamwork, a signifying process that evades conscious censorship through displacement and that produces texts marked by condensation and overdetermination. Something similar happens when I read of a hero who bears a saint's name but does not know it, who wears metaphoric armor from the Book of Ephesians but thinks he is an elf, and who has embarked on a quest that resembles both the exploits of Perseus and events in the Book of Revelation, though along the way he will encounter figures from pagan myth, classical epic, folklore, *The Canterbury Tales*, and chivalric as well as Italian romance, many of whom will behave like figures in a morality play. Lewis Carroll was that kind of allegorist.

We rationalize allegories by tracking correspondences among the registers from which their elements come: the adventures of Redcrosse recapitulate the salvation of Everyman, which resembles the history of the early church, which parallels the fortunes of the reformed church in

England, which corresponds to events in the Book of Revelation, and so on. These analogies are marked by "the telling substitution that we call the 'allegorical interpolant,' the sign that gives allegory away" (Nohrnberg 1976, ix)—a special form of allusion. They are virtually innumerable, since each new allusion opens yet another set of potential correspondences; and they are theoretically openended, since in principle each new set is infinitely extensible, although sooner or later it will always break down in practice. In this way the text continually invites *and* frustrates the tracing of its "continued Allegory, or darke conceit" (Hamilton 2001, 714).

* * *

RICHARD HELGERSON

[The New Poet Presents Himself]†

Among his immediate contemporaries, Spenser was doubly unique. Not only was he the best poet, he was the only poet of distinctly laureate ambition. Other men did, of course, write verse. But he alone presented himself as a poet, as a man who considered writing a duty rather than a distraction. With the exception of a few rare and little-respected hirelings, Spenser's literary contemporaries were gentlemen for whom poetry was a mere ribbon in the cap of youth, a ribbon which, if paraded too ostentatiously, threatened to expose its wearer to ridicule and shame. Their poetic self-indulgence (for self-indulgence it was generally admitted to be) was, in consequence, usually of short duration and was marked, whatever its duration, by much self-conscious defensiveness, leading quite often to repentance. A Sidney, a Lodge, or a Harington might defend poetry in the highest terms, proclaiming its divine origin and advertising its civilizing effect, but when these men spoke of their own work it was either with humorous and graceful disdain or with some more serious uncertainty. At such moments, the various elevated notions of the poet as counselor of kings and monarch of all sciences, as first bringer-in of civility, best teacher of virtue, and most potent inspirer of courage—notions that had filled their defenses of poesy, their apologies, and their honest excuses—failed them, leaving no refuge but self-depreciation or recantation. * * * And often the repentant admission of self-destructive prodigality was coupled with a condemnation of poetry, or of the wit that made it possible, or of the love that inspired it. * * * Whether their excuse was "the unnoble constitution of the age that denies us fit employments" or the overmastering sway of some amorous passion, they did agree that poetry required an excuse, and most felt that the best proof of contrition was a promise not to offend in like sort again—a promise that they usually kept.[1]

† From *Self-Crowned Laureates: Spenser, Jonson, Milton, and the Literary System* by Richard Helgerson, 55–100. The essay has been condensed.

1. For a fuller discussion of this pattern and its place in the lives and works of Spenser's contemporaries, see my *Elizabethan Prodigals* (Berkeley: Univ. of California Press, 1976).

But so long as Englishmen offered their poems as mere "idle toys proceeding from a youngling frenzy," England could hardly hope to have a poet of the laureate sort. . . . [2]

How then did he manage to distinguish himself as laureate from his amateur coevals? At first glance, particularly when the glance is taken in retrospect, the formula for his success seems absurdly simple. It consisted of two steps. The first was publicly to abandon all social identity except that conferred by his elected vocation. He ceased to be Master Edmund Spenser of Merchant Taylors' School and Pembroke College, Cambridge, and became Immerito, Colin Clout, the New Poet. No other writer of his generation was willing to take such a step. His contemporaries all hung on to some higher hope or expectation. But where they were lowered by poetry, Spenser, who never tired of insisting on his personal humility, was raised by it. This strategy had, of course, a certain autobiographical plausibility. Unlike Sidney, heir apparent to the earldoms of Leicester and Warwick, or Harington, the Queen's godson, or even Lodge, son of a knighted Lord Mayor of London, Spenser was, whatever his connection with the Spencers of Althorp, a gentleman only by education. He had attended Merchant Taylors' School as a "poor scholar," and Cambridge as a sizar. In presenting himself as a shepherd-poet, he suffered no major *déclassement.*

The second step was the accomplishment of virtuous action through poetry. Though the poet may not himself be an actor in the world, his poetry does make others act. Having abandoned his own public pretension to gentility and its obligations, he proposes nevertheless that "the general end" of his major work is "to fashion a gentleman or noble person in virtuous and gentle discipline." Now other writers, of course, also argued for the didactic value of their work, but rarely did they go beyond expressing the self-defeating hope that other young gentlemen might learn from the poet's experience to avoid the like excess. The lesson of poetry was thus to stay away from poetry and from everything associated with it. * * * But not only did Spenser maintain his view with a resolutely sage seriousness, as Sidney never did, he also illustrated it triumphantly in the first three books of *The Faerie Queene.*

Yet skirting about the periphery is a slight, but ominous, reminder of the more usual Elizabethan estimate of poetry and its relation to the active life of public service. It emerges most clearly in the dedicatory sonnet to Lord Burghley, the leader of the Queen's government and a man notoriously unsympathetic to poets and to poetry.

> To you right noble Lord, whose carefull brest
>   To menage of most grave affaires is bent,
>   And on whose mightie shoulders most doth rest
>   The burdein of this kingdomes governement,
> As the wide compasse of the firmament,
>   On Atlas mighty shoulders is upstayd;
>   Unfitly I these ydle rimes present,
>   The labor of lost time, and wit unstayd.

2. Thomas Watson, *Hekatompathia or Passionate Centurie of Love*, ed. S. K. Heninger, Jr. (Gainesville, Florida: Scholars' Facsimiles, 1964), p. 5.

Confronted with the statesmanlike gravity of Lord Burghley, Spenser forces himself back into the mold of the prodigal poet, the unstaid wit whose work is the product of idleness and lost time. The pressure on Spenser to define himself and his work in these conventional terms was considerable, for they provided, as I have been arguing, the clearest and most widely understood notion of what a poet was and did. The triumphant realization of another idea of the poet in the first three books of *The Faerie Queene* can hardly be appreciated without some sense of those pressures. * * *

As everyone knows, the publication of *The Shepheardes Calender* was a carefully planned literary event. Not merely another collection of poems, the *Calender* marked the debut of the New Poet. The argument supposed by the poems and by E. K.'s introduction to them was already familiar in 1579 and was to become still more familiar in the decade between this promise and its realization in the first books of *The Faerie Queene*. England lacked a poet. "There are many versifiers," as one contemporary remarked, "but no poet."[3] Italy and France had theirs, as did Greece and Rome before them. Why not England? The English language was as fit for poetry, the glory of the English nation as worthy of celebration. Yet there was no English Homer or Virgil, no English Ariosto or Ronsard. Englishmen could, of course, look back to Chaucer, but Chaucer had lived in a time and written in a language too remote from their own to be more than a distant inspiration. But now, at last, the English Poet had appeared. His fledgling work could not yet fully validate his claim to laureate greatness, and so his identity, like that of a still unproven knight of chivalric romance, was for a time to remain hidden. But he was, E. K. assured his audience, clearly beginning in the right way, with the pastoral,

> following the example of the best and most ancient poets, which devised this kind of writing . . . So flew Theocritus, . . . Virgil, . . . Mantuan, . . . Petrarch . . . Boccace . . . Marot, Sanazarus, and also diverse other excellent both Italian and French poets. . . . So finally flyeth this our new poet, as a bird, whose principals be scarce grown out, but yet as that in time shall be able to keep wing with the best.

An extraordinary claim, but there was much in the volume to support it. Not only do the poems contain, as Sidney was to say, "much poetry, . . . indeed worthy the reading," they constitute a deliberate *défense et illustration*[4] of the English language—a restoration of true English diction and a display of the range of poetic forms that English could handle.

Yet for all its pretension and real accomplishment, the book is rife with intimations of failure, breakdown, and renunciation—intimations that arise most often in conjunction with the commonplace Elizabethan notion of the poet as a youth beguiled by love. Even E. K., in defining "the general drift and purpose of [these] eclogues," falls back on the

3. *Sola quia interea nullum paris Anglia vatem? / Versifices multi, nemo poeta tibi est.* C. Downhale in Watson's *Hekatompathia*, p. 12.
4. The phrase echoes the title of the "manifesto," *Deffence et illustration de la langue françoise*, composed in ca. 1553 by Joachim du Bellay (1522–60), one of a group of young French poets (the "Pléade") who wished to enrich and elevate the French language [*Editors*].

usual etiology and the usual defense: "Only this appeareth," he tells us, "that his unstaid youth had long wandered in the common Labyrinth of Love, in which time to mitigate and allay the heat of his passion, or else to warn (as he saith) the young shepherds . . . his equals and companions of his unfortunate folly, he compiled these xii eclogues." Here too poetry derives from the youthful folly of love and serves either to relieve its author of the effects of that folly or to warn others against it. But if this cure prove successful, why should he ever write again? What is to be his new source of inspiration and what is to be his purpose? These are not questions that occur to E. K. He is content to repeat the commonplace without considering its implications. But clearly they do occur to Spenser. He knows his power and has no hesitation in declaring it. He does not, however, know quite how else to use it, or whether indeed it can be put to any further use. Though *The Shepheardes Calender* is meant to distinguish the New Poet from all other writers of English verse, it finds no role for him to play other than the familiar self-defeating one that limited the poetic careers of all his contemporaries.

The series opens with Colin Clout, "under whose person," as we are repeatedly told, "the author self is shadowed," breaking his pipe and abandoning his muse, and it ends twelve eclogues later with a near echo of this gesture of renunciation, as Colin declares his muse hoarse and weary and hangs his pipe upon a tree.[5] Whatever may be true of Spenser, Colin seems destined for no further accomplishment. There is no prospect here of a tomorrow promising "fresh woods, and pastures new," as there will be in Milton's pastoral of poetic self-consecration. On the contrary, having wasted his year on the love that began in January, Colin will have no second chance. Winter has come again, "And after Winter commeth timely death." His experience thus confirms that common moral admonition so fundamental to the Elizabethan pattern of a poetic career: "All the delights of love, wherein wanton youth walloweth," as E. K. puts it in glossing the March eclogue, "be but folly mixed with bitterness, and sorrow sauced with repentance." The pattern finds perhaps its most explicit application to poetry midway through the *Calender* in the June eclogue, where Colin talks of how he sang of love until

> yeeres more rype,
> And losse of her, whose love as lyfe I wayd,
> Those weary wanton toyes away did wype.
> (11. 46–48)

* * *

Yet played against this conventional image of wanton youth is a suggestion of responsibility neglected—responsibility that in Colin's case is specifically poetic. Love may inspire lyric poetry, but it keeps the poet from other, more worthy, kinds–didactic, panegyric, historical, and divine. * * * *The Shepheardes Calender* thus contains a forceful critique of

5. John W. Moore, Jr., "Colin Breaks His Pipe: A Reading of the 'January' Eclogue," *ELR*, 5 (1975), 3–24, reviews previous criticism of this aspect of *The Shepheardes Calender* and suggests that the January eclogue and, more particularly, Colin's breaking of his pipe with which it ends "introduces us to the issue which gives unity to the *Calender*"—the nature of Colin's poetic vocation and the question of his fitness for it. I agree and would further suggest that the series as a whole fails either to resolve the issue or to answer the question.

the conventional poet-as-lover, revealing that poetry written under such a guise is solipsistic, self-indulgent, and fruitless—that it leads inevitably to its own renunciation. Though the point is hardly less familiar than the role itself, we may be surprised to find it here in the book that launched the New Poet. We may be still more surprised to find it associated particularly with the New Poet's pastoral persona, Colin Clout. A great many other works of Spenser's generation teach the same lesson, but they usually announce, not the author's consecration of himself to poetry, but rather his renunciation of poetry in favor of some more serious pursuit. Spenser also talks of more serious pursuits, but these too, as I have said, are literary. Are we then to conclude that in the end Spenser separates himself from Colin, "cast[ing] off his shepherd's weeds," to "emerge as England's heroic poet"?[6] E. K. does deliver a clarion blast worthy of such an epiphany, but the poems fail to echo it. On the contrary, they express, along with a towering ambition and a sense of unique poetic power, much uncertainty about both the practical and the moral implications of a poetic vocation.

Particularly in the October eclogue, the one that deals most directly with these matters, we find a formidable array of barriers in the way of a modern poet. In the first place, poetry does not pay. Unlike a pastime, a vocation requires financial support. "But ah Mecoenas is yclad in claye" (1. 61). And were money forthcoming, support of another, still more vital, sort would nevertheless be lacking. As an art of imitation, heroic poetry requires heroic models. But "great Augustus long ygoe is dead: / And all the worthies liggen wrapt in leade" (11. 62–63). In a stooped and fallen age, poetry must either follow fashion and "rolle with rest in rymes of rybaudrye" or "it wither must agayn" (11.73–78). In the Renaissance, such complaints are legion. E. K. tells us that Spenser borrowed his from Mantuan and Theocritus. But they are no less relevant for that. If Spenser was to "emerge as England's heroic poet," he did need money and he did need to believe that his age was capable of something approaching heroic accomplishment. Not that the age had to furnish all his material. The true poet makes his time as well as mirrors it, for he is the repository of "a certain . . . celestial inspiration." Such, E. K. tells us, was the argument of Spenser's own "book called the *English Poet.*" But in the October eclogue, inspiration is a matter more of uncertainty than of confident assertion. We have already noticed what short work Cuddie makes of Piers's argument that love and the "immortall mirrhor" of beauty should raise the poet's mind "above the starry skie." Cuddie's own claim for Bacchic inspiration fares no better; his comically bombastic, mock-heroic flight ends, rather, with an inglorious fall: "But ah my corage cooles ere it be warme" (1. 115).

* * *

Lacking financial support, at odds with his age, unsure of his inspiration, the New Poet seems less securely set on his way than E. K. would have us think. And underlying his particular uncertainties is a more general and more serious doubt, that poetry of the sort that he was prepared to write could, whatever his inspiration, ever be lifted to the vatic heights of religious, political, and moral perfection.

6. A. C. Hamilton, "The Argument of Spenser's *Shepheardes Calender*," *ELH*, 23 (1956), 175.

* * *

Yet, though he did not earn his living by writing, he, rather than [Ben] Jonson, deserves to be called England's first professed, if not fully professional, poet. Through all the years of minor civic occupation, and well past the age when most men of his generation stopped writing, he pursued his poetic ambition. So that in 1590 he could complete his imitation of Virgil and emerge indeed as his nation's heroic poet, as the first English laureate.

> Lo I the man, whose Muse whilome did maske,
> As time her taught in lowly Shepheards weeds,
> Am now enforst a far unfitter taske,
> For trumpets sterne to chaunge mine Oaten reeds.

To leap, as I must now do, from the beginning of Spenser's poetic career to its end is to leave out much of the most important part. I count on the reader's acquaintance with the great accomplishment of the 1580s, the first books of *The Faerie Queene*, to keep the picture I am drawing from distortion. In these books there is little of the struggle between the love poet and the vatic poet that we have observed in *The Shepheardes Calender.* Both dissolve into the poem, which contains the passion of the one and the vision of the other in a romance that is also a prophecy. Of the poet's self we hear only the humble fear that he may prove unworthy of his great argument or that his audience may mistake his work for mere "painted forgery, . . . th' aboundance of an idle brain." But these are minor doubts. Properly understood, the poem justifies both itself and its maker. This self-justifying union does not, however, hold together. Although the last books show no radical change in character and certainly no lessening of poetic power, the two poets, or the two ideas of poetry, no longer cohere. The private poet rebels against his public duty; the public poet can find no use for his private inspiration. * * *

Nor is it surprising, given what may well have been a double sense of failure—the practical failure of the policies he favored and the moral failure of the beauty he celebrated—that Spenser should have wearied of his epic task. Through the first books of *The Faerie Queene* fatigue had been the greatest burden, ease after toil the greatest temptation. Redcross was overcome when, like Diana's nymph, he "sat downe to rest in middest of the race" (I.vii.5); Guyon weakened when he heard fair ladies singing of "the Port of rest from troublous toil" (II.xii.32); and even Britomart could be surprised, though not tempted, when "through . . . weary toil she soundly slept" (III.i.58). And most often, as in each of these instances, sensual pleasure combines with rest to oppose heroic activity. So in the Bower of Bliss, Verdant, the green youth (think of Spenser talking of "the greener times of [his] youth" when he wrote his hymns of Love and Beauty), sleeping in the arms of Acrasia, emblematically represents the courtly lovers, and by extension the courtly makers, the prodigal love poets, of Spenser's generation.[7]

7. Though Spenser does not identify himself with Verdant or with any other victim of Acrasia's sensuality, there is an echo of the conflict central to Spenser's laureate self-presentation in the violence of Guyon's destruction of the Bower of Bliss. Here the poet apparently felt compelled to overreact. His integrity and perhaps the integrity of the very culture that he, as laureate,

* * *

In two of the *Amoretti* he refers to his unfinished poem, and each time it is with a sense of weariness. "Taedious toyle," he calls it. The two sonnets do, however, divide on the question of what relation his private love has to his public poetic duty, one taking the position that Cuddie had argued in the October eclogue, the other agreeing with Piers. In *Amoretti* 33 love cancels duty while in *Amoretti* 80 it raises the poet's "spirit to an higher pitch," thus preparing him to return to *The Faerie Queene* with renewed inspiration. But even here, the amorous resting place is sharply cut off from the world of "strong endevour"; it is a "pleasant mew" where he can "sport [his] muse and sing [his] loves sweet praise," a "prison" from which he "will break anew." The "anew" refers, I would suspect, to his first escape from the prison of private poetry in the early 1580s. But this second time he seems not to have made good his promised escape, at least not as a poet. In *Amoretti* 80 he says that his work on *The Faerie Queene* is "halfe fordonne," six books having been completed. Though he had still some five years to live, he seems never to have finished another. His last "useful" work was not a poem but, rather, a treatise on the *Present State of Ireland*. Thus the end of his literary career does have the bifurcated look that we observe in the careers of his contemporaries. Once again poetry serves the truant passion of love, while expository and argumentative prose does the work of the active world.

The split was never, of course, absolute or irrevocable. In *Prothalamion*, the last of Spenser's minor poems and perhaps, depending on the date one assigns to the Mutability Cantos, the last poem he wrote, he casts a valedictory glance back over his career—his birth in London, his service to Leicester, his "long fruitless stay" at court—with the regretful air of a man who would still join in the affairs of the great world if the great world would have him. When he says that "some brave muse may sing" the glories of the new champion, Essex, it is hard to tell whether he is putting himself definitively out of contention or bidding for the job. But in the refrain, with its insistence that the day is short and that his song will continue only while the Thames runs softly, we hear the sound of an ending, an impending withdrawal from the public world that this poem still celebrates. Spenser's magnificently unique "both/and," which had made it possible for him to be England's New Poet, had not wholly given way to the familiar "either/or," but disappointment was clearly pushing in that direction.

If he were to satisfy through poetry the humanist expectation that learning would be turned to the useful work of the world, he had to command the respect and attention of those in power. By the time he finished Book VI, Spenser evidently felt he had lost both. The result was a renewed self-consciousness about his role as poet and a backward and inward turn toward "the sacred noursery of vertue," which is both garden and mind. In making this turn, Spenser once again opened the breach between the poet of the inner pastoral world and the poet of heroic accomplishment, between the love poet and the laureate.

---

sought to embody depended on it. For a discussion of the threat posed by Acrasia and the Bower of Bliss, see Stephen Greenblatt, *Renaissance Self-Fashioning from More to Shakespeare* (Chicago: Univ. of Chicago Press, 1980), pp. 157–192.

The center of Spenser's retreat is found in canto x of Book VI, where he and we and Calidore surprise Colin Clout on Mt. Acidale. Calidore and his creator, the epic poet, have wandered far out of the way of duty (the image and the judgment are Spenser's, and he applies them equally to both knight and poet), only to encounter in the secretmost recesses of the pastoral land an image of themselves. For Calidore, that image is the ideal vision of the courtesy which he is meant to embody. For the poet, it is Colin Clout, in whose guise he had formerly masked. Some critics would argue that this meeting merely reunites the pastoral and the epic strains of Spenser's poetry after the arid division of Book V, while others would claim, rather, that it presents once again what has always been united, though now one side and now the other may have predominated. But such arguments neglect the dramatic construction of the episode and indeed of the whole of Book VI. Calidore comes on the scene as an intruder, an outsider whose very presence causes Colin's vision to dissolve. Moreover, the knight of courtesy fails to understand what he has seen and must have it explained to him by the shepherd-poet. And yet, even given the didactic explanation, Calidore's experience on Mt. Acidale, unlike Redcross's in the House of Holiness, seems not to contribute to his formation as a knight. It neither enhances his courtesy, which was innate, nor moves him to heroic action. On the contrary, he remains in seclusion until called forth by the brigands' destruction of his pastoral retreat.[8] * * *

Though in a more subtle way, the scene on Mt. Acidale bears still further testimony to the disjunction between the two sides of Spenser's poetic identity, for it is here that the union of heroic activity and amorous contemplation breaks down. They had been joined in the figure of the Faerie Queene, "in whose fair eyes," as Harvey wrote, "love linked with virtue sits,"[9] and throughout the poem, devotion to Gloriana had directed and inspired the accomplishment of the epic poet. She had raised his thoughts "too humble and too vile" and provided "the argument of [his] afflicted style." She had been to him, as the various proems proclaim, the "mirror and grace of majesty," the living image of "Faerie lond," the model of rule and chastity, "the Queene of love, and Prince of peace," the "Dread Soveraign Goddesse" whose justice informs his discourse, the source from which "all goodly vertues well." From the April eclogue, where the shepherds' queen, Eliza, figured as a fourth Grace and where Hobbinoll and Thenot lamented that Colin's private love had turned him from the singing of such songs, devotion to the Queen had been Spenser's touchstone of poetic responsibility. What then are we to think when in the midst of *The Faerie Queene* Colin and the Graces reappear in a scene closely reminiscent of the April eclogue, with "a country lasse" in the place of the Queen, particularly when Spenser himself calls attention to the substitution? The form of his remark is, naturally enough, an apology. "Pardon thy shepheard," he begs of the great Gloriana, "to make one minime of thy poore handmayd" (VI.x.28). But this self-conscious plea only compounds the fault by breaking the fiction and revealing the

8. For the opposing argument—i.e., that Calidore does undergo an education in true courtesy on Mt. Acidale—see Humphrey Tonkin, *Spenser's Courteous Pastoral* (Oxford: Clarendon Press, 1972), pp. 111–155.
9. Gabriel Harvey printed in the *Variorum*, III, 186.

historical Spenser behind the pastoral mask of Colin Clout. As in the *Amoretti*, the poet speaks in his own person to associate visionary delight with his private love and wearisome duty with the Faerie Queene.[1] Here the dissociation between his pastoral and his heroic personae is very nearly complete. The conclusion of Book VI makes it still more so. The epic poet ends with the bitter regret that because of the Blatant Beast—the image of the great world's hostility to heroic accomplishment—poetry must be reduced to mere pleasure. "Seeke to please," he tells his verse, "that now is counted wisemens threasure." But for Colin on Mt. Acidale—a place designed "to serve all delight"—pleasure had been sufficient unto itself.

Whether by accident or design, the final shape of Spenser's career resembles the shape of old Melibee's. Each begins with the pastoral and then, as Melibee says, "When pride of youth forth pricked [his] desire," each attaches himself to the court and its public concerns. But after years "excluded from native home," each ruefully returns to the pastoral world (VI.ix.24–25). As Isabel MacCaffrey has remarked, "Spenser evidently attached important meanings to this pattern."[2] It recurs, as she notes, in *Colin Clouts Come Home Againe*, and the title of that poem might well serve as the heading to the final chapter of Spenser's creative life. In his last works, in Book VI of *The Faerie Queene*, in the *Amoretti* and the *Epithalamion*, in the hymns of Divine Beauty and Love, and, to an extent, in the two Mutability Cantos, particularly in their setting on Arlo Hill, Spenser does come home, as he did in the last section of *Colin Clout*. He comes home to the pastoral, the personal, and the amorous. That these are also among his most resonant works, among those which engage the cosmic shape of things most confidently, is testimony to the poetic richness of that home. Whatever the laureate's obligations to the public world, it is in this private realm that he finds the source of his inspiration. And though Spenser's turning back to the self and the secret springs of poetry may be in part the result of that unhappy encounter with the world represented by the threatening of the Blatant Beast, it is no repentance. Unlike the other poets of his generation, Spenser responds to such pressure not by renouncing, but rather by reaffirming, the value of poetry. The sometimes hostile active world belongs, he lets us see, to the realm of mutability. Poetry alone has access to the unchanging forms of moral and aesthetic perfection, to "the sacred noursery of vertue" whose ways "none can find, but who was taught them by the Muse" (VI. proem.2–3). Others may have claimed for poetry a similar superiority to those "serving sciences" that depend on nature rather than on the grace of inspiration, but only Spenser turned that claim into a career. He thus gave to the idea of the laureate poet a local habitation and a name. The "Edmund Spenser" of literary history—"the New Poet," the "first . . . great reformer," "our Virgil"—was for later writers perhaps Spenser's most significant creation. It is in this sense that he particularly deserves to be called "the poets' poet."

1. Cf. VI. proem. 1.
2. Isabel MacCaffrey, *Spenser's Allegory: The Anatomy of Imagination* (Princeton: Princeton Univ. Press, 1976), pp. 366–370. The examples of retirement mentioned in my next few paragraphs were suggested by MacCaffrey.

If there is any tendency toward repentance at the end of his career, what he repents is not poetry but his engagement with the active world. Melibee may speak for this side of Spenser when he castigates the vanity of the court and regrets that he "spent [his] youth in vaine" seeking public position. As in *Colin Clouts Come Home Againe*, the great world is presented as a place of hollow aspiration and inevitable repentance, a place opposed to the virtuous tranquillity of the pastoral world. But this is only one side of Spenser, and, even at the end, perhaps not the dominant one. Whatever his ultimate disillusionment with the active life, Spenser never unequivocally restricts the poet to private contemplation. The poet's pastoral mask is, after all, a mask. Though he may, by virtue of his gift and his art, present himself as a native resident of the land of poetry, he is by education, if not by birth, a gentleman, a man of whom public service is rightfully expected.

The Hermit, another retired wiseman in Book VI, but one "of gentle race," better represents the doubleness of Spenser's view. He too "from all this worlds incombrance did himselfe assoyle," but only after dutifully spending his youth and strength in the "worlds contentious toyle" (VI.v.37). Thus the undercurrent of irony in the exchange between Melibee and Calidore in praise of the shepherd's life. "Fittest is," as Melibee says, "that all contented rest / With that they hold" (VI.ix.29). The shepherd's life may fit Melibee, but not Calidore, who holds and is held by duty of his knighthood. The laureate is both contemplative shepherd and questing knight. In this he resembles Redcross, the "clownishe younge man," raised as a ploughman, who takes on the armor of heroic endeavor but who will, as Contemplation tells him, one day "wash thy hands from guilt of bloudy field: / For bloud can nought but sin, and war but sorrowes yield" (I.x.60).[3] What kept Spenser from something like the Hermit's open declaration of retirement from "this worlds incombrance" was, I suppose, the fear that such promptings might be only the counsel of Despair, "Sleepe after toyle, port after stormie seas, / Ease after warre, death after life does greatly please" (I.ix.40). In no book of *The Faerie Queene* is the lure of the private world more attractive than in the last, but in none are the warnings against resting in "middest of the race" more pressing. For Spenser, the Christian humanist, the race was never clearly over, so he could never join the Roman Horace in saying of his public poetic duties, *Non eadem est aetas, non mens.*[4]

Spenser's idea of a poet was finally an unstable but necessary union of two ideas, embodied in two roles—shepherd and knight, Colin and Calidore—neither of which could be renounced in favor of the other. The first gained him a place in the genus *poetae* as it was understood by his generation. The second defined him as the unique English member of the species of professed national poets. Without the first he would have been no poet at all, however much public verse he had written. Without the second he would have been able to make of poetry no more than a diversion of youth. But not even Spenser could maintain the precarious equilibrium that had made possible his extraordinary accomplishment of the

3. Donald Cheney has suggested the connection between the poet and the Redcross Knight in *Spenser's Image of Nature: Wild Man and Shepherd in "The Faerie Queene"* (New Haven: Yale Univ. Press, 1966), pp. 18–22.
4. "My years, my mind, are not the same": Horace, *Epistle* I.i.4.

1580s, an equilibrium that depended on both roles being subsumed by the poem. Nor could his successors achieve anything approaching that balance. They did not really try. Men like Daniel and Drayton professed themselves poets and stuck to their profession more easily because Spenser had been there first. But while they recognized, praised, and relied on his achievement of a literary career, they neither followed nor dared approve his mixing of the two roles. They wrote in both the pastoral and the heroic guise, but they kept the two nicely separated. A similar hardening of generic distinctions was in process in Italy and France, and it is not surprising that English poets should have responded to it. What is surprising is that, without denying either the humanist or the romantic sides of his cultural and literary heritage and in a country that had known no major poet for two hundred years, Spenser could have created a body of work sufficient to give form and substance to an ideal that other men entertained only in the realm of hypothetical speculation. Despite the pressures of his generation, Spenser took poetry beyond repentance and, in so doing, gave England its first laureate poet.

A. BARTLETT GIAMATTI

Pageant, Show, and Verse†

In his *Observations on the Fairy Queen of Spenser* (1752), Thomas Warton remarks:

> We should remember that, in this age allegory was applied as the subject and foundation of public shews and spectacles, which were exhibited with a magnificence superior to that of former times. The virtues and vices, distinguished by their representative allegorical types, were frequently personified and represented by living actors. These figures bore a chief part in furnishing what they called *pageaunts;* which were then the principal species of entertainment and were shewn, not only in private, or upon the stage, but very often in the open streets for solemnising public occasions, or celebrating any grand event. . . . [Spenser's] peculiar mode of allegorizing seems to have been dictated by those spectacles, rather than by the fictions of Ariosto. (1807 edition, 11,74–75; 76)

Warton, as so often, touches on something very important for *The Faerie Queene.* Certainly there had been pageants before the time of Spenser. In Volume I of the *Variorum* edition of Spenser, the reader will find enumerated the spectacles involving St. George, the dragon, and the King's daughter and her lamb that were presented before or by Henry V and Edward III and that are so reminiscent of the opening and the ending of the first book of *The Faerie Queene.* But Elizabeth's reign saw pageantry, and the enthusiasm for pageantry, reach its peak. Of course, the taste for pageantry did not pass with the coming of a new century and new monarch. * * * The spectacles so crucial to the formation of *The*

† From *Play of Double Senses: Spenser's "Faerie Queene"* (Englewood Cliffs, NJ, 1975), pp. 78–93. The original footnotes have been slightly edited. Reprinted by permission.

Faerie Queene, and its audience, were those, however, that greeted England's queen wherever she went.[1]

On the innumerable progresses by and pageants for Elizabeth, we can note only two and consider them emblematic of the form and spirit of the rest. These two are the series of images that greeted her on the day before her coronation, held on Sunday, January 15, 1559, and the spectacles presented during her nineteen-day visit to her favorite, the Earl of Leicester, at Kenilworth Castle in July of 1575. In his *Chronicles of England, Scotland and Ireland*, Raphael Holinshed tells of Elizabeth's progress through London to Westminster on January 14, 1559. Holinshed compares London to "a stage" (London edition, 1808, IV, 159f.)—a crucial element in the idea of pageantry. At Fanchurch, a child sang and Elizabeth saw two figures, representing Henry VII and his wife Elizabeth, daughter of Edward IV. This pageant represented "The uniting of the two houses of Lancaster and York," the union of the White and the Red roses after the War of the Roses. The chronicler explains the significance of this scene:

> It was devised, that like as Elizabeth was the first occasion of concord, so she another Elizabeth, might mainteine the same among hir subjects, so that unitie was the end whereat the whole devise shot . . .

In a kingdom divided by religious dissension, disturbed by the questions of royal legitimacy and (increasingly) of royal succession, and threatened from beyond the channel, concord and unity were overriding concerns of the people and their monarch. Concord and unity, as we know and will see, were also the concern of Elizabeth's greatest poets.

At Cornhill, she saw a pageant on "The seat of worthy government"; at Cheape, two shows: Promises of God to People, and A Flourishing Commonwealth. The last representation came at Fleetstreet. Here was a pageant showing Deborah (Judges, 4–5) as a good ruler consulting with her people, another reminder by the citizens of London to their future Queen of their hopes for her and for themselves. At Temple Bar, there was another oration from a child, verses in Latin and English from "Gogmagog the Albion and Corineus the Briton, two giants" that explained the whole procession, and farewell verses from children. Then Elizabeth went to Westminster where, next day, she took the crown. Deborah had come, the heir to Brut and Arthur, she who would be in the next forty-odd years celebrated under many guises, among them Astraea, the virgin of Justice who fled the earth when the Golden Age ended, and Belphoebe and Gloriana, the Faery Queen.

The passage through London was very much of the people, a progress which displayed their desires for peace and which drew its figures and significance from British and Biblical history. The glittering royal visit to Leicester's Kenilworth Castle in Warwickshire from Saturday, July 9, to Wednesday, July 27, 1575, was a very different occasion. It was aristocratic, chivalric, and complex. A retainer of Leicester's, one Robert (?)

1. On Pageantry, see Sidney Anglo, *Spectacle, Pageantry and Early Tudor Policy* (Oxford, 1969); David Bergeron, *English Civic Pageantry, 1558–1642* (London, 1971); for a fine overview of where this impulse went, in the drama, see E. Waith, "Spectacles of State," *Studies in English Literature* XIII, 2 (1973), pp. 317–30. Neither Anglo nor Bergeron is concerned to know precisely what the word "pageant" meant.

Laneham, has left us a famous account of the Queen's visit in his *Letter* (ed. F. J. Furnivall, The New Shakespeare Society [London, 1890]), and there we can see the Queen did not lack for the more traditional amusements and delights, such as morris dancing, bearbaiting, an Italian tumbler, and a play by the Coventry Men. But tournaments, knightings, and "literary" pageants were in the main fare. * * *

Yet while the mythological and literary pageants of Kenilworth are more sophisticated than the spectacles presented to Elizabeth in London in 1559, the earlier series of images, enacted as Holinshed said upon the "stage" of the city, is closer to the original meaning (and spirit) of the word *pageant.*

A word of disputed origin, *pageant* derives immediately from the late Middle English *pagyn,* which was contemporary with the Anglo-Latin *pagina.* It is a word with four primary and several secondary meanings. A pageant is (1) a scene acted on a stage, a usage applied particularly to the Mystery Plays (late fourteenth century) with (a) the figurative meaning of a part in the drama of life. This primary meaning is implicit in Holinshed's account of Elizabeth's progress in 1559, and both primary and figurative senses exist in Duke Senior's famous words in *As You Like It:*

> This wide and universal theater
> Presents more woeful pageants than the scene
> Wherein we play in.
> (II,vii,137–39)

There is also another subsidiary meaning from the late fourteenth century, *pageant* as (b) a deceit or trick, the meaning conveyed by the Venetian Senator when he says in *Othello* that the Turks only feign an attack on Rhodes:

> 'Tis a pageant
> To keep us in false gaze.
> (I,iii,18–19)

The second and third primary meanings of pageant shade into one another. A *pageant* was (2) a stage or platform on which a scene was acted or a tableau presented; it was also (3) any kind of show, device, or temporary structure, exhibited as a feature of a public triumph or celebration, carried on a moving car or erected on a fixed stage. The last primary meaning, which continues 1b and to which we will return, is *pageant* as (4) an empty show, a spectacle without substance or reality.

With the meanings of pageant before us, let us go back to meaning 1a—a scene acted on a stage, used with special reference to Mystery Plays. The Chester Mysteries were called *pagina prima, pagina secunda,* and so on, after the Anglo-Latin root *pagina* for pageant. But Latin *pagina* is also the root of English *page,* and thus *pageant* and *page* derive from the same Latin word. And, etymology aside, it is certainly true that the content of a public spectacle, particularly in procession, is similar to the content displayed and bound in a book.

Pageantry is a way of writing—one can "write" a pageant because pageantry is a language. It is a way of talking about intensely private concerns in a public manner—as in 1559 the people of London spoke to

Elizabeth in the streets about their deepest concerns. A single scene or stage, a pageant, is a static moment, but pageants in a series present cumulative and enriching perspectives, as do stanzas in a poem or pages in sequence in a book. Shakespeare, who understood the nuances (and visual uses) of the word *pageant* so well, also perceived the link between *pages* and *pageant*, the way spectacle is a public form of writing (and reading) [cites *Richard III* 4.4.84–85]. * * *

To consider pageantry as a public language signifying private concerns is to approach an idea of allegory. For allegory is a way of talking about substances by way of surfaces, a means of focusing on the private, inner, and hidden through the public, available, and open. Such an approach to allegory (or to pageantry) means we must always absorb the surface, the literal level, in order to penetrate to the substance. We must learn to read the public writing of pageantry in order to grasp the common but submerged private significance. In allegory or in pageantry, the surface is never sacrificed to the substance; surface is, rather, at the service of substance. We must learn, as spectators, as readers, to read back from what is available to what is hidden. We must learn to read out of and into ourselves.

Spenser used the term "pageant" in a variety of ways. In his gloss to *"Many Graces"* in the "June" eclogue, E. K., annotator of *The Shepheardes Calender*, says that Spenser wrote a work called *Pageaunts*. It is now lost, but one can assume that some of it made its way into *The Faerie Queene*. In the epic, there are numerous individual pageants: the procession of the Seven Deadly Sins (I,iv, 18–37), the Masque of Busirane (III,xii,6–25), Mutability's progress of seasons, months, hours, life, and death (VII,vii, 28–41), to name but a few. But we are urged to see whole books as pageants as well. Redcross says to Guyon and the Palmer:

> His be the praise, that this atchiev'ment wrought,
> Who made my hand the organ of His might:
> More then goodwill to me attribute nought;
> For all I did, I did but as I ought.
> But you, faire sir, whose pageant next ensewes,
> Well mote yee thee. . . .
>
> (II,i,33)

Book II and Book I are by implication pageants, and immediately after Redcross's words, at II,i,36, Guyon's adventure begins with one of those "sad pageaunts of mens miseries," the tableau of Mordant, Amavia, and Ruddymane. Later in the poem, the poet muses.

> Wonder it is to see in diverse mindes
> How diversly Love doth his pageaunts play,
> And shewes his powre in variable kindes.
>
> (III,v,1)

Not only is variability and diversity always the subject of the poem, but the matter of Books III and IV is precisely the multiple forms of Love in progressive pageant before (and within) the reader's mind. * * * Finally, however, it is the epic that is the great pageant. To borrow Shakespeare's phrase, the dedicatory sonnets are only the "flattering index" to the public, triumphal procession of England and her founding heroes.

In the *Amoretti*, his sonnet sequence published in 1595, Spenser presents his most traditional and interesting use of the word pageant. This is the first eight lines of sonnet 54:

> Of this worlds theatre in which we stay,
> My love, lyke the spectator, ydly sits,
> Beholding me, that all the pageants play,
> Disguysing diversly my troubled wits.
> Sometimes I joy, when glad occasion fits,
> And maske in myrth lyke to a comedy:
> Soone after, when my joy to sorrow flits,
> I waile, and make my woes a tragedy.

Through the image of the theater, and in the writing of pageants-pages, we catch the sense of "play," of pretense and illusion that animates the whole poem. *The Faerie Queene* is a spectacle of the various moods and modes of a man's life in the theater of the world. Here we, the reader-spectator, sit watching our private self, our inner being, figured forth in public, and readily understandable, terms.

Thus far we have focused on pageants-pages as a public language that is significant and truly indicative of private concerns. I have suggested that pageantry is like allegory, a surface spectacle leading and urging us through itself to hidden areas of individual moral concern. In this way, Spenser's "spectacular" way of writing, his allegorical mode, is admirably summed up by Isis' gesture to Britomart. The idol, inclining her wand,

> with amiable looke,
> By outward shew her inward sense desining.
> (V,vii,8)

Her outward signs truly reveal her inward sense, just as the poet tells the reader that

> Of Faery Lond yet if he more inquyre,
> By certein signes, here sett in sondrie place,
> He may it fynd.
> (II, proem 4)

So pageantry is itself a system of signs, a language, revealing inward sense.

Such a view, however, is only part of the story. From the beginning, pageant also conveyed those subsidiary and, in the sixteenth century, primary meanings of deceit, of empty show, of hollow or false spectacle. This, for instance, is Juliet's meaning when she hears Romeo has wounded Tybalt, and she calls her beloved "Despised substance of divinest show" (III,ii, 77). All pageants are shows, but not all shows are true or wholesome, and thus not all pageants are edifying or trustworthy. Let us recall that Puck also produced "pageants," which only proved "What fools these mortals be" (*Midsummer Night's Dream*, III,ii,115).

Pageants can be empty or deceptive as pages (or books) can be deceiving or misleading, as language itself, notoriously unstable, can destroy as well as create. We must school ourselves to recognize the difference between a surface, a pageant, or a word that celebrates something real, and a surface, a show, or a word that only hides a deceptive or empty core. We need to learn, finally, how far to trust pages, or books, or any form of language, by reading the procession of images with an eye to distinguishing surface which misleads from surface which reflects substance.

In *The Faerie Queene*, Spenser gives us ample evidence of the deceptive side of pageantry, ample warning about trusting anyone's pages or words. The word "show" conveys constantly the deceptive side of public activity, or social behavior, [cites V.v.35, II.v.34] * * * It is a constant motif in *The Faerie Queene* . . . that the trickster is tricked, that falsity always contaminates its source, and that vice is its own reward. The easy moralism of this motif is always qualified, however, by the constant, underlying implication that only evil will defeat evil in this world, that, finally, good is powerless to do more than stand by and watch, and hope.

Of course, we can do more than stand passively by. We can actively press the issue and probe appearances with the mind. Indeed, we must. True Courtesy, for instance, must always distrust show. Therefore, when Calidore sees the sight on Mount Acidale and does not understand it,

> Whether it were the traine of Beauties Queene,
> Or nymphes, or faeries, or enchaunted show,
> With which his eyes mote have deluded beene.
> Therefore resolving, what it was, to know
> (VI,x,17)

he presses strenuously towards it, only to have the vision disappear. The rhyme (and episode) are instructive: (enchanted) "show" is rhymed with "know"—the possibility of falsity impels one, properly, to certainty, and yet the quest for knowledge, tragically, leads to loss.

The Knight of Courtesy's instinctive distrust of vanity and appearances results in the shattering of one of the most authentic moments of vision in the poem, and yet Calidore was in a sense correct. One must see face to face, for so much of the world of the poem is reflected through a glass darkly.

> Her purpose was not such as she did faine,
> Ne yet her person such as it was seene;
> But under simple shew and semblant plaine
> Lurkt false Duessa secretly unseene,
> As a chaste virgin, that had wronged beene;
> So had false Archimago her disguysed,
> To cloke her guile with sorrow and sad teene;
> And eke himselfe had craftily devisd
> To be her squire, and do her service well aguised.
> (II,i,21)

This pair, whose essence is falsity and whose goal is division and decay, is everywhere. The spirit of Archimago and Duessa is as ubiquitous in this world as their chivalric trappings are commonplace. It is precisely because what they represent is so commonplace, so much a part of us, that one must guard against show. With Arthur, we as readers must learn when to begin "to doubt [our] dazeled sight" (II,xi,40), for as the poet constantly tells us and shows us, "forged things do fairest shew" (IV,v,15). * * *

Like the world, the poem is full of beauty but also of "an outward shew of things that onely seeme" (*Hymn in Honour of Beautie*, 1,1.91). Thus the poem warns against the poem itself. While like Arthur, gazing at the Faery Queen's image emblazoned on Guyon's shield, we should see the "vertue in vaine shew" (II,ix,3), we must also remember this grand pageant of pages can be seen as only a "painted forgery" (II, proem 1). Even Spenser, recognizing how impossible it is to figure forth the glory of his queen, begs her pardon with an ambiguous term:

> That I in colourd showes may shadow itt,
> And antique praises unto present persons fitt.
> (III, proem 3)

The poet is always aware that his poem, like that other artifact, Acrasia's Island, may only "painted colours shew" (II,vi,29), though he hopes, like Calidore, our sojourn in the genuine world of Faery will render us wise: never more to delight

> in painted show
> Of such false blisse, as there is set for stales,
> T' entrap unwary fooles in their eternall bales.
> (VI,x,3)

Pageant in *The Faerie Queene*, or pageant as *The Faerie Queene*, means both images of the truth and deceptive illusion. So pageantry leads us back to that dual impulse within the poem and * * * within all epic. But even more, it leads us back to the dual nature of the reader and of reading. As we move through the pages and the pageant proceeds before us, as what happens without also happens within, the reader is a spectator or *voyeur* and protagonist. As a spectator, the reader must shape himself for moral action; as a *voyeur*, he must learn to become a *voyant*, that is, learn to pass from spying at the edges, like Calidore, to seeing at the core, like Colin Clout. As we watch versions of the truth pass publicly without, we need to learn to recognize the private, personal truth within. Great poems are not only relevant to readers; readers must strive to become relevant to great poems. In the mediative activity of reading, we expand our humanity by engaging a world wholly new to us.

The double thrust of pageantry is the dual impulse of the poem. As pageant gives either wholesome spectacle or empty show, so the poem, like daylight, "doth discover bad or good" (VI,viii,51) in us, in the world. Made of words, the poem, like the prophecies of Proteus, is ambiguous:

> So tickle be the terms of mortall state
> And full of subtile sophismes, which doe play
> With double sences, and with false debate,
> T' approve the unknowen purpose of eternall fate.
> (III,iv,28)

In his pageants, and pages, the poet plays "with double sences" because that is his sense of the way life plays with us. And because of these mutable "termes of mortall state," he will finally cry at the end that Mutability's sway

> makes me loath this state of life so tickle,
> And love of things so vaine to caste away.
> (VII,viii,1)

Because of language's, and life's, "tickleness," its instability, the poet by the end will have lost faith in the power of pageants to please and to indicate permanence, and will crave a Sabbath's sight, which is true, a Sabbath's site which is unchanging.

The poet will lose faith in the power of language to encompass and maintain a vision of ideal truth. He will never doubt that his picture of the antique time offers a better guide to life than the present scene but, as Harry Berger has done so much to remind us, Spenser will find it increasingly difficult to maintain his pageants.[2] He tells us in the proem (1) to Book V that "the world is runne quite out of square":

> Right now is wrong, and wrong that was is right,
> As all things else in time are chaunged quight.
> Ne wonder; for the heavens revolution
> Is wandred farre from where it first was pight,
> And so doe make contrarie constitution
> Of all this lower world, toward his dissolution.
> (V, proem 4)

Images fail. We cannot depend upon a public language if the public is depraved and the language is unstable. To escape the terror and frustration of the play of double senses, the poet goes inward. He places the sources of ethical wisdom less and less in the public vocabulary of pageantry and more and more within man, within the manageable world of his private self, [cites V.i.7, ii.47] * * * *The Faerie Queene* enacts before us that gradual loss of faith in public norms which eventually darkens the view of Jacobean dramatists, for instance, where the only choices to be made and acts to be pursued are desperate and private ones. Finally, Milton may have borrowed extensively from Spenser for his gardens and his heavens, but it was Spenser's deepening moral inwardness and his unshakable Christian convictions that attracted Milton most.

In the fifth stanza of the proem to Book VI we are told that Courtesy today is

> nought but forgerie
> Fashion'd to please the eies of them that pas,
> Which see not perfect things but in a glas.

Now Courtesy is simply chic, and only important to those who see indirectly rather than face to face. It is interesting only to the *voyeurs*, not the seers:

> But Vertues seat is deepe within the mynd,
> And not in outward shows, but inward thoughts defyned.
> (VI, proem 5)

All is forgery that is not within. The mind is the source and seat of virtue; there exists no longer a public system to communicate a common morality, no longer an "outward shew . . . inward sense desining" (V,vii,8). Spenser has come to the end of pageantry as it extends to allegory, and Book VI is not "allegorical" in the way earlier books were. No great pools of significance gathered around a Despair, or Charissa, or Mammon, or Alma, or

2. Books decline in length after II, sharply after III.

Garden of Venus and Adonis, or Busirane, or marriage of rivers; now a story after the courtesy books and Greek Romances, with one great vision but all ethical wisdom, all virtue, deep in the minds of solitary hermits and shepherds. Only the Blatant Beast remains as an impulse from the earlier parts of the poem. And this remnant of the pageantry of the past serves only to embody the harsh truth that no matter how deep in the mind the line of conscience or the doom of right, no matter how far into the self one drives the self, language always bears within it the seeds of monstrosity as well as beauty. As long as men use words, they must risk letting slip the Beast.

Perhaps this view of pageantry and pages overstresses the dark side of Spenser's sense of language. What, after all, kept him writing with any sense of accomplishment if his view of the present state of life was so melancholy, and his faith in words to sustain a better vision so frail? Why did not he cease before he did?

The answer may be partly that for Spenser, in his own particular form of exile in Ireland, writing had become somehow synonymous with living. The long poem, instinct with a better time, peopled with the glistening creations of his imagination, sustained him despite the profound disappointments and frustrations of creating and living. To stop one would have meant stopping the other. That the attraction of ceasing was strong is attested by the temptation to give in that assails his epic protagonists; that he saw no final reconciliation of the images in his head and what he saw around him, or even what he could write, is evident from his own words and from the fact that all ideal moments of vision vanish and all the lovely ladies and brave knights meet only to part with promises of future bliss.

The poem must have filled his life as he put all his humanity into it; its ideal landscapes must have become the far country of his mind, deep in the interior of his being. Certainly he saw the poet as a gardener, working the soil of the soul, a sovereign planter reordering his own inner paradise. From the beginning of his career, Spenser had understood what it meant to write a verse; that is, he knew the English word *verse* was derived from Latin *versus*, the past participle of *vertere*, "to turn," meaning the turn of a plow, a furrow, line or row. Hence (as we know from pageant and page), a line of verse was the mark of the poet on the page, similar to the mark of cultivation made by the ploughman in the earth. If a page is a plot of land, growing its vine-trellis of writing, Spenser is the careful husbandman, tending, pruning, arranging.

Spenser began early to exploit the radical meaning of "verse." In *The Shepheardes Calender*, after Cuddie sings a complex *sestina* composed by Colin Clout, Perigot says:

> O Colin, Colin, the shepheards joye,
> How I admire ech turning of thy verse!
> ("August," 11. 190–91)

Later he muses on how difficult it is to cram every furrow with the seeds of all he knows. In the midst of narrating the marriage of Thames and Medway, the poet pauses:

> How can they all in this so narrow verse
> Contayned be, and in small compasse hild?
> (IV,xi,17)

And yet the small space, or the container, rammed with life's plenitude and energy, is the basic image of *The Faerie Queene*, and here the "narrow verse," the furrow, swells with the names of rivers, is irrigated with the very stuff of life.

Finally, the poet-planter wished to leave no plot unturned.

> Now turne againe my teme, thou jolly swayne,
> Back to the furrow which I lately left;
> I lately left a furrow, one or twayne,
> Unplough'd, the which my coulter hath not cleft:
> Yet seem'd the soyle both fayre and frutefull eft,
> As I it past, that were too great a shame,
> That so rich frute should be from us bereft.
> (VI,ix,1)

He then returns to the story of Calidore; he returns to his main "plot."

Spenser did not stop writing for the reason that cultivation of his poem was cultivation of his mind. Public language could become increasingly difficult to sustain; the conviction would grow that virtue lived only deep within the individual mind. But he would never abandon language, or the mind itself. He continued to sow in that green place, continued to turn the soil of his page, and as long as he did, there could be, in the mind and in the poem:

> continuall spring, and harvest there
> Continuall, both meeting at one tyme.
> (III,vi,42)

* * *

NORTHROP FRYE

The Structure of Imagery in *The Faerie Queene*†

To demonstrate a unity in *The Faerie Queene*, we have to examine the imagery of the poem rather than its allegory. It is Spenser's habitual technique, developing as it did out of the emblematic visions he wrote in his nonage, to start with the image, not the allegorical translation of it, and when he says at the beginning of the final canto of Book II:

> Now ginnes this goodly frame of Temperaunce
> Fayrely to rise

one feels that the "frame" is built out of the characters and places that are clearly announced to be what they are, not out of their moral or historical shadows. Spenser prefaces the whole poem with sonnets to possible patrons, telling several of them that they are in the poem somewhere, not specifying where: the implication is that for such readers the allegory

† From "The Structure of Imagery in *The Faerie Queene*," *UTQ* 30 (1961): 109–27. Reprinted by permission of University of Toronto Press.

is to be read more or less *ad libitum*. Spenser's own language about allegory, "darke conceit," "clowdily enwrapped," emphasizes its deliberate vagueness. We know that Belphoebe refers to Elizabeth: therefore, when Timias speaks of "her, whom the hevens doe serve and sew," is there, as one edition suggests, a reference to the storm that wrecked the Armada? I cite this only as an example of how subjective an allegorical reading can be. Allegory is not only often uncertain, however, but in the work of one of our greatest allegorical poets it can even be addled, as it is in *Mother Hubberds Tale*, where the fox and the ape argue over which of them is more like a man, and hence more worthy to wear the skin of a lion. In such episodes as the legal decisions of Artegall, too, we can see that Spenser, unlike Milton, is a poet of very limited conceptual powers, and is helpless without some kind of visualization to start him thinking. I am far from urging that we should "let the allegory go" in reading Spenser, but it is self-evident that the imagery is prior in importance to it. One cannot begin to discuss the allegory without using the imagery, but one could work out an exhaustive analysis of the imagery without ever mentioning the allegory.

Our first step is to find a general structure of imagery in the poem as a whole, and with so public a poet as Spenser we should hardly expect to find this in Spenser's private possession, as we might with Blake or Shelley or Keats. We should be better advised to look for it in the axioms and assumptions which Spenser and his public shared, and which form the basis of its imaginative communication.[1] Perhaps the *Mutabilitie Cantos*, which give us so many clues to the sense of *The Faerie Queene* as a whole, will help us here also.

The action of the *Mutabilitie Cantos* embraces four distinguishable levels of existence. First is that of Mutability herself, the level of death, corruption, and dissolution, which would also be, if this poem were using moral categories, the level of sin. Next comes the world of ordinary experience, the nature of the four elements, over which Mutability is also dominant. Its central symbol is the cycle, the round of days, months, and hours which Mutability brings forth as evidence of her supremacy. In the cycle there are two elements: becoming or change, which is certainly Mutability's, and a principle of order or recurrence within which the change occurs. Hence Mutability's evidence is not conclusive, but could just as easily be turned against her. Above our world is upper nature, the stars in their courses, a world still cyclical but immortal and unchanged in essence. This upper world is all that is now left of nature as God originally created it, the state described in the Biblical story of Eden and the Classical myth of the Golden Age. Its regent is Jove, armed with the power which, in a world struggling against chaos and evil, is "the right hand of justice truly hight." But Jove, however he may bluster and threaten, has no authority over Mutability; that authority belongs to the goddess Nature, whose viceroy he is. If Mutability could be cast out of the world of ordinary experience, lower and upper nature would be reunited, man would re-enter the Golden Age, and the reign of "Saturn's son" would

1. In what follows the debt is obvious to A. S. P. Woodhouse, "Nature and Grace in *The Faerie Queene*," *ELH* (Sept. 1949), but there are some differences of emphasis owing to the fact that I am looking for a structure of images rather than of concepts.

be replaced by that of Saturn. Above Nature is the real God, to whom Mutability appeals when she brushes Jove out of her way, who is invoked in the last stanza of the poem, and who appears in the reference to the Transfiguration of Christ like a mirage behind the assembly of lower gods.

Man is born into the third of these worlds, the order of physical nature which is theologically "fallen" and under the sway of Mutability. But though in this world he is not of it: he really belongs to the upper nature of which he formed part before his fall. The order of physical nature, the world of animals and plants, is morally neutral: man is confronted from his birth with a moral dialectic, and must either sink below it into sin or rise above it into his proper human home. This latter he may reach by the practice of virtue and through education, which includes law, religion, and everything the Elizabethans meant by art. The question whether this "art" included what we mean by art, poetry, painting, and music, was much debated in Spenser's day, and explains why so much of the criticism of the period took the form of apologetic. As a poet, Spenser believed in the moral reality of poetry and in its effectiveness as an educating agent; as a Puritan, he was sensitive to the abuse and perversion of art which had raised the question of its moral value in the first place, and he shows his sense of the importance of the question in his description of the Bower of Bliss.

Spenser means by "Faerie" primarily the world of realized human nature. It is an "antique" world, extending backward to Eden and the Golden Age, and its central figure of Prince Arthur was chosen, Spenser tells us, as "furthest from the daunger of envy, and suspition of present time." It occupies the same space as the ordinary physical world, a fact which makes contemporary allusions possible, but its time sequence is different. It is not timeless: we hear of months or years passing, but time seems curiously foreshortened, as though it followed instead of establishing the rhythm of conscious life. Such foreshortening of time suggests a world of dream and wishfulfilment, like the fairylands of Shakespeare's comedies. But Spenser, with his uneasy political feeling that the price of authority is eternal vigilance, will hardly allow his virtuous characters even to sleep, much less dream, and the drowsy narcotic passages which have so impressed his imitators are associated with spiritual peril. He tells us that sleep is one of the three divisions of the lowest world, the other two being death and hell; and Prince Arthur's long tirade against night (III.iv) would be out of proportion if night, like its seasonal counterpart winter, did not symbolize a lower world than Faerie. The vision of Faerie may be the *author's* dream, as the pilgrimage of Christian is presented as a dream of Bunyan, but what the poet dreams of is the strenuous effort, physical, mental, and moral, of waking up to one's true humanity.

In the ordinary physical world good and evil are inextricably confused; the use and the abuse of natural energies are hard to distinguish, motives are mixed and behaviour inconsistent. The perspective of Faerie, the achieved quest of virtue, clarifies this view. What we now see is a completed moral dialectic. The mixed-up physical world separates out into a human moral world and a demonic one. In this perspective heroes and villains are purely and simply heroic and villainous; characters are either white or black, for the quest or against it; right always has superior might in the long run, for we are looking at reality from the perspective of man as he was originally made in the image of God, unconfused about the difference between heaven and hell. We can now see that physical nature is a source of energy, but that this energy can run only in either of two opposing directions: toward its own fulfilment or towards its own destruction. Nature says to Mutability: "For thy decay thou seekst by thy desire," and contrasts her with those who, struggling out of the natural cycle, "Doe worke their owne perfection so by fate."

Spenser, in Hamlet's language, has no interest in holding the mirror up to nature unless he can thereby show virtue her own feature and scorn her own image. His evil characters are rarely converted to good, and while there is one virtuous character who comes to a bad end, Sir Terpine in Book V, this exception proves the rule, as his fate makes an allegorical point about justice. Sometimes the fiction writer clashes with the moralist in Spenser, though never for long. When Malbecco offers to take Hellenore back from the satyrs, he becomes a figure of some dignity as well as pathos; but Spenser cannot let his dramatic sympathy with Malbecco evolve. Complicated behaviour, mixed motives, or the kind of driving energy of character which makes moral considerations seem less important, as it does in all Shakespeare's heroes, and even in Milton's Satan—none of this could be contained in Spenser's framework.

The Faerie Queene in consequence is necessarily a romance, for romance is the genre of simplified or black and white characterization. The imagery of this romance is organized on two major principles. One is that of the natural cycle, the progression of days and seasons. The other is that of the moral dialectic, in which symbols of virtue are parodied by their vicious or demonic counterparts. Any symbol may be used ambivalently, and may be virtuous or demonic according to its context, an obvious example being the symbolism of gold. Cyclical symbols are subordinated to dialectical ones; in other words the upward turn from darkness to dawn or from winter to spring usually symbolizes the lift in perspective from physical to human nature. Ordinary experience, the morally neutral world of physical nature, never appears as such in *The Faerie Queene*, but its place in Spenser's scheme is symbolized by nymphs and other elemental spirits, or by the satyrs, who may be tamed and awed by the sight of Una or more habitually stimulated by the sight of Hellenore. Satyrane, as his name indicates, is, with several puns intended, a good-natured man, and two of the chief heroes, Redcrosse and Artegall, are explicitly said to be natives of this world and not, like Guyon, natives of Faerie. What this means in practice is that their quests include a good deal of historical allegory.

In the letter to Raleigh Spenser speaks of a possible twenty-four books, twelve to deal with the private virtues of Prince Arthur and the other twelve with the public ones manifested after he was crowned king. But this appalling spectre must have been exorcized very quickly. If we look at the six virtues he did treat, we can see that the first three, holiness, temperance, and chastity, are essentially private virtues, and that the next three, friendship, justice, and courtesy, are public ones. Further, that both sets seem to run in a sort of Hegelian progression. Of all public virtues, friendship is the most private and personal; justice the most public and impersonal, and courtesy seems to combine the two, Calidore being notable for his capacity for friendship and yet able to capture the Blatant Beast that eluded Artegall. Similarly, of all private virtues, holiness is most dependent on grace and revelation, hence the imagery of Book I is Biblical and apocalyptic, and introduces the theological virtues. Temperance, in contrast, is a virtue shared by the enlightened heathen, a prerequisite and somewhat pedestrian virtue (Guyon loses his horse early in the book and does not get it back until Book V), hence the imagery of Book II is classical, with much drawn from the *Odyssey* and from Platonic and Aristotelian ethics. Chastity, a virtue described by Spenser as "farre above the rest," seems to combine something of both. The encounter of Redcrosse and Guyon is indecisive, but Britomart, by virtue of her enchanted spear, is clearly stronger than Guyon, and hardly seems to need Redcrosse's assistance in Castle Joyeous.

We note that in Spenser, as in Milton's *Comus*, the supreme private virtue appears to be chastity rather than charity. Charity, in the sense of Christian love, does not fit the scheme of *The Faerie Queene*: for Spenser it would primarily mean, not man's love for God, but God's love for man, as depicted in the *Hymn of Heavenly Love*. Charissa appears in Book I, but her main connexions are with the kindliness that we associate with "giving to charity"; Agape appears in Book IV, but is so minor and so dimwitted a character that one wonders whether Spenser knew the connotations of the word. Hence, though Book I is the only book that deals explicitly with Christian imagery, it does not follow that holiness is the supreme virtue. Spenser is not dealing with what God gives to man, but with what man does with his gifts, and Redcrosse's grip on holiness is humanly uncertain.

In one of its aspects *The Faerie Queene* is an educational treatise, based, like other treatises of its time, on the two essential social facts of the Renaissance, the prince and the courtier. The most important person in Renaissance society to educate was the prince, and the next most important was the courtier, the servant of the prince. Spenser's heroes are courtiers who serve the Faerie Queene and who metaphorically make up the body and mind of Prince Arthur. To demonstrate the moral reality of poetry Spenser had to assume a connexion between the educational treatise and the highest forms of literature. For Spenser, as for most Elizabethan writers, the highest form of poetry would be either epic or tragedy, and the epic for him deals essentially with the actions of the heroic prince or leader. The highest form of prose, similarly, would be either a Utopian vision outlined in a Platonic dialogue or in a romance like Sidney's *Arcadia*, or a description of an ideal prince's ideal education, for which the classical model was Xenophon's *Cyropaedia*. Spenser's preference of Xenophon's form to Plato's is explicit in the letter to Raleigh. This high view of education is inseparable from Spenser's view of the relation between nature and art. For Spenser, as for Burke centuries later, art is man's nature. Art is nature on the human plane, or what Sidney calls a second nature, a "golden" world, to use another phrase of Sidney's, because essentially the same world as that of the Golden Age, and in contrast to the "brazen" world of physical nature. Hence art is no less natural than physical nature—the art itself is nature, as Polixenes says in *The Winter's Tale*—but it is the civilized nature appropriate to human life.

Private and public education, then, are the central themes of *The Faerie Queene*. If we had to find a single word for the virtue underlying all private education, the best word would perhaps be fidelity: that unswerving loyalty to an ideal which is virtue, to a single lady which is love, and to the demands of one's calling which is courage. Fidelity on the specifically human plane of endeavour is faith, the vision of holiness by which one lives; on the natural plane it is temperance, or the ability to live humanely in the physical world. The corresponding term for the virtue of public education is, perhaps, concord or harmony. On the physical plane concord is friendship, again the ability to achieve a human community in ordinary life; on the specifically human plane it is justice and equity, the foundation of society.

In the first two books the symbolism comes to a climax in what we may call a "house of recognition," the House of Holiness in Book I and the House of Alma in Book II. In the third the climax is the vision of the order of nature in the Gardens of Adonis. The second part repeats the same scheme: we have houses of recognition in the Temple of Venus in Book IV and the Palace of Mercilla in Book V, and a second *locus amoenus* vision in the Mount Acidale canto of Book VI, where the poet himself appears with the Graces. The sequence runs roughly as follows: fidelity in the context of human nature; fidelity in the context of physical nature; fidelity in the context of nature as a whole; concord in the context of physical nature; concord in the context of human nature; concord in the context of nature as a whole. Or, abbreviated: human fidelity, natural fidelity, nature; natural concord, human concord, art. Obviously, such a summary is unacceptable as it stands, but it may give some notion of how the books are related and of how the symbolism flows out of one book into the next one.

The conception of the four levels of existence and the symbols used to represent it come from Spenser's cultural tradition in general and from the Bible in particular. The Bible, as Spenser read it for his purposes, describes how man originally inhabited his own human world, the Garden of Eden, and fell out of it into the present physical world, which fell with him. By his fall he lost the tree and water of life. Below him is hell, represented on earth by the kingdoms of bondage, Egypt, Babylon, and Rome, and symbolized by the serpent of Eden, otherwise Satan, otherwise the huge water-monster called Leviathan or the dragon by the prophets. Man is redeemed by the quest of Christ, who after overcoming the world descended to hell and in three days conquered it too. His descent is usually symbolized in art as walking into the open mouth of a dragon, and when he returns in triumph he carries a banner of a red cross on a white ground, the colours typifying his blood and flesh. At the end of time the dragon of death is finally destroyed, man is restored to Eden, and gets back the water and tree of life. In Christianity these last are symbolized by the two sacraments accepted by the Reformed Church, baptism and the Eucharist.

The quest of the Redcross knight in Book I follows the symbolism of the quest of Christ. He carries the same emblem of a red cross on a white ground; the monster he has to kill is "that old dragon" (quatrain to Canto xi; cf. Rev. xii, 9) who is identical with the Biblical Satan, Leviathan, and serpent of Eden, and the object of killing him is to restore Una's parents, who are Adam and Eve, to their kingdom of Eden, which includes the entire world, now usurped by the dragon. The tyranny of Egypt, Babylon, and the Roman Empire continues in the tyranny of the Roman Church, and the Book of Revelation, as Spenser read it, prophesies the future ascendancy of that church and its ultimate defeat in its vision of the dragon and Great Whore, the latter identified with his Duessa. St. George fights the dragon for three days in the garden of Eden, refreshed by the water and tree of life on the first two days respectively.

But Eden is not heaven: in Spenser, as in Dante, it is rather the summit of purgatory, which St. George goes through in the House of Holiness. It is the world of recovered human nature, as it originally was and still can be when sin is removed. St. George similarly is not Christ, but only the English people trying to be Christian, and the dragon, while he may be part of Satan, is considerably less Satanic than Archimago or Duessa, who survive the book. No monster, however loathsome, can really be evil: for evil there must be a perversion of intelligence, and Spenser drew his dragon with some appreciation of the fact mentioned in an essay of Valéry, that in poetry the most frightful creatures always have something rather childlike about them:

> So dreadfully he towards him did pas,
> Forelifting up aloft his speckled brest,
> And often bounding on the brused gras,
> As for great joyance of his newcome guest. (I, xi, 15)

Hence the theatre of operations in the first book is still a human world. The real heaven appears only in the vision of Jerusalem at the end of the tenth canto and in a few other traces, like the invisible husband of Charissa and the heavenly music heard in the background of the final betrothal. Eden is within the order of nature but it is a new earth turned upward, or sacramentally aligned with a new heaven. The main direction of the imagery is also upward: this upward movement is the theme of the House of Holiness, of the final quest, and of various subordinate themes like the worship of Una by the satyrs.

We have spoken of the principle of symbolic parody, which we meet in all books of *The Faerie Queene*. Virtues are contrasted not only with their vicious opposites, but with vices that have similar names and appearances. Thus the golden mean of temperance is parodied by the golden means provided by Mammon; "That part of justice, which is equity" in Book V is parodied by the anarchistic equality preached by the giant in the second canto, and so on. As the main theme of Book I is really faith, or spiritual fidelity, the sharpest parody of this sort is between Fidelia, or true faith, and Duessa, who calls herself Fidessa. Fidelia holds a golden cup of wine and water (which in other romance patterns would be the Holy Grail, though Spenser's one reference to the Grail shows that he has no interest in it); Duessa holds the golden cup of the Whore of Babylon. Fidelia's cup also contains a serpent (the redeeming brazen serpent of Moses typifying the Crucifixion); Duessa sits on the dragon of the Apocalypse who is metaphorically the same beast as the serpent of Eden. Fidelia's power to raise the dead is stressed; Duessa raises Sansjoy from the dead by the power of Aesculapius, whose emblem is the serpent. Of all such parodies in the first book the most important for the imagery of the poem as a whole is the parody of the tree and water of life in Eden. These symbols have their demonic counterparts in the paralysed trees of Fradubio and Fraelissa and in the paralysing fountain from which St. George drinks in the seventh canto.

Thus the first book shows very clearly what we have called the subordinating of cyclical symbols to dialectical ones: the tree and water of life, originally symbols of the rebirth of spring, are here symbols of resurrection, or a permanent change from a life in physical nature above the animals to life in human nature under God. The main interest of the second book is also dialectical, but in the reverse direction, concerned with human life in the ordinary physical world, and with its separation from the demonic world below. The Bower of Bliss is a parody of Eden, and just as the climax of Book I is St. George's three-day battle with the dragon of death, so the narrative climax of Book II is Guyon's three-day endurance in the underworld. It is the climax at least as far as Guyon's heroism is concerned, for it is Arthur who defeats Maleger and it is really the Palmer who catches Acrasia. * * *

Having outlined the dialectical extremes of his imagery, Spenser moves on to consider the order of nature on its two main levels in the remaining books. Temperance steers a middle course between care and carelessness, jealousy and wantonness, miserliness and prodigality, Mammon's cave and Acrasia's bower. Acrasia is a kind of sinister Venus, and her victims, Mordant wallowing in his blood, Cymochles, Verdant, have something of a dead, wasted, or frustrated Adonis about them. Mammon is an old man with a daughter, Philotime. Much of the symbolism of the third book is based on these two archetypes. The first half leads up to the description of the Gardens of Adonis in Canto vi by at least three repetitions of the theme of Venus and Adonis. First we have the tapestry in the Castle Joyeous representing the story, with a longish description attached. Then comes the wounding of Marinell on his "precious shore" by Britomart (surely the most irritable heroine known to romance), where the sacrificial imagery, the laments of the nymphs, the strewing of flowers on the bier are all conventional images of Adonis. Next is Timias, discovered by Belphoebe wounded in the thigh with a boar-spear. Both Belphoebe and Marinell's mother Cymoent have pleasant retreats closely analogous to the Gardens of Adonis. In the second half of the book we have three examples of the old man and young woman relationships: Malbecco and Hellenore, Proteus and Florimell, Busirane and Amoret. All these are evil: there is no idealized version of this theme. The reason is that the idealized version would be the counterpart to the vision of charity in the *Hymn of Heavenly Love*. That is, it would be the vision of the female Sapience sitting in the bosom of the Deity that we meet at the end of the *Hymn to Heavenly Beauty*, and this would take us outside the scope of *The Faerie Queene*, or at any rate of its third book.

The central figure in the third book and the fourth is Venus, flanked on either side by Cupid and Adonis, or what a modern poet would call Eros and Thanatos. Cupid and Venus are gods of natural love, and form, not a demonic parody, but a simple analogy of Christian love, an analogy which is the symbolic basis of the *Fowre Hymnes*. Cupid, like Jesus, is lord of gods and creator of the cosmos, and simultaneously an infant, Venus' relation to him being that of an erotic Madonna, as her relation to

Adonis is that of an erotic Pietà. Being androgynous, she brings forth Cupid without male assistance,[2] she loses him and goes in search of him, and he returns in triumph in the great masque at the end as lord of all creation.

The Garden of Adonis, with its Genius and its temperate climate, is so carefully paralleled to the Bower of Bliss that it clearly represents the reality of which the Bower is a mirage. It presents the order of nature as a cyclical process of death and renewal, in itself morally innocent, but still within the realm of Mutability, as the presence of Time shows. Like Eden, it is a paradise: it is nature as nature would be if man could live in his proper human world, the "antique" Golden Age. It is a world where substance is constant but where "Forms are variable and decay"; and hence it is closely connected with the theme of metamorphosis, which is the central symbol of divine love as the pagans conceived it.

* * *

Just as Book III deals with the secular and natural counterpart of love, so Book VI deals with the secular and natural counterpart of grace. The word grace itself in all its human manifestations is a thematic word in this book, and when the Graces themselves appear on Mount Acidale we find ourselves in a world that transcends the world of Venus:

> These three to men all gifts of grace do graunt,
> And all that Venus in herself doth vaunt
> Is borrowed of them
>
> (VI, x, 15)

The Graces, we are told, were begotten by Jove when he returned from the wedding of Peleus and Thetis. This wedding is referred to again in the *Mutabilitie Cantos* as the most festive occasion the gods had held before the lawsuit of Mutability. For it was at this wedding that Jove was originally "confirmed in his imperial see": the marriage to Peleus removed the threat to Jove's power coming from the son of Thetis, a threat the secret of which only Prometheus knew, and which Prometheus was crucified on a rock for not revealing. Thus the wedding also led, though Spenser does not tell us this, to the reconciling of Jove and Prometheus, and it was Prometheus, whose name traditionally means forethought or wisdom, who, according to Book II, was the originator of Elves and Fays—that is, of man's moral and conscious nature. There are still many demonic symbols in Book VI, especially the attempt to sacrifice Serena, where the custom of eating the flesh and giving the blood to the priests has obvious overtones of parody. But the centre of symbolic gravity, so to speak, in Book VI is a pastoral Arcadian world, where we seem almost to be entering into the original home of man where, as in the child's world of Dylan Thomas's *Fern Hill*, it was all Adam and maiden. It is no longer the world of Eros; yet the sixth book is the most erotic, in the best sense, of all the books in the poem, full of innocent nakedness and copulation, the surprising of which is so acid a test of courtesy, and with many symbols of the state of innocence and of possible regeneration like the Salvage Man and the recognition scene in which Pastorella is reunited to her parents.

2. This detail is not in *The Faerie Queene*: see *Colin Clouts Come Home Againe* 800ff. [*Editors*].

Such a world is a world in which the distinction between art and nature is disappearing because nature is taking on a human form. In the Bower of Bliss the *mixing* of art and nature is what is stressed: on Mount Acidale the art itself is nature, to quote Polixenes again. Yet art, especially poetry, has a central place in the legend of courtesy. Grace in religion implies revelation by the Word, and human grace depends much on good human words. All through the second part of *The Faerie Queene*, slander is portrayed as the worst enemy of the human community: we have Ate and Sclaunder herself in Book IV, Malfont with his tongue nailed to a post in Mercilla's court, as an allegory of what ought to be done to *other* poets; and finally the Blatant Beast, the voice of rumour full of tongues. The dependence of courtesy on reasonable speech is emphasized at every turn, and just as the legend of justice leads us to the figure of the Queen, as set forth in Mercilla, who manifests the order of society, so the legend of courtesy leads us to the figure of the poet himself, who manifests the order of words.

When Calidore commits his one discourteous act and interrupts Colin Clout, all the figures dancing to his pipe vanish. In Elizabethan English a common meaning of art was magic, and Spenser's Colin Clout, like Shakespeare's Prospero, has the magical power of summoning spirits to enact his present fancies, spirits who disappear if anyone speaks and breaks the spell. Nature similarly vanishes mysteriously at the end of the *Mutabilitie Cantos*, just as the counterpart to Prospero's revels is his subsequent speech on the disappearance of all created things. Colin Clout, understandably annoyed at being suddenly deprived of the company of a hundred and four naked maidens, destroys his pipe, as Prospero drowns his book. Poetry works by suggestion and indirection, and conveys meanings out of all proportion to its words; but in magic the impulse to complete a pattern is very strong. If a spirit is being conjured by the seventy-two names of God as set forth in the *Schemhamphoras*, it will not do if the magician can remember only seventy-one of them. At the end of the sixth book the magician in Spenser had completed half of his gigantic design, and was ready to start on the other half. But the poet in Spenser was satisfied: he had done his work, and his vision was complete.

GORDON TESKEY

Thinking Moments in *The Faerie Queene*†

Poetic thinking in Spenser's *Faerie Queene* is not what it would be for poets in a later age. Even Donne, who was of the next generation, made thinking differently from Spenser the intellectual program of his verse, brittle where Spenser is supple, caustic where Spenser is cool, fiercely articulate where Spenser is mythopoeic and obscure. We might ask, brittle, caustic and articulate at what? Supple, cool and obscurely mythopoeic at what? What is this poetic thinking? The grammar of the phrase, "poetic

† From *Spenser Studies: A Renaissance Poetry Annual*, Volume XXII. Reprinted by permission of the author and AMS Press.

thinking," in which *poetic* is the modifying adjective, suggests one is speaking of a nonstandard, dubiously legitimate species of thinking that is peculiar to poetry. It would seem reasonable to proceed by defining unmodified, proper thinking first, philosophical thinking. Only when that has been done will we be ready to examine its impure imitation in verse: *poetic* thinking. But as readers of *The Faerie Queene* know, the obvious starts are often the false ones, leading to early and easy but unfruitful conclusions. The early and easy conclusion is that the philosophy of *The Faerie Queene* is a bastard blend of inexactly-remembered Aristotle, crude, Calvinist polemic, vacuously complicated star-lore and second-rate Neoplatonism, which as its prefix suggests is already second-rate. That, or something like it, is what we get by supposing that thinking is not proper to Spenser's poetry, is not its very substance, but finds its way into the poetry in a secondary way—on the grey wings of the owl of Minerva.

"The poet's poet," as Leigh Hunt called Spenser, is hardly someone we are likely at first to regard as a thinker, as we might, say, George Chapman, or Sir John Davies, neither of whom one would ever call a poet's poet.[1] There is in them too much admixture of prosaic thinking for us to regard their works—as Spenser's are so often regarded—as effusions of the purely poetical. A poet's poet, we suppose, doesn't think, for thinking is something that may be *in* poetry but is always other with respect *to* poetry. * * *

The unthinking aesthetic purity that is still associated with Spenser today was fastened on him by William Hazlitt in the second of his *Lectures on the English Poets* (1818), when he says that "of all poets. [Spenser] is the most poetical" because "the love of beauty . . . and not of truth, is the moving principle of his mind."[2] * * * "Spenser was the poet of our waking dreams, lulling the senses into a deep oblivion of the jarring noises of the world, from which we have no wish to be ever recalled."

* * *

Inasmuch as Spenser was regarded by the romantics as being even learned, he is learned in the quaint way Southey describes, or rather the fictional Southey we encounter in Landor's *Imaginary Conversations* relishing Spenser's allegory, though with much condescension, as a spacious but low-ceilinged chamber copiously furnished in charming disarray, a cabinet of curiosities. * * *

If Milton inhibited the romantics as a towering fortress of thought, Spenser was to them a friendly, enabling presence, like Keats's teacher, Charles Cowden Clarke, "who had," as his grateful pupil said, "by Mulla's stream / Fondled the maidens with the breasts of cream."[3] No one ever compared reading the sage and serious Milton to fondling maidens with breasts of cream. * * *

Finally, there is the Spenser who is a friend to the romantics because he makes it easier for them to write, inspiring rather than intimidating

1. Paul Alpers, "The Poet's Poet," *The Spenser Encyclopedia*, ed. A. C. Hamilton et al. (Toronto: University of Toronto Press, 1990), 551b.
2. *The Complete Works of William Hazlitt*, ed. P. P. Howe, vol. 5 (London: Dent, 1930). The quotations from Hazlitt are taken from the discussion of Spenser on pp. 34–44. See David Bromwich, "Hazlitt, William," *Spenser Encyclopedia*, 349–50.
3. "To Charles Cowden Clarke," line 33–34. See Greg Kucich, *Keats, Shelley, and Romantic Spenserianism* (University Park: State University of Pennsylvania Press, 1991), 142.

them, and this power to aid and to inspire is the best reason for calling Spenser "the poet's poet," This Spenser is evoked in an aside in the introduction to *The Revolt of Islam*, where Shelley states that he composed that enormous poem in Spenserian stanzas because they caused the poem more or less to write itself without forethought, whereas you can't write blank verse—and by "blank verse" Shelley really means "Milton."

* * *

If it is still a popular error (one hears it among students) to suppose Spenser is purely poetical, where poetry has nothing to do with thinking, the opposite error, into which specialists are in more danger of straying, is to suppose the thinking in Spenser's *Faerie Queene* consists of the philosophical content that went into the poem and that can be led out again by *exegesis*, which means "a leading out." I have mentioned a Platonism that is already *neo-neo* before Spenser takes it in hand, to which may be added—from the *Letter to Ralegh*—an Aristotelian poetics so much mediated by Italian critical theory that the Stagirite would hardly recognize it as his own. In the poem itself we find another Aristotle acquired by Spenser at Cambridge, where he was central to a curriculum that a later graduate of that university, Milton himself, would deride as "an asinine feast of sow thistles and brambles."[4]

This Aristotle, derived from commentary on the *Ethics*, lies behind what we think of as the most simplistic allegorical episodes, such as the House of Alma, wherein the teeth bow to the Soul, or the setup episode for the Legend of Temperance, in which three sisters inhabit the castle of Medina, "an ancient worke of antique fame" (II.ii.12); which is to say, the ancient castle represents the accumulated moral thought, unaided by any Christian revelation, on the wisdom of keeping to the golden mean. The castle is therefore inhabited by Medina herself and the extremes of excess and defect which her sisters represent: her younger sister, Perissa, and her older sister, Elissa, Little Miss Too Much Sex, and Little Miss Too Little.

* * *

Elissa and Perissa (we will not learn their names for another twenty two stanzas) are courted by another pair of opposites: the melancholy Huddibras, suitably matched with Elissa, she of "froward countenance" and sullenly unassailable virtue (II.ii.35), and Sans Foy, that "boldest boy," as Spenser calls him, for "warlike weapons" and for "lawless lust" (II.ii.18), who enjoys Perissa's lavish favors, she being "quite contrary to her sisters kind" (II.ii.36): "a mincing minion, / Who in her loosenesse tooke exceeding joy." Even at table, she is to the eager hands of Sans Loy a "frank franion," or wanton sharer, "of her lewd parts," which spectacle is grievous to the unrelieved Huddibras, who "hardly could . . . endure his [Sans Loy's] hardiment, / Yet still he sat, and inly did him selfe torment" (II.ii.36).[5]

4. John Milton, "Of Education," in *The Complete Prose Works of John Milton*, vol. 2 (New Haven: Yale University Press, 1959), 277.
5. *Franion* usually means a wanton male companion (OED). Spenser applies it to a woman here and also, as OED notes, at V.iii.22, where it refers to the False Florimell.

The moral setup in the castle of Medina is permutatively unstable and mindlessly repetitive, like the game of scissors, paper, and rock.[6] After all, the advice, "not too little, but not too much!", which leaves us still unable to tell whether we are nearer the Gulf of Greediness or the Rock of Vile Reproach, is about as useful in any particular situation as "buy low and sell high!" It is true in theory, but it is nearly useless in practice, and starts us oscillating between extremes as we search for the nonexistent middle. Circumstances in the Castle of Medina are so hermetically sealed, like the Second Empire décor of the infernal room in Sartre's *Huis Clos*, where alliances likewise continually change with victous alteration, that when Guyon arrives and Huddibras and Sans Loy rush out to fight him, urged thereto by their ladies, they fail to reach Guyon because they start fighting each other instead.

* * *

When the "straunger knight," Guyon, hears the uproar, he rushes to the scene and attempts by "goodly meanes" to pacify the combatants, who immediately turn on him "without remorse, / And on his shield like yron sledges bet" (II.ii.22). Guyon defends himself so well that Huddibras and Sansloy must take out their frustration on each other; but when Guyon again tries to make peace, they turn again on him:

* * *

"Straunge sort of fight," Spenser says, as well he might, after three more stanzas of inextricable altercation between parties whose alliances continually change. It is evidently intended as psychological allegory, but if we think of the stages of the fight as unfolding over decades instead of minutes, and between nations instead of individuals, it begins to look less strange. It begins to look rather like Europe from the seventeenth century to the twentieth or, in Spenser's day, like the continually changing alliances of two parties against one in the foreign relations of France, Spain, and England, it being Elizabethan policy wherever possible to keep the other two at each other's throats, and always to side with the weaker. In any event, it appears at this moment as if nothing can ever enter into the Castle of Medina and alter the structure of its interlocking, violent compulsions. The changes are rung endlessly, but the situation remains the same.

Yet simple as it appears (and I confess to taking much pleasure from the mechanics of this episode and others like it), it is richly entangled in its widening contexts and flows into them like the ripples from a stone dropped in a pool. It is entangled with the earlier history of Sansloy, who in the Legend of Holiness attacks Una. It is entangled with the brothers of Sans Loy, especially Sans Joy, whose character is recapitulated in Huddibras. It is entangled, moreover, with what we suppose lies outside it, the history of the English Church and of the Elizabethan *via media*. * * * The episode is, of course, entangled with Guyon himself, with Guyon's Palmer and perhaps even with Guyon's hobbled horse [·]

* * *

6. Sean Kane, *Spenser's Moral Allegory* (Toronto: University of Toronto Press, 1989), 57–59.

For the allegory of Temperance in the Castle of Medina is still more strangely entangled with events in the following canto, when Braggadocchio, who seems to have been assembled from warring elements in Sansloy and Huddibras, encounters that paragon of moral completeness, Belphoebe. I leave aside Belphoebe's blood-lust and its possible relevance to the blood on Ruddymane's hands. I leave it aside because I don't understand it. What I think I do understand is that Belphoebe, who represents the perfection of the body, shows us how the virtue with which Spenser is truly concerned in Book II is not Temperance after all but rather something that is sublimely in excess of that simple moderation for which we strive throughout life and for which Medina, not Belphoebe, is the model. In the very effort to think Temperance as moderation, something far beyond moderation is revealed when Belphoebe unexpectedly enters the tale, though she has little to do there except to be gazed on in wonder. * * *

Matters are complicated and deepened in Spenser's verse by continually widening contexts and by what I have called *entanglement*, a term I prefer to the medieval, hermeneutic notion of *polysemy* "having many significations," and to Bishop Butler's term, *analogy*, which has so much enriched Spenser studies in the work of James Nohrnberg.[7] But like *polysemy, analogy* suggests an harmoniousness and logocentric order, like combed as opposed to tangled hair, that is not true to the real conditions of thinking in *The Faerie Queene*. The conditions of thinking in *The Faerie Queene* are more material, and therefore more complex, than abstractions such as *polysemy* and *analogy* allow. Meaning in *The Faerie Queene* is like meaning in life: it is always entangled with the real. Such entanglement in Spenser is the condition of the possibility of meaning. It may therefore be asked, what larger, more flexible concept of system could embrace both the scale of *The Faerie Queene*, its sheer bigness, and the noetic entanglement of the episodes in it? How may we speak of the poem thinking?

* * *

By "thinking *moments* in *The Faerie Queene*" I mean *moment* in the two meanings of the word that are distinguished in Hegel's German by the use of the neuter and the masculine articles: first, there is a moment in our usual sense of the word, a *moment* of arrest, an instant within which, so long as it lasts, nothing seems to move or change, inviting us to grasp some state of affairs before it slips away, and to subject it to careful analysis. "Just a moment!" we say, when we are in the heat of discussion, "Hold on! Not so fast! Let's look carefully at what you just said." We wish to make time stand still (and in a sense we do) so that we may examine the argument synchronically at one of its stages, its moments. This arresting moment is, of course, not peculiar to Hegel but rather to philosophy: it happens all the time in Plato's dialogues, which is why Socrates was compared to the torpedo fish, with its paralyzing sting. * * *

7. James Nohrnberg, *The Analogy of "The Faerie Queene"* (Princeton: Princeton University Press, 1976). Joseph Butler, *Analogy of Religion, Natural and Revealed* (1736), in which it is argued that there is "a general analogy between the principles of divine government, as set forth by the biblical revelation, and those observable in the course of nature," warranting the conclusion "that there is one Author of both."

It is the other sense of *moment*, the more technically philosophical term for a destabilizing element in a totality, which has peculiar force in the Hegelian philosophy. For it derives from the Latin *moveo* and implies motion of development within a larger whole, effecting some change in that whole. The two meanings of *moment* twist together opposite things in a dynamic situation: instability and stasis, movement and arrest. * * * It is what every moment in any poem feels like, where each image, each word, each moment, may seem to be perfectly itself even as it is becoming something other than itself. But it is especially true of *The Faerie Queene*, with its continual oscillation between narrative movement and symbolic tableau. What does it mean to say Spenser thinks in this way or, more strangely still, to say that *The Faerie Queene* thinks in and through such pulsatile moments? These moments may be reducible as far down as the stanza, with its longer final line forcing us to pause and hear each passing stanza as a unit, in contrast with the headlong rush of the ottava rima used by the Italian narrative poets. This brings us back to the question raised at the outset. Does it make sense to say that poets think as poets and not in some secondary, decorative way?

* * *

What begins as thinking about holiness becomes thinking about substance, purity, and danger. What begins as thinking about temperance as a middle way becomes thinking about the mysterious boundary between the living and the dead. What begins as thinking about chastity becomes thinking about sexual violence but also, more importantly, about the paralyzing fear of all sexual feeling, indeed of all touching, as violence. What begins as thinking about friendship becomes thinking about nature, exchange, and ecology. What begins as thinking about justice becomes thinking about what we would suppose to be quite irrelevant to justice, courtesy. What begins as thinking about courtesy becomes an anthropological thinking about culture. What begins as thinking about constancy and mutability—the two senses of *moment*—becomes thinking about thinking itself.

We commonly suppose two things about thinking. The first thing we suppose, as I suggested earlier when I spoke of a destination to thinking that is not itself thought, is that thinking is about something outside itself; thinking is orientated towards that which is not itself thought. The second thing we suppose is that thinking takes place in the head, from which executive commands are sent through unthinking nerves to mechanical organs and limbs. When we consider Spenser's poetic thinking both these statements must be reversed so as to affirm, first, the identity of the poem with its thinking and, second, the identity of this identity with the movement of thinking in circuit between the head, the hand, the text, the material remains appropriated by this text, and ultimately with the thinking of readers. How could Spenser's thinking be confined to his head if the poem he is making is not a representation of his thinking but simply *is* his thinking?

A still more important issue follows from this circulatory movement of Spenserian thought through its moments. It is that Spenser's poetic thinking is *material*, in the sense that everything the poet tears apart and subsumes in his poem is composed of the material remains of the past. What I would call "the objectifiable, but non-objectified other" in Spenser's creative process is composed of all previous poems, commentaries, and historical documents—in short, *texts*—with which the poet is concerned. I have used the term, *texts*, but Spenser's word for them was *ruins* and, later, *moniments*, a word that makes the passage of time visible in the materials with which the poet is engaged. The material remains of the past with which Spenser worked included classical and medieval poetry, the spiritual and intellectual culture of the Christian tradition, and the imaginary, Arthurian lore of Britain. By deploying those materials kaleidoscopically to represent such abstract ideas as holiness, temperance, chastity, friendship, and so on, Spenser repeatedly found his dead materials seeming to take on a life of their own and speaking to him, driving his thoughts into unexpected channels. Spenser was a prophetic poet because he was willing to listen to the voice of a material other emerging from the process of making his poem.

* * *

Spenser, by contrast, is not an archaic but an *archeological* thinker. He is temperamentally an investigator and a haunter of ruins, the remains of high cultures, marked, and indeed half-effaced with the passage of time. I don't believe Spenser ever held a book—whether it was Homer, or Petrarch, or Sidney—without thinking of it as an index of the passage of time, and without finding the poetical spirit in this temporal aura that the book seems to exhale.

Spenser is not a seeker of origins, therefore, but a seeker without a definite goal. Starting from where he is, he works patiently through the strata of historical remains because turning them over and meditating upon them stimulates his thinking and sends it down unexpected, improvisatory and even supernatural paths, to places where he encounters in the deposits a consciousness that is hard to distinguish from his own—so it seems, for example, in *The Ruins of Time*, when the genius of a place—of Verulam and Troynovant and Rome—appears among its ruins, and speaks. The overriding tone of lament—Spenser published an entire volume called *Complaints*—is the registration in consciousness of the passage of time. The tone of lament is also the registration in consciousness of the material remains of the past, for it is by lament that those remains are made conscious and so absorbed into thinking. In such thinking Spenser does not direct his eye to an object set at a fixed distance across which nothing intervenes. There is for him no "object," no thing impinging on consciousness from without (which is what the very word *object* implies), because the material remains of the past already belong to consciousness. What consciousness? We may call it the consciousness of the Muses, who are daughters of Memory, the mind of the poetic tradition into which Spenser's mind enters and with which it blends.

There is one especially conspicuous thinking moment in *The Faerie Queene*. It comes at the end. Mutabilitie is winding up her spectacular case against Jove, in which she has shown us the pageant of the seasons and months, followed by a survey of changeableness in the heavenly bodies, in the planetary spheres, and in the sphere of the fixed stars, which "even itself is mov'd, as wizards saine" (VII.vii.55). Mutabilitie could have read about those wizards in the proem to the fifth book of the very poem she is in: "those Egyptian wizards old, / Which in Star-read were wont have best insight" (V.Proem.8). In every motion—and I remind you that this word, from Latin *moveo*, lies behind the word *moment*—Mutabilitie spies a moment of arrest, where her trophy might be raised:

> Then since within this wide great *Universe*
> Nothing doth firme and permanent appeare,
> But all things tost and turned by transverse:
> What then should let, but I aloft should reare
> My Trophee, and from all, the triumph beare?
> Now judge then (o thou greatest goddesse trew!)
> According to thy self doest see and heare,
> And unto me adoom that is my dew;
> That is the rule of all, all being rul'd by you.
> (VII.vii.56)

Mutabilitie wants a swift, unthinking, favorable decision from Dame Nature, having told the goddess not only what to think but how to think: judge from what you see, from what appears, and you will see that appearance itself is uncertain and wavering: "within this wide great *Universe* / Nothing doth firme and permanent appeare." Such a statement would seem to discredit seeing, but for Mutabiltie seeing is the guarantee of truth: "But what we see not, who shall us perswade?" (VII.vii.49).

* * *

When Mutabilitie concludes her harangue there is a protracted and tense moment of silence: "silence long ensewed, Ne *Nature* to or fro spake for a space, / But with firme eyes affixt, the ground still viewed." Of course, Nature is not *viewing* the ground at all; she is turning her eyes to the ground so that her ear will be turned toward what, as in a balance, she will weigh, which is not the spectacle she has seen but the voice she has heard: "What then should let, but I aloft should reare / My Trophee, and from all, the triumph beare?" In aristocratic cultures, with their indirect and even unconscious systems of signaling, close attention is paid to how things are said, to what we call *tone*, and the tone of Mutabilitie, as we should expect of a titaness, is pushy. She's a thruster. In the face of such pushiness, deliberate and unhurried calm must be shown. It is not a question of justice, in our more egalitarian sense of the word, but of desert: Mutabilitie doesn't deserve to rule all things. I would go so far as to say that it is also a question of aesthetics: for Mutabilitie to rule all things would be nauseating, arousing what the poet will call, in the first of the two stanzas of the "canto unperfit," *loathing*. So Nature, looking down, is not doing what Mutabilitie tells her to do. Nature is not thinking about the visual spectacle of the whirling motions of the stars or of the tormented gyres of the planets, or of the waning of the moon, or of the turning of the year, or of growing things fading in autumn and flourishing in spring, or even of the fish wavering in the currents of the sea as grass wavers in an uncertain wind. Nor is Nature thinking of the pageant of the life of man from birth to death and of the labors and terrors between. Nature is doing something that takes a moment: she is absorbing and testing, weighing in the balance of the ear the tone with which Mutabilitie speaks, which is why, when Nature answers at last, she does not say, "I well consider all that ye have *shown*"; she says, "I well consider all that ye have *sayd*" (VII.vii.58). She's considering *how* it was said, too.

During Nature's thinking moment, when "silence long ensewed," all the creatures present look anxiously at Nature's downturned face, impatiently awaiting what will follow, like the birds in Chaucer's *Parlement of Foules*: "Meanewhile, all creatures, looking in her face, / Expecting th'end of this so doubtfull case, / Did hang in long suspence what would ensew" (VII.vii.57). I am struck by the repetition of the word *ensue* because, although Dame Nature seems to consider the matter in a state of calm arrest that could continue indefinitely, she is also doing something from which something must *ensue*. I mean that there resides in her very stability and calm a moment of instability that necessitates development from one state to another. This is not a question whether or not the moment of arrest could ever be broken, although it is interesting to imagine the action stopping here, in this moment, for ever, so that centuries would pass as the creatures stare fixedly at Nature as she stares at the ground. The creatures would be blanketed by leaves falling in autumn and by the snows of innumerable winters, and like statues, their very forms would erode in the wind and rain until Arlo Hill itself, on which they stand, is washed down into the valley and carried off in Mulla or Bregog, or the silver, shining Shure, in which, even in that future epoch, when human beings have disappeared from the earth and their ruins are no longer haunted, "are thousand Salmons bred" (VII.vi.55).

We should imagine such a scene of arrest as part of the anxiety that the creatures feel: they're worried that Mutabilitie may be right, but they are also worried about the opposite condition of the world, which is the giant's unacknowledged goal: that nothing may ever change again, that everything will freeze. It's therefore not so much a question about change as it is a question of time signature—and of tempo. It is above all a question of who is in control of the tempo of thought, which is why it is important that Nature not be seen to be forced to give an answer in any fixed period of time, still less that she answer when Mutabilitie says she should, which is immediately. The very silence that ensues, in that moment of thinking, is like an isolating, transparent container. That is why Nature must *break* it, like a foetus in its caul: "At length, she looking up with chearefull view, / The silence brake, and gave her doome in speeches few" (VII.vii.57).

* * *

Listen to how the rhymes come chiming in on one another at the end, imitating the effect of a sestina:

> I well consider all that ye have sayd
> And find that all things stedfastnes doe hate
> And changed be: yet being rightly wayd
> They are not changed from their first estate;
> But by their change their being doe dilate:
> And turning to themselves at length againe,

Doe worke their owne perfection so by fate;
Then over them Change doth not rule and raigne;
But they raigne over Change, and doe their states maintaine.
(VII.vii.58)

* * * Where consciousness modulates and changes, thinking advances. Where consciousness is passive, thinking is active and vigilant, perhaps most of all when it seems to be relaxed, tentative, or playful. Poetic thinking does this work, which is at once relaxed in its attentiveness to the other and rigorous in its attention to itself, to accomplish several things: to find something out about our moral nature; to enrich the wisdom we bring to reflection on that nature; to be in communion with the presences in the earth where we live—we might now say, to be "ecologically aware"—and to build a temple of song to the gods, whether or not there are, objectively speaking, any gods to sing to. For it is of our thinking nature to do so. Doing this asks much more of the poet, and of the poet's audience, than merely being conscious in a poetical way. It demands the tougher work of the thinking Spenser does in every moment of *The Faerie Queene*.

PAUL ALPERS

How to Read *The Faerie Queene*†

Despite the recent flood of books on Spenser, the common reader can still find little to help him read *The Faerie Queene* with pleasure, or understand how, in its alien mode, it has the complexity and human importance we expect of great poetry. Donald Cheney's *Spenser's Image of Nature: Wild Man and Shepherd in 'The Faerie Queen'* (Yale University Press) should provide such help; the fact that it does not can at least let us see some of our difficulties with the poem. Cheney's sense of the poem is most neatly stated in his conclusion:

> The poet's triumph over a recalcitrant reality lies in his imitation of its complexity, in his celebration of the endless pattern of oppositions by which the worlds of physical nature and of man's moral nature are to be conceived. Critics who tend to dismiss Spenser's allegory as an incomplete or onesided presentation of reality seem radically insensitive to this aspect of the poem. It is the poem's richness, its refusal to reduce its world to any neat conceptual pattern, or to exclude any discordant impulse when it arises, which must in the end constitute its chief claim to imaginative validity. (p. 247)

These ideas seem to me true, and they should provide a fruitful way of reading *The Faerie Queene*. They put in their true light a passage like Spenser's commentary on Calidore's stay among the shepherds (6.10.1–3), in which Spenser—by first blaming, then excusing, then commending

† From *Essays in Criticism* 18.4 (1968): 429–43. Reprinted by permission of Oxford University Press Journals.

the 'truant' knight—deliberately makes us see a moral question from all sides, and deliberately avoids the casuistry which fills the critical and scholarly literature on this episode. Cheney's frank acceptance of the poem's contradictions is exactly right for this passage or for the dialogue between the hermit Contemplation and the Red Cross Knight (1.10.57–67), in which Spenser feels perfectly free to let his characters contradict themselves as he lays forth the conflicting claims of heavenly and earthly glory, and the complexities inherent in a Christian's attitude towards earthly endeavour. And Cheney knows that the continually shifting perspectives of *The Faerie Queene* are to be found not only in passages of explicit moral dialectic, but in the details and texture of the verse. His arguments are always based on close analysis of individual stanzas, and the book has many felicitous and useful observations—for example, that the description of Arthur's armour 'insists on those details which had earlier seemed to be the indices of evil' (p. 69). Yet for all its real and potential virtues, *Spenser's Image of Nature* has most of the faults of most books on *The Faerie Queene*—most importantly, rigid interpretations and the distortion of details in the interest of a previously determined point of view or argument. The book is an exceptionally striking, and therefore instructive, instance of the gaps that can exist between intelligent general statements and particular critical analyses and demonstrations.

Cheney begins at the beginning, when a storm drives the Red Cross Knight and Una into the wandering wood:

> Enforst to seeke some couert nigh at hand,
> A shadie groue not far away they spide,
> That promist ayde the tempest to withstand:
> Whose loftie trees yclad with sommers pride,
> Did spred so broad, that heauens light did hide,
> Not perceable with power of any starre:
> And all within were pathes and alleies wide,
> With footing worne, and leading inward farre:
> Faire harbour that them seemes; so in they entred arre.
>
> And foorth they passe, with pleasure forward led,
> Ioying to heare the birdes sweete harmony,
> Which therein shrouded from the tempest dred,
> Seemd in their song to scorne the cruell sky.
> Much can they prayse the trees so straight and hy,
> The sayling Pine, the Cedar proud and tall,
> The vine-prop Elme, the Poplar neuer dry,
> The builder Oake, sole king of forrests all,
> The Aspine good for staues, the Cypresse funerall.
>
> (1.1.7–8)

This catalogue of trees, which continues for another full stanza, is a great stumbling block for critics of the poem. Students always see perfectly clearly that its point and function are indicated by the first line of the stanza that follows it: 'Led with delight, they thus beguile the way' (1.1.10). The simple pleasures of the verse—an expert performance in which Spenser self-consciously rivals earlier poets—carry us along, until, having also been 'led with delight', we share the plight in which the knight and lady find themselves:

> When weening to returne, whence they did stray,
> They cannot finde that path, which first was showne,
> But wander too and fro in wayes vnknowne.
>
> (1.1.10)

All this seems a wonderfully appropriate development of the image of the wood of life—the point of which is that it represents the life of man in general, all not some of us—and thoroughly in the nature of allegory, which does not respect individuals, but examines and brings to life universal realities. But Spenserians make heavy weather of the passage because they think that the main point of allegory is to pass moral judgments, and the student who finds that this opening passage is fun to read will be told, for example, that the catalogue of trees shows that the Red Cross Knight is guilty of succumbing to a visual allurement that weakens his rational powers. Now Cheney's view of the poem seems directly intended to prevent this kind of desiccating distortion. He introduces his discussion of this passage by warning us against 'the reductive reading which [Spenser] has too frequently received' (p. 22), and by insisting on finding the poem's meaning by following its sequence—thus warning us against looking ahead to discover that 'This is the wandring wood, this *Errours den*' (1.1.13). The whole point of postponing Una's announcement (though presumably she knew it all along) is that the 'label' serves us as a moral recognition of what we have undergone, participated in, rather than as a shield, or as wax to plug our ears against the siren song of 'the birdes sweete harmony'. The postponed naming of the wood is a variant of something Cheney points out, also by way of introducing this passage, about the names of characters in *The Faerie Queene*: Spenser 'repeatedly gives his characters names symbolic of their roles but announces those names only after showing them in action, so that the names themselves become capsule summaries or mottoes' (p. 22).

And now, alas, let us see what Cheney actually says about this passage:

> In fleeing the shower, they have abandoned one kind of nature for another. On the plain they are exposed to the elements and almost ludicrously unprepared to confront them. To see how far this is from the 'tempest' of epic or tragedy—in the sense of the hostile environment which tests man's capacity to endure—one need only compare this shower with the storm which confronts Aeneas in Book I of the *Aeneid*. Spenser makes no attempt here to develop a theme of divine wrath—his allusion to 'angry *Ioue*' seems the shallowest of epithets for the darkened sky—and the abruptness of the rain is such that everyone has fled before the question of any possible resistance to it can arise. If there is any similarity here to a Virgilian storm, it is more likely to the shower that drives Dido and Aeneas together, for in Virgil too the absence of any extended description of that later storm suggests the instinctive nature of the lovers' flight from it. Redcross and Una do not hesitate to take cover, and they find themselves in a wood which they seem to know all too well: willfully shrouding themselves from the light as well as the rain, they praise the trees in a catalogue which reflects man's confident moral dissection of his universe. In such a context it is ominously appropriate that the foliage of the trees should be their 'sommers pride', and that the birds whose song 'seemd . . . to scorne the cruell sky' provide the background

> for the human praise of the trees: man seems to share with the lower creatures this false sense of a security which ignores the changing seasons. (pp. 23–24)

Almost every one of these statements seems to me totally without foundation in the poem. How can it possibly be relevant to say that Una and the knight are 'almost ludicrously unprepared' to face the elements, when Spenser says:

> And angry *loue* an hideous storme of raine
> Did poure into his Lemans lap so fast,
> That euery wight to shrowd it did constrain.
> (1.1.6)

Cheney is simply inventing reasons for a moral judgment against the knight and Una: thus the remark about 'angry *loue*' is an attempt to dismiss the fact that this storm is sent by God, or at least by the powers that rule nature. Although the remarks about the *Aeneid* are not the mere fancy footwork they seem in isolation—Cheney has plausible and interesting ideas about the way allusion works in *The Faerie Queene* (cf. pp. 7, 148, 201)—their irrelevance reveals his inability to put his general theories into critical practice.

It is not that Spenser does not call for moral awareness as we read these stanzas, but that our awareness does not take the form that Cheney assumes it must. Like every moralistic interpreter, he singles out the phrase 'sommers pride' and the following line about hiding heaven's light. He ignores the fact that 'sommers pride' can be a valid descriptive epithet for the trees' leaves,[1] and that 'heauens light did hide' is followed by 'Not perceable with power of any starre', which suggests immunity from malignant powers.[2] Cheney has told us to look for ambiguities of exactly the sort found in 'sommers pride' and for shifts of perspective such as occur in the two following lines. But he cannot reveal the poem he knows is there, because he assumes that moral awareness consists of judging characters in action. Thus he accuses Una and the knight of 'willfully [because of "fain" in 1.1.6?] shrouding themselves from the light as well as the rain', and later, turning allegorical description into narrative action that simply does not occur, says 'they have abandoned the sunlight as well as the storms of the plain' (p. 24). But this stanza is an allegory, unfolding, under the pastoral image of a 'shadie groue', the attractions and dangers of the sublunary world. We are to feel the weight of all the words, not just the last, in the phrase, 'Faire harbour that them seemes'. The stanza calls not for judgments, choices, or moral actions—no one person could act coherently on the basis of the multifarious feelings and awarenesses aroused—but contemplation of human nature and the human condition. By the same token, the steady listing of the tree catalogue makes us take in all aspects of man's life—the noble ('The Laurell, meed of mightie Conquerours'), the ordinary ('The Birch for shaftes, the Sallow for the mill'), the frail or corrupt ('the Maple seeldom inward sound'). Moralistic critics who try to size up the wood by noticing only

1. Cf. Shakespeare, sonnet 104, which imitates Horace, *Epodes* 11.6, which in turn imitates Virgil, *Georgics* 2.404. In the Latin poets the word is *honor*.
2. Like Milton's 'branching elm star-proof' (*Arcades* 89), this line adapts Statius's description of Sleep's grove as *nulli penetrabilis astro* (*Thebaid* 10.85).

the last category are telling us, in the first instance, to deny our actual reading experience and ultimately to deny that the human condition is our own.

Cheney consistently reduces moral issues to judgments of character—thus going, as Rosemond Tuve has brilliantly shown, against the nature of allegory as Spenser inherited it and the nature of *The Faerie Queene* itself. Throughout his chapter on the Garden of Adonis, he simply assumes that one of his main tasks is to decide what is 'wrong' with Amoret and her upbringing that she should be imprisoned and tortured by Busyrane, five cantos later. But Amoret is an extreme instance of the way Spenser handles his characters—not as coherent dramatic individuals, about whom ethical judgments would be appropriate, but as congeries of characteristics which he can exploit to reveal fundamental realities of all human personality. Thus his interest in the House of Busyrane is not the ethical question, 'Why is Amoret tortured?' but the fact that human love is always painful; his whole poetic endeavour centres not on Amoret as a personality, but on the traditional emblem produced by her torture—the heart transfixed with a dart. Even in Book VI, where he is directly concerned with the type-figures of the wild man and the shepherd, Cheney cannot conceive that Spenser puts us in possession of truths about courtesy by any means other than making us prefer one character to another. The adventures of Calepine, who takes over from Calidore as the hero of the middle cantos, show, he says, 'the difficulties and perils confronting man in his social role' (p. 202). A very good way, one would think, of seeing Calepine's first adventure: forced to walk in his armour as he supports his beloved Serena, who has been wounded by the Blatant Beast, he is cruelly mocked by a strange knight (later identified as Sir Turpine), who simply refuses to acknowledge chivalric obligations, either to help Calepine or to accept his challenge to battle when help is refused (6.3.27 ff.). All Cheney can do with this well-conceived and sometimes moving episode is to make it show Calepine's moral inferiority to Calidore: 'his difficulties arise from his inability to elicit courteous responses from others' (p. 204), and his 'inability to defend himself against Turpine demonstrates his failure to appreciate the full responsibilities of the courtesy which he attempts to practice' (p. 205). (The real reason he cannot defend himself is that he is on foot and Turpine is on horseback.) And lest we think Calepine's situation shows that 'All flesh is frayle, and full of ficklenesse, / Subject to fortunes chance, still chaunging new' and draw Calidore's moral, 'Who will not mercie vnto others shew, / How can he mercy euer hope to haue?' (6.1.41–42), we are told that 'such a man [as Turpine] can menace only those who put their faith in the appearances of rank' (p. 207).

One is struck not only by Cheney's insistence on moral judgments, but also by the terms in which these judgments are stated. They are as unreal as they are untraditional, and they show why Cheney's actual readings and interpretations are so disappointing: he cannot take *The Faerie Queene* on its own terms. The catalogue of trees is said to be an image of this world and its limitations not because Spenser gives a full range of human use and significance to the trees, but because it 'reflects man's confident moral dissection of his universe'. When the Red Cross Knight meets Duessa (Book I, canto 2), Cheney speaks not of lust and infidelity, but says the knight is 'ludicrously unprepared to read images' (p. 35). The Red Cross Knight's aims—'To winne him worship, and her [Gloriana's] grace to haue' and 'To proue his puissance in battell braue' (1.1.3)—are said to be stated in 'transcendent terms', but 'such transcendence implies a consequent lack of concrete definition' (p. 41). In such formulations, Cheney no doubt seeks to avoid 'obvious' or 'reductive' readings. But in this he reveals an attitude towards moral discourse that is totally foreign to Spenser, who is genuinely interested in moral terms and the truths they contain and does not regard them as naive simplifications of experience. The famous descriptive passage—

> his glistring armor made
> A litle glooming light, much like a shade,
> By which he saw the vgly monster plaine (1.1.14)

is not merely verbal painting, but a testing of the truth of the Red Cross Knight's confident aphorism, 'Vertue giues her selfe light, through darkenesse for to wade' (1.1.12). To juxtapose the dimming of this light in Error's murky den with its showing her plain both criticises and confirms the aphorism, and thus makes us aware that man's native spiritual strengths are genuine, yet are of the earth, involved in their element. It is 'an ironic comment', as Cheney says, but it is the true Spenserian irony, that of a poised intelligence seeing all around a spiritual phenomenon, and not the presumed sophistication that presents 'a transition from complacent philosophizing to a frantic search for the appropriate tag-ends of philosophy' (p. 26).

How could a man like Cheney, to whom aphorisms are always 'naive' or 'easy', even read the stanza in which Spenser renders Una's deception by Archimago disguised as the Red Cross Knight?

> His louely words her seemd due recompence
> Of all her passed paines: one louing howre
> For many yeares of sorrow can dispence:
> A dram of sweet is worth a pound of sowre:
> She has forgot, how many a wofull stowre
> For him she late endur'd; she speakes no more
> Of past: true is, that true loue hath no powre
> To looken backe; his eyes be fixt before.
> Before her stands her knight, for whom she toyld so sore.
> (1.3.30)

Where a poet like Ariosto would make Una's deception persuasive by a physical description of Archimago's disguise, Spenser produces 'Before her stands her knight' from the general truth of the preceding line. Aphorism, which at first serves for a knowing, though entirely generous, commentary on Una's willingness to believe, becomes at the end of the stanza the statement of a truth whose force we must acknowledge. As in any great poet, technical mastery manifests itself as moral intelligence: the interlacing of aphorism and narration and the turn on 'before' are the means by which Spenser makes us both see around and participate in Una's deception. It is so frank and lucid that one wonders how anyone could ever fail to admire and enjoy it and the hundreds and hundreds of stanzas like it in *The Faerie Queene*.

The answer, of course, is that *The Faerie Queene* is radically undramatic, and that it therefore defeats all the modern reader's expectations about the primacy of dramatic narration, about the relation of moral generalisation to the specific instances and 'evidence' offered, and about the nature of 'concrete' details in the verse: Cheney, for example, continually explains moral and psychological matters in terms of the ontological and epistemological status of physical images. Consider the first description of the Bower of Bliss:

> Thus being entred, they behold around
> A large and spacious plaine, on euery side
> Strowed with pleasauns, whose faire grassy ground
> Mantled with greene, and goodly beautifide
> With all the ornaments of *Floraes* pride,
> Wherewith her mother Art, as halfe in scorne
> Of niggard Nature, like a pompous bride
> Did decke her, and too lauishly adorne,
> When forth from virgin bowre she comes in th'early morne.
> (2.12.50)

The interest in this stanza is neither in concrete description nor in abstract moral judgment, but in unfolding—Cheney well remarks how literally explicable *The Faerie Queene* is (p. 15)—the conventional locution 'all the ornaments of *Floraes* pride'. As we come to it, this line expresses the natural attractiveness of a pastoral landscape. But the next line turns the apparently casual personification of Flora into a decisive one; at the same time, the conventional metaphor in 'ornaments' is taken seriously and is made to render a sense of artificial excess. We might argue that these lines make the true meaning of line 5 apparent, were it not for the alexandrine, which again represents '*Floraes* pride' as natural and wholesome. All this is clear enough when pointed out, but it is still difficult to get used to the conditions of our perceiving, taking in, and mentally possessing the movement and point of the stanza. Just as the 'description' is incoherent as fictional narration (what is the relation between 'goodly beautifide' and 'too lauishly adorne' or of the last line to the previous description of Flora?), so the narrator of the poem and the reader attending to it do not have a dramatic relation to the verse. The subject and point of the stanza are similar to those of Marvell's 'The Mower against Gardens', but whereas in Marvell's poem it is essential to catch the precise tone of scorn and wonder in which the mower speaks, here it is positively wrong to specify the tone in which one says, 'With all the ornaments of *Floraes* pride'. The line includes meanings that would dictate very different tones of voice in a speaker dramatically conceived. The verse obviously requires and rewards attention, yet at the same time we must be passive and selfless. We do not even maintain the control given by syntax. Despite the apparently strong enjambments in lines 6–8, we read them line by line, and it is clear—e.g. from the way line 8 rings so independently, and in the collocation of 'niggard' and 'pompous' to produce a sense of false bounty—that Spenser meant us to read that way.

There are essential difficulties in establishing a right relation to Spenser's verse, and they are best stated by Empson, in chapter 1 of *Seven Types of Ambiguity*:

> The size, the possible variety, and the fixity of this unit [the Spenserian stanza] give something of the blankness that comes from fixing your eyes on a bright spot; you have to yield yourself to it very completely to take in the variety of its movement, and, at the same time, there is no need to concentrate the elements of the situation into a judgment as if for action. As a result of this, when there are ambiguities of idea, it is whole civilisations rather than details of the moment which are their elements; he can pour into the even dreamwork of his fairyland Christian, classical, and chivalrous materials with an air, not of ignoring their differences, but of holding all their systems of values floating as if at a distance, so as not to interfere with one another, in the prolonged and diffused energies of his mind. (3rd edn., 1953, p. 34)

The importance of this aside (it was unfortunately no more than that) is that it treats Spenser's and the reader's passivity not as a specialised aesthetic sensuousness, but as the manifestation of a full, humane intelligence. The critic who should have revealed this intelligence to us was Lewis, but his hostility to modern aesthetics and modern morals turned his profound understanding of Spenser from disinterested criticism into proselytising. His celebrated discussion of the Bower of Bliss consists too much of attaching hostile labels, as when he vulgarly names the girls in the fountain (whom Spenser compares to Venus rising from the sea) Cissie and Flossie. He dismisses the following stanza with the remark (*Allegory of Love*, p. 325), 'Whether those who think that Spenser is secretly on Acrasia's side, themselves approve of metal vegetation as a garden ornament, or whether they regard this passage as a proof of Spenser's abominable bad taste, I do not know; but this is how the poet describes it':

> And ouer all, of purest gold was spred,
> A trayle of yuie in his natiue hew:
> For the rich mettall was so coloured,
> That wight, who did not well auis'd it vew,
> Would surely deeme it to be yuie trew:
> Low his lasciuious armes adown did creepe,
> That themselues dipping in the siluer dew,
> Their fleecy flowres they tenderly did steepe,
> Which drops of Christall seemd for wantones to weepe.
> (2.12.61)

Lewis rightly said that Spenser's descriptions are not poetical gossamer but have a moral feel, but to make his case he had to pretend that the final lines here are simply repugnant. But we apprehend the moral clarity of those lines precisely when we respond to the richness and felicity of the verse, and by empathetic participation understand the self-indulgence and self-dissipation of 'wantones'. However, the really difficult aspect of this stanza lies in lines 4 and 5. The modern reader would treat them as an unsuccessful attempt to ward off, with moralistic terms, the powerful sensuousness of the final lines. But to attribute this kind of motive, and the resultant confusion, to Spenser is to assume that his verse should—and would if it could—express a mind that is concentrated into a judgment as if for action. On the contrary, the stanza is an exceptionally clear example of the habit of mind Empson describes. What is so hard to grasp and trust is that Spenser could state these lines so flatly, almost as a warning, and then confirm the persuasiveness of the 'yuie trew' by the sudden sensuousness of the next line. By the same token, the first three lines do not make us 'well auis'd' in the sense Lewis wants them to. They indeed tell us the facts of the case, but they create a vague assent to the deception simply by the kinds of assent involved in the act of reading. The sensuous appeal of 'purest gold' and 'rich mettall' gets what we may call moral support from the plain and strong meaning of 'natiue hew', and 'trayle' (which is an architectural term for a metal ornament) acquires its usual meaning from the line in which it appears. These effects keep 'wight' a truly open term, as it should be in allegory.

Trust the verse—that is what the reader of *The Faerie Queene* must learn to do. The last stanza suggests how hard this is for the modern reader, even though it shows how frankly and generously Spenser's verse offers itself. One can readily imagine that Cheney, seeing what was involved in single stanzas, did not trust the verse, or perhaps did not trust himself, enough to see the poem through to the end on its own terms. The deepest fault of his book is that he seeks to interpret and organise what he perceives in the terms that are familiar to him—terms that are damagingly provincial in time, and perhaps too in place. With a book so elliptically written that the wild man and the shepherd of the subtitle are not mentioned until p. 174, one may be excused for quoting the dust-jacket: '[Mr. Cheney] views allegory as a means by which the poet embraces a vast array of expanding knowledge and gives it unity based not upon objective categories but upon a common involvement in the dialectical processes of the reader. The result, Mr. Cheney suggests, is a poem of infinite complexity, offering endless opportunity for explication, a poem which derives unity and intelligibility from the figure of the poet who strives through his art to create meaning, an epic of imagination'. This summarises an aspect of Cheney's thought more clearly than anything in the book. It puts together a number of things one notices about the book: the lack of substantive content in moral analysis, the consistent speaking of Spenser's multifariousness in terms of paired opposites and dialectic, the dwelling on Spenser's 'personal' appearances in the poem. Most important, it explains why this book about an open-ended poem is itself so rigid—in its moral interpretations, in its account of the continuities that exist in the poem, in its notion that Spenser's allusions entitle one to transfer directly to *The Faerie Queene* points made about Elizabethan history or other poems (e.g. pp. 45, 143–44, 173–4, 225). All this comes from thinking that a poem creates its own meanings—not simply in the broad and truistic sense, but in the sense that poetic usages and processes are uniquely meaningful in a meaningless world. Very similar notions underly the search for structural, ideological, and iconographic keys to *The Faerie Queene*, even when their proponents rightly insist that Spenser's idea of his poem was totally different from one like Cheney's. For the insistence on Spenser's absolute beliefs bears witness to our own lack of them, and we simply assume that a poet who views the universe as ordered from top to bottom will embody that order in a poem. But this is not necessarily so. It is precisely when a poet trusts that the universe really is ordered and assumes that the source of order is God, not the individual poet, that he can allow his poem to expatiate freely. It is no accident that Lewis, the critic who most deeply understood Spenser's trusting habit of mind, has also most encouraged us to take *The Faerie Queene* as it comes.

When we do, when we accept the offer of the verse, we unquestionably become different from what we are when we read almost everything else that gives us pleasure and illumination. But to do this is not to learn to 'think like an Elizabethan' in the narrow sense too often urged on us by scholars. Quite the contrary, it is liberating and restorative to enter the mind of a man who could so trust man's traditional wisdom about himself and the ultimate goodness of his world. Consider the following stanza:

> The third [almoner] had of their wardrobe custodie,
> In which were not rich tyres, nor garments gay,
> The plumes of pride, and wings of vanitie,
> But clothes meet to keepe keene could away,
> And naked nature seemely to aray;
> With which bare wretched wights he dayly clad,
> The images of God in earthly clay;
> And if that no spare cloths to giue he had,
> His owne coate he would cut, and it distribute glad.
> (1.10.39)

This is really ordinary Spenserian verse, from a canto usually dismissed as the most tediously traditional sort of allegory. But when we consider what happens to these formulas in *King Lear*, where agony and destruction come from insisting that they be mutually consistent and answerable to experience, we can understand the value of a poet for whom taking them seriously simply meant registering their human point and value in line after line, stanza after stanza. We are all children of Shakespeare, and no one today could write a poem like *The Faerie Queene*. But in an age so bewilderingly compounded of pleasures, opportunities, and achievements, and at the same time of brutality, tedium, moral horror, and spiritual disaster, it would be tragic to lose so luminous an exemplar of clear-sightedness and acceptance.

JEFF DOLVEN

The Method of Spenser's Stanza†

Let me begin by quoting from the story of a clownish young man who sets out on a great quest for which he is not very well prepared. You may find that the details come back to you with a certain alienated majesty:

> A Worthy Knight was riding on the Plain,
> In Armour Clad, which richly did Contain
> The Gallant Marks of many Battels fought,
> Tho' he before no Martial Habit sought;
> How Warlike ere his Person seem'd to Sit
> On a Bold Steed, that scarce obey'd the Bit:

† From *Spenser Studies: A Renaissance Poetry Annual*, Volume XIX. Reprinted by permission of the author and AMS Press.

Upon his Breast a Bloody Cross display'd,
The Precious Drops for him his Saviour paid;
And on his Mighty Shield the same did bear,
To shew his Faith was his Valours Care.[1]

I could go on—as Edward Howard did, at length, casting the whole of Book I into heroic couplets and publishing the results in 1687 as *Spenser Redivivus: Containing the First Book of the Faery Queen, His Essential Design preserv'd, but his obsolete Language and manner of Verse totally laid aside.* In his preface Howard declares himself to be especially concerned with saving his readers from what he called Spenser's "tedious stanza" (A3v). The couplet he prefers may be a tacit slap at rhymeless John Milton, whose *Paradise Lost* goes conspicuously unmentioned in the preface's brief history of English poetic ambition.[2] But that couplet is also a means by which Spenser's great matter might be more "genuinely and succinctly convey'd" (A3v), "abreviated and, as I conceive, improv'd" (A4r).

Howard's claims for his chosen form might remind us of those made by another turner of couplets, Alexander Pope, almost fifty years later. Pope prefaced his *Essay on Man* by arguing that couplets allowed him to treat his subject "more *shortly* [. . .] than in prose itself; and nothing is more certain, than that much of the *force* as well as *grace* of arguments or instructions, depends on their *conciseness* . . ." Couplets served him as a compositional method, a way of thinking and presenting his "principles, maxims, or precepts": their "chain of reasoning" is among the chief means by which (to quote now the *Essay on Criticism*) "*Nature*" may be "*Methodiz'd*."[3] Compared with Pope, Howard's amateur and uncompressed rhymes cannot be said to show a particularly strong methodizing hand. What I want to ask here is whether method might be exactly the word for what is missing in his rewriting of Spenser; whether it might be the best word for one particular kind of work that the stanza he banishes actually does in its nearly four thousand instances over the length of *The Faerie Queene*.

This is a question I will shortly put to one stanza in particular, Arthur's advice to Una after Red Cross has been haled up from Orgoglio's dungeon. But first I want to consider what that word "method" might have meant to Spenser. The idea of a rational program by which unfounded knowledge might be discarded and new learning built from the foundations—something close to what we might now call scientific method—had to wait for the Royal Academy. The authorities behind the word circa 1590 were as various as Aristotle, the Stoics, Galen, and above all the Protestant educational reformer Petrus Ramus; it was most often understood as a means for bringing systematic order and concision to existing fields of study. A method was a *modus operandi*—*via* and *ordo*

1. Subsequent citations by page number in parenthesis in the text. For a much more thoughtful and thorough examination of Howard than I attempt here, see Clare R. Kinney, "'What s/he ought to have been': Romancing Truth in *Spenser Redivivus*," *Spenser Studies* XVI (2002): 125–38.
2. The book was licensed by Roger L'Estrange, the Surveyor of the Press, on September 21, 1686; author of a broadside against Milton entitled "No Blinde Guides" (1660, L'Estrange presumably would have had no objection to Howard's tactical omission.
3. Alexander Pope, *The Poems of Alexander Pope*, ed. John Butt (New York: Routledge, 1989), 502, 146. On compression, wit, and method in Pope's *Essays*, see Patricia Meyer Spacks, "Imagery and Method in *An Essay on Criticism*," *PMLA* 85 (1970): 97–106.

were common synonyms—by which diffuse materials could be approached, organized, and conveyed to others. It offered a model of thinking and a procedure for teaching:[4] Spenser himself never used the word in his poetry, but he lived in the midst of a great fashion for it, and his friend Gabriel Harvey was among its early English enthusiasts. When both men were still at Cambridge Harvey wrote an elegy for Ramus called Ode Natalia in which a heavenly virgin named Method presides over the goddesses of the arts of grammar, rhetoric, logic, arithmetic, and geometry, all reformed by Ramus, and offers consolation to their unmethodized sisters, music, astronomy, theology, jurisprudence, and medicine. The work is a peculiar and—for a mind like Spenser's—suggestive compound of method and allegory.[5]

The counsel Arthur gives to Una may bias the case that there is something methodical or methodizing about the Spenserian stanza itself. It is one of the most concerted instances of instruction between characters in the poem, and it puts the peculiar pressure on the representation of thinking that teaching always does. Still I hope it will set some general features in high relief. It comes in the forty-fourth stanza of canto viii, Book I:

> Faire Lady, then said that victorious knight,
> The things, that grieuous were to doe, or beare,
> Them to renew, I wote, breeds no delight;
> Best musicke breeds delight in loathing eare:
> But th'only good, that growes of passed feare,
> Is to be wise, and ware of like agein.
> This daies ensample hath this lesson deare
> Deepe written in my heart with yron pen,
> That blisse may not abide in state of mortal men.
> (I.viii.44)[6]

The opening lines are highly controlled. The victorious Arthur begins with the rhetorician's distinction between doing and suffering, a topos of analysis implying that what follows will be carefully structured argument. "I wote" reinforces this deliberateness. It concedes to Una her desire to forget, but also asserts that the wisdom Arthur imparts is already known, already thought or thought out. That wisdom might be paraphrased roughly as follows: the past is painful; it is hard (as always in Spenser) to recognize the difference between agent and victim, particularly in oneself; renewing the past renews its pain and confusion. The compound of remembering and repeating in that word "renew" comes from Aeneas' famous *renovare*, and for a moment it is as though Arthur were giving advice to Virgil's hero too—the hero who fears, at the beginning of *Aeneid* II, that in retelling the Fall of Troy he will suffer it again.[7]

4. On the range of Renaissance definitions of method and their sources, see Neil W. Gilbert, *Renaissance Concepts of Method* (New York: Columbia University Press, 1960).
5. For an account of the Ode Natalia and Harvey's interest in method generally, see Kendrick W. Prewitt, "Gabriel Harvey and the Practice of Method," *SEL* 31:1 (1990): 19–39.
6. Edmund Spenser, *The Faerie Queene*, ed. Thomas P. Roche (Penguin, 1980), I.viii.44. Subsequent citations in parentheses in the text.
7. Virgil, *Eclogues, Georgics, Aeneid I–VI*, tr. H. Rushton Fairclough (Cambridge: Harvard University Press, 1994), II.3.

The problem is old and intractable, but at least Spenser's victorious knight speaks with the authority of one who knows his mind.

The fourth line, then, sounds a kind of preliminary closure: it is syntactically autonomous, and finishes the opening ABAB quatrain with a sententious ring. The next two lines would seem to open up a new unit of thought. The "but" of "but th'only good" is not the unsettling double-take of "Yet armes till that time did he neuer wield" (I.i.1); instead it inaugurates a new quatrain, one that will be a room as fit for its own stage of argument as was the last. But this impression depends upon a hasty reading of that decisive-sounding fourth line, "Best musicke breeds delight in loathing eare," one that (as Hamilton's edition testifies) has provoked more than its share of commentary and emendation.[8] I would suggest the paraphrase, "It is music that best restores delight to an ear poisoned by loathing," and argue that part of the line's difficulty is that it does *not* in fact complete the thought of lines 1 to 3. Instead it is part of lasting good that can come of what you have been through is to remember it well enough to recognize its like in the future. Now the stanza seems to have fallen into three groups of three lines each: not an arrangement abetted by the rhyme scheme, though there are plenty of other examples of it in the poem. What is important for my purposes is that the effect of readjustment I have just described is typical of the unstable relations generated by the couplet at the center of the stanza. Because, as Empson observed, this couplet can be troped both as a moment of disruption and of closure, it introduces a regular-as-clockwork schedule for microcosmic reflection on the cosmic problems of the poem's order and ideas of order.[9]

"Ware of like agein" marks the first full stop in the stanza, and the next line takes a still more decisive didactic turn. "This daies ensample hath this lesson deare / Deepe written in my heart with yron pen, / That blisse may not abide in state of mortal men." It is important to remember the visceral horror of the previous stanzas, Orgoglio's castle awash with the blood of innocent babes, and the spectacle of the emaciated and obdurately silent Red Cross, his flesh dried up like withered flowers. Like the description of the disrobed Duessa that will follow, the vividness of the details seems to exceed the requirements of the emblem: this is the grim *experience* that Arthur must transmute to useful knowledge. He works by stages. The first is "ensample," etymologically poised between "sample," a piece of the original experience, and *exemplum*, an epitome of it. The next stage is a "lesson," still more abstract, another insulating remove. But we have already seen Arthur's concern for the discplacement of memory by music: music which is the perfect threat, in its resistance to representation, to being ware of like again. The next line seems to be driven by the same anxiety. The lesson must be written on the heart with an iron pen, and the pain lost in translation—the grievousness of what was done and borne—is renewed in the violence of the act of inscription itself. Arthur is wrestling with the impossible balance between the lesson as comfort and punishment.

8. Hamilton notes eighteenth-century emendations of "delight" to "dislike" or "no delight"; he goes on, "If the text is kept, possible paraphrases are: 'music best breeds delight, not a recital of grievous matters'; or 'only the best music, not a recital etc., may breed delight.'" Edmund Spenser, *The Faerie Queene*, ed. A. C. Hamilton (Toronto: University of Toronto Press, 2001), 111n.
9. William Empson, *Seven Types of Ambiguity* (New York: New Directions, 1966), 33–34.

And for all this scrupling, still the last word is the maxim of the hexameter, self-balanced on its medial caesura, ripe for the commonplace book. "That blisse may not abide in state of mortal men."

How does Howard manage the same stanza?

> Then to Lady gallant Arthur said,
> All grief repeated is more grievous made:
> Nor can the softest sounds delight the Ear
> Of him that loathing does the Musick hear.
> From actions past no Counsel can arise,
> Other than future Care of being more wise.
> And in my heart this Maxim fix'd I find,
> That constant Bliss abides not with Mankind.
> (L4r)

Howard's complaint against Spenser's form is that "the Writing in Stanza's must render Verse sententious and contrain'd, the most weighty part of their meaning still being to be expected at the Period of the Stanza; so, in that consideration, their Composure must needs be less difficult than where the force of each single Line is to be weigh'd apart" (A3v). He seems to mean that Spenser's verse is "sententious and contrain'd" because it leaves the last line to do all the moral work, rather than distributing the burden evenly; there is a note of self-congratulation in his claim that his couplets—which are less sententious, one assumes, only because no one sententia particularly stands out from the throng of its neighbors—are more difficult to write. His own interest in their autonomy (and in their "composure," in a double sense) means that Howard cannot hear the excruciated second-thoughts of Arthur's instruction. He does, however, recognize the peculiar force and authority of the hexameter. Once again Empson is the canonical guide to "possible variety" (34) of effects that this final line achieves, but so often there is something reflective, summary, or even epigrammatic about it. In a poem so wary of rest it repeatedly proposes itself as a moment of provisional rest (even if that rest is only the formulation of a prayer: "God helpe the man so wrapt in *Errours* endlesse traine" [I.i.18]). * * *

So: a double-take in the middest; a final, elongated, balanced (or notably unbalanced) sententia; a system of rhymes that proposes a variety of relations between them. Is this enough to speak of the stanza as a method? In order to answer this question I want to step a little further back and consider the poem and the stanza in particular as a mimesis of thinking. This is a topic that has long occupied Spenser's critics in one form or another: Isabel MacCaffrey's wonderful book on Spenser's Allegory describes *The Faerie Queene* as "a model of the mind's life in the world"; more recently, both Kenneth Gross and Gordon Teskey have been thinking about Spenserian thinking.[1] Angus Fletcher's wrestle in *Colors of the Mind* with what he calls "noetics"—a poetics of thinking—also has Spenser much on its mind.[2] What makes this topic so elusive and compelling is

1. Isabel McCaffrey, *Spenser's Allegory: The Anatomy of Imagination* (Princeton: Princeton University Press, 1976), 6; Gross and Teskey's work has been presented at recent conferences (e.g., Teskey's "'And therefore as a stranger give it welcome': Courtesy and Thinking," presented at the conference "The Place of Spenser," Cambridge, England [July 2001]; and Kenneth Gross, "Shapes of Time: On the Spenserian Stanza," *Spenser Studies* XIX (2004): 27–35.
2. Angus Fletcher, *Colors of the Mind* (Cambridge: Harvard University Press, 1991), 169–70.

that thinking itself seemed to be, for want of a better word, too *big* to think about: if a given mind were to compass thought in its entirety, what space would be left over for thinking *about* it? Wouldn't that just be more thinking, still to be reflected upon? Reflection is a supplement always being subsumed. One recourse is to admit that when we think about thinking what we imagine are reductions or schemes or, in McCaffrey's phrase, "models" (6), or, in Fletcher's "iconographies of thought" (15–34). And this is precisely what method is. We may take method primarily to be a tool, a cognitive procedure by which some desired order may be brought to new materials. But it is also a picture of the mind at work on those materials: in the ordering of the object, we see the order of the mind. This order may be understood as a subset of mental activity, or (by a mistake either consoling or terrifying) as just what the mind does, ideally or actually. Logic and rhetoric are among the Renaissance disciplines that work this way: the five stages of composing an oration, for example, were often taught by schoolmasters as though they might come to be coextensive with the ideal student's mental life. The stanza too has an analogous power to filter and render all experience, imposing on it a particular shape, deriving from it a particular kind of lesson. Certainly *The Faerie Queene* never thinks without it.

At bottom this is only an analogy: I cannot say more than that it might help us understand how the stanza works, and, more tenuously, that the intellectual fashion for the one method might have contributed to Spenser's turn away from the variety of *The Shepherdes Calender* to the unflagging regularity of *The Faerie Queene*. Still I can make the analogy a little more specific. The basic procedure of Ramus's method was to resolve a field of knowledge into its constituent elements by a technique of dichotomizing analysis: this is the operation that yields the ramifying trees of his diagrams, each branch splitting into two and then splitting again. In matters of literary analysis, however, the point was to isolate the "dialectical ratiocination" or maxim at the heart of the discourse; method becomes a matter of stripping away ornament to arrive at essence. So Cicero's *Pro Milo*, for example, can be reduced to the formula "It is permissible to kill a criminal."[3] The application of the method is complete when it yields this fecund minimum; the process has two separate moments, the first unfolding in time, the other finished, timeless. The Spenserian stanza might likewise be understood as an engine for deriving some kind of concrete result in the form of that sententious hexameter: for making, out of thinking, a thought. Gordon Teskey has distinguished broadly between *The Faerie Queene* as a poem in which thinking actually happens and *Paradise Lost* as poem that teaches what has already been thought. I would suggest that a play between thinking and thought is constantly dramatized within *The Faerie Queene* itself, particularly as a problem of teaching; a play, as Arthur defines it, among experience, memory, and maxim. The stanza is built to raise the problem of their relation continually.

3. See Walter Ong, *Ramus, Method, and the Decay of Dialogue* (Cambridge: Harvard University Press, 1958) 191. On this double movement in Ramist method—dichotomous exfoliation and analytic reduction—see Martin Elsky, "Reorganizing the Encyclopedia: Vives and Ramus on Aristotle and the Scholastics," *The Cambridge History of Literary Criticism: Volume 3, The Renaissance*, ed. Glyn P. Norton (Cambridge: Cambridge University Press, 1999), 406.

This is not to say that the hexameter is inevitably to be identified with fossilized thought. Nor does every stanza work the way I am describing: there are plenty that defy these structural generalizations. But the incidence of conformity is high enough to generate an expectation, and when that expectation is violated—or transcended—the difference is meaningful. On analogy with Teskey's thinking about allegory one might speak of a kind of "stanzaic capture," the fiction that the stanza is imposed upon some antecedent matter that once had a shape of its own. Stanzas that do not fit, particularly those that do not crystallize in their final line, cast doubt on the capacity of the method to process the full range of experience. * * *

I would like to think that Gabriel Harvey could have been persuaded to recognize in Spenser's device the promise of method, though the two men seem to have talked more about lines than about stanzas. It is at all events a more flexible instrument than Ramus ever had, building in as it does a moment of disruption and perhaps of doubt; in this it may even anticipate the programmatic doubt that became essential to the seventeenth century's version of the concept. Spenser applied his method more than thirty-eight hundred times over the course of *The Faerie Queene*, pouring the welter of ideas and events in his massive poem into its idiosyncratic shape again and again; day, we must imagine, after day; year after year. The contest staged there between thinking and thought is parallel to—though it cannot simply be mapped onto—the contest between narrative (or romance) and allegory, forces in the poem that often collaborate but tend fundamentally in different directions. Allegory too might fruitfully be considered under the rubric of method, particularly in those templar moments when it seems most like a mode of analysis. The notorious trick of saving the revelation of a character's name for the end of an episode is a little like the consolidating closure of the hexameter writ large. But none of this is to say that *The Faerie Queene* is a methodical poem: rather, that there is method in it, on a variety of levels: the ambivalent search for a structure of thinking that could be widely and recurrently applied to help us understand and fashion other understanders. In this at least Spenser was a characteristic if ever skeptical citizen of an intellectual moment avid after such reliable, programmatic access to the truth. He may have sleepwalked through the rooms of his accumulating memory palace, and he may have dithered over every threshold, turning forward, then back, but we have to allow that he had the peculiar presence of mind to shut the door behind him, every time.

DAVID WILSON-OKAMURA

The Aesthetic of Spenser's Feminine Rhyme†

One of Spenser's greatest experiments—which does not seem like an experiment anymore—was to flood the second installment of his *Faerie Queene* (1596) with feminine rhymes, such as *gotten*: *soften*: *often*.[1] In

Adapted from "The French Aesthetic of Spenser's Feminine Rhyme," *Modern Language Quarterly* 68.3 (2007).
† Reprinted by permission of the author.

1. *FQ* 4.proem.5. In Books 1–3, there is only one feminine rhyme (2.9.47); in Books 4–6 and

English, feminine rhymes have to be worked at; and yet they have the reputation, perversely, not of being earnest, but of being frivolous or affected. Marlowe, for example, uses feminine rhymes for comic effect in *Hero and Leander* (1593).[2] Spenser, although he uses feminine rhyme in all of his poetry, uses it most frequently in his couplet satire, *Mother Hubberds Tale* (1591).[3] This trend would continue: by the middle of the seventeenth century, feminine rhymes in English were relegated almost exclusively to comedy or satire.

Yet the great majority of Spenser's feminine rhymes are resolutely unfunny. Consider, for instance, this stanza from *Mutabilitie*:

> When I bethinke me on that speech whyleare,
> Of *Mutability*, and well it way:
> Me seemes, that though she all vnworthy were
> Of the Heav'ns Rule; yet very sooth to say,
> In all things else she beares the greatest sway.
> Which makes me loath this state of life so tickle,
> And loue of things so vaine to cast away;
> Whose flowring pride, so fading and so fickle,
> Short *Time* shall soon cut down with his consuming sickle.
> (*Mut.* 8.1)

Spenser's rhymes can be funny (e.g., *raught her*: *distraught her* in *FQ* 5.4.41). But they are not all funny, and the unfunny ones are an irritation unless we can formulate—and internalize, while we are reading him—a theory to account for them.

Maureen Quilligan has argued that Spenser's use of feminine rhyme in Books 4 through 6 of *The Faerie Queene* echoes a negative shift in his assessment of the Virgin Queen, and that he associates feminine endings with emasculation and with different forms of female rulership (motherly for Britomart, rebellious for Radigund and Mutabilitie).[4] Quilligan discusses 18 different cases, but even that is only a fraction: in the whole *Faerie Queene*, there are at least 164 feminine rhymes, not counting ambiguous rhymes such as *powre*: *towre* and *frowned*: *drowned*. To understand feminine rhyme as a category, we need to cast a wider net. This could be done in two ways: by analyzing, rhyme by rhyme, the other 146 examples of feminine rhyme in Spenser's epic; or since that would be unreadable, by examining how feminine rhyme was discussed in the period, and what it was used for.

Medieval Latin was friendly to rhyme, and cultivated feminine rhyme as a special ornament, not only in comic poems, but also in hymns. In Italian poetry, feminine rhyme is the norm; Ariosto and Tasso's epics are full of it. But the term *feminine rhyme* is adapted from French prosody, where it refers to the falling rhythm produced by an otherwise-mute *e*: for example, *faconde*: *monde*. Beginning with Du Bellay and Ronsard, *la rime féminine* is used for poems on every theme and in every genre.[5] According

Mutabilitie there are 169 feminine rhymes according to Josephine Waters Bennett, *The Evolution of* The Faerie Queene (Chicago: University of Chicago Press, 1942), p. 158 and appendix 1.

2. See Elizabeth Bieman, "Comic Rhyme in Marlowe's *Hero and Leander*," *English Literary Renaissance* 9 (1979): 69–77.
3. Floyd Stovall, "Feminine Rimes in the *Faerie Queene*," *JEGP* 26 (1927): 91–95, at 94.
4. "Feminine Endings: The Sexual Politics of Sidney's and Spenser's Rhyming," in *The Renaissance Englishwoman in Print: Counterbalancing the Canon*, ed. Anne M. Haselkorn and Betty S. Travitsky (Amherst: University of Massachusetts Press, 1990), pp. 311–26.
5. On masculine and feminine rhyme in French poetry up to Du Bellay, see Georges Lote, *Histoire*

to critics of the period, this has nothing to do with feminine subject matter, but stems from a desire to increase variety (something that was valued all over Europe) and to reunite music and poetry (one of the special, though not peculiar, goals of French poetry in the Renaissance).[6]

In French prosody, feminine rhyme is a subcategory of *la rime riche*. The concept of rich rhyme is one that goes back to the Troubadors, who classified rhyme into two categories, plain and costly. Plain rhymes (also known as *rimes ruralles, rimes communes*, or *rimes pauvres*) are rhymes that consist of a vowel or diphthong plus a final consonant (e.g., *chat*: *climat*). Costly or dear rhymes are plain rhymes that have been "enriched" with the addition of a secondary echo (for example, the *m* in *charmant*: *calmant*). Leonine rhymes—such as *vanter*: *chanter, vantera*: *chantera*, and *publira*: *oublira*—are a development of the same idea: rich rhyme plus.[7] Indeed, for at least one critic, the terms were interchangeable.[8]

The point of *la rime riche* is not to write sonnets about wealth, but to make poetry itself more splendid, and even (as Du Bellay will argue) to enrich the French language. And it is this concept of richness, more than anything else, that accounts for Spenser's feminine rhymes; that, and Spenser's reading of French poetry. In Italian poetry, rhymes of more than one syllable are so common that they simply do not register. Spenser's reading of Italian would have softened him on feminine rhyme, but nothing more. In French poetry, *les rimes riches et féminines* are ostentatious, because they are difficult, because they are costly. To borrow a metaphor from Puttenham, they are to the poet what gold leaf is to the painter, or lapis lazuli from beyond the sea, ground up to make the pigment called ultramarine. The cost of the materials does not just contribute to the value of the artwork; it is part of the artistry itself.

John Ruskin, in *The Seven Lamps of Architecture* (1849), explains the logic of this position, through what he calls the Lamp of Sacrifice. This, says Ruskin, is the aesthetic impulse that

> prompts us to the offering of precious things, merely because they are precious, not because they are useful or necessary. It is a spirit, for instance, which of two marbles, equally beauitful, applicable and durable, would choose the more costly, because it was so, and of two kinds of decoration, equally effective, would choose the more elaborate because it was so, in order that it might in the same compass present more cost and more thought.[9]

Ruskin goes on to say that the Lamp of Sacrifice has two forms, the first of which is "self-denial for the sake of self-discipline." The author of *The Faerie Queene* (not to mention that argosy of prosody, *The Shepheardes Calender*) was well versed in artistic self-discipline. But that is only the first candle, as it were, of the Lamp.

du vers français (Paris: Boivin, 1949–), 2:111–24.

6. See François Mouret, "Art poétique et musication: De l'alternance des rimes," in *À haute voix: Diction et prononciation au XVI*e et XVIIe siècles, ed. Olivia Rosenthal (Paris: Klincksieck, 1998), pp. 103–17.
7. See Henri Chamard, *Histoire de la Pléiade*, 4 vols. (Paris: Didier, 1939), 4:122–23 and Lote, *Histoire du vers français*, 2:137–48.
8. Thomas Sébillet, *Art poétique françoys* 1.7, sec. 2, in *Traités de poétique et de rhétorique de la Renaissance*, ed. Francis Goyet (Paris: Librairie générale française, 1990), pp. 78–79. See also Goyet's long note, pp. 163–64.
9. *The Seven Lamps of Architecture* (1849; rev. 1880) 1.3, rept. Mineola, NY: Dover, 1989, pp. 10–11.

In addition, Ruskin says there is also "the desire to honour or please someone else by the costliness of the sacrifice." This is the second form of Sacrifice, and it is this form that is on display in Spenser's wedding song, which he offers to his bride "in lieu of many ornaments / With which my loue should duly haue beene dect" (*Epithalamion* 427–28). A poem in place of a jewel: what did she make of it, we wonder, the substitution of vocables for carbuncles? Words, they say, are cheap. But Spenser's rhymes—

> Her cheekes lyke apples which the sun hath rudded,
> Her lips lyke cherryes charming men to byte,
> Her brest like to a bowle of creame vncrudded,
> Her paps lyke lyllies budded,
> Her snowie necke lyke to a marble towre,
> And all her body like a pallace fayre,
> Ascending vppe with many a stately stayre,
> To honors seat and chastities sweet bowre (*Epith.* 173–80)

—those rhymes were sumptuous, rare, expensive,

> unto her a goodly ornament,
> And for short time an endlesse moniment. (*Epith.* 433–34)

In 1875, the American poet and critic James Russell Lowell said that the best word to describe Spenser's style is *costly.* According to Lowell, Spenser "chooses his language for its rich canorousness rather than for its intensity of meaning."[1] Looking back, we can probably agree that the noun *canorousness* needs to be revived and its use extended to all fields of knowledge, including the natural sciences. But when he insinuates that Spenser may have subordinated meaning to sound, we assume the *en garde* position. Spenser must be defended!

For example, it might be argued that the real theme—the latent meaning—of all these rich and feminine rhymes is nationhood: defending English as a language and making it respectable, even glorious. But this is a factor, not a theme. Other factors that encouraged a rich sound were subject matter (according to Tasso, love scenes were supposed to be more ornamental than battle scenes) and the character of the various vernaculars (English, for example, was thought to have an inherently robust sound compared with French). To isolate one of these factors and call it the theme seems arbitrary. Better to call all of them *causes* (final or efficient) and save *theme* for something more specific, what a poem is about.

Poems do have themes, meanings, even messages. But finding those messages, producing "readings" of poems, should not be the sole purpose of literary criticism. New Historicism has been criticized for ignoring aesthetics and treating texts as if they were mere repositories for theme. But much formal criticism, both new and old, is also in a hurry to get rid of form by translating it into something more conceptual—as if the form of a poem were merely an analogy for its content. It is not that form cannot have meaning, but some forms lose their meaning (when they had one to begin with) through repetition. Feminine rhyme is an example. In Spenser, it is used for feminine subjects and for masculine, for love

1. "Spenser" (1875), in *Spenser's Critics: Changing Currents in Literary Taste*, ed. William R. Mueller (Syracuse: Syracuse University Press, 1959), p. 96.

poems, epic, and satire. In French poetry from the same period, feminine rhyme, alternating with masculine, gets used for everything and, in consequence, doesn't mean anything. According to Paul J. Hecht, it is the same with Spenser's alliteration.[2]

This is not a call to stop interpreting. We have had those before and they don't work. More than forty years ago, in "Against Interpretation" (1964), Susan Sontag got to the end of her manifesto and proclaimed, "In place of a hermeneutics we need an erotics of art."[3] That sounds bold but, in fact, it's another substitution, sex in place of statement. Spenser, when he opened the floodgates of feminine rhyme, was not trying to make a statement, or even be sexy; he was trying to make a big, rich sound.

JUDITH H. ANDERSON

"Pricking on the plaine": Spenser's Intertextual Beginnings and Endings[†]

The opening line of the first canto of the first Book of *The Faerie Queene*, "A Gentle Knight was pricking on the plaine," introduces the Chaucerian intertext and does so problematically.[1] I doubt the Spenserian exists who has not heard some medievalist declare, "I could never get over, or never forgive Spenser, his opening line." Yet for years Spenserians themselves, as if conspiring to accept the poet's insensitivity to his own words, totally ignored the "hard begin" of Spenser's best-known Book. By recalling Chaucer's comic *Tale of Sir Thopas*, knight prickant, this remarkably bold and witty beginning serves notice of the extent to which the writings of the medieval poet to whom Spenser affirmed his affinity will pervade, and complicate, his poem.

The problem in Spenser's first line centers on the word "pricking," which has, of course, the perfectly straightforward, innocent meaning, "To spur or urge a horse on; to ride fast," and the *OED* rightly cites Spenser's line as an instance of this meaning.[2] I am unpersuaded, however, that this is the full range of meaning of the word in this line. My argument that it is not so will be circumstantial and eventually circuitous, but such is the difference between lexical definition and poetic usage: literature—especially poetry and even more especially Spenser—is contextual, that is, circumstantial in the extreme.

The work "pricking," already conspicuous as the first verbal action in the opening line of Spenser's story, occurs in a context designed to render its meaning specifically problematical. Pricking emphatically means *fast* riding, even galloping, rather than ambling. It causes some logical distraction, not to mention visual consternation, to learn that "faire beside"

2. "Letters for the Dogs: Chasing Spenserian Alliteration," *Spenser Studies* 25 (2010): 263–85.
3. *Against Interpretation and Other Essays* (New York: Noonday-Farrar, 1966), p. 14.

† Originally published in *English Literary Renaissance* 15.2 (1985): 166–74. Reprinted by permission of John Wiley and Sons.

1. All Spenserian references in this chapter are to *The Works of Edmund Spenser: A Variorum Edition*, ed. Edwin Greenlaw et al, II vols. (Baltimore: Johns Hopkins Press, 1932–1957), cited as *Var.*; *The Faerie Queene* is cited as *FQ*.
2. *OED*, s.v. *Prick v*, 11.

the pricking knight a lovely lady rode "Vpon a lowly Asse" and that "by her" side she in turn led a white lamb on a leash and that lagging, but still within sight, a dwarf, loaded down with sleeping bags and provisions, followed on foot. The time is out of joint, or if not the narrative time, then surely the narrative distance and rate. Within the first stanza of canto i alone, the knight's pricking or spurring on his steed is also narratively discontinuous with the steed's displeasure at the "foming bitt." The steed's disdaining control suggests that restraining pressure is being or at least could be applied to the reins and thus that Redcrosse's rear view mirror might eventually show him that he has outpricked Una, her lamb, and her dwarf—left them, I might add allegorically, in his dust.

Besides being narratively incongruous, the word "pricking" has, like the word "shroud" five stanzas later, a resonance and potentially a doubleness of signification that words like "trot," "gallop," or "amble" simply lack.[3] To begin again with the *OED*, the verb "prick" has also the *figurative* meaning "To drive or urge as with a spur; to impel . . . stimulate, provoke."[4] This meaning commonly carries a generalized association with the agency of nature, appetite, or desire. One of Chaucer's best-known lines in the first sentence of *The Canterbury Tales* describes the lovesick little birds that sleep all night with open eye—"So prycketh hem nature in her corages"—and it thereby affords both an example in point and an instance of the fertile and fundamentally Chaucerian association of such pricking with courage or "corage," the seat of vitality, spirit, lustiness, and vigor.[5]

Although the primary source of the lover's song in Spenser's Temple of Venus is Lucretius' hymn to the Goddess of Love, Lucretian sentiments merge more than once with relevant Chaucerian memories of pricking:

> the merry birds, thy prety pages
> Priuily *pricked* with thy *lustfull* powres,
> Chirpe loud to thee out of their leauy cages,
> And thee their mother call to coole their kindly rages.
> (IV.x.45: my emphasis)

Spenser's lines recall the earlier English poet's association of sexual appetite and desire with nature's pricking. Statistically, the greatest numbers of forms of the word "prick" occur in Spenser's second and fourth Books, and it is reasonable that they should do so. Book II is centrally concerned with the tempering of appetite, and Book IV, with the frustration and fulfillment of desire and, more fundamentally, with the natural force and energy of which love is in good part an expression.

Even at a glance through the Spenser *Concordance*, however, two other occurrences of the word "prick" in Book I are particularly striking, both for the suggestiveness of their immediate verbal contexts and for their Chaucerian flavor or resonance. Conveniently, these occurrences associate the Redcrosse Knight with Prince Arthur, an association eventually to prove of some interest for a reading of the first line of canto i in

3. Cf. *FQ* I.i.8. *OED*, s.v. *Shroud* v^1 2c, 3–7.
4. *OED*, s.v. *Prick v*, 10.
5. *OED*, s.v. *Courage sb*, 1,3, 4. Unless otherwise specified, all Chaucerian references in this chapter are to *The Works 1532, supplemented by material from the editions of 1542, 1561, 1598, and 1602* (London: Scolar, 1969): I have changed the solidi to commas and expanded the contractions in Thynne's text.

this Book. In canto ix, Arthur comments on the circumstances that led to his dream of the Queen of Faeries:

> It was in freshest flowre of youthly yeares,
> When courage first does creepe in manly chest,
> Then first the coale of kindly heat appeares
> To kindle loue in euery liuing brest.
>
> (I.ix.9)[6]

Nearing the dream itself, Arthur explains how on that fateful day he was "prickt forth with iollitie / Of looser life, and heat of hardiment" (12). Arthur's comments align "courage" and "iollitie of looser life" with the force that "pricks" him into his defining experience, the erotic dream of an elf queen. Like *courage, jollity* is a richly suggestive word meaning cheerfulness, pleasure, bravery, or lust.[7] Interestingly, it occurs in Chaucer's *Sir Thopas* (lxxxiv^{v}) and, in adjectival form—"Full iolly knight he seemd"—in the first stanza of Spenser's story that begins with a description of Redcrosse's "pricking on the plaine." The second occurrence of the word "prick" in Book I that is particularly striking in relation to Redcrosse's initial pricking comes in canto x, when Contemplation describes Redcrosse's route from plowman's state to Faerie court: "Till prickt with courage, and thy forces pryde, / To Faery court thou cam'st to seeke for fame" (66). Here again the word "prickt" is aligned with richly charged words—"courage" and "forces pryde"—implying prowess and desire.

A seemingly inevitable extension of lexical meanings of the word "prick" is persuasively documented by Eric Partridge in *Shakespeare's Bawdy.*[8] Counting substantive and verbal examples, Partridge finds that *prick* appears as a pun eight times in Shakespeare's works. Likely the most familiar instance of this Shakespearean pun occurs when Mercutio observes in *Romeo and Juliet*, "the bawdy hand of the dial is now upon the prick of noon" (II.iv.112–13).[9] And somewhere elusively, richly, naughtily, and comically in-between Chaucer's description of those little love sick birds pricked "in her corages" by nature and Shakespeare's more pointed bawdy is Chaucer's notoriously persistent employment of the verb "prick" in the *Tale of Sir Thopas*: for example,

> Sir Thopas fyl in loue longyng,
> And whan he herde the throstel syng
> He pricked as he were wode
> His faire stede in his prickyng
> So swette, that men might him wring
> His sydes were al blode.
> Sir Thopas eke so wery was
> For prickyng on the softe gras
> So fiers was his corage
> That doun he layde him in that place

6. See Lucretius, *De Rerum Natura*, trans. W. H. D. Rouse (London: Heinemann, 1924), 2–4, esp. vs.12–13, 18–20 of Book 1. Cf. also J. A. W. Bennett, *The Parlement of Foules: An Interpretation* (Oxford: Clarendon, 1957), 119–20.
7. *OED*, s.v. *Jollity*, 1, 3, 5.
8. *Shakespeare's Bawdy*, rev. ed. (New York: E. P. Dutton, 1969), 167 (*prick, n, v; prick out*), 176 (rose), 153 (needle).
9. *The Riverside Shakespeare*, ed. G. Blakemore Evans et al. (Boston, Mass.: Houghton Mifflin, 1974).

to dream of the elf queen who will be his "lemman," he hopes, and will sleep, oddly enough, under his "gore" (lxxxiv[v]). Inspired, or at least awakened, by the dream, Sir Thopas climbs gracelessly into his saddle and once more "pricketh ouer style and stone / An Elfe quene for to espye." Examples could be multiplied—mercilessly.

For a reader of Chaucer, the word "pricking" has special resonance and, given a suitable context, a particularly strong, metrically mnemonic potential for association with *The Tale of Sir Thopas.* Excepting the *Treatise on the Astrolabe,* in which *prick* has technically delimited meanings, forms of this word occur eight times in *Sir Thopas,* more often than in any other Chaucerian piece. In view of the relative brevity of *Sir Thopas*—roughly two hundred lines—the association of pricking with this *Tale* is readily available, always possible where relevant, and irresistible when invited.

Spenser's own knowledge of Chaucer's *Tale of Sir Thopas* is indisputable, and the ease, detail, and pervasiveness of his borrowings indicate a thorough assimilation of it. In the March Eclogue of *The Shepheardes Calender,* a tale about two comic boors, he uses one of the two (or more) forms of the tail-rhyme stanza found in *Sir Thopas,* and throughout *The Faerie Queene,* he takes individual words or phrases from it—for example, the Squire of Dames's phrase "many a lane" in Book III (vii.58) and the Giant Disdain's jacket of "checklaton" in Book VI (vii.43).[1] Spenser finds the name Ollyphant in *Sir Thopas,* plausibly also the name Blandamour (spelled Blayndamour in Thynne's *Thopas*) and, probably, by way of Ollyphant's name and lustful nature, the inspiration for Lust's elephantine ears.[2] In addition, of course, there is mention of Sir Thopas as the confounder of Ollyphant in the 1590, although not in the 1596, edition.[3] And finally, there is Prince Arthur's dream of the Faerie Queene in Book I, for which *Sir Thopas* offers as close a source or analogue as centuries of researchers determined to find a more dignified candidate have been able to unearth.[4] I shall return somewhat later to Arthur's dream, which, to my mind, *Sir Thopas* underlies but underlies complexly, for it seems to me most unlikely that Spenser missed the outrageous humor in a Chaucerian *Tale* he knew so well—humor, incidentally, to which Wyatt, Lyly, Drayton, and Shakespeare all responded.[5] Nor do I think the view that

1. The March Eclogue rhymes aabccb. In Thynne's edition, the first stanza of *Sir Thopas* rhymes aabaab; c. 79ff. rhyme aa[II] bccb (tail rhyme added to verse 3, i.e., c-rhyme internalized in verse 3); vs. 142ff. rhyme aabccb. (Thynne's vs. 142 is vs. 146 in Donaldson's 2nd edition and vs. 857 in Robinson's 2nd edition.) See *Var.,* III, 267; VI, 225–26, and A. Kent Hieatt, *Chaucer, Spenser, Milton: Mythopoeic Continuities and Transformations* (Montreal: McGill–Queen's University Press, 1975), 19–24. (On page 23, Hieatt mistakenly assumes that the rhyme scheme of *Sir Thopas* is uniform.)
2. *Var.,* IV, 170–71. Ollyphant signifies "elephant" and "destructive fantasy."
3. *FQ* III.vii.48, vs. 4; *Var.,* III, 412.
4. Edwin Greenlaw, "Britomart at the House of Busirane," *Studies in Philology,* 26 (1929), 124–27, suggests that Arthur of Little Britain is the source of Prince Arthur's dream in *The Faerie Queene.* A glance at Arthur's dreams in chapters 16 and 46 of *Little Britain* will show that, while they might be a distant analogue to Spenser's episode, they are an unlikely source: *The History of the Valiant Knight Arthur of Little Britain,* trans. John Bourchier, Lord Berners ([1555?]; rpt. London: White, Cochrane, 1814). The motto of an older generation of Spenserians appears to have been "anything but Chaucer": cf. chapter 9 on "Chaucer's *Parliament of Fowls* and Refractions of a Veiled Venus in *The Faerie Queene*" in part 2 of this volume.
5. See Josephine Waters Bennett, *The Evolution of "The Faerie Queene"* (1942; rpt. New York: B. Franklin, 1960), 11–15. For Drayton, see also *Works,* ed. J. William Hebel (Oxford, Shakespeare Head, 1961), I, 88–91; V, 11–12. On Chaucer's humor in *Sir Thopas,* see E. Talbot Donaldson, "The Embarrassments of Art: *The Tale of Sir Thopas,* 'Pyramus and Thisbe,' and *A Midsummer Night's Dream,*" in *The Swan at the Well: Shakespeare Reading Chaucer* (New

Spenser either ignored this humor or simply moralized it out of existence is remotely adequate to the wit and subtlety of *The Faerie Queene.*

Given the persistence of a misconception of Spenser as moralistic and humorless, a momentary digression is in order. In the twentieth-century revival of interest in Spenser, this misconception starts, representatively but by no means exclusively, with Josephine Waters Bennett's *Evolution of "The Faerie Queene"* (1942), a volume important enough in its time to have been reprinted in 1960. Although Bennett does not suppose Spenser unaware of Chaucer's humor in *Sir Thopas,* she observes that Gabriel Harvey, Spenser's slightly older and somewhat patronizing friend, considered *Sir Thopas* "morall" and that Harvey so labeled it in his marginalia.[6] She also suggests that Harvey's understanding of *Sir Thopas* was influenced by *The Faerie Queene* (19*n*32). Unfortunately, however, Bennett misinterprets Harvey's marginalium ("morall") on "Chaucer's Tale" in Speght 1598, taking it to refer to *Sir Thopas* rather than to the *Melibeus.* But it is the *Melibeus* that is consistently labeled "Chaucer's Tale" in both Speght and the earlier Thynne family of editions. With equal consistency *Sir Thopas* is called "the Rime of Sir Thopas." In sum, Spenser's alleged moralizing of *Sir Thopas* has no basis in evidence external to the poem, and Bennett's error might be passed over in silence had it not been more recently resuscitated by J. A. Burrow to become a recurrent reference in discussions of the Chaucer-Spenser intertext.[7] On this note, I want to return to the opening of Spenser's first canto to ask what sense a distant echo of *Sir Thopas*—an available resonance, as I have termed it—would make here and in the subsequently unfolding context of Redcrosse's story.

To begin with, a reader who considers the possibility of an echo can do little more with it at the outset of canto i than I already have: that is, to notice resonance and discontinuities and to be mildly puzzled. A similar effect occurs a few stanzas later when a sudden rainstorm is poured by an angry Jove "into his Lemans lap": we have questions and hints, not answers. But once we have grasped the relation of Archimago to Redcrosse and the specifically erotic nature of the dream Archimago provokes, the incongruous—indeed disunified—aspects of our initial impression of Redcrosse become increasingly significant. Increasingly, we realize their potential. Archimago, persistently termed the old man or aged sire, is no more an exclusively external tempter of Redcrosse than the nature of old Adam—the old man as opposed to the new—is external to humankind. The dream Archimago provokes rises out of Redcrosse's own nature, and it reveals the knight's failure to reconcile the pricking of his "corage" with his faith, the force and the energy of his human nature with the form and purity of truth. The word "prick"—conspicuous in the first line of Redcrosse's story and discontinuous with the immediate narrative context—foreshadows this larger, moral discrepancy, making it

Haven, Conn.: Yale University Press, 1985), 7–29. (Shakespeare's *MND* is indebted to John Lyly's *Endymion,* whose comic *Sir Thopas* derives from Chaucer's.)

6. Bennett, 15; also *Gabriel Harvey's Marginalia,* ed. G. C. Moore Smith (Stratford-upon-Avon, U.K.: Shakespeare Head, 1913), 228.

7. J. A. Burrow, citing Bennett, implies that Harvey's marginalium confirms a strictly "morall" interpretation of *Sir Thopas* by Spenser: "*Sir Thopas* in the Sixteenth Century," in *Middle English Studies Presented to Norman Davis,* ed. Douglas Gray and E. G. Stanley (Oxford: Clarendon, 1983), 81–88, esp. 87. Unfortunately, electronic searches turn up Burrow's essay, since it exists in an anthology analyzed by bibliographies such as the MLA's, without turning up corrections of it in other essays that do not feature *Sir Thopas* in their titles.

both more comprehensible and more inevitable—ironically, if perversely enough, more natural.

Prince Arthur's dream of the Faerie Queen adds another dimension to our initial impression of Redcrosse. As Patricia Parker has shown, Arthur's dream is loaded with verbal memories of Redcrosse's earlier dream of a false Una.[8] Within Spenser's first Book itself, therefore, an element of parody, asking for interpretation, underlies Arthur's dream. Allusions to three of Chaucer's stories increase this parody and simultaneously our awareness of the human complexity—possible futility and positive comedy—that underlie, enrich, and also threaten the ideal vision. Perhaps the most striking of the Chaucerian allusions in Arthur's experience is to *The Tale of Sir Thopas*, but there are also pervasive recollections of Chaucer's *Troilus and Criseyde* and one strong echo of *The Wife of Bath's Prologue*. The recollections of *Troilus* glance at a love story with a bright beginning and a blighted end.[9] The echo of the Wife's *Prologue*—"no fort can be so strong / Ne fleshly brest can armed be so sound, / But will at last be wonne with battrie long" (ix.11)—recalls her mock harangue on behalf of hapless husbands one through three: "She may no while in chastite abyde / That is assayled on euery syde . . . men may nat kepe a castel wal / It may so long assayled be ouer all" (xli^{r}).[1] The memory of Chaucer in Spenser's lines thus glances both at the failure of human virtue and at the comic vitality of a thoroughly untamed virago.

Skeptical distancing of Arthur's ideal vision is to an extent inevitable in these Chaucerian allusions, but rather than merely mocking this vision, the delicate layering of parody that underlies it also deepens our awareness of its human relevance. Much the same kind of ironic resonance and specifically Chaucerian parody underlie both outset and end of *The Faerie Queene*, both the ambiguously "gentle" knight's "pricking on the plaine" and the poet's farewell to this world and this poem in the final stanzas of the Mutability Cantos. Like Arthur's dream, the Chaucerian resonance that thus frames the entirety of the poem we have is informed with the ambivalent potency of the physical world, the potency of natural appetite and natural time.[2]

In the interest of a specifically Spenserian closure, which is, like circle and cycle, properly circuitous, I want to extend these observations on the Chaucerian frame of *The Faerie Queene* to the Chaucerian character of Spenser's poetical career as he himself evidently framed it. Spenser's poetic début, *The Shepheardes Calender*, like his grand finale, *The Faerie Queene*, recalls Chaucer at its outset and again at its end, and together these two poems, one pastoral and one romance epic, enclose the poet's progress.[3] In *The Calender*, Immerito's initial address and final farewell to his poem—"Goe little booke" and "Goe lyttle Calender"—allude simply and umistakably to Chaucer's *Troilus*: "Go lytel booke, go my lytel tregedye"

8. Patricia A. Parker, *Inescapable Romance: Studies in the Poetics of a Mode* (Princeton, N.J.: Princeton University Press, 1979), 83–86.
9. See *Troilus and Criseyde*, lxxi–lxxii (Bk. 1.183–239, 316–57, in E. T. Donaldson's or F. N. Robinson's 2nd editions).
1. *Var.*, I, 267.
2. "Arthur and Argante: Parodying the Ideal Vision," part 2, chapter 8, in this volume, returns to ambivalent nuances that accrue to Arthur's figure, exploring these in other passages of Book I.
3. Again, "grand finale": in 1596, Spenser also published *Fowre Hymnes*, two of which are earlier pieces, and the occasional *Prothalamion*.

> But subiecte ben vnto al poesye
> And kysse the steppes, where as thou seest pace
> Of Vergyl, Ovyde, Homer, Lucan, and Stace.
> (ccxviii^{v})

Spenser similarly cautions his *Calender* not to match with the "poesye" of his predecessors "But [to] followe them farre off, and their high steppes adore."

In the penultimate stanza of the Mutability Cantos, as John Pope, quoting Talbot Donaldson, has written, Spenser's profoundly ambiguous lines on the doubleness of the human condition again recall the ending of Chaucer's *Troilus.*[4] But with benefit of a fuller Chaucerian intertext, they do so more subtly and richly. Condemning the world in lines which, in Donaldson's words, "poignantly enhance the very thing that he is repudiating," Chaucer cautions "yonge fresshe folkes, he or she" to think "al nys but a fayre / This worlde that passeth sone, as floures fayre" (ccxviii^{v}).[5] Spenser's lines speak similarly of loveliness and loss, of pleasure and futility:

> Which makes me loath this state of life so tickle
> And loue of things so vaine to cast away;[6]
> Whose flowring pride, so fading and so tickle,
> Short *Time* shall soon cut down with his consuming sickle.

Thus alluding at once to the ending of Chaucer's *Troilus* and recalling, through the further significance of such allusion, the end of Spenser's own *Calender*, the final stanzas of Mutability come full circle, even as they appear to signal the conscious nature of the poet's intention to end. These stanzas simultaneously continue and conclude, defeat time and acknowledge its destructive power.[7] Their irreducible ambiguity is far distant from the narrative discontinuities at the outset of the poem, but circuitously, through a matrix of association and resonance, they lead us back to beginnings.

4. "The Existential Mysteries as Treated in Certain Passages of Our Older Poets," in *Acts of Interpretation: The Text in Its Contexts 700–1600*, ed. Mary J. Carruthers and Elizabeth D. Kirk (Norman, Okla.: Pilgrim, 1982), 345–62, here 345–47, 360–62. Pope quotes E. Talbot Donaldson's "Ending of 'Troilus,'" in *Speaking of Chaucer* (London: Athlone, 1970), 98: "All the illusory loveliness of a world which is man's only reality is expressed in the very lines that reject that loveliness."
5. The interpretive quotation earlier in this sentence is from E. T. Donaldson, ed., *Chaucer's Poetry: An Anthology for the Modern Reader*, 2nd ed. (New York: Ronald, 1975), 1144.
6 In the preceding line, I have eliminated the comma after *tickle* in *Var.* In these profoundly ambiguous lines, *loath* is either an adjective or a verb, and *vain* is either an adjective modifying *love* or *things* or else it is an adverb modifying the infinitive *to cast:* see Harry Berger, Jr., "The *Mutabilitie Cantos:* Archaism and Evolution in Retrospect," in *Spenser: A Collection of Critical Essays*, ed. Harry Berger, Jr. (Englewood Cliffs, N.J.: Prentice-Hall, 1968) 146–76, esp. 172–73; and my *Growth of a Personal Voice: "Piers Plowman" and "The Faerie Queene"* New Haven, Conn.: Yale University Press, 1976), 200–202, cf. 48–49.
7. My position differs from Jonathan Goldberg's sense of Spenser's helplessness—indeed, his dark despair—in the face of time: *Endlesse Worke: Spenser and the Structures of Discourse* (Baltimore: Johns Hopkins University Press, 1981). Goldberg's book greatly renewed interest, including my own, in the relation of Spenser to Chaucer.

JENNIFER SUMMIT

[At the Limits of Memory: Imagination and the Bower of Bliss]†

Like the post-Reformation library that I argue it echoes, Eumnestes's library, with its visibly incomplete holdings, results from a process of distinction and culling. Just as Leland advocates a process of "casting awaye trifles, cutting off olde wiues tales, and superfluous fables" from those matters that one should "reade, scanne vpon, and preserve in memorie," so Spenser upholds the library-worthiness of *Briton moniments* and *Antiquitez of Faerie lond*—and, by extension, the category of memorial writing that they exemplify—by implicitly contrasting them with "th'aboundance of an idle braine" and "painted forgery" that book 2's proem distinguishes from "iust memory." The material that is excluded from Eumnestes's library exists on the other side of its threshold: in the forecourt of the headlike tower of the castle of Alma, the chamber of Phantastes, the imaginative faculty is filled with

> idle thoughts and fantasies
> Deuises, dreames, opinions unsound,
> Shewes, visions, sooth-sayes, and prophesies,
> And all that fained is, as leasings, tales, and lies.
> (*FQ*, 2.9.51)

With their emphasis on imaginative feigning and deception, these "idle thoughts" recall the proem's anxious invocation of "th'aboundance of an idle brain" and "painted forgery," while translating that anxiety into the realm of Reformation anti-Catholicism. "Opinions unsound / Shewes, visions, sooth-sayes, and prophesies" name precisely the dangerous fabrications that Protestant readers chastised in the medieval books they salvaged from the monastic libraries: thus Bale castigates the "vision of the Monk of Evesham" by naming it a "false and fabulous vision" ("*visio fallax et fabulosa*"), just as Robert Burton's later *Anatomy of Melancholy* would debunk Catholic visions or "extasies" such as appear "in Bede and Gregory, Saint Bridgets revelations," and so forth by classifying them as "common apparitions" belonging to "the force of the imagination."[1] For Protestant library makers, no less than for Protestant theological writers such as Tyndale, the imagination was the realm of idolatry: thus Tyndale insists that nothing "bringeth the wrath of God so soon and sore on a man, as the idolatry of his own imagination."[2] Excoriations of fantasy and imagination run through Protestant polemic: a work reprinted by Foxe called "The Phantasy of Idolatry" accuses papists of misleading believers with false shows; Archbishop Cramner attacks idolatrous "images and phantasyes"; and the iconoclastic Royal Visitor's Injunctions of Edward VI in 1547 targeted for

† From "Monuments and Ruins: Spenser and the Limits of the English Library" in *ELH* 70.1 (2003), 20–26, 33–3. Notes have been renumbered.

1. Robert Burton, vol. 1 of *The Anatomy of Melancholy*, ed. Thomas C. Faulkner (Oxford: Clarendon, 1989), 251.
2. Tyndale, cited by Greenblatt, *Renaissance Self-Fashioning: From More to Shakespeare* (Chicago: University of Chicago Press, 1980), 113.

destruction images "devysed by mennes phantasies."[3] In this Reformation discourse, the antidote to the idolatrous imagination and fantasy was memory: thus the very injunctions that forbid the works "devysed by mennes phantasies" permit the uses of images as objects of "remembraunce, whereby, men may be admonished, of the holy lifes and conversacion of theim, that the sayd images do represent."[4] Likewise, while Cramner dismissed idolatrous fantasy, he helped retain holy communion in the Protestant service by defining it as an act of "remembraunce."[5] The terms "imagination" and "memory," as Spenser anatomizes them in the castle of Alma, cannot help but recall the Reformation contexts that charged them with political as well as religious meaning in the sixteenth century.

What separates imagination from memory in the castle of Alma is the unnamed middle chamber, which performs the culling function of reason or judgment, determining which thoughts are to pass from the imagination into the memory. This function is consistent with the medieval and Renaissance theories of mind that distinguish the three faculties of imagination, reason, and memory. As Stephen Batman writes in his 1582 translation of Bartholomaeus Anglicus's *De Proprietatibus Rerum*, Reason performs the role of a judge: "For what the vertue imaginatiue shapeth & imagineth, she sendeth it to the iudgement of reason. And what that reason taketh of the imagination, as a Judge, iudgeth & defineth it sending to the memory."[6] The contents of memory are determined by a process of judgment understood through its extractive powers: the defining action that Batman assigns to Reason indicates the power to reduce to or extract an essential nature, looking forward to a later meaning, to distinguish.[7] The exclusive nature of this process recalls Leland's own reading practices, of which he describes the aim "to reade, scanne upon, and preserve in memorie those things which are consonant with Authoritie" by "casting awaye trifles, cutting off olde wiues tales, and superfluous fables." In describing this action of Reason who "iudgeth & defineth," Batman may well have had in mind the material processes of the post-Reformation library's construction: the translator of *De Proprietatibus Rerum* was the same man who collected books for Parker, whom he describes in terms similar to Reason when he notes the Archbishop's construction of his own library through a process of elimination, of "choyse being taken."[8]

In Spenser's tripartite model of the brain, the middle chamber that intervenes between the chambers Imagination and Memory is represented by a room whose walls are painted in murals "of laws, or iudgments, and of decretals" (*FQ*, 2.9.53). There its unnamed guardian exercises his sole

3. On these examples, see John N. King, *English Reformation Literature: the Tudor Origins of the Protestant Tradition* (Princeton: Princeton Univ. Press, 1982), 146; and King, *Spenser's Poetry and the Reformation Tradition* (Princeton: Princeton University Press, 1990), 78. On the Royal Visitor's Injunctions and English iconoclasm in general, see Ernest B. Gilman, *Iconoclasm and Poetry in the English Reformation: Down Went Dagon* (Chicago: University of Chicago Press, 1986), esp. 7–8.
4. King, *Spenser's Poetry*, 78; see also King, *English Reformation Literature*, 146.
5. King, *English Reformation Literature*, 146.
6. *Batman uppon Bartholome, his Booke de Proprietatibus Rerum*, trans. Stephen Batman (London, 1583), book 3, chap. 16; see *The Works of Edmund Spenser: a Variorum Edition*, ed. Edwin Greenlaw (Baltimore: The Johns Hopkins Univ. Press, 1933), 465.
7. See *OED*, under "Define."
8. Batman, *The Doome Warning all men to the Iudgemente*, 394. Anne Lake Prescott identifies Batman as the author of another possible source for *The Faerie Queene*; see her "Spenser's Chivalric Restoration: from Bateman's *Travayled Pilgrime* to the Redcrosse Knight," *Studies in Philology* 86 (1989): 166–97.

function: to "meditate all his life long" (*FQ*, 2.9.54), an action that, as David Lee Miller points out, involves "the reduction of images to ideal essences."[9] As a center for extraction and purification, the chamber of Reason thus performs a digestive function similar to the stomach described in stanzas 29 through 31, in which nourishment is separated from waste.[1] This function both recalls and recasts "the activities of digestive meditation" that Mary Carruthers identifies with monastic readers who took written texts into their memories through such meditative practices.[2] Spenser's turret of the brain in the castle of Alma takes over the activities of monastic reading by appropriating them on behalf of a decidedly antimonastic aim: if the library of Memory recalls the monastic library and scriptorium, it Protestantizes its memorial function by excluding "shewes, visions, sooth-sayes, and prophesies" (*FQ*, 2.9.51), as did Bale and Prise, to the realm of Imagination, classifying them under the rubric of "all that fained is, as leasings, tales, and lies" (*FQ*, 2.9.51). This principle of exclusion is responsible for what I have noted above as the library's incompleteness, as exemplified in the rupture of Arthur's *Briton moniments*. The chamber of Reason or Judgment, which produces memory through the extraction and exclusion of Imagination, also models a form of reading as rupture. This reading is the lesson that Guyon learns in the castle of Alma and enacts, I want to suggest further, in the Bower of Bliss.

The Bower's presiding figure, Genius, is a personification, like Gower's Genius, of Imagination.[3] But here Imagination is inflected with dangers: he "secretly doth vs procure to fall, / Through guilefull semblaunts, which he makes vs see" (*FQ*, 2.12.48). In its emphasis on deceitful imaginings, Spenser's description of the Bower recalls Bale's earlier fulmination against the "fryvolous fables and lyes" that mislead readers into "depe errours": "we fynde for true hystoryes, most fryvolous fables and lyes, that we myghte the sonner by the deuyls suggestion, fall into most depe errours, and so be lost, for not beleuynge the truthe" (*L*, Diiiir). The Bower of Bliss embodies the very qualities of Imagination that are excluded from the library of memory, the "idle thoughts and fantasies . . . leasings, tales, and lies" (*FQ*, 2.9.51)—and, by extension, the "painted forgery" and "aboundance of an idle brain" that the proem juxtaposes with "iust memory." Where these were Catholicised in the Chamber of Phantasies, in the Bower of Bliss they are secularized and abstracted. As Ernest Gilman observes, the dangerous attractions of the Idol are displaced onto the "Idle."[4]

If the library of Eumnestes is a seat of memory, the Bower of Bliss is a seat of forgetting. Its centerpiece is the postcoital *pietà* formed by Acrasia and Verdant; through them, sensual surfeit, whatever its other dangers, is

9. David Lee Miller, *The Poem's Two Bodies: The Poetics of the 1590 Faerie Queene* (Princeton: Princeton Univ. Press, 1988), 188; on meditation as a key route toward memory, see Mary Carruthers, *The Craft of Thought: Meditation, Rhetoric, and the Making of Images, 400–1200* (Cambridge: Cambridge Univ. Press, 1998), esp. 60–63.
1. On the digestive processes in the Castle of Alma, see Michael Schoenfeldt, "The Construction of Inwardness in *The Faerie Queene*, Book 2," in *Worldmaking Spenser: Explorations in the Early Modern Age*, ed. Patrick Cheney and Lauren Silberman (Lexington: Univ. Press of Kentucky, 2000).
2. Carruthers, *Book of Memory*, 165–6.
3. On Genius as a figure of imagination, see James Simpson, *Sciences and the Self in Medieval Poetry: Alan of Lille's Anticlaudianus and John Gower's Confessio Amantis* (Cambridge: Cambridge Univ. Press, 1995), 167, 266–67.
4. Gilman, 77.

shown to be specifically a threat to memory.[5] Thus Verdant is overcome with forgetfulness of his own origins:

> His warlike armes. the idle instruments
> Of sleeping praise, were hong vpon a tree,
> And his braue shield, full of old moniments,
> Was fowly ra'st, that none the signes might see.
> (*FQ*, 2.12.88)

The "ra'st" monuments on Verdant's shield, emblems of a failed Virgilian ekphrasis, embody historical amnesia and forgetting of origins. Fear of such forgetting prompted the post-Reformation book collectors to attempt to restore "old moniments" to legibility. For Parker's secretary Joscelyn, textual criticism offered a way to undo this corruption: as he writes in the preface to *The Testimonie of Antiquitie*, the texts that were recovered after the Dissolution bore the marks of corruption by ignorant readers and writers. In one, "a very auncient boke of Cannons of Worceter librarye," a key passage has been "rased out by some reader," an action that demonstrated the negligence of pre-Reformation religious libraries, which allowed the corruption of written "moniments" either by neglect—such as Bale charged when he accused monks of storing manuscripts "among wormes and dust" (*L*, Eviir)—or design, as Joscelyn charges here. Yet through textual collation, Joscelyn purports to undo "the corruption of hym, whosoeuer he was," by enabling the "rased" passage to be restored, a process he put to work in the Parker library.[6] The "moniments . . . fowlly ra'st" on Verdant's shield instigate a similarly restorative effort, which I argue Guyon carries out in his destruction of the Bower of Bliss.

Guyon's response to his discovery of Verdant and Acrasia is to bind them in what Maurice Evans calls (in a term that recalls Batman's discussion of Reasons defining powers) "fetters of reason."[7] He releases Verdant after delivering "counsell sage" (*FQ*, 2.12.12), the substance of which is undisclosed, but it is perhaps embodied in the stanza that immediately follows, when Guyon applies himself to the Bower itself. Guyon's destruction of the Bower has been read as a scene of iconoclastic fury which replays the Dissolution's most destructive excesses.[8] Yet the climactic moment itself reveals few direct religious references: rather than seeing it as a literal description of Dissolution iconoclasm, I read the passage's Reformation resonance in its effort to correct and purify a source of corruption, and thereby to restore the forgotten knowledge of origins first signalled in the "moniments . . . fowlly ra'st" on Verdant's shield:

5. Greenblatt notes that the scene suggests a parodic *pietà* (*Renaissance Self-Fashioning*, 189). Of relevance to my argument about the Bower of Bliss as a seat of forgetting is Roland Greene's observation that "within the Bower, of course, the boundaries between self and other, immanence and embassy, can scarcely be discriminated." Greene, "A Primer of Spenser's Worldmaking: Alterity in the Bower of Bliss," in *Worldmaking Spenser*, 25. My reading would extend this boundary-blurring to the distinction of past and present.
6. *Testimonie of Antiquity* (London, 1566), sig. Avr. On Joscelyn's method, see Benedict Scott Robinson, "'Darke Speech': Matthew Parker and the Reforming of History," *Sixteenth Century Journal* 29 (1998): 1061–82."
7. Maurice Evans, cited by ed. A. C. Hamilton, *Spenser: The Faerie Queene* (London: Longman, 1977), 297 n.
8. See Greenblatt, *Renaissance Self-Fashioning*, 189; Alan Sinfield, *Literature of Protestant England, 1560–1660* (Toyowa, NJ: Barnes & Noble Books, 1983), 37; Harry Berger, Jr., *The Allegorical Temper: Vision and Reality in Book II of Spenser's Fairie Queene* (New Haven: Yale Univ. Press, 1957), 218.

all those pleasant bowres and Pallace brave,
Guyon broke down, with rigour pittilesse;
Ne ought their goodly workmanship might saue
Them from the tempest of his wrathfulnesse,
But that their blisse he turn'd to balefulnesse.
Their groues he feld, their gardins did deface,
Their arbers spoyle, their cabinets suppresse,
Their banket houses burne, their buildings race,
And of the fairest late, now made the fowlest place.
(*FQ*, 2.12.83)

While the objects of Guyon's violence—bowers, groves, arbors, and so forth—are emphatically secular, the verbs owe their historical and moral force to the Reformation: "broke," "feld," "spoyle," "suppresse," "burn," and, especially the final act, "race."[9] The repetition of the word "race" in this crucial passage suggests to A. C. Hamilton that Guyon's destruction of the Bower is "fitting revenge" for the "'moniments . . . fowlly ra'st on Verdants shield."[1] Similarly, Guyon's "defacement' of the Bower's gardens ("Their groues he feld, their gardins did *deface*") recalls and responds to Verdant's self-defacement: "certes it great pittie was to see / Him his nobilitie so foule *deface*" (*FQ*, 2.12.79).[2] But in chastising defacement through defacement, razing through razing, Guyon's destruction appears to be less an act of revenge than an attempted reversal. Where Verdant's "ra'st" monuments and defaced nobility represent a historical amnesia, Guyon's razing of the Bower of Bliss aims to recall its denizens to their forgotten origins. Thus, after this orgy of destruction, Guyon is moved to observe,

See the mind of beastly man,
That hath so soone forgot the excellence
Of his creation, when he life began.
(*FQ*, 2.11.87)

If the Bower is a seat of forgetting, in other words, Guyon's destruction of it is an act of violent remembering. In this, Guyon recalls the textual acts of post-Reformation readers and library makers like Leland and Bale, who sought to recuperate England's lost origins in its "monuments of antiquity" by purifying those monuments of the corrosive accretions of monastic influence. Thus Bale seeks to purge "fryvolous fables and lyes" that threaten the "true history" of the Protestant nation, just as Leland advocates "casting awaye trifles, cutting off old wiues tales, and superfluous fables," in order "to reade, scanne upon, and preserve in memory." Like Leland's and Bale's acts of polishing or purifying the written records of the past, Guyon's destruction of the Bower of Bliss is an act of unmaking, whereby "painted forgery" is castigated in order to produce "iust memorie." But the "memory" that Guyon instigates does not produce a positive knowledge of origins; indeed, despite Guyon's command, "Let them returned be vnto their former state" (*FQ*, 2.12.85), the Bower's former denizens never quite recover their original human identities: "being men they did vnmanly looke" (*FQ*, 2.12.86). Instead, Guyon produces

9. On the forcefulness of these verbs, see Gilman, 69–70.
1. Edmund Spenser, *The Faerie Queene*, ed. Hamilton, 296 n.
2. My emphasis.

ruins—a broken landscape that offers neither knowledge nor enchantment—as the locus of post-Reformation memory.[3]

In the Bower of Bliss, Guyon performs the very action of which the proem to book 2 expresses fear, when it worries how it will be "iudged," and whether or not it will be dismissed as "th'aboundance of an idle braine" and "painted forgery / Rather then matter of iust memory" (*FQ*, 2.proem.l). By tracing Guyon's training, through his progress through Eumnestes's library and the Bower of Bliss, in the castigation of "forgery" and the production of "memory," book 2 innoculates against the very judgment it fears by offering itself up as a lesson in such judgment, rather than judgments object. In so doing, it reveals how the preoccupations with distinction, chastisement, and correction established by post-Reformation book collectors and library makers shaped the conditions of reading in *The Faerie Queene*. If, as I have argued, the new English library institutes a *lectio* of suspicion whose object is less the recovery of positive knowledge than the endless castigation of error, *The Faerie Queene* is the first work after the Reformation to be written for its shelves.

READINGS OF THE HOUSE OF BUSYRANE

THOMAS P. ROCHE, JR.: [Love, Lust, and Sexuality]†

* * *

Busyrane is trying to transfer Amoret's love for Scudamour to himself by charms, but the conventional romance structure of this episode should not blind us to its real meaning. He is literally trying to kill Amoret. His love is not sexual but destructive—destructive of the will to love within Amoret herself. Amoret is afraid of the physical surrender which her marriage to Scudamour must entail. The wedding mask crystallizes this fear, and she turns from a joyful acceptance to a cold rejection of the claims of the physical. This is why Busyrane is the great enemy to chastity; he represents a negative force of which chastity is the positive ideal. He represents the negation of chastity, and this for Spenser did not mean lust.

Although Spenser gives no iconographical details to identify his Busyrane, we may learn much from the etymology of his name. Warton suggested long ago that Busyrane is derived from Busiris, "The king of Egypt, famous for his cruelty and inhospitality."[1] Warton, I believe, is correct. The history of Busiris is too complicated to relate. It must suffice to say that Busiris originally was the location of the chief tomb of Osiris, and that in later writers Busiris became the king of the place where Osiris was killed. The complicated traditions agree that Busiris is a loca-

3. Aston, "English Ruins and English History," argues that monastic ruins spurred sixteenth-century historical consciousness. Spenser's preoccupation with ruins is usually read in conjunction with classical ruins; see Judith Anderson, "The Antiquities of Rome and *The Faerie Queene*," *JEGP* (1987): 199–214; and Margaret Ferguson, "'The Afflatus of Ruin': Meditations on Rome by Du Bellay, Spenser, and Stevens," in *Roman Images*, ed. Annabel Patterson (Baltimore: The Johns Hopkins Univ. Press, 1984), 23–50. But see Maryclaire Moroney, "Spenser's Dissolution," for a consideration of the importance of medieval ruins to Spenser.

† From *The Kindly Flame: A Study of the Third and Fourth Books of Spenser's "Faerie Queene"* (Princeton, 1964), pp. 80–83.

1. *Var.*, 3.287.

tion or an agent of sacrificial destruction and is associated with the sacrifice of Osiris.[2] The connection may seem remote, but we must recall the identification of Britomart and Arthegall with Isis and Osiris in Book V and remember that Britomart triumphs over Busyrane before she encounters Arthegall. Even more important is Ovid's retelling of the Busiris legend in the first book of the *Ars Amatoria*. This relates Busiris to the qualities I have been trying to establish as the traits of Busyrane:

"If you are wise, cheat women only, and avoid trouble; keep faith save for this one deceitfulness. Deceive the deceivers; they are mostly an unrighteous sort; let them fall into the snare which they have laid. Egypt is said to have lacked the rains that bless its fields, and to have been parched for nine years, when Thrasius approached Busiris, and showed that Jove could be propitiated by the outpoured blood of a stranger. To him said Busiris, 'Thou shalt be Jove's first victim, and as a stranger give water unto Egypt.' Phalaris too roasted in his fierce bull the limbs of Perillus, its maker first made trial of his ill-omened work. Both were just; for there is no juster law than that contrivers of death should perish by their own contrivances. Therefore, that perjuries may rightly cheat the perjured, let the woman feel the smart of a wound she first inflicted."[3]

Ovid's ironic advice to his hypothetical lover throws a new light on the Busiris legend and brings us back to Warton's suggested etymology. These lines betray an attitude toward love and women; it is the same attitude that underlies the conceit of love as war, and it is of particular interest that the well-known Ovidian treatise should link this attitude with the figure of Busiris. Here, it would appear, is the nexus between the conventional figure of Busiris and Spenser's Busyrane; here is the deceit, the sadism, and the destruction, which we associate with Amoret's plight.

But there are further possibilities in Busyrane's name, possibilities that suggest the sixteenth century usage of the word *abuse* as imposture, ill-usage, delusion. For example, Sidney's sentence from the *Arcadia* quoted in the OED is entirely appropriate: "Was it not enough for him to have deceived me, and through the deceit abused me, and after the abuse forsaken me?" or we might use the obsolete form *abusion*, which the OED defines as "perversion of the truth, deceit, deception, imposture," giving as an example Spenser's lines, "Foolish delights and fond Abusions, Which do that sence besiege with fond illusions." All of these meanings are implicit in the etymology of Busyrane—the illusion, the deceit, the sadism, the destruction.

What then does this make of Busyrane? Is he not the abuse of marriage just as his house is the objectification of Amoret's fears of marriage? He is the abuse of marriage because his mask of Cupid presents an image of marriage as a sacrifice just as Busiris was a place of sacrifice. He is an abuse of marriage because the mind he possesses cannot distinguish

2. See Sir Ernest A. T. Wallis Budge, *Osiris and the Egyptian Resurrection*, 2 vols., London, 1911. Ancient writers who deal with this story include Plutarch, Diodorus Siculus, Apollodorus, Isocrates, Herodotus, and Ovid. See also Heywood's dumbshow in *The Brazen Age, Dramatic Works of Thomas Heywood*, ed. John Pearson, 6 vols., London, 1874, vol. 3, p. 183; Ralegh, *The History of the World*, London, 1614, sig. S2; *Paradise Lost*, 1. 307, and Isabel Rathborne, *The Meaning of Spenser's Fairyland*, pp. 86–90. Professor Rosemond Tuve has kindly pointed out to me the significant appearance of Busiris in Christine de Pisan, *The Epistle of Othea to Hector*, ed. James D. Gordon, Philadelphia, 1942, pp. 68–69.
3. Ovid, *Ars Amatoria*, Book I. 643–658.

between the act of marriage and adulterous love. He is an abuse of marriage because the falsity of his view of love can lead only to lust or death. His power is derived from the *abusion* of the mind in distorting the image of love. The meaning he presents to the wedding guests is trivial, at the most, lust; the meaning he presents to Amoret is the sacrifice of personal integrity. Lust is the least complex of his perversions; he is the image of love distorted in the mind, distorted by lascivious anticipation or horrified withdrawal. He becomes the denial of the unity of body and soul in true love. And in all these respects he is the chief adversary of Britomart as the knight of chastity. Britomart's response to the mask and to Busyrane is that of the intelligent moral reader, who can detect the difference between true and false love.

This interpretation of Busyrane and his power over Amoret explains why Scudamour cannot rescue her. Amoret's fears are based on moral and physical grounds. Scudamour can dispel neither. Unwillingly he is the cause of these fears, and any attempt on his part to dispel them would be self-defeating since it would mean her eventual surrender, the basis of her fears. Britomart, on the other hand, can attack these fears on both the moral and physical grounds. As a woman she understands Amoret's attitude toward the physical side of love, and as the exemplar of chastity she is able to make the moral distinction between marriage and adulterous love. Her entry through the wall of flame gives her an intimate knowledge of the House of Busyrane, and her understanding finally allows her to release Amoret from her fears.

* * *

A. KENT HIEATT: [Sexual Adventurism]†

Most centrally * * * this Masque of Cupid as it relates to Amoret marshals the temptations and horrors of the life of loose sexual commitments, of frequent passion, and of angling for domination of a lover and for deception of a husband or other lovers, as these activities would be seen by a chaste woman, fully committed to one man but tortured by his jealous and insistent dominance over her, as over a sexual prize—a woman, that is, with whom he should have gently and gradually created an entirely different kind of relationship. Such love * * * is really hate, close to the state of the Knight's Tale's Cupid, 'out of alle charitee'. The adulterous temptations begin for Amoret in the fancy and the artificially stoked desire of a life of ease and leisure. They progress through the doubt, dangers, and fearful delights of secret assignations and amours. Such love dangles hopes, but less often satisfactions, before its victims. All of these concepts, personified, pass before us in turn in the Masque of Cupid. Dissemblance and Suspect, Grief and Fury, Displeasure and Pleasure, attend on an unfaithful beloved and a jealous lover. Despite and Cruelty are the lot of an unfaithful wife as conceived by Amoret but also of Amoret herself, a chaste woman, who insists on maintaining her

† From *Chaucer Spenser Milton: Mythopoeic Continuities and Transformations* (Montreal and London, 1975), pp. 129–133. Reprinted by permission of the publisher, McGill-Queen's University Press.

chastity in spite of all temptations and the provocations of a jealous and dominating lover: her heart is taken from her body and bedevilled, yet she will not surrender her love. Like Florimell, she remains love's martyr. As for the remaining figures of the Masque, a woman's ultimate fate in a life of superficial adultery, is, in Amoret's vision, not orgasmic bliss among lusty satyrs but rather something belonging to middle-class ideas, like the final stages of Hogarth's 'Marriage à la Mode', or, less familiarly but more accurately, like what is warned against in certain Continental and English morality plays and interludes:[1] Reproach, Repentance, Shame, Strife, Anger, Care, Unthriftihead, Loss of Time, Sorrow, Change, Disloyalty, Riotise, Dread, Infirmity, Poverty, and Death with Infamy.

All, or almost all, the figures in the Masque exist in Amoret's imagination, but this imagination is one that bodies forth the real consequences of a certain course of action for a chaste woman to whom frivolous surrender has for the first time become a live option, so that she knows what it is to waver ('wavering' being equivocally applied to both 'wemen' and 'wit'):

> There were full many moe like maladies,
> Whose names and natures I note readen well;
> So many moe, as there be phantasies
> In wavering wemens wit, that none can tell,
> Or paines in love, or punishments in hell.
> [xii. 26]

These are quite different from the images of Hellenore's mind, facilely submitting to the Love God's pains and fashioning worlds of fancies 'In her fraile wit' (ix. 52). They are also different from the counterfeits which are the stock-in-trade of the spirit who had fallen with the Prince of Darkness and who animates the body of the false Florimell: he 'all the wyles of wemens wits knew passing well' (viii. 8).

Amoret's torturer, an element in Scudamour himself, is a destroyer of the concord between man and wife. The most advanced embodiment of this concord in *The Faerie Queene* is the relation in V. vii between Britomart-Isis-moon and Artegall-Osiris-crocodile-sun in the Temple of Isis, running 'in equal justice' and achieving a freely offered and freely accepted love and friendship * * *. Certainly then, the explanation of this torturer's name—Busirane—suggested by Professor Roche,[2] is the most apposite one. The key to Roche's etymological explanation is the association of 'Busiris' with the death of Osiris. In the light of Spenser's usual masterful way with mythology, the partly contradictory late Classical and post-Classical lore concerning these two figures, the town of Busiris, and Typhon * * * would have easily permitted him to identify the murderer of Osiris as Busiris. 'Busiris' in this sense, then, furnishes the root of the name 'Busirane', although this name no doubt embodies other phonetic felicities.

* * *

1. John Rastell's *Calisto and Melebea* is an English example. Jean Bretog, *Tragedie françoise à huict personnages: traictant de l'amour d'un serviteur envers sa maitress, et de tout ce qui en advint* (Lyon, 1571; Chartres, 1831) is closer to what is meant here, although of little literary significance. Less to the point but far better than either of these, and well worth translating into English, is the work published as *De Spiegel der Minnen door Colijn van Rijssele*, ed. Margaretha W. Immink (Utrecht, 1913).
2. Thomas P. Roche, Jr., *The Kindly Flame* (Princeton, 1964), p. 81.

One further reason for believing that in the House of Busirane Amoret is being importuned unintentionally by the masterful practices of her husband to turn from her constant love of him to the life of sexual adventurism is that a kind of reduplicative allegory overtakes Amoret in Book IV. While Britomart sleeps, Amoret is captured by Lust himself—Lust who 'could awhape an hardy hart' (vii. 5): that is, who ostensibly is powerful enough to stupefy a strong heart with fear but in fact (considering the singularity of this image) is strong enough to snatch the strongest hearts, just as the Love God joys to see Amoret's heart removed from her bosom and carried before her in the Masque of Cupid. * * * Amoret, like Aemylia, is not simply preyed on by a lustful being, but is herself in some fashion invaded by desire, although she will not perform the acts which desire calls for. She successfully resists both importunities—those of Busirane and Lust—and is finally rescued by the chaste amity of Britomart in the one case and by Belphoebe's virginity in the other.

* * * It is probably true that this episode of Amoret, Timias, and Belphoebe in Book IV is required by Spenser's emergency measures in squaring the accounts of his friend Ralegh with the Queen after the revelation of Ralegh's relations with Elizabeth Throgmorton, but it is equally true that Spenser would not have chosen Amoret for this ambiguous role unless she had been suitable for it. She is readied for pleasure, not overpudicity. Spenser is apparently saying to the Queen that her maid of honour and her favourite Ralegh were touched, but not dominated by, Lust. So with Amoret. In the House of Busirane she is being driven by her lover to become part of the usual courtly round of love that Spenser so strongly condemns elsewhere:

> And is love then (said *Corylas*) once knowne
> In Court, and his sweet lore professed there?
> I weened sure he was our God alone:
> And only wonned in fields and forests here,
> Not so (quoth he) love most aboundeth there.
> For all the walls and windows there are writ,
> All full of love, and love, and love my deare,
> And all their talke and studie is of it,
> Ne any there doth brave or valiant seeme,
> Unlesse that some gay Mistresse badge he beares:
> Ne any one himselfe doth ought esteeme,
> Unlesse he swim in love up to the eares.
> But they of love and of his sacred lere,
> (As it should be) all otherwise devise,
> Then we poore shepheards are accustomd here,
> And him do sue and serve all otherwise,
> For with lewd speeches and licentious deeds,
> His mightie mysteries they do prophane,
> And use his ydle name to other needs,
> But as a complement for courting vaine,
> So him they do not serve as they professe,
> But make him serve to them for sordid uses,
> Ah my dread Lord, that doest liege hearts possesse,
> Avenge thy selfe on them for their abuses.
> [*Colin Clouts Come Home Againe*, 771–94]

The allegory of Lust in Book IV is simply an intensification of what we have already seen in the House of Busirane. For purposes of Spenser's defending his friend and patron, and Elizabeth Throgmorton, and of maintaining the allegorical locus of Amoret, it was not intended that Timias and Amoret should be punished, but that the unclean cleaving thing, amorous desire without constancy to one lover, should be extirpated.

The friendship which Britomart brings to Amoret is what reverses the charms of Busirane, so that Amoret's wound becomes whole and the chains drop from her body, in the inner room where the magician had held her in thrall. Busirane must not be destroyed (III.xii. 34) because he is a part of Scudamour. As a masterful principle of hate, he is ready to destroy Amoret finally (xii. 32), and he wounds Britomart superficially as the masterful principle of Malecasta had done in canto i. In Book IV Britomart and Amoret now go forth in amity, in spite of Amoret's suspicions of what she takes to be a male's intentions—suspicions which are soon allayed in the formation of the first four-group of that book, with Britomart as knight to Amoret and as lady to another knight, so that they may all be lodged in a castle with a custom. * * *

SUSANNE LINDGREN WOFFORD: [The Bold Reader in the House of Busyrane]†

* * *

In the final episodes of Book III, Britomart is confronted with a figure of the male artist who is inscribed deep within her mind, an artist/magician whom she resists and overcomes. Her exploring of the House of Busyrane is glossed by Spenser as an activity like reading, and like other inner worlds, the House of Busyrane is treated as textual space, furnished with a multiplicity of intertextual references. Britomart serves as a reader who is urged by Busyrane in his inscriptions to be bold but not too bold in her interpretations. Her imagined depth of character is represented in the text by means of the analogy established between her and the imagined figure of the reader whom she resembles.

With its three chambers, the House of Busyrane resembles in structure the picture of the human mind given in the House of Alma. There we learned that the mind's three chambers correspond to the faculties of Foresight, Reason and Memory (II,ix,49). The mind Britomart explores in III,xi–xii is a tortured version of this temperate mind, though it too contains in its own way the shows and visions of Phantasies, the "wisards" (here evil) of the chambers of reason, and the library of memory, here a library containing mostly Ovid and Petrarch, but also fragments of the works of other love poets. The place that Britomart explores, then, serves as a figure for an imaginative mind, either Britomart's own which she explores and then purges, or Amoret's, or Busyrane's, a horrific version of her author's mind.

† From "Gendering Allegory: Spenser's Bold Reader and the Emergence of Character in *The Faerie Queene* III." *Criticism* 30 (1988). 9–16, 20. Original footnotes have been reduced and slightly edited.

The episode of the House of Busyrane notoriously calls out for multiple readings, as an allegory of female fantasy ("So many moe, as there be phantasies/In wauering wemens wit" [III,xii,26])[1] and as an allegory of male violence against women, of the kinds of torture to which males have subjected females in their literary and erotic imaginings.[2] If the House represents her own mind, Britomart can be understood to be exploring the sources of her own imagination and therefore of her quest in the previous male poetry that has penned women in stereotypes revealed in the House as torturing and pornographic. Finding his love behind the wall of fire, Scudamour laments, "Why then is Busirane with wicked hand / Suffred . . . My Lady and my loue so cruelly to pen?" (III,xi,10). The pun in this repeated line (to pen is to write about and to pen up) suggests that to write of women at all may be to pen them into some stereotype or allegorization: the line suggests that any male poet—and perhaps any poet—will run this risk, that to use words to describe an other is necessarily to reduce him or her to some limiting image or form.[3]

The torment that Busyrane's version of courtly love produces in the theater of canto 12 is appropriately enough the forced revelation of the inner self in this abusive world. Such forced revelation, Spenser's poem suggests, objectifies and freezes, leaving only the reified image of the heart, but bringing no emotion with it. In spite of this violence, Amoret remains closed to Busyrane, resistant, her innerness as character inviolate. In refusing to give in to Busyrane, she refuses to become object of this torturing, reifying love poetry. Britomart, a knight who can rescue Amoret partly because she herself is also a woman, represents in her heroic energy and power a choice on Spenser's part: here he reverses the male poetic tradition of making women serve only as the passive objects of erotic poetry. In different ways, Britomart and Amoret struggle against this male tradition, personified by Busyrane, a perverse figure of the poet who tries to place them in a stereotypically "male" poetry.

Like Merlin, Busyrane is presented writing "characters," letters which magically bind and unbind the daemonic figures before him:

> And her before the vile Enchaunter sate,
> Figuring straunge characters of his art,
> With liuing blood he those characters wrate,
> Dreadfully dropping from her dying hart. . . .
> (III,xii,31)

Busyrane's magic letters, written in blood, serve to transform women (in this case, Amoret) into allegorical figures. The literalization of writing with "liuing blood" marks out the implicit violence of his poetic praxis, and

1. See Thomas Roche, Jr., *The Kindly Flame: A Study of the Third and Fourth Books of Spenser's Faerie Queene* (Princeton, 1964), pp. 72–87, as a representative of the line of argument which concludes "the mask that takes place at the House of Busyrane is Amoret's interpretation of the wedding mask" (p. 77). See Maureen Quilligan, *Milton's Spenser* (Ithaca, 1983) p. 198, for a feminist version of this interpretation.
2. For an example of this interpretation, see Harry Berger, Jr., "Busirane and the War Between the Sexes: An Interpretation of *The Faerie Queene* III, xi–xii," *English Literary Renaissance*, 1 (1971). See also Lauren Silberman, 1986, pp. 266–67, who argues that Amoret is able to elude Busyrane's "forcible troping" because Busirane's sadomasochism is "an archetypal dualism" of the sort that Spenser seeks to transcend in his own poetic language.
3. Spenser may even bring a third pun to the fore by punning on the link between pen and phallus and thereby suggesting that the male poet at issue here not only pens up his female characters in these stereotypes or allegorical figures but abuses them as he does so.

shows that Busyrane's art functions by denying the woman any interiority. Though Merlin's plot does so benignly, both Merlin and Busyrane pen the female character into a specific plot that depends not only on female stereotypes but also on making female characters serve allegorical ends.

Spenser isolates one aspect of his art and represents it in the figure of Busyrane, while Britomart in her victory is associated with another incipient aspect of his own technique, one which, at this moment in the dialectic, points the way out of allegory. In his highly allegorical house, where all human emotions are represented in reified terms, and where even figures of speech have become objectified and frozen in time, Busyrane comes to stand for the potential abuses of allegory itself. In this limit case, it is allegory that is challenged here, not simply the failures of courtly love as an imaginative scheme. Allegory in its most extreme form is the pen from which Britomart strives to save the daemonic Amoret, a rescue that can only be partially successful, as both endings of the story suggest.

In this self-interrogation, then, Spenser looks at Busyrane's art from the point of view of a woman and condemns it. He uses a more fictional mode of writing to challenge and reveal the limitations of allegory in its most static and extreme form. The struggle between Britomart and Busyrane—a struggle in which Britomart defends herself as well as Amoret—suggests that the dialectic of allegory and fiction is not a comfortable nor perhaps even a resolvable one. Spenser's self-interrogations in other Books of *The Faerie Queene* are also uncomfortable; what is distinctive here is not the intensity of the self-doubt, but the aesthetic and gender-specific formulations that Spenser gives to the uncertainty and ideological tension at the heart of his poetics.

The nearly obsessive puns on "read" in cantos 11 and 12 prepare the reader for the emphasis on interpretation. Britomart is consistently represented in the House as a reader of allegory. A typical case occurs in canto 11 where she sees the Idol of Cupid and then encounters the first of the inscriptions on the House itself:

> Tho as she backward cast her busie eye,
> To search each secret of that goodly sted
> Ouer the dore thus written she did spye
> *Be Bold:* she oft and oft it ouer-red,
> Yet could not find what sense it figured:
> But what so were therein or writ or ment,
> She was no whit thereby discouraged
> From prosecuting of her first intent,
> But forward with bold steps into the next roome went.
> (III,xi,50)

Here Britomart stands in the same place as the reader, who also overreads (in both senses) and yet cannot easily interpret these passages. Who wrote "Be Bold" over the door? Busyrane, to encourage his innocent victims? The author, eager for Britomart to discover and unmask Busyrane? The conventions of society and literature which encourage the chaste woman to continue to be bold at this stage of a courtship? Britomart cannot find what sense it figures, but her uncertainty does not keep her from prosecuting her first intent; the reader goes with her into the next room.

Britomart is represented as a reader when she views the Ovidian tapestries, when she studies the Idol of Cupid, and when she watches the Masque of Cupid, but, as the previous example suggested, she is most particularly so in her efforts to "read" the House itself. In the second chamber she is everywhere encouraged to be bold, but only at the far end of the chamber is she told to "be not too bold."

> And as she lookt about, she did behold,
> How ouer that same dore was likewise writ,
> *Be bold, be bold*, and euery where *Be bold*,
> That much she muz'd, yet could not construe it
> By any ridling skill, or commune wit.
> At last she spyde at that roomes vpper end,
> Another yron dore, on which was writ,
> *Be not too bold;* whereto though she did bend
> Her earnest mind, yet wist not what it might intend.
> (III,xi,54)

Words like "construe" and "writ" once again emphasize that Britomart and the reader interpret in parallel here. She "bends" her mind to interpret this last command, but she still cannot understand the warning in the inscription. If Busyrane represents at least an aspect of her society's conventions about love, Britomart is being told here exactly how much demystification she should indulge in: the female character is to be drawn in by the snare of "be bold," only to be stopped at the final chamber and prevented from seeing the inmost workings of the male mind. Busyrane blocks her way: when she first tries to enter the chamber, she finds the door locked (III,xii,27) and has to use "sleights and art" to find a way in.[4]

When she finally does enter the inmost chamber, disobeying the injunction over the door, Britomart finds the male abuser of her fantasy, a figure of the male poet who has drawn her into a pornographic love poem (a love poetry that abuses women by literalizing the cliches of Petrarchan sonnets).[5] She opposes the kind of eroticism represented by Busyrane's reifying art, forcing him "his charmes backe to reuerse" (III,xii,36), but she also opposes Busyrane by entering the chamber in the first place. Britomart succeeds in rescuing Amoret then, precisely because she is "too bold" in prosecuting her first intent: she is not stopped by the male commands that would pen her into the second room, nor is she stopped because she is unable to reach a conclusive interpretation of the inscription.

This final scene can be understood metaphorically as a figurative representation or animation of the struggle between one type of male poet and a female character whom his poetry would control or destroy. Spenser's narrator is left in an ambiguous position: to the extent that he attempts to attach specific allegorical meanings to Britomart's quest, he

4. See Lesley Brill, "Chastity as Ideal Sexuality in the Third Book of *The Faerie Queene*," *Studies in English Literature*, 11 (1971) for an interpretation of the "Be Bold, Be Bold" inscription that links it to Britomart's lament in III,iv,9. See Iris Tilman Hill, "Britomart and Be Bold, Be Not Too Bold," *ELH*, 38 (1971), 173–78, for an interpretation of the inscription as an explicit allusion to the myth of Venus and Adonis.

5. See Mark Rose, *Heroic Love* (Cambridge, 1968) pp. 121ff., on the tortures in the house of Busyrane as literalizations of the conventions of Petrarchan sonnets.

is allied with Busyrane, even as he represents Britomart's victory over the evil magician sympathetically. Throughout this episode Britomart as character makes such allegorizing more and more difficult. Moreover, she searches out the character who, fictionally speaking, created this section of the plot, and overthrows him, thereby undoing—"reversing," as Spenser says—the plot. Spenser the author in these scenes brings to the surface an evil anti-type to what we should imagine to be the ideal figure of the poet, but here as elsewhere (most notably in the case of Archimago), the poem reveals an uncomfortable liaison between Spenser's poetry and the evil form of art that it attempts to exorcise.

In the 1590 ending of Book III, Britomart brings Amoret out of the House to the embrace of Scudamour, metaphorically making possible the consummation of their marriage as their two bodies blend into one. In the moment of this much desired embrace, the readers see Amoret's more partial side, one reason why she may have been "penned" by Busyrane. As Donald Cheney has shown, the Ovidian subtext of the Hermaphrodite story, to which Spenser explicitly alludes in several lines, speaks of the losses as well as the gains in such an embrace.[6] As Amoret and Scudamor become Scudamoret, the emblem of marriage in the figure of the Hermaphrodite, they also make evident their daemonic nature. Their embrace represents both a gain and a loss: they are reunited, but for them, as for Malbecco, the process of becoming an emblem brings also a loss of human form.

Although this embrace produces the much desired ending of the story, Britomart is excluded from it and from the closure it produces. She stands outside, as does the reader, "halfe enuying their blesse" (III,xii,46a). Britomart is alien in their highly conventional world: as heroine of an epic-romance, she stands outside the lyric; as protonovelistic heroine with her own originality and force of character, she stands outside the allegorical tableau they create. She attempts to read it, she half envies them its relative simplicity, but finally she is left outside it.

Britomart stands outside this closural embrace of Scudamoret particularly because she has stood against one version of the male poet, and thereby resisted the type of conventional characterization of love in which he had attempted to entangle her. Amoret and Scudamour, on the other hand, have clearly not left their conventionality behind.[7] Their daemonic nature is not something Britomart can rescue them from, and they blend together to produce an emblem to balance the emblem of jealousy which begins the episode (III,xi,1–2). Amoret and Scudamour are characters who cannot escape destructive conventionality because they partly symbolize it—or at least, they symbolize the allegorical fragmentation of characteristics that produces in the individual (though not necessarily in the composite) a less complicated picture of human action than does a more multiple characterization. Given such fragmentation, it takes many daemonic or partial characters to create a complex analysis, while the individual daemon remains penned in his or her limited, "obsessive" identity. In the conclusion to Book III, then, Spenser opposes two methods of

6. See Donald Cheney, "Spenser's Hermaphrodite and the 1590 *Faerie Queene*," *PMLA*, 87 (1972).
7. Cheney, "Spenser's Hermaphrodite," stresses the Petrarchan clichés in the rhymes of stanza 44a, and suggests that Scudamour cannot transcend the Petrarchan problematic on his own.

achieving a complexity of character and of moral analysis while revealing through the dialectic between them the limitations and powers of each. Each mode alone allows for a less complex "analysis" than does the dialectical combination of the two.

The figurative struggle between a female character and an evil male artist, then, points to a struggle between modes of writing, modes which in this episode are associated with male and female perspectives. Britomart stands against one version of allegory itself, and rescues Amoret from it; afterwards, she stands outside the allegorical representation of the promised marriage, and finds it only half satisfying. In her gesture of liberation, she moves against one version of male authority, positing an alternative female authority that reverses the male plot and creates a different kind of female character.

The interpretive openness of the poem in general, and especially of this episode, stands as an image of that aspect of Britomart which is not "penned" up in her allegorical significance: she has an openness of character that leads her into unexpected adventures and makes her respond in unpredictable ways. She tries to live up to an ideal, which in her quest she may also adumbrate—hence her function in the allegory—but she also has a character which cannot be contained by that or any other closural allegorical significance. Only in the figure of the reader are her two roles able to merge, but to the extent that she becomes a figure of reading she is excluded from what she reads. Britomart's wholeness as a reader, and by extension our own, is gained at the expense of a coherent allegorical or ideological structure within which she herself is a signifies.

In Book III Spenser exposes the epistemological dilemma present throughout his poem through the sexual tension which animates the narrative: this sexual tension undermines the absoluteness of the authority of the narrative voice. Spenser's narrator may tell his readers what his allegory means, but his readers continually find that his inscribed interpretations do not reflect the experience of the characters in their dimension as characters. In Book III Spenser uses female characters to dramatize this disjunction; moreover, Britomart's actions, in serving to tie the idea of depth of character to the figure of the reader, suggest that the interpreter of Spenser also necessarily takes up an oppositional position, searching for the countertext, and reading against as well as with the allegory.

In the 1596 ending of Book III, Spenser again suggests that his own narrative strategies may defile the characters whose virtues he wishes to represent and to praise. As Amoret comes out of the House hoping to see her knight, Spenser tells us that "Being thereof beguyld," she "was fild with new affright" (III,xii,44). Amoret's "perfect hole," her healed inner self, is both "filled" and "defiled" with fright once again, for the denial of closure is a torture to her daemonic self. It constitutes yet another version of the frozen postures of delay that she has experienced within the House. The word "beguyld" associates Spenser's narrative art with Busyrane's imagistic and theatrical art; Spenser's art can either fill or defile, the danger being that these two may amount to the same thing. Breaking off closure is a defiling of the allegorical figure at the same time as it may allow the filling in of the character. As in every case of broken endings that Spenser provides, the lack of plot closure re-emphasizes that there can be no absolute closure to the allegory. Spenser's poem may desire to reach that promised end, but until that time it acts out the impossibility of expressing absolute meaning in a poem. In Book III, Spenser dramatizes this impossibility as the disjunction between the male meanings imposed by narrator or magician and the female understandings represented and acted upon within the story as story, as Britomart, being too bold for the allegory, steps forward to save Amoret from the tortures her author had devised.

JANE GROGAN

[Romancing the Reader (in Book VI)]†

Doctrine by Rule?

Very soon after the Proem's high-minded declarations, readers are directed to the verbal facility and social mores of 'civil conversation', exemplified in a knight of Courtesy noticeably scant on inward thoughts and repeatedly unable to penetrate beyond outward shows. Calidore is cut out of the mould of the *cortegiano* and follows 'outward' principles of seemliness and pragmatism, decorum and opportunism, delicacy and resourcefulness, just as the courtesy tradition prescribed. He wanders from situation to marvellous situation, improvising temporary resolutions to local conflicts by evaluating how best to re-order or put a gloss on matters. Spenser identifies Calidore with the courtesy tradition rather than—and in opposition to—his own didactic poetics in three ways: in his belief in the sufficiency of his courtesy, in the consequent shape of his romance quest, and in the nature of his arts of words. The three converge in Calidore's encounter with Spenser's own persona, Colin Clout, at Acidale.

'Many are the aids (among the first is self-confidence) / of which no one will be a professor, everybody a master.'[1] Just such self-confidence marks Calidore's every action. Calidore rests conspicuously assured in his own courtesy. Whereas Spenser's didactic strategies in previous books had made use of flawed exemplars on the Xenophontic model, the knight of Book VI follows the sparkling exemplars of courtesy books. 'But mongst them all was none more courteous Knight, / Then *Calidore*, beloved over all' (VI. i. 2).[2] Calidore is a perfected ideal—albeit one who necessarily falls short of the rigorous standards of inward virtue that Spenser invokes in the Proem. Nothing he does will be regarded by him as a mistake, nor will the values of his romance world indict him either. Thus, Calidore's courtesy is about stamina rather than standards, application rather than principles, repetition with endless variation rather than tempering skills in encounters with the opposing vice. This quality of self-confidence threatens to obstruct the wary reader's identification with Calidore; Redcrosse's hard-won lesson that virtue does not give sufficient light to

† From *Exemplary Spenser: Visual and Poetic Pedagogy in* The Faerie Queene (Farnham, Surrey: Ashgate, 2009), pp. 149–55. Reprinted by permission of Ashgate Publishing.

1. Gabriel Harvey, *Gratulationes Valdinenses*, p. 156.
2. Compare the 'tall clownishe younge man' Redcrosse (Letter to Ralegh) or even the highest praise of Arthegall, chosen by the Faery Queen to undertake Irena's quest 'For that to her he seem'd best skild in righteous lore' (V. i. 4).

negotiate the darkness of error has been repeated throughout the first five Books, and endlessly re-played through the volatilities of the reading experience. Where the strivings and evident flaws or mistakes of other Spenserian knights allowed for both sympathy and critical distance, seeing Calidore star again and again in a range of situations without recourse to any discernible external principles makes it no easier for readers to learn how to be courteous.

The Book features other perfected exemplars of courtesy, but they, too, fall short of Spenser's demand that courtesy be defined by inward thoughts rather than outward shows. In his courteous hospitality, Aldus tempers his grief and 'turned it to cheare, / To cheare his guests' (VI. iii. 6), the attempt at false jocosity poetically rendered through *anadiplosis*. A later scene of hospitality retreats from this false cheer. Arthur, Serena and Timias are welcomed at the hut of a hermit deep in the forest, where he entertained them 'Not with such forged showes, as fitter beene / For courting fooles, that curtesies would faine, / But with entire affection and appearaunce plaine' (VI. v. 38). The hermit's hospitality fulfils the symbolic function of bolstering courteous values, particularly in light of the discourtesies endured (and the false courtesies Arthur will soon endure) at the court of Turpine and Blandina.[3] And yet, the hermit's plainness is itself a deliberate expression of a courteous instinct, and his choice to renounce chivalric ways to dwell in the woods is a continuation of those principles:

> For well it seem'd, that whilome he had beene
> Some goodly person, and of gentle race,
> That could his good to all, and well did weene,
> How each to entertaine with curt'sie well beseene.
> (VI. v. 36)

Hospitality is a key feature of conduct manuals and is accordingly emphasised in this Book, but it is a measure of Spenser's continued struggle to separate courtliness and courtesy that he gives such perfected incarnations of it to woodsmen and hermits.

The Endless Quest

The effects of Calidore's belief in his own sufficiency on his quest are startlingly new. A strong instinct for self-preservation replaces the drastic corrective action we might expect of a Spenserian knight: in his first battle, for example, he quite reasonably 'instructs' Crudor that 'What haps to day to me, to morrow may to you' (VI. i. 41). At one point he reneges on his quest and the whole chivalric ethos to take what some have called a pastoral 'holiday', disappearing for nearly five cantos. Unlike previous knights, he never meets Prince Arthur, the superlative exemplar and vehicle of Spenser's moral doctrine. In his absence Calepine and Arthur act as his acolyte and surrogate respectively, more traditional 'errant knights, that did inquire / After adventure where they mote them get' (VI. v. 11). Where they seek adventure, adventure pursues Calidore. His quarry, the Blatant Beast, is less a fixed threat than a moving target,

3. Blandina 'fayrely entertayned / With all the courteous glee and goodly feast,' but in an unusual piece of irony at Arthur's expense, the narrator tells us that 'Yet were her words but wynd, and all her tears but water' (VI. vi. 42).

'with . . . pursuit incited more' (VI. iii. 25). They are locked in a perpetual and irresolvable cycle of pursuit and temporary capture, bound in an enduring struggle where the Beast knows Calidore's 'fatall hand by former feare' (VI. xii. 25) but feeds happily close by.

Calidore's quest is tedious, guideless, thankless and endless. Recognisably a romance quest, its idiosyncrasies exceed the literary boundaries of genre and show further debts to the dictates of courtesy books. Previously Spenser had used a teleological trajectory to dramatise the evolution of the knight's virtue: the initially naive hero was guided on his predetermined way, strengthened by a series of minor tussles and some instructive experience, which equipped him finally to defeat the monstrous incarnation of the vice threatening the book's virtue. But both Calidore and his quest bear the imprint of the courtesy tradition, an imprint which can be traced in their divergence from Spenser's established patterns up until Book VI: because he is convinced of his virtue from the beginning, Calidore is resigned to a non-teleological quest, a series of repetitive acts to execute and apparently nothing to learn. In turn, his quest is endless, inscrutable and displays little development. It is no surprise, then, that after he captures the Blatant Beast it manages to escape.

The path or quest is a standard figure for reformation ('the right path of vertue' in Christian thought), and the primary vehicle of Spenser's didactic 'historicall fictions'.[4] But Spenser's focus on the quest and its strikingly new shape in Book VI also evoke the ways in which courtesy books were received in England. Castiglione had famously described his work as a 'purtraict in peinting' of the court of Urbino, an image of an ideal enacted during the discussion. His translator, Thomas Hoby, amended that, describing his translation of Castiglione as a pathway to virtue.[5] Dedicating his translation of *Galateo*, Robert Peterson offers the Earl of Leicester 'This worke, if it please your honour to vouchsafe as a companion of ease to *trace the pathes*, which you haue already so well beaten' although, as he hastily adds, he 'presumeth not to be a guide for conduction'.[6] The path of courtesy is necessarily less exalted than a Christian or epic quest, lacking a grand climax which rewards the traveller for cleaving to the route. Rather, the path itself is the sole object of courtesy.

The 'strange waies' (VI. Pr. 2) of Courtesy's quest become clear by comparison with that of the Legend of Holiness. At the start of Book I, Una and Redcrosse struggle to find their true path through the Wandering Wood, eventually escaping by the most beaten path. Throughout the book the measure of Redcrosse's success is spatial, culminating in Heavenly Contemplation's counsel to 'seeke this path, that I to thee presage, / Which after all to heauen shall thee send' (I. x. 61). But in Book VI there is no predetermined or preferred path. Calidore tells Arthegall that

> . . . where ye ended haue, now I begin
> To tread an endlesse trace, withouten guyde,
> Or good direction, how to enter in,
> Or how to issue forth in waies vntryde.
>
> (VI. i. 6)

4. Bryskett, *A Discourse of Ciuill Life* (London: [R. Field] for William Aspley, 1606), sig. D1.
5. Hoby, *The Book of the Courtier*, pp. 10, 3.
6. Delia Casa, *Galateo*, trans. Peterson, sig. [A4]; emphasis mine.

Reinforcing this are multiple instances of blocked passages or obstructed entrances in Book VI: jammed doors, churning rivers, unpassable undergrowth, darkened caves. The decapitated Maleffort's head rolls to block the door to Briana's castle as he failed to do alive, and Calidore's brigand-victims pile up in their cave so that 'all the entry was with bodies mand' (VI. xi. 46). More traditionally, we have the 'hardly passable' river that Calepine and Serena reach, and the frustrating landscape of hidden caves, pathless woods and 'couert . . . so thicke, that did no passage shew' (VI. v. 22). Emphasising the hostility of this landscape, the narration is peppered with reminders of the protagonists' efforts to return to their 'first quest'. Calidore's sense of his obstructed quest contrasts with the spatial significance of quests in the earlier books: Redcrosse's course was clearly defined, and no guide comes more true than Una. Arthegall 'for nought would swerve / From his course' (V. xii. 43), with Talus as the 'true guide of his way and vertuous government' (V. viii. 3). By contrast, digressions (never clearly identifiable as such) typify the quest of Courtesy, and the Blatant Beast's recidivism is a direct function of the courteous man's difficulty in identifying his quest. The distended shape of the romance quest also takes its toll on the poem's commitment to didactic images: tellingly, Yeats's selections from his pictorial Spenser included excerpts from every book in *The Faerie Queene* except Book VI. There are few significant sights made available to the protagonists, and where such visions are supplied—Acidale, Serena amongst the cannibals—the protagonists show no capacity to understand them.

Thus the epistemological configuration of the quest is subverted in Book VI. The *telos* of the quest, the structure that allows time and space measure progress, becomes redundant in a book whose quest is acknowledged from the start to be not just unidentifiable but endless. An endless quest also compromises the narrative structure that allows for reforming protagonist and reader: Calepine finds and rescues his lost love 'by chance more then by choyce' (VI. viii. 46). Calidore happens upon the dance of the Graces one day as he is out hunting. An ever-changing, apparently random quest eludes the usual moral and visual markers of space and narrative available to Spenser's readers. Instead, a new set of moral cues prevails: where travel is fruitless and endless travail, speed and diligence lose importance. Calidore wanders with moral impunity as no other knight could. Space, stripped of the task of symbolising progress, is left value-free, at Calidore's disposal. This allows him, for example, to retrace his steps to retrieve evidence for Priscilla's father. This allows Calidore a surprising reprieve from the widespread critical condemnation of his pastoral 'holiday' as a moral lapse. Ambiguities in the mind of the poet are evident in the discrepancy between the Argument and action of Canto x: in the Argument Calidore's glimpse of the Graces dancing to Colin's melody is said to occur '*The whiles* his Pastorell is led / Into captivity' (emphasis mine), which contradicts the Canto's clearly separated accounts of the episodes. Given the mutation of the quest figure and its attendant moral values, Calidore must be exonerated from censure for swerving from his quest to join the shepherd community. Although Redcrosse's dallying by a fountain with Duessa while Una searched for him was obviously reprehensible, the narrative structure of Calidore's quest ensure that he cannot be chastised for his lengthy holiday in pursuit of

Pastorella on similar temporal or spatial grounds, especially as he remains infallibly courteous throughout. The narrator confirms this, declaring that Calidore's delaying of his quest 'Though out of course, yet hath not bene missayd, / To shew the courtesie by him profest' (VI. xii. 2). Responding to digression, not vice, is courtesy's forte.

That this frustration of the semantic framework of the heroic quest is closely allied to courtesy is prefigured in the episodes involving Phaedria in Book II. Joseph Parry writes of Guyon's failure to overcome Phaedria at any point in Book II.[7] 'Phaedria is not a piece of knowledge that Guyon masters. She lives and moves right on the boundaries of what Guyon can and perhaps should know and be able to control.'[8] As an avatar of the immobilising Acrasia, whom Guyon in turn needs to immobilise, Phaedria's danger to Guyon lies in her ability to travel whimsically, frustrating Guyon's 'controlled, careful style of progress'.[9] Guyon, temporarily as guideless as Calidore, wanders on the Idle lake with Phaedria and is forcibly distracted on a pleasant island. Twice his baffled response to this uncontrollable and unfathomable quest-wrecker is described as 'courteous' (II. vi. 21) and Phaedria as 'courteous seeming' (II. vi. 26).[1] By the end of Book II, Guyon has still not managed to contain her. She catches up with him on the final leg of his voyage but floats away again and, like the Blatant Beast, is left free to continue her pernicious tour of Faeryland.

The mobile heroes and villains of courtesy repeatedly escape the moral-allegorical and epistemological confines of Faeryland. Calidore is suited to victories which look substantial but are rather adjustments which avoid loss of face: no knowledge ensues from them, and redress is temporary, protean and inscrutable. This curious heroic impotence affects another disciple of the traditional quest: the narrator. Back in the opening lines of the Proem to Book VI, the narrator complains:

> The waies, through which my weary steps I guyde,
> In this delightful! land of Faery,
> Are so exceeding spacious and wyde,
> And sprinckled with such sweet variety,
> Of all that pleasant is to eare or eye,
> That I nigh rauisht with rare thoughts delight,
> My tedious travell doe forget thereby
>
> (VI. Pr. 1)

Momentarily distracted, the narrator seeks to forget the tedious imperatives of his quest in the marvelous romance world and self-pleasing thoughts of Faeryland courtesy. But throughout the Book the narrator shares Calidore's sense of frustrated, ineffectual wandering, culminating in the disconsolate closing lines of Canto xii. This is unsurprising given

7. 'Phaedria and Guyon: Traveling Alone in *The Faerie Queene*, Book II', *Spenser Studies*, 15 (2001): 53–77. See also David Quint, 'The Boat of Romance and Renaissance Epic' in Kevin Brownlee and Marilyn Scordilis Brownlee, ed., *Romance: Generic Tranformations from Chrétien de Troyes to Cervantes* (Hanover: University Press of New England, 1985), pp. 178–202, and Philip Edwards, *Sea-Mark: The Metaphorical Voyage from Spenser to Milton* (Liverpool: Liverpool University Press, 1997).
8. Parry, 'Phaedria and Guyon,' p. 54.
9. Ibid., p. 58.
1. II. vi. 21: 'The knight was courteous and did not forbeare / Her honest merth and pleasaunce to partake;' and II. vi. 36: 'such is the might / Of courteous clemencie in gentle hart' (where her 'pleasing words' (II. vi. 36) of courteous clemency calm the struggle between Guyon and Cymochles).

that he describes his narration as a quest in the very book in which the heroic quest is undermined.[2] Ultimately, the narrator is struck by introspection and despair in his task, finally rejecting the didactic principles of his poem, bitterly concluding that it may have been more useful to him to have written verse that 'seeke[s] to please' (VI. xii. 41). The narrator's insecurities, too, impede readers in their endeavours to learn from this book. It is not his misleading prompts that are missed but rather what readerly confidence remains in the narrator's role as facilitator and guarantor of the morally improving experience of reading the poem. Despite his protestations in the exordium to Canto xii, the core movement of that experience is paralysed in Book VI. Courtesy's endless quest disables the usual narrative cues and epistemological structures of Spenser's poem before Book VI.

One of those key epistemological structures was repetition, specifically the repetition of plots and language across the poem's surface of 'historicall fictions'. Such repetitions were an important aspect of Spenser's cultivation of the reader's narrative intelligence, forcing an attention to the surface narrative and guarding against prescriptiveness or hasty emblematising. In Book VI, Spenser plunders his storehouse of poetic images and ideas more vigorously than ever. No other book 'quotes' itself and the rest of the poem so repeatedly, and Book VI has been seen by Isabel MacCaffrey and others to be, essentially, a meditation on its own past in the earlier books and on the ideal past of antiquity out of which the poem grows.[3] And yet, the repetitions destabilise in increasingly ominous ways. Serena, for example, is stripped like Duessa but worshipped by forest cannibals as Una was by wood-folk. She also parallels panicky Florimell as she flees through the forest; with Una when accompanied by the Salvage Man (a version of Satyrane); with Priscilla when she and Calepine are originally disturbed by Calidore; with Amoret when snatched by the Blatant Beast, as Amoret was by lust. Other obvious repetitions include Tristram greedily despoiling a dead knight of his arms, which recalls Pyrocles and Cymochles's plunder of the unconscious Guyon; the unknown pathless ways to the Salvage's glade, which recall those of Mammon's den; and the fable of Mirabella's female pride, which confirms that lamented by the Squire of Dames. That the stripping of villainous Duessa can return as the shocking crimes of the cannibals against Serena, or the discourteous robbery of a helpless victim reappear as Tristram's admirable seizure of arms suggests that these recapitulations are uninflected deployments of earlier material. But this goes against the readers' previous experience of the poem, which has repeatedly taught them to investigate echoes and parallels of diction or plot for vital clues about the moral colouring of the events narrated. With the deforming of the quest structure, however, the readers are all at sea as to what these repetitions might mean.

* * *

2. The quest conceit, mostly in the form of the metaphor of a voyage by ship, was prominent at the close of Books I and II, but the 'weary steps' on dry land in Book VI are closer to the chivalric quests.
3. Nohrnberg, too, has noticed the repetition in Book VI and 'quotation' is his term for it in *The Analogy of 'The Faerie Queene'* (Princeton, N.: Princeton University Press, 1976), p. 704. Isabel G. MacCaffrey sees Book VI as being about a return *ad fontes* in *Spenser's Allegory: The Anatomy of Imagination* (Princeton, NJ: Princeton University Press, 1976), pp. 417–18.

ANDREW D. HADFIELD

["Two Cantos of Mutabilitie"]†

'Two Cantos of Mutabilitie', a fragment of an apparently never completed 'Legend of Constancie', first appeared in the 1609 folio edition of *The Faerie Queene*, published by Matthew Lownes, who had attempted to publish *A View* in 1598. Nothing is known of the date of composition of the cantos, whether they were a relatively early piece which was not incorporated into *The Faerie Queene*, or whether they were, as one critic has argued, 'Spenser's last testament of faith', composed in the final year of his life.[1] It is improbable that they were written before 1586, as Spenser refers to Arlo Hill, which he would have been unlikely to have known of before he took up his Kilcolman estate. The allusion to the Bregog and Mulla story told in *Colin Clouts come home againe* (lines 104–55), in VII. vi. 40, would suggest a date after 1590, and if the reference to Cynthia abandoning Ireland to wolves and thieves (VII. vii. 55) is a 'tactful reference to the rout of the English during Tyrone's rebellion', or the figure of Faunus is an allegorical depiction of Hugh O'Neill, a later date would be confirmed (at least, of the extant text).[2] It is quite possible that the cantos were discovered posthumously; equally, their publication by Lownes might suggest that they had come into his possession, perhaps via Spenser himself, at the same time as he acquired the manuscript of *A View* that he attempted to have published. It must remain no more than the most tentative form of speculation, but it is conceivable that Spenser—or someone acting for him with or without his permission—was intending to make a stronger impact as a New English writer, a role he performed posthumously.[3]

The cantos can be read as a coda, a reinforcement of the fears surrounding the status of the court and its attendant virtue, courtesy, or else as a fable which encapsulates the fundamental message of the whole poem.[4] The ability of the court to transform nature and shape it (an Orphic function) has been continually challenged throughout the poem by the converse fear of a regression to an infinite relativization of difference which will engulf even the most seemingly stable centres of authority

† From *Spenser's Irish Experience: Wilde Fruit and Salvage Soyl* (Oxford: Clarendon Press, 1997), pp. 185–202. Reprinted by permission of Oxford University Press.

1. Judah L. Stampfer, 'The *Cantos of Mutability*: Spenser's Last Testament of Faith', *University of Toronto Quarterly* 21 (1951–2), 140–56. On the dating of the cantos, see Helen Hackett, *Virgin Mother, Maiden Queen: Elizabeth I and the Cult of the Virgin Mary* (Basingstoke: Macmillan, 1995), 269. Most critics believe they were a late composition, with the exception of Alice Fox Blitch; 'The Mutabilitie Cantos: "In Meet Order Ranged"', *English Language Notes* 7 (1969–70), 179–86.
2. Edmund Spenser, *The Mutability Cantos*, ed. Sheldon P. Zitner (London: Nelson, 1968), 2–4; Helena Shire, *A Preface to Spenser* (London: Longman, 1978), 64; Sheldon P. Zitner, '*The Faerie Queene*, Book VII', *Sp. Enc.*, 287–9, at 287, 289. See also Russell J. Meyer, "'Fixt in heauens hight": Spenser, Astronomy, and the Date of the *Cantos of Mutabilitie*', *Sp. Stud.*, 4 (1983), 115–29.
3. Nicholas Canny, 'Edmund Spenser and the Development of an Anglo-Irish Identity', *Yearbook of English Studies* 13 (1983), 1–19. Willy Maley, 'How Milton and Some Contemporaries Read Spenser's *View*' in Brendan Bradshaw, Andrew Hadfield and Willy Maley, eds., *Representing Ireland: Literature and the Origins of Conflict, 1534–1660* (Cambridge: Cambridge University Press, 1993), 191–208.
4. Elizabeth Fowler argues that the cantos display 'a shift in register' in restating the fundamental legal problems which underlie the poem: 'Failure of Moral Philosophy', 'The Failure of Moral Philosophy in the Work of Edmund Spenser,' *Representations* 51 (1995), 47–76, 49.

(a protean nightmare).[5] Here, on Arlo Hill, just outside Spenser's Irish estate in Kilcolman, the leader of the Gods, Jove, meets the challenge of the Titaness, Mutabilitie, for an argument to determine who holds sway over the universe. Mutabilitie's claim, which she substantiates at great length, is that Jove's exalted position is rightly hers because everything in the realm under the moon is subject to the perpetual change that she causes. Nature, who is appointed judge, grants that there is much reason behind Mutabilitie's allegations, but detects what she argues is a fatal flaw in Mutabilitie's arguments. It is true, Nature admits, that 'all things stedfastnes doe hate', the main point of Mutabilitie's speech on Arlo Hill, but:

> being rightly wayd
> They are not changed from their first estate;
> But by their change their being doe dilate:
> And turning to themselues at length againe,
> Doe worke their owne perfection so by fate:
> Then ouer them Change doth not rule and raigne;
> But they raigne ouer change, and doe their states maintaine.
> (VII. vii. 58)

The canto ends on an apocalyptic note, with Nature asserting that Jove can continue to rule the universe because change is subject to change; Mutabilitie cannot escape the logic of her own premisses, and 'time shall come that all shall changed bee, | And from thenceforth, none no more change shall see' (59).

These lines have often been interpreted as philosophical maxims, yet the neat caesura of the final alexandrine and the carefully signalled inversion of the chiasmus, might suggest that they are better read as metaphysical poetry than as philosophical speculation (metaphysics), comparable to Donne's 'Divine Meditation', 10. That sonnet concludes with the couplet, 'One short sleep past, we wake eternally, | And death shall be no more, Death thou shalt die'; the suppressed premises of Nature's speech might be interpreted as 'Change thou shalt change'.[6] It clearly does not follow that, because change has to change, Jove can rule as a figure of constancy nominated by Nature. Nature herself is a shadowy figure about whom we learn little except that he or she is an elusive creature of disguise: 'Whether she man or woman inly were, | That could not any creature well descry: | For, with a veile that wimpled euery wherer, | Her head and face was hid, that mote to none appear' (VII. vii. 5), recalling the troubling hermaphrodite figures of Books II and III. This remote figure becomes yet another type of Elizabeth in the following stanza:

> That some doe say [her veil] was so by skill deuized,
> To hide the terror of her uncouth hew,
> From mortall eyes that should be sore agrized;

5. John Guillory, *Poetic Authority: Spenser, Milton and Literary History* (New York: Columbia University Press, 1983), 48.
6. John Donne, *The Complete English Poems*, ed. A. J. Smith (Harmondsworth: Penguin, 1971), 313. For such judgements of the poem, see Sheldon P. Zitner, '*Faerie Queene*, Book VII', *Sp. Enc.*, pp. 287–89, 288, where he describes the cantos as a 'celebration of life in process', a 'reconcil[iation] of the world of change and the unaltered spirit', 'eternal unchanging grace'. See also Kathleen Williams, '"Eterne in Mutabilitie": The Unified World of *The Faerie Queene*', *E.L.H* 19 (1951), 115–30; J. E. Holland, 'The Cantos of Mutability and the Form of *The Faerie Queene*', *ELH* 35 (1968), 21–31; Robin Headlam Wells, *Spenser's* Faerie Queene *and the Cult of Elizabeth* (London: Macmillan, 1983), ch. 7.

> For that her face did like a Lion shew,
> That eye of wight could not indure to view:
> But others tell that it so beautious was,
> And round about such beames of splendor threw,
> That it the Sunne a thousand times did pass,
> Ne could be seene, but like an image in a glass.
> (vii. vii. 6)

The image of Nature's face as a reflection in a mirror recalls the descriptions in the proem to Book VI of courtesy as a shadowy virtue which could only be imperfectly realized and the queen's mind as a mirror of the apotheosis of that virtue. Nature, who judges this vital debate in Ireland, appears as remote from those who witness her performance as the queen did after she abandoned Ireland in Book VI. During the long silence that ensues before she makes her judgement, the expectant crowd of creatures try to gain clues from her face, but she keeps her eyes firmly on the ground (57). The mirror image of her face may well be splendid, but it is equally mysterious. Once the judgement has been delivered, 'was that whole assembly quite dismist | And *Natur's* selfe did vanish, whither no man wist' (59). Like Astrea, and, in the 'Two Cantos of Mutabilitie', Diana, Nature abandons the world to live with her decisions, taking no further part in enforcing the order she wishes to affirm as right, consulting with no one and keeping her subjects waiting to find out her decision. The suggestion is that Mutabilitie may not be quite so easy to banish, partly because, Nature herself appears as a protean figure whose only existence is in the eyes and minds of those who observe her. It is by no means clear that she has the right or the power to defeat Mutabilitie.[7]

In the imperfect last canto (viii), which contains only two stanzas, the narrator appears to be quite impressed by Mutabilitie's arguments: 'When I bethinke me on that speech why leare; | Of *Mutability*, and well it way, | Me seemes, that though she all unworthy were | Of the Heav'ns Rule; yet very sooth to say, | In all things else she beares the greatest sway' (vii. viii. 1).[8] The narrator attempts to offset such doubts with a metaphor: 'Then gin I thinke on that which Nature sayd, | Of that same time when no more *Change* shall be, | But stedfast rest of all things firmely stayd | Upon the pillours of Eternity' (2). All that remains to counter Mutabilitie's arguments is the comparsion, 'pillours of Eternity', a lack of substantial form which not only recalls the elusive figure of Nature herself, but also the problems of representing truth in the first place: Una, like Nature, wears a veil. Ideology, as Barthes recognized, is where the play of language stops and meaning is fixed by an authority.[9]

The problem with Nature is not the only irony haunting an affirmative reading of the poem. At the start of canto vi Mutabilitie is already described as having displaced Nature from the earth, 'That all which Nature had establisht first | In good estate, and in meet order ranged, | She did pervert, and all their statutes burst' (vii. vi. 5). The use of the

7. See Harry Berger, Jr., 'The Mutabilitie Cantos: Archaism and Evolution in Retrospect', in id., *Revisionary Play*, 242–73, at 249. John Guillory, *Poetic Authority: Spenser, Milton and Literary History* (New York: Columbia University Press) 1983 61–2.
8. See Lewis J. Owen, 'Mutable in Eternity: Spenser's Despair and the Multiple Forms of Mutabilitie', *JMRS* 2 (1972), 49–68.
9. Roland Barthes S/Z, trans. Richard Miller (New York: Hill and Wang, 1976) 100.

legal term, 'statutes' refers the cantos to the extensive discussion of the rule of law in *A View* (another reason, perhaps, to connect the two to Lownes?), a conjunction continued in the next stanza: 'Ne shee the lawes of Nature onely brake, | But eke of Iustice, and of Policie; | And wrong of right, and bad of good did make | . . . And all this world is woxen daily worse' (6). Such lines link the world of Mutabilitie to the state of the world left behind by Astrea at the start of Book V, implying that Mutabilitie stands as a figure of Ireland opposed to the figure of Elizabeth as Nature.[1]

Mutabilitie proceeds to challenge Cynthia for supremacy under the moon and forces the goddess down to face her. It is quite clear that Cynthia stands as yet another figure for Elizabeth, quite apart from the evidence of the letter to Raleigh which made such a connection explicit:

> Thence, to the Circle of the Moone she clambe,
> Where *Cynthia* raignes in euerlasting glory,
> To whose bright shining palace straight she came,
> All fairely deckt with heauens goodly story;
> Whose siluer gates (by which there sate an hory
> Old aged Sire, with hower-glasse in hand,
> Hight *Tyme*) she entred, were he liefe or sory:
> Ne staide till she the highest stage had scand,
> Where *Cynthia* did sit, that nuer still did stand.
>
> (VII. vi. 8)

The proximity of the figure of Time to Cynthia's throne, is a *memento mori*, an aggressively situated *dopplegänger*, like the poet Bon | MalFont outside the throne room of Mercilla, who points to the reality of Elizabeth's rule. Cynthia is described as never standing still, a double-edged reference to Elizabeth's inconstant policies and the mutability of her own body, which had been beyond childbearing age since the 1580s, leaving the succession uncertain.[2] The point is repeated towards the end of canto vii when Mutabilitie addresses Cynthia directly: 'Euen you faire *Cynthia*, whom so much ye make | *Ioues* dearest darling . . . Then is she mortall borne, how-so ye crake' (50). Both stanzas are warnings to Elizabeth that, although she might appear invincible in her public role as a mighty empress, she is also subject to the ravages of time in her private person, a studied ambiguity which neatly reflects the paradox of the queen's two bodies highlighted in the letter to Raleigh.[3] In itself such stanzas make it that much harder to read Nature's argument against Mutabilitie as anything other than a neat trick, as Mutabilitie's effects were available for all to see in the in the extra-fictional world to which the poem refers.

Both stanzas also link Cynthia's rule directly to the conquest of Jove, so that the description of Cynthia reigning in 'euerlasting glory' cannot but be ironic when placed alongside the account of the degeneration of the world from the age of Saturn whom Jove overthrew, especially given the echo strategically placed in stanza 6 that 'this world is woxen daily worse'. Cynthia's very status as a ruling goddess depends upon what she and Jove wish to deny, the very process of change and decay they are now

1. A resemblance strengthened if one recalls the mutable (Irish) figure of Malengin in v. ix.
2. Andrew Hadfield, *Literature, Politics and National Identity: Reformation to Renaissance* (Cambridge, Cambridge University Press, 1996) 200.
3. Hackett, *Virgin Mother, Maiden Queen*, 193.

forced to oppose. In Book V, Artegall was given the very sword, Chrysaor, which Jove used to defeat the Titans. With this he was remarkably successful until he was thwarted in his ultimate goal of pacifying Ireland. Mutabilitie is a Titaness, returning to claim her due revenge, because the forces appointed by Jove failed to finish their task. Once again, we are faced with the prospect that there is no just order in the universe, simply the law of conquest. Spenser's political vision might seem to verge on the Hobbesian. While Cynthia and Mutabilitie struggle in the heavens, a portent appears to 'the lower World', when the sky turns black and people worry 'least *Chaos* broken had his chaine' (14). Jove and Cynthia may not have natural justice on their side (the fact that the initial struggle is between a goddess and a Titaness could be a further attack on female rule), but if they are displaced the alternative could well be significantly more frightening.

The location of the debate between Jove and Mutabilitie (established at great length in vi. 36–55), lends further weight to demands that the cantos be read topically and politically, rather than as 'the comic minor plot' which foregrounds the major philosophical interest of the debate itself.[4] This takes place on Arlo Hill, Spenser's name for Galtymore, which overlooked his estate at Kilcolman and was 'a notorious resort of outlaws in Spenser's day'.[5] In *A View*, Irenius cites Arlo as one of the areas 'which lyinge neare unto anye mountaines or Irishe desertes had bynne planted with Englishe weare shortelye displanted and loste' (p. 57), after the chaos of the Wars of the Roses had reduced English government to disarray. Such intertextual connections establish the mutable nature of the geographical setting and also suggest that Arlo Hill is a borderland over which the savages of Book VI might well stray.[6]

The setting of the debate on a hill recalls Irenius' description of the Irish custom of assembling on a rath (hill) to debate 'aboute matters and wronges betwene Towneshipp and Towneshippe or one private persone and another' (p. 128), a practice which once expressed a rudimentary democracy when first established under English control, but which now leads to rebellion, anarchy, and murder:

> But well I wote and trewe it hathe bene often times aproued that in these metinges manye mischiefs haue bene bothe practised and wroughte ffor to them doe Comonlye resorte all the scum of lose people wheare they maye frelye mete and Conferr of what they liste which else they Coulde not doe without suspicion or knowledge of others Besides at those parlies I haue diuerse times knowen that manye Englishemen and other good Irishe subiectes haue bene villanouslye murdered by movinge one quarrell or another amongest them. (pp. 128–9)[7]

4. Zitner, '*Faerie Queene*, Book VII', 288; Richard N. Ringler, 'The Faunus Episode', *MP* 63 (1965–6), 12–19, at 12–13. For a reading of the cantos in terms of property rights, see Julia Reinhard Lupton, 'Mapping Mutability: Or Spenser's Irish Plot', in Bradshaw *et al.* (eds.), *Representing Ireland*, 93–115.
5. See William Keach, 'Arlo Hill', *Sp. Enc.* 60. See also Pauline Henley, *Spenser in Ireland* (Cork: Cork University Press, 1928) 87–8; Roland M. Smith, 'Spenser's Irish River Stories', *PMLA* 50 (1935), 1047–56, at 1049; and more generally, Rudolf Gottfried, 'Irish Geography in Spenser's. *View*, *ECH* 6 (1939), 114–37, at 132–3.
6. On the concept of the 'borderland' in early modern British history, see Steven G. Ellis, 'Crown, Community and Government in the British Territories, 1450–1575', *History*, 71 (1986), 187–204.
7. For analysis, see Samuel Kliger, 'Spenser's Irish Tract and Tribal Democracy', *SAQ* 49 (1950), 490–7.

In a crucial sense, the debate on Arlo Hill could be said to establish the borderland itself: the result could either affirm that there is a civilized order to the universe or allow matters to descend into chaos, depending on who actually wins the verbal battle. More immediately, and granted a potent irony in the light of the imminent destruction of the Minister Plantation—including Spenser's own estate—the encounter will establish either English or Irish hegemony. The stately dispute of gods and Titans might appear to some as an uncivilized squabble, a dangerous and absurd parody of proper debate. The other literary references of the poem, Chaucer's *Parlement of Foulys* and Ovid's *Metamorphoses*, which establish a native English and Classical heritage, only serve to throw the Irish context into starker relief.[8]

The seemingly humorous incongruity of the situation is highlighted by the rhetorical question, 'Who knowes not *Arlo-hill*?' (VII. vi. 36), a question which recalls the similar interrogative form during the Dance of the Graces (VI. x. 16), 'who knowes not *Colin Clout*?'. The resemblance is underlined by the almost exact repetition of the structures of each line, with the question appearing in brackets after the mention of the name.[9] Both demand to be read ironically, rather than as affirmations of a stable identity, given that Galtymore/Arlo Hill was hardly likely to have been known to any but a few other Munster undertakers and officials concerned with the Plantation, especially in the light of the care with which Spenser appears to have established his New English persona as that of a neglected sage ignored by the metropolitan authorities.[1] Yet here is the very centre of the universe, the place where the fate of civilization will be decided, whatever more lofty minds might think.

The following stanza (37), signals that the setting of the debate within the Irish landscape—not Faerieland—is of a different order to the rest of the poem (whether the cantos themselves or the whole of *The Faerie Queene* is left unclear); either it is a passing interlude or an aetiological and etymological fable:

> And, were it not ill fitting for this file,
> To sing of hilles and woods, mongst warres and Knights,
> I would abate the sternenesse of my stile,
> Mongst these sterne sounds to mingle soft delights;
> And tell how *Arlo* through *Dianaes* spights
> (Beeing of old the best and fairest Hill
> That was in all this holy-Islands hights)
> Was made the most unpleasant, and most ill.
> Meane while, O *Clio*, lend *Calliope* thy quill.
>
> (VII. vi. 37)

The stanza is riddled with irony and ambiguity. The narrator claims that he would change his style to suit the narration of this episode, but that he

8. Chaucer's work is explicitly mentioned at the start of canto vii (3–10); see Alice Miskimin, *The Renaissance Chaucer*, (New Haven: Yale University Press, 1973) 35–41. On the Ovidian analogues of the poem, see Julia Lupton, 'Mapping Mutabilitie: or, Spenser's Irish Plot' in Bradshaw *et al.*, eds., *Representing Ireland*, pp. 93–115, 102–11; Ringler, 'Faunus Episode'; Michael Holahan, '*Iamque opus exegi*: Ovid's Changes and Spenser's Brief Epic of Mutabilitie', *ELR* 6 (1976), 244–70.
9. See Hadfield, *Literature, Politics and National Identity*, 171–2; Berger, 'Mutabilitie Cantos', 264.
1. For an alternative reading see Luptun, 'Mapping Mutabilitie', 110.

cannot because his poem demands that he does not. It is hot clear at this stage whether this means that he will not tell the story, or whether he will tell the story of Arlo Hill, but in a style fitting to the poem as it has been narrated so far. Either way, the stanza becomes, retrospectively, an example of the trope of *occupatio*, defined by Abraham Fraunce as 'A kind of irony, a kind of pretended omitting or letting slip of that which indeed we elegantly note out in the very show of praetermission', because the story is actually told.[2] Indeed, the bare bones are outlined in stanza 37, namely the story of the fall of Arlo Hill from 'the best and fairest' on the island, to 'the most unpleasant, and most ill', a further suggestion that the subsequent story will be far from a tale of 'soft delights' and, in fact, exactly in keeping with what has gone before, particularly in the second half of *The Faerie Queene* (the ubiquitous story of the Fall recalls the abandonment of the world by Astrea, a narrative repetition which becomes more obvious as the canto continues). The final lines, which appear precise and in line with the change signalled at the start of the stanza, are similarly problematic. It is not clear why Calliope, the Muse of heroic poetry, should be more fitted than Clio, the Muse of history, to inspire the story, especially given that Calliope is presumably inspiring the story anyway (I, proem, 2).[3] The letter to Raleigh defines the poem, along Sidneyan lines, as 'an historicall fiction', further suggesting that any distinction made between Clio and Calliope, history and historical fiction, is an arbitrary one. However it is read, the stanza invokes the co-operation of the two Muses, drawing the reader's attention to the significance of the episode as a key to the mythology of the poem; in a sense, its myth of origin.

Stanza 38 starts the story proper, following on from the appellation of Ireland as 'this holy-Island', with a description of the land—significantly emphasized in capitals in the folio—as the most desirable part of Britain:

> Whylome, when *IRELAND*, florished in fame
> Of wealths and goodnesse, far aboue the rest
> Of all that beare the *British* Islands name,
> The Gods then us'd (for pleasure and for rest)
> Oft to resort there-to, when seem'd them best:
> But none of all there-in-more pleasure found,
> Then *Cynthia*; that is soueraine Queene profest
> Of woods and forrests, which therein abound,
> Sprinkled with wholsom waters, more then most on ground.
> (vii. vi. 38)

The stanza invokes a distant mythical time, presumably contemporary with the debate, although we are not actually told, when Ireland was the centre of the universe and was sought out by the gods, rather than neglected by them. Ireland was a pastoral *locus amoenus*, centred on Arlo Hill, a land of pleasure not work, akin to the garden of Adonis, or, more dangerously, the Bower of Bliss, rather than the hard anti-pastoral land observed now. Here nymphs and satyrs 'loue to play and sport' (39), a prelapsarian harmony exists before their names and identities become invested with significance,

2. *Arcadian Rhetoric* (1588), fo. 13, cited in Lee A. Sonnino, *A Handbook to Sixteenth-Century Rhetoric* (London: Routledge, 1968), 135–6.
3. Assuming that this is how the lines should be read; see *FQ*, 720, 28. See also Berger, 'Mutabilitie Cantos', 256–7.

as they have in the earlier faerie landscape when they both harboured Una (I. vi. 7–33), or the satyrs practised a less harmless sport with Hellenore, Malbecco's estranged wife (III. x. 44–7).[4] There is a forecast of Ireland's current state in the description of Cynthia as 'soueraine Queene profest | Of woods and forrests' which becomes an ironic prophecy of Cynthia's (Elizabeth's) current rule over an ungovernable land of forests. Just as Ireland has fallen from its state of grace, so has the significance of the queen's mythological identity as Diana.[5]

However, there is a serpent in this Garden of Eden: Faunus, the 'Foolish God', 'though full many a day | He saw her clad, yet longed foolishly | To see her naked mongst her Nymphes in priuity' (42). To achieve this forbidden desire, he decides to bargain with one of her nymphs, Molanna. He will help her to satisfy her unrequited love for Fanchin if she will tell him where Diana bathes. The deal is made and Faunus sees Diana naked in a 'sweet spring' (45). However, he is unable to contain the 'great ioy' he feels at this sight and remain silent, so he breaks 'forth in laughter' and 'loud profest | His foolish thought' (46). Diana, suitably abashed and understandably a little cross, seizes him and discusses with her nymphs the exact mode of punishment to be inflicted upon the transgressor.[6] Various suggestions are made, but eventually Faunus is dressed like a stag and chased by their hounds, from whom he escapes, spurred on by fear. Molanna weds Fanchin, even though Diana knows of her complicity in Faunus' voyeurism.[7]

As a result, Diana decides that Ireland is no longer the place for her to reside, and 'full of indignation, | Thence-forth abandoned her delicious brooke', which had previously given her 'So much delight' (54). Instead, she leaves behind 'an heauy haplesse curse':

> To weet, that Wolues, where she was won't to space,
> Should harbour'd be, and all those Woods deface,
> And Thieues should rob and spoile that Coast around.
> Since which, those Woods, and all that goodly Chase,
> Doth to this day with Wolues and Theues abound:
> Which too-too true that lands in-dwellers since haue found.
> (VII. vi. 55)

Ireland becomes the land that Cynthia rules in Spenser's time after she has fled the world like her other *alter ego*, Astrea.

The myth is a combination of three stories from Ovid's *Metamorphoses*, most importantly that of Actaeon (referred to in stanza 45) with the crucial alteration that whereas Actaeon is devoured by his own hounds, Faunus escapes from Diana's, making him into a figure like Duessa and the Blatant Beast, always likely to return.[8] The story of Faunus can be read as an allegory of English rule over Ireland, a counterpart to *A View*'s analysis of the helplessness of attempts to assert control unless viceregal

4. Richard D. Jordan, 'satyrs', *Sp. Enc.*, 628.
5. On Elizabeth as Diana, see Philippa Berry, *Of Chastity and Power: Elizabethan Literature and the Unmarried Queen* (London: Routledge, 1989) ch. 3.
6. Contrast Diana's reaction to Serena's (VI. viii. 50–1).
7. On the historical and topological significance, see Smith, 'Spenser's Irish River Stories', 1052–6.
8. See Lars-Hakan Svensson, 'Actaeon', *Sp. Enc.*, 6–7; Ringler, 'Faunus Episode'; Holahan, '*Imaque opus exegi*'; Ovid, *Metamorphoses*, trans. Mary M. Innes (Harmondsmith: Penguin, 1955) 77–80.

authority is re-established. * * * Ireland is the place where Elizabeth/ Diana is seen naked, exposed like Serena before the salvage nation, the mysterious power of her regal body rendered helpless.

The incident has a precedent—quite apart from the blazon representing Serena's body—in the similar depiction of Belpheobe observed by Braggadocchio and Trompart hidden within the bushes (II. iii. 21–30). This episode, which contains the longest description of a female body in the poem, clearly refers back to the myth of Actaeon. Braggadocchio, inflamed with lust, attempts to assault her, but flees when she threatens him with her spear. Belphoebe runs off and subsequently disappears form the book (like Astrea, Diana, Serena, the Graces).[9] Braggadocchio and Trompart 'shrowd themselues from causelesse feare' (II. iii. 20); when Faunus hides in the bushes, the relationship is made explicit:

> The simple maid [Molanna] did yield to him anone;
> And eft him placed where he close might view
> That neuer any saw, saue onely one;
> Who, for his hire to so foole-hardy dew,
> Was of his hounds devour'd in Hunters hew.
>
> (VII. vi. 45)

Actacon has transgressed and seen what no one should see, the naked body behind the masks of power.

Other textual clues demand that the two incidents be read in terms of each other, quite apart from the letter to Raleigh informing us that Belphoebe is a type of Diana/Cynthia. At the end of the blazon, Belphoebe is compared to Diana who 'on *Cynthus* greene, | Where all the Nymphes haue her unwares forlore, | Wandreth alone with bow and arrowes keen' (II. iii. 31); this prefigures not simply the wandering of the nymphs on Arlo Hill, but also the description of Cynthia as '*Ioues* dearest darling, she was bred and nurst | On *Cynthus* hill' (VII. vii. 50), so that a direct link is made between the three separate figures; Belphoebe, Diana in Ireland, and Diana seen by Actaeon.

Such links strengthen the perception of a carefully constructed attack on the queen that the second edition of the poem activates what is latent within the first. The description of Belphoebe contains a missing half-line, the only one in the poem, which is of crucial significance:

> [she] was yclad, for heat of scorching aire,
> All in a silken Camus lylly whight,
> Purfled upon with many a folded plight,
> Which all aboue besprinckled was throughout
> With golden aygulets, that glistred bright
> Like twinckling starres, and all about the skirt about
> Was hemd with golden fringe
>
> Below her ham her weed did somewhat traine,
> And her streight legs most brauely were embayld
> In gilden buskins.
>
> (II. iii. 26–7)

9. Louis A. Montrose, 'The Elizabethan Subject and the Spenserian Text', in David Quint and Patricia Parker, eds., *Literary Theory/Renaissance Texts* (Baltimore: The Johns Hopkins University Press, 1986), pp. 303–40, 328–9.

The description moves from the skirt to the legs, not with undue haste, but, rather, leaving a gaping hole in the centre of Belphoebe's body, the elaborate account of the gorgeous clothes drawing attention to the absence at the centre. Appearing keen to hide the mystery of female power, as Serena's sex was wrapped up in a conceit, the narrator's loquaciousness simply draws our attention to it. We do and do not 'glimpse the naked goddess in her radical otherness'.[1] Such is the constant threat to the multiple guises of the Faerie Queene throughout the poem; by the end of the poem we can be in no doubt that the most significant challenge to her power comes from Ireland, where Actaeon-figures lurk, not yet picked off by the Crown forces.

Although Cynthia is waiting for her own body's demise at the end of the 'Two Cantos of Mutabilitie', the effect of Faunus' forbidden vision of the queen's vagina is the downfall of Ireland rather than his own demise. Cynthia/Diana preserves her power by retreating into an untouchable political void and Faunus remains at large. Those who suffer are the subjects of the queen who have to live in the dangerous pastoral world of Book VI and post-lapsarian Ireland. When Diana departs, Ireland falls both in terms of its physical landscape and etymologically; it ceases to be a 'holy island', a *locus amoenus* connoting concord, and becomes instead, the '*Banno* or *sacra Insula* takinge *sacra* for accursed' of *A View* (p. 145), the ordinary meaning of everyday usage having to give way to another root which reverses the normal understanding.[2] Language has split and become duplicitous so that one cannot trust exactly where words lead to or from, a problem which overshadows the allegorical narrative of the whole poem and which is here seen to result from the problem of governing Ireland.[3] Two Cantos of Mutabilitie' repeat what has developed into the fundamental political message of *The Faerie Queene*, that the queen's masks of power/authority are most in danger of slipping in Ireland and that her rule is threatened by her failure to intervene there, as much as it is by her own fading physical form, reliance upon which, at the expense of developing a durable public sphere, has also cost her subjects dear. Furthermore, the cantos transform that message into a myth of origins which is also the conclusion of the poem's allegorical content, physically, in terms of being appended as a fragment to what is already a fragment, and chronologically, both pre- and post-dating the time-scale of the poem's action.[4] The cantos announce an aporia, simultaneously describing how events came to be as they are (an etiological reading) and revealing the result of mistaken actions (a reading in terms of the historical allegory); they are both the end and the beginning of *The Faerie Queene*, haunting the poem like the banished, unhappy ghosts of 'A Brief Note'.[5]

Although 'Two Cantos of Mutabilitie' can be read alongside *A View* as a demand for greater intervention in Ireland on the part of the Crown,

1. Montrose, 'Elizabethan Subject', 328.
2. See also the note in *Variorum*, x. 372.
3. See Martha Craig, 'The Secret Wit of Spenser's Language', in Paul Alpers (ed.), *Elizabethan Poetry: Modern Essays in Criticism* (Oxford: Oxford University Press, 1967), 447–72.
4. See Geoffrey Bennington, 'Postal Politics and the Institution of the Nation', in Homi K. Bhabha (ed.), *Nation and Narration*, (London: Routledge, 1990) 121–37.
5. See Jacques Derrida, 'Passions: "An Oblique Offering"', in David Wood (ed.), *Derrida: A Critical Reader* (Oxford: Blackwell, 1992), 5–35. On the concept of 'aporia', see Christopher Norris, *Deconstruction: Theory and Practice* (London: Methuen, 1982), 49–50, 100.

and a demand that the voices of the disaffected New English be heard in court circles, they hint at a much more sinister reality, and one at odds with what has been asserted in that attempt to intervene in contemporary politics. The cantos also serve to undercut the ideal of transformation so vital to Spenser's political discourse. Nature might award Jove sovereignty over the universe, but she has no more implicit right to rule than Mutabilitie, the daughter of the Titans who fought Jove for mastery, but lost. The usurpation of Jove can, of course, be read as a parallel event to the Fall, which is linked specifically to Ireland, so that allegorically Jove's victory can be seen to be the counterpart to the triumph of Faunus in Ireland: mythical events overlap with each other and contradict themselves so that Mutabilitie's claim to hold sway over them appears to have been vindicated.[6] Jove's brief argument against Mutabilitie bears this problem out:

> Then thus gan *loue*; Right true it is, that these
> And all things else that under heauen dwell
> Are chaung'd of *Time*, who doth them all disseise
> Of being: But, who is it (to me tell)
> That *Time* himselfe doth moue and still compell
> To keepe his course? Is not that namely wee
> Which poure that vertue from our heauenly cell,
> That moues them all, and makes them changed be?
> So them we gods doe rule, and in them also thee.
> (vii. vii. 48)

There are many ways in which the poem signals that we should not accept Jove's argument (it is worth noting the gap between Nature's eventual judgement and Jove's defence); but, most obviously, it is immediately undercut by Mutabilitie's reply. Jove claims that Time is subject to the power of the gods: Mutabilitie counters that his conclusion is based upon an assumption that what cannot be understood is caused by them: 'The things | Which we see not how they are mov'd and swayd, | Ye may attribute to your selues as Kings' (49). The problem is that this only appears to be the case and Jove is far too confident that everything is ordered by his power. Mutabilitie asks, 'what if I can proue, that euen yee | Your selues are likewise chang'd, and subiect unto mee?' (49), offering as her defence the example of Cynthia's decay and so moving the allegory back from the general to the historically specific. The attach works on two interrelated levels: on the one, Cynthia/Elizabeth has been foolish to have placed her political faith in the wiles of her mutable body; on the other, Jove, a usurper, who has elevated Cynthia/Elizabeth to her current position of eminence, has to be wrong to claim that the gods have power over Time.[7] He, and his main charge, both belong to the world of change below the moon, however strenuously they attempt to deny this stubborn state of affairs. Just as there was no natural law which granted Irena easy sovereignty over the salvage land/Ireland, neither is there any which will keep rulers perpetually alive and in power. Mutabilitie stands as yet another of Elizabeth's guises, a demonic inversion which reveals that

6. See Clark Hulse, Andrew D. Weiner, and Richard Strier, 'Spenser: Myth, Politics, Poetry', *SP* 85 (1988), pp. 378–411, 382–4.
7. Guillory, *Poetic Authority*, 63–4.

she has become more like Duessa than Una, a figure of untruth rather than truth. This is the essence of Mutabilitie's warning to Cynthia, one which short-circuits the fictional surface, of the text in order to address the monarch directly 'her face and countenance euery day | We changed see, and sundry forms partake, | Now hornd, now round, now bright, now brown and gray: | So that *as changefull as the Moone* men use to say' (VII. vii. 50, emphasis in text). Cynthia thinks that she is defined as Jove's 'dearest darling', but time and her own failings have led her to become Mutabilitie's *doppelgänger*, a situation which will cost her subjects dear unless the violent order of the masculine god can be re-established.

Jove, as the current leader of the gods, gains Nature's approval by default, as he is not forced to make a convincing defence of his rule, which implies that he could really be anyone, possessing no more inherent authority than that obtained through victorious conquest. Nature's statement that things are not changed from their first state because they turn 'to themselves at length againe' and 'worke their owne perfection so by fate' (58), whatever its truth-value as an analysis of the nature of matter, simply does not apply to the problem of Elizabeth's succession or to the ghostly and substantial menace of Ireland threatening to explode the desired unity of Britain and its attendant civilization. Once again, taking Nature at face value is to take the writing as witty but inconsequential metaphysical poetry.

In the same way, the Irish setting of the debate serves further to reinforce the fact that the real victory goes to Mutabilitie, whatever the arguments used against her triumph by Nature, Jove, and Cynthia. If Ireland cannot be absorbed and fixed into a stable form, then the masks of power, the points at which interpretation has to stop and give way to an authority, will be thrust aside and the world of Proteus and Mutabilitie will take over. *The Faerie Queene* emerges as a desperate poem, the problem being that even seemingly fixed and abstract figures like Error, Grantorto, or Duessa easily revert into more subversive, mutable forms, threatening to reveal that the queen's robes of state are no more than the emperor's new clothes, so that the actual locus of power is merely a vacuum.[8] What is really dangerous is 'the blind and mobile flaw in the system' of the text, the problem that if the queen's authority has to be represented as a series of figures in order to confront and combat the multiplicity of enemies ranged against her, then that authority will also become fragmented.[9] The supposed unity of Book I will fail to escape from the difference it is defined against, an inescapable paradox.[1] In the end, only an irruption of violent action can solve matters, like that produced by Artegall, the salvage knight who bears an uncomfortable resemblance to those he is supposed to be subduing and civilizing. Only when a figure like Malengin can be made to disappear, an episode in the poem which has its counterpart in the apparent belief of Irenius that evil elements can be rooted out of Ireland without the slaughter of evil people, can Irena rule in peace and fulfil the meaning of her name, guaranteeing (and being guaranteed

8. See the comments on Thomas More, in Stephen J. Greenblatt, *Renaissance Self-Fashioning,: From More to Shakespeare* (Chicago: Chicago University Press, 1980) 14.
9. Barthes, S/Z, 36.
1. Jonathan Goldberg, *Endlesse Worke: Spenser and the Structures of Discourse* (Baltimore: The Johns Hopkins University Press, 1981), ch. 1.

by) a subservient and transparent group of subjects. When these resist and demand a voice, power ceases to be monolithic, a state of affairs Spenser both recognizes and demands in his work, acknowledging that neither political nor literary representation can ever—or should ever—be pure. Words will never correspond exactly to things in the fallen world, so that allegory can never reach a straightforward, satisfactory conclusion; power must always be a diverse and complex phenomenon in the age of iron, which no one will ever fully control.

Ireland as represented in *The Faerie Queene* is a body of overlapping and conflicting texts which presents a whole series of figures: good and bad savages, pliable loyalists, disgruntled colonizers. The poem is a vast colonizing work trying to absorb all the representations it can and subject them to its own structure, familiarize and absorb the alien.[2] At the same time, there is a recognition that this is an impossible process (an endless work) and that the vast series of dichotomies produced—Una/Duessa, truth/error, savage/civil, queen/subjects, and so on—will never be held together at a final allegorical point. The teleological goal of the allegory is ultimately reduced to a series of inter- and intra-textual references which do not necessarily lead any where.

The Faerie Queene is caught within the paradox of announcing a political programme or definite allegorical message, and dealing with the problem of representation *per se*.[3] The text is as much a refusal of power, a surrender to the 'endlesse trace withouten guyde' which Calidore fears will be his lot, as it is a fashioning agent producing the gentlemanly reader or ideal queen. The fiction is an evasion of power, distanced from other discourses which have to induce action in an extra-textual world or describe an external 'reality' (legal, political, medical, historical), so that it can contain all codes and none, refusing action as much as inciting it.[4] Ireland, as a literary representation, is both scattered throughout *The Faerie Queene* as series of traces and, in so far as it is the locus of chaos, represents what the allegory surrenders to (its content) and becomes dissolved by (its linguistic form), a relationship which demonstrates the symbiotic relationship between questions of everyday government and cosmic fate which the poem articulates.

'Two Cantos of Mutabilitie' articulate what a political tract like *A View* can never admit, that it may be impossible ever to control and govern Ireland, to transform it into a 'West England'; that Ireland is the place where chaos originates and which will absorb and consume all attempts to redeem it in the name of an Anglocentric civilization.[5] It is where (the English) language turns against itself and ceases to be able to transform its 'other'; the master tropes of *A View* have no privileged status in Faerieland, which adds a certain poetic justice to that text's failure to appear in the public sphere of print until 1633. Conquest is shown to be an arbitrary

2. A Bartlett Giamatti, 'Primitivism and the Process of Civility in *Spenser's Faerie Queene*' in Fredi Chiappelli, ed., *First Images of America: The Impact of the New World on the Old* (Berkeley: University of California Press, 1978), 71–82.
3. A brilliant discussion of the problem of representation is contained in Suzanne Kappeler, *The Pornography of Representation* (Cambridge: Polity Press, 1986).
4. Derek Attridge, 'Introduction: The Peculiar Language of Literature', in id., *Peculiar Language: Language as Difference from the Renaissance to James Joyce* (Ithaca: Cornell University Press, 1988), 1–16.
5. On Ireland as a 'West England', see Hadfield and McVeagh (eds.), *Strangers to that Land*, 52.

act devoid of distinction and significance (but no less necessary for that). The conclusion of *The Faerie Queene*, whether that be taken as the end of Book VI or includes the surviving ruins of Book VII, reiterates the experimental and inconclusive nature of that work, because, for Spenser, even the cruel power of Jove may be unable to halt the tide of endless change.

Lewis's charge that Ireland corrupted Spenser's imagination is truer than he meant. *The Faerie Queene* is a project of purported national focus which exposes the problematic nature of national identity and its implicit relationship with colonial expansion. *The Faerie Queene* moves from an English to a British context and, in doing so, has to confront front the loss of its aesthetic and political unity because in the borderlands of the expanding and divergent English/British state there were numerous peoples who had no desire to fit easily into the narrow range of identities constructed for them by their would-be rulers. Spenser's writings catalogue the resistance of the Irish—in the 1590s, the most threatening opposition to the spread of English government—to the encroaching power of the hegemonic English monarch as well as the creation of a colonial class within the supposed boundaries of the state whose own English identity and loyalty to the Crown were challenged and eventually transformed by their experiences in trying to govern the Irish. *The Faerie Queene* is not a work which deals incidentally with Ireland but one which is framed by its author's own Irish experience, a fact registered in the development of both the form and the content of its allegorical design. The poem and its author ceased to be 'mere English' when both left England in the late 1570s or 1580 and were 'corrupted' by their relationship with Ireland. *The Faerie Queene* demands to be read alongside *A View of the Present State of Ireland*; while the latter proposes a solution to Spenser's fears of the apocalypse which he probably realized were too costly ever to be implemented,[6] the former would appear to recognize that the English could never govern Ireland properly or successfully and that the unhappy relationship between the two countries would permanently hobble England's political and moral hopes after the Reformation.

* * *

COLIN BURROW

[On *The Shepheardes Calender*][†]

* * *

Spenser's first collection of verse was *The Shepheardes Calender*, published anonymously, and tentatively dedicated to Sir Philip Sidney in 1579. The book is elaborately crafted in order to create maximum impact and mystery, and to cut across the literary expectations of its audience. Its title is drawn from a popular handbook called *The Kalender of Shepherds*, which

6. Ciarán Brady, 'Spenser's Irish Crisis: Humanism and Experience in the 1590s', *Past & Present* 111 (1986): 17–49, 31.

† From *Edmund Spenser* (Plymouth, UK: Northcote House, 1996, pp. 12–19). © Colin Burrow. Reprinted by permission of Northcote House Publishers Ltd, Tavistock, Devon, UK.

was first translated from French in 1503. This was a rustic almanac cum medicine cabinet cum prayerbook of Catholic leanings, which was reprinted so frequently that copies of it must have sat next to Bibles in houses and hovels throughout the land. Woodcuts ensured that its appeal would not be limited to the literate. Spenser's volume is designed to have the popular appeal of its model. Each of his eclogues is accompanied by a woodcut, some of which might remind the illiterate of a popular book, others of which might recall schoolroom editions of Virgil. The black letter type in which the poems are set would have looked decidedly old fashioned in 1579. A potential buyer, flipping through a copy, would find recurrent references to Colin Clout, who was a satirical and popular persona adopted by the early sixteenth-century poet John Skelton. The physical form of the book is nourished by the early stages of the English Reformation, and the whole work is designed to seem embedded in the popular energies of the nation. The volume is, however, also designed to exhibit the grandeur of a scholarly edition of a classical text. Each eclogue is preceded by an 'argument', or summary, and is followed by a learned, sometimes comically learned, set of notes by 'EK'. A would-be purchaser browsing over the stalls of Hugh Singleton, its printer, in 1579 would have been puzzled and excited by *The Shepheardes Calender*: here was a book which was modelled on the humblest kind of semi-literate chapbook, but which looked completely new in the grandeur with which it presented the work of an anonymous vernacular poet. It was an edgy work, one which straddled the boundaries between élite and popular forms of publication.[1]

The Shepheardes Calender also has the faint flavour of political opposition which so often emanates from Spenser's works. Its publisher was Hugh Singleton, who, five months before, had nearly had one of his hands chopped off for publishing *The Discoverie of a Gaping Gulf* . . . by the militant puritan John Stubbes. *The Gaping Gulf* was an attack on the Queen's flirtation with the Catholic Duc d'Alençon, which, had it developed into a marriage, might have returned the English Church to Roman Catholicism. Spenser's 'November' eclogue, with its lament for an unidentified princess called Dido (whose identity, EK nervously protests, 'is unknowen and closely buried in the Authors conceipt' (p.196)) has been seen as a representation of the nation's mourning for a queen who was in danger of dying to the faith (in Virgil's *Aeneid* Dido is also called 'Elissa'—not quite, but almost, Eliza). *The Shepheardes Calender* also repeatedly praises a shepherd called Algrind, whose purity is presented as a model for all pastors. Algrind is a transparent representation of Archbishop Grindal, who had been suspended from his duties as Archbishop of Canterbury in 1577 for his refusal to suppress lay preaching in his diocese. He had also written to the Queen protesting that royal influence on the Church and on lay piety had its limits. Grindal, was a model for all those who wished that the Queen's conservative ecclesiastical policies would soften; and this popular religious hero, at odds with the will of the court, is the hero of the *Calender*'s ecclesiastical eclogues. For all its scent of opposition, and perhaps partly because of it, *The Shepheardes Calender* was the most popular of Spenser's works. It went through five editions in

1. George Puttenham, *The Arte of English Poesie*, ed. G. Willcock and A. Walker (Cambridge, 1936), 21.

his lifetime, and rapidly inspired admiring and, occasionally, envious comment. It was *the* literary event of the 1570s.

The excitement is hard to recapture now. *The Shepheardes Calender* is partly designed to signal the emergence of a new poet, who, like Virgil before him, uses the sophisticatedly humble form of pastoral to initiate his career. The *Calender* contains many pre-echoes of Spenser's later style. Cuddie in 'September' promises to sing of 'fierce warres', as Spenser himself was to promise in the proem to *The Faerie Queene* that 'Fierce warres and faithful loues will moralize my song'. Hobbinol in 'June' recalls a song 'Whose Echo made the neyghbour groves to ring' (1.52), and which joyously pre-echoes the varied chorus of Spenser's own *Epithalamion*, 'The woods shall to me answer and my Eccho ring'. But the bulk of *The Shepheardes Calender* is humbler fare, which, rather than pointing to the future, now has the musty flavour of second-hand bookshops. A modern reader will encounter shepherdly archaisms and dialect words throughout the volume. Sometimes, as in the start of 'Aprill', one is plunged straight into Middle English: 'what garres thee greete?', asks Thenot, and EK's gloss is as necessary now as it was to his first readers: what 'causeth thee weepe and complain'. Why write a poem which needed glossing even on its first publication? Spenser was partly imitating the theories of the French poet Du Bellay, whose *Défense et illustration de la langue Française* (1549) argues that the vernacular should be augmented by antique tongues and new coinages. Spenser was, that is, *innovating* by using old words. And many of the words which appear to be antiquated in *The Shepheardes Calender* are in fact words which Spenser introduced into the printed, literate language of his day. The *Oxford English Dictionary* attributes to Spenser the first usages of 'bellibone' (beautiful lady), 'wimble' (thought to be a northern dialect word for 'nimble'), and 'swink' (to work). Spenser can make powerful poetic use of the faintly antiqued resonances of these words. He writes in 'July' of hay which is 'frowie' ('musty'). A word which is itself mustily agricultural is used with brilliant precision to describe old hay. The word is not actually an archaism, but a word which Spenser brought into the language: like hay, its apparent oldness is potentially living and new. There are some howlers in Spenser's antiquey language: he invents the false archaic noun 'derring-do' (heroic deeds) from the Chaucerian verb 'derring-don' ('daring to do'); he also mistakenly thought that Chaucer's phrase 'The tigre yond in Inde' ('the tiger a long way away in India') meant 'the fierce tiger in India', and so can use 'yond' to mean 'ferocious'. These examples give some substance to Ben Jonson's accusation that 'Spenser, in Affecting the ancients, writ no Language';[2] but the overwhelming impact of *The Shepheardes Calender* is of amazing verbal innovation, in which even mistakes renovate the language, and extend its official sphere into new ranges of dialect. As EK's introduction says, the *Calender* is a work of renewal: 'he hath laboured to restore, as to theyr rightfull heritage such good and naturall English words, as have been long time out of use and almost cleare disherited'. Richard Mulcaster, Spenser's schoolmaster, had used a similarly political vocabulary when he described the expansion of English by the 'enfranchisement' of foreign

2. Ben Jonson, *Works*, ed. C. H. Herford and P. and E. Simpson (11 vols; Oxford: Oxford University Press, 1925–1953), VIII, p. 618.

words.[3] EK's suggestion that Spenser's language marks a liberation for native English words is worth taking seriously. A decade after the publication of *The Shepheardes Calender*, George Puttenham's *Arte of English Poesie* sought to close down the social inclusiveness of the *Calender's* vocabulary by insisting that would-be poets 'shall therefore take the usuall speach of the Court, and that of London and the shires lying about London within lx miles and not much above'.[4] The *Calender* has no such exclusivity: this, work by a successful poor scholar welcomes northern and Kentish forms into the language.

The most obvious thing to say about *The Shepheardes Calender* is that it is a calendar. It encompasses the whole year, from the deep-frozen buds of January, through the fitful warmth of March, the showers and flowers of April, into summer, and out into a withering September, a deadly November, and chill December. At every stage of the process the collection is aware that each stage *is* only a stage in a process. A welter of internal correspondences and recurrent images glance through the volume: tears are like frozen icicles in 'Januarye', by 'Aprill' they fall, promising fertility, into furrows. In 'June' they flow like overabundant sap from the leaves of trees; in 'November' they drop in unrelieved mourning, and finally in 'December' they dewily preserve the withered flowers of Colin Clout. 'Buds' are wasted with wailing in 'Januarye', are 'bloosming' (both blossoming and blooming) in 'Maye', and have turned into 'buddes of Poetrie', freeze-dried vitality, by 'October'. These running images invite a reader to recall, and to flip back to, earlier occurrences of them in order to build up an extended, seasonally adjusted, view of the year and its variety. A bud is both a frightened thing, securely enclosing itself against winter frosts, and a thrusting sign of spring. A tear can be icily isolating, or it can mark a sociable and reviving sorrow for another person. *The Shepheardes Calender*, that is, uses its extended structure to build deep patterns of association, aimed to persuade that sorrow and joy, cold and life, are not antitheses but aspects of a continuing process. The governing rhetorical trope of the volume is oxymoron, a phrase which apparently contradicts itself. *The Shepheardes Calender* offers vital images of death, moments of chill which promise warmth—and presents itself as offering new oldness. There is no better evocation in English of what it feels like to live through a year, and to half-remember in January that dry twigs will eventually burgeon.

The *Calender* aims to create a coincidence of opposing moods. Its speakers are often grouped in opposing pairs, and seldom agree with each other. In 'August', for instance, Perigot has a singing-contest with Willye; while Perigot sings of his wounding by love's arrow, Willye answers him in incongruously jolly vein: 'There it rankleth more and more', laments Perigot, 'Hey ho the arrowe', chirrups Willye in reply. Moods interlace with one another, as the chilly old Thenot counters the youthful Cuddie in 'Februarie', but they never entirely overlap. The *Calender* is multiperspectived art: what seems vital and optimistic in one character is at the same moment a source of melancholy for another. In 'Maye' Piers tells the Aesopian fable of a kid who is devoured by a wolf. The kid has a thrusting energy which suits the energy of the month:

3. Richard Mulcaster, *The First Part of the Elementarie* (London, 1582), 80.
4. Puttenham, *Arte*, 145.

> His Vellet head began to shoote out,
> And his wreathed hornes gan newly sprout,
> The blossomes of lust to bud did beginne,
> And spring forth ranckly under his chinne.
> (ll. 185–8)

The verbs 'shoote', 'sprout', 'bud', and 'spring' link the life of the lamb with the vegetative energies of May. But for the kid's mother, signs of life prompt memories of sadness.

> A thrilling throbbe from her hart did aryse,
> And interrupted all her other speache,
> With some old sorowe, that made a newe breache:
> Seemed shee sawe in the younglings face
> The old lineaments of his fathers grace.
> (ll. 208–12)

'Thrilling' is one of Spenser's favourite words. He often uses it to evoke a sudden pang of emotion, the violent irruption of an unexpected voice into silence, or the sudden stab of Cupid's arrow. Here it catches the sharp anguish of being reminded of an old sorrow by something new and fresh. Newness and life are celebrated in the *Calender*, but are tied in with sadness: rebirth of a new generation depends upon the death of the old. William Ponsonby, the printer of *Complaints*, reports that Spenser paraphrased Ecclesiastes. Whether or not he did so, the mingling of life and death, and the dependency of the one on the other, which Ecclesiastes so mournfully explores, is the founding principle of much of Spenser's most painfully fresh writing. EK's Epistle notes that *The Shepheardes Calender* applies 'an olde name to a new worke'. That line 'With some old sorowe, that made a newe breache' could stand as an epigraph for the whole: old pain makes new wounds; the new painfully recalls the old.

The central figure in *The Shepheardes Calender* is the poet Colin Clout, whom Spenser adopted as his own persona throughout his literary career. He is not a successful shepherd: when we meet him in 'Januarye' his sheep are starving, and he is bewailing the hardheartedness of his mistress Rosalind. When we leave him in 'December' he is on the brink of death. His poems include only one moment of joyous control, and only one moment when poet and court seem to be identified, when he sings of Eliza, Queene of Shepheardes, in 'Aprill':

> See, where she sits upon the grassie greene,
> (O seemely sight)
> Yclad in Scarlot like a mayden Queene
> And Ermines white.
> Upon her head a Cremosin coronet,
> With Damaske roses and Dafadillies set.
> (ll. 55–60)

At this moment Colin seems almost himself to be making the Queen, directing our gaze towards her, and shaping her garments to reflect the image of her which he wishes to convey. It is the first of many Spenserian moments of framed vision (which abound in *The Faerie Queene*), when the poet fashions a pageant with a woman at its centre. But this moment of poetic centrality is evanescent: Colin is not present in 'Aprill' to sing his poem (his friend Hobbinol sings it for him), since he has devoted his life to the solitary business of bewailing his unsuccessful love; His role as a court poet is placed in the past. He has become a poet whose idiom is lament, who listens to the melancholy echoes of his own voice from the woods and rocks through which he wanders. He complains in 'June', sings a plaintive sestina (a stanzaic poem in which each of the six rhyming words is repeated at the end of a different line in each stanza) in 'August', and returns in 'November' to bemoan the death of Dido. In 'December' he describes how his life dwindles towards a wintry isolation, cut off from the court, and insulated from the sources of life. Moralizing critics have been hard on Colin, and have argued that he is a representative of a self-obsessed, inward-looking poetry which was anathema to Spenser. But throughout his career Spenser pressed for a virtual equivalence between the sources of poetry and a sense of loss. Indeed perhaps the chief goal of his shorter works is to create a poetic which attaches significance to poets who lack either patronage or an active role in court. The argument to 'October' states that 'In Cuddie is set out the perfecte paterne of a Poete, which finding no maintenaunce of his state and studies, complayneth of the comtempte of Poetrie, and the causes thereof'. Cuddie himself is obsessed by the loss of past patrons ('But ah *Mecœnas* is yclad in claye, | And great *Augustus* long ygoe is dead' (ll. 61–2)) in a way that suggests he is not quite 'the perfecte paterne of a Poete'. But he does share a sense of loss with the *Calender*'s plaintive central persona, Colin Clout. Colin Clout's melancholy, however, is seldom without a consoling power. His laments, like the whole *Calender*, mingle a sense of loss with joyful renewal. When Colin laments the death of the ideal English poet, Chaucer, his plaintful elegy is aware that the death of a predecessor can generate life for the poets who follow him:

> Nowe dead he is, and lyeth wrapt in lead,
> (O why should death on hym such outrage showe?)
> And all hys passing skil with him is fledde,
> The fame whereof doth dayly greater growe.
> But if on me some little drops would flowe,
> Of that the spring was in his learned hedde,
> I soone would learne these woods, to wayle my woe,
> And teache the trees their trickling teares to shedde.
> ('June', ll. 89–96)

At first this seems simply glum. But the whole stanza has just the paradoxical combination of gloom and vitality which runs through *The Sheepheardes Calender* as a whole. Chaucer's fame still grows, along with the vegetative life of June, and his liquid influence (springs in the *Calender* are as life-giving as the season with which they share their name) nourishes Colin's mournful song. Learning from the dead how to lament the dead is how poetry continues to grow. *The Shepheardes Calender* is often seen as a work which straddles the boundary between 'medieval' and 'Renaissance'. Its interest in the power and immortality of verse, and its determined construction of a powerful persona for Colin Clout, have been seen as its most distinctively 'Renaissance' aspects, since, it is often thought, the key element in Renaissance attitudes to poetry is a sense of the power and dignity of the poet. Precedent for all these things can be found in Chaucer and his successors, however.[5] Rather, what makes the collection distinctively the work of a Renaissance poet is the feature which seems at first to be its most medieval element: its conscious oldness, and its conscious identification of the power of a modern poet with his capacity to complain about the loss of the past. *The Shepheardes Calender* makes its readers aware that there is a space between the present and a literary past, and that a poet is growing anew from his efforts to bridge that gap. The word 'Renaissance', of course, is not used in English before the nineteenth century, and certainly would not have been used by Spenser himself. But it is an appropriate term to describe the period between Petrarch and Milton, since poetry in that period is preoccupied with a desire to revive dead classical learning. This desire permeates the literary criticism of the period, which frequently uses metaphors of disinterring, of raising the dead to life, and of biological reproduction to describe how new poets grow from old. *The Shepheardes Calender* is a deliberate attempt to mark a poetic rebirth in England; but that rebirth comes, oddly, from the death of the old. Death and life feed each other reciprocally.

* * *

LYNN STALEY

[Februarie]†

Spenser's Moral Eclogues

The Moral eclogues comprise an elaborate dialogue upon the nature of social bodies. Both formally and thematically, they function as a unit, emerging from two contexts, one literary, the other historical. Like many contemporary tracts, speeches, and sermons, the five eclogues chide the age, suggesting that it is dominated by commerce, that a corrupt notion of trade underpins human institutions and relationships.[1] The eclogues

5. See A. C. Spearing, *Medieval to Renaissance in English Poetry* (Cambridge UK, 1985).

† From *The Shepheardes Calender: An Introduction* (University Park: Pennsylvania State University Press, 1990), pp. 62–71. Notes have been edited. Copyright © 1991 by The Pennsylvania State University Press. Reprinted by permission of The Pennsylvania State University Press.

1. For official comments upon the tensions of the age, see *All Such Proclamations, as were Published During the Reign of Elizabeth.* For sermons that convey the uneasiness that seemed to characterize the seventies, see William James, "A Sermon Preached Before the Queenes Maiestie at Hampton Court the 19. of February laste paste" (London: 1578). The text for this sermon was Ezra 4, and James expanded upon the need to rebuild the Temple, an act that he linked to the sovereign's will and to the obedience of the citizenry. See also John Knewstubb, "A Sermon preached at Paules Crosse the Fryday before Easter . . . in the yeere of our lorde, 1579" (London, 1579). Knewstubb urged contentment, exhorting his hearer to find ease in the estate in which God had placed him. John Stockwood's "A Sermon Preached at Paules Crosse on Bartholomew Day, being the 24. of August, 1578" (London, 1578) is 174 pages long and decidedly lugubrious. It is a warning to England, a call to repentance, and a mild effort to nudge Elizabeth towards a more active Protestant stand. In "A Sermon No lesse fruitfull then famous. Made in the yeare . . . 1388. And founde out hyd in a wall" (London, 1579), R. Wimbleton bases his remarks on the Parable of the Vineyard and urges his hearer to "see to what state God hath called hym." He then goes on to emphasize the theme of judgment. John Young's "A Sermon preached before the Queenes Maiestie, the second of March. 1575" (London, 1576?) is possibly a contemporary source for both *Mother Hubberds Tale* and the fable of the Oak and the Briar. Young focused upon the evils of ambition as detrimental to the commonweal. He ended by asking God for humility with no immoderate desires for Englishmen. [See also the appendix to Louis Thorn Golding, *An Elizabethan Puritan: Arthur Golding* (New York: R. R. Smith, 1937).]

therefore treat the traditional subjects of moral literature—conflict between the generations; the need for clerical discretion, purity, and poverty; and the poetic vocation—by drawing upon the metaphors of a mercantilist society. As some of the speakers insist and the five eclogues imply, only when the citizens of this pastoral world transfer their allegiance from earthly to spiritual profits can they begin to realize the harmony of the Golden Age. Spenser's literary guides in these eclogues, which could be described as an extended and particularly graceful bow to his literary heritage, are the revered authorities of moral literature—Mantuan, Aesop, Barclay, and, most importantly, Chaucer.[2] As Chaucer borrowed from the authorities of his literary age, so Spenser recast Chaucerian debates, problems and situations, creating pieces that, in the truest sense, are Chaucerian. Like *The Canterbury Tales*, the Moral eclogues are meant to capture English voices, presenting us with figures who are both timely and timeless, figures whose very problems identify them as Elizabethans, but in whose voices echo the language and the rhetorical stances found in works like *Reynard the Fox*, Aesop's *Fables*, the eclogues of Barclay and Mantuan, and *The Canterbury Tales*.

"Februarie," the first of the Moral eclogues, provides us with important clues to Spenser's perspective upon the body politic and his attitude toward the conventions and possibilities of moral literature.[3] The eclogue is a deceptively simple altercation between two shepherds, Thenot and Cuddie, upon the traditional subject of youth and age. In response to Cuddie's complaint over the raw winter weather, Thenot counsels stability—or equanimity—in the face of Fortune, going on to warn the young and sexually active Cuddie that he, too, will find himself old someday. Under the guise of offering Cuddie some of his hard-won wisdom, Thenot recounts the fable of the Oak and the Briar, a fable that he mistakenly attributes to Chaucer. Thus, in the eclogue, Spenser not only presents a debate, but encloses a tale within the eclogue itself. Like Chaucer's pilgrims, who exist within one fiction and go on to create secondary fictions, Thenot and Cuddie reveal their lack of sympathy for one another in their diverging perspectives upon the fable Thenot tells. They are the first in a series of paired shepherds who can have no sympathy for one another because they do not understand one another. Throughout the Moral eclogues Spenser suggests that the language that should be a common medium of exchange is not even legal tender in the *Calender*'s pastoral world: like those dwelling in the suburbs of Babel, Spenser's shepherds do not use and understand language in the same way. Within the frame of the *Calender*, words that should be symbols of higher values and that find their highest form in poetry are useless. Spenser prepares us for a world whose broken chain of

2. Harvey's correspondence suggests his interest in Chaucerian imitation. Thus, in a series of letters to John Young that inform Young about Harvey's troubles at Pembroke, Harvey adopted a Chaucerian tone, employed a number of homely similes and tags, and evoked Chaucer by dropping the name Jynkin (a name immortalized by the Wife of Bath). He specifically alluded to the *Miller's Tale* in lines like "But by youre leave a litle her must first goe pisse" and "Tho arte so queynte felt" or tags like "piggesnye" ["*Letter-book of Gabriel Harvey*, ed. Edward J. L. Scott for the Camden Society n.s. 33 (1884), 90]. Though Harvey's efforts are heavy-handed attempts to echo one of the most innocent bawdy tales in English literature, they nonetheless suggest his (possibly Spenser's) interest in Chaucer's verbal dexterity and Chaucerian turns of phrase.
3. For discussions of "Februarie," see Ronald B. Bond, "Supplantation in the Elizabethan Court: The Theme of Spenser's February Eclogue," *Spenser Studies* 2 (1981), 55–66; Patrick Cullen, *Spenser, Marvell, and Renaissance Pastoral* (Cambridge MA: Harvard University Press, 1970); and Montrose 1979.

commerce signals its disorder by his account in the first of the Moral eclogues of the conflict between Cuddie and Thenot, a conflict that is heightened, rather than resolved, by the tale Thenot tells.

Like Chaucer's Reeve and Miller, Thenot and Cuddie enjoy a relationship characterized by envy and scorn.[4] The Miller, a relatively uncomplex character though a brilliant storyteller, gives the Reeve, a carpenter by trade, occasion for malice by telling a tale about old carpenter John who, despite his care for his young wife, is nonetheless hoodwinked by a young student living in his home. While the *Miller's Tale* cuts many ways and, in fact, says more about Robin the Miller than John the Carpenter, Oswald the Reeve takes the tale personally as a slap at his declining sexual prowess. What therefore ensues is a good deal more complex than the Miller's tale of cuckoldry, for Oswald "requites" Robin, opening his own tale by stressing his continuing sexual vigor and by feigning a sagacity and a forebearance that he uses as a cover for malice. He goes on to recount a tale of a miller who loses both his wife and daughter to the lechery of students. More importantly, he paints a picture of the Miller that is a grotesque and judgmental version of Chaucer's own portrait of Robin in the General Prologue and, while purporting to offer wisdom to Robin, instead offers only the harsh justice of the law. Oswald's spitefulness is far more serious than Robin's annoying but relatively harmless dig. The one is merely instinctive and provocative, the other premeditated and well-aimed. Where Robin is hot, Oswald is cool; where Robin is drunk, Oswald is sober; where Robin is boisterous, Oswald is malicious.

A similar dynamic underpins Spenser's characterization of Cuddie and Thenot. Cuddie opens the contest by complaining about winter: he feels himself too young and lusty to have to endure "rancke winters rage." Thenot replies to what is Cuddie's private quarrel with winter, using language that signals the outbreak of hostilities, "Lewdly complainest thou laesie ladde." The line's alliteration and pattern of stress force our attention to *lewdly, laesie*, and *ladde*, none of them terms designed to promote rational discourse. Thenot goes on to take cover behind sagacity, discussing the rotations of Fortune and the weather in more general terms, but what we in fact hear is Oswald the Reeve's equally hypocritical balm applied to the unquiet brow of Robin the Miller. Thus the Reeve's initial reaction to the Miller's tale and the Miller's sexual exuberance suggests his intention of using his age as a screen for his anger:

> "So theek," quod he, "ful wel koude I thee quite
> With bleryng of a proud milleres ye,
> If that me liste speke of ribaudye.
> But ik am oold, me list not pley for age;
> Gras tyme is doon, my fodder is now forage;[5]
> (I, 3864–68)

4. Harry Berger also links Chaucer's Reeve to Spenser's image of age; see his "The Aging Boy: Paradise and Parricide in Spenser's *Shepheardes Calender*," in *Poetic Traditions of the English Renaissance* ed. Maynard Mack and George deForest Lord (New Haven: Yale University Press, 1982), pp. 25–46. On the relationship between the Miller and the Reeve see Paul A Olson, "The Reeve's Tale: Chaucer's Measure for Measure." *Studies in Philology* 59 (1962): 1–17.

5. *The Riverside Chaucer*, ed. Larry Dean Benson (Oxford: Oxford University Press, 1988). All references to the works of Chaucer refer to this edition and will be designated in the text by line number.

Oswald here admits his age, linking age with sagacity and forebearance. But in the remainder of his speech, he dwells on the issue of sexual vigor, denying that age has had any effect on his abilities. He in fact offers us an emblem for old age in the leek, a vegetable with a "hoor head and a grene tayl" that suggests folly and weakness rather than wisdom and strength. Thenot's remarks to Cuddie follow much the same pattern, for, though he purports to offer counsel, his comments reveal his envy of Cuddie's youth and sexual prowess.

In Thenot's two opening speeches, of about fifty lines total, Spenser demonstrates the deleterious effects of envy upon social relations, for Thenot very swiftly moves Cuddie from his initial, and desultory, dissatisfaction with the cold weather to wrath, Thenot begins by saying that when he was young he, unlike Cuddie, never complained about the weather. This opening speech is especially interesting, for it provides us with the outlines of Thenot's characteristic rhetorical habits in the eclogue. Thenot's speech falls into two parts, the first containing general remarks about fortune, the second focusing our attention on his own prudence. Thus his first query, "Must not the world wend in his commun course / From good to badd, and from badde to worse" ("Februarie," ll. 11–12), serves as a preamble to

> Selfe haue I worne out thrise threttie yeares,
> Some in much ioy, many in many teares:
> Yet neuer complained of cold nor heate,
> Of Sommers flame, nor of Winters threat:
> Ne euer was to Fortune foeman,
> But gently tooke, that vngently came.
> ("Februarie," ll. 17–22)

As laudable as this advice may be when taken out of context, it is advice that nonetheless should be seen as coming from a spokesman whose opening remarks to Cuddie suggest not charity but scorn. Furthermore, the ensuing conversation reveals Thenot as less than objective about his "thrise threttie yeares," making it hard for us to believe in his portrait of his own youthful equilibrium. His remarks become more pointed in his second speech to Cuddie, for he describes Cuddie and his fellows as "little heardgroomes" and "fond flyes," filled with "careless corage" and "surquedrie," who keep their beasts in the "budded broomes" and spend time "crowing in pypes made of greene corne." The language he uses to describe the youthful sexual vigor of Cuddie and his friends has the effect, not of undercutting Cuddie, but of turning our attention to the depths of his own envy for the younger shepherds. Thenot reaps what he sows when Cuddie responds in kind, pointing out that Phyllis, whom Cuddie "wonne" with a "gyrdle of gelt," is the Abushag Thenot needs in his dry old age. From there on, the debate disintegrates into name-calling until Thenot offers to tell one of Chaucer's tales. If Phyllis is Cuddie's remedy for Thenot's age, then the tale should be seen as Thenot's remedy for Cuddie's youth. However, like the *Reeve's Tale*, Thenot's is merely a tale of revenge masquerading as one of wisdom and balance.

When we approach Thenot's tale of the Oak and the Briar, which is usually viewed as embodying the moral lessons of the eclogue as a whole, we need to recall the lessons in sleight-of-hand *The Canterbury Tales* might have offered to the young Spenser. The *Tales* demand a reader who is alive to the various perspectives Chaucer creates within the frame of his Canterbury pilgrimage. We need to know which pilgrim is telling a tale, and seek to understand why he tells it and what he thinks it means. We must then consider what the teller reveals about himself, judging whether or not he is in control of his own fiction and if he understands the implications of his own tale. Spenser seems to be aware of Chaucer's mastery of narrative perspective, for those same issues are central to the underlying purpose of the fable of the Oak and the Briar. Through the tale, Thenot purports to counsel Cuddie's heedlessness and scorn; however, he uses it to disguise his real purpose, which is revenge.

Although Thenot loudly proclaims his good intentions, his introductory description of youth suggests that he is less concerned with the idea of mercy than with the realities of justice:

> *Cuddie*, I wote thou kenst little good,
> So vainely t'aduaunce thy headlesse hood.
> For Youngth is a bubble blown vp with breath,
> Whose witt is weakenesse, whose wage is death,
> Whose way is wildernesse, whose ynne Penaunce,
> And stoopegallaunt Age the hoste of Greeuance.
> ("Februarie," ll. 85–90).

The fact that Cuddie will eventually get what he deserves—becoming old and withered himself someday—obviously charms Thenot. His desire for strict justice informs the fable, for Thenot tells a tale where age turns out to be right about the world and is even belatedly valued for its usefulness. Ironically, however, his wishful tale of the quarrel between an Oak and a Briar simply reveals the depth of his own frustration with change and fortune.[6]

Thenot characterizes the Oak and the Briar in terms of age, humility, and forebearance and youth, pride, and spite; as a storyteller, Thenot tells more than he knows. From the eclogue itself we know few facts about Cuddie: he is young, dislikes bad weather—or is unwilling to endure its adversities—glories in his sexual vigor, and, like Aesop's grasshopper, seems unaware that his green youth will decline to Thenot's withered age. As such, his high spirits and lack of foresight certainly contribute to one of the *Calender's* central lessons, which Colin's declen-

6. The motif of the tree and the briar or the tree and the vine was used in several ways: as an illustration of the interdependence of tree and vine, as a portrait of the decay (frequently "Romish") of the old tree, or as a depiction of the evils of ambition. Spenser's use of this motif is his own: it reveals his ability to recast and thereby transform those traditional elements that made up his literary heritage in ways that served the needs of a poetic designed both to transmit and transmute the past. For positive uses of this motif, see Geffrey Whitney, *A Choice of Emblemes* (1586) p. 62 and Henry Peacham, *Minerva Britanna* (1612), p. 39. *The Dialoges of Creatures Moralysed* (1530) by Pergaminus Nicolaus] depicts a number of pairs whose apparent conflict is used to demonstrate the necessity for concord. For negative or hortatory uses of the emblem, see Whitney's *Choice*, p. 34; a 1575 letter of disputed authorship describing the entertainment for Elizabeth at Kenilworth Castle (Robert Langham, *A Letter*, ed. R. J. P. Kuin, Leiden: Brill, 1983); and John Young's 1575 "Sermon Preached Before the Queens Majestie". (On the relationship between Young's sermon and "Februarie," see [Brents Stirling, "Spenser and Thomas Watson, Bishop of Lincoln," *Philological Quarterly* 10 (1931), 321–28. On the other hand, Roger Ascham in *The Scholemaster* (1570, p. 56) linked the Oak to Marian decay (see Sidney Rosenzweig, "Ascham's Scholemaster and Spenser's February Eclogue," *Shakespeare Association Bulletin* 15 (1940), 103–109.]).

sion from potential to waste, from January to December, illustrates all too forcefully. Though Cuddie appears foolishly vulnerable to the threat of time, he hardly deserves the transformation he undergoes at the hands of Thenot. Thenot's briar is not only foolhardy, it is bragging (l. 115), proud (ll.116, 160, 223, 228), foolish (l. 127), spiteful (l. 148), determined to stir up strife (l. 150), crafty (l. 162), ambitious, and slanderous. Only one of Thenot's observations seems to fit, for he links the Briar's boastfulness with what, in effect, is its sexuality:

> Yt was embellisht with blossomes fayre,
> And thereto aye wonned to repayre
> The shepheards daughters, to gather flowres,
> To peinct their girlonds with his colowres.
> And in his small bushes vsed to shrowde
> The sweete Nightingale singing so lowde
> ("Februarie," ll. 118–23)

The blossoms, the songs of the nightingale, the garlands—all suggest sexual exuberance. Foolish and boastful Cuddie may be, but we only have Thenot's word that he is spiteful, contentious, crafty, and ambitious. These are serious accusations, and would seem to demand more than the sort of nonevidence Thenot offers.[7]

Thenot's description of the Oak reveals even more about how he sees himself. He describes the Oak as goodly (l.102), strongly built (l.105), once fruitful, and rooted in the practices of the past. Thenot, however, seems not to realize that in describing the Oak he describes his own blindness and incapacity. First, he portrays the Oak as silent in the face of the Briar's spiteful verbosity, a silence that the fable itself exposes as a fanciful bit of self-fashioning. Although Thenot describes the Oak's forebearance as a means of pointing up the Briar's mean lineage ("Little him answered the Oake againe, / But yielded, with shame and greefe adawed, / That of a weede he was ouerawed" ["Februarie," ll. 140–42]), he in fact reveals more about his own illusions about himself. Furthermore, despite his eagerness to expose Cuddie in his characterization of the Briar, Thenot inadvertently reveals his own insecurities by going on to praise the Oak's former service to the ungrateful Husbandman:

> For it had bene an auncient tree,
> Sacred with many a mysteree,
> And often crost with the priestes crewe,
> And often halowed with holy water dewe.
> ("Februarie," ll. 207–10)

In this one detail, a detail, by the way, that does not appear in other contemporary versions of this fable, Thenot gives himself away, undercutting his entire argument. The suggestion that the Oak had once been sacred to the rites of England's old religion seems designed to evoke Lucan's description of Pompey in the *Pharsalia*: "The mere shadow of a mighty name he stood. Thus an oak-tree laden with the ancient trophies of a nation and the consecrated gifts of conquerors, towers in a fruitful field; but the roots it clings by have lost their toughness, and it stands by

7. See Bond [, "Supplanation."].

its weight alone, throwing out bare boughs into the sky and making a shade not with leaves but with its trunk."[8] This passage is central to Lucan's characterization of Pompey as a figure from the past whose worth cannot be translated into the present; for Lucan contrasts Pompey's age and position to Caesar's energy and ambition. If Pompey is the ancient oak, Caesar is the bolt of lightning that will inevitably fell the old and unsound tree. DuBellay adapted Lucan's conceit, applying it to the idea of Rome in Sonnet 28 of his important *Antiquitez de Rome*, the sequence of sonnets that Spenser translated as *The Ruines of Rome* and published in *The Complaints* in 1591. Since Spenser probably made this translation fairly early in his career, perhaps as an undergraduate, it is likely that Lucan's description of the Oak served as the subtext for Thenot's description of himself as a wasted but venerable oak.[9]

Thenot, however, misses the point of Lucan's conceit or DuBellay's sonnet. By ignoring the underlying message of decay and illusory strength and honor that the emblem conveys, Thenot glories in the description of himself as an oak, heightening our sense of the glories of the past and thus of the pathos of the oak's present condition:

> But now the gray mosse marred his rine,
> His bared boughes were beaten with stormes,
> His toppe was bald, and wasted with wormes,
> His honor decayed, his braunches sere.
> ("Februarie," ll. 111–14)

Thenot omits any hints of the Oak's responsibility for his advanced state of decay, hints that inform both Lucan's and DuBellay's handling of the Oak as a figure for diseased honor. Later, after describing the Oak as sacred to the old religion, Thenot admits that "sike fancies weren foolerie, / And brougthen this Oake to this miserye" ("Februarie," ll. 211–12). However, he shies away from any moral that might apply to his own condition, instead turning our attention to the Briar and its likely and deserved end. In his eagerness to malign Cuddie for his youth, energy, and impatience, Thenot inadvertently undermines his own position as a figure of wisdom and authority. Not only does Thenot's description of the Oak suggest the depths of his own self-delusion, but his fable reveals him as the spiteful, contentious, slanderous, and vengeful member of the debate.

He pretends to speak for Cuddie's own good, but in fact he tells a tale whose strict justice leaves little room for either amendment or appease-

8. Lucan, *The Civil War*, ed. and trans. J. D. Duff (Cambridge MA: Harvard University Press, 1969), I:135–43.

9. See [Thomas M. Greene, *The Light in Troy: Imitation and Discovery in Renaissance Poetry* (New Haven: Yale University Press, 1982), p. 225.] On Du Bellay's importance to English poets, see Prescott, *French Poets and the English Renaissance*, 37–75. On the *Antiquitez de Rome*, see [Margaret Ferguson, "'The Afflatus of Ruin,' Meditations on Rome by Du Bellay, Spenser, and Stevens," in *Roman Images*, ed. Annabel Patterson (Baltimore: Johns Hopkins University Press, 1984), pp. 23–50. See also Daniel Russell, "Du Bellay's Emblematic Vision of Rome," *Yale French Studies* 47 (1972), 98–109.] For Spenser's translation of Du Bellay's sonnet, see [*The Works of Edmund Spenser* ed. Greenlaw et al., VIII, pp. 152, 389–90. See also the text of the *Ruines of Rome* in this Norton Critical Edition—*Editors*]. It is possible that Spenser intended his description of the Oak in the fable as his contribution to an elaborate literary dialogue with Du Bellay and Lucan, especially since Du Bellay used the *topos* as a means of exploring the nature of the body politic and the future of France. Spenser's use of the *topos* in the first of the Moral eclogues suggests his awareness of the need to incorporate the past into the present.

ment. The moral he draws is singularly flat: "Such was thend of this Ambitious brere, / For scorning Eld." Cuddie interrupts, breaking Thenot's line after the second foot and leaving us with a tag whose didacticism resonates with all the self-righteous morality that young people generally associate with their peevish elders. Thenot's remedy for Cuddie's youth is suspect; like the Wife of Bath, who recommends old women for young men, Thenot self-servingly advises that the young should give place to the old. Since Thenot is hardly humble himself, the tale turns round on its teller, revealing him to be the divisive character he accuses Cuddie of being. For it is Thenot who speaks for most of the eclogue, and it is Thenot's wagging tongue that slanders Cuddie, praises his own virtues, and stirs up Cuddie to wrath. Moreover, since Thenot implies a vision of the world not unlike that found in the world of the *fabliaux*, where each man "gets his," the justice Thenot anticipates for Cuddie is just as likely to fall on himself, or the ax we see in the woodcut to "Februarie" is just as likely to hack at his own ancient roots. Both the tale he tells and the woodcut to "Februarie" evoke Saint John the Baptist's well-known forecast of doom for a corrupt Jerusalem ("Now also is the axe laid vnto the roots of the trees: therefore euerie tre which bringeth not forthe good frute, shalbe hewen downe and cast into the fyre." [Luke 3:9]). It is a lesson frequently applied to England's perceived weaknesses.[1] Thenot fails to understand the more serious, metaphoric lesson hidden in his own tale: Envy is a worse crime than lust, conscious malice far worse than simple anger. If the tree is known by its fruit, then Thenot should look to his own harvest, figured in the tale he tells, and let Cuddie tend to his own fragile spring bloom.

Spenser's handling of his various sources and analogues for his first Moral eclogue, however, offers us more than a series of narrative ironies. Like *The Canterbury Tales*, which cannot be fixed in topical or political allegory, the "Februarie" eclogue nonetheless offers a fundamental—and fundamentally Chaucerian—social commentary in its figuration of social tension. Rather than suggesting that we side with either member of the debate, the eclogue suggests that we affirm not one of the polarities of their verbal conflict, which reveals the utter lack of sympathy between Thenot and Cuddie, but a good outside the actual world the eclogue portrays. That good is implicit in the fable of the Oak and the Briar, for Spenser, like Chaucer before him, uses the device of the tale-within-a-tale to depict truths upon which all truly lasting social bodies are founded. It is Spenser the tale-maker and not Thenot the tale-teller who emerges as the genuinely moral center of the "Februarie" eclogue.[2]

* * *

1. See, for example, Arthur Golding's "Discourse vpon the Earthquake that hapned throughe this Realme of England . . . the first of Aprill, 1580," in Golding 195.
2. This is one of the problems in reading Thenot's tale as a strict political allegory (see Paul E. McLane, *Spenser's Shepheardes Calender: A Study in Elizabethan Allegory* [Notre Dame: Notre Dame University Press, 1961, repr. 1970], pp. 61–76). First, such a reading inevitably ignores the frame that the conversation between Thenot and Cuddie provides for the fable. Second, it makes no sense to identify Leicester with an oak that Spenser links to the Roman rite. Given the fable's components and the relationship between the fable and the eclogue, it seems more potentially fruitful to investigate Spenser's attitude toward and exploitation of traditional materials.

LAUREN SILBERMAN

Aesopian *Prosopopoia:* Making Faces and Playing Chicken in *Mother Hubberds Tale*†

Mother Hubberds Tale, best known for having caused its author political trouble,[1] has received relatively little critical attention.[2] A notable exception is Annabel Patterson, who places *Mother Hubberds Tale* in the Aesopian tradition of covert political engagement.[3] I should like to extend consideration of *Mother Hubberds Tale* as Aesopian fiction in a way that locates the political engagements of the poem within a very complex Aesopian tradition.[4] In reflecting and reflecting on this tradition, the poem registers political resentments and hostility under the cover of Aesopian deniability: generic beast fable figures can seem to conceal specific human targets while making the conclusive identification of those targets impossible. At the same time, the poem's meta-level examination of its own rhetorical tools is revealed as potentially one more defensive strategy: just as an attack on Burleigh or a critique of Elizabeth can masquerade as a fable about a fox or a lion, so sedition can purport to be discourse *about* sedition. Is Spenser venting his own political grudges in the course of writing *Mother Hubberds Tale*? Is he committing to print sedition against the Crown? One or both possibilities might be true, but the reciprocal reflection of politics and poetics in *Mother Hubberds Tale* makes it impossible to know for sure. At stake, I think, in the elaborate game of hide-and-seek Spenser is staging in his poem is an exploration of the political subject in relation to the multiplicity of cultural and political forces in which that subject is enmeshed.[5] Just as beast fables are ulti-

† Adapted and condensed from an essay on the same title in *SSt* 27 (2012), 221–47. Reprinted by permission of the author and AMS Press.

1. Richard S. Peterson has discovered a contemporary reference to the calling-in of Spenser's *Complaints*. See Richard S. Peterson," Laurel Crown and Ape's Tail: New Light on Spenser's career from Sir Thomas Tresham," *SSt* 12 (1991), 16. See also H. S. V. Jones, *A Spenser Handbook* (New York: Appleton-Century-Crofts, 1930), 74–75; and Harold Stein, *Studies in Spenser's Complaints* (New York: Oxford University Press, 1934), pp. 81–83.
2. In "Still Reading Spenser After All These Years," *ELR* 25 (1995): 432–44, Annabel Patterson aptly characterizes *Mother Hubberds Tale* as "An extremely peculiar poem, which has . . . been assiduously avoided by literary scholars" (436) and then goes on to comment perceptively about the ways in which *Mother Hubberds Tale* presents poetry as a safe-conduct passport for satire. On the esoteric quality of the *Complaints* volume in general, see Katherine A. Craik, "Spenser's 'Complaints' and the New Poet" *HLQ* 64 (2001): 63–79. For a summary of earlier criticism of the poem, see Kenneth John Atchity, "Spenser's *Mother Hubberds Tale*: Three Themes of Order," *PQ* 52 (1973): 161–172.
3. Annabel Patterson, *Fables of Power: Aesopian Writing and Political History* (Durham: Duke University Press, 1991: "Post Contemporary Interventions").
4. For a discussion of how the medieval Renard the Fox material underlies the anti-court satire in the poem, see Edwin Greenlaw, "The Sources of Spenser's 'Mother Hubberds Tale," *MP* 2 (1905): 411–32.
5. In many respects, I am taking the argument by Kent Van den Berg, in "The Counterfeit in Personation: Spenser's Prosopopoia, or Mother Hubberds Tale," *The Author in his Work: Essays on a Problem in Criticism*, ed. Louis Martz and Aubrey Williams (New Haven: Yale University Press, 1978), pp. 85–102, that in "Mother Hubberds Tale," Spenser "sets the poet's power to personify against his disdain for the counterfeit self, and thereby exemplifies his struggle to maintain moral and aesthetic integrity in the face of a fragmented and deceptive world" (86) and suggesting that Spenser is engaging in a much more risk-taking, metamorphic performance. For an illuminating study of how literature of the period can explore political subjecthood in the guise of treating erotic subject matter, see Melissa E. Sanchez, *Erotic Subjects: The Sexuality of Politics in Early Modern English Literature* (New York: Oxford University Press, 2011).

mately about what it means to be human, so *Mother Hubberds Tale* examines what it means to be a political animal.

By framing his Aesopian *prosopopoeia* as "Mother Hubberds tale," Spenser presents the adventures of his talking animals as the oral production of a female speaker. In so doing, Spenser follows the example of Wyatt in his second satire. Like Wyatt, Spenser engages in strategic misdirection with this presentation. In sixteenth-century English culture, Aesop's Fables belonged, not to the feminine realm of fairy tales, but to the male world of Greek and Latin study.[6]

Mother Hubberds Tale reflects Wyatt's opening gambit of assigning an Aesopian fable to a female voice as it as it engages with and contests the satiric subject position Wyatt constructs in both Satire 1 and Satire 2.[7] In Satire 2, Wyatt's initial misdirection in presenting an Aesop Fable as a fairy tale told by "my mother's maids" signals the poet's manipulation of gender position as he claims for himself the role of self-sufficient male observer. Wyatt revises Horace's expansion of the Fable of the Town and Country Mouse.[8] In Satire 2.6, Horace transforms Aesop's straightforward parable of how it is better to live simply in security than to live luxuriously in fear into a complex meditation on point of view and the place of philosophical discussion. Horace presents himself as an urban sophisticate whose country retreat offers a venue for discussing Stoic and Epicurean views of the good life. Wyatt's talking mice are both gendered female, and neither mouse enjoys the security of a simple life on the one hand or the precarious pleasures of luxury on the other. Philosophical reflection is reserved for the first-person male speaker, who draws a Stoic moral significantly divergent from the fable attributed to "my mother's maids" and irrelevant to the vulnerable female mice in the fable. Projecting vulnerability onto the female mice enables the detachment with which Wyatt as speaker comments to his friend John Poins.

Spenser follows Wyatt in assigning a beast fable to a female speaker as he contests the pose of Stoic detachment that Wyatt constructs for himself through gendered voices. In his more overtly biographical satire,

6. *See Aesop's Fables* would likely have been among the first Latin texts studied by a Tudor schoolboy. T. W. Baldwin, *William Shakespere's Small Latine and Lesse Greeke* (Urbana: University of Illinois Press, 1944), Vol. I, 607; Patterson, 52.

7. "Mine Owne John Poynz" and "Of the Mean and Sure Estate, written to John Poins."

8. In Spenser's time, there were multiple collections of fables, printed in England and on the continent attributed to Aesop. The question of what edition or editions Spenser might have consulted is a vexed one, to say the least. For a sense of how difficult it is to determine what, exactly, an Elizabethan poet might have used as a source, see Baldwin, I, 610–16. Very briefly, Tudor schoolboys would use a Greek/Latin collection of prose fables by Aesop and verse fables by Babrius, geared towards the study of grammar, imitation and paraphrase (correspondence, William P. Weaver). An English translation was done by Caxton of (a French translation of) the German version by Steinhowel. In 1585, there was another English version by William Bullokar. For more information on collections of Aesopian fables, see Paul Thoen, "Les grands recueils ésopiques des XVe et XVIe siècles et leur importance pour les littératures des temps modernes," *Acta Conventus Neo-Latini Lovaniensis: Proceedings of the First International Congress of Neo-Latin Studies, Louvain 23–28 August 1971*, eds. J. Ijswijn and E. Kessler (Louvain: Leuven University Press, 1971), pp. 659–79. See also, *Caxton's* Aesop, ed. with introduction and notes R. T. Lenaghan (Cambridge, MA: Harvard University Press, 1967). Also of interest is the extensive introduction to Ben Edwin Perry's edition and translation of *Babrius and Phaedrus* (Cambridge, MA: Harvard University Press, 1965). I shall be citing tale numbers and any English translations from the edition by Laura Gibbs, *Aesop's Fables* (New York: Oxford University Press, 2002), as well as the numbers given in Gibbs's edition from the monumental modern edition by Perry entitled *Aesopica* as well as the other editions cited by Gibbs. A complete listing of the numbers, along with the Greek and Latin texts, may be found at http://www.aesopica.net. In Gibbs, the Fable of the Town and Country Mouse is number 408, and Fable 352 in the modern edition by Perry and Fable 13 in the medieval Ademar of Chabannes.

"Mine Own John Poynz," Wyatt reveals his pose of autonomy as a cultivated response to political subjection as he creates poetically a state of liberty "in Kent and Christendom" while under house arrest on his own estate. In *Mother Hubberds Tale*, Spenser manipulates Aesopian materials in order to destabilize and reconfigure the relationship between the poet-satirist and the world, which is both an object of critique and a source of constraint. Spenser systematically undermines the possibility of inhabiting a position "in Kent and in Christendom" either as poet or as reader. In place of the urbane exchange Wyatt stages between himself and his cultivated auditor, Spenser takes his reader on a political and literary thrill ride.

The descent of Mercury at the conclusion of *Mother Hubberds Tale* seems to balance the flight of Astraea that inaugurates the poem and to restore order and justice to a decadent world. Nevertheless, the apparent closure brought as Mercury rouses the Lion to restore royal justice to the animal kingdom reflects and accentuates the instabilities of the opening by alienating the reader retrospectively from the experience of reading the poem. In a final act of retribution, the Lion punishes the ape with mutilation for the crime of impersonating the king. There is a certain poetic justice that as the Lion claims his rightful identity as king, the Ape becomes the Ape as we know it. Nevertheless, this final transformation manifestly severs readers from the local time of the narrative—a time when Apes had tails and much larger ears. We are estranged from our own experience of reading *Mother Hubberds Tale* when the generic Ape whose adventures we imagine we are following as the narrative goes along is replaced retroactively by the exotic creature with big ears and a tail who only at the very end becomes our own image of the Ape in *Mother Hubberds Tale*.[9] At the same time that the Ape's mutilation produces a disorienting experience of Spenser's poem, it points beyond the poem to remind its readers of actual mutilations carried out in Elizabethan England in the name of public justice.

The flight of Astraea in the first lines of *Mother Hubberds Tale* opens up a poem of metamorphic change in a world of instability.[1] Mother Hubberd begins her tale by establishing a setting that is at once the distant past and the mirror of Elizabethan England.[2] The poem combines the "Mirror of Princes" tradition, in which rulers and authority figures are shown idealized images of themselves to emulate and negative images to avoid, with the specular dynamic of the beast fable, in which human characteristics are projected onto animals and reflected back to the audience, as political and social criticism is subjected to metamorphic instability.

9. A similar shift in which readers must revise significantly their mental picture occurs in Apuleius's *Metamorphoses* (*The Golden Ass*). A character named Thelyphron tells a first-person story that culminates in his realization that his own ears and nose have been stolen by witches and replaced with wax substitutes (2.20–31). The audience within the work, fellow guests at a dinner party, laugh cruelly when Thelyphron describes first discovering his deformity, while the reader of the work learns for the first time that the narrator has a piece of linen glued where his nose once was. See Apuleius, *Metamorphoses*, ed. and trans. J. Arthur Hanson (Cambridge, MA: Harvard University Press, 1989), 98–121.

1. For a reading of the poem that focuses on order and harmony, see Atchity.

2. See *The Yale Edition of the Shorter Poems of Edmund Spenser*, ed. William A. Oram, Einar Bjorvand, Ronald Bond, Thomas H. Cain, Alexander Dunlop, and Richard Schell (New Haven: Yale University Press, 1989), p. 336, note to line 45.

As the Foxe and Ape undergo their transformations, how the talking animals are being represented changes as well.[3] Let me take some modern examples to illustrate the way modes of beast fable can shift. In general, beast fables, ancient or modern, can engage in varying degrees of anthropomorphism, running the gamut from something like Richard Adams' novel *Watership Down*, in which animals speak to one another but otherwise act in ways consistent with what one might observe of actual animals, to something like Kenneth Grahame's *Wind in the Willows*, in which animals wear clothes, take tea, and drive motorcars. In this regard, one might think of a variety of Disney cartoons from *Lady and the Tramp* and *101 Dalmations*, in which dogs converse with other dogs but bark at humans, to *Robin Hood*, in which the familiar folk characters are represented by various talking animals in medieval dress. *The Lion King* veers very far into anthropomorphism, with animals performing elaborate musical numbers. One scene, however, destabilizes the mode of representation prevailing in the rest of the cartoon. The hero's wicked uncle, voiced by Jeremy Irons, torments a mute, naturalistic mouse: the anti-Mickey *mise en abyme*.

As the Foxe and Ape proceed from one adventure to another and from one disguise to another, the way in which they are presented shifts along the continuum from naturalistic to anthropomorphic—from the pole of "mouse" to the pole of "Mickey," if you will. This process of morphing leads up to the politically charged masquerade of the Ape as the monarch, which scrutinizes the doctrine of the monarch's two bodies in the guise of a rewriting of the Aesopian fable of the ass in a lion's skin.[4]

The first disguises assumed by the Foxe and Ape disrupt the prevailing mode of beast fable representation in ways subtler than, but not unlike, the introduction of a naturalistic mouse into the extravagantly anthropomorphic Disney cartoon. The opening exposition of Mother Hubberd's fable presents both protagonists as fully anthropomorphized figures. When the Foxe disguises himself as a dog, however, the rules of representation change: some animals turn out to be more human-like than others. Although the accent on canine appearance seems to move the Foxe's disguise as a *faux* sheepdog away from the pole of anthropomorphism and towards the pole of naturalism, the apparent naturalism of this version of Beast fable representation becomes more problematic when the Foxe displays a wolf-like appetite for sheep and leads the Ape to share in the slaughter. Granted that foxes are carnivores and Spenser may not have been aware that apes are not, Aesopian fables about a wolf playing the role of a sheepdog underlie the fiction at this point and subtly destabilize it, "For that disguised Dog lov'd blood to spill, / And drew the wicked Shepheard to his will" (319–20).[5] Are we seeing a fox or a wolf or a dog in our mind's

3. Stein observes the shift but ascribes it to Spenser's carelessness, 56–62. In "Poets, Poetry and Mercury in Spenser's *Prosopopoia: Mother Hubberds Tale*" *Costerus* 5 (1972): 27–33, Robert Bryan argues more judiciously that a shift from the world of men to the world of animals organizes the poem in a devolutionary pattern. See also van den Berg, 91. I will argue that these transformations are very radical and highly intentional.
4. Gibbs, 322 and 323; Perry 188 and 358. The first, in which the donkey reveals itself when it brays, is found in Chambry's edition of anonymous Greek fables as number 267 (*Aesopi Fabulae*, recensuit Aemilius Chambry. 2 vols. [Paris: Société d'édition "Les Belles lettres," 1925–1926]). The second, in which a wind reveals the disguised donkey, is Aphthonius 10. See also Erasmus *Adages* 1.7.12 and 1.3.66, which cite Lucian's *Fisherman*.
5. Gibbs 38, Chambry 229, Perry 234; Gibbs 36, Chambry 314, Perry 366.

eye? Is the Foxe yielding to his canine nature as he goes after prey that, by the way, outweighs him by a considerable margin, or is he channeling his Aesopian precursor, the wolf?

As the beasts' masquerade modulates from shepherd and sheepdog to Pastor and Parish Clerk in the second of the four major episodes of the poem, the mode of beast fable representation shifts from the naturalistic to the anthropomorphic pole. In this case, the Foxe assumes the role of Priest not because of his physical appearance, but because of his wily nature.

As the Foxe and Ape go through various metamorphoses in the course of their adventures, the individual episodes that constitute those adventures alter the shape of the fables they adapt.[6] Not only do the Foxe and Ape shape-shift along a continuum from Mickey to Mouse, but the nature and extent of the engagement or detachment solicited from the reader shifts as well. By expanding the scope of Aesop's terse fables, Spenser introduces an element of suspense: how long can his rogues maintain their masquerade until they are caught at it?[7] This allows issues of authority to be explored in a context of reader engagement, as our sympathies are divided between the Foxe and Ape, whose rogueries are entertaining, and the forces of order, which are increasingly needful as the pair pursues its depredations.

The final two episodes complicate the pleasures of the text considerably and engage the reader in more problematic fashion as they rework and expand Aesopian fables in complex ways. The talking mule that initiates the third episode recalls Aesop's fable of the Wild and the Domestic Ass, in which the wild ass envies the sleekness of the domestic ass until it observes the domestic ass being beaten by its master. In Aesop's fable, the contrast between wild and domestic expresses a trade-off between freedom and privation, on the one hand, and material comfort and subjection, on the other. Spenser transforms Aesop's straightforward beast fable into a dark allegory of court intrigue as the initially disdainful Mule warms to the invitation to share court gossip.

The Mule's speech intimates secret knowledge. He speaks of "wild beasts" and insinuates a determinate, but hidden, reference to some public figure in Spenser's own world.[8] Contributing to the impression that the Mule's cryptic account incorporates an allegory of contemporary politics is the gender identification of the figure presiding over the court: as the focus narrows to one "wild beast," his Liege is distinguished as "she," which invites identification with Elizabeth. Spenser exploits the metamorphic quality of beast fable representation throughout his poem to slip into a potential allusion to the reigning monarch and then slip away from it.

6. See particularly van den Berg.
7. As William P. Weaver points out in his "Marlowe's Fable: *Hero and Leander* and the Rudiments of Eloquence," *SP* 105 (2008): 388–408, taking Aesop's fables and expanding them was a standard grammar school exercise in imitation recommended by Quintilian. Weaver describes how Marlowe expands on this rhetorical exercise as he revises Musaeus in his *Hero and Leander*, particularly in amplifying the descriptions of the lovers. Spenser may well be doing something analogous in expanding the narrative scope of the fables.
8. On this point, see Richard Rambuss, *Spenser's Secret Career* (New York: Cambridge University Press, 1993).

Spenser's slipperiness here goes beyond teasing the reader with possible allusions to public figures. In fact, the very provocativeness of presenting a reigning Queen and particular courtiers in Aesopian guise directs attention from what is arguably more subversive in Aesop's fable of the wild and the domesticated ass, namely the premise that the state of nature is to be free of political subjection. Spenser executes a rhetorical pirouette on the term "wild" as he shifts away from the generic political implication of "wild" as natural and free to use "wild" as a code word for unnamed political insiders. Just as the representation of the ass's harness as courtly trappings supersedes its original Aesopian significance as shackles, so the dangerous glamor of courtly gossip diverts attention from the far more audacious political implications of Aesop's unembellished imagery.[9] To the extent that readers identify themselves as privileged consumers of political information, they are distracted from seeing their own political circumstances mirrored by Aesop's wild and domestic asses.

As with previous episodes, the final masquerade begins as a revision of an Aesop fable. The Ape's donning the pelt of the sleeping Lion at the urging of the Foxe recalls Aesop's fable of the Ass clothed in the skin of the lion while amending the fable's essentialist point.[1] In doffing his skin, the Lion has effected a separation between the monarch's two bodies. In successfully masquerading in the discarded lion's skin, Spenser's Ape undermines the essential legitimacy of the monarch's body natural, that is to say, Elizabeth. Having flirted with a highly inflammatory identification of the fictional Ape and the reigning monarch, Spenser retreats from the extremes of political danger. As the identification of the Foxe with some extra-literary figure becomes increasingly audacious, the Ape fades from view as a satiric target. The poem shifts generically from a covert critique of monarchy in the Aesopian mode to an Elizabethan poem of personal destruction in the manner of, say, *Leicester's Commonwealth*. Although the charges that the Foxe plundered the kingdom to "fe[e]d his cubs" (1151) invites identification with Burleigh, who was frequently accused of using his office to enrich his relatives, any self-serving politician fits the description well enough. As in the previous episode, hints of personal attack on a specific contemporary political figure function as a diversionary strategy: the seeming specificity and genuine indeterminacy of the poison-pen portrait grafted onto the Foxe shift focus from the critique of the Lion.

The temerity of the reproach directed to the Lion is one more of the poem's defensive gestures. In bidding him to redeem himself and his honor, Mercurie confirms the essential royalty of the Lion. The criticism

9. In making the word "wild" a focus of politically charged ambiguity, Spenser echoes a crux in Wyatt that he fascinatingly revisits in *Amoretti* 67. Although one can take the wild beast that provokes his Liege's displeasure with "his late chayne" as a reference to any number of courtiers who displeased Elizabeth by marrying, the coded language of "wild" and "tame" and the image of the chain recall the sonnet by Sir Thomas Wyatt "Who so list to hunt," a poem from which has been read veiled allusion to the sexual politics of an earlier Tudor court. The conclusion of Amoretti 67, "Strange thing me seemd to see a beast so wyld, / so goodly wonne with her owne will beguyld" recalls the inscription worn around the neck of Wyatt's anthropomorphic deer, "'*Noli me tangere*, for Cæsar's I am, / And wild for to hold, though I seem tame'" and transforms the play of female chastity and political subjecthood in Wyatt's poem to a private interplay between courting lovers.

1. Gibbs 322, Chambry 267, Perry 188.

voiced by Mercurie is in the traditional mirror-of-princes mode as it posits distance between individual monarch and the ideal of monarchy in order to offer the monarch an image of his (or her) ideal self and effaces more subversive understandings of how the monarch's two bodies are figured by Spenser's Lion and his detachable skin. Just how much Spenser might have been committed to the more radical implications of the Aesopian fictions put in play throughout *Mother Hubberds Tale* and how much he puts them in play for rhetorical effect is impossible to know for certain since Aesopian political deniability is part of the subject of the poem and cultivating political indeterminacy is an important strategy. At the same time, the way *Mother Hubberds Tale* adapts and revises its myriad subtexts hints that the political intentions of an individual poet, even if knowable, do not account for all of the political consequences of a particular poem.[2] It was the great intuition of Sir Isaac Newton that the planets in their motions are *falling*. The moment Newton articulated that insight, earlier studies of falling bodies became part of Newtonian mechanics. Spenser manipulates Aesopian imagery and tropes with conscious, indisputable skill and makes them more fully available to anyone who would use them as an instrument of political thought. As *Mother Hubberds Tale* enmeshes poet and reader in a metamorphic world of Aesopian political discourse, it intervenes in the political conversation of the English-speaking world and beyond in ways that are unpredictable but genuine.

A. E. B. COLDIRON

[How Spenser Excavates Du Bellay's *Antiquitez*]†

"O Apolon! O Muses! prophaner ainsi les sacrés reliques de l'Antiquité!"[1]

With these words Du Bellay condemns poetic translation in his *Deffence et illustration de la langue francoyse.* It is hard to take his exclamation seriously, for not only is the *Deffence* a slippery and idiosyncratic work, the *Antiquitez* itself is a collection of relics that in many cases draw their power from translation. Yet even if Du Bellay's hyperbolic exclamation invites a wry smile, his reasons for condemning poetic translation are worth understanding in greater detail. To translate poetry is a profanation

> à cause de ceste divinité d'invention qu'ilz ont plus que les autres, de ceste grandeur de style, magnificence des motz, gravité de sentences, audace & varieté de figures, & mil'autres lumieres de poësie: bref ceste energie, & ne sçay quel esprit, qui est en leurs ecriz, que les Latins appelleroient *genius.*

2. In this regard, see Andrew Hadfield, *Shakespeare and Republicanism* (Cambridge: Cambridge University Press, 2005). See also the exchange between Hadfield and David Scott Wilson-Okamura in *SSt* 17 (2003): 253–292.

† From *JEGP* 101.1 (2002): 41–67. Reprinted by permission.

1. 'Oh Apollo, oh Muses, thus to profane the sacred relics of antiquity!' For further discussion of Du Bellay's condemnations of translation, see Alexandre Lorian, "Du Bellay, un traducteur contre les traducteurs?" in *Du Bellay: Actes du Colloque International d'Angers du 26 au 29 mai 1989*, ed. Georges Cesbron (Presses de l'Université d'Angers, 1990), II, 477–84. All translations here except Spenser's are mine. In notes and parenthetical citations, I abbreviate *Antiquitez* as *Ant* and *Ruines of Rome* as *RR*.

('because of this divinity of invention that they [the poets] have more than others, this greatness of style, magnificence of words, gravity of aphorisms, boldness and variety of figures, and a thousand other lights of poetry: in short, that energy, and I-don't-know-what spirit that is in their writings, which the Latins would call *genius*'.)

These sacred features of poetry—invention, style, diction, *gravitas*, rhetorical boldness and variety, *genius* in its several senses—one cannot translate, he says, nor should one try. For our purposes, Du Bellay's list of untranslatables can stand either as specific challenges to Renaissance poet/translators' powers, or, in retrospect at least, as another example of the gaps early modern translation tends to open between poetic theory and poetic practice. For not only does Du Bellay try in his own poetry to translate these untranslatables; Edmund Spenser attempts similar sacrileges on Du Bellay's *Antiquitez* and *Songe*. Spenser's *Ruines of Rome* and *Visions of Bellay* do clearly seek to translate Du Bellay's "mille lumières"—invention, grand style and magnificent lexicon, his *gravitas*, his *énergie* (implying either *energeia* or *enargeia*), the boldness and variety of his rhetorical figures. Whether Spenser achieves a similar or parallel *genius* is not the point of this essay, and would depend anyway on whether we take *genius* in its imperial sense to mean something like inspiration (Martial, *Epigrams* VI.61.10) or in its earlier sense to mean the *genius loci*, the governing spirit that presided at the birth of the *Antiquitez*. The other features Spenser may recreate, but Du Bellay's untranslatable *genius loci*, or rather the governing spirit of the poem's literary and cultural milieux, Spenser ultimately must create anew. Even as he replicates closely Du Bellay's content and "mille lumières," Spenser also creates a new way of writing the lyric sequence, and a newly optimistic view of the poet's role in history. Translation as Spenser practices it on Du Bellay becomes not a "profanation" but both enactment and thematization of the central Renaissance project of *renovatio*, of bringing Antiquity to English readers. Although Spenser's translations look remarkably "close" (theoretically speaking, "replicative," "equivalent," or "faithful"[2]), his way is nevertheless distinctly different from Du Bellay's. Spenser scholars are coming to agree that these translations significantly shaped certain images, phrases, and uses of form in Spenser's other work (specifically, the *Shepherdes Calender*, the *Amoretti*, and *The Faerie Queene*).[3]

2. Translation theorists before our century tended to focus on "fidelity," implying a moral or theological criterion for the likeness between source and target items (Jerome, Horace, Seneca, Dryden); Jakobson's "equivalence" is a related term, but the impossibility of identity between source and translation has generally been widely accepted in the wake of poststructuralism; more recent theorists like Rita Copeland (*Rhetoric, Hermeneutics, and Translation in the Middle Ages* [Cambridge: Cambridge Univ. Press, 1991]) and Lawrence Venuti (*The Translator's Invisibility: A History of Translation* [London: Routledge, 1995]) tend instead to regard translation as hermeneutic (Copeland) or appropriative (Venuti). For a short taxonomy of "replicativity" as a better way than "fidelity" of talking about the kinds of closeness possible between source and translation, and a proposal for some new terms, see my "Thomas Watson and Renaissance Lyric Translation," *Translation and Literature*, 5 (1996), 3–25.

3. Anne Lake Prescott, "Du Bellay in Renaissance England: Recent Work on Translation and Response," *Oeuvres et Critiques*, 20 (1995), 121–28; M. L. Stapleton, "Spenser, the *Antiquitez de Rome*, and the Development of the English Sonnet Form," *Comparative Literature Studies*, 27 (1990), 259–74; A. Kent Hieatt, "The Genesis of Shakespeare's Sonnets," *PMLA*, 98 (1983), 800–814; Prescott, *French Poets and the English Renaissance* (New Haven: Yale Univ. Press, 1978), a foundational work establishing that the relation between Du Bellay and Spenser was significant, and that Spenser was one of the English poets who "respond most fully" to Du Bellay (p. 60). Other poets include Gorges, Soowthern, Daniel, et al. See also *Complaints*, ed. W. L. Renwick (London: Scholartis, 1928), pp. 179–87, 244–48, 257–60; A. Satterthwaite,

Clearly, too, the early thematic concerns adopted from Du Bellay and Marot beginning about 1569 continue to appear in *Shepherdes Calender, The Faerie Queene*, and most of the rest of the *Complaints* volume: themes of ruined empire, time, and mutability.[4] For these reasons alone, Spenser's translations from French deserve greater prominence in canon and curriculum. But my particular point here is that the translations show Spenser's direct, early engagement with several of what were then unresolved, even contested issues in English poetics: the perceived role of the poet or translator especially in the on-going wars against time; the modal and rhetorical innovations required in writing England's first real historiographic sonnet sequence; the rupture between oneiric and historiographic voice (and the concomitant theoretical problem of a deictic rather than an epideictic "lyric I"); and the material and cultural decontextualization of the source poems (or, how Renaissance *imitatio* implies and makes use of recontextualization). In other words, over the course of his most formative decades—the 1570s and 1580s—Spenser takes on with these translations a central thematic preoccupation with re-birthing the Classical world, pitting empire against eternity with a more-optimistic poet as mediator. He also finds his own answers to some extremely timely "how-to" problems of sixteenth-century English poetics—modal, rhetorical, aesthetic, theoretical. His is an excavation not just of Rome, not just of Du Bellay's Rome, but of Du Bellay's way-of-excavating. In this highly selective and subtle project, the intertextuality that counts is "not so much . . . the scattered bones of individual sources as the suggestive skeleton of a once living cultural context."[5]

* * *

What exactly did Spenser translate from French, and how important are these excavations to students of the English Renaissance? The first poems we have from Spenser are translations from French,[6] and his largest translations are of entire French lyric sequences. Spenser translated poems from the *Visions* sequences for Jan Van der Noodt's 1569 *A Theatre for Voluptuous Worldlings*, a book of emblems with religious commentary. In the *Complaints* volume (1591), Spenser includes three sonnet sequences: his *Ruines of Rome: by Bellay* translates Du Bellay's *Antiq-*

Spenser, Ronsard and Du Bellay (Princeton: Princeton Univ. Press, 1960; rpt. Port Washington, NY: Kennikat, 1972); and Margaret Ferguson, "'The Afflatus of Ruin': Meditations on Rome by Du Bellay, Spenser, and Stevens," in *Roman Images*, ed. Annabel Patterson (Baltimore: Johns Hopkins Univ. Press, 1984), pp. 23–50.

4. Prescott, "Spenser (Re)Reading Du Bellay: Chronology and Literary Response," in *Spenser's Life and the Subject of Biography*, ed. Judith Anderson, Donald Cheney, and David Richardson (Amherst: Univ. of Massachusetts Press, 1996), pp. 131–45, establishes that Spenser was reading Du Bellay during the middle years, 1569–79, pre-*Shepherdes Calender,* in other words. She also explains that Spenser was likely using a kind of "multiple reading" method across his writing years that includes the re-reading of his own translations as well as of Du Bellay's and others' texts.

5. George H. Tucker, *The Poet's Odyssey: Joachim du Bellay and the Antiquitez de Rome*. (Oxford: Clarendon Press, 1990), p. 4.

6. Jan Van der Noodt, *A Theatre for Voluptuous Worldlings* (London: Henry Bynneman, 1569; Delmar, NY: Scholars' facs. & rpts., 1977). A reprint of the Dutch first edition (np, nd) with another work is *Het Bosken en Het Theatre*, ed. W. A. P. Smit and W. Vermeer (Amsterdam and Antwerp: Wereldbibliotheek, 1953; rpt. Utrecht: HES, 1979). The edition of 1568 is *Le theatre auquel sont exposés* . . . (London: J. Day; STC 18603); I can find no modern edition of this particular item. Carl Rasmussen ("'Quietnesse of Minde': *A Theatre for Worldlings* as as Protestant Poetics," *Spenser Studies*, 1 [1980], 3–27) sees it as a religious sequence; but its protestantism, as Anne Prescott points out, resides mostly in the prose. Prescott also notes that this early work gives an impression very different from a sonnet sequence, since it comprises two hundred pages of polemic accompanied by a handful of pictures with brief remarks (private commentary, Spring 1999).

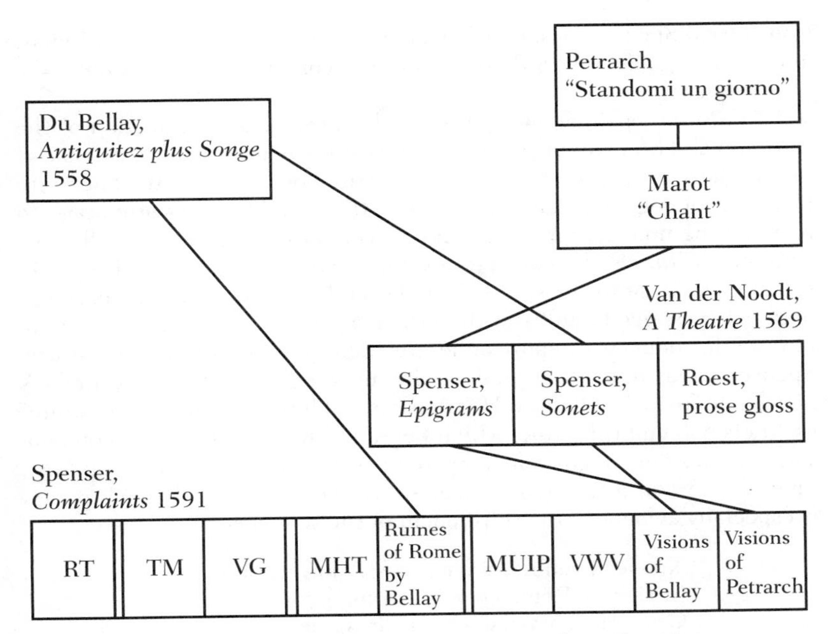

Figure 1. Genealogy of Spenser's lyric translations from French

uitez, the *Visions of Bellay* translates his *Songe*, and the *Visions of Petrarch formerly translated*, despite its title, is wrought from Marot's *Chant des Visions* (see fig. 1, a genealogy of these poems).[7] Between the 1569 *Theatre for Voluptuous Worldlings* and the 1591 *Complaints*, some important poetic growth took place—both in the English literary milieu and in Spenser's own work—which his translations and his later revisions of them register. Any translation is of course a revision, an interpretation, but the apparent replicativities of Spenser's *Ruines* sequence are less significant than are the sequence's non-replicativities, the subtler gaps, shifts, and tensions in the translation. Next, the essay examines the cultural and print contexts of the two sequences, finding further gaps and tensions that show us Spenser's efforts to navigate some modal difficulties in the English and thereby to reshape the English sonnet sequence. Finally, these transla-

7. Unless otherwise noted, Spenser's poems are cited from the variorum, *The Works of Edmund Spenser*, ed. Edwin Greenlaw, et al., vol. 7, pt. 2, *The Minor Poems* (Baltimore: The Johns Hopkins Univ. Press, 1947); Du Bellay's are from the edition of Daniel Aris and Françoise Joukovsky, *Oeuvres poétiques*, t. 2 (Paris: Bordas, 1993). A facing-page edition of the French and English poems is available with introduction and notes by Malcolm C. Smith: *Joachim du Bellay*, Les Antiquitez de Rome, *translated by Edmund Spenser as* Ruines of Rome (Binghamton, NY: MRTS, 1994). Other editions consulted include the *Yale Edition of the Shorter Poems of Edmund Spenser*, ed. William Oram, et al. (New Haven: Yale Univ. Press, 1989); *Complaints*, ed. W. L. Renwick (London: Scholartis, 1928); microfilm of the 1591 *Complaints*; Henri Chamard's edition of Du Bellay's *Oeuvres poétiques* (Paris: Société d'éditions d'enseignement supérieur, 1908–31, 6 tomes, t.2); 4ème ed. H. Weber, 1961; rééd. STFM, 1982–86; édition Droz, 1974, and a microfilm *Antiquitez . . . plus un Songe* (Paris, 1558) courtesy of the British Library. Marot's dizains are expanded from Petrarch's "Standomi un giorno," *Rime* 323, in *Petrarch's Lyric Poems*, ed. and trans. Robert M. Durling (Cambridge, Mass.: Harvard Univ. Press, 1976). Marot's poem is "Le Chant des Visions de Pétrarque," in *Oeuvres complètes*, ed. C. A. Mayer, vol. 6, *Les Traductions* (Genève: Slatkine, 1978); relevant material on pp. 13, 41, 63, 215–25.

tions reveal Spenser's vision of history as distinct from that of Du Bellay, and some possible ways Spenser found to accommodate that vision in the lyric sequence.

* * * *Ruines of Rome* looks at first like a very close replication of the *Antiquitez.* The content of the thirty-two sonnets in each sequence is nearly the same, and even at line level, the poems are close. There are instances of cognate rhyming (e.g., *Ant/RR* 6), and Spenser often tries to recreate the nuance, force, and inner dynamics of a poem as well as its content. In *Ruines of Rome* 7, for example, Spenser closely replicates Du Bellay's caesurae in lines 1, 3, 5, 8, 11, and 12. The caesurae mark the organizing principle and the rhetorical rhythm of the poem: key noun phrases introduced in apostrophe are then qualified after the caesura. Spenser seems to try to reproduce the meaningful stress on Du Bellay's bi-syllabic "peine" in line 14. He translates "Il finira la peine que j'endure" as "It als will end the paine, which I endure," using a comma to compensate for heavier English feet by requiring a slight pause at "paine." Spenser's aim at a full, many-faceted replicativity of Du Bellay's poetry is especially evident in the third poem of the sequence:[8]

> Nouveau venu, qui cherches Rome en Rome,
> Et rien de Rome en Rome n'apperçois,
> Ces vieux palais, ces vieux arcs que tu vois,
> Et ces vieux murs, c'est ce que Rome on nomme.
> Voy quel orgueil, quelle ruine: et comme
> Celle qui mist le monde sous ses loix
> Pour donter tout, se donta quelquefois,
> Et devint proye au temps, qui tout consomme.
> Rome de Rome est le seul monument,
> Et Rome Rome a vaincu seulement,
> Le Tybre seul, qui vers la mer s'enfuit,
> Reste de Rome. O mondaine inconstance!
> Ce qui est ferme, est par le temps destruit,
> Et ce qui fuit, au temps fait resistence.

Spenser, tolling the word "Rome" at nearly the same places (ll. 1, 2, 9), translates Du Bellay's ploce. * * * Line 10 repeats "onely" similarly, if without the extra edge of Du Bellay's epizeuxis ("Rome Rome") and without the polyptoton of "seul/seulement." Nor can Spenser play with the echoing bisyllabification of the word "Rome" in lines 2, 9, and 10 made possible by romance metrics. Spenser enjambs lines 6–7 for a momentum less striking than, but still like, Du Bellay's. Alliteration at line 5 is not much compensation for the lost "orgueil," an essential concept in the larger sequence. Yet "Tam'd" (l. 7) captures the reflexiveness and positioning of "donter/se donta," and more: in translating the verb this way Spenser does more than solve a syllabic problem. Elsewhere he translates

8. *Antiquitez* 3 is itself a translation of Janus Vitalis's epigram, "Qui Romam in media queris, novus advena, Roma." See G. H. Tucker, "Du Bellay, Janus Vitalis et Lucain," in *Du Bellay: Actes du Colloque International d'Angers du 26 au 29 mai 1989,* ed. Georges Cesbron (Presses de l'Université d'Angers, 1990), I, 149ff, on how Du Bellay decontextualized Vitalis. M. L. Stapleton also reads this translation as an instance of Spenser's subtle development of the sonnet form; see her reading of *RR* 3, "Spenser, the *Antiquitez de Rome,* and the Development of the English Sonnet Form," p. 268. The italics in the English text add to the effects I discuss here.

"donter" as "subdue" (*RR* 8), but here, choosing "tam'd," he extends the animal suggestion in Du Bellay's images of a predatory "devouring time."[1] The lovely "qui vers la mer s'enfuit" Spenser loses, but his choices of "funerall" (for 'monument') and "fall" work well with internal rhyme at "all" (l. 12) for a sonority consistent with the French poem's knelling sonorities and a finality that prepares at least as well for the break in line 12.

We could say that it is no surprise that the translation is replicative in so many ways, since this poem is especially well suited to some of Spenser's characteristic tendencies. It reflects on mutability using two images, the river and the ruins, whose juxtaposition includes a philosophically instructive paradox, which Spenser renders neatly in an epigrammatic couplet.[2] Or we could say, with Prescott, that such tendencies in Spenser had to come from somewhere, and that translating fifty-five such sonnets so closely and revising twenty-three of them may have helped Spenser develop his characteristic (and influential) habits of poetry. "What [Spenser] saw in Du Bellay was . . . central to his own sensibility; indeed it may have shaped that sensibility, for Spenser came to Du Bellay young."[3] * * *

However, Spenser seems deliberately to ignore or alter a few aspects of Du Bellay's work. Chief among these, one of only two such significant aspects to be treated here, is a revised conception of the poet/translator's role in history: Spenser takes a more optimistic attitude toward the poet's potential role in reviving the Classical past. First we need to understand the considerable doubts about that role that Du Bellay's sequence reveals. Despite his theoretical calls for "deffence" and "illustration," Du Bellay is not optimistic about the poet's powers over time in the *Antiquitez*, the work in his oeuvre most concerned with Renaissance *renovatio*. He wonders if his verses will endure and never finally asserts that they will. In fact over the course of the sequence he noticeably diminishes the powers of the poet. When the sequence starts these are quite strong. The sister-arts metaphors in the opening sonnet "Au Roy" rather confidently announce the power of his poems to substitute for "ces ouvrages antiques / Pour vostre Sainct-Germain, ou pour Fontainebleau." * * * *Antiquitez* 25 expresses the poet's unfulfilled, now seemingly unfulfillable yearnings to "rebastir au compas de la plume / Ce que les mains ne peuvent maçonner"—a long fall from the confident *ut architectura poesis* of the dedicatory sonnet. *Antiquitez* 26 immediately corrects, nearly chastises the poet. "Qui voudrait figurer la Romaine grandeur," snaps Du Bellay back at himself, must eschew the builder's tools, the material measures of map and square, for "Rome fut tout le monde, et tout le monde est Rome." All, including poetry, *is* as vulnerable as Rome. *Antiquitez* 27 next turns, commanding the reader to "regarder" and "juger" while giving advice on interpreting landscape; the poet had hoped to be an architect of new-old

1. One of several French epithets that seem to have entered our poetry via Spenser. A. Kent Hieatt discusses several in "The Genesis of Shakespeare's Sonnets." Prescott reminds me of its Latin origin: *tempus edax*.
2. See Lawrence Manley, "Spenser and the City: the Minor Poems," *MLQ* 43 (1982), 203–27; on the wider implications of rivers in Spenser, see Gordon Braden, "riverrun: An Epic Catalogue in the *Faerie Queene*," *ELR*, 5 (1975), 25–48.
3. Prescott, *French Poets*, p. 41.

glory but has had to settle for being a critic, an interpreter.[4] Then *Antiquitez* 30 figures the poet as gleaner, using what was sometimes a metaphor for translators. The figure as it is placed here stresses the belatedness and meagreness of the poet's possibilities, not the transcendence or promise in the role. The reaper in *Antiquitez* 30 scythes away most hope for poetic gleaning (nothing, in Du Bellay's poem, comes "après le moissonneur," l. 14). By the final poem in the sequence, *Antiquitez* 32, Du Bellay is in the grip of doubt as he addresses his own poetry (his long scrutiny of the Roman landscape having yielded no eternizing promise):

> Esperez-vous que la posterité
> Doive (mes vers) pour tout jamais vous lire?

* * *

Over the course of the *Ruines of Rome*, however, Spenser reverses that erosion of belief in the powers of the poet, or at least mitigates its progress, with a few slight changes in translation and one big addition at the end. First, there is no "Au Roy" dedication in which to raise hopes of a poetic monument or to imply poetic durability in sister-arts metaphors, an absence that suits Spenser's quiet de-politicization of the topic. And the poem Spenser places first cedes a good bit more of the poet's power.* * * In *Ruines* 26, Spenser shows his hand by altering that important present-tense verb. Prescott thinks the verb here might matter to Du Bellay;[5] I think it *must* matter to Spenser, a poet translating past poetry about past poetry. Where Du Bellay includes everything in the Roman fate—"Tout le monde fut Rome et Rome *est* tout le monde"—Spenser writes "Rome was th' whole world, and al the world *was* Rome" (emphases mine). Rome's fate mapped, but does not now map, that of the "whole world." Spenser's verb tense leaves room to hope for England's empire and poetic immortality, so the question he then asks of his verses in the closing poem (*RR* 32) does not sound ironic, or defeatist as it does in Du Bellay's sequence.

In poem 32, Spenser asks his verses what only looks like, but is in fact not, the same question Du Bellay asked his:

> Hope ye my verses that posteritie
> Of age ensuing shall you ever read?

* * *

Spenser acknowledges the apparent reasonableness of Rome's claim to immortality, which the marble "might well have hop'd to have obtained" (l. 8). Even beyond that line, the English poem on the whole is not as pessimistic as the French poem (previously quoted) for several reasons. One is grammatical: English allows the indicative after "hope" where French requires the subjunctive (when "esperer" is interrogative or negative). A somatic theorist might propose that the long-*e* sounds in the English version keep us smiling as we read ("ye," "posteritie," "read," "ye," "immortalite," "meane," "meed," seven long *e*'s just in the first quatrain). More likely it has to do with the loss of the disturbing desrobbe-robe rhyme.

4. There is much more to this complex and important poem than can be treated here; for one thing, *Antiquitez* 25–26–27 form a group that invokes poet, critic, reader, in turn and in corrective fashion and may balance group 10–11–12.
5. Prescott notes "Du Bellay's perhaps significant shift in tense" within the line (*French Poets,* p. 49).

Spenser's couplet takes a more reassuring—more Virgilian?—view of the poet's eternizing powers (song/long), without Du Bellay's implied stripping of all glory (desrobbe/robbe). Into the *Antiquitez*'s doubting view of the poet's place in history, Spenser has translated a subtle and gradual optimism.

He also mitigates Du Bellay's related view of translation. Translation, of course, is a primary means of creating poetic immortality and of passing on poetic glory. And "as a theory of history, as a hermeneutic tool, and as a linguistic practice, translation is at the heart of Du Bellay's and Spenser's meditations on Rome."[6] Beyond a medieval *translatio imperii*, the imperatives of which were fairly clear (to reproduce or transmit older empires' successes in the new language and culture), Renaissance translation was coming to include not only what Karlheinz Stierle has called a newly "horizontal" translation but also a potentially revisionist practice.[7] * * *

Spenser's replicative practice of translation, then, has implicitly countered Du Bellay's condemnation of poetic translation in the *Deffence* while effacing the doubts about the poet's role in history expressed in the *Antiquitez* poems themselves. And Spenser's final word on the matter of translation as an instrument of poetic immortality comes in the final poem of the *Ruines*, a sonnet not translated from Du Bellay. By adding this new poem, "L'Envoy," Spenser sends his sequence out, confidently declaring his belief in future readers and in a poet's power over time, as well as in a translator's power to sing for his nation. * * * Poetry, adds Spenser to Du Bellay's doubting meditations on the Roman past, is not sacrilege or necromancy but resurrection. By implication Spenser sees that his own poetic translation can to Bellay "give eternall dayes." This final, original word from Spenser caps the series of small shifts he made in the poems' translations. The idea that poetry can confer immortal fame is a Renaissance commonplace (and translation is the idea's common implement), but here the idea is particularly dependent on the pragmatic powers of translation to breathe new life into old texts and to cross the boundaries of time, language, culture. Spenser states the commonplace most openly in the final poem he adds, setting his view rather pointedly against Du Bellay's in ways consistent with his translations of Du Bellay's sonnets.

All three of Spenser's sonnet sequences translated from French, although they are in several senses "close" translations (substantive, variously replicative) containing like matter expressed in like forms, are in another sense not the same poems at all. Removed from their original print contexts, their meaning changes. This removal is a significant, though silent, part of the effect of Spenser's translations.

* * *

6. Ferguson, "The Afflatus of Ruin," p. 25.
7. Stierle, "*Translatio studii* and Renaissance: From Vertical to Horizontal Translation," in *The Translatability of Cultures*, ed. Sanford Budick and Wolfgang Iser (Stanford: Stanford Univ. Press, 1996), pp. 55–67. For the *locus classicus* of the idea of the *translatio imperii*, see Sallust, *Bellum Catilinae* (trans. J. C. Rolfe; Cambridge, Mass.: Harvard Univ. Press, 1971), 11.6. For an Old English discussion, see Alfred the Great's Preface to Gregory's *Pastoral Care*; Étienne Gilson, *Les Idées et les lettres* (Paris: Vrin, 1932), pp. 183–89, begins the discussion in the twentieth century.

Reading the poems according to the visual organization of the page is enlightening, as is reading the four poems on any two open pages as related groupings. Yet Spenser rejected Du Bellay's considerably complex rhetoric of visual form and spatial arrangement in favor of numbered, uniform, pentameter sonnets presented in a linear rather than architectural fashion. It is not the case that English habits in such things were fixed by 1591. English poets (Sidney, for instance) were capable if not of alexandrines at least of hexameters. Nor was arrangement on a page a fixed matter; Spenser's own—or Ponsonby's—practice varied in this regard. Spenser perhaps reveals that he wants for English readers something other than the French way of reading and writing sonnets in sequences, which of course varied considerably. * * *

In rejecting so thoroughly such signifying print contexts, he also rejects a foundational connection between the two sequences: the *Antiquitez* and *Songe* poems originally appeared together as two parts of the same work, *Le premier livre des Antiquitez de Rome contentant une generale description de sa grandeur, et comme une deploration de sa ruine . . . plus un Songe, ou vision sur le mesme subject . . .* [8] Du Bellay's sequences form a unity that fulfills the promise of its title and of its publication as one work. They appear as two parts of one volume, with all the poems presented on the page as described above. There is evidence of numerological and architectural design in the volume.[9] The numerous verbal links and recurring images between the *Antiquitez* and *Songe* sequences enhance the reader's sense of continuity: many of the recurring images are icons of greatness such as oaks, eagles, towers, and Titans. Most of all, the *Antiquitez . . . plus Songe* takes two approaches to the one idea of inexorable human loss in the face of time. The volume thus seems a kind of two-sided cultural elegy. * * * The *Antiquitez-Songe* volume as a whole thus explores two dimensions or capacities of lyric—the historiographically-meditative and the oneiric—and connects two ways of "seeing" catastrophic losses both in and outside of historical time.

* * * In *Complaints* the two sequences, translated as the *Ruines of Rome* and the *Visions*, are placed in separate sections. This separation of the two ways of seeing is curious, since Spenser tends to weave the two ways together in the *Faerie Queene*, or at least tends to put history with prophecy and narrative alongside the more-mystical or nearly-oneiric (in the New Jerusalem vision, the House of Holiness, and the prophecies about Britomart and the kingdom, for instance). But these translations break the connection between historiographic vision and oneiric vision. It is curious that such an ostensibly "faithful" or replicative set of transla-

8. The two sequences appeared together in every early issue I have been able to find: two issues in 1558; in 1562; in posthumous *Oeuvres* of 1568, 1569, and after. Modern editions usually keep them together, but the edition of Aris and Joukovsky (*Oeuvres poétiques,* t.2 [Paris: Bordas, 1993]) is superior in this regard because it reproduces the order and placement of the poems on the page, an important signifying feature of the work.

9. Richard A. Katz, *The Ordered Text: The Sonnet Sequences of Du Bellay* (New York: Peter Lang, 1985), and Doranne Fenoaltea and David Lee Rubin, *The Ladder of High Designs: Structure and Interpretation of the French Lyric Sequence* (Charlottesville: Univ. Press of Virginia, 1991), among others, find such French lyric sequences' architectural design to be a chief signifying method for Renaissance poets. On the general principles, see also Alastair Fowler, *Triumphal Forms: Structural Patterns in Elizabethan Poetry* (Cambridge: Cambridge Univ. Press, 1970), and Prescott, *French Poets*, pp. 46–47 and 51.

tions simultaneously exists in such a state of rupture. This rupture matters to readers of Spenser, for to separate oneiric vision (*Songe*) from historiographic vision (*Antiquitez*) involves Spenser's developing ideas about lyric genre and voice, for one thing, and about English sonnet decorum, for another. * * *

The *Ruines of Rome* is kept apart from the two *Visions* sequences, which appear in separate subsections at the end of the volume. The order of visions in the *Theatre* is here reversed, so that in 1591 *Visions of Petrarch* follows *Visions of Bellay* and ends the *Complaints* volume: this matters considerably to Spenser's oneiric vision, as the order of dreaming and waking is reversed.[1] Although at least one scholar doubts the degree of Spenser's involvement with the *Complaints* volume,[2] surely he had more say in the matter in 1591 than he'd had in 1569; at very least we can say that the disposition of the poems in *Complaints* (1591) confirms their prior separation and advertizes it under Spenser's authorship.

* * *

This topical expansion of the English sonnet, to include historiography, dream-vision, and landscape meditation, has implications for the construction of the much-contested lyric "I."[3] Lyric historiography, at least as Du Bellay and Spenser practice it, is less a matter of "telling" or narration than of presenting a set of vivid (though partial) allusive images; the speaker's role is as presenter of the images, not as narrator or verifier of historical events. This speaker is a presenter and implicit *interpreter of* images, that is. It works oddly: since the lyric "I" operates in the expressive, not the narrative, mode, we are to see and to feel historical loss as the speaker sees and feels it. In the more usual, narrative forms of writing history (epic or Falls of Princes narratives), the expressive dimension is less prominent, aired in asides, exclamations ("Alas!"), invocations, or moral tags. Instead, with the "I" foremost, lyric becomes a vehicle for interpreting history. Readers' identification with the "I" is essential to this technique, and a powerful tool for lyric historiography: if one can get one's readers to identify with the speaker they may be more likely to adopt one's particular view of matters historical. What looks like a replicative translation, again, turns out in fact to be Spenser's significant expansion of English possibilities for historiography and for the sonnet.

1. Each section has a title page and dedication. The *Ruines of Rome* is in section 2, following *Mother Hubberds Tale*, dedicated to Lady Compton and Mountegle. The two *Visions* sequences appear in a section dedicated to Lady Carey, along with Spenser's *Muiopotmos* and his *Visions of the Worlds Vanitie*. The *Theatre*'s prose gloss is gone, as are van der Noodt's apocalyptic sonnets; Spenser apparently returned to Du Bellay's *Songe* for poems to translate in their place.
2. While Harold Leo Stein (*Studies in Spenser's Complaints* [Folcroft, PA: Folcroft Press, 1972], pp. 4, 12–20, and Appendix of Variants) and Renwick (pp. 179–80) think Spenser was heavily involved in putting together the 1591 *Complaints*, Jean Brink has questioned that involvement, in "Who Fashioned Edmund Spenser?: The Textual History of *Complaints*," *Studies in Philology*, 88 (1991), 153–68. She argues that Ponsonby assembled the volume. The evidence now available, I think, is insufficient for certitude. The poems came to English readers arranged this way under Spenser's name, regardless of whose idea it first was. If we were to speak of the arranging of the poems in terms of a contribution to Spenser's poetic development, certitude on this point would matter more.
3. Theorists like Joel Fineman see epideixis as the single most important mode in Renaissance lyric, but Spenser's translations tend to emphasize a deictic rather than an epideictic lyric "I." See Fineman, *Shakespeare's Perjured Eye: The Invention of Poetic Subjectivity in the Sonnets* (Berkeley: Univ. of California Press, 1996).

On the other hand, *not* replicating Du Bellay's sonnet *form* lets Spenser affirm the newer English or Elizabethan sonnet form. M. L. Stapleton has argued that the *Ruines* translation is an experiment in form (p. 261), focusing especially on changes of rhyme scheme and the way that Spenser "expedites the material of the poem" (p. 263). I would agree that Spenser creates advantages for the English couplet. Du Bellay writes French sonnets, that is, *abba cddc eefgfg* or some variant, two quatrains and two tercets. Sometimes the two tercets are distinct (*Ant* 1, 7, 12), sometimes they flow together as one sestet (*Ant* 4, 10, 15), and sometimes they more resemble a sixain (*ee: fgfg* or *fggf, Ant* 2, 6, 18). Spenser consistently translates these continental forms into Elizabethan sonnets, or some version of three quatrains plus a couplet, *abab cdcd efef gg.*[4] Poets who do this, it could be argued, are reacting to the relative paucity of English rhymes when moving from Romance languages. Or they are following the formal pattern set by Wyatt and Surrey; but we should not overestimate the fixed character of the Elizabethan sonnet form in England, by thinking that after Surrey it was the main form. Consider the persistence of other forms for the sonnet, during and after the 90s quatorzain craze: think of the writers of eighteen-line sonnets, of Petrarchan 8/6 forms, of Sidney's maniform *Certaine Sonets*, even of sonnets in seven couplets, like Habington's *Castara*. The form, like the term, was not firmly fixed until our critical canon made it so and in fact contained a fair amount of variation.

But even if Spenser chooses the Elizabethan arrangement of 3Q+2 because he feels compelled to follow Surrey, or because our language lacks rhyme-words, he makes a virtue of necessity. He usually creates rhetorical advantages in the new scheme.[5] For instance, in *Antiquitez/Ruines* 10, 11, and 12, Spenser achieves epigrammatic couplets where there were none in French by rearranging Du Bellay's unified sestets in 10 and 11 and his neat tercets in 12:

> Tel encor' on a veu par dessus les humains
> Le front audacieux des sept costaux Romains
> Lever contre le ciel son orgueilleuse face:
>
> Et telz ores on void ces champs deshonnorez
> Regretter leur ruine, et les Dieux asseurez
> Ne craindre plus là hault si effroyable audace.

Spacing on the page adds to the chief effect, created in many cases like this one when Spenser changes the conjunction between syntax and lineation.

> So did that haughtie front which heaped up was
> On these seven Romane hills, it selfe upreare
> Over the world, and lift her loftie face
> Against the heaven, than gan her force to feare,
> But now these scorned fields bemone her fall,
> And Gods secure feare not her force at all.

4. Enclosed quatrains are of course another main pattern. His only "Spenserian" or interlaced sonnet, *abab bcbc cdcd ee*, is "L Envoy," discussed briefly above.

5. Usually, but not always: rhetorical losses accrue, it seems to me, in *RR* 6, 9, and 15, and perhaps 18, which seeks an interesting 4+10 flowing effect that is stopped short with an almost inappropriately sententious last line.

In poems 23, 29, and 31, Spenser similarly reshapes Du Bellay's content into the English sonnet form to good advantage.[6] *Ruines* 13, for another example, is a stronger statement than *Antiquitez* 13 partly because of its couplet, or rather because its form and content join forces.

Ny la fureur de la flamme enragee,
Ny le trenchant du fer victorieux,
Ny le degast du soldat furieux,
Qui tant de fois (Rome) t'a saccagee,

Ny coup sur coup ta fortune changee,
Ny le ronger des siecles envieux,
Ny le despit des hommes et des Dieux,
Ny contre toy ta puissance rangee

Ny l'ebranler des vents impetueux,
Ny le débord de ce Dieu tortueux
Qui tant de fois t'a couvert de son onde,

Ont tellement ton orgeuil abbaissé,
Que la grandeur du rien, qu'ilz t'ont laissé,
Ne face encor' esmerveiller le monde.

Nor the swift furie of the flames aspiring,
Nor the deep wounds of victours raging blade,
Nor ruthlesse spoyle of souldiers blood-desiring.
The which so oft thee (*Rome*) their conquest made;
    Ne stroke on stroke of fortune variable,
Ne rust of age hating continuance,
Nor wrath of Gods, nor spight of men vnstable,
Nor thou opposed against thine owne puissance;
    Nor th' horrible vprore of windes high-blowing,
Nor swelling streames of that God snakie-paced,
Which hath so often with his overflowing
Thee drenched, haue thy pride so much abaced:
    But that this nothing, which they haue thee left,
    Makes the world wonder, what they from thee reft.

* * * [T]hese translations offer, at a crucial moment for Spenser's oeuvre and for English lyric more generally, a truly unusual set of claims and possibilities. What has been least well understood is that at the same time Spenser appears to replicate Du Bellay's poems, in fact, his excavation of Du Bellay involves significant refusals and revisions. Refusing the original contexts of the *Antiquitez . . . plus un Songe*, Spenser suggests some productive possibilities for English poetry, demonstrating that lyric, specifically the sonnet sequence, can be a new vehicle for a new kind of historiographic vision in England. Moreover, Spenser's translations also subtly revise Du Bellay's doubts about the efficacy of the poet/transla-

6. See Stapleton's discussion of poem 23 and the excellent analysis of the acceleration Spenser creates in the 12–2 arrangement of certain sonnets (pp. 261–63). The article is less clear about tonal changes: Spenser's new "urgency" (p. 264) seems consistent with the new "expediting of the material" Stapleton's discussion of form establishes, but I would disagree that Spenser's tone is as pessimistic as Du Bellay's (p. 268) and that no change of vision results (p. 270).

tor's role: while still writing the mutability of empires, Spenser grants poets much greater powers against time. He participates in the wider, tension-filled early modern project, the excavation of excavations, about which his source author expresses doubts and anxieties. But Spenser uses the archaeological tool of translation in precise, original, and optimistic ways, despite the sequences' vague, pessimistic, even horrific content. His decontextualized *Ruines* appropriate for new English use a method of historiographic lyric and an altered set of possibilities for the English sonnet at a crucial moment in its development. In doing so, Spenser effectively disarms any of Du Bellay's own prohibitions against the "profanations" of translators. The translations do not "profane the sacred relics" but instead handle them, and declare the re-handling of them—the poet/translator's work in history—to be both necessary and productive.

MUIOPOTMOS: A MINI-CASEBOOK

D. C. ALLEN: [The Butterfly-Soul]†

The literal reading of the "Muiopotmos" may now be made with a certain assurance. The butterfly Clarion, unaware of his symbolic history and of the great cause between Venus and Minerva, is slain by the spider who is well tutored in traditional antipathy. A conflict on high affects the humble ones below. The moral may be pondered: when great men or goddesses quarrel, lesser innocents suffer. This may be all that the poem means; but I am inclined to think that it has a higher seriousness than this, that it is an allegorical account of the eternal struggle between Good and Evil, and, on a subordinate plane, between Wisdom and Pleasure as partisans of these great forces. To discover this seriousness we can make an excursion into the history of the legend of Cupid and Psyche to which Spenser alludes. * * * The myth of Cupid and Psyche, hallowed by the Platonic associations of its author, was read during the Renaissance as an allegory of the rational soul bound in marriage to Divine Love but disturbed in its marital duties by the lower levels of the mind. * * *

The Psyche legend, like that of the Phoenix, was one of the few pagan myths accepted by early Christians. The myth is represented on many Christian monuments, gravestones, catacomb frescoes, and sarcophagi; and the Christian Psyche is usually painted with the wings of a butterfly.[1] The reason for these symbolic wings is that the Greeks represented the human soul as a butterfly.* * * Spenser had only to look up the word for "soul" in any Greek lexicon such as the 1586 edition of Scapula's dictionary to read: "ψυχή spiritus, flatus . . . Item papilio."

The title, then, is not so ironic as it seems, for "πὀτμο," as Spenser surely knew, was reserved by the Greeks for the fatal destiny of great heroes: "πὀτμον ἐπισπειν" as Homer is accustomed to say. On the literal

† From "*Muiopotmos*, or The Fate of the Butterflie," *Image and Meaning* (Baltimore, 1968) 20–41. The essay has been condensed.

1. M. Collingnon, *Essai sur les Monuments Grecs et Romains relatifs au Mythe de Psyché* (Paris, 1877).

level there is irony, but it washes away as the allegory unfolds. The clear soul, faultless and sinless, sponsored by piety and wisdom (Minerva), yet ballasted and weighed down by the senses (Venus), can come through spiritual heedlessness into the web of evil. For this tragedy, "πὸτμο" is an exact term and Melpomene the proper Muse. * * * Patterned after this garden of the fleshly way of life, the "gay gardins" where Clarion wanders are those in which Art aspires

> T'excell the naturall, with made delights:
> And all that faire or pleasant may be found
> In riotous excess doth there abound. (166–68)

The permissible world of experience is left behind, and Clarion yields to the senses. As yet he has not sinned, but his spiritual weakness will carry him into the web of evil. Spenser now begins to warn the reader, to suggest by adjectives that the butterfly-soul is in trouble. Clarion has a "curious busie eye" (171); he attempts to satisfy "his glutton sense" (179); he preys "greedily" (204) on the flowers, and then he rests in "riotous suffisaunce" (207). The hero, in spite of his Christian armor and the good hopes of his "Sire," is slipping into heedlessness. The butterfly-soul that cannot distinguish between "flowres" and "weed of glorious feature" will easily succumb to the eye-sins that hide behind "what ever thing doth please the eie."

It is just at this point, too, that Clarion is doomed, for we are instantly informed that Jove has woven the fate of the butterfly. "Heavens avengement," "πότμο," is at hand. Both Destiny and Providence are aware that the butterfly must fall. "Careles Clarion" (375) flutters sinward while Spenser provides us with two passages that comment on his "unstaid desire" and the heedless independence that is mutually possessed by the butterfly and the Red Cross Knight. Directed by desire, reckless Clarion feeds hither and yon in the garden of sensation,

> And whatso else of vertue good or ill
> Grewe in this Gardin, fetcht from farre away,
> Of everie one he takes. (201–203)

His inability on this fair morning to distinguish between good and evil, his love of foreign pleasures (any normal Englishman would see the fault in this), his eagerness to possess all that the spring brought forth comes, perhaps, from the spiritual vanity that ruined the Red Cross Knight. This suggestion is strengthened by a suite of lines that ushers in the actual tragedy,

> [Clarion] walkt at will, and wandred too and fro,
> In the pride of his freedome principall:
> Litle wist he his fatall future woe,
> But was secure, the liker he to fall.
> He likest is to fall into mischaunce,
> That is regardles of his gouvernaunce. (379–84)

This is a poetical restatement of the advice given by St. Paul to the men of Corinth, when he reminded the Church of the pride that brought Lucifer down and would overthrow them, too. "Let him that thinketh he standeth take heed lest he fall." Through heedlessness as much as through the "troublous winde," through pride of self-surety as much as through the hate of the spider, Clarion, brightest and fairest of souls, descends to the realm of the senses. With this fall, we return to a Christian reading of the Psyche myth.

It is time now, since the cue has been heard, for Aragnoll, son of Arachne and foe by tradition of Minerva's butterfly, to enter. Thanks to Job 8.14 (His trust shall be like the spider's web) and Isaiah 59.5 (They have eaten the eggs of asps and woven the webs of spiders), Aragnoll and his house embodied a Christian symbolism that associated them with impiety, heresy, hypocrisy, worldliness, and the very Devil himself. * * * An early commentary on the eleventh century *Physiologus* of Theobaldus combines all of these meanings into a spiritual discourse on the nature of Aragnoll.

> The Devil catches us as if we were flies; he is always putting traps, nets, and loops in our way so that he can take us through sin. When he takes someone in mortal sin, then he eviscerates and deprives them of grace unless the sinner is rescued by confession and penitence. So the chief snare of the devil is man's own will and it is only by repentance that he can avoid it. The spider fears the sun just as the devil fears the Holy Church and the just man, who can also be compared to the sun. Usually the spider weaves his web at night; so the devil weaves his when the just man is less watchful.[2]

Thus Aragnoll, the destroyer of the butterfly-soul, is unmasked.

RONALD B. BOND: [The Workings of Envy][†]

* * *

Allen's interpretation is paradoxically reductive in that it enlarges the meaning of the poem to a point where more exact analysis has seemed redundant. I want to suggest, however, that as well as being a story embodying disillusionment, as well as being about the fall, "Muiopotmos" is an allegorical story about the workings of envy. Even the normal rivalry between art and nature becomes in this poem part of a spirit of contentiousness which permeates Clarion's world. In considering this competitiveness, we should recall that one of the most frequently used synonyms for *invidia* is *aemulatio*. Cooper's *Thesaurus* defines *aemulor* thus: "With a certayne enuy and ambition to indeuour to passe & excell an other man: to folowe, or study to be like an other: to imitate or counterfaite."[1] The first meaning given here, the common one, lies behind Spenser's use of conceptual cognates for the central idea of envy:

2. Auber, *Histoíre et Théorie du Symbolisme Religeux* (Paris, 1884), III. 496.

† From "*Invidia* and the Allegory of Spenser's *Muiopotmos*," *English Studies in Canada* 2 (1976): 144–55. The original footnotes have been reduced and edited. Reprinted by permission of *English Studies in Canada* and the author.

1. Cooper, *Thesaurus Linguae Romanae et Britanniae* (1565; facs rpt Menston 1969), s.v. *aemulor.* The confusion between in *bono* and in *malo* senses of emulation is noted frequently by late medieval exegetes, particularly when glossing 1 Corinthians 13:4 where Paul includes among the attributes of charity the phrase, "charitas non aemulatur." Commentators distinguished between the meaning of *aemulor* here and its other meaning exemplified in 1 Corinthians 14:1.

witness the prominence of words such as "contend," "challenge," and "excell" in the poem.

Spenser's primary allegorical symbol for envy in the poem is Aragnoll. With considerable cumulative force Spenser calls him "a wicked wight / The foe of faire things, th'author of confusion, / The shame of Nature, the bondslaue of spight" (243–45). Traditionally spiders and scorpions had been associated not just with evil in general, but specifically with the envious and detracting. Aragnoll's web is linked with another significant trap, moreover, in the simile which compares the spider's web with Vulcan's net [369–74]. Vulcan, his forge, and his home on Mount Aetna had become convenient symbols for jealousy and *invidia*, and it is unlikely, therefore, that Spenser's recollection of Vulcan at this juncture is simply fortuitous.

The conjunction of the envious spider with the poem's prominent weaving image suggests that a further moralization may apply. Drawing on the literal and derived meanings of the Latin verb *texere*, from which our words "text" and "textile" come, and on the fact that *exordium* can mean either the warp of a web, or the beginning of a speech, Erasmus had written about the nature of the spider and its human counterparts in "Ex se fingit velut araneus," one of the *Adagia*. Included under the rubric "Inconstantiae perfidiae versutiae," the passage suggests that, as the spider brings its web out of itself, so detractors spin their insubstantial tales. I would suggest, then, that the whole weight of the iconographical tradition which associates envy and detraction with spiders lies behind Spenser's poem. To regard Aragnoll as Satan simply because the spider is "traditionally an obnoxious creature"[2] is surely to assume too readily the correctness of Allen's thesis and to make Spenser unnecessarily oblivious to aspects of his culture lesser writers did not ignore.

But what of the spider's victim? He is not just a butterfly, he is a butterfly called Clarion [i.e., trumpet]. * * * The trumpet's designation as Fame's instrument is a commonplace: the Pléiade poets extolled Homer as the "Buccinateur" of Achilles' praise;[3] Valeriano and Ripa both affiliate *tuba* and *fama*, and there are many iconographic representations of Fame's clarion;[4] Puttenham says that poets are "in deede the trumpetters of all praise,"[5] while E.K., in the letter to Harvey, assures us that Spenser will be raised from oblivion when his praises have been broadcast in the "tromp of fame." In the light of this image's conventionality, it is reasonable to assume that in naming his butterfly, Spenser used metonymy, fully expecting his readers to identify properly the nuances of Clarion's name.

If we think of Clarion as representing the man hungry for fame, many of the poem's details have additional significance. The gathering of flowers to make a garland for Venus is itself germane to the quest for fame and should be compared with Serena's picking of flowers in book VI of *The Faerie Queene*: in both cases, envy's incursions are not long in coming. The praise and "blazed fame" (266) accorded Arachne, moreover,

2. Franklin E. Court, "The Theme and Structure of Spenser's *Muiopotmos*," *SEL* 10 (1970), p. 12.
3. *Variorum Spenser*, *VII*. 297.
4. See Guy de Tervarent, *Attributs et symboles dans l'art profane 1450–1600*: Diction langue perdu (Geneva, 1958–59), col. 397.
5. George Puttenham, *The Arte of English Poesie*, ed. G. D. Willcock and Alice Walker (Folcroft, Pa., 1969), p. 15.

prompt Minerva's descent to earth and finally provoke the presumptuous Arachne's challenge. The happiest consequence of treating Clarion in this way, however, is that throughout the whole of Spenser's work and, indeed, most of Renaissance poetry, the famous man, recipient of worldly praise, is most susceptible to envy. * * *

The historical pressures which complement this philosophical theme add another dimension to the fact that Clarion is a butterfly. "Muiopotmos," published in 1591 after Spenser's visit to England, reflects the same disillusionment with the court and courtiers which we find in "Colin Clouts Come Home Againe" and parts of "Mother Hubberds Tale," and the butterfly who is first envied "in Court" (105) epitomizes, in fact, the vain trifling activity in which courtiers were engaged. In late Elizabethan and Jacobean literature the comparison between courtiers and butterflies becomes a commonplace to be repeated in satires such as *The Scourge of Villanie*, *Skialetheia*, *The Time's Whistle*; it is repeated in Marston's *Antonio and Mellida;* both Dekker and Nashe use it.[6] But surely Clarion is the most conspicuous (and perhaps the first) example of this tendency to identify the butterfly with the courtier: decked in all his finery, he is a pregnant reminder of the fame-thirsty courtier who is brought low by his own carelessness and his rivals' envy.

ROBERT A. BRINKLEY: [The Politics of Metamorphosis][†]

If the Arachne-Pallas episode in *Muiopotmos* rereads Ovid in terms of the Elizabethan court, if it uses a reading of Ovid to read the art of the Fairy Queen, the butterfly in *Muiopotmos* involves a rereading of Vergil as well. * * *

Muiopotmos concludes with a fresco from the *Aeneid*; Clarion dies as Turnus dies: "His deepe groning spright / In Bloudie streames foorth fled into the aire, / His bodie left the spectacle of care" (11. 438–40). Like Turnus, Clarion's corpse is a Vergilian sign: as a spectacle, the corpse represents care (in Vergil, *cura*), but what the corpse also represented in the *Aeneid* was the careful labor (the labors of Aeneas, of Caesar and of Vergil) for which—like force in Homer—mortal things are indices. In *Muiopotmos*, on the other hand, as a spectacle of care, Clarion, a parody of a hero, is an index only of envy. Turnus is killed by Aeneas, the founder of the Roman world. Clarion is killed by a spider, a rival victim. The hero's fate—drained of meaning—has become no more relevant than an insect's.

Such insignificance involves political perspectives. William Nelson suggests that in *Muiopotmos* Spenser "directs his "readers to sit in a god-like seat, to look upon the little world of butterflies and spiders so that he may understand how Olympus sees mankind."[1] The poem recreates us

6. For Marston, see *The Poems*, ed Arnold Davenport (Liverpool 1961), p 121 and *The Works*, ed A. H. Bullen (London 1887); Everard Guilpin, *Skialetheia* (1598), Shakespeare Association Facsimiles No. 2 (Oxford 1931), sig. B4r, R. C., Gent., *The Time's Whistle: or New Daunce of Seven Satires and Other Poems*, ed. J. M. Cowper, *EETS* os 48, p 136; for Nashe and Dekker, see the reference in John Carey, "Sixteenth and Seventeenth Century Prose," *English Poetry and Prose*, 1540–1674, ed. Christopher Ricks (London 1970), pp 381–82.

† From Robert A. Brinkley, "Spenser's *Muiopotmos* and the Politics of Metamorphosis," *ELH* 48 (1981): 668–76. The essay has been condensed.

1. William Nelson, *The Poetry of Edmund Spenser* (New York and London, 1963), p. 72.

both as gods and insects, and for Spenser's immediate audience, the Elizabethan court, the poem mirrors positions at court. Courtiers may take a godlike perspective and regard Clarion and Aragnoll as insects; courtiers may identify themselves with the insect world and discover that they themselves participate in epic parodies. As gods we celebrate the artistry which produces Clarion and Aragnoll; as insects we feel diminished by that artistry. Yet Spenser's poem may involve a third perspective as well, that of a reader-narrator who, by understanding the fate of the butterfly, absents himself from that fate.

In *Muiopotmos*, Pallas's artistry recreates the artistry of the poem, but as Vergil's temple in the *Georgics* centers on an image of Caesar, so Spenser's text in *Muiopotmos* centers on an image of Elizabeth. As such the focus of his epyllion recreates the focus of *The Faerie Queene*, a poem consecrated "to live with the eternitie of her fame," * * * [and] even as the *mortalia* in Vergil's temple are glorifications, so Spenser's epic parodies are frescoes which decorate his poem and glorify the power of his Queen. That the parodies glorify Spenser's own power seems to me less clear. * * * The narrator observes, wanders in, and explores a poetic domain which he claims to have discovered. He rarely seems in possession of it. At times he seems possessed by it, but possessed, in particular, by its foreignness: "My weary steps I guyde/In this delightfull land of Faery . . . strange waies," Spenser writes (VI, Proem, i). In the Mutability Cantos he explicitly separates his own vision from the vision he relates. In *Muiopotmos* he finds himself driven toward a conclusion which he does not seek but which the poem's creativity requires. While we may interpret such a stance as mere convention, if we imagine a master rhetorician behind this convention, manipulating our responses, we create a figure for the poet which the poetry itself does not envision. * * * Spenser pictures himself wandering through a landscape of recreations, an explorer of a metamorphic world, who encounters parodies but is not recreated as one of them. Rather than become a sign in the text of the poem, the narrator who reads what he envisions and relates what he reads, makes of his poem an index of his freedom to read—even as what he reads is an index of the presence of the Fairy Queen. The narrator who reads distinguishes himself both from the characters in his poem and from his poetry's metamorphic force. Unlike Arachne or the butterfly, Spenser is not a figure in Pallas's text. Having become its narrator, he evades the politics which has silenced them.

ANDREW D. WEINER: [Butterflies, Men, and the Narrator in *Muiopotmos*][†]

* * *

The problem may be stated simply enough: if we accept Allen's notion (however modified) of the butterfly as the rational soul, we must then proceed to see in his destruction either a just punishment for his "fall," the unjustness of a universe that destroys what is beautiful, fragile, and inno-

† From Andrew D. Weiner, "Spenser's *Muiopotmos* and the Fates of Butterflies and Men," *JEGP* 84 (1985): 203–20.

cent for no good reason, or blind chance randomly striking out against a handy target. In any case, though, the equation of the butterfly with the soul creates a problem of poetic representation. After all, a butterfly, whatever meaning we may impose upon it, *is* an irrational creature of the "lower order," and it is not likely to be able to act other than naturally. * * *

If, however, the butterfly is an emblem of the soul, he must be doing something wrong to merit the destruction the gods visit upon him—if we are not to be left with the blinded Gloucester's despairing analogy: "As flies to wanton boys are we to the gods; / They kill us for their sport" (*King Lear*, IV. i. 36–37). On other occasions, the narrator apparently adopts this position and, consequently, we are offered (more or less simultaneously) another vision of the psyche's decline and fall. That the butterfly can be a representation of the soul is clear. * * * [But] if commentaries on the legend of Cupid and Psyche attest to the symbolic meaning of the butterfly, marginal illustrations in medieval and Renaissance manuscripts—at least as late as the Grimani Breviary—abound in butterflies, frequently full of sound and fury, yet apparently signifying absolutely nothing. With little effort, one finds them (in the pages of Lilian Randall's census of *Images in the Margins of Gothic Manuscripts*) sitting still, flying, or being held on strings; fighting men with swords and bucklers, being shot at by men with crossbows and by centaurs, or having shawms blown at them; riding in carts; being pursued by women, nude men, and apes; ringing bells; and being viewed as lunch by storks.[1]

In the fifteenth century, butterflies leave the margins and move into panel paintings as well. In addition to being presented more or less innocently for decorative purposes, as in the Louvre portrait of an Este Princess by Pisanello or the Baldovinetti Annunciation (c. 1460) in the Uffizi, there are Renaissance butterflies whose meaning is precisely that they mean nothing.[2] * * *

If we now return to consider Spenser's ambiguous butterfly not as a necessary fixed emblem for the human soul, the rock upon which we must build an allegory, but as a "creature wilde" by whom man "in somme thinges may be taughte," * * * we must first decide whether the fate of the butterfly in fact has the slightest relevance for us. The narrator seems to think so, but if we look at him objectively we might well wonder how objectively he is looking at the butterfly. His description of Clarion arming himself to fly abroad may serve as a possible test. While it may begin as a light parody of an epic arming scene, this description (along with the butterfly's "furnitures") quickly becomes too bizarre to comprehend. Clarion's breastplate "of substance pure" is perhaps easily allegorized as the soul guarding itself with righteousness (cf. Ephesians 6:14), although "righteousness" is perhaps not most optimistically viewed as

> framed, to endure
> The bit of balefull steele and bitter stownd,
> No lesse than that, which *Vulcane* made to sheild
> *Achilles* life from fate of *Troyan* field. (ll. 61–64)

1. Lilian M. C. Randall, *Images in the Margins of Gothic Manuscripts* (Berkeley: Univ. of California Press, 1966), pp. 62, 74, 76, 136, 146–47, 166, and 227.
2. For Pisanello, see Enio Sindona, *Pisanello* (New York: Harry N. Abrams, 1963), Plate 104. For Baldovinetti, see Paolo Lecaldano, *I Grandi Maestri della Pittura Italiana Del Quattrocento*, II (Milan: Rizzoli Editore, 1963), Plate 52.

From this point, the narrator's hold on reality seems to become increasingly tenuous. What are we to do with a butterfly who wears "about his shoulders broad" the "hairie hide of some wilde beast, whom hee / In saluage forrest by aduenture slew" (ll. 65–67), and what are we to think about those who, seeing him "so horrible," believe him to be "*Alcides* with the Lyons skin / When the *Naemean* Conquest he did win" (ll. 70–72)? Displaying no sense of the incongruity of his description, the narrator goes on to talk about Clarion's "glistering Burganet" that "could both *Phoebus* arrowes ward, / And th'hayling darts of heauen beating hard" (ll. 79–80). Nor is it easier to accept his comparison of the butterfly's antennae, those "two deadly weapon's fixt," to the "threatfull pikes" of a "warlike Brigandine," which this "flie" outstretched "so as him their terrour more adornes" (ll. 81, 84–85, 87–88). Not only is it hard to see in this an allegory of the soul—Dante's "angelic butterfly / that flieth to judgment without defence"—it is hard to see anything that can possibly be taken as seriously as the narrator quite obviously does.

* * * We are more likely, it seems to me, to get a sense of what *Muiopotmos* is about by considering the butterfly as if it were merely a butterfly and the narrator as though he were a Chaucerian narrator and not Colin Clout in disguise. * * * Like Sir Terwin, who also loves in vain a lady who "ioyd to see her lover languish and lament" (*Faerie Queene*, I.ix.27), the narrator seems to see the world through the eyes of that "Cursed wight," the "man of hell, that cals himselfe *Despaire*" (I.ix.28). All "hope of due reliefe" (I.ix.29) has evidently been plucked from him, and the fate of the butterfly is for him a confirmation of this state of affairs.

Instead of seeing the butterfly's death as totally unrelated to his own or as emblematic of the transitoriness of earthly things—like the love over which "The Archer God . . . / That ioyes on wretched louers to be wroken, / and heaped spoyles of bleeding harts to see" (ll. 98–100) presides—he takes it as a sign of the destruction that will come to all "fraile, fleshly wight[s]" (l. 225). Una's consolation to another "fraile, feeble, fleshly wight" (*Faerie Queene*, I.ix.53) suffering at the hands of *Despaire*, "In heauenly mercies hast thou not a part?" (I. ix. 53), is evidently beyond his comprehension since the only "grace" of which he can conceive is the grace to be gained by stealing Clarion's wings and bringing "So precious a pray" (ll. 110, 112) to his love.

If the narrator's psychological state explains *why* he has misunderstood his story, it does not explain *how* he "misread" the events he saw—a butterfly flying through a garden until he became entangled in a spider's web and perished. To say that he turned a simple narrative into an allegory, while true, does not explain how he came to do such a bad job of it. After all, he too presumably had the emblem books and the commentators to tell him how to interpret: what went wrong? * * * Calvin notes that God, "to manifest his perfection in the whole structure of the universe, and daily place himself in our view," has forever engraved his "glory . . . in characters so bright, so distinct, and so illustrious" on all of his works that "none, however dull and illiterate, can plead ignorance as their excuse."[3]

3. Jean Calvin, *The Institutes of the Christian Religion*, trans. Henry Beveridge (Grand Rapids, Mich., Wm. B. Eerdmans, 1970), I.vi. 1. I cite Calvin simply as a representative of Reformed Protestant opinion in the second half of the sixteenth century, not to suggest that Spenser was a Calvinist.

As he goes on to add, however, "Bright . . . as is the manifestation which God gives both of himself and his immortal kingdom in the mirror of his works, so great is our stupidity, so dull are we in regard to these bright manifestations, that we derive no benefit from them" (I.v.ii). * * *

Protestant exegetics thus downgrades allegory to the status of "examples or similitudes borrowed of strange matters" or excludes it altogether. As Tyndale comments, "Allegories prove nothing."[4]

The narrator's attempt to find meaning in the life and death of the butterfly is doomed to failure from the beginning. As he seeks to understand allegorically the connection between the butterfly's fate and his own and to comprehend the cause of its fall, his only chance of success lies in his coming to recognize that he must fail. Yet despite his confusion—he vacillates between feeling that the butterfly has done nothing to deserve its fate and assuming that everything it did must have been wrong—he never seems able to confess to himself or to us that he has not the faintest notion why the butterfly died or what its death might mean. The narrator, hoping to find some visible cause for the butterfly's fate, tries his best to condemn the insect for doing what it was created to do, to "cast his glutton sense to satisfy" (l. 179). But if so strict a moralist as Calvin would not find fault in the butterfly's enjoyment in the garden, why should we?

AMORETTI

A. LEIGH DENEEF: The *Amoretti*[†]

In the *Amoretti*, Spenser again tries "rightly to define" the nature and the power of love. We might expect, therefore, that the ways of misperceiving and falsely expressing love that have engaged the poet in the *Calender*, the *Daphnaida*, and *Colin Clout* will once more serve as dramatic foils to his own right speaking. As those poems have taught us, the obligation to express correctly predicts a double commitment—to remain faithful to the fact that poetry speaks metaphorically, and to defend the poetic metaphors against those intelligences that would reduce them to literality.

The descriptive title Spenser accords his collection of sonnets is evidence of the poet's consciousness of these obligations. Love, or *Amor*, is the Idea lying behind and shaping the sequence. The eighty-nine sonnets, or *amoretti*, that comprise the sequence are literary acts of loving, textual metaphors of the abstract Idea. The task of the poet is to reveal the fore-conceit by which these *amoretti* are metaphorically figured forth. By conceiving the whole in these Sidneyan terms, we can redirect the critical energies usually spent in charting the narrative progression of the sequence or in describing the individualized personalities of its lover and his beloved.[1]

4. William Tyndale, "Prologue to Leviticus," in Tyndale's *Doctrinal Treatises and Introductions to Different Portions of the Holy Scriptures*, ed. Henry Walter (Cambridge: Cambridge Univ. Press, 1848), p. 425.

† From *Spenser and the Motives of Metaphor* (Durham, NC: Duke University Press, 1982), pp. 62–76.

1. The critical studies of the *Amoretti* I have found most useful are: P. M. Cummings, "Spenser's *Amoretti* as an Allegory of Love," *TSLL* 12 (1970): 163–179; O. B. Hardison, "*Amoretti* and the Dolce Stil Nuovo," *ELR* 2 (1972): 208–216; William C. Johnson, "Amor and Spenser's *Amoretti*," *ES* 54 (1973): 217–226; Louis Martz, "The *Amoretti*: 'Most Goodly Temperature'," in *Form and*

For regardless of how these elements are defined, narrative progress is nothing more than a Sidneyan groundplot, and the lover and his lady are but "notable images." Both must be unfigured along the linguistic stages of mimetic making in order to learn how they speak metaphorically.

Much has been written about the groundplot of the *Amoretti*, and some of it is relevant to our concerns. The most obvious thing to say is that Spenser habitually repeats whole poems, parts of poems, or specific image patterns in different contexts throughout the sequence. In fact, these repetitions—actually transformations—are so consistent that almost all of the individual sonnets could be arranged in identifiable mini-sequences within the sequence as a whole.[2] It is also clear that such minor sequences are themselves subjected to three large structural and thematic divisions. Generally speaking, the first twenty-two sonnets are controlled by a broadly sketched Petrarchan context, and sonnets of several distinct groups (calendric sonnets, sonnets on the "cruel fayre," pride sonnets, eye sonnets) are all focused through the Petrarchan perspective. In the middle forty-five sonnets, Spenser seems intent upon complicating the terms by which love is defined. The singleness of the Petrarchan view gives way to a context in which Petrarchan, neo-Platonic, Ovidian, and Christian perspectives all compete with and clash against one another. In the final twenty-two sonnets, the multiplicity of viewpoints seems again to resolve into one as Spenser tries to articulate a Christian synthesis.[3]

All of this is obvious enough, but the precise nature of the divisions—whether they are thematic, calendric, liturgical—is not as important-as the necessity which gives rise to them. Rather than thinking of the divisions as a narrative fact, we should ask whether they answer to a particular poetic problem. * * *

* * * Spaces that remain open are guaranteed to be metaphorical; those that are closed are reduced to the literal. The various divisions of the *Amoretti*, then, are rhetorical safeguards by which Spenser keeps his semantic sites open to metaphoric extension. Our task, therefore, is not to name a given place, or even to name the kind of loving that is set to work in that place, but to learn the relations the poet makes between places. "Rightly to define" is to demonstrate how the text is made to speak metaphorically of a site that is beyond it.

We can begin this work by looking yet once more at the obviously calendric sonnets. The first of these is Sonnet 4, a New Year's poem, set in January, but looking forward to the awakening of spring and Cupid,

---

Convention in the Poetry of Edmund Spenser, ed. William Nelson (New York, 1961), pp. 146–168; J. W. Lever, *The Elizabethan Love Sonnet* (London, 1956); Hallett Smith, *Elizabethan Poetry* (Cambridge, Mass., 1966); and Alexander Dunlop, "The Unity of Spenser's *Amoretti*," in *Silent Poetry*, ed. Alastair Fowler (London, 1970), pp. 153–169.

2. The difficulties of actually naming or classifying such sonnet groups are immense, for not only do the groupings range from as few as two to as many as seventeen poems, but they are also developed by different means. Some groups are imagistic (variations on eye conceits or hair conceits), some rhetorical (varieties of blazon or *carpe diem* poems), some thematic (pride sonnets, cruel mistress sonnets), some structural (calendric sonnets) and so on. The problem is even more complicated when we realize how Spenser interlaces motifs. Thus a quatrain from a sonnet in group A may be expanded into a full sonnet belonging to group B. Despite the risks, however, a full study of such groupings would demonstrate the complexity of Spenser's *entrelacement* and act as a positive corrective to presumptions that we can understand this sequence by means of a few numerological keys.

3. A more comprehensive discussion of these three divisions and the contexts they create can be found in Hardison's "*Amoretti* and the Dolce Stil Nuovo." Hardison's argument seems strongest on the Petrarchan context of the first division.

and calling upon the beloved to "prepare [her] selfe new loue to entertaine." Although Spenser has some original fun with the diction and the puns, the sonnet itself is perfectly conventional and heavily dependent upon the classical *carpe diem* motif. Despite the fact that it is still winter, the promise of spring is seemingly fulfilled within the poem as the flowers quite literally take over the final eight lines. Fifteen sonnets later, Sonnet 19, spring formally arrives. Like Ronsard before and Herrick after him, Spenser affirms the sanctity of seasonal love by directing a "quyre of Byrds" to sing "anthemes" and "lays" in its honor, and by having "all the woods" reecho those hymns. Again the *carpe diem* urge lies behind the poem, even though the major focus is on the lady's rebellion from Love's law, her willful disobeying of the natural "precepts."

In Sonnet 62, after "one year is spent," New Year's comes round again. As in Sonnet 4, the temporal change leads the lover to envision a more hopeful season of clear weather, fresh joys, and reciprocated love. Yet the tone of this poem is very different from that of Sonnet 4. The eagerness, the confident word-play, even the rather bold, brash challenge of the final "prepare your selfe," have given way in Sonnet 62 to a more somber pleading and a greater awareness that some of winter's gloom is likely to linger on:

> The weary yeare his race now hauing run,
> the new begins his compast course anew:
> with shew of morning mylde he hath begun,
> betokening peace and plenty to ensew.
> So let vs, which this chaunge of weather vew,
> chaunge eeke our mynds and former liues amend,
> the old yeares sinnes forepast let vs eschew,
> and fly the faults with which we did offend.
> Then shall the new yeares ioy forth freshly send,
> into the glooming world his gladsome ray:
> and all these stormes which now his beauty blend,
> shall turne to caulmes and tymely cleare away.
> So likewise loue cheare you your heauy spright,
> and chaunge old yeares annoy to new delight.

How inappropriate the *carpe diem* injunction of Sonnet 4 would be to this poem. Fresh youth and wanton love are not addressed at all. Instead of awakening a lusty hour, these more exprienced lovers are both enjoined to amend their lives, eschew old faults, and cheer their heavy and possibly sinful spirits.

Sonnet 70 repeats the spring song of Sonnet 19, and although the *carpe diem* urge reappears in one of its strongest forms, its meaning is fundamentally altered again by the changed tone:

> Fresh spring the herald of loues mighty king,
> in whose cote armour richly are displayd
> all sorts of flowers the which on earth do spring
> in goodly colours gloriously arrayd:
> Goe to my loue, where she is careless layd,
> yet in her winters bowre not well awake:
> tell her the ioyous time wil not be staid
> vnlesse she doe him by the forelock take.

Bid her therefore her selfe soone ready make,
to wayt on loue amongst his louely crew:
where euery one that misseth then her make,
shall be by him amearst with penance dew.
Make hast therefore sweet loue, whilest it is prime,
for none can call againe the passed time.

As in Sonnet 19, the lady is threatened with a penalty if she does not "wayt on loue." But here the call to love, to seize the day, is chastened by the speaker's own wry smile at the conventional injunction and by the strong biblical overtones of lines 5–6. Sonnet 70 is one of a small group of climactic sonnets drawing on the Song of Songs[4] and on the coming of spring that blesses the lovers in the biblical text (2: 10–12):

> My welbeloued spake & said vnto me, Arise, my loue, my faire one, & come thy way. For beholde, winter is past: the raine is changed, and is gone away. The flowers appear in ye earth: the time of the singing of birdes is come, & the voice of the turtle is heard in our land.[5]

The *carpe diem* exhortation, therefore, is focused through the perspective of the symbolic marriage celebrated in the Song. The beloved in this sonnet is not asked, as she was in Sonnet 19, to wait upon Cupid's crew, but to love as she ought, as "the Lord vs taught."

How are we to articulate the relationships between these four sonnets? If we suppose a sequential progress through the "sequence," then the obvious calendric pairing (Sonnets 4 and 62; Sonnets 19 and 70) is a secondary structure abstracted from a prior pairing within contextual sites (Sonnets 4 and 19; Sonnets 62 and 70). The kind of loving expressed in Sonnet 4, for example, is determined by a sequence of semantic situations: first, by the Petrarchan context in which the poem is initially perceived; second, by calendric analogy to the second poem in that context (19); and third, by a calendric analogy to a third poem situated in a different context (62). Each poem in the sequence alters the perspective and the placement of the initial calendric sonnet. And in this way, Spenser ensures that the terms of that initial sonnet remain open to metaphoric extension. Sonnet 4 "speaks metaphorically" Sonnets 19, 62, and 70.

We could draw the same conclusion by observing how the poet-lover perceives his own terms. In Sonnets 4 and 19, King Cupid and the *carpe diem* injunction pronounced in his name are both interpreted literally by the poet-lover. His sense of the poetic and ethical dimensions of his words is limited by the equally literal seasons in which the poems are situated. Sonnets 62 and 70 transform both the literal seasons and their literal terms into metaphors. The threshold of New Year's Day becomes a metaphor for personal reformation and renewed commitments of all kinds, and the promise of spring becomes a metaphor for the spiritual uniting of all existence. The repetition of the seasonal site thus discloses the error of the poet-lover's initial perceptions, for we now see that even

4. The only study of Spenser's use of the Song of Songs is Israel Baroway's "The Imagery of Spenser and the Song of Songs," *JEGP* 33 (1934): 23–45. In the light of more recent studies of the Song, such as Stanley Stewart's *The Enclosed Garden* (Madison, 1966), a reexamination of the sequence in terms of its biblical—rather than liturgical—imagery is long overdue.
5. Cited from *The Geneva Bible: A Facsimile*, ed. Lloyd Berry (Madison, 1969), p. 281.

Sonnets 4 and 19 are metaphoric adumbrations of the broader perspectives in 62 and 70. The "mighty king" of Sonnet 70 is not only itself metaphoric, but also redefines the "King" of Sonnet 19 as a metaphor; and the metaphoric confession-contrition-amendment of Sonnet 64 rewrites the *carpe diem* of Sonnet 4 as a metaphoric prefiguration of itself. The speaker has learned, in the later poems, to open his earlier terms and places to new and larger accommodations which are themselves metaphoric extensions of those earlier terms. He has learned, in short, to speak metaphorically.

Sonnets 22 and 68 form another calendric pairing and provide another opportunity for metaphoric transformation. But in this instance Spenser complicates the interpretive problems of both his speaker and his reader by revealing that even metaphoric speech is susceptible to falsifying closure. At first glance, the relationship between these two sonnets seems to duplicate those we have already drawn. The enclosed and literal place of worship in Sonnet 22 is radically opened to metaphoric extension in 68: the "holy day" of interiorized devotion in the early poem becomes, in the later one, "this day" which reaches back to "death and sin" and forward to eternal life "in felicity." Similarly, the temple within the mind in Sonnet 22 is opened in 68 to admit not only worship of the lady, but also man's devotion to God as well as God's love for man.

But if we ask how the lover of Sonnet 22 goes wrong, it is clear that his error does not result from the kind of literalizing we have seen in Sonnets 4 and 19. He is perfectly conscious of the fact that both his "seruice" and his "sacrifice" are metaphors fashioned by imitating the devotions of "this holy season." In effect, what the speaker here has forgotten is the heart of his own metaphors. By failing to see how such metaphors point beyond themselves, he has again settled for an incomplete definition.

Sonnet 68 presents the action from which all of love's metaphors derive: Christ's sacrifice is not a fictional metaphor but a literal fact. As a result of that sacrifice, all other loving is metaphorically situated. Man's love of God metaphorically imitates Christ's love of man: "thy loue we weighing worthily, / may likewise loue thee for the same againe." Man's love of man metaphorically imitates God's love of man: "and for thy sake that all lyke deare didst buy, / with loue may one another entertayne." The speaker's love of his mistress must find its metaphoric site among these loving relationships. The "gentle deare" whose "owne goodwill" allows the lover to capture her in Sonnet 67 not only reenacts Christ's sacrificial act, but also is allowed to do so because Christ has defined her as one of "all lyke deare." Similarly, the "entertainment" to which the lady is called in the first calendric sonnet is here redefined not as the closed metaphoric devotion of Sonnet 22 but as the radically metaphoric entertainment by which loving "one another" participates in loving God and being loved by God.[6] Even the structure of Sonnet 68 enforces this open-

6. The problem can be posed in linguistic terms by seeing the conventional "devotion" of Sonnet 22 as the signifier and the Christian devotion of Sonnet 68 as the signified. But as in all linguistic signs, signifier and signified can be reversed. The interpretive problem is the same as that defined by Tzvetan Todorov's discussion of *La Quest de Sanct Graile*: "For us . . . combat must occur either in the material world or else in the world of ideas; it is earthly or celestial, but not both at once. If it is two ideas which are in combat, Bors's blood cannot be shed, only his mind is concerned. To maintain the contrary is to infringe upon one of the fundamental laws of our logic, which is the law of the excluded middle. X and its contrary cannot be true at the

ing of the metaphoric places. The mistress is addressed only through and in proper subordination to the prayer of the first eight lines. Unlike Sonnet 22, which replaces heavenly love with a narrowly conceived, even if metaphoric, earthly love, Sonnet 68 insists that the metaphoric relations between all forms of loving inform the activity of any one of them.

The profundity of Sonnet 68 does not lie simply in its Christian dogma, but in its radical transformation of all the metaphors of loving that appear in the *Amoretti*. It defines the literal act by which all such metaphors arise and to which all such metaphors must be referred. All acts of loving are metaphoric imitations, and it is precisely Spenser's continual reformulation of those metaphoric acts, his constant opening of them to ever larger metaphoric relation, that reveals the mimetic principle.[7] We hardly need add, perhaps, that this poetic activity is itself metaphoric of appropriate ethical action.

We have dealt thus far with only the most obvious of the metaphoric recreations in the *Amoretti*, but if our conclusions are valid, we should find a similar strategy at work in other mini-sequences. Sonnet 7 begins a series of sonnets treating the mistress's eyes:

> Fayre eyes, the myrrour of my mazed hart,
> what wondrous vertue is contaynd in you
> the which both lyfe and death forth from you dart
> into the obiect of your mighty view?
>
> [ll. 1–4]

As we might expect, the contextual placement of the poem within the sequence predicates a semantic commonplace. The poet-lover merely elaborates the Petrarchan contrariety: when the lady smiles, he is "inspired"; when she frowns, he is "fyred." Apparently unable to conceive the eyes in any other terms, he can only keep repeating the simplistic life-death dichotomy the commonplace gives rise to. Spenser's own wry judgment on such reductive literalizing implies not that the Petrarchan trope is wrong, but that to the speaker it has become a semantic trap.

That the speaker's perspective is arbitrarily limited is revealed in the very next poem:

> More then most faire, full of the liuing fire,
> kindled aboue vnto the maker neere:
> no eies but ioyes, in which al powers conspire,
> that to the world naught else be counted deare.
> Thrugh your bright beams doth not the blinded guest
> shoot out his darts to base affections wound;
> but Angels come to lead fraile mindes to rest
> in chast desires on heauenly beauty bound.

same time, says the logic of ordinary discourse. The Quest of the Holy Grail says exactly the contrary. Every event has a literal meaning *and* an allegorical meaning." See *The Poetics of Prose*, tr. Richard Howard (Ithaca, 1977), pp. 128–129. In Spenser's terms, the spiritual can as easily be the signifier of the material as the material can be the signifier of the spiritual. The sign-system of love thus depends upon a recognition that all forms are *significant*, revelatory of the signified truth.

7. It may be noted, especially in light of the paradigm linking Maker and maker we observed in the Introduction, that only God can figure forth without reduction, hence without the need for metaphor. Christ's act is a literal bodying forth of the divine Idea, but it neither distorts nor limits that Idea and it does not cease to participate directly in the Idea.

You frame my thoughts and fashion me within,
you stop my toung, and teach my hart to speake,
you calme the storme that passion did begin,
strong thrugh your cause, but by your vertue weak.
Dark is the world, where your light shined neuer;
well is he borne, that may behold you euer.

Here the lady's eyes serve only reforming functions—framing, fashioning, teaching, and calming—and the poet-lover seems to have corrected the Petrarchan excesses of Sonnet 7 by invoking a new semantic convention, here loosely neo-Platonic. He seems also to understand in this sonnet that "rightly to define" the lady's eyes means finding a suitable metaphor. Hence the eyes are not eyes, but "ioyes"; and the lover gazing into them sees not affections' dart, but "heauenly beauty." It is clear, however, that this positive reading of the eyes arises not by metaphorically accommodating the contraries of the preceding sonnet, but by excluding half of its terms.

Sonnet 9 takes the speaker a step further:

Long-while I sought to what I might compare
those powrefull eies, which lighten my dark spright,
yet find I nought on earth to which I dare
resemble th'ymage of their goodly light.
Not to the Sun: for they doo shine by night;
nor to the Moone: for they are changed neuer;
nor to the Starres: for they haue purer sight;
nor to the fire: for they consume not euer;
Nor to the lightning: for they still perseuer;
nor to the Diamond: for they are more tender;
nor Vnto Christall: for nought may them seuer;
nor vnto glasse: such basenesse mought offend her;
Then to the Maker selfe they likest be,
whose light doth lighten all that here we see.

What was implicit in Sonnet 8 here becomes explicit as Spenser parodies his speaker's quest for an adequate metaphor by mocking the intelligence that seeks such a metaphor in literal-minded equivalences. Throughout the first section of the sequence, and well into the second, the speaker tries out the various literary conventions by which he might express the lady's eyes. Most of these are broadly Petrarchan, as Sonnets 7, 10, 12, and 16; some are loosely neo-Platonic, as 8 and 21; and some potentially Christian, as 9 and 24. But in every case, the speaker pursues the conventions only to reductive ends. Even when he recognizes that the contextual tropes are metaphoric, he does not see that they are metaphors for the other contextual tropes as well. In a sense, we could say that the conventional models provide the poet-lover with literal situations in which he can act out differing ways of loving. But like the shepherds in the *Calender*, or Alcyon, or Colin, he merely substitutes one semantic site for another and thus fails to conceive the relationship between them.

For Spenser, however, the interplay between discrete texts of loving discloses a broader metaphor from which all textual figures have been "figured forth." And this metaphor, rather than excluding specific contextual options, seeks to accommodate them all. By reading the conceit *to love* or the Idea *Love* behind the different texts of *loving*, we learn that those texts speak metaphorically. As we get on in the sequence, the speaker too learns to read in this way. In fact, it is exactly his growing ability to perceive metaphorically that charts his progress within the sequence. By the end of the middle section, he has learned to appropriate and approximate the voice of the poet by using conventional tropes to explore what remains constant in the varieties of loving rather than abusing them by assuming that one kind of loving precludes another. Like the Shepheard of the Ocean [Raleigh, eds.], he becomes "faithfull" to the metaphoric nature of his discrete sites of loving and begins to avoid the kind of dichotomizing his earlier literal-mindedness gave rise to.

The rhetorical interplay between metaphors that close by literal reduction and those that open by metaphoric extension shapes another mini-sequence on capture and captivity. The series begins with the very first sonnet:

> Happy ye leaues when as those lilly hands
> which hold my life in their dead doing might
> shall handle you and hold in loues soft bands,
> lyke captiues trembling at the victors sight.
> [ll. 1–4]

Captivity is clearly metaphoric in these lines, a sign of the mistress's acceptance and prophetic of the speaker's future love and happiness. Sonnet 10 repeats the metaphor but situates it within a literalized Petrarchan context. The literal implications of tyranny, massacre, and vengeance control the next several appearances of the trope and thus occasion the speaker's growing complaint. In Sonnets 11, 12, 14, 29, and 37, the metaphoric captivity the speaker initially desired has become a literal place from which he wishes to escape. Sonnet 37 presents the altered perspective in its clearest terms:

> Fondness it were for any being free,
> to couet fetters, though they golden be.
> [ll. 13–14]

The initial trope has again become a semantic trap and the speaker's escape is made to depend upon his recovery of the metaphoric sense of his term.

His reformed image of captivity comes dramatically in Sonnet 65, but Spenser prepares very carefully for this new image by once again making the contextual site an opportunity for speaking metaphorically rather than a condition of semantic reduction. In Sonnet 62, as we have seen, the speaker prays that both he and his mistress will "chaunge old yeares annoy to new delight," and in Sonnet 63 he sights "the happy shore" which promises "the ioyous safety of so sweet a rest." As Sonnet 64 shows, this shore is the mistress herself, now perceived as "a gardin of sweet flowres." Because this biblical metaphor is so crucial to understanding the metaphoric speech of Sonnet 65, it is worth a slight digression.

The central metaphor of the Song of Songs is, of course, the enclosed garden, the *hortus conclusus:* "My sister my spouse is as a garden inclosed, as a spring shut vp, and a fountaine sealed vp" (4:12, Geneva Bible).

Enclosure, shutting up, is not a negative or life-denying act here, for it is precisely because the garden is enclosed that it flourishes; because it is sealed, the lover is unafraid to enter it, to taste "the ioyous safety of so sweete a rest."

> My welbeloued is gone downe into his garden to the beds of spices, to fede in the gardens, and to gather lilies. [Song 6:1]

The Great Bible combines the description of the sealed garden and the lover's entry into it in its translation of the fourth chapter:

> A garden well locked is my syster, my spouse, a garden well locked, and a sealed well. The frutes [that] are planted in the, are lyke a very Paradyse of pomgranates with swete frutes . . . a well of gardens, a well of lyuinge waters, which renne down from Libanus. . . . yee [that] my beloved maye come into this garden and eate of the swete frutes that growe therein.

In an annotation on the word "locked" in this passage, Henry Ainsworth writes: "*Barred*: that is, close shut . . . which is for safetie and defense, that no evill should come thereon, no enemies should enter."[8] Captivity, therefore, is neither destructive nor delimiting; it is instead a guarantee of safety and productivity if correctly viewed. The Song of Songs thus gives the lover the means of transforming his previously literal understanding of captivity. As we shall see, this enables the lover not only to "offer" captivity to his mistress, but also to explain to her exactly what such captivity means.

But there may be even more behind Spenser's use of the Song of Songs at this dramatic point in the sequence. The repeated incident of the maid's taking hold of her love and bringing him into her house not only furthers the notion that captivity is productive, but foreshadows both the climactic Sonnet 67, in which the deer-love returns willingly to be caught and led in by the reformed lover, and the *Epithalamion*, where the lover first takes his bride by the hand and later leads her into the bridal chamber to consummate their union. In the third chapter of the Song, the maid says:

> I founde him whome my soule loued: I toke holde on him and left him not, til I had broght him vnto my mothers house into the chamber of her that concieved me. [Geneva 3:4]

John Dove explains this passage: the maid does not grab her lover as Potiphar's wife grabbed Joseph, for he was able to slip away from her. The maid holds the lover as the Christian must hold Christ, "as Iacob did, which held not the Angels garment, but the Angell himself; not the shadow but the substance."[9] Although the lover loses his freedom to captivity, the result is nourishment:

> I wil lead thee & bring thee into my mothers house: there thou shalt teache me: & I wil cause thee to drinke spiced wine, & newe wine of the pomegranate. [8:2]

8. *Annotations upon the Five Bookes of Moses, the Booke of the Psalms, and the Song of Songs, or Canticles* (London, 1627), p. 34.
9. *The Conversion of Salomon* (London, 1613), p. 148.

Captivity is thus doubly sustaining: as in Sonnets 76 and 77, the lover is fed with the "sweet fruit of pleasure"; the lady, as in Sonnets 65 and 68, is taught the sweet fruit of Christian doctrine.

Sonnet 65, then, demonstrates not only that the lover's literalizing and reductive perception of captivity has been strikingly altered, but also that he has now adopted the role of the instructor sanctioned by the biblical text:

> The doubt which ye misdeeme, fayre loue, is vaine,
> that fondly feare to loose your liberty,
> when loosing one, two liberties ye gayne,
> and make him bond that bondage earst dyd fly
> Sweet be the bands, the which true loue doth tye,
> without constraynt or dread of any ill:
> the gentle birde feeles no captiuity
> within her cage, but singes and feeds her fill.
> There pride dare not approach, nor discord spill
> the league twixt them, that loyal loue hath bound:
> but simple truth and mutuall good will,
> seekes with sweet peace to salue each others wound:
> There fayth doth fearlesse dwell in brasen towre,
> and spotlesse pleasure builds her sacred bowre.

The lover admits, in lines 3–4, that he had formerly misconstrued bondage as a literal captivity, loss of freedom as dreaded constraint. But now, understanding the metaphor of the "true loue knot," the sweet bands of love, he argues that only in such captivity is the soul completely free. "The gentle birde feeles no captiuity / within her cage, but singes and feeds her fill." Singing and feeding are metaphorically related again to the two roles the lover now assumes: the teacher of the mistress and partaker of her sweet fruits. As in the enclosed garden of the Song of Songs, there is multiple nourishment within the captivity of love in the *Amoretti*.

In Sonnet 67 the mistress, apparently having learned the lesson given her by the lover in Sonnet 65, allows herself to be "gotten hold of" as the bridegroom in the Song. Both lover and lady have learned to interpret captivity metaphorically. No longer reducing it to falsifying dichotomies, they open the term to accommodating paradox. The validity of their new perspective is immediately affirmed in Sonnet 68: Christ, triumphing over sin and death, "didst bring away / captiuity thence captiue vs to win." Man's captivity to sin is rewritten by his full acceptance of his greater captivity to Christ, a captivity both educating and nourishing:

> being with thy deare blood clene washt from sin,
> may liue for euer in felicity.

Even Christ here proves a mimetic lover: adopting the literal role of man's captivity, Christ captures captivity itself, rendering it only metaphoric. The lovers' love, insofar as it reflects, imitates, Christ's own act, reflects as well Christ's freeing love.

Two final sonnets measure the lovers' success. In Sonnet 71 the lover tells the lady that just as her needlework "is wouen all aboue / With woodbynd flowres and fragrant Eglantine," so shall what seemed a prison in which love has trapped her be "with many deare delights bedecked."

The reference to the spider in line 3 of this poem recalls the description of the spider in Sonnet 23. There the lover compared his labor to win the lady to a spider whose web was merely "fruitlesse worke . . . broken with least wynd." Now, however, the spider and the bee live in peace and safety in the enclosure of the garden, aware of the necessity for captivity. And the web is full of fruit for both of them.

In Sonnet 73, the lover plays true and false views of captivity against one another. Captive within his own prison of the self, the lover breaks free to give himself over to the "seruile bands" of the "fayre tresses" of the lady's "golden hayre." Spenser once again doubles back upon his own poems, here on the literal interpretation given in Sonnet 37 of the net of hair as entangling and entrapping. Then, expanding the image he had already used in Sonnet 65, Spenser has the lover fly as a bird "to feed his fill" on the lady's eyes. Those eyes, seen throughout the early stages of the sequence as literal sources of destruction, now are metaphoric nourishment. Finally, the lover prays to be encaged as a bird in the mistress's bosom, where, as he said in Sonnet 65, captivity is not captivity at all but the freedom to learn, to feed, and to sing:

> perhaps he there may learn with rare delight,
> to sing your name and praises ouer all
> That it hereafter may you not repent,
> him lodging in your bosome to haue lent.
> [ll. 11–14]

The strategy by which Spenser opens his textual metaphors to other and more encompassing accommodations is remarkably similar to the kind of *entrelacement* Rosemond Tuve describes in the continued metaphor of *The Faerie Queene.* As specific images or motifs are repeatedly placed in distinct contextual situations and shown to fulfill the semantic requirements of each place, their metaphoric nature is both ensured and illustrated. The textual transformations, in other words, guarantee the openness of all semantic places. Such freeing of place and of the literal vocabularies that places give rise to is itself a poetic imitation of Christ's redemptive act. For the Christ who frees love opens the space in which love is imprisoned in literal dichotomies, transforms that place into a metaphor that voids all dichotomy. Christ's freeing of love thus frees as well all ways of expressing love. "In Christ," Erasmus tells us, "everything is created anew, and vocabulary is wholly transformed."[1] The conventional vocabularies of Petrarchan or neo-Platonic love need not, therefore, be denied or even satirized, only opened to metaphoric status. The languages of traditional loving speak metaphorically of the divine injunction "to love," and the poet's task is to reveal the mimetic process by which such speaking has been "created anew." Such poetic reformation proposes a model, moreover, for ethical action. Lovers within and without the poetic narrative must learn that the various forms of loving available to them are legitimate only insofar as they are metaphorically accommodated to the lesson which "the Lord vs taught"—"to love" one another as we love Him and as He loves us.

It is precisely in these terms that Spenser opens even the site of Christ's loving to further metaphoric extension. Christ enters the textual

1. *Enchiridion*, in *Ausgewählte Werke*, ed. Hajo and Annemarie Holborn (Munich, 1964), p. 96.

sequence in order to force all literal narrative places into accommodating Him; but His action is itself metaphoric of the Idea of Love which He too imitates. The reformation which Christ accomplishes is thus a model rather than an end, and the poet's new task at the conclusion of the sequence is to reveal how such a model resolves all places into one, or frees all desire to love to aspire to the divine Idea of Love.

The typical Elizabethan sonnet sequence ends in a separation. In the terms of the present discussion, separation would necessarily involve a return to reductive dichotomies: lover and beloved, presence and absence, this place and that. At first glance, Spenser seems to confirm this sense of separation by placing his lover in the conventional condition:

> Lackying my loue I go from place to place,
> lyke a young fawne that late hath lost the hynd:
> and seeke each where, where last I sawe her face,
> whose ymage yet I carry fresh in mynd.
> I seeke the fields with her late footing synd,
> I seeke her bowre with her late presence deckt,
> yet nor in field nor bowre I her can fynd:
> yet field and bowre are full of her aspect.
> [Sonnet 78, 1–8]

In the normal sequence, such spatial separation would imply the lady's final rejection of the persistently physical lover.[2] Here, however, the spatial terms are again opened to the metaphoric condition of the beloved in the Song of Songs: separation is not rejection, and those who seek will find. This separation does not question but affirms the success of the narrative lovers.

The final separation is very different from this traditional pattern. The lovers are still in love, but are driven apart by lies and slanders. In other words, once the lovers try to broaden their private, internal dialogue of love to include an external, public community, mistrust and misunderstanding result. Spenser sketches this outward movement clearly and precisely. Sonnet 85[3] laments that "the world . . . cannot deeme of worthy things"; nonetheless, says the poet-lover, he will continue to trumpet abroad his lady's praise and the world can choose whether "to enuy or to wonder." As the next sonnet, the first of the separation group, demonstrates, the world chooses to envy:

> Venemous toung tipt with vile adders sting,
> Of that selfe kynd with which the Furies fell
> theyr snaky heads doe combe, from which a spring
> of poysoned words and spitefull speeches well.
> Let all the plagues and horrid paines of hell,
> vpon thee fall for thine accursed hyre:
> that with false forged lyes, which thou didst tel,
> in my true loue did stirre vp coles of yre.[4]

2. Sidney's *Astrophel and Stella* (1582, pub. 1591) may be taken as the standard Elizabethan model in this regard.
3. I am following the Variorum numbers here, hence Sonnets 35 and 83, although identical, are retained.
4. Cf. Spenser's descriptions of the Blatant Beast, *FQ* VI.i.8; VI.xii.27–28.

Six sonnets after Spenser tells us he has completed Book VI of *The Faerie Queene*, the Blatant Beast, having already escaped from Calidore's iron chains and threatened the poet himself, enters the sonnet sequence and forces the lovers apart by interpreting their reformed love as a lie. In the face of that public slander, the lover fails to be consoled even by contemplating "the Idaea playne," and he ends the sequence mourning his absent beloved.

Although it may not be possible to understand the full import of the "venemous toung" to Spenser without examining Books V and VI of *The Faerie Queene*, some tentative suggestions may be offered.[5] The Beast represents the public world, the community, within which the lovers must find their ultimate success. What the lovers have thus far achieved is not denied, but it is seriously qualified.[6] One measure of that qualification is the surprise by which we suddenly realize how closed a space the lovers have inhabited to this point. Once their private place is opened, however, we see that their loving must now be figured forth in an act of marriage affirmed and sanctified by the human community called upon to witness that sacrament. Without that public sanctification by what the Prayer Book calls "his congregation," the activity of Christian loving and the reformation it should occasion would literally be displaced. The deformative slanders of the Beast, therefore, separate not only the lovers from each other, but also the entire community from the unfolding and regenerating love of God.

It is ultimately the metaphoric place of human loving within divine Love that leads Spenser to both the Christ of Sonnet 68 and the Song of Songs throughout the concluding section of the *Amoretti*. The redemption which Christ offers and the spiritual union of which the Song speaks establish the obligations that right loving must fulfill. Like the Song itself, the state of matrimony, as the Prayer Book defines it, is a metaphoric participation in "the spiritual marriage and unity betwixt Christ and his Church."[7] By breaking off his sequence prior to this moment of private, public, and divine unity, Spenser seems to imply that the success of each place depends upon the others. The lovers' final achievement, therefore, is measured not only by their metaphoric relation to Christ's act of redeeming love, but also by our metaphoric relation to their reforming love. The Idea of Love accommodates all three places and all three metaphoric imitations. And unless we imitate the lovers' imitation we, like the "venemous toung," deprive them of their due place in the figuring forth of divine Love. We also, of course, deprive ourselves of a place in the redemption love offers. We are the community that must sanctify the lovers' love, and we can do so only by now metaphorically transferring their poetic re-formation into our own ethical reformation.

At this point, we may begin to measure one aspect of Spenser's achievement in the *Epithalamion* to follow. Just as he there calls upon all the

5. For a fuller analysis of the "venemous toung," see my "'Who now does follow the foule Blatant Beast': Spenser's Self-Effacing Fictions," *Renaissance Papers 1978* (1979), pp. 11–21.
6. Carol V. Kaske, "Spenser's *Amoretti* and *Epithalamion* of 1595: Structure, Genre, and Numerology," *ELR* 8 (1978): 271–295, also argues a qualification on the lovers' success in the concluding sonnets. But Kaske sees the failure here as occasioned by the period of sexual frustration following their betrothal and preceding the marriage. Such literal terms seem to me to limit the process of loving that Spenser is exploring here.
7. Cited from *The Book of Common Prayer 1559*, ed. John E. Booty (Charlottesville, 1976), p. 296.

muses, nymphs, young maids and virgins, fresh boys, minstrels, merchants' daughters, and even the high heavens to come and celebrate the public moment of the wedding, so he calls upon the community of the poem's readers to stand with the couple before the holy priest and bless their matrimonial union. We become, in effect, the participating congregation, praising the happy pair and sanctifying through the poetic ritual the public success of their "tymely ioyes."[8] Our engagement in this poetic sacrament is precisely the ethical activity for which the lesson of the *Amoretti* prepares us, and to which it incites us. Only our active participation in the rite of this loving can assure the lovers and ourselves that the poem is "for short time an endlesse moniment."

ANNE LAKE PRESCOTT:
[Allegorical Deer and *Amoretti* 67][†]

As the huntsman of *Amoretti* 67 sits resting in the shade, alone with his hounds and the approaching hind, he is in fact accompanied by the literary ghosts of deer and hunters past. One hunter is Petrarch, of course (see *Rime* 190), and, although less often noted, Tasso's "fera gentil" (a wild animal now tame enough to be caught) is probably around somewhere.[1] But behind Petrarch and Tasso lies an immense body of literature comparing a relationship to that of hunter and hunted. Renaissance readers would know the most famous deer. One appears in Horace's lovely reassurance to Chloë, a poem sometimes cited as a source for *Am.* 78 but with a fawn more closely resembling the beguiled and trembling hind of *Am.* 67 observed at an earlier stage in the process of persuasion. "You avoid me," he tells the girl, "like a fawn seeking its timid mother on the pathless mountains, not without vain fear of the breezes and forest; if the coming spring rustles the light leaves or the green lizards disturb the bramble, the fawn trembles in heart and limb. Yet I do not chase you in order to mangle you like a fierce tiger or Gaetulian lion. Cease then at last to follow your mother, now that you are ready (*tempestiva*) for a man" (*Odes* 3.23).

Despite Horace's seductive mildness, hunting imagery like this hints at an anxiety about captivity and dismemberment. Deer are not wrong to tremble, after all, and the ancient metaphor touches on one of *Amoretti*'s major themes: a (supposedly) feminine fear of imprisonment and wounding that must be put by when it is timely to do so. Indeed the hunt in *Am.* 67 may itself be "timely," because the capture, death, or even sighting of deer has often meant, at least in literary texts, a new beginning. True, such moments of transition can be unhappy. When Virgil compares the lovelorn Dido to a pierced hind wandering in anguish through the city (*Aeneid* 4.66–73), he indicates something about the cost of refounding a dynasty, for her lover Aeneas must choose between two quarries: the

8. I am indebted to Professor John N. Wall for first suggesting this point to me.

† From "The Thirsty Deer and the Lord of Life: Some Contexts for *Amoretti* 67–70," *Spenser Studies* 6 (1985): 33–76. This excerpt has been somewhat revised and the notes severely minimized. Sources for information on deer, their symbolism, and hunting poems are cited in the original article. I quote the Bible in the 1560 Geneva translation. Reprinted by permission of the author and AMS Press.

1. Dasenbrock 1991 briefly discusses "Questa fera gentil" in the context of Spenser's quarrel with Petrarchism.

stricken deer and the Italic shores. Dido finds just what many animals fear—death—and in Italy the hero will again have trouble with deer when the killing of a pet fawn starts a war between the natives and the Trojans, a savagery once more associating empire with blood and sorrow.

Renaissance English poetry is likewise crowded with deer, sometimes indicating the poet and sometimes the object of his desire, while puns on *deer/dear* or *hart/heart* proliferated so that sometimes it is difficult to know if the author intends his metaphor as anatomical imagery, hunting allegory, or both. Among the hundreds of Renaissance (and medieval) hunting poems there may be several in which the hunter chases the deer with dogs, gives up, sits down by water to rest, and then finds that the deer comes to him to be bound. So far, however, I have found only one precedent for *Am.* 67 that contains all these elements. It is the sixth lyric in the *Chansons spirituelles* (1547) of Marguerite de Navarre, sister of King Francis I, grandmother of Henry IV (Sir Burbon in Book V of *The Faerie Queene*), and famous in England.[2] In it a young hunter asks a happy and wise old woman if the deer he seeks is in that forest, for he is willing to devote all his strength to hunting it. He is a bad hunter, she replies, for this deer is not to be captured by hard work, well-equipped hounds, and fancy paraphernalia. Rather, she informs the at first skeptical huntsman, if he will merely rest by a spring and spread the net of a humble heart, the deer will turn back and let itself be caught by love. Marguerite makes it clear that the deer in her witty evangelical allegory is the crucified Christ (the next song in the volume is, like *Am.* 68, a Resurrection poem). Some readers have also found the deer in *Am.* 67 Christlike, and this poem may offer further evidence that they are right—and also support a reading of *Amoretti* that stresses the utterly free nature of the lady's surrender, not the merit, education, or psychological development of the lover/speaker.[3]

Like Marguerite, moreover, Spenser may want us to recall some biblical harts and hinds, all thought by one or another authority to represent Christ, the Christian, or the Church, and by some to signify more than one of these. These deer, to be sure, have shifty and multiple identities. Harts in one translation are hinds in another, and it can sometimes be difficult to divide the deer from the goats. In any case, though, deer had a reputation for habits that explain their usefulness to scriptural exegesis, art, and poetry. Even after the Reformation, when biblical commentary had for some time been sobering up after what now seemed its allegorical excesses, the purported behavior of deer remained familiar. As almost any reader of classical science, the church fathers, and bestiaries knew, deer are thirsty by nature. Their thirst increases after contact with their mortal enemies, serpents, which they force from their holes with saliva or warm breath and then either snuffle up in their nostrils and swallow (from hatred or as rejuvenating medicine) or trample under foot. Snake-killing is thirsty work; so, filled with venom, deer race to a spring or brook whose waters will refresh and renew them. Deer move quickly, leaping on the hills and rocky places. Although timid, they may be lured by music. Extremely long-lived, they know that to eat dittany will

2. Ed. Georges Dottin (Geneva, 1971) 17–20.
3. DeNeef 1982, 67, and Bernard 1989, 174, call her behavior Christlike.

make an arrow fall out. They cross a wide river by swimming in single file, each deer's head resting on the rump of the preceding one; when the leader is exhausted it retires to the rear of the line and the next one takes over. Spenser would have come across this deer lore in any number of places, while for advice on how to catch them he could have consulted George Gascoigne's *Noble art of venerie* (1575), which also suggests uses for leftover bits of animal (dried deer pizzle, for example, helps stop bleeding) and gives the proper time to hunt each sort of deer: as a hind, the lady of *Am.* 67 is indeed in season in late March, at least if she is "fatte or in good plight."[4]

Of all biblical deer the one with the most obvious significance to a lover with respectable intentions is that in Proverbs 5.18–19: "Let thy fountaine be blessed, and rejoyce with the wife of thy youth. Let her be as the loving hinde and pleasant roe: let her breasts satisfie thee at all times, and delite in her love continually." The Geneva editors say merely that this shows that "God blesseth marriage and curseth whordome," but to the church fathers the loving hind was above all a symbol of Christ or of Christian love and celestial contemplation. God tells us to bear each other's burdens (see Galatians 6.2), says Augustine, and since deer do just that when crossing a river, perhaps Solomon was thinking of their habits when he wrote Proverbs 5.19.[5] Other commentators agreed; Ambrose, for example, calls the deer our lover, Christ (*PL* 14.849–50), and Origen says it signifies the love of a God who makes us not his servants but his friends (*PG* 87¹. 1266).

Also relevant to *Am.* 67, despite their gender, are the amorous roes and harts of the Song of Solomon (e.g., 2.9: "My welbeloved is like a roe, or a yong heart"). The wedding of such a hart (usually allegorized as Christ) to his beloved bride sanctifies human unions and the love that sustains or inspires them. More of a puzzle is Psalm 22, the psalm Christ quoted from the cross and which was assumed to foretell the crucifixion. The psalmist was, says the headnote in the Geneva Bible, "past all hope" but now "recovereth him self from the bottomles pit of tentations and groweth in hope," just as Christ "shulde marvelously, and strangely be dejected and abased, before his Father shulde raise and exalte him againe." The psalm, assigned in the Edward VI prayerbook for Good Friday, is certainly about a victim; is it also about a deer? Many thought it was, for its traditional title is "The Hind of the Morning" (probably in fact referring to the name of the tune). As Richard Sampson's 1539 commentary on the first fifty psalms put it, Christ is not absurdly called a hart or hind, for as deer snuffle up serpents and kill them, so Christ killed the serpent when he harrowed Hell and freed the human race from captivity (cf. *Am.* 68).

Commentators on deer, however, more often liked to cite Psalm 42, which for centuries had been sung at baptismal ceremonies on Easter Saturday (the day to which *Am.* 67 corresponds in Spenser's calendrical scheme); in its opening verse David's soul groans for God just as "When lyke in chase the hunted Hynde the water brookes doth glad desire."[6] The thirsty deer's gender varied from psalter to psalter, so like Matthew

4. Sigs. C4ff, P7v; listed under Turberville in Pollard and Redgrave but ascribed to Gascoigne.
5. *Patrologia Latina*, ed. J. P. Migne (Paris, 1844–64) 40.80–81, henceforth *PL*; *PG* is *Patrologia Graeca*, ed. J. P. Migne (Paris, 1857–86).
6. Bieman 1983 and Johnson 1991 also hear an echo of Psalm 42 in *Am.* 67.

Parker, whose 1567 translation I quote, Spenser may well have imagined a panting hind. In any case, this deer, too, was associated with Christ, although it more often represented apostles, saints, and the faithful. Like many exegetes, Augustine is content to equate it with the faithful, especially those penitents who have killed the serpents of vice and now race to the waters of baptism and the fountains of life. Let us love like deer, he urges, who help each other (*PL* 36.464–67). John Chrysostom, whose writings may have influenced *The Faerie Queene*, goes further. In an impassioned meditation of the sort that earned him his name "Golden Mouth," he turns over and over to this verse. The implied serpents are vices, and we too should eat the "intelligible serpent" so as to acquire a holy thirst. After all, we are contracted to God, having promised to cherish him more than others and to burn with love. So when in the forum you see silver or golden clothes or other wealth, say to yourself, "Just a little while ago I sang, 'As the hart thirsts . . .' " (*PG* 55.155ff). In other words, the verse is a mnemonic to recall a contract, an engagement; as in the Song of Solomon and Proverbs 5.19 the deer is our partner in a love affair. Reformation commentary, however, tended to stress the exiled David's longing for water as a metaphor for his frustrated desire to worship in the temple. Perhaps this reading has some relevance to *Am.* 67, for Spenser's lovers are indeed soon found at public worship, probably in the next sonnet with its liturgical rhythms and certainly in the *Epithalamion*. The point, says Calvin, is to remind us that we are not to live in spiritual isolation, ignoring ceremonies and the congregation: "For he biddeth us not clymb straight up into heaven, but favouring our weaknes, he commeth down neerer untoo us" (*Commentaries*, trans. A. Golding, 1571). To Calvin, the deer is the suffering historical David, not Christ, but this argument, too, moves the discouraged human lover toward union with a beloved who comes voluntarily and whose love is not private and separate but sociable, joining the soul, in the words of *Am.* 70, to Love's "lovely crew."

One discussion of the thirsty deer seems particularly germane to Spenser: Victorinus Strigelius's often delightful *A proceeding in the harmonie of King David's harpe* (trans. R. Robinson, 1582 to 1598). The commentary on Psalm 42 (1593) paraphrases the opening verse in words that strikingly anticipate Spenser's own: "As the Hart in *chase* fleeth, and in *long pursute* made *wearie*, doth most greedily covet and *thirst* after the lively running springs," so I thirst not for puddles but for "springs of livelie Water" (my italics). This curative water is true consolation, the forgiveness of sin through Christ, for "The acknowledgement of Gods presence in calamaties, and the hope of the very last deliveraunce and of eternall salvation, doo call back languishing soules, as it were from the jawes of hel, and effectually heale the woundes of the hart." Sometimes, he adds, we feel abandoned (cf. the end of *Amoretti*), but we must learn to wait.

It seems clear, then, that *Am.* 67 resonates with scriptural echoes, all the more audible because Psalm 42 had long been associated with the evening before Easter. But why should Spenser think of a captured deer and not some other pre-Easter symbol? To provide a pastoral moment, maybe, or to help show up Petrarch. To sound again the theme of binding and loosing, of constraint that is liberating because freely chosen and mutual. Also, I think, to acknowledge that erotic love is like divine love also in its experience of pain and sacrifice. Spenser's sonnet nowhere mentions the dismemberment Marguerite's deer will experience, but the implication may be there, and feminine anxieties (whether widespread in real life is probably beside the point) about the consequences of even loving capture certainly receive sympathetic exploration in Books III and IV of *The Faerie Queene*. By accepting the risk of suffering, either as physical intrusion and later parturition or, also scary, as the penetration of an emotional and psychological perimeter, and by taking on an inevitable sense of some loss, the half-trembling deer assures for herself and for others—her lover, her family—a future triumph over doubt, bondage, and fear. It is hard to imagine what deeper or wiser compliment a poet could give a young woman.

HELENA MENNIE SHIRE: [On *Amoretti* 78]†

* * *

Sonnet lxxviii

Lackyng my love I go from place to place,
lyke a young fawne that late hath lost the hynd:
and seeke each where, where last I sawe her face,
whose ymage yet I carry fresh in mynd.
I seeke the fields with her late footing synd, 5
I seeke her bowre with her late presence deckt,
yet nor in field nor bowre I her can fynd:
yet field and bowre are full of her aspect.
But when myne eyes I thereunto direct,
they ydly back returne to me agayne, 10
and when I hope to see theyr trew obiect,
I fynd my selfe but fed with fancies vayne.
Ceasse then myne eyes, to seeke her selfe to see,
and let my thoughts behold her selfe in mee.
(1595)

This is Spenser at his simple best. The state of restless hungry seeking in the lover whose beloved is gone away is vividly rendered in the 'likening' to the fawn that has lost its mother: the image is of physical deprivation but the tone is tender. Bewildered seeking is felt in the line of 'each where, where . . .'. A hind is traced by footprints and has a 'bowre'; 'fynd' gathers force from the likening as it is the word in hunting for establishing contact with the quarry, a force it retains when it appears again in line 12. The likening operates delicately throughout the first eight lines and is still in play, with 'fynd' and 'fed', as the argument draws to a close.

The shape of the sonnet—three quatrains interlinked by the rhyme scheme which runs on, then a summing couplet—is Spenser's particular choice from among a number of possible sonnet patterns; he uses it throughout the *Amoretti*. The three quatrains here record three phases: a statement, a particularising and unfolding of it into two (fields/footing and bowre/presence, which are beautifully balanced), then confrontation with the negative result. The couplet then interprets the experience, summing, balancing and penetrating to the 'truth' of it. Alliteration is used lightly and subtly to link words that the author wishes us to think of together so that their meanings may intensify one another: lacking love, late lost last, field footing fynd—and there are others.

But is it so simple? Look at the spelling; 'synd' for signed may be so spelt to make clear its perfect rhyme with 'hynd' (as is the case in Sonnet LXXXIII), but 'ymage' is not the usual spelling and makes one pause to think about the word's whole range of meaning. So too with 'ydly': 'ydlesse' of Book VI, canto ii stanza 31 is not the same as the idleness of Idle Lake in Book II, canto vi stanza 10 of *The Faerie Queene*. And 'behold', key-word in the summing couplet? The form directs us to balance 'eyes . . . see' against 'thoughts . . . behold'. Behold is a powerful form of 'hold', and Spenser spells it 'be-hold' when he means it as 'retain, capture' as in the September Eclogue line 229. To behold is to regard with concentration of eyes and mind, capturing and retaining by a mental and spiritual process. It is done by thoughts.

In the phrase of the excellent complimentary sonnet Spenser is here exercising his learned quill in his poetry for his lovely mistress. For the sonnet marks a learning by the lover, a progress from blind seeking of the physical—the face recorded in memory—through the denial of satisfaction by the traces of her physical presence (aspect) moving on to the need to find 'the trew obiect' (the goal love's desire ought to be making for) and the revelation that the object of love is the 'idea', the very self of the beloved, which is within the lover's mind. The progress is upward, along the way defined by Neoplatonism, from actual/physical to ideal, which is reality. We, reading the sonnet, learn too.

In the sonnet itself can be found 'rare invention, bewtified by skill', unity of form and meaning, relation of part to part and to the whole, and aptness in likening and in language. As a part of a larger whole the sonnet comes in the wonderfully varied but always onward-moving sequence of the *Amoretti*. Before it ran two sonnets, couched in richer language, of sensuous delight in the beloved's physical presence and beauty. In LXXVI frail thoughts may be led astray to wanton in her lovely breast, a nearness of touch the lover is not allowed. In LXXVII the breasts of the beloved are a vision of glorying sensuous delight, echoing the scriptural 'apples of gold in dishes of silver', 'exceeding sweet, yet voyd of sinfull vice'—a table spread at which the thoughts are guests, and would fain have fed. After these the sonnet of sudden absence, with the fawn deprived of food and comforting presence, takes the stronger hold on the imagination. And the sonnet that follows after that is on true beauty, not perishable as is beauty of the body, but unfading because of the mind—'deriv'd from that fayre Spirit from whom al true/and perfect beauty did at first proceed'.

As a gloss, read 'The Song of Songs, which is Solomon's'. There are the hind and the lover, the loss and the seeking, and the banquet of sense.

List of Abbreviations

CL	Comparative Literature
EIC	Essays in Criticism
ELH	English Literary History
ELR	English Literary Renaissance
ES	English Studies
ESC	English Studies in Canada
HLQ	Huntington Library Quarterly
IUR	Irish University Review
JBS	Journal of British Studies
JEGP	Journal of English and Germanic Philology
JMEMS	Journal of Medieval and Early Modern Studies
JWCI	Journal of the Warburg and Courtauld Institutes
MLA	Modern Language Association
MLN	Modern Language Notes
MLS	Modern Language Studies
MLR	Modern Language Review
MP	Modern Philology
MRTS	Medieval and Renaissance Texts and Studies
N&Q	Notes and Queries
PBA	Proceedings of the British Academy
PMLA	Publications of the Modern Language Association of America
PQ	Philological Quarterly
RES	Review of English Studies
RQ	Renaissance Quarterly
SB	Studies in Bibliography
SEL	Studies in English Literature, 1500–1900
SLI	Studies in the Literary Imagination
SP	Studies in Philology
SR	Sewanee Review
SSt	Spenser Studies
TP	Textual Practice
TSLL	Texas Studies in Language and Literature
UTQ	University of Toronto Quarterly
YES	Yearbook of English Studies

Selected Bibliography

• indicates a work excerpted or included in this Norton Critical edition.

GENERAL OVERVIEW

Editions: *The Works of Edmund Spenser: A Variorum Edition*, ed. Edwin Greenlaw, Charles Grosvenor Osgood, and Frederick Morgan Padelford. 11 Vols. (Baltimore: Johns Hopkins University Press, 1932–49). Although fairly dated now, the annotations contain a wealth of useful material. The best edition of *The Faerie Queene* is that edited by A. C. Hamilton (text by Hiroshi Yamashita and Toshiyuki Suzuki [Harlow: Longman, 2001, rev. ed. 1977]). Also useful is *The Faerie Queene*, gen. ed. Abraham Stoll. 5 Vols. (Indianapolis: Hackett, 2006), which has individual editions of each book (Books III and IV as one, as are Books VI and VII).

The best edition of the shorter poems is *The Shorter Poems*, ed. Richard McCabe (Harmondsworth: Penguin, 1999); also worth consulting is *The Yale Edition of the Shorter Poems of Edmund Spenser*, ed. William A. Oram, Einar Bjorvand, Ronald Bond, Thomas H. Cain, Alexander Dunlop, and Richard Schell (New Haven: Yale University Press, 1989). Other useful editions include *Edmund Spenser's* Amoretti *and* Epithalamion*: A Critical Edition*, ed. Kenneth J. Larsen (Tempe, AZ: MRTS, 1997), a useful edition of the sonnets and marriage hymn with an emphasis on their religious and liturgical significance. *Selected Letters and Other Papers*, ed. Christopher Burlinson and Andrew Zurcher (Oxford: Oxford University Press, 2009), contains a selection of letters in Spenser's hand and has an excellent introduction with information on Spenser's career in Ireland as a secretary.

There are two serial publications dedicated to the study of Spenser: *The Spenser Review*, published three times a year by the International Spenser Society, which contains abstracts and summaries of recent Spenser scholarship and lists of future events, and *Spenser Studies* (New York: AMS Press, 1980–), an established and widely read annual forum with a series of articles and "gleanings" (notes and discoveries) contributed by Spenserian and other Renaissance scholars.

Useful Internet resources are The Edmund Spenser Home Page http://www.english.cam.ac.uk/spenser/biography.htm, which provides a succinct overview of Spenser's life, reading lists, and a variety of easily explained guides to other resources online, as well as links to many sites; and Edmund Spenser World Bibliography (http://bibs.slu.edu/spenser/index.html), which provides access to a searchable archive of Spenser bibliographies, with summaries, reviews, and abstracts taken from the *Spenser Newsletter*.

The standard biography is Andrew Hadfield, *Edmund Spenser: A Life* (Oxford: Oxford University Press, 2012). Biographical studies that cover known information are in Judith H. Anderson, Donald Cheney, and David H. Richardson, eds., *Spenser's Life and the Subject of Biography* (Amherst: University of Massachusetts Press, 1996); Willy Maley's excellent and informative *A Spenser Chronology* (Basingstoke: Macmillan, 1994); and Gary F. Waller, *Edmund Spenser: A Literary Life* (Basingstoke: Palgrave, 1994). See also Andrew Hadfield, "Secrets and Lies: The Life of Edmund Spenser," in Kevin Sharpe and Steven Zwicker, eds., *Writing Lives: Biography and Textuality, Identity and Representation in Early Modern England* (Oxford: Oxford University Press, 2008), pp. 55–73. Those interested in the excavations at Kilcolman Castle, Spenser's Irish home, should consult Eric Klingelhöfer, *Castles and Colonists: An Archaeology of Elizabethan Ireland* (Manchester: Manchester University Press, 2010).

Bibliographical analysis should start with Francis R. Johnson, *A Critical Bibliography of the Works of Edmund Spenser printed before 1700* (London: Dawsons, 1966, rpt. of 1933); and Hiroshi Yamashita, Haruo Sato, Toshiyuki Suzuki, and Akira Takano, *A*

Textual Companion to The Faerie Queene *1590* (Tokoyo: Kenyusha, 1993). See also the historical study, Jewel Wurtsbaugh, *Two Centuries of Spenserian Scholarship (1609–1805)* (Port Washington: Kennikat, 1970, rpt. of 1936). Charles Grosvenor Osgood, *A Concordance to the Poems of Edmund Spenser* (Washington: Carnegie Institute, 1915) is worth using if access to a complete text of the poem on the Internet proves difficult.

The best reference guides are A. C. Hamilton, ed., *The Spenser Encyclopedia* (Toronto and London: University of Toronto Press/Routledge, 1990), and Richard A. McCabe, ed. *The Oxford Handbook of Spenser* (Oxford: Oxford University Press, 2011). Others worth consulting include Frederick Ives Carpenter, *A Reference Guide to Edmund Spenser.* (New York: Peter Smith, 1950, rpt. of 1923), which, although dated, is still a valuable resource.

Studies of Spenser's influence include R. M. Cummings, ed., *Edmund Spenser: The Critical Heritage* (London: Routledge, 1971); David Hill Radcliffe, *Edmund Spenser: A Reception History* (Columbia: Camden House, 1996); William Wells, *Spenser Allusions in the Sixteenth and Seventeenth Centuries.* 2 Vols. (Chapel Hill: University of North Carolina Press, 1972); Greg Kucich, *Keats, Shelley, and Romantic Spenserianism* (University Park, PA: Pennsylvania University Press, 1991); William R. Mueller, *Spenser's Critics: Changing Currents in Literary Taste* (Syracuse: Syracuse University Press, 1959). There is also the important study of Spenser's most celebrated reader: Maureen Quilligan, *Milton's Spenser: The Politics of Reading* (Ithaca: Cornell University Press, 1983). For another study of a major reader, see James A. Riddell and Stanley Stewart, *Jonson's Spenser: Evidence and Historical Criticism* (Pittsburgh: Duquesne University Press, 1995). More specific influences on seventeenth-century poetry are contained in Joan Grundy, *The Spenserian Poets: A Study in Elizabethan and Jacobean Poetry* (London: Arnold, 1969); and Michelle O'Callaghan, *The 'Shepheardes Nation': Jacobean Spenserians and early Stuart political culture, 1612–1625* (Oxford: Clarendon Press, 2000).

Needless to say, and to our regret, our bibliography must omit much on Spenser and his contemporaries that is useful; luckily, the MLA database and the Internet as well as the websites listed here are available for further browsing.

SPENSER'S POETRY: GENERAL STUDIES AND COLLECTIONS

Anderson, Judith H., *Reading the Allegorical Intertext: Chaucer, Spenser, Shakespeare, Milton.* New York: Fordham University Press, 2008.

Baker, David J., *Between Nations: Shakespeare, Spenser, Marvell, and the Question of Britain.* Stanford: Stanford University Press, 1997.

Bates, Catherine. *The Rhetoric of Courtship in Elizabethan Language and Literature.* Cambridge: Cambridge University Press, 1992.

Bender, John B. *Spenser and Literary Pictorialism.* Princeton: Princeton University Press, 1972.

Bennett, Josephine Waters. "Spenser and Gabriel Harvey's 'Letter-Book,'" *MP* 29 (1931): 163–86.

Berry, Philippa. *Of Chastity and Power: Elizabethan Literature and the Unmarried Queene.* London: Routledge, 1989.

• Burrow, Colin. *Edmund Spenser.* Plymouth, UK: Northcote House, 1996.

———. *Epic Romance: Homer to Milton.* Oxford: Clarendon Press, 1993.

Carroll, Clare. *Circe's Cup: Cultural Transformation in Early Modern Ireland.* Cork: Cork University Press, 2001.

Chamberlain, Richard. *Radical Spenser: Pastoral, Politics and the New Aestheticism.* Edinburgh: Edinburgh University Press, 2005.

Cheney, Patrick. *Spenser's Famous Flight: A Renaissance Idea of a Literary Career.* Toronto: University of Toronto Press, 1993.

——— and Lauren Silberman, eds. *World Maxing Spenser:* Explorations in the Early Modern age. Lexington KY: University Press of Kentucky, 2000.

Coughlan, Patricia, ed. *Spenser and Ireland: An Interdisciplinary Perspective.* Cork: Cork University Press, 1989.

• DeNeef, A. Leigh. *Spenser and the Motives of Metaphor.* Durham: Duke University Press, 1982.

Dolven, Jeff. *Scenes of Instruction in Renaissance Romance.* Chicago: University of Chicago Press, 2007.

Ellrodt, Robert. *NeoPlatonism in the Poetry of Spenser.* Geneva: Droz, 1960.

Escobedo, Andrew. *Nationalism and Historical Loss in Renaissance England: Foxe, Dee, Spenser, Milton*. Ithaca: Cornell University Press, 2004.
Flinker, Noam. *The Song of Songs in English Renaissance Literature: Kisses of their Mouths*. Woodbridge: Boydell, 2000.
Fowler, Elizabeth. *Literary Character: The Human Figure in English Writing*. Ithaca: Cornell University Press, 2003.
Gilman, Ernest B. *Iconoclasm and Poetry in the English Reformation: Down went Dagon*. Chicago: The University of Chicago Press, 1986.
Goldberg, Jonathan. *Sodometries: Renaissance Texts, Modern Sexualities*. Stanford: Stanford University Press, 1992.
• Grogan, Jane. *Exemplary Spenser: Visual and Poetic Pedagogy in* The Faerie Queene. Aldershot: Ashgate, 2009.
• Hadfield, Andrew D. *Spenser's Irish Experience: Wilde Fruit and Salvage Soyl*. Oxford: Clarendon Press, 1997.
———, ed. *The Cambridge Companion to Spenser*. Cambridge: Cambridge University Press, 2001.
Hamlin, Hannibal. *Psalm Culture in Early Modern English Literature*. Cambridge: Cambridge University Press, 2004.
• Helgerson, Richard. *Self-Crowned Laureates: Spenser, Jonson, Milton and the Literary System*. Berkeley: University of California Press, 1983.
———. *Forms of Nationhood: the Elizabethan Writing of England*. Chicago: The University of Chicago Press, 1992.
Heninger, S. K. *Sidney and Spenser: The Poet as Maker*. University Park: Pennsylvania State University Press, 1989.
Henley, Pauline. *Spenser in Ireland*. Cork: Cork University Press, 1928.
Herman, Peter C. *Squitter-Wits and Muse-Haters: Sidney, Spenser, Milton, and Renaissance Anti-Poetic Sentiment*. Detroit: Wayne State University Press, 1996.
Herron, Thomas. *Spenser's Irish Work: Poetry, Plantation and Colonial Reformation*. Aldershot: Ashgate, 2007.
Highley, Christopher. *Shakespeare, Spenser, and the Crisis in Ireland*. Cambridge: Cambridge University Press, 1997.
Hume, Anthea. *Edmund Spenser: Protestant Poet*. Cambridge: Cambridge University Press, 1984.
Javitch, Daniel. *Poetry and Courtliness in Renaissance England*. Princeton: Princeton University Press, 1978.
Joyce, P. W. "Spenser's Irish Rivers." In *The Wonders of Ireland and other papers on Irish subjects*. Dublin: Longman, 1911, pp. 72–114.
Kaske, Carol V. *Spenser and Biblical Poetics*. Ithaca: Cornell University Press, 1999.
King, Andrew. The Faerie Queene *and Middle English Romance: The Matter of Just Memory*. Oxford: Clarendon Press, 2000.
King, John N. *Spenser's Poetry and the Reformation Tradition*. Princeton: Princeton University Press, 1990.
Knapp, Jeffrey. *An Empire Nowhere: England, America, and Literature from* Utopia *to* The Tempest. Berkeley: University of California Press, 1992.
———. "Spenser the Priest." *Representations* 81 (Winter 2003): 61–78.
Koller, Katherine, "Spenser and Ralegh." *ELH* 1 (1934): 37–60.
Lees-Jeffries, Hester. *England's Helicon: Fountains in Early Modern Literature and Culture*. Oxford: Oxford University Press, 2007.
Lamb, Mary Ellen. *The Popular Culture of Shakespeare, Spenser, and Jonson*. Abingdon: Routledge, 2006.
Lethbridge, J. B., ed. *Edmund Spenser: New and Renewed Directions*. Madison: Fairleigh Dickinson University Press, 2006.
———, ed. *Shakespeare and Spenser: Attractive Opposites*. Manchester: Manchester University Press, 2008.
Lever, J. W. *The Elizabethan Love Sonnet*. London: Methuen, 1956.
Lewis, C. S. *The Allegory of Love: A Study in Medieval Tradition*. Oxford: Oxford University Press, 1936.
• ———. *English Literature in the Sixteenth Century, excluding drama*. Oxford: Oxford University Press, 1954, Book III, Ch. 1, "Sidney and Spenser."
Loewenstein, Joseph. "Echo's Ring: Orpheus and Spenser's Career." *ELR* 16 (1986): 287–302.
McCabe, Richard A. "Edmund Spenser, Poet of Exile." *PBA* 80 (1993): 73–103.
———. *The Pillars of Eternity: Time and Providence in* The Faerie Queene. Dublin: Irish Academic Press, 1989.

———. *Spenser's Monstrous Regiment: Elizabethan Ireland and the Poetics of Difference.* Oxford: Oxford University Press, 2002.
———. "Edmund Spenser." In *The Cambridge Companion to English Poets.* Ed. Claude Rawson. Cambridge: Cambridge University Press, 2011, pp. 53–71.
McEachern, Claire. *The Poetics of English Nationhood, 1590–1612.* Cambridge: Cambridge University Press, 1996.
Maley, Willy. *Salvaging Spenser: Colonialism, Culture and Identity.* Basingstoke: Palgrave, 1997.
Mallette, Richard. *Spenser and the Discourses of Reformation England.* Lincoln: University of Nebraska Press, 1997.
Manley, Lawrence. *Literature and Culture in Early Modern London.* Cambridge: Cambridge University Press, 1995.
Mikics, David. *The Limits of Moralizing: Pathos and Subjectivity in Spenser and Milton.* Lewisburg: Bucknell University Press, 1994.
Miller, David Lee, and Alexander Dunlop, ed. *Approaches to Teaching Spenser's* Faerie Queene. New York: MLA, 1999.
Miskimin, Alice S. *The Renaissance Chaucer:* New Haven: Yale University Press, 1975.
Montrose, Louis A. "The Elizabethan Subject and the Spenserian Text." In *Literary Theory / Renaissance Texts.* Ed. David Quint and Patricia Parker. Baltimore: The Johns Hopkins University Press, 1986, pp. 303–340.
———. "Spenser and the Elizabethan Political Imaginary." *ELH* 69 (2002): 907–46.
Mueller, William R., and Don Cameron Allen, eds. *That Soueraine Light: Essays in Honor of Edmund Spenser, 1552–1952.* Baltimore: Johns Hopkins University Press, 1952.
Myers, Benjamin P. "The Green and Golden World: Spenser's Rewriting of the Munster Plantation." *ELH* 76 (2009): 473–90.
Nelson, William. *The Poetry of Edmund Spenser.* New York: Columbia University Press, 1963.
Norbrook, David. *Poetry and Politics in the English Renaissance*, rev. ed. Oxford: Oxford University Press, 2002.
Oram, William. "Spenser's Audiences, 1589–91." *SP* 100 (2003): 514–33.
Owens, Judith. *Enabling Engagements: Edmund Spenser and the Poetics of Patronage.* Montreal: McGill-Queen's University Press, 2002.
Palmer, Patricia. *Language and Conquest in Early Modern Ireland: English Renaissance Literature and Elizabethan imperial expansion.* Cambridge: Cambridge University Press, 2001.
———. "Missing Bodies, Absent Minds: Spenser, Shakespeare and a crisis in criticism." *ELR* 36 (2006): 376–95.
Partridge, A. C. *The Language of Renaissance Poetry.* London: Andre Deutsch, 1971.
Pask, Kevin. *The Emergence of the English Author: Scripting the Life of the Poet in Early Modern England.* Cambridge: Cambridge University Press, 1996.
Pattison, Bruce. *Music and Poetry of the English Renaissance.* London: Methuen, 2nd ed., 1970.
Prescott, Anne Lake. *French Poets and the English Renaissance: Studies in Fame and Transformation.* New Haven: Yale University Press, 1978.
Pugh, Syrithe. *Spenser and Ovid.* Aldershot: Ashgate, 2005.
Quitslund, Jon A. *Spenser's Supreme Fiction: Platonic Natural Philosophy and The Faerie Queene.* Toronto: University of Toronto Press, 2001.
Rambuss, Richard. *Spenser's Secret Career.* Cambridge: Cambridge University Press, 1993.
Richards, Jennifer. *Rhetoric and Courtliness in Early Modern Literature.* Cambridge: Cambridge University Press, 2003.
Rivers, Isabel. *Classical and Christian Ideas in English Renaissance Poetry.* London: Routledge, 1975.
Rix, Herbert David. *Rhetoric in Spenser's Poetry.* State College, PA: Pennsylvania State College, 1940.
• Shire, Helena Mennie. *A Preface to Spenser.* London: Longman, 1978.
Snyder, Susan. *Pastoral Process: Spenser, Marvell, Milton.* Stanford: Stanford University Press, 1998.
Stevens, Paul. "Spenser and the End of the British Empire." *SSt* XXII (2007): 5–26.
Suzuki, Mihoko. *Critical Essays on Edmund Spenser.* New York: G. K. Hall & Co., 1996.
• Teskey, Gordon. "Thinking Moments in *The Faerie Queene.*" *SSt* XXII (2007): 103–125.

Tilmouth, Christopher. *Passion's Triumph Over Reason: A History of the Moral Imagination from Spenser to Rochester.* Oxford: Oxford University Press, 2007.

Tuve, Rosamund. *Essays by Rosamund Tuve: Spenser, Herbert, Milton.* Ed. Thomas P. Roche, Jr. Princeton: Princeton University Press, 1970.

Van Es, Bart. *Spenser's Forms of History.* Oxford: Oxford University Press, 2002.

———, ed. *A Critical Companion to Spenser Studies.* Basingstoke: Palgrave, 2006.

Williams, Kathleen. *Spenser's* Faerie Queene: *The World of Glass.* London: Routledge, 1966.

Woolf, Jessica. *Humanism, Machinery, and Renaissance Literature.* Cambridge: Cambridge University Press, 2004.

Yates, Frances A. *Astrea: The Imperial Theme in the Sixteenth Century.* London: Routledge, 1975.

Yeats, W. B. "Edmund Spenser." In W. B. Yeats, *Essays and Introductions.* London: Macmillan, 1961, pp. 356–83.

Zurcher, Andrew. *Spenser's Legal Language: Law and Poetry in Early Modern England.* Cambridge: Brewer, 2007.

THE FAERIE QUEENE: GENERAL

• Alpers, Paul J. "How to Read *The Faerie Queene.*" *EIC* 18 (1968): 429–43.

Bennett, Josephine Waters. *The Evolution of 'The Faerie Queene.'* Chicago: University of Chicago Press, 1942.

Brink, Jean R. "Materialist History of the Publication of Spenser's *Faerie Queene.*" *RES*, n.s., 54 (2001): 1–26.

Cain, Thomas H. *Praise in* The Faerie Queene. Lincoln, NB.: University of Nebraska Press, 1978.

Campana, Joseph. *The Pain of Reformation Spenser, Vulnerability, and the Ethics of Masculinity.* New York: Fordham University Press, 2012.

Cavanagh, Sheila T. *Wanton Eyes and Chaste Desires: Female Sexuality in* The Faerie Queene. Bloomington: Indiana University Press, 1994.

• Craig, Martha. "The Secret Wit of Spenser's Language." In *Elizabethan Poetry: Modern Essays in Criticism.* Ed. Paul J. Alpers. London: Oxford University Press, 1967, pp. 447–72.

• Dolven, Jeff. "The Method of Spenser's Stanza." *SSt* 19 (2004): 17–25.

Dundas, Judith. *The Spider and the Bee. The Artistry of Spenser's* Faerie Queene. Urbana-Chicago: University of Illinois Press, 1985.

Erikson, Wayne C., ed. *The 1590* Faerie Queene: *Paratexts and Publishing. SLI* 38.2 (2005).

Evans, Frank B. "The Printing of Spenser's *Faerie Queene* in 1596." *SB* 18 (1965): 50–69.

Evans, Maurice. *Spenser's Anatomy of Heroism.* Cambridge: Cambridge University Press, 1970.

Fleck, Andrew. "Early Modern Marginalia in Spenser's *Faerie Queene* at the Folger." *N&Q* 55 (2008): 165–70.

Fowler, Alastair. *Spenser and the Numbers of Time.* London: Routledge, 1964.

Fowler, Elizabeth. "The Failure of Moral Philosophy in the Work of Edmund Spenser." *Representations* 51 (1995): 47–76.

• Frye, Northrop. "The Structure of Imagery in *The Faerie Queene.*" *UTC* 30 (1961): 109–127.

• Giamatti, A. Bartlett. *Play of Double Senses: Spenser's* Faerie Queene. New York: Norton, 1990; rpt. of 1975.

Gless, Darryl J. *Interpretation and Theology in Spenser.* Cambridge: Cambridge University Press, 1994.

Hadfield, Andrew D. "Spenser and Religion—Yet Again." *SEL* 51.1 (2011): 21–46.

Hamilton, A. C. *The Structure of Allegory in* The Faerie Queene. Oxford: Clarendon Press, 1961.

Headlam Wells, Robin. *Spenser's* Faerie Queene *and the Cult of Elizabeth.* London: Croom Helm, 1983.

Heale, Elizabeth. *The Faerie Queene: A Reader's Guide.* Cambridge: Cambridge University Press, rev. ed., 1999.

• Hieatt, A. Kent. *Chaucer, Spenser, Milton: Mythopoeic Continuities and Transformations.* Montreal and London: McGill-Queen's University Press, 1975.

Hough, Graham. *A Preface to* The Faerie Queene. London: Duckworth, 1962.

Leslie, Michael. *Spenser's "Fierce Warres and Faithfull Loves": Martial and Chivalric Symbolism in "The Faerie Queene."* Cambridge: Brewer, 1983.

MacCaffrey, Isabel G. *Spenser's Allegory: The Anatomy of Imagination.* Princeton: Princeton University Press, 1976.

• Miller, David Lee. "*The Faerie Queene* (1590)." In *A Critical Companion to Spenser Studies.* Ed. Bart van Es. New York: Palgrave Macmillan, 2006, pp. 139–65.

———. *The Poem's Two Bodies: The Poetics of the 1590* Faerie Queene. Princeton: Princeton University Press, 1988.

Nohrnberg, James. *The Analogy of* The Faerie Queene. Princeton: Princeton University Press, 1976.

O'Connell, Michael. *Mirror and Veil: The Historical Dimension of Spenser's* Faerie Queene. Chapel Hill: The University of North Carolina Press, 1977.

Owen, W. J. B. "The Structure of *The Faerie Queene.*" *PMLA* 68 (1953): 1079–1100.

Parker, Patricia. *Inescapable Romance: Studies in the Poetics of a Mode.* Princeton: Princeton University Press, 1979.

Pearce, Roy Harvey. "Primitivistic Ideas in *The Faerie Queene.*" *JEGP* 44 (1945): 138–51.

Sandison, Helen E. "Spenser's 'Lost' Works and Their Probable Relation to His *Faerie Queene.*" *PMLA* 25 (1910): 134–51.

Sandler, Florence. "*The Faerie Queene*: An Elizabethan Apocalypse." In *The Apocalypse in English Renaissance Thought and Literature* Ed. C. A. Patrides and Joseph Wittreich. Manchester: Manchester University Press, 1984, pp. 148–74.

Scott Warren, Jason. "Unannotating Spenser." In *Renaissance Paratexts.* Ed. Helen Smith, and Louise Wilson. Cambridge: Cambridge University Press, 2011, pp. 153–64.

Shaheen, Naseeb. *Biblical References in* The Faerie Queene. Memphis: Memphis State University Press, 1976.

Smith, Roland M. "Spenser's Irish River Stories." *PMLA* 50 (1935): 1047–56.

Suttie, Paul. *Self-Interpretation in* The Faerie Queene. Cambridge: Boydell and Brewer, 2006.

Teskey, Gordon. *Allegory and Violence.* Ithaca: Cornell University Press, 1996.

Watkins, John. *The Specter of Dido: Spenser and Virgilian Epic.* New Haven: Yale University Press, 1995.

Weatherby, Harold L. *Mirrors of Celestial Grace: Patristic Theology in Spenser's Allegory.* Toronto: University of Toronto Press, 1994.

West, Michael. "Spenser's Art of War: Chivalric Allegory, Military Technology, and the Elizabethan Mock-Heroic Sensibility." *RQ* 41 (1988): 654–704.

Wilson-Okamura, David Scott. *Virgil in the Renaissance.* Cambridge: Cambridge University Press, 2010.

Woodcock, Matthew. *Fairy in* The Faerie Queene: *Renaissance Elf-Fashioning and Elizabethan Myth-Making.* Aldershot: Ashgate, 2004.

Zurcher, Andrew. *Edmund Spenser's* The Faerie Queene: *A Reading Guide.* Edinburgh: Edinburgh University Press, 2011.

THE FAERIE QUEENE: BOOKS I AND II

Brooks-Davies, Douglas. *Spenser's* Faerie Queene: *A critical commentary on Books I and II.* Manchester: Manchester University Press, 1977.

Butler, Christopher. "'Pricking' and Ambiguity at the Start of *The Faerie Queene.*" *N&Q* 55 (2008): 159–61.

Greenblatt, Stephen. "To Fashion A Gentleman: Spenser and the Destruction of the Bower of Bliss." In *Renaissance Self-Fashioning: From More to Shakespeare.* Chicago: University of Chicago Press, 1980.

Hughes, Merritt Y. "Spenser's Palmer." *ELH* 2 (1935): 151–64.

Kaske, Carol V. "'Religious Reuerence Doth Buriall Teene': Christian and Pagan in *The Faerie Queene*, II, 1–3." *RES* 30 (1979): 129–43.

Magill, A. J. "Spenser's Guyon and the Mediocrity of the Elizabethan Settlement." *SP* 67 (1970): 167–77.

Phillips, James E. "Spenser's Syncretistic Religious Imagery." *ELH* 36 (1969): 110–30.

Prescott, Anne Lake. "Spenser's Chivalric Restoration: From Bateman's 'Travayled Pylgrime' to the Redcrosse Knight." *SP* 86 (1989): 166–97.

Robinson, Benedict S. *Islam and Early Modern English Literature: The Politics of Romance from Spenser to Milton.* Basingstoke: Palgrave, 2007.

Shanley, James Lyndon. "Spenser's Temperance and Aristotle." *MP* 43 (1946): 170–74.
Smith, Roland M. "Origines Arthurianae: The Two Crosses of Spenser's Red Cross Knight." *JEGP* 54 (1955): 670–83.
• Summit, Jennifer. "Monuments and Ruins: Spenser and the Limits of The English Library." *ELH* 70.1 (2003): 1–34.
Waters, D. Douglas. *Duessa as Theological Satire.* Columbia: University of Missouri Press, 1970.
Werth, Tiffany Jo. *The Fabulous Dark Cloister: Romance in England After the Reformation.* Baltimore: The Johns Hopkins Press, 2011.
Wesley, John. "The Well-Schooled Wrestler: Athletics and Rhetoric in *The Faerie Queene, Book II.*" *RES* 60 (2009): 34–60.
Wheatley, Chloe. *Epic, Epitome, and the Early Modern Historical Imagination.* Farnham: Ashgate, 2011.

THE FAERIE QUEENE: BOOKS III AND IV

Goldberg, Jonathan. *Endlesse Work: Spenser and the Structures of Discourse.* Baltimore: Johns Hopkins University Press, 1981.
Oruch, Jack B. "Spenser, Camden, and the Poetic Marriage of Rivers." *SP* 64 (1967): 606–24.
Pichaske, David R. "*The Faerie Queene* IV.ii and iii: Spenser and the Genesis of Friendship." *SEL* 17 (1977): 81–93.
• Roche, Thomas P., Jr. *The Kindly Flame: A Study of the Third and Fourth Books of Spenser's* Faerie Queene. Princeton, NJ: Princeton University Press, 1964.
Silberman, Lauren. *Transforming Desire: Erotic Knowledge in Books III and IV of* The Faerie Queene. Berkeley: University of California Press, 1995.
Tuell, Anne K. "The Original End of *Faerie Queene*, Book III." *MLN* 36 (1921): 309–11.
• Wofford, Susanne Lindgren. "Gendering Allegory: Spenser's Bold Reader and the Emergence of Character in *The Faerie Queene* III. *Criticism* 30 (1988): 1–21.

THE FAERIE QUEENE: BOOKS V, VI, AND MUTABILITIE CANTOS

Aptekar, Jane. *Icons of Justice: Iconography and Thematic Imagery in Book V of* The Faerie Queene. New York: Columbia University Press, 1969.
Coughlan, Patricia. "The Local Context of Mutabilitie's Plea." *IUR: Spenser in Ireland, 1596–1996.* Ed. Anne Fogarty (Autumn/Winter 1996): 320–41.
Cumming, William P. "The Influence of Ovid's *Metamorphoses* on Spenser's 'Mutabilitie' Cantos." *SP* 28 (1931): 241–56.
Dunseath, T. K. *Spenser's Allegory of Justice in Book Five of* The Faerie Queene. Princeton: Princeton University Press, 1968.
Grogan, Jane, ed. *Celebrating Mutabilitie: Essays on Edmund Spenser's Mutabilitie Cantos.* Manchester: Manchester University Press, 2010.
Holohan, Michael. "'*Iamque opus exegi*': Ovid's Changes and Spenser's Brief Epic of Mutability." *ELR* 6 (1976): 244–70.
Hughes, Merritt Y. "Spenser's 'Blatant Beast.'" *MLR* 13 (1918): 267–75.
Lupton, Julia Reinhard. "Mapping Mutability: or, Spenser's Irish plot." In *Representing Ireland: Literature and the Origins of Conflict, 1534–1660.* Ed. Andrew Hadfield and Willy Maley. Cambridge: Cambridge University Press, 1993, pp. 93–115.
McCabe, Richard A. "The Masks of Duessa: Spenser, Mary Queen of Scots, and James VI." *ELR* 17 (1987): 224–42.
McNeir, Waldo F. "The Sacrifice of Serena: *The Faerie Queene*, VI, viii. 31–51." In *Festschrift Für Edgar Mertner.* Ed., Bernhard Fabian and Ulrich Suerbaum. Munich: W. F. V. Munchen, 1968, pp. 117–56.
Manning, R. J. "'Deuicefull Sights': Spenser's Emblematic Practice in *The Faerie Queene*, V.1–3." *SSt* V (1984): 65–89.
Meyer, Russell J. "'Fixt in heauens hight': Spenser, Astronomy, and the Date of the *Cantos of Mutabilitie.*" *SSt* IV (1983): 115–29.
Neuse, Richard. "Book VI as Conclusion to *The Faerie Queene.*" *ELH* 35 (1968): 329–53.
Northrop, Douglas A. "Spenser's Defense of Elizabeth." *UTQ* 38 (1968–9): 27–94.

Patterson, Annabel. "The Egalitarian Giant: Representations of Justice in History/ Literature." *JBS* 31 (1992): 97–132.
Pindell, Richard. "The Mutable Image: Man-in-Creation." In *Eterne in Mutabilitie: The Unity of* The Faerie Queene: *Essays Published in Memory of Davis Philoon Harding*. Ed. Kenneth John Atchity. Hamden, CT: Archon Books, 1972, pp. 158–79.
Phillips, James E. *Images of a Queen: Mary Stuart in Sixteenth-Century Literature*. Berkeley: University of California Press, 1964.
Ringler, Richard N. "The Faunus Episode." *MP* 43 (1966): 12–19.
Snare, Gerald. "Spenser's Fourth Grace." *JWCI* 34 (1971): 350–55.
Staines, John D. "Elizabeth, Mercilla, and the Rhetoric of Propaganda in Spenser's *Faerie Queene*." *JMEMS* 31 (2001): 283–312.
———. *The Tragic Histories of Mary Queen of Scots, 1560–1690*. Aldershot: Ashgate, 2009.
———. "Pity and the Authority of Feminine Passions in Books V and VI of *The Faerie Queene*." SSt XXV (2010): 129–61.
Steinberg, Glenn A. "Chaucer's Mutability in Spenser's *Mutabilitie Cantos*." *SEL* 46 (2006): 27–42.
Tonkin, Humphrey. *Spenser's Courteous Pastoral: Book Six of* The Faerie Queene. Oxford: Oxford University Press, 1972.
Villeponteaux, Mary. "'Not as women wonted be': Spenser's Amazon Queen." In *Dissing Elizabeth: Negative Representations of Gloriana*. Ed. Julia M. Walker. Durham: Duke University Press, 1998, pp. 209–25.
Weixel, Elizabeth M. "Squires of the Wood: The Decline of the Aristocratic Forest in Book VI of *The Faerie Queene*." *SSt* XXV (2010): 187–213.
Williams, Arnold. *Flower On A Lowly Stalk: The Sixth Book of* The Faerie Queene. East Lansing: Michigan State University Press, 1967.
Wind, Edgar. *Pagan Mysteries in the Renaissance*. London: Faber, 1967.
Woodworth, Mary K. "The Mutability Cantos and the Succession." *PMLA* 59 (1944): 985–1002.

THE SHEPHEARDES CALENDER AND PASTORAL POETRY

Adler, Doris. "Imaginary Toads in Real Gardens." *ELR* 11 (1981): 235–60.
Alpers, Paul J. *What Is Pastoral?* Chicago: The University of Chicago Press, 1996.
Bernard, John D. *Ceremonies of Innocence: Pastoralism in the Poetry of Edmund Spenser*. Cambridge: Cambridge University Press, 1989.
Bradner, Leicester. "The Latin Translations of Spenser's 'Shepheardes Calender.'" *MP* 33.1 (1935): 21–26.
Cain, Thomas H. "The Strategy of Praise in Spenser's 'Aprill.'" *SEL* 8 (1968): 45–58.
Chapman, Alison. "The Politics of Time in Edmund Spenser's English Calendar." *SEL* 42 (2002): 1–24.
Dees, Jerome S. "Colin Clout and the Shepherd of the Ocean." *SSt* XV (2001): 185–96.
Galbraith, Steven K. "'English' Black-Letter Type and Spenser's *Shepheardes Calender*." *SSt* XXIII (2008): 13–40.
Heninger, S. K. "The Implications of Form for *The Shepheardes Calender*." *SR* 9 (1962): 309–21.
Higinson, James Jackson. *Spenser's* Shepheardes Calender *in Relation to Contemporary Events*. New York: Columbia University Press, 1912.
Hoffman, Nancy Jo. *Spenser's Pastorals:* The Shepheardes Calender *and "Colin Clout."* Baltimore: Johns Hopkins University Press, 1977.
Kinney, Clare R. "Marginal Presence: Lyric Resonance, Epic Absence: *Troilus and Criseyde* and/in *The Shepheardes Calender*." *SSt* XVIII (2004): 25–39.
Koller, Katherine. "Identifications in *Colin Clouts Come Home Againe*." *MLN* 50 (1935): 155–158.
Lindheim, Nancy. "Spenser's Virgilian Pastoral: The Case for September." *SSt* XI (1990, pub. 1994): 1–16.
Marot, Clément. *Oeuvres complètes*. Ed. François Rigolot. Paris: Flammarion, 2007–2009.
McCabe, Richard A. "'Little booke: thy selfe present': The Politics of Presentation in *The Shepheardes Calendar*." In *Presenting Poetry: Composition, Publication, Reception: Essays in honour of Ian Jack*. Ed. Howard Erskine-Hill and Richard A. McCabe. Cambridge: Cambridge University Press, 1995, pp. 15–40.

McCanles, Michael. "*The Shepheardes Calender* as Document and Monument." *SEL* 22 (1982): 5–19.
McLane, Paul E. *Spenser's* Shepheardes Calender: *A Study in Elizabethan Allegory.* Notre Dame: Notre Dame University Press, 1961.
Meyer, Sam. *An Interpretation of Edmund Spenser's* Colin Clout. Cork: Cork University Press, 1969.
Montrose, Louis Adrian. "'The Perfecte Paterne of a Poete': The Poetics of Courtship in *The Shepheardes Calender.*" *TSLL* 21 (1979): 34–67.
Piepho, Lee. "*The Shepheardes Calender* and Neo-Latin Pastoral: A Book Newly Discovered to Have Been Owned by Spenser." *SSt* XVI (2002): 17–86.
Reamer, Owen J. "Spenser's Debt to Marot—Re-examined." *TSLL* 10 (1969): 504–27.
Schleiner, Louise. "Spenser's 'E. K.' as Edmund Kent (Kenned/of Kent): Kyth (Couth), Kissed, and Kunning-Coning." *ELR* 20 (2008): 374–407.
Sessions, W. A. "Spenser's Georgics." *ELR* 10 (1980): 202–38.
Shinn, Abigail. "'Extraordinary discourses of vnnecessarie matter': Spenser's *Shepheardes Calender* and the Almanac Tradition." In *Literature and Popular Culture in Early Modern England.* Ed. Matthew Dimmock and Andrew Hadfield. Aldershot: Ashgate, 2009, pp. 137–49.
• Staley, Lynn. *The Shepheardes Calender: An Introduction.* University Park: The Pennsylvania State University Press, 1990.
Steinberg, Theodore L. "'E. K.'s *Shepheardes Calender* and Spenser's." *MLS* 3 (1973): 46–58.

COMPLAINTS

• Allen, D. C. "*Muiopotmos*, or The Fate of the Butterflie." In *Image and Meaning.* Baltimore: Johns Hopkins University Press, 1968 pp. 20–4
———. "On Spenser's 'Muiopotmos.'" *SP* 53 (1956): 141–58.
Aston, Margaret. "English Ruins and English History: The Dissolution and the Sense of the Past." *JWCI* 36 (1973): 231–55.
Atchity, Kenneth John. "Spenser's *Mother Hubberds Tale*: Three Themes of Order." *PQ* 52 (1973): 161–72.
• Bond, Ronald B. "Invidia and the Allegory of Spenser's *Muiopotmos.*" *ESC* 2 (1976): 144–55.
Brink, Jean R. "Who Fashioned Edmund Spenser? The Textual History of *Complaints.*" *SP* 88 (1991): 153–68.
• Brinkley, Robert A. "Spenser's *Muiopotmos* and the Politics of Metamorphosis." *ELH* 48 (1981): 668–76.
Brown, Richard Danson. *"The New Poet": Novelty and Tradition in Spenser's* Complaints. Liverpool: Liverpool University Press, 1999.
• Coldiron, A. E. B. "How Spenser Excavates Du Bellay's *Antiquitez*: Or, The Role of the Poet, Lyric Historiography, and the English Sonnet." *JEGP* 101 (2002): 41–67.
Court, Franklin E. "The Theme and Structure of Spenser's *Muiopotmos.*" *SEL* 10 (1970): 1–15.
Danner, Bruce. *Furious Muse: Edmund Spenser's War on Lord Burghley.* Basingstoke: Palgrave, 2011.
Dundas, Judith. "'Muiopotmos': A World of Art." *YES* 5 (1975): 30–38.
Harris, Brice. "The Ape in 'Mother Hubberds Tale.'" *HLQ* 4 (1941): 191–203.
———. "The Butterfly in Spenser's *Muiopotmos.*" *JEGP* 43 (1944): 302–16.
Helgerson, Richard. *Joachim du Bellay.* Philadelphia: University of Pennsylvania Press, 2006.
Herron, Thomas. "Reforming the Fox: Spenser's 'Mother Hubberds Tale,' the Beast Fables of Barnabe Rich, and Adam Loftus, Archbishop of Dublin." *SP* 105 (2008): 336–87.
Hieatt, A. Kent. "The Genesis of Shakespeare's *Sonnets:* Spenser's *Ruins of Rome: by Bellay.*" *PMLA* 98 (1983): 800–814.
Kerrigan, John, ed. *Motives of Woe: Shakespeare & "Female Complaint": A Critical Anthology.* Oxford: Clarendon Press, 1991.
Leubner, Jason. "Temporal Distance, Antiquity, and the Beloved in Petrarch's *Rime sparse* and Du Bellay's *Les Antiquitez de Rome.*" *MLN* 122 (2007): 1079–1104.
Luborsky, Ruth Samson. "The Allusive Presentation of *The Shepheardes Calender.*" *SSt* I (1980): 29–67.
———. "The Illustrations to *The Shepheardes Calender.*" *SSt* II (1981): 3–53.

Lucas, Scott. "Diggon Davie and Davy Dicar: Edmund Spenser, Thomas Churchyard, and the Poetics of Public Protest." *SSt* XVI (2001): 151–65.
Manley, Lawrence. "Spenser and the City: The Minor Poems." *MLQ* 43 (1982): 203–227.
Melehy, Hassan. *The Poetics of Literary Transfer in Early Modern France and England.* Farnham: Ashgate, 2010.
Muir, Tom. "Without Remainder: Ruins and Tombs in Shakespeare's *Sonnets*." *TP* 24 (2010): 21–49.
———. "Specters of Spenser: Translating the *Antiquitez*." *SSt* XXV (2010): 327–61.
Peter, John Desmond. *Complaint and Satire in Early English Literature.* Oxford: Clarendon Press, 1956.
Peterson, Richard. "Laurel Crown and Ape's Tail: New Light on Spenser's Career from Sir Thomas Tresham." *SSt* XII (1989): 1–36.
Rebhorn, Wayne. "Du Bellay's Imperial Mistress: *Les Antiquitez de Rome* as Petrarchist Sonnet Sequence." *RQ* 33.4 (1980): 609–622.
Smith, Malcolm, ed. *Antiquitez* and *Ruines of Rome*. Binghamton NY: MRTS, 1994.
Stein, Harold. *Studies in Spenser's Complaints.* New York: Oxford University Press, 1934.
Van Den Berg, Kent T. "'The Counterfeit in Personation': Spenser's *Prosopopoia, or Mother Hubberds Tale*." In *The Author in His Work: Essays on a Problem in Criticism.* Ed. Louis L. Martz and Aubrey Williams. New Haven: Yale University Press, 1978, pp. 85–102.
• Weiner, Andrew D. "Spenser's *Muiopotmos* and the Fates of Butterflies and Men." *JEGP* 84 (1985): 203–20.
Wells, William. "'To Make a Milde Construction': The Significance of the Opening Stanzas of *Muiopotmos*." *SP* 42 (1945): 544–54.

OTHER POETRY

Brown, Ted. "Metapoetry in Edmund Spenser's *Amoretti*." *PQ* 82 (2003): 401–17.
Cheney, Donald. "Spenser's Fortieth Birthday and Related Fictions." *SSt* IV (1984): 3–31.
———. Review of Judith Dundas's *The Spider and the Bee.* In *RS* 39.4 (1986): 798–801.
Chinitz, David. "The Poem as Sacrament: Spenser's *Epithalamion* and the Golden Section." *JMRS* 21.2 (1991): 251–68.
Cirillo, A. R. "Spenser's *Epithalamion*: The Harmonious Universe of Love." *SEL* 8 (1968): 19–34.
Cummings, L. "Spenser's *Amoretti* VIII: New Manuscript Versions." *SEL* 4 (1964): 125–35.
Dasenbrock, Reed Way. "The Petrarchan Context of Spenser's *Amoretti*." *PMLA* 100 (1985): 38–50.
Eade, J. C. "The Pattern in the Astronomy of Spenser's *Epithalamion*." *RES* 23 (1972): 173–178.
Fleming, James. "A View from the Bridge: Ireland and Violence in Spenser's *Amoretti*." *SSt* XV (2001): 135–64.
Fowler, Alastair. "Spenser's Prothalamion." In *Conceitful Thought: The Interpretation of English Renaissance Poems.* Edinburgh: Edinburgh University Press, 1975.
Greene, Thomas M. "Spenser and the Epithalamic Convention." *CL* 9 (1957): 215–28.
Helfer, Rebeca. *Spenser's Ruins and the Art of Recollection.* Toronto: University of Toronto Press, 2012.
Hieatt, A. Kent. *Short Time's Endless Monument: The Symbolism of the Numbers in Edmund Spenser's "Epithalamion."* New York: Columbia University Press, 1960.
Hutton, James. "Cupid and the Bee." *PMLA* 56 (1941): 1036–58.
Loewenstein, Joseph. "A Note on the Structure of Spenser's Amoretti: Viper Thoughts." *SSt* VIII (1987): 311–29.
Johnson, William C. *Spenser's* Amoretti: *Analogies of Love*. Lewisburg: Bucknell University Press, 1990.
———. "Gender Fashioning and the Dynamics of Mutuality in Spenser's *Amoretti*." *ES* 74 (1993): 503–19.
Kaske, Carol V. "Spenser's *Amoretti* and *Epithalamion* of 1595: Structure, Genre, and Numerology." *ELR* 8 (1978): 271–95.